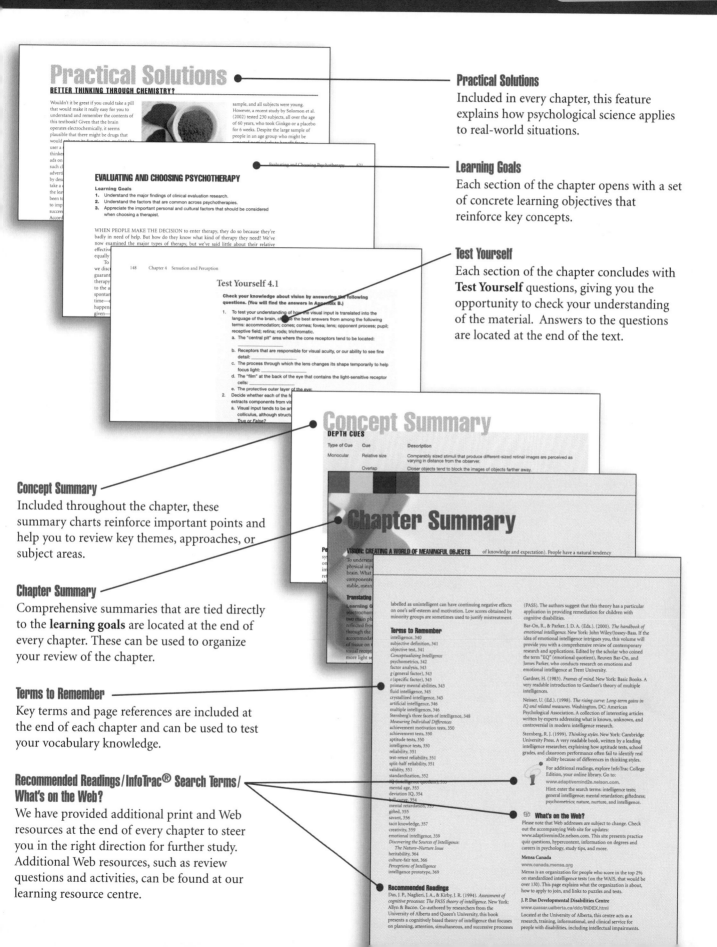

P9-AGK-885

Practical Solutions
Included in every chapter, this feature explains how psychological science applies to real-world situations.

Learning Goals
Each section of the chapter opens with a set of concrete learning objectives that reinforce key concepts.

Test Yourself
Each section of the chapter concludes with **Test Yourself** questions, giving you the opportunity to check your understanding of the material. Answers to the questions are located at the end of the text.

Concept Summary
Included throughout the chapter, these summary charts reinforce important points and help you to review key themes, approaches, or subject areas.

Chapter Summary
Comprehensive summaries that are tied directly to the **learning goals** are located at the end of every chapter. These can be used to organize your review of the chapter.

Terms to Remember
Key terms and page references are included at the end of each chapter and can be used to test your vocabulary knowledge.

Recommended Readings/InfoTrac® Search Terms/ What's on the Web?
We have provided additional print and Web resources at the end of every chapter to steer you in the right direction for further study. Additional Web resources, such as review questions and activities, can be found at our learning resource centre.

Second Canadian Edition

Psychology

THE ADAPTIVE MIND

James S. Nairne
Purdue University

D. Stephen Lindsay
University of Victoria

Delroy L. Paulhus
University of British Columbia

Martin S. Smith
University of Victoria

THOMSON

NELSON

Australia   Canada   Mexico   Singapore   Spain   United Kingdom   United States

Psychology: The Adaptive Mind
Second Canadian Edition

by James S. Nairne, Stephen Lindsay,
Delroy L. Paulhus, and Martin S. Smith

Editorial Director and Publisher:
Evelyn Veitch

Executive Editor:
Joanna Cotton

Marketing Manager:
Murray Moman

Developmental Editor:
Liz Radojkovic

Production Editor:
Carrie Withers

Senior Production Coordinator:
Hedy Sellers

Copy Editor:
Valerie Adams

Proofreader:
Marcia Miron de Gallego

Indexer:
Belle Wong

**Photo Researcher/Permissions
Coordinator:**
Indu Ghuman

Creative Director:
Angela Cluer

Interior Design Modifications:
Katherine Strain

Cover Design:
Angela Cluer

Cover Image:
Katherine Hollinrake

Senior Composition Analyst:
Zenaida Diores

Printer:
Transcontinental

**National Library of Canada
Cataloguing in Publication**

Psychology: The adaptive mind /
James S. Nairne... [et al.]—2nd
Canadian ed.

Includes bibliographical references
and index.

ISBN 0-17-622474-2

1. Psychology—Textbooks. I.
Nairne, James S., 1954–

HM586.K45 2003   301
C2003-903035-0

About the Authors

James S. Nairne

Jim Nairne received his Ph.D. in Human Memory and Cognition from Yale University. He is a professor at Purdue University, where he specializes in cognition and human memory. He is a member of the American Psychological Association, American Psychological Society, and the Psychonomic Society. He was an Associate Editor of the *Journal of Memory and Language* from 1997 to 2001 and has served on the board of that journal since 1993. He was recently awarded the distinguished Outstanding Undergraduate Teaching Award, in memory of Charles B. Murphy, from Purdue University.

D. Stephen Lindsay

Steve Lindsay is Professor of Psychology at the University of Victoria. He conducted his undergraduate work at Reed College (B.A. 1981) and his graduate training at Princeton University (Ph.D. 1987). Specializing in the study of human memory, much of his research has focused on memory source monitoring (e.g., studies of conditions under which people mistake memories of suggestions as memories of witnessed events). He has published numerous articles in scholarly journals, as well as chapters in edited professional books, and has co-edited two books on memory. Steve is the editor of the *Journal of Experimental Psychology: General.* He is on the editorial board of *Applied Cognitive Psychology* and has also served on the editorial boards of the *Journal of Experimental Psychology: Learning, Memory, and Cognition; Journal of Memory and Language,* and the *Psychological Bulletin.*

Delroy L. Paulhus

Joining the author team for the Second Canadian Edition, Del Paulhus is Professor of Psychology at the University of British Columbia. His undergraduate degree is from Carleton University (B.A. 1974) and his M.S. and Ph.D. are both from Columbia University. He was also a visiting professor at the University of California (Berkeley). Del conducts research in a variety of areas of personality and social psychology. Topics include self-presentation (e.g., self-deception, faking, and impression management), aversive personalities, (e.g., narcissism and subclinical psychopathy), and social judgment (e.g., perceptions of intelligence and personality). He has edited several books and published a number of psychological test manuals. Del was recently an associate editor for the *Personality and Social Psychology Bulletin.* He was also a member of the review committee for the Canadian federal granting agency, the Social Science and Humanities Research Council.

Martin S. Smith

Martin S. Smith is a faculty member in the Department of Psychology at the University of Victoria. He was previously Associate Professor of Psychology and Director of the Child Studies Program at Brock University. Martin received his undergraduate training at Simon Fraser University and his M.A. and Ph.D. at York University. He is a family and developmental psychologist with specific interests in undergraduate teaching and instructional development, and the evolutionary psychology of the human family. He is currently interested in developing innovative ways of teaching large university classes, the use of technology, and undergraduate peer tutors in undergraduate instruction.

Brief Contents

Contents

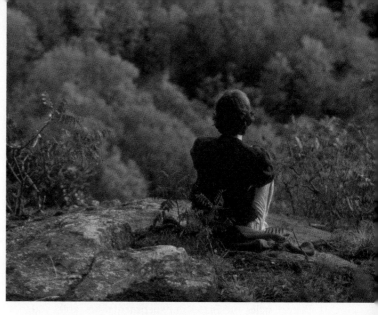

Chapter 3
Biological Processes   74

Chapter 5
Consciousness   172

Chapter 8
Thought and Language   298

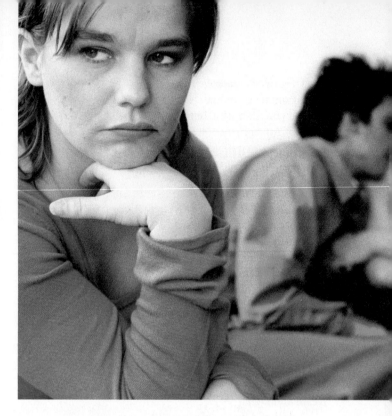

Chapter 13
Social Psychology   508

Chapter 14
Abnormal Psychology   556

*Previewing the Scientific and
Practical Problems   558*

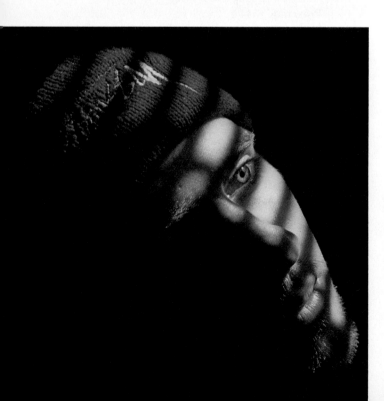

Chapter 15
Therapy   596

*Previewing the Scientific and
Practical Problems   598*

TREATING THE BODY: BIOMEDICAL THERAPIES   599

Preface

TO THE INSTRUCTOR

Our work on *Psychology: The Adaptive Mind*, Second Canadian Edition, focused on several objectives:

- Our most important aim was to explain the basic principles and findings of modern psychology in a text that is engaging for readers and that clearly and accurately communicates the original scientific research that underlies our discipline.
- A second objective was to make the text particularly appealing and interesting for Canadian students. To this end, the text highlights the work of Canadian psychologists, many of whom have played substantial roles in shaping modern psychology. The text also reviews how the discipline and profession of psychology is structured in Canada. More generally, throughout the text we have anchored the discussion of psychological topics to real-world examples that will be familiar and meaningful to Canadian students. In our experience, Canadian students have a strong preference for learning from texts that deal with issues, examples, and references relevant to their own experiences as Canadians, rather than from texts that might be topical in other countries.
- A third goal was to produce a text that affords some conceptual "hooks" for students—that is, core ideas that help students structure and organize the numerous theories and findings reviewed in the text. The adaptive problem-solving approach, originally developed by James Nairne and outlined below, provides a pedagogically effective means of understanding how the various aspects of modern psychology fit together.
- A fourth goal was to convey the dynamic nature of contemporary research in active and emerging areas, such as cognitive science and evolutionary psychology. We've added numerous new references to the second edition (many from 2000 and beyond).
- As a fifth aim, we strove to produce a volume that is aesthetically pleasing. The art, figures, and layout of this text all contribute to a lucid, enjoyable, and absorbing learning experience.
- Finally, we worked to develop a package of ancillaries that provides as much assistance as possible to instructors in teaching this challenging course, and to students in learning about this diverse discipline.

The Adaptive Problem-Solving Approach

One of the first hurdles we face as instructors of introductory psychology is convincing students that psychology is more than just the study of abnormal behaviour. Introduce yourself as a psychologist and you're likely to get a response such as "Don't analyze me!" or "I'd better watch what I say around you!" It takes time for students to realize that psychology is a vast interdisciplinary field that includes all aspects of both normal and abnormal behaviour. Even after exposure to its breadth, students may still find the topics of psychology mysterious and forbidding. Take a look at a typical chapter on learning, for example, and its contents seem to bear little resemblance to our everyday understanding of what it means to "learn." There are extended discussions of drooling dogs and key-pecking pigeons, but little about the connection between conditioning procedures and the learning problems we face on a daily basis.

In *Psychology: The Adaptive Mind*, Second Canadian Edition, we focus extensively on the function and purpose of psychological processes. Instead of leading with findings, methods, and theories specific to a topic, we introduce each topic as a "solution" to an adaptive or scientific "problem." For example, as one way of understanding how people and other animals learn about the signalling properties of events (problem), one can look to classical conditioning (solution). Notice the shift in emphasis: Instead of topic followed by function, it's function followed by topic. This is what we call the adaptive problem-solving approach, and it offers a number of advantages:

1. The student has a reason to follow the discussion; understanding the problem to be solved enables the student to appreciate the value of seeking a solution.

2. Because the discussion is about an adaptive or scientific problem, it naturally promotes critical thinking. The student sees the connection between the problem and the solution.

3. The adaptive problem-solving theme extends across chapters, enabling us to draw connections between what are typically treated as separate topics.

Thus, the adaptive problem-solving approach provides an effective learning framework.

Each chapter is organized around a set of adaptive or scientific problems that (1) focus the discussion on the functional relevance of the material and (2) demonstrate that people think and act for adaptive reasons. For example, electrochemical transmission in the nervous system is introduced as the solution to the adaptive problem of communicating internally, the experimental method is introduced as a solution to the conceptual problem of determining the causes of behaviour, and so on.

When behaviour is viewed as the product of adaptive systems, psychology begins to make more sense to students. They learn that behaviours (including the methods of psychologists!) are reactions to particular problems. Through the emphasis on adaptiveness, students relax their egocentric view of the world and increase sensitivity to why behaviour is so diverse, both within and across species. Appreciation of individuality and diversity is enhanced by the understanding that differences are natural consequences of adaptations to the environment.

Changes in the Second Canadian Edition

Below we've listed the major changes in this edition. In addition to these specific changes, we have improved the clarity of the narrative throughout the text and updated the science. Although we have kept primary and classic references in place where appropriate, we have included many new references from 2000 and beyond—both Canadian and international. Another important addition to this edition is the substantial increase in practical applications. Each chapter now contains new features entitled "Practical Solutions" that explain how psychological science applies to real-world situation that are of interest to students.

Chapter 1: An Introduction to Psychology

- New introduction to chapter focusing on psychologists' contributions in responding to the events of September 11, 2001
- Section on women psychologists has been moved and now includes new material on Doreen Kimura and Brenda Milner, as well as a reference to Storm and Gurevich's special issue of *Canadian Psychology* on the status of women in psychology
- New section on "How to Become a Psychologist"

Chapter 2: The Tactics of Psychological Research

- Improved definition of scientific method
- Clarified introduction to inferential statistics
- Enhanced treatment of and extended discussion of the issue of generalizing from experimental research

- Extended discussion of ethical issues related to deception in research
- Sharpened focus of section on ethics of animal research

Chapter 3: Biological Processes
- Extensive reorganization of the first section entitled "Communicating Internally: Connecting World and Brain"
- New section and accompanying figure on the resting potential
- Improved definitions of somatic nervous system and EEG
- New material on transcranial magnetic stimulation (TMS)
- New discussion of event-related potentials (ERP)
- New Practical Solutions feature on scientific investigations of Gingko biloba as a memory enhancer
- Streamlined discussion of evolutionary and genetic psychology

Chapter 4: Sensation and Perception
- New Practical Solutions feature entitled "Creating Illusions of Depth"
- New information on the decibel scale and hearing damage caused by exposure to loud music
- Expanded and updated section on taste, including discussion of umami

Chapter 5: Consciousness
- Newly integrated and expanded discussion of subliminal perception
- New Practical Solutions feature on cell phones and driving
- Expanded and updated discussion of REM sleep
- New research on substance abuse, including material from several recent Canadian studies

Chapter 6: Learning from Experience
- New chapter introduction
- Streamlined discussion of habituation
- Improved clarity of section entitled "Acquiring the Conditioned Stimulus–Unconditioned Stimulus Connection"
- Additional material on conditioned inhibition
- Clarified explanation of radical behaviourism

Chapter 7: Memory
- Updated treatment of flashbulb memories
- New Practical Solutions feature on studying for exams
- Shortened discussion of mnemonic devices
- Expanded coverage of childhood amnesia

Chapter 8: Thought and Language
- New section on confirmation bias and illusory correlations
- New material elaborating on the development of language comprehension in childhood

Chapter 9: Intelligence
- Revised introduction including examples highlighting three issues: the idiosyncratic nature of intelligence judgments, the effects of language testing on IQ estimates, and the relation between personality and intelligence
- Incorporated discussion of measuring brain speed into section on cognitive approaches

- Revised and expanded section on multiple intelligences to include exemplar nomination approach
- New discussion of savants within the section on extremes of intelligence
- New section on perceptions of intelligence including material on judging intelligence and abuses of intelligence testing
- New material on artificial intelligence
- Addition of Gardner's eight and ninth types of intelligence
- Addition of split-half reliability to the reliability section
- New Practical Solutions feature entitled "Does Intelligence Predict Success in the Workplace?"
- Revised nurture section to reflect fact that twin and adoption studies support both nature and nurture perspectives

Chapter 10: Human Development
- Improved introduction
- Revised section on environmental hazards
- Memory and age section updated with addition of work by Graf and Uttl
- Addition of evolutionary explanation for deterioration of short-term memory in the aged
- More complete treatment of temperament
- New Practical Solutions feature entitled "Do Parents Really Matter?"

Chapter 11: Motivation and Emotion
- Expanded section on human instincts
- Revised section on evolutionary influences: more emphasis on sex difference literature with social learning alternatives to evolutionary explanations
- New Practical Solutions feature entitled "Does the Polygraph Work?"
- Integration of material on disgust into the narrative
- Expanded discussion of anorexia nervosa
- Expanded discussion and clarification of Schachter's two-factor theory

Chapter 12: Personality
- Reorganized and revised section on the Big Five personality dimensions, including a new section on the interpersonal circle and recent alternatives to the Big Five
- Nonverbal inventories now included under indirect methods
- New Practical Solutions box entitled "Does Your Room Give Away Your Personality?"
- New material on the defence mechanism of denial
- Shortened section on neo-Freudians
- Section on multiple and possible selves integrated into the narrative
- New material on the self in flux
- Section on personality and the problems of life
- New material on the pure cognitive approach
- Reorganized and revised section on culture
- New section on levels of analysis of personality theories

Chapter 13: Social Psychology
- Expanded discussion of attributional biases including new discussion of the actor-observer effect and cross-cultural differences
- New discussion on social loafing and deindividuation under the section on the power of the group
- New section on group decision making with a discussion of group polarization and groupthink

- Addition of level of arousal under the section on the determinants of liking and loving; now includes the famous Capilano Bridge study
- New and revised material on prosocial (helping) and antisocial (aggression) behaviour
- New Practical Solutions feature entitled "How Can Hostility and Aggression Be Reduced?"

Chapter 14: Abnormal Psychology
- New definitions of abnormal behaviour and psychological disorders
- New discussion of the medical model versus the sociological model
- New discussion of research on social phobia and perfectionism by Canadian researchers
- Two new Practical Solutions features entitled "The Insanity Defence" and "Are Creative People Mad?"
- Revised discussion of the DSM-IV

Chapter 15: Therapy
- Expanded and updated discussion of biomedical therapies including new coverage of the medications risperidone and buspirone
- Updated discussion of shock therapy (ECT)
- New section on the use of punishment to change behaviour
- Revised and updated Practical Solutions feature entitled "Social Skills Training in Schizophrenia"
- Revised discussion of choosing a therapist

Chapter 16: Stress and Health
- Revised discussion of Type A personality to accommodate new research
- New section on pain as a major stressor
- Updated research on immune system consequences of stress
- New discussion of work by Canadian researchers (Conrod, Pihl, Stewart, and Peterson) on substance abuse
- New section on gender differences in the stress response—tending-and-befriending instead of fight-or-flight
- New coverage of stress and the September 11, 2001, terrorist attacks
- Expanded section on external sources of stress, adding physical pain as a class
- Introduction of the term hardy personality within the section on internal sources of stress
- New section on burnout as a psychological consequence of stress
- New Practical Solutions feature entitled "Pet Support"

Learning Aids
- Each chapter section begins with Learning Goals and ends with a Test Yourself review to give students regular opportunities to check their understanding of the material.
- Concept Summaries are located throughout the chapter to help students review important themes, approaches, or subject areas.
- Comprehensive Chapter Summaries encourage students to review important points without having to take extensive notes or wade through the entire text again. The summaries have been thoroughly revised to reflect the learning goals and content within each chapter.
- New to this edition are connections to Psyk.trek 2.0, the leading multi-media CD-ROM in Canada for introductory psychology. The Psyk.trek icon, located next to appropriate headings, directs students to specific interactive learning modules and simulations.

- Annotated Recommended Readings and What's on the Web sections are located at the end of each chapter and offer brief descriptions of relevant books, articles, and Web sites to steer students toward further investigation.
- Suggested search terms and the URL for InfoTrac® College Edition are listed at the end of each chapter. Further suggestions for using InfoTrac®, including possible research projects, are found on both the student and instructor sections of the book site: www.adaptivemind2e.nelson.com

Teaching and Learning Supplements

Psychology: The Adaptive Mind, Second Canadian Edition, is supported by a state-of-the-art teaching and learning package.

Study Guide (0-17-622475-0)

Revised for this edition by Sue Burns of Grant MacEwan College, this useful supplement is tied directly to the Learning Goals of each chapter in the text and includes exercises for mastering the vocabulary, fill-in-the-blank exercises, and multiple-choice test items for each major concept. It also includes short essay questions, matching exercises, and two additional sets of multiple-choice questions per chapter. Also included is a language enhancement guide that explains nontechnical terms and idioms that may be unfamiliar. The second edition also includes phonetic pronunciations of some of the more challenging words in each chapter.

Instructor's Resource Manual (0-17-641645-5)

The Instructor's Resource Manual, adapted by Jeff Pfeifer of the University of Regina, includes detailed chapter outlines, learning goals, lecture elaborations, "Focus on Research" sections, demonstrations and activities, responses to Critical Thinking questions from the text and additional Critical Thinking questions, extensions for the Practical Solutions boxes, suggested readings, InfoTrac® College Edition key words, film and video suggestions, Web sites, and Web activities. An electronic version of the Instructor's Resource Manual is also available through our instructor's Web site.

Test Bank (0-17-640544-5)

This fully revised Test Bank was adapted by Megan Easterbrook of Grant MacEwan College, and it provides over 4000 multiple-choice, sentence completion, and essay questions. The multiple-choice test items are organized into different categories: text definition, applied definition, factual, text application, new application, and conceptual. Ten questions are drawn directly from the Study Guide and an additional ten questions are taken from the Web site. Psyk.trek questions have been added to this edition.

Computerized Test Bank (0-17-641644-7)

An electronic version of the Test Bank is available for both Windows and Macintosh. The ExamView software is a user-friendly program that allows instructors to insert their own questions and customize those provided.

Transparency Acetates (0-17-640546-1)

Approximately 100 text figures and illustrations from the Second Canadian Edition are available in this acetate package.

Multimedia Manager PowerPoint Presentation (0-17-641614-5)

This CD-ROM includes text-specific lecture outlines, a high-resolution digital version of each figure and illustration from the text, videos, animations, and Web content. These graphics can be combined with your own material to create powerful, personal, media-enhanced presentations.

Web Site: www.adaptivemind2e.nelson.com

This Web site is tied directly to the text. Chapter resources include practice quizzes, Web links from the text as well as additional links, crossword puzzles, glossary terms, InfoTrac® exercises, and animations and simulations (MediaWorks). The student site also includes study tips, information on degrees and careers in psychology, and further resources designed to enhance the learning experience. The password-protected instructors-only area of the site includes downloadable ancillaries, suggestions for additional activities, and information to help instructors incorporate technology into their teaching.

CNN Today Videos: Introductory Psychology

Exclusive to Nelson Thomson Learning, *CNN Today Videos* are course-specific to help instructors launch lectures and to encourage discussion. Organized by topics covered in a typical course, these 60-minute videos contain many exciting clips. Contact your publisher's representative for more information.

Digital Video Library CD-ROM (0-534-17899-5)

This CD-ROM helps enliven lectures by offering access to a range of digital materials, including classic video footage of prominent psychologists, demonstrations and simulations of important experiments, and selections from our *CNN Today Videos.*

Psyk.trek 2.0 (0-534-37062-4)

Psyk.trek is a multimedia supplement that provides students with new opportunities for active learning. It consists of four components. The main component is a set of 62 Interactive Learning Modules that present the core content of psychology in a dynamic new way. These tutorials feature thousands of graphics, hundreds of photos, hundreds of animations, approximately four hours of narration, 35 carefully selected videos, and about 160 uniquely visual concept checks and quizzes. Simulations allow students to explore complex psychological phenomena in depth through highly interactive, experiential demonstrations. A Multimedia Glossary allows students to look up over 800 psychological terms, access hundreds of pronunciations of obscure words, and pull up hundreds of related diagrams, photos, and videos. The Video Selector allows students to directly access 35 video segments.

InfoTrac® College Edition

A free subscription to this extensive online library is enclosed with every new copy of the book, giving students access to the latest news and research articles online. This easy-to-use database features thousands of reliable, full-length articles from hundreds of top academic journals and popular sources.

ACKNOWLEDGMENTS

We thank the superb team at Nelson Thomson learning—especially Joanna Cotton, Liz Radojkovic, Valerie Adams, Carrie Withers, Marcia Miron de Gallego, and Murray Moman. Producing a text like this is a team undertaking, and the Nelson Thomson professionals deserve a great deal of the credit for the final product. They've been unfailingly encouraging and friendly, prompt and effective, and highly skilled. Steve thanks Moira and Duncan for their personal support, patience, and good humour. Del would like to thank Ngaere, Jean, and Shirley for their support and inspiration.

Reviewers

Many instructors across Canada were involved in helping us develop this Second Canadian Edition. We offer special thanks to the following professors for their insightful reviews. Their contributions can be seen throughout this Second Canadian Edition:

Glen Bodner, University of Calgary

Ken Cramer, University of Windsor

Dianne Crisp, Kwantlen University College

Kathy Denton, Douglas College

Robert Moore, University of Regina

David Reagan, Camosun College

Sonya Symons, Acadia University

The following individuals played an invaluable role in the development of the First Canadian Edition and for that we extend our thanks. Ken Cramer for his essential contribution to Chapter 12, Deborah Hunt Matheson for her timely help with Chapter 16, and Jennifer Lloyd and Laura-Lyn Stewart for their friendly and efficient research assistance.

First Canadian Edition Reviewers and Contributors

Catherine Salmon, Simon Fraser University

Sally Walters, Simon Fraser University

Doug McCann, York University

Enrico DiTommaso, University of New Brunswick—Saint John

Bruce Bolster, University of Winnipeg

Robert Huxtable, Okanagan University College

Russell Powell, Grant MacEwan College

Michael MacNeill, Capilano College

Sonya Symons, Acadia University

Ken Cramer, University of Windsor

Jody Bain, University of Victoria

Bram Goldwater, University of Victoria

James Plant, University of Victoria

TO THE STUDENT

Psychology is the scientific study of behaviour and mind. It can be a tough subject, but we think you'll find it rewarding and fascinating. Throughout this book there are dozens of specific studies and hundreds of isolated facts, but our main goal is for you to understand psychology in a way that will be useful throughout your life. Toward that end, we try hard to show you how particular behaviours, cognitive processes, and emotions help you solve important adaptive problems every day.

What Do We Mean by "The Adaptive Mind"?

We take the view that everything people do is influenced by their need to solve or adapt to problems in their environment. By "problems" we mean the threats people encounter and the various demands they need to meet as they navigate through everyday life. People are constantly digging into their psychological "tool kit" to solve one problem or another. For example, the sight of a charging enemy is a serious problem to be solved. To solve it, the body instantly creates extra energy in the form of general arousal that makes fighting or escaping more effective. A more long-term example is the continual threat to an organism's survival created by an inability to communicate with others of its species. Survival would be greatly enhanced by improved communication abilities. In this case, the solution—or adaptation—was the evolution of sophisticated verbal and nonverbal language in our species.

Furthermore, each chapter in this book may be viewed as a set of scientific problems that need to be tackled by rigorous psychological research. Some have been solved but, for many of these scientific problems, we have only partial solutions. We know, for example, that certain drug can treat certain forms of mental illness but we don't yet know why.

We believe that viewing human behaviour and scientific research as short-term problem solving or long-term adaptions to recurring problems will facilitate your learning of psychology. Therefore, each chapter begins with three or four adaptive, practical, or, scientific problems like the ones described above, and throughout the chapter we show you how these particular problems are solved by the human body and mind.

We hope that some of what you learn in this book will help you with situations in your daily life. The study of psychology is challenging but it is most certainly relevant to everything you do.

How to Read This Book

Inexperienced students often read textbooks in a passive way. They start at the first assigned page, drag their eyes along each sentence until the end of the assignment, and then close the book and go do something else. Some students do this while listening to music or TV. Some students do it with a highlighter, assiduously marking all of the bold and italic text (as if the fluorescent ink will somehow transmit the material to the brain).

If you're used to having background music or TV on when you study, you'll miss it at first. Music and TV are entertaining, and studying can be boring (especially if you're studying difficult and unfamiliar material in a passive way). But distracting background noises interfere with cognitive processing and hence are likely to make it harder for you to learn and retain what you're reading (see Chapter 6). Why make studying harder and less effective?

Studying will be more entertaining and valuable if you do it actively, striving to understand and think about the material rather than merely letting the words roll across your mind. You spontaneously read in an active manner if the text is something you care about and are interested in. If you're a hockey fan, for example, when you read an article about your favourite team, you don't just take in the words, but rather actively relate the new information to things you already know, form images of what the writer describes, question the author's claims, and so on. Reading in that way supports understanding and retention. It's easy when you are already an expert on and care about the topic, because you have a wealth of experience that supports this sort of intellectual engagement with the writing. It's harder with an introductory textbook, but with effort you can do it and it will pay off.

Our text includes numerous features designed to encourage students to work with the text in an actively engaged, thoughtful manner. We've included those features because we know that using them will benefit students (in the form of better understanding and retention of the material, not to mention better grades). The features are there: Now it's up to you to use them.

We suggest that you begin each chapter by reading through the chapter outline. This will give you a general overview of the material to be covered. Also, ask yourself questions about the headings in the outline (e.g., "What is the difference between a clinical psychologist and an applied psychologist?" or "What does Darwin have to do with psychology?"). Generating these questions gets you actively engaged in thinking about the material, and primes your mind to take in the parts of the text that address those questions.

As you read, strive to understand each sentence. If you don't understand it as you read it, you're not likely to remember it when tested. Also, understanding of many later points of the text requires understanding of earlier ones; if you don't make the effort to understand in the beginning, it will likely get harder as you go along.

When the text describes something concrete (such as a real-world example or the procedures of an experiment), form mental images of what the text is describing, or call to mind similar examples from your own experience. Forming mental images and relating new knowledge to things you know will support understanding and subsequent recall. It will also help if you take notes as you read, especially if you write those notes in your own words; there is little value in simply copying material from the text, but paraphrasing key points in your own words can have substantial value.

Early in each chapter is a box titled "Previewing the Adaptive, Scientific, or Practical Problems," and toward the end of each chapter is another box titled "Solving the Adaptive, Scientific, or Practical Problems." It is important to read and think about these carefully. Doing so will help you grasp and hold on to the main points of the chapter.

The text includes a variety of materials in the margins: Almost every page has some sort of picture, drawing, definition, or exercise in the margin. There are also materials presented in boxes, such as Concept Summaries. Do not ignore any of these. They partly overlap with the text, but their purpose is to encourage you to think about centrally important points in ways that are slightly different from how you thought about them when reading the main body of the text. Research has shown that thinking about material in multiple ways improves performance on subsequent memory tests.

Speaking of tests, each chapter includes several "Test Yourself" exercises, and you would be wise to do these as you go along and to assess your accuracy by checking your answers against Appendix B. It's easy to fool yourself into thinking you know and understand the material, but if you want to do well in the course then it's crucial to find out whether you do know and understand it.

Each chapter also includes several "Critical Thinking" questions in the margins. As a student, your aim is not merely to memorize material, but also to develop intellectual skills that enable you to go beyond the information given. Don't just passively accept whatever the text says, but think critically about it; that is, question the text, think through the wider implications of its claims, note parallels between different issues raised in the text, and so on. The Critical Thinking items are designed to spark this sort of active, questioning approach to the text. Taking such an approach will simultaneously help you develop intellectual skills and encourage you to think about the ideas in the text in ways that support long-term memory.

When you finish reading a chapter, don't forget the end-of-chapter material. Go through the Chapter Summary and the list of Terms to Remember with care. With regard to the latter, don't just look at the terms and decide whether or not they are familiar; rather, write down brief definitions of each term. If you cannot answer those questions right after reading the chapter, how will you answer questions about them later, when you are given a test? If you encounter questions you cannot answer, review the relevant parts of the chapter until you can answer them. If questions remain after your best efforts, then seek help from your instructor, the course teaching assistant, or whatever other resources may be available to you. Talking to other students about what you've read can also be very productive.

If you read the text in the ways we've suggested, you'll probably find that you don't need to do a lot of cramming the night before a test. Although cramming can be effective for improving performance on an immediate test, it isn't great for long-term memory. The best approach is to keep up with the reading in a deep and thoughtful way as the course goes along, and then spend time shortly before the test reviewing the material.

People differ from one another in terms of which study techniques work best, but a general principle is that learning and retention are enhanced when readers engage with the material in an active, dynamic way (see Chapter 8). We hope these comments will help you take advantage of the features of this book, and that these in turn will enable you to learn a great deal about psychology.

James S. Nairne
D. Stephen Lindsay
Delroy L. Paulhus
Martin S. Smith

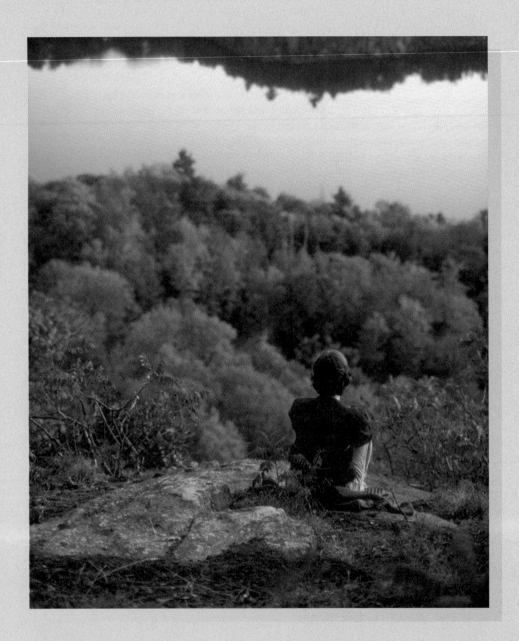

It was the best of times, it was the worst of times, it was the age of wisdom, it was the age of foolishness, it was the epoch of belief, it was the epoch of incredulity, it was the season of Light, it was the season of Darkness, it was the spring of hope, it was the winter of despair.…

Charles Dickens, *A Tale of Two Cities*

Chapter 1 An Introduction to Psychology

n the quotation with which we begin this book, Dickens was speaking of pre-revolutionary France, but the contrasting extremes of his description capture the current moment as well. Today's Canadians enjoy an extraordinarily high quality of life (among the top three countries in the world in terms of education, health and life expectancy, wealth, and quality of life). Yet our fast-paced, increasingly urban and technologized lifestyles, and the bewildering array of choices and options that are open to us, can be very stressful and unsettling. Many Canadians suffer from symptoms ranging from anxiety to depression, and despite its many fine points and advantages, our culture is plagued with problems such as drug abuse and violence.

There is a sense in which it is always both the best and worst of times. At any given moment, some people are brimming with joy and others are drowning in sorrow. Also, to paraphrase Dickens, humans are the best of animals and the worst of animals. We are a species capable of discovering the principles of flight, unlocking the secrets of the atom, and raising graceful, glittering towers hundreds of metres into the air. Yet we are also capable of deliberately flying loaded passenger jets into skyscrapers, dropping atom bombs on cities, and enslaving our fellow humans. We create moving works of art and heaps of garbage. We soar at times, crash at others, and everything in between.

The events of September 11, 2001, dramatically illustrate the spectrum of human behaviour. Some individuals sought to unleash terror by killing thousands of people; others courageously struggled to save lives and to provide shelter and support for those in need. Among the latter, residents of Gander, Newfoundland (population nearly 10 000) gained international fame for their generous hospitality to hundreds of passengers from the 50 international flights grounded at Gander International Airport. Also among those providing support to persons traumatized by the terrorist acts were clinical psychologists, such as Anna B. Baranowsky, who earned an honours bachelor of arts degree at the University of Victoria and a doctoral degree in clinical psychology at the University of Ottawa, and now directs Toronto's Traumatology Institute and York University's certificate program in Trauma Response. We will discuss psychological trauma and its treatment later in this book; for now, the point is that the human animal is capable of an enormous range of behaviours.

What makes us humans tick? Why and how do we do the things we do? Why are some people so different from others? What can be done to enhance the human potential to do good and to be well, and to curtail the human potential to do harm and to suffer? Answers to such questions (and many others) can be sought through the study of **psychology,** the scientific study of behaviour and mind. This book is an introduction to that scientific discipline.

psychology
The scientific study of behaviour and mind.

Although many psychologists work to help people cope with trauma and other psychological problems, the science of psychology focuses just as much on normal behaviour as on abnormal or problem behaviour. Why focus on everyday, normal behaviour as well as abnormal behaviour? For one thing, to understand the abnormal it's essential that we understand normal functioning first, just as medical doctors must understand the healthy body before they can understand sickness and disease. For another, the "normal" human animal is a marvellous scientific mystery, a great puzzle that is fascinating to study in its own right.

Psychology seeks to understand the essentials of behaviour and mind: how people act, think, and feel. Psychologists have gradually built a knowledge base about this subject, and they're continually using this knowledge to build a systematic science of behaviour and mind. By studying psychology, you will receive several tangible benefits:

4

1. *You will see how psychologists have learned to predict behaviour in various situations.* By observing the world, psychologists have discovered the causes of many different behaviours, both normal and abnormal. What you learn will help you to better understand your own actions as well as those of the people around you.

2. *You will learn about techniques that can help you modify your own behaviour.* Modern psychology has something to say about everything from the treatment of irrational fears (such as the fear of spiders) to the development of effective study skills to the design of technologies ranging from kitchen stoves to telephones to computers.

3. *You will encounter a method of inquiry that will help you constructively analyze your own behaviour and that of other people.* You will learn how researchers ask questions about behaviour, how they draw conclusions about cause and effect, and how they develop theories that allow them to predict when particular behaviours will occur.

4. *You will discover why people differ in their actions, thoughts, and feelings.* Most psychologists believe that human actions are governed by general principles, but any given instance of behaviour—such as how you will act at dinner tomorrow night—is determined by multiple causes. Your actions are shaped by your current environment, the culture in which you were raised, and the genetic material passed along to you by your biological parents. Much of psychology is concerned with studying how people differ from one another in their thinking and behaviour.

From psychology, you may learn things about yourself that conflict with your familiar view of everyday experience. For example, you will discover that your personal memories are not always accurate; instead, what you remember is an elaborate—and fallible—reconstruction of the past created by adaptive memory mechanisms in your brain. You will learn that some beliefs you hold about yourself—how you act and treat others—are not rock solid and unchanging, as you might think; instead, they can be easily changed in the face of a demanding environment. You may even start to question the amount of control you have over your own behaviour. We'll consider the possibility (although with a critical eye) that your actions are controlled by unconscious forces, evolutionary dispositions, biological drives, and external stimuli that are not under direct willful control.

So be forewarned: The content of this textbook may make you feel uncomfortable at times. What you'll learn may change the way you view yourself, the world, and others around you. That may seem rather unlikely at the moment, but it's a possibility we hope you find intriguing as you begin your journey into the adaptive mind.

Most psychologists believe that human thoughts and emotions arise from complex interactions between the brain, other organs of the body, and the environment.

Previewing the Scientific Problems

To help tackle the subject matter of psychology, each of the chapters in this textbook is organized around groups of problems that relate to everyday life. The purpose of this organizational scheme is to show you how people use psychological processes to help them adapt to their environment.

For example, one of the most important things that you learn about in your environment is that certain events are reliable predictors, or signals, of other events. If you're walking along a mountain path and hear a sudden rattling sound, it's useful to know that a dangerous snake might be lurking nearby. In Chapter 6, "Learning from Experience," you'll learn about a procedure that psychologists use to study how people learn about signals in their environment. This procedure, called *classical conditioning*, is a solution to an important problem: how we learn about events in the environment that can help us or hurt us. Similarly, in Chapter 3, "Biological Processes," you'll learn how we communicate information internally through the vast communication network of the nervous system. Internal communication is a crucial problem for your body to solve: If a cyclist suddenly weaves into the path of your car, the message needs to be communicated quickly and efficiently to the muscles controlling the foot-to-brake connection. The body uses its internal neural networks to solve this problem of internal communication.

When you encounter each new topic in a chapter, it is useful to ask yourself the following question: How does the psychological process under discussion help me solve an adaptive problem in my life? Each of us is constantly adjusting our actions, often in a flexible and strategic way, to meet the needs of new conditions as they arise. We each carry around with us a psychological tool kit that has evolved over millions of years and been sharpened and refined by our own personal learning experiences. Those tools enable us to initiate and control our behaviour in situation-appropriate ways. In the coming chapters, you'll see how these adaptive tools can be used to solve the obstacles and survival problems we face. (For a look ahead, you can find some of these tools listed in Table 1.1.)

In some instances, our focus will shift from adaptive problems that each of us solves toward particular problems that psychologists seek to solve, either to advance basic knowledge or to help

Table 1.1
Examples of Adaptive, Scientific, and Practical Problems

	Chapter	Problem to Be Solved	Example	Solution Tools
Adaptive problems	3	Communicating internally	A cyclist suddenly weaves into the path of your car.	Electrochemical transmission in the nervous system
	6	Learning what events signal	You hear a rattling tail on a mountain path.	Associations between events acquired through classical conditioning
	7	Remembering over the short term	You try to remember a telephone number as you cross the room.	Rehearsal in short-term memory
	13	Interpreting the behaviour of others	A shadowy figure emerges suddenly from an alleyway.	Knowledge-based social schemas used to predict outcomes
Scientific and practical problems	2	Determining the causes of behaviour	Sally watches a violent TV program and later behaves aggressively.	Experimental research
	9	Conceptualizing intelligence	Andy is excellent at fixing mechanical devices but is terrible at reading and math.	Psychometric tests designed to measure the mind
	14	Defining abnormality	Lucinda hears voices and thinks she's immortal.	*Diagnostic and Statistical Manual of Mental Disorders*
	15	Treating the mind	Ralph is mired in the depths of depression.	Psychoactive drug therapy and/or psychotherapy

Note: The solution tools shown in the far right column will be discussed in detail in the relevant chapters.

individuals in need. For instance, what are the best strategies to use to understand the cause of a behaviour (Chapter 2)? What are the best ways to conceptualize and then measure something as abstract as intelligence (Chapter 9)? Intelligence is not something that can be measured directly, like height or weight; it can only be inferred by measuring aspects of observable behaviour. How can abnormal behaviour be classified, and how can it be treated (Chapter 14)? These are practical problems that psychologists attempt to solve, and learning about the solutions and how they're reached is key to understanding how modern psychology works.

In this first chapter, you'll be exposed to three broad topics, which you can think of as conceptual problems that psychologists have attempted to solve. Each is designed to help acquaint you with the scientific study of behaviour and mind.

First, how do we define and describe psychology? That is, what are the topics with which this field is concerned, what methods are used to address those topics, and what are the goals of psychological study?

Second, how did current psychological perspectives develop? As you'll see, psychology as a scientific field has a short history, but the issues explored by psychologists have long captured the interest of scholars in other, older disciplines (especially philosophy and physiology). Understanding these historical roots will help you understand contemporary psychology.

Third, what is the dominant theoretical orientation of modern psychology? Over the course of more than 100 years since psychology first emerged as a distinct scientific field, various schools of thought have dominated psychological theory for periods of time. Such theoretical perspectives influence the questions psychologists ask, the methods they use, and the ways they apply their research. To anticipate, nowadays most psychologists combine multiple theoretical approaches, rather than adhering dogmatically to any single approach.

DEFINING AND DESCRIBING PSYCHOLOGY

Learning Goals
1. Learn the modern definition of psychology.
2. Be able to discuss the different ways of studying the mind scientifically.
3. Learn about what psychologists do, distinguishing between clinical, applied, and research psychologists.
4. Learn about the schooling and qualifications required to become a psychologist.

AS DEFINED EARLIER, psychology is the scientific study of behaviour and mind. The word comes from the Greek *psyche,* which translates as "soul" or "breath," and *logos,* which means the study or investigation of something (as in biology or physiology). The word *psychology* was not in common use before the 19th century, and it did not become an independent subject matter of science until around the middle of the 19th century (Boring, 1950). Until then, "the study of the mind," as psychology was widely known, was conducted mainly by philosophers and physiologists. Neither Sigmund Freud nor Ivan Pavlov, for example, was trained in psychology, despite their contributions to psychological theory and practice.

Notice that psychology is not simply the study of the mind; rather, it is the *scientific study of behaviour and mind.* The emphasis on science, and particularly the scientific method, helps to distinguish psychology from the related field of philosophy. An essential characteristic of the scientific method, as you'll see in Chapter 2, is *systematic observation:* Scientific knowledge is always based on some kind of direct or indirect observation. Psychologists collect observations, look for regularities, and then generate and test predictions based on what they've observed.

By **mind,** psychologists usually mean the contents and processes of subjective experience: sensations, thoughts, and emotions. Behaviour and mind are kept separate in the definition because only behaviour, not mind, can be directly measured by the scientific observer. Psychologists interpret the term **behaviour** in a quite general way. Besides referring to obvious actions such as moving, talking, and gesturing, many psychologists consider the activities of cells within the brain (as measured through

mind
The contents and processes of subjective experience: sensations, thoughts, and emotions.

behaviour
Observable actions such as moving, talking, gesturing, and so on; behaviours can also refer to the activities of cells, as measured through physiological recording devices, and to thoughts and feelings, as measured through oral and written expression.

The term *behaviour* can mean many things to a psychologist: overt actions, verbal reports of thoughts and feelings, and even activities of brain cells as measured by recordings of physiological activity in the brain.

Critical Thinking

Do you think it's possible to study behaviour independently of the mind? Or does all behaviour result from the actions of a willful mind? Cockroaches, snails, and starfish all behave, but do they have minds?

physiological recording devices) and the expressions of thoughts and feelings (as revealed through oral and written responses) to be types of "behaviour."

The Invisible and Dynamic Mind: How Can It Be Studied?

How can psychologists scientifically study the mind, given that it is invisible and largely intangible? Asking people to report their own subjective impressions about how their minds work provides us with some interesting and potentially valuable data (Ericsson & Simon, 1993), but a science of the mind and behaviour cannot rest solely on such subjective self-reports. As will be further discussed later in this chapter, such subjective self-reports may be inaccurate, and many mental processes are simply inaccessible to self-observation (Nisbett & Wilson, 1977).

What about looking inside the brain as a way of studying the invisible mind? Many research psychologists do measure brain structures and activities as a way of exploring psychological questions, as you'll see in Chapter 3. However, a complete understanding of the human mind cannot be obtained solely by examining the physical structures and processes of the brain. Similarly, if you wanted to understand how your computer's spellchecker works, prying the cover off your computer and looking at the hardware wouldn't get you very far. Instead, measurements of the brain must be taken in the context of studies that also measure people's responses to carefully constructed questions and tasks. Therefore, research psychologists often study human behaviour in controlled settings, measuring things such as reaction times and response accuracy (e.g., on tests of memory) to make inferences about how the mind works. Some researchers include measurements of the brain and/or people's subjective self-reports in their studies, whereas others focus exclusively on people's behaviour responses while performing tasks. A complete science of mind and behaviour requires a combination of all three of these sorts of measures: subjects' self-reports of their subjective impressions, their behavioural responses, and their physiological (including neurological) processes.

Figure 1.1 illustrates the above discussion by asking you to imagine the mind as a black box that you want to understand; it also illustrates the different ways you might attempt to understand how the box works. The black-box metaphor is useful because it is easy to understand; if the box emitted complex and sophisticated messages and you wanted to understand how it worked, you'd need to use a variety of converging methods to figure it out.

The black-box metaphor is limited, because the human brain and mind are not simple mechanical devices; rather, they are active, dynamic, living systems. Thus, understanding and predicting human behaviour is akin to understanding and predicting atmospheric phenomena such as rainstorms. Meteorologists have been studying the science of weather systems for a very long time, developing sophisticated

FIGURE 1.1
Studying the Mind

It is difficult to study the mind because mental events are not directly observable. Using the analogy of a black box, these three panels depict some of the ways that one might attempt to study the mind: (a) ask the box itself for insight (*self-report measures*); (b) pry the box open to see what's inside (*physiological measures*); or (c) measure the box's behaviour and look for regularities (*behavioural measures*). If the box's "behaviour" was sophisticated and complex, you'd probably need to combine all three of these methods to figure out how it worked.

instruments and elegant theories. Yet it remains difficult to forecast the weather with precision and accuracy, because the systems that control it are vast and dynamic, and they interact in extraordinarily complex ways. So, too, psychologists are far from developing a complete understanding of the human mind and behaviour but, as you'll see, we have made substantial progress toward revealing these intriguing mysteries.

What Psychologists Do

What do psychologists do on a daily basis? How do they earn a living? Where do they work? As shown in the Concept Summary on page 12, we can divide the job description into three main categories: *clinical psychologist, applied psychologist,* and *research psychologist.* These are not meant to be exclusive "either-or" categories—for example, clinical psychologists often work in applied settings and conduct research. The categorization scheme is designed merely to provide a useful way of subdividing the profession.

Clinical Psychologists Most people believe that all psychologists work at treating psychological problems such as depression, anxiety, phobias, or schizophrenia. Some psychologists, namely **clinical psychologists,** do indeed work in clinics or in private practice providing psychotherapy to individuals with psychological problems. Distinctions are often made between clinical and counselling psychologists, although the dividing line between the two is not clear and firm. **Counselling psychologists** generally deal with adjustment problems (e.g., marriage and family problems), whereas clinical psychologists tend to work with those kinds of problems as well as with more severe psychological disorders such as schizophrenia. Together, clinical and counselling psychologists make up the majority of psychologists: Over half of all the professionals working in psychology are actively involved in the treatment of people with psychological problems.

In most provinces, only clinical psychologists who have been certified by a regulatory body can call themselves "psychologists" to describe their professional services.

clinical psychologists
Professional psychologists who specialize in the diagnosis and treatment of psychological problems.

counselling psychologists
Professional psychologists who deal with milder problems, such as family and personal adjustment issues.

Several provinces require a doctoral-level degree, such as a Ph.D., to be certified as a psychologist, and the rest require at least a master's degree (see the subsequent section on "How to Become a Psychologist" for more information about such degrees). Almost all provinces require that clinical and counselling psychologists complete internships or supervised practice periods of one to four years, and achieve acceptable standards on professional psychology examinations. If you wish to check on the accreditation status of someone claiming to be a psychologist, you can contact your provincial Association of Professional Psychologists, or you can check his or her status with the Canadian Register of Health Service Providers in Psychology (www.crhspp.ca).

Not all individuals who help people with psychological problems have advanced training or degrees. For example, **counsellor** is a term used to describe individuals who provide some type of therapy or support-related service to clients. The term *counsellor* is not regulated by law in most provinces, and there are generally no minimum educational requirements for people who describe themselves as "counsellors" or "therapists." Most counsellors do not have doctoral-level degrees in their specialties, and many have not completed an internship or period of supervised practice. Some such individuals are highly skilled, but others are not. There are attempts underway in some provinces to set minimum professional requirements for specific counsellor designations such as "Registered Clinical Counsellor."

Psychiatrists are medical doctors who specialize in treating psychological and psychiatric problems. To become a psychiatrist you must graduate from medical school and then complete further specialized training in diagnosing and treating psychological/psychiatric disorders. Like clinical psychologists, psychiatrists are involved in the diagnosis and treatment of mental disorders, but unlike psychologists, they are licensed to prescribe drugs (although some states in the U.S. recently passed laws allowing psychologists with special training to prescribe a limited range of drugs; for commentaries on whether or not psychologists should be able to prescribe drugs, see DeNelsky, 1996; Hayes & Heiby, 1996; Sammons et al., 2000). Sometimes clinical psychologists, psychiatrists, and general practitioners work together. A clinical psychologist, for example, might refer a client to a psychiatrist or GP if he or she suspects that a physical problem might be involved or that drug therapy might be useful.

Applied Psychologists   Not all psychologists are concerned with understanding and treating abnormal behaviour or with helping people adjust. Many professional psychologists focus on "normal" people (we'll consider what it means to be normal or abnormal in Chapter 14). The goal of **applied psychologists** is to apply the principles of scientific psychology to practical, everyday problems in the real world. Applied psychologists work in various settings. For example, a *school psychologist* might work with students in primary and secondary schools to help them perform well academically and socially; an *industrial/organizational psychologist* might be employed in industry to help improve employee morale, train new recruits, or help managers establish effective lines of communication with their employees. *Human factors psychologists* play a key role in the design of new products: Why do you think telephone numbers are seven digits long, grouped in three, then four (e.g., 555-9378)? How about traffic lights—why red and green? Does it make a difference whether the word *delete, remove,* or *erase* is used in a word processing program? These are examples of practical problems that have been studied by human factors psychologists (Proctor & Van Zandt, 1994). See the Practical Solutions box for more information about human factors research in psychology.

Research Psychologists   Research psychologists conduct experiments and collect systematic observations in an effort to discover the basic principles of behaviour and mind. Research psychologists specialize in a variety of areas. *Biopsychologists,* for instance, seek to understand how biological or genetic factors influence and determine behaviour. *Personality psychologists* focus on the internal factors that lead people to act

counsellor
An individual who provides some sort of therapy or support to clients, but who (typically) does not have advanced training in providing psychological treatment. Some counsellors (or "therapists") are skilled and effective, but others are not.

psychiatrists
Medical doctors who specialize in the diagnosis and treatment of psychological problems. Unlike psychologists, psychiatrists are licensed to prescribe drugs.

applied psychologists
Psychologists who apply the principles of scientific psychology to practical, everyday problems in the world.

research psychologists
Psychologists who conduct experiments or collect observations designed to discover the basic principles of behaviour and mind.

Practical Solutions

THE PSYCHOLOGY OF STOVES AND DOORS

At the beginning of the chapter, we mentioned that psychologists have something to say about a variety of topics—even the design of the kitchen stove. You may not have thought too much about the role of psychology in stove design, but remember: Between every machine and its successful operation is a user, a human being. It's this human factor that often determines whether the product will be a success or a disaster. Let's see how a modern psychologist might analyze proper and improper stove design.

Does your stove look like the one depicted in the left panel of Figure 1.2? One of the authors of this textbook (JSN) has such a stove. There are four burners, arranged in a rectangle, and four control knobs that line up horizontally along the front (or sometimes the back). Your job as a user is to learn the relationship, or what psychologists call the *mapping,* between the control knobs and each burner. In this case you need to learn that the far left knob controls the back burner on the left. Or is it the front burner on the left? If you have a stove like this, which is psychologically incorrect, the odds are that you have trouble remembering which knob controls which burner. The reason is simple: The stove has been designed with an unnatural mapping between its controls and the burners. (By the way, the stove came with the house.)

"Mapping" is easier to understand when you look at a psychologically correct

design, as depicted in the middle panel of Figure 1.2. Notice in this case that the arrangement of the burners naturally aligns with the controls. The left-to-right display of the control knobs matches the left-to-right arrangement of the burners. There is no need to learn the mapping in this case: It's obvious at first sight which knob controls which burner. Alternatively, if you want to keep the rectangular arrangement of the stove top, then simply arrange the control knobs in a rectangular manner that matches the burners, as shown in the far right panel. The point is that there are natural and unnatural ways to express the relationship between product control and product function. Taking advantage of the natural mapping requires that you consider the human factor—in this case, the fact that humans tend to rely on spatial similarity (left knob to left burner; right knob to right burner).

As we've stressed in this chapter, humans interact with the world with an adaptive tool kit—we tend to use certain strategies that have evolved over countless generations of interacting with objects in our natural environment. The stove example is a very simple one, yet it illustrates our natural tendency to map or link objects that share spatial nearness or similarity to one another. The more general point to be made is that it is crucial to take people's natural tendencies into account when designing devices for human use. As another example of that point, have

Examples of psychologically incorrect and correct door designs.

you ever encountered a door like that shown in the top photo? The "push bar" clearly signals you to push, but you may have slammed your shoulder into such doors because they fail to signal which side opens. Likewise, the middle door has a large flat plate, which invites a natural response of pushing, not pulling. The fact that this door has a large "PULL" sign indicates how poorly it is designed. The bottom door, in contrast, is well designed: The large flat shape invites a natural pushing response, and the top plate on the left indicates which side should be pushed. The same issues arise in the design of more complex devices, such as cars and computers. Good design requires consideration of the human factor.

FIGURE 1.2
The Human Factors of Stove Design
The stove on the left does not provide a natural "mapping" between the control knobs and the burners and is therefore difficult to use. The stoves in the middle and on the right provide psychologically correct designs that reduce user errors.

11

Concept Summary

TYPES OF PSYCHOLOGISTS

Type of Psychologist	Guiding Focus	Primary Workplace	Examples of What They Do
Counselling psychologists	Treatment of adjustment problems	Clinics Private practice Universities and colleges	Counsel clients suffering from adjustment problems.
Clinical psychologists	Diagnosis and treatment of psychological problems	Clinics Private practice Universities and colleges	Counsel clients suffering from adjustment problems or more severe psychological problems; evaluate diagnostic techniques and therapy effectiveness.
Applied psychologists	Applying psychological principles to practical problems in the world	Private industry Schools Universities and colleges	Help performance of students in school; improve employee morale and performance at work; design computers so that humans can use them efficiently.
Research psychologists	Conduct research to discover the basic principles of behaviour and mind	Academic settings Private industry	Conduct experiments on the best study method for improving memory; assess the impact of daycare on children's attachment to their parents; observe the effects of others on a person's helping behaviour.

consistently in different situations, and that make people behave differently from each other. *Cognitive psychologists* research higher mental processes such as memory, learning, and reasoning. *Developmental psychologists* study how people's behaviour and thinking change over the course of a lifetime. *Social psychologists* are interested in how people think about, influence, and relate to each other. These are just a few of the specialties that research psychologists adopt. As you work your way through the chapters of this text, you will be exposed to a wide range of research interests.

How to Become a Psychologist

These days, most people who become psychologists majored in psychology as undergraduates, so if you are interested in a career in psychology then majoring in psychology is a sensible first step. Many students do not appreciate that the decisions they make during their first few years in university have long-term consequences. If you want to do well in the long run, it is important to learn the requirements of various potential majors. It is also important to earn good marks, even in your first-year courses, partly because admission to higher-level courses may be contingent on good marks in the earlier courses. Most, if not all, Canadian psychology departments have optional honours programs; earning an honours degree will give you a substantial advantage if you decide that you want to go on in psychology. Honours programs have quite stringent criteria; every year we encounter third-year students who would like to be in an honours program but are rejected because their grade-point averages are too low.

It also helps to get to know individual faculty members and advanced students. To go on for further education or get a skilled job after earning your undergraduate degree, you are likely to need letters of reference from several professors. Those letters will be much better if the professors who write them have had a chance to get to know you and can comment in detail about your skills and abilities. Ask questions in class. If your professors have office hours, go to them occasionally. If your department offers independent studies courses (sometimes called directed studies), consider taking such a course. Look for opportunities to work in professors' laboratories (or in community settings that are related to psychology) as a volunteer. Doing these things will make it easier to get good letters of reference, and will also enhance your résumé.

As Dr. Margaret Lloyd explains in her extraordinarily helpful Web site Careers in Psychology (www.psywww.com/careers/index.htm), students who earn a bachelor's degree in psychology typically develop analytical thinking skills, "people" skills, and writing skills that prepare them for a wide variety of entry-level jobs. These include jobs related to counselling, social work, business, corrections, health, recreation, and education. It is possible to find work in these areas with a bachelor's degree, but those positions have certain limitations (e.g., you would likely work under supervision, with limited authority and pay).

To become a clinical psychologist, you would first need to earn a bachelor's degree and then gain admittance to a graduate program in clinical psychology. Canadian clinical psychology graduate programs have extremely stringent criteria for admission (as do programs in the U.S.); only students with very strong academic records are likely to be admitted. Completing a graduate degree in clinical psychology is a major undertaking: Students typically take two to three years to complete their master's degree, and then go on to spend another three or more years completing their doctoral degree, followed by an internship in which they further hone their clinical skills by working under supervision. Note that, as mentioned above, psychiatrists get their postgraduate training in medical school.

Qualifications for a career in research or applied psychology also begin with a bachelor's degree followed by graduate school. There is less competition for spaces in nonclinical psychology graduate programs, and therefore it is somewhat easier to gain admission (although only students with quite strong academic records are likely to be admitted). Here too, graduate school begins with two to three years of work toward a master's degree. Some graduate programs in nonclinical psychology are designed to terminate with the master's degree, and it is certainly possible to find a variety of good jobs with a master's degree in psychology. Most psychology graduate programs, however, are oriented toward a doctoral degree, which typically requires another two to three years of study and research beyond the master's. Almost all Canadian psychology professors, for example, have doctoral degrees.

You can see that it takes quite a commitment to earn the necessary qualifications for a career in psychology. We hope you'll also come to see, through reading this book, how incredibly rewarding and interesting such a career can be.

Test Yourself 1.1

Test your knowledge about how best to define and describe psychology by deciding whether each of the following statements is true or false. (You will find the answers in Appendix B.)

1. Psychologists use the term *behaviour* to refer only to observable responses, such as moving, talking, gesturing, and electrical activity in brain cells. Subjective internal events, such as thoughts and feelings, are not studied within scientific psychology. *True or False?*

2. Psychology did not exist as a separate subject matter of science 150 years ago. Until then, questions having to do with the mind were explored primarily by philosophers. *True or False?*

3. Clinical psychologists restrict themselves to diagnosing and treating psychological problems such as depression or anxiety disorders, and do not conduct basic research. *True or False?*

4. Psychiatrists differ from clinical psychologists primarily in their focus of interest. Psychiatrists tend to work on severe and chronic problems, such as schizophrenia, whereas psychologists restrict their practice to milder problems, such as phobias and relationship problems. *True or False?*

5. The highest level of formal training in psychology is the master's degree. *True or False?*

TRACING THE EVOLUTION OF PSYCHOLOGICAL THOUGHT

Learning Goals

1. Be able to explain what is meant by the mind–body problem.
2. Understand differing viewpoints on the origins of knowledge.
3. Be able to outline the development of the first scientific schools of psychology: structuralism, functionalism, and behaviourism.
4. Discuss the early clinical contributions of Freud and the humanistic psychologists.
5. Learn about some of the contributions women researchers have made to the science of psychology.

THE FIELD OF SCIENTIFIC PSYCHOLOGY may have a relatively short past, but the study of psychological issues has a long and distinguished intellectual history. Thousands of years ago, the Greek philosopher Aristotle (384–322 B.C.) wrote extensively on such topics as memory, sleep, and sensation. Today, these topics form an important part of the subject matter of psychology. Aristotle argued that the mind of a baby could be seen as a kind of *tabula rasa*—a blank slate—upon which experiences are written to form the basis of knowledge. The idea that knowledge arises directly from experience, a philosophical position known as **empiricism,** continues to be an important aspect of modern psychological thought (although few modern psychologists would agree with the idea that we are born with "blank" minds).

empiricism

The idea that knowledge comes directly from experience.

Critical Thinking

Psychology is the scientific study of behaviour and mind. Is it really surprising, then, that its intellectual roots lie in physiology and philosophy?

Mind and Body: Are They the Same?

As mentioned earlier, the intellectual roots of modern psychology lie in the disciplines of *philosophy* and *physiology*. Psychology has always occupied a "middle ground" between these two areas (Bolles, 1993; Hunt, 1993). Ancient philosophers such as Aristotle and Plato helped to frame many of the fundamental questions that occupy the attention of psychologists today: Where does knowledge come from? What are the laws that govern sensory processes? How do we learn and remember?

Physiologists, on the other hand, focus on the workings of the human body. Years of research on the mechanics of physical movement and the anatomy of sensory systems produced volumes of data that were later used to develop a *scientific* understanding of behaviour and mind. In 1833, the German physiologist Johannes Müller published the enormously influential *Handbook of Human Physiology* that proposed links between the nervous system and psychological effects. By the 1860s, clear connections had been established between brain damage and the loss of mental functions, such as language ability. Advances in brain research continue to influence psychological theory. We'll discuss some of these advances in Chapter 3 and later in this chapter.

Descartes' Solution   A fundamental problem in psychology involves the relationship between the physical *body,* as studied by the physiologists, and the *mind,* as studied by philosophers. Are the mind and body separate and distinct, or are they one and the same? Do they interact in ways we can understand? Can we learn anything about one by studying the other? In the 17th century, the French philosopher René Descartes (1596–1650) argued that the mind and body are separate: The physical body, he claimed, cannot "think," nor is it possible to explain "thinking" by appealing to physical matter. He did allow for the possibility, however, that one could significantly influence the other. The *mind,* he argued, controls the actions of a mechanical *body* through the pineal gland, a small structure at the base of the brain; Descartes did not, however, explain exactly how this would work (see Figure 1.3).

Descartes stated the mind–body problem clearly, and his description of the human body in machine-like terms had an important influence on generations of physiologists. His specific ideas about the body turned out to be largely incorrect—the pineal gland, for example, plays a role in producing hormones, not muscle movements—but some of his ideas remain influential today. It was Descartes, for instance, who first introduced the concept of a *reflex*. Reflexes are automatic, involuntary reactions of the body to events in the environment. As you'll see in Chapter 3, reflexes play a very important role in our survival. But his solution to the mind–body problem did little to advance the scientific study of the mind. Talking about the mind as something separate from the physical world places the subject matter of psychology outside the boundaries of science. The scientific method is based on observation, and it's impossible to study something scientifically unless it is lawfully related to observable phenomena.

Mind as a Product of Brain Activity   Most modern psychologists reject Descartes' separation of mind and body and assume there is no essential division between the two. The mind is considered to be a direct product of brain activity; put simply, the mind is what the brain does. Although we are still far from a complete understanding of how subjective mental states arise from physical processes in the brain and body, most psychologists believe that psychology is making progress toward solving this fascinating problem (e.g., Damasio, 2000; Pinker, 1997a; Searle et al., 1997). As you'll read in this text, there is an extremely close link between the operation of the brain and behaviour. Many psychological problems appear to come directly from problems in the operation of the brain, and many of the symptoms can be treated effectively through biological means (usually the administration of drugs).

Nature and Nurture: Where Does Knowledge Come From?

Philosophers and psychologists have long sought to determine the origins of knowledge. Where does knowledge come from? As noted earlier, Aristotle adopted an empiricist position: He believed that knowledge comes entirely from our day-to-day experiences. Empiricism can be contrasted with a philosophical position called **nativism,** which holds that certain kinds of knowledge are inborn, or innate.

Nativists believe that babies arrive into the world knowing certain things, prior to any experience. For example, the German philosopher Immanuel Kant (1724–1804) believed that humans are born with a certain mental "structure" that determines how they perceive the world. He argued that people are born with a natural tendency to see things in terms of cause and effect and to interpret the world in terms of space and time (Bolles, 1993; Wertheimer, 1987). Nativists do not believe that all knowledge is present at birth, but they reject the idea that all knowledge comes directly from experience.

Darwin's Theory of Evolution   Charles Darwin (1809–1882) provided some of the most important conceptual foundations of modern thinking about the human mind. Darwin proposed that all living things are products of an extended period of evolution, guided by the principles of natural selection. Cats have fur, seals have thick skin, and babies cry because these physical and behavioural traits have been selected for during the evolutionary history of the species. By *natural selection,* Darwin meant that some individuals survive and reproduce more than others because the successful individuals have heritable traits that make them better than others at overcoming obstacles and solving the problems present in their environment. For example, if an inborn tendency to cry helps to communicate feelings about hunger effectively, then crying increases the likelihood that one will live long enough to pass this natural tendency on to offspring. Such tendencies are selected for naturally because they are *adaptive*—they improve the chances for meeting the needs demanded by the environment (Darwin, 1859, 1871).

Darwin believed that the principles of natural selection apply to characteristics that pass from parents to their offspring—not only physical traits, but behavioural and psychological traits as well. By emphasizing the adaptive value of inherited characteristics, including psychological characteristics, Darwin's ideas greatly influenced psychological theorizing (Dennett, 1995). Psychologists now generally agree, for example, that humans have an inherited predisposition to acquire language, much as birds have an inherited predisposition to fly (Pinker, 1994).

FIGURE 1.3
Descartes and Reflex

René Descartes introduced the concept of the reflex, which he described as an automatic, involuntary reaction of a mechanical body to an event in the world. He erroneously thought the mediating structure was the pineal gland, shown here as a tear-shaped object in the back of the head.

nativism
The idea that certain kinds of knowledge and ideas are innate, or present at birth; innate ideas do not need to be learned.

Charles Darwin believed that both physical and psychological characteristics were selected for their adaptive value.

Certain physical characteristics, such as camouflage, are selected for in nature because they are adaptive; they improve the chances of an organism surviving and reproducing.

Nature Plus Nurture Today, it is widely recognized that most psychological phenomena—intelligence, emotion, personality—are influenced by innate genetic factors. At the same time, psychologists also agree that personal experience also plays a critically important role in thought, emotions, and behaviour. How a genetic message is expressed depends on an interaction between the genetic information and environmental influences during development. Recognition of this interaction has led virtually all psychologists to the following generalization: Human mind and behaviour are influenced by both nature (innate factors) and nurture (experience). So, the solution to the nature versus nurture debate isn't nature *or* nurture; it's nature *plus* nurture. A continuing challenge for psychologists is to discover the respective roles that innate and learned factors play in any given instance of behaviour.

The First Schools: Psychology as Science

The first psychological laboratory was established in 1879 at the University of Leipzig by a German professor named Wilhelm Wundt (1832–1920). Wundt was a medical doctor by training, and early in his career he worked with some of the great physiologists of the 19th century. Fittingly, Wundt was a professor of philosophy when he established his psychology laboratory. (Remember, the intellectual roots of psychology lie at the union of philosophy and physiology.) Wundt is traditionally recognized as the founder of modern scientific psychology, and 1879 is seen as the year that psychology finally emerged as a unique field separate from philosophy and physiology. Prior to Wundt, there were no independent psychology departments or officially recognized psychologists (Bolles, 1993).

It is noteworthy that the birth of psychology is identified with the establishment of an experimental laboratory. Wundt's background in physiological research convinced him that the proper approach to the study of mental events was to conduct experiments. He believed that controlled observations should be collected about the phenomena of mind in the same way that one might observe twitching frog legs in an effort to understand the principles of nerve conduction. Wundt wasn't sure that all mental processes could be studied in this way, but he committed himself wholeheartedly to the use of scientific techniques.

Structuralism Wundt (1896) believed that psychology should be the study of immediate conscious experience, by which he meant the things that people sense and perceive when they reflect inward on their own minds. Wundt analyzed conscious experience in terms of *elements*—primarily sensations and feelings—and he suggested

Wilhelm Wundt, circa 1912, established the first psychological laboratory at the University of Leipzig in 1879.

it was the job of the psychologist to identify these elements and discover how they combine to produce meaningful wholes. This general approach was later named **structuralism** by one of Wundt's students, Edward Titchener (1867–1927). Structuralists believe that psychologists should seek to understand the *structure* of the mind by breaking it down into elementary parts, much like a chemist might try to understand a chemical compound (Titchener, 1899).

The structuralists amassed volumes of data about subjects' reports of their elementary sensory experiences. Titchener's laboratory, for example, was one of the first to document that complex tastes could be broken down into combinations of four elementary tastes: salty, bitter, sour, and sweet (Webb, 1981; as you'll see in Chapter 4, researchers have recently confirmed the existence of a fifth elementary taste, called *umami*).

Functionalism Once pioneer researchers such as Wundt helped establish psychology as an independent scientific discipline, psychology departments began to spring up rapidly throughout the world. This was particularly true in North America, where dozens of psychological laboratories were established in the two decades from 1880 to 1900 (Hilgard, 1987). In Canada, James Mark Baldwin established a psychological laboratory at the University of Toronto in 1891; this event is generally considered to signify the beginning of an independent science of psychology in Canada (Hoff, 1992). By 1890, psychologists had established several journals for reporting research results, and influential psychology textbooks had been published (e.g., James, 1890).

North American psychologists quickly departed from the strict structuralist approach advocated by many European psychologists. Whereas structuralists focused on the *content* of immediate experience, dissecting the mind into parts, North American psychologists worried more about the *function* of immediate experience. What is the *purpose* of the mental operations that underlie immediate experience? How are the components of mind used to achieve this end? Because the emphasis was on function rather than content, this school of thought became known as **functionalism.** Functionalists believe that it's not the analysis of structure but the analysis of function and purpose that should occupy the attention of psychologists (Dewey, 1896; James, 1890).

Functionalists such as William James (1842–1910) were convinced that it's not possible to understand a system like the mind by simply looking at its parts; that's like trying to understand a house by analyzing its bricks and mortar (James, 1884). It's necessary to first understand the goal—what the mental operation is designed to achieve—then you can try to decipher how the individual parts work together to achieve that goal. For example, to understand how memory works, you must first consider the purpose of memory: What specific problems do our memory systems help us solve in our everyday environments?

Darwin's ideas about evolution through natural selection were extremely influential in the development of functionalist thinking. If you want to analyze the colour markings on a butterfly's wings, a Darwinian theorist would argue, you must ask how those markings help the butterfly survive. Similarly, when analyzing the operations and processes of mind, a functionalist would argue, we need to focus first on the adaptive value of those operations—how they help people solve the problems they face.

Functionalism had a liberalizing effect on the development of psychology in North America. It greatly expanded the range of topics that scientific psychology could approach. For example, it became important to study how an organism interacts with its environment, which led to an early emphasis on learning (Thorndike, 1898) and to the study of individual differences (how people differ from one another). Later, some functionalists turned their attention to applied issues, such as how people solve practical problems in industry and in educational settings (e.g., Taylor, 1911). To a functionalist, just about any aspect of behaviour or mind was considered fair game for study, and psychology in Canada and the United States boomed.

structuralism

An early school of psychology; structuralists attempted to understand the mind by breaking it down into its basic constituent parts, much like a chemist might try to understand a chemical compound.

James Mark Baldwin opened the first Canadian psychology research laboratory in 1891 at the University of Toronto.

functionalism

An early school of psychology; functionalists believe that the proper way to understand mind and behaviour is to analyze their function and purpose. You can only truly understand a mental process, functionalists argue, by first knowing the purpose of that process.

William James, shown here in 1868, was convinced that to understand a mental process, it's important to consider its function: How does the process help the individual solve problems in the environment?

John B. Watson rejected the study of the mind in favour of the study of observable behaviour.

B. F. Skinner championed the behaviourist approach and was one of the most influential psychologists of the 20th century.

behaviourism
A school of psychology proposing that the proper subject matter of psychology is directly observable behaviour and the situations that lead to changes in behaviour, rather than immediate conscious experience.

Behaviourism Psychology changed even more radically from 1900 to 1920. Although functionalism and structuralism differed in their emphases, both perspectives considered that the fundamental aim of psychology was to understand immediate conscious experience. The great functionalist William James, in particular, is well known for his superb analysis of the content and purpose of consciousness, which he compared to a flowing and ever-changing stream (see Chapter 5). Around 1900, the technique of *introspection*—looking inward to observe one's own mind—was the primary research method of the experimental psychologist. That is, researchers would present certain stimuli and tasks to subjects and ask them to introspect and report about their perceptions, thoughts, and feelings while doing those tasks.

Yet not all psychologists were convinced that self-observation could produce valid scientific data. By definition, self-observations are private, and there is no way to be certain that a person's reports accurately reflect their mental experiences. It was also recognized that introspection might change the mental operations being observed. If you're concentrating intently on introspecting about your perceptions of, say, a banana, you are probably experiencing "banana" in an atypical way—not as something to eat, but rather as a complex collection of sensations. Also, people lack introspective awareness of how their minds accomplish certain tasks (e.g., what are the mental processes that enable you to read these words?). Because of these problems, different laboratories often reported conflicting findings. The introspective method also limited the people and topics that could be studied; it's difficult to ask someone with a severe mental disorder, for example, to introspect and report systematically on his or her condition (Marx & Cronan-Hillix, 1987).

Starting around 1910, psychologists began to question the usefulness of studying immediate conscious experience. A shift began toward studying behaviour, rather than consciousness. The spokesperson of this new movement was a young professor at Johns Hopkins University named John B. Watson (1878–1958). Watson believed that psychology should discard all references to consciousness or mental events. Such events cannot be publicly observed, he argued, and therefore fall outside of the proper domain of science. Observable behaviour should be the proper subject matter of psychology, and the aim of the scientific researcher is to discover how changes in the environment can lead to changes in measurable behaviour. Because of its emphasis on behaviour, Watson called this new way of thinking **behaviourism** (Watson, 1913, 1919).

Behaviourism had an enormous impact on the development of psychology, particularly in North America. Remember, the psychology of Wundt and James was the psychology of mind and immediate experience. Yet by the 1920s, references to consciousness or immediate experience had largely vanished from the psychological vocabulary, as had the technique of systematic introspection. Researchers now concerned themselves with measuring behaviour, especially in animals, and studying how controlled laboratory conditions could change behaviour (Hull, 1943; Skinner, 1938). Influential psychologists such as B. F. Skinner (1904–1990) provided repeated demonstrations of the practical value of the behaviourist approach. Skinner discovered principles of behaviour modification—how behaviour changes in response to reinforcement and nonreinforcement—that are now widely used in such settings as mental hospitals, schools, and the workplace (Skinner, 1969). We'll discuss these principles in some detail in Chapter 6.

The behaviourist approach dominated psychology for decades. However, as you'll see later in this chapter, its influence was not to last forever. To help you put things in perspective, the Concept Summary on page 20 summarizes the three main schools of psychology's early days.

1a, 10a, 10c

Freud and the Humanists: The Influence of the Clinic

At roughly the same time psychology in North America was undergoing its behaviourist reformation, a medical doctor practising in Vienna was mounting his own psychological revolution. Sigmund Freud (1856–1939) was trained as a neurologist (someone who studies the nervous system), but his psychological insights came not from the laboratory but from his experiences as a clinician. Freud regularly encountered patients whose physical problems appeared to him to be psychological in origin. Freud's efforts to treat these disorders led him to a comprehensive theory of mind that influenced legions of future psychologists and psychiatrists (Freud, 1900, 1910, 1940).

Psychoanalysis Freud called his theory of mind and system of therapy **psychoanalysis.** He believed that the mind and its contents—the *psyche*—must be *analyzed* extensively before effective treatments can begin. In his view, psychological problems need to be solved through *insight:* The patient needs to understand exactly how his or her mental processes lead to problem behaviours. For this reason, psychoanalysis is often referred to as a form of "insight" therapy.

Among Freud's major contributions were his ideas about unconscious determinants of behaviour. Freud believed each person has a hidden reservoir in the mind, filled with memories, urges, and conflicts that influence actions but that are not accessible to conscious awareness. Freud proposed that the conscious mind blocks people from consciously experiencing certain feelings and memories. If you accept Freud's reasoning, it follows that psychology should not be based solely on the study of immediate experience because thoughts and behaviours are influenced by unconscious forces.

Although Freud worked outside of mainstream developments in scientific psychology, he too would have rejected systematic introspection as a viable technique for the analysis of mind—but for reasons different from the behaviourists. Freud believed that recording immediate experience was of interest, but only as a way of discovering hidden conflicts and desires. Freud relied instead on the analysis of dreams—which he believed were largely symbolic—slips of the tongue, and free associations as his primary investigative data (although he also asked patients to report their conscious recollections of childhood). Freud spent hours listening to his patients relate their latest dreams or fantasies in the hope of discovering some symbolic key that would unlock the contents of his patients' unconscious minds. His complex analyses of the mind and its symbols led him to develop a theory of how the unconscious mind defends itself from those seeking to unlock its secrets. We'll consider this theory, as well as its applications for the treatment of psychological disorders, in more detail in Chapters 12 and 15.

In addition to emphasizing unconscious influences on behaviour, Freud believed that childhood experiences play an important role in shaping adult behaviour. He suggested that children go through stages of psychological development that involve a complex interplay between innate sexual urges and experience. He proposed, for example, that boys become erotically attached to their mothers during childhood and consequently experience anxiety about potential castration by their father. These urges and anxieties are unconscious, of course, so the adult male is unlikely consciously to remember these conflicts. Freud's theory was considered shocking when it was first introduced (during the highly moralistic Victorian era), and it continues to be criticized today. For example, Freud has been criticized for being biased against women (Lerman, 1986; Masson, 1984). However, there is no denying the impact of psychoanalytic thought. Psychodynamic theories of human personality—those that stress unconscious but emotionally charged forces in determining behaviour—continue to influence modern psychology.

The Humanistic Response Freud's influence was substantial, especially among clinicians seeking to treat psychologically disturbed patients. The familiar image of the client lying on a couch talking about his or her childhood, while the therapist silently jots down notes, is a fairly accurate description of the way early psychoanalysis was performed. However, not all psychologists were comfortable with this approach. Freudian psychology paints a pessimistic view of human nature. It presents human

Sigmund Freud, developer of psychoanalysis, is shown here in the early 1920s.

psychoanalysis
A term used by Freud to describe his theory of mind and system of therapy, which involves analyzing the conscious mind to discover underlying unconscious influences.

Critical Thinking

Although Freud was not technically a psychologist—he was a medical doctor—would you classify him as a clinical, an applied, or a research psychologist?

humanistic psychology
A movement in psychology that emerged largely as a reaction against the pessimism of Freud. Humanistic psychologists focus on people's unique capacity for choice, responsibility, and growth.

Carl Rogers helped develop the humanistic perspective, which focuses on our unique capacity for self-awareness, responsibility, and growth.

actions as the product of unconscious animalistic urges related to sex and aggression. Moreover, it dismisses any awareness that people might have about why they act the way they do as symbolic and misleading; instead, people's actions are really motivated by deeply hidden conflicts of which they are unaware.

In the 1950s, negative reactions to Freud's view of therapy and mind led to the development of a new movement known as **humanistic psychology.** Humanistic psychologists such as Carl Rogers (1905–1987) and Abraham Maslow (1908–1970) rejected the pessimistic views of Freud and focused instead on the unique human capacity for self-awareness, choice, responsibility, and growth. The humanists argued that people are not helpless unknowing animals, controlled by unconscious forces; they are ultimately in control of their own destinies and can rise above innate sexual or animalistic urges. Humans are built for personal growth, to seek their fullest potential, to become all they are capable of being (Maslow, 1954; Rogers, 1951).

The optimistic message of the humanists played a significant role in theories of personality development as well as in the treatment of psychological disorders. Carl Rogers, for example, promoted the idea of *client-centred therapy,* in which the therapist is seen not as an analyst or judge, but rather as a supporter and friend. Humanistic psychologists believe that all individuals have untapped potential that can be nurtured by an empathic therapist. This idea remains influential among modern psychological approaches to therapy (see Chapters 12 and 15).

Pioneers: The Influence of Women

The American Psychological Association (APA) was founded in 1892 and quickly became an important and influential professional organization. Mary Whiton Calkins was elected president of the APA in 1905. It's worth drawing special attention to this accomplishment because women have often been overlooked in historical treatments of psychology (Scarborough & Furumoto, 1987). The success of Mary Calkins is espe-

Concept Summary

EARLY APPROACHES TO THE STUDY OF PSYCHOLOGY

General Focus	Specific Approach	Important Figure(s)	Focuses of Approach
Research	Structuralism	Wundt, Titchener	Determining the structure of immediate conscious experience through the use of *systematic introspection,* in which one attempts to describe the fundamental elements associated with simple thoughts and sensations.
	Functionalism	James, Dewey	Determining the *functions* of conscious experience through the use of introspection, naturalistic observation, and the measurement of individual differences. Influenced by Darwin, it greatly expanded the range of topics studied in psychology.
	Behaviourism	Watson, Skinner	Establishing laws of observable *behaviour*. The approach rejects the study of immediate conscious experience and mental events, unless they are defined in terms of observable behaviour. It was the dominant approach to scientific psychology until the "cognitive revolution" of the 1950s.
Clinical	Psychoanalytic	Freud	Analyzing personality and treating psychological disorders by focusing on *unconscious* determinants of behaviour. Also contends that childhood experiences play an important role in shaping adult behaviour.
	Humanistic	Rogers, Maslow	Each person's unique *self*, and capacity for growth. Developing partly as a reaction against Freud, it emphasized that humans are basically good and have a unique capacity for self-awareness, choice, responsibility, and growth.

cially noteworthy, considering the significant discrimination against women in the early days of psychology. Calkins, for example, was denied admittance to Harvard University (as were all women), and she was only allowed to take classes with William James as a "guest" graduate student. She passed the final examinations for the Ph.D., but was never officially awarded the degree.

Calkins made a number of contributions to the science of psychology, including the development of the paired-associate learning technique (a method for studying memory that is still in use today); she was also a major contributor to philosophy. The first woman to receive a Ph.D. in psychology was Margaret Floy Washburn (in 1894), who in 1921 went on to become the second woman president of the American Psychological Association. Washburn's early contributions were in the structuralist tradition—she published her dissertation in one of Wundt's journals—and later she became very well known for her book *The Animal Mind* (1908) and for her behavioural views on consciousness.

Canada has a long and impressive history in the science of psychology, and that history includes important contributions from many women psychologists. One of the best known and most influential Canadian women psychologists was Mary Salter Ainsworth (1913–1999). Ainsworth was a major in the Canadian Women's Army Corps during World War II and returned to the University of Toronto after the war to resume a position as a faculty member (Wright, 1992). Her early contributions were important; for example, she helped validate the famous Rorschach inkblot projective test. However, it was while working with her English colleague, John Bowlby, that she made pioneering contributions to our understanding of the process by which children become socially and emotionally attached to their parents (e.g., Ainsworth & Bowlby, 1954; Ainsworth & Wittig, 1969).

Canadian women have continued to play major roles in modern scientific psychology. For example, Brenda Milner of the Montreal Neurological Institute and McGill University is highly celebrated as one of the pioneers of neuropsychology, famed for her brilliant studies of patients with various kinds of brain damage. Another leading Canadian woman psychologist is Doreen Kimura, who has had tremendous impact on the study of biological influences on human cognition and behaviour. Professor Kimura, who was on the faculty of the University of Western Ontario for some 30 years and now holds a position at Simon Fraser University, is particularly known for her studies of gender-related hormones and of differences between right- and left-handed individuals.

In the coming chapters, you'll read more about the contributions of women to psychology, and you'll find that the influence of women researchers has grown decade by decade, so that today women researchers are represented in virtually all areas of psychology (see Storm & Gurevich, 2001, for critical reviews). Over the years, the study of the psychology of women has also grown dramatically (e.g., Boehnert, 1993), as has the examination of gender differences and similarities in many areas of psychological functioning (e.g., Kimura, 1999; Silverman & Phillips, 1998).

Mary Whiton Calkins was the first female president of the American Psychological Association. She passed the final examinations for the Ph.D., but was never officially awarded the degree.

Mary Salter Ainsworth, a pioneer Canadian psychologist and an important contributor to the study of child–parent attachment.

Test Yourself 1.2

Test your knowledge about how thinking in psychology developed by answering the following questions. (You will find the answers in Appendix B.)

1. Most modern psychologists believe that the mind and the body are:
   a. controlled by different sections of the pineal gland.
   b. best considered as one and the same.
   c. separate, but both can be studied with the scientific method.
   d. best studied by philosophers and physiologists, respectively.

2. Fill in the blanks in the following paragraph. Choose your answers from the following set of terms: behaviour; behaviourism; emotions; empiricists; functionalists; introspection; structuralists; thoughts.

Functionalists and structuralists used the technique of _____ to understand immediate conscious experience. The _____ believed that it was best to break the mind down into basic parts, much like a chemist would seek to understand a chemical compound. The _____ were influenced by Darwin's views on natural selection and focused primarily on the purpose and adaptive value of mental events. _____, founded by John Watson, steered psychology away from the study of immediate conscious experience toward an emphasis on _____.

3. Freud's psychoanalysis differs from Rogers's humanistic approach in which of the following ways?
   a. Psychoanalysis is "client centred" rather than "therapist centred."
   b. Psychoanalysis is designed to promote self-awareness and personal growth.
   c. Psychoanalysis minimizes the influence of early childhood experiences.
   d. Psychoanalysis is designed to reveal hidden urges and memories related to sex and aggression.

4. Who was Mary Salter Ainsworth, and for what research was she particularly well known?

UNDERSTANDING THE FOCUS OF MODERN PSYCHOLOGY

Learning Goals

1. Understand what it means to adopt an eclectic approach to psychology.

2. Be able to discuss the origins and central premises of the cognitive revolution.

3. Learn about recent developments in biology and neuroscience and how they have influenced modern psychology.

4. Understand how natural selection contributed to the evolution of the adaptive human mind.

5. Appreciate why psychologists believe that cultural factors are important determinants of behaviour and mind.

6. Grasp how psychologists strive to use their own adaptive minds to understand how and why people do and feel the things they do.

PSYCHOLOGY HAS CHANGED SUBSTANTIALLY since Wundt established the first psychological laboratory in 1879 (see Robins et al., 1999, for an empirical analysis of trends in modern psychology). Psychologists have argued—often for decades—about the proper focus for psychology (mind or behaviour?), about how to conceive of human nature (e.g., is there free will?), and about which research methods and forms of theorizing are appropriate for a science of psychology. Remember, the discipline is only a little over a century old; psychology is still getting its theoretical feet wet.

As we enter the 21st century, most psychologists have turned away from a strict allegiance to one theoretical orientation, such as behaviourism or psychoanalysis, and have adopted a more **eclectic approach.** This means that contemporary psychologists generally integrate from many different sources of ideas rather than rely entirely on one theoretical perspective. Eclecticism is common among both clinical psychologists helping people with psychological problems and research psychologists working primarily in the laboratory.

In the case of the clinical psychologist, the best technique often depends on the preferences of the client and on the particular problem at hand. For instance, some

eclectic approach

The position adopted by many psychologists that it's useful to integrate information from several sources; one need not rely exclusively on any single theoretical perspective.

kinds of phobias—irrational fears of things like heights or spiders—can be treated effectively by focusing on the fearful behaviour itself and ignoring its ultimate origin. (We don't need to know why you're afraid of snakes; we can just try to deal with the fear itself.) Other psychological problems may require the therapist to determine how childhood factors influenced adult dysfunction. Modern clinical psychologists integrate perspectives in an effort to find the best solution for their clients' problems, and they increasingly rely on scientific evaluations of the efficacy of various treatment options rather than relying exclusively on their intuitions and casual observations.

Modern research psychologists also take an eclectic approach. For example, a researcher might try to determine the genetic or biological origins of a behaviour or seek simply to describe the conditions under which the behaviour occurs. If it is possible to determine how the environment causes a behaviour to occur, the behaviour can be modified positively. Researchers recognize that it's possible to understand behaviour and mind from many different perspectives, at many different levels of analysis.

Four additional perspectives have become quite influential in recent years. Modern psychologists remain eclectic, but they generally refer to cognitive, biological, evolutionary, and cultural factors to explain behaviour. Because of the special emphasis these factors currently receive, we highlight them briefly in the following sections.

The Cognitive Revolution

By the 1950s, many psychologists had grown uncomfortable with the behaviourist idea that behaviour is the only proper subject matter for psychology. Researchers showed renewed interest in the study of consciousness and internal mental processes (Miller et al., 1960; Neisser, 1967). A shift away from behaviourism began, and this movement, which is still going strong, is known as the **cognitive revolution.** The word *cognitive* refers to the process of knowing or perceiving; as you may remember from our earlier discussion, cognitive psychologists are research psychologists who study phenomena such as memory, learning, and reasoning.

cognitive revolution
The shift away from strict behaviourism, begun in the 1950s, characterized by renewed interest in the study of consciousness and internal mental processes.

There are several reasons why psychologists returned to studying internal mental phenomena. One factor is the development of research techniques that enable investigators to infer cognitive processes from observable behaviour. Regularities in behaviour such as reaction times or forgetting rates can provide detailed information about internal mental processes, provided the experiments are conducted properly. You'll learn about specific tactics of psychological research in Chapter 2, and in subsequent chapters you'll see how those techniques have been used to study the mind as well as behaviour.

Another important factor that helped fuel the cognitive revolution was the development of the computer. Computers function through an interplay between *hardware*—the fixed structural features of the machine such as the internal chips and disk drives—and *software*, the programs that tell the hardware what to do. Although the human mind cannot be compared directly to a computer, it's useful to conceive of behaviour as reflecting the interplay between biological (or genetic) factors—that is, the hardwired structures of the brain and nervous system—and the tactics and strategies (the software) we learn from interactions with the environment. Cognitive psychologists have developed explanations of human behaviour as reflecting the operation of *information processing systems*—internal structures in the brain that manipulate information from the environment in ways that solve problems (see Chapters 7 and 8).

As you'll discover throughout this book, behaviour is often influenced by people's beliefs and mental strategies. Everything—from perceptions and memories to decisions about what foods to eat to our choice of friends—is critically influenced by prior knowledge and beliefs. Many psychologists believe that the key to understanding psychological disorders such as depression lies in the analysis of an individual's thought patterns. Depressed individuals tend to think rigidly and inflexibly, and some forms of therapy are directed specifically at challenging these entrenched thoughts and beliefs.

Canadian psychologist Donald O. Hebb of McGill University made important contributions to the cognitive revolution and to our understanding of the biological bases of behaviour.

You'll see many references to thoughts and cognitions as we investigate a range of psychological phenomena.

Developments in Biology

The focus of modern psychology has also been greatly shaped by the wealth of recent discoveries relating to the biological underpinnings of behaviour. One of the most important researchers to attempt to understand the biological processes that underlie thought and action was the Canadian psychologist Donald O. Hebb. His 1949 book, *The Organization of Behavior: A Neuropsychological Theory*, is one of the most influential volumes in the history of psychology (Fentress, 1999; Klein, 1999), and has just been republished (thanks largely to the efforts of Professor Richard Brown of Dalhousie University's Neuroscience Institute). As a professor at McGill University, Hebb had a significant influence on fostering the cognitive revolution of the 1950s and 1960s (Wickelgren, 1999). He is the only psychologist to date to serve as president of both the Canadian Psychological Association and the American Psychological Association. Each year since 1998, the Canadian Society for Brain, Behavioural, and Cognitive Science has celebrated Hebb's contributions by conferring the Hebb Award on a prominent Canadian researcher. The most recent honouree is Professor Bryan Kolb of the University of Lethbridge; you will see numerous references to Kolb's research in subsequent chapters (see psych.mcmaster.ca/bbcs/hebb.html for a complete list of Hebb Award winners).

Since Hebb, researchers have uncovered fascinating links between structures in the brain and the phenomena of behaviour and mind (see Figure 1.4). It is now possible to record the activity of brain cells directly, and it's been discovered that individual brain cells often respond to particular kinds of events in the environment. For example, there are cells in the "visual" part of the brain that respond actively only when particular colours, or patterns of light and dark, are shown to the eye. Other cells respond to inadequate supplies of nutrients by "motivating" a person to seek food.

Moreover, technology is now allowing psychologists to take "snapshots" of mental life in action. As you'll see in Chapter 3, it is now possible to create images of how activities in the brain change as the mind processes different things. These images of the brain in action help researchers understand normal as well as abnormal brain activity. For example, it's possible to record brain activity during depression, during extreme anxiety, or even during auditory and visual hallucinations. This information is useful in determining where in the brain specific psychological disorders originate and in providing a "road map" for treatment.

FIGURE 1.4

Specificity in the Brain

Researchers have discovered that bodily functions are largely controlled by specific areas of the brain. Developments in the biological sciences continue to have an enormous impact on the thinking of psychologists.

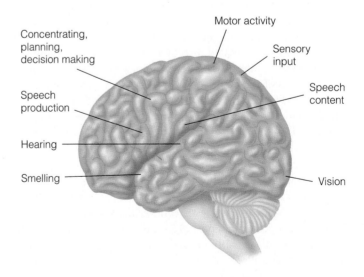

Great strides have also been made in understanding brain chemistry, that is, how natural drugs inside the brain influence many behaviours. It turns out that certain psychological problems, such as depression and schizophrenia, may be related to imbalances among the chemical messengers in the brain. Cognitive neuroscientists have also learned a great deal about the functions of various parts of the brain, and how those parts are interconnected. These developments, which we'll discuss in detail in Chapters 3, 14, and 15, are shaping the way psychological theories are constructed and how psychological problems are treated.

Evolutionary Bases of Thought and Behaviour

Another category of "biological" influence on modern psychological thinking involves researching the evolutionary origins of mind and behaviour. You will remember that Darwin's ideas influenced the early development of psychological thought, being particularly important in the development of functionalism. Darwinian ideas have recently re-emerged as a significant source of concepts and insights in understanding human psychology. This contemporary Darwinian perspective has been labelled **evolutionary psychology** (Barkow et al., 1992; Buss, 1999; Crawford & Krebs, 1998; Daly & Wilson, 1999); it views human thought and behaviour as comprising somewhat independent "modules" that evolved to solve specific problems that repeatedly arose in the ecology of our evolutionary ancestors. In this perspective, the human mind evolved to include cognitive and social mechanisms to solve delineated adaptive problems, such as how to find and reproduce with an appropriate mate (Buss, 1994), how to nurture and invest in offspring in a way that makes best use of limited resources (Daly & Wilson, 1998), and how to quickly make judgments and predictions about people's actions and motives (Krebs & Denton, 1997). The contemporary Darwinian perspective in psychology does not view evolutionary explanations as opposed to cognitive or cultural explanations of behaviour, but as complementary, providing a level of analysis of human behaviour using many of the same explanatory models used to understand the adaptive behaviour of nonhuman animals.

evolutionary psychology
The study of the human mind and behavioural processes as products of natural selection.

The Importance of Culture

Modern psychological thinking also emphasizes the concept of culture and the role it plays in shaping people's thoughts and behaviours. By **culture,** psychologists mean the shared values, customs, and beliefs that characterize a group or community. Cultural groups can be based on obvious things, such as ethnicity, geography, or socioeconomic class, but also on political, religious, or other factors (e.g., those who share the same sexual orientation might be considered a cultural group). Culture is a broad construct, and its influences can be found in virtually all aspects of behaviour and mind.

culture
The shared values, customs, and beliefs that are characteristic of a group or community.

Cultural groups can be based on numerous dimensions, such as ethnicity, geography, socioeconomic class, or political or religious allegiance.

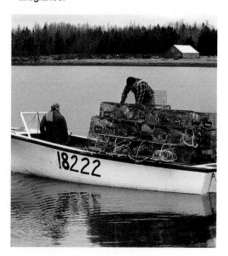

Recognizing that culture exerts a strong influence on our thoughts and actions may seem obvious to you, but it was largely ignored in mainstream psychology for many years. In the introductory textbook used by one of this textbook's authors as an undergraduate student, group influences were not discussed except for a mere three paragraphs covering why individuals might differ in intelligence. Psychologists have always recognized that behaviour is influenced by the environment, which can mean one's culture, but it was the behaviour of individuals in isolation rather than the behaviour of individuals in groups that received the most attention. Researchers spent their time looking for universal principles of behaviour, those that cut across all people in all groups, rather than exploring how the shared values of a community might affect how people think and act. The search for universal principles continues today, but cross-cultural factors are now considered to be an integral part of the story of psychology, as shown in the recent *Handbook of Cross-Cultural Psychology,* compiled by Queen's University's cross-cultural psychologist John Berry and his colleagues (1997).

There were a few notable psychologists who paid attention to culture early on, especially in attempting to explain cognitive and social development. Over half a century ago, the Russian psychologist Lev Vygotsky proposed that children's thoughts and actions originate from their social interactions, particularly with parents. Vygotsky believed that it's not possible to understand the mind of a child without carefully considering the child's social and cultural world. In an important sense, the properties of a child's mind are created by his or her social and cultural interactions. At first, these ideas were not very influential in psychology, partly because Vygotsky died young in the 1930s, but they've been rediscovered by psychologists in the last few decades and are now being actively pursued. (You'll read a bit more about Vygotsky in Chapter 10.)

Why have cultural factors become so important to psychologists? Most importantly, studies have demonstrated that culture matters, even when studying basic psychological principles such as memory (DiMaggio, 1997; Mullen, 1994), perception (Davies & Corbett, 1997), self-presentation (Heine et al., 1999), and reasoning (Li et al., 1996). For example, in research conducted in New Zealand, MacDonald et al. (2000) asked adults from three different cultural backgrounds to report their earliest childhood memory: Maoris (the indigenous people of New Zealand), European New Zealanders, and Chinese people. The Maori culture places a strong emphasis on memory for the past, and Maori adults reported memories of significantly earlier childhood events than did individuals from the other cultures.

Most psychologists agree that a full understanding of behaviour and mind cannot be achieved without considering the individual in his or her social and cultural context. Although evolution has provided humans with a basic set of adaptive mental modules for solving problems that were important for the survival of our ancestors, cultural factors also play major roles in how we think, in how we interact with each other, and even in how we see the world.

Solving Problems with the Adaptive Mind

We began this chapter by emphasizing the tremendous range of human behaviour, from acts of brutal violence to works of subtle genius. That range, from one person to another and from one moment to the next within individuals, is a telling characteristic of our species. Telling because it illustrates the unusual (compared to other animals) extent to which our behavioural repertoire is determined by experiential and environmental factors as opposed to being genetically fixed and determined. As noted earlier (and elaborated in subsequent chapters), genes play important roles in the human experience, but our major evolutionary genetic endowment is of a mind/brain capable of an astounding flexibility and adaptiveness.

The ultimate aim of psychology is to develop a science of mind and behaviour, and an understanding of how and why people do, feel, and experience the things they do. Psychologists strive to use their own adaptive minds to unravel the mind's complex and mysterious nature. This science, and its practical application by clinical psychologists and applied psychologists, is still at an early stage of development. To put it another way, the science is still evolving, responding adaptively to new empirical evidence and new theoretical ideas. The following 15 chapters will introduce you to some of what we have discovered so far.

As we mentioned at the beginning of the chapter, each of the chapters in this textbook is organized around a set of adaptive or practical *problems.* The problem-solving approach is designed to promote the idea that we think and act for adaptive reasons; we use our psychological tool kit to help us solve problems every day. But this theme is also designed to provide you with a direct link between the topic discussions and the real world. For instance, in Chapter 13 you'll learn about a topic in social psychology called *attribution theory.* Why? Because attribution theory deals with a very important everyday problem: How do we assign a cause to someone's behaviour? You constantly need to interpret the behaviour of others, whether it's the sudden anger of a friend or the disapproving look of a professor. At first glance, attribution theory may seem like an abstract topic, but it's really quite relevant to your life.

The problem-solving approach is also intended to encourage you to think critically about the material. Rather than just memorizing the facts about a topic, you will learn more if you try to make the connection between the topic under discussion and solving the adaptive or practical problem. For example, how does a procedure like classical conditioning help psychologists understand how people learn about the signalling properties of events? (We'll discuss this in Chapter 6.)

Finally, the problem-solving approach is designed to provide some continuity across the different chapters. Human behaviour is easier to comprehend when it is viewed as the product of an adaptive mind. You are encouraged to understand that behaviours, as well as the methods of psychologists, are reactions to problems faced. Focusing on adaptiveness will sensitize you to the diversity of behaviour, both among people and across species. Although constrained by their shared evolutionary heritage, individuals respond to unique situations and use strategies that are influenced by culture and by transient biological states. The wide array of different behaviours and personal styles you encounter in daily life testifies to the diverse outcomes of our adaptive minds.

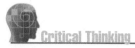

Critical Thinking

Behaviour can be difficult to predict but can still be governed by understandable principles. Think about how difficult it is to predict the weather or even the movement of a ball rolling down an inclined plane. Would you claim that these activities are not controlled by principled "laws of nature"?

Test Yourself 1.3

Test your knowledge about the focus of modern psychology by answering the following questions. (You will find the answers in Appendix B.)

1. According to the eclectic approach, in choosing the best technique to use in therapy, you should consider the:
   a. specific unconscious urges that are driving behaviour.
   b. training and biases of the therapist/researcher.
   c. preferences of the client and the particular problem under investigation.
   d. availability of relevant monitoring equipment.

2. Fill in the blanks in the following paragraph. Choose your answers from the following set of terms: biology; cognitive; computer; cultural; philosophy.

   Over the past several decades, psychologists have returned to the study of internal mental phenomena such as consciousness. This shift away from strict behaviourism has been labelled the _____ revolution. An important factor that helped fuel this revolution was the development of the _____, which became a model of sorts for the human mind. Developments in _____ are also playing an important role in shaping modern psychology and in creating effective treatments for psychological problems.

3. Psychologists are increasingly appealing to cultural factors to help explain human behaviour. Which of the following statements about culture and psychology is *false*?
   a. Psychologists largely ignored cultural influences for many years.
   b. Culture influences social processes but not basic psychological processes such as memory and reasoning.
   c. A few notable psychologists, such as Lev Vygotsky, studied cultural influences many decades ago.
   d. By culture, psychologists mean the shared values, customs, and beliefs that are characteristic of a group or community.

Solving the Scientific Problems

At the end of every chapter, you'll find a section that summarizes the main points of the chapter from the perspective of our "problems to be solved." This is a good point to stop and think about the facts and theories you've read about and to try to see how they relate to the particular problems we've discussed. In this chapter, our primary goal was to introduce you to the science of psychology. Our discussion involved three main issues.

First, how do we define and describe psychology? Psychology is the scientific study of behaviour and mind. Notice that this definition makes no specific reference to psychological problems or abnormal behaviour. Although many psychologists (especially clinical psychologists) work to promote mental health, applied psychologists and research psychologists work primarily to understand "normal" people. The goal of the scientific study of behaviour and mind is to discover general principles that can be applied widely to help people adapt more successfully—in the workplace, in school, or at home—and to unravel the great scientific mystery of how and why people do the things they do.

Second, how did current psychological perspectives develop? Psychology has existed as a separate subject matter of science for a little more than a century, but people have pondered the mysteries of behaviour and mind for thousands of years. Psychology has its roots in philosophy and physiology. Thinkers in these fields addressed several fundamental psychological issues, such as the relation between the mind and the body, and the origins of knowledge. Most modern psychologists solve the mind–body problem by assuming that the two are essentially one and the same—thoughts, ideas, and emotions arise out of the biological processes of the brain (although we are still far from a complete understanding of how this works). Most psychologists also assume that basic kinds of behaviours originate from natural evolved dispositions (nature) as well as from lifetime experiences (nurture).

Once the discipline of psychology was established by Wundt in 1879, vigorous arguments ensued over the proper way to characterize and study the mind. Structuralists like Wundt believed the world of immediate experience could be broken down into elements, much like how a chemist analyzes a chemical compound. In contrast, the functionalists argued that psychology should focus on the function and purpose of behaviour. The behaviourists rejected the world of immediate experience in favour of studying behaviour, without reference to consciousness. Sigmund Freud's psychoanalytic view outlined a quite different perspective on human psychology, with its emphasis on the unconscious mind. The pessimism of the Freudians was one factor that led to the reaction of the humanistic psychologists, who strongly advocate free will and the power of personal choice.

Third, what is the dominant theoretical orientation of modern psychology? Each of the earlier psychological perspectives has some continuing influence on psychological ideas today. But most modern psychologists adopt an eclectic approach: They choose from the perspectives based on the problem at hand. Many psychologists still focus on behaviour as a research strategy, but the world of inner experience is also a prime target for study, as evidenced by the cognitive revolution and by recent developments in the biological sciences. Recently, there has been a resurgence in efforts to use evolutionary ideas to help understand the functioning of the modules of the mind, and psychologists also increasingly include cultural factors in their explanations of behaviour and mind.

The problem-solving approach in this book is based on the concept of the adaptive mind: People, as well as other animals, use their mental machinery—forged in evolutionary history and rooted in the biological processes of the brain—to achieve certain fundamental ends. Individuals continually adjust their actions in an effort to solve the problems that arise from a complex and changing environment.

Chapter Summary

DEFINING AND DESCRIBING PSYCHOLOGY

Learning Goal: Learn the modern definition of psychology. *Psychology* is the scientific study of *behaviour* and *mind* and of how people differ as a result of biological and environmental influences and cultural context. Psychological understanding lets us predict, control, and improve behaviour.

The Invisible and Dynamic Mind: How Can It Be Studied?

Learning Goal: Be able to discuss the different ways of studying the mind scientifically. Psychologists use three types of measures to assess mental events. With *self-report* measures, people describe their own thoughts and feelings. With *biological* measures, scientists assess physiological processes, including brain activities. With *behavioural* measures, psychologists infer how the mind works from how the body behaves under particular conditions.

What Psychologists Do

Learning Goal: Learn about what psychologists do, distinguishing between clinical, applied, and research psychologists. *Clinical psychologists* diagnose and treat psychological problems, and they give advice. *Psychiatrists* also diagnose and treat psychological problems, but unlike clinical psychologists they receive their training in medical school and are able to prescribe drugs. Some *counsellors* also provide services to people with psychological problems, but they vary widely in the kind and amount of training they have received. *Applied psychologists* help normal people in practical settings improve their performance. *Research psychologists* collect data on basic and applied issues through research and observation.

How to Become a Psychologist

Learning Goal: Learn about the schooling and qualifications required to become a psychologist. The first step is to do well in your undergraduate years. There are a variety of psychology-related jobs that can be held by an individual with a bachelor's degree in psychology, but to be classified as a psychologist per se, more advanced training is required. To provide therapy as a licensed psychologist, you need to complete a bachelor's degree (often, but not necessarily, in psychology) followed by a doctoral degree in clinical psychology (usually, a master's degree is earned en route to a doctoral degree). Most people working as applied psychologists have a master's degree and/or doctoral degree in psychology. Most research psychologists have a doctoral degree in psychology.

TRACING THE EVOLUTION OF PSYCHOLOGICAL THOUGHT

The primary intellectual roots of psychology are in philosophy and physiology.

Mind and Body: Are They the Same?

Learning Goal: Be able to explain what is meant by the mind–body problem. *Descartes* believed that the mind is separate from the body, which it controls through the pineal gland. *Modern psychologists* believe that the mind and body are different aspects of the same thing, because the mind is a product of what the brain does.

Nature and Nurture: Where Does Knowledge Come From?

Learning Goal: Understand differing viewpoints on the origins of knowledge. *Empiricism* holds that we learn everything through experience (Aristotle). *Nativism* holds that some knowledge is inborn (innate), including ideas regarding cause and effect, and space and time. *Darwin* proposed that natural selection guides evolution, and that some behavioural tendencies are inherited.

The First Schools: Psychology as Science

Learning Goal: Be able to outline the development of the first scientific schools of psychology: structuralism, functionalism, and behaviourism. *Structuralism* was founded by Wundt, who established an experimental laboratory to study the components of immediate experience, and how they sum to a meaningful whole. *Functionalism* was developed by North American psychologists who studied the adaptive purpose *(function)* of immediate experience. *Behaviourism,* led by Watson, was based on the premise that because immediate conscious experience cannot be observed, behaviour is the proper subject of psychology.

Freud and the Humanists: The Influence of the Clinic

Learning Goal: Discuss the early clinical contributions of Freud and the humanistic psychologists. *Freud* was a neurologist and clinician who used dreams and free association to analyze both the mind and the unconscious determinants of behaviour. According to Freud, much of human behaviour reflects unconscious drives to gratify sensual urges. Humanist psychologists such as *Rogers* and *Maslow* rejected Freud's pessimism and focused instead on positive traits. According to humanistic psychologists, people control their destinies and can attain their full potential through insight and personal growth.

Pioneers: The Influence of Women

Learning Goal: Learn about some of the contributions women researchers have made to the science of psychology. *Mary Calkins,* who developed a paired-associate learning technique, was the first female president of the American Psychological Association (APA). Calkins completed the work for a Ph.D. in psychology, but was denied the degree by Harvard on the basis of her gender. *Margaret Washburn* was the first woman to receive a doctorate in psychology, and the second female president of the APA. *Mary Salter Ainsworth* was a pioneer Canadian woman psychologist and an important contributor to our understanding of child–parent attachment. *Brenda Milner* of the Montreal Neurological Institute and McGill University is highly celebrated as one of the pioneers of neuropsychology, famed for her brilliant studies of patients with various kinds of brain damage. *Doreen Kimura,* another leading Canadian woman psychologist, has had tremendous impact on the study of biological influences on human cognition and behaviour.

UNDERSTANDING THE FOCUS OF MODERN PSYCHOLOGY

Learning Goal: Understand what it means to adopt an eclectic approach to psychology. An *eclectic approach* draws from diverse sources and theoretical perspectives and uses various methods to investigate psychological issues and to apply psychology in clinical and/or applied settings.

The Cognitive Revolution

Learning Goal: Be able to discuss the origins and central premises of the cognitive revolution. The *cognitive revolution* was a shift away from strict behaviourism, characterized by a renewed interest in the study of consciousness and internal mental processes. The word *cognitive* refers to the process of knowing or perceiving that involves learning, memory, and reasoning, and underlies much human behaviour.

Developments in Biology

Learning Goal: Learn about recent developments in biology and neuroscience and how they have influenced modern psychology. *Biology* has always played an important role in psychology, but that role has increased in recent years with the development of new knowledge concerning genetics and the anatomy and physiology of the brain, and new methods for studying the physiology of the brain in action. Psychological research informed by such knowledge and methods has led to new understandings of how human behaviour and experience are influenced by chemicals in the brain, and of how various components within the brain interact to give rise to mental phenomena.

Evolutionary Bases of Thought and Behaviour

Learning Goal: Understand how natural selection contributed to the evolution of the adaptive human mind. Natural selection—the tendency for more successful organisms to survive to reproduce and hence pass their genes on to future generations—shaped specific modules of mind and behaviour to address problems faced by our evolutionary ancestors.

The Importance of Culture

Learning Goal: Appreciate why psychologists believe that cultural factors are important determinants of behaviour and mind. *Culture*—the shared values, customs, and beliefs that characterize a group or community—plays a major role in contributing to the diversity of human experience and behaviour. Differences between cultures affect not only relatively superficial things, such as clothing styles and language, but also more fundamental psychological processes such as memory.

Solving Problems with the Adaptive Mind

Learning Goal: Grasp how psychologists strive to use their own adaptive minds to understand how and why people do and feel the things they do. Natural selection has endowed the human animal with a mind/brain capable of great flexibility and adaptiveness. Our behaviour and our understanding can shift dramatically with experience and we are capable of solving (as well as creating!) a huge array of problems. Psychological scientists use their adaptive, problem-solving minds to explore fundamental questions of human behaviour and experience. By using your own *adaptive mind* in an actively engaged, problem-solving manner, you can enrich your understanding and retention of this (and other) texts.

Terms to Remember

psychology, 4
Defining and Describing Psychology
mind, 7
behaviour, 7
clinical psychologists, 9
counselling psychologists, 9
counsellor, 10
psychiatrists, 10
applied psychologists, 10
research psychologists, 10

Recommended Readings

Hunt, M. (1993). *The story of psychology*. New York: Anchor Books. A highly entertaining look at the history of psychology from the musings of the ancient Greek philosophers to modern theoretical approaches.

James, W. (1890). *The principles of psychology*. New York: Holt. (Reprinted Harvard University Press, 1983.) It's worth taking a look at James's classic work. The writing is poetic, the insights are many, and remember—this was once used as an introductory textbook in psychology!

Pinker, S. (1997a). *How the mind works*. New York: W. W. Norton. A witty and lucid exploration of some of the basic concepts in contemporary cognitive and evolutionary psychology. Explains the "modules of mind" idea in some detail.

Wright, R. (1994). *The moral animal*. Toronto: Random House/New York: Pantheon. Clearly explains the basic principles of modern evolutionary psychology, interweaves the story of Charles Darwin's life and ideas, and discusses which of Darwin's ideas have the most influence today.

For additional readings, explore InfoTrac® College Edition, your online library. Go to:

www.adaptivemind2e.nelson.com

Hint: enter the search terms: psychologist; psychoanalysis; behaviourism; history of psychology; cognitive psychology.

What's on the Web?

Please note that Web addresses are subject to change. Check out the accompanying Web site for updates: www.adaptivemind2e.nelson.com. This site presents practice quiz questions, hypercontent, information on degrees and careers in psychology, study tips, and more.

The History of Psychology in Canada

www.cpa.ca/history.html

Articles from a special section of the journal *Canadian Psychology*. The site includes topics such as the establishment of the first psychological laboratory in Canada at the University of Toronto, the role of Canadian psychologists in training pilots during World War II, and pioneering women psychologists in Canada.

Classics in the History of Psychology

psychclassics.yorku.ca/

York University psychologist Christopher Green has made available full text versions of many classic writings in the history of psychology, including contributions from Darwin, Wundt, Baldwin, James, Freud, Skinner, and Hebb.

Canadian Psychological Association

www.cpa.ca

The national association for psychologists in Canada. The site includes information on careers for psychologists, provincial licensing requirements, educational opportunities, and links to Canadian psychology journals.

Bad Human Factors Designs

www.baddesigns.com/examples.html

Ever get frustrated with the stupid way that someone designed the things you work with every day? Have trouble telling the difference between the buttons on your stereo? Can't figure out which side of the door to push to get out? This site is full of stupid human factors designs, complete with pictures. Surf around, and see if you can do some intelligent redesigning!

History of Psychology Web Site

elvers.stjoe.udayton.edu/history/welcome.htm

This is a comprehensive site, with a list of over 100 "clickable" names that will give you a description of how that person contributed to psychology. The list ranges from Aristotle to St. Thomas Aquinas to B. F. Skinner. You can even sort the list of historical figures according to their birth date. See if any famous figures share your birthday!

You can observe a lot by watching.
Yogi Berra

Chapter 2 The Tactics of Psychological Research

Todd leaned back on his bed, headphones firmly in place, and cranked up the volume. He couldn't hear the message playing backward on the tape, the one announcing the arrival of Satan. He noticed nothing at all in particular, in fact, but he didn't feel much like going to church either.

Is it possible to influence people with messages that they do not consciously see or hear? Some believe that such messages are everywhere, hidden from the naked eye by evil advertisers and dark-natured rock stars. What do you think? Are there secret messages lurking in advertisements, or flowing backward on the soundtrack of your favourite CD? People who believe in such subliminal influences (subliminal means "below threshold," or too weak to be perceived consciously) assume these messages are responsible for many of society's ills, ranging from impulse purchases to acts of violence (Key, 1973).

Fortunately, research psychologists have investigated the topic of subliminal influence and have discovered very little need for concern. We'll return to this fascinating topic later (in Chapter 5), but for the moment we note that there's almost no evidence that subliminal messages are actually used by advertisers—and even if they are, their influence is probably minimal at most. The topic is of interest to us here, however, because the subject of this chapter is the strategies and tactics of psychological research. How do psychologists determine whether events in the environment, such as subliminal messages, affect mind and behaviour?

As you may remember from Chapter 1, psychology is a scientific enterprise. Its methods rely on observation, on information gathered through the senses. Because observation is the ultimate authority in psychology, psychologists use the **scientific method** as their main tool for investigating behaviour and mind. This means that if you want to understand the effect of subliminal messages on the mind, your first step is to employ the scientific method. Reduced to its barest essentials, the scientific method contains four important steps (see Figure 2.1):

scientific method
A method for acquiring knowledge by combining (a) the principles of rational thought (that is, logic) with (b) information derived from systematic measurements of the object of study (that is, empirical research).

FIGURE 2.1
Steps in the Scientific Method
The four major steps in the scientific method. The first step is observation; in step 1, the rat is observed jumping toward a checkerboard panel on the left. In step 2, the researcher looks for regularities in behaviour and notes that the rat, over repeated trials, consistently jumps to the checkerboard on the left. In step 3, the researcher generates a hypothesis (If I move the checkerboard to the right, the rat will jump to the right), and in step 4, the researcher tests the hypothesis. Here the hypothesis has turned out to be wrong. The rat is jumping left rather than following the checkerboard.

Observe	Detect Regularities	Generate Hypothesis	Observe
The rat receives food for jumping through the checkerboard panel on the left.	Over trials, the rat consistently chooses to jump toward the checkerboard panel on the left.	The rat has learned to associate the checkerboard with food, so if the checkerboard is moved to the right, the rat will jump to the right.	The rat jumps to the left, suggesting it has learned that jumping left produces food.

Previewing the Scientific Problems

The primary goal of most psychologists is understanding. Psychologists want to know what causes behaviour; they want to understand how external events in the environment and internal processes in the individual conspire to produce the remarkable diversity of human thought, feeling, and action. However, understanding is not always easy to achieve, nor is it the only acceptable goal of psychology. Sometimes it is enough merely to describe and predict. Consider TV sets, refrigerators, and computers. Most of us have no idea how these things work, nor can we fix them when they break, but we do know how to use them. The same might be said of psychology; we may not always understand why people act the way they do, but if we can predict when people will act in a particular way then we gain a degree of control over our environment.

In this chapter you'll be introduced to the basic techniques of psychological research. The discussion focuses on four practical problems that researchers investigating behaviour and mind often attempt to solve. In each case, we'll discuss the technical solutions to these problems, and we'll pay particular attention to the pitfalls that can hinder the research process.

First, what are the best techniques for observing and describing behaviour? One of the most important steps in any psychological research project is to choose a behaviour of interest and begin recording its characteristics. Observation in research is more than just casual looking or listening; to yield reliable data, the methods of observation must be systematic.

Second, how can one predict behaviour? Descriptive research yields facts about behaviour, but psychologists are often interested not only in describing how people behaved at one time, but also in predicting their future behaviour. A different set of techniques can be used to predict (with varying degrees of confidence) future behaviour. Prediction is of value because it allows for more effective control of future environments.

Third, how can psychologists determine the underlying causes of behaviour? Most psychologists want to understand *why* people behave as they do—that is, they want to understand the *causes* of particular behaviours. To determine causality it is necessary to use the *experimental method*. That is, the researcher must systematically manipulate aspects of the environment to determine the effect of that manipulation on behaviour. If conducted properly, experiments provide powerful evidence regarding what causes behaviours to occur or change in particular situations.

Fourth, what procedures ensure that research participants are treated ethically? Psychologists seeking to describe, predict, and understand behaviour must grapple with the important practical problem of how to pursue these goals while treating research participants ethically. The vast majority of psychology research with humans consists of straightforward, nonstressful procedures that do not put participants at risk, but even with such procedures psychologists must take care to ensure that participants are aware of their rights. Some research procedures do expose participants to risks (e.g., of stress or embarrassment) and laboratory research with animals raises many ethical issues. How can the value of such research be weighed against the potential costs to participants?

1. *Observe.* The scientific method usually begins, appropriately, with observation. In psychology, we choose the behaviour of interest and begin recording its characteristics as well as the conditions under which the behaviour occurs.

2. *Detect regularities.* Next, the researcher looks for regularities in the observations that have been collected: Are there certain consistent features that the behaviours show, or conditions under which the behaviours commonly appear?

3. *Generate hypothesis.* In step 3, the researcher forms a hypothesis, which is essentially a prediction about the behaviour under study. Hypotheses are expressed in the form of testable if-then statements: If some set of conditions is present, then a certain kind of behaviour will occur.

4. *Observe.* Finally, the predictions of the hypothesis are checked for accuracy, once again through observation under controlled conditions. If new data are consistent with the prediction of the hypothesis, the hypothesis is supported.

Notice that the scientific method is anchored on both ends by observation. The kinds of observations that are collected in the first and last steps aren't always the same, but some kind of observation or measurement always plays a key role in the scientific process. Of course, observations or measurements are valuable only if they are accurate. To help ensure the accuracy of their measurements, research psychologists use **operational definitions** to define the behaviours or responses under investigation. An operational definition defines a to-be-measured variable in terms of the steps or operations used to measure that variable (Levine & Parkinson, 1994; Stevens, 1939). For example, "intelligence" might be defined operationally as performance on a particular IQ test; "impatience" might be defined as the number of times the subject looks at his or her watch during a set period. One of the major challenges of psychological research is developing operational definitions that capture the underlying concepts explored in empirical investigations (e.g., creating IQ tests that measure what we have in mind when we think of "intelligence"). If your goal is to investigate the topic of subliminal influence, for example, you must develop an operational definition of "subliminal influence." Can you think of one? We'll return to the topic of subliminal messages later in the chapter and in Chapter 5.

operational definition
Concept defined in terms of how it is measured.

OBSERVING BEHAVIOUR: DESCRIPTIVE RESEARCH

Learning Goals

1. Understand the goals, techniques, and challenges of descriptive research.
2. Learn how psychologists conduct naturalistic research.
3. Appreciate the strengths and weaknesses of case studies.
4. Understand the advantages and limitations of surveys.
5. Learn the major purpose of psychological tests.
6. Be able to explain how statistics can summarize and help interpret data.

BECAUSE OBSERVATION IS SO IMPORTANT to psychological research, we begin with a discussion of descriptive research. We note at the outset, however, that psychologists are usually not satisfied with purely descriptive research because they want to know not only *what* people do but *why* they do it. As will become clear as we go along, descriptive research by itself cannot provide compelling evidence of causal relationships (i.e., evidence about what factors cause certain behaviours). Nonetheless, before we can attempt to understand *why* people do the things they do, we must know *what* they do; hence descriptive research plays a vital role in psychological research.

Descriptive research consists of the methods used to observe and describe behaviour. At face value, the act of observation seems simple enough; after all, people observe one another all the time. However, it's actually easy to be misled, even when the goal is simply to record behaviour (Rosenthal & Rosnow, 1969; Rosnow & Rosenthal, 1996).

descriptive research
The tactics and methods that underlie the direct observation and description of behaviour.

Psychologists want to understand what causes people to do the things they do.

Let's suppose that you want to observe the behaviour of preschoolers in a local daycare centre. You arrive with cameras and recording devices in hand and begin systematic observations of the children at play. Right away, you notice that the children distract easily—many seem uneasy and hesitant to engage in the activities suggested by the teacher. Several children show outward signs of fear and eventually withdraw, crying, to a corner of the room. Later, in describing your results, you conclude that children in daycare centres adjust badly, and some even show early signs of poor psychological health.

It shouldn't take much thought to recognize that your research strategy may suffer from a basic problem. Whenever you observe the actions of someone else, the very act of observing can affect the behaviour you're recording. In the case of the daycare centre, it's likely that your unexpected presence in the centre (with cameras and the like) made the children feel uncomfortable and led them to act in ways that were not representative of their normal behaviour. Psychologists refer to this phenomenon as reactivity. **Reactivity** occurs whenever an individual's behaviour is changed in some way by being observed. It's called "reactivity" because the subject's behaviour is altered in *reaction* to the observation (Orne, 1969; Webb et al., 1981). It may be that the children in the daycare centre are not normally hesitant and distracted; those behaviours may have been a reaction to you and your recording devices.

Reactivity can lead research to lack external validity. **External validity** refers to how well the results of a research study generalize to other situations or are representative of real life (Campbell & Stanley, 1966; Cook & Campbell, 1979). If the children's behaviour is largely a reaction to your presence as an observer, it's clearly not representative of their everyday behaviour. Moreover, even if these children are generally fearful, your observations may not be representative of children at other daycare centres. To improve external validity, you must minimize reactivity and record the behaviour of children at several daycare centres to see whether similar patterns of behaviour emerge.

Naturalistic Observation: Focusing on Real Life

One way that researchers try to reduce the problem of reactivity and improve external validity is to observe behaviour in natural settings using noninterfering measures (Martin & Bateson, 1993; Timberlake & Silva, 1994). In **naturalistic observation,** the researcher records naturally occurring behaviour in the everyday environment, as

Psychologists need to consider the problem of reactivity: Are the observed behaviours simply a reaction to the observation process? If the behaviour of these children is changed as a result of the observer's presence, then the observations may not generalize well to other situations.

reactivity
The extent to which an individual's behaviour changes as a result of being observed; the behaviour is altered in reaction to being observed.

external validity
The extent to which the results of an observation generalize to other situations or are representative of real life.

naturalistic observation
A research technique that involves recording only naturally occurring behaviour, as opposed to behaviour produced in the laboratory.

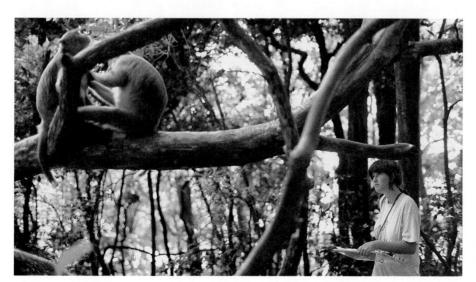

In naturalistic observation, the researcher records only naturally occurring behaviour, as opposed to behaviour produced in the laboratory, and a concerted effort is made not to interfere with the behaviour.

opposed to behaviour produced in the laboratory, and tries not to interfere with the behaviour in any way. If the recorded behaviour is natural and has not been affected by the researcher, then the recorded data are representative of real life (of course, it is also necessary to repeat the observations in different settings to be sure the results generalize). One way to avoid reactivity is to observe subjects without them knowing they are being observed: If the subjects are unaware of being observed, their behaviour cannot be a reaction to the observation process. Naturalistic observation has been used with great success by psychologists as well as by *ethologists,* biologists who study the behaviour of animals in the wild (Goodall, 1990; Lorenz, 1958).

To observe natural behaviour while minimizing reactivity, researchers sometimes use a technique called *participant observation,* in which the observer attempts to become a part of the activities being studied. For example, in the 1950s a group of psychologists infiltrated a doomsday cult by passing themselves off as believers. This particular cult preached the impending end of the United States, on a particular date, from a natural disaster. Once they were on the inside, the psychologists recorded and studied the reactions of the cultists when the inevitable day of doom failed to materialize (Festinger et al., 1956). In another classic project about which you'll read more in Chapter 14, a group of researchers had themselves committed to local mental hospitals—they complained of hearing voices—in an effort to obtain an honest record of patient life inside an institution (Rosenhan, 1973). Participant observation could easily be used in our daycare centre example: You could simply introduce yourself as a new teacher, rather than as a researcher, and hide your cameras or other recording equipment.

Another useful technique is to measure behaviour indirectly, by looking at *indicators* of a behaviour rather than the behaviour itself. For example, you might be able to learn something about the eating or shopping habits of teenagers at the local mall by measuring the content and quality of the litter they leave behind. Administrators at museums have determined the popularity of various exhibits by noting how quickly floor tiles in front of each exhibit wear out (Webb et al., 1981) (see Figure 2.2). Neither of these examples requires direct observation of behaviour; it is the aftereffects—the products—of the behaviour that provide the insightful clues.

Naturalistic observation is an effective technique for measuring natural behaviour, and it can also be used to verify the results of laboratory experiments (Miller, 1977; Timberlake & Silva, 1994). As we'll discuss later in the chapter, experiments are the best way to gain knowledge about *why* people do the things they do. It is difficult to con-

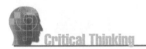

Critical Thinking

Do you see any ethical problems with the technique of participant observation?

FIGURE 2.2

Naturalistic Observation of Behavioural Results

In a study conducted at the Chicago Museum of Science and Industry, researchers gauged the popularity of exhibits by noting how quickly the vinyl floor tiles in front of each display needed to be replaced. The live chick–hatching exhibit proved to be extremely popular.

duct experimental research in natural settings, so most experiments are conducted in the lab. Questions can be raised, however, regarding the external validity of laboratory research. For instance, many studies of human memory have been conducted in the laboratory by having subjects learn lists of words (Bruce, 1985; Neisser, 1978). To what extent are the psychological principles gleaned from such studies relevant to learning and remembering in natural settings? To answer this question, psychologists also record natural instances of remembering and forgetting, such as eyewitness accounts of naturally occurring events, to determine whether the patterns resemble those collected in the lab (e.g., Conway et al., 1994; Neisser & Hyman, 1999; Yuille, 1993). For reasons that will become clear later in this chapter, naturalistic observation, by itself, is a poor vehicle for determining the causes of behaviour. It can, however, be used effectively to gather basic information about a phenomenon and to test the generality of psychological principles discovered in the lab.

Case Studies: Focusing on the Individual

Another descriptive research technique is the case study. In a **case study,** the researcher focuses on a single case and studies that case in great detail and depth (Bromley, 1986; Elmes et al., 1995; Heiman, 1995). Usually the "case" is an individual person, although there are also case studies of small groups. Because a great deal of information is collected about the background and behaviour of one person, case studies give the researcher a very important historical perspective that aids in forming hypotheses about the possible causes of a behaviour or psychological problem.

case study

A descriptive research technique in which the research effort is focused on a single case (usually an individual, although case studies can also be conducted on small groups).

One of the most influential psychological theories of the 20th century, the psychoanalytic theory of Sigmund Freud, was based primarily on descriptive data derived from case studies. Clinical psychologists continue to report and be influenced by case studies. Some case studies have gained substantial popular interest as well. For example, you may have heard of Chris Sizemore, popularized in the movie *The Three Faces of Eve,* who coped with emotional distress by apparently shifting among three quite different personalities (Thigpen & Cleckley, 1957). *Sybil,* depicted in a television miniseries of the same name, was the subject of another famous case study of multiple personality disorder (now known as dissociative identity disorder).

Like naturalistic observation, the case study methodology suffers from some limitations (Yin, 1998). By focusing on just a single case, researchers essentially place all of their theoretical eggs in one basket. This means that questions are often raised about external validity: Are the experiences of the individual subject truly representative of others (Liebert & Liebert, 1995)? For example, Sybil's frightening descent into dissociative identity disorder may or may not be representative of how psychological disorders normally develop (see Rieber, 1999, for a skeptical discussion of the Sybil case; for critiques of the whole idea of dissociative identity disorder, see Piper, 1997, and Spanos, 1994). Another problem with case studies is that the claims of the individual under study are often difficult to verify. If the observations of the single subject are somehow tainted with inaccuracies—if the subject is lying, for example—the entire study must be viewed with suspicion (see Horton et al., 1992; Iverson et al., 2001; Strauss et al., 2002; and Tombaugh, 1997, for techniques for catching people who are pretending to have symptoms that they don't really have). Once again, as with naturalistic observation, case studies are excellent vehicles for generating hypotheses but are not effective for determining cause-and-effect relationships.

Surveys: Describing Populations

Whereas a case study focuses on a single individual, psychologists use a **survey** to sample reported behaviour or opinions broadly by gathering responses from many people. Most surveys are administered in the form of a questionnaire: Individuals, or groups of individuals, are asked questions about some behaviour, psychological characteristic, or belief. You are, of course, familiar with the opinion surveys conducted by

survey

A descriptive research technique designed to gather limited amounts of information from many people, usually by administering a questionnaire.

FIGURE 2.3

Opinions about Memory Techniques in Psychotherapy

Selected results from the Poole et al. (1995) survey of psychotherapists show the percentage of respondents who reported using various techniques to help adult clients remember childhood sexual abuse and the percentage of respondents who indicated that those techniques should not be used to help clients remember childhood sexual abuse.

political campaigns or by the news media to capture the current attitudes of voters. Surveys can also be used for research purposes, to gain valuable descriptive information about behaviour and mind. For example, researchers can use a survey to examine the relationship between personality characteristics and health problems in air traffic controllers (MacLennan & Peebles, 1996) or between perfectionism and stress in school teachers (Flett et al., 1995).

Figure 2.3 shows some of the results of a survey conducted to assess U.S. psychotherapists' beliefs and practices regarding therapeutic techniques that may help adult clients remember long-forgotten childhood sexual abuse. Poole et al. (1995) sent surveys to a randomly selected sample of psychotherapists and reported results from 145 respondents. What is most striking about the findings depicted in Figure 2.3 is the extent to which respondents disagreed with one another regarding the use of the techniques. For example, 29% reported that they used hypnosis to help clients remember childhood sexual abuse, but 27% indicated that hypnosis should not be used in this way. Similarly, 44% reported using dream interpretation as a way of helping clients remember childhood sexual abuse, but 26% judged that dream interpretation should not be used in this manner.

Surveys can be informative, if conducted properly, because they can provide researchers with valuable insights into individuals' opinions and beliefs. In this case, the Poole data are worrisome because they reveal substantial disagreements among psychotherapists with regard to the appropriateness of various therapeutic techniques. Such disagreements indicate a need for further research to develop widely agreed-upon guidelines for which treatments are effective and appropriate and which are not. Moreover, a minority of the Poole respondents reported a constellation of beliefs and practices regarding ways of encouraging clients to remember childhood sexual abuse that many memory researchers view as suggestive (see Lindsay & Read, 1994; Loftus, 1993). As you'll see shortly, however, results of surveys such as this must be interpreted with caution because a variety of methodological problems can lead surveys to produce misleading results.

Sampling from a Population   The aim of a survey is to gather many observations to help determine the characteristics of a large group. Usually the group of interest is too large for researchers to measure everyone in it (such as all Canadians between 18 and 25 years of age), so researchers must decide how to select a representative subset of individuals to measure. The complete group that the researcher wants to learn about is called a *population*. The subset of individuals from the target population who are measured (e.g., those who complete and return a questionnaire) is referred to as a *sample.*

A researcher needs to consider a number of technical details when sampling from a population. This is because it is easy to end up with an unrepresentative, or biased, sample unless the proper precautions are taken (Weisberg et al., 1989). Let's imagine that a researcher named Rosa wants to study Canadian university students' sexual behaviours. She places an ad with a toll-free telephone number in selected university newspapers. Her hope is that students will call the number and answer questions about their sexual practices. However, not every university-aged student in the country will choose to participate, so Rosa will end up with only a subset, or sample, of the population of interest. Do you think the data collected from her subset will be truly representative of university students?

In this case, the answer is clearly "no" because the method of sampling depends on people volunteering to participate. Volunteers tend to produce biased samples, because people who volunteer usually have strong feelings or opinions about the study (Rosenthal & Rosnow, 1975). This tends to be especially problematic if the survey deals with an emotionally charged or sensitive topic. Think about it: Would you call in and tell a researcher about your sex life? Which of your friends would do so?

Representative samples can be produced through **random sampling,** which means that everyone in the target population has an equal likelihood of being selected for the survey. In principle, for Rosa to achieve a truly unbiased sample she would need to sample randomly from the entire population of Canadian university students—everyone in the population must have an equal chance of being selected. Because this is difficult to achieve in practice, Rosa will probably need to limit herself to sampling randomly from the population of students going to her particular university. Even obtaining a truly random sample from a single university can be difficult. If you randomly selected survey recipients from a complete list of students, you might find that those who return the survey differ systematically from those who don't. The point is that survey researchers must strive to obtain representative samples; when representativeness is in doubt, survey researchers must be cautious in generalizing their results to the population of interest.

Now let's return to the Poole et al. (1995) survey of psychotherapists' reports regarding therapeutic techniques for helping adult clients remember childhood sexual abuse. The researchers sent their survey to a random sample from a large national list of qualified psychotherapists, so the sample of therapists who received the survey was very likely representative of the larger population of qualified psychotherapists. However, only 43% of the sample completed and returned the questionnaire. This raises the possibility that those who returned the survey had different views on the therapeutic techniques in question than those who did not; that is, it is possible that the sample was not representative of the population of qualified psychotherapists (although Poole et al. offered arguments against this concern).

Even if a proper representative sample of the population has been obtained, surveys can suffer from other problems (Taylor, 1997; Weisberg et al., 1989). A very general limitation of surveys is that they rely on respondents' verbal self-reports. This is a problem because people do not always respond truthfully and openly on questionnaires; they may exaggerate or disguise their views for any of a variety of reasons. Furthermore, survey respondents may not know the answers to the questions they are asked and may therefore guess or infer incorrect answers or leave questions blank. The results of a survey can depend on the particular wording of the questions, and even on the order in which the questions are asked (Ellard & Rogers, 1993). Also, there is often room for debate about exactly what respondents mean when they give particular answers (see Lindsay & Poole, 1998, for discussion of debates about the interpretation of the Poole et al. survey, and see Gore-Felton et al., 2000, for a more recent survey on the same topic). Surveys can be written in ways that minimize these problems—for example, particular questions can be asked several times with slightly different wording

random sampling
A procedure for selecting a representative subset of a target population; the procedure guarantees that everyone in the population has an equal likelihood of being selected for the sample.

Concept Summary

DESCRIPTIVE RESEARCH METHODS

Specific Method	Description	Advantages and Disadvantages
Naturalistic observation	Record naturally occurring behaviour.	A: Behaviour is natural; results are generalizable. D: Research lacks control; can't determine cause.
Case studies	Gather a great deal of information on a single case.	A: Gives historical perspective. D: Difficulties in generalization based on one case; can't determine cause.
Surveys	Gather responses from many participants.	A: Can easily gather information from many people. D: Sampling bias; inaccurate self-reports; can't determine cause.
Psychological tests	Measure individual differences between people.	A: Practical predictions; assess basics of mind. D: Difficulties in test construction and validation; can't determine cause.

to check on the consistency of each participant's responses—but inaccuracies and ambiguities in responses are difficult to eliminate entirely.

If conducted properly, surveys can be great vehicles for obtaining information from a target population. But as with the other descriptive research methods that we've discussed, surveys rarely provide definitive information about behaviour and mental processes. They are best used in conjunction with other techniques, such as case studies, naturalistic observation, and experimentation, in a broadly based research effort. As will be discussed later in this chapter, when researchers want to understand what *causes* behaviours (e.g., what factors lead therapists to use or to disapprove of certain techniques), the best research approach is the experimental method.

Psychological Tests: Assessing Individual Differences

A major area of descriptive research in psychology is psychological testing. Psychological tests, which come in a variety of forms, are designed primarily to measure individual differences between people. For example, *achievement tests* measure a person's current level of knowledge or competence in a particular subject (such as mathematics or psychology) compared to others'; *aptitude tests* are designed to measure a person's potential for success in a given profession or area of study; *neuropsychological tests* (e.g., Spreen & Strauss, 1998) assess effects of various kinds of brain damage on cognitive performance. Researchers also use various kinds of intelligence and personality tests to classify ability, or to characterize a person's tendency to act in particular ways.

Psychological tests have enormous practical value and can help to advance basic research (Anastasi, 1985). For example, Anderson and Walsh (1998) reported evidence that IQ test performance of juvenile offenders is related to the likelihood of subsequent criminal behaviours; Ree and Earles (1992) showed that IQ is a good predictor of job performance; and Kuncel et al. (2001) summarized evidence that the Graduate Record Examination (GRE) predicts students' performance in graduate school.

Psychologists also analyze test performance to answer fundamental questions about the mind. For example, data collected from psychological tests have been used to tackle questions such as: Do people have a single and fixed amount of intelligence, present at birth, or do they have multiple kinds of intelligence that rise and fall with experience? Do people have consistent personality traits, such as honesty or pleasantness, or do their behaviours change haphazardly across situations? You'll hear more about these specific questions when we treat psychological tests in more detail in Chapters 9 and 12.

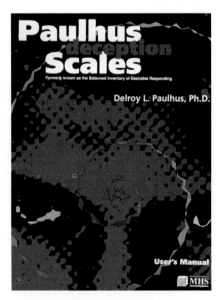

Psychologists use psychological tests to predict individuals' future behaviour as well as to help decipher the fundamental components of mind.

Statistics: Summarizing and Interpreting the Data

At the end of most research projects, regardless of the method used, the researcher is faced with lots of observations to analyze. When observing children in a daycare centre, for instance, an investigator normally collects information from many children, with repeated observations of each child, in an effort to make certain that the results can be generalized. These observations, or data, need to be organized and summarized into a form that allows for interpretation. It would be inappropriate to simply pick and choose from the results, based on what looks interesting, because selective analyses of data can introduce systematic biases into the interpretation (Barber, 1976; Rosenthal, 1994). Instead, the psychologist needs a principled way of describing and summarizing all the data.

Central Tendencies If the recorded observations can be expressed in the form of numerical scores, it is possible to calculate statistics to summarize the results. For any set of numerical observations, such as how often daycare providers wash their hands during a fixed period of diaper changing, it is useful to begin with a measure of *central tendency,* or the value around which most of the scores tend to cluster. You are probably familiar with the **mean,** which is the arithmetic average of a set of scores. To calculate a mean, you simply add up the numbers representing each observation and divide the total by the number of observations. So, if Jack washed his hands 4 times, Sally 9 times, Kim 4 times, Jessica 5 times, and Rowena 8 times, the mean of these five scores would be 6 ($4 + 9 + 4 + 5 + 8 = 30$; $30 \div 5 = 6$). The mean summarizes the observations with a single representative number: On average, daycare workers in your study washed their hands 6 times. Notice that in this case none of the workers actually washed his or her hands exactly 6 times. The mean provides only an estimate of central tendency; it does not indicate anything about particular scores.

Another measure of central tendency is the **mode,** which is the most frequently occurring score (in the hand washing example the mode is 4). The mode has the advantage that it always represents a real score—someone actually washed his or her hands 4 times—and it is easy to calculate. Yet another measure of central tendency is the **median,** which is the middle score when scores are arranged in rank order. To calculate the median, order the scores from smallest to largest (4, 4, 5, 8, 9), then look for the middle score. With the hand washers, half the scores fall below 5, and half fall above, so 5 is the median. If the number of scores is even, with no single middle score (e.g., 4, 4, 5, 6, 8, 9), the median is calculated as the mean of the two middle scores (e.g., $[5 + 6] \div 2 = 5.5$).

Researchers often compute several measures of central tendency for a set of scores. The mean is an excellent summary of the average score, but it can sometimes be misleading. Suppose, for example, that Sally is replaced at the daycare centre by Anthony, who suffers from an abnormal compulsion to wash his hands. Anthony washes his hands 29 times during the recording period. If we replace Sally with Anthony, we now have the following set of scores: 4, 4, 5, 8, 29. The arithmetic average, or mean, will shift rather dramatically—from 6 to 10—because of Anthony's extreme score, but neither the mode nor the median will change at all (see Figure 2.4). Because of the way they are calculated, means are very sensitive to extreme scores: The value shifts in the direction of the extreme score. On the other hand, the mode and the median are less affected by extreme scores. In our example, when Anthony is included the median or the mode is probably a better summary of the average amount of hand washing than the mean. Researchers usually use the median or mode to summarize the central tendency of a set of data that includes a few very extreme, unusual scores that would distort the mean.

Variability In addition to measuring the central tendency of a set of data, researchers are also interested in summarizing **variability,** or how much the scores in the set differ from one another. The mean indicates the average, but it provides no information about how far apart the individual scores are from each other. A good way to get a

mean
The arithmetic average of a set of scores, obtained by dividing the sum of all scores by the number of scores.

mode
The most frequently occurring score in a set of scores.

median
The middle point in an ordered set of scores; half the scores fall below the median score, and half fall above the median score.

Critical Thinking

Grade point average is typically calculated using the mean. Suppose the mean was replaced with a grade point mode or a grade point median. What would be the advantages and disadvantages of calculating grade point in these ways?

variability
A measure of how much the scores in a distribution of scores differ from one another.

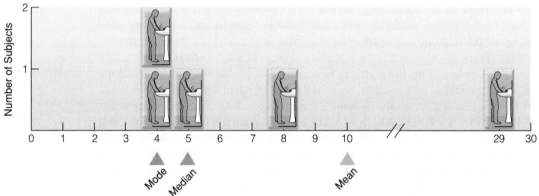

FIGURE 2.4

Comparing the Mean, the Median, and the Mode

The top row shows the differences between the *mean* (arithmetic average), the *median* (middle point in a set of scores), and the *mode* (most frequently occurring score) for hand washing behaviour at a daycare centre. The bottom row shows how the mean can be affected by an extreme score, someone who washes his or her hands 29 times. Notice that the extreme score has no effect on the median or mode.

sense of how much variability there is in a set of data is to look at a frequency histogram of those data. A frequency histogram is a chart that displays the number (i.e., frequency) of cases that received various scores on the measurement scale used in a study. The horizontal axis of the chart represents different levels of the measurement scale, and the vertical axis represents the number of cases. For example, in the frequency histogram on the left side of Figure 2.5, about 30 students had a score of 75 and about 27 students had a score of 83. In the frequency histogram on the right side of Figure 2.5, in contrast, about 45 students had a score of 75, and only about 7 had a score of 83. There is much more variability in the scores depicted on the left of Figure 2.5 than in those depicted on the right of Figure 2.5.

To see why variability is important, think about your last exam score. Let's assume that you received an 83 and the average score was 75. What can you conclude about your performance? You might think that you did only slightly above average because your score was relatively close to the mean. But perhaps not. If the scores were all bunched toward the middle, your performance might have been spectacular; in fact, a grade of 83 could have been the highest in the class. Thus, researchers need to know more than the average of a set of scores; they also need to know something about variability.

Several measures of variability are available to researchers. A simple one is the **range,** which measures the difference between the largest and smallest scores in the distribution. If the highest score in the class was a 90 and the lowest score a 50, the range

range

The difference between the largest and smallest scores in a distribution.

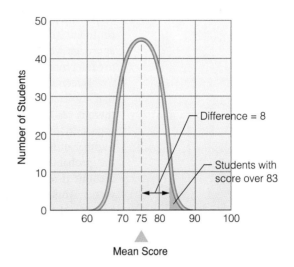

FIGURE 2.5
Variability

Researchers are often interested in variability, or the extent to which scores in a set differ from one another. Each of these two distributions has the same average, or mean, but the distribution on the left has more variability. Notice that the raw difference between the mean (75) and a particular score, such as 83, is the same in the two cases. But scoring 8 points above the mean is highly unusual in the distribution on the right, and fairly common in the distribution on the left. If you received a score of 83, which class would you rather be in? How about if you received a score of 67?

would be $90 - 50 = 40$. A more widely used index is the **standard deviation,** which provides an indication of the average extent to which individual scores vary from the mean score. If all of the scores are very close to the mean score, then the average distance from the mean will be small, whereas if many scores differ dramatically from the mean then the average distance from the mean will be large (see Appendix A for more detail). The standard deviation is larger for the data set depicted in the frequency histogram on the left of Figure 2.5 than in that on the right. We'll return to the concept of standard deviation later in the text, particularly in Chapter 9, because psychologists often describe an individual's score on a psychological test, such as an IQ test, in terms of the extent to which that score deviates from the mean relative to other individuals' scores.

Inferential Statistics Statistics such as the mean and the standard deviation help researchers describe their data; as such, they form a part of what is generally called **descriptive statistics** (so named because they describe the data in a sample). But it is also possible to use a different sort of statistics, called **inferential statistics,** to estimate (1) the likelihood that the behaviours recorded in a sample are representative of some larger population and (2) the likelihood that the differences or relationships between observations are due to chance. Inferential statistics enable researchers to make inferences, based on sample data, regarding the larger population of which the sample is representative.

Suppose that after a day of observation you find that male daycare providers washed their hands 5.8 times on average, whereas female providers washed 6.2 times a day (a difference of 0.40). Is there really a gender difference in hand washing behaviour at this daycare centre? It could be that the difference you observed between men and women was just a fluke. Maybe if you had recorded hand washing behaviour on a different day you would have found no gender difference, or that male daycare providers washed their hands more often. How could you determine whether your data are truly representative of hand washing behaviour at this daycare centre? One way would be to collect lots and lots of data (e.g., observing all of the daycare providers full-time for

standard deviation
An indication of how much individual scores differ or vary from the mean in a set of scores.

descriptive statistics
Mathematical techniques that help researchers describe and summarize their data.

inferential statistics
Mathematical techniques that help researchers estimate the likelihood that recorded behaviours are representative of a population or the likelihood that differences or relationships between observations are due to chance.

several months). The more consistently you observed a gender difference, the more confident you would be that there really is a gender difference. Unfortunately, this approach would be very time consuming and expensive. An alternative approach is to use inferential statistics.

Inferential statistics enable researchers to estimate the likelihood, or probability, that a collected pattern of data came out the way it did by chance alone. For example, if there is really no gender difference in hand washing behaviour, how often would you expect to find, after a particular day's observation, a 0.40 difference in the mean number of times women versus men washed their hands? Inferential statistics estimate the probability of getting a result by chance alone by simultaneously taking into account three factors: (1) the size of the obtained difference (e.g., how much men versus women daycare workers differed in hand washing in the sample), (2) the amount of variability within each group (e.g., how much the men differed from one another and how much the women differed from one another, in terms of hand washing), and (3) sample size (e.g., how many daycare workers of each gender were measured). All else being equal, a large difference between groups is less likely to have occurred by chance alone than a small one; a difference between groups is less likely to have occurred by chance alone if the variability within the groups is small; and a difference between groups is less likely to have occurred by chance alone if the samples are large.

Take a moment and think through these three factors; you should be able to get an intuitive sense as to why the combination of these three factors could be used to estimate the probability that an observed difference occurred merely as a fluke of chance. Inferential statistics use the mathematics of probability theory to combine these three factors to yield a specific numerical estimate of the likelihood that an observed difference would occur by chance alone. As discussed in the Practical Solutions feature on Intuitive Statistics, people make statistical inferences about all sorts of things in their daily lives, but they often do so in ways that fail to take into account the statistical factors that affect the reliability of an observation, relationship, or difference. By learning about these things, you can make better decisions in your daily life.

If inferential statistics indicate that the observed difference in men's versus women's hand washing is very unlikely to have occurred by chance alone, then your findings can be treated as statistically reliable (i.e., you can rely on getting the same findings if the study is repeated under the same conditions). In most psychological studies, the probability that an outcome is due to chance alone must be lower than 0.05 (5%) for the outcome to be accepted as being statistically reliable. This means that you can treat a male–female difference in hand washing of 0.40 as statistically reliable only if that difference would occur by chance alone less than 5 times out of 100. Because the absolute size of the difference in our example is fairly small (0.40), it would be statistically reliable only if the variability in hand washing among each sex was small and the sample sizes were large.

Practical Solutions

INTUITIVE STATISTICS

Most people are intuitive statisticians, whether they recognize it or not. For example, when you meet someone new, you may try to determine which of his or her actions represent the "real" person and which are only momentary quirks. You try to figure out the collective beliefs of your friends, and you worry about how your beliefs might differ from theirs. It's natural and reasonable to act in this way because everyday statistical intuitions help you describe and summarize your environment.

Unfortunately, evidence suggests that we're often not very good everyday statisticians. Let's consider an example taken from a study by Fong, Krantz, and Nisbett (1986) involving a statistical principle called the *law of large numbers.* Imagine that you recently went to a particular restaurant for the first time and that the meal was superb. You confidently recommend the place to your friends, and you all decide to visit there as a group. But this time the meal is mediocre; not terrible, but neither you nor your friends are impressed. What conclusion would you draw? If you're like most people, you will give a *deterministic* answer, which means that you come up with some simple explanation for why the restaurant went from being great to being mediocre. You might speculate, for example, that the chef has changed.

Let's consider another example that demonstrates the same point. Suppose you're a hockey fan and that you've been following the career of your favourite NHL team's new goalie. The guy had a spectacular first year and won Rookie of the Year honours. In the off-season, he was awarded a huge new contract, and expectations are high when the new season rolls around. But his second year turns out to be disappointing, and his play is no better than average for the league. How would you explain this?

Asked such a question, most people come up with simple, deterministic answers for why the goalie performed poorly in the second season (e.g., the success of his first year put him under more pressure than he could handle). Such explanations are not necessarily wrong, but the need for them is questionable from a statistical perspective. The problem arises from assuming that the original small sample of behaviour provided a reliable indication of true characteristics. Dozens of variables affect how well a particular hockey player performs in a given season (e.g., which teams are played when, how well teammates perform, travel schedules, ice conditions, coaching, health, and home life). The player who wins a Rookie of the Year award is likely to have had lots of luck that year in terms of such variables, and it

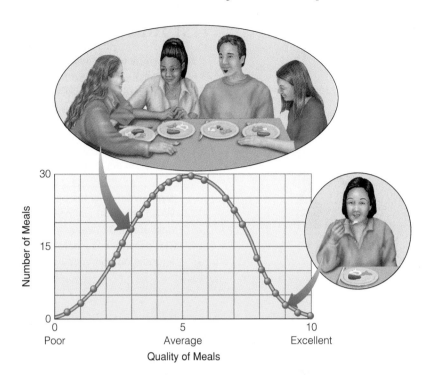

FIGURE 2.6

The Law of Large Numbers

The larger the sample size, the more likely it is that the sample will accurately represent the true average of the population. Any single small sample may or may not reflect the average. If you have a great meal one time at a restaurant, that doesn't mean it represents the average meal at that restaurant.

is unlikely that chance will continue to be so kind in the second year. Moreover, an NHL player who has a spectacular season may well be playing above his own average ability. You can be above your own average some of the time, but not consistently!

Behaviour varies dramatically as a consequence of a huge number of factors, whether you're talking about the behaviour of a restaurant kitchen or the behaviour of a person. Statistically, small samples of behaviour—such as one meal in a restaurant or one season in the NHL—cannot be expected to provide reliable indications of true quality or average ability. To achieve an accurate representation, you need lots of observations. This is the law of large numbers: The larger the sample size, the more likely the conclusions will accurately represent the population of interest (see

Figure 2.6). Yet people tend to err by assuming that a small sample of behaviour is representative; consequently, they believe that any subsequent change in behaviour must be explained in terms of some simple cause.

Is there any way to avoid these kinds of errors? One answer is education: If you ask doctoral-level scientists with training in statistics to comment on the restaurant or rookie examples, they tend to give statistical rather than simple deterministic answers. They point to the concept of variability and say things like, "There are probably more instances of mediocre restaurants that serve an occasional excellent meal than exceptional ones that serve only excellent meals" or "You hit it lucky at an average restaurant" (Fong & Nisbett, 1991). So there's hope for us all— as long as we take some stats courses!

Test Yourself 2.1

To test your knowledge of descriptive research methods, fill in the blanks with one of the following words or terms: reactivity; external validity; case study; random sampling; survey; mean; median; mode; standard deviation. (You will find the answers in Appendix B.)

1. The middle point in a rank-ordered set of scores is the _____.
2. The _____ technique, in which one or a few individuals are studied in depth, is open to criticism because its results may lack _____; that is, the results may not generalize or be representative of the population as a whole.
3. When behaviour changes as a result of the observation process, the recorded data are said to suffer from a problem of _____.
4. The descriptive research technique used to gather limited amounts of information from many people is called a _____.

PREDICTING BEHAVIOUR: CORRELATIONAL RESEARCH

Learning Goals

1. Learn to define correlation and discuss how correlations can be used to predict behaviour.
2. Be able to explain why correlations cannot normally be used to determine the cause of behaviour.

WHEN DONE PROPERLY, descriptive research provides psychologists with facts about people's behaviour. Psychologists are rarely satisfied, however, with simply describing the facts of behaviour. At minimum, we would also like to be able to predict behaviour. For example, educational psychologists would like to be able to predict which high school graduates are likely to do well versus poorly in university. Similarly, a psychologist working with prison inmates would like to be able to predict which prisoners will do well on parole and which will not.

Correlational Research

One step toward predicting behaviour is to determine whether a *relationship* exists between two measures, such as scores on an aptitude test and scores on a measure of job performance. Psychologists often use a statistical measure called a **correlation** to assess the relationship between a pair of measures. A correlation tells you whether two *variables,* or measures that can take on more than one value (such as test scores), tend to vary together systematically. Correlations are computed by gathering observations on both measures of interest from a sample of individuals and then computing a mathematical index called a *correlation coefficient.* A correlation coefficient indicates how accurately the value of one variable, such as job success, can be predicted by the value of the other variable, such as an IQ test score.

When there is a correlation between two measures, those two variables tend to vary together in some way. In the daycare example, there is probably a strong correlation between the number of diapers changed during the day and the number of times the caretakers wash their hands: the more diapers changed, the more frequently hands are washed. In this particular case, it is a *positive correlation,* which means that the two measures tend to vary in the same direction: the more of one, the more of the other. A *negative correlation* exists when the two measures vary together but in opposite directions. For example, there is a negative relationship between the number of hours that

correlation

A statistic that indicates whether two variables are related or vary together in a systematic way; correlation coefficients vary from +1.00 (perfect positive relationship) to 0.00 (no relationship) to −1.00 (perfect negative relationship).

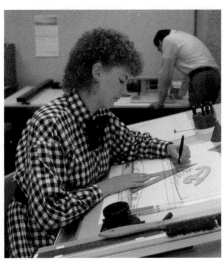

The building skills of the young girl on the left may or may not be predictive of a professional career in architecture.

Beverly practises on the piano and the number of errors she makes during her recital performance. The more she practises, the fewer errors she makes. A relationship still exists—we can roughly predict one when we know the other—but the correlation is negative because increases in one variable tend to co-occur with decreases in the other variable.

The strength of the correlation between two variables can be represented by a mathematical value called a correlation coefficient. Calculating a correlation coefficient requires measurement of a relatively large number of individuals. Moreover, you need to collect data on *both* measures. Correlation coefficients range between +1.00 and −1.00. The absolute value of the coefficient (the difference from 0, regardless of the sign) indicates the *strength* of the correlation. A correlation coefficient of 0 indicates no relationship between the two variables. The closer the value is to 1.00 (either positive or negative), the stronger the relationship between the two measures and the more likely you are to be able to predict one variable correctly if you know the other. As a trivial example, the correlation between weight measured in kilograms and weight measured in pounds is +1.00. The sign of the coefficient indicates whether the correlation is positive or negative. For example, a correlation coefficient of +0.30 indicates a fairly weak positive correlation (e.g., among a sample of university undergraduates, those who get high scores on a spelling test might also tend to get high scores on a math test, but there would be many exceptions to that general rule, resulting in a fairly weak positive correlation). Similarly, a correlation coefficient of −0.74 indicates a quite strong negative correlation (e.g., it might be that individuals who had consumed more alcohol would do less well on a test of manual dexterity—the relationship would not be perfect, but depending on the characteristics of the sample and the specifics of the dexterity test, it might be quite a strong negative correlation).

Figure 2.7 shows how positive and negative correlations can be represented graphically, in the form of *scatter plots*. Looking at the figure will help you understand how correlations work. Each point in a scatter plot represents a person's scores on both of two measures. Figure (a) depicts data from 40 individuals, showing for each one the number of diapers changed and the number of times hands were washed. In (b) you can find, for each of 40 individuals, how many hours he or she spent practising and the number of errors made during the recital. Once the correlation has been computed, it can then be used to make predictions about a new subject's score on one variable based on his or her score on the other variable. So, if a correlation is present, you can predict (with some degree of confidence and accuracy) how many errors Nathan will make during his recital by knowing how many hours he practised. Given that the correlation coefficient was calculated based on accurate measures of a large and representative sample, then the closer the correlation is to 1.00 (positive or negative), the more

FIGURE 2.7

Positive and Negative Correlation Depicted in Scatter Plots

Two examples of scatter plots. Each point shows an individual's scores on each of the two variables. (a) In a strong positive correlation, the values for both variables move in the *same* direction; that is, as more diapers are changed, the more times hands are washed. (b) In a negative correlation, the values for the two variables move in *opposite* directions; that is, as more time is spent practising, fewer errors are made during the recital.

a Strong Positive Correlation

b Strong Negative Correlation

accurate your prediction is likely to be. This is the reasoning used by most university admissions committees: They know there is a strong positive correlation between high school marks and university performance, so they predict how well people will do in university by looking at their high school marks.

Zero Correlations   When a correlation coefficient is not statistically different from zero, the two behavioural measures are said to be *uncorrelated*. Technically, this means that knowing the value of one measure does not allow you to predict the value of the second measure with an accuracy greater than chance. Imagine, for example, trying to predict university grade point average by measuring how many times people wash their hands during the day. In this case, the correlation is almost certainly zero—you can't use hand washing behaviour to predict GPA. It's important not to confuse the concept of a zero correlation with negative correlation. If the correlation between two variables is zero, no statistical relationship is present; the value of one variable reveals nothing about the other. In a negative correlation a clear relationship exists; it's just that the value of one variable tends to increase when the value of the other decreases (and vice versa).

It is worth emphasizing that even when there is zero correlation between two variables, there are likely to be some cases with high scores on both of those variables (and some cases with high scores on one variable and low scores on the other, and yet others with low scores on both variables). Suppose, for example, that each day for two weeks you read your daily horoscope and scored its prediction for your day on a scale from 0 (a really bad day) to 10 (a really great day), and then each night before bed you scored your actual day on the same scale (see Figure 2.8). Suppose further that it turns out that there is no correlation between the horoscope predictions and the actual days. Does that mean that the horoscope's prediction would never agree with the actual day? No—indeed, there would have to be something magical about horoscopes if they always managed to be wrong! In this example, a zero correlation means that sometimes the horoscope predicts that the day will be good and it turns out to be bad, other times it predicts the day will be bad and it is good, other times it predicts the day will be good and it is indeed good, and yet other times it predicts that the day will be bad and it is indeed bad.

FIGURE 2.8

Zero Correlation

This scatter plot shows a near-zero correlation between (a) daily horoscope predictions (rated on a scale of 0 for a very bad day to 10 for a really great day) and (b) ratings of actual days. Overall, it is not possible to predict the value of one of the variables by knowing a value on the other—the correlation is very near zero—even though there are some days on which the horoscope's predictions happen to agree perfectly with the actual day.

The point to remember is that if there is no significant correlation between two variables, then we cannot predict one variable on the basis of the other. People sometimes err in daily life by paying attention only to cases in which two variables appear to be related, ignoring the equally numerous cases in which the lack of relationship is obvious, leading them to perceive a correlation that isn't there.

Psychological measures rarely correlate perfectly; most correlations are only moderate. For example, the correlation between scores on the Scholastic Aptitude Test (SAT) and the grade point average of first-year university students is only about +0.40

(Donlon, 1984). This means that when researchers make predictions about behaviour based on correlations, the accuracy of their predictions will usually be limited. University admissions officers can use SAT scores to predict university performance at greater than chance levels, but the test's predictive abilities are far from perfect (Stricker et al., 1996). Similarly, the correlation between adults' height and weight is only about +0.60; on average, taller people tend to weigh more than shorter people, but obviously there are exceptions to this general rule. Correlation coefficients give researchers some important predictive ability, but they rarely enable exact predictions because correlations are rarely perfect.

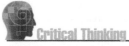

Critical Thinking

Pat doesn't make any decisions in her life without consulting a psychic. She's convinced that most of what the psychic tells her about her future comes true. Given what you know about correlations and causality, how might you convince her otherwise?

Correlations and Causality

Determining if a relationship (correlation) exists between two variables is important in everyday life because it helps people make predictions about their environment. It is useful to know, for example, whether someone who acts in a certain way at time 1 is likely to act in another certain way at time 2. Evidence of predictive relationships between variables can also have important real-world implications. Suppose, for example, that psychologists demonstrated a substantial positive correlation between the amount of violence children watch on television and how aggressively those children act later in life. Knowing about such a relationship would probably influence the behaviour of parents and might even lead to a social outcry for the monitoring of televised violence (Bushman & Anderson, 2001).

We must, however, be cautious when interpreting correlational evidence. Correlations are useful devices for describing patterns of relationships between variables, but they are of limited value when it comes to understanding why behaviours occur and co-occur. The presence of a correlation between two behaviours may help psychologists predict one behaviour based on another, but correlations do not enable them to determine causality. For example, a correlation between watching violence on television and later aggression does not necessarily mean that television violence causes aggression, even if the correlation is very strong.

Third Variables   The main reason why it's not possible to determine causality from a correlation has to do with the presence of other factors in the situation. Two variables can appear to be connected—they might rise or fall together in a regular, predictable way—but the connection could be due to a common link with some third variable. Let's consider an example close to home. On average, people who graduate from university end up with higher incomes than people who don't. Put in terms of a correlation, annual income is positively correlated with years of schooling. Does that mean that a university education *causes* better jobs and higher income? Perhaps, but not necessarily. There could be other variables that explain part or even all of the relationship.

Think for a moment about the kinds of people who go to university. Do they represent a random sample of the population as a whole? Of course not. University students tend to be brighter, they tend to come from better high schools, they tend to be people who have worked hard and succeeded in high school, and they also tend to come from families that are in the higher income brackets (partly because attending university is expensive). None of these other factors is controlled for in the calculation of a correlation. You can predict with a correlation, but the mere presence of a correlation doesn't tell you what causes the relationship. University students might end up with higher incomes because they're smarter, richer, more hard working, and/or because they're better educated. Any or all of these factors could be contributing to the relationship that the correlation describes (Cook & Campbell, 1979).

Now let's return to the example of the relationship between TV violence and aggression. Can you think of any third variable that might explain the correlation? Try to answer that question before reading on. One possibility is that parents who allow their children to watch lots of violence on TV tend to be more aggressive than parents who do not let their children watch such shows. If so, the children who watch a lot of

Do children model what they see on television? Many psychologists believe they do.

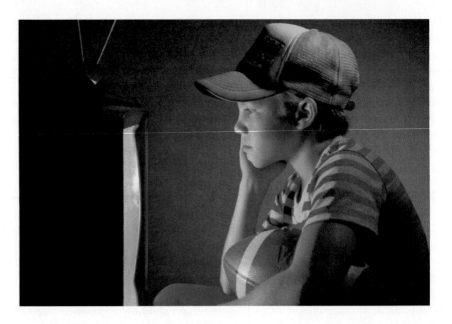

violent TV and later turn out to be aggressive might have grown up to be highly aggressive anyway, even if they had never seen a television set. That is, perhaps it's the parents' aggressiveness that is causing the children's aggressiveness, and exposure to violent TV just happens to co-occur with having more aggressive parents.

Even if there is a causal relationship between two variables, the direction of that relationship is not always obvious. For example, it might be that aggressive children simply like to watch violent programs on television. If so, then perhaps it's not that TV violence is causing the aggression, but rather that the children's aggressive tendencies are influencing their choice of programs. Once again, correlations describe relationships, but by themselves they cannot establish cause and effect. To determine causality, as you'll see shortly, researchers cannot simply describe and predict behaviour; they must manipulate it.

Concept Summary

CORRELATIONAL PATTERNS

Question to Be Addressed	Pattern of Correlation	Description
How does the number of diaper changes *relate to* the number of hand washings?	Positive	The more diaper changes, the more hand washings; the fewer diaper changes, the fewer hand washings.
How does performance in high school *relate to* university GPA?	Positive	The higher the high school GPA, the higher the university GPA; the lower the high school GPA, the lower the university GPA.
How does the amount of piano practice *relate to* the number of errors during a recital?	Negative	The more practice, the fewer errors are made; the less practice, the more errors are made.
How does the amount of time spent partying *relate to* university GPA?	Negative	The more time spent partying, the lower the GPA; the less time spent partying, the higher the GPA.
How does a person's shoe size *relate to* his or her score on an intelligence test?	No correlation	Knowing someone's shoe size tells you nothing about his or her IQ test score and vice versa.

Test Yourself 2.2

Test your understanding of correlations by identifying whether the following statements represent positive, negative, or zero correlations. (You will find the answers in Appendix B.)

1. The more Larry studies his psychology, the fewer errors he makes on the chapter test: _____

2. As Sadaf reduces her rate of exercising, her heart rate begins to slow: _____

3. The longer Yolanda waits for her date to arrive, the higher her blood pressure rises: _____

4. Eddie finds no relationship between his horoscope's predictions and what actually happens to him during the day: _____

DETERMINING WHY BEHAVIOUR OCCURS: EXPERIMENTAL METHOD

 1b, SIM 1
Psyk.trek

Learning Goals

1. Grasp the differences between independent and dependent variables.
2. Be able to explain what is meant by experimental control and how it allows for the determination of causality.
3. Appreciate the problems created by expectancies and biases and be able to explain how these problems are avoided.
4. Understand the key issues regarding generalizing the results of an experiment.

AS NOTED EARLIER, psychologists want to understand the *causes* of behaviour. For example, psychologists studying teenagers' health-related behaviours are not satisfied by merely describing teens' patterns of drug use, unprotected sex, or risk taking; they want to know *why* some teens develop drug problems, contract sexually transmitted diseases, or take dangerous risks, whereas others do not. Understanding why people do the things they do entails understanding causal relationships; that is, knowing the factors that influence people toward or away from performing particular behaviours or having certain thoughts and feelings. Given such an understanding, one can both predict behaviour (e.g., predict which high school graduates are likely to do well in university) and, more importantly, influence it (e.g., develop programs that effectively reduce teenage drug abuse).

If the ultimate goal of most psychologists is to establish the causes of behaviour, what research strategy will enable them to do so? Suppose you wanted to determine whether watching violent TV shows causes an increase in later aggression. What specific steps should you take? You must create a situation in which you can be confident that if aggressive behaviour increases after exposure to violent television, then it is indeed the television violence that is responsible for the change. Alternative possibilities need to be eliminated before you can confidently conclude that things are causally related. As you've just seen, the mere description of a relationship is not sufficient; correlation does not imply causation. Establishing causality requires *control,* one of the most important functions of an experiment.

In research using the **experimental method,** the investigator actively manipulates or alters some aspect of the environment and observes the effect (if any) of that manipulation on behaviour. By the term *environment,* psychologists can mean just about anything. For instance, they might manipulate the external setting (room temperature, lighting, time of day), a person's internal state (hunger, mood, motivation to perform),

experimental method

A technique in which the investigator actively manipulates or alters some aspect of the environment (defined broadly) and observes the effect of the manipulation on behaviour.

Descriptive Method	Correlational Method	Experimental Method
Purpose Observing and describing behaviour	Predicting and selecting behaviour	Determining why behaviour occurs: Establishing cause and effect
Research Tactics Naturalistic observation Case studies Survey research Psychological tests	Statistical correlations based on two or more variables	Experiments manipulating an independent variable to note effects on a dependent variable

(The Purpose and Research Tactics labels appear at left of the respective rows.)

FIGURE 2.9

Summary of Major Research Methods

The chart summarizes the purpose and research tactics for the three major research methods: descriptive research, correlational research, and experimental research.

or social factors (presence or absence of an authority figure or popular peer group). The particular manipulation is determined by the researcher's hypothesis. As mentioned earlier, hypotheses in psychology are usually expressed in the form of if-then statements about behaviour: If some set of conditions is present, then a certain kind of behaviour will occur. The purpose of the experiment is to set up the proposed conditions and see what happens.

To examine the role of television violence on aggressive behaviour, an experimenter might directly manipulate the amount of TV violence children watch. Perhaps one group of children would be picked by the experimenter to watch a violent superhero cartoon while a second group watches the playful antics of a lovable purple dinosaur (if one could be found!). The experimenter would then measure the effect of the manipulation (if any) on the behaviour of interest: aggression. This strategy of directly *manipulating* the viewing habits, rather than simply observing them, is the essential feature of the experimental approach. Notice the difference from correlational research, in which the investigator simply records the viewing habits of a sample of children and then measures later aggressive acts. It is only through a direct manipulation by the experimenter that control over the environment can be exercised and causality determined. Figure 2.9 compares experimental research to the other two approaches we've discussed: descriptive and correlational research.

Independent and Dependent Variables

independent variable

The aspect of the environment that is manipulated in an experiment. It must consist of at least two conditions.

The aspect of the environment that is manipulated in an experiment is called the **independent variable.** Because it is a *variable* (i.e., something that can take on more than one value), any experimental manipulation must consist of at least two different conditions. In our example, the independent variable is the amount of television violence observed by the children, and the two conditions are (1) watching a violent program and (2) watching a nonviolent program. The aspect that is manipulated is called an *independent* variable because the experimenter produces the change, independently of the subjects' wishes, desires, personality, or behaviour.

Hypothesis   If people are exposed to advertising that contains a hidden message, product sales will increase.

FIGURE 2.10

The Major Components of an Experiment

The hypothesis is tested by manipulating the independent variable and then assessing its effects on the dependent variable. If the only thing changing systematically in the experiment is the independent variable, then the experimenter can assume that changes in the independent variable are likely *causing* any changes measured by the dependent variable.

Manipulation of Independent Variable

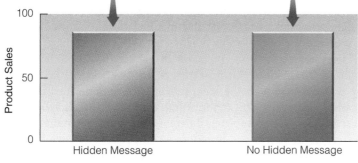

Subjects are asked to study an ad with a hidden message.

Other subjects are asked to study the same ad without the hidden message.

Measurement of Dependent Variable

Product Sales — Independent Variable: Hidden Message / No Hidden Message

The behaviour that is measured in an experiment is called the **dependent variable.** In our example, the dependent variable is the amount of aggressive behaviour that is seen following exposure to the violent or nonviolent program. The experimenter manipulates the independent variable (exposure to TV violence) and observes whether the behaviour measured by the dependent variable (aggression) changes. Notice that the experimenter is interested in whether or not the dependent variable *depends* on the experimental manipulation (hence the name *dependent variable*).

Now let's return to the topic that opened this chapter: subliminal perception. Can evil advertisers improve product sales by hiding messages such as "BUY NOW" in their advertising material? Remember: A subliminal message is presented below a person's normal threshold for perception, but it might exert an effect nonetheless. Let's begin by forming the hypothesis: If people are exposed to advertising material containing a hidden subliminal message, then product sales will increase (see Figure 2.10). To test this prediction, you might give two groups of people an advertisement to study. One group receives an ad containing a hidden message; the other group receives the same advertisement without the hidden message. Later, you check to see how likely the people in each group are to purchase the product described in the ad.

What is the independent variable in this experiment? To answer this question, look for the aspect of the environment that is being manipulated: The independent variable is the presence or absence of the secret subliminal message (half of the subjects see an

dependent variable
The behaviour that is measured in an experiment.

ad that contains a hidden message, whereas the remaining subjects see an ad that does not contain a hidden message). What is the dependent variable? In this case, the researcher wants to know whether sales of the advertised product will depend on the presence of the subliminal message. The dependent variable is defined as the number of times the people in each group buy the advertised product during some set period of time. Results of experiments like this are described in Chapter 5.

Experimental Control

To conclude that changes in the dependent variable are really *caused* by the independent variable, you need to be certain that the independent variable is the only thing changing systematically in the experiment. This is the main reason why at least two conditions are needed in an experiment. Researchers compare subjects who get the special treatment, called the *experimental group,* with those who do not, called the *control group.* In the subliminal perception experiment, the experimental group consisted of the subjects who received the hidden message, and the control group consisted of those receiving an ad without the message. If sales of the product subsequently differ between these two groups, and we know that the only systematic difference between them was the presence of the hidden message in the ad, then we can conclude that subliminal messages likely can cause changes in sales.

Confounding Variables   The determination of cause and effect hinges on the ability to be certain that the experimental and control groups are equivalent in all respects except for the critical independent variable manipulation. But how can you be certain that this is indeed the case? If some other factor differs across the groups, besides the independent variable, then interpretation of the results will be hopelessly compromised (Levine & Parkinson, 1994; Rosenthal & Rosnow, 1991). Uncontrolled variables that vary systematically with the independent variable are called **confounding variables** (the word *confound* means to throw into confusion or dismay). Suppose, for example, that researchers used completely different advertisements in the experimental and control conditions. This would introduce a confounding variable because any differences in sales could be due to differences between the ads other than the presence or absence of the subliminal message. Changes in the dependent variable could not then be attributed uniquely to the manipulation of the hidden message.

One solution to the problem of confounding variables is to equate the groups by holding constant all the factors that might vary along with the experimental manipulation. You could give everyone the same advertisement (except for the presence versus absence of the subliminal message) and test both groups under the same conditions (e.g., same time of day, same experimenter, same instructions). Any factor that might affect the likelihood of purchase, other than the independent variable manipulation, should be controlled—that is, held constant—across the different groups. When potential confounding variables are effectively controlled, allowing for the determination of cause and effect, the experiment is said to have high **internal validity.**

Random Assignment   Even in a perfectly controlled experiment, the problem of subject differences remains: How can experimenters ever be certain that their two groups of subjects are equivalent? People differ in many ways: intelligence, affection for certain products, motivation to perform, and so on. Researchers cannot hold all of these factors constant. Just think about the task of finding two or more groups of subjects with exactly the same intelligence, the same likes and dislikes, and equal motivation to perform. It would be impossible. The solution to the problem of intrinsic subject differences lies in the concept of random assignment, which is similar to the use of random sampling in survey research. In **random assignment,** the experimenter ensures that each participant has an equal chance of being assigned to any of the groups or conditions in the experiment. Each subject is assigned randomly to a group. Neither the sub-

confounding variable
An uncontrolled variable that changes along with the independent variable.

internal validity
The extent to which an experiment has effectively controlled for confounding variables; internally valid experiments allow for the determination of causality.

random assignment
A technique that ensures that each participant in an experiment has an equal chance of being assigned to any of the conditions in the experiment.

ject nor the experimenter chooses who gets assigned to which conditions; the assignment is governed by chance.

Random assignment does not eliminate differences between people: Some subjects will still be more intelligent than others, and some will be more naturally inclined to buy an advertised product than others. Random assignment simply increases the likelihood that these differences will be equally represented in each of the groups (see Figure 2.11). When participants are randomly assigned to conditions, only flukes of

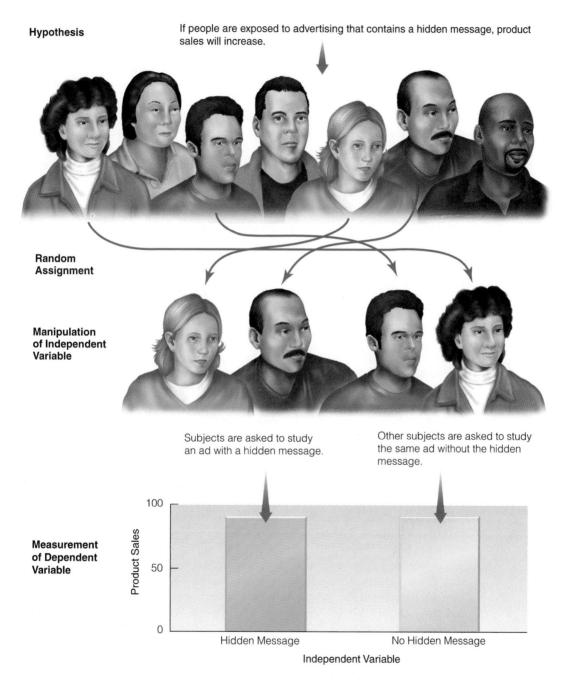

Hypothesis   If people are exposed to advertising that contains a hidden message, product sales will increase.

Random Assignment

Manipulation of Independent Variable

Subjects are asked to study an ad with a hidden message.

Other subjects are asked to study the same ad without the hidden message.

Measurement of Dependent Variable

Product Sales

100

50

0

Hidden Message   No Hidden Message

Independent Variable

FIGURE 2.11

Random Assignment

In random assignment, the experimenter ensures that each participant has an equal likelihood of being assigned to any of the groups or conditions in the experiment; that is, people are randomly assigned to the different levels of the independent variable. Random assignment increases the chances that unique subject characteristics will be represented equally in each condition.

chance could lead to systematic differences between the people in each condition. Importantly, inferential statistics enable researchers to estimate the likelihood of such flukes (review page 47).

Expectancies and Biases in Experimental Research

People are rarely passive participants in research; they almost always have expectations about the purpose of the research study and try to act accordingly. These expectations can sometimes affect subjects' behaviour in ways that cloud interpretation of the results (Barber, 1976; Rosenthal & Rosnow, 1969). Let's suppose, for example, that on the first day of class your teacher randomly selects half the students, including you, to participate in a special enrichment program. You receive instruction in a special room, with carefully controlled lighting and temperature, to see whether your learning will improve. The rest of the students, forming the control group, are left in the original classroom. The end of the semester arrives and, sure enough, the enrichment group has statistically reliably performed better than the control group. What can you conclude from these results?

In some ways, this seems to be a well-designed experiment. It includes both an experimental and a control group, the subjects were randomly assigned to groups, and let's assume that many potentially confounding variables were carefully controlled. But there is still a problem. The subjects in the enrichment group *expected* to perform better, based on their knowledge of the experiment. After all, they knew they were in an enrichment group. Consequently, these students may have simply tried harder, or studied more, in an effort to live up to the perceived expectations of the researcher. At the same time, subjects in the control group were aware that they were failing to get special treatment; this knowledge may have lowered their motivation to perform, leading to poorer performance. The fact that the groups differed in how much they learned doesn't necessarily mean that the enrichment program itself caused that difference.

There are two main ways that researchers can control for these kinds of *expectancy effects*. First, the investigator can be somewhat misleading in initially describing the study. Subjects can be deceived, or misled, in a way that disguises the true purpose of the experiment. This approach raises obvious ethical questions, although it is possible, under some conditions, to omit telling the subjects some critical feature of the study without severely violating ethical standards. (We'll return to the topic of research ethics later in the chapter.)

Second, the investigator can try to equate the expectations of the experimental and control groups. For example, the researchers can lead the control group to believe that they, too, are receiving an experimental treatment. This technique is often used in drug studies, in which participants in both the experimental and control groups receive a pill or an injection, but the drug is actually present only in the substance given to the experimental group. The control subjects are given a **placebo**—an inactive, or inert, substance (e.g., a "sugar pill") that looks just like the drug (Shapiro, 1960; White et al., 1985). (By the way, even though placebos are used precisely because there is no reason they should have an effect, people sometimes report effects of placebo treatments, presumably because they expect the treatment to work; for studies of the neurophysiological bases of such placebo effects, see de la Fuente-Fernandez & Stoessl, 2002, and Mayberg et al., 2002.)

Blind Controls The kind of experimental procedure described above is often used in a **single-blind study;** that is, the subjects are kept "blind" about the condition in which they have been placed (e.g., they don't know whether they are getting the drug or the placebo). Single-blind studies effectively control for subject expectancies because the subjects don't know which group they are in. This means that any expectations that might be present are likely to be equivalent in both groups. Notice that the single-blind technique does not eliminate subject expectancies; it simply reduces the chances that

Critical Thinking

As noted in the text, people sometimes experience effects of placebo treatments. If a placebo has an effect, how can it be described as a control condition?

placebo
An inactive, or inert, substance or treatment that resembles an experimental substance or treatment.

single-blind study
An experimental design in which the participants do not know to which of the conditions they have been assigned (e.g., experimental vs. control); it's used to control for subject expectancies.

Subjects who participate in research studies usually have expectations about the research. They expect certain things to happen, and these expectations can influence the results.

expectancies will differ systematically between the experimental and control groups and hence reduces the chances that any difference observed in the two conditions is due solely to expectations.

The individuals participating in the experiment as subjects aren't the only ones who expect certain things to happen; the experimenter does too (Rosenthal, 1966). Experimenters may expect that behaviour will be affected by the independent variable in a certain way, and that expectation might influence the results. Imagine, for example, that a researcher has developed a drug designed to cure influenza. The researcher has worked hard to develop the drug and needs convincing scientific evidence that it is effective. So the researcher designs a single-blind experiment composed of two groups of flu-suffering subjects. One group receives the drug and the other a placebo. The researcher is pleased to find that indeed people in the experimental group recovered reliably more quickly than those in the control group.

There are two ways that the experimenter's expectations might have influenced these results. First, unscrupulous investigators can deliberately "fudge" their data. Such intentional dishonesty is rare, but cases of scientific fraud have been documented on occasion in most fields of science, including psychology (for discussion, see Barber, 1976; Broad & Wade, 1982). Second, researchers can unknowingly influence their results in subtle ways. Perhaps, for example, the researcher gave slightly more attention to the people in the experimental group, and was more sympathetic and encouraging to them than to the people in the control group, and perhaps those subtle and unintended differences affected subjects' health. Or perhaps the researcher measured recovery in a subjective way and was biased to score people who got the treatment as recovered even when they weren't (or vice versa). Such biases are not deliberate on the part of the researcher, but they can cloud interpretation of the results.

The solution to experimenter expectancy effects is similar to that for controlling subject expectancies: Keep the researcher blind to the assignment of subjects to conditions. If those administering the study do not know which subjects are receiving the experimental treatment, they are unlikely to treat members of each group differently. Obviously, someone needs to know the group assignments, but the information can be coded in such a way that the person doing the direct observations remains blind to the condition. To control for both experimenter and subject expectancies in the same

double-blind study

An experimental design in which neither the participants nor the research observers are aware of who has been assigned to the experimental and control groups; it's used to control for both subject and experimenter expectancies.

context, a **double-blind study** is conducted, in which neither the subject nor the observer is aware of who is in the experimental and control conditions. Double-blind studies, often used in drug research, effectively eliminate bias effects.

Generalizing Experimental Conclusions

Properly designed experiments enable investigators to test hypotheses about the causes of behaviour in the context of the experiment. The determination of causality is possible if the experimenter has sufficient control over the situation to eliminate factors other than the experimental manipulation as contributors to a change in behaviour. But experimental control sometimes carries a cost. Sometimes, in the effort to control potentially confounding variables, the researcher creates an environment that is sterile or artificial and not very representative of everyday situations. The results of such an experiment may not generalize to real-world situations. As you learned previously, researchers use the term *external validity* to refer to how well results generalize across subjects and situations.

Consider again the issue of television violence and aggression: Does exposure to violent TV cause an increase in aggression? A number of experimental studies have explored this question (Bushman & Anderson, 2001; Friedrich-Cofer & Huston, 1986), but most have been conducted in the laboratory under controlled conditions. Subjects are randomly assigned to groups who watch violent programs or neutral programs, and their behaviour is then observed for aggressive tendencies, again under controlled conditions. In one recent study, preschool children were exposed to neutral or aggressive cartoons and then were given the opportunity to play with aggressive toys (such as guns); more aggressive acts were recorded for the children who watched the violent cartoon (Sanson & di-Muccio, 1993). These results clearly demonstrate that witnessed violence can increase the likelihood of aggressiveness. But this does not necessarily mean that these children would act similarly in their homes or that the effects of the brief exposure to violence were long lasting. In short, the experiment may lack external validity (for a discussion of what can and cannot be concluded from research on the effects of TV on aggression, see Freedman, 1992).

Concerns about the generalizability of laboratory results should not be exaggerated—results of laboratory experiments very often *do* generalize to real-world environments (see, for example, Banaji & Crowder, 1989). But it's legitimate to question

Critical Thinking

Many psychology experiments test introductory psychology students as subjects, raising questions about the generalizability of the findings of such research to the broader population. Do you think problems with generalizing from studies of undergraduates to a broader population may be worse for some research questions than for others? Can you think of a research question for which it is probably reasonable to generalize from undergraduate subjects to the wider population?

Concept Summary

THE EXPERIMENTAL METHOD

Research Question (variables in bold)	Independent Variable (experimenter manipulates)	Dependent Variable (experimenter measures)
Does **watching television violence** increase **aggression**?	Experimenter *manipulates* the amount of exposure to TV violence.	Experimenter *measures* the amount of aggression displayed.
Does **exposure to subliminal messages** have an effect on **product sales**?	Experimenter *manipulates* whether or not subjects receive a hidden message.	Experimenter *measures* product sales.
Does **forming images of words** enhance **memory for those words**?	Experimenter *manipulates* whether or not subjects form images of words as they're being presented.	Experimenter *measures* memory for the words.

whether the findings of a particular laboratory experiment apply to the real world. The degree of skepticism regarding generalizing from laboratory research to everyday situations depends in part on the topic of the research. For example, if you studied basic sensory processes (say, the visual mechanisms involved in detecting a briefly presented, faint flash of light) in university undergraduates, your results would probably generalize to the wider population (because there probably are no qualitative differences in the basic sensory mechanisms of undergraduates versus other people). In contrast, if you explored hypotheses regarding social behaviours by testing undergraduates, you would want to be cautious about generalizing your results to others who differ in age, education, and other characteristics, because the principles that govern social behaviours on campus may well differ from those in force in other populations and other life situations. Ultimately, of course, the issue of generalizability must be addressed empirically by conducting follow-up research with various samples and in various situations.

Test Yourself 2.3

Answer the following questions to test your knowledge of experimental method. (You will find the answers in Appendix B.)

1. Fill in the blanks with the term *independent* or *dependent*.

    In experimental research, the researcher actively manipulates the environment to observe its effect on behaviour. The aspect of the environment that is manipulated is called the _____variable; the behaviour of interest is measured by the _____ variable. To draw conclusions about cause and effect, the experimenter must make certain that the _____ variable is the only thing changing systematically in the environment.

2. Jean-Paul wants to determine whether the presence of Tom Cruise in a movie increases the box office take. He randomly forms two groups of subjects. One group sees *Minority Report,* starring Cruise, and the other group sees *Barney's Big Adventure,* without Cruise. Sure enough, the Tom Cruise movie is rated as more enjoyable than the movie starring the purple dinosaur. Jean-Paul concludes that the presence of Tom Cruise in a film causes increased enjoyment. What's wrong with this experiment?
    a. The dependent variable—Tom Cruise versus Barney—is confounded with the content of the movie.
    b. The independent variable—Tom Cruise versus Barney—is not the only factor changing across the groups.
    c. Nothing has been manipulated; it's really a correlational study.
    d. Experiments of this type require independent variables with at least three levels.

3. Random assignment is an important research tool because it helps the researcher control for potential confounding variables. Which of the following statements about random assignment is true? Random assignment:
    a. eliminates individual differences between people.
    b. ensures that some participants will get the experimental treatment and others will not.
    c. increases the likelihood that subject differences will be equally represented in each group.
    d. controls for bias by ensuring that biased subjects will be placed in the control group.

TREATING RESEARCH PARTICIPANTS ETHICALLY: HUMAN AND ANIMAL GUIDELINES

Learning Goals

1. Grasp the principle of informed consent.

2. Be able to summarize the roles of debriefing and confidentiality in research.

3. Understand some of the key ethical issues involved in animal research.

AS YOU'VE SEEN, knowledge in psychology comes from observation, but observing others requires that psychologists intrude, to some extent, into the personal environment of the research participants. Earlier you were introduced to the problem of *reactivity:* Knowing they are being observed can importantly change the way people behave. Although psychologists have developed techniques for reducing reactivity—designing noninterfering measures, keeping subjects blind to their actual role in the study, fooling subjects into thinking the observer is really a part of the environment—each method raises ethical questions. Is it appropriate to deceive people into thinking their behaviours are not being recorded? Is it appropriate to withhold treatment from some participants, through the use of placebos, in the interest of achieving proper experimental control?

To deal with such issues, professional organizations such as the Canadian Psychological Association (CPA) have developed and published ethical guidelines and codes of conduct that members are expected to follow (Canadian Psychological Association, 1991; Fisher & Younggren, 1997; Sales & Folkman, 2000). Canadian granting agencies that fund psychological research (e.g., the Canadian Institutes for Health Research, the Natural Sciences and Engineering Research Council, and the Social Sciences and Humanities Research Council) also require researchers to conform to strict ethical guidelines articulated in the Tri-Council Policy Statement (1998).

All psychologists have a professional responsibility to respect the rights and dignity of other people. This responsibility is recognized around the world (Leach & Harbin, 1997), and it goes beyond research activities; the code of conduct applies to all psychologists' professional activities, from providing therapy to working in the laboratory or field to giving testimony in the courtroom. First and foremost, respecting the rights of others means showing concern for their health, safety, and welfare; no treatments or research procedures that are likely to harm people are allowed. Clinical psychologists are also expected to act responsibly in how they advertise their services, how they represent themselves in the media, and how they charge and collect their fees.

Informed Consent

informed consent

The principle that before consenting to participate in research, people must be fully informed of any significant factors that might affect their willingness to participate.

The cornerstone of the code of ethical conduct is the principle of **informed consent.** Participants in any form of research or therapy must be informed, in easy-to-understand language, of any significant factors that might affect their willingness to participate (Mann, 1994; Meisel & Roth, 1983). Physical and emotional risks must be explained, along with the general nature of the research project or the therapeutic procedures that will be used, and only those who willingly give their consent in writing can be treated or tested (Charney, 2000). Clients or research subjects must also be informed that if they choose not to participate, for whatever reason, they will suffer no negative consequences.

But informed consent can raise problems for researchers. It can be argued that individuals cannot give truly informed consent unless they understand all of the details of the project. Yet, as we've discussed previously, it is often necessary to keep subjects blind about group assignments and hypotheses so that their expectations won't affect their behaviour in the study. Most often, this can be done without deceiving subjects about what is involved in participating in the experiment. Suppose, for example, that you tested the hypothesis that Ginkgo biloba (an herbal extract sold in health food stores) enhances memorization by having some subjects take Ginkgo biloba and others take a placebo, then asking them to memorize a story, and then testing their ability to recall the story. To avoid problems with reactivity, you would not tell subjects whether they were receiving the Ginkgo biloba or the placebo, but there would be no need to deceive them by telling them they were taking one substance when they were actually taking the other or to mislead them as to what they would be asked to do during the experiment. If, however, you were interested in assessing the effects of Ginkgo biloba on spontaneous or "incidental" memory (i.e., learning without intentional memorization), then you would not inform participants about the memory test until after they had taken the Ginkgo biloba or placebo and read the story. In a case like this, ethical problems can be reduced by using a two-stage consent procedure: You would first ask subjects to consent to participate in a study that involves taking Ginkgo biloba or a placebo and then reading a story, and then you would ask their consent to participate in the test phase. (See the Practical Solutions feature on page 89 of Chapter 3 for research on the effects of Ginkgo biloba on memory.)

Most psychological research topics can be studied rigorously without grossly deceiving subjects about what participating in the study will be like—they may not know all of the details of the procedure, but they have an accurate understanding of what will be involved in participating. Some hypotheses, however, cannot be tested without deceiving subjects. Imagine, for example, that you were interested in studying why bystanders at an accident often fail to offer assistance to the victim. To gain experimental control, you might stage a mock accident in the laboratory, in front of waiting research subjects, to see how they react under various conditions (e.g., when the victim is a man versus a woman). To conduct this research in a meaningful way, you would have to mislead the subjects—you certainly could not fully inform them about the procedure by telling them that they will see a fake accident!

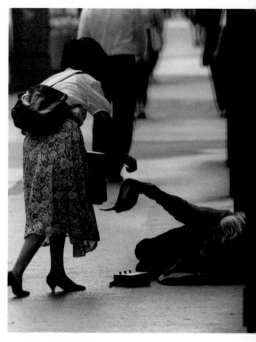

Studying the behaviour of people in natural settings, such as the willingness of bystanders to help others in need, sometimes requires that the researcher mislead or withhold information from the people being observed.

Most members of the psychological research community agree that it is sometimes justifiable to use deception in research procedures. Not all psychologists concur with this view (Baumrind, 1985; Ortmann & Hertwig, 1997), but it is the majority opinion. According to the CPA code of ethics, deception in research is justified only if the prospective scientific, educational, or applied value of the study is clear and substantial and there is no way to answer the research questions adequately without deceiving the subjects. It is also agreed that deception must not be of a type that could cause subjects lasting physical or emotional harm, and that subjects should not be deceived into doing things they would not consent to do. Experimenters have a responsibility to respect the rights and dignity of research participants at all times. Most universities ensure that subjects' rights are protected by requiring investigators to submit detailed descriptions of their studies to oversight committees before any human or animal subjects can be tested. If a study fails to protect subjects adequately, permission to conduct the study is denied.

Debriefing and Confidentiality

Two other key ingredients of the psychologist's code of ethical conduct are the process of *debriefing* and the maintenance of *confidentiality*. Psychologists are expected to debrief subjects fully at the end of the experimental session, meaning that everyone involved is to be informed of the purpose of the study. **Debriefing** is intended to clear up any misunderstandings that the subject might have about the research and to explain in detail why certain procedures were used (Gurman, 1994; Holmes, 1976). If deception was a part of the study, the full nature of the deception must be disclosed during the debriefing process. Debriefing gives the researcher an opportunity to counteract any anxieties that the subject might have developed as a result of the research. If the subject failed to help the victim of a staged accident, for example, the experimenter could explain that bystander passivity is a characteristic of most people (Darley &

debriefing

At the conclusion of an experimental session, informing the participants about the purpose of the experiment, including any deception that was involved.

Latané, 1968). It is worth emphasizing that the vast majority of psychological research does not involve deception (that is, subjects are given an accurate idea of what participating will involve before the study begins). Research indicates that most people who participate in psychology experiments come away with positive views of the experience (e.g., Landrum & Chastain, 1995).

After participation is completed, the subject's right to privacy continues. Psychologists are obligated to respect the privacy of the individual by maintaining **confidentiality**—the researcher or therapist is not to discuss or report confidential information obtained in research or in therapy without the permission of the individual. Confidentiality makes sense for more than just ethical reasons. Research subjects, as well as people seeking help for psychological problems, are likely to feel more comfortable with the process, and to act more naturally, if they are convinced that their right to privacy will be respected.

confidentiality
The principle that all personal information obtained from a participant in research or therapy should not be revealed without the individual's permission.

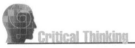

Critical Thinking

Can you think of any circumstances in which it might be ethical to conduct research with animals even though the results won't generalize to humans?

The Ethics of Animal Research

The psychology departments of many universities in Canada and throughout the world include psychologists who study nonhuman animals. Although some psychologists study animals by observing them in their natural environments, most do so in laboratory research. Animals are probably used in less than 10% of all current psychological research studies, but animal research has been and continues to be a very important source of psychological knowledge (Coile & Miller, 1984). As you'll see in later chapters, many of the most significant psychological principles were originally discovered through the study of animal behaviour (Domjan & Purdy, 1995).

Why use animal subjects? The most often cited reason is experimental control: Animal researchers can control the genetic background, diet, and experience of their subjects and thereby eliminate many of the potentially confounding variables that plague research with human subjects. Researchers can also study phenomena such as life-span development in ways that cannot be accomplished with human subjects. Studies of aging that would take 70 or 80 years with humans take only a few years with rats. Some research explores mechanisms of recovering from damage or stressors (e.g., testing treatments for brain injury): To develop effective interventions, researchers can cause and then treat damage in animals in ways they could not ethically do with human subjects. Yet another reason for studying nonhuman animals is that they have

Many important insights in psychology have come from the study of animals, but using animals as laboratory subjects raises serious ethical questions.

relatively simple internal structures and systems. The basic biological mechanisms that underlie learning, for example, have been studied extensively with sea slugs; the number of neural connections in a sea slug is tiny compared with the billions of connections residing in a human brain. Research with nonhuman subjects often serves as a vehicle for developing hypotheses that are later elaborated and tested with humans.

But researchers cannot ask nonhuman animals for informed consent, and even if they could, the animals would likely decline. Can animal research be justified by its scientific value? For example, is it okay to destroy a part of a rat's brain to test the efficacy of treatments for brain damage? Obviously, the use of animals in research is a highly controversial subject. Many millions of dollars are spent every year by animal rights groups, some of which oppose all forms of animal research (see Hubbel, 1990). In one survey of animal rights activists, 85% advocated the complete elimination of all animal research (Plous, 1991). Other critics question the intrinsic value of animal studies, arguing that an understanding of animals reveals little about human functioning and may even mislead researchers into drawing inappropriate conclusions (see Ulrich, 1991).

While acknowledging these concerns, most psychologists believe that animal research has enormous value. They base their belief on the fact that animal studies have repeatedly led to significant breakthroughs in the understanding of behaviour and psychological disorders and in medical and biological research (see Johnson & Morris, 1987; Miller, 1985, 1991). To cite one instance, animal research has led to breakthroughs in our understanding of depression and to the development of drugs that lessen the symptoms of this disorder (see Chapters 14 and 15). In virtually every chapter in this textbook, you will be exposed to psychological principles that have been gained from research with nonhuman subjects.

Controversy regarding animal research has sometimes been inflamed by misinformation. For example, experiments that deliberately inflict pain and suffering on animals are extremely rare (see Coile & Miller, 1984). The CPA and agencies that fund psychological research (e.g., the Canadian Institutes for Health Research) enforce strict guidelines for the ethical treatment of nonhuman subjects. Psychologists who conduct research using animals are expected to treat their subjects humanely. They are responsible for ensuring the animals' proper care and for minimizing their discomfort, pain, or illness. When surgical procedures are performed, the animals must be given the appropriate anesthesia, and proper medical procedures must be followed to eliminate infections and minimize pain. Failure to follow these standards can result in censure, loss of research funding, or termination of membership by the governing body of the association. Animal research raises legitimate and complex ethical issues about which reasonable people may disagree, but our opinion is that testing animal subjects is justifiable provided (a) the research has genuine potential to advance knowledge in important ways and (b) researchers minimize the distress experienced by their animal subjects.

Test Yourself 2.4

You can test what you've learned about ethics and research by answering the following questions. (You will find the answers in Appendix B.)

1. Fill in the blanks.

    All psychologists have a responsibility to respect the rights and dignity of other people. To ensure that research participants are treated ethically, psychologists use (a) _____, which means that all potential participants are fully informed about the potential risks of the project, (b) _____, which ensures that the subject's right to privacy will be maintained, and (c) _____, which is designed to provide participants with more information about the purpose and procedures of the research.

2. Sometimes it is necessary to deceive research participants in some way, such as keeping them blind to group assignments, so that expectations won't determine the outcome. Most psychologists believe that deception:
    a. is always justified as long as it furthers scientific knowledge.
    b. is never justified unless the research involves clinical treatment.
    c. is justified, but only under some circumstances.
    d. is not necessary if you design the project correctly.

3. The majority of psychologists believe that animal research has enormous value. But some question the ethics of using animals, primarily because:
    a. no real scientific advancements have come from animal research.
    b. animals are often treated cruelly.
    c. animals can give no informed consent.
    d. animal research is too expensive.

Solving the Scientific Problems

The facts and theories that make up the discipline of psychology have arisen from the systematic application of a set of research tools. Consequently, to understand the field of psychology you must learn about these methodological tools. In this chapter we divided our discussion of the methods of psychological research into four main problem areas.

First, what are the best techniques for observing and describing behaviour? Psychologists use systematic techniques to observe and describe behaviour. In *naturalistic observation,* the researcher observes behaviour in natural settings rather than in a laboratory environment. Naturalistic observation is a useful technique for generating research ideas and for verifying whether conclusions reached in the lab generalize to more realistic settings. In *case studies,* the focus is on a single example of a behaviour or psychological phenomenon. This technique allows the researcher to obtain lots of background information on the individual being studied, but the results may not always generalize to wider populations. In *survey research,* behaviour is sampled broadly, usually by gathering questionnaire responses

from many people. Finally, through *psychological tests,* differences between individuals can be quantified.

Once the observational data have been collected, they are summarized through the application of *descriptive statistics.* Such statistics include measures of the average or central tendency of a set of observations and measures of the extent to which individual scores in the set of observations vary from each other. Researchers also use *inferential statistics,* based on the laws of probability, to test hypotheses. Inferential statistics can help the researcher decide whether a difference between an experimental and a control group, for example, is likely to have occurred by chance.

Second, how can one predict behaviour? In *correlational research,* the researcher tries to determine whether a relationship exists between two measures of behaviour. For instance, do high school grades predict university performance? Correlation coefficients are statistics that provide an index of how well one measure predicts another: If two variables are highly correlated, then one can predict a person's score on one variable on the

basis of knowing that person's score on the other variable. Correlations are useful tools for predicting, but they do not allow the researcher to draw conclusions about what causes behaviour.

Third, how can psychologists determine the underlying causes of behaviour? If researchers want to know whether an activity, such as watching violence on television, *causes* a change in behaviour, they must conduct an *experiment.* In an experiment, the researcher manipulates the environment in a systematic way and then observes the effect of that manipulation on behaviour. The aspect of the environment that is manipulated is called the *independent variable;* the measured behaviour of interest is called the *dependent variable.* To determine that the independent variable is really responsible for the changes in behaviour, the researcher must exert experimental control—the only thing that can vary systematically between conditions is the experimenter's manipulation of the independent variable. Researchers conducting experiments encounter a variety of potential pitfalls, including subject and experimenter expectancies, that need to be controlled. Control strategies include the use of random assignment and blind research designs.

Fourth, what procedures ensure that research participants are treated ethically? Scientific psychology is based on observation, and observing others requires that researchers invade, to a certain extent, the personal environment of their subjects. As a result, it is important that all researchers follow a strict code of ethical conduct. An important safeguard is informed consent, which is designed to guarantee that participants are informed of any significant factors that could influence their willingness to participate. Other ethical standards govern proper debriefing and the maintenance of confidentiality. The same sorts of standards also apply to clinical psychologists when they provide psychological therapy. All psychologists have a professional responsibility to respect the rights and dignity of their research subjects and clients. This applies not only to human participants but also to animals used in research.

Chapter Summary

Rather than relying solely on intuition or speculation, psychologists develop and test theories by using the *scientific method*: (1) observe; (2) detect regularities; (3) generate a hypothesis; (4) test the hypothesis by observation under controlled conditions.

OBSERVING BEHAVIOUR: DESCRIPTIVE RESEARCH

Learning Goal: Understand the goals, techniques, and challenges of descriptive research. Descriptive research consists of tools and procedures for observing and recording behaviour systematically. One major challenge of descriptive research is minimization of reactivity (i.e., the tendency for research participants to alter their behaviour when they know they are being observed).

Naturalistic Observation: Focusing on Real Life

Learning Goal: Learn how psychologists conduct naturalistic research. Behaviour is observed in natural settings with noninterfering measures.

Case Studies: Focusing on the Individual

Learning Goal: Appreciate the strengths and weaknesses of case studies. Intense focus on a single case yields richly detailed historical information that can be used to generate hypotheses. Unfortunately, however, it is often unclear whether the results of a case study can be generalized to other cases.

Surveys: Describing Populations

Learning Goal: Understand the advantages and limitations of surveys. Responses can be gathered relatively easily from a large number of people, which helps establish generality. It is important to ensure that the sample of respondents to a survey is representative of the population to which the results are to be generalized. A major limitation of surveys is that they rely on verbal self-reports, which are not always accurate and are sometimes ambiguous.

Psychological Tests: Assessing Individual Differences

Learning Goal: Learn the major purpose of psychological tests. Psychological tests measure individual differences on variables such as intelligence and various dimensions of personality.

Statistics: Summarizing and Interpreting the Data

Learning Goal: Be able to explain how statistics can summarize and help interpret data. Descriptive statistics summarize or "describe" the findings of systematic research.

Inferential statistics enable researchers to estimate the likelihood that the results of a study are representative of the larger population and the likelihood that observed differences (e.g., between groups of subjects) are due solely to chance.

PREDICTING BEHAVIOUR: CORRELATIONAL RESEARCH
Correlational Research

Learning Goal: Learn to define correlation and discuss how correlations can be used to predict behaviour. Correlational research involves measuring each of a number of individuals on two variables and then determining whether or not the two variables are correlated (i.e., related) to one another. A positive correlation is observed if cases with high scores on one of the measures also tend to have high scores on the other (e.g., years of education and annual income). A negative correlation is observed if cases with low scores on one measure tend to have high scores on the other (e.g., test marks and hours spent watching TV the day before the exam). No correlation is observed if the two measures are unrelated to one another (e.g., shoe size and musical aptitude). Knowing that two variables are correlated means that an individual's score on one variable can be predicted on the basis of his or her score on the other.

Correlations and Causality

Learning Goal: Be able to explain why correlations cannot normally be used to determine the cause of behaviour. A correlation between two measures of behaviour helps prediction, but does not determine causality. For example, if IQ and income are correlated that might be because having a higher IQ leads to better income, or because greater income leads to better education, or because some third variable (e.g., family background or motivation) has a causal influence on both IQ and income.

DETERMINING WHY BEHAVIOUR OCCURS: EXPERIMENTAL METHOD
Independent and Dependent Variables

Learning Goal: Grasp the differences between independent and dependent variables. The *independent variable* is the aspect of the environment that is manipulated in an experiment. The independent variable must consist of at least two conditions (e.g., experimental and control conditions). A *dependent variable* is the behaviour or response that is measured in an experiment.

Experimental Control

Learning Goal: Be able to explain what is meant by experimental control and how it allows for the determination of causality. *Experimental control* is achieved by ensuring that the only systematic difference between conditions in an experiment is the independent variable. If, for example, the only systematic difference between two groups of subjects is whether they received the experimental or control treatment, then any difference in the dependent variable can be attributed to the manipulation of the independent variable.

Expectancies and Biases in Experimental Research

Learning Goal: Appreciate the problems created by expectancies and biases and be able to explain how these problems are avoided. Researchers must control for expectations and biases that can affect subjects' and researchers' behaviour in ways that might distort an experiment's results. Blind experiments are often used to control for expectancies on the part of subjects (single-blind) and experimenters (double-blind).

Generalizing Experimental Conclusions

Learning Goal: Understand the key issues regarding generalizing the results of an experiment. The effort to maximize experimental control can lead researchers to test hypotheses in quite artificial contexts, and this raises questions regarding the generalizability of the findings. Such questions are especially justified if the research explores an aspect of behaviour that is likely to differ across situations. Ultimately, conclusions from laboratory experiments must be confirmed by converging evidence obtained in naturalistic situations.

TREATING RESEARCH PARTICIPANTS ETHICALLY: HUMAN AND ANIMAL GUIDELINES
Informed Consent

Learning Goal: Grasp the principle of informed consent. Research participants must be informed of any factors that could affect their willingness to participate in psychological research or receive psychological treatment.

Debriefing and Confidentiality

Learning Goal: Be able to summarize the roles of debriefing and confidentiality in research. *Debriefing* is the process of explaining to research participants the purpose and details of a study after their participation. *Confidentiality* protects the participant's privacy.

The Ethics of Animal Research

Learning Goal: Understand some of the key ethical issues involved in animal research. Although CPA guidelines require that animals be treated humanely, controversy remains over their use in psychological research. One fundamental issue is that nonhuman animals cannot give informed consent (and would be unlikely to do so if they could). Balancing this issue is the fact that animal research has been tremendously valuable in advancing psychological knowledge, including in the development of treatments that have greatly enhanced humans' lives.

Terms to Remember

scientific method, 36
operational definition, 38
Observing Behaviour:
    Descriptive Research
descriptive research, 38
reactivity, 39
external validity, 39
naturalistic observation, 39
case study, 41
survey, 41
random sampling, 43
mean, 45
mode, 45
median, 45
variability, 45
range, 46
standard deviation, 47
descriptive statistics, 47
inferential statistics, 47
Predicting Behaviour:
    Correlational Research
correlation, 50
Determining Why Behaviour Occurs:
    Experimental Method
experimental method, 55
independent variable, 56
dependent variable, 57
confounding variable, 58
internal validity, 58
random assignment, 58
placebo, 60
single-blind study, 60
double-blind study, 62
Treating Research Participants Ethically:
    Human and Animal Guidelines
informed consent, 64

Recommended Readings

Stanovich, K. E. (2001). *How to think straight about psychology* (6th ed.). Reading, MA: Addison-Wesley. University of Toronto researcher Keith Stanovich provides an in-depth discussion of how to evaluate empirical evidence in psychology and avoid faulty conclusions.

Snodgrass, J. G., Levy-Berger, G., & Haydon, M. (1985). *Human experimental psychology.* New York: Oxford University Press. An excellent resource for designing experiments, setting up apparatus, testing subjects, analyzing and interpreting data, and writing up the results of research.

Pelham, B. W. (1999). *Conducting experiments in psychology: Measuring the weight of smoke.* Pacific Grove, CA: Brooks/Cole. An interesting book that describes the essentials of research methods using many real-life examples and hands-on activities.

 For additional readings, explore InfoTrac® College Edition, your online library. Go to:

www.adaptivemind2e.nelson.com

Hint: enter the search terms: participant observation; survey research; psychological tests; experimental design; psychological research methods.

What's on the Web?

Please note that Web addresses are subject to change. Check out the accompanying Web site for updates: www.adaptivemind2e.nelson.com. This site presents practice quiz questions, hypercontent, information on degrees and careers in psychology, study tips, and more.

The Natural Sciences and Engineering Research Council (NSERC)

www.nserc.ca/index.htm

NSERC is one of the largest Canadian federal agencies that provides grants for scientific research and is a major source of funding for research in scientific psychology. The NSERC Web site includes information about scholarships and grants for students and faculty in psychology as well as information about research ethics.

The Junk Science Homepage

www.junkscience.org

This page presents "all the junk that's fit to debunk." It's a very interesting site, chock full of phony claims and questionable science—a veritable feast for skeptical types—along with explanations of the flaws in the claims. Although many of the articles do not relate specifically to psychology, it's still a great site to visit to get a feel for the dogged skepticism of a scientist.

Psychology Research on the Net

psych.hanover.edu/Research/exponnet.html

This page is part of the American Psychological Society Web site and offers links to a dizzying array of research projects that will give you an idea of the range of phenomena that psychologists investigate. The projects linked to this site run the gamut of every area in psychology, from clinical to social to cognitive. Participate in projects on decision making, giving directions, anger, irrational food beliefs, and dozens of others.

CSICOP On-Line

www.csicop.org

This is the official home page of the Committee for Scientific Investigation of Claims of the Paranormal. CSICOP "encourages the critical investigation of paranormal and fringe-science claims from a responsible scientific point of view."

To discover that a particular feeling depends on activity in a number of specific brain systems interacting with a number of body organs does not diminish the status of that feeling as a human phenomenon. Neither anguish nor the elation that love or art can bring about are devalued by understanding some of the myriad biological processes that make them what they are. Precisely the opposite should be true: Our sense of wonder should increase before the intricate mechanisms that make such magic possible.

Antonio Damasio, *Descartes' Error: Emotion, Reason and the Human Brain*

What a piece of work is man!
How noble in reason.
How infinite in faculties.
In form and moving, how express and admirabl
In action how like an angel.
In apprehension, how like a god.
The beauty of the world.
The paragon of animals.

William Shakespeare, *Hamlet*, Act II, Scene II

Chapter 3 Biological Processes

ou, dear reader, are an amazing object. You are a specimen of the most complex thing in the known universe. One of the aims of this book is to help you appreciate that you (like the other 7 billion humans on planet Earth) are a marvel. Consider, for example, what you are doing now: As you'll learn in more detail in Chapter 4, light is bouncing off this page, sending a reflected pattern of shades and hues into the environment, with some of that reflected light entering your eyes and being transformed, through a remarkably complex cascade of processes, into thoughts, ideas, images, and feelings sparked by the black squiggles on this page. As another example, reach out and pick something up, such as a pen or a cup. Really—stop and do it. Now do it again, but this time notice the elegance of the trajectory of your reach (swiftly accelerating to a peak velocity, following a graceful arc, then smoothly braking as your hand nears the object, with your fingers oriented almost perfectly to grasp the object appropriately before your hand even reaches it).

The most remarkable thing about you, as a physical object, is your brain. This is an organ of bewildering complexity, with billions of intricately interconnected micro-components, and it plays the lead role in all of your skills and abilities, from controlling the performance of physical acts (picking up a pencil, dancing, snowboarding) to constructing your experience of the world around you to giving rise to your innermost thoughts and feelings.

This chapter introduces the field of **neuroscience,** which studies the connection between the brain, the mind, and behaviour. Although we'll focus primarily on the brain, your behaviour is controlled by a broader system that includes the spinal cord as well as neural connections to muscles, sensory organs, hormone-secreting glands, and other internal structures in the body. More specifically, the brain and spinal cord comprise what is called the **central nervous system** (see Figure 3.1). An additional network

neuroscience
An interdisciplinary field of study directed at understanding the brain and its relation to behaviour.

central nervous system
The brain and the spinal cord.

FIGURE 3.1
The Central Nervous System
The central nervous system consists of the brain and the spinal cord.

Previewing the Adaptive Problems

Biological processes address four central problems of adaptation. Each problem can be viewed as a challenge to be solved by the systems of your body to help you survive and adapt to the environment. These biological solutions provide important insight into the workings of the adaptive mind.

First, how does your body communicate with the environment and internally? One reason behaviour is often adaptive is that people are able to monitor their environment continuously and produce quick responses that fit the needs of the situations they face. If a child suddenly runs into the path of your car, you slam on the brakes and the child is saved. These rapid world-to-behaviour links are possible because of a complex communication network linking the outside world to the brain and linking the brain to the rest of the body.

Second, how does your brain initiate and coordinate behaviour? The nervous system handles the complicated task of receiving and communicating information, but information by itself does not translate into hand movements, quick reactions, or artistic creativity. The brain assigns meaning to the information it receives and coordinates the appropriate responses.

Third, how does the body regulate growth and other internal functions? Besides relying on the rapid transmission of information from one point to the next, the systems in your body also have widespread and long-term internal communication needs. To resolve these needs, structures in the body control the release of chemicals into the bloodstream that serve important regulatory functions, influencing growth and development, sexual behaviour, appetite, and emotions.

Fourth, how and why did evolution select the kind of brain structures and nervous system that humans have today, and how does the body store and transmit the genetic code? Natural selection has provided the human species with a unique set of physical, mental, and behavioural "solution tools" for solving the problems that our ancient ancestors encountered in their natural environments. The transmission of physical and behavioural characteristics from one generation to the next via genetics played a crucial role in our evolution, and your genetic inheritance continues to influence you today. The environments we live in today are quite different from those of our evolutionary ancestors, yet our genetically coded "solution tools" have probably not changed very much, and this can cause problems.

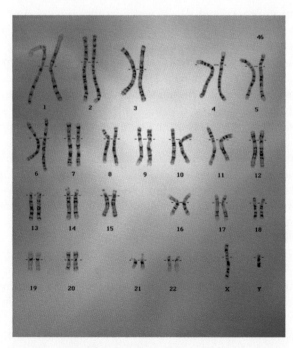

The genetic code is inherited from the mother and father and importantly shapes our physical and psychological characteristics.

A vast communication network in the body helps us monitor the environment and produce quick adaptive responses when they're needed.

peripheral nervous system
The network of nerves that link the central nervous system with the rest of the body.

of nerves, the **peripheral nervous system,** acts as the communication link between the central nervous system and the rest of the body. Later in this chapter, we'll expand on these basic divisions of the nervous system and outline their various functions in greater detail.

COMMUNICATING INTERNALLY: CONNECTING WORLD AND BRAIN

Learning Goals

1. Learn the basic structure of neurons and the three major kinds of neurons.
2. Understand how information is transmitted along a neuron and from one neuron to another.
3. Grasp how neurons work together in communication networks.

neurons
The cells in the nervous system that receive and transmit information by generating an electrochemical signal; neurons are the basic building blocks of the nervous system.

sensory neurons
Neurons that make initial contact with the environment and carry the message inward toward the spinal cord and brain.

interneurons
Neurons that make no direct contact with the external world but rather convey information from one neuron to another.

motor neurons
Neurons that carry information away from the central nervous system to the muscles and glands that directly produce behavioural responses.

glial cells
Cells in the nervous system that do not transmit or receive information but perform a variety of functions, such as removing waste, filling in empty space, and helping neurons to communicate efficiently.

myelin sheath
An insulating material that protects the axons of some neurons and helps to speed up neural transmission.

dendrites
The branchlike fibres that extend outward from a neuron and receive information from other neurons.

soma
The cell body of a neuron.

axon
The long tail-like part of a neuron that serves as the cell's transmitter device.

nodes of Ranvier
Space separating the segments of the myelin covering of the neuron; they help speed the nerve impulse along the axon.

The Anatomy of Neurons

The main components of the nervous system are individual cells, called **neurons,** that receive, transmit, and integrate information. Before it's possible to understand how the nervous system accomplishes communication between the external world and the body, you need to know the basic anatomical hardware of these cells. Neurons come in three major types—*sensory neurons, interneurons,* and *motor neurons*—that differ physically from one another and serve quite different functions.

1. **Sensory neurons** make the initial contact with the environment and are responsible for carrying the message inward toward the spinal cord and brain.

2. **Interneurons,** the most plentiful type of neuron, make no direct contact with the world but rather convey information from one neuron to another.

3. **Motor neurons** carry information from the central nervous system to the muscles and glands that directly produce behavioural responses.

The nervous system also contains **glial cells,** which greatly outnumber neurons (by a factor of about ten to one) but do not directly communicate messages. Glial cells perform several functions in the nervous system, such as removing waste, filling in empty space, and surrounding neurons with a physical environment that helps them to function efficiently (see Kimelberg & Norenberg, 1989). Some types of glial cells wrap around the axons of neurons, creating a **myelin sheath** that insulates the neuron from interference and that helps speed neural transmission (we'll have more to say about this shortly). Problems with glial cells play major roles in some kinds of brain dysfunction, including brain cancer and Alzheimer's disease (Saitoh et al., 1997).

As shown in Figure 3.2, neurons typically have four major structural components: *dendrites,* a *soma,* an *axon,* and *terminal buttons.* For any communication system to work properly, it must have a way to receive information, a way to process any received messages, and a means for transmitting information. The four structural components of the neuron play these distinct roles in the communication chain.

The **dendrites,** which look like tree branches extending outward from the main body of the cell, are the primary information receivers. One neuron passes information to another neuron by stimulating its dendrites. A particular neuron may have thousands of these dendritic branches, allowing the cell to receive input from many different sources. Once received, the message is processed in the **soma,** the main body of the cell.

The **axon** is the cell's transmitter device. When a neuron transmits a message, it sends an electrical signal called an *action potential* from its soma along its axon. In many neurons (like that depicted in Figure 3.2), the axon is often covered with an insulating sheath of myelin, with small gaps in the myelin sheath called **nodes of Ranvier.** Axons vary dramatically in size and shape; in some cases, they can be more than a

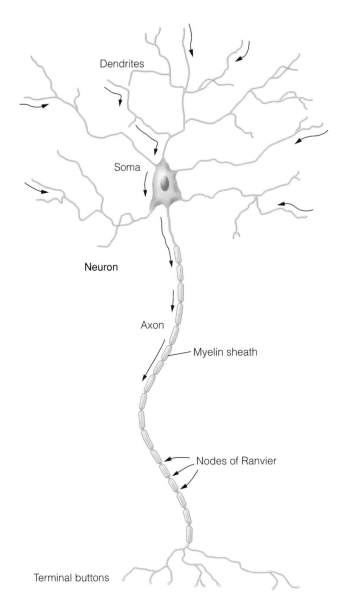

FIGURE 3.2
The Components of a Neuron

The *dendrites* are the primary information receivers, the *soma* is the cell body, and the *axon* is the cell's transmitter device. The myelin sheath that surrounds the axon of some neurons helps speed up neural transmission, as do the *nodes of Ranvier.* At the end of the axon are the *terminal buttons,* which contain the chemical messengers.

metre long (e.g., sensory and motor neurons between your feet and spinal cord). Near its end, the axon branches out in preparation to make contact with other cells. At the tip of each branch are tiny swellings called **terminal buttons.** Chemicals released by these buttons pass the message on to the next neuron.

Neurons don't actually touch one another. The **synapse** is a small gap between a terminal button of one neuron and a dendrite of another. When an action potential arrives at a terminal button, mechanisms in the terminal button release a chemical into the synaptic cleft. That chemical is taken up by the dendrites of the next neuron.

Neural Transmission: The Electrochemical Message

2a, 2b, 4d

Neurons differ in size and shape, but the manner and direction of information flow are consistent across all neurons:

$$\text{Dendrites} \rightarrow \text{Soma} \rightarrow \text{Axon} \rightarrow \text{Terminal buttons}$$

Information usually arrives at the dendrites from multiple sources—many thousands of synaptic connections might be made to the dendrites of a single neuron—and is passed along to the soma. Here, all the messages that have been received sum together;

terminal buttons
The tiny swellings at the end of a neuron's axon that contain chemicals important to neural transmission.

synapse
The junction, or small gap, between a terminal button of one neuron and a dendrite of another neuron.

if sufficient energy is present, an action potential will be generated. The action potential travels down the axon toward the terminal buttons, where it causes the release of chemicals into the synapse. These chemicals move the message from the end of the axon to the dendrites of the next neuron, starting the process all over again. That's the general sequence of information flow: Messages travel electrically from one point to another within a neuron, but the message is transmitted chemically between neurons. Because the language that neurons use to communicate is part electrical and part chemical, it is referred to as electrochemical.

resting potential

The tiny electrical charge in place between the inside and outside of the resting neuron.

The Resting Potential   Neurons possess electrical properties even when they aren't receiving or transmitting messages. Specifically, a tiny electrical charge, called the **resting potential,** exists between the inside and outside of the cell. This resting potential is created by the presence of electrically charged atoms and molecules, called *ions,* that are distributed unevenly between the inside and outside of the cell. The main ions in neural transmission are positively charged *sodium* and *potassium* ions and negatively charged *chloride* ions.

Normally, ions will distribute themselves evenly in an environment, through a process called *diffusion.* However, they are unable to do so around a resting neuron because free movement is blocked by the neuron's cell wall, or *membrane.* The membrane of a neuron is selectively permeable, which means that it only allows certain ions to pass in and out through special ion "channels." As shown in Figure 3.3, when the neuron is resting, the sodium and chloride ions are concentrated outside of the cell and the potassium ions are largely contained inside. These unequal concentrations are maintained, in part, by a sodium-potassium pump that actively moves the ions into and out of the cell. If you measured the electrical potential of the neuron with an electrode, you would find that the fluid inside the cell is *negative* with respect to the outside (between –60 and –70 millivolts). This negative charge defines the resting potential for the cell. Most of the negative charge comes from large protein molecules inside the cell, which are too big to pass through ion channels.

Why is it adaptive for neurons to have a resting potential? It's likely that the resting potential helps the cell respond quickly when it's contacted by other neurons. When one neuron communicates with another, it releases chemicals that change the nature of the contacted neuron's membrane. Ions that are normally outside the cell can rush in

FIGURE 3.3
The Resting Potential

Neurons possess electrical properties even when they are neither receiving nor transmitting messages. The resting potential, a tiny negative electrical charge across the inside and outside of a resting cell, is created by an uneven distribution of ions across the cell membrane.

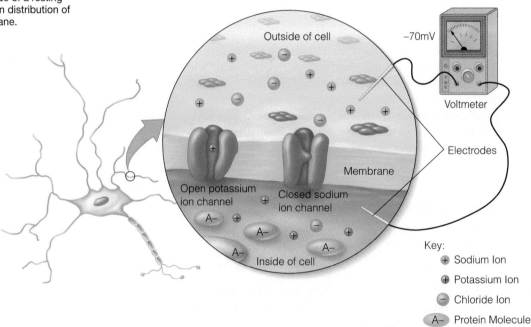

quickly through newly opened channels. This changes the electrical potential inside the cell, which, as you'll see shortly, can lead to the production of an action potential.

Generating Action Potentials   For a neuron to stop resting and generate an **action potential,** the electrical signal that travels down the axon, the electrical potential inside the cell must become less negative. This necessary change occurs primarily as a result of contact from other neurons. Two types of messages can be passed from one neuron to the next: Excitatory messages and inhibitory messages. If the message is excitatory, the membrane of the contacted neuron changes and sodium ions begin to flow into the cell. This process, called *depolarization,* moves the electrical potential of the cell from negative toward zero and increases the chances of an action potential. When the message is inhibitory, the opposite happens: The cell membrane either pushes more positive ions out of the cell or allows negative ions to move in. The result is *hyperpolarization:* The electrical potential of the cell becomes more negative, and the chances of an action potential decrease.

It's important to remember that any given neuron in the nervous system is in contact with many other neurons. As a result, small changes in potential regularly occur in many input regions of the neuron as messages are received (see Figure 3.4). Near the point where the axon leaves the cell body, in a special trigger zone called the *axon hillock,* all of the excitatory and inhibitory potentials combine. If enough excitatory messages have been received—that is, if the electrical potential inside the cell has become sufficiently less negative—an action potential will be initiated. If not, the resting potential of the axon will be maintained.

Action potentials are the electrical signals that travel down a neuron's axon. They are generated in an *all-or-none* fashion; that is, the action potential will not begin until sufficient excitatory input has been received, but once the firing threshold is reached, they always travel completely down the length of the axon to its end. The process is somewhat analogous to the firing of a gun: Bullets don't travel farther or faster if you pull the trigger harder. Likewise, an action potential travels along the axon at the same rate regardless of the intensity of the messages that caused the firing. Also, the basic characteristics of action potentials are the same regardless of the type of information being transmitted: It doesn't matter whether the neuron is carrying a message about pleasure or pain, thought or reflex, the basic characteristics of action potentials are the same.

There are many different kinds of neurons, and although all action potentials are all-or-none, the speed of transmission does vary across different kinds of neurons. Transmission speed depends partly on the size and shape of the axon; in general, the thicker the axon, the faster the message will travel. Another feature that increases the speed of transmission in many neurons is the myelin sheath, which, as mentioned earlier, is made from a type of glial cell. Myelin provides an insulating wrap for the axon, like the plastic around the copper electrical wiring in a house, thereby protecting the

action potential
The all-or-none electrical signal that travels down a neuron's axon.

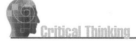 **Critical Thinking**

The speed of neural transmission is quite slow, at least relative to the speed of processing in a computer chip. How do you think it's possible for people to make very quick decisions? *Hint:* Could large groups of neurons acting together be involved?

FIGURE 3.4
Summing Excitatory and Inhibitory Messages

Each neuron is in contact with many other neurons. Some contacts initiate excitatory messages, or *depolarization,* and others initiate inhibitory messages, or *hyperpolarization.* A neuron generates its own action potential only if the summed messages produce sufficient depolarization (the negative potential moves close enough to zero).

neuron from interference from other nearby neurons. At regular points are the nodes of Ranvier—gaps in the insulation—which permit the action potential to jump down the axon from gap to gap rather than travelling more gradually along the whole length of the axon. This method of transmission from node to node is called *saltatory conduction* (from the Latin word *saltare,* which means "to jump"). Due to variations in size and in mylenination, transmission speed varies across different sorts of neurons from about 3 to 300 km/h (which is much slower than the speed of electricity through a copper wire).

Although action potentials are all or none, the nervous system can code the intensity of a stimulus through the frequency or rate at which neurons generate action potentials. The *firing rate* of a neuron is defined by the number of action potentials it generates per unit of time. The firing rate is subject to some natural limitations. For instance, a very brief **refractory period** follows the generation of an action potential, during which another action potential cannot be generated.

Many neurons have spontaneous firing rates; they generate a steady series of action potentials even without input from other neurons or the environment. A continuously active cell is adaptive for the nervous system because different information can be communicated by decreasing as well as by increasing the spontaneous firing rate. The colour red, for example, might be experienced when particular cells in the brain increase their frequency of firing, whereas green may be linked to a decrease in the rate of action potentials in the same cells (see Figure 3.5). In this way, the system can code more information. (You'll learn more about how colour is processed in the visual system in Chapter 4.) Patterns of changes in firing rate, across large groups of interconnected neurons, give rise to complex psychological phenomena.

Neurotransmitters: The Chemical Messengers
When the action potential reaches the end of the axon, it triggers the release of chemical messengers from small sacs, or vesicles, in the terminal buttons (see Figure 3.6). These chemical molecules, called **neurotransmitters,** spill out into the synapse and interact chemically with the cell membrane of the next neuron (called the *postsynaptic membrane*). Depending on the particular characteristics of the postsynaptic membrane, the neurotransmitter will

refractory period
The period of time following an action potential during which more action potentials cannot be generated.

neurotransmitters
Chemical messengers that relay information from one neuron to the next. They are released from the terminal buttons into the synapse, where they interact chemically with the cell membrane of the next neuron; the result is either an excitatory or an inhibitory influence on the recipient neuron.

FIGURE 3.5
Changes in Firing Rates
Information is communicated through changes in the firing rates of neurons. Here, certain neurons in the monkey's brain increase their firing rate (relative to baseline) when a red stimulus appears and decrease their firing rate (relative to baseline) when a green stimulus appears. Thus the same neurons can code both red and green.

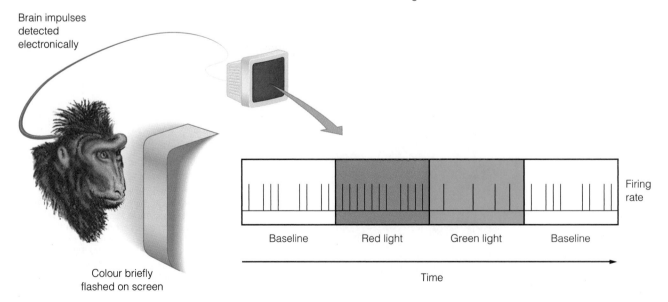

Brain impulses detected electronically

Colour briefly flashed on screen

Baseline   Red light   Green light   Baseline

Firing rate

Time

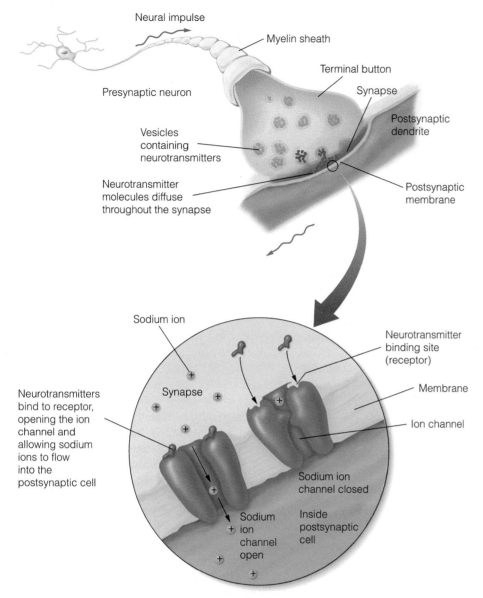

Neural impulse

Myelin sheath

Terminal button

Presynaptic neuron

Synapse

Postsynaptic dendrite

Vesicles containing neurotransmitters

Neurotransmitter molecules diffuse throughout the synapse

Postsynaptic membrane

Sodium ion

Neurotransmitter binding site (receptor)

Synapse

Membrane

Neurotransmitters bind to receptor, opening the ion channel and allowing sodium ions to flow into the postsynaptic cell

Ion channel

Sodium ion channel closed

Inside postsynaptic cell

Sodium ion channel open

FIGURE 3.6
Releasing the Chemical Messengers

When the action potential reaches the terminal buttons at the end of the axon, it causes the release of chemical messengers—neurotransmitters—into the synapse. The neurotransmitters interact with the postsynaptic membrane of the next neuron, opening or closing its ion channels. Here, the neurotransmitter is opening sodium channels, which will increase the chances of the receiving cell initiating its own action potential. In other synapses, neurotransmitters have inhibitory effects, decreasing the likelihood that the recipient neuron will generate an action potential.

either excite the recipient neuron toward generating an action potential or will inhibit it away from generating an action potential.

Each neurotransmitter molecule acts as a kind of key in search of the appropriate lock. The substance moves quickly across the synapse—it takes only about 1/10 000 of a second—and activates receptor molecules contained in the postsynaptic membrane. Depending on the particular type of receptor molecule that is present, the neurotransmitter will then either increase or decrease the electrical potential of the receiving cell. When the message is excitatory, the neurotransmitter causes channels in the postsynaptic membrane to open, allowing positive sodium ions to flow into the receiving cell. When the message is inhibitory, negative chloride ions are allowed to enter the cell and positive potassium ions are allowed to leave. It's worth emphasizing that neurotransmitters, by themselves, are neither excitatory nor inhibitory. It is really the nature of the receptor molecule that determines whether a particular neurotransmitter will produce an excitatory or inhibitory effect; the same neurotransmitter can produce quite different effects at different sites in the nervous system.

Dozens of neurotransmitters have been identified in the brain, along with their various functions. The neurotransmitter **acetylcholine** is a major messenger in both

acetylcholine
A neurotransmitter that plays several roles in the central and peripheral nervous systems, including the excitation of muscle contractions.

For much of recorded history, psychological disorders were attributed to possession by evil spirits. Today, psychologists recognize that many disorders are the result of brain malfunctioning.

dopamine

A neurotransmitter that often leads to inhibitory effects; decreased levels have been linked to Parkinson's disease, and increased levels have been linked to schizophrenia.

serotonin

A neurotransmitter that has been linked to sleep, dreaming, and general arousal and may also be involved in some psychological disorders such as depression and schizophrenia.

gamma-amino-butyric acid (GABA)

A neurotransmitter that may play a role in the regulation of anxiety; it generally produces inhibitory effects.

the central and peripheral nervous systems; it acts, for example, as the primary transmitter between motor neurons and muscles in the body. When released into the synapse between motor neurons and muscle cells, acetylcholine tends to create excitatory messages that lead to muscle contraction. The neurotransmitter **dopamine** often produces inhibitory effects that help dampen and stabilize communications in the brain and elsewhere. Inhibitory effects help keep the brain on an even keel and allow us to do things such as produce smooth voluntary muscle movements, sleep without physically acting out our dreams, and maintain posture. If neurotransmitters had only excitatory effects, there would be an endless chain of communication, producing an explosion of overactivity in the brain and resulting in confused and chaotic thoughts and behaviours.

Dopamine is of particular interest to psychologists because it's thought to play a role in schizophrenia, a serious psychological disorder that disrupts thought processes and produces delusions and hallucinations. When schizophrenic patients take drugs that inhibit the action of dopamine, their hallucinations and delusions are sometimes reduced or even eliminated. It has been speculated that perhaps an excess supply of dopamine is partly responsible for the disorder (O'Donnell & Grace, 1998; Sigmundson, 1994; Snyder, 1976). Further evidence linking dopamine and schizophrenia has come from the study of Parkinson's disease. This movement disorder apparently results from the underproduction of dopamine. Parkinson's patients are often given the drug L-dopa, which increases the levels of dopamine in the brain, to reduce the tremors and other movement problems that result from the disease. For some patients, however, L-dopa causes thought disorders characteristic of schizophrenia (Braff & Huey, 1988). Dopamine also plays an important role in the "reward pathway" of the brain, the parts of the brain that are most involved in transmitting feelings of pleasure.

Neurotransmitters in the brain fundamentally affect people's thoughts and actions, but the particular mechanisms involved are not well understood. We know, for example, that people with Alzheimer's disease have damage to cells that play a role in producing acetylcholine (Mash et al., 1985; Quirion, 1993). Because memory loss is a common problem for Alzheimer patients, this suggests a connection between acetylcholine and certain kinds of memory functioning (Degroot & Parent, 2001; Hasselmo et al., 1996; McDonald & Crawley, 1997; Pappas et al., 2000). We also know that **serotonin,** another neurotransmitter that often acts in an inhibitory fashion, affects sleep, dreaming, and general arousal and may also be involved in such psychological disorders as depression, schizophrenia, and obsessive-compulsive disorder (Alda, 2001; McAllister-Williams et al., 1998; Potter & Manji, 1993; Thomsen, 1994, 1998). As you'll learn in Chapter 15, some medications used to treat depression, such as Prozac, act by modulating the effectiveness of serotonin. Similarly, many researchers believe that a neurotransmitter called **gamma-amino-butyric acid (GABA)** plays an important role in the regulation of anxiety (Adamec, 2000). Many oft-prescribed medications for anxiety (e.g., tranquillizers such as Valium) regulate GABA in the brain (Stock et al., 2001).

In each of these cases, however, researchers still face the difficult task of determining the specific neural pathways and mechanisms involved. At this point, much of the evidence is correlational rather than experimental, so we cannot be certain about the causal roles of particular neurotransmitters (see Chapter 2). We know that as the levels of particular neurotransmitters vary in the body, so too do the symptoms of various disorders. This is useful information for treatment, but it doesn't establish a definitive cause-and-effect link between neurotransmitters and psychological characteristics (e.g., it could be that some unknown mechanism has parallel influences on both neurotransmitters and psychological characteristics).

Drugs and the Brain Because the transmission of messages between neurons is chemical, chemicals that are ingested into the body can affect the communication networks in the brain. Some drugs, called *agonists,* mimic the action of neurotransmitters. For example, the nicotine in cigarette smoke can act like the neurotransmitter acetylcholine. Nicotine has a general stimulating effect in the body (e.g., increases heart rate) because it produces excitatory messages in much the same way as acetylcholine.

Other drugs act as *antagonists,* which means that they oppose or block the action of neurotransmitters. The lethal drug curare, which South Americans sometimes use on the tips of hunting arrows and blow darts, is antagonistic to acetylcholine. Curare blocks the receptor systems involved in muscle movements, including the muscles that move the diaphragm during breathing. The result is paralysis and death from suffocation.

In the early 1970s, membrane receptor systems were discovered in the brain that react directly to *morphine,* a pain-killing and highly addictive drug derived from the opium plant (Pert & Snyder, 1973). It turns out that we have receptor systems that are sensitive to morphine because the brain produces its own morphine-like substances called **endorphins.** Endorphins serve as natural painkillers in the body. They are thought to act as *neuromodulators,* or chemicals that modulate (increase or decrease) the effectiveness of neurotransmitters. Apparently, the brain has evolved systems for releasing endorphins under conditions of stress or exertion to reduce pain and possibly to provide pleasurable reinforcement (Hoffmann, 1997; Schedlowski et al., 1995). As shown by Christina Gianoulakis (2000) of McGill University, endorphins may also interact with ingested chemicals such as alcohol. We'll return to the study of drugs, particularly their effects on conscious awareness, in Chapter 5.

endorphins
Morphine-like chemicals that act as the brain's natural painkillers.

Many natural substances, such as coffee, curare, and the common groundcover St. John's wort, contain ingredients that affect the action of neurotransmitters.

Concept Summary

NEUROTRANSMITTERS AND THEIR EFFECTS

Neurotransmitter	Nature of Effect	Involved in ...
Dopamine	Generally inhibitory*	Dampening and stabilizing communication in the brain and elsewhere; helps ensure smooth motor function; plays a role in both schizophrenia and Parkinson's disease.
Acetylcholine	Generally excitatory*	Communication between motor neurons and muscles in the body, leading to muscle contraction; may also play a role in Alzheimer's disease.
Serotonin	Generally inhibitory*	Regulating sleep, dreaming, and general arousal; may also play a role in some psychological disorders, including depression.
GABA	Generally inhibitory*	The regulation of anxiety; tranquillizing drugs act on GABA to decrease anxiety.

*Note: No neurotransmitter, on its own, is excitatory or inhibitory; the specific nature of a neuron's action depends on specific characteristics of the receiving cell's membrane.

The Communication Network

Up to this point, you've seen how information is transmitted electrically within a neuron, via the flow of charged ions that makes up an action potential, and how one neuron signals another through the release of chemical messengers. But the dynamics of activity within a neuron, and the way one neuron passes activation to another, are only small parts of the story. The nervous system consists of many millions of neurons, and billions upon billions of synaptic connections. No perceptions, thought, feeling, or action arises from the activation of a single neuron; rather, *patterns of activation* across large groups of interconnected neurons operating together underlie conscious experiences and complex behaviours. You may have heard claims to the effect that most people use only 10% of their brains, but this is a nonsensical myth: Everyone uses 100% of his or her brain (although some to greater effect than others!), and it is the fine-grained detail of how neurons are interconnected that, researchers believe, underlies what people can do with their brains. It is therefore necessary to pay attention to the specific ways in which neurons are interconnected.

Reflexes   As a first step toward understanding the role of neural interconnectivity, let's consider the mechanisms that give rise to the simplest form of neurally mediated behaviour, known as a **reflex.** If you inadvertently put your right index finger in a candle flame, you withdraw your finger very quickly, automatically. This may not seem like much of an accomplishment, but it's obviously pretty important that organisms be able to do this sort of thing. Further, the problem is not as trivial as it may at first appear: Imagine trying to build a robot such that holding a match to part of its body would cause it to very quickly jerk that part of its body away.

Here's how your body does it (see Figure 3.7). First, the flame stimulates sensory receptor neurons in your finger that are specialized to respond to pain, causing those cells to begin creating action potentials. Thus a form of physical energy in the world (heat) is coded into the electrochemical language of the body. Those action potentials travel along the sensory cells' axons to specific sites in your spinal cord, where they synapse on to short interneurons in the spinal cord. The reflex is "wired" in such a way that when these interneurons receive activation they in turn pass activation directly to motor neurons with which they synapse. Moreover, the system is set up so that those motor neurons control muscles that effect movements of the body part from which the pain signals originated (i.e., the system "knows" the pain is in your right finger rather than somewhere else in the body). The action potentials travel along the axon of the motor neurons from the spinal cord to the muscles of your hand and arm, causing those muscles to contract such that your hand quickly jerks away.

You may have noticed that the brain hasn't figured into our discussion of fingers and flames. This is because a reflex requires no input to or from the brain. The message

reflex

A largely automatic body movement, such as the knee jerk, that is controlled by a simple network of sensory neurons, interneurons in the spinal cord, and motor neurons.

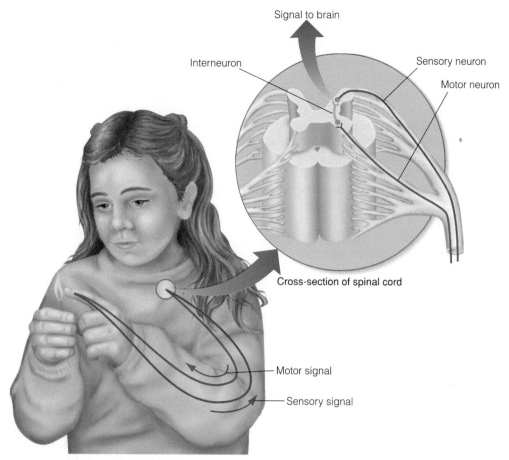

Signal to brain

Interneuron

Sensory neuron

Motor neuron

Cross-section of spinal cord

Motor signal

Sensory signal

FIGURE 3.7
A Simple Reflex Pathway
As the flame touches flesh, the information travels through a sensory neuron to the spinal cord, where it's passed to an interneuron and then on to a motor neuron. The motor neuron then contacts muscles in the hand and arm, causing a quick withdrawal. Other interneurons pass the information from the spinal cord upward to the brain, where the experience of pain occurs.

normally *is* passed upward from the spinal cord to the brain via other interneurons, and it is in the brain that you consciously experience the heat of the flame, but the reflexive jerking away of your finger does not rely on the brain. If your spinal cord were cut near your neck, blocking communication between most of the body and brain, you wouldn't feel the pain or react with a facial grimace, but your hand would still twitch (although if you had been paralyzed for a long time the action would be greatly attenuated, partly due to muscle atrophy). Reflex pathways allow the body to respond very quickly to environmental events in a simple and direct way. People don't think or feel with their spinal cords, but reflex pathways are an important part of our ability to adapt successfully to the world.

Neural Plasticity Of course, reflexes make up only a tiny fraction of human behaviour, and the sorts of psychological events that most people find especially interesting are driven primarily by the brain. Nonetheless, reflexes serve to illustrate two key points. First, even the simplest behaviours (e.g., reflexes) don't reflect the operation of a single neuron, but rather interconnected systems of neurons; more complex behaviours involve even more extensive collaborations of large numbers of neurons. Second, the effect of a given neuron depends largely on which other neurons and/or organs it synapses with. For example, what makes an interneuron an interneuron is that it receives activation from and sends activation to other neurons, rather than receiving

Critical Thinking

A reflex is a type of adaptive behaviour that does not arise directly from activity of the brain. If you were building a body from scratch, what types of reflexes would you build in and why?

activation from the external environment or sending it to muscles, glands, or other organs. More specifically, what makes a particular interneuron code information about, say, pain in the right index finger, is the fact that it synapses with pain-specialized receptor cells from the right index finger and with other neurons that control reactions to pain.

The same is true (but in a more indirect and complex way) when it comes to the brain. For example, the interneurons that carry information about the pain from the spinal cord to the brain project to and synapse with other cells in specialized areas of the brain, thereby coding information about the location and intensity of the pain in ways that eventually give rise (through mechanisms that remain mysterious) to the subjective experience of being burned. This is why neuroscientists are particularly interested in discovering how neurons are connected to one another, and the means through which those connections can be modified by experience (Hebb, 1949, 2002; Kandel, 1991; Shaw & McEachern, 2001).

When you learn new things (e.g., right now, we hope!) the physical structure of your brain shifts in very subtle but crucial ways as the strength and even patterns of synaptic interconnections change to implement the new knowledge. Also, if you have the misfortune to damage your brain, cellular processes will work toward repairing the damage; depending on the nature and extent of the damage, the recovery may not be complete, but recent evidence shows that the brain is better able to repair itself than once was thought. Indeed, anecdotal reports claim that Christopher Reeve (famed for starring as Superman in several successful movies) has regained some voluntary movement after years of complete paralysis following an accident in which he broke his neck. These are examples of **neural plasticity,** or the ability of neural systems to change. Neural plasticity has been extensively studied by University of Lethbridge neuropsychologist Bryan Kolb and his co-workers, primarily by studying changes in the brains of rats as a consequence of experience or during recovery from brain damage (e.g., Kolb, 1995, 1999; Kolb et al., 2001). For research on rehabilitation programs that foster recovery from brain damage, see Raskin and Mateer (2000) and Stuss et al. (1999).

neural plasticity
Ability of neurons to alter synaptic connections during learning and during recovery from brain injury.

Test Yourself 3.1

Test your knowledge about neurons and how they communicate. Select your answers from the following list of terms: dendrites; soma; axon; sensory; terminal buttons; spinal cord; action potential; interneurons; neurotransmitters; motor; refractory period. (You will find the answers in Appendix B.)

1. The main body of the cell, where excitatory and inhibitory messages combine: _____

2. The long tail-like part of a neuron that serves as the cell's main transmitter device: _____

3. The all-or-none electrical signal that travels to the end of the axon, causing the release of chemical messengers: _____

4. The branchlike fibres that extend outward from a neuron and receive information from other neurons: _____

5. Acetylcholine, serotonin, GABA, and dopamine are all examples of: _____

6. In a reflex response, _____ neurons carry information about a stimulus (such as intense heat) to the _____, where they synapse on to _____ neurons, which in turn synapse with _____ neurons that stimulate muscles to contract.

Practical Solutions

BETTER THINKING THROUGH CHEMISTRY?

Wouldn't it be great if you could take a pill that would make it really easy for you to understand and remember the contents of this textbook? Given that the brain operates electrochemically, it seems plausible that there might be drugs that would enhance its functioning, making the user a smarter, faster, and more retentive thinker. And you've probably encountered ads on TV and other media making just such claims. Often, the attractiveness of the advertised substance is further enhanced by describing it as completely "natural." To take a case in point, an extract made from the leaves of the Ginkgo biloba tree has been touted as a natural and effective way to improve memory. Advertising has succeeded in making Ginkgo a big seller: According to the Nonprescription Drug Manufacturers Association of Canada, Ginkgo sales totalled $9.1 million in 1999. Of course, that might be a bargain if the drug dramatically enhances memory.

As you may recall from Chapter 2, the best way to test the effectiveness of a drug or other experimental treatment is to conduct a double-blind, placebo-controlled experiment. In such an experiment, some subjects receive the drug and others receive an inert pill that looks and tastes identical to the drug, with neither the subjects nor the person administering the experiment knowing which subjects receive the drug and which receive the placebo. Only a few such experiments have assessed the effects of Ginkgo on human memory, and the results are mixed.

Wesnes et al. (2000) reported what appears to be the first large double-blind, placebo-controlled study that yielded clear evidence of effects of Ginkgo (combined with ginseng) on memory-test performance. This study involved 256 healthy middle-aged volunteers, who took the drug (or a placebo) daily for 12 weeks.

Some studies indicate that Ginkgo biloba may live up to its popular reputation as a memory enhancer. Unfortunately, other studies suggest it has no such effects.

Small but significant effects were found on several measures of memory. Similarly, a study by Strough et al. (2001) involved 61 volunteers who took either Ginkgo or a placebo over a 30-day period. Statistically significant benefits of Ginkgo were found on tests of the speed and flexible control of mental processing.

The Wesnes and Strough findings are encouraging, and there are also other studies reporting beneficial effects of Ginkgo (e.g., Mix & Crews, 2002). Support seems to be particularly strong for beneficial effects among elderly people with age-related cognitive impairments (see Beaubrun & Gray, 2000, for a review). Unfortunately, however, there are also a number of studies reporting null effects. For example, Moulton et al. (2001) tested 30 healthy young men who took Ginkgo or a placebo daily for 5 days and then completed a variety of standardized memory tests. Their results indicated that the extract was ineffective in enhancing memory. An obvious criticism of this study is that 5 days may simply not be long enough for effects to be detected. The Moulton study also had a relatively small

sample, and all subjects were young. However, a recent study by Solomon et al. (2002) tested 230 subjects, all over the age of 60 years, who took Ginkgo or a placebo for 6 weeks. Despite the large sample of people in an age group who might be expected particularly to benefit from a memory enhancer, no reliable benefits of Ginkgo were observed in this study. Similarly, van Dongen et al. (2000) tested 123 elderly individuals with dementia or age-associated memory impairments, with subjects randomly selected to receive either a placebo or Ginkgo daily over a 12-week period; the results did not support the efficacy of Ginkgo as a memory treatment.

What are we to make of these results? On the one hand, it is possible that the experiments supporting the efficacy of Ginkgo biloba were flawed by undetected confounds or were mere flukes of chance (see Chapter 2). On the other hand, it may be that Ginkgo has effects, but those effects are relatively small and/or occur only in some people and/or only under particular test conditions. Of these two kinds of accounts for the inconsistent findings, the latter seems the more likely. In any case, two things are sure. One is that the extract does not have large and general memory-enhancing effects on all people. The other is that further research is needed. Those same two conclusions also hold for other substances promoted and sold as sure-fire ways to increase intelligence or bolster memory. Many neuroscientists are optimistic that drugs eventually will be developed that improve mental functions such as memory. Our recommendation, however, is to wait until solid scientific evidence supports the efficacy and safety of such substances before buying and trying them (and also to consult a physician before taking such supplements, as they can have dangerous side effects, especially when combined with other drugs).

INITIATING AND COORDINATING BEHAVIOUR: A DIVISION OF LABOUR

Learning Goals

1. Know the basic organization of the nervous system.
2. Become familiar with some of the techniques that researchers use to study the brain.
3. Be able to describe the major structures of the brain and the functions associated with each structure.
4. Learn how the two hemispheres divide and coordinate brain functions.

THE NERVOUS SYSTEM has many complex problems to solve through its communication network of neurons. In addition to generating physical behaviours and mental processes such as thinking and feeling, the brain keeps constant track of more basic things, such as maintaining a beating heart, controlling breathing, and signalling the body that it's time to eat. If your body is deprived of food or water, or if its constant internal temperature is compromised, something must motivate you to seek sustenance or shelter. Moreover, although you may not have thought about it too much, even the most common everyday activities—speaking, walking, seeing—require a great deal of coordination between the muscles and sensory organs of the body. To accomplish such different functions, the nervous system divides its labour.

The Central and Peripheral Nervous Systems

2a, 2b, 8c
Psyk.trek

As explained at the beginning of the chapter, the nervous system is divided into two major parts: the central nervous system and the peripheral nervous system. The central nervous system, consisting of the brain and spinal cord, acts as the central executive of the body. Decisions are made here, and messages are then communicated to the rest of the body through bundles of axons called **nerves.** The nerves outside the brain and spinal cord form the peripheral nervous system.

nerves
Bundles of axons that make up neural "transmission cables."

It is through the peripheral nervous system that muscles are moved, internal organs are regulated, and sensory input is moved toward the brain. As you can see in Figure 3.8, the peripheral nervous system is further subdivided into the *somatic* and *autonomic systems.* Information travels toward the brain and spinal cord through *afferent* (sensory) nerve pathways; *efferent* (motor) nerve pathways carry central nervous system messages outward to the muscles and glands. The **somatic system** consists of the nerves that transmit sensory information toward the brain as well as the nerves that connect to the skeletal muscles to initiate movement. Without the somatic system, information about the environment could not reach the brain, nor could we move voluntarily. The **autonomic system** controls the more automatic needs of the body, such as heart rate, digestion, blood pressure, and the activities of internal glands. These two systems work together to ensure that information about the world is communicated to the brain for interpretation, movements are carried out, and the life-sustaining internal activities of the body are performed.

somatic system
Nerves that transmit information from sensory organs to the brain, and from the brain to the skeletal muscles; part of the peripheral nervous system.

autonomic system
Nerves that control the more automatic needs of the body, such as heart rate, digestion, blood pressure, and so on; part of the peripheral nervous system.

One critical function of the autonomic system, besides performing the automatic "housekeeping" activities that keep the body alive, is to affect the body's ability to handle and recover from emergency situations. The *sympathetic division* of the autonomic system helps the body respond to emergencies by triggering the release of chemicals that put it in a state of readiness to act quickly and vigorously (such as by increasing heart rate, blood pressure, and breathing rate). After the emergency has passed, the *parasympathetic division* calms the body down by slowing the heart rate and lowering the blood pressure. Parasympathetic activity also helps increase the body's supply of stored energy that may have been depleted as a result of dealing with an emergency situation.

FIGURE 3.8

The Nervous System

The human nervous system is subdivided into two major systems: the central nervous system, which consists of the brain and the spinal cord, and the peripheral nervous system, which includes the somatic system and the autonomic system. (Based on Kalat, 1996.)

Research Techniques for Exploring Brain Function

Before we embark on a detailed examination of the structure and function of the brain, let's consider some techniques that researchers use to explore what functions the different parts of the brain serve. The anatomical features of the nervous system as a whole—the various nerve tracts and so on—can be studied through dissection of the body. But the dissection of brain tissue, which contains billions of neurons, tells only a limited story. To determine the architecture of the brain, researchers need to draw on a broader set of tools. We'll briefly consider three general techniques: (1) the study of brain damage from injury or disease; (2) methods that allow the researcher to activate the brain directly; and (3) methods that allow researchers to monitor the brain in action.

Brain Damage The study of brain damage is one of the oldest methods for investigating brain function. A patient with some specific, localized region of damage—such as a blow to the right side of the head—typically complains of a particular problem, such as trouble moving the left side of his or her body. In this way, a link is established between a brain area and a behaviour or function. By the middle of the 19th century it was known that damage to specific areas on the left side of the brain creates distinct patterns of linguistic difficulties. Destruction of *Wernicke's area* results in a patient who

Researcher Cindy Bukach of the University of Victoria (right) demonstrates some of the tests used to detect brain damage.

speaks very quickly and incoherently and who cannot easily understand spoken language (Wernicke, 1874); damage to *Broca's area* results in a patient who can understand others' speech but whose own speech is very slow, halting, and effortful (Broca, 1861). Damage to other brain regions causes other problems (e.g., amnesia). Such cases suggest that particular psychological and behavioural functions are controlled by specific areas of the brain.

Unfortunately, relying on case studies of people who accidentally sustain brain damage has its limitations. For one thing, researchers must wait for the specific injury of interest to present itself for their inspection. Also, most instances of brain damage, either from an accident or from a tumour or a stroke, produce very general and widespread damage, making it difficult to know exactly which portion of the damaged brain is responsible for particular behavioural or psychological problems. Furthermore, it is difficult to determine the precise areas and extent of brain damage without performing an autopsy. Finally, as we saw in Chapter 2, case studies can be rich sources of information, but the researcher typically lacks important controls (e.g., an individual who sustains brain damage may have differed from most people even before the damage occurred).

To establish a structure–function relationship, it is necessary to observe in a controlled way the effects of systematic and localized removal of tissue. Researchers have used surgical techniques to explore brain function in lower animals, particularly rats. It's possible to destroy, or *lesion*, particular regions of an animal's brain by administering an electric current, injecting chemicals, or cutting tissue. Even here it is often difficult to pinpoint the damage exactly (because everything in the brain is interconnected), but lesioning techniques have become increasingly accurate in recent years. There are chemicals, for example, that can selectively damage specific kinds of neurons in the brain without damaging neighbouring nerve pathways (Bergvall et al., 1996; Jarrad, 1993). The lesioning procedure is then followed by controlled examination of the animal's behaviour to see how it is affected. Animal research using brain lesioning techniques has provided much valuable information regarding brain functioning (e.g., Arvanitogiannis et al., 1999; Barnes et al., 2000; Crowne & Wah, 1998; Ellard, 2000; Mumby et al., 2002; Whishaw et al., 2001).

Talking to the Brain   It is also possible to "talk" to the brain directly by capitalizing on the electrochemical nature of the communication network. Essentially, neural activity can be induced artificially. One means of doing this is to inject chemicals that excite

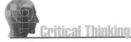

Critical Thinking

Does it bother you when researchers generalize the results of studies of rats to humans? If so, does it also bother you that the basic principles of genetics were initially derived from studies of pea plants?

Electrical stimulator

Connection to stimulator

Rotating drum

Pen

Connection to recorder

Cumulative response recorder

FIGURE 3.9
Electrical Stimulation

A rat presses a bar and a small pulse of electric current is delivered to the brain. Stimulation of certain brain areas appears quite rewarding to the rat, leading it to press the bar at a very rapid rate.

neurons in a particular area of the brain. Alternatively, researchers can insert tiny wire electrodes into brain tissue, allowing an area's cells to be stimulated electrically.

Electrical stimulation techniques have been used primarily with animals. It is possible to implant an electrode in ways that allow an animal to move freely about in its environment (see Figure 3.9). A small pulse of current can then be delivered to various brain regions whenever the researcher desires. Studies have shown that electrical brain stimulation can cause animals to suddenly start eating, drinking, engaging in sexual behaviour, or preparing for an attack, with the response depending primarily on what brain area is stimulated. In a classic study conducted at McGill University, researchers stimulated specific areas of rats' brains with electricity and found that certain areas in the brain act as pleasure centres in rats, leading them to engage repeatedly in whatever behaviour led to the stimulation (Olds & Milner, 1954). For example, if rats are taught that pressing a metal bar leads to electrical stimulation of a reward area, they will press the bar thousands of times an hour.

The electrical stimulation technique is often used by researchers to link behaviour to patterns of activity in specific areas in the brain. For example, a behaviour that is produced by stimulation of brain region X but not by stimulation of brain region Y suggests that region X plays some role in the overall behaviour. Nonetheless, the precise mapping of behaviours to brain locations remains a difficult task. It is always possible to argue, for example, that a stimulated area is required to produce a particular behaviour but that it does not act alone—it might serve only as a communication link, or relay connection, to some other brain region that actually starts the behaviour.

Under some circumstances, it is possible to stimulate cells in the human brain and note the behavioural effects. Famed Canadian neurosurgeon Wilder Penfield, working at the Montreal Neurological Institute at McGill University, developed what became known as the "Montreal procedure" for mapping the functions of specific areas of the human brain. During certain kinds of brain surgery (such as surgery to reduce epileptic seizures), the patient was kept awake and the brain was stimulated with a tiny electrode. The primary purpose of the procedure was to determine the functions of particular brain areas before deciding whether or not to remove those areas to treat the disorder that the surgery was intended to correct. The procedure also revealed interesting things about the functions of the brain. Electrical stimulation under these conditions caused patients to produce involuntary movement, hear buzzing noises, and in some rare instances even experience what they reported to be memories (Penfield & Perot, 1963).

Direct electrical stimulation of brain tissue is a difficult and invasive procedure. An alternative method is known as **transcranial magnetic stimulation (TMS)**. In

Canadian neurosurgeon Wilder Penfield established the Montreal Neurological Institute at McGill University and pioneered open brain stimulation techniques with human patients that helped establish the function of specific areas of the brain.

transcranial magnetic stimulation (TMS)
Powerful pulses of magnetic energy applied to the scalp stimulate action potentials in regions of the cortex; behavioural responses cast light on the function of the stimulated brain region.

TMS, an electrical coil pressed to the scalp creates powerful magnetic pulses over the brain area of interest, causing the neurons in that area to propagate action potentials. Researchers can then observe the behaviours associated with action potentials in a particular brain area. For example, stimulating one area might cause the subject to move his or her right hand, whereas stimulating another area might lead the person to "see" a flash of red light. Although this technique is still quite new, research to date demonstrates that it has potential both as a research tool and as a therapeutic intervention for, among other things, major depression (George et al., 1999; Grafman & Wassermann, 1999; Lisanby et al., 2000; Nguyen, 2001).

Listening to the Brain   Brain lesioning and direct electrical stimulation are effective research tools, but they are *invasive* in the sense that they require making contact with (or even destroying) actual brain tissue. Transcranial magnetic stimulation is less invasive than the other two techniques, and studies indicate that the procedure is safe, but some people might nonetheless be reluctant to undergo it. Fortunately, there are other techniques that essentially eavesdrop on the brain without any penetration of the skull.

The **electroencephalograph (EEG)** is a device that simply monitors the gross electrical activity of the brain. Recording electrodes attached to the scalp measure global changes in the electrical potentials of thousands of brain cells (brain waves), representing those changes in the form of line tracings. The EEG is useful not only as a research tool (e.g., Doucet & Stelmack, 1999), but also for diagnostic purposes (Barcelo & Gale, 1997). Brain disorders, including psychological disorders and brain seizures, can sometimes be detected through abnormalities in brain waves (John et al., 1988; Lee, 1998; Sponheim et al., 1994). Most researchers who use EEG do so in the context of **event-related potentials (ERP)**: A computer is used to time-lock changes in the EEG to computer-presented stimuli (events), allowing researchers to assess brain responses to different sorts of stimuli.

An actual picture of the brain's anatomical structures, including abnormalities in brain tissue, can be obtained through a **computerized tomography scan (CT scan).**

electroencephalograph (EEG)
A device used to monitor the electrical activity of the brain by measuring minute changes in the electrical fields on the scalp.

event-related potentials (ERP)
EEG patterns observed shortly after presentation of a stimulus.

computerized tomography scan (CT scan)
The use of highly focused beams of X-rays to construct detailed anatomical maps of the living brain.

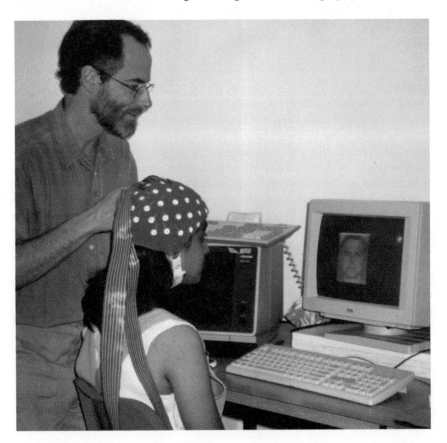

Developmental neuropsychologist Sid Segalowitz of Brock University and a subject are shown here using an event-related potential (ERP) apparatus.

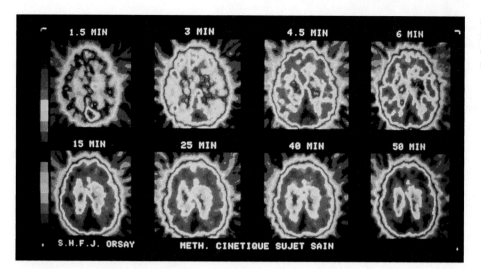

A series of eight PET scans demonstrates how a harmless radioactive substance is absorbed into the cells of active brain regions.

CT scanners use computers to detect how highly focused beams of X-rays change as they pass through the body at various angles and orientations. CT scanners are most often used by physicians to detect tumours or injuries to the brain, but they can also be used to determine whether there is a physical basis for a chronic behavioural or psychological disorder.

Other imaging devices are designed to obtain a snapshot of the active brain at work. These techniques help the researcher determine how various tasks, such as reading, involve particular parts of the brain. In **positron emission tomography (PET),** the patient ingests a harmless radioactive substance, which is absorbed into the cells of brain regions that are metabolically active. When the person performs a specific kind of task, such as speaking or reading, the active areas of the brain absorb more of the ingested radioactive material. The PET scanner reveals which brain regions are more versus less active during performance of a particular task. It is assumed that the parts of the brain with the most concentrated traces of radioactive material probably play significant roles in the task that the subject is performing.

positron emission tomography (PET)
A method for measuring how radioactive substances are absorbed in the brain; it can be used to detect how different tasks activate different areas of the living brain.

(a) Researcher Helen Mayberg of the Rotman Research Institute at the University of Toronto assists a patient undergoing an MRI procedure. The MRI is capable of providing information on both structure and function in the brain. (b) MRIs produce extremely detailed images of the brain and are therefore excellent diagnostic tools for spotting damage, tumour growth, and other physical abnormalities.

Concept Summary

BRAIN INVESTIGATION TECHNIQUES

Technique	Overview	What Can It Show?
Brain damage	Associate areas of brain damage with changes in behavioural function.	The area of the brain that may be responsible for different functions.
Electrical brain stimulation	Use direct electrical or chemical stimulation to excite brain areas.	How activation of certain brain regions affects behaviour.
Transcranial magnetic stimulation (TMS)	Use a magnetic coil pressed to the scalp to excite brain areas.	How activation of certain brain regions affects behaviour.
Electroencephalograph (EEG)	Use electrodes to record gross electrical activity of the brain.	How overall activity in the brain changes during certain activities, such as sleeping, and may allow for detection of disorders.
Event-related potentials (ERP)	Time-locks EEG records to computer-presented stimuli.	How brain activity changes in response to particular kinds of stimuli (events).
Computerized tomography (CT) scan	X-rays are passed through the body at various angles and orientations.	Tumours or injuries to the brain, as well as the structural bases for chronic behavioural or psychological disorders.
Positron emission tomography (PET)	A radioactive substance is ingested; active brain areas absorb the substance; PET scanner reveals distribution of the substance.	How various tasks (such as reading) involve different parts of the brain.
Magnetic resonance imaging (MRI)	Monitors systematic activity of atoms in the presence of magnetic fields and radio wave impulses.	A three-dimensional view of the brain, serving as a diagnostic tool for brain abnormalities, such as tumours.

magnetic resonance imaging (MRI)
A device that uses magnetic fields and radio wave pulses to construct detailed, three-dimensional images of the brain.

Another technique that can be used to isolate both structure and function in the brain is **magnetic resonance imaging (MRI).** MRI is capable of producing extremely detailed, three-dimensional images of the brain. MRI technology capitalizes on the fact that atoms behave in systematic ways in the presence of magnetic fields and radio wave pulses. Although expensive to build and use, MRIs have proven to be excellent diagnostic tools for spotting brain damage, tumour growth, and other abnormalities.

Perhaps the most sophisticated brain-imaging technique is "functional magnetic resonance imaging" (fMRI). fMRI produces a very detailed map of the blood oxygen levels in the brain. More active areas use more oxygen, so this map is used to infer which areas of the brain are particularly important in performance of various tasks. fMRI has been used to identify brain regions associated with visual processing, visual imaging, language, attention, and memory (Gabrieli, 1998; Schacter et al., 1998). For example, Schacter (2001) reported fMRI evidence that brain activities differ when a person is experiencing a false memory (i.e., remembering something that hadn't really occurred) versus an actual memory. As with all brain-imaging techniques, precise interpretation of fMRI data is a matter of heated debate (Bub, 2000), but there is wide agreement that brain-imaging techniques are very useful tools.

Brain Structures and Their Functions

Having discussed some of the research tools that scientists use to map out brain structure and function, let's now turn our attention to the brain itself. Mental processes arise in the brain through the simultaneous activities of millions of densely interconnected individual neurons. Particular regions in the brain underlie unique aspects of an experience, collectively creating a psychological whole. Thus, your perception of a cat is not controlled by a single cell, or even by a single group of cells, but rather by different brain areas that detect the form, colour, texture, and movement of the beast, recognize a characteristic meow, and generate the expectation that the cat will saunter into the room because you just put down the food dish. As discussed earlier, knowledge about which brain areas perform particular mental functions comes, in part, from studies of patients with damage to specific parts of the brain. For instance, a patient might lose knowledge about living things but not about inanimate things (Dixon et al., 2000), or a person might lose the ability to see moving objects but not objects that are stationary (Zeki, 1992).

Our discussion of the brain is divided into sections that correspond to the brain's three major anatomical regions: the *hindbrain,* the *midbrain,* and the *forebrain.*

The Hindbrain: Basic Life Support

The **hindbrain,** which is the most primitive part of the brain, sits at the juncture where the spinal cord and brain merge (see Figure 3.10). "Primitive" is an appropriate term for two reasons. First, structures in the hindbrain act as the basic life-support system for the body—no creative thoughts or complex emotions originate here. Second, from the standpoint of evolution, the hindbrain is the oldest part of the brain. Similar structures, with similar functions, can be found throughout the animal kingdom. You can think of the hindbrain as a kind of base camp, with higher structures situated farther up into the brain controlling increasingly complex mental processes. Not surprisingly, damage to the hindbrain seriously compromises the ability of the organism to survive.

As you can see in Figure 3.10, the hindbrain contains several important anatomical substructures. The *medulla* and the *pons* are associated with the control of heart rate, breathing, blood pressure, and reflexes such as vomiting, sneezing, and coughing. Both areas serve as pathways for neural impulses travelling to and from the spinal cord (the word *pons* means "bridge"). These areas are particularly sensitive to the ill effects of drugs such as alcohol, barbiturates, and cocaine.

The hindbrain also contains the *reticular formation,* a network of nerves linked to the control of general arousal, sleep, and possibly certain movements of the head (Robbins, 1997). Damage to the reticular formation can lead to the loss of consciousness. Finally, at the base of the brain sits a structure that in general appearance resembles a smaller version of the brain. This is the **cerebellum** (which means "little brain"), a structure involved in the preparation, selection, and coordination of complex motor movements such as hitting a golf ball, playing the piano, or writing (Yamaguchi et al., 1998). No one is certain about the exact role the cerebellum plays in movement—it may help guide movement through the integration of sensory information—but it

hindbrain
A primitive part of the brain that sits at the juncture where the brain and spinal cord merge. Structures in the hindbrain, including the medulla, pons, and reticular formation, act as the basic life-support system for the body.

cerebellum
A hindbrain structure at the base of the brain that is involved in the coordination of complex motor skills.

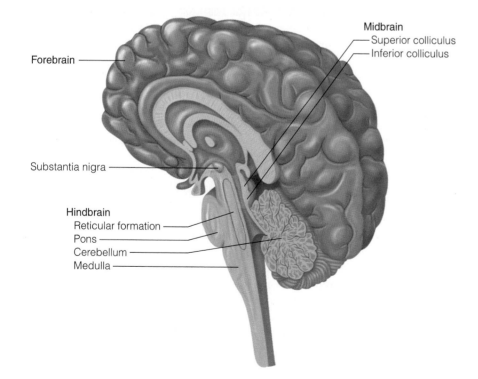

FIGURE 3.10

The Hindbrain and Midbrain

Shown here are the various structures of the human hindbrain and midbrain. The hindbrain (blue) acts as the basic life-support system for the body, controlling such things as heart rate, blood pressure, and respiration. The midbrain (orange) relays some of the information from the spinal cord to higher brain regions.

midbrain

The middle portion of the brain, containing such structures as the tectum, superior colliculus, and inferior colliculus; midbrain structures serve as neural relay stations and may help coordinate reactions to sensory events.

forebrain

The outer portion of the brain, including the cerebral cortex and the structures of the limbic system.

cerebral cortex

The outer layer of the brain, considered to be the seat of higher mental processes.

thalamus

A relay station in the forebrain thought to be an important gathering point for input from the senses.

hypothalamus

A forebrain structure thought to play a role in the regulation of various motivational activities, including eating, drinking, and sexual behaviour.

clearly serves a vital function. The cerebellum may be involved in other functions as well; for instance, evidence suggests that the cerebellum becomes active during language, memory, and reasoning tasks (Schmahmann & Sherman, 1998).

The Midbrain: Neural Relay Stations The **midbrain,** which lies deep within the brain atop the hindbrain, is enveloped by other structures that make up the forebrain. Perhaps because of its central position, the midbrain and its accompanying structures receive input from multiple sources, including the sense organs. The *tectum* and its component structures, the *superior colliculus* and *inferior colliculus,* serve as important relay stations for visual and auditory information and help coordinate reactions to sensory events in the environment (such as moving the head in response to a sudden sound).

The midbrain also contains a group of neurons, collectively called the *substantia nigra,* which release the neurotransmitter dopamine from their terminal buttons. As you learned earlier in the chapter, dopamine tends to produce inhibitory effects in the body, and it seems to be involved in a number of physical and psychological disorders (e.g., schizophrenia and Parkinson's disease). There is evidence that Parkinson's disease is caused by the death of neurons in the substantia nigra (Jenner, 1990; Keller & Rueda, 1998; Mendez et al., 2000). Exactly why this portion of the midbrain degenerates is not known, although environmental toxins may be contributors (Kuhn et al., 1998; Snyder & D'Amato, 1986).

A number of important developments in the understanding and treatment of Parkinson's-like disorders have resulted from investigating the substantia nigra. A disturbing example comes from some recreational drug users who mistakenly ingested a substance called MPTP, which destroys the substantia nigra. Their minds remained active, but they lost the ability to communicate or move about freely. Ironically, this tragic accident proved to be of great value to researchers of Parkinson's disease. By studying these individuals, researchers were able to confirm the link between the production of dopamine in the substantia nigra and the rigidity of movement that characterizes Parkinson's disease. It has even been possible to mimic Parkinson's disease in animals through the administration of MPTP (Schneider et al., 1994; Snyder & D'Amato, 1986).

The Forebrain: Higher Mental Functioning Moving up past the midbrain, we encounter the **forebrain** (see Figure 3.11). The most recognizable feature of the forebrain is the **cerebral cortex,** the greyish matter full of fissures, folds, and crevices that covers the outside of the brain (*cortex* is the Latin word for "bark"). The cortex is quite large in humans; it accounts for approximately 80% of the total volume of the human brain (Kolb & Whishaw, 2002). We'll look at the cerebral cortex in depth after a review of the other structures of the forebrain.

Beneath the cerebral cortex are subcortical structures, including the thalamus, the hypothalamus, and the limbic system. The **thalamus** is positioned close to the midbrain, and it's an important gathering point for input from the various senses. Indeed, the thalamus is thought to be the main processing centre for sensory input before that information is sent out to areas in the upper regions of the cortex. Besides acting as an efficient relay centre, information from the various senses is probably combined in some way here.

The **hypothalamus,** which lies just below the thalamus, is important in the regulation of eating, drinking, body temperature, and sexual behaviour. In experiments on lower animals, administering an electric current to different regions of the hypothalamus initiates a variety of behaviours. For example, male and female rats show characteristic sexual responses when one portion of the hypothalamus is stimulated (Marson & McKenna, 1994), whereas damage to another region of the hypothalamus can seriously affect regular eating behaviour (Sclafani, 1994). (There is more

Neuroscientist Sandra Witelson of McMaster University has conducted extensive research on the relationship between human brain anatomy and human behaviour. She is shown here with part of her collection of over 100 human brains.

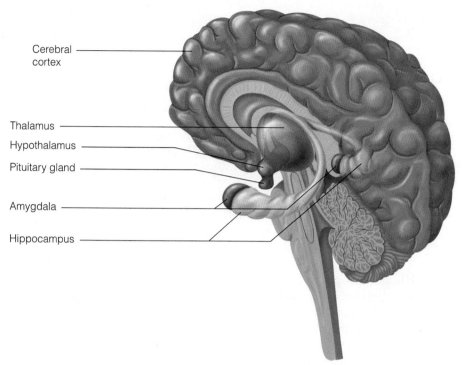

Cerebral cortex

Thalamus

Hypothalamus

Pituitary gland

Amygdala

Hippocampus

FIGURE 3.11
The Forebrain
Shown here are the various structures of the forebrain, including parts of the limbic system and the cerebral cortex. Structures in the limbic system are thought to be involved in motivation, emotions, and memory. The cerebral cortex is the seat of higher mental processes.

information about the neural basis of hunger in Chapter 11.) The hypothalamus also plays a key role in the release of hormones by the pituitary gland; you'll read about the actions of hormones when we discuss the endocrine system later in this chapter.

The **limbic system** is composed of several interrelated brain structures, including the amygdala, the hippocampus, and the septum. The *amygdala* is a small, almond-shaped piece of brain (*amygdala* means "almond") that has been linked to a variety of motivational and emotional behaviours, including fear, aggression, and defensive behaviours (Aggleton, 1993; Davis & Lee, 1998). Destruction of portions of the amygdala in lower animals, through brain lesioning, can produce an extremely passive animal—one that will do nothing in response to provocation. The *hippocampus* (Greek for "sea horse," which it resembles anatomically) is thought to be important to the formation of memories (Eichenbaum et al., 1994). People with severe damage to the hippocampus sometimes live in a kind of perpetual present—they are aware of the world around them, and they recognize people and things known to them prior to the damage, but they recall almost nothing new. These patients act as if they are continually awakening from a dream; experiences slip away, and they recall nothing from only minutes before (Milner et al., 1968). (We'll return to disturbances of this type, and memory loss in general, in Chapter 7.) It should also be noted that the limbic system is the site of most epileptic seizures (Wada, 1991). The *septum* is also part of the limbic system. Lesions in the septum can lead to "septal rage syndrome"; a colleague of one of the authors (MS) reported that a rat with this condition bit right through his thumb, bone and all (Plant, personal communication) (see also Treit & Menard, 2000).

limbic system

A system of structures thought to be involved in motivational and emotional behaviours (the amygdala) and memory (the hippocampus).

The Cerebral Cortex The cerebral cortex is considered the seat of the higher mental processes. Thoughts, the sense of self, reasoning—each arises primarily as a result of neurons firing in patterns in specialized regions of the cerebral cortex. The cortex is divided into two *hemispheres,* left and right. The left hemisphere controls the sensory and motor functions for the right side of the body, and the right hemisphere controls these functions for the left side of the body. A structure called the *corpus callosum,* which we'll discuss later, serves as a communication bridge between the two hemispheres.

FIGURE 3.12
The Cerebral Cortex
The cerebral cortex is divided into two hemispheres—left and right—and each hemisphere can be divided further into four parts, or lobes. The lobes appear specialized to control particular functions, such as visual processing by the occipital lobe and language processing by the frontal and temporal lobes.

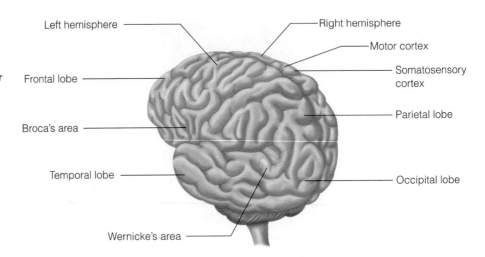

Left hemisphere

Right hemisphere

Motor cortex

Somatosensory cortex

Frontal lobe

Broca's area

Parietal lobe

Temporal lobe

Occipital lobe

Wernicke's area

Critical Thinking

Do you think it's possible that personality is completely localized in one portion of the brain? If so, how could you explain the fact that someone's personality can seem to change depending on the situation?

After a blasting accident substantially damaged the frontal lobe of Phineas Gage's brain, he was "no longer Gage" in the opinion of his friends and acquaintances.

Each hemisphere can be further divided into four parts, or *lobes:* the *frontal, temporal, parietal,* and *occipital* lobes (see Figure 3.12). These lobes (or at least parts of them) appear to control particular body functions, such as visual processing by the occipital lobe and language processing by the frontal and temporal lobes. A slight warning is in order here, however: Although researchers have discovered that particular areas in the brain seem to control highly specialized functions, there is almost certainly considerable overlap of function in the brain. Most brain regions are designed to play multiple roles in helping us think, act, or remember.

How can we possibly assign something like a "sense of self" to a specific area of the cerebral cortex? Once again, the evidence is primarily correlational—some portion of the cortex is damaged, or stimulated electrically, and behavioural changes are observed. We know, for example, that damage to the frontal lobe of the cerebral cortex can produce dramatic changes in an individual's personality. In 1850, a railroad foreman named Phineas Gage was packing black powder into a blasting hole when the powder accidentally discharged, driving a thick iron rod through the left side of his head (entering just below his left eye and exiting the left-top portion of his skull). The result was a 7-cm hole in his skull and the complete shredding of a large portion of the left frontal lobe of his brain. Remarkably, Gage recovered, and with the exception of the loss of vision in his left eye and some slight facial paralysis, he was able to move about freely and perform a variety of tasks. But according to his friends and family he was "no longer Gage"; his personality had completely changed. Whereas prior to his injury he was known as someone with "a well-balanced mind" and as "a shrewd businessman," after the meeting of brain and iron rod he became "fitful, irreverent, indulging at times in the grossest profanity (which was not previously his custom)" (Bigelow, 1850).

The **frontal lobes** are the largest lobes in the cortex and are thought to be involved in a variety of functions including planning and decision making, certain kinds of memory (particularly developing strategies for remembering), and personality (as our discussion of Phineas Gage indicated). The frontal lobes were once the site of a famous surgical operation, the prefrontal lobotomy, which was performed on people suffering from severe psychological disorders (prior to the development of modern psychopharmacological medications). The operation was performed to calm the patient and reduce symptoms, which it sometimes did, but the side effects were severe. Patients lost their ability to take initiative or make plans, and they often appeared to lose their social inhibitions (like Gage). For these reasons, the operation fell out of favour as an acceptable treatment for psychological disorders (see Valenstein, 1986, for a fascinating and accessible treatment of the history of lobotomy).

The frontal lobes also contain the *motor cortex,* which controls the initiation of voluntary muscle movements, as well as areas involved in language production and, possibly, higher-level thought processes (Baldo & Shimamura, 1998; Butler et al., 1993). Broca's area, which is involved in speech production, is located in a portion of the left frontal lobe in most people. The motor cortex sits at the rear of the frontal lobe in both hemispheres; axons from the motor cortex project down to motor neurons in the spinal cord and elsewhere. If neurons in this area of the brain are stimulated electrically, muscle contractions—the twitch of a finger or the jerking of a foot—can occur. Even more interesting, researchers have discovered an intriguing relation between body parts and regions of the motor cortex. It turns out that there is a mapping, or *topographic* organization, in which adjacent areas of the body, such as the hand and the wrist, are activated by neurons that sit next to each other in the motor cortex (Penfield & Boldrey, 1958).

This topographic organization is found in many regions of the cerebral cortex. For example, the **parietal lobe** contains the topographically organized somatosensory cortex, through which people experience the sensations of touch, temperature, and pain. Thus, the brush of a lover's kiss on the cheek excites neurons that lie close to neurons that would be excited by the same kiss to the lips. In addition, as Figure 3.13 demonstrates, there is a relationship between sensitivity to touch (or the ability to control a movement) and the size of the representation in the cortex: Those areas of the body that show particular sensitivity to touch or are associated with fine motor control (such as the face, lips, and fingers) have relatively large areas of neural representation in the cortex.

The **temporal lobes,** which lie on either side of the cortex, are involved in processing auditory information received from the left and right ears. As you'll see in Chapter 4, there is a close relationship between the activities of particular neurons in the temporal lobe and the perception of certain frequencies of sound. As noted earlier, one region of the temporal lobe, Wernicke's area, appears to play a large role in language comprehension (the ability to understand what someone is saying). A person with damage to Wernicke's area might be able to repeat a spoken sentence aloud with perfect diction yet not understand a word of it. Converging evidence comes from brain-imaging studies revealing that Wernicke's area becomes active when people are asked to perform tasks that require meaningful verbal processing (Abdullaev & Posner, 1998). For most people, the speech area is localized in the temporal lobe of the *left* cerebral hemisphere.

frontal lobe
One of four anatomical regions of each hemisphere of the cerebral cortex, located on the top front of the brain; it contains the motor cortex and may be involved in higher-level thought processes.

parietal lobe
One of four anatomical regions of each hemisphere of the cerebral cortex, located roughly on the top middle portion of the brain; it contains the somatosensory cortex, which controls the sense of touch.

temporal lobe
One of four anatomical regions of each hemisphere of the cerebral cortex, located roughly on the sides of the brain; it's involved in certain aspects of speech and language perception.

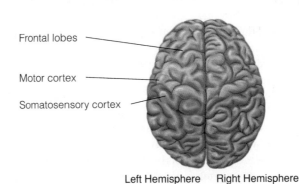

FIGURE 3.13

Specialization in the Motor and Somatosensory Cortex

The motor cortex is located at the rear of the frontal lobes in each cerebral hemisphere. In a systematic body-to-brain relationship, adjacent parts of the body are activated by neurons in adjacent areas of the motor cortex. The somatosensory cortex, which controls the sense of touch, is located in the parietal lobes of each hemisphere; again, there is a systematic mapping arrangement. Notice that for each type of cortex, the size or amount of the representation relates to the degree of sensitivity and/or dexterity of the body part.

occipital lobe

One of four anatomical regions of each hemisphere of the cerebral cortex, located at the back of the brain; visual processing is controlled here.

Finally, at the back of the brain sit the **occipital lobes,** where most visual processing occurs. We'll consider the organization of this part of the brain in more detail in Chapter 4; for now, recognize that it is here, in the far back of the brain, that the information received from receptor cells in the eyes is analyzed and turned into visual images. The brain represents the visual world through a remarkable division of labour—there appear to be separate processing stations in the occipital lobe designed to process colour, form, and motion independently (Shapley, 1990). Not surprisingly, damage to the occipital lobe tends to produce highly specific visual deficits—the person might lose the ability to recognize a face, a contour moving in a particular direction, or a colour (Zeki, 1992).

The Divided Brain

Nowhere is the division of labour in the brain more evident than in the study of the two separate halves, or hemispheres, that make up the cerebral cortex. Although the brain is designed to operate as a functional whole, the hemispheres are *lateralized,* which means that each side is responsible for performing different functions (Hellige, 1990). As you've seen, the right hemisphere of the brain controls the movements and sensations of the left side of the body, whereas the left hemisphere handles the body's right side. This means that stimulating a region of the motor cortex in the left cerebral hemisphere would cause a muscle on the right side of the body to twitch. Similarly, if cells in the occipital lobe of the right cerebral hemisphere are damaged or destroyed, a blind spot develops in the left portion of the visual world. **Lateralization** undoubtedly serves some adaptive functions. For example, it may allow the brain to divide its labour in ways that produce more efficient processing.

lateralization

Asymmetry in the functions of the right and left hemispheres of the cerebral cortex (e.g., in most individuals, most language skills are lateralized to the left hemisphere).

Figure 3.14 shows how information received through the eyes travels to one side of the brain or the other. If you are looking straight ahead, an image originating from the

Concept Summary

BRAIN AREAS, STRUCTURES, AND FUNCTIONS

Brain Area	General Function	Structures and Specific Function
Hindbrain	Basic life support	**Medulla** and **pons:** associated with the control of heart rate, breathing, and certain reflexes. **Reticular formation:** control of general arousal, sleep, and some movement of the head. **Cerebellum:** involved in preparation, selection, and coordination of complex motor movement.
Midbrain	Houses neural relay stations	**Tectum** (components are **superior colliculus** and **inferior colliculus**): relay stations for visual and auditory information. **Substantia nigra:** group of neurons that release the neurotransmitter dopamine.
Forebrain	Higher mental functions	**Thalamus:** initial gathering point for sensory input; information combined and relayed here. **Hypothalamus:** helps regulate eating, drinking, body temperature, and sexual behaviour. **Amygdala** (part of **limbic system**): linked to fear, aggression, and defensive behaviours. **Hippocampus** (part of **limbic system**): important to the formation of memories. **Cerebral cortex:** the seat of higher mental processes, including sense of self and the ability to reason and solve problems.

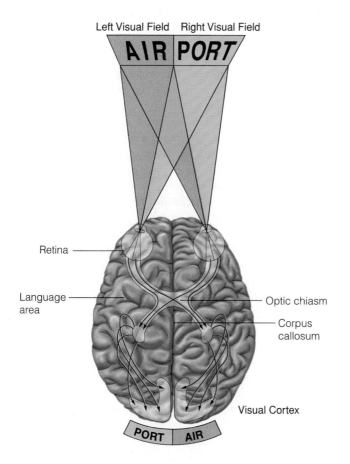

Left Visual Field   Right Visual Field

AIR PORT

Retina

Language area

Optic chiasm

Corpus callosum

Visual Cortex

PORT AIR

FIGURE 3.14

Visual Processing in the Two Hemispheres

Images originating in the left visual field fall on the inside half of the left eye and the outside half of the right eye and are then projected to the right hemisphere. Information appearing in the right visual field, in contrast, projects to the left hemisphere. Because most language processing occurs in the left hemisphere, split-brain patients can vocally report only stimuli that are shown in the right visual field. In this case, the subject says only "port" because that is the word available for processing in the left hemisphere.

left side of your body (the left visual field) falls on the inside half of the left eye and the outside half of the right eye; receptor cells in these locations transmit their images to the back of the *right* cerebral hemisphere. Both eyes project information directly to each hemisphere, as the figure shows, but information from the left visual field goes to the right hemisphere and vice versa. By capitalizing on the nature of these neural

corpus callosum
The collection of nerve fibres that connect the two cerebral hemispheres and allow information to pass from one side to the other.

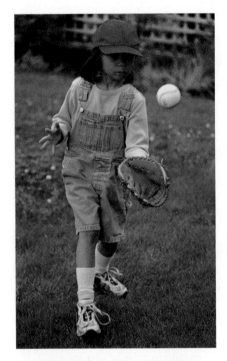

It's adaptive for both sides of the brain to process information from the environment; otherwise, this child would probably have difficulty developing a coordinated response to this rapidly arriving ball.

Critical Thinking

Besides as a treatment for epilepsy, can you think of any situations in which having a split brain might be beneficial?

pathways, as you'll see in a moment, researchers can present information initially to one side of the brain or the other.

Under normal circumstances, a visual object presented in only one visual field is eventually represented in both sides of the brain. This is because, as we noted earlier, a major communication bridge—the **corpus callosum**—connects the two brain halves. Information arriving in the right hemisphere, for example, is transported to the left hemisphere through the corpus callosum in just a few thousandths of a second (Saron & Davidson, 1989). This transfer process occurs automatically and requires no head or eye turning.

Splitting the Brain   If you think about it, you'll realize that it's important for both sides of the brain to receive information about objects in the environment. To see why, imagine what visual perception would be like for someone without a corpus callosum—someone with a "split brain." Suppose an object appears suddenly, with great velocity, in the person's left visual field. There's no time to move the head or eyes, only time for a kind of reflexive response. Our patient would be incapable of a coordinated response, because the right side of the brain contains the machinery to control only the left side of the body. Moreover, the split-brain patient would be unable to name the menacing object, because the language comprehension and production centres are located, typically, on the left side of the brain.

Let's consider another experiment for our hypothetical patient. Suppose that we flash the word AIRPORT on a screen, very quickly, but arrange it so that the first part of the word, AIR, appears in the left visual field and the second part, PORT, appears in the right visual field. What do you think the patient will report seeing? The answer is the word PORT, because that's the image received by the left hemisphere—the place where the language centres are located. The language part of the brain wouldn't even know that AIR had been presented, because the image would remain locked in the visual centres of the right hemisphere.

Actually, our hypothetical patient, as well as a version of the study we just described, is *real* (Gazzaniga, 1970). There are a number of individuals who have split brains. Some were born without a corpus callosum (Lassonde & Jeeves, 1994; Sanders, 1989); others had their communication gateway severed on purpose by surgeons seeking to reduce the spread of severe epileptic seizures (Springer & Deutsch, 1989). Epilepsy is a kind of electrical firestorm in the brain that spreads across the cortex, producing convulsions and sometimes loss of consciousness. Cutting the communication gateway from one hemisphere to another limits epileptic seizures to one half of the brain. Severing the corpus callosum is a rarely used procedure because modern antiepileptic drugs control seizures for most patients. However, it has proven effective in some instances for patients who fail to respond to medication.

The two hemispheres of split-brain patients are not broken or damaged by the operation; information simply cannot easily pass from one side of the brain to the other. In fact, the behaviour of split-brain patients appears to be remarkably normal. It's extremely unlikely that you would be able to identify one of them in a crowd. Their behaviour appears normal because most input from the environment still reaches both sides of their brain. These patients can turn their heads and eyes freely as they interact with the environment, allowing information to fall on receptor regions that transmit to both hemispheres. The abnormal nature of their brains becomes apparent only under manufactured conditions like those described above and through the personal anecdotes that these patients sometimes report.

Much of the work on split-brain individuals was conducted by the late Nobel Prize–winning neuroscientist Roger Sperry and his colleagues. In one classic study by Gazzaniga, Bogen, and Sperry (1965), several images (pictures, words, or symbols) were presented visually to either the left or right visual fields of split-brain subjects. When an image was shown to the right visual field, it was easily named because it could be processed by the language centres of the left hemisphere. For left visual field presentations, the patients remained perplexed and silent. It was later learned, however, that their silence did not mean that the brain failed to process the image. If split-brain patients were asked to *point* to a picture of the object just shown, they could do so, but only with the *left* hand (e.g., Gazzaniga & LeDoux, 1978). The brain had received the input but could not respond verbally.

Although split-brain patients behave relatively normally after surgery, they do report that sometimes their right and left hands act as if they have minds of their own. These reports are anecdotal, of course, and need to be viewed with some caution. Patients have claimed that it is difficult to read something, such as a newspaper or a book, unless it is held by the right hand; the left hand, which maps to the nonverbal right hemisphere, apparently has no interest in reading as a leisure activity (Preilowski, 1975). It has been claimed that the two hemispheres occasionally compete, sometimes over bizarre things such as what clothes to wear. One patient reported buttoning a blouse with one hand while, at the same time, unbuttoning the blouse with the other. Again, it's difficult to know what to make of these claims, or to know how accurately they have been reported, but it does seem likely that independent processing activities can go on simultaneously in the two hemispheres of the brain. Some researchers have even suggested that each side may have its own kind of separate consciousness (Kandel, 1991; Victor, 1996).

Hemispheric Specialization The available evidence strongly indicates that the two hemispheres of the cerebral cortex are specialized to perform certain kinds of tasks. The right hemisphere, for example, appears to play a more important role in spatial tasks, such as fitting together the pieces of a puzzle or orienting oneself spatially in an environment. Patients with damage to the right hemisphere characteristically have trouble with spatial tasks, as do split-brain patients who must assemble a puzzle with their right hand (Kalat, 1992). The right hemisphere may also be involved in some important aspects of emotional processing (Spence et al., 1996). The left hemisphere—perhaps in part because of the lateralized language centres—clearly contributes more to verbal tasks such as reading and writing.

There is little, if any, scientific evidence to support claims of the type made in this advertisement. (From Kalat, 1996.)

Still, you should understand that a great deal of cooperation and collaboration goes on between the hemispheres. They interact continuously, and most mental processes, including language, depend on activity that arises in both sides of the brain. You think and behave with a whole brain, not a fragmented one. Moreover, if one side of the brain is damaged, regions in the other hemisphere can sometimes take over the lost functions (Gazzaniga et al., 1996). Finally, it is worth noting that people vary in how specialized their right and left hemispheres are, and there is some indication that these variations in the degree of brain lateralization are related to individual differences on dimensions such as creativity (e.g., Weinstein & Graves, 2002).

Over the last two decades or so, there has been an explosion of interest—often by people operating at the fringe of scientific psychology—in assigning a variety of psychological phenomena to the different sides of the brain. It has been suggested, for example, that the right side of the brain is holistic rather than analytic and accounts for such varied activities as fantasy, dance, and music appreciation. The left side of the brain is argued to be the rational mind, controlling not only language but also mathematical and scientific abilities. One of the authors once encountered a man who offered his left hand in greeting, explaining, "I'm trying to develop my right hemisphere." He apparently felt that shaking with his left hand would promote right brain thinking. Some companies even market packages designed to teach people to become more right brained in their approach to the world, or to develop ways to synchronize the two sides of the brain.

At present, there is little scientific evidence to support such claims. It's extremely unlikely that people can learn to develop a particular side of the brain or that individuals can be properly classified as "right brained" or "left brained." There is also no scientific rationale for proposing that a particular thinking style can be attributed to one hemisphere and not to the other (Hellige, 1990). Far too often the striking and newsworthy claims are based on anecdotal reports or poorly designed studies. For example, students who listened to tapes designed to stimulate synchronization of the hemispheres were found to perform better on a variety of tasks than students who weren't exposed to the tapes. But the students who participated were fully informed about the potential benefits of the tapes, so their task improvements could easily be attributed to a placebo effect (for further discussion, see Druckman & Swets, 1988).

Test Yourself 3.2

Test what you've learned about research into brain structures and their functions. Fill in each blank with one of the following terms: EEG; PET scan; hindbrain; midbrain; forebrain; cerebellum; hypothalamus; cortex; frontal lobes; limbic system; corpus callosum. (You will find the answers in Appendix B.)

1. A "primitive" part of the brain that controls basic life-support functions such as heart rate and respiration: _____

2. A structure thought to be involved in a variety of motivational activities, including eating, drinking, and sexual behaviour: _____

3. The portion of the cortex believed to be involved in higher-order thought processes (such as planning) as well as the initiation of voluntary motor movements: _____

4. A structure near the base of the brain that is involved in coordination of complex activities such as walking and playing the piano:

    _____

5. A device that is used to monitor the gross electrical activity of the brain:

    _____

REGULATING GROWTH AND INTERNAL FUNCTIONS: EXTENDED COMMUNICATION

Learning Goals

1. Learn how the endocrine system controls long-term and widespread communication needs.
2. Be able to discuss the roles that hormones play in establishing sexual identity and how they may contribute to gender differences on psychological measures.

THE HUMAN BODY actually has two communication systems. The first, the connective network of the nervous system, starts and controls most behaviours—thoughts, voluntary movements, and sensations and perceptions of the external world. Electrochemical activity, forming the neural impulse, moves rapidly down axons, like sparks traversing the fuses of firecrackers tied in series, forcing the release of neurotransmitters that affect activity in the postsynaptic cells. But the body also has long-term communication needs. For example, the body must initiate and control growth and provide long-term regulation of numerous internal biological systems. A second communication system serves these needs: a network of glands called the **endocrine system** (see Figure 3.15), which uses the bloodstream, rather than neurons, as its main

endocrine system
A network of glands that uses the bloodstream, rather than neurons, to send chemical messages that regulate growth and other internal functions.

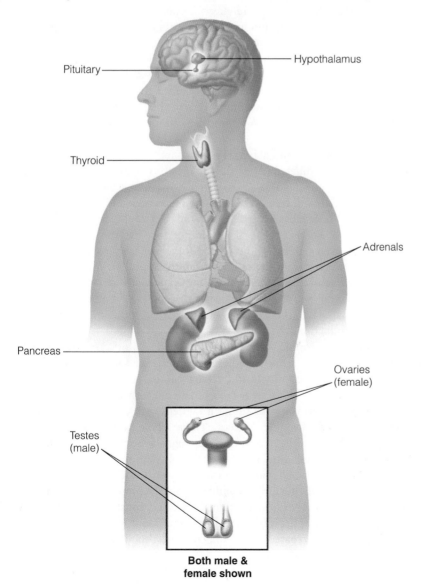

Pituitary

Hypothalamus

Thyroid

Adrenals

Pancreas

Ovaries (female)

Testes (male)

Both male & female shown

FIGURE 3.15

The Endocrine System

The major glands of the human endocrine system. Collectively, they secrete more than 20 different hormones, or chemical messengers, into the bloodstream. Each hormone has specific effects on particular types of cells in the body, often at locations quite remote from the gland itself.

hormones

Chemicals released into the blood by the various endocrine glands to help control a variety of internal regulatory functions.

information courier. Chemicals called **hormones** are released into the blood by the various endocrine glands and serve to control a variety of internal functions.

The word *hormone* comes aptly from the Greek *hormon,* which means "to set into motion." Hormones play a role in many basic, life-sustaining activities in the body. Hunger, thirst, sexual behaviour, and the "fight or flight" response are all regulated in part by an interplay between the nervous system and hormones released by the endocrine glands. Again, the fact that the body has two communication systems rather than one makes sense from an adaptive standpoint. One system, communication among neurons, governs transmissions that are quick and detailed; the other, the endocrine system, initiates slower but more widespread and longer-lasting effects. In the following section, we'll consider the endocrine system in more detail and then consider how hormones influence some fundamental differences between men and women.

The Endocrine System

The chemical communication system of the endocrine glands differs in some important ways from the rapid-fire electrochemical activities of the nervous system. On the one hand, communication in the nervous system tends to be *localized,* which means that a given neurotransmitter usually affects only cells in a small area. On the other hand, hormones have widespread effects. Because they are carried by the blood, they travel throughout the body and interact with numerous target sites. Also in contrast to neurotransmitters, hormones have long-lasting effects. Whereas neural communication operates in time scales bordering on the blink of an eye, the endocrine system can produce effects lasting minutes, hours, or even days. In some animals, for example, circulating hormones prepare the organism for seasonal migration or for hibernation. Thus, the endocrine system provides the body with a mechanism for both widespread and long-term communication that cannot be produced by interactions among neurons.

Although the endocrine and nervous systems communicate in different ways, their activities are closely coordinated (Anisman et al., 2001; Cooper, P.E., 1991). Structures in the brain (especially the hypothalamus) stimulate or inhibit the release of hormones by the glands; once released, these chemicals then feed back and affect the firing rates of neural impulses. The feedback loop balances and controls the regulatory activities of the body. The hypothalamus is of particular importance because it controls the *pituitary gland.* The **pituitary gland** can be thought of as a master gland that controls the secretion of hormones in response to signals from the hypothalamus; these hormones, in turn, regulate the activity of many of the other vital glands in the endocrine system. For example, the pituitary gland signals the testes in males to produce *testosterone* and the ovaries in females to produce *estrogen*—both of critical importance in sexual behaviour and reproduction.

pituitary gland

A kind of master gland in the body that controls the release of hormones in response to signals from the hypothalamus.

adrenal glands

Secrete norepinephrine and epinephrine into the bloodstream.

norepinephrine and epinephrine

Cause a surge of energy that increases the heart rate; blood is shunted to areas that require it, away from the stomach and intestine; glucose is made available to the muscles.

Let's consider one example of the endocrine system at work. You leave a party late, convinced that you can walk the two kilometres home without incident. The streets, quiet without the noise of midday traffic, exert a calming influence as you walk along. But suddenly two shadowy figures emerge from an alleyway and move in your direction. You draw in your breath, your stomach tightens, and your rapidly beating heart seems ready to explode from your chest. These whole-body reactions, critical in preparing you to fight or flee, are created by signals from the brain that lead to increased activity of the endocrine glands. The hypothalamus, acting through the pituitary gland, signals the **adrenal glands** (located above the kidneys) to begin secreting the hormones **norepinephrine** and **epinephrine** into the blood. These hormones produce energizing effects on the body, increasing heart rate, constricting the blood supply to the stomach and intestines, and increasing the amount of glucose (sugar) in the blood. The body is now prepared for action, enhancing the likelihood of survival (see Figure 3.16).

Critical Thinking

Initiation of the fight-or-flight response clearly has adaptive value. But can you think of any circumstances in which this response might lower the chances of an adaptive response?

Hypothalamus
Stimulates adrenal glands.

Adrenal Glands
Secrete norepinephrine and epinephrine into bloodstream.

Norepinephrine and Epinephrine
Cause energy surge; heart rate increase; blood is shunted away from the stomach and intestine to areas that require it; glucose is made available to the muscles.

FIGURE 3.16

The Fight-or-Flight Response

In potentially dangerous situations the endocrine system generates a fight-or-flight response. Hormones are released that produce energizing effects on the body, increasing our chances of survival.

Gender, Hormones, and Psychology

Prior to birth, hormones released by the pituitary gland initiate developments in the fetus's reproductive anatomy, determining whether a child ends up with male or female sex organs. At puberty, an increase in sex hormones (testosterone and estrogen) leads males to develop facial hair and deep voices and females to develop breasts and to begin menstruation. It is now suspected that hormones released during development may even affect basic patterns of neuronal connections within men's and women's brains. Evidence suggests that men and women may think differently as the result of gender-specific activities of the endocrine system.

Simon Fraser University psychologist Doreen Kimura and her colleague Elizabeth Hampson (1994), for example, reported that the performance of women and men on certain tasks changes significantly as the levels of sex hormones in the body increase or decrease. Women typically perform better than men on some tests of verbal ability, and their performance on these tasks improves with high levels of estrogen in their body. Similarly, men tend to show slightly better performance on some kinds of spatial tasks (such as imagining that three-dimensional objects are rotating), and their performance seems to be related somewhat to their testosterone levels. The evidence is correlational, which means that we cannot be sure that the hormones are causing the performance changes, but the data are suggestive of endocrine-based gender differences in thought (Collins & Kimura, 1997). York University evolutionary psychologist Irwin Silverman and colleagues have suggested that, although men tend to do well on spatial tasks such as mental rotation of objects and map reading, women tend to do better than males in remembering the contents and locations of arrays of objects (Silverman & Eals, 1992; Silverman & Phillips, 1998). These researchers suggest that these gender differences are linked to hormonal changes during puberty and may reflect the likelihood that human male brains were selected more by evolution to produce cognitive skills associated with hunting, and female brains evolved more for the cognitive skills associated with foraging for food. Obviously, social and cultural factors are also likely to play roles in producing such gender differences, but there is some evidence that hormones also play a role.

Although gender differences in brain anatomy and functioning may influence cognitive and behavioural differences between boys and girls, environmental factors also play a role.

It's also the case that girls who have been exposed to an excess of male hormones during the initial stages of prenatal development, either because of a genetic disorder or from chemicals ingested by the mother during pregnancy, tend to be particularly tomboyish during development (Resnick et al., 1986), preferring to engage in play activities that are more traditionally associated with boys. In one study reported by Kimura (1992), researchers at the University of California, Los Angeles, compared the choice of toys by girls who either had or had not been exposed to excess male hormones during early development. The girls who had been exposed to the male hormones tended to prefer typical masculine activities—smashing trucks and cars together, for example—more than the control girls did.

There is evidence that male and female brains differ somewhat anatomically, although such differences have often been exaggerated historically (Shields, 1975). Animal studies have confirmed that male and female rat brains differ anatomically and that these differences in rat brains are due, in part, to the early influence of hormones (see Hines, 1982, for a review). For humans, the data are less clear and more controversial. It's been reported that the right cortex of males tends to be slightly thicker than the right cortex of females (Boone & Lu, 2000; Kimura, 1992, 1999), but whether this anatomical difference accounts, even in part, for the superiority that males show in performing certain spatial tasks is unclear. Other studies have reported that sections of the corpus callosum are more elaborate in women, suggesting that the two hemispheres communicate more effectively in females (de Lacoste-Utamsing & Holloway, 1982). However, McMaster University neuropsychologist Sandra Witelson (1992) has reported failure to replicate this particular result.

There is also evidence supporting gender differences in mental functioning (e.g., Kimura, 1999), and some of those differences may be due to hormones. Hormones released by the endocrine system produce permanent changes early in human development, and actions later in life may be influenced by these changes. However, it should be noted that there are many psychological and cognitive measures on which men and women do not differ, and that even on those tasks in which gender differences are observed, the differences are usually very small, with a great deal of overlap between the performance of men and women (Hyde & Lin, 1988). There is also evidence that some such differences can be eliminated with relatively brief training interventions.

To repeat a theme discussed in Chapter 1, it is difficult to separate the effects of biology *(nature)* from the ongoing influences of the environment *(nurture)* (see Karmiloff-Smith et al., 1998). Men and women undoubtedly faced some differing problems of adaptation during our evolutionary history, and evolution likely selected for somewhat different "solution tools" in the brains of men and women. Furthermore, men and women are currently faced with different environmental pressures and cultural expectations during their lifetimes. These pressures also shape the actions they take, thereby influencing behavioural differences between the sexes. We will return to gender issues often in later chapters of this text.

Test Yourself 3.3

Test your knowledge about the differences between the endocrine system and the nervous system. For each statement, decide whether the *endocrine* or *nervous* system is the most appropriate term to apply. (You will find the answers in Appendix B.)

1. Communication effects tend to be localized, affecting only a small area: _____

2. Responsible for whole-body reactions, such as the fight-or-flight response: _____

3. The major determinant of sexual identity: _____

4. Communicates through the release of epinephrine and norepinephrine: _____

5. Operates quickly, with time scales bordering on the blink of an eye: _____

ADAPTING AND TRANSMITTING THE GENETIC CODE: EVOLVED PSYCHOLOGICAL TRAITS

Learning Goals

1. Be able to explain what it means to say that a trait evolved through the process of natural selection.
2. Learn the basics of genetic transmission.
3. Become familiar with how psychologists study the role of genetics in psychological traits.
4. Understand how evolutionary mechanisms may have influenced human thinking, feelings, and behaviours, and appreciate the concept of the "environment of evolutionary adaptedness."

THE HUMAN BODY, including the brain, developed over the course of thousands of millennia through the process of organic evolution. To understand humans and how and why they do and feel the things they do, it is important to understand the mechanisms of evolution that shaped that development. You are probably already familiar with the idea that plants and animals evolved via natural selection. In this section, we provide a brief introduction to evolutionary processes, and discuss reasons for believing that our evolutionary heritage influences not only how our bodies look and operate, but also how we think, feel, and act.

Natural Selection

Darwin proposed the mechanism of **natural selection** to explain how species change, or evolve, over time. He recognized that having certain **traits,** or characteristic features of body or behaviour, can help an organism survive and reproduce in its environment.

natural selection
The differential production and survival of offspring by species members with advantageous traits.

trait
A distinguishable characteristic of an organism.

The zebra's stripes presumably evolved because they benefit the zebra's survival and reproduction. Similarly, genetically coded tendencies toward loving offspring may constitute evolutionary adaptations that contributed to human survival and reproductive success in our evolutionary past.

Further, he assumed that some such features are passed from one generation to the next. For example, if a sparrow is born with a special capacity to find seeds, then its chances of living long enough to mate and produce offspring increase relative to other sparrows. If that special capacity is heritable, then that sparrow's offspring will have a chance of sharing that evolutionary advantage. Over many generations, the special seed-finding trait may become a stable characteristic of all sparrows. The seed-finding trait in this example is an **evolutionary adaptation,** a characteristic selected by nature because it increases the odds of survival. As illustrated in this example, natural selection refers to the differential production and survival of offspring by members of a species who differ in some advantageous way from other members of that species (Crawford, 1998a).

For natural selection to produce evolutionary adaptations, there needs to be a mechanism for producing variation within a species. If all the members of a species were exactly the same, then obviously there could be no special trait for nature to select. In addition, there needs to be some mechanism by which an adaptive trait can pass from one generation to the next. During Darwin's time, the mechanism for creating variability and inheritance was unknown; Darwin made his case by documenting the abundance of variability and inherited characteristics that exist in nature. It was later learned that the mechanism that enables natural selection is the genetic code.

evolutionary adaptation
A heritable trait that provided an organism with an advantage in surviving and/or reproducing during its evolutionary history.

Genetic Principles

Let's briefly review some of the important principles of genetics. What are genes, what do they do, and what are the factors that produce genetic variability? The genetic message resides within chromosomes, which are thin, threadlike strips of DNA. Every cell in your body (except sperm cells and unfertilized egg cells) contains 46 chromosomes, arranged in 23 pairs. Half of each chromosome pair came from your mother through one of her eggs, and the other half arrived in you from one of your father's sperm cells when it fertilized that egg. **Genes** are segments of chromosomes that contain chemically coded instructions telling cells how to manufacture various substances that, in turn, give rise to particular hereditary traits. Your genes, interacting with the environment, controlled the development of your body from a fertilized egg to whatever age you have attained, and they will continue to play roles in making you who you are throughout your life. For example, each person has genes that help determine height,

genes
Segments of chromosomes that contain chemically coded instructions for creating particular hereditary characteristics.

other genes that help determine eye colour, and yet others that influence susceptibility to specific heritable diseases.

There are two genes for most heritable characteristics, or traits. People have two genes, for example, for hair colour, blood type, and the possible development of facial dimples. If both genes are designed to produce the same trait (such as nearsightedness), there's little question the characteristic will develop (you'll definitely need glasses). But what if the two genes differ—for example, the father passes along the gene for nearsightedness, but the corresponding gene from the mother is for normal distance vision? Under these conditions, the trait is determined by the dominant gene; in the case of vision, the **dominant** "normal" **gene** will dominate the **recessive gene** for nearsightedness, such that the child will have normal vision.

The fact that a dominant gene masks the effects of a recessive gene means that everybody has genetic material that is not actually expressed in their physical and psychological characteristics. A person may see perfectly but still carry the recessive gene for nearsightedness. This is why parents with normal vision can produce a nearsighted child, or two brown-haired parents can produce a child with blond hair—it is the particular combination of genes that determines the inherited characteristics.

Another important distinction is between the **genotype,** which is the genetic code in an individual's chromosomes, and the **phenotype,** which is the individual's observable characteristics. The phenotype, such as good vision, is influenced by the genotype, but it can also be influenced by the environment. A person's height and weight, for example, are strongly influenced by the genotype, but environmental factors such as diet also contribute significantly to these aspects of the phenotype. This is an important point to remember: Genes provide the materials from which characteristics develop, but the environment often shapes the final product. Exactly how a genotype is expressed into a phenotype defines the nature–nurture issue in its purest form.

Across individuals, variations in the genetic message arise partly because there are trillions of different ways that the genetic information from each parent can be combined at fertilization. Each egg or sperm cell contains a random half of each parent's 23 chromosome pairs. According to the laws of probability, this means that there are some 8 million (2^{23}) different combinations that a given individual could produce in his or her reproductive cells. The fertilization of a particular egg by a particular sperm is also a matter of chance, which means that there are some 64 trillion ways that the genetic material of a given pair of parents can be combined. Thus a very wide variety of traits (and combinations of traits) can emerge via reproduction, thereby contributing to variability across individuals. If a particular genetically coded trait produces a survival advantage, then individuals with that trait will be more likely to reproduce and their offspring will be more likely to have the trait. This is one way in which evolution proceeds.

Variation in the genetic code can also occur by chance via mutations. A **mutation** is a spontaneous change in the genetic material that occurs due to an error during the gene replication process. Genetic mutations are essentially random errors in the biological mechanisms by which chromosomes are copied, and most mutations are harmful to the organism. Occasionally, however, by a fluke of chance a mutation leads to a new trait that confers a survival advantage to the organism. Mutations, along with the variations produced by unique combinations of genetic material, are key ingredients for natural selection because they introduce novelty into nature. Via natural selection, nature tends to discard novel organisms that are unfit, and to favour those that are fit.

dominant versus recessive genes
For many traits there are two genes, with one of them being dominant and the other recessive. If the two such genes for a given trait differ, it is the dominant gene that influences the observable characteristic.

genotype
The genetic information inherited from one's parents.

phenotype
A person's observable characteristics, such as red hair. The phenotype is controlled partly by the genotype and partly by the environment.

mutation
Error in the process by which chromosomes are copied that changes the genotype specified by those chromosomes.

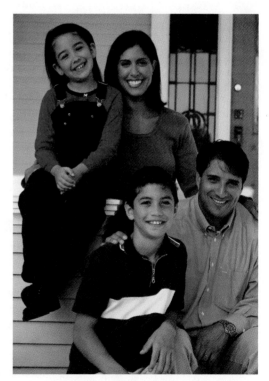

Genetic background plays an important role in determining physical appearance, but many researchers believe that it also helps shape certain psychological characteristics.

Genes and Behaviour

You probably find it pretty easy to accept the idea that your height and eye colour reflect your genes. But you may be less open to the idea that your genetic makeup affects your thoughts, feelings, and behaviours. However, as you'll see throughout this book, it is sometimes possible to predict (not perfectly, but above chance) things about the psychology of an individual by knowing something about his or her genes. Susceptibility to the psychological disorder schizophrenia is a case in point. Natural children of parents who have schizophrenia have a greater chance of developing the disorder themselves, when compared to children of parents without schizophrenia, even if the children were adopted by non-schizophrenics at birth (Gottesman, 1991; Moldin & Gottesman, 1997). Thus, genes probably play some role in susceptibility to schizophrenia. (We will return to this issue in more detail in Chapter 14.)

One way that psychologists study the link between genes and behaviour is to investigate family histories in detail. In **family studies,** researchers look for similarities and differences between biological (blood) relatives as a way of determining whether heredity has an influence. As you've just learned, the chances of schizophrenia increase with a family history, and there are many other traits that seem to run in families as well (e.g., intelligence and personality). The trouble with family studies, however, is that members of a family share more than just common genes. They are also exposed to similar environmental experiences, so it's difficult to separate the relative roles of nature and nurture in behaviour. Family studies can be useful sources of information—it helps to know, for instance, if someone has a greater than average risk of developing schizophrenia—but they can't be used to establish cause-and-effect links between genes and behaviour.

In **twin studies,** a somewhat better technique, researchers compare behavioural traits between *identical* twins, who share the same genetic material, and *fraternal* twins, who were born at the same time but whose genetic overlap is only roughly 50% (fraternal twins can even be of different sexes). In studies of intelligence, for example, identical twins tend to have much more similar intelligence scores than fraternal twins, even when environmental factors are taken into account (Bouchard, 1997; Bouchard et al., 1990). Kerry Jang of the University of British Columbia and Phillip Vernon of the University of Western Ontario and their co-workers have collaborated on many such studies, emphasizing the interaction between genes and environment in, for example, susceptibility to alcoholism (Jang et al., 2001). Identical twins make ideal research subjects because researchers can control, at least in principle, for genetic factors. Because these twins have the same genetic makeup, any physical or psychological differences that emerge during development must be attributable to environmental factors. Similarly, if identical twins are raised in different environments but still show similar traits, it's a strong indication that genetic factors are involved in expression of the trait. It's worth noting, though, that when identical twins are raised apart, they are often raised by close relatives (e.g., one twin with the mother and another with the mother's sister) and hence in similar environments, making it difficult to determine whether similarities between the twins are purely genetic (Kamin, 1974).

Evolutionary Adaptations and Human Behaviour

Having reviewed the basics of genetics, let's return to the issue of evolution. Evolutionary psychologists propose that humans evolved tendencies to think, feel, and behave in certain ways, and not others, because humans (or prehuman hominids) who thought and behaved in certain ways survived and reproduced better than those who did not. An example of this is the human tendency for fathers to love, nurture, and protect their children. Presumably, this tendency exists across the human species because, among ancient humans (and our prehuman ancestors), loving and protective fathering conferred a survival advantage. Note that we refer to a *tendency* here; although some human fathers do not demonstrate much loving behaviour toward their offspring, most do, and as a species, humans show much more fathering motivation and behaviour than males in closely related species such as chimpanzees and orangutans (Smuts et al., 1987). This is what we mean when we say humans may have *evolved* a tendency for males in the species to love and protect their offspring. Males

family studies
The similarities and differences between biological (blood) relatives are studied to help discover the role heredity plays in physical or psychological traits. Family studies rarely provide conclusive evidence because genes and the environment are usually entangled.

twin studies
Identical twins, who share genetic material, are compared to fraternal twins in an effort to disentangle the roles of heredity and environment in giving rise to psychological traits.

Critical Thinking

In what ways are the environmental experiences of identical twins more similar than those for fraternal twins? Why might this still be true if both sets of twins were raised apart from birth?

who had genes that built brains that disposed them toward fathering behaviours left more offspring than males who did not have such genes, so genes for some degree of paternal love became "standard equipment" in the genetic complement of human males, just like genes coding for facial hair in males.

As is the case for facial hair, the claim that a trait evolved to be standard equipment across the human species does not mean that it shows no variability. Just as some men have a lot of facial hair and some have very little, some men show a great deal of fatherly love and some show very little. Although both traits are virtually universal across the human species (among adult males) and likely arose via natural selection, this does not mean that the expression of each trait will be similar in every man. Particularly in the case of psychological traits, what was likely selected was a *tendency* to respond in a certain way, not an invariant behavioural pattern. Such a tendency can be overridden by environmental or developmental circumstances (see Karmiloff-Smith et al., 1998).

A related point is that although human psychology may have been sculpted by evolution, those evolutionary adaptations are general and flexible, rather than specific and rigid. Humans have not, for example, evolved to understand a specific language such as English or French. Instead, humans have evolved a tendency to learn the language or languages that they are exposed to in their environments, especially during childhood (Pinker, 1997b). We do not have genes for speaking English or French, but we do have genes that code for the construction of brain/mind mechanisms for learning whatever human language is present around us during childhood. Evidently, natural selection favoured such genes in human evolution because language gave our ancestors an advantage in surviving and reproducing.

Evolutionary psychologists have suggested a number of aspects of human thought and behaviour that are likely evolutionary adaptations (Barkow et al., 1992; Bock & Cardew, 1997). These include the two examples discussed above: language mechanisms (Pinker, 1997b) and parenting motivations and behaviours (Wilson & Daly, 1997). Other examples include our tendency to find certain problems easier to solve if they are posed in a social context rather than in a nonsocial or abstract context (Cosmides & Tooby, 1997), and the tendency for people to feel jealous if they think a romantic partner is sexually attracted to or involved with someone else (Buss, 2000). Many of the "solution tools" to adaptive problems discussed in Chapter 1 are also likely evolutionary adaptations. For instance, the reason that our minds have the ability to form associations using classical conditioning is that this ability helped some of our distant ancestors to survive and reproduce better than those who did not have that ability.

How do we identify which human traits are evolved adaptations, as opposed to learned adaptations? This is a tricky and controversial topic among evolutionary biologists and psychologists, particularly with respect to mental processes. To be considered an evolutionary adaptation, a trait must be (a) *adaptive*, meaning it contributed to survival or reproduction in the ancestral environment of a species; (b) *heritable*, meaning that it can be passed from parents to offspring via genes; and (c) *universal*, meaning it occurs (if appropriate environmental conditions are present) in all genetically normal individuals of a species. It follows that not all human abilities evolved via natural selection. Consider, for example, your ability to read. This is a highly adaptive psychological ability, yet it could not have evolved through natural selection. Reading developed relatively recently in human history—too short a time period for evolutionary change—and emerged long after the human brain had achieved its current size and form (Gould, 2000). We evolved eyes and a brain that is capable of learning to read (Dawkins, 1987), but reading itself did not evolve via natural selection.

There are a number of aspects of human behaviour that probably reflect evolutionary adaptations but do not increase people's survival and reproduction in contemporary human environments. An example is humans' preferences for sweet foods. Although there is individual and cultural variability in people's fondness for sweets, some degree of fondness for sweet tastes is universal, and there is evidence of a genetic basis for sweet preference (e.g., Looy & Weingarten, 1992). This preference for sweet tastes probably evolved to encourage our ancestors to expend energy searching for foods that tasted sweet, which in our ancestral environments would usually be fruits. Fruits are high in nutrients that our bodies cannot get from other sources, so it was advantageous for our ancestors to have a "sweet tooth" that encouraged them to search for fruits as compared to more readily available but less nutritious foods. And in a natural environment, there was little danger of people "overdosing" on too many fruits.

The situation is quite different today. Modern humans have learned to refine sugar and other highly concentrated sources of sweet tastes so that people can indulge their sweet tooth by consuming cookies, pies, candies, and thousands of other very sweet and non-nutritious concoctions. Our evolved fondness for sweetness, which was adaptive in our ancestral environments, was not designed to function in an environment where sweet tastes could be found in foods other than nutritious ones such as fruits. So our evolved adaptation of a fondness for sweet tastes, which helped us survive in natural environments, backfires in contemporary environments and contributes to poor health, obesity, dental problems, and so on.

When considering the usefulness of a human trait, we must always consider how such adaptations would have contributed to human survival and reproduction in the human **environment of evolutionary adaptedness,** or **EEA** (Bowlby, 1969; Crawford, 1998b). The EEA refers to the environments in which our ancestors lived for millions of years prior to the rise of agriculture. Human evolutionary adaptations were selected to help people survive and reproduce in the human EEAs, but not necessarily in other environments. The human EEAs that shaped most human adaptations probably included a hunting–gathering lifestyle, living within small groups of mostly related individuals, and considerable degrees of conflict between neighbouring groups. Evolutionary adaptations (especially in large, complex mammals such as humans) take very long periods of time to evolve and change, so the human brain today is partly composed of modules that evolved in and were adapted to our ancient environment of evolutionary adaptedness, rather than our modern environment of cities, cars, and computers. Incompatibilities between our evolved minds and the modern environment may contribute to the frequency of some psychological disorders, as we shall see in Chapter 14.

environment of evolutionary adaptedness (EEA)

Environment, or environments, in which a species' evolutionary adaptations were selected.

Test Yourself 3.4

Test your knowledge of the evolution of human psychological adaptations. Select your answers from the following list of terms: EEA, mutation; natural selection; heritable; trait; evolutionary adaptation; identical; recessive; universal; fraternal; adaptive. (You will find the answers in Appendix B.)

1. The differential reproduction of offspring by genetically different members of a population: _____
2. Any distinguishable aspect of a species: _____
3. Neither Eugene nor Kelly has red hair, but their daughter Colleen does. This suggests that the gene for red hair is _____.
4. An error in the process by which chromosomes are duplicated:

   _____
5. To the extent that a trait is inherited, _____ twins would be expected to be more similar to one another on that trait than _____ twins.
6. To qualify as an evolutionary adaptation, a trait must be _____, _____, and _____.
7. Some human evolutionary adaptations may create problems for us due to differences between our modern environments and our _____.

Solving the Adaptive Problems

Psychologists believe that human thoughts, feelings, and actions are products of active biological systems. The human brain, along with the rest of the nervous system and all of the other parts of our bodies, is a biological solution to problems produced by the natural environment. Out of these biological solutions arise the attributes that make up the human mind, including intellect, emotion, and artistic creativity. In this chapter we've considered four central problems of adaptation that were solved through the evolution of our biological systems.

First, how does your body communicate with the environment and internally? Networks of interconnected individual cells, called neurons, constitute the nervous system. To communicate internally, the nervous system has developed an electrochemical language. Messages travel electrically within a neuron, usually from dendrite to soma to axon to terminal button, and then chemically from one neuron to the next at a synapse. Combining electrical and chemical components creates a quick, efficient, and extremely versatile communication system. Neurotransmitters regulate the rate at which neurons fire, by producing excitatory or inhibitory messages, and the resulting global patterns of activation underlie behaviours, feelings, and thought processes.

Second, how does your brain initiate and coordinate behaviour? To accomplish the remarkable variety of functions it controls, the nervous system divides its labour. Through the use of sophisticated techniques, including brain-imaging devices, researchers have begun to map out the localized regions of brain tissue that support particular psychological and life-sustaining functions. At the base of the brain, in the hindbrain region, structures control such basic processes as respiration, heart rate, and the coordination of muscle movements. Higher up are regions that control motivational processes such as eating, drinking, and sexual behaviour. Finally, in the cerebral cortex more complex mental processes—such as thought, sensations, and language—arise. Some functions in the brain appear to be lateralized, which means that they are controlled primarily by one cerebral hemisphere or the other.

Third, how does the body regulate growth and other internal functions? To solve its widespread and long-term communication needs, the body uses the endocrine system to release chemicals called hormones into the bloodstream. These chemical messengers serve a variety of regulatory functions, influencing growth and development, hunger, thirst, and sexual behaviour, in addition to helping the body prepare for action. Hormones released early in development and on into adulthood may underlie some of the behavioural differences that are found between men and women.

Fourth, how and why did evolution select the kind of brain structures and nervous system that humans have today, and how does the body store and transmit the genetic code? Humans (and our prehuman ancestors) faced many threats to survival over the millions of years of our evolutionary history. Certain genetically coded brain structures provided solutions to the survival problems our ancestors faced, and these became part of the human makeup via natural selection. Physical and behavioural characteristics are passed on to offspring via portions of chromosomes called genes. The phenotypes an individual displays reflect interactions between his or her genotype and environment. Psychologists often try to disentangle the relative contributions of genes and the environment by conducting twin studies, comparing the behaviours and abilities of identical and fraternal twins who have been raised in similar or dissimilar environments. Discrepancies between our contemporary environments and those in which we evolved may cause problems for humans.

Chapter Summary

Most scientists believe that all behaviour arises from the activities of the brain. Every time you think, act, or feel, biological activity in your brain is playing a critical role. *Neuroscience* is the study of how the brain, mind, and behaviour are interconnected. Evolutionary processes shaped the human brain and nervous system, and the genetic code transmits information about how to construct the human body and mind to the next generation.

COMMUNICATING INTERNALLY: CONNECTING WORLD AND BRAIN

Information is received, transmitted, and integrated by *neurons*, interconnected cells that communicate electrochemically.

The Anatomy of Neurons

Learning Goal: Learn the basic structure of neurons and the three major kinds of neurons. Each neuron has *dendrites*, a *soma* or cell body, an *axon*, and a *terminal button*. *Sensory neurons* carry information from sensory receptors to the spinal cord and brain. *Interneurons* convey information between internal processing sites. *Motor neurons* carry messages from the central nervous system to muscles and glands.

Neural Transmission: The Electrochemical Message

Learning Goal: Understand how information is transmitted along a neuron and from one neuron to another. Messages travel electrically from one point to another within a neuron and chemically, through *neurotransmitters,* from the terminal button of one neuron to the dendrites of another at a synapse.

The Communication Network

Learning Goal: Grasp how neurons work together in communication networks. The pattern of activation produced by groups of neurons operating at the same time underlies both conscious experiences and complex behaviours.

INITIATING AND COORDINATING BEHAVIOUR: A DIVISION OF LABOUR

The nervous system consists of several subparts that coordinate with one another (and with other systems in the body) to give rise to thinking, feeling, and behaving.

The Central and Peripheral Nervous Systems

Learning Goal: Know the basic organization of the nervous system. The *central nervous system* consists of the brain and spinal cord, which communicate with the rest of the body through bundles of axons (nerves). The *peripheral nervous system* is subdivided into the *somatic system* (which sends information from sensory receptors to muscles) and the *autonomic system*, which controls the more automatic needs of the body such as respiration and heartbeat.

Research Techniques for Exploring Brain Function

Learning Goal: Become familiar with some of the techniques that researchers use to study the brain. Studies of brain damage have revealed much about which areas of the brain perform particular functions. Researchers have also "talked" to the brain by way of *chemical injections, electrodes,* and *transcranial magnetic stimulation* (TMS). They can also "listen" to the brain with noninvasive techniques such as *electroencephalography* (EEG and ERP) and *magnetic resonance imaging* (MRI and fMRI).

Brain Structures and Their Functions

Learning Goal: Be able to describe the major structures of the brain and the functions associated with each structure. The *hindbrain* provides basic life support through the *medulla, pons, reticular formation,* and *cerebellum.* The *midbrain* relays sensory messages. Higher mental functioning arises in the *forebrain,* using the *cerebral cortex, thalamus, hypothalamus,* and *limbic system.*

The Divided Brain

Learning Goal: Learn how the two hemispheres divide and coordinate brain functions. The two *hemispheres* (halves) of the cerebral cortex are *lateralized*: Each side is responsible for somewhat different functions, but the two normally coordinate together by communicating via the *corpus callosum.*

REGULATING GROWTH AND INTERNAL FUNCTIONS: EXTENDED COMMUNICATION

Long-term communication requirements are provided by the endocrine system, which uses the bloodstream as its communication corridor.

The Endocrine System

Learning Goal: Learn how the endocrine system controls long-term and widespread communication needs. *Endocrine glands* release *hormones* into the blood that interact with the nervous system to regulate basic activities such as the fight-or-flight response.

Gender, Hormones, and Psychology

Learning Goal: Be able to discuss the roles that hormones play in establishing sexual identity and how they may contribute to gender differences on psychological measures. Hormones released by the *pituitary gland* determine sexual identity before birth and direct sexual maturing at puberty. Endocrine activities may contribute to some differences in the way males and females think and behave.

ADAPTING AND TRANSMITTING THE GENETIC CODE: EVOLVED PSYCHOLOGICAL TRAITS

Humans evolved over millions of years, and our ancestral environments shaped our bodies and brains.

Natural Selection

Learning Goal: Be able to explain what it means to say that a trait evolved through the process of natural selection. If a physical or behavioural *trait* enhances an individual's chances of producing viable offspring, and if that trait is heritable, then by *natural selection* that trait may gradually become characteristic of the species.

Genetic Principles

Learning Goal: Learn the basics of genetic transmission. Most cells of the human body contain 23 pairs of *chromosomes*. *Genes* are segments of chromosomes that contain chemical instructions that influence the development of hereditary traits. Genes can be *dominant* or *recessive*.

Genes and Behaviour

Learning Goal: Become familiar with how psychologists study the role of genetics in psychological traits. *Family studies* identify similarities and differences that may reveal the influence of heredity. In *twin studies*, researchers compare the traits of *identical twins*, who have the same genes, and *fraternal twins*, who have only about half of their genes in common. Differences between identical twins can be attributed to the environment; similarities between identical twins are partly genetic, but may also partly reflect similarities in twins' environments.

Evolutionary Adaptations and Human Behaviour

Learning Goal: Understand how evolutionary mechanisms may have influenced human thinking, feelings, and behaviours, and appreciate the concept of the "environment of evolutionary adaptedness." Gene-based physical and behavioural traits that increase the chances of producing viable offspring can, via natural selection, evolve as adaptations. Psychological traits are tendencies, with considerable flexibility and variability across individuals in how and the extent to which those tendencies are realized. Our bodies (including brains) evolved over millions of years, shaped by natural selection to the demands of a natural environment vastly different from that of most modern humans. Discrepancies between the environments in which we evolved and those in which we live may be a source of difficulty for humans.

Terms to Remember

Recommended Readings

Ingram, J. (1994). *The burning house: Unlocking the mysteries of the human brain.* Toronto: Penguin. Winner of the Canadian Science Writers' book award, this is an easy-to-read tour of contemporary brain research with an emphasis on Canadian research centres at the University of Ottawa, McGill University, and the University of Toronto.

Pinel, J. P. J., & Edwards, M. E. (1997). *A colorful introduction to the anatomy of the human brain: A brain and psychology coloring book.* Needham Heights, MA: Allyn & Bacon. University of British Columbia biopsychology researcher John Pinel and collaborator Maggie Edwards constructed this intriguing interactive method of learning about the brain and its functions.

Sacks, O. (1985). *The man who mistook his wife for a hat.* New York: Summit Books. A witty example of the case study approach applied to the neurosciences. Sacks presents examples and anecdotes from patients suffering from various

forms of brain damage. All of Sacks's books are interesting, but this one is a classic.

Gazzaniga, M. S. (1992). *Nature's mind: The biological roots of thinking, emotions, sexuality, and intelligence.* New York: Basic Books. This book is written by a leading neuroscientist, Michael Gazzaniga, who is one of the pioneers in the study of split-brain patients. He provides a fascinating and readable account of the role that biological processes play in mind and behaviour.

Buss, D. M. (1999). *Evolutionary psychology: The new science of the human mind.* Needham Heights, MA: Allyn & Bacon. Clearly and comprehensively reviews the origins and empirical findings regarding human evolved psychological adaptations.

Ridley, M. (2000). *Genome: The autobiography of a species in 23 chapters.* New York: HarperCollins. Ridley picks one newly discovered gene from each of the 23 pairs of chromosomes that humans have and uses these genes as a device to explore the history and structure of the human genome.

Kolb, B., & Whishaw, I. Q. (2001). *An introduction to brain and behavior.* New York: Worth. Written by two world-renowned neuroscientists at the University of Lethbridge, this introductory-level text explores the biological basis of behaviour, communicating the excitement of the tremendous advances in the field in recent years. Drawing on their teaching and research experiences, the authors organize this text around the key questions that intrigue brain researchers and students (e.g., "Why do we have a brain?" "How is the brain organized?"). A strong focus on clinical issues and innovative art is incorporated.

For additional readings, explore InfoTrac® College Edition, your online library. Go to:

www.adaptivemind2e.nelson.com

Hint: enter the search terms: neural transmission; sympathetic nervous system; cerebral cortex; brain imaging; behavioural genetics.

What's on the Web?

Please note that Web addresses are subject to change. Check out the accompanying Web site for updates: www.adaptivemind2e.nelson.com. This site presents practice quiz questions, hypercontent, information on degrees and careers in psychology, study tips, and more.

Rotman Research Institute

www.rotman-baycrest.on.ca

Canada's renowned centre for the study of basic brain processes as well as associated functions of learning and memory. The Web site includes lists of publications and research projects and links to the home pages of the Rotman research scientists. If you have a QuickTime-equipped browser, you can even listen to audio clips of some of Canada's most distinguished neuroscientists explaining their research findings.

Discovery Channel Neuroscience Conference Coverage

www.beemnet.com/dana/discovery.html

A summary of lectures given at a conference on the function of the frontal lobes. Includes graphics and tests such as the Stroop test.

Neurosciences on the Internet

www.neuroguide.com

If you want to find information related to the brain or neurosciences, this is the place to do it! A very impressive site that serves as a sort of "clearinghouse" for information on the brain and nervous system. It provides information on neurosurgery and brain disorders as well as psychiatry and psychology.

Neuroscience for Kids

faculty.washington.edu/chudler/neurok.html

Yes, the title says "for kids," but this site isn't just for children. It provides information on the brain and nervous system

presented in a straightforward, engaging, and interesting fashion. Think of it as "Sesame Street Meets Chapter 3." Included are exercises to let you explore the nervous system, experiments, and activities as well as links to other neuroscience resources. The site is part of a larger neuroscience site based at the University of Washington.

Human Behavior and Evolution Society

www.hbes.com

Includes essays introducing evolutionary psychological ideas, a list of recent books, publications, and conferences in this area, and RealAudio interviews with many of the leading researchers examining the evolved mechanisms underlying human social and cognitive behaviour.

Behavior Genetics Association

www.bga.org

News and messages relating to the genetics of human behaviour and behaviour by other species. Especially useful is the collection of links to human genetic research from around the world.

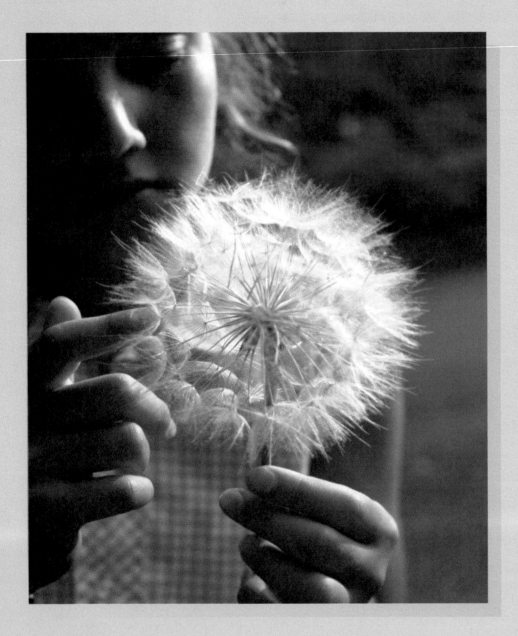

Whilst part of what we perceive comes through our senses from the object before us, another part (and it may be the larger part) always comes out of our own mind.
William James

Chapter 4   Sensation and Perception

At the end of this sentence, stop reading for a moment and pay attention to what you can see and hear around you, the odours you smell, the tastes in your mouth, and what you can feel on your skin and inside your body. Really, take a moment and check it out. Maybe you are reading this in a frantically busy environment such as a cafeteria at noon, with people moving all around you, the babble of many voices, and a complex mixture of powerful odours. Or maybe you are in the library, with its more muted sounds, the subtle dusty-gluey smell of books, and the slight discomfort of a too-hard chair. Or perhaps you are in your own room, flopped on your bed on top of a scratchy blanket, with some music on the stereo. Wherever you are at the moment, you are being bombarded with stimulation from your environment. Even if you were reading this in the seclusion of an abandoned monastery, your sensory systems would be receiving many sorts of stimulation at every moment.

If asked to describe the input your sensory system is currently receiving, you would probably mention meaningful objects. You might say, "I smell the fish that someone is warming in the microwave," or "I see lots of shelves full of books," or "I hear people talking and laughing on the television," or "I feel the band of my baseball cap on my forehead." These might be perfectly good descriptions of your perceptions, but notice that they are not really descriptions of the sensory stimulation itself. In the case of vision, for example, the sensory input is patterns of coloured light and dark: Light energy from some source—such as the sun or a light bulb—bounces in all directions off objects in the environment, and some of that reflected light enters your eyes and stimulates the visual system. Similarly, when you hear a voice or other sound, the sensory input to the auditory system consists of patterns of changes in air pressure.

Each sensory system transduces, or translates, the pattern of physical input it receives into electrochemical neuronal activities that code the characteristics of the sensory stimulation. This transduction, and other brain processes involved in interpreting its products, are the central topics of this chapter. We turn now to the important psychological processes of sensation and perception. It is through sensation and perception that we create our immediate experience of the world around us.

To help understand the difference between the psychological terms *sensation* and *perception*, consider the image shown in Figure 4.1. It depicts a three-dimensional geometric figure—a cube—but it exists at another, more objective level of description as well. At that more objective level of description, the figure consists of two-dimensional lines, angles, patterns of light and dark, colours, and so on. These elementary features—the building blocks of the meaningful image—are processed by the visual system, through reasonably well-understood physiological systems, and the products of that processing are visual **sensations**. Psychologists have historically thought of sensations—such as a pattern of light and dark, a bitter taste, a change in temperature—as the fundamental, elementary components of experience. **Perception** is the collection of processes used to arrive at a meaningful interpretation of sensations. Through perception, the simple components are organized and interpreted by higher-order brain activities (which are less well understood) into a recognizable, meaningful form. In this case, you perceive a three-dimensional *cube*.

Now, let's think more closely about what "interpretation" means in this context. Look closely at the cube in Figure 4.1. Stare at it for a while. The lines, the angles, and the colours remain fixed, but the cube appears to shift its orientation from moment to moment. For a time, the shaded surface of the figure is the front of the cube; then, in

sensations
The elementary components, or building blocks, of perception, such as a pattern of light and dark, a bitter taste, or a change in temperature.

perception
The processes used to arrive at a meaningful interpretation of sensations; through perception, the simple component sensations are organized and interpreted into meaningful, recognizable forms.

FIGURE 4.1
The Necker Cube

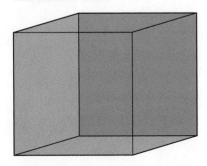

Previewing the Adaptive Problems

To appreciate how the brain creates its internal representation of the physical world, we'll discuss each of the sensory systems from the perspective of three important adaptive problems. Each is a fundamental problem that each of our sensory systems needs to solve, regardless of whether the system is trying to interpret light, sound, or some other kind of physical energy (see Figure 4.2).

First, how does the external input from the environment get translated into the language of the nervous system?
As you learned in Chapter 3, communication in the nervous system is fundamentally an electrochemical process. Input from the outside world arrives in a variety of forms, but none of it arrives in the electrochemical "language" of the nervous system. For example, you see by means of reflected light, which arrives in the form of electromagnetic energy; you hear by interpreting sound waves, which are rhythmic changes in air pressure. In a sense, it's like trying to listen to someone who speaks a language other than your own. The brain needs an interpreter, a process through which the incoming input is changed into an understandable form. The translation process is called **transduction,** and it's accomplished in a different way for each of the sensory systems.

Second, how are the elementary components—the sensations—extracted from the input? Once the environmental input has been successfully translated—represented now in the form of neural impulses—the important input components need to be extracted or pulled out of the complex sensory pattern. For example, a given region of the scene depicted in Figure 4.2 contains a great deal of overlapping information, which must be decomposed into information about simple shapes and colours (e.g., a curved green line, a straight vertical grey line). To accomplish this feat, the newly formed neural code is transferred from the transduction sites to processing stations deep within the brain. For each sensory system, there is a different pathway from the sensory receptors through particular brain regions. Along each pathway there are specialized regions of the brain that transform the initial neural coding of the input into elementary component sensations.

Third, how does the brain build and maintain a meaningful interpretation of these component sensations once they've been extracted? How, for example, does information about "green" and "curved" give rise to perception of a leaf? You see objects, not patterns of coloured light and dark; you hear melodies or speech, not sequences of irregularly timed sounds. The biological and psychological mechanisms of perception—the processes that produce the interpretation that we experience as reality—are still under investigation, but we know a good deal about the principles of organization by which the brain interprets sensory input.

transduction
The process by which external inputs are translated into the internal language of the brain.

FIGURE 4.2
Adaptive Problems of Sensation and Perception
To create its internal representation of the physical world, the brain needs to solve three fundamental adaptive problems for each of its sensory systems: (1) translating the input from the environment into the language of the nervous system; (2) extracting the elementary components of the input, such as sounds of particular pitches and particular patterns of coloured light and dark; and (3) creating a meaningful interpretation of those component sensations as objects of perception.

the next instant, it forms the back of the cube. First you see the cube from one perspective, and then from another. Why is this happening? Certainly the figure on the page remains fixed; the reflected light is not changing systematically with time. The answer lies in the *interpretation* of the sensory image. When you look at the Necker cube, the sensory input—the pattern of lines and colours that is stimulating your visual receptors—is ambiguous. Because the sensory input supports two quite different interpretations equally well, the brain engages in a perceptual dance, shifting from one interpretation to the other (Gaetz et al., 1998). The extreme ambiguity of the Necker cube is not typical of real-world objects; usually, the pattern of light bouncing off an object and its surrounding environmental context provides the visual system with many cues as to the appropriate interpretation or perception of that object (Gibson, 1966). Nonetheless, the brain does a great deal of active work to interpret those cues to create our perceptions of the world around us.

VISION: CREATING A WORLD OF MEANINGFUL OBJECTS

Learning Goals

1. Learn how light gets translated into the electrochemical language of the brain.
2. Grasp how the essential features of the visual input, such as colour, are extracted by the brain.
3. Understand how a stable, meaningful interpretation of visual information is created and why the interpretation process sometimes leads to visual illusions.

OUR DISCUSSION OF SENSATION and perception begins with vision, the sense of sight. To understand vision, it's first necessary to know how the physical input—light—is translated into the language of the brain. Next, we'll trace some of the pathways in the brain that are used to extract the basic components of the visual input. Finally, we'll tackle the topic of visual perception: How does the brain create a stable, meaningful interpretation of the light information it receives?

Translating the Input: Visual Transduction

3a, 3b
Psyk.trek

The physical input delivered to visual receptors, **light,** is a form of electromagnetic energy. Visible light is only a very small portion of an electromagnetic spectrum that includes other energy forms, such as X-rays, ultraviolet rays, and even radio and television waves (see Figure 4.3).

Light can be classified by two main physical properties. The first is wavelength, which corresponds to the physical distance from one energy cycle to the next. Changes in the wavelength of light are generally experienced, psychologically, as changes in colour, or **hue.** If you look at Figure 4.3, you'll discover that humans see wavelengths ranging from only about 400 to 700 nanometres (nm, billionths of a metre). Psychologically, these wavelengths are experienced as colours ranging roughly from violet to red. Of course, light of other wavelengths also enters your eyes, but you cannot sense those wavelengths. The second physical property is intensity, which corresponds to the amount of light falling on an object. Changes in intensity are generally experienced as increases or decreases in **brightness.**

Light originates from a source, such as the sun or a light bulb, and usually enters the eye after bouncing off objects in its path. Most light is a mixture of many different wavelengths; after hitting an object, some of these wavelengths are absorbed by the object—which ones depends on the physical properties of the object—and the remaining wavelengths reflect outward. When you look at an object, some of the light bouncing off it enters your eyes through your pupils. It is here, in the eyes, that the important translation process occurs.

light

The small portion of the electromagnetic spectrum that is processed by the visual system. Light is typically classified in terms of *wavelength* (the physical distance from one energy cycle to the next) and *intensity* (the amount of light falling on an object).

hue

The dimension of light that produces colour; hue is typically determined by the wavelength of light reflecting from an object.

brightness

The aspect of the visual experience that changes with light intensity; in general, as the intensity of light increases, so does its perceived brightness.

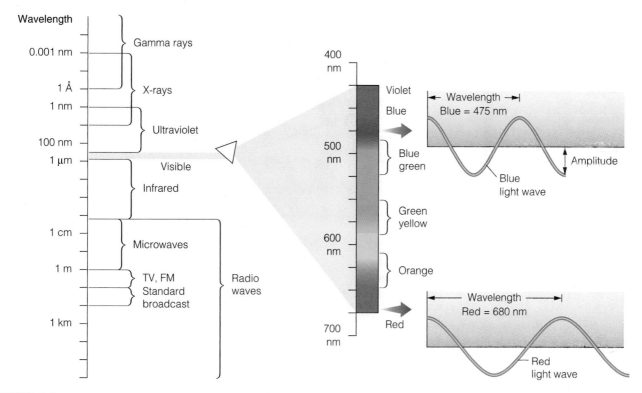

FIGURE 4.3

Light and the Electromagnetic Spectrum

Visible light is only a small portion of the electromagnetic spectrum, which includes other forms of energy such as X-rays, radio and TV waves, and light waves (such as infrared) that are not sensed by the human eye. Changes in the wavelength of light from about 400 to 700 nm are experienced as changes in colour; short wavelengths are seen as violets and blues; medium wavelengths as yellows and greens; and long wavelengths as reds.

Entering the Eye The first step in the translation process is to bring the incoming light energy to the light-sensitive receptor cells at the back of each eye. When light bounces off an object, the reflected wavelengths are scattered about. They then need to be brought back together—focused—for a clear image to be processed. In the human eye, the focusing process is accomplished by the **cornea,** the protective outer layer of the eye, and by the **lens,** a clear, flexible piece of tissue that sits behind the pupil.

As shown in Figure 4.4, light first passes through the cornea and the pupil before travelling through the lens. The **pupil,** which looks like a black spot, is actually a hole in a ring of coloured tissue called the **iris.** The iris gives the eye its distinctive colour (a person with brown eyes has brown irises), but the colour of the iris plays no real role in vision. Relaxing or tightening muscles around the iris changes the size of the pupil, thereby regulating the amount of light that enters the eye. In dim light the pupil gets larger, which allows more light to get in; in bright light the pupil gets smaller, allowing less light to enter. As light passes through the pupil, it is also restricted to the central portions of the lens, where there are fewer optical distortions (Thibos et al., 1990).

The lens focuses the light on the sensory receptors at the back of the eye, much like the lens in a camera focuses light on film. In a camera, focusing typically involves changing the distance between the lens and the film; however, in the human eye, focusing is accomplished by changing the shape of the lens itself. The adjustment of the shape of the lens, known as **accommodation,** depends on the distance between the lens and the object being viewed. When an object is far away, the lens is relatively long and thin; as the object moves closer, muscles attached to the lens contract and the lens becomes thicker and rounder. As people age, the lens loses some of this flexibility, making the accommodation process less efficient (Fukuda et al., 1990). This is one of

cornea
The transparent and protective outer covering of the eye.

lens
The flexible, transparent disk of tissue that helps focus light toward the back of the eye.

pupil
The hole in the centre of the iris through which light enters the eye; the size of the pupil changes with light intensity.

iris
The ring of coloured tissue surrounding the pupil. If you have brown eyes, your irises are brown.

accommodation
In vision, the process by which the lens changes shape temporarily to help focus light on the retina.

 Critical Thinking

It's been reported that pupil size increases with interest or level of emotional involvement. What do you think the adaptive value of this phenomenon might be?

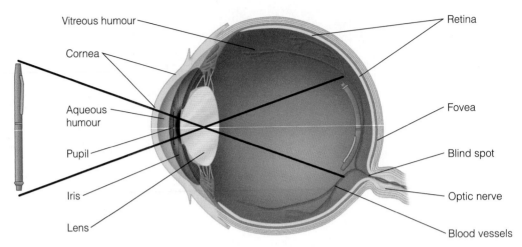

FIGURE 4.4
The Human Eye
Light enters the eye through the cornea, pupil, and lens. As the lens changes shape in relation to the distance of the object, the reflected light is focused on the retina at the back of the eye, where the visual input is transduced into electrochemical neural activity.

retina
The thin layer of tissue that covers the back of the inside of the eye and contains the light-sensitive receptor cells for vision.

rods
Receptor cells in the retina, located mainly on the periphery of the retina, that transduce light energy into neural inputs; these visual receptors are highly sensitive and are active in dim light.

cones
Receptor cells in the central portion of the retina that transduce light energy into neural activity; they operate best when light levels are fairly high, and they are primarily responsible for the ability to sense fine detail and colour.

fovea
The "central pit" area in the centre portion of the retina where most of the cone receptors are located.

the reasons people typically require reading glasses or bifocals when they reach middle age. The corrective lenses in the glasses partially substitute for the accommodation process, which the eyes can no longer successfully perform on their own.

Light completes its journey when it reaches a thin layer of tissue, called the **retina,** that covers the back of the inside of the eye. Here the electromagnetic energy of light is translated into the electrochemical language of the brain. Embedded in the retina of each eye are about 126 million light-sensitive receptor cells that transduce, or change, the light energy into the electrochemical impulses of neural processing. The translation process is chemically based. Each of the receptor cells contains a substance, called a *photopigment,* that reacts to light. The light causes a chemical reaction in the cell that ultimately leads to a neural impulse, completing the transduction process. Thus, what begins as a pattern of electromagnetic information becomes a pattern of electrochemical signals, the language of the brain.

You may have noticed in Figure 4.4 that the image on the retina is upside down. The inverted image is created by the optical properties of the lens: The upper part of whatever we look at projects light to the lower part of the retina and vice versa. This may seem strange, given that we don't see an upside-down world. It's important to remember that we don't see with our eyes. Our perceptual world is built in our brains. The main function of the eyes is simply to solve the problem of transduction and pass the information on to the brain. The brain later corrects the inversion problem and we see a sensible, right-side-up world.

Rods and Cones   There are two types of receptor cells in the retina: **rods** and **cones.** Of the roughly 126 million receptor cells within each eye, about 120 million are rods and 6 million are cones. Each receptor type is named for its appearance: Rods are generally long and thin, whereas cones are short, thick, and tapered to a point. Rods are the more sensitive visual receptors; they can generate signals when very small amounts of light strike their surface. This makes rods useful at night and in any situation in which the overall level of illumination is low. Indeed, because of the sensitivity of the rods people can detect a single photon of light. Rods tend to be concentrated along the periphery, or sides, of the retina. This is one reason that dim images can sometimes be seen better out of the "corners" of your eyes.

Cones tend to be concentrated mostly in the very centre of the retina, bunched in a small central pit called the **fovea** (which means "central pit"). Unlike rods, cones need relatively high levels of light to operate efficiently, as further discussed below. Cones perform a number of critical visual functions. For example, cones are used for processing fine detail, an ability called **visual acuity.** Cones also play an extremely important role in the early processing of colour, as we'll discuss later.

Dark Adaptation When you move from a brightly lit environment to a dark one, at first you can see very little, but after a while your vision improves. It takes about 25 minutes for your eyes to adjust fully to very dim light, a process known as **dark adaptation.** As mentioned earlier, visual transduction occurs when light reacts chemically with photopigments in the receptor cells. Photopigments break down, or become "bleached," in the process of reacting to light, which makes them less able to generate a neural impulse. The receptor cells constantly regenerate photopigments, but in bright light the regeneration process cannot keep up with the rate at which photopigments are bleached. As long as there is plenty of light around, your vision is fine because your eyes never completely run out of photopigment, but when the amount of light is suddenly reduced, your receptor cells don't have enough viable photopigments to detect the low levels of illumination. When there is little light, the rate at which photopigments are bleached is less than the rate at which the cells regenerate photopigments, so as time goes by the receptor cells become more and more sensitive and you can see more and more. Your eyes have adapted to the low light level.

The timing of the adaptation process is shown in Figure 4.5. This "dark adaptation curve" depicts the smallest amount of light that people can reliably see, plotted as a function of time spent in the dark. Over time, smaller and smaller amounts of light can be detected. Sensitivity increases because the visual receptor cells are recovering from earlier interactions with bright light, which broke down many of the visual pigments, by regenerating photopigments and hence becoming more sensitive.

Notice that there is a discontinuity at about the 8-minute mark in the dark adaptation curve. This is because the rods and the cones adapt to the dark at different rates. Early in the dark adaptation function, the cones rapidly increase in sensitivity, but they achieve their maximum responsiveness rather quickly. After about 7 or 8 minutes in the dark, the rods, which can detect quite low levels of illumination, begin to take over, gradually becoming more and more sensitive as they maximize the amount of viable photopigments they contain. Things look grey and lack fine detail in a very dim environment—only the rods are sufficiently sensitive to respond to very low levels of illumination, and rods do not detect colours, and the large receptive fields in the peripheral parts of the retina (where most of the rods are located) are not sensitive to fine details.

Early Processing in the Retina Once an electrochemical signal is generated by a rod or a cone, it's passed along to other cells in the retina, particularly *bipolar cells* and

Each human retina contains two types of photoreceptor cells: rods and cones. As shown in this colour-enhanced photo, the rods are rod-shaped in appearance and the cones are cone-shaped.

visual acuity
The ability to see fine detail.

dark adaptation
The process through which the eyes adjust to dim light.

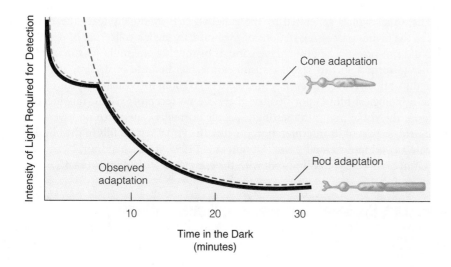

FIGURE 4.5
The Dark Adaptation Curve
The photoreceptors in your eyes gradually adjust to the dark and become more sensitive; that is, you are able to detect light at increasingly low levels of intensity. The rods and cones adapt at different rates and reach different final levels of sensitivity. The dark adaptation curve represents the combined adaptation of the two receptor types. Notice that after about 8 minutes there is a point of discontinuity; this is where further increases in sensitivity are due to the enhanced functioning of the rods.

FIGURE 4.6
Rods, Cones, and Receptive Fields
Rods and cones send signals to other cells in the retina, such as bipolar cells and ganglion cells. Each ganglion cell has a receptive field. Ganglion cells in the fovea, which receive input from cones, tend to have smaller receptive fields than ganglion cells in the periphery, which receive input from rods. The fovea provides better detail, and the periphery of the retina is more sensitive to low levels of light.

receptive field

In vision, the portion of the retina that, when stimulated, causes the activity of a higher-level neuron (such as a ganglion cell or an even higher-level neuron in the visual cortex) to change.

blind spot

The point where the optic nerve leaves the back of the eye; there are no rods or cones in the blind spot.

ganglion cells, where further processing occurs (see Figure 4.6). Even at this early stage in visual processing, cells in the retina are beginning to interpret patterns in the incoming visual input. For example, the ganglion cells have what are called **receptive fields,** which means they receive input from a group of receptor cells and respond only to particular patterns of light shining on that group of receptors (Shapley, 1990). For example, the ganglion on the left side of Figure 4.6 might increase its firing rate only when one of the bipolar cells with which it synapses is firing and the other is not firing.

This concept of receptive fields is very important. The fact that a neuron, such as a ganglion cell, receives input from several receptor cells, and responds only to a particular pattern across those receptor cells, means that it can represent information about how light is spread out across the retina. One byproduct is that we can easily detect edges in visual scenes: Ganglion cells help the visual system tell where light stops and starts. As you'll discover shortly, the complexity of receptive fields increases at later stages of the visual processing pathway in the brain.

The visual signals generated by the ganglion cells eventually leave the retina, en route to the higher processing stations of the brain, through a collection of nerve fibres called the *optic nerve.* The optic nerve consists of roughly one million axons that wrap together to form a sort of visual transmission cable. Because of its size, at the point where the optic nerve leaves each retina there is no room for visual receptor cells. This creates a biological **blind spot** because there are no receptor cells in this location to transduce the visual input. Interestingly, people normally experience no holes in their visual field; as part of its interpretation process, the visual system fills in the blind spots to create a continuous visual scene (Durgin et al., 1995; Ramachandran, 1992; Sekuler, 1994). You can locate your blind spot with the exercise described in Figure 4.7.

Extracting the Input Components: Visual Pathways

After leaving the retina, the neural activity coding the input to each eye flows along each optic nerve until it reaches the *optic chiasm* (from the Greek word meaning

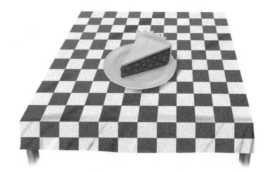

FIGURE 4.7
The Blind Spot

To experience your blind spot, hold this book a few centimetres from your face; close your left eye and focus with your right eye on the boy's face. Then slowly move the book away until the pie mysteriously disappears. Notice that your brain fills in the spot—complete with the checkerboard pattern!

Concept Summary

COMPARING RODS AND CONES

Characteristic	Rods	Cones
Number	Approximately 120 million per retina	Approximately 6 million per retina
Shape	Generally long and thin	Short, thick, tapered to a point
Location	Concentrated in the periphery of the retina	Concentrated in the centre of the retina, the *fovea*
Sensitivity		
—Light	Sensitive at low levels of illumination	Not very sensitive at low levels of illumination
—Detail	Not sensitive to visual detail	High level of sensitivity to detail; high *visual acuity*
—Colour	Not sensitive to differences in wavelength	Three types, each maximally sensitive to a different wavelength

"cross"), where the information splits into different tracts leading to the separate hemispheres of the brain (see Figure 4.8). Information that has been detected on the right half of each retina (from the left visual field) is sent to the right hemisphere, and information falling on the left half of each retina (from the right visual field) projects to the left hemisphere. The majority of the visual signals then move directly toward a major relay station in the thalamus called the *lateral geniculate nucleus;* other signals, perhaps 10% of the total, detour into a midbrain structure called the *superior colliculus.*

Significant processing and interpretation of the visual input occur along these pathways. Neuroscientists believe that there are two primary visual pathways from the retina through the lateral geniculate nucleus. One pathway, called the P-channel, is specialized to process colour, texture, and possibly depth; the other, called the M-channel, seems to process movement (Livingstone & Hubel, 1988; Schiller et al., 1990; Shapley, 1990). At the same time, processing in the superior colliculus, a somewhat more primitive structure, controls our ability to localize objects in space by moving the head and eyes (Sparks, 1988). Many of these activities are carried out simultaneously, through what is called **parallel processing.** Many different brain regions work together, in parallel, to pull the essential features out of visual input.

parallel processing
Processing that occurs in many different brain regions at the same time, in parallel.

Feature Detectors From the lateral geniculate nucleus, the neural coding of the visual input moves toward the back of the brain, primarily to portions of the occipital lobe. Here, in the primary visual cortex, further elements of the transduced visual input are picked out and identified. For example, Hubel and Wiesel (1962, 1979) discovered **feature detectors** in the visual cortex of cats and monkeys. Feature detectors are cells that respond best to very specific visual events, such as a pattern of light and dark of a particular shape. One type of feature detector, which Hubel and Wiesel called a *simple cell,* responds actively only when a small bar of light is shone onto a particular

feature detectors
Cells in the visual cortex that respond to very specific visual events, such as bars of light at particular orientations.

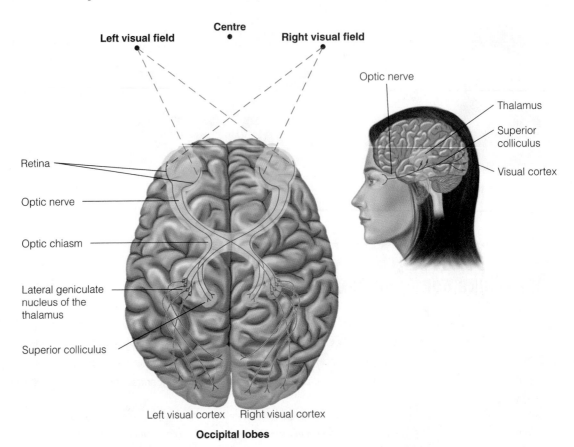

Centre

Left visual field   **Right visual field**

Optic nerve

Thalamus

Superior colliculus

Visual cortex

Retina

Optic nerve

Optic chiasm

Lateral geniculate nucleus of the thalamus

Superior colliculus

Left visual cortex   Right visual cortex

Occipital lobes

FIGURE 4.8
The Visual Pathways

Input from the left visual field falls on the inside half of the left retina and on the outside half of the right retina and projects to the right hemisphere of the brain; input from the right visual field projects to the left hemisphere. Visual processing occurs at several places along the pathway, ending in the visual cortex, where highly specialized processing takes place.

region of the retina. Cells of this type are orientation specific, which means that the visual bar needs to be presented at a particular angle for the cell to respond.

The properties of these cells were discovered by measuring neural impulses in individual cells, using implanted recording electrodes. An example of this type of experiment, and the equipment used, is shown in Figure 4.9. Remember: There are no pain receptors in the brain, which makes it possible for researchers to explore the reactions of brain cells without causing an animal severe discomfort. The recorded cells were found to increase, decrease, or show no changes in their firing rates in response to specific visual stimuli shown to the eye. In Figure 4.9, experimenters are recording the reaction to the presentation of a small bar of light presented at a particular angle. Again, Hubel and Wiesel found that certain feature detectors in the monkey's brain would react to this stimulus, and not to others, and only when the bar was shown at this particular angle.

Higher-Level Detection Obviously, the brain is sensitive to more complex visual inputs than orientation-specific bars. Hubel and Wiesel also found cells that responded selectively to more complex patterns, such as corners, edges, bars that moved through the visual field, and bars of a certain length. Other researchers have found cells—once again in monkey brains—that respond most actively to realistic monkey faces; if the face was distorted or cartoonish, the cells did not respond as actively (Perrett & Mistlin, 1987). There's even evidence suggesting that some cells are "tuned" to respond selectively to certain facial expressions (Hasselmo et al., 1989). It is also clear that visual

Critical Thinking

Can you think of any reason why it might be adaptive for the brain to first break the visual pattern down into basic features—such as a pattern of light and dark—before recombining those features into a unified whole?

Stimulus

No light | Vertical line | Horizontal line | Diagonal line

Recording

Baseline firing rate | Rapid firing rate | Low firing rate | Moderate firing rate

object-identification performance depends in part on experience: People with extensive expertise in a given domain (e.g., bird watchers) develop qualitatively different skills at identifying objects in that domain (Tanaka, 2001).

One way that researchers have collected evidence of how the brain parses the visual input is by studying brain-damaged patients. When certain parts of the human brain are damaged by stroke or injury, the result is often very selective, and sometimes bizarre, visual problems. For example, one kind of damage in the brain can produce a condition called *prosopagnosia,* in which a person loses the ability to recognize faces (Farah, 1994). An afflicted person can fail to recognize acquaintances, family members, or even his or her own reflection in a mirror, but his or her ability to identify other sorts of objects is fine. Patients with a related disorder, *visual agnosia,* have great difficulty recognizing everyday objects such as fruits and vegetables (see Figure 4.10). In some such cases the disorder is specific to particular categories; for example, the person might be unable to recognize fruits and vegetables but have little difficulty recognizing tools (Arguin et al., 1996). Some patients cannot identify the names of colours, even

FIGURE 4.9

Feature Detectors in the Visual Cortex

Hubel and Wiesel discovered feature detectors in the brains of animals. Feature detectors are cells that increase their firing rates in response to particular patterns. Here a cell in a monkey's brain fires a lot when the monkey looks at a vertical line, very little when it looks at a horizontal line, and an intermediate amount in response to a diagonal line.

FIGURE 4.10

Drawings by a Patient with Visual Agnosia

The right-hand side of each column shows the performance of a brain-damaged patient who was asked to copy the particular letter, number, or shape. The patient had normal visual acuity and motor coordination, but great difficulty perceiving even simple shapes.

though their colour perceptions seem normal (e.g., Woodward et al., 1999). In another condition, called *akinetopsia*, patients possess normal vision only for objects at rest; if an object is placed in motion, it seems to vanish, only to reappear if it becomes stationary once more. Conversely, patients with a lesion in another cortical location show the most sensitivity to objects that move rather than stay stationary (Zeki, 1992).

Additional evidence for specialization in the human brain has come from studies using PET (positron emission tomography) brain-scanning procedures. In this procedure, the subject ingests a harmless radioactive substance that is then absorbed into the brain cells; the more active a brain cell is, the more of the substance it will absorb. A visual stimulus is presented, and the researcher measures which areas of the brain increase their activity. Using this technique, researchers have discovered that certain areas of the brain respond selectively to patterns of dots that move across the visual field (Dupont et al., 1994). Other areas respond selectively to particular tasks, such as matching faces or finding dots in an array (McIntosh et al., 1994). Still other areas of the brain may be selectively involved in the processing of mental images (Kosslyn et al., 1993). Behrmann, Winocur, and Moscovitch (1992), of Toronto's Rotman Research Institute, described a brain-damaged patient who had severe visual agnosia yet had preserved visual imagery (see Servos & Goodale, 1995, for a second such case). Mel Goodale and his colleagues at the University of Western Ontario have demonstrated that brain-damaged patients who are grossly impaired in their ability to identify objects nonetheless reach for, grasp, and manipulate them in object-appropriate ways, suggesting that different visual systems underlie describing versus acting upon visual stimuli (Goodale & Humphrey, 2000).

Results like these suggest that the human brain, like the monkey brain, divides its labour. Certain regions of the cortex are specifically designed to process particular parts of the transduced visual input. In other words, there is specificity in the organization and function of the brain. The exact role that each of these parts plays in vision remains to be worked out, and it is likely that particular cells or regions of the brain perform more than one function (Schiller, 1996), but the mysteries of how the brain solves the basic problems of vision are beginning to unravel.

Colour Vision: Trichromatic Theory   One of the most significant things the brain pulls out of the visual input is colour. It turns out that colour information is processed along the entire visual pathway: retina → lateral geniculate nucleus → visual cortex. In the retina, as you'll see shortly, early colour information is extracted by comparing the relative activations of different types of cone receptors; higher up in the brain, neuronal representations of visual input encounter cells that are "tuned" to respond only to particular colours.

Many areas in the human brain appear to respond selectively to visual motion. The highlighted regions, derived from PET scanning, show areas of the human brain that react more to a moving visual stimulus than to a stationary one.

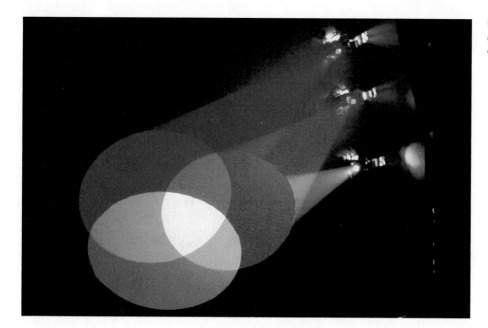

Mixing lights with different wavelengths can create a variety of perceived colours—even white.

Earlier you learned that colour is determined primarily by the wavelength of light reflected back into the eye. In general, short wavelengths (around 450 nm) produce blues, medium wavelengths (around 530 nm) produce greens, and long wavelengths (around 670 nm) produce reds. White light, which most people would classify as colourless, is actually a combination of all the wavelengths of the visible spectrum. The reason your neighbour's shirt looks red is because its fabric absorbs all but the long wavelengths of light; the long wavelengths are reflected back into the environment and you see the shirt as red. But in a sense the object itself, the shirt, has no colour; you perceive it as red only because it selectively "rejects," by reflecting outward, red light waves. In the dark, all objects are black.

When reflected wavelengths reach the retina, they stimulate the photoreceptor cells. Stimulation of the cones plays a key role in colour perception. Physiological analysis of the human eye has revealed three types of cone receptors: One type generates neural impulses primarily to *short* wavelengths (420 nm); another type responds most energetically to *medium* wavelengths (530 nm); and a final type responds most to *long* wavelengths (560 nm) of light. The sensitivity of a particular cone type actually spreads across a relatively broad range of individual wavelengths and is determined by the photopigment that the receptor contains (Bowmaker & Dartnall, 1980; Schnapf & Baylor, 1987). Figure 4.11 shows the sensitivities for each of the types of cones, as well as for the rods.

The **trichromatic theory** of colour vision proposes that colour information is extracted through the activations of the three types of cones (*trichromatic* means "three-colour"). An early version of the trichromatic theory was proposed in the 19th century by Thomas Young and Hermann von Helmholtz, long before modern techniques had verified the existence of the different cone types.

As the basis for their theory, Young and Helmholtz used the fact that most colours can be made by mixing three basic, or *primary*, colours. They speculated that the brain must determine the colour of an object by comparing the relative activation levels of three primary receptors. When just one receptor type is strongly activated, you see one of the primary colours. For example, when a short wavelength cone is strongly activated, you might see something in the violet to blue region of the spectrum; when a medium cone is active, you would see green. For long wavelengths, which activate the third type of cone, you sense the colour red. All other colours, such as a pumpkin orange, are sensed when more than one of the receptor types is activated. According to the trichromatic theory, most colours correspond to a mixture of wavelengths and are sensed by comparing the activations of the three receptors.

trichromatic theory

A theory of colour vision proposing that colour information is extracted by comparing the relative activations of three different types of cone receptors.

FIGURE 4.11
Receptor Sensitivity Curves

Blue-sensitive cones are most likely to respond to short wavelengths of light; green-sensitive cones respond best to medium wavelengths; red-sensitive cones respond best to long wavelengths. On the sensitivity curve for rods, notice that rods are not sensitive to long wavelengths of light. (Based on Jones & Childers, 1993.)

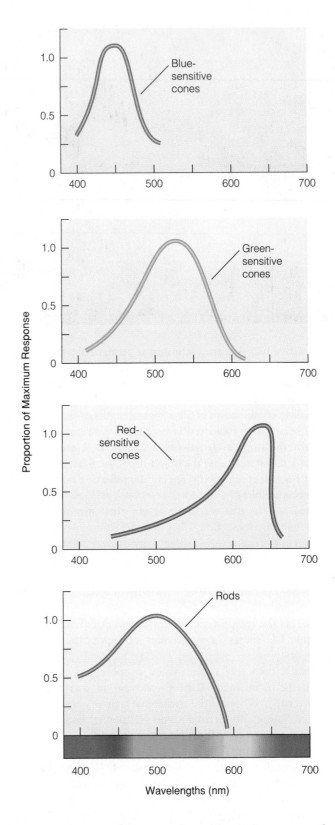

The trichromatic theory explains a number of interesting aspects of colour vision. For example, it explains certain kinds of colour blindness. At times, nature makes a mistake and fills a person's red cones with green photopigment or the green cones with red photopigment (Boynton, 1979). Under these rare conditions, which affect more males than females, individuals are left with two rather than three operational cone receptors. The trichromatic theory predicts that *dichromats*—people with two rather than three cone types—should lose their ability to discriminate between certain colours. Indeed, people who lack either the red or green cone type have a great deal of trouble distinguishing red from green. Other types of cone loss can produce trouble with blue–green discriminations. The particular type of colour deficiency depends on the particular type of lost receptor.

Colour Vision: Opponent Processes The physiological evidence, combined with the colour mixing and colour blindness patterns, provides strong support for the trichromatic theory. But the theory is not a complete account of colour vision. For one thing, the trichromatic theory has a problem with *yellow*. There are no cones that are uniquely sensitive to yellow, but people perceive yellow as every bit as "pure" a colour as red, green, and blue; even 4-month-old infants prefer dividing the colour spectrum into four colour categories rather than three (Bornstein et al., 1976). In addition, most people often report perceiving a yellowish-red or a bluish-green but rarely report seeing a yellowish-blue or, for that matter, a greenish-red. Why?

It turns out that certain colours are specially linked, such as blue and yellow, and red and green. You can discover this for yourself: If you stare at a patch of vivid colour (e.g., bright red) for a while and then switch your focus to a blank white space, you will see an **afterimage** of its *complementary* colour (e.g., green). Exposure to red produces an afterimage of green; exposure to blue results in an afterimage of yellow. The fact that people perceive yellow as a pure colour and that blue light can produce a yellow afterimage is quite difficult for the trichromatic theory to explain.

The McCollough effect (named after its discoverer, Celeste McCollough) is a particularly interesting kind of afterimage. The effect, which has been extensively studied by Lorraine Allan and Shep Siegel at McMaster University (Allan & Siegel, 1997) and by Keith Humphrey and his co-workers at the University of Western Ontario (Humphrey et al., 1999), is unusual in two ways. First, as you'll see if you try the demonstration in Figure 4.12, the afterimage is specific to the orientation of the edges in the grid (once you have the afterimage, try rotating the book 45 degrees and notice how the illusory colours "move" to different grids). Second, the effect can last for hours (if you have a strong afterimage now, try it again when you finish reading the chapter). The mechanisms of the McCollough effect are as yet unknown—another of the many mysteries of perception—but it likely has to do with fairly high-level parts of the visual system rather than with the cells in the retina (partly because it involves the integration of information about colour and information about form).

The difficulties with the trichromatic view were recognized in the 19th century by the German physiologist Ewald Hering. Hering proposed an alternative view of colour

afterimage
A sensation experienced after removal of a stimulus. For example, after staring at a red maple leaf for several seconds, when you shift your focus to a blank part of the page you will have a green afterimage.

FIGURE 4.12
The McCollough Effect

Look at the two coloured grids (alternating back and forth between them every few seconds) for at least 2 minutes. Then look at the black and white grid. You should see a greenish haze around the horizontal lines and a magenta haze around the vertical lines. If it doesn't work, try looking at the coloured grids for a longer period, and then return your gaze to the black and white grid.

opponent process theory
A theory of colour vision proposing that certain cells in the visual pathway increase their activation levels to one colour and decrease their activation levels to another colour (e.g., increasing to red and decreasing to green).

Based on what you've learned about colour vision, why do you think traffic lights change between red and green?

vision: **opponent process theory.** He suggested that there must be cells in the visual system that respond positively to one colour type (such as red) and negatively to another (such as green). Instead of three primary colours, Hering proposed six: *blue,* which is linked to *yellow* (therefore solving the problem with yellow); *green,* which is linked to *red;* and finally, *white,* which is linked to *black.* According to the opponent process theory, people have difficulty perceiving a yellowish-blue because activation of, say, the blue mechanism is accompanied by inhibition, or decreased activation, of the yellow mechanism. A yellowish-red does not present a problem in this scheme because yellow and red are not linked in an opponent fashion.

Like Young and Helmholtz, Hering was operating in a kind of physiological vacuum—there was no solid physiological evidence for either a three-receptor system or for specially linked opponent process cells. Such evidence now exists. For example, in addition to discovering different cone photopigments, researchers have found brain cells at various points in the visual pathway that do indeed code colour information in an opponent process fashion (DeValois & DeValois, 1980). The activity of these cells increases in response to one type of colour (e.g., red) and decreases to another (e.g., green).

So what underlies our ability to detect such a vast array of colours in the world? The visual system pulls colour information out of the visual input by relying on multiple processing stations. Colour information is extracted first at the retinal level through the activations of different cone types; farther up in the brain, opponent process cells fine-tune and further process the visual information. Thus a combination of the trichromatic and opponent process views best characterizes our current knowledge about colour extraction.

Producing Stable and Meaningful Interpretations: Visual Perception

Let's return, for a moment, to the cube in Figure 4.1 (page 124). You've seen how the electromagnetic energy bouncing off the page gets translated into an electrochemical signal, and how specialized regions of the visual pathway break the visual information down—the brain extracts lines, edges, colours, and even angles of orientation from the visual scene. But your perception is of seeing a cube—a particular object form—not a collection of elementary features.

To understand how the brain can generate perceptions of whole objects with visual machinery that seems designed to analyze parts, it helps to remember that perception is only partly determined by what comes in through the eyes. People also rely a

Concept Summary

COMPARING TRICHROMATIC AND OPPONENT PROCESS THEORY

Theory	Stage of Processing	Processing Mechanism	Basic Description
Trichromatic	Early in the retina	Three different cone types, maximally sensitive to short, medium, or long wavelengths of light, respectively.	The brain compares the relative activity levels between the three cone types to determine the colour of a stimulus; helps to explain certain types of colour blindness (e.g., *dichromats*).
Opponent process	Later in the visual pathway	Three types of mechanisms (e.g., cells) that respond positively and negatively to certain colour pairs (red–green; blue–yellow; black–white).	Mechanism responds positively to one member of a particular colour pair (e.g., blue) and negatively to the other (e.g., yellow); helps to explain complementary colour afterimages and prominence of yellow as a primary colour.

(a)

(b)

FIGURE 4.13
Prior Knowledge and Perception
Whether you detect meaningful images in (a) and (b) depends on how much prior knowledge you bring to your perceptual interpretation of these stimuli. (From Coren et al., 1999.)

great deal on their knowledge and expectations to construct what they see. Let's consider a simple example: Take a look at the two images depicted in Figure 4.13. You probably have no trouble seeing the image in panel (a): It's the word SKY, written in white against a black background (although note that none of the letters is fully defined, and the figure could instead be seen as a series of irregular black shapes). Panel (b) probably looks like a meaningless collection of black shapes (unless you read Chinese). Panel (b) also shows the word SKY, but it's written in Chinese. People who can read English but not Chinese see panel (a) as a meaningful image; those who can read Chinese but not English see panel (b) as the meaningful image (Coren et al., 1999). Thus, prior knowledge plays a critical role in how the brain interprets and organizes visual input.

People often use parts of a visual display to help interpret other parts. For example, take a look at each of the following lines of text:

A 13 C D E F G

10 11 12 13 14 15 16

The "B" in the first line is identical to the "13" in the second, but you "see" the letter B in the first line and the number 13 in the second because the other symbols in each line act as context that guides the perceptual interpretation of the ambiguous stimuli. In some cases, how the elements are arranged in a visual display can even cause people to see things that aren't really there. Is there a white triangle embedded in the middle of Figure 4.14? It sure looks like there is, but the perception is really an illusion—there is no physical stimulus, no reflected pattern of electromagnetic energy on the retina, that corresponds to the triangular form. Yet you interpret the pattern as a triangle.

There is more to perception than what meets the eye. Our perceptual world is constructed through a combination of two important kinds of mental activities. First, as we've been discussing throughout the chapter, the visual system analyzes the sensory input, the pattern of electromagnetic information on the retina. Psychologists refer to this as **bottom-up processing**—processing that starts with the raw physical input contacting the sensory receptors and works its way up to higher brain areas. Second, we also use our knowledge, beliefs, and expectations about the world to interpret and organize information from lower-level sensory systems, something psychologists call **top-down processing.** Perception always reflects a combination of these two kinds of processes. What you see is determined by what's out there in the world, but also by what you *expect* to be out there.

bottom-up processing
Processing that is driven by the physical input contacting the sensory receptors.

top-down processing
Processing that is driven by one's beliefs and expectations about how the world is organized.

Principles of Organization You may recall that in Chapter 1 we briefly discussed the possibility that people are born with certain organizing principles of perception. This point of view was championed by a group of researchers known as *Gestalt psychologists* (the word *Gestalt* translates from the German as "configuration" or "pattern"). According to the Gestalt psychologists, people see objects as well-structured and organized wholes because they are born with tendencies to *group* the incoming visual input

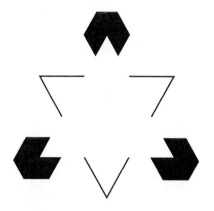

FIGURE 4.14
Illusory Contours

Can you see the white upright triangle embedded in this figure? No physical stimulus corresponds to that triangular form. Nonetheless, people interpret the pattern as a triangle.

FIGURE 4.15
Separating Figure from Ground
We have a natural tendency to divide any visual scene into a discernible "figure" and "ground." This task can be easy but ambiguous, as in the black and white image on the left (which do you see, a vase or a pair of profiles?), and it can be difficult, as in the painting on the right (how many faces can you find in the "ground" of the painting? We've found 10 so far!).

Gestalt principles of organization

The organizing principles of perception proposed by the Gestalt psychologists. These principles include the laws of proximity, similarity, closure, continuation, and common fate.

in sensible ways. For example, people have a natural, automatic tendency to divide any visual scene into a *figure* and a *ground*—we see the wine glass as separate from the table, the printed word as separate from the page. As you can see from Figure 4.15, the task of separating figure from ground is easy or difficult depending on whether strong or weak cues are available to guide the interpretation.

The Gestalt psychologists outlined a number of compelling and systematic regularities in human perception, known generally as the **Gestalt principles of organization,** that describe how people organize visual input to create the perception of whole objects:

1. *The law of proximity.* If the elements of a display are close to each other—that is, they lie in close spatial proximity—they tend to be grouped together as part of the same object. Here, for example, you see three groups of dots rather than a single collection.

Proximity

2. *The law of similarity.* Items that share physical properties—that physically resemble each other—tend to be perceived as belonging together. Thus, here you see rows of Xs and rows of Os rather than mixed-letter columns.

Similarity

3. *The law of closure.* If a figure has a gap, or a small amount of its border is missing, people nonetheless tend to perceive the object as complete. Below, for example, you likely perceive each figure as a circle, even though neither is a complete circle.

Closure

4. *The law of good continuation.* If lines cross or are interrupted, people tend to see continuous lines that flow in a continuous direction. In this figure you perceive two lines intersecting to form an X, but the figure could just as well be described as two angles with their vertices touching.

Continuation

5. *The law of common fate.* If several objects appear to be moving in the same direction, people tend to group them together. Try this demonstration: With a black felt-tipped pen, put several dots in a random pattern on a piece of clear plastic (such as a CD cover with the paper insert removed), and put several dots in a different pattern on a piece of paper. If you hold the paper under the plastic, it is difficult to tell which dots are on the paper and which are on the plastic, but as soon as you slide the paper along the plastic, the dots instantly become perceptually separated into two groups because the dots in each group share "common fate."

Object Recognition By imposing organization on a visual scene, the natural grouping tendencies described by the Gestalt principles simplify the problem of recognizing objects. Psychologist Irving Biederman (1987, 1990) suggested that the Gestalt principles of organization help the visual system break down complex visual inputs into components called *geons* (short for "geometric icons"). Geons are simple geometrical forms, such as blocks, cylinders, wedges, and cones. From a collection of only 36 geons, Biederman argues, more than 150 million possible very distinct complex and meaningful objects can be created—far more than people would ever need to capture the richness of their perceptual world. This means that once the brain is familiar with the basic geons, it can recognize the basic components of any perceptual experience. Just as the 26 letters of the alphabet form the basis for a huge variety of words and an infinite variety of sentences, geons could form the alphabet for building any object a person might see.

One of the attractive features of Biederman's theory, which he calls **recognition by components,** is its ability to explain how people can successfully identify degraded or incomplete objects. In everyday life, parts of objects in the environment are often occluded by other objects. For example, when you are driving, the other vehicles you see are typically partially hidden behind other cars, and at the dinner table the cutlery may be obscured by your plate. Yet you have no trouble recognizing the car or the fork. According to Biederman (1987), only a few geons are needed for the rapid identification of most objects.

To illustrate, Biederman asked subjects to identify degraded drawings of objects such as those shown in Figure 4.16. Some of the drawings were degraded by removing bits of lines that defined geons, so that the geons themselves were disrupted (drawings 1, 3, and 5 in Figure 4.16), whereas others were degraded by removing bits of lines that did not define geons, leaving the geons intact (drawings 2 and 4 in Figure 4.16). Consistent with the recognition by components theory, people had little difficulty recognizing the objects in drawings like 2 and 4, in which the geons were preserved, but had considerably more trouble identifying the objects in drawings like 1, 3, and 5, in which the geons were disrupted (even though the amount of line information was comparable in both conditions).

Biederman's theory of object recognition is quite successful in explaining the results of experiments like the one just described (Biederman, 2000). But not all researchers are convinced that a relatively small set of basic shapes is sufficient to allow us to discriminate between all objects (Liu, 1996). Many objects share basic parts, yet we are able to quickly and efficiently tell them apart. Moreover, there may be certain

recognition by components
The idea proposed by Biederman that people recognize objects perceptually through smaller components called *geons.*

FIGURE 4.16
Recognition by Components
Biederman proposed that we recognize visual forms in part by extracting simple geometric forms—geons—from the visual input. Above are degraded versions of drawings of common objects. Can you identify them? In drawings 1, 3, and 5, bits of lines that define geons have been removed, whereas in drawings 2 and 4 other bits of lines that do not define geons have been removed. You will likely find it easier to identify the objects in the even-numbered rows (intact geons) than those in the odd-numbered rows (disrupted geons). See page 142 for the answers. (From Biederman, 1990.)

1.

2.

3.

4.

5.

kinds of objects in the world, such as faces, that are perceived and remembered immediately as wholes, without any breaking down or building up from parts (Farah et al., 1998). There are cells in the brain that respond selectively to faces, and damage to some brain regions impairs face recognition without affecting perception of other sorts of objects. We are capable of recognizing an enormous range of objects in our world, and it may well be that our brains solve the problems of object recognition in several different ways.

The Perception of Depth The ability to perceive depth is one of the most amazing capabilities of the visual system. Think about it: The input to the visual system is a two-dimensional pattern of light falling on the surface of the retina. Yet, somehow, people extract a rich three-dimensional world from the "flat" image on the retina. As we will discuss in Chapter 10, the ability to perceive depth develops early in life (see also Tychsen, 2001): Infants as young as a few months can clearly tell the difference between the shallow and deep sides of a visual cliff (Campos et al., 1970; Gibson & Walk, 1960) and can even perceive depth in at least some kinds of two-dimensional displays (Schmuckler & Proffitt, 1994). How does the visual system create such a rich and vivid perceptual experience from the two-dimensional pattern of light falling on the retina?

The ability to extract depth from the visual input results from a combination of bottom-up and top-down processing. People use their knowledge about objects, in combination with bottom-up processing of the visual input, to create the perception of a three-dimensional visual world. For example, the brain knows and adjusts for the fact that distant objects produce smaller reflections on the retina. Thus, if you see two people whom you *know* to be of comparable height, but the retinal images they produce are of different sizes, your brain figures out that one person must be standing closer to you than the other. Experience also makes it clear that closer objects tend to block the images of objects that are farther away: If your view of a TV screen is blocked by a human form, you can be reasonably certain that the person is standing in *front* of the television and is therefore closer to you than is the television.

Another cue for distance, one that artists often use to depict depth in paintings, is *linear perspective*. As shown in the accompanying photos, parallel lines that recede into the distance converge toward a single point. Generally, the farther away two lines are, the closer together those lines will appear to be. The relative shading of objects in a scene can provide important cues as well: If one object casts a shadow on another, you can often tell which of the two is farther away. Objects that are far away also tend to look blurry and slightly bluish. If you look at a realistic painting of a mountain scene, you'll see that the distant hills lack fine detail and are painted with a tinge of blue.

Can you identify the types of cues present in these "flat" pictures that allow us to perceive depth?

In everyday environments, the ground stretches away from the viewer to the visual boundaries of the environment (the wall of a room or the horizon line out of doors). The ground—whether it's a leaf-strewn lawn or a linoleum floor—has visual texture; that is, there are variations of light and dark and (usually) of colour across the surface of the ground. The texture of nearby ground appears relatively coarse or rough, and the texture of more distant ground looks progressively finer and finer. For example, kneel on a carpet and look across its surface toward the far wall: The visual texture of the carpet close to your eyes appears coarse, whereas that far away appears fine. Gibson (1966) proposed that such **texture gradients** provide the visual system with a great deal of information about the distance between a viewer and objects on the ground.

Recently, Shaun Vecera and co-authors (2002) documented another cue to figure–ground discrimination, which they call "**lower region**": All else being equal, the lower part of a scene tends to be perceived as "figure," and the upper part as "ground." Figure 4.17 provides a simple example. In a natural setting, regions below the horizon line are usually closer to the observer than regions above the horizon line, and the objects with which people typically interact (rocks, plants, animals) are more often below than above the horizon line; presumably, the visual system has adaptively developed a bias to interpret stimuli in the lower region of a scene as "figure" rather than ground.

The depth cues that we've been considering so far are called **monocular depth cues,** which means they can work even if there is only input from one eye. A person can close one eye and still see a world full of depth, based on the use of monocular cues such as the ones we discussed above. But the brain also uses **binocular depth cues;** these are cues produced by two eyes, each with a slightly different view of the world. Hold your index finger up a few centimetres in front of your eyes. Now close and open each eye in alternation. You should see your finger jumping back and forth as you switch from one open eye to the other. The finger appears to move because each eye has a slightly different angle of view on the world (because the eyes are about 5 cm apart), producing different images in each retina. The difference between the images in the two eyes is called **retinal disparity.** The brain derives depth information, in part, by calculating the amount of disparity between the image in the left eye and the image in the right eye. Move your finger farther away and try looking at it with one eye and then the other; the amount of disparity is now much less than it was when your finger was close to your eyes. The brain also uses the degree that the two eyes turn inward, called **convergence,** to derive information about depth. The closer an object is to the face, the more the two eyes need to turn inward, or converge, for the object to be seen in focus.

We have described only some of the more important depth cues. Psychologists have identified many other kinds of information that the visual system also uses to infer the distance of objects and to create the compelling three-dimensional experience of seeing the world around us (see Coren et al., 1999). We hope that, in addition to learning about the cues to depth that we have discussed, you have developed an appreciation for the sophistication and complexity of visual perception. What to most people seems an effortless task—looking around and perceiving a three-dimensional

texture gradient
Gradual reduction, with increasing distance, of the apparent coarseness of a surface (such as the ground or floor); provides a powerful cue to the distances of objects located on that surface.

lower region
Bias to perceive the lower part of a visual scene as the "figure" (meaningful object of perception) rather than "ground" (background).

monocular depth cues
Cues for depth for which input from one eye is sufficient.

binocular depth cues
Cues for depth that depend on comparisons between the two eyes.

retinal disparity
A binocular cue for depth that is based on location differences between the images in each eye.

convergence
A binocular cue for depth that is based on the extent to which the two eyes move inward, or converge, when looking at an object.

FIGURE 4.17
"Lower Region" Depth Cue
Most people see this drawing as consisting of black stalagmite-like figures raising up against a white background, but the drawing can also be perceived as white stalactite-like figures hanging down against a black background. Turn the page upside down: If you are like most people, you will still be biased to see the "lower region" (now coloured white) as the figure.

Practical Solutions

CREATING ILLUSIONS OF DEPTH

To survive in a 3-D environment, animals that move rapidly must perceive depth. Yet the pattern of light falling on the retina is only 2-dimensional: It has height and width, but not depth. As you've read in this chapter, the visual system solves this problem by using multiple cues to depth (the dimension not directly represented on the retina).

The same processes that have evolved to enable us to perceive the depth of the real 3-D world can also give rise to illusions of depth in certain kinds of 2-D pictures. For example, 3-D movies are made by filming each scene twice, from slightly different angles, then projecting both versions simultaneously to viewers wearing special glasses with lenses that selectively deliver one image to the right eye and the other to the left eye. If done just right, this arrangement simulates the *retinal disparity* (discussed in the section "The Perception of Depth") that would occur if the viewer were really looking at a 3-D object. Our two eyes are separated by several centimetres, and that means that when we look at a 3-D scene each eye gets a slightly different view (e.g., looking at a cup on the desk, your left eye sees more of the cup's left side and less of its right side than does your right eye [and vice versa], and the amount of disparity is systematically related to the distance of the object). By using two cameras to record a scene, two projectors to present them, and a device (such as special glasses) to separate the projected images so that one image goes to each eye, 3-D movies mimic this natural retinal disparity, thereby giving rise to an illusion of depth from the 2-D stimulus of the movie. Some 3-D movies use red and green lenses to separate the signal to each eye, whereas others use polarized lenses, which selectively filter the light according to its angle.

The once-popular children's toy called a ViewMaster works on the same principle: When you look through the ViewMaster you are viewing two pictures of the same scene, taken from slightly different perspectives, and the device delivers one image to each eye, thereby producing the illusion of depth.

Neither 3-D movies nor the ViewMaster are currently in fashion, and you may never have seen either of them. But you almost certainly *have* seen single-image random-dot stereograms like that shown in Figure 4.18. These have enjoyed prolonged popularity for the last decade or so, despite the fact that it is somewhat difficult to experience a 3-D effect with them. The nifty thing about stereograms is that you don't need special glasses or any other device to make them work—just a little patience. The pattern consists of two systematic patterns of dots that are slightly offset. When you look at the images in the right way, your brain fuses separate pairs of points in the image as though they were slightly different perspectives on the same point, thereby giving rise to a 3-D illusion.

Make sure you are in a brightly lit environment. Hold the book in front of your face, with Figure 4.18 several centimetres from your nose. Imagine that you are focusing on an object more than a metre in front of you. The stereogram will be blurry because it is very close but you are focused as though looking at something in the distance. Keep staring blankly forward as you gradually and smoothly move the book away from your eyes. What you are trying to do is set up a situation in which (a) the convergence of your eyeballs is appropriate for looking at a relatively distant object but (b) the image of the figure is in fairly good focus. If you achieve this, a 3-D image will arise. As in the other examples described above, this illusion arises from the adaptive mechanisms that enable us to perceive the depth of the real world around us. In turn, studies of stereograms have provided new insights into the nature and operation of those adaptive mechanisms (e.g., Grove et al., 2002).

FIGURE 4.18
Random-Dot Stereogram
An example of a single-picture random-dot stereogram.

world of people and objects—is in fact an enormous accomplishment. Interestingly, as described in the Practical Solutions box, the same mechanisms that enable us to perceive the three-dimensional depth of the world around us can also give rise to illusory perceptions of depth in two-dimensional images.

Concept Summary

DEPTH CUES

Type of Cue	Cue	Description
Monocular	Relative size	Comparably sized stimuli that produce different-sized retinal images are perceived as varying in distance from the observer.
	Overlap	Closer objects tend to block the images of objects farther away.
	Linear perspective	Parallel lines that recede into the distance appear to converge on a single point.
	Shading	Shadows cast by objects on other objects assist in depth perception.
	Haze	Distant objects tend to look blurry and slightly bluish.
	Texture gradient	The texture of the ground on which an object is sitting will appear relatively coarse if the object is near and relatively fine if the object is distant.
Binocular	Retinal disparity	The differences between the locations of the images in the two eyes; the amount of disparity changes with distance from a point of fixation.
	Convergence	The closer the stimulus, the more the eyes turn inward toward one another.

Perceptual Constancies Yet another rather remarkable feature of the human visual system is its capacity to recognize that an object remains the same even when the image on the retina changes. As a case in point, consider how the size of an object's retinal image decreases with distance. As you walk away from a parked car, the size of its retinal image becomes smaller and smaller—so that it eventually resembles the image that might be reflected from a toy car held at arm's length. Do you ever wonder why your car has mysteriously been transformed into a toy? You don't, of course, because your visual system maintains a stable interpretation of the image—as a normal-sized car—despite the changes in retinal size.

When you perceive an object, or its properties, as remaining the same even though the physical input received by the eyes is changing, you are showing what is called a **perceptual constancy.** In the car example, it is *size constancy*—the perceived size of the car remains constant even though the size of the reflected image is changing with distance. Figure 4.19 provides an example of *shape constancy.* Consider how many changes occur in the reflected image of a door as it slowly moves from closed to open. Yet you still recognize it as a door, not as some bizarre shape that changes over time. Size and shape constancies are related. Both result, at least in part, from the visual system's use of cues to determine distance. Both are also extremely adaptive characteristics, because most of the time the size and shape of an object does, in fact, remain constant—only its reflected image changes.

To see what kind of cues might be used to produce constancy, take a look at Figure 4.20. Take particular note of the rectangular shapes on the ground marked as A, B, and C. You see these planters as being the same size and shape, in part, because of

perceptual constancy
Perceiving the properties of an object as remaining the same even though the physical properties of the sensory input are changing.

FIGURE 4.19
Shape Constancy

Think about all the changes in the image of a door as it moves from closed to open. Yet we perceive it as a constant rectangular shape.

FIGURE 4.20
Constancy Cues

We see these three planters, marked A, B, and C, as matching in size and shape partly because of depth cues in the environment: Each covers three tiles in length and three in width.

the texture patterns covering the ground. Each of the open boxes covers three texture tiles in length and an additional three in width. The retinal image, however, differs markedly for each of the shapes (take a ruler and measure the physical size of each shape). You interpret and see them as the same because your experiences in the world have taught you that size and distance are related in systematic ways.

People experience perceptual constancies for a variety of object dimensions. In addition to size and shape constancy, the brightness and colour of an object typically appear to remain constant, even though the intensity and wavelength of the light change when ambient lighting conditions vary. Once again, these characteristics help us maintain a stable and orderly interpretation of a constantly changing sensory input. Think about how chaotic the world would appear if you saw a new and different object every time the physical properties of its reflected image changed. For example, instead of seeing a dancer gliding across the floor, you might see a series of dancers, each striking a unique and unusual pose.

Perceptual Illusions   The processes by which the brain interprets the ambiguous and incomplete information that reaches the retina can also give rise to **perceptual illusions,** or inaccurate interpretations of physical reality. For example, look at the two girls sitting in the room depicted in Figure 4.21. The girl on the right appears to be much taller than the girl on the left. In reality, the two girls are approximately the same size. You're tricked because your brain uses cues in the environment—combined with the assumption that rooms are vertically and horizontally rectangular—to interpret the size of the occupants. Actually, as the rest of the figure shows, it is the room (known as the Ames room), not the sizes of the girls, that is unusual.

Based partly on your expectations about the shape of rooms and partly on the unique construction of the Ames room, as you look through the peephole you think you're looking at two people who are the same distance from your eyes. But the person on the left is actually farther away, so a smaller image is projected onto the retina (and onto the page). Because the brain assumes the two are the same distance away, it also assumes that the person on the right is larger (Dorward & Day, 1997). A related phenomenon is called the moon illusion: The full moon often looks huge as it rises over the horizon, and appears to dwindle in size as it gradually mounts higher into the sky, but neither the size of the moon nor the size of its reflected image entering your eyes changes (see Coren, 1992).

The Ponzo illusion, shown in Figure 4.22(a), operates in a similar way. You see two lines that are exactly the same size as quite different because the linear perspective

perceptual illusions

Inappropriate interpretations of physical reality. Perceptual illusions often occur as a result of the brain's use of otherwise adaptive organizing principles.

FIGURE 4.21

The Ames Room

The girl on the right appears to be much taller than the girl on the left. But this is an illusion induced by the visual system's assumption that the room is rectangular. The sloping ceiling and floors and the angle of the back wall, along with systematic distortions of the shape and size of details in the room, provide misleading depth cues. For example, neither of the windows is really rectangular, and the window on the left is larger than that on the right. To the viewer looking through the peephole, the room appears perfectly normal. The misleading cues lead the visual system to perceive the two girls as being approximately the same distance away from the viewer; hence the girl on the right, who (because she is nearer) projects a larger image on the retina (and on the page), is perceived as larger. Here you see only a photo of an Ames room; the effect is even more compelling when you peep into an actual Ames room.

cue—the converging parallel lines—tricks the brain into thinking that the horizontal line near the top of the display is farther away. Because it has the same size retinal image as the bottom line (remember, the two are physically the same size), the brain compensates for the "distance" by making the top line appear larger. Figure 4.22(b) shows a similar illusion: The monsters are really the same size (measure them with a ruler), but the one on the top appears to be much larger. This is yet another example of a key theme of this text: What you see is more than meets the eye!

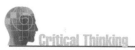
Critical Thinking

Our perceptual systems give rise to certain illusions (such as the Ponzo illusion illustrated in Figure 4.22(a)). How can this be squared with the idea that our brains have evolved adaptively?

(a)   **(b)**

FIGURE 4.22

Illusion of Depth

These two figures, based on the Ponzo illusion, show that depth cues can lead to perceptual errors. In (a) the horizontal lines are actually the same size, as are the monsters in (b). (From Shepard, 1990.)

Test Yourself 4.1

Check your knowledge about vision by answering the following questions. (You will find the answers in Appendix B.)

1. To test your understanding of how the visual input is translated into the language of the brain, choose the best answers from among the following terms: accommodation; cones; cornea; fovea; lens; opponent process; pupil; receptive field; retina; rods; trichromatic.
   a. The "central pit" area where the cone receptors tend to be located: _____
   b. Receptors that are responsible for visual acuity, or our ability to see fine detail: _____
   c. The process through which the lens changes its shape temporarily to help focus light: _____
   d. The "film" at the back of the eye that contains the light-sensitive receptor cells: _____
   e. The protective outer layer of the eye: _____

2. Decide whether each of the following statements about how your brain extracts components from visual input is true or false.
   a. Visual input tends to be analyzed primarily by structures in the superior colliculus, although structures in the lateral geniculate are important too. *True or False?*
   b. It's currently believed that information about colour and movement is probably processed in separate pathways in the brain. *True or False?*
   c. The opponent process theory of colour vision makes it easier to understand why most people think there are four, rather than three, primary colours (red, green, blue, yellow). *True or False?*
   d. Some feature detectors in the brain are "tuned" to respond only when certain patterns of light stimulate the retina. *True or False?*

3. Test your knowledge about visual perception by filling in the blanks. Choose your answers from the following terms: binocular depth cues; bottom-up processing; convergence; monocular depth cues; lower region; perceptual constancy; perceptual illusion; retinal disparity; recognition by components; top-down processing.
   a. The part of perception that is controlled by our beliefs and expectations about how the world is organized: _____
   b. Perceiving an object, or its properties, to remain the same even though the physical input received by the eyes is changing: _____
   c. The depth cue that is based on calculating the degree to which the two eyes have turned inward: _____
   d. The view that object perception is based on the analysis of simple building blocks called geons: _____
   e. People have a bias to perceive the _____ of a scene as the figure rather than ground.

HEARING: IDENTIFYING AND LOCALIZING SOUNDS

Learning Goals

1. Understand how physical sound input is translated into the electrochemical language of the brain.
2. Learn how pitch information is pulled out of the auditory input.
3. Comprehend how the auditory input is interpreted to localize the source of a sound.

IMAGINE THE WORLD without sound. You wouldn't hear music, speech, or laughter. Hearing enriches our life and, like vision, it serves a variety of very adaptive functions. For example, sounds help us identify and locate objects, and it is through sound that we produce and comprehend the spoken word. Even our most private sense of self—the world inside our heads—often appears in the form of an inner voice, an ongoing speech-based monologue (see Chapter 7).

Translating the Input: Auditory Transduction

The physical input received by the auditory system, **sound,** is a form of energy that, like light, travels as a wave. However, sound—unlike light—is mechanical energy and requires a *medium* (such as air or water) through which to move. Sound cannot travel in a vacuum. Sound begins with a vibrating object, such as the movement of vocal cords, the plucking of a guitar string, or the pounding diaphragm of a woofer speaker. The vibration pushes air molecules out into space, where they collide with other air molecules, and a kind of travelling chain reaction begins.

    The rate of vibration of the object that is the source of a sound determines the *frequency* of the sound, defined as the number of times the pressure wave moves from peak to peak per second (measured in units called *hertz*, where 1 Hz = 1 cycle per second). Psychologically, when the frequency of a sound varies, people hear changes in **pitch,** which corresponds to how high or low a tone sounds. For example, middle C on a piano has a frequency of 262 Hz, whereas the highest note on a piano corresponds to about 4000 Hz. Humans are sensitive to frequencies from roughly 20 to 20 000 Hz, but we are most sensitive to frequencies in the 1000 to 5000 Hz range (Gulick et al., 1989; Sivian & White, 1933). Many important sounds fall into this range of maximum sensitivity, including the sounds that make up speech.

    The other major dimension of sound is *amplitude,* the height a sound wave reaches. Psychologically, increases in amplitude are experienced as increases in **loudness.** The amplitude of a wave is measured in units called *decibels* (dB). The decibel scale is logarithmic: A 10-dB sound is 10 times more intense than the weakest sound a human can hear, a 20-dB sound is 10 × 10 (that is, 100) times more intense than the weakest audible sound, and so on. To give you some perspective, normal conversation is around 60 dB, whereas an incredibly loud rock band can produce sounds over 120 dB in the front row.

    It is not unusual for dance clubs to have ambient sound levels at or above 100 dB. Repeated and prolonged exposure to sounds 90 dB or higher can produce permanent hearing loss: The louder, longer, and more frequent the exposure, the more likely it will cause both short- and long-term hearing loss. As a rule of thumb, if the music is loud

sound
The physical input to the auditory system, a mechanical energy travelling in waves that requires a medium such as air or water through which to move.

pitch
The psychological experience that results from the auditory processing of a particular *frequency* of sound.

loudness
The psychological experience that results from the auditory processing of a particular *amplitude* of sound.

Dr. Mark A. Schmuckler, Professor of Psychology at the University of Toronto, examines a computer-generated spectogram, which records the pattern of variation in the intensity and frequencies of sounds over time. For example, the spectogram on the screen might depict the sounds of the word "relish" (with the "r" sound on the left and the "ish" sound on the right). If you have a PC, it may have a digital sound recorder that displays crude spectograms (e.g., Windows Sound Recorder).

enough that you have to really raise your voice to be understood by someone less than a metre away, you are at risk. Many smart and cool people wear earplugs to clubs (by the way, stuffing tissue in your ears doesn't cut it).

Entering the Ear Let's follow a sound as it enters the auditory pathway (see Figure 4.23). We saw that in the visual system, an optical pathway through the cornea, pupil, and lens focuses the light energy onto the visual receptors. In the auditory system, sound travels toward the auditory receptor cells through the ears. The external flap of tissue usually referred to as the "ear" is known technically as the **pinna;** it helps capture the sound, which then funnels down the auditory canal toward the *eardrum*, or **tympanic membrane.**

The tympanic membrane responds to the incoming sound wave by vibrating. The particular vibration pattern, which differs for different sound frequencies, is then transmitted through three small bones in the **middle ear:** the *malleus* (Latin for "hammer"), the *incus* (anvil), and the *stapes* (stirrup). These bones intensify the vibration pattern and prepare it for passage into the fluid-filled inner ear. Within the inner ear lies a bony, snail shell–shaped sound processor called the **cochlea;** here, the sound energy is transduced into the internal language of the nervous system—electrochemical activity in neurons.

Transduction in the Cochlea The third bone in the middle ear, the stapes, is connected to an opening in the cochlea called the *oval window*. As the stapes vibrates, it causes fluid inside the cochlea to displace a flexible membrane, called the **basilar membrane,** that runs throughout the cochlear shell, somewhat like a long carpet. Transduction takes place through the activation of tiny auditory receptor cells, called *hair cells*, that lie along the basilar membrane. As the membrane starts to ripple—like a cat moving under a bed sheet—in response to the wave of pressure flowing through the fluid in the cochlea, tiny hairs called *cilia*, which extend outward from the hair cells,

pinna
The external flap of tissue commonly referred to as the "ear"; it helps direct sounds toward the tympanic membrane.

tympanic membrane
The eardrum, which responds to incoming sound waves by vibrating.

middle ear
The portion of the ear between the eardrum and the cochlea containing three small bones (the malleus, incus, and stapes) that intensify and prepare the sound vibrations for passage into the inner ear.

cochlea
The bony, snail shell–shaped sound processor in the inner ear, where sounds are transduced into nerve impulses.

basilar membrane
A flexible membrane running through the cochlea that, through its movement, displaces the auditory receptor cells (hair cells).

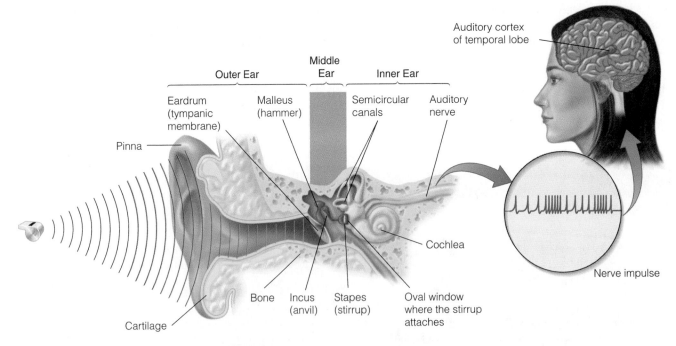

FIGURE 4.23

The Structures of the Human Ear

Sound enters the auditory canal and causes the tympanic membrane to vibrate in a pattern that is then transmitted through three small bones in the middle ear to the oval window. The oval window vibrates, causing fluid inside the cochlea to be displaced, which moves the basilar membrane. The semicircular canals and vestibular sacks are not involved in audition; rather, they are part of the vestibular system, which senses the position and movement of the head.

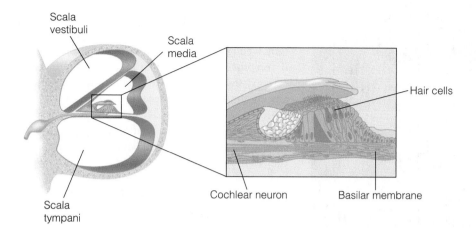

Scala vestibuli

Scala media

Hair cells

Cochlear neuron

Basilar membrane

Scala tympani

FIGURE 4.24
The Basilar Membrane
This figure shows an open slice of the cochlea. Sound vibrations cause fluid inside the cochlea to displace the basilar membrane that runs throughout the cochlear shell. Different frequencies trigger different patterns of movement along the membrane. Transduction takes place through bending hair cells. The hair cells nearest the point of maximum displacement will be stimulated the most, which helps the brain code information about pitch.

are displaced. The bending of these hairs causes the auditory receptor cells to fire, creating a neural impulse that travels up the auditory pathways to the brain (see Figure 4.24). (By the way, it is these delicate cilia that can be permanently damaged by frequent prolonged exposure to loud noises.)

Different sound frequencies trigger different movement patterns along the basilar membrane. Higher frequencies of sound cause the membrane to be displaced the most near the oval window; low frequencies produce a travelling wave that reaches its peak deep inside the spiralling cochlea. As you'll learn shortly, the receptor cells that are activated the most by any particular sound pattern help the brain detect pitch. If hair cells near the oval window are responding the most, the incoming sound is perceived as high in pitch. If many cells along the membrane are active, and the most active ones are far away from the oval window, the incoming sound is perceived as low in pitch.

Extracting the Input Components: Auditory Pathways

Less is known about the auditory pathways than about the visual route toward the cortex, but there are some general similarities worth noting. The neural impulses generated by the hair cells leave the cochlea in each ear along the *auditory nerve*. Neural codings of sounds that have been received in the right ear travel mainly along pathways leading to the left hemisphere of the brain; left-ear sounds go primarily to the right hemisphere. As in the visual system, auditory nerve fibres also appear to be "tuned" to transmit a specific kind of input. In the visual system, the ganglion cells transmit information about regions of light and dark on the retina. In the auditory system, fibres in the auditory nerve pass on rough *frequency* information. Electrophysiological measurements of individual auditory nerve fibres show tuning curves—for example, a particular fibre might respond best to an input stimulus of around 2000 Hz and less well to others (Ribaupierre, 1997).

Extracting Pitch Complex sounds, such as speech, consist of combinations of simple sound frequencies. The auditory system pulls out information about the simple frequencies, which correspond to different pitches, in several ways. Pitch is determined, in part, by the particular place on the basilar membrane that is most active. For example, as we discussed earlier, activation of hair cells near the oval window leads to the perception of a high-pitched sound. This is called the **place theory** of pitch perception (Békésy, 1960): "Place" in this instance refers to the location of the activated hair cell along the basilar membrane. We hear a particular pitch partly because certain hair cells are responding actively.

Place theory helps to explain certain kinds of hearing loss. For example, as people grow older they typically have trouble hearing the higher frequencies of sound (such as those in whispered speech). Why might this be? Most sounds that enter the auditory system activate, to at least some extent, those hair cells nearest the oval window, which

place theory
The idea that the *location* of auditory receptor cells activated by movement of the basilar membrane plays a role in the perception of pitch.

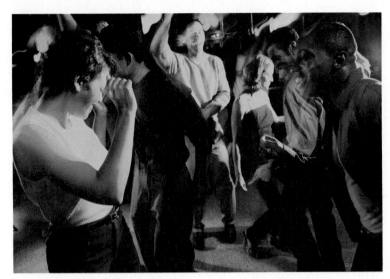

Prolonged exposure to intense noise can cause permanent hearing loss.

frequency theory
The idea that pitch perception is determined partly by the *frequency* of neural impulses travelling up the auditory pathway.

are most sensitive to high-frequency sounds. Cells in the interior portions of the cochlea respond actively only when low-frequency sounds are present. Thus, if receptor cells wear out from years of prolonged activity, those nearest the oval window should be among the first to go. Place theory thus explains, in part, why older people have difficulty hearing high-pitched sounds (especially if they went to lots of rock concerts or operated noisy equipment when they were younger!).

Despite its successes, place theory does not offer a complete account of pitch perception. One problem with place theory is that hair cells do not act independently; often, many are activated in unison. As a result, it's thought that the brain also relies on the *rate* at which cells fire their neural impulses. According to **frequency theory,** pitch is determined partly by the frequency of neural impulses travelling up the auditory pathway: The higher the rate of firing, the higher the perceived pitch. This makes sense (so to speak) because high-pitched sounds are carried by high-frequency sound waves (i.e., ones in which peaks occur very frequently).

In summary, the brain uses several kinds of information to extract pitch. Remember that for colour vision the brain uses information from multiple cone receptors as well as from opponent process cells located in the upper regions of the brain. Similarly, to detect pitch the brain uses information about where on the basilar membrane activation is occurring *(place theory)* as well as the rate at which signals are generated *(frequency theory)*. Neither place nor frequency information, by itself, is sufficient to explain our perception of pitch—both kinds of information are needed and used.

The Auditory Cortex   The neural activity caused by auditory input eventually reaches the auditory cortex, which is located mainly in the temporal lobes of the brain. Cells in the auditory cortex are frequency-sensitive, which means that they respond best to particular frequencies of sound. There is a well-defined organizational scheme: Cells that respond to low-frequency sounds are clustered together in one area of the auditory cortex, whereas cells responsive to high-frequency sounds sit in another area (Scheich & Zuschratter, 1995).

There also appear to be cells in the auditory cortex that respond best to complex combinations of sounds. For example, a cell might respond only to a sequence of tones that move from one frequency to another in a rising series (Pickles, 1988). In non-human animals, cortical cells have also been discovered that respond only to sounds that exist in the animal's natural "vocabulary," such as a particular shriek, cackle, or trill (Wollberg & Newman, 1972). In people, PET scans have shown that specific areas of the brain "light up" when complex auditory sequences are played, such as eight-note melodies (Zatorre et al., 1994). Much remains to be learned, though, about how complex sounds—such as patterns of speech—are represented in the cortex.

Producing Stable and Meaningful Interpretations: Auditory Perception

Say the phrase "kiss the sky" several times in rapid succession. Now do the same thing with the word "stress" or "life." Your perception of what you're saying may undergo some interesting changes. "Kiss the sky" may begin to sound like "kiss this guy"; "stress" will probably turn into "dress" and "life" into "fly." Even if the way you say the sounds doesn't change, your perception of it may. Indeed, the "kiss the sky/kiss this guy" example follows from a story about audiences' misperceptions of a lyric in the

When you listen to a band, you can separately pick out the sounds different musicians are creating, selectively attending to the guitar, vocals, or bass.

Jimi Hendrix song "Purple Haze." This is an auditory analogue to the Necker cube that we discussed at the beginning of the chapter. Input to the auditory system is ambiguous and must be interpreted by the brain.

Organizing the Auditory Input As with the ever-changing Necker cube, there is not always a straightforward mapping between the physical and the psychological interpretation of a sound event. The brain is often faced with auditory ambiguity—it seeks meaning where it can, partly by relying on established organizational rules (Bregman, 1990; Hirsh & Watson, 1996). As with vision, the brain separates the incoming auditory stream into figure and ground. For example, at a party you focus on one voice (making it the "figure") and other people's voices become part of the auditory background. The auditory system tends to group sounds that are similar and that occur close together in time. Sound frequency, for example, can be used as a grouping cue to distinguish between voices. Females generally speak at higher frequencies than males, and as a result, it is usually easier to separate the signals of two people talking simultaneously if they are of different sexes (see Chapter 5).

The ability to identify and organize sounds increases with experience. People use their knowledge and expectations, through top-down processing, to interpret the incoming auditory sequence. Experienced car mechanics, for example, can often identify an engine problem simply by listening to the particular "knocking" that the engine makes; cardiologists, as a result of experience, can use the intricacies of the heartbeat to diagnose the health of a patient's cardiovascular system.

Prior knowledge not only influences how we perceive sounds; it also influences how we produce sequences of sounds. Read the following silently, then say it aloud while listening closely to the sounds:

Marzi doats n doze edoats n lidul lamzey divey.

Recognize anything familiar? The line is a lesson on the dietary habits of familiar barnyard animals; it's taken from a popular 1940s song (Sekular & Blake, 1990). (Here's a hint: Mares eat oats and....) With a little knowledge and some expectations about the content of the input, you should eventually arrive at an agreeable interpretation of the lyric. Notice that once you've arrived at that interpretation, the same groupings of letters produce quite a different auditory experience when they are read aloud.

Sound Localization Another adaptive characteristic of the auditory sense is the ability to identify the spatial location from which sounds emanate. For example, if you're driving down the street and hear a sudden screech of brakes, you very quickly identify the direction from which the sound came. How do you accomplish this feat? Just as

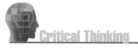

Critical Thinking

Can you think of any songs that you like now but didn't like when you first heard them? One possibility is that you've learned to organize the music in a way that makes it more appealing.

comparisons between the retinal locations of images in the two eyes provide information about visual depth, comparisons between the auditory input to the right and left ears help people *localize* objects in space.

Let's assume that the braking car is approaching yours from the left side. Because your left ear is closer to the source of the sound, it receives the sound vibrations slightly sooner than your right ear. If an object is directly in front of or behind you, the input will arrive at both ears simultaneously. By comparing the arrival times between the left and right ears, the brain is able to localize the sound fairly accurately. What's amazing is that these arrival time differences are extremely small. For example, the maximum arrival time difference, which occurs when an object is directly opposite one ear, is only about 600 *microseconds* (a microsecond is 1/10 000 of a second).

Another important cue for sound localization is *intensity* differences between the ears. The sound that arrives first—to either the left or right ear—will be somewhat louder, or more intense, than the sound arriving second. Again, these intensity differences are not large, and they depend partly on the frequency of the arriving sound, but they are useful cues for sound localization. Thus, your brain calculates the difference in arrival times between the two ears, plus any differences in intensity (or loudness), and uses this information to localize the source (Giguere & Abel, 1993). Just as infants demonstrate depth perception at an early age, they also demonstrate the ability to localize sounds (Morrongiello et al., 1994), although the precision of localization and the ability to integrate auditory and visual cues to localization improve during infancy (Fenwick & Morrongiello, 1998).

Test Yourself 4.2

Check your knowledge about the auditory system by determining whether each of the following questions is true or false. (You will find the answers in Appendix B.)

1. Sound is a form of mechanical energy that requires a medium, such as air or water, through which to move. *True or False?*
2. According to the frequency theory of pitch perception, the location of activity on the basilar membrane is the primary cue for determining pitch. *True or False?*
3. Sound pressure causes tiny hair cells, located in the pinna, to bend, thereby generating a neural impulse. *True or False?*
4. The separation of a sensory input into figure and ground occurs for vision but not for hearing. *True or False?*
5. We use multiple cues to help us localize a sound, including comparisons of arrival times and intensity differences between the two ears. *True or False?*

THE SKIN AND BODY SENSES: EXPERIENCING TOUCH, TEMPERATURE, PAIN, AND MOVEMENT

Learning Goals

1. Understand how touch information is translated and interpreted within the brain.
2. Learn how sensory receptors in the skin code information about temperature, and understand the basis of the subjective experience of temperature perception.
3. Know how we perceive and interpret pain.
4. Understand the sensory systems that give rise to (nonvisual) awareness of the position and movement of parts of your body (e.g., your arms).
5. Learn about the sensory systems that underlie the perception of the movement of your body through space.

OUR PERCEPTUAL EXPERIENCES might appear to be driven primarily by what comes in through our eyes and ears. We communicate through the spoken word; we usually identify objects through vision. But imagine a world without physical contact. Touch, such as a lingering kiss or the brush of a hand against a cheek, is obviously an important perceptual experience. Skin contact builds its own perceptual world: You can detect the location of a light switch in the dark, feel the warmth of a fire, or experience the pain of an accident in the mosh pit.

It's relatively easy to appreciate the adaptive significance of the skin and body senses. You need to be able to detect the presence of a spider crawling up your leg; if a blowing ember from the fireplace happens to land on your forearm, it is certainly adaptive for you to respond quickly. It's also important for us to be able to detect and control the movement and position of our bodies. We need to know, for example, if we're hanging upside down and the current positions of our arms and legs. Human sensory systems have developed not only to detect the presence of objects in the environment but also to provide accurate information about the body itself.

In this section you'll learn about three skin senses—touch, temperature, and pain—as well as the body senses related to the perception of movement and balance. In each case, as in our earlier discussions, the environmental input needs to be translated, transmitted to the brain, and interpreted in a meaningful fashion.

Touch

In the case of touch or pressure, the physical input delivered to the skin is mechanical. An object makes contact with the body, and receptor cells embedded in the skin are disturbed. The mechanical pressure on the cell (it is literally deformed) produces a neural impulse, and the input is then transmitted to the spinal cord and up into the brain.

There are several different types of pressure-sensitive receptor cells in the skin. Some respond to constant pressure; others respond best to intermittent pressure, such as a tapping on the skin or a stimulus that vibrates at a particular frequency (Bolanowski et al., 1994). As with vision and hearing, touch information is transmitted up the neural pathway through distinct channels to processing stations in the brain, where the inputs received from various points on the body are combined (Bolanowski, 1989). One kind of nerve fibre might carry information about touch location; other fibres might transmit information about whether the touch has been brief or sustained.

At the level of the *somatosensory cortex,* located in the parietal lobe of the brain, a close connection is found between regions of the skin and representation in the cortex (Prud'homme et al., 1994). As you learned in Chapter 3, the somatosensory cortex contains multiple "body maps," where adjacent cortical cells have areas of sensitivity that correspond to adjacent areas on the skin. Moreover, as in the visual cortex, some areas of the body are represented more elaborately in the somatosensory cortex than others. For example, a relatively large amount of cortical tissue is devoted to the hands and lips, whereas the middle portion of the back, despite its size, receives little representation in the cortex. Maybe that's the reason why we kiss to display intense affection rather than simply pat someone on the back. There's a lot more cortex devoted to the lips than to the back. Recent research suggests that different regions of somatosensory cortex are involved in representing different kinds of touch-related information (e.g., one region represents information about the texture of an object, whereas another represents information about the firmness of that object) (Servos et al., 2001).

People can recognize complex objects through touch. When blindfolded, people show near-perfect identification of common objects (such as toothbrushes and paper clips) after examining them by active touch (Klatzky et al., 1985). Andrea Kilgour and Susan Lederman (2002) of Queen's University showed that people can often identify another person by exploring his or her face with the fingertips. Active skin contact with an object produces not only shape information but information about firmness,

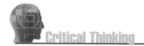

Critical Thinking

Can you tell the difference between the touch of a loved one and the touch of a stranger? If so, how?

Humans use the sense of touch to acquire information about shape, firmness, texture, and weight.

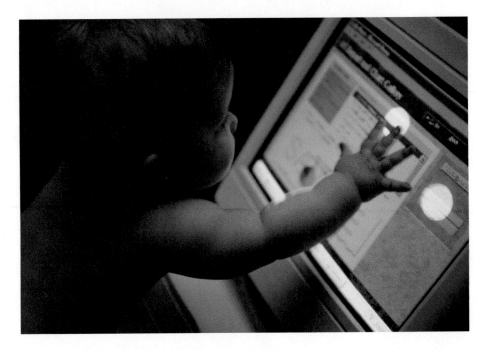

texture, and (if the object is held in the hand) weight. As with seeing and hearing, a person's interpretation of an object depends on a mixture of what the person feels and what he or she expects to feel. For instance, beliefs about objects' weights affect perceptions of weight (Ellis & Lederman, 1998). Similarly, if you expect to be touched by an object on a particular finger, you are more likely to identify the object correctly if it touches that finger than if it touches another (Craig, 1985). There are also changes in blood flow in the somatosensory cortex when a person expects to be touched (Drevets et al., 1995).

Temperature

At present, researchers have only a limited understanding of how the body records and processes the temperature of an object. Electrophysiological research has detected the presence of **cold fibres** that respond to a cooling of the skin by increasing the production of neural impulses, as well as **warm fibres** that respond vigorously when the temperature of the skin increases. But the behaviour of these temperature-sensitive receptor systems is not yet well understood (Zotterman, 1959).

We do know, however, that the perception of warm and cold is only indirectly related to the temperature of the real-world object. To demonstrate, try plunging one hand into a bowl of cold water and the other hand into a bowl of hot water. After 30 seconds, place both hands into a third bowl containing room-temperature water. The hand that was in the cold water will sense the water as warm; the other hand will register it as cool. Same water, same temperature, but two different perceptual experiences. The secret behind this perceptual enigma lies in understanding that it is temperature *change* that determines your perception. When your cold hand touches warmer water, your skin begins to warm; it is the increase in skin temperature that you perceive as warmth.

These perceptual processes can lead to temperature "illusions." For instance, pick up a metal spoon and a wooden spoon. The two are exactly the same temperature, but if that temperature is below body temperature, the metal spoon will feel cooler. Why? Because metal is a better conductor of heat than wood, so it absorbs more warmth from the skin. Consequently, the brain perceives the loss of heat as a cooler physical temperature. Similarly, if both spoons were heated above body temperature, the metal spoon would feel hotter to the touch.

cold fibres
Neurons that respond to a cooling of the skin by increasing the production of neural impulses.

warm fibres
Neurons that respond vigorously when the temperature of the skin increases.

The fact that these people can take a "polar bear swim" in the middle of winter demonstrates that the perception of temperature can be influenced by psychological factors.

Experiencing Pain

Pain is an adaptive reaction that the body generates in response to any stimulus that is intense enough to cause tissue damage. The stimulus can come from outside or inside the body; it does not need to be particularly intense (consider the effect of salt on an open wound). Animals lacking pain sensations rarely live for long.

Little is known about pain receptors in the skin, although cells have been discovered in some animals that react to painful stimuli (such as intense heat) by sending signals to the cortex (Dong et al., 1994). Pain is a complex psychological experience, and it often relies on much more than just a physical stimulus. For example, amputees often report experiencing feelings of itching or pain in the limb they no longer have; clearly such sensations do not arise from receptors in the absent limb, but rather from the central nervous system (Melzack, 1992). At the opposite extreme, there are well-documented examples of soldiers who report little or no pain after receiving serious injuries in battle; the same is true of many individuals entering an emergency room. In addition, some non-Western cultures use rituals that should, from a Western perspective, inflict great pain but apparently do not (Melzack, 1973).

Gate-Control Theory The interplay between the physical and the psychological in pain perception forms the basis for the **gate-control theory** of pain (Melzack & Wall, 1965, 1982). The basic idea is that the neural impulses generated by pain receptors can be blocked, or gated, in the spinal cord by signals produced in the brain. If you've just sliced your finger cutting carrots on the kitchen counter, you would normally feel pain. But if a pan on the stove suddenly starts to smoke, the pain of that cut seems to evaporate while you try to prevent your house from burning down. According to the gate-control theory, the brain can "close the gate" and block pain signals from reaching higher neural centres when it is important to do so.

How is the gating action carried out? The details of the mechanisms are still under investigation, but there appear to be two types of nerve fibres that are responsible for opening and closing the gate. So-called "large" fibres, when stimulated, produce nervous system activity that closes the gate; other "small" fibres, when stimulated, inhibit the effects of the large fibres and open the gate. Presumably, higher-level brain processes can stimulate the large fibres to gate out further processing of pain sensations. External stimulation—such as rubbing or placing ice on a wound—can also stimulate the large fibres, thereby reducing transmission of pain signals to the brain. The details of the neural circuitry remain to be worked out, but the idea of a pain gate that opens and closes remains popular.

pain
An adaptive response by the body to any stimulus that is intense enough to cause tissue damage.

gate-control theory
The idea that neural impulses generated by pain receptors can be blocked, or gated, in the spinal cord by signals produced in the brain.

In addition to gating pain signals, the brain can also control the experience of pain through the release of chemicals called *endorphins* (as we discussed in Chapter 3), which have pain-killing effects similar in some ways to morphine. The release of endorphins is thought to account, in part, for instances in which pain should be experienced but is not. For example, sometimes swallowing a sugar pill can dramatically reduce pain even though there is no physical reason why sugar should be effective (a "placebo" effect). The locus of such effects, and other analgesic procedures such as acupuncture, might lie in the brain's internal production of its own anti-pain medication.

The Kinesthetic Sense

kinesthesia

In perception, the ability to sense the position and movement of one's body parts.

The word **kinesthesia** literally means "movement"; when used in connection with sensation, the term refers to the ability to sense the position and movement of one's body parts. For example, as you reach toward a blossoming flower, feedback from your skin, tendons, muscles, and joints helps you maintain the correct line toward the target. The kinesthetic sense shares many properties with the sense of touch—a variety of receptor types in the muscles that surround the joints react to the physical forces produced by moving the limbs (Gandevia et al., 1992; Verschueven et al., 1998).

The nerve impulses generated by the kinesthetic receptors travel, as in touch, to the somatosensory cortex. It is presumed that at the level of the cortex there are increasingly complex cells that respond only when particular body parts, such as the right arm, are placed in certain positions (Gardner & Costanzo, 1981). But the psychological experience of movement is most likely influenced by multiple factors, as with other kinds of perception (Jones, 1988). The visual system, for example, provides additional feedback about current body position, as does the sense of touch.

The Vestibular Sense

semicircular canals

A receptor system attached to the inner ear that responds to movement and acceleration and to changes in upright posture.

vestibular sacs

Small organs in the inner ear that contain receptors responsible for the sense of balance.

We have another complex receptor system, attached to the cochlea of the inner ear, that responds not only to movement but also to acceleration and changes in upright posture. Each ear contains three small fluid-filled **semicircular canals** that are lined with hair cells similar to those found in the cochlea. If you quickly turn your head toward some object, these hair cells are displaced and nerve impulses signalling acceleration are transmitted throughout the brain. Some of the nerve fibres project to the cortex; others direct inputs toward the eye muscles, so you can accurately adjust your eyes as your head is turning.

The vestibular system is also responsible for the sense of balance. If you tilt your head, or hurtle through a 360-degree loop on a roller coaster, receptor cells located in other inner-ear organs, called **vestibular sacs,** quickly transmit the appropriate orientation information to the brain. Continual disturbance of the semicircular canals or the vestibular sacs can produce dizziness and nausea, as in motion sickness (Lackner & DiZio, 1991). When you were a kid, did you ever spin yourself around and around to experience the subsequent rush of dizziness? Or have you ever spent several hours on a boat on the ocean, and later noticed the apparent heaving of the earth when you returned to walk on land? Both of these examples are aftereffects of prolonged stimulation of the vestibular sense receptors.

The vestibular sense helps people maintain balance by monitoring the position of the body in space.

The absence of gravity experienced by astronauts in a spaceship disables parts of the vestibular system, thereby impairing astronauts' perceptions of their own body movements. One effect is that most astronauts suffer "space sickness" (akin to motion sickness) for the first few days in space. Another consequence is that they experience a variety of interesting perceptual illusions when they first return to earth and the previously disabled aspects of the vestibular system start working again (Young & Shelhamer, 1990).

Test Yourself 4.3

Check your knowledge about the skin and body senses by answering the following multiple-choice questions. (You will find the answers in Appendix B.)

1. Alicia holds her left hand in a bowl of cold water and her right hand in a bowl of hot water. She then transfers both hands to a bowl of room-temperature water. She finds that her left hand now feels warm and her right hand cool. Why?
    a. Cold and hot fibres rebound after continued activity.
    b. It's temperature change that determines perception.
    c. She expects a change; therefore, a change is experienced.
    d. Opponent process cells in the cortex are reacting.
2. According to the gate-control theory, psychological factors can influence the perception of pain by:
    a. channelling pain signals to the occipital lobe.
    b. reducing the supply of endorphins in the body.
    c. blocking pain signals from reaching higher neural centres.
    d. blocking pain receptors from relaying sensory information to the spinal cord.
3. The vestibular sacs contain receptor cells that help us maintain our sense of balance. Where are they located?
    a. in the lateral geniculate nucleus
    b. in the superior colliculus
    c. in the joints and limbs of the body
    d. in the inner ear

THE CHEMICAL SENSES: SMELL AND TASTE

Learning Goals

1. Understand how chemical stimuli lead to neural activity that gives rise to the perception of odours.
2. Learn about the sensory mechanisms that give rise to the perception of the taste or flavour of foods.

WE END OUR REVIEW of the individual sensory systems with the chemical senses, smell and taste. We receive a vast array of stimulation from the environment, but few carry as much emotional impact as chemically based input. You can appreciate the touch from a loving caress or the visual beauty of a sunset, but consider your reaction to the smell of decaying meat or to the taste of milk left too long in the sun. Smells and tastes are enormously adaptive because they possess powerful signalling properties; like other animals, humans learn to avoid the off-odours or bitter tastes typical of noxious substances.

chemoreceptors

Receptor cells that react to molecules in the air or dissolved in liquids, leading to the senses of smell and taste.

The perception of both smell and taste begins with the activity of receptor cells, called **chemoreceptors,** that react to molecules in the air or dissolved in liquids. These receptors solve the translation problem and project the newly formed neural impulses toward the brain. Psychologically, the two senses are related: Anyone who has ever had a cold knows that things "just don't taste right" with a plugged nose. You can demonstrate this for yourself by pinching your nostrils closed, closing your eyes, and trying to taste the difference between an apple and a piece of raw potato. In fact, people can identify a taste far more efficiently if they are also allowed a brief sniff (Mozell et al., 1969). Let's consider each of these chemical senses in more detail.

Smell

olfaction

The sense of smell.

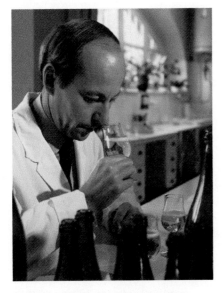

A taster's ability to identify the smell, or "bouquet," of a fine wine depends on the constellation of airborne chemicals produced by the wine, as well as on the experiences of the taster.

The technical name for the sense of smell is **olfaction,** which comes from the Latin word *olfacere,* meaning "to smell." Airborne molecules enter through the nose or the mouth and interact with receptor cells embedded in the upper region of the nasal cavity (Lancet et al., 1993). Like the receptor systems that are used to hear and detect motion, the olfactory receptor cells contain tiny hairs, or *cilia.* The airborne molecules bind with the cilia, causing the generation of a neural impulse. Receptor fibres then send the message forward to the *olfactory bulb,* located at the bottom front region of the brain. From here, the information is sent to several areas in the brain.

People have a thousand or more different kinds of olfactory receptor cells (Buck & Axel, 1991). It's not yet known whether each receptor type plays a special role in the perception of a particular odour, but there's almost certainly no simple one-to-one connection. For one thing, individual olfactory receptor cells are often activated by more than one kind of chemical stimulus. In addition, most odours are complex psychological experiences (Carrasco & Ridout, 1993; Kauer, 1987). People have no problem recognizing the smell of frying bacon or the aroma of fresh coffee, but a chemical analysis of these stimuli fails to reveal the presence of any single defining molecule. Clearly, the ability to apply the label "frying bacon" to a set of airborne chemicals arises from complex perceptual processes. It's even possible to produce smell illusions—if you are led to expect that a particular odour is present, even though it is not, you are likely to report detecting its presence (O'Mahony, 1978).

The neural pathway for smell is somewhat unusual, compared with the other sensory systems that we've discussed, because connections are made with forebrain structures such as the amygdala, the hippocampus, and the hypothalamus (Buck, 1996). As you learned in Chapter 3, these areas have been linked with the regulation of feeding, drinking, sexual behaviour, and even memory. It's speculation, but part of the emotional power of olfactory cues might be related to the involvement of this motivational pathway. Certainly in lower animals, whose behaviour is often dominated by odour cues (e.g., Brown, 1992), brain structures such as the hypothalamus and the amygdala seem to play a major role in the animal's reaction to odours in its environment.

Critical Thinking

Some smells and tastes are truly disgusting and lead to characteristic facial expressions and reactions. Can you think of any adaptive reasons why we might have such reactions?

Many animals release special chemicals, called *pheromones,* that cause highly specific reactions when detected by other members of the species. Often pheromones can provoke sexual behaviour or characteristic patterns of aggression, but a variety of reactions can be produced. Ants, for example, react to the smell of a dead member of the colony by carrying the decaying corpse outside the nest (Wilson, 1963). So far, much to the disappointment of the perfume industry, no solid support has been found for human pheromones; at least, no scents have been discovered that reliably induce sexual interest (although scents can certainly become associated with people who are perceived as arousing).

Taste

gustation

The sense of taste.

Smell's companion sense, taste, is known by the technical term **gustation,** which comes from the Latin *gustare,* meaning "to taste." Most textbooks tell students that there are four basic tastes: sweet, bitter, salty, and sour. Recent research supports the existence of a fifth basic taste, called *umami* (Chaudhari et al., 2000; Halpern, 2002). Umami was

Taste buds, which contain the receptor cells for taste, are embedded within the folds of the papillae (shown here as the large, circular objects).

first proposed by Professor Kikunae Ikeda of Tokyo Imperial University in the early 1900s. Tastes are difficult to describe; the most common term used to describe umami is "savoury." Umami taste is often prominent in Japanese foods (dried seaweed and fish are particularly rich in umami), but cheese and tomatoes also have umami (think of a savoury tomato sauce).

When psychologists use the term *taste,* they are referring to the sensations produced by stimulation of the taste receptors, not to the overall richness of the experience of eating. The term **flavour** is used to describe the complete meal experience. Flavour is influenced by taste, smell, and the visual appearance of the food, as well as by expectations about the quality of the meal.

Taste receptors are distributed throughout the mouth, but mainly occur across the tongue. If you coat your tongue after a sip of milk and glance at it in a mirror, you'll see that your tongue is covered with tiny bumps called *papillae.* The **taste buds,** which contain the receptor cells, are embedded within the folds of the papillae. Many questions remain about how the transduction process for taste occurs. One possibility is that taste stimuli directly penetrate the membrane of the receptor cell, causing the cell to fire; another idea is that taste stimuli alter the chemical structure of the cell membrane without entering the cell itself (Shirley & Persaud, 1990; Teeter & Brand, 1987). In any case, the neural impulse is generated and passed up toward the brain.

Compared to the neural pathway for olfaction, that for taste is more similar to the pathways for vision and audition: Information is passed toward the thalamus and then to the somatosensory area of the cortex (Rolls, 1995). Little work has been done on how cortical taste cells function, although taste-sensitive cells (analogous to visual feature detectors) have been discovered (Scott et al., 1994; Yamamoto et al., 1981). Stronger evidence for taste "tuning" has been found in analyses of the receptor neurons, but a given receptor cell seems to react to a broad range of gustatory stimuli. The neural code for taste is probably determined, to some extent, by the particular receptor cell that happens to react and by the relative patterns of activity across large groups of receptors. For an accessible article on the physiology of taste, see Smith and Margolskee (2001).

The brain can produce stable interpretations of taste stimuli, but the identification process is complex. For one thing, prior exposure to one kind of taste often changes the perception of another. Anyone who has ever had a drink of orange juice after brushing his or her teeth understands how tastes interact. To some extent, the interaction process

flavour

A psychological term used to describe the overall gustatory (eating) experience. Flavour is influenced by taste, smell, the visual appearance of food, and expectations about the food's quality.

taste buds

The receptor cells on the tongue involved in taste.

depends on the similarity of successive tastes. For example, a taste of a sour pickle will reduce the "sourness" of lemon juice, but a taste of salty cracker will not. There are even natural substances that can completely change the normal perception of taste. A substance extracted from berries, called "miracle fruit," turns extremely sour tastes (such as from raw lemons) sweet. Another substance, taken from the leaves of a plant found in India and Africa, temporarily eliminates the sweet taste of sugar. It is also clear that expectations play a profound role in taste perceptions. Have you ever reached for one beverage and accidentally picked up and swallowed another? The discrepancy between your expectation and the taste is experienced as distinctly unpleasant.

Test Yourself 4.4

Check your knowledge about smell and taste by filling in the blanks. Choose the best answer from among the following terms: chemoreceptors; flavour; gustation; hypothalamus; olfaction; olfactory bulb; pheromones; taste; taste buds. (You will find the answers in Appendix B.)

1. The general term for receptor cells that are activated by molecules in the air or dissolved in liquids: _____

2. One of the main brain destinations for odour stimuli: _____

3. A psychological term used to describe the entire gustatory experience: _____

4. The technical name for the sense of smell: _____

5. The technical name for the sense of taste: _____

FROM THE PHYSICAL TO THE PSYCHOLOGICAL

Learning Goals

1. Learn the psychology of stimulus detection, including the technique of signal detection.
2. Learn about difference thresholds and understand Weber's law.
3. Comprehend sensory adaptation and its adaptive value.
4. Understand that perceptual experiences involve the interaction of multiple sensory systems.

THROUGHOUT THIS CHAPTER, you've learned that there is a transition from the physical to the psychological. Sensory stimuli originate in the physical world, but our conscious experiences of those inputs are influenced by expectations and beliefs about how the world is organized. We interpret the physical message, and this means that our conscious experience of the sensory input can be different from the one that is delivered by the environment.

In the field of **psychophysics,** researchers search for mathematical laws that describe the transition from the physical to the psychological. By quantifying the relationship between the physical properties of a stimulus and its subjective experience, psychophysicists hope to develop general laws that apply across all kinds of sensory input. Let's consider some examples of how such laws are established.

psychophysics

A field of psychology in which researchers search for ways to describe the transition from the physical stimulus to the psychological experience of that stimulus.

Stimulus Detection

Psychophysics is one of the oldest research areas in psychology; it dates back to the work of Wilhelm Wundt, Gustav Fechner, and others in the 19th century. One of the first questions these early researchers asked was: What is the minimum amount of

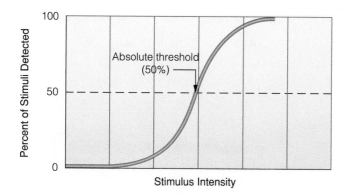

FIGURE 4.25
Absolute Threshold
The more intense the stimulus, the greater the likelihood that it will be detected. The absolute threshold of detection is defined as the intensity level at which the presence of the stimulus can be detected 50% of the time.

stimulus energy needed to produce a sensation? Suppose we present you with a very faint pure tone—so faint that you cannot hear it—and gradually make it louder. At some point you will hear the tone. This point is known as the **absolute threshold** for the stimulus; it represents the level of intensity that lifts the stimulus over the threshold of conscious awareness. One of the early insights of psychophysicists such as Fechner was the realization that absolute thresholds are really *not* absolute; that is, there is no single point in an intensity curve at which detection reliably begins. For a given intensity level, sometimes the person will hear the tone, other times not (the same situation applies to detection in all the sensory modalities, not just auditory). For this reason, absolute threshold is redefined as the intensity level at which a person detects the presence of a stimulus 50% of the time (see Figure 4.25).

It might seem strange that a person's detection abilities change from moment to moment. Part of the reason is that trial-to-trial observations are "noisy," in that they are influenced by all sorts of essentially random factors. It is virtually impossible for a researcher to control all the things that can potentially affect someone's performance. For example, a subject might have a momentary lapse of attention that causes him or her to miss a presented stimulus on a given trial. Some random activity in the nervous system might even create brief changes in the sensitivity of the receptor systems. Experimenters try to take these factors into account by presenting the subject with many detection opportunities and averaging performance over trials to determine the threshold point.

Psychologists have also developed sophisticated statistical techniques to pull the truth out of noisy data. Human observers often have built-in biases that influence how they respond in a detection environment. For example, people will sometimes report the presence of a stimulus even though none has been presented. Why? Sometimes the observer is simply worried about missing a presented stimulus, so he or she says "Yes" on almost every trial. To control for these tendencies, which are called "response biases," researchers use a technique called **signal detection,** which mathematically compares *hits*—in which a stimulus is correctly detected—to *false alarms*—in which the observer claims a stimulus was presented when it was not.

Four types of outcome can occur in a detection situation. Besides hits and false alarms, the subject can also fail to detect a stimulus when it was actually presented—called a *miss*—or correctly decide that a stimulus was not presented—called a *correct rejection*. These four outcomes are shown in Figure 4.26. Take a moment to think through why the names for the four outcomes make sense. Researchers compare the rates of hits and false alarms (over a large number of trials) to infer a subject's true detection ability.

To see why it's important to compare hits and false alarms, imagine that Lois is participating in a simple detection experiment and that her strategy is to say, "Yes, a stimulus occurred" on almost every trial (even when she is not sure that a stimulus was actually presented). If the researcher pays attention only to hits, it will appear as if Lois has almost perfect detection ability—she almost always correctly identifies a stimulus

absolute threshold
The level of intensity that lifts a stimulus over the threshold of conscious awareness; it's defined as the intensity level at which a person detects the presence of the stimulus 50% of the time.

signal detection
A technique that can be used to determine an individual's ability to detect the presence of a stimulus and to measure the individual's response bias.

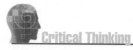

Critical Thinking

Can you think of any occupations requiring detection—such as air traffic controller—in which it might be advantageous to be biased toward saying "Yes" that a stimulus has occurred?

FIGURE 4.26

Signal Detection Outcomes

There are four possible outcomes in each trial of a signal detection experiment. If the stimulus is present and correctly detected, it's called a *hit;* if the stimulus is absent but the observer claims it's present, it's a *false alarm.* A *miss* is when the stimulus is present but not detected, and a *correct rejection* is when the observer correctly decides that the stimulus was not presented.

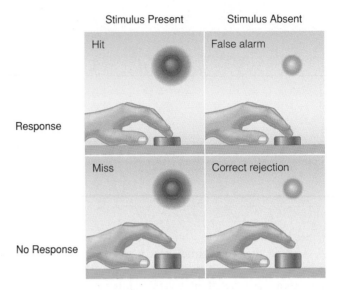

when it occurs. But saying "Yes" on every trial will also lead to lots of false alarms: She will often say "Yes" on trials when no stimulus was actually presented. By comparing hits and false alarms, the researcher is able to determine whether her high number of "hits" is really due to detection ability or to a strategic bias on her part. If Lois can truly detect the stimulus when it occurs, she should show lots of hits and very few false alarms (for an in-depth review of signal detection theory, see Macmillan & Creelman, 1991).

Difference Thresholds

difference threshold

The smallest difference in the magnitude of two stimuli that an observer can reliably detect.

Researchers in psychophysics have also been concerned with the measurement of **difference thresholds:** the smallest difference in the magnitude of two stimuli that an observer can detect. Suppose we present you with two tones in immediate succession, each equally loud. We then gradually increase the intensity of one of the tones until you notice it as being louder than the other (called the *standard*). How much of a change in magnitude do we need to make for you to detect the difference? As with absolute thresholds, the required amount changes slightly from one moment to the next, but an important general principle emerges.

It turns out that detection of a *just noticeable difference* (or *jnd*) in magnitude depends on how intense the standard was in the first place. If you're at a rock concert and your friend Gillian wants to tell you something, she needs to yell; if you're in a library, a whisper will do. We can state this relationship more formally as follows: The jnd for stimulus magnitude is a constant proportion of the magnitude of the standard stimulus. In other words, the louder the standard stimulus, the more volume will need to be added (or subtracted) before a difference in loudness will be detected. This general relationship, called **Weber's law,** works not only for loudness; it applies across all the sensory systems. If the lights in your house go off, lighting a candle will make a big difference; if the lights are on, the addition of a candle will lead to little, if any, noticeable increase in brightness (even though the candle emits the same amount of light in both situations). Weber's law demonstrates once again that the relationship between the physical and the psychological is not always direct: Increases in the magnitude of a physical stimulus will not always lead to increases in the psychological experience.

Weber's law

The principle stating that the ability to notice a difference in the magnitude of two stimuli is a constant proportion of the intensity of the standard stimulus. Psychologically, the more intense a stimulus is to begin with, the more intense it will need to become for a person to notice a difference.

Sensory Adaptation

Another feature of all sensory systems also interested early researchers in psychophysics. Sensory systems are more sensitive to a particular kind of input when it

Burning candles in a brightly lit room would have little effect on perceived brightness (left photo); but lighting candles in a dimly lit room (right photo) would noticeably increase brightness.

first occurs than to its continued presence. Through **sensory adaptation,** the body quickly adapts, by reducing sensitivity, to input that remains constant—such as the feel of a shirtsleeve on your forearm or the hum of computers in the background. Think about what the world would be like without sensory adaptation. The water in the pool would never seem to warm up; the slightly musty smell of your friend's basement apartment would remain a pervasive force throughout your visit; you would be constantly reminded of the texture of your socks pressing on your ankles.

Adaptation is a feature of each of the sensory systems. Images that remain stable on the retina vanish after awhile; this doesn't normally occur because the eyes are constantly moving and refreshing the retinal image. Our sensitivity to many odours decreases by 70% over the course of a few minutes of exposure (one of the reasons your neighbour is probably not aware of his or her own BO!). If you are presented with a continuous tone, your perception of its loudness decreases over time (Evans, 1982). Sensory systems evolved to detect changes in the incoming input; sensitivity is reduced to those aspects of the input that remain the same, perhaps because they are not telling us anything new.

sensory adaptation
The tendency of sensory systems to reduce sensitivity to a stimulus that remains constant.

Interactions between Sensory Systems

In this chapter we've mostly considered the sensory systems one by one, in isolation, but in everyday life they act together. Within a particular sensory system, the components of a stimulus (such as the shape and colour of a visual object) are picked out of the input and ultimately integrated (e.g., so that you see shape and colour as different aspects of the same visual object). Similarly, the internal representations of different sensory systems are also integrated, giving rise to a multifaceted but coherent perceptual experience. For example, you experience the smell, appearance, and texture of a pizza simultaneously as attributes of the same object.

It's not just that we see things at the same time as we are hearing, smelling, or feeling them, but also that the operations of different sensory systems influence one another. For example, we mentioned earlier that the flavour of food arises from a complex interaction of the taste, aroma, texture, and appearance of the food, together with higher-level psychological and social processes (such as expectations and mood). The same pizza that is delicious in one situation may be distasteful in another, partly because of interactions between different sensory systems.

Multiple sensory systems, such as audition and vision, often work together to help us localize and identify objects in the environment. For example, sounds and other sensations often capture our attention, leading us to direct our visual receptors toward some interesting object. As mentioned previously, even newborn infants look toward unexpected sounds. (Interestingly, studies at Queen's University by Symons et al., 1998, found that 21-month-old babies are very sensitive to small shifts in adults' gazes, as though they realize that shifts of gaze reveal shifts of attention.) Even if no eye movements are required, sounds can be used to facilitate visual processing. For example, it is easier to detect a briefly presented visual stimulus if its onset is accompanied by a sound (McDonald & Ward, 2000; Woods et al., 1998).

We benefit from interactions between sensory modalities, but they also sometimes produce illusions. For example, objects that look heavy tend to be perceived as weighing more than they really do (Ellis & Lederman, 1999). Similarly, misleading visual cues can produce an astonishingly vivid illusion of motion (you may have had the experience of sitting in a stopped car when a car beside yours rolls backward a few metres, giving you the illusion that your car is moving forward) (Telford & Frost, 1993). A related phenomenon can occur when people use "virtual reality" systems. In a driving simulator, for example, the visual, auditory, and kinesthetic sensory systems receive information that indicates that the driver is moving (accelerating, braking, turning) but the vestibular system is not receiving the stimulation that it would if the driver's body really was moving through space, and that incompatibility can make the person in the simulator feel nauseated (you may have experienced a weaker reaction of this sort from playing video games).

A small proportion of people experience a phenomenon called synesthesia. Synesthesia occurs when a perceptual experience triggered by one kind of sensory processing is also accompanied by a perceptual experience associated with a different sensory system (e.g., sounds might be experienced as having colours as well as auditory properties). A synesthete known as C, for example, perceives digits as having colours (e.g., C reports that a black digit 9 looks orange, whereas 3 looks purple) (Dixon et al., 2000).

Your everyday perceptual experiences of the world around you arise through interactions of the various sensory systems. Each sense is an exquisitely complex and sophisticated system that has evolved to create rich and vivid internal representations of reality, in ways that are consistent with prior experiences and beliefs. These systems sometimes err, but for the most part they serve us well.

Test Yourself 4.5

Check your understanding of psychophysics by deciding whether each of the following statements is true or false. (You will find the answers in Appendix B.)

1. The intensity level that is required to barely perceive a stimulus varies across individuals, but remains constant for any given individual. *True or False?*
2. A "false alarm" occurs in signal detection when an observer claims a signal was present when, in fact, it was not. *True or False?*
3. According to Weber's law, the detection of a just noticeable difference (jnd) in magnitude is constant across all intensity levels. *True or False?*
4. Sensory adaptation is a characteristic of all sensory systems. *True or False?*
5. Sensory systems interact with one another, such that the operation of one system can be altered by that of another. *True or False?*

Solving the Adaptive Problems

To interact successfully with the world, and to experience its richness, we rely on multiple sensory systems. The external world bombards the body with complex and ever-changing physical stimuli, but none arrives in the same form as the electrochemical neuronal language of the brain. Thus, the body faces three fundamental problems of adaptation: How can the external input be translated into the internal language of the nervous system? How do the elementary components get extracted from the input? Finally, how does the brain build a stable and meaningful interpretation of the input components once they've been extracted?

First, how does the external input from the environment get translated into the language of the nervous system? To solve the translation problem, the body relies on specialized receptor cells that transduce particular forms of physical energy input into neural impulses. In the visual system, receptor cells—rods and cones—react to light; in the auditory system, sound energy leads to movement of the basilar membrane, which in turn causes tiny hair cells to generate neural impulses. Other specialized receptors react to pressure on the skin, free-floating chemicals in the air, and the relative position or movement of the body. Each of these receptor systems acts as a "translator," changing the input delivered by the external world into the electrochemical language of the nervous system.

Second, how are the elementary components—the sensations—extracted from the input? Once translated, the initial neural coding of the sensory input receives further processing in the brain to extract the components. A variety of neural pathways are specialized to process particular kinds of sensory information. For example, opponent process cells in the lateral geniculate region of the brain are specialized to process colour; they signal the presence of one kind of colour by increasing the rate at which they generate neural impulses, and they signal another kind of colour by decreasing their firing rate. Similarly, highly specialized cells in the visual cortex respond only to particular patterns of light and dark on the retina. One kind of cell might respond only to a bar of light presented at a particular orientation; another cell might respond only to a pattern of light that moves in a particular direction across the retina.

In the auditory cortex, the brain extracts information about the frequencies and amplitudes of sound in an auditory message. Psychologically, changes in frequency correspond to changes in perceived pitch, whereas changes in amplitude are experienced as variations in loudness. The brain detects frequency information by noting the particular place on the basilar membrane where hair cells are stimulated and by noting the rate at which neural impulses are generated over time.

The brain often relies on multiple kinds of processing to extract a particular component or aspect of a stimulus. The perception of colour, for instance, relies not only on opponent process cells but also on the relative activations of three different cone types that reside in the retina.

Third, how does the brain build and maintain a meaningful interpretation of these component sensations once they've been extracted? To establish a coherent, stable, meaningful interpretation of sensory input, people use a combination of bottom-up and top-down processing—beliefs and expectations work with the sensory input to create perceptions of the external world. The fact that people are able to maintain a stable perception of objects and actions in the world is really quite a remarkable accomplishment. As we noted at the beginning of the chapter, the pattern of light reflected from a moving object changes continuously with time, yet you perceive it as the same object with the same properties. You can also recognize the voice of a friend in a crowded room, even though the auditory input reaching your ears also includes sound information from many different voices.

The brain solves the problems of perception, in part, by relying on organizational "rules." For example, we are born with built-in tendencies to group input components in particular ways. Figures are separated from ground, items that share physical properties are perceived together, and so on. But we also rely on prior knowledge for help in the interpretation process. The perceptual systems use knowledge about how cues are related in the environment to arrive at sensible interpretations of ambiguous objects. For instance, if two parallel lines converge in the visual field, the brain assumes that the lines are stretching off into the distance. Such top-down processing is usually extremely adaptive—it helps us maintain a stable interpretation—although in some cases, these same top-down processes can lead to perceptual illusions.

Chapter Summary

VISION: CREATING A WORLD OF MEANINGFUL OBJECTS

To understand vision, it's necessary to understand how the physical input—light—is translated into the language of the brain. What pathways in the brain are used to extract the basic components of the visual input? How does the brain create a stable, meaningful interpretation?

Translating the Input: Visual Transduction

Learning Goal: Learn how light gets translated into the electrochemical language of the brain. Light is classified by two main physical properties: *wavelength* and *intensity*. Light reflected from an object passes through the *cornea,* and then through the *pupil* (the middle of the *iris*). The *lens* undergoes accommodation, focusing the incoming light onto a thin layer of tissue on the inside of the back of the eye, the *retina.* The visual receptors (rods and cones) are located here. The rods are more light sensitive but less able to detect fine details, are located primarily in the periphery of the retina, and are useful at low levels of illumination. The cones are concentrated in the centre of the retina (in the *fovea*), need more light to operate, and are responsible for processing fine detail and colour. *Bipolar* and *ganglion* cells process the activity of the receptor cells and send it to the brain through the *optic nerve.*

Extracting the Input Components: Visual Pathways

Learning Goal: Grasp how the essential features of the visual input, such as colour, are extracted by the brain. From the retina, patterns of activation flow to the *optic chiasm,* after which most of the incoming visual neurons project to a relay station in the thalamus, the *lateral geniculate nucleus.* Many processing activities are carried out simultaneously, through *parallel processing.* In the visual cortex, feature detectors respond to particular aspects of a stimulus, such as orientation and patterns of light and dark. The *trichromatic theory* of colour vision proposes that colour information is extracted through the activation of three different types of cones. The *opponent process theory* proposes mechanisms in the visual system that respond positively to one colour type and negatively to others. Both theories account for certain aspects of colour vision.

Producing Stable and Meaningful Interpretations: Visual Perception

Learning Goal: Understand how a stable, meaningful interpretation of visual information is created and why the interpretation process sometimes leads to visual illusions. Perception involves both *bottom-up* processing (which starts with the physical input) and *top-down* processing (application of knowledge and expectation). People have a natural tendency to group incoming visual inputs according to *Gestalt principles of organization,* which include the laws of *proximity, similarity, closure,* and *good continuation.* Depth is perceived with the aid of *monocular depth cues* (such as *linear perspective, texture gradients,* and the bias to perceive the *lower region* of a scene as the figure rather than ground) and *binocular depth cues* (such as *convergence* and *retinal disparity*). Visual perception also demonstrates perceptual constancy; perceived properties (such as size) remain the same even when the physical input to the eye changes. *Perceptual illusions* are inappropriate interpretations of physical reality.

HEARING: IDENTIFYING AND LOCALIZING SOUNDS

Hearing enriches our lives, and like vision, it serves a variety of adaptive functions. Sound helps us identify and locate objects in the environment. It allows us to produce and comprehend the spoken word. Even our private self often appears in the form of an inner voice.

Translating the Input: Auditory Transduction

Learning Goal: Understand how physical sound input is translated into the electrochemical language of the brain. The auditory system receives *sound,* which is composed of waves of energy (moving through a medium such as air) that vary in *frequency* and *amplitude.* Sound is funnelled by the *pinna* into the auditory canal and travels through the *tympanic membrane,* which it causes to vibrate. Vibration of the tympanic membrane causes patterns of movement to be transmitted through the three tiny bones in the *middle ear,* which in turn transmit the signal to the *cochlea* in the inner ear. Vibrations propagating through the fluid in the cochlea displace the *basilar membrane,* which causes auditory receptors (*cilia,* or *hair cells*) to be activated.

Extracting the Input Components: Auditory Pathways

Learning Goal: Learn how pitch information is pulled out of the auditory input. According to the *place theory* of pitch perception, we hear a particular pitch because certain hair cells are responding actively. According to *frequency theory,* pitch is determined in part by the frequency of neural impulses travelling up the auditory pathway. Both theories explain aspects of pitch perception. Final processing of the input occurs in the *auditory cortex* of the brain.

Producing Stable and Meaningful Interpretations: Auditory Perception

Learning Goal: Comprehend how the auditory input is

interpreted to localize the source of a sound. Prior knowledge helps the brain organize and impose structure on incoming sound input. *Sound localization* involves comparisons between the auditory stimuli reaching the ears (arrival time and intensity).

THE SKIN AND BODY SENSES: EXPERIENCING TOUCH, TEMPERATURE, PAIN, AND MOVEMENT

Although perceptual experiences seem to be driven primarily by seeing and hearing, sensory receptors in the skin and other parts of the body are also extremely important, allowing us to experience touch, temperature, pain, and movement.

Touch

Learning Goal: Understand how touch information is translated and interpreted within the brain. There are several types of pressure-sensitive receptors in the skin. Touch information is transmitted through distinct channels to processing stations in the brain. There, the somatosensory cortex (in the *parietal lobe*) further processes the input.

Temperature

Learning Goal: Learn how sensory receptors in the skin code information about temperature, and understand the basis of the subjective experience of temperature perception. *Cold fibres* respond to cooling of the skin by increasing the production of neural impulses; *warm fibres* respond vigorously when the temperature of the skin increases. Temperature change determines temperature perception.

Experiencing Pain

Learning Goal: Know how we perceive and interpret pain. *Pain* is an adaptive reaction that the body generates in response to any stimulus intense enough to cause tissue damage. According to the *gate-control theory* of pain, neural impulses generated by pain receptors are gated in the spinal cord by signals produced by the brain; the brain can block critical signals from reaching higher neural centres when appropriate. The brain also controls the experience of pain through the release of chemicals called *endorphins,* which produce morphine-like effects.

The Kinesthetic Sense

Learning Goal: Understand the sensory systems that give rise to (nonvisual) awareness of the position and movement of parts of your body (e.g., your arms). *Kinesthesia* refers to the ability to sense the position and movement of one's body

parts. Nerve impulses generated by kinesthetic receptors travel to the somatosensory cortex.

The Vestibular Sense

Learning Goal: Learn about the sensory systems that underlie the perception of the movement of your body through space. The *vestibular sense* responds to movement, acceleration, and changes in posture. Each ear contains fluid-filled *semicircular canals* that help us detect the position of the head: When your head moves, fluid within these structures moves, triggering action potentials in receptor cells. The *vestibular sacs,* also in the inner ear, are primarily responsible for our sense of balance.

THE CHEMICAL SENSES: SMELL AND TASTE

Smells and tastes are adaptive because they possess powerful signalling properties; like other animals, humans learn to avoid bad odours and very bitter tastes. The perception of smell and taste begins with *chemoreceptors*.

Smell

Learning Goal: Understand how chemical stimuli lead to neural activity that gives rise to the perception of odours. *Olfaction* occurs as airborne molecules enter the nose or mouth and interact with receptors in the nasal cavity. The input travels to the olfactory bulb in the brain. People have up to 1000 different types of olfactory receptor cells. Many animals release *pheromones,* chemicals that cause highly specific (often sexual) reactions when detected by other members of a species.

Taste

Learning Goal: Learn about the sensory mechanisms that give rise to the perception of the taste or flavour of foods. *Gustation* is smell's companion sense. There are at least four basic tastes: sweet, salty, bitter, and sour; recent evidence supports the existence of a fifth basic taste, called *umami* (savoury). *Taste buds* containing the taste receptors are embedded within *papillae* (tiny bumps) on the tongue. Neural codes representing taste stimuli travel toward the thalamus and then to the somatosensory area of the cortex.

FROM THE PHYSICAL TO THE PSYCHOLOGICAL

Sensory stimuli originate in the physical world, but our conscious experience of them is also influenced by expectations and beliefs about how the world is organized. In the field of *psychophysics,* researchers try to describe the transition from the physical to the psychological in the form of mathematical laws.

Stimulus Detection

Learning Goal: Learn the psychology of stimulus detection, including the technique of signal detection. The *absolute threshold* for a stimulus is the level of intensity that lifts it over the threshold of conscious awareness. *Threshold* is defined as the intensity level at which a person can detect the presence of a stimulus 50% of the time. To account for response biases, researchers developed a technique known as *signal detection* that mathematically compares *hits* to *false alarms*.

Difference Thresholds

Learning Goal: Learn about difference thresholds and understand Weber's law. A *difference threshold* is the smallest difference in the magnitude of two stimuli that an observer can detect. Detection of a *just noticeable difference (jnd)* between two stimuli depends on the intensity of the standard stimulus. According to *Weber's law*, the jnd for stimulus magnitude is a constant proportion of the intensity of the standard stimulus.

Sensory Adaptation

Learning Goal: Comprehend sensory adaptation and its adaptive value. One important adaptive function of sensory systems is sensory adaptation, through which the body quickly adapts to a stimulus by reducing sensitivity to input that remains constant, such as the feel of a shirtsleeve on your arm.

Interactions between Sensory Systems

Learning Goal: Understand that perceptual experiences involve the interaction of multiple sensory systems. In everyday life, perceptual experience reflects the interactive operation of numerous sensory systems; messages processed by one system (e.g., vision) often influence the simultaneous operation of other systems (e.g., olfaction and gustation).

Terms to Remember

Recommended Readings

Goldstein, E. B. (1999). *Sensation and perception* (5th ed.). Pacific Grove, CA: Brooks/Cole. This is an excellent undergraduate textbook filled with interesting demonstrations. It covers most of the material presented in Chapter 4, but in much greater depth.

Shepard, R. N. (1990). *Mind sights*. New York: W. H. Freeman. This provocative book is full of wonderfully original visual tricks and illusions. Accompanying the drawings are concise scientific explanations of the illusions. The two "monsters" shown in Figure 4.22(b) come from this book.

Ramachandran, V. S. (1992). Filling gaps in perception: I. *Current Directions in Psychological Science 1*, 199–205. This article, written for a general audience, describes fascinating research on how the visual system "fills in" information in the blind spot, along with numerous demonstrations of this filling-in phenomenon (and its limits).

 For additional readings, explore InfoTrac® College Edition, your online library. Go to:

www.adaptivemind2e.nelson.com

Hint: enter the search terms: motor development; cognitive development; moral development; psychosocial development; death and dying.

What's on the Web?

Please note that Web addresses are subject to change. Check out the accompanying Web site for updates: www.adaptivemind2e.nelson.com. This site presents practice quiz questions, hypercontent, information on degrees and careers in psychology, study tips, and more.

Cow's Eye Dissection

www.exploratorium.edu/learning_studio/cow_eye

Yes, you read that right. This site, part of the wonderful Exploratorium site, provides you with the opportunity to dissect the eye of a cow online—it turns out there's a fair amount of similarity between our eyes and a cow's eyes. A fun way to find out more about the eye.

Illusionworks

psylux.psych.tu-dresden.de/i1/kaw/diverses%20Material/ www.illusionworks.com/

Nothing's quite as fascinating as visual illusions. They're fun to look at and intriguing to learn about. This superb site, winner of numerous awards, presents a variety of visual illusions and interesting and informative explanations of the processes that are responsible.

Seeing, Hearing, and Smelling the World

www.hhmi.org/senses

While many Web sites enable you to learn more about vision, relatively few are devoted to the other major senses. This site allows you to investigate these more "neglected" senses, with articles such as "A Secret Sense in the Human Nose?" and "Locating a Mouse by Its Sound."

H.E.A.R (Hearing Education and Awareness for Rockers)

www.hearnet.com

In addition to lots of information about the relationship between loud music and hearing damage (including inside info about musicians who wear earplugs and those who wish they had because they're now partially deaf), this site includes a simple way to test the effect of a night in a club on your own hearing.

Mondegreens

www.kissthisguy.com

Mondegreens are misperceptions of song lyrics, as in the "kiss the sky/kiss this guy" example discussed on page 152. This fun site is an archive of hundreds of anecdotal accounts of these perceptual errors, such as the man who thought the Rolling Stones were singing "I'll never be your big Suburban" (instead of "beast of burden"). Another one is a woman who misheard the line "the girl with kaleidoscope eyes" (from "Lucy in the Sky with Diamonds" by the Beatles) as "the girl with colitis goes by."

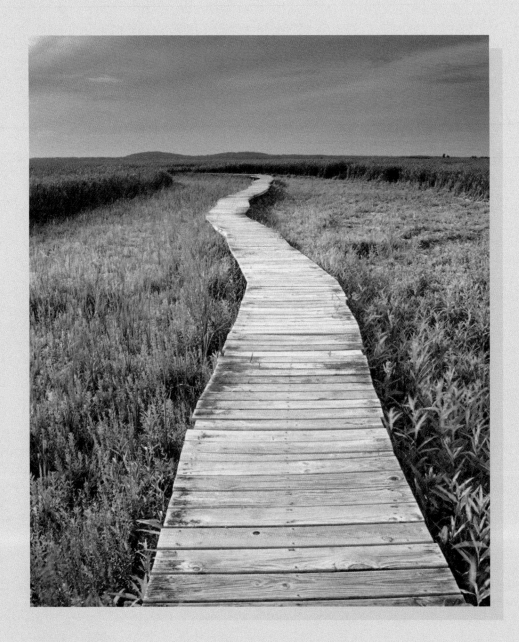

*When asked the question, what is consciousness? we become
conscious of consciousness. And most of us take this consciousness of
consciousness to be what consciousness is. This is not true....
Consciousness is a much smaller part of our mental life than we are
conscious of, because we cannot be conscious of what we are not
conscious of.*
Julian Jaynes, 1976

Chapter 5   Consciousness

Stop for a moment and take a look inside your own head. Just let your thoughts go, and see where they take you. Pay attention to the movement from thought to thought to thought. Notice the transitions, the way that ideas and feelings and images spring forth, only to disappear a moment later, replaced by new thoughts. Does your "stream of consciousness" (James, 1890) flow smoothly and steadily along a single coherent line or thought, or do you find the content of your mental states to shift sharply, thinking about psychology one moment, then focusing briefly on the discomfort of the chair in which you are sitting, then shifting to thoughts of food before being grabbed by some interesting noise?

Studying the characteristics of **consciousness,** which can crudely be defined as our subjective awareness of internal and external events, was one of the main jobs of psychologists in the 19th century. In fact, if you had taken a psychology course at the turn of the last century, the subject matter would likely have been defined as "the science which describes and explains the phenomena of consciousness" (Ladd, 1896, p. 1). At that time, the main research technique for studying psychology was introspection, in which research subjects were asked to look inward and report on their own internal thoughts. With the rise of behaviourism, however, psychologists shifted away from the study of internal experience toward an emphasis on behaviour. Techniques such as introspection fell strongly out of favour. Most psychologists became convinced that internal observations were difficult, if not impossible, to confirm objectively. Behaviourists argued forcefully that "psychology must discard all reference to consciousness" (Watson, 1913, p. 163) because it is impossible to measure conscious experience directly and objectively.

It's easy to understand why the behaviourists were dissatisfied with the study of internal subjective experience. Turning inward and asking questions about the contents of consciousness is "like asking a flashlight in a dark room to search around for

consciousness
The subjective awareness of internal and external events.

Technologies such as ERP, shown here, are providing psychologists with a "window" through which the internal activities of the brain can be observed, but we do not yet know how electrochemical activity gives rise to consciousness.

174

Previewing the Adaptive Problems

Consciousness can be defined as the subjective awareness of internal and external events. But what does it mean to be aware? Intuitively, everyone has a reasonably good idea of what the term means. To be aware is to experience the here and now, to re-experience the past in the form of memories, to think and feel internally and create a "view of the world" (Klatzky, 1984). Awareness has the additional property that it can be focused: You can choose to attend to that bug walking up the page of your text, to the beautiful sunset outside your window, or to the voice of your roommate talking on the phone. You can also be consciously aware of developing strategies for future behaviour; you can think about what you want to say or do, and you can imagine the outcomes of those actions without actually performing them. You can also consciously imagine the content of other minds—and hence predict the behaviour of other people and understand (or at least think you understand) their motivations (Nickerson, 1999; Weiskrantz, 1992).

Despite the importance of consciousness, many human actions are controlled by processes that operate without awareness. To take an extreme case, you're not aware of the processes controlling your heartbeat or (usually) your breathing rate, yet these functions carry on like clockwork in the body. You also lack awareness of many basic cognitive processes, such as the perceptual processes described in Chapter 4. (For example, your brain is doing a phenomenal amount of sophisticated work to read the words on this page. You are probably aware that you are reading, but you lack awareness of the basic processes that are separating the black marks from the white background of the paper, identifying the letters and words, etc.) As you'll see later in this chapter, the brain can accomplish a lot without conscious awareness.

Your awareness also takes on different properties when you sleep, when you're hypnotized, when you take certain types of drugs, or when you are in different social settings or moods. As you'll see later in the chapter, altering awareness can help people solve certain adaptive problems. For a visual summary of the problems that will be addressed in this chapter, take a look at Figure 5.1.

First, how do people set priorities for mental functioning? There are limits to the number of things that a person can think about at the same time and to the number of tasks that can be performed simultaneously. Have you ever tried to solve a difficult thought problem while someone talks nearby? Obviously, it's critical for people to be selective about what they focus on. How do we set those priorities from moment to moment, and what mechanisms enable us to focus mental processing on some tasks or stimuli while ignoring others?

Second, what roles do sleep and dreaming play for the adaptive mind? Sleep clearly serves an adaptive function, as does dreaming. Some researchers believe that we sleep in order to give the brain a chance to rest and restore itself from the day's activities. Others believe that sleep protects us during periods when our sensory equipment is likely to function poorly (such as at night). Dreaming, *(continued)*

FIGURE 5.1
Adaptive Problems of Consciousness
Here are the four adaptive problems that we consider in this chapter.

Setting priorities for mental functioning

Sleeping and dreaming

Altering awareness:
Psychoactive drugs

Altering awareness:
Induced states

with its sometimes bizarre imagery, may help us work out hidden conflicts, or it may simply exercise the neural circuitry of the brain.

Third, how do certain chemicals, or drugs, produce profound alterations in awareness? You probably know about the mind-bending alterations of consciousness that are produced by

psychoactive drugs, such as LSD or mescaline. What you may not know, however, is that the biological processes that produce those effects are natural and important ingredients of the adaptive mind. Psychoactive drugs can have long-lasting harmful consequences, but it's important to understand that artificial drugs operate, in part, by tapping natural adaptive systems.

Fourth, what happens under hypnosis and meditation, two other techniques

that seem to alter awareness? Hypnosis is a social interaction that induces a heightened state of suggestibility in a willing subject. How can it serve an adaptive purpose? Well, for one thing, hypnosis can dramatically reduce the experience of pain (e.g., during dental treatments). Similarly, meditation may reduce stress and anxiety. Thus, you'll discover that both hypnosis and meditation can have adaptive benefits.

something that doesn't have any light shining upon it. The flashlight, since there is light in whatever direction it turns, would have to conclude that there is light everywhere" (Jaynes, 1976, p. 23). William James, too, was aware of the inherent difficulty of introspectively analyzing consciousness. He wrote: "The attempt at introspective analysis ... is ... like seizing a spinning top to catch its motion, or trying to turn up the gas quickly enough to see how the darkness looks." It's tough to study the properties of something when your only tool of discovery is the object itself!

In recent decades, however, the study of consciousness has emerged from its intellectual Dark Age and has regained a measure of respectability (Cohen & Schooler, 1997; Milner & Rugg, 1992). One major contributor to the renewed interest in the scientific study of consciousness was the development by cognitive psychologists in the 1950s and 1960s of clever experimental procedures that enable researchers to test hypotheses about the nature of mental events (e.g., Broadbent, 1952; Brooks, 1968; Miller, 1956; Sperling, 1960). Examples of such procedures will be described later, but for now the point to appreciate is that they provide an alternative to introspection: Rather than asking participants to report on their own mental events, cognitive psychologists can make strong inferences about participants' mental processes by objectively measuring performance in such experiments.

Another contributing factor to the re-emergence of scientific studies of consciousness has been the development of technologies such as the electroencephalograph (EEG) and positron emission tomography (PET) (see Chapter 3). These devices provide a window into the activities of the living brain, enabling researchers to measure how internal activity changes over time. Most neuroscientists are convinced that consciousness is linked directly to patterns of neural activity in the brain, although the biological basis of consciousness is not yet known (Revonsuo, 2001; van Loocke, 2001) and the interpretation of data from EEGs and PET scans is not as straightforward as is sometimes implied (Bub, 2000). Nonetheless, as our tools of discovery have broadened, psychologists' willingness to explore the workings of the inner world of the mind has increased.

SETTING PRIORITIES FOR MENTAL FUNCTIONING: ATTENTION

Learning Goals

1. Learn how experiments on dichotic listening can be used to study attention.
2. Understand the concept of "automaticity."

3. Learn about attention disorders such as visual neglect and attention deficit/hyperactivity disorder.

4. Understand research on the influence of subliminal messages.

AS YOU LEARNED IN CHAPTER 4, the world is a teeming smorgasbord of sensory information, offering an astonishing variety of sensory input. You don't consciously experience every stimulus at any given time; you sample selectively from the table, based partly on your current interests and needs. If you're searching desperately for a child lost in a shopping mall, you focus on the familiar sound of the child's voice or the colour of his or her shirt, and largely ignore other stimuli, such as the items displayed for sale. If you're trying to determine what's for dinner tonight, you sniff the air for the smell of cooking pot roast or simmering spaghetti sauce, selecting food aromas from the other scents stimulating your olfactory receptors. You tend to notice those things that are important to the task at hand, selecting them from the vast array of stimuli in the environment.

Psychologists use the term **attention** to refer to the internal processes people use to set and follow priorities for mental functioning. For adaptive reasons, the brain uses attention to focus selectively on certain parts of the environment while largely ignoring others. Obviously, the concepts of attention and consciousness are closely linked—you are consciously aware of only those things that receive some measure of attention. But why is attention selective? One reason is that any individual's mental resources are limited: Given the particular cognitive skills (both conscious and unconscious) that a person has developed, he or she will be limited in the number and kinds of cognitive tasks that can be performed simultaneously (Spelke et al., 1976). Furthermore, some cognitive psychologists believe that certain kinds of cognitive operations can only be performed one at a time, which would prevent us from performing those operations on different stimuli simultaneously (e.g., Pashler, 1992; Shapiro & Raymond, 1994). These limitations require us to make choices about which parts of the environment to process deeply and extensively (Broadbent, 1958; Kahneman, 1973).

Even if mental resources were unlimited, it would still be in our interest to select information that is relevant to our goals. In a mystery novel, certain events are relevant clues for solving the murder and others are "red herrings," irrelevant points that lead the reader in the wrong direction and delay solving the crime. The trick is to be selective in deciding which components are worth selecting for focused attention. A first-rate detective knows not only what to look for, but also what information to avoid. The same is true for even the simplest kind of action, such as walking across the room or reaching for a cup. The visual and motor systems must focus on the objects in the person's *path*, not every object in the room. If you tried to focus on and think about everything in the environment, you would suffer interference from irrelevant input. Prioritizing mental functioning is an important part of the coordination and control of human action (Allport, 1989).

Experiments on Attention: Dichotic Listening

Experiments on attention began in the 1950s with the development of the **dichotic listening** technique (Broadbent, 1952; Cherry, 1953). As shown in Figure 5.2, in a dichotic listening experiment subjects are exposed to two messages spoken simultaneously, each presented to one ear through headphones. To promote selective attention, the subject is asked to "shadow," or repeat aloud, one of the two messages as it goes along while essentially ignoring the other. This kind of listening is called *dichotic*, meaning "divided into two," because two messages are involved, delivered separately into each of the two ears.

A dichotic listening experiment requires the subject to listen to two voices at the same time. Have you ever tried to listen to a lecture while someone next to you is filling you in on the details of his or her latest escapade? Not an easy task. In fact, you may

attention
The internal processes people use to set and follow priorities for mental functioning.

Critical Thinking

Can you think of any circumstances in which your brain attends to things that you are not aware of?

dichotic listening
A technique in which two different auditory messages are simultaneously presented, one to each ear. Usually the subject's task is to shadow, or repeat aloud, one of the messages as it goes along while ignoring the other.

FIGURE 5.2
Dichotic Listening Technique

In dichotic listening, two different spoken messages are presented simultaneously, one to each ear; usually the subject is required to shadow—or repeat aloud—one of the messages while ignoring the other. The task taps the ability to *attend selectively*.

Shadowed channel:
"Emily Carr was known for her eccentricity as well as for her art...."

Nonshadowed channel:
"When asked the question, 'what is consciousness?' we become conscious of consciousness...."

"Emily Carr ... was known for her ... ah ... eccentricity as well as for her art...."

cocktail party effect
The ability to focus on one auditory message, such as a friend's voice at a noisy party, and largely ignore others, yet notice when one's name is spoken among the auditory stimuli that one has been "ignoring."

have found yourself either ignoring one of the two or switching back and forth from one message to the other. This is essentially what happens in a dichotic listening experiment. Subjects attend selectively on the to-be-shadowed message, based on both the spatial location and the sound qualities of that message (Mondor et al., 1998). Consequently, they process the other message poorly. For example, if at the end of the experiment subjects are given a surprise test for the nonshadowed message, they can usually remember very little about its content. They might be able to report whether the speaker of the nonshadowed message was male or female, but they recall virtually nothing else about that message, even if it repeated the same statements over and over (Cherry, 1953; Moray, 1959).

People don't just completely shut off the part of the world that is not bathed in the spotlight of attention. If they did, their actions wouldn't be very adaptive because the world is constantly changing. Some new, possibly critical, situation could suddenly arise, and we need to be able to switch our attention to such events quickly and flexibly when they occur. This means that the brain must monitor many things at the same time, although the monitoring may be minimal and below your current awareness.

A case in point is something called the **cocktail party effect.** Imagine you're at a large and noisy party, engaged in conversation with your date. In all likelihood, you won't be consciously aware of the content of the conversations around you; you'll be aware of hearing the babble of voices as background noise, but if asked to say what the couple standing next to you had been discussing, you probably couldn't do it. You successfully select the sound of your date's voice from all the other sounds that are stimulating your auditory receptors by using the processes of selective attention. Now suppose that someone across the room speaks your name. The odds are that you'll turn your head immediately. People in dichotic listening experiments have shown the same effect: They appear to ignore the contents of the nonshadowed message, but if their name is spoken in the nonshadowed channel they notice and remember it later. This is the cocktail party effect, and it suggests that our brains are aware of more things than we think: You could not recognize the particular pattern of sounds that is your name unless your brain was analyzing *all* of the auditory input.

Another compelling example of how people monitor auditory input that they appear to be ignoring comes from a dichotic listening experiment by Anne Treisman (1960), one of the pioneers of cognitive psychology. People were presented with compound sentences, such as "Against the advice of his broker, the naive investor panicked" in one ear and "Released from his cage, the little lamb bounded into the field" in the other (see Figure 5.3). Subjects were to shadow the message in one of the ears. In the middle of some of the sentences, Treisman switched things around—the second half of each sentence moved to the opposite ear. Thus, in the to-be-shadowed ear the subject heard a sentence such as, "Against the advice of his broker, the little lamb bounded into the field," whereas in the other ear the message was "Released from his cage, the naive investor panicked." The interesting finding was that about 30% of the time subjects continued to repeat the meaningful sentence ("Against the advice of his broker, the naive investor panicked") smoothly and without hesitation, even though the message had switched midway from the to-be-shadowed ear to the to-be-ignored ear. Moreover, many of the subjects reported that they hadn't even realized that they had switched to shadowing the to-be-ignored ear.

The cocktail party effect and the findings of the ear-switching experiments suggest that the brain does not completely ignore stimuli that are not the focus of attention. Compare (a) what the brain does when we selectively attend to a source of stimuli to (b) what a TV does when tuned to a particular channel: For the TV, it doesn't matter what happens on the other channels; as long as it is tuned to MuchMusic, that's all you're going to see. In contrast, the brain focuses the spotlight of attention on the task at hand, but it carries on at least some unconscious monitoring of the rest of the environment as well. If something else important happens, the brain shifts the spotlight of attention and the new event becomes the focus of conscious awareness. In Treisman's experiment, the brain must have been following the meaning of the messages in both ears, even though the people who participated were only aware of monitoring one message. Exactly how all this works has been the subject of considerable debate over the last several decades (Cowan, 1995; Hirst, 1995; Pashler, 1998), but the process itself is clearly adaptive. Humans wouldn't survive for long if they processed only those things in the realm of immediate awareness.

The cocktail party effect. By using the processes of attention, it's possible to attend selectively to one of many conversations in a noisy environment. But if someone across the room speaks your name, you'll probably notice it.

Processing without Attention: Automaticity

The idea that the brain and body are doing things beyond current awareness may seem strange at first, but not if you think about it. After all, when's the last time you thought about breathing, or keeping your heart beating, or walking, or even forming words from your repertoire of spoken sounds? You can drive a car and carry on a conversation at the same time; you don't need to focus an attentional spotlight on every turn of

Attended Channel
"Against the advice of his broker the little lamb bounded into the field."

Unattended Channel
"Released from his cage the naive investor panicked."

"Against the advice of his broker, the naive investor panicked."

FIGURE 5.3
Treisman's "Ear-Switching" Experiment

At one point in a dichotic listening experiment by Treisman, the to-be-shadowed message was suddenly switched to the to-be-ignored ear. Interestingly, subjects often continued to repeat the meaningful sentence without even noticing that they were now shadowing the message they were supposed to be ignoring.

Practical Solutions

CELL PHONES AND DRIVING

You've seen that there are limitations on the brain's capacity to perform mental work. We attend selectively to current priorities, because there are limitations on how much information we can process at a given time. As we've discussed, with sufficient practice certain tasks (even quite complex ones) can become largely automatic, such that performing them has relatively little impact on our ability to perform another task simultaneously, and vice versa. Yet real-world tasks, such as driving, never become 100% automatic, partly because of unpredictable variations in the demands of driving. If something unexpected happens while you are driving (e.g., a child or an animal darts into the path of your car, or the driver in front of you suddenly slams on the brakes), you cannot rely on well-practised routines but must respond very quickly in a way that fits the needs of that specific situation. Consequently, driving demands vigilance at all times. Yet studies suggest that a very substantial percentage of accidents involve lapses of drivers' attention.

According to a 2001 study, approximately half of Canadian adults use cellular phones occasionally, and about three-quarters of those who own cell phones report at least occasional use of them while driving (Leger, 2001). Studies have established a strong correlation between cell phone use and traffic accidents. In fact, it's been claimed that talking on a cell phone increases the risk of accident to levels comparable to those of driving with a blood alcohol level above the legal limit (Redelmeier & Tibshirani, 1997). The presence of a correlation between cell phone use and accidents, however, is not sufficient to infer that cell phone use *causes* accidents. It could be that people who use cell phones while driving are just bad drivers. As you know, correlations do not imply causality (see Chapter 2).

To determine a causal link, you must have experimental control. A number of experiments have been conducted examining the link between cell phone use and driving. Typically, these studies manipulate the type and extent of cell phone use during simulated driving—either in a driving simulator or by requiring people to perform a tracking task on a computer. In a recent study by Strayer and Johnston (2001), people were asked to use a joystick to move a cursor on a computer screen; the task was to keep the cursor aligned as closely as possible to a moving target (meant to correspond roughly to maintaining location on a road). At random intervals, either a red or a green light flashed on the computer screen. The subjects were instructed to react to the red light by pressing a "brake" button on the joystick.

Strayer and Johnston found that when people were engaged in a cell phone conversation while performing the simulated driving task, they missed twice as many red lights. Even when the red light was detected, and the brake applied, people talking on a cell phone were considerably slower to respond. Moreover, the impairments were found regardless of whether the cell phone was a hand-held or a hands-free model. Importantly, simply listening to the radio did not impair performance.

A study commissioned by Transport Canada and conducted by Harbluk et al. (2002) yielded similar findings. The Harbluk study used actual driving performance, with technology that enabled measurement of a large range of driving-related behaviours (braking, accelerating, eye movements). Even though the drivers in this study used hands-free phones, their performance was impaired when they were participating in a cognitively demanding phone conversation. For example, they spent more time looking centrally (and hence less time checking the sides of the road and their mirrors), and they more often braked hard.

The theoretical implications of these and other recent studies are clear: Cell phones are particularly distracting because (unlike other distractions, such as the radio or food or a companion in the car) they require the user to commit substantial cognitive resources to interacting with another person who is not "there" in the driving situation. The practical implications are equally clear: Turn off the cell phone when you drive. If the call is important, then it's worth getting off the road.

---

the wheel or pressing of the brake. You perform such tasks largely automatically (but see the Practical Solutions box for limits on the automaticity of driving).

Psychologists use the term **automaticity** to refer to fast and nearly effortless processing that requires little or no focused attention (Logan, 1991). When you practise a task, such as playing Mozart on the piano, overall speed steadily improves. You may even reach a point at which performing the task seems automatic—Mozart rolls off your fingertips with such ease that you're not even consciously aware of controlling your own finger movements. Automatic processes, once they develop, no longer seem to require much conscious control. The mind is free to consider other things, while the task itself is performed without a hitch. Many of the activities that people take for granted—such as reading, talking, and walking—are essentially automatic processes.

It's possible to measure how automaticity develops through what is called a *divided attention task* (Logan, 1988). In a typical experiment, people are asked to perform two

automaticity
Fast and almost effortless processing that requires little or no focused attention.

tasks at the same time, such as playing a piece by Mozart on the piano while simultaneously trying to remember a short list of unrelated words. Automaticity is demonstrated when one task, the automatic one, doesn't interfere with performance on the other task (Hasher & Zacks, 1979; Shiffrin & Schneider, 1977). Clearly, if you've just learned to play the Mozart piece, you'll have enough trouble just getting through it without error, let alone memorizing a list of words at the same time. But if you're an accomplished pianist—if your Mozart performance has become largely automatic—you can let your fingers do the playing and your mind can concentrate on remembering the word list.

The relationship between automaticity and awareness tells us something important about the function of consciousness. The better you are at performing a task—the more automatic the task has become—the less likely you are to be aware of the processes involved in performing the task. This is a very important characteristic of mental functioning: Performance of novel tasks seems to require conscious awareness of each step in performing the task, whereas highly practised tasks can be performed without conscious monitoring of all of their component processes. Environmental conditions can change at any moment, so we need to be able to initiate new and adaptive behaviours when the unexpected occurs. It appears that people use consciousness for handling the new and demanding, while relying on the nearly effortless processes of automaticity to continue performing routine tasks.

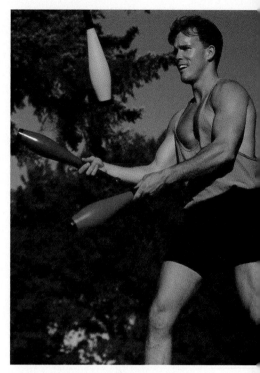

If you practise a task, such as juggling, for extended periods, your performance may become largely automatic. Automatic processes, once acquired, no longer require much conscious control.

Disorders of Attention

We've stressed the link between attention and consciousness because, in many respects, attention is the gateway to consciousness: We only become conscious of things that receive some measure of attention. It follows that if the brain systems that control attention were damaged in some way, there will be corresponding loss in conscious awareness. Brain researchers have used clinical cases of brain damage to examine this possibility, and they are in the process of mapping out what appear to be attention-related areas of the brain (Kiernan & Hudson, 1994; Park et al., 1999; Posner & Rothbart, 1992; Stuss et al., 1999). Other researchers are developing treatment strategies for people who suffer from attention disorders as a consequence of brain injury (e.g., Mateer et al., 1997). Let's briefly consider two attention disorders that are related to brain dysfunction: *visual neglect* and *attention deficit/hyperactivity disorder*.

Visual Neglect Damage to the right parietal lobe of the cerebral cortex can produce an odd and complex attention disorder called **visual neglect** (see Figure 5.4). People suffering from visual neglect tend to ignore things on the left side of the body (remember from Chapter 3 that the right side of the brain processes most information on the left side of the body). Visual neglect can cause people to read only from the right side of pages and copy only the right side of pictures; patients with visual neglect may even dress, shave, or apply makeup to only the right side of the body (Arguin & Bub, 1993; Bisiach & Rusconi, 1990; Graves & Jones, 1992). It's as if an entire side of their visual field has vanished from awareness. Fortunately, the condition typically diminishes with time (Kerkhoff et al., 1994; Mesulam, 1987).

Is the brain of patients with visual neglect really shutting off all visual information from one side of the body? Probably not. In one study, a patient suffering from visual neglect was shown drawings of two houses. One house was normal in appearance; the other was normal on the right side but had bright red flames and smoke billowing out from a window on its left side. The patient was asked to choose which of the two houses she would prefer to live in. "The houses look the same to me," she reported, presumably because she was attending only to the right side of each picture. Nevertheless, when forced to indicate which of the two she would prefer to live in, she consistently chose the house without the flames (Marshall & Halligan, 1988). This suggests that even though the brain mechanisms underlying conscious awareness had been damaged, her brain was still able to use information from the left visual field (Bisiach, 1992; Schweinberger & Stief, 2001). Based on their studies of many cases of visual neglect

visual neglect

A complex attention disorder characterized by a tendency to ignore things that appear on one side of the body, usually the left side.

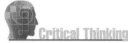

Critical Thinking

In what ways are the symptoms of visual neglect similar to the symptoms of the split-brain patients discussed in Chapter 3?

FIGURE 5.4
Visual Neglect
Patients suffering from visual neglect might consciously detect no differences between these two houses. But if pressed to choose, they would probably opt to live in the house without the flames.

and related phenomena, Goodale and Humphrey (1998) of the University of Western Ontario proposed that there are two distinct but interacting visual systems: one for the conscious perception of objects and the other for involuntary actions upon objects. According to this view, phenomena such as visual neglect arise from damage to the former system.

Attention Deficit/Hyperactivity Disorder The right hemisphere of the brain may also be involved in **attention deficit/hyperactivity disorder,** or ADHD, a psychological condition characterized by difficulties in concentrating and by high levels of fidgety physical activity. Individuals with ADHD have trouble sustaining attention for extended periods; they're easily distracted and have difficulty completing tasks. They also tend to squirm and fidget continuously and often act impulsively (e.g., blurt out answers to questions before the questions have even been completely asked) (Barkley, 1997). Attention deficits sometimes occur without hyperactivity (in which case the disorder is known simply as attention deficit disorder) (Barlow & Durand, 2002). ADHD and attention deficit disorder are among the most common psychological problems in school-aged children, although only about 3% to 5% of all children meet criteria for either of these diagnoses (Cantwell, 1996).

Research by Kerns and Price (2001) at the University of Victoria tested children's performance on a "prospective memory" task embedded in a computer game called CyberCruiser. The game involved controlling a "car" on a computer screen, and the player had to remember to check the "gas" level at appropriate times as the game went along. Compared with control children, children diagnosed with attention deficit dis-

attention deficit/hyperactivity disorder

A psychological condition marked by difficulties in concentrating or in sustaining attention for extended periods and by high levels of fidgety physical activity; occurs most often in children.

order more often forgot to check the gas, suggesting that they had difficulty keeping that intention in mind while playing the game.

There is some evidence that attention deficit disorder might be caused by mild damage to, or malfunctioning of, the right hemisphere of the brain. But the brain mechanisms involved in attention deficit disorder are still largely unknown, with different studies yielding differing results. PET scan studies, for instance, have indicated that various regions of the brain may be selectively involved (Zametkin et al., 1990). It's unlikely that any single brain location is responsible, because the disorder is quite complex and can manifest itself in a variety of ways. There are even ongoing debates about the disorder's proper definition (Barkley, 1997; Shaywitz et al., 1994). So, it may take some time before researchers arrive at a complete neurological understanding of the problem. As one might expect, experience and social influences play roles in the onset and maintenance of the disorder (DeGrandpre, 2000).

What about treatment? The news on this front is promising. It turns out that a majority of children who have attention problems can be helped with a combination of medication and training. Children with attention problems need to learn coping strategies to help them perform well in school and in social settings. A complete training program typically includes teaching study skills, such as learning to write down important information (rather than relying on memory) and offering rewards for sitting still and not being disruptive in social interactions. Medications, such as Ritalin, seem to help concentration and they often reduce hyperactivity and disruptive behaviour. It's interesting to note that Ritalin, as well as many other drugs that are used to treat attention deficit disorder, comes from a class of drugs—called stimulants—that generally serve to increase nervous system activity. You'll read more about stimulants later in this chapter, but for present purposes the point to remember is that, in low doses, certain stimulants such as Ritalin appear to increase the ability to concentrate and focus attention in children with attention deficits (Mattay et al., 1996). Finally, it's worth mentioning that there is some concern among psychologists that attention deficit disorder has been overdiagnosed in recent years and that drugs such as Ritalin have been overprescribed.

Attention deficit/hyperactivity disorder involves distractibility, hyperactivity, and impulsive behaviour.

Subliminal Perception

Can people be influenced by stimuli of which they are entirely unaware? We briefly considered this topic in Chapter 2, when experimental methods were discussed, but it's worthwhile to examine the topic again in greater detail as we discuss attention. You've seen how the brain uses attention to prioritize mental functioning; automatic processes can also develop that lead to fast and nearly effortless behaviours that require little or no conscious thought. So, from an adaptive perspective, it's reasonable to assume that people might be influenced by stimuli that bypass conscious awareness. But do subliminal messages really work?

It's not known whether advertisers really try to influence people subliminally (the advertisers deny it) or, in fact, whether the subliminal tapes that some people buy to lose weight or gain confidence really do present the promised embedded messages (some evidence suggests that the messages are often not even present). It is possible, however, to conduct controlled experiments in which messages are purposely embedded in print advertisements or on audiotapes. Dozens of such studies have been conducted (Druckman & Bjork, 1991; Merikle et al., 2001; Rosen & Singh, 1992); the general consensus seems to be that such subliminal messages have little if any effect.

It is sometimes claimed that subliminal messages lead to enhanced memory for the supraliminal material in which they are embedded. In a study conducted at the University of Lethbridge by Vokey and Read (1985), several instances of the word *SEX* were inserted into vacation slides; the words were placed into the pictures in such a way that they were not noticeable but could be detected if pointed out by the experimenters. Subjects viewed the slides (without being told about the hidden word) and then were tested on their ability to recognize them. Subjects did no better in recognizing the slides than control subjects who viewed the slides without the embedded words.

As another example, Rosen and Singh (1992) had people view one of three visually embedded subliminal messages: (1) the word *SEX,* (2) a picture of a naked woman and several phallic symbols, or (3) the word *DEATH* combined with pictures of skulls. The "embeds" were placed in print ads for liquor or cologne, and subjects viewed the ads as part of an experiment on advertising effectiveness. No mention was made of the embeds, which were present in some of the ads but not in others. This study is noteworthy because it used a variety of measures of advertising effectiveness to check for effects of the subliminal messages. None of these measures was affected by the hidden information.

With regard to self-help tapes, again the data are clear. For example, Moore (1995) reported a study conducted at York University in which subjects listened to pairs of subliminal tapes and tried to discriminate between them; even after 400 trials, subjects scored no better than chance. Similarly, Greenwald and his colleagues (1991) at the University of Washington recruited subjects for a study of the effectiveness of subliminal tapes designed to improve either memory or self-esteem. Unknown to the subjects, the labels on the tapes had sometimes been switched, such that some subjects who thought they were listening to a self-esteem tape were actually given a memory tape, and vice versa. After regular listening, subjects improved on post-tests of self-esteem or memory (depending on which tape they thought they had been listening to), but it didn't matter which tape they had actually been given.

Why the improvement? From a psychological perspective, it's important to remember that people who buy such tapes (and those who participate in studies of memory or self-esteem enhancement) are *motivated* to improve. Thus, we might expect to see some improvement over the course of a study, even if the tapes themselves have no effect at all. It is also possible that subliminal tapes act as a kind of *placebo,* leading to improvement because the listener believes in their magical powers. If subliminal self-help is placebo related, all that's necessary is that subjects *think* they are receiving something that will work. Consequently, we would expect the subject to improve regardless of whether or not the appropriate message was actually embedded in the background, just as occurred in the Greenwald study.

Such placebo effects are not always obtained, however. For example, in research conducted at the University of Waterloo by Merikle and Skanes (1992), subjects who had volunteered to participate in a study of the effects of subliminal messages on weight loss were randomly assigned to one of three conditions: Some listened to tapes with subliminal messages promoting weight loss, others listened to similar tapes but without any subliminal messages, and yet others did not listen to any tape. Participants in all three conditions tended to lose weight over the course of the study, but the average amount lost was the same regardless of condition.

What about backwards speech, such as that supposedly included in some rock music? Can the unconscious mind somehow reverse the backwards speech, leading people to be influenced by it unawares? Vokey and Read (1985) reported several studies of backwards speech: Their results indicate that people cannot tell the difference between innocent and sinister messages played backwards and, just as important, they showed that giving people suggestions about what they would hear in backwards speech often led people to report hearing what was suggested. A 1993 study at McMaster University by Begg and colleagues also found no effect of backwards audio messages. In summary, there is no reason to believe that the unconscious mind can translate backwards speech (a feat that would have had no adaptive value until the advent of audio recording devices). It's also worth noting here that there is no convincing evidence of long-term memory for forward speech presented to people while they are asleep (Wood et al., 1992).

So what can we conclude about subliminal messages? Is it possible to alter behaviour without awareness? Perhaps. Most psychologists believe that a person's behaviour

Critical Thinking

Many people seems to want to believe in the ill effects of subliminal messages. Do you have any ideas about why this might be?

can be affected in small and transient ways without subjective conscious awareness of the source of the influence (Cheesman & Merikle, 1986; Greenwald et al., 1995). For example, Debner and Jacoby (1994) conducted a study at McMaster University in which subjects were asked to complete word fragments (e.g., "M O T _ _") presented on a computer screen. Immediately before each fragment appeared, a word was briefly flashed on the screen; on some trials, the briefly presented word could be used to complete the fragment (e.g., "MOTEL"). Subjects were warned about the briefly flashed words and told *not* to use them to complete the fragments, and instead to come up with different completions (e.g., "MOTOR"). If the briefly presented word was shown long enough for subjects to be consciously aware of it, they successfully avoided using it, but if its presentation was very brief they often did use it. The beauty of this design is that we can be sure that use of the briefly flashed word was mediated by unconscious influences, rather than by conscious perception of the word, because when subjects were aware of the word (i.e., when the word was flashed for a long enough time for subjects to see it) they avoided using it. This is strong evidence of an unconscious influence of the very briefly presented words. Thus we probably can be influenced by stimuli of which we are unaware, but there's not much evidence that such messages exist in advertisements—and even if they do, their influence is minimal at best.

Test Yourself 5.1

To test your knowledge about how we set priorities for mental functioning, decide whether each of the following statements about attention and its disorders is true or false. (You will find the answers in Appendix B.)

1. The "cocktail party effect" suggests that we cannot attend to more than one message at a time; we focus our attention on one thing and the rest of the environment is effectively blocked out. *True or False?*
2. In dichotic listening tasks, people are presented with two auditory messages, one in each ear, and the task is to repeat one of the messages aloud while essentially ignoring the other. *True or False?*
3. If a task—such as playing Mozart on the piano—has become automatic, then you can perform a second task—such as remembering a list of letters—with little or no interference with performance on the first task. *True or False?*
4. When visual neglect is caused by damage to the right side of the brain, people seem not to notice things that appear on the right side of the body. *True or False?*
5. Attention deficit/hyperactivity disorder is primarily a learned disorder that can easily be treated by special skills training. *True or False?*
6. Research has proven that there is no such thing as subliminal perception. *True or False?*

SLEEPING AND DREAMING

Learning Goals

1. Understand biological rhythms and how they are controlled.
2. Be able to describe the various stages and characteristics of sleep.
3. Be able to discuss the function and adaptive significance of sleep.
4. Learn about current theories of dreaming and its function.
5. Learn about the major sleep disorders.

SUPPOSE YOU SET OUT to design the perfect animal. What would such an animal look like? What characteristics would it have? You'd probably make it smart, strong, and perhaps swift, but would you design your animal so that it would sleep? If so, what purposes would that serve, and what mechanisms would regulate the timing and duration of sleep? What would go on inside the animal while it slept? Psychologists are not in the business of designing ideal animals, but we do strive to understand how and why existing animals—including humans—function as they do; hence we seek answers to these same sorts of questions. Why do we sleep? What mechanisms regulate when and for how long we sleep? What is going on inside us as we sleep?

Biological Rhythms

To understand sleep, you first need to appreciate that we live in a world of many rhythms and cycles, both in the environment (day to night, new moon to old, low tide to high, winter to spring to summer to fall, etc.) and within our bodies. The regular daily transition from waking awareness to sleep is an example of a cycle, or *biological rhythm,* in the body. Many body functions work in cycles, in humans as well as in other members of the animal kingdom. Sleep and waking vary daily, along with body temperature, hormone secretions, blood pressure, and other processes (for a review, see Aschoff & Wever, 1981). Activities that rise and fall along a 24-hour cycle are known as **circadian rhythms** (*circa* means "about," and *dias* means "day"). Other biological activities may follow other cycles that are either shorter or longer. The human menstrual cycle operates on an approximately 28-day cycle, for example, whereas changes in appetite and the ability to perform certain tasks may change several times throughout the day.

What controls these internal rhythms? You don't consciously alert the endocrine system that it's time to secrete hormones or actively instruct some portion of your brain that your body temperature needs to start rising. These functions are controlled automatically by structures in the brain, called **biological clocks,** that trigger the needed activities at just the right time. These clocks schedule the internal functions of the body and make sure that everything is performing as it should. Animal research has determined that a particular area of the hypothalamus, called the *suprachiasmatic nucleus,* may play a key role in regulating the clock that controls circadian rhythms (Ralph et al., 1990; Schwartz, 1996). But it's thought that the human brain probably has several clocks, each controlling its own function such as body temperature or activity level (Johnson & Hastings, 1986).

The environment plays a critical role in helping our brains synchronize their internal biological clocks. Light is a particularly important controller, or *zeitgeber* (meaning "time giver"), of the pacing of internal clocks (Czeisler et al., 1989). If you were forced to live in a continuously dark or light environment without knowing the time of day, you would still sleep regularly (although your sleep might be disrupted somewhat). But the timing of the sleeping and waking cycles would likely drift and lose connection with night and day (see Figure 5.5). Rather than falling asleep at your usual 11:00 p.m. and waking at 7:00 a.m., after a while you might find yourself becoming sleepy at 2:00 a.m. and rising at 10:00 a.m. People use light during the day, as well as the absence of light at night, as a way of setting their internal sleep clock.

The fact that the environment is so important in maintaining internal body rhythms makes considerable adaptive sense. On average, the sun rises and sets approximately every 12 hours. There are daily changes in air pressure and temperature caused, in part, by the continuous rotation of the earth about its axis. It's perfectly reasonable to assume that animals, including humans, have adapted to remain in harmony with these natural environmental cycles. As the cold of winter approaches, birds fly south for warmer temperatures and more plentiful food supplies; other animals stay put and prepare for hibernation. These changes in behaviour are sensible adaptations to cyclic changes in the environment that are not under the animal's control.

circadian rhythms
Biological activities that rise and fall in a 24-hour cycle.

biological clocks
Brain structures that schedule rhythmic variations in bodily functions by triggering them at the appropriate times.

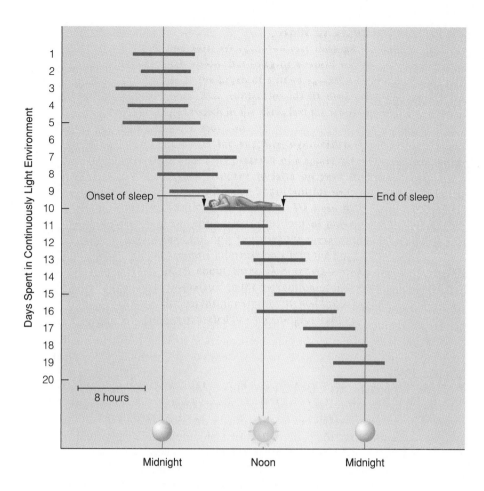

FIGURE 5.5
Pacing the Internal Clock
Light strongly influences our biological clocks. If you were forced to live without darkness and without knowing the time of day, you would still sleep a normal 8 hours (shown by the length of the bar). But sleep onset times would probably drift. For example, if you usually fall asleep at 11:00 p.m. and wake at 7:00 a.m., after a while you might find yourself becoming sleepy at 2:00 a.m. and rising at 10:00 a.m.

Jet lag is a good example of how the environment can play havoc with our internal clocks. When you travel to a new time zone, especially if you move east (which shortens your day), your usual signals for sleeping and waking become disrupted: It gets light and dark at unusual times for you. The net result is that you have trouble going to sleep, you get up at the "wrong" time, and you generally feel lousy. Your body needs to reset its clocks, in line with your new environment, and this process takes time. This is one reason why diplomats and business travellers often arrive at their destinations a few days before an important event or meeting; it gives them time to adjust their internal clocks and shrug off the jet lag.

Critical Thinking

Can you think of any workplace environments that might lead to symptoms similar to jet lag?

The activity levels of many animals are controlled by internal clocks that are "set," in part, by the environment. Bears are active during the warm summer months and hibernate during the winter.

The Characteristics of Sleep

The transition from waking to sleep is sometimes described as a change in one's state or level of consciousness. Rather than being "death's counterfeit" (as Shakespeare called it), sleep involves some awareness, although the focus of that awareness no longer connects so directly to events in the world as does our waking awareness. The problem facing researchers trying to understand the nature of consciousness during sleep is that they cannot collect reports of what sleep feels like to the sleeper (because the subject is unresponsive). Researchers can, however, measure what people say about a prior period of sleep after they awaken from it. Moreover, through EEG recordings and other physiological measures, scientists can eavesdrop on the electrical activity of the brain during sleep and infer things about changes in the sleeper's state of consciousness by looking at how the patterns of brain activity change over time.

As you may recall from Chapter 3, the *electroencephalograph*, or EEG, is a device that monitors the electrical activity of the brain. Electrodes are attached to the scalp, and changes in the electrical potentials of large numbers of brain cells are recorded in the form of line tracings, or brain waves. The EEG was first applied to the sleeping brain in the 1930s, and by the 1950s researchers had discovered some very intriguing and unexpected things about the sleep process. For example, EEG tracings revealed that sleep is characterized by cyclic changes in brain activity and that at certain points the electrical activity of the sleeping brain bears a striking similarity to the brain activity of a person who is wide awake (Aserinsky & Kleitman, 1955; Dement & Kleitman, 1957).

Figure 5.6 presents typical EEG recordings made during waking and sleep states. The main things to notice are (1) the *height*, or amplitude, of the brain waves; (2) the *frequency*, or number of cycles per second (usually described in Hertz); and (3) the *regularity*, or smoothness, of the pattern. Regular high-amplitude waves of low frequency reflect neural synchrony, meaning that large numbers of neurons are firing together. In the first row of tracings, measured when the subject was awake, you'll see no evidence of neural synchrony—the EEG pattern is fast and irregular, and the waves are of low amplitude. Presumably, when people are awake and focusing their attention on some task, the brain is busy dividing its labour; lots of cells are working on specialized individual tasks, so the combined brain activity looks irregular. In contrast, when the brain is in a relaxed state, it produces **alpha waves,** which have a higher amplitude and cycle in a slower, more regular manner.

alpha waves
The pattern of brain activity observed in someone who is in a relaxed state with eyes open.

theta waves
The pattern of brain activity observed in stage 1 sleep.

Stages 1 to 4 of Sleep   As you settle down for the night and prepare for sleep, the fast and irregular wave patterns of the waking state are gradually replaced by slower, more synchronized alpha waves. You're not really asleep at this point, just relaxed and perhaps a little drowsy. The first stage of sleep—called *stage 1* sleep—is marked by a return to waves that are a bit lower in amplitude and slightly more irregular. The dominant wave patterns of stage 1 sleep are called **theta waves;** as you can see in Figure 5.6, they're different from the patterns found in the waking state. Scientists take the occurrence of theta waves, along with other physiological indicators, as evidence that stage 1 sleep truly is a stage of sleep, yet if people are awakened after entering stage 1 sleep they are likely to report that they had not really been asleep; instead, they usually claim that their thoughts were simply drifting.

The second stage of sleep, *stage 2* sleep, is defined by another change in the EEG pattern. Specifically, the theta activity that defines stage 1 sleep begins to be interrupted occasionally by short bursts of activity called *sleep spindles.* There are also sudden, sharp waveforms from time to time called *K complexes.* You're definitely asleep at this point, although your brain still shows some sensitivity to events in the external world. Loud noises, for example, tend to be reflected immediately in the EEG pattern by the triggering of a

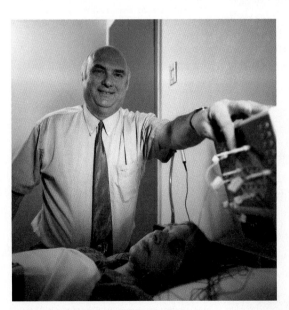

In sleep disorder clinics, patterns in the electrical activity of the brain are monitored throughout the night.

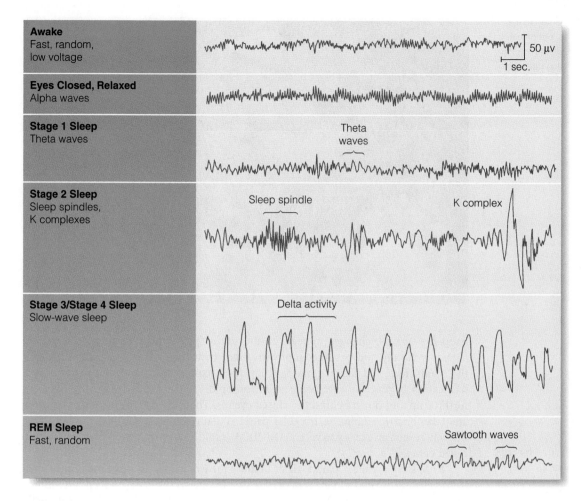

FIGURE 5.6

EEG Patterns Associated with Sleeping and Wakefulness

As we move from a waking state into sleep, characteristic changes occur in the electrical activity of the brain. Generally, as we become drowsy and move through the first four stages of sleep, our brain waves become slower and more regular and show more amplitude. But during REM sleep, when we are presumed to be dreaming, the EEG shows a pattern more closely resembling the waking state. (From Hauri, 1982.)

K complex (Bastien & Campbell, 1992; Cote et al., 2001). Your brain reacts, as revealed by the K complex, but you're not really consciously aware of the environment. For instance, you'll do a very poor job of responding to prearranged signals delivered by an experimenter (such as instructions to raise your hand if you hear your name).

The next two stages of sleep, *stage 3* and *stage 4,* are progressively deeper states and show more synchronized slow-wave brain patterns called **delta activity;** for this reason, these stages are sometimes called delta or *slow-wave sleep.* Notice that the wave patterns for stage 3/stage 4 sleep in Figure 5.6 appear large (high in amplitude) and cycle slowly compared to the patterns of the earlier sleep stages. You're deeply asleep now and difficult to awaken (Kelly, 1991). If someone shakes you awake during slow-wave sleep, you'll be confused and disoriented, and it'll take quite some time for you to reach a normal state of conscious awareness.

delta activity

The pattern of brain activity observed in stage 3 and stage 4 sleep; it's characterized by synchronized slow waves. Also called *slow-wave sleep.*

REM Sleep It's fair to characterize the transition from stage 1 to stage 4 sleep as moving from a light to a deep sleep. Not surprisingly, measures of arousal, such as breathing rate, heart rate, and blood pressure, decline regularly as you progress through each of the stages. But about 70 to 90 minutes into the sleep cycle something very odd

Why do people sleep? It could be to restore or repair depleted resources, but research suggests that vigorous activity during the day has little effect on sleeping patterns.

REM

A stage of sleep characterized by rapid eye movements and low-amplitude, irregular EEG patterns similar to those found in the waking brain. REM is typically associated with dreaming.

happens: Abrupt changes appear in the entire physiological pattern. Heart rate increases rapidly and becomes more irregular; twitching movements might begin in the hands, feet, and face; in males, the penis becomes erect, and in females vaginal lubrication begins; the eyes begin to move rapidly and irregularly, darting back and forth or up and down behind the closed eyelids. The EEG pattern loses its synchrony and takes on low-amplitude, irregular patterns that resemble those of the waking state. But you're not awake—you've entered **REM** (rapid eye movement) sleep, sometimes called *paradoxical sleep.*

REM sleep is called "paradoxical" because the electrical activity of the brain during REM sleep resembles the "awake" pattern, yet the person is deeply asleep. The muscle tone is extremely relaxed, and the person is relatively difficult to awaken. But, as the EEG indicates, the brain is extremely active during this period; if the person is jostled awake from REM sleep, he or she will seem instantly alert. As noted above, this contrasts sharply with the reaction of people who are awakened from stages 3 and 4 of sleep, when they're likely to act confused. Perhaps most interesting, people who awaken from REM sleep are very likely to report an emotional and story-like dream. In fact, dreaming is reported well over 80% of the time among people awakened during REM sleep, even in people who previously denied that they dream (Goodenough, 1991; Snyder, 1967).

There is still some debate among sleep researchers about the exact relationship between the REM state and dreaming. People usually report dreaming if they're awak-

FIGURE 5.7
Sleep Cycles

During an average night, most adults pass through the various stages of sleep four or five times. A complete cycle usually takes about 90 minutes. As the figure shows, as morning approaches, we tend to spend more time in REM sleep, presumably dreaming. We also tend to spend brief intervals awake (indicated by the letter A in the figure) during the last hour or two of sleep. (Based on Kalat, 1996.)

| | 11 P.M. | | | 12 A.M. | | | | 1 A.M. | | 2 A.M. | | |

Sleep Stage   A 1 2 3 4 3 2 REM 1 2 3 4 3 2 3 2 REM 1 ened during REM, but dreaming also sometimes occurs during the earlier stages of sleep. Haven't you ever experienced a dream moments after going to sleep? Most people have, but it's unlikely that your brain was in the REM state. Systematic studies of dreaming and the sleep stages have revealed conflicting results. Some studies report low levels of dreaming during non-REM stages (Dement, 1978); other studies have found the percentages to be fairly high (over 50%; Foulkes, 1985).

The Sleep Cycle   Over the course of an average night, most adults cycle through the various stages of sleep, including REM sleep, about four or five times. Each sleep cycle takes about 90 minutes: You progress from stage 1 through stage 4, then back from stage 4 toward stage 1, ending in REM (see Figure 5.7). This sequence remains intact throughout much of the night, but the amount of time spent in each stage changes as morning approaches. During the first cycle of sleep, the majority of time is spent in stages 3 and 4 (slow-wave sleep), but REM sleep tends to dominate the later cycles. Over the course of the typical night, the amount of time spent in REM sleep, presumably dreaming, increases and the interval between successive REM states becomes shorter (Ellman et al., 1991). In fact, by the end of the night, stage 4 seems to disappear and you end up spending almost all of your time in REM sleep (Webb, 1992). As you're aware, many dreams seem to occur toward the end of the sleep period, and these are the dreams you're most likely to remember.

Critical Thinking

Can you think of any adaptive reasons why sleep occurs in stages? What might be the advantage to starting off in a light sleep and moving to a deeper sleep?

The Function of Sleep

If you sleep 8 hours a night and you live to the ripe old age of 75, you'll have spent a quarter century with your eyes closed, your limbs lying useless at your sides, and your outstretched body open to attack. Doesn't this seem a bit strange? Think about it. What could be the adaptive value of regularly entering a state in which the organism is unaware of resources and threats in the environment?

Repairing and Restoring   At one level, it seems pretty obvious: People sleep because they get tired. The daily activities of waking life produce wear and tear on the body, and some mind/body "down time" may be needed to put things back in order. During sleep, especially slow-wave sleep, the metabolic activity of the brain and the rest of the body is dramatically lowered (Sakai et al., 1979), and these decreased demands on use of the body may enable cellular processes to recover from fatigue. Consistent with that idea, if people are deprived of sleep for an extended period of time, their ability to perform complex tasks, especially those requiring problem solving, deteriorates (see below).

The trickier question is whether or not the brain actively performs special restorative processes during sleep. Many restorative activities do go on during sleep, but such activities also go on regularly throughout the waking day, and it is not clear if sleep is special in this regard (Horne, 1988). Despite people's intuitions, there also doesn't appear to be a strong relationship between the amount of activity in a day and the depth and length of the sleep period that follows (Horne & Minard, 1985). Rest and restoration are important consequences of a good night's sleep and, as discussed in a subsequent section, REM sleep may play special active roles in consolidating new learning, but there may be another important value to sleep as well.

Survival Value Sleep may be an adaptive response to environmental conditions, a behaviour that increases the likelihood of survival. Primates rely heavily on their visual systems; as a result, they aren't very efficient outside at night in low levels of illumination. Our ancestors could have moved about at night, groping around for food while trying to avoid being eaten by some lurking predator, but it was probably better for them to stay put in a tree or cave until dawn. Sleep at night thus may have been adaptive because it stopped our ancestors from venturing forth into a hostile environment.

We can find evidence supporting this idea by examining the sleeping patterns of animal species in the wild. If sleep is an adaptive reaction to light–dark cycles and susceptibility to predators, then we might expect animals that rely on senses other than vision to be active primarily at night, when vision-based predators would be at a hunting disadvantage. This is indeed the case for mice, rats, and other rodents. Second, large animals that must eat almost continuously and can't easily find places to hide should sleep very little. And, indeed, grazing animals such as sheep, goats, horses, and cattle, which are vulnerable to surprise attack by predators, sleep only a few hours a day (see Figure 5.8). In one study, researchers found that body weight and susceptibility to attack could explain the majority of the differences among the sleeping patterns of different species (Allison & Cicchetti, 1976).

Sleep Deprivation Earlier we mentioned that our ability to perform complex tasks is disrupted if we haven't received much sleep. This shouldn't come as too much of a surprise—you've probably pulled an all-nighter at some point, finding yourself irritable and not good for much the next day. But how serious is prolonged sleep deprivation? Some individuals have tried to remain awake for very long periods—approaching two weeks—and the results have been generally negative: Some of the symptoms were slurred speech, sharp declines in mental ability, and even symptoms of paranoia and hallucinations. Although severely sleep-deprived individuals can appear normal for brief periods, prolonged sleep deprivation generally wreaks havoc on virtually all aspects of normal functioning.

The harmfulness of extreme sleep deprivation has been dramatically demonstrated in animal studies. When rats and dogs are deprived of sleep for extended periods, their ability to regulate internal functions, such as temperature, is grossly impaired, leading to considerable loss of weight (despite an increased intake of food). The immune system also starts to fail, along with various organs in the body. After roughly three weeks of no sleep, the survival rate among these animals is virtually zero—most of them die (Rechtschaffen et al., 2002).

FIGURE 5.8
Sleep Times for Various Species

Large grazing animals, such as cows and horses, eat frequently and are quite vulnerable to surprise attacks from predators. As the figure shows, such animals tend to sleep very little. Small, quick animals, such as cats and rodents, are less vulnerable to attack and sleep a great deal.

Fortunately, people rarely if ever reach these levels of sleep deprivation, because we simply can't stay awake. Nonetheless, less extreme sleep deprivation contributes to thousands of deaths each year, mostly through traffic accidents and job-related mishaps. University of British Columbia professor Stanley Coren published a provocative and popular book on this subject (1996), arguing that most members of our culture are chronically sleep deprived. William Dement (a pioneer in the scientific study of sleep) made similar arguments in another engaging and accessible book with co-author Christopher Vaughan (1999). The bottom line is this: One of the easiest, simplest, and most effective things you can do to improve your daily life is to get an adequate amount of sleep each night (see also Horne, 2001).

The Function of REM and Dreaming

It's easy to see how sleep itself might have developed as an adaptive response, to repair, restore, and protect the organism struggling to survive. But why are there stages of sleep? Why, if people want to protect or rest the body, do they spend a significant amount of time in such an internally active state as REM sleep? Does dreaming serve some unique biological or psychological function? Unfortunately, we have no definitive answers to these questions.

It's not clear whether REM sleep is even a necessary component of normal functioning. It's possible to deprive people selectively of REM sleep by carefully monitoring the EEG and then waking the person whenever characteristic REM patterns appear in the recordings. Unlike the findings for sleep loss in general, losing significant amounts of REM sleep usually does not lead to dramatic effects. People may show a bit more irritability (compared to controls who are awakened during non-REM periods), and their performance on tasks requiring logical reasoning and problem solving is hurt, but the level of impairment is not large (Ellman et al., 1991). Some forms of severe depression even appear to be helped by REM sleep deprivation (Boivin, 2000), and some effective antidepressant drugs suppress REM sleep (Vogel et al., 1990).

On the other hand, an intriguing change does occur in sleep *patterns* after periods of REM deprivation. Sleep researchers have noticed that on the second or third night of REM deprivation it is necessary to awaken the subject with much greater frequency. When people lose REM sleep, their brains attempt to make up for the loss during the next sleep period by increasing the proportion of time spent in the REM stage. The more REM sleep lost, the more the brain tries to make it up the next night. This tendency, known as **REM rebound,** is one reason why many researchers remain convinced that REM sleep serves some unknown but extremely important function in the brain.

REM rebound
The tendency to increase the proportion of sleeping time spent in REM sleep after a period of REM deprivation.

Memory Consolidation   One possibility is that REM sleep plays a role in strengthening or consolidating new memories. Several recent studies provide evidence for this idea. For example, Karni and colleagues (1994) asked subjects to solve a perceptual task that required detecting a small target pattern in a complex visual array. Subjects practised the perceptual task shortly before going to sleep, and were retested the next morning. The key finding was that subjects who had a normal night's sleep, and those whose sleep was disturbed only when they were in stage 3 or 4 sleep, benefited from the practice session, but subjects who were deprived of REM sleep did not. Mednick and colleagues (2002) used the same perceptual task and showed that performance across blocks of trials was enhanced if subjects napped for 30 to 60 minutes during the breaks between blocks.

These results, and others reviewed by Stickgold and co-authors (2001), suggest that activities during REM sleep are needed to consolidate some forms of learning overnight. But what are these activities? It's unclear at this point, but one possibility is that the neurotransmitter *acetylcholine* (ACh) may be involved. Studies with animals have shown that ACh increases in the brain during REM sleep. This important neurotransmitter is thought to play a role in storing memories. As we mentioned in Chapter 3, memory problems are common in patients suffering from Alzheimer's disease, and it's known that neurons in the brain that produce ACh often degenerate during the disease. Thus, ACh may be needed to consolidate the storage of experience, which may in turn explain why REM activity is important in the consolidation process. Unfortunately, at this point this account is purely speculative, and researchers even question the evidence that REM sleep is important for consolidating memories (e.g., Vertes & Eastman, 2000).

Wish Fulfillment   Historically, many psychologists viewed dreaming as an extremely important psychological phenomenon. Sigmund Freud believed that dreams, once interpreted, could serve as a "royal road to the unconscious." Freud believed that dreaming was a psychological mechanism for *wish fulfillment,* a way to satisfy forbidden wishes and desires, especially sexual ones. He believed that dreams often look bizarre because the objects within our dreams are often symbolic. We hide our true feelings because our wishes and desires are too disturbing to be allowed to come to consciousness directly. To Freud, for example, a cigar or a gun (or any elongated object) in a dream might represent a penis, whereas a tunnel (or any entryway) could stand for a vagina. To establish the true meaning of the dream, Freud believed, it was necessary to distinguish between the dream's **manifest content**—the things seen and otherwise experienced by the dreamer—and its **latent content,** those hidden desires that are too disturbing to be confronted directly.

Compared to Freud, most modern psychologists are more reluctant to search for hidden meaning in dreams. Although certain kinds of dream events cut across people and cultures (e.g., people often dream of flying or falling or of having their teeth fall out), there is little evidence that particular dream contents (such as cigars) have any universal symbolic meaning. The interpretation of dreams is in the eye of the dreamer. Indeed, far from focusing on unconscious wishes, dreams often relate to the dreamer's waking concerns (Marquardt et al., 1996; Nielsen & Powell, 1992). For example, students who care about their studies in their waking lives quite often report dreams with scholastic themes, such as trying to take an exam but not having anything to write with. In addition, there is no compelling evidence that dreams are a reliable source of accurate memories of childhood events (Brenneis, 1994). Even recurrent dreams don't necessarily have any hidden psychological significance. A troubling dream might lead you to wake up suddenly and think about the dream, so that it becomes firmly ingrained in memory and consequently is likely to occur again. It is also of interest to note that virtually all mammals experience REM, as do birds and some reptiles, such as turtles (Durie, 1981). Moreover, human infants spend a remarkable amount of time in REM sleep; even human fetuses show REM patterns in the womb. It seems very unlikely that the fetus or mouse in REM sleep is working out some hidden sexual desire or conflict. But if dreams are not about wish fulfillment, then what is the function of dreams?

Activation-Synthesis Hypothesis   An alternative to the notion that dreams are vehicles for imaginative wish fulfillment is the **activation-synthesis hypothesis** of Hobson and McCarley (1977; Hobson et al., 2000). This view proposes that the initial seeds of dreams are random activity in the brain. During REM sleep, for reasons that are not particularly clear, cells in the hindbrain spontaneously activate the higher centres of the brain. This activity could arise simply to exercise the brain circuitry (Edelman, 1987), or it could be a consequence of random events in the room (e.g., the cat snoring or a mosquito buzzing around your face). Whatever the reason, the higher brain centres have evolved to interpret lower brain signals in meaningful ways. According to the activation-synthesis hypothesis, the brain creates a story in an effort to make some sense out of the signals that it's receiving. But in the activation-synthesis view, there's little of psychological significance here: Dreams are assumed to represent only a synthesis of random neurological activity (Weinstein et al., 1991).

The activation-synthesis hypothesis has received a lot of attention among sleep researchers because it takes into account how biological activity in the brain changes

manifest content
According to Freud, the objects and events experienced in a dream.

latent content
According to Freud, the true psychological meaning of objects and events in dreams, which are said to represent hidden wishes and desires that are too disturbing to be confronted directly.

activation-synthesis hypothesis
The idea that dreams represent the brain's attempt to make sense out of random patterns of neural activity generated during sleep.

during sleep. It also provides another explanation for why dream content is often bizarre: Since the activated signals that produce dreams are random in nature, the higher centres of the brain have a tough time creating a storyline that is meaningful and consistent. Ironically, this view implies that there may be some psychological significance to reported dreams after all, but not for the reasons suggested by Freud. The biological mechanisms that generate the REM state may not be psychologically driven, but the brain's *interpretations* of those purely physiological activities may have psychological meaning. The story your brain creates probably tells us something about how you think when you're awake (Antrobus, 1991; Foulkes, 1985).

The activation-synthesis hypothesis is an intriguing alternative to the traditional Freudian view, but much remains to be worked out. The theory is a bit vague and consequently difficult to test. Also, in its present form the theory focuses primarily on brain activity that occurs during REM sleep but, as noted earlier, we also dream during non-REM states.

We've discussed two prominent views of dreaming—Freudian wish fulfillment and activation-synthesis—but there are others. For example, some psychologists have suggested that dreams serve a problem-solving function. We may dream to focus our attention on particularly troubling current problems in order to work toward possible solutions (Cartwright, 1991; Fiss, 1991). But the evidence for the problem-solving view is weak, relying mainly on anecdotes rather than systematic research (Blagrove, 1996; Domhoff, 1996). Yet another recent view comes from evolutionary psychologists who have speculated that dreaming allows us to simulate threats from the environment and mentally practise the skills needed to avoid those threats (Revonsuo, 2000). People often do dream about aggressive events and threatening situations, but whether dreaming

Critical Thinking

The activation-synthesis hypothesis proposes that dreams arise from the interpretation of random neural activity. Yet many people dream of flying, falling, or being unprepared for a test. How do you explain the fact that people have similar dreams if dreaming results from the interpretation of random neural activity?

Concept Summary

FUNCTIONS OF SLEEP AND DREAMING

Why Do We Sleep?

Theory	Description	Evaluation
Repair and restoration	Sleep restores and/or repairs the body and brain.	Not strongly supported by data; restorative activities of the body are not limited to sleep. Changes in physical activity do not lead to consistent changes in subsequent sleep patterns.
Survival value	Sleep increases chances of survival.	Receives some support from sleep patterns in different species of animals.

Why Do We Dream?

Theory	Description	Evaluation
Wish fulfillment (Freud)	Dreaming is a psychological mechanism for fulfilling wishes, often sexual in nature. Dreams include both manifest and latent content.	Difficult to assess; most modern psychologists are reluctant to ascribe hidden meaning to dreams. The meaning of dreams is in the eye of the dreamer.
Activation-synthesis	Dreaming is a consequence of random activity that occurs in the brain during REM sleep. The brain creates a story to make sense of these random signals.	Theory is vague and difficult to test. Dreaming is not limited to REM sleep.
Problem solving	Dreaming helps us focus on our current problems to find solutions.	Evidence is weak and anecdotal.
Threat simulation	Dreaming evolved to help us practise the skills needed to avoid threats.	Still speculation at this point.

really evolved to help us handle real-world threats remains highly speculative (Flanagan, 2000). It's safe to assume that REM sleep and dreaming reflect some important property of the adaptive mind, but at the moment major questions remain unanswered.

Sleep Disorders

We end our review of sleep and dreaming with a brief discussion of sleep disorders. Psychologists and other mental health professionals divide sleep disorders into two main diagnostic categories: (1) *dyssomnias*, which are problems associated with the amount, timing, and quality of sleep, and (2) *parasomnias*, which are abnormal disturbances that occur during sleep. Let's consider some prominent examples of each type.

Dyssomnias The most common type of dyssomnia is **insomnia,** a condition marked by difficulties in initiating or maintaining sleep. Everyone has trouble getting to sleep from time to time, and most people have awakened in the middle of the night and been unable to get back to sleep. For the clinical diagnosis of insomnia, however, these difficulties must be chronic—lasting for at least a month. It's been estimated that perhaps 30% of the population suffers from some degree of insomnia, although the percentage of severe cases is thought to be closer to 15% (Bootzin et al., 1993; Gillin, 1993). Sutton and co-authors (2001) reported on a survey of 11 924 Canadian adults, of whom 24% reported suffering from insomnia. There are many potential causes for the condition, including stress, emotional problems, alcohol and other drug use, as well as medical conditions. Some kinds of insomnia may even be learned; for example, children who regularly fall asleep in the presence of their parents often have trouble getting back to sleep if later they wake up alone (Adair et al., 1991). Presumably, these children have learned to associate going to sleep with the presence of a parent and consequently cannot return to sleep without the parent present.

Whereas insomnia is characterized by an inability to sleep, in **hypersomnia** the problem is *too much* sleep. People who are diagnosed with hypersomnia show excessive sleepiness—they're often caught catnapping during the day, and they complain of being tired all the time. The cause of this condition is unknown, although genetic factors may be involved (Parkes & Block, 1989). Excessive sleepiness can also be caused by infectious diseases, such as mononucleosis, and by a sleep disorder called *sleep apnea*. Sleep apnea is a relatively rare condition in which the sleeper repeatedly stops breathing, usually for short periods lasting up to a minute or so. The episodes typically end with the person briefly waking up, gasping for breath. Because these episodes occur frequently throughout the night, the affected person feels tired during the day. Significant sleep apnea problems are found in perhaps 1% to 2% of the population, although a much higher percentage of individuals experience occasional or briefer episodes (Kales & Kales, 1984).

Narcolepsy is a very rare sleep disorder, characterized by sudden extreme sleepiness. Sleep attacks can occur at any time during the day and can last from a few seconds to several minutes. What makes this disorder unusual is that the person seems to directly enter a kind of REM sleep state. He or she loses all muscle tone and can even fall to the ground in a sound sleep. Fortunately, not all instances of narcolepsy are this extreme, but it can be a disabling condition. There is some evidence that the disorder has a genetic link (Barlow & Durand, 2002).

Parasomnias The second category of sleep disorders, parasomnias, includes such abnormal sleep disturbances as nightmares, night terrors, and sleepwalking (Silber, 2001). **Nightmares** are frightening dreams that occur primarily during the REM stage of sleep. They inevitably cause the sleeper to awaken; if they recur frequently, they can lead to symptoms of insomnia. What causes nightmares? No one is certain at this point, although very frequent nightmares may indicate the presence of a psychological disorder.

insomnia
A chronic condition marked by difficulties in initiating or maintaining sleep, lasting for a period of at least one month.

hypersomnia
A chronic condition marked by excessive sleepiness.

nightmares
Frightening dreams that occur primarily during the REM stage of sleep.

Night terrors, which occur mainly in children, are terrifying experiences in which the sleeper awakens suddenly in an extreme state of panic. The child may sit in bed screaming and will show little responsiveness to others who are present. Night terrors are not considered to be serious indicators of psychological or medical problems, and they tend to go away with age.

Finally, **sleepwalking** occurs when the sleeper rises during sleep and wanders about. Sleepwalking happens mainly in childhood, tends to vanish as the child reaches adolescence, and is not thought to result from a serious psychological or medical problem. It's interesting to note that both night terrors and sleepwalking occur during periods of non-REM sleep, which suggests that neither is related to dreaming (although it remains possible that they are related to non-REM dreaming).

night terrors
A condition in which the sleeper, usually a child, awakens suddenly in an extreme state of panic; not thought to be associated with dreaming.

sleepwalking
A condition in which the sleeper rises during sleep and wanders about; not thought to be associated with dreaming.

Test Yourself 5.2

To check your understanding of sleep and dreaming, answer the following questions. (You will find the answers in Appendix B.)

1. Choose the EEG pattern that best fits the following descriptions. Choose from the following: alpha waves; delta activity; K complex; sleep spindles; theta waves; REM.
   a. The characteristic pattern found in stage 1 sleep: _____
   b. Often triggered by loud noises during stage 2 sleep: _____
   c. Another name for the slow-wave patterns that are found during stage 3 and stage 4 sleep: _____
   d. The characteristic pattern of paradoxical sleep: _____
2. Which of the following statements is most consistent with the view that we sleep because it keeps us away from hostile environments during times when we can't see well?
   a. Sleep deprivation leads to a breakdown in normal functioning.
   b. Fearful dreams make us wary of venturing outside.
   c. Cats sleep more than cows.
   d. People sleep less as they age.
3. Diagnose the following sleep disorders based on the information provided. Choose from the following: hypersomnia; insomnia; nightmare; night terror; sleep apnea; sleepwalking.
   a. Difficulty initiating and maintaining sleep: _____
   b. Sleeper awakens suddenly, screaming, but the EEG pattern indicates a period of non-REM sleep: _____
   c. Sleeper repeatedly stops breathing during the night, usually for short periods lasting less than one minute: _____
   d. A frightening dream that usually occurs during the REM stage of sleep: _____

ALTERING AWARENESS: PSYCHOACTIVE DRUGS

Learning Goals
1. Understand the relationship between neurotransmitters and psychoactive drugs.
2. Learn the different categories of psychoactive drugs, and provide examples of each.
3. Be able to discuss the psychological factors that influence the effects of psychoactive drugs.

THE RHYTHMIC CYCLES OF SLEEP reveal how conscious awareness can shift in dramatic ways as the electrical activity of the brain changes. We haven't talked much about the biological factors that control these brain changes, but it shouldn't surprise you to learn that the brain's chemical messengers, the neurotransmitters, are primarily responsible. The start of REM sleep, for example, appears to be controlled by neurons in the hindbrain, particularly the *pons,* which release acetylcholine (Amzica & Steriade, 1996). In studies with animals, it's been found that levels of acetylcholine in the cortex are highest during REM and waking states and drop to lower levels during the stages of slow-wave sleep (Jasper & Tessier, 1969). Exactly when we fall asleep and how long we sleep may be affected by the actions of the neurotransmitter *GABA;* wakefulness and general arousal have been linked to *norepinephrine* and *dopamine.* Thus, the mind's own chemicals play important roles in controlling changes in consciousness through the sleep–wake cycle.

The brain is a kind of biochemical factory, altering moods and shifting awareness by moderating the release of its various neurotransmitters. For example, we've previously mentioned that the brain sometimes reacts to stress or injury by releasing brain chemicals called *endorphins,* which reduce pain and elevate mood. Altering awareness chemically in such a fashion is highly adaptive, because the delay of pain can enable an organism to escape from a life-threatening situation.

If an external chemical agent enters your body, it too can radically alter the delicate chemical balance that controls awareness and other mental processes. Obviously, drugs can have tremendously beneficial effects, especially in the treatment of psychological and medical disorders (see Chapter 15). But drugs can have negative effects as well, even if their short-term effects are pleasant. As you probably know, drug abuse, particularly of alcohol and tobacco, is directly or indirectly responsible for tens of thousands of deaths annually in Canada (MacNeill & Webster, 1995; Single et al., 1996). Single and co-authors estimated that premature mortality due to drugs accounts for about one in five of the total number of deaths each year. In this section, we'll consider the actions of drugs labelled **psychoactive drugs,** those that alter conscious experience.

Drug Actions and Effects

Psychologists are interested in psychoactive drugs for three main reasons. First, some psychoactive drugs are effective in the treatment of psychological disorders, such as attention deficit/hyperactivity disorder, schizophrenia, and depression. Treating such disorders is a primary goal of many clinical psychologists and psychiatrists. Second, the

psychoactive drugs
Drugs that affect behaviour and mental processes, and produce alterations of conscious awareness.

This series of PET scans shows how an opium-like drug affects general activity in the brain. The first PET scan in the top row shows a normal active brain; the last PET scan in the bottom row shows diminished activity after the drug has taken full effect.

abuse of some psychoactive drugs has tremendously destructive real-world consequences, harming users, their families, and the wider society. Many psychologists are interested in the development of scientifically validated approaches to discourage people from abusing psychoactive drugs and to treat and support those who have developed drug problems. Third, psychoactive drugs have powerful effects on behaviour and mental processes, and such effects are interesting in their own right and can help us understand the normal workings of the mind.

Psychoactive drugs, like the natural chemicals produced by the brain, exert their effects primarily by changing the normal communication channels of neurons. Neuron-to-neuron communication can be affected in a variety of ways. Some drugs, such as *nicotine,* duplicate the action of neurotransmitters by attaching themselves to neuronal receptor sites; this mimicking action allows the drug to produce the same effect as the brain's natural chemical messenger. Other drugs depress or block the action of neurotransmitters; some sleeping pills, for instance, decrease norepinephrine or dopamine stimulation. The psychoactive drug *fluoxetine* (known commercially as Prozac) is widely used to treat depression; it (as well as a wide variety of related drugs) slows the process through which the neurotransmitter serotonin is broken down and taken back up into the transmitting cell (Kramer, 1993; for a critique of Prozac, see Kirsch & Sapirstein, 1999).

Over time, repeated use of a drug can change the way the body reacts to that chemical. For example, a drug **tolerance** can develop, which means that increasing amounts of the drug are needed to produce the same physical and behavioural effects. Tolerance is a kind of adaptation that the brain makes to compensate for the effects of the drug. **Drug dependency** is manifested as either a physical or a psychological need for continued use (Woody & Cacciola, 1997). With physical dependency, the person experiences **withdrawal** symptoms when he or she stops taking the drug. These are clear, measurable physical reactions such as sweating, vomiting, changes in heart rate, or tremors. Drug dependency is the primary cause of substance abuse, although the mechanisms that lead to dependency are still a matter of some debate. At this point, it's not certain whether dependency develops as a consequence of "urgings" produced by biological withdrawal or whether people essentially learn to become dependent on the drug with repeated use (Tiffany, 1990).

Categories of Psychoactive Drugs

It's useful to classify psychoactive drugs into four categories—depressants, stimulants, opiates, and hallucinogens—based on their specific mind-altering characteristics. We'll briefly examine each type and then conclude with a discussion of some psychological factors involved in drug use.

Depressants In general, drugs classified as **depressants** slow, or depress, the ongoing activity of the central nervous system. *Ethyl alcohol,* which is present in beer, wine, and distilled drinks, is a well-known example of a depressant. Biochemically, alcohol appears to lead to an increase in either the secretion or effectiveness of the neurotransmitters GABA and dopamine. Both usually act as inhibitory messengers in the brain, so neurons in a number of vital brain centres become inhibited (Suzdak et al., 1986). Drinkers feel "high" after a few drinks in part because the drug produces a calming effect on the body, which leads to a reduction in anxiety (Oscar-Berman et al., 1997). By the way, animals also find the effects of alcohol quite reinforcing; they will perform tasks that yield small amounts of alcohol as a reward (Wise & Bozarth, 1987).

As the consumption of alcohol increases, more complex psychological effects emerge because those brain centres that control judgment become sluggish from inhibition. As you're undoubtedly aware, after a few drinks people often start acting in ways that are contrary to their normal behavioural tendencies (Steele & Josephs, 1990). The normally demure may become loud and aggressive; the sexually inhibited may become flirtatious and provocative. These behavioural changes are produced, in part, because

tolerance

An adaptation that the body makes to compensate for the continued use of a drug such that increasing amounts of the drug are needed to produce the same physical, psychological, and behavioural effects.

drug dependency

A condition in which an individual experiences a physical or psychological need for continued use of a drug.

withdrawal

Clear and measurable physical reactions, such as sweating, vomiting, changes in heart rate, or tremors, that occur when a person stops taking certain drugs after continued use.

depressants

A class of drugs that slow or depress the ongoing activity of the central nervous system.

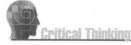

Critical Thinking

Do you believe that all psychoactive drugs should be legalized for recreational use? If not, how can you justify the availability of alcohol, nicotine, and caffeine?

Moderate drinking can be pleasurable, but consuming too much alcohol can have severe negative consequences on your health and well-being.

stimulants

A class of drugs that increase central nervous system activity, enhancing neural transmission.

alcohol reduces self-awareness. Drinkers are less likely to monitor their behaviours and actions closely, and they tend to forget about their problems (Hull & Bond, 1986).

These carefree moments are stolen at a cost, of course, because the body eventually reacts to the drug in a more negative way. Nearly one in every ten Canadian respondents to the General Social Survey of 1993 reported having problems with their drinking, and nearly a quarter reported exceeding the low-risk guidelines for alcohol consumption (1 or 2 units a day). Overconsumption leads to impaired judgment, coordination, and reaction time while under the influence, and fatigue, nausea, and depression afterward. Every year, numerous Canadians die by pure and simple alcohol overdose: If enough alcohol is consumed in a short period of time, the result is death. Even consumption far short of a lethal overdose increases the likelihood of accidents. The Canadian Centre on Substance Abuse estimates that over 6500 Canadians lost their lives as a result of alcohol consumption in 1995, and nearly 81 000 were hospitalized due to alcohol in 1995–96. A disproportionate number of alcohol-related deaths are young people. Many such cases involve the combination of drinking and driving: Among Canadian drivers killed in automobile accidents in 1996, 35% had blood alcohol concentrations over the legal limit. A study by Single et al. (1996) estimated that overconsumption of alcohol by Canadians cost us $7.5 billion per year (or about $265 per Canadian). There is evidence that moderate drinking (1 to 2 units per day) has certain health benefits (e.g., reduced risk of heart attack; see Gronbaek, 2002), but it is tragically clear that overconsumption causes a great deal of harm.

Barbiturates and *tranquillizers* are also classified as depressant drugs. Both are widely prescribed for the treatment of anxiety and insomnia, and they produce effects in the brain similar to those induced by alcohol (the neurotransmitter GABA is again involved; Gardner, 1997). Like alcohol, at low doses tranquillizing agents tend to produce pleasurable feelings of relaxation. But at higher doses the ability to concentrate is lost, memory is impaired, and speech becomes slurred. Barbiturate use also commonly leads to tolerance and dependency. With continued use, larger and larger doses of the drug are required to obtain the same effect, and the user becomes physically and psychologically dependent on the drug. Tranquillizers (such as the widely prescribed Valium and Xanax) are less habit forming than barbiturates.

Stimulants A **stimulant** is a drug that increases central nervous system activity. Examples of stimulants include *caffeine, amphetamines, cocaine, nicotine,* and *Ecstasy.* These agents generally increase alertness and can affect mood by inducing feelings of pleasure. The morning cup of coffee is an excellent example of how low doses of a stimulant—caffeine—can improve your mood and enhance concentration and attention. Other effects of stimulants include dilated pupils, increased heart and respiration rate, and decreased appetite. In large doses, stimulants can produce extreme anxiety and even convulsions and death.

Both amphetamines and cocaine produce their stimulating effects by increasing the effectiveness of the neurotransmitters norepinephrine and dopamine. Dopamine seems to be primarily responsible for the positive, reinforcing qualities of these drugs (Wise & Rompre, 1989). Research has shown that animals will work hard to administer themselves drugs that increase the activity of dopamine-based synapses. Cocaine, which is derived from the leaves of the coca plant, blocks the reabsorption of both norepinephrine and dopamine. When reabsorption is blocked, these transmitter substances are able to exert their effects for a longer period of time. Cocaine produces intense feelings of euphoria, although the effects of the drug wear off relatively quickly. A half hour or so after the drug enters the body, the user "crashes," in part because the drug has temporarily depleted the user's internal supply of norepinephrine and dopamine. Regular use of cocaine leads to dependence and tolerance and produces a number of very harmful side effects, including intense episodes of paranoia and delusions (Stein & Ellinwood, 1993), insomnia, impotence, and even death from heart attack, stroke, or seizure. "Crack" cocaine is a particularly powerful and dangerous form of this drug.

Nicotine, the psychoactive drug in tobacco, is also a stimulant. Approximately 100 000 Canadian teenagers take up smoking each year. Nicotine is highly addictive, and tobacco delivers a powerful mix of lethal substances to the user. It's estimated that smoking costs the Canadian economy $15 billion a year, and more than 30 000 Canadians die from tobacco each year (Single et al., 1996).

The psychoactive drug that has gained the most popularity in recent years is *methylenedioxymethamphetamine* (or MDMA), better known as *Ecstasy* (also called X, XTC, and a variety of other names). The RCMP reports that law enforcement officers seized nearly 4 million doses of Ecstasy in 2000–2001, and Canada Customs seized 120 kilograms of the drug (enough to make about 1.5 million pills, with an estimated street value of $52.5 million) in a single bust in October of 2002. It is likely that only a small fraction of the Ecstasy entering Canada is stopped by authorities, so these numbers suggest that tremendous quantities of this drug are being used by Canadians. This drug combines characteristics of stimulants and hallucinogens (although hallucinations are likely to be experienced only when dangerously high doses are taken). Users report feelings of euphoria, interpersonal closeness with others, and boundless energy. That sounds great, but new evidence of the long-term ill effects of Ecstasy use is frightening. For example, Ricaurte and colleagues (2002) gave nonhuman primates doses of MDMA comparable to what a human recreational user would take at an all-night rave. Animals exposed to several sequential doses of MDMA suffered severe neurotoxicity, meaning that there was very extensive death of brain cells (especially among neurons that use the neurotransmitter dopamine). These animals also had evidence of impaired motor control. To quote the Ricaurte study, "MDMA users may unwittingly be putting themselves at risk ... for developing neuropsychiatric disorders related to brain dopamine and/or serotonin deficiency" (see Gowing, 2002, and Hegadoren, 1999, for comprehensive reviews of human and animal research on the risks of Ecstasy).

Opiates Drugs classified as **opiates** (also sometimes called *narcotics)* depress nervous system activity, thereby reducing anxiety, elevating mood (with small doses), and lowering sensitivity to pain. Well-known examples of opiates include opium, heroin, and morphine. As you learned previously, morphine, which is derived from the flowering opium plant, acts on existing neuronal receptor sites in the nervous system. Its pain-killing effects and pleasurable mood shifts (it's named after Morpheus, the Greek god of dreams) apparently arise from the fact that it mimics the brain's own chemicals, specifically *endorphins,* which are involved in reducing pain. Opiates, however, can quickly produce strong physical and psychological dependence. The brain is changed with continued use; once usage is stopped, the body rebels with intense and prolonged withdrawal symptoms.

People who are regular users of opiates such as heroin or morphine suffer in many ways, greatly overshadowing the fleeting pleasures that immediately follow drug use. Kicking an opiate habit is extremely tough because the physical withdrawal symptoms—which can include everything from excessive yawning, to extreme nausea, to severe chills—last for days. Users who opt for the typical method of administration—intravenous injection—run additional risks of contracting diseases such as HIV and hepatitis C. Longitudinal studies of heroin addicts paint a grim picture: Addicts tend to

opiates

A class of drugs that reduce anxiety, lower sensitivity to pain, and elevate mood; opiates often act to depress nervous system activity.

The flowering opium plant.

hallucinogens

A class of drugs that tend to disrupt normal mental and emotional functioning and produce distorted perceptions.

die young (at an average age of about 40 years) from a variety of causes, including suicide, homicide, and overdose (Hser et al., 1993).

Hallucinogens For the final category of psychoactive drugs, **hallucinogens** (sometimes called *psychedelics*), the term "psychoactive" is particularly apt. *Hallucinogens* play havoc with your normal internal construction of reality. Perception itself is fractured, and the world may become awash in fantastic colours, sounds, and tactile sensations. Two of the best known examples of these drugs, *mescaline* and *psilocybin*, occur naturally in the environment. Mescaline comes from a certain kind of cactus, and psilocybin is a type of mushroom. Both of these drugs have been used for centuries, primarily in the context of religious rituals and ceremonies. Since the 1960s, they have served as potentially dangerous recreational drugs for those seeking alternative realities.

Lysergic acid diethylamide (LSD) is a synthetic psychedelic drug. LSD is thought to mimic the action of the neurotransmitter serotonin (Strassman, 1992); the drug acts on specific serotonin-based receptor sites in the brain, producing stimulation. For reasons that are not particularly clear, variations in sensation and perception are produced. A typical LSD experience, which can last for up to 16 hours, consists of profound changes in perception. Some users report a phenomenon called *synesthesia,* which is a blending of sensory experiences—colours may feel warm or cold, and rough textures may begin to sing. Also for unknown reasons, a user's experience can turn sharply wrong. Panic or depression can develop, increasing the likelihood of accidents and personal harm. Users also sometimes report the occurrence of "flashbacks," in which the sensations of the drug are re-experienced long after the drug has presumably left the body.

Marijuana, which comes from the naturally occurring hemp plant *Cannabis,* can also be classified as a hallucinogenic drug. It is unusual to see profound distortions of perceptual reality with this drug, however, unless large amounts are ingested. Marijuana can be smoked or swallowed, and its effects last around 4 hours. THC, the active ingredient in marijuana, inhibits release of a variety of neurotransmitters, and may suppress inhibitory synaptic transmission involving the neurotransmitter GABA (Davies et al., 2002). Users often report a melting away of anxiety, a general sense of well-being, and an intensification of normal sensations. Changes in the perception of time and its passage are sometimes reported, along with increased appetite. As with other hallucinogenic drugs, marijuana does not always produce a pleasant experience. Indeed, reactions to marijuana vary dramatically, both across individuals and within an

Concept Summary

PSYCHOACTIVE DRUGS

Category	Examples	General Effects
Depressants	Ethyl alcohol Barbiturates Tranquillizers	Believed to enhance the effectiveness of GABA and dopamine, which often act as inhibitory messengers in the brain. Produce pleasurable feelings of relaxation, but at high doses concentration and memory are impaired.
Stimulants	Caffeine Amphetamines Cocaine Nicotine Ecstasy	Amphetamines and cocaine may work primarily by increasing the effectiveness of dopamine and norepinephrine. Stimulants tend to increase alertness, elevate mood, and produce physical changes such as increased heart and respiration rates.
Opiates	Opium Morphine Heroin	Depressing of nervous system activity, resulting in reduced anxiety, mood elevation, and lower sensitivity to pain. Tend to produce strong physical and psychological dependence.
Hallucinogens	LSD Mescaline Psilocybin Marijuana	Produce variations in sensation and perception. LSD is believed to mimic the action of serotonin. Some users report *synesthesia,* a blending of sensory experiences. Marijuana often leads to a general sense of well-being and heightened awareness of normal sensations. Negative side effects can include anxiety, fearfulness, and panic.

individual on different occasions. Some users report anxiety, extreme fearfulness, and even panic; others experience flat affect and doziness (Fackelmann, 1993). The effects of the drug are usually followed by feelings of mild fatigue.

A number of studies have shown that marijuana use impairs concentration, memory, motor coordination, and the ability to track things visually (Moskowitz, 1985; Sullivan, 2000); these side effects probably increase the likelihood of traffic accidents when driving under the influence. Less is known about the long-term effects of regular use (partly because it is not ethically possible to randomly assign people to long-term dope-smoking versus control conditions), but there's some evidence that marijuana may impair a variety of cognitive functions, including memory (Solowij, 2002; Millsaps et al., 1994; Pope et al., 2001). A study by Croft and co-authors (2001) indicates that combined use of Ecstasy and marijuana has particularly deleterious effects on cognition. There is also evidence that smoking marijuana can contribute to a variety of serious respiratory problems (Ashton, 2001). On the positive side, marijuana may help reduce some of the negative symptoms of chemotherapy (e.g., nausea), and in some cases it's proved helpful in treating eye disorders such as glaucoma (Watson et al., 2000).

Psychological Factors

Among the more interesting characteristics of psychoactive drugs, especially to psychologists, are the sharp differences that can be seen in the effects of any particular drug on different individuals. Two people can take the same drug, in exactly the same quantity, but experience completely different effects. A small amount of LSD consumed by Teo produces a euphoric "religious experience"; the same amount for Jane produces a frightening descent into a whirlpool of terror. Why? Shouldn't the pharmacological effects on the neurotransmitters in the brain produce similar psychological effects?

The answer is that the psychological effects are influenced by many factors. The environmental setting in which a drug is taken, for example, is known to affect the experience. Smoking marijuana for the first time in a car speeding at 120 km/h might limit the anxiety-reducing effects of the drug. Many users report that familiarity with the drug's effects is also important—users claim that you need to "learn" to smoke marijuana or take LSD before the innermost "secrets" of the drug are revealed. In fact, experienced users of marijuana have been found to experience a "high" after smoking a cigarette they only thought was marijuana; similar effects did not occur for novice users (Jones, 1971). Both familiarity and the environment affect the user's *mental set*, his or her expectations about the drug's harmful and beneficial consequences. Likely there are also individual differences in users' physiological metabolism and in their psychological reactions. For instance, some people develop resistance or tolerance to a drug faster than others do. The experience of a drug may even depend on such mundane things as whether the person has eaten recently or is well rested.

Test Yourself 5.3

Test your knowledge about psychoactive drugs by picking the category of drug that best fits each of the following statements. Choose from among these terms: caffeine; depressant; hallucinogen; opiate; stimulant. (You will find the answers in Appendix B.)

1. Increases central nervous system activity: _____
2. Reduces pain by mimicking the brain's own natural pain-reducing chemicals:

    _____
3. Tends to produce inhibitory effects by increasing the effectiveness of the neurotransmitter GABA: _____
4. Distorts perception and may lead to flashbacks: _____
5. The active ingredient found in your morning cup of coffee:

    _____

ALTERING AWARENESS: INDUCED STATES

Learning Goals
1. Become familiar with the physiological and behavioural effects of hypnosis.
2. Learn the scientific status of hypnosis as a memory-retrieval technique.
3. Be able to describe the dissociation and role-playing accounts of hypnosis.
4. Understand the physical, behavioural, and psychological effects of meditation.

THE SETTING IS PARIS, late in the year 1783. Dressed in a lilac silk robe, German-born physician Franz Anton Mesmer works to restore the delicate balance of universal fluids within his patients. He attaches large magnets to each patient—the better to affect their animal magnetism—and then rhythmically passes an iron rod, in large wavelike motions, over their outstretched bodies. His patients fall into a trancelike state: They can still talk and move their limbs on command, but each appears to have lost all forms of voluntary control. Upon later awakening, many feel better, apparently cured of their various physical and psychological problems.

Although Mesmer eventually fell into disrepute, rejected by the scientific community of his time, the phenomenon of "mesmerizing" did not. Today, of course, we recognize that the unusual behaviours he induced in his patients had nothing to do with magnets or universal fluids. Modern psychologists would explain the bizarre behaviour of Mesmer's patients as an example of hypnosis. **Hypnosis** can be defined as a social interaction between a person perceived to be a hypnotist and a person who perceives himself or herself as a hypnotic subject; the interaction produces a *heightened state of suggestibility* in the subject. It is of interest to psychologists partly because, like the related topic of meditation, it's a technique that is specifically designed to alter conscious awareness. As you'll see shortly, hypnosis has some highly adaptive properties.

hypnosis

A social interaction between a person perceived to be a hypnotist and a person who perceives himself or herself to be a hypnotic subject; the interaction produces a heightened state of suggestibility in the subject.

The Phenomena of Hypnosis

Despite some two centuries of work on the topic, our understanding of hypnosis remains incomplete. Researchers are not sure whether hypnosis is truly a unique state of awareness, qualitatively different from that of normal waking consciousness, or a kind of social role-playing in which the subject takes on the part of a hypnotized person. But we do know a few things about what hypnosis is *not*. For one thing, people who are hypnotized do not enter into anything resembling a deep sleep. The word *hypnosis* does come from the Greek *hypnos,* meaning "to sleep," but hypnosis bears little physiological relation to sleep. The EEG patterns of a hypnotized subject, along with other physiological indexes, more closely resemble those of someone who is relaxed rather than asleep (Graffen et al., 1995). Moreover, certain reflexes that are commonly absent during sleep, such as the knee jerk, are still present under hypnosis (Pratt et al., 1988).

Another myth is that only weak-willed people are susceptible to hypnotic induction. Everyone appears to be susceptible to a degree, in the sense that we all show heightened suggestibility under some circumstances. There are individual differences among people—hypnotic suggestibility scales indicate that only about 20% of the population are highly hypnotizable (Hilgard, 1965)—but it's not clear what factors account for these differences. Personality studies have shown that people who are easy to hypnotize are not generally weak willed or highly conforming, although they may have more active imaginations than people who resist hypnosis (Nadon et al., 1991).

Yet another myth is that hypnosis can only be induced by going through a particular induction ritual. It is true that hypnotists do use such rituals, but a wide variety of methods can be used to induce hypnotic behaviour. The most popular induction technique is one in which the hypnotist, acting as an authority figure, suggests to the subject that he or she is growing increasingly more relaxed and sleepy: "Your eyes are getting heavier and heavier, you can barely keep your lids open," and so on. Often the to-be-hypnotized person is asked to fixate on something, perhaps a spot on the wall or a swinging pendulum. The logic here is that eye fixation leads to muscle fatigue, which helps convince clients that they are indeed becoming increasingly relaxed. Other approaches to induction rely on more subtle suggestions (Erickson, 1964), including ones that many people would not recognize as hypnotic induction procedures at all. No one method is necessarily better than any other. In the words of one researcher, "The art of hypnosis relies on not providing the client with grounds for resisting" the hypnotist's suggestions (Araoz, 1982, p. 106).

Once hypnotized, a person becomes highly suggestible, responding to instructions from the hypnotist in ways that seem involuntary. The hypnotist can then use his or her power of suggestion to achieve adaptive ends, such as helping the subject to reduce anxiety or increase self-esteem. Research indicates that hypnosis can be a significant adjunct to other forms of therapy in achieving such aims (Kirsch et al., 1995). Anesthetic effects are also possible at deep stages of hypnosis. Hypnotized patients report less pain during childbirth (Harmon et al., 1990) and dental work (Houle et al., 1988). It has even been possible to perform major surgeries (such as appendectomies) using hypnosis as the primary anesthesia (Kihlstrom, 1985). Research is ongoing to determine the biological bases for these striking analgesic effects. It was once thought, for example, that the release of endorphins by the brain might be responsible, although this now seems unlikely (Moret et al., 1991).

If you ever see a stage hypnotist, you're likely to witness an astonishing variety of hypnotically induced behaviours. One impressive demonstration is **catalepsy:** One of the hypnotized person's limbs is placed in some unusual position (perhaps raising a leg or an arm in the air), and the subject then retains this position rigidly for long periods of time without signs of tiring. In a related demonstration, the hypnotized person lies with his or her head on one chair and heels on another, remaining rigid in a way that seems miraculous. Apparent perceptual illusions are also common: The volunteer appears to see or hear things that are not really there or ignores loud noises that would

Critical Thinking

Under what circumstances do you think it might be adaptive for someone to enter a heightened state of suggestibility?

catalepsy

A hypnotically induced behaviour characterized by an ability to hold one or more limbs of the body in a rigid position for long periods without tiring. Motivated nonhypnotized subjects can enact catalepsy as well as hypnotized subjects.

normally cause someone to jump. Hypnotized individuals may also perform a variety of ridiculous behaviours, such as flapping their arms and quacking like a duck, in response to the hypnotist's suggestions. As you'll learn later in this chapter, these phenomena are less bizarre (and less specific to hypnosis) than they seem. First, however, we highlight a particularly important question regarding hypnosis: Does it enable people to recall things that they otherwise could not have remembered?

Hypnosis and Memory

It is popularly believed that hypnosis can dramatically improve recall performance through a phenomenon called **hypnotic hypermnesia.** Perhaps you've heard of crime investigations in which hypnosis apparently enabled witnesses to recall minute details of a horrific crime. In one famous kidnapping case from the 1970s, a bus driver was buried two metres underground along with 26 children inside a tractor trailer. Later, under hypnosis, he was able to recall the kidnapper's licence plate. There is a longstanding belief among some psychotherapists that hypnosis is an excellent tool for uncovering hidden memories of childhood abuse or other forms of psychological trauma (Poole et al., 1995; Pratt et al., 1988; Yapko, 1994). There have even been a number of well-publicized examples of *age regression* under hypnosis, in which the subject appeared to mentally travel backward to some earlier place (such as his or her grade 2 classroom, the experience of being born, or even a past life).

Unfortunately, there is little hard evidence supporting the idea of hypnotic hypermnesia. A person's memory may indeed improve after a hypnotic session, but this fact does not allow us to conclude that hypnosis was responsible for the improvement (Spiegel, 1995). One possibility is that the hypnotic session simply provided the subject with another opportunity to recall the to-be-remembered material; everyone has had the experience of being unable to remember a particular piece of information at one time and then later recalling it. It is also possible that hypnotic procedures create effective and supportive environments in which to remember (Geiselman et al., 1985). Another problem is that it's often difficult to judge whether memories recovered during hypnosis are, in fact, accurate representations of what actually occurred. You may "remember" a particularly unpleasant experience from your grade 2 classroom, but can you be sure that this traumatic episode indeed occurred as you remember it (Lindsay & Read, 1994; Loftus, 1993)?

As you'll see in a moment, evidence suggests that hypnotizable subjects adopt the role of being hypnotized. If the hypnotist suggests that the subject will be able to recall previously forgotten material, the subject will try to comply. What appear to be memories, then, may sometimes be fabrications—stories that the subject unintentionally makes up to please the hypnotist. To put this another way, the hypnotized individual may report as memories thoughts and images that are too vague or incomplete to normally be reported as memories; some of these may indeed be accurate, but many of them will be fabrications (Dywan & Bowers, 1983). If the hypnotist convincingly suggests that the subject will be able to remember a past life, highly hypnotizable subjects may comply with the suggestion and give a detailed report, but there is no reason to believe that the report corresponds to any real past event (Spanos, 1996). Controlled experiments in the laboratory have failed to find good evidence that hypnosis improves the ability to recall past experiences, but it sometimes increases false memories and sometimes inflates confidence in memory reports (Dinges et al., 1992; Lynn et al., 1997; Steblay & Bothwell, 1994). For this reason, the use of hypnotic testimony in criminal court cases is rarely allowed. It's simply too difficult to tell whether the memory recovered after hypnosis is accurate or a product of suggestion by the hypnotist.

Explaining Hypnosis

There is considerable debate over how the phenomena of hypnosis should be explained. As noted earlier, the EEG patterns of someone in a deep hypnotic trance

hypnotic hypermnesia
The supposed enhancement of memory that is said to occur under hypnosis; there is little evidence to support the existence of this effect.

Critical Thinking

Can you think of any situations in which memories accessed through hypnosis should be admitted in court? Why or why not?

resemble the patterns of someone in a relaxed waking state, and there do not appear to be any other physiological indicators that are unique to hypnosis. So how do we explain the heightened suggestibility? Currently, there are two prominent interpretations of hypnosis: (1) Hypnosis is a kind of dissociation, or true splitting of conscious awareness, and (2) hypnosis represents a kind of social role-playing. Let's consider each of these ideas in more detail.

Hypnotic Dissociations Some researchers believe that hypnosis produces **hypnotic dissociations.** By "dissociations" it is meant that the hypnotized individual experiences a splitting of consciousness in which two forms of awareness coexist (Hilgard, 1986, 1992): One stream of consciousness follows the commands of the hypnotist, such as feeling no effects of painful stimulation, while another stream, called the "hidden observer," retains a more objective awareness of what is really going on (e.g., is painfully aware of the true stimulation) but does not reveal this awareness.

Hilgard supported his position with experiments in which subjects were hypnotized and asked to submerge one arm into a bucket of extremely cold ice water (a procedure to test for the analgesic effects of hypnosis). "You'll be aware of no pain," the subject was told, "but that other part of you, the hidden part that is aware of everything going on, can signal any true pain by pressing this key with your nonsubmerged hand." Subjects pressed the key repeatedly—reporting the pain—and the key presses became more frequent the longer the arm was kept submerged. During hypnosis, as well as afterward, the subjects claimed not to experience pain and to have no awareness of the nonsubmerged hand's behaviour. There is a hidden part of consciousness, Hilgard argued, that maintains realistic contact with what's going on; it is the other hypnotized stream of awareness that feels no pain. For a recent defence of the concept of hypnotic dissociation, see Spiegel (1998).

This idea that conscious awareness is divided or split during hypnosis may seem mystical, strange, and worthy of skepticism. Yet you may have had everyday experiences that might reasonably be characterized as divided consciousness. At a movie theatre, for example, you can be deeply absorbed in the film yet be aware, at another level, of the theatre around you. As another example, you may have attended a party at which everyone, including you, seemed to be having a good time (animatedly laughing and chatting) but "deep down" you felt sad or troubled about something in your life. Some psychologists would characterize this as an example of split or divided consciousness; as you'll see below, others would describe it as an example of social role-playing.

hypnotic dissociation
A hypothesized, hypnotically induced splitting of consciousness during which two streams of awareness are said to coexist: one that is fully under the sway of the hypnotist's suggestions and one that remains more aloof and objective.

Hypnosis is often used for entertainment purposes. It can also have considerable clinical value.

Social Role-Playing By definition, the behaviour of a hypnotized person is easily modified by the suggestions of the hypnotist. Such suggestions need not be blatant, and they do not need to be given while the person is hypnotized. Indeed, the suggestions do not even have to come from the hypnotist per se, but can be based on the subject's beliefs and expectations regarding hypnosis. For example, if people are told prior to being hypnotized that a rigid right arm is a prominent feature of the hypnotized state, then rigid right arms are likely to be demonstrated during hypnosis even when no such specific suggestion is made during the induction process (Orne, 1959). It often appears as if highly hypnotizable subjects are trying hard to "do whatever they can to achieve the suggested effects" (Kihlstrom & McConkey, 1990; Kirsch, 1999).

A number of researchers have suggested that hypnotic behaviour is a kind of social role-playing. Everyone has some idea of what hypnotized behaviour looks like: To be hypnotized, you must fall into a trance and slavishly obey the all-powerful hypnotist. So when people agree to be hypnotized, they implicitly agree to take on this role (Barber et al., 1974; Sarbin & Coe, 1972; Spanos, 1982). According to this view, people have not actually lost voluntary control over their behaviour; rather, they follow the lead of the hypnotist and obey his or her every command because they think, perhaps unconsciously, that involuntary compliance is an important part of what it means to be hypnotized (Lynn et al., 1997). The claim is not that people are merely "faking it"; rather, the idea is that hypnosis is a phenomenon of "creative role engagement, where people generate the sensations, subjective experiences, and mental representations scripted by the hypnotic context" (Lynn et al., 1997, p. 172).

Quite a bit of evidence supports this role-playing interpretation of hypnosis. One compelling finding is that essentially all hypnotic phenomena can be reproduced with *simulating subjects*—people who are not actually hypnotized but who are told to act as if they are hypnotized as part of an experiment. These issues were extensively explored by the late Nick Spanos of Carleton University (e.g., Spanos, 1986, 1996). For example, catalepsy looks very impressive, but it turns out that motivated nonhypnotized individuals can enact it just as well as hypnotized individuals. Moreover, many of the classic phenomena of hypnosis—such as posthypnotic suggestions—turn out to be controlled mainly by subject expectations. For example, if subjects are told to respond to some cue after the hypnotic session ends, such as tugging on their ear every time they hear the word *psychology,* they will often do so after hypnosis. However, posthypnotic suggestions of this kind are effective only if the subjects believe they are still participating in the experiment; if the hypnotist leaves the room or if the subjects believe the experiment is over, they stop responding appropriately to the cue (see Lynn et al., 1997, and Spanos, 1996, for reviews).

What can we conclude about hypnosis? Do hypnotic induction procedures produce a unique state of mind, qualitatively different from all other forms of awareness, in which the hypnotized part of consciousness slavishly follows the hypnotist's suggestions? Or do hypnotizable individuals merely take on a socially constructed role? Debate continues among psychologists, but we suggest that the two positions may not be very different from each other: If part of the role of hypnotized subjects is entering a peculiar state of mind, then individuals who truly "get into" that role will indeed experience a peculiar state of mind.

Meditation

There are a number of parallels between hypnosis and meditation. For example, both are often said to produce an altered state of mind, both entail relaxation, and both typically involve some sort of induction ceremony. Most **meditation** techniques require practitioners to perform some time-honoured mental exercise, such as concentrating on repeating a particular string of words or sounds called a *mantra,* while focusing on breathing in a particular manner and making efforts to clear and calm the mind.

The variations in awareness achieved through meditation, as with hypnosis, are often described in mystical or spiritual ways. Meditators often report that they are able

meditation
A technique for self-induced manipulation of awareness, often used for relaxation and self-reflection.

Daily meditation sessions can likely produce significant reductions in anxiety.

to obtain an expanded state of awareness, characterized by a pure and calm form of thought unburdened by self-awareness. There are many forms of meditation and numerous induction procedures; most trace their roots back thousands of years to the practices of a variety of Eastern religions.

The general idea of meditation is to step back from the ongoing stream of mental activity and set the mind adrift in the oneness of the universe. Advocates claim numerous benefits of daily meditation, including spiritual insights, improved physical health, and release from desire. Scientifically, it's not clear that meditation produces significant changes in physiological functions, compared to simple relaxation. Arousal is lowered, and heart rate, respiration rate, and blood pressure tend to decline (Seer, 1979), and EEG recordings of brain activity during meditation have typically revealed what appears to be a relaxed mind; specifically, there is a significant increase in alpha wave activity (Benson, 1975). Such changes are, of course, to be expected during any kind of relaxed state and do not necessarily signify any special state of consciousness. Indeed, although some researchers have reported differences between the physiological patterns of accomplished meditators and those of nonmeditators who are simply relaxing, or between meditators when they are meditating versus when they are simply relaxing, such findings have been inconsistent (Holmes, 1987; Travis & Wallace, 1999). At this point, researchers have little to say about the subjective aspects of the meditative experience—whether, in fact, the meditator has indeed merged with the oneness of the universe—but most researchers agree that inducing a deeply relaxed state once or twice a day is likely to have genuinely beneficial effects.

Test Yourself 5.4

Check what you've learned about hypnosis and meditation by deciding whether each of the following statements is true or false. (You will find the answers in Appendix B.)

1. The EEG patterns of a hypnotized person resemble those of non-REM sleep. *True or False?*

2. Hypnosis improves memory under some circumstances because it reduces the tendency to fabricate, or make things up, to please the questioner. *True or False?*
3. The concept of hypnotic dissociation refers to a kind of splitting of consciousness, in which more than one kind of awareness is present at the same time. *True or False?*
4. Hilgard described his "hidden observer" experiments as providing support for the social role-playing explanation of hypnosis. *True or False?*
5. Meditation leads primarily to alpha wave rather than theta wave EEG activity. *True or False?*

Solving the Adaptive Problems

Studying conscious awareness is not an easy task. Consciousness is by its very nature a subjective, personal experience. It is a difficult concept to define objectively, and the scribblings of an EEG pattern or a pretty picture from a PET scanning device may, in the minds of many, fail to capture the complexities of the topic adequately. Is consciousness some classifiable thing that can change its state, like water as it freezes or evaporates? For the moment, psychologists are working with a set of rather loose ideas about the topic, although conscious awareness is agreed to have many adaptive properties. We considered four adaptive characteristics of consciousness in this chapter; each revealed ways that the adaptive mind adjusts to solve problems faced in the environment.

First, how do people set priorities for mental functioning? The processes of attention allow the mind to prioritize its functioning. Faced with limited resources, the brain needs to be selective about the enormous amount of information it receives. Through attention, people can focus on certain aspects of the environment while largely ignoring others, adapting their thinking in ways that allow for selective and deliberate movement toward a problem solution. Attentional processes also enable the brain to divide its processing. People don't always need to

be consciously aware of the tasks they perform; automatic processes allow one to perform multiple tasks—such as driving a car and following a conversation—at the same time. Certain disorders of attention, including visual neglect and attention deficit disorder, provide some insights into attention processes. In both of these conditions, which may be caused by malfunctioning in the brain, the person's ability to adapt to the environment is compromised.

Second, what roles do sleep and dreaming play for the adaptive mind? Sleep is one part of a daily (circadian) rhythm that includes wakefulness, and sleep itself turns out to be composed of regularly changing cycles of brain activity. Studies using the EEG reveal that people move through several distinct stages during sleep. Sleeping may allow the brain a chance to rest and restore itself from its daily workout, or it may simply be adaptive as a safe period of time out. Lying relatively motionless in the dark recesses of some shelter may have protected our ancestors at night when their sensory equipment was unlikely to function well. The function of dreaming, which occurs during the REM period of sleep (and sometimes during other stages of sleep), remains unclear. Some psychologists believe that dreaming may reveal conflicts that

are hidden from conscious awareness or that dreaming may be one way to work out currently troubling problems. A third possibility is that dreaming is simply a manifestation of the brain's attempt to make sense of its own spontaneous neural activity.

Third, how do certain chemicals, or drugs, produce profound alterations in awareness? Psychoactive drugs alter behaviour and awareness by tapping into natural brain systems that have evolved for adaptive reasons. The brain, as a biochemical factory, can react to stress or injury by releasing chemicals (neurotransmitters) that help reduce pain or that shift mood in a positive direction. Many of the drugs that are abused in our society activate these natural systems. As a result, the study of psychoactive drugs has enabled researchers to learn more about communication systems in the brain. There are four main categories of psychoactive drugs. *Depressants,* such as alcohol and barbiturates, lower the ongoing activity of the central nervous system. *Stimulants,* such as caffeine, nicotine, and cocaine, stimulate central nervous system activity by increasing the likelihood that neural transmissions will occur. *Opiates,* such as opium, morphine, and heroin, depress nervous system activity by mimicking the chemicals involved in the brain's own pain-control system. Finally, *hallucinogens,* such as LSD, play havoc with the user's normal internal construction of reality. Although the mechanisms involved are not known, it's believed that LSD mimics the actions of the neurotransmitter serotonin.

Fourth, what happens under hypnosis and meditation, two other techniques that seem to alter awareness? Two techniques have been designed specifically to alter conscious awareness: hypnosis and meditation. Hypnosis is a form of social interaction that induces a heightened state of suggestibility in the subject. Hypnotic techniques usually promote relaxation, but brain activity under hypnosis more closely resembles the waking rather than the sleeping state. In meditation, the participant manipulates awareness, often by mentally repeating a particular word or string of words, focusing on breathing in a particular way, and making efforts toward clear and calm thoughts. The biological mechanisms of both hypnosis and meditation are poorly understood at present, but each has some positive consequences. Pain and discomfort can be significantly reduced through hypnotic suggestion, and the regular practice of meditation has been linked to the reduction of stress and anxiety.

Chapter Summary

SETTING PRIORITIES FOR MENTAL FUNCTIONING: ATTENTION

Attention refers to the internal processes we use to set and follow priorities for mental functioning. The brain uses attention to focus selectively on certain parts of the environment and not others.

Experiments on Attention: Dichotic Listening

Learning Goal: Learn how experiments on dichotic listening can be used to study attention. Different messages are presented simultaneously to each ear, and the subject tries to repeat one message aloud while ignoring the other.

Processing without Attention: Automaticity

Learning Goal: Understand the concept of "automaticity." *Automaticity* refers to mental processing that, due to extensive skill development via practice, is fast and easy, requiring little or no focused attention.

Disorders of Attention

Learning Goal: Learn about attention disorders such as visual neglect and attention deficit/hyperactivity disorder. *Visual neglect* is a tendency, caused by damage to one side of the parietal lobe, to ignore everything on the other side of the body. *Attention deficit/hyperactivity disorder* is a psychological condition characterized by extreme distractibility, often with impulsivity and/or hyperactivity.

Subliminal Perception

Learning Goal: Understand research on the influence of subliminal messages. *Subliminal messages* are stimuli that are presented so briefly, or in such a disguised fashion, that we cannot consciously perceive them. Contrary to popular beliefs, scientific research indicates that such messages can only affect behaviour in small and transient ways.

SLEEPING AND DREAMING
Biological Rhythms

Learning Goal: Understand biological rhythms and how they are controlled. The internal cycles that regulate sleep, waking, and other physical processes are controlled by structures in the brain that trigger rhythmic variations at appropriate times.

The Characteristics of Sleep

Learning Goal: Be able to describe the various stages and characteristics of sleep. During sleep, we experience repeated cycles of brain activity, each complete cycle being about 90 minutes long. *Stage 1:* "Drifting." *Stage 2:* Asleep but still dimly sensitive to the external world. *Stages 3 and 4:* Progressively deeper sleep. *REM sleep:* Abrupt physiological changes, brain waves look "awake," but motor movements are minimized; most dream activity occurs during this stage.

The Function of Sleep

Learning Goal: Be able to discuss the function and adaptive significance of sleep. Sleep helps to *repair* and *restore* the body and brain. It also helps us respond adaptively to environmental conditions for the sake of survival.

The Function of REM and Dreaming

Learning Goal: Learn about current theories of dreaming and its function. REM sleep may serve an important function in the brain, such as strengthening certain kinds of memories. Dreams may be a form of *wish fulfillment* (Freud); the *activation-synthesis hypothesis* holds that dreaming is a product of random activity in the brain.

Sleep Disorders

Learning Goal: Learn about the major sleep disorders. *Dyssomnias* are problems associated with the amount, timing, and quality of sleep, such as *insomnia, hypersomnia,* and *narcolepsy. Parasomnias* are abnormal sleep disturbances such as *nightmares, night terrors,* and *sleepwalking.*

ALTERING AWARENESS: PSYCHOACTIVE DRUGS
Drug Actions and Effects

Learning Goal: Understand the relationship between neurotransmitters and psychoactive drugs. Like neurotransmitters, psychoactive drugs alter behaviour and mental processes by affecting the operation of neurons in the brain. Use of psychoactive drugs can produce lasting changes in the brain. These changes may include *tolerance*, a decreased susceptibility to the effects of the drug, and *dependence*, a physical or psychological need to use the drug. *Withdrawal* refers to physical and psychological symptoms when drug use stops. Many popular recreational drugs have been shown to impair mental functioning.

Categories of Psychoactive Drugs

Learning Goal: Learn the different categories of psychoactive drugs, and provide examples of each. *Depressants,* such as alcohol and barbiturates, slow the activity of the central nervous system. *Stimulants,* such as caffeine, amphetamines, cocaine, nicotine, and Ecstasy, increase central nervous system activity. *Opiates (narcotics),* such as opium, heroin, and morphine, depress nervous system activity and reduce anxiety and sensitivity to pain. *Hallucinogens (psychedelics),* such as LSD, mescaline, psilocybin, and marijuana, dramatically alter mood and perception.

Psychological Factors

Learning Goal: Be able to discuss the psychological factors that influence the effects of psychoactive drugs. Among the factors that can influence reactions to psychoactive drugs are *environmental setting, familiarity* with the effects of the substance, *physical state,* and *expectations and mental attitude.*

ALTERING AWARENESS: INDUCED STATES
The Phenomena of Hypnosis

Learning Goal: Become familiar with the physiological and behavioural effects of hypnosis. Hypnosis is social interaction that produces a *heightened state of suggestibility* in a willing subject. It bears little physiological relation to sleep.

Hypnosis and Memory

Learning Goal: Learn the scientific status of hypnosis as a memory-retrieval technique. People sometimes remember things under hypnosis that they had previously failed to remember, and some such memories are accurate, but there is no convincing evidence that the hypnotic state gives people remarkable powers of memory.

Explaining Hypnosis

Learning Goal: Be able to describe the dissociation and role-playing accounts of hypnosis. Some psychologists believe that hypnosis induces a true dividing of consciousness, with one stream of consciousness fully under the hypnotist's sway and the other more aloof and independent, but other psychologists describe hypnosis as a powerful form of *social role-playing* in which the subject enters into the role of being hypnotized.

Meditation

Learning Goal: Understand the physical, behavioural, and psychological effects of meditation. Meditation is characterized by self-induced altered awareness achieved by calming, relaxing, and concentrating on breathing or on a *mantra* (repetition of specific sounds). Daily meditation may reduce anxiety.

Terms to Remember

consciousness, 174

Recommended Readings

Coren, S. (1996). *Sleep thieves.* New York: The Free Press. Written for the layperson by a top research psychologist at the University of British Columbia, this book presents a convincing case for the importance of a good night's sleep.

Jaynes, J. (1976). *The origin of consciousness in the breakdown of the bicameral mind.* Boston: Houghton Mifflin. This is a fascinating and provocative book, full of speculations about the origins of consciousness. Jaynes argued that conscious awareness developed relatively recently in human history and that ancient peoples from Mesopotamia to Peru were unable to think as we can today.

Dennett, D. C. (1991). *Consciousness explained.* Boston: Little, Brown and Company. Written by a philosopher, this book challenges the traditional common-sense view of consciousness. Generally easy to read—Dennett is a great writer—and it contains much food for thought.

 For additional readings, explore InfoTrac® College Edition, your online library. Go to:

www.adaptivemind2e.nelson.com

Hint: enter the search terms: visual neglect; altered states of consciousness; stages of sleep; REM sleep; drugs and behaviour; hypnotic effects.

What's on the Web?

Please note that Web addresses are subject to change. Check out the accompanying Web site for updates: www.adaptivemind2e.nelson.com. This site presents practice quiz questions, hypercontent, information on degrees and careers in psychology, study tips, and more.

The Need for Attention to See Change

www.psych.ubc.ca/~rensink/flicker/

viscog.beckman.uiuc.edu/djs_lab/demos.html

In Chapter 4 you read about vision, and in this chapter you've read about attention. As you might expect, there are many interactions between attention and vision. A particularly interesting example is a phenomenon called "change blindness." The first of the two sites listed above, by Dr. Ronald A. Rensink (formerly of Nissan Technical Center, now at UBC), provides several demonstrations of the phenomenon and links to articles about it. The second site, by Professor Daniel J. Simons of the University of Illinois, provides a wide variety of demonstrations of the change-blindness phenomenon. The effect is quite amusing, as well as intriguing.

Canadian Centre on Substance Abuse

www.ccsa.ca/

The Canadian Centre on Substance Abuse is a nonprofit organization working to minimize the harm associated with the use of alcohol, tobacco, and other drugs. The site is well designed and packed with authoritative and on-target information and useful resources.

Sleeping Better

www.healthyresources.com/sleep/apnea/index.html

www.stanford.edu/~dement

www.sleepnet.com

Some of the best sites on the Web for finding out more about sleep. Find out about snoring, dreams, insomnia, sleep aids, and much more.

Dream Sites

www.rider.edu/users/suler/dreams.html

psych.ucsc.edu/dreams

Few topics pique the curiosity of the psychology student more than dreams. Why do we dream? What do dreams mean? These two sites will allow you to explore the question in depth. They provide information about ongoing research on dreams as well as information for those who wish to explore their own dreams.

And you may find yourself living in a shotgun shack

And you may find yourself in another part of the world

And you may find yourself behind the wheel of a large automobile

And you may find yourself in a beautiful house, with a beautiful wife …

And you may ask yourself—Well … How did I get here?

And you may ask yourself, How do I work this?

Talking Heads, "Once in a Lifetime"

Chapter 6 Learning from Experience

magine that you, a university student studying in Canada, suddenly traded places with someone from a radically different time and culture. You might, for example, awaken in a *ger* (a felt tent, also known as a *yurt*) on the steppes of Mongolia, home of a great horse-based, nomadic culture, perhaps in the time of Genghis Khan. If you're like most Canadian undergraduates, you won't know a word of the language, nor will you be an expert in the care of horses (let alone yaks and goats) and the handling of weapons. Indeed, even the most basic tasks of everyday living, such as finding water and food, will be challenging mysteries. Your counterpart, transported from the Mongolian camp to your university, would probably be similarly discomfited. Yet, given time, effort, and a bit of luck, each of you would learn to adapt to your new environment reasonably well. After all, each of you had learned to adapt to your initial cultures as children. You are genetically endowed with the ability to adapt to a very wide range of physical and cultural environments by learning from experience. The question explored in this chapter is how you do so.

Historically, much of scientific psychology's investigations of learning have focused on learning in relatively simple situations, often using nonhuman species such as rats, pigeons, or sea snails as subjects. Indeed, much of what you'll read about in this chapter comes from animal research. Using animals as models to understand human psychology makes sense when you consider that all species—even sea snails—need to learn to survive. Many psychologists believe that all organisms, including humans, share similar learning mechanisms (Roitblat & von Ferson, 1992). Different species differ in important ways, and humans are extraordinary in the extent to which they can adapt via learning from experience. Nonetheless, there appear to be common principles, or laws, of learning that apply widely across species.

Previewing the Adaptive Problems

What exactly is learning? Most people view learning as simply the process of acquiring knowledge and skill. In broad terms, psychologists would agree with this general description but, as you learned in Chapter 2, psychologists like to define concepts in terms of how those concepts are measured (i.e., operational definitions). "Knowledge" cannot be measured directly—if you looked inside someone's brain, you'd see neurons, glial cells, and so on, but not any accurate index of specific pieces of knowledge or skill. Instead, psychologists define **learning** in terms of behaviour—specifically, as a relatively permanent change in behaviour that results from experience.

(Keep in mind that speaking and writing are behaviours.) To determine that learning has occurred, one must observe a change in behaviour (Wasserman & Miller, 1997). Thus psychologists make inferences about learning and the acquisition of knowledge and skill by observing behaviour and noting how behaviour changes with experience.

In this chapter our discussion revolves around four simple adaptive problems that are solved by our ability to learn from experience.

First, how do we recognize consequential events when they occur and react to them appropriately? We

need to recognize consequential events when they occur and react to them appropriately. We also need to learn to ignore events that occur repeatedly but have no consequences of interest to us. The cry of an infant, the screech of automobile brakes—these sounds demand our attention and cause us to react. Humans and animals note sudden changes in their environment; they notice those things that are new and potentially of interest. However, our reactions to these novel events

learning
A relatively permanent change in behaviour, or potential to respond, that results from experience.

The bright colours and screeching sirens of a fire engine are designed to draw our attention and to signal the need for us to get out of the way.

It's clearly adaptive to learn about the signalling properties of events. A distinctive rattle on a mountain trail signals the potential strike of the western diamondback rattlesnake.

This family dog has learned about the consequences of hanging around the dinner table. She's learned that her begging behaviour is instrumental in producing a tasty reward.

change with repeated experience, and these changes are controlled by basic learning processes.

Second, how do we learn about the signalling properties of stimuli or events in the environment? When does one event predict that a second event is likely to follow? For instance, you know that lightning precedes thunder and that the rattling of a tail can signal the bite of a venomous snake. Often, you can't *do* anything about the co-occurrence of such events, but if you recognize the relationship, you can respond accordingly (you can take cover or move to avoid the snake).

Third, how do we learn about the consequences of our own behaviour? All species, sea snails as well as people, need to learn that when they act in a certain way in a particular situation, their behaviour is likely to have consequences. The child who flicks the tail of a cat once too often receives an unwelcome surprise. The family dog learns that if she hangs around the dinner table, a scrap of food might very well come her way. Behaviours often result in either rewards or punishments, and learning about such consequences plays a key role in adaptation via learning.

Fourth, how can we learn by observing others? People (as well as many other kinds of animals) often learn by observing the actions of others and the consequences those actions bring. Observational learning has considerable adaptive significance: A teenager learns about the consequences of drunk driving, one hopes, not from direct experience but from observing others whose fate has already been sealed. A young monkey in the wild learns to be afraid of snakes not from a deadly personal encounter but from observing her mother's fear.

It's adaptive for all living things to notice sudden changes in the environment. In this case, the unexpected appearance of a red-tailed hawk elicits distinctive orienting reactions from an opossum family.

LEARNING ABOUT EVENTS: NOTICING AND IGNORING

Learning Goals

1. Learn about the concept of the orienting response, and discuss its adaptive value.

2. Understand and compare habituation and sensitization.

LET'S BEGIN WITH THE FIRST PROBLEM: How do we learn to notice consequential stimuli or events, and to ignore inconsequential ones? We're constantly surrounded by sights, sounds, and sensations—from the sound of traffic outside the window, to the colour of the paint on the wall, to the feel of denim jeans against our legs. As further discussed in Chapter 5, it's not possible to attend fully to all of these stimuli at once. Instead, you need to prioritize your mental functioning because the human nervous system has limited resources. And this is not just a human problem: Animals, too, have limited resources, and they constantly need to decide whether events in their environment are important or unimportant. Not surprisingly, there are basic psychological processes that help people and other animals determine which events deserve our attention and which do not.

Orienting Responses, Habituation, and Sensitization

orienting response
An inborn tendency to shift one's focus of attention toward a novel or surprising event.

Humans are programmed from birth to notice novelty; when something new or different happens, we pay close attention. Suppose you hear a funny ticking noise in your car engine when you press the gas pedal. When you first notice the sound, it occupies your attention. You produce an **orienting response,** which is an automatic shift of attention toward the event. Perhaps you lean forward and listen; you may even repeatedly press the gas pedal to establish a link between acceleration and ticking. But suppose you keep driving, and the car performs as usual. After a while, your behaviour changes—the ticking becomes less bothersome, and you may even stop reacting to it altogether. Your behaviour in the presence of the event changes with repeated experience, which is the hallmark of learning.

habituation
The decline in the tendency to respond to an event that has become familiar through repeated exposure.

When you reduce the extent to which you respond to an event that has become familiar through repeated presentation, you are demonstrating **habituation.** (This process will be discussed in more detail in Chapter 10.) Most birds are startled and become agitated when the shadow of a hawk passes overhead, but their level of alarm rapidly declines if the shadow occurs repeatedly and there is no subsequent attack (Tinbergen, 1951). It makes sense for animals to produce a strong initial orienting response to a sudden change in their environment. If a bird fails to attend quickly to the shape of a potential predator, it's not likely to survive. Through the process of habituation, organisms learn to be selective about the things they orient toward. They attend initially to the new and unusual events but subsequently ignore events that occur repeatedly without significant consequence.

sensitization
An increase in the tendency to respond to an event that has been repeated; sensitization is more likely when a repeated stimulus is intense.

Sensitization occurs when responsiveness to an event increases with repeated exposure. Sensitization, like habituation, is a general learning phenomenon found throughout the animal kingdom. Both habituation and sensitization are natural responses to repeated events—they help us respond appropriately to the environment. Whether you become more or less responsive in any specific situation depends on the relative strengths of the habituation and sensitization processes (Groves & Thompson, 1970). Generally, increases in responsiveness—sensitization—are more likely when the repeated stimulus is intense. For example, if you are exposed to repetitions of a very loud noise, you become "sensitized" to the noise—your reactions become more intense and prolonged with repeated exposure. If the noise is relatively modest in intensity, repeated exposure may lead to decreases in responsiveness (i.e., habituation). Habituation and sensitization also depend importantly on the timing of presentations—that is, whether the repetitions occur close together or are widely separated in time (Haerich, 1997; Staddon, 1998).

Habituation and sensitization are both examples of learning because they produce changes in behaviour as a function of experience. The effects of sensitization generally tend to be short lived (Domjan, 1998), whereas habituation can produce quite long-term effects. For example, when placed in a new environment cats are often skittish when they eat. The slightest sound or movement is likely to send them scurrying under the nearest piece of furniture. With time the animal learns, and the adjustment is typically long lasting (see Figure 6.1). Drug tolerance, which we discussed in more detail in Chapter 5, can also be described in terms of long-term habituation. In humans, an initial dose of 100 to 200 mg of morphine produces profound sedation or even death, but morphine-tolerant subjects are capable of receiving over 100 times that amount without negative effects (Baker & Tiffany, 1985). The body's response to the drug changes after repeated use—that is, the body *habituates* to the drug. Most interestingly, drug tolerance depends, in part, on environmental context: A dose that would be effective when taken in the context in which the individual has often previously taken the drug may produce a lethal overdose if taken in a novel environment. This suggests that the organism has learned to produce physiological responses that attenuate the influence of the drug (Siegel, 1988). The exact nature of the learning that occurs as tolerance develops is still a matter of some debate (Krank & O'Neill, 2002; Siegel, 1989), but tolerance shows clearly how responsiveness to an event can change as a consequence of repeated exposure.

Because it is a general kind of learning process that occurs throughout the animal world, habituation is often used as a psychological model for understanding how behaviours change with experience. Some learning theorists, for example, have used habituation as the basis for proposing theories about the structure of basic learning and memory systems (Staddon, 1998; Wagner, 1981). A number of neuroscientists have used habituation and sensitization as tools for mapping out the fundamental neural mechanisms of learning (Cleary et al., 1998; Groves & Thompson, 1970). As another example, developmental psychologists have used habituation as an experimental technique for making inferences about infants' perceptions (Bornstein, 1992). For example, Easterbrook and colleagues (1999) at Nipissing University repeatedly presented pictures of faces to 1- to 3-day-old infants. At first, the infants tended to look at each face quite a bit, but after a while they habituated to faces and spent little time looking at them. The researchers then presented either another picture of a face or a picture that included facial features but in scrambled positions (i.e., an eye below an ear, with a mouth to the side, etc.). The infants who were shown another normal face appeared uninterested, but those shown the scrambled face looked at it for quite a while, revealing that they perceived it as different from a non-scrambled face.

As adaptive organisms, humans rely on simple learning processes such as habituation to adapt to the environment. The world is full of events to be noticed, far more than anyone can ever hope to monitor. Orienting responses help people notice the new

Critical Thinking

In Chapter 4 you learned about sensory adaptation, which refers to the tendency of sensory systems to stop or reduce responding to a stimulus source that remains constant. Do you suppose there's any connection between sensory adaptation and habituation?

FIGURE 6.1

Long-Term Habituation

Organisms notice sudden changes in the environment, but they learn to ignore them if they occur repeatedly. For an eating cat, a novel sound leads initially to panic and escape, but if the sound is repeated over days, the cat gradually habituates and continues eating without the slightest reaction.

Day 1   Day 2   Day 3   Day 4   Day 5

and unusual, but through habituation we learn to ignore things that are repeated but are of no significant consequence. People are thereby able to solve a very important problem—how to be selective about the events that occur and recur in the world. However, there is more to learning than just noticing and ignoring events; it is equally important to learn about relationships between events, as you'll see in the next section.

eque

Test Yourself 6.1

Check your knowledge about noticing and ignoring by choosing the best answer for each of the following descriptions. Choose from the following terms: habituation; orienting response; sensitization. (You will find the answers in Appendix B.)

1. When Shawn practises his trumpet, he tries repeatedly to hit a high C note. The first time he tries, his roommate says nothing. By the third try, his roommate is banging on the door telling him to be quiet: _____

2. First-time driver Alonda reacts by screaming and slamming on the brakes when a passing car horn sounds: _____

3. Kesha loves clocks and has six different varieties in her apartment. Strangely, she rarely notices the ticking noises: _____

4. Your cat Comet used to jump about a metre in the air whenever you ground your gourmet coffee beans in the morning. Now he never seems to notice: _____

5. Drug users often develop tolerance, which means that after repeated use they need larger doses of the drug to achieve the same effects. Tolerance may be considered an example of: _____

LEARNING WHAT EVENTS SIGNAL: CLASSICAL CONDITIONING

Learning Goals

1. Learn the basic elements of classical conditioning.
2. Be able to describe how the connection between the conditioned stimulus and the unconditioned stimulus is acquired.
3. Understand and discuss how and why conditioned responding develops.
4. Be able to explain the concept of second-order conditioning.
5. Understand and be able to differentiate between the concepts of stimulus generalization and stimulus discrimination.
6. Understand and explain the extinction of a conditioned response.
7. Learn about conditioned inhibition.

WHAT HAPPENS SHORTLY AFTER A BOLT OF LIGHTNING flashes across a stormy sky? If you pour milk into your coffee and little white lumps float to the top, how's it going to taste? If you drink it anyway, how will your stomach react? In each of these cases, you've learned an association between two events; more specifically, you've learned that one event signals the likely subsequent occurrence of the other. This knowledge is adaptive because it allows you to prepare yourself for future events: You know to cover your ears or to avoid drinking the brew. In this section, we'll consider how simple associations like these are learned and reflected in performance.

The scientific study of associations began in the early years of the 20th century in the laboratory of a Russian physiologist named Ivan P. Pavlov (1849–1936). Pavlov developed a technique, now known as **classical conditioning,** that proved useful for investigating how associations are formed. Pavlov didn't start off with a plan to study learning. His main interest was in digestion, including salivation. Mammals (including humans) salivate when they eat, and saliva contains chemicals that help in the initial stages of digestion. Pavlov aimed to investigate the relation between various kinds of food and saliva production, by putting particular kinds of food in dogs' mouths and measuring their salivary responses. Much to his annoyance, however, Pavlov found that his dogs often began to drool long before the food was placed in their mouths. Pavlov referred to these premature droolings as "psychic" secretions, and he began to study why they occurred, in part with the hope of learning how to eliminate this phenomenon in future studies of digestion.

The Terminology of Classical Conditioning

Pavlov observed that "psychic" secretions developed as a result of experience. At the same time, he assumed that drooling in response to food is not a learned response. He recognized that the presentation of certain kinds of stimuli, which he called **unconditioned stimuli** (**US**), automatically lead to responses, which he called **unconditioned responses** (**UR**s). For example, food is an unconditioned stimulus that automatically produces salivation as an unconditioned response. Neither dogs nor humans need to be taught to drool when food is placed in their mouths; this response is a reflex similar to the jerking of your leg when tapped just below the knee. The occurrence of an unconditioned response (salivation) after presentation of an unconditioned stimulus (food in the mouth) is *unconditioned*—that is, no learning, or conditioning, is required.

The problem facing Pavlov was that his dogs began to drool merely at the *sight* of the food dish or even at the sound of a food-bearing assistant entering the room. Food dishes and the footsteps of arriving assistants are not unconditioned stimuli that automatically cause a dog to salivate. Drooling in response to such stimuli is learned; it is *conditioned*, or acquired as a result of experience. For this reason, Pavlov began referring to the "psychic" secretions as **conditioned responses** (**CR**s) and to the stimuli that produced them as **conditioned stimuli** (**CS**).

Let's take footsteps as an example. The sound of an approaching feeder leads to drooling because the dog has learned that the sound *signals* the appearance of the food. Over time, footsteps and food come to bear a special relation to each other: When the footsteps are heard, the food is soon to arrive. To use Pavlov's terminology, the footsteps are acting as a conditioned stimulus that produces salivation, a conditioned response, in anticipation of food. This is not unlike what happens to you when your

classical conditioning

A set of procedures, initially developed by Pavlov, used to investigate how organisms learn about the signalling properties of events. Classical conditioning leads to the learning of relations between events—conditioned and unconditioned stimuli—that occur outside of one's control.

 Critical Thinking

Can you think of any reason why it might be adaptive to begin the digestive processes before food actually gets into the mouth?

unconditioned stimulus (US)

A stimulus that automatically produces—or elicits—an observable response prior to any training.

unconditioned response (UR)

The observable response that is produced automatically, prior to training, on presentation of an unconditioned stimulus.

conditioned response (CR)

The acquired response that is produced to the conditioned stimulus in anticipation of the arrival of the unconditioned stimulus. Often, the conditioned response resembles the unconditioned response, although not always.

conditioned stimulus (CS)

A neutral stimulus (one that does not produce the unconditioned response prior to training) that is paired with the unconditioned stimulus during classical conditioning.

In the summer of 1934, the Russian physiologist Ivan Pavlov watched one of his experiments on "psychic" secretions in dogs. Notice the dog's cheek, which is fitted with a device for measuring salivation.

mouth begins to water as your waiter arrives with a delicious-looking meal. Conditioned stimuli typically lead to conditioned responses after the conditioned stimulus and the unconditioned stimulus have been paired together in time—the footsteps (the CS) reliably occur just before presentation of the food (the US). However, as you'll see shortly, simply pairing two events together does not always lead to the formation of this kind of association.

Acquiring the Conditioned Stimulus– Unconditioned Stimulus Connection

What conditions lead to the *acquisition* of an association between a conditioned stimulus and an unconditioned stimulus? That is, what determines whether an animal will come to respond to a previously neutral stimulus in ways that are related to the animal's automatic responses to an unconditioned stimulus? It helps to remember the following general rule: A conditioned stimulus will acquire signalling properties, leading to the production of a conditioned response, whenever it provides information about the occurrence of the unconditioned stimulus (Rescorla, 1992). If a bell (CS) is struck just before the delivery of food (US), and the bell–food pairings are continued over time, the dog will begin to salivate (CR) whenever the bell (CS) is struck (see Figure 6.2). An association is formed in this case because the bell provides *information* about the delivery of the food—the dog knows that food will be arriving soon after it hears the bell. This rule helps to explain a wide variety of experimental findings:

1. For an effective association to form, the conditioned stimulus needs to be presented before the unconditioned stimulus. If the two are presented at the same time *(simultaneous conditioning)*, or if the conditioned stimulus is presented after the unconditioned stimulus *(backward conditioning),* little evidence of conditioning will be found. In both of these cases, the conditioned stimulus provides no information about when the unconditioned stimulus will appear, so conditioned responding does not develop. There are some exceptions to this general rule (e.g., Matzel et al., 1988; Rescorla, 1980), but usually the conditioned stimulus needs to be presented first, before the unconditioned stimulus, for effective conditioning.

2. The unconditioned stimulus needs to follow the conditioned stimulus *closely in time.* Pavlov found that if there is a long delay between when the bell (CS) is struck and when the food (US) is delivered, dogs usually don't form a connection between the bell and the food. As the gap between presentation of the conditioned stimulus and presentation of the unconditioned stimulus increases, one becomes a less efficient signal for the arrival of the other—that is, the conditioned stimulus provides less useful information about the appearance of the unconditioned stimulus. Once again, there are exceptions to the rule (DeCola & Fanselow, 1995; Gallistel & Gibbon, 2000; Williams et al., 1991), but generally if the gap between the conditioned stimulus and the unconditioned stimulus is long, only a weak association forms.

3. The conditioned stimulus needs to provide *new* information about the occurrence of the unconditioned stimulus. If there are already stimuli in the environment that signal the unconditioned stimulus, then presenting yet another stimulus before the unconditioned stimulus leads to little or no learning. When rats are exposed to mild electrical shock, their unconditioned, automatic response is to freeze. Suppose you teach some rats that a tone is a reliable signal for the shock. Now, after the rats have learned to freeze to the tone, you start turning on a light at the same time as you sound the tone, such that both the light and the tone are followed by the shock. Under these conditions, rats don't typically learn that the light, too, is a reliable signal for the shock, as was shown in a classic study by Leon Kamin at McMaster University (Kamin, 1968). This result is called *blocking* because the tone appears to block acquisition of a CR to the light. The light is

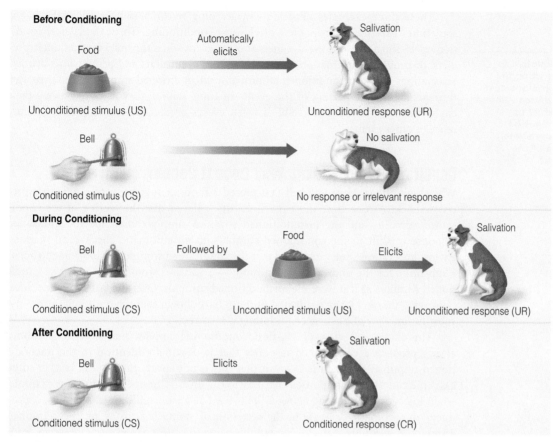

FIGURE 6.2

Classical Conditioning

Through classical conditioning, organisms learn about the signalling properties of events. The presentation of an unconditioned stimulus (US) leads to an automatic unconditioned response (UR) prior to training. A neutral stimulus (one that does not produce a relevant response before conditioning) is paired closely in time with a US. Eventually, the animal learns that this conditioned stimulus (CS) predicts the occurrence of the US and begins to show an appropriate conditioned response (CR) on presentation of the CS. Although here the CR and the UR are the same, they needn't be.

Concept Summary

FACTORS AFFECTING CLASSICAL CONDITIONING

Factor	Relation to Conditioning Effectiveness
Timing relationship between conditioned stimulus and unconditioned stimulus	Conditioned stimulus should usually be presented *before* the unconditioned stimulus. The unconditioned stimulus should usually follow the conditioned stimulus closely in time.
Informativeness of conditioned stimulus	The conditioned stimulus should provide new information about the occurrence of the unconditioned stimulus (to avoid blocking).

always presented just before the shock, but no conditioning occurs. Why? Because the light provides no new information about the occurrence of the shock—the tone already tells the rat that the shock is about to occur, so the rat learns nothing about the light.

Critical Thinking

Why do you think it's adaptive to learn associations only when the conditioned stimulus provides new information about the unconditioned stimulus? Can you think of any situations in which it might be useful to learn that many stimuli predict the appearance of the unconditioned stimulus?

These three examples illustrate why learning researchers have adopted what is sometimes called a *cognitive* view of classical conditioning. Through classical conditioning we learn that one event signals another event when the first event uniquely predicts, or provides information about, the second event. Rats and people don't acquire associations between conditioned stimuli and unconditioned stimuli in a *passive* way, through the simple pairing of the events in time. Rather, they actively process their environment—they seek to establish when events predict, or even cause, the occurrence of other events.

Conditioned Responding: Why Does It Develop?

Why should dogs drool to a bell that precedes food, or rats freeze to a tone that precedes shock? At one time most psychologists believed that the pairing of the conditioned stimulus and the unconditioned stimulus simply caused the unconditioned response to shift to the conditioned stimulus, in an automatic, mechanical manner. Pavlov, for example, was convinced that the conditioned stimulus would come to act as a substitute for the unconditioned stimulus—organisms would respond to the conditioned stimulus as if it were the unconditioned stimulus. Over the last several decades, however, a number of experimental findings have shown that the traditional stimulus-substitution view of classical conditioning is incorrect.

The traditional view of classical conditioning implies that organisms should always produce a conditioned response that is essentially identical to the unconditioned response. Research has shown that this is not always the case. In fact, in some cases the conditioned response is *opposite* to the unconditioned response. For example, when injection of the drug *epinephrine* is used as an unconditioned stimulus, it produces an automatic decrease in the secretion of stomach acids as an unconditioned response. A stimulus that signals the impending injection of this drug, however, leads to an *increase* in secretions as a conditioned response. When a conditioned response acts in the opposite direction from an unconditioned response, it is called a *compensatory response.* Shephard Siegel at McMaster University has conducted extensive research examining learned responses to drugs, and he and his colleagues have suggested that compensatory responses help offset a drug's effects, perhaps playing a role in the development of drug tolerance (Siegel, 1983, 1999; Siegel & Allan, 1998). (As we discussed earlier, drug tolerance can also be viewed as an example of habituation; it is not yet clear whether tolerance develops from the learning processes involved in classical conditioning, from habituation, or from both.)

A second challenge to the traditional view of conditioning is that the response to the conditioned stimulus depends not only on the unconditioned stimulus, but also on the properties of the conditioned stimulus itself (Holland, 1977; Rescorla, 1988). We mentioned earlier that rats learn to freeze in response to a tone that signals impending shock; interestingly, however, if the cue that signals shock is a localized object, then rather than freezing in the presence of that object, rats will try to bury or cover up the object. As shown in Figure 6.3, for example, if rats learn that touching a bar in the cage means they will get shocked, they will try to cover the bar with material from the bottom of the cage (Pinel & Treit, 1979). As another example, pigeons will peck a lighted disk that signals food but will show little or no change in behaviour to a tone that predicts food (Nairne & Rescorla, 1981). In both of these cases, the conditioned response depends on the nature of the conditioned stimulus, suggesting that conditioning cannot be explained in terms of a passive, mechanical process by which the CS becomes a substitute for the US.

Yet another challenge to the idea that conditioned responses arise in a passive, mechanical manner comes from evidence that the nature of the CR depends on the organism's current "attitude" toward the unconditioned stimulus. For example, animals that have just gorged themselves on food show little or no response to a conditioned stimulus that signals the delivery of yet more food (Holland & Rescorla, 1975).

(a) US produces UR

(b) Localized CS produces a CR
that is different from the UR

FIGURE 6.3
Form of the Conditioned Response

In classical conditioning, the form of the CR depends not only on the expected US but also on the CS itself. In an experiment by University of British Columbia researchers John Pinel and Dallas Treit (1979), rats attempted to bury an electric prod that produced shock on contact. When the prod was first introduced to the cage, rats tended to explore it by touching it, thereby getting shocked (a US), which automatically elicits withdrawal (a UR) (left panel). Subsequently, the presence of the prod acts as a CS, but the CR it elicits is burying (right panel), which is quite a different response from the UR, withdrawal.

Findings such as these have led most psychologists who study classical conditioning to embrace what is sometimes called the "cognitive" account of conditioning. By this view, animals learn that the CS signals the US, and they use this information to prepare to respond appropriately. Because the conditioned stimulus informs the animal that a significant event is about to occur, the animal responds in a way that is appropriate for the upcoming event. Robert Rescorla (1988) put it this way: "Pavlovian conditioning is not the shifting of a response from one stimulus to another. Instead, conditioning involves the learning of relations among events that are complexly represented, a learning that can be exhibited in various ways" (p. 158). Learning such relations among events can be quite adaptive, as the Practical Solutions box discusses.

Second-Order Conditioning

In addition to discovering the basic phenomenon of classical conditioning, Pavlov found that a conditioned stimulus can be used to condition a second signal. In **second-order conditioning** an established conditioned stimulus, such as a tone that predicts food, is presented immediately after a new event, such as a light; the unconditioned stimulus itself is never actually presented. In such a case, the pairing of the tone with the light can be sufficient to produce conditioned responding to the light.

An example from Pavlov's laboratory helps to illustrate the procedure. One of Pavlov's associates, Dr. Frolov, first taught a dog that the sound of a ticking metronome signalled the application of meat powder in the mouth. The dog quickly started to drool in the presence of the ticking. A black square was then presented, followed closely by the ticking. After a number of these black square–metronome pairings, even though the ticking was never followed by food powder on these trials, the dog began to drool in the presence of the black square. The dog drooled in response to the square because it signalled the ticking, which the dog had previously learned signalled the food (see Figure 6.4).

The fact that conditioned stimuli can be used to condition responses to other events is important because it greatly expands the number of situations in which classical conditioning applies. It is not necessary for an unconditioned stimulus to be physically present in a situation for you to learn something about the relationship between that situation and the likely occurrence of that US. Advertisers regularly use second-order conditioning to sell products. One example is the use of celebrities to endorse products. If the celebrity is an expert on the product being sold (e.g., Wayne Gretzky selling hockey equipment), then the endorsement makes sense on rational grounds. Often, however, the celebrity has no particular expertise related to the product being sold (e.g., Wayne Gretzky selling cars), and advertisers hope that prior associations between the celebrity and good feelings (e.g., from Wayne to winning Olympic gold) will, via second-order conditioning, create associations between their product and those good feelings.

second-order conditioning

A procedure in which an established conditioned stimulus is used to condition a second neutral stimulus.

Practical Solutions

DEVELOPING TASTE AVERSIONS

On St. Thomas in the Virgin Islands, researchers Lowell Nicolaus and David Nellis encouraged captured mongooses to eat eggs laced with carbachol, a drug that produces temporary illness. The mongooses were hungry, but over a period of days they dramatically reduced their consumption of the tainted eggs (Nicolaus & Nellis, 1987). In research conducted in a different domain, children undergoing treatment for cancer ate ice cream flavoured with quinine (which has a very bitter taste) just before the onset of chemotherapy. Chemotherapy typically causes nausea and vomiting. Several weeks later, when offered the ice cream, only 21% of the children were willing to taste it again (Bernstein, 1978).

Both of these situations represent naturalistic applications of classical conditioning. Can you identify the critical features of each? How do these two examples involve the learning of a relation between two events, a conditioned stimulus and an unconditioned stimulus, that largely occurs outside the organism's control? First, let's look for the unconditioned stimulus—the stimulus that unconditionally produces a response prior to training. In both of these cases, the unconditioned stimulus is the illness-producing event, either the drug carbachol or the cancer-fighting chemotherapy. The response that is automatically produced, unfortunately for the participants, is stomach distress. Children don't need to learn to vomit from chemotherapy; a mongoose doesn't need to be taught to be sick after receiving carbachol. These are inevitable consequences that require no prior conditioning.

Now, what is the conditioned stimulus—the event that provides information about the occurrence of the unconditioned stimulus? In these examples, it is the taste of the food (the eggs or the ice cream) that signals the later onset of nausea. A conditioned response, feelings of queasiness to the food, was produced whenever the opportunity to eat that food was presented. Taste aversions are

easy to acquire, and are sometimes learned after a single pairing of a distinctive, novel food and illness. You may have conditioned taste aversions of your own.

Why would anyone want to do research studies like these? What possible value or relevance would such studies have? For one thing, it is extremely adaptive for people and mongooses to acquire taste aversions to potentially dangerous foods—it is in their interest to avoid those events that signal something potentially harmful—and discovering the principles and mechanisms that underlie such learning is a legitimate scientific aim. Moreover, in the two studies we've just considered the researchers investigated the aversions for particular reasons. Mongooses often eat the eggs of endangered species (such as marine turtles). By baiting the nests of mongoose prey with tainted eggs and establishing a taste aversion, scientists reduced the overall rate of egg predation. Similar techniques have also been used to prevent sheep from eating dangerous plants in the pasture (Zahorik et al., 1990).

In the case of chemotherapy, Illene Bernstein was interested in developing

methods for *avoiding* the establishment of taste aversions: Cancer patients who are undergoing chemotherapy also need to eat, so it's critical to understand the conditions under which aversions are formed. Taste aversions often develop as a side effect of chemotherapy. Patients tend to avoid foods that they consumed just before treatment, potentially leading to weight loss that impedes recovery. Researchers have found that associations are particularly likely to form between *unusual* tastes and nausea. Broberg and Bernstein (1987), for example, found that giving children an unusual flavour of candy just before treatment reduced the likelihood of their forming aversions to healthy parts of their normal diet. These children formed a taste aversion to the candy rather than to their normal diet. Another helpful technique in preventing taste aversions from developing is to ask the patient to eat a very familiar, preferably bland, food before every treatment. Foods that do not have distinctive tastes and that people eat regularly (such as bread) are less likely to elicit taste aversions.

For children undergoing the rigours of chemotherapy, like this young boy suffering from leukemia, it's important to prevent taste aversions to healthy foods from developing as a negative side effect of the treatment. Broberg and Bernstein (1987) found that giving children an unusual flavour of candy just prior to treatment reduced the chances of a taste aversion forming to their normal diet.

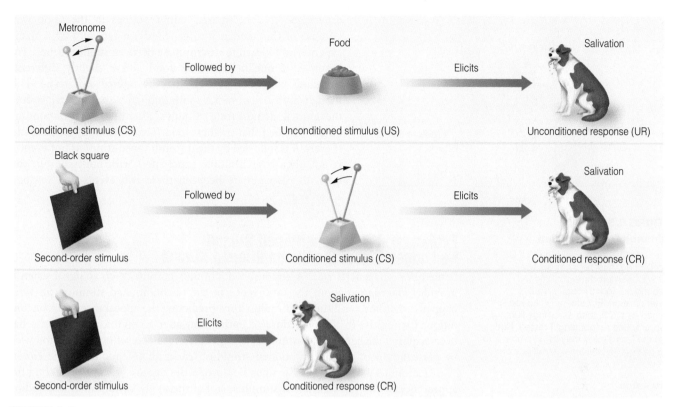

FIGURE 6.4

Second-Order Conditioning

In second-order conditioning, an established CS is used in place of a US to condition a second signal. In Dr. Frolov's experiment, a ticking metronome was first paired with food; after repeated pairings, the ticking elicited salivation as a CR. Next, a black square—which did not produce salivation initially—was paired with the ticking (no US was presented). After repeated pairings, the presentation of the black square produced salivation.

Stimulus Generalization

Pavlov also discovered that a response conditioned to one stimulus tended to generalize to other, similar stimuli. If a bell with a particular pitch was conditioned as a signal for food, another bell that sounded similar also produced salivation—even though the dog had never before heard the second bell. When a new stimulus produces a response similar to the CR produced by the conditioned stimulus, **stimulus generalization** has occurred.

As a rule, stimulus generalization occurs when a new stimulus is similar to the conditioned stimulus (see Figure 6.5). If you get sick after eating clams, there's a good chance you'll avoid eating oysters; if you've had a bad experience in the dentist's chair, the sound of the neighbour's high-speed drill may make you uncomfortable. Generalization makes adaptive sense: Things that look, sound, or feel similar often share significant properties. It really doesn't matter whether it's a tiger, a lion, or a panther leaping at you—you should run all the same.

Stimulus Discrimination

Stimulus discrimination occurs when you respond to a new stimulus in a way that is different from your response to the original conditioned stimulus. Through stimulus discrimination, you reveal that you can distinguish between stimuli, even when those stimuli are quite similar.

When stimuli do share properties—for example, two tones of a similar pitch—people often need experience to teach them to discriminate. The natural tendency is to

stimulus generalization
Responding to a new stimulus in a way similar to the response produced by an established conditioned stimulus.

Critical Thinking

After reading about stimulus generalization, can you understand why some psychologists believe that certain psychological problems, such as specific fears called phobias, might result from learning experiences?

stimulus discrimination
Responding to a new stimulus differently from the way one responds to an established conditioned stimulus.

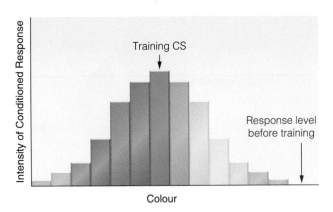

FIGURE 6.5

Stimulus Generalization

After conditioned responding to a CS is established, another stimulus similar to the CS will often produce conditioned responding, too, through stimulus generalization. For example, if a red light is trained as a CS, then an orange light will also produce responding if tested. Notice that the less similar the new stimulus is to the trained CS, the less generalization occurs.

extinction

Presenting a conditioned stimulus repeatedly, after conditioning, without the unconditioned stimulus, resulting in a gradual loss of the conditioned response.

spontaneous recovery

The recovery of an extinguished conditioned response after a period of nonexposure to the conditioned stimulus.

conditioned inhibition

Learning to associate a previously neutral stimulus with the non-occurrence of an unconditioned stimulus.

generalize—that is, to treat similar things in the same way. Because of this tendency to generalize, it typically takes many experiences to learn to discriminate between similar stimuli. For example, if one bell predicts food and a slightly different-sounding bell does not, at first the animal will respond as though both bells predict food; only after multiple trials does the animal demonstrate stimulus discrimination, responding only to the bell that predicts food. The same holds for humans. If event A is followed by the unconditioned stimulus but event B is not, then over multiple experiences with both stimuli, you learn to discriminate between these two events and respond accordingly.

Extinction: When Conditioned Stimuli No Longer Signal the Unconditioned Stimuli

Remember our general rule: A conditioned stimulus becomes a good signal when it provides *information* about the occurrence of the unconditioned stimulus. So what happens when the conditioned stimulus stops predicting the appearance of an unconditioned stimulus? In the procedure of **extinction,** after a conditioned response has been acquired the conditioned stimulus is presented repeatedly without being followed by presentation of the unconditioned stimulus. Under these conditions, the conditioned stimulus gradually loses its signalling properties because it stops predicting the appearance of the unconditioned stimulus. Not surprisingly, conditioned responding gradually diminishes as a result.

Notice the similarity between the procedure of extinction and the concept of habituation. Both involve the repeated presentation of an event accompanied by a gradual loss in responding. The difference between them is that extinction involves a loss in responding that has been acquired as a result of conditioning—you change your behaviour because the conditioned stimulus no longer signals the presence of another significant event. In habituation, no prior learning or conditioning is required to produce the changes that result from repeated exposure. You naturally orient toward sudden changes in your environment—no learning is required—but you'll learn to ignore those events that repeatedly occur without significant consequence.

Spontaneous Recovery Sometimes conditioned responding that has disappeared as a result of extinction will recover spontaneously with the passage of a period of time during which the CS is not presented. This phenomenon is known as **spontaneous recovery** (see Figure 6.6). For example, Pavlov's dogs stopped drooling if a bell that had previously signalled food was repeatedly presented alone, but when the bell was rung again the day after extinction, the conditioned response reappeared (although often not as strongly). Spontaneous recovery is another example of why it is important to distinguish between learning and performance. At the end of extinction, the conditioned stimulus seems to have lost its signalling properties, but when it is tested after a delay, we see that at least some of the learning remained (see also Bouton, 1991; Brooks, 2000).

Conditioned Inhibition: Signalling the Absence of an Unconditioned Stimulus

In the conditioning phenomena discussed so far, the organism learns that a previously neutral stimulus predicts the subsequent occurrence of an unconditioned stimulus (or, via extinction, gradually loses that association). Animals can also acquire **conditioned inhibition;** that is, they can learn to associate a previously neutral stimulus with the non-occurrence of an unconditioned stimulus. In the procedure illustrated in Figure 6.7, for example, a pigeon has been trained to associate the presence of a green

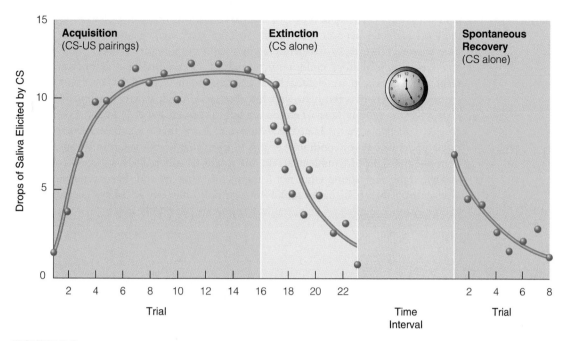

FIGURE 6.6

Training, Extinction, and Spontaneous Recovery

During training, Pavlov found that the amount of salivation produced in response to the CS initially increased and then levelled off as a function of the number of CS–US pairings. During extinction, the CS is repeatedly presented without the US, and conditioned responding gradually diminishes. If no testing of the CS occurs for a rest interval following extinction, spontaneous recovery of the CR will often occur if the CS is presented again.

FIGURE 6.7

Conditioned Inhibition

The top panel illustrates a standard classical conditioned response: A green light has been repeatedly paired with the presence of food, and the pigeon has learned to associate the green light with availability of food and so approaches the hopper when the green light is on. The lower panel illustrates a conditioned inhibition response: A red light has repeatedly been paired with the absence of food, and the pigeon has learned to associate the red light with the non-availability of food and so moves away from the hopper when the red light is on.

light with the availability of food (a standard conditioned response), and so approaches the food hopper whenever it is hungry and the green light is on; the pigeon has also been trained, however, to associate a red light with the absence of food.

Typically, inhibitory conditioning produces a response that is opposite to the response that would be elicited by a CS that predicts the US. For example, after repeated pairings of a red light with the absence of food, a pigeon will actively move away from the food hopper when the red light is on (Hearst & Franklin, 1977; Jenkins et al., 1978). Note that it is just as adaptive to learn that a significant event will *not* occur under one set of conditions as it is to learn that it will occur under another. For example, the sight of troublemaker Randy might usually make Justin quake with fear and avoid the playground—but not if there's a teacher around. The teacher signals the absence of a threat. In nature, inhibitory stimuli often act as "safety" signals, telling people or other animals when potential dangers are likely to be absent.

Concept Summary

MAJOR PHENOMENA OF CLASSICAL CONDITIONING

Phenomenon	Description	Example: Pavlov's Dogs
Second-order conditioning	An established conditioned stimulus is presented immediately following a new event; after several pairings, the new event elicits the conditioned response.	After a dog has been conditioned to salivate in response to a conditioned stimulus (tone), the conditioned stimulus is presented immediately following a new signal (e.g., a light). After several pairings, the light then may come to elicit responding.
Stimulus generalization	A new stimulus that is similar to a conditioned stimulus produces a response similar to the one produced by the conditioned stimulus.	After a dog has been conditioned to salivate in response to a conditioned stimulus (e.g., a red light), the same response may be produced by a similar stimulus (e.g., an orange or purple light).
Stimulus discrimination	The response to a new stimulus is different from the response to the original conditioned stimulus.	After a dog has been conditioned to salivate in response to a conditioned stimulus (light), the response does not occur to a different stimulus, such as a ringing bell.
Extinction	Conditioned responding diminishes when the conditioned stimulus (after conditioning) is presented without being followed by the unconditioned stimulus.	After a dog has been conditioned to salivate in response to a conditioned stimulus (tone), the tone is presented repeatedly without the unconditioned stimulus (food). Responding to the conditioned stimulus lessens.
Spontaneous recovery	Conditioned responding that has disappeared in extinction recovers spontaneously with the passage of a period of time during which the conditioned stimulus is not presented.	After extinction, a dog no longer responds to the conditioned stimulus (tone). After a rest period, the dog once again will respond when presented with the conditioned stimulus (tone).
Conditioned inhibition	A stimulus that is repeatedly paired with the absence of an unconditioned stimulus leads to responding that is opposite in direction to that of the conditioned response that would be elicited by a conditioned stimulus that signals the presence of that unconditioned stimulus.	After repeated trials in which a red light signals the absence of meat powder, the dog produces even less saliva when a red light is turned on than it would normally do in the absence of any relevant stimuli.

Test Yourself 6.2

Check your knowledge about classical conditioning by answering the following questions. (You will find the answers in Appendix B.)

1. Growing up, your little sister Leah had the annoying habit of screaming, at the top of her lungs, every time she stepped into her bath water. Her screaming always made you wince and cover your ears. Now, years later, you still wince every time you hear running water. Identify the
    a. unconditioned stimulus: _____
    b. unconditioned response: _____
    c. conditioned stimulus: _____
    d. conditioned response: _____

2. Every two years when you visit the optometrist, you get a puff of air blown into your eye to test for glaucoma. It always makes you blink. Just before the puff is delivered, the doctor typically asks you if you're "ready." Now, whenever you hear that word, you feel an urge to blink. Identify the
    a. unconditioned stimulus: _____
    b. unconditioned response: _____
    c. conditioned stimulus: _____
    d. conditioned response: _____

3. A boy is repeatedly frightened by his neighbour's large dogs and soon begins to cry whenever he looks at the neighbour's yard, even if the dogs are not there. The neighbours (and their dogs) move away, and within a year the boy does not cry anymore when he looks at the yard. Which of the following probably best accounts for this development?
    a. Habituation
    b. Stimulus generalization
    c. Spontaneous recovery
    d. Extinction
    e. Inhibitory conditioning

4. You used to give your dog Rascal scraps from the table, except when your grandmother (who thought this was deplorable manners) was visiting. Normally, Rascal stays close to the table at dinnertime, but when Grandma visits, Rascal sprawls in the kitchen. Which of the following best fits this phenomenon?
    a. Habituation
    b. Stimulus generalization
    c. Spontaneous recovery
    d. Extinction
    e. Inhibitory conditioning

LEARNING ABOUT THE CONSEQUENCES OF BEHAVIOUR: INSTRUMENTAL CONDITIONING

5c, SIM 4
Psyk.trek

Learning Goals

1. Be able to define instrumental conditioning, and discuss the law of effect.
2. Learn about B. F. Skinner's theoretical approach to psychology, which he called "radical behaviourism."
3. Be able to explain what is meant by the discriminative stimulus.
4. Understand the concept of reinforcement, and be able to distinguish between positive and negative reinforcement.

5. Be able to discuss different schedules of reinforcement, and compare their effects on behaviour.
6. Grasp how complex behaviours can be acquired through shaping.
7. Be able to describe the practical applications of instrumental conditioning and shaping.
8. Understand how biological factors may limit the responses that can be learned.
9. Be able to define punishment, and learn to distinguish between positive and negative punishment.
10. Be able to describe the practical applications of punishment.

instrumental conditioning

A procedure for studying how organisms learn about the consequences of their own voluntary actions; they learn that their behaviours are instrumental in producing rewards and punishments. Also called **operant conditioning**.

FIGURE 6.8
Classical versus Instrumental Conditioning

In classical conditioning, panel (a), food is delivered independently of the rat's behaviour. The light (CS) signals the automatic arrival of the food (US). In instrumental conditioning, panel (b), the rat must press the bar in the presence of the light in order to get the food (i.e., food is delivered to the hopper when the bar is pressed when the light is on). The light serves as a *discriminative stimulus* telling the rat that pressing the bar will now produce the food.

CLASSICAL CONDITIONING answers an important survival question: How do we learn that certain events signal the presence or the absence of other events? Through the processes tapped by classical conditioning, we learn to expect that certain events will or will not occur under certain conditions, and we react accordingly. Note that our actions under these conditions don't necessarily have any effect on the pairing of the signal and the unconditioned stimulus. Usually, occurrences of the conditioned stimulus and the unconditioned stimulus are outside our control. For example, you can't change the fact that thunder will follow lightning; all you can do is prepare for an event (thunder) when a prior event (lightning) tells you it's coming.

In another type of learning, studied through a procedure called **instrumental conditioning** (or **operant conditioning**), we learn that our own *actions,* rather than conditioned stimuli, lead to outcomes. If a child is allowed to watch an hour of television as a reward for cleaning her room, she learns that her behaviour is *instrumental* in producing rewards; by *operating* on her environment, she produces a pleasing consequence. Instrumental (or operant) learning involves learning about the consequences of one's own behaviour. Notice how classical conditioning differs from instrumental conditioning: In the former, you learn that events signal outcomes; in the latter, you learn that your own actions or behaviours produce outcomes (see Figure 6.8).

The Law of Effect

The study of instrumental conditioning predates Pavlov's historic work by several years. In 1895, Harvard graduate student Edward Lee Thorndike (1874–1949), working in the cellar of his mentor William James, began a series of experiments on "animal

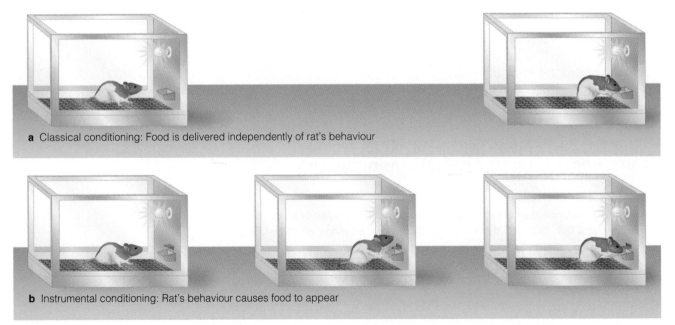

a Classical conditioning: Food is delivered independently of rat's behaviour

b Instrumental conditioning: Rat's behaviour causes food to appear

FIGURE 6.9
Instrumental Conditioning

In Thorndike's famous experiments on animal intelligence, cats learned that some kind of unusual response—such as pressing a lever or tilting a pole—allowed them to escape from a puzzle box. The graph shows that the time required to escape gradually diminished over learning trials. Here the cat is learning that its behaviour is instrumental in producing escape. (Based on Weiten, 1995.)

intelligence" using cats from around the neighbourhood. He built a puzzle box, which resembled a kind of tiny prison, and carefully recorded the time it took for the cats to escape. The boxes were designed so that escape was possible only through an unusual response, such as tilting a pole, pulling a string, or pressing a lever (see Figure 6.9). On release, the cats received a small amount of food as a reward.

Thorndike specifically selected escape responses that were unlikely to occur when the animals were first placed in the box. In this way, he could observe how the cats learned to escape over time. Through trial and error, the cats eventually learned to make the appropriate response, but the learning process was gradual. Thorndike also found that the time it took for an animal to escape on any particular trial depended on the number of prior successful escapes. The more times the animal had successfully escaped in the past, the faster it could get out of the box on a new trial.

The relationship between escape time and the number of prior successful escapes led Thorndike to formulate the **law of effect:** If a behaviour in a particular situation is followed by a satisfying or pleasant consequence, it will be strengthened (i.e., the probability of the animal performing that behaviour in that situation will increase); if a response in a particular situation is followed by an unsatisfying or unpleasant consequence, it will be weakened (i.e., its probability will decrease). According to the law of effect, all organisms learn to make certain responses in certain situations; the responses that regularly occur are those that have produced positive consequences in the past. If a response tends to occur initially (e.g., scratching at the walls of the cage) but is not followed by something good (such as freedom from the box), the chances of that response occurring again in the situation diminish.

law of effect

The idea that if a response in a particular situation is followed by a satisfying or pleasant consequence, it will be strengthened; if a response in a particular situation is followed by an unsatisfying or unpleasant consequence, it will be weakened.

B. F. Skinner and "Radical Behaviourism"

As you may recall from Chapter 1, from the late 1920s to the late 1950s psychological science was dominated by behaviourism. Behaviourists built on the work of pioneers such as Pavlov and Thorndike in an effort to develop a science of psychology based solely on observable environmental events and measurable behaviours. Behaviourists disdained attempts to explain psychological phenomena in terms of internal mental constructs such as "consciousness" or "insight," preferring to conduct research (often

radical behaviourism

A perspective on the analysis of human and animal behaviour that emphasizes explaining behaviour in terms of environmental events and that minimizes the use of internal explanations like thoughts, beliefs, and intentions.

with animal subjects) aimed at establishing lawful relationships between environmental stimuli and behavioural responses.

Probably the most influential behaviourist after Thorndike was B. F. Skinner (1904–1990). Skinner was responsible for major advances in our understanding of the details of animal and human learning. He developed a perspective regarding the explanation of behaviour that he called **radical behaviourism** (Skinner, 1974). Unlike earlier behaviourists, Skinner did not completely rule out referring to private events like thoughts and feelings in explaining behaviour. Skinner argued that it is acceptable to speculate about the events that take place "within the skin," as he put it, the things that only the person experiencing them can observe, as long as we treat them the same way we treat observable, public events—as physical in nature and subject to the same laws as external stimuli and behaviours.

As an example, Skinner talked about "conditioned seeing," as when a person listening to a particularly good recording of waves hitting a beach might "see," that is, imagine, the ocean waves crashing down on the shore. This "seeing" would be understood as involving some of the same brain activity as when we actually see waves when we're at the ocean. Skinner suggested that an event such as a person "seeing" an ocean when there is no ocean there to see should be treated just like any other behaviour. In this case, Skinner would claim that this covert "behaviour" is determined by exactly the same laws as the conditioned salivation in Pavlov's dogs, except that it's private rather than public.

Although Skinner allowed for a role of mental events in human behaviour, he was very cautious about making inferences about them. Instead, radical behaviourism emphasized the role of external, observable stimuli in influencing the behaviour of human and nonhuman animals. The idea was that behaviour can be understood as the product of an individual animal's history of reinforcement, as governed by the principles of classical and, especially, instrumental conditioning.

The Discriminative Stimulus: Knowing When to Respond

The law of effect tends to be situation specific. For example, if you are praised for raising your hand in class, your rate of raising your hand in class is likely to increase, but you're not likely to start raising your hand while walking down the street. What you've learned is something like the following: If some stimulus situation is present (the classroom) and you act in a certain way (raising your hand), then some reinforcing consequence (praise) is likely to follow.

discriminative stimulus

The stimulus situation that sets the occasion for a response to be followed by reinforcement or punishment.

Skinner (1938) referred to the situation as the **discriminative stimulus.** He suggested that a discriminative stimulus "sets the occasion" for a response to be rewarded. Being in class—the discriminative stimulus—sets the occasion for question-asking to be rewarded. In some ways, the discriminative stimulus shares properties with the conditioned stimulus established in classical conditioning. For example, you often find *stimulus generalization* of a discriminative stimulus: If a pigeon is trained to peck a key in the presence of a red light, the bird will later peck the key whenever a light of a similar colour is turned on. If you're rewarded for asking questions in psychology, you might naturally generalize your response to another course, such as economics, and raise your hand there, and you might even find yourself raising your hand when you want to break into an animated conversation with friends outside of the classroom. Conversely, *stimulus discrimination* also occurs, usually after experiencing reward in one situation but not in another. You may learn, for instance, that raising your hand in psychology class leads to positive consequences, but not in your economics class. In such a case, one setting (psychology) acts as an effective discriminative stimulus for a certain instrumental response, but another setting (economics) does not.

Over the years, learning researchers have argued about exactly what is learned about the discriminative stimulus in instrumental conditioning, especially in studies with animal subjects. For example, if a rat is taught to press a lever to receive food, does the rat learn simply to press the lever whenever it is there? Does the reward merely "stamp in" an association between a discriminative stimulus (the lever) and a response (pressing)? For many years, this was the traditional view in psychology: Instrumental conditioning leads to the formation of associations between stimuli and responses (Hull, 1943).

However, most psychologists now believe that more is learned in instrumental conditioning than simple connections between discriminative stimuli and responses. For example, it seems likely that the animal also learns something about the reward itself. Just as in classical conditioning, responding in the presence of the discriminative stimulus depends on how the animal feels about the reward—if a rat is taught to press a lever for a reward, and then the value of the reward is somehow changed, the rat will change its behaviour accordingly (Colwill & Rescorla, 1986). This suggests that the animal learns not only about the discriminative stimulus and the response, but also about the specific reward that follows the response (Colwill, 1994; Colwill & Delameter, 1995).

Similarly, in recent years researchers have used instrumental conditioning procedures to explore other aspects of the animal's "cognitive" processing of the learning experience. For instance, Marcia Spetch and Douglas Grant of the University of Alberta (1993) and Angelo Santi and colleagues of Wilfrid Laurier University (1995) have used variations in the timing of the experimental procedures during conditioning trials to learn significant details about the memory systems of rats and pigeons. As another example, Cohen and colleagues (2002) at Windsor University tested rats in sequences of operant conditioning trials, with reinforcement being provided on some trials but not on others (e.g., a rat might get reinforced for running a maze on trials 1 and 2, but not on trial 3 of a 3-trial sequence). After several such sequences, the rats run the maze more slowly on the nonreinforced trials, indicating that they have learned something about the temporal sequence of trials.

The Nature of Reinforcement

The law of effect states that responses will be strengthened if they are followed by a pleasant or satisfying consequence. By "strengthened," Thorndike meant that a response was more likely to occur in the future in that particular situation. But what defines a pleasant or satisfying consequence? This is a tricky problem because the concept of a "pleasant" or "satisfying" event is highly personal—what's pleasant for me might not be pleasant for you. Moreover, something that's pleasing at one time might not be pleasing at another. Food, for example, is "positive at the beginning of Thanksgiving dinner, indifferent halfway through, and negative at the end of it" (Kimble, 1993). For these reasons, psychologists use a technical term—**reinforcement**—to describe consequences that increase the likelihood of responding. As you'll see, behavioural psychologists distinguish between two major types of reinforcement: *positive* and *negative*.

reinforcement
Response consequences that increase the likelihood of responding in a similar way again.

Positive Reinforcement

When the presentation of an event after a response in a certain situation increases the likelihood of the response occurring again in that situation, **positive reinforcement** has occurred. Usually, the presented event is an *appetitive stimulus*—something the organism likes, needs, or has an "appetite" for. Food and water are obvious examples, but behaviours can be reinforcing too (such as sexual activity or painting a picture). Remember, though, it's not the subjective qualities of the consequence that matter from the behaviourist perspective—what matters in defining positive reinforcement is an *increase* in the frequency of the behaviour that led to the reinforcement. As long as you're more likely to act in a certain way again after a consequence has been delivered, then the consequence qualifies as positive reinforcement.

Psychologists have discovered that it's sometimes possible to predict when the presentation of an event will be reinforcing by appealing to the concept of a behavioural *bliss point*. By bliss points psychologists mean baseline tendencies to respond to events. Everyone has a certain desire to eat, drink, listen to music, play volleyball, study

positive reinforcement
An event that, when *presented* after a response in a certain situation, increases the likelihood of that response occurring again in that situation.

Critical Thinking

Can you think of a case in which an unpleasant event increases the likelihood of the response that produces it?

for school, and so on. These baseline levels of satisfaction, which presumably differ from one person to the next, are called bliss points. According to the *response deprivation theory* of reinforcement, an event will be reinforcing as long as presenting it allows someone to move toward his or her natural bliss point for that event (Allison, 1989; Timberlake, 1980). If you have been deprived of eating for a while, you have fallen below your natural bliss point for eating and therefore will find the presentation of food to be positively reinforcing. Once you've eaten, food loses its reinforcing value because you've already reached your natural bliss point for eating. This is the reason why food is no longer reinforcing shortly after you finish a large meal.

Importantly, the response deprivation theory predicts that the presentation of any event or response, in principle, can serve as positive reinforcement (see also Premack, 1962). If you have been deprived of responding to an event for long enough (i.e., you have fallen below your bliss point), the presentation of that event should be reinforcing. Most children, for example, would rather colour than do math problems (presumably because the bliss point for colouring is naturally high). However, if children are deprived of doing math problems for long enough, so that they fall below their natural bliss point for math, the opportunity to do math can serve as positive reinforcement (see Konarski, 1985; Timberlake, 1980).

Negative Reinforcement

negative reinforcement
An event that, when *removed* after a response in a situation, increases the likelihood of that response occurring in that situation again.

Negative Reinforcement With **negative reinforcement,** the removal of an event after a response in a given situation increases the likelihood of that response occurring in that situation again. In most cases, negative reinforcement occurs when a response allows you to eliminate, avoid, or escape from an unpleasant situation. For instance, you hang up the phone on someone who is criticizing you unfairly, shut off the blaring alarm clock in the morning, or walk out of a movie that is boring you to tears. These responses are more likely to occur again in the future, given the appropriate circumstance, because they lead to the removal of something negative—criticism, noise, or boredom. But, as you may have guessed, the event that is removed doesn't have to be unpleasant—it simply has to increase the likelihood of the "contingent" response (the response that led to the removal).

Critical Thinking

When you study for an examination or try to do well in school, are you seeking positive reinforcement or negative reinforcement?

Students are often confused by the term *negative reinforcement* because they think negative reinforcement is a bad thing. Whenever psychologists use the term *reinforcement,* both positive and negative, they are referring to outcomes that increase the probability of responding. The terms *positive* and *negative* simply refer to whether the response decreases due to the presentation of something (positive) or due to the removal of something (negative). In both cases, the result is to reward or reinforce the contingent behaviour, and we can expect the response that produced the reinforcement to occur again in that situation.

Concept Summary

POSITIVE AND NEGATIVE REINFORCEMENT

Consequence	Description	Example
Positive reinforcement	The *presentation* of an event after a response increases the likelihood of the response occurring again.	Jean-Claude's parents reward him for cleaning his room by giving him $5. The presentation of $5 increases the likelihood that Jean-Claude will clean his room again.
Negative reinforcement	The *removal* of an event after a response increases the likelihood of the response occurring again.	Hannah's parents nag her continually about cleaning up her room. When she finally cleans her room, her parents stop nagging her. The removal of the nagging increases the probability that Hannah will clean her room again.

Conditioned Reinforcers   Sometimes a stimulus can act like a reinforcer even though it seems to have no intrinsic value. For example, money will serve as a powerful reinforcer even though it's only a well-made piece of paper marked with interesting engravings. However, having money predicts something of intrinsic value—you can buy things—and this is what gives it its reinforcing value. In the same way, if a stimulus predicts the removal of something negative, then its presentation is also likely to be reinforcing. Stimuli of this type are called **conditioned reinforcers** because their reinforcing properties are acquired through learning (they are also sometimes called "secondary" reinforcers to distinguish them from more "primary" reinforcers such as food or water). These stimuli are reinforcing because they signal the presence or absence of other events that are themselves reinforcing.

Schedules of Reinforcement

The law of effect implies that behaviours are more likely to be repeated if they are *followed* by positive or negative reinforcement. As in classical conditioning, however, the development of an instrumental response depends greatly on how often, and when, the reinforcements are delivered. It is necessary to teach someone that his or her behaviour uniquely predicts the reward—if you deliver the reward in a haphazard way, or when the behaviour in question has not occurred, learning can be slow or nonexistent (Dickinson & Charnock, 1985).

Most of the research done on the acquisition of instrumental responding has been concerned with the scheduling of reinforcements. A **schedule of reinforcement** is simply a rule used by the experimenter to determine when particular responses will be reinforced (Ferster & Skinner, 1957). If a response is followed rapidly by reinforcement every time it occurs, the reinforcement is said to be on a *continuous* schedule. If reinforcement is delivered only some of the time after the response has occurred, this is called a **partial reinforcement schedule.** There are four major types of partial reinforcement schedules: fixed-ratio, variable-ratio, fixed-interval, and variable-interval. Each produces a distinctive pattern of responding (see Figure 6.10).

Fixed-Ratio Schedules   *Ratio* schedules of reinforcement require that you produce a certain *number* of responses before receiving reinforcement. In a **fixed-ratio schedule,** the number of required responses is fixed and doesn't change from one trial to the next. Suppose you are paid a dollar for every 100 envelopes you stuff for a local marketing firm. This schedule of reinforcement is referred to as an "FR 100" (fixed-ratio 100) because it requires 100 responses (envelopes stuffed) before the reinforcement is delivered (a dollar). You can stuff the envelopes as quickly as you like, but you must produce 100 responses before you get the reward.

Fixed-ratio schedules typically produce steady, consistent rates of responding because the relationship between the instrumental response and the reinforcement is clear and predictable. For this reason, assembly-line work in factories is often reinforced on a fixed-ratio schedule. The only behavioural quirk occurs when the number of required responses is relatively large. For example, if you have to pick 10 bushels of grapes for each monetary reward, you are likely to pause a bit in your responding immediately after the tenth bushel. This delay in responding after reinforcement is called the *postreinforcement pause.* Pausing after reinforcement is easy to understand in this situation—after all, you have to do a lot of work before you receive the next reward. But it can be an important factor to consider when choosing the most appropriate schedule for a given work environment.

If you stop delivering the reinforcement after the fixed number of responses has occurred, you can expect the individual to change his or her behaviour accordingly. Eventually, the individual will simply stop responding. Similar to what happens in classical conditioning, the introduction of nonreinforcement following a period of training is called *extinction.* How quickly subjects stop responding, or extinguish their behaviour, when reinforcements are no longer delivered is determined partly by the

conditioned reinforcer
A stimulus that has acquired reinforcing properties through prior learning.

schedule of reinforcement
A rule that an experimenter uses to determine when particular responses will be reinforced. A continuous reinforcement schedule is one in which a reward is delivered each and every time the target behaviour is performed. Partial reinforcement schedules, in contrast, can be fixed or variable, and ratio or interval.

partial reinforcement schedule
A schedule in which reinforcement is delivered only some of the time after the response has occurred.

fixed-ratio schedule
A schedule in which the number of responses required for reinforcement is fixed and does not change from trial to trial.

FIGURE 6.10

Schedules of Reinforcement

Schedules of reinforcement are rules that the experimenter uses to determine when responses will be reinforced. Ratio schedules tend to produce rapid rates of responding because reinforcement depends on the number of responses. Interval schedules tend to produce lower rates of responding because reinforcement is delivered only for the first response after a specified time interval. In the cumulative response functions plotted here, the total number of responses is plotted over time. The short dark lines indicate delivery of reinforcement.

variable-ratio schedule

A schedule in which a certain number of responses is required for reinforcement, but the number of required responses typically changes from trial to trial.

reinforcement schedule in effect. Fixed-ratio schedules typically produce rapid rates of extinction because it quickly becomes clear that the schedule has changed—the reinforcement no longer occurs after the required number of responses has been produced.

Variable-Ratio Schedules A **variable-ratio schedule** also requires that a certain *number* of responses be made before a reward is given. However, with a variable-ratio schedule, the number of responses required varies over trials. Reinforcement may be delivered after the first response on trial 1, after the seventh response on trial 2, after the third response on trial 3, and so on. It's called a variable-ratio (VR) schedule because the number of responses required to earn a reward *varies* (often in a random fashion).

Variable-ratio schedules differ from fixed-ratio schedules in that you can never predict which response will get you the reward. These schedules typically produce high rates of responding, and the postreinforcement pause, seen in fixed-ratio schedules, is usually absent (after all, the next response might get you the reward again). Gambling is an example of a variable-ratio schedule; because of chance factors, a gambler wins some bets and loses others, but the gambler never knows what to expect on a given bet.

The unpredictability of reward during a variable-ratio schedule makes it difficult to eliminate a response trained on this schedule when the response is no longer reinforced. Consider the typical compulsive slot machine player: Dollar after dollar goes into the machine; sometimes there's a payoff, more often not. Even if a machine was rigged so that rewards are never delivered (thus placing the responder on extinction), many established gamblers would continue playing long into the night. On a variable-ratio schedule, it's hard to see that extinction is in effect because you've never been able to predict when reinforcement will occur.

Fixed-Interval Schedules   In an *interval* schedule of reinforcement, the reward is delivered for the first response that occurs following a certain interval of time; if a **fixed-interval schedule** (FI) is in effect, the time period remains constant from one trial to the next. Suppose we reward a pigeon with food when it pecks a lighted response key after 2 minutes have elapsed. In this case, we would be using an "FI 2 min." schedule. Note that the pigeon must still produce the response to receive the reward. (Otherwise, the learning procedure would not be instrumental conditioning.) Pecking just doesn't do any good until at least 2 minutes have elapsed.

You shouldn't be surprised to learn that fixed-interval schedules typically produce low rates of responding. Because no direct association exists between how much you respond and the delivery of reinforcement—you're rewarded only when you respond after the interval has passed—it doesn't make sense to respond all the time. Another characteristic of fixed-interval schedules is that responding slows down after reinforcement and gradually increases as the end of the interval approaches. If the total number of responses is plotted over time in a cumulative response record, the net effect is a *scalloping* pattern of the type shown in Figure 6.10.

To appreciate scalloping, consider how people generally study in school. Because "reinforcement" occurs only on fixed test days, students often wait until the week (or night) before the test to start studying the material. Studying behaviour increases gradually throughout the test-to-test interval and peaks on the night before the exam. (Actually, studying is not reinforced on a true fixed-interval schedule because you must take the test on a specific day; in a true fixed-interval schedule, you can respond at any time after the fixed interval has elapsed and still get reinforcement.)

Variable-Interval Schedules   When a **variable-interval schedule** (VI) is in effect, the allotted time before a response will yield reinforcement changes from trial to trial. For example, we may deliver reinforcement for a response occurring after 2 minutes on trial 1, after 10 minutes on trial 2, after 30 seconds on trial 3, and so on. Variable-interval schedules are common in everyday life. Suppose you are trying to reach someone on the telephone, but every time you dial you hear a busy signal. To be rewarded, you know that you have to dial the number and that a certain amount of time has to elapse, but you're not sure exactly how long you need to wait.

Learning—that is, the increase in the rate at which the animal performs the target behaviour—tends to be slow in variable-interval schedules; the contingency between performing the behaviour and earning a reward is difficult to detect, because it is contingent on a randomly varying amount of time since the last rewarded response. Like variable-ratio schedules, however, variable-interval schedules help eliminate the pause in responding that usually occurs after reinforcement in fixed reinforcement schedules. The rate of extinction also tends to be slower in a variable-interval schedule because of the uncertainty created about when the next reinforcement will be delivered. From the responder's point of view, the next response could very well produce the desired reward, so it makes sense to continue steady responding. For responding to cease, you need to recognize that the relationship between responding and reinforcement has changed.

There are many different types of reinforcement schedules. The four partial schedules we have considered here are representative and demonstrate that different reinforcement schedules produce strikingly different patterns of behaviour. Moreover, as Skinner (1956) argued, these principled behaviours are universal—the postreinforcement pause, for example, occurs regardless of the specific response, the nature of the

fixed-interval schedule
A schedule in which the reinforcement is delivered for the first response that occurs following a fixed interval of time.

variable-interval schedule
A schedule in which the allotted time before a response will yield reinforcement changes from trial to trial.

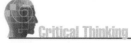
Critical Thinking

Do you think fishing is reinforced on a variable-interval schedule of reinforcement or a variable-ratio schedule? How might the answer depend on the skill of the person doing the fishing?

Concept Summary

SCHEDULES OF REINFORCEMENT

Type of Schedule	Description	Example	Effect on Behaviour
Continuous	Response is followed rapidly by reinforcement every time it occurs.	Every time Jean-Claude cleans his room, his parents give him $5.	Leads to fast acquisition of response, but response is easily extinguished.
Partial	Response is followed by reinforcement only some of the time.	Sometimes, Jean-Claude gets $5 after he cleans his room.	Acquisition is slower, but learned response is more resistant to extinction.
—fixed ratio	The number of responses required for reinforcement is fixed.	Jean-Claude gets $5 every three times he cleans his room.	Jean-Claude cleans his room consistently with a pause in cleaning after each $5; he stops quickly if reward stops.
—variable ratio	The number of responses required for reinforcement varies.	Jean-Claude gets $5 after cleaning his room a certain number of times, but the exact number varies.	Jean-Claude cleans his room consistently with few pauses; he continues to clean his room even if the reward isn't delivered for a while.
—fixed interval	Reinforcement is delivered for the first response after a fixed interval of time.	Every Tuesday, Jean-Claude's parents give him $5 if his room is clean.	Jean-Claude doesn't do much cleaning until Tuesday is approaching; he stops quickly if reward stops.
—variable interval	Reinforcement is delivered for the first response after a variable interval of time.	On some random weekday, Jean-Claude gets $5 if his room is clean.	Jean-Claude cleans his room consistently and doesn't stop even if the reward isn't delivered for a while.

reinforcement, or the species receiving the training. Reward, and the pattern with which it is delivered, exerts a powerful influence on everyday actions.

Acquisition: Shaping the Desired Behaviour

5c, SIM 4
Psyk.trek

In principle, you should be able to gain control over any behaviour, such as getting your dog to sit or shake hands, by reinforcing the appropriate response according to a specified schedule. For example, if you use a variable-ratio schedule to train your dog to sit and you use food as a reward, then your dog should continue to sit on command even when food is not available as a reward. In this case, the dog knows that sitting is reinforced only some of the time, so failure to receive a reward doesn't necessarily weaken the response.

In practice, however, it can be difficult to train a behaviour if that behaviour is unlikely to occur initially. How do you reward your dog for sitting if the dog never sits on command in the first place? Most people try to train a dog by saying "Sit," then pushing the dog's bottom down and promptly giving the dog a food reward. This approach amounts to a kind of classical conditioning procedure—the dog is taught that having his bottom pushed downward is a *signal* for an inviting (food) unconditioned stimulus. If this was all you did, the dog would learn to salivate in response to the word "sit," but it would not learn that its own behaviour is instrumental in producing the outcome. What you want your dog to learn is that the word "sit" is a discriminative stimulus that signals that a behaviour (sitting) is instrumental in producing a reward.

To solve this problem, Skinner (1938) developed a procedure called **shaping,** in which reinforcement is delivered for successive *approximations* of the desired response. Instead of waiting for the complete response—here, sitting to the command "Sit"—to occur, you reinforce some part of the response that is likely to occur initially. For instance, at an early stage of training you might give a dog a reward if it makes even a small movement toward sitting when you say "sit." As each part of the response is acquired, you become stricter in your criteria for what behaviour will be rewarded. Skinner and others have shown that a variety of animals (e.g., pigeons, rats, dogs, dolphins) can learn incredibly complex sequences of behaviours through the successive-

shaping

A procedure in which reinforcement is delivered for successive approximations of the desired response.

approximation technique of shaping. For example, chickens can be taught to peck out a simple melody on a toy piano, with the chicken playing one tune if a red light comes on and another if a blue light comes on.

Practical Applications Not surprisingly, shaping also works quite well as a technique for modifying behaviour in people. (In Chapter 15, you'll see how shaping can be applied in therapy to modify maladaptive thoughts, lessen fears, and help individuals handle stressful situations.) Children with developmental disabilities that grossly impair their language skills have been taught to speak by reinforcing verbal sequences with candy or cereal. Whereas the child might be reinforced initially for any kind of verbal utterance, gradually the reward is withheld until the child produces a more natural flow of sounds.

The same kind of training can be used with adult patients who are suffering from severe psychological disorders. Patients with serious mental problems sometimes lack normal living skills—for example, they might lose the ability to clean or bathe themselves properly or communicate effectively with others. Social skills can be trained, through shaping, leading to a significant improvement in the quality of the patient's life (e.g., Benton & Schroeder, 1990; Wong et al., 1993). For a more detailed review of how shaping and other behavioural interventions can help people control problematic behaviours and increase desirable ones, see Martin and Pear (1999).

Shaping also has enormous applications for teaching, both inside and outside of the classroom. B. F. Skinner and others long advocated for the use of shaping as a technique for learning. Mastery of subject matter can be broken down into small steps accompanied by lots of positive reinforcement. Many computer programs used in schools and at home follow the shaping format—start small and gradually increase the requirements for reward. Shaping is also a great technique for sports activities. To teach someone an effective golf swing, it's best to begin by rewarding simple contact between the club and the ball. Later, the teacher can fine-tune the person's swing by offering praise only when the mechanics of the swing are more technically correct.

So far, we've described shaping procedures in which a teacher or experimenter deliberately arranges contingencies, reinforcing some responses and not others and thereby gradually shaping a desired behaviour. But shaping can also be influenced by chance events that happen, by fluke, to coincide with reinforcement. As discussed in the Practical Solutions box, this can lead to the shaping of some quite odd behaviours.

Biological Constraints on Learning

Is it really possible to train any behaviour, in any situation, provided that you have enough time and an effective reinforcer? No, because there are biological constraints

Through shaping—in which reinforcements are delivered for successive approximations of a desired behaviour—it is possible to produce some unusual behaviours in animals. These rabbits are shown in the early stages of training for an advertisement that featured them popping out of top hats (circa 1952).

Practical Solutions

SUPERSTITIOUS BEHAVIOUR

If you are a sports fan, you know that many professional athletes perform ritual actions in preparation for a game or an important shot. For example, basketball legend Michael Jordan wore his "lucky" North Carolina Tarheels trunks under his Bulls uniform. Similarly, New York Yankees' baseball star Wade Boggs is said to believe that he hits better after eating chicken, and consequently, to have eaten chicken every day for the last 20 years. Boggs also avoids stepping onto the foul line when running onto the field, and steps onto it each time he leaves the field. Individual baseball players may make ritualistic movements each time they step up to the plate, and the same holds true for basketball players at the free-throw line. Such regular patterns are a player's signature—you can often identify who's in the batter's box or up at the line by watching these ritualistic preparation patterns.

Let's analyze these behaviours from the perspective of instrumental conditioning. According to the law of effect, these odd patterns of behaviour must have been reinforced—they occurred, perhaps by chance, and were followed by a reward (a hit or a successful free throw). But because the pairing of the behaviour with its consequence was really accidental, psychologists refer to this kind of reinforcement as *accidental* or *adventitious reinforcement*. In the player's mind, however, a cause-and-effect link has been formed, and he acts in a similar fashion

Many athletes perform odd rituals on a regular basis. This baseball player feels the need to brush his teeth vigorously before every time up at the plate. A learning theorist might argue that the player's bizarre behaviour was somehow accidentally reinforced in the past, forming a superstitious cause-and-effect link between teeth brushing and successful performance.

again. Once the player starts to perform the behaviour on a regular basis, it's likely that the behaviour will continue to be accidentally reinforced, although on a partial schedule of reinforcement. (Can you identify the particular schedule?) The result is called a superstitious behaviour, and because of the partial schedule (a variable-ratio one) it is difficult to eliminate.

In 1948, B. F. Skinner developed an experimental procedure to mimic and gain control over the development of

superstitious acts. He placed hungry pigeons in a chamber and delivered bits of food every 15 seconds, irrespective of what the bird happened to be doing at the time. In his own words: "In six out of eight cases the resulting responses were so clearly defined that two observers could agree perfectly in counting instances. One bird was conditioned to turn counterclockwise about the cage, making two or three turns between reinforcements. Another repeatedly thrust its head into one of the upper corners of the cage. A third developed a 'tossing' response, as if placing its head beneath an invisible bar and lifting it repeatedly" (Skinner, 1948, p. 168).

Remember, from the experimenter's point of view, no cause-and-effect relationship existed between these quirky behaviours and the delivery of food. From the responder's point of view, illusory connections can form between behaviours and outcomes. By chance alone, a particular behaviour (typically, one that the responder is likely to perform in the situation) happens to be followed closely by reward, and this leads the responder to perceive a systematic relationship where there is really only a fluky one. Once these connections have been made, if the animal comes to perform the behaviour frequently, then it is likely to continue to be accidentally reinforced every now and then (again, by chance alone) and this occurrence serves as the basis for a superstitious behaviour.

Critical Thinking

Do you perform any superstitious behaviours (in sports or school)? Why might a person who has read about superstitious behaviours, and accepts the explanation for them described in the Practical Solutions box, nonetheless decide to keep performing them?

that limit the responses that can be taught. For one thing, animals of a given species are simply unable to make certain kinds of responses (e.g., you cannot condition a fish to fly).

More interestingly, even certain kinds of responses that an animal can make are very resistant to condition. For example, in his studies of cats in puzzle boxes, Thorndike found that he could not increase the probability of yawning or of certain reflexive scratching responses in cats through the application of reinforcement. Similar observations were reported later by animal trainers Keller and Marion Breland (1961). The Brelands, who were former students of Skinner, encountered some interesting difficulties while attempting to train a variety of species to make certain responses. In one case, they tried to train a pig to drop large wooden coins into a piggy bank (for a bank commercial). They followed a shaping procedure, where successive approximations of the desired sequence are reinforced, but they could not get the pig to complete the

244

response. The animal would pick up the coin and begin to lumber toward the bank but would stop midway and begin "rooting" the coins along the ground. Despite using punishment and nonreinforcement of the rooting response, the Brelands could never completely eliminate the response. They encountered similar problems trying to teach a raccoon to put coins in a bank:

> We started out by reinforcing him for picking up a single coin. Then the metal container was introduced, with the requirement that he drop the coin into the container. Here we ran into the first bit of difficulty: he seemed to have a great deal of trouble letting go of the coin. He would rub it against the inside of the container, pull it back out, and clutch it firmly for several seconds…. [With two coins] not only could he not let go of the coins, but he spent seconds, even minutes, rubbing them together (in a most miserly fashion) and dipping them into the container. He carried on this behavior to such an extent that the practical application that we had in mind—a display featuring a raccoon putting money into a piggy bank—simply was not feasible. The rubbing behavior became worse and worse as time went on, in spite of nonreinforcement. (Breland & Breland, 1961, p. 682)

In the cases of the pig and the raccoon, biological tendencies connected with feeding and food reinforcement interfered with the learning of certain response sequences. Pigs root in connection with feeding, and raccoons rub and dunk objects related to food (Domjan, 1998). These natural tendencies are adaptive responses for the animals—at least with respect to feeding—but they limit what the animals can be taught. Behaviour is a joint product of biology (nature) and experience (nurture), and both must be taken into account in a full description or account of learning.

Punishment: Lowering the Likelihood of a Response

Up to now, we have considered how the chances of a response increase, in the presence of a discriminative stimulus, when the response leads to reinforcement. If your behaviour is instrumental in producing an appetitive event (positive reinforcement) or in removing something unpleasant (negative reinforcement), you're likely to behave in a similar fashion in the future. But the law of effect has another side: Thorndike claimed that if a response is followed by an unsatisfying or unpleasant consequence, it will be weakened. The term **punishment** is used to refer to consequences that decrease the likelihood of responding in the presence of a discriminative stimulus. Like reinforcement, punishment comes in two forms: *positive* and *negative*.

punishment
Consequences that decrease the likelihood of responding in a similar way again.

Positive Punishment When a response leads to the *presentation* of an event that lowers the likelihood of that response occurring again, this is **positive punishment**. Notice, as with reinforcement, the concept is defined in terms of its effect on behaviour—lowering the likelihood of responding—rather than on its subjective qualities. Usually, however, positive punishment occurs when a response leads to an *aversive* outcome. If you hassled the family cat with a new toy when you were a child, your parents might scold you. The scolding qualifies as positive punishment. If the aversive event— the scolding—is intense enough, the instrumental response that produced the punishment—hassling the cat—will tend to disappear rapidly or become *suppressed*.

positive punishment
An event that, when *presented* after a response, lowers the likelihood of that response occurring again.

Negative Punishment When the removal of an event after responding lowers the likelihood of that response occurring again, **negative punishment** has occurred. For example, if a response leads to the removal of a positive outcome, you are unlikely to respond in that way again. Instead of scolding you for hassling the cat, your parents could simply take your toy away. They would be removing something you like when you engage in an inappropriate behaviour—this qualifies as negative punishment. Similarly, if they withheld your weekly allowance because your room was messy, they

negative punishment
An event that, when *removed* after a response, lowers the likelihood of that response occurring again.

punished you by removing something good—money. As with positive punishment, negative punishment can rapidly suppress an undesirable response.

What accounts for the rapid suppression of the response that is punished? People simply learn the associative relationship between their behaviour and the particular outcome. You learn about the consequences of your actions—that a particular kind of behaviour will lead to an unpleasant consequence. In this sense, we don't really need two different explanations to account for the behaviour changes produced by reinforcement and punishment; the only major difference is that behaviour increases in one situation and declines in the other. In both cases, people simply use their knowledge about a behaviour and its consequences to maximize gain and minimize loss in a particular situation.

Practical Applications In principle, punishment is an effective technique for suppressing an undesirable behaviour. However, difficulties often arise in everyday practice. For example, it can be hard to gauge the appropriate strength of the punishing event. When the punishment is aggressive or violent, such as the forceful spanking of a child, you run the risk of hurting the child either physically or emotionally. At the same time, if a child feels ignored, yelling at him or her can be reinforcing because of the attention it provides. Children who spend a lot of time in the principal's office may be causing trouble partly because of the attention that the punishment produces. In cases such as this, punishment leads to the exact opposite of the intended result.

You also need to recognize that punishment only suppresses an undesirable behaviour; it does not teach someone how to perform desirable behaviours. For instance, spanking a child for lying might reduce the lying behaviour, but it will not teach the

Concept Summary

COMPARING PUNISHMENT AND REINFORCEMENT

Reinforcement: Consequences That Increase the Likelihood of Responding

Outcome	Description	Example
Positive reinforcement	Response leads to the presentation of an event that increases the likelihood of that response occurring again.	Little 5-year-old Skip helps his dad do the dishes. Dad takes him to the store and lets him pick out any candy bar he wants. Letting Skip pick out a candy bar increases the likelihood that he'll help with the dishes again.
Negative reinforcement	Response leads to the removal of an event that increases the likelihood of that response occurring again.	Little Skip has been such a good helper all week that his parents tell him that next week he doesn't have to do any of his scheduled chores. Relieving Skip of his scheduled chores increases the likelihood that he'll be a good helper.

Punishment: Consequences That Decrease the Likelihood of Responding

Outcome	Description	Example
Positive punishment	Response leads to the presentation of an event that decreases the likelihood of that response occurring again.	Little Skip nearly runs into the street; his mother pulls him back from the curb and gives him a brief scolding. This decreases the likelihood that Skip will run into the street.
Negative punishment	Response leads to the removal of an event that decreases the likelihood of that response occurring again.	Little Skip keeps teasing his 3-year-old sister at the dinner table. His parents send him to bed without his favourite dessert. Withholding the dessert decreases the likelihood that Skip will tease his sister at the dinner table.

child how to deal more effectively with the social situation that led to the initial lie. To teach the child about more appropriate forms of behaviour, you would need to reinforce some kind of alternative response. You must teach the child a positive strategy for dealing with situations that can lead to lying. That's the main advantage of reinforcement over punishment: Reinforcement teaches you what you should be doing—how you should act—whereas punishment only teaches you what you shouldn't be doing.

Punishment can also produce undesirable side effects, most notably anger, resentment, and aggression. Studies with animals in the laboratory have shown that aggressive behaviour is often a consequence of punishment procedures. Animals that are shocked together in the same experimental context will often attack one another throughout the shock duration (Domjan, 1998). Parents who punish their children regularly, without alternative reinforcement, invite future resentment and a loss in the quality of the relationship with their children. Few psychologists deny that punishment can be an effective means for stopping a behaviour, and it may even be appropriate in some circumstances (e.g., running into the street or sticking a fork into an electrical outlet). But punishment, by itself, is rarely a sufficient technique for teaching children—it needs to be supplemented with alternative strategies for behaving that provide the opportunity for a little tender loving care (positive reinforcement).

Test Yourself 6.3

Check your knowledge about instrumental conditioning by answering the following questions. (You will find the answers in Appendix B.)

1. For each of the following statements, decide which term best applies: negative punishment; positive punishment; negative reinforcement; positive reinforcement.
    a. Stephanie is grounded for arriving home well past her curfew: _____
    b. Greg receives a bonus of $500 for exceeding his sales goal for the year: _____
    c. Nikki gets a ticket, at double the normal rate, for exceeding the posted speed limit in a school zone: _____
    d. Little Mowrer cries all the time when her mom is home because Mom always comforts her with a kiss and a story: _____
    e. With Dad, Mowrer is a perfect angel because crying tends to be followed by a stern lecture: _____
2. Identify the schedule of reinforcement that is at work in each of the following situations. Choose from the following: fixed-interval; fixed-ratio; variable-interval; variable-ratio.
    a. Rowena feels intense satisfaction after she calls the psychic hotline, but only when a psychic named Darlene reads her future: _____
    b. Prana likes to visit the Monster Truck rally because they always have good corn dogs: _____
    c. Sinéad constantly watches music television because her favourite show, "Puck Live," comes on from time to time at odd hours: _____
    d. Mohamed has just joined a coffee club—he gets a free pound of gourmet coffee after the tenth pound that he buys: _____
    e. Charlie hangs around street corners for hours at a time. Occasionally, a pretty woman walks by and gives him a smile: _____

LEARNING FROM OTHERS: OBSERVATIONAL LEARNING

Learning Goals

1. Be able to describe observational learning, and to specify the conditions that lead to effective modelling.
2. Be able to describe the practical applications of observational learning.

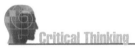

Critical Thinking

Do you think monkeys raised in captivity, such as in a zoo, will also show a strong fear of snakes?

observational learning

Learning that occurs as a result of observing the experiences of others. Also called **social learning** or **modelling.**

THE WORLD WOULD BE A VERY UNPLEASANT PLACE if you could only learn about the consequences of your behaviour through simple trial and error. You could learn to avoid certain foods through positive punishment, but only after eating them and experiencing an unpleasant consequence. Through conditioning, children might learn not to play in the street, provided their initial injuries were not fatal. You could learn to avoid risky drugs, but only if you have a bad experience, such as an arrest or a risky overdose. Clearly, it's sometimes best not to undergo the experiences that lead to classical or instrumental conditioning.

In the wild, rhesus monkeys show an adaptive fear response in the presence of snakes. Because snakes are natural predators of monkeys, it makes sense for monkeys to avoid them whenever possible. But how do you suppose that fear is originally acquired? According to a strict interpretation of the law of effect, the animal must learn its fear through some kind of direct reinforcement or punishment—that is, through trial and error. This means that a monkey would probably need to approach a snake and be bitten (or nearly bitten) before it could learn to fear the snake; unfortunately, this single learning experience is likely to be fatal much of the time. This suggests that trial-and-error learning is not always adaptive, especially when you're learning about something dangerous or potentially harmful.

Fortunately, it turns out that it's possible to learn a great deal without trial and error—by simply observing the experiences of others. People and animals can learn by example, and this kind of learning, called **observational learning, social learning,** or **modelling,** has considerable adaptive value. For instance, McMaster University researcher Bennett Galef has demonstrated that in the wild, newly weaned rats acquire food habits by eating what the older rats eat (Galef, 1985). Similarly, red-winged blackbirds will refuse to eat a certain food if they have observed another bird getting sick after it has eaten the food (Mason & Reidinger, 1982), and chimpanzees in the wild learn how to use stone tools to crack open nuts by observing older chimpanzees eating (Inoue-Nokamura & Matsuzawa, 1997). Rhesus monkeys, it turns out, acquire their fear of snakes partly through social learning rather than through direct experience (Mineka, 1987). They watch other monkeys in their environment showing fear in the presence of a snake and thereby acquire the tendency to show fear themselves. It's also possible to learn by observing the mistakes of others—if one bird watches another bird consistently choosing an incorrect response for food, the bird doing the observing is more likely not to make the same mistake (Templeton, 1998).

Modelling: Learning through Example

What conditions produce effective observational learning? One important factor is the presence of a significant role model. People naturally tend to imitate, or *model,* the behaviour of significant others, as do most members of the animal kingdom. You probably learned a lot of things by watching your parents or your teachers—even though you may not have been aware of doing so. Research has shown that observational learning is particularly effective if the model is perceived as having positive characteristics, such as attractiveness, honesty, perceived competence, and some kind of social standing (Bandura, 1986; Brewer & Wann, 1998). It's also more likely if you observe the model being rewarded for a particular action, or if the model's behaviour is particularly successful.

The scientific study of learning from models was pioneered by Albert Bandura, who was born in Alberta and earned his B.A. degree at the University of British Columbia (we'll discuss his work further in Chapter 12). Bandura termed his approach "social learning theory." In one classic study, Bandura and his colleagues showed nursery school children a film that portrayed an adult striking, punching, and kicking a large, inflatable, upright "Bobo" doll. Afterward, when placed in a room with Bobo, many of these children imitated the adult and violently attacked the doll (Bandura et al., 1963). In addition, the chances of the children kicking the doll increased if the adult was directly praised in the film for attacking Bobo ("You're the champion"). Bandura (1986) has claimed that the responses acquired through observational learning are strengthened through *vicarious reinforcement,* which occurs when the model is reinforced for an action, or weakened through *vicarious punishment,* in which the model is punished for an action. A clear parallel therefore exists between the law of effect and observational learning; the difference, of course, is that the behaviour of others is being reinforced or punished rather than one's own.

Bandura believes that much of what we learn from an experience depends on our existing beliefs and expectations. You are unlikely to learn much from a model, for example, if you believe that you are incapable of ever performing the model's behaviour. You can watch a great pianist, singer, or athlete, but you're not likely to imitate his or her behaviour if you feel that you're incapable of performing the task. Our beliefs about our own abilities—which Bandura refers to as "self-efficacy"—significantly shape and constrain what we gain from observational learning.

Practical Applications

It's easy to see how the techniques of observational learning might be used to improve or change unwanted behaviours. Many studies have shown that observation of a model performing some desirable behaviour can lower unwanted or maladaptive behaviour. Children have been able to reduce their fear of dental visits (Craig, 1978) or impending surgery (Melamed & Siegel, 1975) by observing films of other children effectively handling their dental or surgical anxieties. Clinical psychologists now use observational learning as a technique to deal with specific fears and as a method for promoting cooperative behaviour among preschoolers (Granvold, 1994).

At the same time, it's just as important to recognize that observational or social learning can lead to undesirable effects. For example, it's been estimated that children now witness thousands of reinforced acts of violence just by watching Saturday

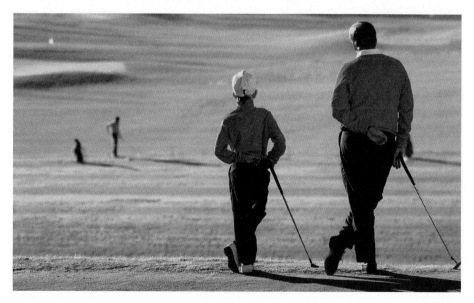

We naturally tend to imitate, or model, the behaviour of significant others. Modelling is adaptive because it allows us to learn things without always directly experiencing consequences.

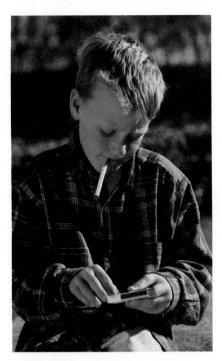

Observational learning has powerful consequences that are not always what we intend. Children model the behaviour of significant role models, even when the model acts in a way that lacks adaptive value.

Critical Thinking

Given what you've learned about modelling, do you now favour the passage of laws that will control the amount of violence shown on television? Might you change your own viewing behaviours? Why or why not?

morning cartoons. Although the causal connection between TV violence and personal aggression has not been firmly established (Freedman, 1988), the consensus among psychologists clearly supports a link (Bushman & Anderson, 2001; Hearold, 1986). In addition, it can be difficult for a society to overcome unproductive stereotypes if they are repeatedly portrayed through the behaviour of others. Many gender-related stereotypes, such as submissive or helpless behaviour in females, continue to be represented in TV programs and movies. By the age of 6 or 7, children have already begun to shy away from activities that are identified with members of the opposite sex. It's widely believed that television and other mass media play important roles in this trend (Blair & Sanford, 1999; Ruble et al., 1981).

Even if people don't directly imitate or model a particular violent act, it's still likely that the observation itself influences the way they think. For instance, witnessing repeated examples of fictional violence distorts people's estimates of realistic violence—they are likely to believe, for example, that more people die a violent death than is actually the case. This can lead individuals to show irrational fear and to avoid situations that are in all likelihood safe. People who watch a lot of television tend to view the world in a fashion that is coloured by what they see on the screen. They tend to think, for example, that a large proportion of the population are professionals (such as doctors or lawyers) and that few people in society are elderly (Gerbner & Gross, 1976). It's not just the imitation of particular acts we need to worry about: Television and other vehicles of observational learning can literally change or determine our everyday view of the world (Bandura, 1986; Bushman & Anderson, 2001).

Test Yourself 6.4

Check your knowledge about observational learning by deciding whether each of the following statements is true or false. (You will find the answers in Appendix B.)

1. Observational learning, like classical conditioning, typically involves learning about events that occur outside of your control. *True or False?*
2. People are more likely to imitate the behaviour of a role model if the model is observed being rewarded for his or her behaviour. Bandura refers to this reward process as vicarious reinforcement. *True or False?*
3. Observational learning is usually a passive process. Our beliefs and expectations about how well we can perform the model's behaviour play little or no role. *True or False?*
4. Most psychologists believe that television is a powerful vehicle for observational learning. *True or False?*
5. Clinical psychologists now use observational learning to treat specific fears, such as phobias. *True or False?*

Solving the Adaptive Problems

As organisms strive to survive and flourish in their environments, their capacity to learn—that is, to change their behaviour as a result of experience—represents one of their greatest adaptive tools. Psychologists have long recognized the need to understand how behaviour changes with experience; historically, research on learning predates research on all other topics except for basic sensory and perceptual processes.

The study of learning continues to be important in many areas of psychology. In attempting to understand and treat mental disorders, clinical psychologists often seek their answers in an individual's prior experiences. To understand the dynamics of group behaviour, social psychologists examine the effects of prior experience. Cognitive psychologists, as you'll see in the next two chapters, consider experience to be an important determinant of thinking and other mental processes. Indeed, learning is considered fundamental in most areas of psychology.

In this chapter, we've concentrated on relatively basic learning processes. To meet the needs of changing environments, all organisms must solve certain types of learning problems, and the principles of behaviour that you've learned about apply generally across animal species. Although humans differ from other animals in that they are uniquely able to change their behaviour as a result of experience, many scientists believe that the same basic mechanisms of learning (habituation, sensitization, classical conditioning, operant conditioning, and modelling) play important roles in how all animals, including humans, learn to adapt to their physical (and for some animals,

cultural) environments. Studying how individuals learn from experience can help us understand both similarities in the behaviour of individuals across cultures and differences between cultures.

First, how do we recognize consequential events when they occur and react to them appropriately? Everyone—people and animals—needs to *recognize* new events when they occur. Novel, or unusual, events lead to an orienting response, which helps ensure that we'll react quickly to sudden changes in our environment. The sound of screeching automobile brakes leads to an immediate reaction; you don't have to stop and think about it. At the same time, you cannot attend to all the stimuli that surround you, so you must learn to ignore events that are of little adaptive significance. Through the process of habituation, characterized by the decline in the tendency to respond to an inconsequential event that has become familiar, you become selective about responding to events that occur repeatedly in your environment.

Second, how do we learn about the signalling properties of stimuli or events in the environment? We also need to learn about what events *signal*—it's helpful to know, for example, that when the cat's tail gets all bushy you shouldn't try to play with it. Signals, or conditioned stimuli, can be established through classical conditioning. Events that provide information about the occurrence or non-occurrence of other significant events become conditioned stimuli. A conditioned stimulus elicits a conditioned response, which is a

response appropriate for anticipating the event that will follow.

Third, how do we learn about the consequences of our own behaviour? It's also important to learn about the *consequences* of our own actions. People need to learn that when they act a certain way, their behaviours produce outcomes that are sometimes pleasing and sometimes not. In instrumental conditioning, the presentation and removal of events after responding can either increase or decrease the likelihood of responding in a similar way again. When a response is followed by reinforcement, either positive or negative, the tendency to respond in that way in that situation is strengthened. When a response is followed by punishment, either positive or negative, you are less likely to behave that way again. It's also important to consider the schedule of reinforcement (continuous or partial; ratio or interval; fixed or variable). Schedules affect not only how rapidly you will learn and respond, but also the pattern of responding and how quickly you will change your behaviour if the reinforcement stops.

Fourth, how can we learn by observing others? Through observational, or social, learning we imitate and model the actions of others, thereby learning from example rather than from direct experience. We study how other people behave and how their behaviour is reinforced or punished, and we change our own behaviour accordingly. Observational learning can have both positive and negative effects on the individual and on society.

Chapter Summary

Learning is a relatively permanent *change in behaviour,* or *in potential to respond,* that results from experience. Common principles of learning can be applied widely across situations and species; much of what we know comes from animal research.

LEARNING ABOUT EVENTS: NOTICING AND IGNORING

Because the nervous system has limited resources, we cannot attend to every stimulus in the environment. Basic psychological processes help us prioritize our mental functioning.

Orienting Responses, Habituation, and Sensitization

Learning Goal: Learn about the concept of the orienting response, and discuss its adaptive value. When a novel event suddenly occurs in the immediate environment, animals exhibit an *orienting response,* an automatic turning of attention toward the unusual event.

Learning Goal: Understand and compare habituation and sensitization. *Habituation* occurs when one slows or stops responding to an event that has become familiar through repeated responding. *Sensitization* occurs when responsiveness to an event increases with repeated exposure. These are both general learning phenomena found throughout the animal kingdom. Researchers have focused on habituation, rather than sensitization, and have established that habituation can have either short-term or long-term effects. *Short-term habituation* refers to instances when the loss in responsiveness is short lived. In *long-term habituation,* the loss in responsiveness lasts for an extended period.

LEARNING WHAT EVENTS SIGNAL: CLASSICAL CONDITIONING

It's important to learn about the signalling properties of stimuli, or events in the environment. We need to learn that one event predicts that a second event is likely to follow. It may not be possible to do anything about the co-occurrence of the events, but we can respond accordingly.

The Terminology of Classical Conditioning

Learning Goal: Learn the basic elements of classical conditioning. *Unconditioned stimuli (US)* are stimuli that lead to automatic responses termed *unconditioned responses (UR).* After repeated pairings with an unconditioned stimulus, a *conditioned stimulus (CS)* can come to elicit a *conditioned response (CR).* An association between the conditioned stimulus and unconditioned stimulus has been acquired.

Acquiring the Conditioned Stimulus– Unconditioned Stimulus Connection

Learning Goal: Be able to describe how the connection between the conditioned stimulus and the unconditioned stimulus is acquired. For an effective association to be formed, the conditioned stimulus must be presented *before* the unconditioned stimulus, the unconditioned stimulus must follow the conditioned stimulus *closely in time,* and the conditioned stimulus needs to *uniquely predict* the unconditioned stimulus and provide *new information* about the unconditioned stimulus.

Conditioned Responding: Why Does It Develop?

Learning Goal: Understand and discuss how and why conditioned responding develops. Sometimes the conditioned stimulus and the unconditioned stimulus lead to different responses. The conditioned response depends on both the unconditioned stimulus and the conditioned stimulus. Sometimes a conditioned response is opposite to the unconditioned response, but its form is usually appropriate for the arrival of the unconditioned stimulus.

Second-Order Conditioning

Learning Goal: Be able to explain the concept of second-order conditioning. In *second-order conditioning,* an established conditioned stimulus (e.g., a tone that predicts food) is presented immediately following a new event, such as a light; the unconditioned stimulus itself is never presented. In this case, the pairing of the tone and the light can produce conditioned responding to the light.

Stimulus Generalization and Stimulus Discrimination

Learning Goal: Understand and be able to differentiate between the concepts of stimulus generalization and stimulus discrimination. *Stimulus generalization* occurs when a new stimulus produces a response similar to the one produced by the conditioned stimulus. *Stimulus discrimination* occurs when one responds to a new stimulus in a way that is different from the response to the original stimulus.

Extinction: When Conditioned Stimuli No Longer Signal the Unconditioned Stimuli

Learning Goal: Understand and explain the extinction of a conditioned response. If the conditioned stimulus is presented repeatedly without being followed by the unconditioned stimulus, the conditioned stimulus loses its signalling properties and conditioned responding diminishes.

Conditioned Inhibition: Signalling the Absence of an Unconditioned Stimulus

Learning Goal: Learn about conditioned inhibition. *Conditioned inhibition* occurs when we learn that an event signals the absence of the unconditioned stimulus.

LEARNING ABOUT THE CONSEQUENCES OF BEHAVIOUR: INSTRUMENTAL CONDITIONING

All species need to learn that when they behave in a certain way, the behaviour has consequences. Behaviours play an important role in producing rewards and punishments; people and animals tend to adapt their behaviour to maximize rewards and minimize punishments.

The Law of Effect

Learning Goal: Be able to define instrumental conditioning, and discuss the law of effect. *Instrumental conditioning* is a procedure for studying how organisms learn about the consequences of their own behaviour. In his experiments, Thorndike found that if a response is followed by a satisfying consequence, it will be strengthened; if a response is followed by an unsatisfying consequence, it will be weakened. This is the *law of effect*.

B. F. Skinner and "Radical Behaviourism"

Learning Goal: Learn about B. F. Skinner's theoretical approach to psychology, which he called "radical behaviourism." B. F. Skinner discovered some of the basic principles of instrumental conditioning. He suggested that psychologists should refer mainly to environmental events and not to "internal" events in explaining behaviour, a view known as *radical behaviourism*.

The Discriminative Stimulus: Knowing When to Respond

Learning Goal: Be able to explain what is meant by the discriminative stimulus. The law of effect applies only to responses that are rewarded in *particular situations*. The situation is termed the *discriminative stimulus*.

The Nature of Reinforcement

Learning Goal: Understand the concept of reinforcement, and be able to distinguish between positive and negative reinforcement. When the presentation of an event after a response increases the likelihood of the response occurring again, *positive reinforcement* has occurred. When the removal of an event after a response increases the likelihood of the response occurring again, *negative reinforcement* has occurred.

Conditioned reinforcers are stimuli that acquire reinforcing properties through learning (e.g., money).

Schedules of Reinforcement

Learning Goal: Be able to discuss different schedules of reinforcement, and compare their effects on behaviour. A *schedule of reinforcement* is a rule used to determine when responses will be reinforced. In a *continuous schedule,* every response is followed by reinforcement; in a *partial schedule,* reinforcement is delivered only after some responses. Partial schedules include *fixed-ratio, variable-ratio, fixed-interval,* and *variable-interval.*

Acquisition: Shaping the Desired Behaviour

Learning Goal: Grasp how complex behaviours can be acquired through shaping. Training a behaviour can be accomplished through *shaping,* which refers to reinforcing *successive approximations* of the desired behaviour.

Learning Goal: Be able to describe the practical applications of instrumental conditioning and shaping. Instrumental conditioning and shaping have proven to have numerous and important practical applications, from regulating the behaviour of wild animals to improving the performance of students and athletes. Instrumental conditioning and shaping can be used to promote the acquisition of desirable behaviours and skills and to discourage inappropriate or destructive behaviours.

Biological Constraints on Learning

Learning Goal: Understand how biological factors may limit the responses that can be learned. Many psychologists believe that there are biological constraints, perhaps in the genetic code, that limit the responses that can be taught.

Punishment: Lowering the Likelihood of a Response

Learning Goal: Be able to define punishment, and learn to distinguish between positive and negative punishment. *Punishment* refers to consequences that decrease the likelihood of repeating a response in a situation. *Positive punishment* occurs when the presentation of an event decreases the response. *Negative punishment* occurs when the removal of an event decreases the response.

Learning Goal: Be able to describe the practical applications of punishment. Punishment has long been used to discourage undesirable behaviours in humans and other animals, in part because it is often quite effective.

LEARNING FROM OTHERS: OBSERVATIONAL LEARNING

Often, our most important teachers are the actions of others; people, as well as most of the animal kingdom, learn by example. Learning through observation of others has considerable adaptive significance.

Modelling: Learning through Example

Learning Goal: Be able to describe observational learning, and to specify the conditions that lead to effective modelling. People naturally tend to model the behaviour of significant others. *Observational learning* is especially likely if the model has positive characteristics or is observed being rewarded.

Practical Applications

Learning Goal: Be able to describe the practical applications of observational learning. Observational learning (like punishment), can lead to undesirable effects, as in the case of children *modelling* the violence they see on TV.

Terms to Remember

Recommended Readings

Martin, G., & Pear, J. (1998). *Behavior modification—What it is and how to do it* (6th ed.). New York: Prentice-Hall. Written by Garry Martin and Joseph Pear, experts on behavioural approaches to human performance at the University of Manitoba, this text covers theory, basic principles, and practical applications of learning theory as applied to everyday issues in child development, education, sports, and other areas.

Heyes, C. M., & Galef, B. G. (Eds.). (1996). *Social learning in animals: The roots of culture.* London: Academic Press. Co-edited by McMaster University social learning expert Bennett Galef, this volume examines topics such as how rats copy feeding behaviour, how other animals learn about mate choices through observation, and why yawning and laughing are contagious.

Domjan, M. (1998). *The principles of learning and behaviour* (4th ed.). Pacific Grove, CA: Brooks/Cole. A leading undergraduate textbook on learning. The material discussed in this chapter is covered here in much more detail.

Skinner, B. F. (1948). *Walden two.* New York: Macmillan. This is behaviourist B. F. Skinner's famous work of fiction describing how the principles of behaviour modification might be used to create a utopian society. Interesting and controversial.

For additional readings, explore InfoTrac® College Edition, your online library. Go to:

www.adaptivemind2e.nelson.com

Hint: enter the search terms: habituation; classical conditioning; schedule of reinforcement; consequences of punishment; observational learning.

What's on the Web?

Please note that Web addresses are subject to change. Check out the accompanying Web site for updates: www.adaptivemind2e.nelson.com. This site presents practice quiz questions, hypercontent, information on degrees and careers in psychology, study tips, and more.

Classics in the History of Psychology

psychclassics.yorku.ca

This fascinating Web site is maintained by psychologist Christopher Green of York University and contains the full text of articles by Ivan Pavlov, John B. Watson, Edward Thorndike, B. F. Skinner, and other key researchers in the history of learning theory.

Animal Training at Sea World

www.seaworld.org/infobooks/Training/home.html

After reading this chapter, you are no doubt aware that the basic principles of learning are instrumental (pun intended) in training animals to do the fantastic tricks they do at parks like Sea World. This Web site provides an overview of basic learning principles, presented within the context of the training done at Sea World. It's a very interesting explanation of basic learning principles in an applied context.

B. F. Skinner Foundation

www.bfskinner.org/

This Web site is devoted to the legendary learning researcher. It provides a wealth of information about B. F. Skinner and his legacy, as well as a biography penned by Skinner's daughter, Julie S. Vargas.

Dr. P's Dog Training

www.uwsp.edu/psych/dog/dog.htm

Like the Sea World site described above, this site allows you to see the principles of learning applied to animal training. Learn how to teach an old dog new tricks with a visit to this site. It provides a wealth of information about dog training, including selections on assistance dogs, martial arts for dogs, and dog sledding.

It's a poor sort of memory that only works backwards.
Lewis Carroll

Chapter 7   Memory

What if the flow of time suddenly fractured and you were forced to relive the same 10 minutes over and over again in an endless cycle? You might be driving your car or reading this book; it wouldn't matter—at the end of the interval you'd begin again, back at the same fork in the road or the same word on the page. Think about what this would be like. Would you notice that something was wrong? No; if your memories were truly erased before each new 10-minute interval, you'd be unaware of your hopeless plight; each repetition would seem new. It is through **memory,** broadly defined as the capacity to preserve and recover information, that concepts such as the past and the present gain meaning in our lives.

Certain brain injuries and neurological disorders greatly disrupt memory in various ways. Individuals suffering from *anterograde amnesia,* for example, appear normal at first sight. Their social skills and language abilities are largely intact, but they are forever locked in the present and distant past. In extreme cases, anterograde amnesiacs are unable to recognize people they have met since the onset of the disorder, even if they have interacted with those people many times. They can't remember what they ate for breakfast or the year in which they are living. Each morning begins like the previous one, devoid of any sense of recent personal history. They may read the same magazine repeatedly, not remembering their prior readings; each time they are told of the death of a loved one, they mourn anew (Ogden & Corkin, 1991). If you've seen the movie *Memento,* you'll have a sense of what this might be like.

Even individuals with severe anterograde amnesia preserve many components of memory functioning. They retain the ability to communicate, which requires the use of memory for the meaning of words and the rules for stringing words together. They still have a basic understanding of the world and the objects in it, and their learned motor skills remain intact. They can even remember past personal experiences that happened before the brain dysfunction began. A world truly without memory would be devoid of thought and reason. You would never learn; you would not be able to produce spoken language or understand the words of others; your sense of personal history would be lost, and thereby much of your personal identity; even motor skills, such as walking, sitting in a chair, or feeding yourself, require memory for the complex set of muscle controls involved.

memory
The capacity to preserve and recover information.

Previewing the Adaptive Problems

Like learning, memory is not something that can be directly observed. It is an inferred capacity, one that psychologists assume must be operating in situations in which people act on the basis of information that is no longer physically present. To understand how memory works, we need to consider how information is entered into memory (**encoding**), how information is maintained in memory (**storage**), and how the stored information is recovered and translated into performance (**retrieval**). We'll examine each of these psychological processes in more detail as we work through some adaptive problems that memory systems help solve.

First, how does the mind maintain information over the short term?
Consider the interpretation of spoken

encoding
The processes that control the acquisition of information into memory.

storage
The processes that determine how information is maintained over time.

retrieval
The processes that control how information is recovered from memory and translated into performance.

language. Because speech unfolds over time you must remember the early part of a sentence, after it has receded into the past, to comprehend the meaning of the sentence as a whole. Likewise, to perform mental tasks, such as solving math problems, certain bits of information must be retained during the ongoing solution process. By establishing short-term memories, we prolong the incoming information, giving us more time to interpret it properly.

Second, how do we retain accessible long-term memories of past experiences? To establish effective long-term memories, you must process, or think about, information in certain

ways. For example, forming a visual image of to-be-remembered information enhances memory. It also helps to think about the meaning of the material and to relate it to other information you already know. We'll consider these techniques in some detail and provide some tips for improving your ability to remember.

Third, what initiates an act of remembering? What causes you to remember your appointment with the doctor this afternoon, what you had for breakfast this morning, or a fleeting encounter with a stranger yesterday? The retrieval of memories is triggered by an interaction between (a) events or cues encountered in the environment,

(b) current "mindset" (i.e., what you are thinking about when the cues are encountered), and (c) information stored in memory.

Fourth, what mechanisms underlie forgetting? It can be frustrating to forget, but forgetting has considerable adaptive value: It keeps us current and prevents us from being overwhelmed by a flood of irrelevant memories when we encounter cues. Typically, it's today's study assignment that you need to remember to do, not the one from yesterday or the week before; it's your *current* phone number that you need to remember, not the one from a previous residence.

REMEMBERING OVER THE SHORT TERM

Learning Goals

1. Understand the concept of visual sensory memory, be able to describe how it can be measured, and distinguish it from short-term memory.
2. Learn about auditory sensory memory (the echo) and its functions.
3. Be able to define short-term memory and to describe the nature of the code used to represent verbalizable material in short-term memory.
4. Learn about the role of rehearsal in maintaining information in short-term memory, and how quickly information is lost from short-term memory without rehearsal.
5. Be able to explain what has been discovered about the limited capacity of short-term memory, and explain how chunking can increase memory span.
6. Become familiar with the working memory model and its three primary components: the articulatory loop, the visuospatial sketchpad, and the central executive.

THE "CLASSIC" THEORY OF MEMORY is Atkinson and Shiffrin's (1968) multistore model of memory. According to the multistore model, people rely on two memory systems to help prolong incoming sensory information over relatively short terms. The first, called **sensory memory,** maintains the sensory stimuli in a relatively pure, unanalyzed form for a very brief period. Sensory memories are like fleeting snapshots of the world. The external message is represented in detail, as a kind of picture or echo that can last for a few moments (Crowder & Surprenant, 2000). The second system, **short-term memory,** is a limited-capacity "working memory" that we use to hold information after it has been analyzed into a meaningful form, usually for periods ranging from about a second to less than a minute. Short-term memories are usually rapidly forgotten, but they can be maintained for extended periods through rehearsal (internal repetition). We'll take a look at each of these systems and consider some of their important properties.

sensory memory
The capacity to preserve sensory information in a relatively pure, unanalyzed form for a very brief period.

short-term memory
A limited-capacity "working memory" system that people use to hold information, after it has been perceptually analyzed, for periods usually lasting less than a minute. Short-term memory is the system we use to temporarily store, think about, and reason with new information and with information retrieved from long-term memory.

Visual Sensory Memory: The Icon

Imagine that you are a commercial pilot, lazing along peacefully at 40 000 feet, your head in the clouds. Suddenly an alarm buzzer sounds, and you quickly look at the dozens of instruments and indicators in front of you. Quick action is a matter of life and death, and quick action depends on your ability to extract the critical information at a glance.

How much information can the human visual system extract in a single glance? This question gave rise to many studies in the 1950s. Using an apparatus called a *tachistoscope,* which presents visual displays for carefully controlled durations, researchers would briefly flash a matrix of letters (say, for 50 milliseconds, or 1/20 of a second) and ask subjects to report as many of the letters as they could. For example, a 12-letter matrix might look like this:

$$X \quad L \quad W \quad F$$
$$J \quad B \quad O \quad V$$
$$K \quad C \quad Z \quad R$$

Typically, subjects reported only 4 or 5 letters from each matrix, suggesting a severe limitation on the amount of information taken in by the visual system in a single glance. Interestingly, however, subjects often said things like, "I *saw* all the letters in the matrix, but by the time I told you 4 or 5 of them I had forgotten the others." Of course, subjects might have made such claims to make themselves look good or because they had some sort of illusion of having seen more of the letters than they really did.

Sperling's Partial Report Task   Did subjects really see all the letters in the matrix, thereafter forgetting them so quickly that by the time they had reported 4 or 5 they had forgotten the others? Or did they really see only the 4 or 5 letters that they reported? This is a question about what is going on inside people's minds, the very sort of question that behaviourists had argued cannot be studied scientifically.

Over 40 years ago, a psychology graduate student named George Sperling (1960) developed a clever procedure for answering this question. On each trial, a matrix of 12 letters was briefly presented and, *after* the matrix was removed, Sperling presented a tone. If the pitch of the tone was high, medium, or low, the subject was to report the top, middle, or bottom row of the display, respectively (see Figure 7.1). Sperling called this a *partial report* task because subjects were asked to report only a part of each display. Sperling found that subjects were usually able to report all of the letters in the

Critical Thinking

Do you consider the lingering afterimage left by a camera flashbulb to be a type of memory?

The trails of light created by a whirling sparkler are caused by visual sensory memories, which act as "still photographs" of the perceptual scene.

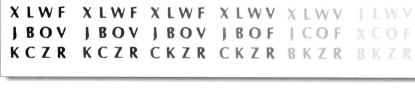

Presentation for 50 msec

Tone sounds after display terminates, indicates line to be remembered, and starts recall.

Memory becomes less clear and more spatially jumbled with time.

```
X L W F   X L W F   X L W F   X L W V   X L W V   J L W V
J B O V   J B O V   J B O V   J B O F   J C O F   X C O F
K C Z R   K C Z R   C K Z R   C K Z R   B K Z R   B K Z R
```

Time (sec)   0.5

"J"   "B"   "O"   "F?"

Recall output

to-be-reported row, even though they had no way of knowing which row they would be asked to report until *after* the matrix was removed. Because subjects never knew in advance which of the three rows they would be asked to report, the fact that they could usually report all of the letters in the appropriate row supported the subjects' claims: They really did see all (or almost all) of the letters in the matrix. If they hadn't, they wouldn't be able to report whichever row of letters they were cued to report after the display was terminated.

Sperling's results suggested the existence of a visual sensory memory, which came to be known as **iconic memory.** Asking subjects to recall only a portion of the display, rather than the entire display, improved performance because subjects could report the relevant information before the iconic image had faded. In further experiments, Sperling measured the duration of visual sensory memory by varying the delay between removing the matrix and sounding the tone. He discovered that the fleeting image—iconic memory—faded in less than a second.

You are not usually aware of iconic memory, because its contents are replaced moment by moment by new incoming visual stimulation. In the Sperling task, the briefly flashed matrix was followed by a blank screen, so that the icon would not be overwritten by new input. You can get a related effect with a flashlight or sparkler on a dark night: Swing it in a quick circle and you will "see" the whole circle even though the light itself does not linger in the air. (For a critical discussion of the role of the icon in everyday perception, see Haber, 1985; for a more recent theoretical account of the nature and function of iconic memory, see DiLollo & Bischof, 1995.)

Auditory Sensory Memory: The Echo

Psychological research indicates we have a separate sensory memory system for each of the sensory modalities. In the auditory system, for example, there is a lingering *echo,* or **echoic memory.** Sounds, unanalyzed for meaning, can be held for brief intervals to help auditory perception. In Chapter 4 you learned that the brain calculates arrival time differences between the ears to help localize sounds. To compare arrival times, the first sound needs to be retained in echoic memory until the second one arrives. As noted earlier, echoic memory is also widely believed to play a key role in language processing by retaining replicas of sounds during sentence and word processing (Crowder, 1976; Nairne, 1990).

You've probably been aware of using your own echoic memory in everyday situations. For example, imagine you're watching TV when someone speaks to you (perhaps saying, "Do you want some pizza?"). You look up, knowing that someone has spoken to you but having no idea what he or she said. But a moment later you "hear" the

FIGURE 7.1
Sperling's Partial Report Task

On each of many trials, a tone sounds *after* the visual display is removed, indicating which row of letters is to be reported on that trial. As soon as the display is turned off, the visual iconic memory of the letters begins to fade and memory for the spatial positions of individual letters becomes error-prone; the icon lasts only long enough for subjects to report about 4 or 5 letters before the image fades completely, but when only one line of letters is to be reported this is usually enough time to report all the letters in that row.

iconic memory
The system that produces and stores visual sensory memories.

Critical Thinking

Can you think of a reason why it might be adaptive for icons to be lost so quickly?

echoic memory
The system that produces and stores auditory sensory memories.

statement in your echoic memory and then understand it (perhaps saying something like, "Huh? Oh, sure!").

Moray et al. (1965) devised a procedure for studying echoic memory that was analogous to Sperling's partial report procedure. Moray and colleagues used stereophonic equipment to present sounds from four distinct spatial locations. On each trial, a short series of spoken digits and letters was presented from each sound source. Subjects in a whole report condition, instructed simply to report as many of the items as they could, usually managed only 4 or 5 of them. For subjects in a partial report procedure, *after* the letters were spoken a flashing light indicated which of the four sound sources they should report: Subjects were usually able to report most of the letters from that source, showing that most of the items were available for report from echoic memory. Whereas visual sensory memory lasts for less than a second, most studies have found that auditory sensory memory can linger for several seconds (Cowan, 1995; Watkins & Watkins, 1980).

Short-Term Memory: The Mental Workspace

According to Atkinson and Shiffrin's (1968) multistore model of memory, attention selects some of the information available in the various sensory memory systems for further processing, transforming the selected information into meaningful representations in short-term memory. Short-term memory is the system we use to think about and consciously focus on information; whatever you are focusing on now is in short-term memory. The term *working memory* is sometimes used because this memory system often acts as a kind of mental workplace, allowing us to store the components of a problem as we work toward a solution (Baddeley, 2000; Nairne, 2002).

We address three important questions about short-term memory. First, what kinds of codes are used to maintain information over the short term? Second, how and why is information forgotten from short-term memory? Third, what is the capacity of short-term memory—that is, how much information can we maintain in short-term memory at any given moment? We'll consider each of these questions in the following sections.

The Short-Term Code Sensory memory maintains a relatively exact representation of the physical stimuli received by the sensory receptors. But, as you know from Chapter 5, the conscious experience of perceiving things in the environment is the end result of perceptual analyses carried out on the contents of sensory memory. Consider the letters M O N E Y. Your iconic memory of that string of letters would represent only the shape, colour, and position of the various lines. But your internal experience when you perceive that string of letters is probably not about curved and straight lines, or even about letters. Your thoughts are likely to be about what the message stands for—in this case, a word that has particular meanings. If you do a little introspection, you'll also notice that you do much of your thinking in a kind of inner voice. Notice that you can repeat the word MONEY silently to yourself, either quickly or slowly; you can even insert internal pauses after each repetition. There is nothing visual about this repetition process; you have recoded, or translated, the visual message into another form, a kind of inner voice.

The notion that people often use an inner voice to store verbalizable information over the short term is supported by the types of errors that people tend to make during short-term recall. When recalling from short-term memory, errors are usually acoustically based. That is, mistakes tend to *sound* like correct items even if the stimulus materials were not presented auditorially (Conrad, 1964; Hanson, 1990). For example, suppose you're given five letters to remember for a few seconds—B X R C L—but you make a mistake and misremember the fourth letter. Your error will probably be a letter that sounds like the correct one; you will probably incorrectly remember something like T or P. Notice that C and T and P all sound alike, but they *look* nothing alike. It is

Short-term memory helps us maintain meaningful information, such as telephone numbers, over relatively brief time intervals.

Input	Recoding Method	Recall
	Inner Voice	**Acoustic Errors**

BXRCL

"Let's see... B... X... R... now, is it P? or T?..."

Inner Eye | **Visual Errors**

BXRCL

BXRCL

"Let's see... B... X... R... now, is it O? or Q?..."

FIGURE 7.2
Recoding and Memory Errors

Short-term memories consist of the results of cognitive processing and analyses. People recode, or translate, the sensory stimuli represented in sensory memory into meaningful representations. For verbalizable material, the recoding is usually from whatever form the stimuli were received into an inner voice. The top row presents a typical case, in which the subject recodes a visually presented message into an inner voice. Notice that recall errors are likely to sound like the letters that were presented. If to-be-remembered information was recoded into a visual form (an inner eye), as shown in the bottom row, recall errors would tend to be visually similar to the sensory input.

believed that errors in short-term recall tend to be acoustic because people recode the original visual input into an inner voice rather than an inner "eye" (see Figure 7.2).

Short-term memories of verbal material are typically stored acoustically, but you are capable of coding information in short-term memory in a variety of ways. For example, information is sometimes stored over the short term in the form of visual images (Baddeley, 1992). To illustrate, stop for a moment, close your eyes, and mentally count the number of windows in your house or apartment. People usually perform this task by visualizing the rooms, one by one, and counting the number of windows they "see." Nevertheless, we often rely heavily on an inner voice when thinking about verbalizable information, partly because language is a handy way of representing ideas and partly because we're often called on to comprehend and produce spoken language. It makes sense to think in a way that is compatible with the way we communicate.

Critical Thinking

Do you believe that nonhuman animals think about things? If so, in what ways would their short-term memories differ from those of humans?

Short-Term Forgetting What about forgetting from short-term memory? You've probably had the experience of looking up a phone number and then forgetting it before you get to the phone. Of course, it's possible to prolong short-term memories by engaging in **rehearsal,** which is a process of internal repetition, for as long as you continue the rehearsal process. (Think about the word *rehearsal* as re-*hear*-sal, as if listening to the inner voice.) Without rehearsal, as you'll see shortly, information is quickly lost from short-term memory.

Researchers at two different psychology labs (Brown, 1958; Peterson & Peterson, 1959) independently developed the same procedure to study forgetting from short-term memory. In the Brown/Peterson task, on each of a large number of trials the subject is asked to remember a triplet of letters (such as CLX) and then to report that triplet after a 3- to 18-second delay. The task sounds easy—remembering three letters for less than half a minute—but subjects were prevented from rehearsing, or thinking about the letters during the delay interval. To prevent rehearsal, the students were asked to count backward by 3s aloud from the time they were given the triplet until a recall signal appeared. You can try this experiment for yourself: Just ask someone to read you three letters, then immediately begin counting aloud backward by 3s from a three-digit

rehearsal

A strategic process that helps maintain short-term memories through the use of internal repetition.

Input		Distraction Interval, Counting Backward	Recall
Trial 1	CLX	". . . 391-388"	"C-L-X"
Trial 2	FVR	". . . 476-473-470"	"F-V-R"
Trial 3	ZQW	". . . 582-579-576-573"	"Z-W-Q ?"
Trial 4	LBC	". . . 267-264-261-258-255"	"L-B- ?"
Trial 5	KJX	". . . 941-938-935-932-929-926"	"K- ? - ?"
Trial 6	MDW	". . . 747-744-741-739-736-733-730"	"? - ? - ?"

0   3   6   9   12   15   18

Time (sec)

FIGURE 7.3

The Brown/Peterson Distractor Task

On each trial, subjects were asked to recall three letters in correct order, after counting backward aloud for from 3 to 18 seconds. The longer the subjects counted, the less likely they were to recall the letters correctly.

number, and have your friend signal you to recall after about 10 to 20 seconds. Try several trials in a row, with a different triplet of letters and a different three-digit number each time. You'll find that you often forget the letters, especially after the first few trials. In the Brown/Peterson experiments, subjects were reduced to guessing after about 10 to 15 seconds of counting backward (see Figure 7.3).

The Brown/Peterson task underestimates how quickly information is forgotten from short-term memory without rehearsal. When people are trying to remember material, as in the Brown/Peterson task, they sometimes "cheat" by turning their attention from the counting task to rehearsal for brief periods of time. If the task is redesigned so that subjects believe that the contents of short-term memory will not be tested but then a surprise test is given, results indicate that nonrehearsed information is lost from short-term memory after only a second or two (Marsh et al., 1997; Muter, 1980; Sebrechts et al., 1989). Thus, short-term memory is an excellent system for maintaining information over the short term, but only while you're paying attention to it. In the absence of rehearsal, short-term memories are quickly lost.

Why is information lost from short-term memory so rapidly in the absence of rehearsal? Some researchers believe that short-term memories are lost spontaneously with the passage of time through a process called *decay,* unless those memories are kept active through rehearsal (Baddeley, 1992; Cowan et al., 1997). Other researchers believe that short-term forgetting is caused by *interference* from new information or because people confuse current memories with past memories (Crowder & Neath, 1991; Keppel & Underwood, 1962; Nairne, 1990, 2002). It is likely that both decay and interference operate together to produce information loss from short-term memory.

Short-Term Memory Capacity   How much information can be stored over the short term—that is, what's the capacity of short-term memory? Research has shown that short-term **memory span**—the largest number of items a person can reliably recall in the exact order of presentation—is typically between five and nine pieces of information (as proposed in George Miller's classic 1956 article, titled "The Magic Number 7+/-2"). Most people find it easy to remember a list of four items, but have great difficulty quickly mastering a list of 10 items.

Some psychologists believe that the capacity of short-term memory is limited because it takes time to execute the process of rehearsal. To illustrate, read the following list of letters aloud:

memory span

The largest number of items that can reliably be recalled from short-term memory in their proper presentation order.

CA TFL YBU G

It probably took you about two to four seconds to read those letters aloud from C to G. Now look at the list again and then close your eyes and try cycling through the list with your inner voice, as if you were preparing for a short-term recall test. It turns out that the C to G cycling takes a similar amount of time when you are saying the words silently inside your head as it does when you are saying the letters aloud (Landauer, 1962). Items are lost from short-term memory in a second or two without rehearsal, so by the time you're finished with the last letter and ready to return to the beginning of the list, the early items may have already been lost from memory. You can think about this relationship between forgetting and rehearsal as roughly like juggling (see Figure 7.4). To juggle successfully, you need to win a constant battle against gravity. You throw the balls up, and gravity pushes them down. To prevent one of the balls from hitting the ground, it's necessary to catch it and toss it back up in the air before gravity pulls it down to the ground. Similarly, to prevent an item from being lost from short-term memory, you need to return to the rapidly fading short-term memory trace and reactivate it through rehearsal before the "force" of forgetting renders the memory unobtainable. It's a race between two opposing forces: rehearsal and forgetting.

This means that there should be a close link between the rate of rehearsal (or internal speech) and memory span. The sooner the rehearsal cycle is completed and begun again, the less chance that information will be lost through decay. This relationship is supported by a number of experimental findings. For example, over the short term, it's more difficult to remember lists of long words (such as "rhinoceros") than it is to remember lists of short words (such as "bat"). It takes longer to cycle through a list of long words using the inner voice, so more of these items are likely to be forgotten (Baddeley et al., 1975; Schweickert et al., 1990; Standing & Curtis, 1989). It also takes longer to count to 10 in Arabic than it does in English; consequently, people who speak English can remember longer lists of digits over the short term than those who speak Arabic (Naveh-Benjamin & Ayres, 1986). Finally, children's ability to remember information over the short term improves with language development; as they learn to speak more fluently, their rate of rehearsal improves, which contributes to an improved ability to recall information from short-term memory (Blake et al., 1994; Hitch & Halliday, 1983).

As a general rule, memory span is roughly equal to the amount of material that can be internally rehearsed in about two seconds (which usually turns out to be about seven plus or minus two items). To improve your ability to remember over the short term, then, it's best to figure out a way to rehearse a lot of information in a short

FIGURE 7.4
The Capacity of Short-Term Memory
The amount of information that can be stored in short-term memory depends partly on the process of rehearsal, which you can think of as roughly analogous to juggling. You need to return to each rapidly fading short-term memory trace and reactivate it through rehearsal before it's forgotten. Forming "chunks" from the to-be-remembered material makes it easier and faster to rehearse and therefore increases the amount of information that can be retained.

Do you think it's an accident that local telephone numbers are seven digits long? Why do you suppose the telephone company encourages you to group the numbers into chunks, for example, 449-5854?

chunking
A short-term memory strategy that involves mentally rearranging many pieces of information into a familiar and meaningful pattern. A single chunk can represent a wealth of information.

amount of time. One effective technique is **chunking,** which involves mentally rearranging the incoming information into meaningful or familiar patterns called *chunks*. A single chunk can represent a wealth of information. Remember that long list of letters presented earlier (CA TFL YBU G)? Perhaps you noticed that the spaces between the nine letters could be rearranged to form three words:

CAT FLY BUG

Forming the letters into words drastically reduces the time it takes to repeat the list internally (try saying CAT FLY BUG internally, compared to saying the list of letters internally). In addition, once you remember a chunk, it's easy to report the letters. In most cases, words are great storage devices for remembering sequences of letters. Of course, the trick lies in finding meaningful chunks in what can initially appear to be a meaningless jumble of information.

The ability to create meaningful chunks, thereby improving memory span, often depends on how much you know about the to-be-remembered material. Expert chess players can re-create most of the positions of a mid-game chessboard after only a brief glance (Chase & Simon, 1973). They recognize familiar attack or defence patterns in the game, which allows them to create easy-to-rehearse chunks of position information, each representing several pieces. Similar results are found when electronics experts are asked to remember complex circuit board diagrams (Egan & Schwartz, 1979). In both cases, if the materials are arranged randomly (e.g., the chess pieces are randomly scattered about the board), experts do no better than novices (see Figure 7.5).

The Working Memory Model

Our discussion up to this point has focused on the characteristics of short-term memories, but we haven't discussed the psychological system that controls memory over the short term. Unfortunately, memory researchers still don't completely agree about the mechanisms that allow us to remember over the short term. Some psychologists believe that memory over the short term is controlled by the same machinery that underlies long-term memory (Melton, 1963; Nairne, 2002). Other psychologists assume we have special equipment for short-term memory. The most popular current account of the short-term memory system is the *working memory model* developed originally by Baddeley and Hitch (1974) and elaborated more recently by Baddeley (1992, 2000).

FIGURE 7.5
Expertise, Chunking, and Memory

Expert chess players recognize familiar configurations in a chess game and can re-create them easily from memory (left); however, when chess pieces are arranged randomly on a board (right), which precludes the chunking of familiar patterns, chess experts show memory similar to novices. (Chase & Simon, 1973.)

Middle game
Black

Random middle game
Black

White   White

3 components

According to the working memory model, several distinct mechanisms are important for short-term retention. First, the temporary storage of acoustic and verbal information is controlled by the *phonological loop*. The phonological loop is the structure we use to temporarily store verbal information and engage in repetitive rehearsal—it corresponds roughly to the inner voice and is believed to play a critical role in language (Baddeley et al., 1998). The short-term retention and processing of visual and spatial information relies on a different system—the *visuospatial sketchpad*. When you try to count the number of windows in your house by moving through it in your mind's eye, you are using something like the visuospatial sketchpad. Finally, Baddeley and Hitch (1974) proposed that there is a *central executive* that controls and allocates how processing is divided across the loop and the sketchpad. The central executive determines when the loop or sketchpad will be used with particular pieces of information and coordinates their actions.

One reason why the working memory model is popular among memory researchers is that it helps to explain the effects of certain types of brain damage. There are patients, for example, who seem to lose very specific verbal skills, such as the ability to learn new words in an unfamiliar language. Other patients retain their language skills but have difficulties with memory for spatial and/or visual information (Baddeley, 2000). These results suggest that we have separate systems controlling verbal and visual storage, just as the working memory model proposes. There have also been studies using neuroimaging techniques, such as PET scanning, which show that different areas of the brain are active when we remember verbal and visual information (Jonides, 2000).

Test Yourself 7.1

Check your knowledge about remembering over the short term by deciding whether each of the following statements best describes sensory memory or short-term memory. (You will find the answers in Appendix B.)

1. Information is stored as a relatively exact copy of the stimuli received by the sensory receptors: _____

2. Information can be stored indefinitely through the process of rehearsal: _____

3. System measured through Sperling's partial report procedure: _____

4. Recall errors tend to sound like the correct item even if the to-be-remembered items were presented visually: _____

5. May help us calculate sound arrival time differences between the two ears: _____

6. Span is roughly equal to the amount of material that you can say to yourself in two seconds: _____

7. Capacity is improved through chunking: _____

8. The working memory model provides a theoretical account of its operation and use: _____

STORING INFORMATION FOR THE LONG TERM 6b, SIM 6 Psyk.trek

Learning Goals

1. Be able to differentiate between episodic, semantic, and procedural memories.

2. Be able to compare and contrast the effects of elaboration and distinctiveness on retrieval from long-term memory.

3. Appreciate how and why repetition influences later retrieval from long-term memory.
4. Understand how and why memory tends to be better for items near the beginning and end of a list than for mid-list items.
5. Learn how visual imagery can be used to improve retrieval from memory.
6. Learn about mnemonic devices.

long-term memory
The system used to maintain information for extended periods of time, from several seconds to a lifetime.

MANY OF THE PROCESSES used to store information in short-term memory also play key roles in the storage of information for the long term. At least some of the information in short-term memory also becomes encoded into **long-term memory.** (Remember, information in short-term memory lasts only for a few seconds without rehearsal, so any memories more than a few seconds post-rehearsal rely on long-term memory.) Most psychologists believe that there is no limit on the amount of material that can be stored in long-term memory. Whether, for how long, and under what circumstances information can later be *retrieved* from long-term memory depends partly on the processing activities performed during encoding, while the information was in short-term memory. To promote effective long-term retention, it's important to think about the information in certain ways during initial presentation. In this section, we'll consider the kinds of encoding activities that lead to effective long-term storage, but first we'll consider the general kinds of information that are stored.

What Is Stored in Long-Term Memory?

episodic memory
Remembering a particular past event or episode that happened to you personally, such as recalling having breakfast this morning or where you went on vacation last year.

Stop for a moment and think about your first romantic kiss. Do you remember the person's name, the situation, the year? Memories of this type, in which you recall a particular moment of your own past experience, are called **episodic memories**—they are composed of particular events, or episodes, that happened to you personally. Most experimental research on remembering involves episodic memory; that is, subjects in most memory studies are asked to remember particular prior events, such as reading a word on a list or seeing a picture presented on a computer screen.

Now think of a capital city in Europe, located on the Seine, famous for its fashion, fine food, and wine. What is the square root of nine, and what is the capital city of Canada? Answering these questions certainly uses memory, in the sense that you must retrieve information from the past, but remembering these answers feels quite different from remembering your first kiss. When you use knowledge about language or the world but have no feeling of remembering a particular episode in your past, you are using **semantic memory** (*semantic* refers to "meaning"). Semantic memory represents knowledge and beliefs.

semantic memory
Knowledge about language and the world, retrieved as abstract facts or beliefs that make little or no reference to any particular episode in one's personal experience.

procedural memory
Memory for how to do things, such as ride a bike or swing a golf club.

Finally, recall how to tie your shoes, drive a car, or ride a bike. The memory for how to *do* things is called **procedural memory.** Most skills,

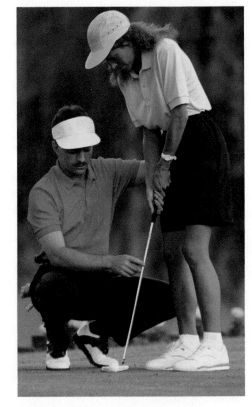

It's difficult to teach skills associated with procedural memory, such as golf, partly because it is difficult to verbalize such skills.

including athletic prowess, rely on the use of procedural memories. Procedural memories differ from episodic memories in that they do not produce a conscious experience of "remembering," and they differ from semantic memory in that they are very difficult to verbalize. Most people have a difficult time reporting how to tie their shoes or ride a bike. For a summary of these three memory types—episodic, semantic, and procedural—see the Concept Summary table.

Critical Thinking

When you take a test in one of your university courses, is the test primarily tapping episodic, semantic, or procedural memory?

Elaboration: Connecting New Material with Existing Knowledge

If you want to remember something over the long term, you should relate the material to your existing knowledge. We all house an incredibly rich collection of information in long-term memory. This existing knowledge can be used to enrich, or elaborate, the new material you're trying to remember. Through **elaboration,** the process of relating new information to well-remembered previously acquired information, meaningful connections can be established that ease later retrieval of the stored material. This is one of the reasons that experts in a given area (say, hockey fans) usually do very well at remembering new information in their domain of expertise (e.g., remembering the name of the captain of last year's Canucks).

elaboration
An encoding process that involves the formation of connections between to-be-remembered input and other information in memory.

Think about Meaning   In its simplest form, elaboration involves thinking about the meaning of information that you want to remember. In a famous experiment by Craik and Tulving (1975) of the University of Toronto, people were asked questions about a long list of words, such as MOUSE. In one condition, the task required judgments about the sound of the word (Does the word rhyme with HOUSE?). In another condition, people were required to think about the meaning of the word (Is a MOUSE a type of animal?). Substantially better memory was obtained in this second condition. Presumably, thinking about meaning, rather than sound, causes people to form more connections between presented events and other information in memory. The "deeper" and more elaborative the processing during study, the better memory performance on most tests of recall or recognition (Craik & Lockhart, 1972).

Notice Relationships   You can also use your existing knowledge to look for relationships between the items that you want to remember, to organize what you need to learn. Suppose you were asked to remember the following list of words:

NOTES   PENCIL   CHOCOLATE   BOOK   PAPER   ERASER   COFFEE

If you think about what the words mean and look for properties that the words have in common—perhaps thinking of them as things that you might take to a late-night

Concept Summary
VARIETIES OF LONG-TERM MEMORY

Type of Memory	Description	Example
Episodic	Memories of moments of one's past experience.	Wanda, the mail carrier, remembers that yesterday 20 cm of snow fell, making the daily mail delivery very difficult.
Semantic	Knowledge about the world, with no specific reference to a particular past episode.	Wanda knows that mailing a letter costs 48 cents; she also knows that it costs more to send something by courier.
Procedural	Knowledge about how to do something.	Wanda drives along the streets of her mail route effortlessly, without really thinking about it.

study session—you are engaging in what psychologists call *relational processing*. Relational processing is a kind of elaboration, and it turns out to be an extremely effective strategy for promoting long-term retention (Hunt & Einstein, 1981).

Relational processing works because you are embellishing, or adding to, the stimulus input. By thinking about how the word PENCIL relates to a study-session scenario, you create a rich, elaborate, and multifaceted memory record. Later, when you try to remember this particular word, several different kinds of cues may help you recall it. Thinking about notes, chocolate, drinking coffee, studying—any of these might lead to correct recall of PENCIL given that you encoded that word by thinking about it in relation to those varied but meaningfully interrelated concepts.

Notice Differences Connections like those just described help memory, but it's also important to think about how the material you want to remember is different from other information in long-term memory. If you simply encode the fact that PENCIL is a writing implement, you might incorrectly recall things such as PEN, CHALK, or even CRAYON when later tested. You need to think about the to-be-remembered item in some detail—such as by thinking about a yellow number 2 pencil—so that the memory record becomes *distinctive*. Distinctive memory records are remembered better because they are easier to distinguish from other related material in memory that might otherwise interfere with retrieval of the appropriate information (Waddill & McDaniel, 1998).

Psychologists use the term **distinctiveness** to refer to how unique or different a memory record is, compared to other information in memory (Neath, 1998; Schmidt, 1991). One of the byproducts of elaboration is a distinctive, and therefore relatively easy-to-retrieve, memory record. By comparing the item that you're trying to remember with other information in memory, you'll notice how the item is both related to other information (elaboration) and is unique or different (Craik & Jacoby, 1979; Hunt & McDaniel, 1993). Generally, if you want to remember something you should concentrate on encoding both its similarities to and its differences from other things you know.

Repetition of To-Be-Remembered Material: Diversify and Distribute

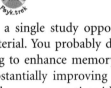

You probably already know that, compared to a single study opportunity, repeated studying improves memory for the studied material. You probably don't know, however, that repetition alone does little if anything to enhance memory. It's possible to encounter an item multiple times without substantially improving memory: If you think about the material in exactly the same shallow way every time it's presented, your memory won't improve very much with repetitions (Challis, 1993; Greene, 1992; Herrmann et al., 1993). This is why rote rehearsal (that is, simply repeating the to-be-remembered material over and over again) is a poor memorization technique. To benefit from multiple study occasions, you must use each opportunity to encode the material in a slightly different way. That is, you must diversify the way you think about the material. Doing so fosters the creation of multiple interrelated memory records, each of which is well elaborated and distinctive.

Many students put off serious studying until shortly before an exam, cramming almost all of their studying into the day or so leading up to the exam. This is known as **massed practice.** It is not a very effective way of learning, especially if you want to retain what you've learned after the exam is over. The better approach is to "distribute" your studying over wide time periods, with other activities interspersed between study sessions. For example, rather than doing all of your psychology studying in one long session, it's better to study a little psychology, do something else, and then return to your psychology (Neath, 1998; Rea & Modigliani, 1988). This is called **distributed practice.**

distinctiveness

A term used to refer to how unique or different a memory record is, compared to other information in memory. Distinctive memory records tend to be recalled well.

massed practice

Clustering repetitions of to-be-remembered information close together in time.

distributed practice

Spacing the repetitions of to-be-remembered information over time.

Why does distributed practice lead to better long-term memory than massed practice? The answer lies in how you process the material while studying it. If you engage in massed practice—where you simply reread the same material over and over again without a break—you're likely to think about the material in almost exactly the same way every time it is presented. If you insert a break between study sessions, when you see the material again there is a better chance that you will notice something new or different. Thus, compared to massed practice, distributed practice leads to memory records that are more diversified, elaborate, and distinctive. Also, distributed study sessions provide you with opportunities to practise retrieving memories of prior study episodes. Finally, distributing study sessions gives you a better sense of which things you have learned well and which things you haven't yet mastered (Metcalfe, 2002).

Effects of Temporal Order

Long-term memory also depends on the temporal order in which items are presented during study. For example, if you are given a long list of items to remember, such as 10 errands to complete, you will tend to remember the items from the beginning and the end of the list best. This pattern is shown in Figure 7.6, which plots how well items are recalled as a function of their temporal, or serial, position in a list (this graph is often called a *serial position curve*). The enhanced memory for items at the beginning of the list is called the **primacy effect;** the end-of-the-list advantage is called the **recency effect.** Memory researchers believe that primacy and recency effects arise partly because items that occur at the beginning and end of a sequence are more naturally distinctive in memory and are therefore easier to recall. Also, the first few items tend to be rehearsed more than later items, and if the memory test is immediate, then the last few items will still be available for report from short-term memory (Murdock, 1960, 1995; Neath, 1993).

Imagery: Remembering through Visualization

Another way to enhance memory is to form visual images of the to-be-remembered materials. **Visual imagery** is the process used to construct an internal vision-like image. Creating images during study can dramatically improve subsequent memory. If you're trying to remember the word COFFEE, for example, try forming a mental picture of a steaming hot, freshly brewed mug. As a more apt example, you might foster memory for a psychology experiment described in this text by forming an image of what the setting, equipment, and procedure of the experiment would look like.

Forming mental images is an effective memory strategy, partly because it naturally leads to elaborate, rich, distinctive encodings. That is, the process of forming an image of a to-be-remembered item leads you to think about various aspects of that item in novel ways that both connect it to things you already know well and make it distinctive and unique. Allan Paivio of the University of Western Ontario has argued that there is a second mechanism by which imagery enhances memory. According to Paivio's "dual code" hypothesis, when you form images as well as verbalize to-be-remembered material, you are creating two qualitatively different kinds of mental representations. When you later attempt to recall the item, either or both of those memory records could be retrieved, thereby increasing your chances of recall (Paivio, 1995).

There is good evidence that, consistent with Paivio's hypothesis, visual imagery involves cognitive codes and processes that are qualitatively different from those that support mental verbalization. For example, a classic study by Lee Brooks (1968) of McMaster University demonstrated that people have great difficulty holding a visual

primacy effect
The better memory seen for items near the beginning of a studied list compared to mid-list items.

recency effect
The better memory seen for items near the end of a studied list compared to mid-list items.

visual imagery
The processes used to construct an internal visual image, using some of the same brain mechanisms as in perception.

FIGURE 7.6
The Serial Position Curve

When we are asked to recall a list of items, our performance often depends on the temporal, or serial, position of the items in the list. Items at the beginning of the list are remembered relatively well (the *primacy effect*) and so are items at the end of the list (the *recency effect*).

image in their mind's eye while performing a spatial pointing task, but have little difficulty holding an image in mind while performing a verbal task. This suggests that imaging and verbalizing involve separate mental machinery. That is, it is difficult to use the same piece of mental equipment to do two different tasks at the same time, but if each task involves a different piece of mental equipment, then it is relatively easy to perform them concurrently (also see Baddeley & Lieberman, 1980).

As evidence that mental imagery is perception-like, Kosslyn and colleagues showed that the time to answer questions that involve mentally "traversing" across imagined space is lawfully related to the distance "travelled" (Kosslyn et al., 1978). Similarly, Shepard and co-authors tested subjects on tasks that required them to mentally rotate an image of an object, and found that response times increased as a function of the number of degrees of mental rotation (Shepard & Cooper, 1986). These sorts of findings suggest that mental images represent spatial relations in ways that are directly analogous to perceptual spatial relations. Further supporting that claim, brain-imaging studies have shown that mental imagery involves some of the same brain areas as visual perception (Farah, 1988; Kosslyn & Koenig, 1992; Loverock & Modigliani, 1995; Raij, 1999). Also, some brain-damaged patients have parallel impairments in perceptual and imagery tasks (Levine et al., 1985). For example, patients whose brain damage has caused them to lose their colour vision may also have difficulty forming a colourful visual image. Results such as these indicate that there are important links between the brain systems involved in visual perception and those involved in mental imagery (Ishai & Sagi, 1997).

Although mental imagery is similar to perception in some ways, imagery differs from perception in other ways. For example, try forming a very clear visual image of the "leaf" side of a penny. You've seen pennies thousands of times, so if you have good imagery skills this will probably seem easy. Now try to reproduce your image on paper—sketch the leaves, indicating the correct orientation, write in the words, and add the other details. Despite the apparent vividness of your mental image, you'll probably have difficulty with this task. Most people cannot reproduce the main features of the coin accurately, despite their belief that they can "see" an accurate representation in their mind's eye. Even more surprisingly, people have difficulty even recognizing the correct coin when it is presented along with incorrect versions, as shown in Figure 7.7 (Nickerson & Adams, 1979; for a British version of this study, see Jones & Martin, 1992).

Another limitation of mental images is that people cannot change their interpretations of images as they can with visual perceptions. For example, if subjects are shown a Necker cube like that in Chapter 4 (see Figure 4.1 on page 124) and are then asked to form a visual image of it and examine their image, the imagined cube does not change perspective the way a visually present Necker cube does. Similarly, try imagining a line drawing of a Star of David (two superimposed upward- and downward-pointing equilateral triangles): Does the imagined line drawing have embedded within it any paral-

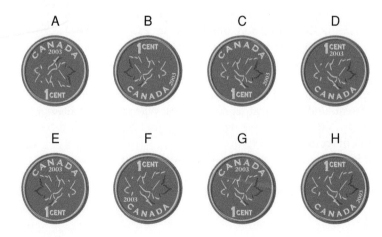

FIGURE 7.7

Can You Recognize a Penny?

Most people think that they can form an accurate mental image of a penny, but few can pick out a true penny from a group of alternatives. Can you find the real penny in this display? (Adapted from Nickerson & Adams, 1979.)

lelograms (a four-sided figure with opposite lines parallel to one another but not meeting at right angles)? Most people are unable to "see" any embedded parallelograms in their images, but if they actually look at a Star of David they easily spot four of them (try it!) (Reisberg & Chambers, 1991).

Findings such as those described in the preceding two paragraphs suggest that visual images are typically fairly vague or fuzzy, not entirely accurate, and different from perceptual images in some important ways. Nonetheless, images do differ from more word-like forms of mental representation. Moreover, mental images can powerfully enhance memory, particularly when combined with other mental strategies, as described in the next section.

Mnemonic Devices

Mnemonic devices are special mental tricks that help people think about material in ways that lead to effective remembering of that material (*mnemonic* means "pertaining to memory"). Many of these devices were originally developed by the ancient Greeks (Yates, 1966). Mnemonic devices combine imagery and elaboration during study with a strategy or structure that guides retrieval when memory is tested.

One of the oldest mnemonic devices is the **method of loci** (*loci* is Latin for "places"). The method of loci (see Figure 7.8) has two primary components: visual imagery and a system for relating pieces of to-be-remembered information to well-remembered previously learned material that simultaneously encourages elaboration (and hence good encoding) and provides a strategy for searching memory. The technique begins with the choice of a familiar real-world pathway, such as a familiar route to work or school, and flawlessly memorizing a set of landmarks encountered along that pathway (e.g., the front hallway of your residence, the front steps, the bush close to the sidewalk, the mail box down the street). The to-be-remembered material is then systematically placed, in your mind's eye, at the various landmarks along the path. So, if you wanted to remember to pay the gas bill, then feed the cat, then put a frozen pizza in the oven, etc., you might form a mental picture of a large cheque made out to the gas company sitting in your front hallway, an image of your cat chowing down on your front steps, an image of your oven opening up to receive a pizza beside the bush close to the sidewalk, and so on. Then, when you want to remember this to-do list, you mentally traverse the pathway, checking each landmark. Ordinary people can remember

mnemonic devices
Special mental tricks that help people think about material in ways that improve later memory. Most mnemonic devices use visual imagery and elaboration during encoding and a systematic strategy for searching memory during retrieval.

method of loci
A mnemonic device in which you first memorize a series of locations along a familiar real-world pathway, such as the route from your residence to the university, and then form visual images of the to-be-remembered items sitting in the various locations along that pathway. To recall the items, you mentally traverse the pathway, checking each location as a retrieval cue.

FIGURE 7.8
The Method of Loci

To-be-remembered items are mentally imaged in various locations along a familiar path. These items will be easy to remember because the use of visual imagery promotes a distinctive and elaborate memory trace and because the pathway is well learned and hence provides a structure for searching memory. In this example, the locations are the kitchen counter, the TV, and the couch of the rememberer's apartment, and the to-be-memorized items are dry cleaning, dog food, and library books.

link-word system

A mnemonic device for remembering foreign language vocabulary in which you (a) think of an English word that sounds similar to the to-be-learned foreign word and (b) form a visual image connecting the meaning of the to-be-remembered word with the similar-sounding English word.

Critical Thinking

Many people say, "I never forget a face, but I'm terrible at remembering names." Based on what you have learned in this chapter, generate several ideas about why people find it harder to remember names than faces.

very long lists with this technique (Bower, 1973; for a more general discussion of the relationship between imagery and memory, see Paivio, 1995).

Another mnemonic device, known as the **link-word system,** can be used to learn foreign language vocabulary (Gruneberg et al., 1994). Suppose you wanted to remember the French word for rabbit *(lapin).* While studying, think of an English word that sounds like the French word; perhaps the word *lap* would do for *lapin.* Next, think about the meaning of the French word, and form a visual image of that meaning linked to the English term. For example, you could imagine a white rabbit sitting in someone's lap. When the word *lapin* later appears on a test, the English word should serve as an effective cue for bringing forth a remembered image of the rabbit (*lap* acts as a kind of peg word for rabbit). Using this method can nearly double the rate of learning vocabulary words (Raugh & Atkinson, 1975).

The method of loci and the link-word technique are just two examples of mnemonic devices—there are many others (see Herrmann et al., 2000). The techniques are not necessarily easy, but diligent use of them can be extremely effective. How do they work? For one thing, most mnemonic techniques require the use of visual imagery. As noted earlier, the formation of a visual image often leads to an elaborate and distinctive memory record. Equally important, mnemonic techniques also require you to link to-be-remembered material to a set of easily available retrieval cues. By associating material to your house, as in the method of loci, you establish retrieval cues that are easy to access at any time: All you need to do is mentally walk through your house, and the stored memory items are likely to come to mind. This illustrates a fundamental point, to be further explored in the next section: Memory performance is greatly influenced by the types of retrieval cues that are available when memory is tested.

Test Yourself 7.2

Check your knowledge of how information is stored over the long term by answering the following questions. (You will find the answers in Appendix B.)

1. For each of the following, decide whether the relevant memory is episodic, semantic, or procedural.
   a. The capital city of British Columbia is Victoria: _____
   b. I had a superb meal at Café Brio last night: _____
   c. My mother's maiden name is Hudlow: _____
   d. Executing a perfect golf swing: _____
   e. Tying your shoelaces: _____
2. Your little brother Eddie needs to learn a long list of vocabulary words for school tomorrow. Which of the following represents the best advice for improving his memory?
   a. Say the words aloud as many times as possible.
   b. Write down the words as many times as possible.
   c. Form a visual image of each word.
   d. Spend more time studying words at the beginning and end of the list than those near the middle of the list.
3. For each of the following, decide which term best applies. Choose from: distinctiveness; massed practice; distributed practice; elaboration; method of loci; link-word system.
   a. Visualize each of the items sitting in a location along a familiar pathway: _____
   b. Notice how each of the items is different from other information in memory: _____

c. Form connections between the items that you want to remember and other things you already know: _____

d. Form an image linking the meaning of a foreign word to the meaning of an English word that sounds similar to that foreign word: _____

e. Study for a while, then do something else for a while, then do some more studying, and so on: _____

f. Concentrate all of your study in a single session: _____

RECOVERING INFORMATION FROM CUES

Learning Goals

1. Understand the ideas of cue-dependent forgetting, the encoding specificity principle, and the notion of transfer-appropriate processing.
2. Understand how reconstructive processes, such as schemas and source monitoring, can lead to inaccurate recollections of past events.
3. Learn about the differences between implicit and explicit memory.

CAN YOU REMEMBER the memory list from a few pages back? You know, the one that included PENCIL? If you remembered the other items, such as BOOK, NOTES, and COFFEE, it's probably because you were able to use the common theme—things to take to a late-night study session—as a retrieval cue. Most psychologists believe that *retrieval,* which is the process of recovering previously stored memories, is guided by the presence of *retrieval cues,* which are either generated internally (thinking of the study session helps you remember PENCIL) or are physically present in the environment (as when the cue was presented here).

The Importance of Retrieval Cues

A classic study conducted by Tulving and Pearlstone (1966) at the University of Toronto illustrates the critical role that retrieval cues play in remembering. People were given lists to remember that contained words from a variety of meaningful categories (types of animals, birds, vegetables, and so on). Later, the participants were asked to remember the words either with or without the aid of retrieval cues. Half the subjects were asked to recall the words without cues (a condition known as **free recall**); the remaining subjects were given the category names to help them remember (an example of a kind of memory test known as **cued recall**). Subjects in the cued-recall condition recalled nearly twice as many words, even though the two groups did not differ in how they had studied the words. Performance was better in the cued-recall condition because the category names helped subjects gain access to memories of the studied list.

Although these results may not seem surprising, they have important implications for how we think about remembering and forgetting. Consider performance in the free-recall condition. Because people performed poorly, it's tempting to conclude that they either never learned the material or simply forgot many of the items from the list. But the performance of the people who were cued shows that the poor memory in the free-recall condition resulted from a failure to access the relevant memory information. With the right retrieval cues, material that seems to have been lost, or never learned, can be remembered with striking clarity. For this reason, many memory researchers believe that most, if not all, instances of forgetting are really

free recall

A testing condition in which a person is asked to remember information without specific retrieval cues. For example, subjects might simply be asked to "recall the words you studied a few minutes ago."

cued recall

A testing condition in which subjects are given specific retrieval cues to help them remember. For example, subjects might be given hints or cues such as "some of the words were fruits; others were vegetables."

Can you name all of your classmates from grade 5? Probably not, but your performance is likely to improve if you're given a retrieval cue in the form of a class photo.

cue-dependent forgetting

The idea that forgetting is caused by a failure to retrieve memories due to lack of appropriate retrieval cues.

encoding specificity principle

The idea that the effectiveness of retrieval cues depends on the extent to which they match the specifics of the to-be-remembered material; the more similar the cue and the testing situation to the to-be-remembered material and the studying situation, the more likely the memories will be accessed.

cue-dependent forgetting. The information, once it's encoded in long-term memory, is available in the brain; you simply need the right kind of retrieval cues to recover it.

The Encoding–Retrieval Match What conditions make retrieval cues effective? Psychologists believe that the effectiveness of a retrieval cue depends on how well and how uniquely the cue matches the memory that was encoded. If you thought about the meaning of the materials while studying them, then retrieval cues having to do with meaning will be most effective, but if you thought only about the sounds of the words while studying them, then sound-alike cues (such as rhymes) will be more effective. This idea is known as the **encoding specificity principle,** which holds that the effectiveness of a retrieval cue depends on the extent to which the cue and testing context match to-be-remembered material (Tulving & Thomson, 1973).

Let's consider an example. Suppose you were asked to remember the two words BANK and WAGON. You know about the effectiveness of elaborative encoding and imagery, so you form a visual image of a WAGON perched on the BANK of a river (see Figure 7.9). Later, BANK is provided as a retrieval cue. Will it help you remember WAGON? Probably, but only if you interpret the retrieval cue BANK to mean "land bordering a river." If for some reason you think about BANK as a financial institution, you probably will not recover WAGON successfully. A retrieval cue will be effective only if you interpret it in a way that matches the original encoding.

The encoding specificity principle has a number of interesting implications for remembering. For example, it helps to explain context- and state-dependent remembering. Context-dependent remembering refers to the fact that memory tends to be better when study and test are performed in the same environmental context. That phenomenon was dramatically demonstrated in a study by Martin and Aggelton (1993), who had students in a skin-diving school study information either on land or under water, and then tested their memory either on land or under water. Those who studied on land did better if tested on land, whereas those who studied under water did better if tested under water. Presumably, there is a better match between encoding and retrieval when information is learned and tested in the same environment. The concept of state-dependent remembering is similar, but here it is the match in internal state (e.g., mood) between study and test that matters (e.g., Eich, 2000).

The encoding specificity principle may also explain the intriguing phenomenon of childhood amnesia. It is clear that very young children soak up new information at a prodigious rate, yet most adults remember few if any of their experiences before the age of 3 or 4 years (as though we were amnesic for early childhood). It's likely that we interpreted the world very differently when we were small. Childhood amnesia may result, then, from a poor match between the adult present and the early-childhood past. We see and interpret events differently now from how we did as children, so we

FIGURE 7.9

The Encoding–Retrieval Match

Memory performance depends partly on how well retrieval cues match the way information was originally studied or encoded. Suppose you're asked to remember the word pair BANK–WAGON. During study, you form a visual image of a wagon teetering on the edge of a riverbank. When later presented with the retrieval cue BANK, you're more likely to remember WAGON if you interpret that cue as land bordering a river than as a place to keep money.

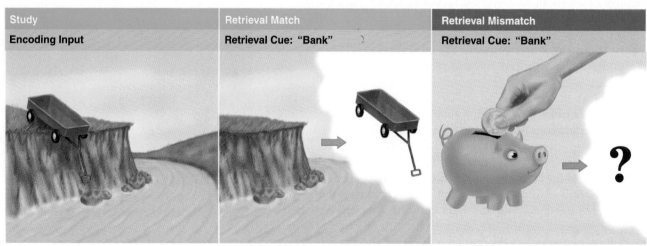

Study — Encoding Input

Retrieval Match — Retrieval Cue: "Bank"

Retrieval Mismatch — Retrieval Cue: "Bank"

have few effective retrieval cues available for remembering childhood events (Howe & Courage, 1993; Newcombe et al., 2000).

Transfer-Appropriate Processing The encoding specificity principle says that for retrieval cues to be effective, they need to match the to-be-remembered material fairly closely. The concept of **transfer-appropriate processing** is a slightly different way of expressing the same basic idea. In this context, "transfer" refers to effects of past performance on current performance. The more similar your current cognitive processes are to those you performed during a prior study session, the more likely the learning that occurred during that session will "transfer" to the present and hence be recollected (Jacoby & Dallas, 1981; Morris et al., 1977; Roediger et al., 1989). This means that if you want to remember something at a certain future place and time, you should study the material using the same kinds of mental processes that will be required during retrieval, as well as in a similar environmental context and emotional state.

To illustrate, you've learned at various points in this chapter that elaboration—relating to-be-remembered material to other information in memory—is a generally effective strategy for remembering. But the effectiveness of any encoding manipulation will depend on what kind of information is required by the memory test and what cues are available in the testing context. Let's assume that you're asked to remember the word TUG (see Figure 7.10). If you form a visual image of a tugboat and you are later specifically asked about a tugboat on the memory test, you will probably perform well.

Later, this couple may find it easier to remember their blissful reunion if they're happy rather than sad when they attempt recall. How does this conclusion follow from consideration of the encoding–retrieval match?

transfer-appropriate processing
The idea that the likelihood of correct retrieval increases as a function of the similarity between mental processes during encoding and those during test.

FIGURE 7.10
Transfer-Appropriate Processing
Study using the same type of mental processes that you'll use when tested. Suppose you form a visual image of a to-be-remembered word during study (panel 1). If the test requires you to recognize an image corresponding to this meaning of the studied word, you should do well (panel 2). But if the test asks how the word sounds (panel 3) or whether the word was studied in upper- or lower-case letters (panel 4), you're likely to perform poorly. It's best to study in a way that is appropriate for the test.

But suppose you are asked instead to remember whether the word TUG was printed in upper- or lower-case letters in the study materials. All the elaboration in the world isn't going to help you answer this question unless it had something to do with encoding the way the letters were shaped ("TUG," not "tug"). The lesson of transfer-appropriate processing is that you need to consider the nature of the test before you can decide how to study most effectively.

You should think about the characteristics of an exam *before* you study for it. Learn the material by reading the chapter and thinking about it in deeply elaborative ways, forming distinctive images and relating the new knowledge to information you already know, and then prepare for the exam by doing the kinds of things that will be required on the test (Herrmann et al., 1993). Often, students prepare for exams by reading their notes and the text over and over again; this would make sense if the test was of reading speed, but exams rarely involve rereading the text. An essay exam, for example, is a kind of *cued-recall* test: You are given a cue in the form of a test question, and you are to recall and write down the most appropriate answer. To study for such a test, it is best to practise cued recall: Make up questions that are relevant to the material, and practise recalling and writing down the appropriate answer. For a multiple-choice test, which is a kind of *recognition* test, it is necessary to discriminate a correct answer from a group of incorrect answers (called *distractors*). The best way to study for a multiple-choice test is to practise with multiple-choice questions; either make up your own or use questions from a study guide. For more hints on how to apply the principle of transfer-appropriate processing when you study for an exam, see the Practical Solutions box.

Reconstructive Remembering

Retrieval cues guide remembering in much the same way as physical stimuli guide perception. As you may recall from Chapter 4, what people "see" depends on both the incoming environmental stimuli and their expectations about what's "out there." In a similar way, remembering depends on more than just encoding processes and retrieval cues—beliefs and expectations can distort recollections of the past just as they can distort what people perceive in the present. Stop for a moment and try to remember what you had for breakfast exactly two weeks ago. It turns out that what you will "remember" in a case like this often corresponds more to habit than to actual fact. If you regularly eat a bowl of cereal in the morning, then you may "recall" eating cereal even if you broke your routine on that particular day and had a bagel.

Memory Schemas   To understand why memory acts in this way, you need to realize that we store more than just events and facts in long-term memory; we also store relationships between events and between facts. You know, for example, that houses contain rooms with walls, require insurance protection, and can catch fire. You know that 2-year-old children drool, fall down, and put things into their mouths. You have a wealth of knowledge about everyday tasks and situations, such as shopping for groceries or doing your laundry. Psychologists refer to these large clusters of related knowledge as **schemas.** Schemas can be about people, places, or activities, such as going to a restaurant, visiting the local drop-in medical clinic, or making breakfast. When you recollect a past experience, you use these organized knowledge clusters to help reconstruct what happened. So when someone asks you what you ate for breakfast two weeks ago, you may confidently answer "cereal" because you know that cereal is what you usually eat for breakfast. You don't have to remember the specific episode; you can rely on your general knowledge. More interestingly, thoughts and images that are based on schemas are sometimes erroneously experienced as if they were episodic memories; that is, you might feel that you are remembering a particular episode but really just be "filling in" from your schemas.

Schema-based remembering is usually reliable, because a schema typically corresponds to what most often happens. But schema-based remembering sometimes leads

We designed this text to encourage readers to process the material in ways that support excellent memory for the content. How many features of the text can you identify that are likely to have this effect?

schema
An organized knowledge structure in long-term memory.

Practical Solutions

STUDYING FOR AN EXAM

Motivation to learn does not, in itself, directly enhance memory. What matters is not how keenly you desire to remember the material, but rather how appropriately you process the material while studying. Here we synthesize the concepts discussed in this chapter in the context of their implications for studying.

An essential starting point is to read the to-be-remembered material in an active, elaborative way. Simply running your eyes over the words will do little to support understanding and subsequent performance on a memory test. Even when a topic area is new to you, by being creative you can note relationships, similarities, and differences between particular pieces of information and other things that you already know well. By pushing yourself to understand the material as you read it, you will process it in ways that create memory records that are distinctive and yet also relate to other knowledge. When the material describes something that has some concrete setting, forming visual images will both test your understanding and support later memory performance. A related point is that paying attention to the various pictures, graphs, quotations, and definitions provided in the margins of

texts like this encourages you to form distinctive memory records that are connected with your memories of the ideas in the main body of the text.

Many texts (including this one) include self-test items, summary review sections, and lists of "words to remember" at the end of the chapter. Some students ignore these, or look at them but without using them. Answering the self-test questions, reading the summaries thoughtfully, and testing yourself on the vocabulary after reading each chapter will have numerous benefits (Herrmann et al., 2000; Willoughby et al., 2000). When you practise remembering by answering self-test questions, you practise exactly what you want to do later. Now that you know about the notion of transfer-appropriate processing, it will be easy to see why integrating self-testing with your studying makes very good sense. Self-testing will also help you identify parts of the material that you did not initially understand and/or process effectively.

Long-term retention is better supported by distributed rather than massed practice. If you keep up with the reading as the school term goes along, and if you do the reading in an actively engaged, elaborative

manner as described above, your need to "cram" at the last minute will be reduced and the likelihood that you will still remember the material months after the exam will increase.

When preparing for an exam, make your studying as similar to the test as you can (as per the encoding specificity principle). Unless they'll be playing tunes or videos while you're taking the exam, don't study with such background distractions. Include self-testing in your exam preparation, and tailor the self-tests to the nature of the real test. For example, if the test is multiple-choice, then your examination preparation should include answering multiple-choice questions, whereas if it will be short answers then you should practise writing short answers to those sorts of questions. Practice questions can be taken from a study guide if one is available for the text, or you can make up your own while looking at the text on one day and then test yourself on them the next. If you have a study partner preparing for the same exam, the two of you can make up practice questions for each other.

---

to inaccurate memories. You can remember something that is completely wrong—it didn't really happen—yet still be convinced your memory is accurate. In a well-known study conducted over 60 years ago, Sir Frederick Bartlett asked English undergraduates to read an unfamiliar North American Indian folk tale about tribe members who battled with some warrior "ghosts" (the story's title was "The War of the Ghosts"). In recalling the story some time later, the students tended to distort facts, omit details, and fill in information that was not included in the original version. These errors were not random; rather, they often systematically changed the story in ways that made it more consistent with the English subjects' schemas. For example, familiar things were substituted for unfamiliar ones, such as the word "boat" being remembered rather than "canoe." Bartlett's subjects used their prior knowledge to reconstruct the story—even though they were often confident that they were remembering the material accurately (Bartlett, 1932).

You can demonstrate how easily schema-based remembering leads to false memories by reading the following list of words aloud to a group of friends:

BED   REST   AWAKE   TIRED   DREAM   WAKE   SNOOZE

BLANKET   DOZE   SLUMBER   SNORE   NAP   YAWN   DROWSY

After you've finished reading the list, ask your friends to write down all the words. The chances are good that someone will falsely remember the word SLEEP. In experiments using lists of related words such as these, people recalled nonpresented items, such as SLEEP, nearly 50% of the time (Deese, 1959; Read, 1996; Roediger & McDermott, 1995). The chances of false memory increase further when recognition memory is tested; that is, when subjects are given the word SLEEP and are asked if it was presented on the list (McDermott & Roediger, 1998). Subjects often indicate that they are highly confident that SLEEP was on the list and that they can recollect details of its presentation such as the sound of the experimenter's voice when the word was read aloud.

What's behind this effect? Obviously, the word SLEEP is highly related to the words on the list. It seems likely that people recognize the relationships between the words and use this knowledge to help them remember, which in turn causes the word SLEEP to come to mind at test. This is a very effective strategy for remembering, but it can lead to false recollections. Other studies show that knowledge and beliefs can lead to false memories of significant life events. For example, research by Michael Ross and colleagues at the University of Waterloo has demonstrated that individuals' current beliefs about themselves can distort their recollections of their own pasts (Ross & Wilson, 2000).

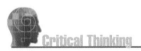

Critical Thinking

Do you think all remembering is reconstructive? What about sensory memory—isn't that a pure kind of remembering?

Eyewitness Testimony   The fact that memory tends to be reconstructive, sometimes leading to false memories, has important implications for eyewitness testimony. Loftus and Palmer (1974) conducted an experiment in which undergraduates were shown a short film depicting an automobile accident. When later questioned about the film, the students were asked to estimate the speed of the cars just prior to the accident. Some students were asked to estimate how fast the cars were going when they *smashed* into each other; others were asked how fast the cars were going when they *contacted* each other. Notice the difference between the words *smashed* and *contacted*. The schema for *smashed* implies that the cars were travelling at a high rate of speed, whereas *contacted* suggests that the cars were moving slowly. As shown in Figure 7.11, subjects who heard the word *smashed* in the question estimated that the cars were travelling about 42 miles per hour (70 km/h); subjects in the *contacted* group gave an estimate about 10 miles per hour (16 km/h) slower.

FIGURE 7.11

Schema-Based Remembering

Loftus and Palmer (1974) found that subjects remembered that cars had been travelling at a faster speed when the test question used the word *smashed* as opposed to *contacted*. All subjects saw the same film, but their different schemas for the words *smashed* and *contacted* presumably caused them to reconstruct their memories differently.

Recall Instructions	Schema	Response
"How fast were the cars going when they **smashed** into each other?"		"About 42 mph"
"How fast were the cars going when they **contacted** each other?"		"About 32 mph"

Results such as these show that remembering is importantly influenced by general knowledge, beliefs, and social pressures. Everyone in the Loftus and Palmer experiment saw the same film, but what people remembered depended on whether the question implied that the cars were going fast or slow. In addition to giving estimates of speed, subjects were asked whether any broken glass was present in the accident scene. When *smashed* was used in the speed question, subjects were much more likely to remember seeing broken glass, even though there wasn't any in the original film. By asking the right kinds of questions during testing, it is possible to make people think they experienced things that did not occur. As Loftus (1979, 1991) has emphasized, these findings suggest that caution must be exercised in interpreting the testimony of any eyewitness—reconstructive factors are always involved, and they can lead to memory errors. Young children may be especially vulnerable to suggestive influences (e.g., Marche, 1999; Poole & Lindsay, 2002).

We have emphasized the errors that can be produced by reconstructive memory processes, partly because the errors are interesting and partly because they reveal the influence of reconstructive processes. Overall, though, there is great adaptive value to schema-based reconstructive remembering. By relying on pre-existing knowledge to "fill in the gaps" and to help interpret fuzzy recollections, people increase the chances that their responses will be appropriate; after all, our knowledge and beliefs are often accurate. People can also use their schematic knowledge to fill in minor details they may have missed during the original exposure. If you already have a pretty good idea of what goes on during a visit to a fast-food restaurant, your mind doesn't need to expend a great deal of effort attending to details when you enter a McDonald's. You can rely on your prior knowledge to capture the gist of the experience, even though, on the downside, you may later recollect a few things that didn't actually happen.

Source Monitoring Have you ever had the experience of believing—if only for a few minutes—that something you had dreamed about had actually occurred? Have you ever remembered doing something (such as locking your door or turning off the oven) and later discovered that you had only *thought* about doing that action, not really performed it? Most people have experienced such memory confusions, and everyone has made similar memory errors such as remembering hearing John say something that was actually uttered by Sean, believing they had seen a movie when really they had read the book, or thinking that a particular event had occurred yesterday when really it had happened two days before. These are examples of what Marcia Johnson and her co-authors refer to as *source-monitoring* errors (Johnson et al., 1993).

Source-monitoring failures (being aware that you cannot identify the source of a memory) and source-monitoring confusions (mistakenly attributing a memory to a source other than its actual source) are among the most common of memory problems. Indeed, all the reconstructive memory errors discussed above can be described as source-monitoring confusions. For example, information retrieved from a schema may mistakenly be attributed to memory for a particular episode. Source-monitoring difficulties can also contribute to certain kinds of illusory memories, such as *déjà vu*, in which you feel a sense of familiarity about a place you've never before visited. You probably encountered a similar place in the past, but you're unable to pinpoint the particular time and place and so you experience only a haunting sense of familiarity (Jacoby & Witherspoon, 1982; Whittlesea & Williams, 2000). Illusory feelings of remembering can also be produced by subtly manipulating the present. For example, if subjects are given "retrieval cues" that don't really correspond to any of the studied materials but that do cause nonstudied items to pop to mind, then they are likely to falsely report that they remember those items (Lindsay & Kelley, 1996; Whittlesea & Leboe, 2000). Here again, such memory illusions can be described as source-monitoring failures: The actual source of the item popping to mind is not apprehended by the subject, who instead erroneously attributes it to memory for the study list. Source monitoring skills improve across childhood (e.g., Lindsay, 2002) but tend to decline in the senior years (e.g., McIntyre & Craik, 1987).

You may have a strong flashbulb memory for the events of September 11, 2001—but is the memory accurate?

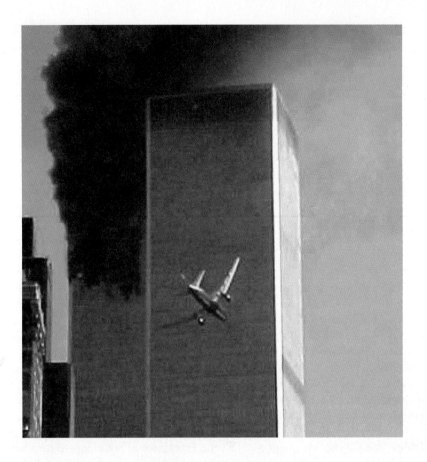

flashbulb memory
Highly detailed and vivid recollections of the circumstances under which one first learned of an emotionally significant and surprising event.

Flashbulb Memories Stop reading for a minute, and recall as much as you can about the moment you first learned of the terrorist attacks on September 11, 2001. Do you remember where you were, the approximate time of day, what you had been doing, and how you learned the news? Now recall as much as you can about where you were, what you were doing, and so on, at about the same time of day on September 10, 2001. We expect that most readers of this text will have very vivid recollections of hearing the news of the terrorist attacks, whereas their recollections of the day before are likely to be quite vague and schematic.

The term **flashbulb memories** refers to highly detailed and vivid recollections of the circumstances surrounding learning about an emotionally significant and surprising event (Brown & Kulick, 1977). Flashbulb memories have been reported for such events as the death of Princess Diana in 1997, the Space Shuttle *Challenger* disaster in 1986, and the verdict in the O. J. Simpson murder trial in 1995 (see Conway, 1995, for numerous studies of flashbulb memories). Several researchers are currently studying flashbulb memories related to the events of September 11, 2001, and there may also be studies of memory for the tragic explosion of the Space Shuttle *Columbus* in 2003.

Flashbulb memories are interesting because of their great vividness and detail and the very strong confidence with which people hold them. People who experience flashbulb memories are convinced they can remember exactly what they were doing when they first heard the shocking news. Even more interesting, however, is that flashbulb memories are *not* necessarily accurate. This has been shown in studies in which people were asked about their memories on two occasions: shortly after the shocking news and months or years later. For example, the day after the *Challenger* exploded (live on TV, 73 seconds after take-off, killing all seven on board), Neisser and Harsch (1992) asked university students to describe how they learned of that accident, and then asked them the same question three years later. Most of the respondents were very confident about their recollections three years after the event, yet the original and delayed memories often differed in substantial ways. For example, one student initially reported being on the phone at work when the news was received, but later said that she first heard the news in class. The students were sure that they were remembering things accurately, but the data proved otherwise.

Why are flashbulb memories so vivid and detailed? Most memory researchers believe that the same basic processes we've discussed throughout this chapter account for the intensity of flashbulb memories: The events that give rise to flashbulb memories are highly distinctive and people tend to mentally elaborate on them extensively in the hours and days after the event, and to rehearse them frequently thereafter. The emotionality of the experiences that give rise to flashbulb memory reports also likely plays an important role. Intense emotion during an event contributes to distinctiveness, and may encourage subsequent elaboration and rehearsal. Also, the fact that the recollections themselves have an emotionally charged quality may contribute to feelings of confidence in their accuracy. (For a recent discussion of the relationship between emotion and memory, including flashbulb memories, see Eich & Schooler, 2000.) Despite that confidence, research indicates that the same sorts of reconstructive memory processes described in other parts of this chapter play roles in sculpting flashbulb memories, producing unusually vivid and detailed but nonetheless error-prone recollections.

Remembering without Awareness: Implicit Memory

Up to this point in the chapter, we've concentrated on conscious acts of remembering; that is, we've emphasized situations in which someone is trying to remember something—such as what he or she ate for breakfast or the words from a memory list—and subsequently has the subjective experience of remembering. But people often use memory without meaning to and without being aware that they are doing so. You speak, walk to work, greet someone you know—all these activities require memory, but when you use memory in these ways you have no subjective experience of remembering the past. Most of the time, your awareness is focused on the present, but you are nonetheless constantly being influenced by your memories of the past.

Psychologists use the term **implicit memory** to refer to this kind of remembering, which occurs automatically and without a subjective feeling of remembering (Graf & Schacter, 1985; Roediger & McDermott, 1993). It turns out that implicit memory is in some ways similar to **explicit memory,** the name researchers use to describe deliberate uses of memory that are accompanied by a feeling of remembering. For example, both implicit and explicit memory are strongly influenced by retrieval cues in the environment. If you look at Figure 7.12, you'll see some examples of word and picture fragments. Your ability to complete fragments like these improves if you've recently read the solution word (e.g., the word fragment E_E_ _AN_ is easier to solve if the word ELEPHANT has been encountered in the prior 24 hours). But you don't need to consciously remember having seen the word to benefit from the fact that you had seen it. Your performance improves even if you don't consciously remember having recently seen the word, which makes the remembering *implicit* rather than *explicit.* The effect of prior exposure on fragment completion varies, depending on how closely the earlier encounter matches the fragment. If you need to solve a picture fragment, then you're helped more if the earlier encounter was in the form of a picture—such as seeing a picture of an elephant—rather than a word (McDermott & Roediger, 1994; Weldon & Roediger, 1987; Yonelinas & Jacoby, 1995). This is similar to what you learned earlier about explicit memory: Performance improves when the testing conditions match the study conditions; indeed, this is even more true of implicit memory than of explicit memory.

There are differences as well as similarities between implicit and explicit memory. For example, study strategies that typically improve explicit remembering often have little or no effect on implicit memory (Roediger et al., 1992). If you elaborate material

implicit memory
Use of memory that occurs automatically and without conscious awareness of remembering.

explicit memory
Deliberate uses of memory with conscious awareness of remembering.

| Picture fragment completion | | | | |

| Word fragment completion | E_ _P_ _ _ _ | EL_P_ _NT | EL_PHANT | ELEPHANT |

FIGURE 7.12

Implicit Memory Tests

Here are two examples of implicit memory tests. The subject's task in each case is to complete the picture or word fragment by identifying it as the object shown on the far right. In the fragments on the far left, the completion process would be difficult. Recent prior exposure to the word "elephant" enables people to complete the fragments more easily than they otherwise would have.

by thinking about its meaning, for example, your ability to remember that information will improve on most explicit tests of memory such as recall or recognition. But the degree of elaborative processing has little or no effect if memory is tested indirectly using an implicit test such as solving word fragments (Graf et al., 1982; Jacoby & Dallas, 1981).

Illusions Produced by Implicit Memory We previously discussed illusions of remembering; that is, cases in which people "remember" a past experience that never in fact occurred, such as hearing the word SLEEP on a list of words associated with the concept sleep. Unconscious, or implicit, uses of memory can produce the opposite kind of illusion; that is, cases in which people's perceptions or judgments are distorted because they are using memory without realizing that they are doing so.

For example, Larry Jacoby and his colleagues at McMaster University (1989) led subjects to believe that made-up names were names of famous people. Subjects first read a list of made-up names (such as Sebastian Weisdorf). Half the subjects studied the list with their full attention, whereas others were required to perform a distracting task at the same time the list of made-up names was presented. Later, a test list was presented that contained three types of items: (1) slightly famous real names (such as Minnie Pearl), (2) made-up names that were presented on the study list, and (3) made-up names that were new to the experiment. The test task was to judge whether each name was famous. Before taking the test, subjects were accurately informed that none of the names on the study list was famous. The researchers found that subjects who had studied the list of made-up names with full attention were less likely to falsely call a made-up name famous if it had been on the study list than if it had not. This is because these subjects usually recognized the made-up names from the study list, and so knew that those names were not famous. Subjects who had been distracted while studying the list of made-up names, in contrast, later often falsely judged those names to be famous. Distracting subjects during the first phase of the experiment, so that they were unable to process the made-up names elaboratively, decreased their ability to later consciously recognize the names as names presented on the study list, but it did not eliminate implicit memory for those names. Thus the studied names seemed familiar and subjects erroneously attributed that familiarity to fame.

The false fame effect shows how prior experience can affect us in ways that escape awareness. Prior experience can make something seem familiar, but if you can't remember the specific time or place that you encountered the person or object, you

Memories of a prior experience can influence a person's behaviour, such as by producing a feeling of *déjà vu,* even though that prior experience is not consciously recollected.

can draw erroneous conclusions. Other studies have shown that unconscious uses of memory can distort perceptual experiences, make difficult problems seem easy, and create illusions of "knowing" that false answers to trivia questions are correct (Kelley, 1999; Whittlesea & Leboe, 2000). Unconscious uses of memory also account for instances of *cryptomnesia*, or unintentional plagiarism (Brown & Murphy, 1989; Marsh et al., 1997; Taylor, 1965). Have you ever discovered that one of your "great ideas" was actually something you had heard or read about some time previously? If so, this is an instance in which you were affected by memories of a prior experience without consciously remembering that experience. The stored memory affected your behaviour, but the memory was misidentified as a new idea (Johnson et al., 1993).

Critical Thinking

Can you think of any ways that advertising agencies might use memory illusions to improve the image of a product?

Test Yourself 7.3

Check your knowledge about how we use cues to help us remember by answering the following questions. Fill in the blanks with one of these terms: cued recall; encoding specificity principle; explicit memory; free recall; implicit memory; schema; flashbulb memory; transfer-appropriate processing. (You will find the answers in Appendix B.)

1. An organized structure of knowledge stored in long-term memory: _____

2. Using memory automatically and without awareness of doing so: _____

3. Studying for a multiple-choice test by writing and answering your own multiple-choice questions: _____

4. Retrieval cues must match the information stored in the original memory record: _____

5. Detailed and vivid recollection of a surprising and consequential event: _____

6. Remembering material without the aid of any specific external retrieval cues: _____

UPDATING MEMORY

Learning Goals

1. Be able to describe the rate at which forgetting tends to occur, and explain why forgetting is adaptive.
2. Learn about the mechanisms that cause forgetting, including decay and retroactive and proactive interference.
3. Learn about motivated forgetting and the case for and against the concept of repression.
4. Be able to define retrograde and anterograde amnesia, and understand why it is unlikely that memories are stored in a single region of the brain.

DO YOU WISH YOU NEVER FORGOT ANYTHING? If you said yes, think again. If cues retained the same retrieval power indefinitely, then most cues would retrieve a flood of memories, challenging your ability to differentiate between memories from different sources. For example, if the cue "Where did you park your car?" was equally effective for retrieving all of your memories of episodes of parking, you'd have to sort through thousands of memories for the one of parking your car this morning. **Forgetting,** the loss in accessibility of previously stored information, is an important and adaptive property of your memory system (Bjork, 1989; Kraemer & Golding, 1997).

forgetting

The loss in accessibility of previously accessible memory information.

FIGURE 7.13
The Ebbinghaus Forgetting Curve

The German philosopher Hermann Ebbinghaus learned lists of nonsense syllables and then measured how long it took to relearn the same material after various delays. Ebbinghaus termed the difference between times to learn the list on the two occasions "savings." Shown here are the percent savings found after the delays. (A 50% savings means it took half as long to relearn the list as it did to learn the list originally; a 0% savings means that it took just as long to relearn the list as it did to learn the list originally.)

Hermann Ebbinghaus (1859–1909).

How Quickly Do We Forget?

How quickly an item is forgotten depends on several factors: how the item was initially encoded, whether it was encountered again at some later time, whether it is relatively unique versus very confusable with other memories, and the kinds of retrieval cues present when memory is tested. Factors such as elaboration, distinctiveness, rehearsal, and retrieval cues affect the absolute rate of forgetting, but the course of forgetting over time usually looks like the curve shown in Figure 7.13. Most of the forgetting occurs early, with the rate of forgetting decreasing gradually for a long period following the initial exposure (Wixted & Ebbesen, 1991). Immediately after hearing a list of eight words, for example, you might be able to recall all eight of them; if recall was instead delayed for several minutes while you are engaged in some other task, you might recall only three or four of the words, yet even hours later you would probably still remember at least a couple of the words.

The forgetting curve shown in Figure 7.13 is taken from classic research by the German philosopher Hermann Ebbinghaus, who was one of the first people to investigate memory and forgetting scientifically (Ebbinghaus, 1885/1964). Ebbinghaus memorized lists of nonsense syllables (such as ZOK) and then measured how long it took to relearn the same material after various delays (his technique is called the *savings method*). As the graph shows, the longer the delay after original learning, the more time Ebbinghaus had to spend relearning the list. The form of the Ebbinghaus forgetting function—a rapid loss followed by a more gradual decline—is typical of forgetting in general. Similar forgetting functions are found for a variety of materials, and even for complex skills such as typing (Baddeley & Longman, 1978) or performing cardiopulmonary resuscitation (McKenna & Glendon, 1985).

Memories of everyday experiences also tend to be forgotten over time, but there is some evidence to suggest that material that has been retained in memory in accessible form without rehearsal for several years may be immune to further forgetting. Psychologist Harry Bahrick coined the term *permastore* to refer to this idea that information that has been retained for a number of years without rehearsal may be retained indefinitely. In one study, Bahrick (1984) looked at memory for a second language (Spanish) that had been studied in high school, with delay intervals ranging from about 1 to 50 years. In another study, Bahrick and Hall (1991) examined the retention of high school mathematics over 50 years. In both cases, the rate of forgetting was very rapid at first, followed by more gradual loss, but after 3 to 6 years the forgetting curve became almost flat (that is, forgetting seemed to stop). What's surprising about these studies is that a fair amount of the knowledge remained, even though the participants claimed to have not rehearsed or thought about the material in over half a century. Bahrick's results suggest that if you can remember an early childhood experience now, you are likely to retain that memory for the rest of your life (see also Lindsay et al., in press). It's worth noting a caveat, though: Bahrick found that students who performed very poorly in the course forgot almost all of the little they had learned very quickly! It was only students who had mastered a fair amount of material who managed to retain some of that material for decades.

Why Do We Forget?

What causes forgetting? As we discussed earlier, most modern memory researchers believe that forgetting from long-term memory is *cue-dependent*—you fail to remember a prior event that had been stored in long-term memory because you don't have the right retrieval cues. Earlier psychologists believed that memories simply fade with the passage of time (through some spontaneous chemical process that happens over time, similar to rusting). But **decay**—the idea that memories fade just because time passes—cannot explain forgetting. For one thing, as you've seen, memories that appear to have been forgotten can sometimes be remembered later under the right retrieval conditions. In addition, people often remember trivial events (such as a joke) years later but forget more important things that once received a great deal of practice (such as knowledge about geography). If forgetting were merely a matter of passive decay, then one would expect that the extensively studied material would be retained longer. These observations suggest that other processes that occur over time must contribute to forgetting.

Retroactive Interference What happens over time that could contribute to forgetting? Part of the answer is that we create new memories every moment and these new memories can compete, or interfere, with the retrieval of old memories. When you get a new apartment, you memorize your new phone number. After you succeed, it becomes more difficult to retrieve your old number. The retrieval cue "telephone number" has now become associated with something new; as a result, its capacity to produce the old number is reduced. Psychologists use the term **retroactive interference** to refer to cases in which the formation of new memories hurts the retrieval of old memories.

In a classic study of retroactive interference, Jenkins and Dallenbach (1924) asked two students from Cornell University to learn lists of nonsense syllables either just before bed or early in the morning. The students were tested 1, 2, 4, or 8 hours after learning. The results, which are shown in Figure 7.14, were clear: When the students slept during the delay interval, they remembered more than when they remained awake. Note that a constant amount of time passed in both conditions, so a decay theory would predict no differences between the conditions. The findings suggest that it was the activities that occurred during the students' waking hours that produced the

decay
The proposal that memories are forgotten or lost spontaneously with the passage of time (or with some passive chemical processes that occur over time, akin to rusting).

retroactive interference
A process in which the formation of new memories hurts the retrieval of old memories.

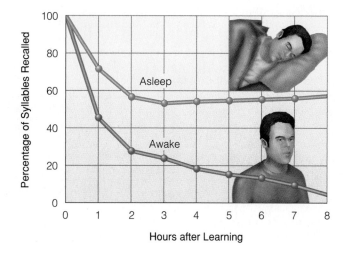

FIGURE 7.14
Interference and Memory
The mental processes that occur after learning affect how well information is remembered. In this classic study by Jenkins and Dallenbach (1924), the students showed better memory if they slept during the retention interval than if they remained awake. Presumably, memories acquired during the waking activities interfered with retrieval of the studied material.

information loss. When awake, the students formed many new memories, which interfered with retrieval of the studied material.

Proactive Interference   It is not only the learning of new information that produces forgetting. For one thing, previously learned information can also produce interference. **Proactive interference** occurs when old memories interfere with the establishment and retrieval of new memories. If you try to remember to think of the word DEATH every time you see the word HAPPY, previously learned associations will interfere with memorizing that association. Seeing the word HAPPY causes you to think of many things that are inconsistent with DEATH. To consider another example, suppose as part of an experiment you're asked to think of FORK as a weapon. You could think about the word in this way for the experiment, but as time passes you will almost certainly revert to thinking about FORK in the usual way. You would find it difficult to remember FORK as a weapon because the word has been used in a different way so many times before. Prior knowledge can interfere with the learning and retention of the new material.

Most memory researchers believe that forgetting from long-term memory is caused by various kinds of interference. Previously learned associations interfere with the acquisition of new ones, and as new memories are encoded, old retrieval cues become less effective because those cues are now associated with new memories. If a particular cue is associated with many memories, that cue will not guide the rememberer uniquely to the relevant stored material. New experiences can also affect how people interpret retrieval cues, rendering those cues less effective (as in the idea of transfer-appropriate processing, discussed earlier). That is, as we learn and change, we are less able to perceive or generate cues in ways that match memories created earlier in our lives (you may recall we made this point earlier, in the context of the phenomenon of childhood amnesia). Remembering depends on retrieval cues that are specific to the to-be-remembered material. Once again, you can see why elaboration is an effective strategy for remembering. If the original event is encoded in an elaborative and distinctive way, the memory record is less likely to be subject to competition from other remembered events.

Although most memory researchers attribute forgetting of material in long-term memory to interference, it is likely that decay—some passive neurochemical processes that occur spontaneously over time—contributes to forgetting over the very short

proactive interference
A process in which old memories interfere with the establishment and retrieval of new memories.

Critical Thinking

Can you think of any ways to lessen the influence of interference? Is there any way that you could study information so as to reduce interference?

Most people recall more pleasant than unpleasant experiences, perhaps partly because they think about and rehearse pleasant experiences more often.

term, that is, in sensory memory and short-term memory (Cowan, 1995; Cowan et al., 1997). Even in sensory memory and short-term memory, however, interference also plays important roles in forgetting. For example, in everyday situations the content of the sensory register is replaced or updated moment by moment by new sensory stimuli, and the content of short-term memory is replaced by new perceptions, thoughts, images, and feelings.

Motivated Forgetting

In our earlier comments about flashbulb memories, we suggested that highly unusual or emotional events tend to lead to distinctive, and therefore easy-to-remember, memory records. The adaptive value of a system that retains significant events is easy to understand—remembering these kinds of events could increase our ability to survive. But what about experiences it might be adaptive to forget, such as childhood abuse or witnessing a violent crime?

The idea that the mind can actively repress threatening memory records is an important ingredient of Freud's psychoanalytic theory, as you'll see when we discuss personality theories in Chapter 12. Freud described repression as a "defence mechanism" that people use, unknowingly, to push threatening thoughts, memories, and feelings out of conscious awareness. According to Freud, repressed memories retain the capacity to affect behaviour, but they cannot be consciously recollected.

The Evidence for Repression Modern researchers are undecided about the scientific validity of repression. There is evidence from laboratory studies that forming an intention to forget a subset of studied materials lowers subsequent memory performance on those materials (e.g., Allen & Vokey, 1998; MacLeod, 1999). When it comes to autobiographical memories, people typically recall more pleasant than unpleasant events (Lindsay et al., in press; Linton, 1975; Wagenaar, 1986), and physically painful experiences, such as childbirth, are often not recollected well with the passage of time (Robinson et al., 1980). There are also many instances, reported mainly in clinical settings, in which people appear to have forgotten traumatic experiences.

In one study, for example, 475 adults who were undergoing psychotherapy and had reported experiencing childhood sexual abuse were asked about their memories. Each was asked the following question: "During the period of time when the first forced sexual encounter happened and your 18th birthday, was there ever a time when you could not remember the forced sexual experience?" (Briere & Conte, 1993). Fifty-nine percent responded "yes," which Briere and Conte took as evidence that the memories had been pushed out of consciousness for some period of time. In another study supporting the same conclusion, Williams (1994) interviewed 129 women who had been medically treated for sexual abuse as children approximately 17 years earlier. The women were not specifically asked about the recorded instance of abuse but rather questioned more generally about any childhood sexual experiences they may have had; 38% did not describe the particular instance of abuse recorded in the medical records, and 12% did not report *any* instance of childhood sexual abuse.

Do these data demonstrate repression? Not necessarily. The fact that painful childhood experiences are sometimes forgotten can be explained in many ways. Many childhood events are forgotten in adulthood, and so far we lack good data on whether or not forgetting of childhood sexual abuse differs from forgetting of other sorts of childhood experiences (Read & Lindsay, 2000). Even if future research shows that childhood abuse is much more likely to be forgotten than neutral or positive childhood experiences, such forgetting might be due to ordinary mechanisms of forgetting rather than to a special repression mechanism. For example, abuse may less often be mentally rehearsed than other sorts of events. Some psychologists (e.g., Brown et al., 1998) are convinced that there is a special forgetting mechanism that is triggered by traumatic events, but the issue remains controversial. Of course, even if failures to recall childhood abuse are not due to a special repression mechanism, such "forgotten" events may nonetheless influence people in ways that bypass awareness (as per our discussion of implicit memory).

There was a lot of controversy throughout the 1990s about cases in which people reported that they had recovered memories of long-forgotten childhood sexual abuse (Lindsay & Read, 1994; Loftus, 1993; Pope, 1996). Debate focused on cases in which such reports emerged in the context of trauma-oriented psychotherapy. Critics argued that some therapists used highly suggestive therapeutic techniques (such as hypnosis) in well-intended but misguided efforts to help clients recover suspected repressed memories of abuse. Given what you have learned in this chapter about the reconstructive nature of remembering and about the effects of suggestive questions on memory, it is easy to appreciate that such approaches to therapy might unintentionally lead some clients to develop false beliefs about abuse that never really happened. This does not mean that all or even most memories of abuse that emerge in therapy are illusory, but some of them may be.

The Neuroscience of Forgetting

To explain the instances of forgetting that we've encountered up to this point, we've appealed largely to the actions of normal, adaptive psychological processes. But forgetting can also be caused by physical problems in the brain due to injury or illness. Psychologists use the term **organic amnesia** to refer to forgetting that is caused by a physical problem. (There is another type of amnesia that is emotional in origin, but we'll delay our discussion of this kind of forgetting until Chapter 14.)

Types of Organic Amnesia   There are two major kinds of organic amnesia: *retrograde* and *anterograde*. **Retrograde amnesia** is memory loss for events that happened *prior* to the time of injury (*retro* means backward in time). People who receive a severe blow to the head often have trouble remembering the events immediately prior to the accident. The memory loss can apply to events that happened only moments before the accident, or the loss can be quite extensive; in some cases, patients lose their ability to recall personal experiences from the last several years leading up to the accident. In most cases, these memory losses are not permanent and recover slowly over time, although the moments immediately before the injury are usually not recovered (Cermak, 1982).

Anterograde amnesia is memory loss for events that happen *after* the physical damage. People who suffer from anterograde amnesia, as we noted at the beginning of

organic amnesia
Forgetting that is caused by physical problems in the brain, such as those induced by injury or disease.

retrograde amnesia
Memory loss for events that happened prior to the brain injury.

anterograde amnesia
Memory loss for events that happen after the physical injury.

Concept Summary

MECHANISMS OF FORGETTING

Mechanism	Description	Example
Cue dependence	Failure to remember due to a lack of appropriate cues.	Although Susan would recognize a definition of semantic memory on a multiple-choice test, she can't think of it for a fill-in-the-blank test.
Decay	Memories fade with the passage of time (or with some passive process that occurs spontaneously over time).	After the letters disappeared from the screen, Sarah's sensory memory of them rapidly faded.
Proactive interference	Old memories interfere with the formation and retrieval of new memories.	Bruce acted in a high school production of *Hamlet,* and he now finds it difficult to memorize *Macbeth*.
Retroactive interference	New memories interfere with the retrieval of old memories.	Filling out a job application, Seth can only remember his most recent address, not the one before it.
Motivated forgetting	Traumatic experiences are forgotten to reduce anxiety.	Jackie remembers almost nothing about the day her parents were seriously injured in an accident.

this chapter, seem to be forever locked in the present and distant past—they have great difficulty recollecting new experiences. The disorder develops as a result of brain damage, which can occur from the persistent use of alcohol coupled with poor nutrition (a condition called *Korsakoff's syndrome*), from brain infections (such as viral encephalitis), or, in some cases, as a byproduct of brain surgery. One of the most thoroughly studied amnesiac patients, known to researchers as H.M., developed the disorder after surgeons removed large portions of his temporal lobes. The operation was performed to reduce the severity of H.M.'s epileptic seizures; the surgery was successful—his seizures *were* dramatically reduced—but severe anterograde amnesia developed as an unexpected side effect.

What's Forgotten in Amnesia? Over the past 25 years, considerable research has been conducted on anterograde amnesia. Patients such as H.M. have been studied in great detail to determine exactly what kinds of memory processing are lost (Milner, 1966). It was originally believed that H.M. and other anterograde amnesiacs were incapable of forming new memories. It is now clear, however, that these patients can learn a great deal but must be tested in particular ways. If a patient like H.M. is tested indirectly, on a task that does not require *conscious* remembering, performance can approach or even match normal levels; that is, performance on implicit tests of memory is preserved in anterograde amnesia.

In one study, Jacoby and Witherspoon (1982) asked Korsakoff's patients with anterograde amnesia to learn homophones for a later memory test. Homophones are words that sound alike but have different meanings and spellings, such as READ and REED. To "bias" a particular interpretation for each homophone, it was presented as part of a word pair, such as BOOK–READ or, for other subjects, SAXOPHONE–REED. (Because the words were presented aloud, the only way to distinguish between the homophones READ and REED was through the accompanying context word BOOK or SAXOPHONE.) Later, the amnesiacs performed an explicit memory test in which they were shown studied words mixed with nonstudied words and asked which words had been presented in the study list. Amnesiacs performed very poorly on this test; they seemed not to have encoded the presented information. In a second test, however, the homophones were read aloud by the experimenter and the subjects' task was simply to spell them. The amnesiacs had a strong tendency to spell the words in a way that was consistent with their presentation during the study phase; for example, they were much more likely to spell "REED" if they had previously heard that word paired with SAXOPHONE than if they had heard it paired with BOOK.

These results demonstrate that the amnesic patients had encoded and retained memories of the study phase of the experiment. Other experiments have revealed similar findings. For example, amnesiacs are more likely to complete a word fragment (such as E_E_ _AN_) correctly if they have seen the word before, but if asked to recall the previously seen words they cannot do so (Graf & Schacter, 1985). Patients who suffer from anterograde amnesia fail on tests that ask them to consciously recollect past experiences; when memory is assessed indirectly, or implicitly, through a task that does not require conscious remembering, amnesiacs often perform at normal levels.

What Parts of the Brain Underlie Memory, Forgetting, and Remembering? The study of brain-damaged individuals, such as Korsakoff's patients, has encouraged researchers to draw tentative conclusions about which parts of the brain underlie particular aspects of memory. We touched on this issue in Chapter 3, when we considered biological processes. At that point special attention was paid to a structure called the *hippocampus,* which most brain researchers believe is critically involved in the formation and storage of memories (Squire, 1992). Damage to the hippocampus, as well as to surrounding structures in the brain, leads to memory problems in a wide variety of species, including humans, monkeys, and rats. Areas surrounding the hippocampus also "light up" in PET scans when subjects are asked to recall past events (Raichle, 1994; Squire et al., 1992) (although it is worth emphasizing that other brain areas also "light

Critical Thinking

What advice would you give to the family of someone suffering from anterograde amnesia?

This PET scan shows regions of brain activity during auditory stimulation. The arrows are pointing to areas inside the temporal lobes that become active after words are heard; these areas are thought to be associated with some kinds of memory.

up" in such studies). A related point is that certain memory disorders, such as those associated with Alzheimer's disease, have been linked to inadequate supplies of particular neurotransmitters (such as acetylcholine) (Albert & Moss, 1992).

However, no single brain structure, or even group of structures, is responsible for all memory functions. The regions of the brain that are involved in memory depend on the type of processing involved. For example, episodic memory appears to involve different brain regions from those involved in procedural memory (i.e., learning and remembering skills) (Gabrieli, 1998; Wheeler et al., 1997). There's also evidence that emotionally charged memories involve a structure in the brain called the *amygdala* (Metcalfe & Jacobs, 2000; Phelps & Anderson, 1997), and different brain regions may contribute to true versus false memories (Johnson et al., 1997; Schacter, 2001). More generally, different areas of the brain are richly interconnected with one another, and activities in one part of the brain often depend on activities in other parts. Similarly, damage to a part of the brain that produces a particular neurotransmitter, such as acetylcholine, probably has consequences for numerous other regions of the brain that depend on that neurotransmitter.

Thus it is unlikely that there is any single "storehouse" for memory in the brain. Different kinds of memory tasks likely draw on different brain mechanisms. Even for a given type of memory, such as episodic recollections of mundane events, remembering draws on numerous regions of the brain. Most people think of remembering a past event as being akin to finding a book in a library, as though all the information about a particular moment in one's past experience were stored in a single record, and as though remembering were merely a matter of locating that record and playing it back. As you've learned in this chapter, remembering is not this simple.

Test Yourself 7.4

Check your knowledge about forgetting and the updating of memory by deciding whether each of the following statements is true or false. (You will find the answers in Appendix B.)

1. Forgetting is usually slow at first and becomes more rapid as time passes. *True or False?*
2. Most psychologists agree that interference rather than decay is primarily responsible for long-term forgetting. *True or False?*
3. Proactive interference occurs when what you learn at time 2 interferes with what you learned previously at time 1. *True or False?*
4. Anterograde amnesia blocks the learning of new information. *True or False?*
5. People tend to recall more pleasant than unpleasant events over time. *True or False?*
6. Psychologists believe that the hippocampus is involved in some, but not all, uses of memory. *True or False?*

Solving the Adaptive Problems

Time flows continuously, so experiences quickly leave the present and recede backward into the past. To understand humans' capacity to preserve and recollect their own pasts, we considered some of the fundamental problems that memory systems help us solve.

First, how does the mind maintain information over the short term? To improve perception and aid ongoing comprehension, people have internal processes that help them maintain information over the short term. In the case of sensory memory, we retain a relatively pure copy of the physical stimuli picked up by our sensory receptors. Sensory memories accurately represent the world as recorded by the sensory equipment, but they are very short lived, lasting between one and a few seconds. Short-term memory, in contrast, is the system used to store, think about, and reason with the products of perceptual analyses and with information retrieved from long-term memory. Verbalizable information is typically maintained in short-term memory in the form of an "inner voice." Information in short-term memory is forgotten rapidly in the absence of rehearsal. The capacity, or size, of short-term memory is determined by a tradeoff between the factors that lead to forgetting over the short term (decay and interference) and the attention-demanding process of rehearsal.

Second, how do we retain accessible long-term memories of past experiences? To remember over the long term, it helps to produce elaborate and distinctive memory records. Focusing on the meaning of the input, relating it to things you already know, and forming visual images all lead to distinctive memory records that are relatively easily discriminated from other information in memory. Forming a visual image is particularly effective, and many memory aids, or mnemonic devices, are based on the use of imagery coupled with strategies for systematically searching memory. In the method of loci, for example, you form a visual image linking the to-be-remembered material to particular locations along a familiar pathway. Long-term memory also depends on the temporal order in which materials are presented: Items presented near the beginning and end of a sequence are remembered well. Repetition also improves memory, especially if the material is processed elaboratively and in slightly different ways across repetitions and is spaced or distributed across time rather than massed.

Third, what initiates an act of remembering? Most memory researchers believe that successful remembering depends largely on having the right kinds of retrieval cues. Most forgetting from long-term memory is cue dependent, which means that stored information is not really "lost"; it's simply inaccessible because the appropriate retrieval cues are not present. According to the encoding specificity principle, effective retrieval cues are those that uniquely match the conditions that were present during original learning. Similarly, the notion of transfer-appropriate processing holds that memory depends on the extent to which the same sorts of mental processes are performed at study and at test. Remembering is not, however, simply a matter of retrieving episodic memory records. People use their general knowledge and beliefs to interpret and fill in gaps in information retrieved from memory. Such reconstructive remembering is adaptive because it is efficient and usually accurate, but it sometimes leads to inaccurate recollections.

Fourth, what mechanisms underlie forgetting? Forgetting is an adaptive process. If retrieval cues retained their efficacy indefinitely, most cues would prompt a flood of irrelevant memories, such as where you parked your car last Wednesday. Although the psychological mechanisms of forgetting are still being investigated, it seems unlikely that long-term memories simply fade or decay passively over time. Rather, older memories can interfere with the retrieval of newer ones (proactive interference), and new memories can interfere with the retrieval of older ones (retroactive interference). Also, as we change and develop over time, our ability to cue ourselves in ways that match earlier memories declines. With the right kinds of cues, however—cues that uniquely match the memory records of a past event—previously forgotten material can often be retrieved.

Chapter Summary

REMEMBERING OVER THE SHORT TERM

It's necessary to have some sort of internal machinery for remembering information over the short term. The performance of most mental tasks requires that certain bits of information be retained throughout the solution process.

Visual Sensory Memory: The Icon

Learning Goal: Understand the concept of visual sensory memory, be able to describe how it can be measured, and distinguish it from short-term memory. The *icon* is a lingering visual sensory memory trace. These images allow visual sensations to be extended in time so the brain can more efficiently process the incoming physical stimuli. In a classic series of studies, Sperling compared *whole report* and *partial report* and found that the icon contains a large amount of information but lasts less than a second.

Auditory Sensory Memory: The Echo

Learning Goal: Learn about auditory sensory memory (the echo) and its functions. Sounds can be held in auditory sensory memory (the *echo*) for brief intervals to aid in auditory perception. Auditory sensory memory maintains a relatively exact replica of the incoming stimulus for a brief interval (on the order of a few seconds). The echo helps us localize sounds and understand spoken language.

Short-Term Memory: The Mental Workspace

Learning Goal: Be able to define short-term memory and to describe the nature of the code used to represent verbalizable material in short-term memory. *Short-term memory* is the system we use to temporarily store, think about, and reason with information. Verbalizable information in short-term memory is typically recoded in the form of an "inner voice."

Learning Goal: Learn about the role of rehearsal in maintaining information in short-term memory, and how quickly information is lost from short-term memory without rehearsal. Information can be maintained in short-term memory as long as it is being *rehearsed* (mentally repeated in the "inner voice"). Information is lost from short-term memory within a few seconds if not rehearsed, due to *decay* and *interference* from other information.

Learning Goal: Be able to explain what has been discovered about the limited capacity of short-term memory, and explain how chunking can increase memory span. Short-term memory capacity is limited, as demonstrated by *memory span*, the number of items a person can reliably recall in their correct order from short-term memory. Memory span is equivalent to the number of items that can be rehearsed in about two seconds. It can be dramatically increased through *chunking*, mentally rearranging many individual pieces of information into a single familiar and meaningful pattern.

The Working Memory Model

Learning Goal: Become familiar with the working memory model and its three primary components: the articulatory loop, the visuospatial sketchpad, and the central executive. According to the *working memory model*, the *central executive* controls which pieces of information are thought about and rehearsed at any given moment. The central executive relies on the *articulatory loop* to rehearse verbalizable information, and on the *visuospatial sketchpad* to rehearse visuospatial information.

STORING INFORMATION FOR THE LONG TERM

Once information is no longer being thought about in short-term memory, we need to store at least some of it internally so that it can later be recovered at the appropriate place and time. Certain types of thinking processes increase the likelihood that material will be remembered later.

What Is Stored in Long-Term Memory?

Learning Goal: Be able to differentiate between episodic, semantic, and procedural memories. *Episodic memories* are those in which we recall a moment of our own past experience, *semantic memory* refers to knowledge and beliefs, and *procedural memory* refers to our tacit knowledge of how to do things.

Elaboration: Connecting New Material with Existing Knowledge

Learning Goal: Be able to compare and contrast the effects of elaboration and distinctiveness on retrieval from long-term memory. *Elaboration* (relating input to other knowledge) allows us to establish meaningful connections that ease later retrieval of the stored material. This can be accomplished by thinking about meaning and noticing relationships between different elements of the to-be-remembered material and between the to-be-remembered material and things that you already know. *Distinctiveness* refers to aspects of a to-be-remembered item or event that are unusual or unique. Attending to and noting distinctive aspects of an item or event facilitate later remembering by helping you differentiate between memories of that event versus memories of other events.

Repetition of To-Be-Remembered Material: Diversify and Distribute

Learning Goal: Appreciate how and why repetition influences later retrieval from long-term memory. Simply thinking about something you want to remember over and over in exactly the same way has little effect on memory, but if you think about the item in different ways then memory improves with repeated rehearsal of to-be-remembered information. Benefits of repeated rehearsal for long-term memory tend to be greater if the repetitions are widely spaced in time, with other activities intervening between rehearsals (i.e., *distributed practice*) than if the repetitions are tightly clustered together in time (i.e., *massed practice*).

Effects of Temporal Order

Learning Goal: Understand how and why memory tends to be better for items near the beginning and end of a list than for mid-list items. Good memory for the first few items in a list is termed the *primacy effect*; good memory for the last few items in a list is termed the *recency effect*. *Repetition* also improves memory, particularly if the material is processed elaboratively each time and if the repetitions are *distributed* over time.

Imagery: Remembering through Visualization

Learning Goal: Learn how visual imagery can be used to improve retrieval from memory. Forming a *visual image* of presented material is a good way to produce an elaborative and distinctive memory trace, which in turn promotes long-term memory. According to Paivio's dual-code hypothesis, imagery also benefits memory simply because it leads to the creation of a second, qualitatively different kind of memory record than does thinking about the to-be remembered material verbally. Research on visual imagery suggests that "mental pictures" are similar to visual perceptions in some ways but not in others. For example, some of the same areas are involved in perceiving and imaging visual objects, but visual images are less detailed than visual perceptions.

Mnemonic Devices

Learning Goal: Learn about mnemonic devices. *Mnemonic devices* are special mental tricks that help people think about material in ways that lead to effective remembering and that provide strategies for searching memory. These techniques include the *method of loci* and the *link-word system.*

RECOVERING INFORMATION FROM CUES

Our interactions with the world require us to retrieve information about both the immediate and the distant past. Retrieval is triggered directly or indirectly by other events, or cues, encountered in the environment.

The Importance of Retrieval Cues

Learning Goal: Understand the ideas of cue-dependent forgetting, the encoding specificity principle, and the notion of transfer-appropriate processing. Many researchers believe that most failures to remember are due to *cue-dependent forgetting.* Once encoded, the information is available in long-term memory, given the right type of cues. According to the *encoding specificity principle,* an effective retrieval cue is one that uniquely matches the encoded material. According to the notion of *transfer-appropriate processing,* material should be studied using the same kind of mental processes that will be used during retrieval.

Reconstructive Remembering

Learning Goal: Understand how reconstructive processes, such as schemas and source monitoring, can lead to inaccurate recollections of past events. Remembering is influenced by beliefs and expectations. Remembering is aided by *schemas,* which are large clusters of related knowledge about people, places, and activities. Although schema-based reconstructive remembering has considerable adaptive value, it can lead to *false memories,* as shown in research on eyewitness testimony and *flashbulb memories. Source-monitoring* skills usually (but not always) enable us to differentiate between memories of a to-be-remembered event versus thoughts and images from other sources such as schemas.

Remembering without Awareness: Implicit Memory

Learning Goal: Learn about the differences between implicit and explicit memory. *Implicit memory* refers to uses of memory that occur automatically and without awareness that one is remembering. *Explicit memory* refers to conscious, willful remembering. Implicit and explicit memory are similarly affected by retrieval cues, but sometimes behave differently; implicit memory is relatively unaffected by encoding strategies that help explicit remembering. Implicit memory can distort our perceptions, such as by leading us to think that we have just come up with a brilliant new idea when we have really merely remembered someone else's idea.

UPDATING MEMORY

Forgetting refers to the loss in accessibility of previously stored material. Forgetting has considerable adaptive value: It reduces the likelihood that retrieval cues in the current environment will lead to retrieval of a flood of irrelevant, outdated information.

How Quickly Do We Forget?

Learning Goal: Be able to describe the rate at which forgetting tends to occur, and explain why forgetting is adaptive. Most forgetting occurs soon after initial exposure. Additional forgetting continues for a long period thereafter, with the rate of forgetting gradually decreasing. If material is retained in accessible form for a number of years without rehearsal, the rate of forgetting may approach zero (*permastore*).

Why Do We Forget?

Learning Goal: Learn about the mechanisms that cause forgetting, including decay and retroactive and proactive interference. The simple passage of time (*decay*) is not sufficient to explain forgetting from long-term memory. *Retroactive interference* (new material interfering with old) and *proactive interference* (old material interfering with new) play major roles in forgetting.

Motivated Forgetting

Learning Goal: Learn about motivated forgetting and the case for and against the concept of repression. An important part of Freud's psychoanalytic theory is the assumption that the mind can actively *repress* certain memories. Modern researchers agree that seemingly memorable traumatic events are sometimes forgotten, but they remain undecided about the scientific validity of the concept of *repression*. Ordinary mechanisms may account for cases in which traumatic events are forgotten.

The Neuroscience of Forgetting

Learning Goal: Be able to define retrograde and anterograde amnesia, and understand why it is unlikely that memories are stored in a single region of the brain. *Organic amnesia* refers to forgetting that is caused by some type of physical problem; *retrograde amnesia* is memory loss for events that happened prior to an injury; *anterograde amnesia* is memory loss for events that happen after the point of physical damage. Although the *hippocampus* is important for memory, no single brain structure is responsible for remembering.

Terms to Remember

Recommended Readings

Neath, I. (1998). *Human memory: An introduction to research, data, and theory.* Pacific Grove, CA: Brooks/Cole. A leading undergraduate textbook on memory. The material discussed in this chapter is covered by Neath in much more detail.

Schacter, D. L. (1996). *Searching for memory.* New York: Basic Books. Written by a top memory researcher for a general audience, this book paints a fascinating portrait of how the brain remembers and reconstructs the past. Covers both the psychology of memory and the biological processes thought to underlie remembering.

Pendergrast, M. (1996). *Victims of memory: Sex, abuse, accusations and shattered lives* (2nd ed.). Hinesburg, VT: Upper Access Books. Pendergrast is an investigative journalist, known for his award-winning book on the history of the Coca-Cola Company. In the early 1990s, his two adult daughters accused him of having sexually abused them during childhood. Although Pendergrast's personal situation understandably created a bias that is sometimes apparent in the book, for the most part he has done a fine job of integrating and discussing a wide range of scientific literature on how suggestive influences can lead to false beliefs and illusory memories.

Tulving, E. (1983). *Elements of episodic memory.* New York: Oxford University Press. This is a semi-autobiographical account of one of Canada's (and the world's) most renowned memory researcher's profound influence on modern memory theory. Although written as a professional book, it contains many personal observations and anecdotes that bring memory theory to life.

For additional readings, explore InfoTrac® College Edition, your online library. Go to:

www.adaptivemind2e.nelson.com

Hint: enter the search terms: short-term memory; long-term memory; autobiographical memory; visual imagery; implicit memory; explicit memory; amnesia.

What's on the Web?

Please note that Web addresses are subject to change. Check out the accompanying Web site for updates: www.adaptivemind2e.nelson.com. This site presents practice quiz questions, hypercontent, information on degrees and careers in psychology, study tips, and more.

The Recovered Memories Controversy

web.lemoyne.edu/~hevern/nr-mem.html

Few topics in psychology have fuelled as much debate as the controversy about "recovered memories" of childhood sexual abuse. Throughout much of the 1990s, the debate was very polarized, with critics on one side claiming that most recovered memories were illusions produced by misguided therapy and countercritics dismissing such claims as antifeminist "backlash." More recently, various "middle-ground" perspectives have come to the fore, according to which some recovered memories are essentially false and others essentially accurate. This Web site offers an impressive array of links to sites presenting both sides (and the middle) of this complex and volatile issue.

Memory (at the Exploratorium)

www.exploratorium.edu/memory

This renowned science museum has an online memory exhibition, with some fun and informative memory demonstrations, facts, and figures. Read about a memory artist, learn more about memories for emotional events, play games with your memory, and explore "tricks" for improving your memory.

NASA Applied Cognition Lab

olias.arc.nasa.gov/cognition/tutorials/index.html

This particular set of pages at the NASA Web site provides some fun demonstrations that allow you to explore how your own memory works. The demonstrations help you learn about the effects of mnemonic devices, interference, and word/picture encoding.

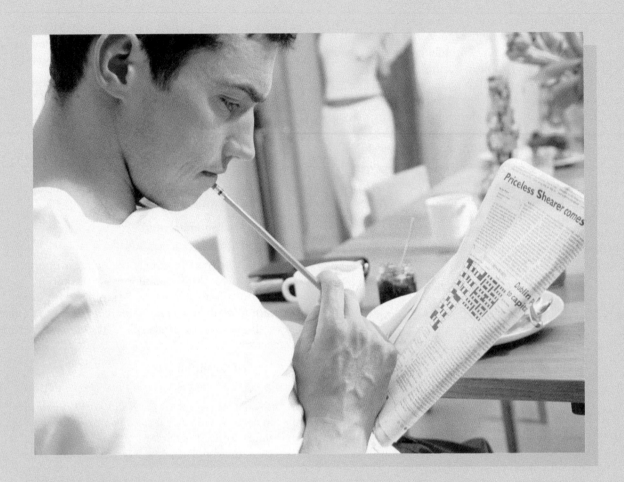

It isn't what people think that is important, but the reason they think what they think.

E. Ionesco

Chapter 8 Thought and Language

Wayne Inges, a devious soul, chuckles silently to himself as he completes the deal. "That's right," he says. "Centre court, floor level—$100 for the pair. Good deal, eh?" Having paid only $50 for the tickets himself, Wayne pockets a tidy little profit. But he knows there are more fools in the world, so he decides to buy the tickets back for $150. Just as game time approaches, he sells the pair for $200. Can you figure out Wayne's total profit for the evening?

Answering such a question requires a bit of thinking. **Thinking,** or cognition, can be broadly defined as the set of processes used to manipulate knowledge, images, and ideas. Through thought we can act on our knowledge in a directed and purposeful way to solve problems, to reason and make decisions, and to understand and communicate with others. Like most other internal psychological phenomena, it's not possible to measure thinking directly, but much can be learned by observing thinkers and listening to their rationales for actions or conclusions.

Let's see, Wayne made $50 on the first transaction but spent $150 to buy the tickets back, so he lost the original $50. He finally sold the pair for $200, so his total profit for the evening must be $50, right? Easy enough. We've used our knowledge about the world, and about mathematics in particular, to work systematically toward a goal. It's easy to see the adaptive value of the process. Thinking increases your ability to survive because you can act on your knowledge in precise, systematic, and purposeful ways.

But, as you may have noticed, our reasoning in this case was completely wrong. We arrived at the wrong answer, as do many others who try this task. Using a slight variation of the same problem, Maier and Burke (1967) found that people come up with the correct answer less than 40% of the time. The correct answer is $100—Wayne paid out a total of $200 ($50 for the first transaction and $150 for the second) and received $300 back from the buyers. Simple subtraction yields the correct answer of $100.

What lies behind the error? The difficulty comes from thinking about Wayne's sales as one continuous event rather than as two separate transactions. This becomes clearer if you frame the problem slightly differently: Wayne bought tickets for Friday night's game for $50 and sold them for $100, then he bought tickets for Saturday's game for $150 and sold them for $200. When the problem is expressed this way, people rarely err. One of the challenges of the modern study of thinking, and of problem solving in particular, is to understand why human thought processes are sometimes led astray. How can illogical thought processes arise from an adaptive mind? In this chapter, we consider scientific evidence regarding the nature of human thinking. We begin with an examination of what may be the single greatest tool for thinking: language. We then turn to research on categorization, problem solving, and decision making. By the end of the chapter, you should have gained new insights into both strengths and weaknesses of human thinking.

thinking
The processes that underlie the mental manipulation of knowledge, images, and ideas, often in an attempt to reach a goal such as solving a problem.

Previewing the Adaptive Problems

The topics of thought and language touch on a wide variety of psychological activities. Thinking relies on learning and involves conscious awareness. To manipulate the knowledge in your head, you need to remember things you learned in the past. When you solve problems or make decisions, you need to come up with criteria for what represents an acceptable solution. To express ideas symbolically in the form of language, you need rules for categorizing objects and guidelines for transforming ideas into the symbols of speech or writing.

For centuries, philosophers have struggled to understand the "higher mental processes" of thought and language. More recently, questions about thought and language have formed the focus of cognitive science, a diverse field that draws on a wide variety of disciplines, including psychology, linguistics, philosophy, biology, and even engineering and computer science. Once again, we'll discuss the insights of psychologists and cognitive scientists by considering a set of adaptive problems (see Figure 8.1).

First, how do we communicate with others? The ability to communicate through language may well be humanity's greatest success story. No other species approaches our ability to transmit knowledge through speech and writing. In fact, the use of language may be the "most pervasive and uniquely human characteristic of the species" (Wasow, 1989). Through language production we transmit thoughts, feelings, and needs to others; through language comprehension we understand and learn from others.

Second, how do we categorize objects in our world? To make sense of our environment, especially the objects in it, we carve the world into *categories.* Can you imagine a world where every encounter was new and unique—a world where no two things shared features in common, where each encounter with a cat, bird, or snake was a new and mysterious experience? The ability to see similarities between things, to classify objects as exemplars of meaningful categories (e.g., to perceive a round, orange-coloured object as a member of the category "orange," part of the larger category "fruit"), enables us to simplify our environment and make predictions.

Third, how do we solve problems such as the ticket-scalping-profit problem posed at the beginning of the chapter? When you do problem solving, you want to reach a goal, such as answering a math problem or hooking up a new VCR, but you don't know exactly how to attain that goal. Think about the dozens of practical problems you face and solve each and every day. Did you have trouble finding your keys this morning, or have a difficult time choosing what to wear or what to eat? The adaptive value of problem solving is obvious: If humans couldn't solve the problem of where to find food and water, *Homo sapiens* would quickly become extinct.

Fourth, how do we make decisions when confronted with a set of alternatives? Should I buy the tickets for $100, use the money to help pay this month's rent, or gamble it on the outcome of tonight's game? Should I keep working on my university education or go travelling? Note that an important ingredient of decision making is *risk*—choices have consequences, and an incorrect decision can lead to an unpleasant or even fatal outcome.

Communicating with others

Classifying and categorizing

Solving problems

Making decisions

FIGURE 8.1
The Adaptive Problems
Thought and language serve a variety of adaptive functions. Summarized here are the four adaptive problems that we'll be considering in this chapter.

COMMUNICATING WITH OTHERS

Learning Goals

1. Be able to evaluate the linguistic relativity hypothesis.
2. Learn about the structure of language and its basic units.
3. Appreciate the role of shared knowledge in language comprehension.
4. Be able to identify the major milestones of language development.
5. Evaluate whether or not nonhuman animals are capable of language.
6. Be able to summarize ideas about the evolution of language.

WE BEGIN OUR EXPLORATION of thinking with an extended discussion of language. It might seem odd to lump language and thought together, but the two are closely linked: Language importantly influences the way we think about and view our world. Remember from Chapter 7 how using the word *smashed* rather than *contacted* in a question changed witnesses' reports of a car accident?

Does Language Determine Thought?

linguistic relativity hypothesis
The proposal that language determines the characteristics and content of thought.

How strong is the connection between language and thought? The **linguistic relativity hypothesis** proposes that language *determines* thought (Whorf, 1956). The idea is that the words and structures of a culture's language determine the perceptions and thoughts of members of that culture. For example, the Hopi language has no past tense for verbs, and Whorf argued that Hopi people consequently had difficulty thinking about the past.

To test the linguistic relativity hypothesis, researchers have turned to nature's laboratory to examine relationships between the idiosyncrasies of language and the way people think in different cultures. In the Philippines, for example, the Hanunoo people have 92 different names for rice (Anderson, 1990). According to the linguistic relativity hypothesis, language determines how people think about and perceive the world. Consequently, you might expect the Hanunoo people to perceive subtle distinctions in rice that members of other cultures, with a more limited "rice" vocabulary, do not.

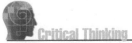

Critical Thinking

Do you think the study of colour perception is a fair way to test the linguistic relativity hypothesis?

The Cultural Evidence In some important cross-cultural research, Eleanor Rosch (publishing under her former name, Heider) travelled to New Guinea to investigate the perceptual abilities of members of a tribe called the Dani. The Dani's language contains only two basic colour terms: *mola* for bright, warm hues, and *mili* for the darker, colder hues. If words completely shape thought, Rosch reasoned, the Dani should have trouble perceiving and remembering colours. Using a wide range of colour chips, Rosch discovered that volunteers from the tribe had no trouble remembering novel colours; moreover, the Dani did particularly well with focal colours (red, green, and blue) as opposed to nonfocal colours (such as teal), just as English speakers do.

Rosch interpreted her results as evidence that English speakers and speakers of the Dani language perceive colour in very similar ways. Colour perception appears to be universal, depending more on the physiology of the visual system than on the vocabulary of the perceiver (Heider, 1972). In research conducted after Rosch's pioneering study, the same general conclusion has been reached: Colour perception seems to be largely universal, regardless of language (Davies, 1998; Davies & Corbett, 1997; for a critique, see Saunders & van Brakel, 1997), although there is also recent evidence that learning new colour categories can subtly influence colour perception (Goldstone, 1998; Oezgen & Davies, 2002).

The cross-cultural evidence has led most psychologists to conclude that linguistic differences across cultures do not cause dramatic differences in the operation of basic perceptual processes, such as colour perception. The evidence is less clear when it comes to the operation of higher-level perceptual and cognitive processes. One problem is that it is difficult to determine causation from cross-cultural comparisons. Suppose, for example, that research showed that Hanunoo people perceive rice differ-

The Quecha, who live in mountainous regions, have no word in their language for "flat." According to the linguistic relativity hypothesis, one might expect them to have a difficult time orienting themselves spatially in a flat environment.

ently from members of Western cultures. Would that mean that the large Hanunoo rice vocabulary *causes* that difference? An alternative explanation is that different cultures place value on different sorts of things, and each culture develops vocabularies to communicate subtle distinctions in those things perceived as important. For example, most Canadians know hundreds of words for "automobile" (e.g., Cadillac, Camry, Camaro, car, and cab). Knowing these words may not, in itself, change the way we perceive automobiles, but may merely go along with living in a culture in which people learn to talk about fine discriminations between automobiles.

Nonetheless, there is little question that language can influence thought. Both perception and memory depend on prior knowledge, and people often use words to summarize and represent prior knowledge. For example, verbal labels can strongly bias the perception of ambiguous pictures like those discussed in Chapter 4. Language—in the form of an inner voice—also plays important roles in more abstract thinking. For example, a study conducted at Mount Allison University indicated that university students use internal speech as a cognitive tool in their studies (Duncan & Cheyne, 1999). Also, as you learned in Chapter 7, memory for an event depends significantly on how you thought about the event when it originally occurred. Furthermore, memory search is often mediated by language; for example, DODGE VIPER would be a powerful retrieval cue for memories of seeing a car for a person with expertise in automobiles. Language is a tool of human thought, useful in many ways, but there is also evidence that in some cases language can interfere with nonlinguistic processes. For example, Jonathan Schooler and his colleagues have shown that when people verbally describe hard-to-describe things (such as their memories of a person's face) their performance on subsequent judgment tasks involving those things (e.g., trying to recognize the person from a set of pictures) is sometimes impaired (Schooler, 2002). Language clearly affects thought in significant ways (Lucy, 1997).

The interplay between thought and language can be insidious: "The secretary hates his boss." Did you find yourself stumbling when you read this sentence? Many people do, which suggests that the "generic" male pronoun ("his") is not truly generic and that people tend to think of secretaries as women. Many words carry such gendered connotations. If used inappropriately, they become weapons, leading people to generate misleading expectations or draw inaccurate conclusions (Ehrlich, 1999; Henley, 1989; Mackay, 1983).

The Structure of Language

We now turn our attention to language itself. What is language? Birds communicate effectively through their songs. Some biologists believe that bees convey information about the exact location of nectar through a tail-wagging dance (von Frisch, 1967, but

Bees do a characteristic "waggle dance" that may communicate information about the location of nectar. But would you say bees have language?

grammar
The rules or procedures of language that allow the communicator to combine arbitrary symbols in an infinite number of ways to convey meaning; grammar includes the rules of phonology, syntax, and semantics.

phonology
The rules and procedures for combining sounds to make words in a language.

syntax
The rules and procedures for combining words to form sentences.

semantics
The rules and procedures for communicating meaning through words and combinations of words.

phonemes
The smallest significant, difference-making sound units in speech.

see also Wenner, 1998). Your neighbour's dog barks incessantly at outdoor noises. But to qualify as a true language, a communication system must have a generative **grammar** that enables the communicator to combine arbitrary symbols in an infinite number of ways to convey meaning.

A generative grammar specifies which combinations of sounds are permissible in a particular language and which are not. Grammar has three aspects: (1) **phonology,** the rules for combining sounds to make words; (2) **syntax,** the rules for combining words to make sentences; and (3) **semantics,** the rules regarding the meanings of words and combinations of words. An English speaker would not normally say something like, "The cautious the at barked nasty man poodle." This particular combination of words violates a number of rules of syntax, such as the rule that articles *(the)* and adjectives *(nasty)* come before nouns *(man).* Most English speakers would also be unlikely to generate a sentence like "Colourless green ideas sleep furiously." Although this is a well-structured sentence with good syntax, it suffers from violations of semantics: It has no coherent meaning, even though the individual words are meaningful. We use our knowledge about semantics to pick the appropriate words to express thoughts (perhaps "people" can sleep furiously, but "ideas" cannot) and to infer connections between words and other information in memory.

Phonemes and Morphemes Language has a hierarchical structure: A fairly small set of simple sounds can be combined in various ways to make thousands of words, and words can be combined in innumerable ways to generate infinitely many sentences. At the base of the hierarchy are **phonemes,** which are the smallest significant, difference-making sound units in a language. Speech sounds are produced through a complex coordination of the vocal cords, lungs, lips, tongue, and teeth. Table 8.1 lists some examples of phonemes in the English language. Notice that there isn't a simple one-to-one mapping between a given letter of the alphabet and a phoneme. The letter *e,* for example, maps onto one phoneme in the word *head* and a different phoneme in the word *heat.*

English speakers use about 40 phonemes; some languages use considerably more, and others use fewer. Within a given language, a range of physically different sounds will be heard by speakers of that language as a single phoneme. For example, English speakers will hear a variety of physically different sounds as all being a "k" sound. Languages differ in where the boundaries between different sounds are drawn. Japanese, for example, does not differentiate between the sounds *r* and *l;* these are just different ways of saying a single phoneme. Similarly, English does not meaningfully distinguish between the initial consonant sounds in *keep* and *cool* (say these two words aloud, and notice how differently your mouth is shaped for each); here again, in English these two quite different sounds are perceived as a single phoneme. For example, if you force yourself to say the "k" sound from *keep* followed by the "ool" sound from *cool,* to an English speaker it will just sound like *cool.* That's what makes them the same

Table 8.1
Some Examples of English Phonemes

Symbol	Examples	Symbol	Examples
b	burger, rubble	ng	sting, ringer
ē	easy, zombie	oy	coil, employ
ĕ	enter, metric	r	rat, crust
f	fungus, phone	s	stodgy, best
ĭ	icky, wig	t	tramp, missed
ī	ice, shy	th	that, other
k	kitty, ache	ŭ	ugly, butter
n	newt, annoy		

phoneme in English, the fact that it doesn't matter which one you say. In Arabic, in contrast, those two "k" sounds correspond to two different phonemes, such that the meaning of a spoken word changes depending on which one is used (just as, in English, the *r* and *l* sounds are treated as different). Part of the challenge of acquiring a foreign language is mastering the phonology of that language; it is difficult to learn to pronounce differences that you cannot hear.

At the next level in the hierarchy are **morphemes,** the smallest units of language that carry meaning. Most morphemes are single words, such as *cool* or *hip*, but prefixes and suffixes are

A spectrogram is a computer-generated visual image that represents sounds in terms of their frequencies (pitches, represented by the height of the lines) and amplitudes (loudness, represented by the darkness of the lines). Time is represented from left to right. The spectogram above was provided by Professor R. Hagiwara of the University of Manitoba (see www.umanitoba.ca/linguistics/robh).

also morphemes. For instance, the word *cool* contains a single morpheme, whereas *uncool* contains two: the root word *cool* and the prefix *un*. The grammar of a language dictates the acceptable order of morphemes within a word—*uncool* has a particular meaning in English; *coolun* does not. Similarly, the morpheme *s* when placed at the end of a word *(oar)* designates plural (two or more *oars*). But the phoneme *s* when placed at the beginning of that same word means something entirely different *(soar)*. All told, the average speaker of English knows and uses somewhere between 50 000 and 80 000 morphemes (see Figure 8.2).

Words to Sentences At the higher levels of the language hierarchy are *words, phrases,* and *sentences*. Words combine to form phrases; phrases combine to form sentences.

morphemes
The smallest units in a language that carry meaning (words, prefixes, suffixes).

FIGURE 8.2
The Units of Language
Languages have a hierarchical structure, building from simple speech sounds to more complex levels of spoken conversation. Complex rules determine how fundamental speech sounds (phonemes) are combined to create the smallest units of meaning (morphemes) and words, and how words are combined into phrases and sentences. A small number of phonemes can be used to create many thousands of different words, and these can be combined to form an infinite number of different sentences.

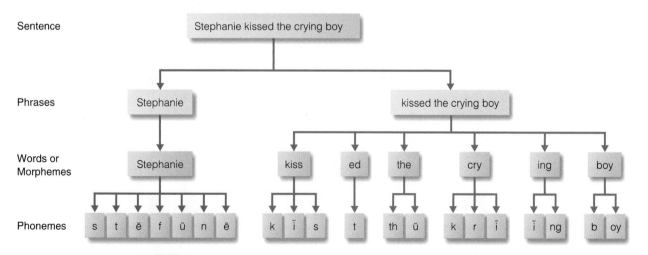

Sentences are not just collections of words, because the meaning of the sentence depends not only on what words it contains but also on how they are organized: "Beth shot John" has a meaning quite different from "John shot Beth." Language researchers have spent decades trying to decipher the rules of syntax that people use to combine words into phrases and phrases into sentences. It turns out that those rules are enormously complex.

Surface and Deep Structure   Noam Chomsky is widely heralded as the most important linguist of recent times. One of Chomsky's (1957) early contributions to the study of language was his distinction between the "surface" structure of a sentence and its more abstract "deep" structure. The **surface structure** of a sentence corresponds to its superficial appearance (the literal ordering of words), whereas **deep structure** refers to the underlying representation of meaning. Thus a single surface structure can have two different deep structures. Chomsky used as an example the following sentence: "Visiting relatives can be a nuisance." Whether it is the relatives or visiting them that is a nuisance depends on the deep structure. Conversely, two different surface structures can represent essentially the same deep structure ("Beth shot John" and "John was shot by Beth").

According to Chomsky, language production requires the transformation of deep structure into an acceptable surface structure (see Figure 8.3), and comprehension involves transforming a surface structure into the appropriate deep structure. Most language researchers agree with Chomsky on this point, although there are disagreements over how the transformation process works (see Wasow, 1989, for a review). Language is clearly more than sets of words or symbols organized in a fixed and rigid way. In the words of Canadian psychologist Steven Pinker (1997b), there are "hundreds of millions of trillions of thinkable thoughts," and each can, in principle, be expressed through language in an understandable way. The challenge for language researchers is to discover how this flexibility arises.

Language Comprehension

How do you understand what a speaker is trying to communicate? This is not a trivial problem because language comprehension presents many difficulties: In normal

surface structure
The literal ordering of words in a sentence.

deep structure
The underlying representation of meaning in a sentence.

Critical Thinking

Based on what you've learned about Chomsky's work, why might it be difficult to program a computer to understand speech?

FIGURE 8.3

Surface Structure and Deep Structure

The surface structure of a sentence is its "surface" appearance, the literal ordering of words. Deep structure is the underlying meaning of the sentence. The left and right panels of this figure show how the same surface structure—"Visiting relatives can be a nuisance"—can reflect two different deep structures. Similarly, the panel on the far right shows how a single deep structure can be transformed into two or more acceptable surface structures.

Surface Structure

"Visiting relatives can be a nuisance."

"Stephanie kissed the crying boy."

"The crying boy was kissed by Stephanie."

Deep Structure

speech, sounds are presented very quickly, without well-defined pauses between words; we don't always hear sounds clearly or correctly; word sounds often have many different meanings (e.g., consider the number of meanings that correspond to the sound of the word "rite"); and language is full of metaphors and other indirect speech acts that complicate the interpretation process (Glucksberg, 1998; Lakoff, 1987; Pinker, 1994).

Effective communication seems to rely a great deal on *common knowledge* among speakers (Clark, 1992; Keysar et al., 1998). When you're having a conversation with someone about a mutual friend, you can say "That's typical of her" and be understood. You both know that "her" refers to your friend, and you can both list examples of your friend's "typical" behaviour. You go beyond the information given in the spoken message by using shared knowledge. Similarly, everyday language is rife with ambiguity, yet we usually resolve the ambiguity without even being aware that it is there. Someone says to you, "They're shooting stars," and in one context you immediately comprehend that this refers to meteorites, in another to expert marksmen, in yet another to victimized movie actors or a scene from *Star Wars*. Like other forms of perception, language comprehension involves a combination of top-down and bottom-up processing (McClelland & Elman, 1986). Sometimes the system breaks down and we become aware of ambiguity or even misunderstand one another, just as we sometimes misperceive objects, but most of the time language comprehension is very fluent.

Pragmatic Rules Language researchers use the term **pragmatics** to describe how practical knowledge is used to comprehend the intentions of speakers and to produce appropriate responses. Consider your response to an *indirect* request such as "Could you close the window?" If you process the request directly—that is, if you take its literal interpretation—you might respond, "Yes, I'm capable of putting enough steady pressure on the window to produce closure." You have answered the question, but clearly you have violated an important pragmatic rule. The speaker was making a request, not asking you about your ability to perform the task. In fact, if you answered the question in this way, the speaker would probably infer that you were using *irony* or *sarcasm* (Gibbs et al., 1995; Kreuz, 2000; Lee & Katz, 1998).

pragmatics
The practical knowledge used to comprehend the intentions of a speaker and to produce an appropriate response.

The pragmatics of language add to its complexity. How you interpret someone's words depends on the shared context of the conversation as well as on the expectations and beliefs that you bring to the exchange. To facilitate effective communication, there are certain pragmatic guidelines, or conversational maxims, that good speakers follow (Grice, 1975):

1. Be informative.

2. Tell the truth.

3. Be relevant.

4. Be clear.

If you choose to answer an indirect request literally ("Yes, I can close the window"), then you're not being relevant; you're violating an accepted guideline for communication. If you don't tell the truth or are purposely vague in answering a request, then you'll soon have trouble finding people who want to talk with you. By following the simple rules listed above, and by assuming the same of your conversational partner, you can enhance the ease and flow of the conversational process.

Language Development

How does language develop? Are humans born with a genetic blueprint that directs and shapes their communication skills? Or do we acquire language exclusively as a product of experience? There are thousands of different languages, so experience must certainly play an important role. But most language researchers are convinced that

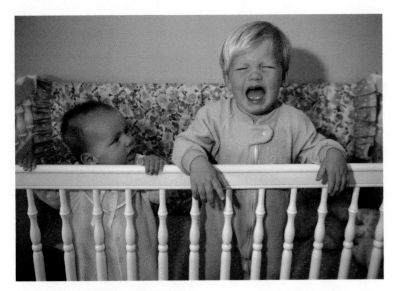

Infants and small children develop rather sophisticated ways to communicate meaningfully (cooing, kicking, looking, pointing, crying, and so on), even though their language skills are limited.

babies are genetically prepared to learn language, much as they are genetically prepared to learn to walk. There is a regularity to language development, as there is to the development of motor skills, that is difficult to explain by appealing solely to the environment (Chomsky, 1986; Pinker, 1994b). Moreover, the complexity of language is so great that some scholars have argued that it would be impossible to learn any language from scratch without innately specified linguistic mechanisms that constrain and guide language development.

The universality of language is apparent even at birth. Most babies cry in similar ways, and they move quickly through vocalization milestones that precede formal language development. By 3 to 5 weeks of age, *cooing*—repeating vowel sounds like "ooooh" and "aaaaah"—has been added to the baby's vocalization patterns. *Babbling*—repeating consonant/vowel combinations such as "kaka" or "baba"—begins in virtually all babies between the ages of 4 and 6 months. It doesn't matter where you look in the world, this same sequence—crying then cooing then babbling—is found. Babbling also progresses through a regular series of stages, beginning with simple sound sequences and culminating with complex and speech-like (but meaningless) vocalizations known as "expressive jargon."

Between the ages of 6 and 18 months, experience begins to play a noticeable role, shaping and fine-tuning the baby's babblings into language-specific sounds. Babies begin to restrict their vocalizations to the phonemes of the language(s) they hear every day; they even acquire a kind of language-specific "accent" by around 8 months of age (de Boysson-Bardies et al., 1984; Locke, 1994). Six-month-old babies perceive subtle phonemic differences from other languages that their parents cannot detect, but by one year children no longer hear those differences (Werker & Tees, 1999; for a more general overview of infants' perceptions of speech sounds, see Werker & Desjardins, 2001). Simple words appear by the end of the first year, and by 24 months most babies have developed a vocabulary of nearly 200 words (Nelson, 1973).

Language comprehension also develops rapidly during this period; in fact, infants develop the ability to understand language faster than they learn to produce it. At first thought, you might assume that learning to understand words would be relatively simple, but deeper consideration shows that here too children's ability to learn is amazing. For example, suppose I point at a dog and say "flug." Is flug the word for dog? Or is it the word for that particular breed of dog (a collie, perhaps) or the name of that specific dog (Flug)? Or maybe it means "bark" or "bite" or refers to some specific part of the dog (collar, nose, whatever), or perhaps it refers to the rug the dog is standing on. Young children use a variety of sophisticated inferential strategies to solve problems like this and hone in on the meanings of new words (Nelson & Shaw, 2002; Welder & Graham, 2001).

Child Speak As every parent knows, infants and young children develop rather sophisticated ways to communicate meaningfully, even though their language skills are limited. An 18-month-old child can point to the jar on the counter and say "ookie," and Mom or Dad immediately knows what the child has in mind. An enormous amount of information can be packed into a single word, even if that word is spoken incorrectly, especially if its utterance is combined with a gesture or occurs in the right context.

As the child approaches the end of his or her second year of life, a phase of *telegraphic speech* begins. Telegraphic speech involves combining two words into simple sentences, such as "Daddy bad" or "Give cookie." It's called telegraphic speech because, as in a telegram, the child characteristically omits articles *(the, a)* and prepositions *(at,*

Concept Summary

HIGHLIGHTS IN LANGUAGE DEVELOPMENT

Age	Linguistic Highlight(s)	Interpretation
3–5 weeks	Cooing, or the repetition of vowel sounds, such as "ooh" and "aah."	Both cooing and babbling are vocalization milestones that occur before formal language development, and their occurrence is similar across cultures, highlighting the universality of language.
4–6 months	Babbling, or the repetition of vowel–consonant combinations, such as "kaka" and "baba."	As above.
6–18 months	Vocalizations become specific to the native language; the first word is spoken by the end of the first year.	Experience plays a role in vocalization as baby's babblings are shaped into language-specific sounds. Language comprehension is rapidly developing.
24 months	Vocabulary of nearly 200 words; child shows telegraphic speech, grammatical two-word combinations.	Speech reflects knowledge of syntax, as words are almost always combined in the proper order.
Preschool years	Ability to produce and comprehend sentences; vocabulary growing at an astounding rate.	Child is now showing most of the important features of adult syntax.

in). But a 2-year-old's first sentences reflect a rudimentary knowledge of the syntax of his or her language: Words are almost always spoken in the proper *order.* For example, a child will say, "Want cookie," not "Cookie want," and "Me push!" will mean something quite different from "Push me!" During the rest of the child's preschool years, up to around age 5 or 6, sentences become increasingly complex, such that the average child of kindergarten age can produce and comprehend sentences that reveal most of the important features of adult syntax.

The linguistic rules children learn during their preschool years are revealed by the errors that they make. For example, preschoolers acquire the rule "Add *ed* to the ends of verbs to make them past tense." Interestingly, children tend to *overgeneralize* this rule— they say things such as "goed" and "falled," which are incorrect in English but represent an application of the rule. Notice that children are not rewarded for saying *goed,* nor do they hear the word being used by their parents. Rather, children appear to be naturally "tuned" to pick up linguistic rules and apply them generally, even if a rule sometimes leads to an incorrect utterance. This natural tendency to learn and apply rules is then further refined and shaped by experience as the child learns the exceptions to the rules.

Language development continues throughout the school years, as children fine-tune their articulation skills and knowledge about grammar. Vocabulary expands at an astounding rate, as does the child's ability to communicate abstract concepts. Ultimately, the sophistication of any child's language ability will depend, at least in part, on his or her level of cognitive development. Children think differently as they mature, and their increasingly sophisticated cognitive abilities are reflected in the conversations they generate. You should keep this fact in mind when we turn our attention to language abilities in nonhuman species.

Acquiring one's first language has been described as "The greatest intellectual feat any of us is ever required to perform" (Bloomfield, 1933). How do children develop such sophisticated language skills so quickly? Few parents sit down with their preschoolers and teach them the rules of grammar (such as the differences between present and past tense). Moreover, as we will discuss further in Chapter 10, children at this age lack the ability to understand most abstract concepts, so they couldn't consciously understand grammatical rules even if parents tried to explain them. Children pick up their language skills implicitly, not through explicit instruction. It's also clear that children do not simply imitate the speech they hear around them. For example, children's first words are *not* the words they most often hear (articles such as *the* and *a,* or perhaps their own names), but rather names for things that move and that they find interesting. Similarly,

Critical Thinking

If imitation played the major role in the development of language, what words would babies first use?

309

children's early telegraphic grammar is not something they hear others use. Also, deaf children raised without exposure to sign language often develop their own gestural languages (Pinker, 1994). It's worth mentioning that manual languages, such as American Sign Language, are just as complex, sophisticated, and generative as spoken languages. Research conducted at McGill University by Pettito and colleagues (Petitto, 2000) showed that the acquisition of sign language by young children follows a developmental trajectory that parallels that of the acquisition of spoken language, and some of the same brain areas are involved in spoken and signed language use.

Most psychologists are convinced that humans have an innate "language acquisition device" that enables them to develop linguistic skills astonishingly quickly. This inherent tendency toward language development must be sufficiently flexible to allow for the acquisition of any of the many thousands of languages used by humans (including sign language). All languages use comparable building blocks (nouns and verbs, subjects and objects, interrogatives and negations, etc.), and although there is considerable variation in surface structure across languages, those variations all fit within certain common constraints. Thus all human languages can be described as dialects or variants of an innate universal grammar.

Language in Nonhuman Species

Anyone who has ever seen a cat indicate that it would rather be inside the house than outside knows that nonhuman animals can communicate. The question is whether such forms of communication should be called *language*. There's no doubt that an animal's actions can convey meaning. But to qualify as having a true language, the animal would need to possess at least a rudimentary grammar, that is, a set of rules or procedures for generatively combining arbitrary symbols to convey innumerable possible messages.

Several teams of researchers have explored nonhuman animals' linguistic skills by attempting to teach them a language. For example, chimps were raised in human homes in an effort to provide the ideal environment for language development. In one case, a chimp named Gua was raised along with the researchers' son, Donald (Kellogg & Kellogg, 1933). Donald and Gua were exposed to the same experiences, and careful attention was paid to rewarding the appropriate vocalizations. But in the end the Kelloggs had merely produced a fine-speaking son and an effectively mute chimp (legend has it that Donald also developed into an excellent tree climber). Later efforts to teach chimps to speak yielded the same discouraging results (Hayes & Hayes, 1951).

Signs and Symbol Communication   Attempts to teach chimps to speak were misguided because chimps' vocal apparatus cannot produce most of the sounds required for human speech (Hayes, 1952). It's like a bird trying to teach a human to fly by raising a child in a nest—without wings, the child just isn't going to fly. For this reason, subsequent researchers turned to visual communication mediums. Allen and Beatrice Gardner tried to teach a simplified form of American Sign Language to a chimp named Washoe (Gardner & Gardner, 1969; Gardner et al., 1989). By 4 years of age, Washoe was capable of producing about 160 appropriate signs, and apparently she understood a great deal more. Even more impressive was her ability to produce various word combinations, such as "more fruit" or "gimme tickle."

Koko, a gorilla trained by Francine Patterson (1978), also demonstrated impressive use of sign language. Similarly, David Premack taught a chimp named Sarah to manipulate plastic shapes that symbolized words (e.g., a plastic triangle stood for the word *banana*). Sarah eventually learned to respond to simple symbol-based sentences that were arranged on a magnetic board (such as "Sarah insert banana into pail"; Premack, 1976). In Georgia, pigmy chimpanzees were taught to communicate by pressing keys that represent objects such as food or toys (Rumbaugh, 1977; Savage-Rumbaugh et al., 1986). Again, not only did these chimps learn to associate particular symbols with

Chimpanzees lack the vocal equipment needed to produce most of the sounds of human speech. But chimps can be taught to communicate in relatively sophisticated ways using American Sign Language or by pressing keys that symbolically represent objects such as food or toys.

words or actions, but they also showed the capacity to generate combinations of words by pressing the symbols in sequence.

Work in Savage-Rumbaugh's Georgia laboratory has also shown that pygmy chimpanzees can understand some spoken English. A chimp named Kanzi can press the appropriate symbol key when a word is spoken (e.g., banana). He can also respond appropriately to a variety of spoken commands. When asked, "Can you pour the ice water in the potty?" Kanzi picks up the bowl of ice water, heads to the potty, and carefully pours it in (Savage-Rumbaugh et al., 1993). When asked to "Hide the toy gorilla," Kanzi picks up the toy gorilla and attempts to push it under a fence.

Is It Really Language?   These are very impressive demonstrations and are quite convincing when you see them on video. But have chimps such as Kanzi really acquired *language*? The jury is still out on this issue. Some psychologists believe that the chimps' behaviour simply reflects reinforced learning—like a pigeon who has been taught to peck a key for food—rather than true language (Terrace, 1986). But this view is challenged by reports that chimps such as Washoe and Kanzi can generate new combinations of words and respond to requests that they have never heard before. Washoe, for example, could apparently respond to environmental events by producing novel signs. On seeing a duck for the first time, she reportedly signed "water bird." Moreover, it's been shown that chimps can acquire these language skills through observing other chimps, without being trained directly (Savage-Rumbaugh et al., 1986).

This debate is nowhere near a firm resolution. Most of the psychologists who work with chimps are firmly convinced that the language abilities are real. Kanzi, for example, doesn't seem to follow rigid scripts; he can respond appropriately to a request that is worded in various ways, which is far beyond what you would expect from a pigeon trained to peck a key. Yet Seidenberg and Petitto (1987) offered strong arguments that Kanzi's behaviours were like the nonlinguistic gestural communication of very young children, not comparable to the generative grammar of language users. Moreover, much of the critical evidence (such as Washoe's "water bird") has come from trainer anecdotes, so there is room for multiple interpretations. For example, some of the novel combinations generated by the chimps may merely be imitations of their trainers or flukes of chance; it is also possible that trainers' beliefs and expectations have sometimes distorted their perceptions (as discussed in Chapter 4). We just don't know at this point. It is clear, however, that even if chimps or other nonhuman animals are capable of acquiring language, their abilities in this regard are qualitatively different from humans. Untutored 3-year-old humans have linguistic skills far beyond those of the most intensively trained nonhuman animals.

The Evolution of Language

Given that human linguistic competence differs qualitatively from the communicative skills of nonhuman animals, how did our species acquire that competence? It's easy to say that language "evolved," but by itself that isn't much of an explanation. Darwinian evolution works through random genetic errors; mutations that turn out to be advantageous tend to be preserved because animals with advantageous mutations are more likely to survive and propagate and their progeny are likely to share the mutation. It is easy to see that language has survival value. The major difficulty is that any given random genetic mutation is likely to produce a subtle variation on its predecessors, not a large and qualitative difference, so evolution occurs gradually. Thus, "There must have been a series of steps leading from no language at all to language as we now find it, each step small enough to have been produced by a random mutation ... and each intermediate grammar useful to its possessor" (Pinker & Bloom, 1992). Where is the evidence of all of these small steps?

Most linguists agree that all known human languages are comparable in terms of complexity and sophistication (as noted earlier, each language appears to be a variant of an underlying "universal grammar" shared by all humans) (Cartwright, 2000). Presumably, then, language evolved gradually in early forms of human life (e.g., *Australopithecus afarensis*) (Pinker & Bloom, 1992). If early forms of human life had survived rather than becoming extinct, then perhaps we would share the planet with creatures with protogrammars of varying degrees of complexity (see Merlin, 1999, for a discussion of what such prehuman protogrammars might have been like).

As you think about this topic for yourself, try to avoid adopting an anthropocentric view of the world. It's important to keep in mind that chimpanzees did not evolve to understand or produce human language. Chimps evolved to solve their own problems, problems that arise from their own unique environments. The human mind has evolved to solve human problems, and those problems may or may not overlap with the challenges faced by other members of the animal kingdom. You would probably have difficulty performing the honeybee's waggle dance effectively, and your climbing skills are likely but a faint echo of those of the chimpanzee.

Test Yourself 8.1

Check your knowledge about language by answering the following questions. (You will find the answers in Appendix B.)

1. Choose the term that best fits the following descriptions. Choose your answers from the following: deep structure; linguistic relativity; morphemes; pragmatics; phonemes; phonology; semantics; surface structure; syntax.
   a. The smallest significant, difference-making sound units in speech:

   _____

   b. The practical knowledge used to understand the intentions of a speaker and to produce an appropriate response: _____
   c. The idea that language determines the characteristics and contents of thought: _____
   d. The rules governing how words are combined to form sentences:

   _____

   e. The smallest units in language that carry meaning: _____
2. Decide whether each of the following statements about language is true or false.
   a. Across the world babies cry, coo, and begin to babble in similar ways. *True or False?*
   b. Children learn the rules of language primarily by copying the words and phrases of their parents. *True or False?*

c. Telegraphic speech begins toward the end of the child's second year of life. *True or False?*

d. Chimpanzees lack the vocal equipment needed to produce human speech. *True or False?*

e. Chimpanzee Kanzi learned to associate symbols with a variety of words, but cannot follow spoken instructions from his trainers. *True or False?*

f. Early (now extinct) forms of human life likely possessed a more primitive grammar than *Homo sapiens. True or False?*

CATEGORIZATION

Learning Goals

1. Understand why psychologists have rejected the idea that natural categories have defining features, in favour of the idea that category members share a "family resemblance."

2. Be able to compare the prototype and exemplar views of categorization.

3. Learn about the hierarchical organization of categories.

WE NOW TURN OUR ATTENTION to another highly adaptive quality of the mind: the ability to categorize objects. By carving the environment into meaningful categories, people create a world that is manageable, predictable, and sensible. Imagine what it would be like if each time you encountered a new ballpoint pen you did not perceive it as a member of the category "pen" but rather as a novel object (after all, you've never encountered that particular pen before). Without categorization, every new object and event would be a one-of-a-kind mystery, and you would have to explore each one to discover its nonapparent properties.

A **category** is a collection of objects (people, places, or things) or events that people in a given culture agree belong together (Smith, 1989). "Vegetables" is a category that contains such things as peas, carrots, and Brussels sprouts; "psychologists" is a category that includes researchers, clinicians, and other professionals working within particular areas of expertise. Categories allow people to *infer* invisible properties of objects. For example, by perceiving a particular object as an orange you immediately access information about what the inside of that object looks, tastes, and feels like, what can be done with it, and so on. Once you have successfully categorized something, you can also make *predictions* about the future. You know, for example, that if you throw an orange against a wall with sufficient force it is likely to splatter, and that if you plant its seeds and tend the soil properly they will sprout.

We'll divide our discussion of categorizing into three main topics. First, what properties of an object make it a member of a particular category? Second, do we form and store an abstract representation of the most typical member (or "prototype") of each category, or are category judgments based on memory for individual encounters with category members? Finally, we'll end the section by considering the structure of categories: When people categorize an object, do they usually do so in a very general or a highly specific manner?

category
A class of objects (people, places, or things) or events that most people in a given culture agree belong together.

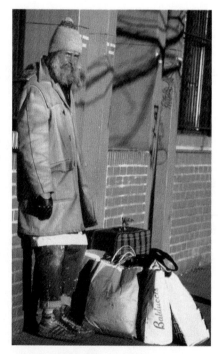

People automatically classify objects, and even other people, into categories. How would you categorize this individual, and what "invisible" properties would you infer about him? Can you predict how he might act in a social situation?

Defining Category Membership

Researchers have spent a lot of time studying how people categorize objects and events in everyday experience. How do we know that a trout is a member of the category "fish"? How is it that we quickly and effortlessly classify a sparrow as a bird? These questions probably sound pretty silly to you at this point, but as you read on you will (we hope) come to appreciate that the question of how people categorize things is quite interesting.

defining features

A set of features that define membership in a category, such that all members of that category (and no nonmembers of that category) have all of those features. For example, the defining features of the category "triangle" might be (1) a two-dimensional figure that is (2) composed of three straight lines with (3) each end of each line joined to an end of one of the other lines.

The intuitively obvious answer is that people classify a sparrow as a "bird" because it has features that all members of the bird category share. We'll refer to this as the **defining-features** account of categorization: If the object in question has all the defining features of a category, it must be a member of that category; if the object lacks one or more of these characteristics, it must be something else (Medin, 1989). For example, to be a member of the category "bird" an object might have to be a living thing that flies, sings, lays eggs, and nests in trees. From this standpoint, categorizing an object is simply a matter of learning and applying the right set of defining features (see Figure 8.4).

As is often the case, the intuitively obvious answer is inadequate. The defining-features account of categorization works fine for mathematical categories such as "triangle," but it breaks down for natural objects. Take the category "vehicle," for example. What are the defining features of a vehicle? Something that moves along the ground, has wheels, and can transport people? That applies well to cars and trucks, but what about monorail trains and snowmobiles, which many would describe as vehicles but which don't run on wheels? What about inline skates, which have all of those "defining" features but which most people would not describe as a vehicle? Research on natural categories such as birds, vehicles, furniture, and games demonstrates that people cannot agree on just what constitutes the defining features of a natural category (Malt & Smith, 1984; Rosch & Mervis, 1975).

Most natural categories have *fuzzy boundaries*. For example, in Figure 8.5 you can see a series of objects within the fuzzy boundaries of the category "cup." In an experiment by Labov (1973), people were presented with a set of these objects, such as objects 1 through 4 in the figure, and were required to name each object as it was presented. As the ratio of width to depth increased (as the object appeared wider), subjects were increasingly likely to reject the "cup" label and categorize the object as a "bowl." But the crossover point was gradual rather than fixed. Subjects who began at the "cup" end of the series (object 1) usually called the object labelled 3 a cup, and a significant number of them also confidently categorized object 4 as a cup. Other subjects, who started at the "bowl" end of the series, almost always called the object labelled 4 a bowl and usually called object 3 a bowl as well. One implication of these results is that category members have typical features that are characteristic of the category rather than fixed defining features.

FIGURE 8.4
Natural Categories Do Not Have Defining Features

According to the defining-features account, all members of a category (and no nonmembers) share a set of defining features. This account works well for certain artificial categories (e.g., geometric forms) but fails for most everyday categories such as birds, furniture, or games. The problem is that members of most categories don't share any unique set of defining features. All of the objects shown here are birds, for example, but they don't all share the same set of "defining" features. (Based on Smith, 1989.)

Properties	Generic bird	Robin	Sandpiper	Vulture	Chicken	Penguin
Flies regularly	+	+	+	+	–	–
Sings	+	+	+	–	–	–
Lays eggs	+	+	+	+	+	+
Is small	+	+	+	–	–	–
Nests in trees	+	+	–	+	–	–

Does this monorail train fit into your category for "vehicle"? If so, what "defining features" does it share with other members of the category?

Family Resemblance Another way to think about the idea of typical features is in terms of what Rosch and Mervis (1975) called **family resemblance.** Members of the same category usually share some of a set of characteristic features, but it isn't necessary for each member to have them all. Within an extended human family there may be a characteristic drooping nose, close-set beady eyes, receding hairlines, and a prominent cleft chin. Cousin Theodore may lack the cleft chin or the beady eyes, but he could still possess a family resemblance in his drooping nose and balding pate that would enable outsiders to identify him as a member of that family. For the category "vehicle," people know that a monorail train doesn't have wheels, and it's not shaped like a car, but in other senses it fits the category so most people agree that a monorail is a vehicle (albeit a somewhat atypical one).

The degree of family resemblance is determined by how many of the characteristic features of the category an object possesses. Again, members of a category share some of a set of characteristic features, but it's unlikely that any single member will have them all. If a given object has most of the family features, it will be seen as a good member of the category; if an object has only a few, it will be seen as a poor member of the category. For North Americans, a car has most of the basic features of the category "vehicle"; an elevator does not. A robin has most of the features of "bird"; an ostrich or a flamingo has just a few. Through the notion of family resemblance, we can begin to see how natural categories achieve their fuzzy status. There is no absolute set of criteria

family resemblance
The idea that categories are defined by a set of characteristic features, which category members share in varying degrees; each member of the category will have some but not necessarily all of these features.

Critical Thinking

Although categories are usually adaptive, can you think of any instance in which categorizing an object or a person might not be adaptive?

| 1 | 2 | 3 | 4 |

FIGURE 8.5

Fuzzy Category Boundaries

Are all of these objects members of the category "cup"? Labov (1973) discovered that as the width of the object increased, people were more likely to label it as a "bowl." But the cup category boundary was fuzzy rather than fixed: When the objects were presented from 1 to 4, a significant number of people confidently judged that the fourth object was a cup. (From Goldstein, 1994.)

Members of the same family often share physical features, creating a family resemblance, but it's unlikely that any single member of the family will have them all.

for what constitutes a vehicle or a bird; there are only good and poor examples of a class of objects that share at least some of a set of features (Rosch et al., 1976).

Do People Store Category Prototypes?

The concept of family resemblance, combined with the idea that there are good and poor members of a category, leads naturally to the concept of a *prototype*. In this context, a **prototype** is the best or most representative member of a category. For most Canadians, a robin is close to the prototype for the category "bird"; an apple resembles the prototype for "fruit." Some psychologists believe that we store abstract representations of category prototypes in long-term memory and use them to help decide category membership. If an object, say a small fuzzy creature with a beak, is similar to the prototype for the category "bird," then we assume that the object must be a bird (Homa, 1984).

Reference to stored prototypes is not the only way people can classify things into categories. We can also store memories of all of the category examples (or **category exemplars**) that we encounter. To decide whether a new object is a member of a specific category, we might compare the object to all of these stored examples (or to a sample of them from memory) rather than to a single prototype. If the object is similar to many examples in a particular category, then we would categorize the object as a member of that category (see Figure 8.6). You should note the main difference between prototype and exemplar views of categorization: In prototype theory, you compare the object to one thing—the stored prototype; in the exemplar view, there is no single stored prototype and the object is compared to many things—the category exemplars.

Whether prototypes or exemplars are used in categorization is currently unknown, although many cognitive psychologists favour the exemplar view (Hintzman, 1986; Jacoby & Brooks, 1984; Medin & Shaffer, 1978; Nosofsky, 1992). One reason for preferring the exemplar view is that people know a lot about the individual members of a category. For example, people know about what features tend to go together—such as the fact that small birds are more likely to sing than large birds—and this kind of knowledge is more easily explained by theories proposing that we store exemplars (because a single prototype could not represent, say, the relationship between size and singing in birds). Another reason for favouring the exemplar account is that the number of categories is boundless because we can make up a category (and judge how well particular items fit that category) on the spot (e.g., "things to save if your house catches fire"; "foods that are good barbecued") (Barsalou, 1983). It's difficult to

prototype
The best or most representative member of a category (such as robin for the category "bird").

category exemplars
Specific examples of category members that are stored in long-term memory.

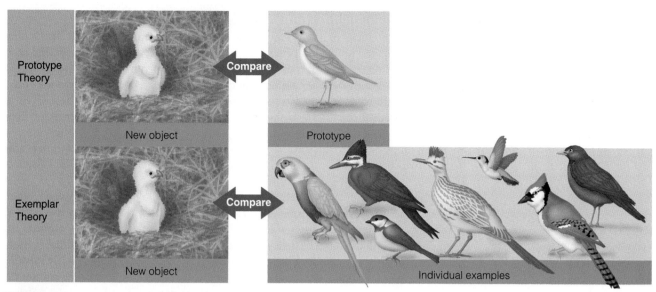

FIGURE 8.6

Prototypes versus Exemplars

How do we decide whether an object is a member of a particular category? According to prototype theory, we compare the object to a stored representation of the abstract "best" example of the category (a generic bird). If the new object is similar to the prototype, it is assigned to the prototype's category. Exemplar theories of categorization propose instead that we compare the new object to the individual examples of the category that have been stored in memory. Category membership is based on the summed similarity between the new object and the exemplars.

imagine that we have abstracted and stored an ideal prototype for every possible category. Also, prototypes are supposed to be quite stable, changing only gradually as a result of experience, but studies have shown that categorization judgments are greatly affected by recent exposure to exemplars. For example, research at McMaster University has shown that physicians are more likely to diagnose an ambiguous set of symptoms as a particular disease if they have recently encountered (or read about) a case of that disease (Hatala et al., 1999).

Given the flexibility of the human mind, it seems likely that people can perform categorization in more than one way. Sometimes we may form prototypes; other times we may rely on rules for deciding category membership; and in many situations we may appeal only to category exemplars (e.g., Erickson & Kruschke, 1998; Smith et al., 1998; Whittlesea et al., 1994).

Concept Summary

DEFINING CATEGORY MEMBERSHIP

View of Categorization	Basis for Categorization	Example
Defining features	Presence of certain features that define membership in the category.	Amiko knows that a particular shape is a triangle because it has all the features that define a triangle, such as three straight lines joined at their ends.
Family resemblance	The degree to which category members share certain core features. A prototype is the most representative member of a category.	James knows that a robin is a bird because it has several features that are characteristic of birds. In North America, "robin" might be considered the prototype for the category "bird."
Exemplars	All category examples (category exemplars) that we encountered in the past are used for categorization.	Sehar knows that a robin is a bird because it matches fairly closely so many of the examples of birds stored in her memory.

The Hierarchical Structure of Categories

Virtually any object or event can be described at numerous levels of abstraction, ranging from very broad and general categorizations to very narrow and specific categorizations. Consider the class of "living things." Under the umbrella of "living things," there are categories such as "animals" and "plants"; under "animals" there are "cats" (and other animals); under "cats" there are "Siamese cats," and so on. These levels of description are hierarchical, in that they differ from one another in terms of their degree of inclusion. The more general the level, the more inclusive it is—the category "living things" is more inclusive (i.e., includes more members) than the category "animals," which is in turn more inclusive than the category "cats" (Murphy & Lassaline, 1997).

Not all levels in the hierarchy of categories are psychologically equivalent. When people refer to an object during an everyday conversation, they tend to use what is called its **basic-level category** name (see Figure 8.7). When a furry feline saunters by, you typically call it a cat (a basic-level category term), not a thing or an animal (a more general, or *superordinate*, category) or a Siamese seal point (a more specific, or *subordinate*, category). Basic-level category terms tend to be short words, yet they communicate a lot of useful and predictive information (Markman & Wisniewski, 1997; Rosch et al., 1976). For example, in most situations the term "cat" provides just the right amount of relevant information: People know you're talking about a medium-sized, four-legged pet that likely has certain characteristic features and behaviours (much more information than would be provided if you used the nondescriptive "animal"), but you haven't burdened the conversation with a needless amount of detail. Typically, people use subordinate terms only when doing so provides additional information that is important in the conversational context (e.g., if there is something important about the cat being a Siamese).

Rosch and her colleagues found that when people were asked to list the distinguishing features of superordinate categories (such as "living things"), they generated only a few features. (Try it yourself: List the properties that characterize "living things.") At the basic level, many more properties were generated, and the generated properties tended to be ones that most subordinate members of the category share (i.e., many of the characteristics of cats are shared by most varieties of cats) (Rosch et

basic-level categories

The level in a category hierarchy that most efficiently provides a lot of useful and predictive information; the basic level is usually an intermediate level in a category hierarchy.

FIGURE 8.7

Category Hierarchies

Most things can be described at a variety of levels of abstraction, ranging from very broad and general category terms (such as "living thing") to very narrow and specific terms (such as "Siamese seal-point cat"). When people refer to something during normal conversation, they often use its intermediate, or *basic-level,* category label. In most everyday contexts, we would refer to an animal like the one depicted in the figure as a "cat" rather than a "living thing" or an "18-year-old Siamese cat who likes salmon."

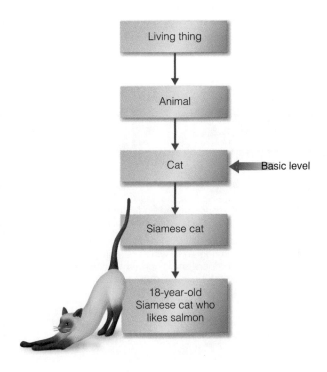

Living thing

↓

Animal

↓

Cat ← Basic level

↓

Siamese cat

↓

18-year-old Siamese cat who likes salmon

al., 1976). It's of interest to note that basic-level categories are also the category names that children first learn to use. It is through basic-level categorization that the adaptive mind most efficiently cuts the world into useful and informative slices.

Test Yourself 8.2

Check your knowledge about how people form categories by answering the following questions. (You will find the answers in Appendix B.)

1. For each of the following statements, decide on the category term that seems most appropriate. Choose from the following: category exemplars; defining features; family resemblance; prototype.
   a. It must be a bird because all birds (and no nonbirds) have wings, feathers, and a beak. _____
   b. It must be a bird because it looks like most of the other birds that I've seen. _____
   c. It must be a bird because it has several features that are typical of birds.
   _____
   d. It must be a bird because it looks a lot like a robin. _____
2. When people refer to an object during normal conversation, they tend to use what kind of category descriptor?
   a. Superordinate ("look, it's an object on the planet Earth")
   b. Basic level ("look, it's a cat")
   c. Subordinate ("look, it's a seal-point Siamese")
   d. Functional ("look, it's something to cuddle")

SOLVING PROBLEMS 6d, SIM 7

Learning Goals

1. Be able to list the steps in the IDEAL problem-solving technique.
2. Describe factors that influence how a problem is identified and defined.
3. Understand the distinction between algorithms and heuristics as problem-solving strategies, and learn about several commonly used problem-solving heuristics.
4. Appreciate the importance of looking back and assessing how well a problem was solved for improving future problem solving.

IN THIS SECTION we'll consider some of the thought processes people use when they solve problems. Obviously, problem solving is an extremely adaptive skill. When you're faced with a problem, such as how to get your car started in the morning, there is a goal, a running motor, and some uncertainty about how to reach that goal. To study the solution process, psychologists often use problems like the following:

> It's early morning, still dark, and you're trying to get dressed. Your 2-month-old baby, snuggled in her crib at the foot of the bed, sleeps peacefully after a night of sustained wailing. You can't turn on the light—she'll wake up for sure—but your five pairs of black socks and four pairs of blue socks are unpaired and mixed up in the drawer. You don't care what colour you wear today, but you want them to match. How many single socks do you need to take out of the drawer to guarantee a pair of matching colours?

Notice there is a goal (selecting a pair of matching socks), and it's not immediately obvious how to attain that goal. Psychologists call this a **well-defined problem** (even though you may have no idea how to solve it) because there is a well-defined starting

well-defined problem
A problem with a clear starting point and a fully specified goal.

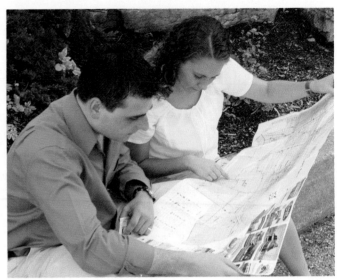

Certain kinds of problems are well defined, such as trying to find the correct route on a map. Other problems are ill defined and may not even have a solution. Can you decipher the true meaning of the artwork on the left?

ill-defined problem
A problem, such as "becoming a better person," for which the starting point and goal cannot be clearly specified.

point and a well-defined goal (i.e., with regard to the problem, you know exactly where you are starting out and you know exactly what goal you want to achieve). Other kinds of problems do not have a clearly defined starting point or a clearly defined goal, and these are called **ill-defined problems.** Maybe, for example, you'd like to become a better person. This can be described as a problem, with a starting point and a goal, but it would probably be difficult to provide an exact specification of either so the problem is ill defined.

Most of the research done on problem solving has examined performance on well-defined problems, such as our sock problem. We'll focus on well-defined problems in this section, but ill-defined problems can be tackled with some of the same strategies. It's believed that ill-defined problems may sometimes require unique cognitive processes (Jausovec, 1997), but generally the same psychological processes are assumed to operate in the vast majority of problem-solving settings.

The IDEAL Problem Solver

Let's start by considering a set of guidelines that highlight the psychological processes relevant to problem solving. These guidelines were developed by psychologists John Bransford and Barry Stein and are recommended in their book *The Ideal Problem Solver* (1993). Bransford and Stein use the letters of the acronym IDEAL to stand for the five major steps that underlie effective problem solving. These steps are briefly described here and are summarized in the Concept Summary table.

1. *Identify* the problem. Before you can solve a problem, you need to recognize that there is, in fact, a problem that needs solving. Strange knocking sounds, little spots of oil, and uneven acceleration are signs of car problems, but they need to be recognized as symptoms before the appropriate diagnosis and repairs can begin.

2. *Define*, or represent, the problem information in the clearest and most efficient way. Not only is it important to define the goal—What exactly are you trying to achieve?—it's also important to conceptualize the problem information in ways that will make it easier for you to generate effective problem-solving strategies. The ticket-scalping problem discussed at the beginning of the chapter is difficult because most people don't describe it to themselves as a situation in which Wayne made two separate ticket transactions. They tend to think about just one pair of tickets, so the cost of the second transaction is applied incorrectly to the first.

3. *Explore* a variety of problem strategies. Once you have identified the problem, defined the goal, and developed an appropriate representation of the information

you have to work with, it's time to try to move forward toward a possible solution. To do this, you must decide on a strategy. Most solution strategies amount to "rules of thumb." They don't guarantee a solution, but they usually move you closer to your goal.

4. *Act* on the problem strategy that you chose in step 3. Work through the solution strategy, and as part of the process try to anticipate any dead ends or obstacles that might prevent you from reaching the goal.

5. *Look back* and evaluate the effectiveness of your selected strategy. Have you in fact solved the problem? It's important to identify and correct any errors that have occurred before moving on and trying something new.

If you follow these five problem-solving guidelines, you will approximate the IDEAL problem solver (Bransford & Stein, 1993). Now let's consider some of the processes involved in greater detail.

Identifying and Defining: Problem Representation

To identify and define a problem correctly, it's essential to represent the problem information in an appropriate way. *Problem representation* refers to your understanding of the starting point, the goal, the difference between them, and the kinds of actions that are appropriate for moving from the starting point to the goal.

Take the sock problem, for example. The correct answer is three. There are only two colours, so with three samples you will get two that match. If you're like most people, you let the math get in your way. Did you start worrying about the four-to-five ratio of blue-to-black? Did you consider calculating some sort of probability? To solve this problem, you must pay attention to the right problem components—you need to see the problem in the right way. Most people fail to detect which information is relevant and which is not. They get hung up with ratios and probabilities and the like. Let's consider another example.

> Dr. Adams is interrupted from his daily rounds by the arrival of a new patient, a child, who has been seriously injured in a fall. "My God!" Adams cries. "It's my son!" Moments later, Dr. Henderson arrives, sees the injured child, and sobs, "My son, my dear son!" Is it a tragic mix-up?

Concept Summary

THE IDEAL PROBLEM SOLVER

State of Problem Solving	Description	Example
Identify	Recognize that a problem exists.	In the basement, Greg notices a small amount of water underneath the washing machine.
Define	Represent the problem information in the most efficient way.	Greg notices that there is water dripping from the ceiling, just under where the bathroom is. He tests and confirms the hypothesis that the shower upstairs is leaking.
Explore	Consider possible solutions.	Greg considers showering at the gym for the rest of the semester; then he considers calling a plumber; then he considers caulking the base of the shower stall.
Act	Employ the chosen strategy.	Greg caulks the base of the shower stall.
Look back	Evaluate the effectiveness of the chosen strategy.	Greg notices that the pool of water is gone and that the ceiling has stopped leaking.

You probably solved this one almost immediately, but it demonstrates the point. The two doctors are the mother and the father of the injured child. The gender connotations of the word "doctor," along with the fact that the two doctors have different last names, lead some people to represent this problem inappropriately, thereby making it difficult. (It is likely that this problem stumped people more often a few decades ago, when the gender connotation of "doctor" was stronger than it is today.) The point to appreciate is that we often make problems difficult for ourselves by making inaccurate assumptions.

Functional Fixedness   The two-doctor problem illustrates a common obstacle to correct problem representation. People often allow their preconceptions and prejudices to lock them into an incorrect view of the problem information (Bassok et al., 1995; Dixon & Moore, 1997). Consider another example, illustrated in Figure 8.8, called the Maier two-string problem (after Maier, 1931). Imagine you are standing in a room with two strings hanging from the ceiling. The strings are hung such a distance apart that, when holding one of the strings, you cannot reach the other. Using only a pair of pliers, which happen to be sitting on a table in the room, can you tie the strings together?

This is a difficult problem because most people have a certain set, or fixed, way of viewing the function of pliers. The solution is to tie the pliers to one of the strings and swing it, like a pendulum, while you hold on to the other string. Solving the problem requires you to change the way that you normally think about pliers. Pliers are designed for gripping, but they can also serve as pendulum weights.

Psychologists use the term **functional fixedness** to refer to this tendency to see objects, and their functions, in certain fixed and typical ways. Doctors are men, pliers are for gripping, and so on. Functional fixedness is an obstacle to problem solving because it prevents you from recognizing the problem-solving tools that are present in the situation. Now try solving the problem illustrated in Figure 8.9. You enter a room in which a candle, a box of tacks, some matches, and a hammer lie on a table. You are told to mount the candle on the wall so that it will burn properly, using only the objects on the table. Work on the problem for a while; we'll return to its solution shortly.

Let's stop for a moment and think about the adaptive significance of functional fixedness. How can such a tendency possibly be adaptive? Wouldn't it be better to con-

Critical Thinking

Think back to the linguistic relativity hypothesis we discussed earlier. Do you think the "doctor" problem supports the hypothesis?

functional fixedness

The tendency to see objects, and their functions, in certain fixed and typical ways, and thereby to fail to see alternative uses of objects that would enable one to solve a problem.

FIGURE 8.8

The Maier Two-String Problem

Can you figure out a way to tie these two strings together? Notice there's a pair of pliers on the table.

FIGURE 8.9
The Duncker Candle Problem
Using only the materials shown, figure out a way to mount the candle on the wall so it will burn properly.

sider all possible object uses? Well, how many possible uses does each object have? If you think about this for a moment, you can see that it would be very inefficient if we went around thinking about every possible use for every object. Most of the time, if you view objects in fixed ways or use fixed strategies that have worked well in the past, you're likely to be successful. After all, pliers usually do solve problems having to do with holding and gripping. Generally, relying on well-established habits of perception and thought (sometimes called **mental sets**) is an efficient and effective problem-solving strategy. Sometimes, however, such habits of thought get in the way of solving problems, as in the problems we've been considering.

Did you solve the candle-mounting problem? The correct solution is to dump the tacks out of the box, mount the box on the wall with some of the tacks, and then stand the candle in the box (Duncker, 1945). The problem is difficult because most people see the box only as a device for holding the tacks, not as a potential problem-solving tool. They become *fixed* in their views about the *functions* of objects and thereby fail to identify and define all the available problem tools correctly.

mental sets
Well-established habits of perception and thought used to solve problems; typically efficient and effective, but sometimes make problem solving more difficult.

Exploring and Acting: Problem Strategies

It's important to represent a problem and the potential mechanisms for solving it correctly (e.g., by avoiding functional fixedness and unhelpful mental sets), but problem representation alone cannot guarantee a solution. You also need an arsenal of problem *strategies*, techniques that allow you to move toward a problem solution. There are two large classes of problem-solving strategies: *algorithms* and *heuristics*.

Algorithms For some well-defined problems you can use **algorithms,** which are step-by-step rules or procedures that guarantee a solution. You can use algorithms to solve simple math problems, for example, because there are fixed rules for addition, subtraction, and so on. As long as you use the rules properly, you will always arrive at the correct solution. Solving anagrams, such as MBLOPRE, is another case in point. There are seven letters in the word, which means there are 5040 possible combinations of the letters. If you systematically work out each of the possible sequences, you will eventually solve the PROBLEM. But it could take a long time.

algorithms
Step-by-step rules or procedures that, if applied correctly, guarantee a problem solution eventually.

Computers are often programmed to use algorithms because computers can perform lots of simple transformations very quickly. But algorithms are not always practical strategies for problem solution, even for computers. Consider chess, for example. In principle, it would be possible to use algorithms to play chess—the computer would simply need to consider all the possible consequences of a particular move. But practically, even the most advanced computers cannot examine all the possible outcomes in a chess game; they can examine only some of them. There are some 10^{40} possible game sequences, so even if a computer could calculate a game in under one-millionth of one-thousandth of a second, it would still require 10^{21} centuries to examine all the game possibilities (Best, 1989). Another problem with algorithms is that they work only for certain kinds of well-defined problems. There is no algorithm, for example, for figuring out how to be happy, choose an appropriate career, or create a great Web site.

Heuristics   In cases in which it's not feasible to use an algorithm, it's possible to use **heuristics,** which are problem-solving "rules of thumb." To solve an anagram, especially one with many letters, it's not expedient to use an algorithmic approach (e.g., the 5040 possible letter sequences for a 7-letter anagram). Instead, you use heuristics. For example, you know that English words don't usually begin with MB, or end with BL, so you don't even check out those possibilities. In other words, you can use your knowledge about English words to make guesses about elements of the most likely solutions. Heuristics are extremely adaptive problem-solving tools because they often open the door to a quick and accurate solution. In natural environments, quick solutions can mean the difference between life and death. An organism cannot spend its time wrapped in thought, systematically working through a long list of solution possibilities. Instead, it's adaptive for the organism to make informed guesses, as long as those guesses are usually at least close to correct. Below we describe some commonly used problem-solving heuristics.

Means–Ends Analysis   One common heuristic that people use to solve problems is **means–ends analysis,** which attacks problems by devising *means,* or actions, that are designed to reduce the gap between the current starting point and the desired goal, or *end* (Newell & Simon, 1972). Usually, this strategy requires breaking the problem down into a series of simpler subgoals, in which the appropriate means to an end are more immediately visible. Let's assume that Peter, an underachieving undergraduate, wants to start a relationship with Jill, the brightest student in his psychology class. Obviously, asking Jill out immediately is unlikely to succeed, so Peter breaks the problem down into more manageable components.

First, he reasons, he'll impress her by making insightful comments during lectures. He now has a new goal, acting intelligently in class, for which there is relatively

heuristics

The rules of thumb we often use to solve problems; heuristics are quick and easy, but they do not guarantee a correct solution.

means–ends analysis

A problem-solving heuristic that involves devising actions, or means, that reduce the distance between the current starting point and the desired end (the goal).

People use heuristics—"general rules of thumb"—when they play chess because the human mind cannot examine all the possible moves and their consequences during a game. Even chess masters do not consider a huge number of potential moves; instead, they usually consider only two or three moves. What makes them masters is that the few moves they consider are among the best possible moves in the given situation.

straightforward means—he needs to study so he can master the material. If he is successful (everyone now thinks he is an amazingly bright guy), he devises a new subgoal: making some kind of sustained contact with Jill. Forming a small study group would be a good means to that end, he surmises, so he approaches the recently impressed Jill with the idea. Notice the key ingredients of the problem-solving strategy: Establish where you are, figure out where you want to be, and then devise a means for effectively getting from here to there. Often, as in Peter's case, means–ends analysis is made more effective by working systematically through a series of subgoals.

Working Backward Another effective heuristic is **working backward**—starting mentally at the goal and moving back toward the starting point. Suppose someone asked you to generate an anagram. How would you proceed? Would you create a random set of letters and then see if they can be rearranged to form a word? Of course not. You would start with the solution, the word, and work backward by mixing up the known sequence.

Let's consider another example. You're working on a biology project tracking the growth of bacteria in a petri dish. You know that this particular strain of bacteria doubles every 2 hours. You discover that the petri dish is exactly full after 12 hours. After how many hours was the petri dish exactly half full? To solve this one, it's better to work backward. If the dish is full after 12 hours, and it takes 2 hours for the bacteria to double, what did the dish look like 2 hours ago? This turns out to be the answer, which is attained fairly easily by working backward.

Searching for Analogies Another useful heuristic for problem solving is **searching for analogies.** If you can see a resemblance between the current problem and some problem that you solved in the past, you can often quickly obtain a solution. Let's test your analogy-searching skills. Imagine that a woman buys a horse for $60 and sells it for $70. Later, she buys the same horse back for $80 and sells it again for $90. How much money did she make in the horse-trading business? The attentive reader will not miss this one. It's a different version of the ticket-scalping problem that opened this chapter. If you see the relationship between the two problems, you're unlikely to suffer the same problem-solving pitfalls you encountered before.

Interestingly, people often fail to detect the relationship between a new problem and analogous past problems. For example, the dance-partner problem described in the Practical Solutions box should serve as an effective analogy for solving the mutilated checkerboard problem, but most people fail to see the connection when the two problems are presented in succession. In research conducted at Carleton University, Gick and McGarry (1992) showed people how to solve the dance-partner problem and later asked them to solve the checkerboard problem. Very few solved the checkerboard problem, even though they all understood the solution to the dance-partner problem; they failed to make the connection between the two problems. It is important, when working on a problem, to look for analogies with other problems you have solved in the past, yet people often fail to do so.

Looking Back and Learning

The ideal problem solver identifies and defines the problem, seeks the best problem representation, and explores and acts on problem strategies. But the process is incomplete unless you also *look back* and *learn* from your experience (Bransford & Stein, 1993). The ideal problem solver "debugs" performance in an effort to maximize the information gained.

By analyzing your performance in detail and noting your mistakes as well as your successes, you can determine whether your strategy helped solve one kind of problem but not another. Through an after-the-fact analysis, you can also gain insight into *why* a particular heuristic failed or succeeded. Look and learn from your experience so that the next time you can do better still.

working backward
A problem-solving heuristic that involves mentally starting at the goal and mentally moving backward toward the starting point to see how the goal can be reached.

searching for analogies
A problem-solving heuristic that involves trying to find a connection between the current problem and some previous problem you have solved successfully.

Practical Solutions

CHANGING HOW PROBLEMS ARE MENTALLY REPRESENTED

Changing the way a problem is represented is often a key step toward solving it. Indeed, for many problems the difficulty evaporates when the problem is properly construed. Unfortunately, however, it is often difficult to think about problems in appropriate ways. Consider the problem involving the checkerboard pattern shown in Figure 8.10.

You are given a checkerboard and 32 dominoes. Each domino covers exactly two adjacent squares on the board. Thus, the 32 dominoes can cover all 64 squares of the checkerboard. Now suppose two squares are cut off at diagonally opposite corners of the board. Can you cover all 62 squares with 31 dominoes? Work on it for a while, and pay attention to how you go about trying to find a solution.

Most people find this a very difficult problem. Now consider a different problem. One Saturday night 40 people—20 men and 20 women—went to a local country dance. The dance was a "contra dance," in which men and women face each other in lines. After a while, two women left, leaving 38 people to dance. Could the dance caller make arrangements so that the remaining people could all dance together in 19 male–female couples?

This problem is quite easy for most people to solve. They immediately realize that 20 men and 18 women cannot be divided into 19 mixed-sex couples. Now, did you notice any relationship between this dancing-partners problem and the mutilated checkerboard problem? In fact, the two problems are essentially identical (these are sometimes called "parity" problems; they are on a par with one another). Just substitute the word

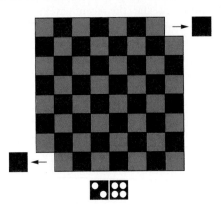

FIGURE 8.10
The Mutilated Checkerboard

In a complete checkerboard, 32 dominoes of the appropriate size will cover the 64 squares. Two diagonally opposite corners of this mutilated checkerboard have been removed. Could you place 31 dominoes on the board so that all of the 62 remaining squares are covered?

"woman" for black and the word "man" for red, and think of each domino as the pairing of a mixed-sex couple. Any domino covering two squares must cover one red square and one black square, just as any pair of different-sex dancers must consist of one woman and one man. Therefore, it is not possible to cover 62 squares (30 black and 32 red) with 31 dominoes.

When people work on the checkerboard problem, they usually focus on the mathematics of the problem (e.g., the number of squares per edge and so forth), which makes it difficult to solve. They rarely realize that the fact that each domino must cover one red and one black square is an important element of the problem. In contrast, the analogue of this important constraint is immediately obvious in the dance-partner problem. The trick, then, is to represent the problem in a way that makes what is relevant to the problem become obvious.

What factors promote successful transfer from one problem-solving situation to another? For one thing, people who have a great deal of experience in a particular area seem better able to draw connections across situations relevant to their expertise than do nonexperts. Experts are able to see what amounts to the deep structure or underlying principles of a problem, and they can therefore map one kind of problem to another by noting how the problems are similar in terms of their underlying principles (Novick, 1988).

It also helps if problem-solving hints are provided. In the checkerboard problem, if subjects are told to try using the dance-partner solution as a way of solving the checkerboard problem, performance improves significantly. Finally, it may even help transfer somewhat if your initial attempts at solving the first problem fail. Gick and McGarry (1992) showed that if people get stuck for a while before solving one problem and then find themselves stuck in a similar way while later working on an analogous problem, their current difficulty is likely to remind them of how they solved the first problem. Similarly, a series of studies at McMaster University by Needham and Begg (1991) showed that subjects were more likely to use the principles learned from one problem to solve a subsequent problem if they had actually worked on solving the first problem rather than merely been told how to solve it.

Test Yourself 8.3

Check your knowledge about problem solving by answering the following questions. (You will find the answers in Appendix B.)

1. Decide whether each of the following problems is well defined or ill defined. Justify your answer.
   a. Finding your way to a new restaurant in town: _____
   b. Receiving an A in your psychology course: _____
   c. Making your lab partner in chemistry fall madly in love with you:

   _____
   d. Baking a delicious cherry cheesecake: _____

2. Try to identify the problem-solving strategy at work in each of the following examples. Choose from the following terms: algorithm; means–ends analysis; working backward; searching for analogies.
   a. On the final exam Myka looks for connections between the physics problem on the test and the ones he solved while studying.

   _____

   b. Rachel needs a three-letter word that begins with R to complete the crossword puzzle. She mindlessly considers all possible two-letter combinations, placing them after R until she arrives at an acceptable word.

   _____

   c. Hector really needs an A in his philosophy class, but he has no idea what it takes. He decides to start by doing the assigned readings before each class. _____

   d. Courtney needs to generate a set of anagrams for a school project. To generate each anagram, she starts with a word and then scrambles the letters. _____

MAKING DECISIONS

Learning Goals

1. Learn about framing effects and their influence on decision making.
2. Understand the human tendency toward confirmation bias and how this bias can contribute to illusory correlations.
3. Learn about two common decision-making heuristics: representativeness and availability.
4. Be able to discuss the pros and cons of using heuristics.

WE TURN OUR ATTENTION now to the topic of **decision making,** which deals with the thought processes involved in evaluating and choosing from among a set of alternatives. Choosing almost always entails risk, because the wrong choice can have long-lasting unpleasant consequences, so it's in your interest to evaluate and select from among the alternatives wisely. Consider a doctor deciding whether or not to prescribe a risky drug that may save a patient but that may also have harmful side effects, or a student whose decisions about which courses to take may have life-long career implications. We make decisions virtually every moment of our waking lives, and some of them have substantial consequences.

Like problem solving, decision making is influenced by how you represent the alternatives in your mind and by the decision-making strategies you use. Let's examine how each of these processes affects the choices we make.

decision making

The thought processes involved in evaluating and choosing from among a set of alternatives; it usually involves some degree of risk.

The Framing of Decision Alternatives

framing

The way the alternatives in a decision-making situation are structured and described.

The way the alternatives are structured and described, called **framing,** can dramatically influence decision making. In a study by Tversky and Kahneman (1987), for example, subjects were asked to choose between two programs designed to combat a deadly disease: If program A is adopted, 200 people will be saved, whereas if program B is adopted, there is a one-in-three probability that 600 people will be saved and a two-in-three probability that no people will be saved. Which program would you choose? There is no right answer to this question—there are good arguments for and against each alternative—but about three-quarters of the subjects preferred the less risky (but potentially less rewarding) program A. Other subjects were asked to choose between the same two programs, but the programs were framed negatively (in terms of who will die). They were told that under program A 400 people will die, whereas under program B there is a one-in-three probability that nobody will die and a two-in-three probability that 600 people will die. This pair of alternatives is mathematically identical to the first pair, but when the question is framed in this way, three-quarters of the subjects preferred the more risky (but potentially more rewarding) program B.

In general, when people are confronted with decisions in ways that emphasize potential gains, they tend to avoid taking risks—they choose certainty or the best approximation to it. But if the choice is framed negatively, in terms of potential losses, people are much more likely to take a gamble to limit or avoid the loss. More generally, the way alternatives are structured and described often affects decisions. Framing effects are commonplace and are used by marketers and public relations firms. For example, people prefer beef that is labelled "75% lean" to beef that is labelled "25% fat" (Levin & Gaeth, 1988), and condoms are perceived as more effective if they are described as having a 95% success rate than if they are said to have a 5% failure rate (Linville et al., 1993). A study by McNeil et al. (1982) revealed analogous effects on decisions made by medical doctors. Thus, human decision making is not always rational, partly because our minds weigh information differently depending on how alternatives are framed (Kahneman et al., 1982).

Critical Thinking

Do you think problem solving is a part of decision making, or is decision making a part of problem solving?

Confirmation Bias and Illusory Correlations

confirmation bias

The tendency to emphasize hypothesis-confirming evidence when making decisions.

Suppose you were offered $100 if you could find out, just by asking a yes-or-no question, whether Jane is socially outgoing. What question would you ask? Think about it for a moment. Now, what if the task was to ask a yes/no question to find out if Jack is introverted? What question would you pose? If you are like most people, you'd ask Jane a question such as "Do you enjoy being the centre of attention?" and you'd ask Jack a question like "Do you like to spend a lot of time quietly by yourself?" That is, in each case you'd seek evidence that would confirm your hypothesis, as opposed to evidence that would disconfirm it. This is an example of **confirmation bias,** the tendency to emphasize hypothesis-confirming evidence when making decisions.

As another example of confirmation bias, Reisberg (2002) noted that roosters might believe that their crowing causes the sun to rise each morning (assuming roosters only crow at dawn, they would have lots and lots of evidence that every time they crow, up comes the sun). To do a better job of testing that hypothesis, the rooster must try NOT crowing some mornings, thereby seeking evidence that something else is responsible for the sunrise (and hence disconfirming his hypothesis). This example is amusing, but it illustrates a serious point: Our human tendency to focus on confirming evidence can lead us to make very poor judgments. For example, there is evidence that medical doctors show a confirmation bias when making diagnoses (e.g., Travis et al., 1989), thereby increasing the likelihood that they will falsely diagnose a condition as being what they initially hypothesized it was rather than as what it really is.

illusory correlation

Perception of a relationship between variables (e.g., handwriting and personality) that does not really exist.

Confirmation bias often leads to **illusory correlations,** perceptions of relationships between variables that do not really exist. In a classic study, Chapman and Chapman (1967) showed psychology students drawings done by psychiatric patients. Each drawing had a psychiatric diagnosis (e.g., schizophrenia, depression, paranoia,

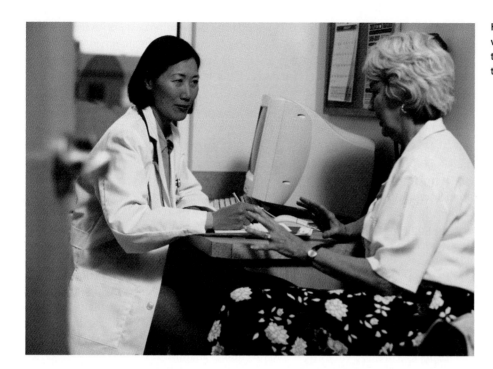

How doctors interpret treatment options, as well as how the information relevant to those treatments is framed, can critically influence the decision-making process.

etc.) attached to it. The students were asked to examine the drawings and determine whether there were any relationships between features or characteristics of drawings and patients' diagnoses. Sure enough, the students detected such relationships. For example, many of them noted that patients diagnosed with paranoia tended to draw faces with exaggerated or otherwise peculiar-looking eyes. What makes this interesting is that, unknown to the students, the researchers had paired the diagnostic labels and drawings randomly; that is, there was no relationship at all between the drawings and the diagnostic labels. Students perceived such relationships, however, because they tended to focus their attention on and remember cases in which, by chance alone, a drawing happened to confirm their hunches about the kinds of drawings patients with particular disorders would make.

Confirmation bias and illusory correlations are powerful influences on human thought. It is very likely that they play important roles in supporting superstitions and beliefs in various paranormal phenomena such as telepathy and astrology. Consider, for example, the pseudoscience of graphology, according to which a person's handwriting reveals important information about his or her personality. Scientific tests of graphology have failed to produce any compelling evidence in support of it, but many people persist in believing in it. In research at the University of Waterloo, King and Koehler (2000) provide evidence that confirmation bias and illusory correlations underlie this persistent belief. As another example, DiBattista and Shepherd (1993) proposed that confirmation bias and illusory correlations support exaggerated beliefs regarding the effects of sugar on children's activity levels.

Critical Thinking

Can you think of any of your own beliefs that might have arisen due to confirmation bias and illusory correlation?

Decision-Making Heuristics

People usually rely on heuristics, or rules of thumb, when making decisions, just as they do when solving problems. Heuristics simplify the decision-making process and often lead to correct judgments, but they sometimes lead to errors.

Representativeness When people are asked to estimate the likelihood that an object or event belongs to a particular class, they often rely on a rule of thumb called the **representativeness heuristic.** They arrive at their decision by comparing the object or event in question to their idea of the average, or prototypical, member of the class. The representativeness heuristic is similar to the idea, discussed earlier in this chapter, that

representativeness heuristic
The tendency to base judgments on similarity to an abstract ideal, expectation, or stereotype. For example, when deciding whether a sequence of coin-toss outcomes is random, people using the representativeness heuristic focus on how irregular the sequence looks, because they think short random sequences should look irregular.

people categorize perceptual objects by comparing them to prototypes, except that the representativeness heuristic is used when people make explicit judgments of probability. Suppose, for example, that you flip a coin six times in a row. Which of the following two sequences of heads (H) and tails (T) is more likely?

1. H H H T T T

2. H T T H T H

If you chose the second sequence as more likely, you're like most people. According to the laws of probability, however, the two outcomes are equally likely. Whether a coin comes up heads or tails has nothing to do with previous (or future) flips. The coin has no memory, and each flip is independent of the others. Nonetheless, people favour the second alternative because the first sequence clashes with their (mistaken) world-view of randomness. The first sequence just doesn't look the way people think the outcome of a random process should look—it's not *representative* of people's ideas of randomness—because it "looks too regular."

People frequently use the representativeness heuristic to make decisions in real-world settings. For example, clerks in stores use the type of products that a shopper buys as a way of judging age. If someone loads his or her shopping cart with products normally thought to be representative of an older consumer, the clerk's estimate of the shopper's age increases (McCall, 1994).

Using a heuristic such as representativeness is adaptive and beneficial most of the time, but it can lead to irrational decisions. Suppose that the public relations office at the University of Toronto randomly selected a faculty member to be interviewed for a newsletter. The faculty member selected is a man who is fairly short, slight, quiet, and somewhat shy, and who enjoys nature. Which do you think is more likely, that the man is a professor of Chinese studies or that he is a professor of psychology? Most people asked this question chose Chinese studies, because the man fits their stereotype of a Chinese studies scholar. But this is an illogical choice, because in Canada professors of psychology vastly outnumber professors of Chinese studies. The University of Toronto, for example, currently has approximately 100 professors in the Department of Psychology, but no Department of Chinese Studies (and the Department of East Asian Studies has only 17 faculty members). In choosing Chinese studies, people have failed to think about the *base rate,* or the proportion of times that an object or event is likely to occur in the population being sampled.

The representativeness heuristic also dupes people into committing what is called the *conjunction error.* Consider the following: Linda is 31 years old, single, outspoken, and very bright. She majored in philosophy. As a student she was deeply concerned with issues of discrimination and social justice and participated in demonstrations against logging. Which of the following alternatives is more likely?

1. Linda is a bank teller.

2. Linda is a bank teller and active in the feminist movement.

In a study conducted by Tversky and Kahneman (1983), 85% of the participants judged alternative 2 to be the more likely. Why? Because Linda's description is more representative of someone active in the feminist movement than it is of a bank teller. But think about it—how can the odds of two things happening together be higher than the odds of either of those events happening alone? Notice that the second alternative is a subset of the first alternative and therefore cannot be more likely. Consequently, it is illogical to choose option 2, but most people do so, presumably because it better fits (i.e., it is more representative of) their impression of Linda.

Availability   When asked to estimate the odds of some event occurring in the future, or the frequency with which it has occurred in the past, people usually rely on the **availability heuristic.** Imagine you're asked to estimate the likelihood that you will forget to turn off your alarm clock on Friday night. If you can easily remember lots of Saturday

availability heuristic

The tendency to base estimates of frequency or probability on the ease with which examples come to mind. For example, if you've just heard about a plane crash, your estimate of the likelihood of plane crashes may increase because the recent plane crash easily comes to mind.

mornings on which your sleep was interrupted by a blasting alarm, your estimate is likely to be high. You have relied on the availability of memories of relevant prior events as a basis for judging probability of a future event.

The availability heuristic is usually reliable: Compared to rare events, common events are more likely to come to mind and more likely to occur in the future, so availability is often a good basis for judging past frequency and for predicting future probability. But, as with the representativeness heuristic, in some situations this decision-making heuristic leads us astray. Which do you think is more common, English words that begin with the letter *K* or English words with *K* as their third letter? By now you're probably justly skeptical about your intuitive choice, but most naïve subjects judge that English words that begin with *K* are more likely (Tversky & Kahneman, 1973). In fact, English words that have *K* in the third position are about three times more common. Which do you think is more likely, someone dying from any kind of accident or someone dying from a stroke? Accidents, right? Nope. It's not even close. More than twice as many people die from stroke than from all kinds of accidents (Slovic et al., 1982). People make the error because examples of the incorrect alternative are more likely to come to mind. It's easier to search your memory for words by first letter, and accidental deaths get much more publicity than deaths due to stroke and so are more memorable.

The Value of Heuristics

We've briefly reviewed evidence of the way reliance on the representativeness and availability heuristics sometimes leads human decision makers astray. Representativeness and availability are not the only heuristics people use when making decisions. Cognitive psychologists have identified several other "mental shortcuts" that decision makers often use and that sometimes lead to erroneous judgments (for some interesting examples, see Buehler et al., 1994; Kunda, 1999; Sharpe & Adair, 1993). What are we to make of such an imperfect decision maker? Well, imperfect as heuristics are, there are several points worth making in their favour. First, the use of heuristics leads to errors under some circumstances but, as Tversky and Kahneman (1974) argued, they are usually quite effective. Second, heuristics are economical. Optimal, or rational, decision making can be a complex, time-consuming activity; indeed, in many situations it is not feasible to make a perfectly rational decision (e.g., the needed data may not be on hand, so we are forced to rely on availability, or the number of potential steps may be too large to allow for a systematic consideration of all of them). Think back to our discussion of perceptual illusions in Chapter 4. Just because your visual system can be tricked by an illusion doesn't mean it's a bad system. Indeed, it is precisely the strengths of the visual system (such as its use of top-down processing) that leads it to create illusions under some conditions. Similarly, when you make decisions you rely on adaptive systems that serve you very well in the majority of situations, even though they sometimes lead you to make errors (Gigerenzer, 1997).

Moreover, the fact that people often make errors in certain situations (as when they judge that Linda is more likely to be a feminist bank teller than she is to be a bank teller) does not mean that people are unable to think rationally. Rather, it appears that people often fail to think about problems or decisions in ways that would lead them to access and use the appropriate rational decision-making rules. In the "Linda is a bank teller" example, for instance, people know that there are more bank tellers in the world than feminist bank tellers. The mistake is made because people focus their thoughts on a single case, Linda, and base their decision solely on representativeness, rather than

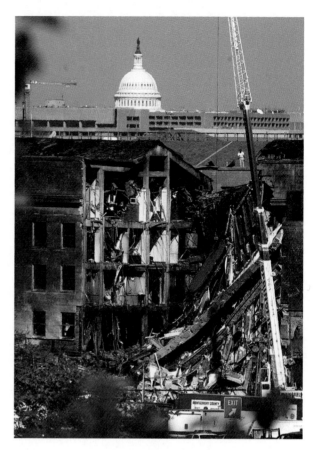

People are much more likely to worry about terrorism if a recently publicized disaster (such as the attack on the Pentagon) is fresh and available in their minds.

Critical Thinking

Try to come up with some examples in your own life in which applying the availability heuristic caused you to change your behaviour in some way.

Concept Summary

DECISION-MAKING HEURISTICS

Heuristic	Description	Example
Representativeness	We arrive at a decision by comparing the object or event in question to our image of the average member of potential categories.	Juan meets his new college roommate, Bryce, who is 208 cm tall and very athletic looking. Juan assumes that Bryce is a basketball player, probably on scholarship.
Availability	We estimate the odds of some event occurring based on the ease with which examples come to mind.	Stella reads so much in the newspaper about car accidents that she believes her chances of dying in a car accident are greater than her chances of dying from a stroke.

thinking about probabilities in general (Fiedler, 1988; Gigerenzer, 1996). Under conditions that encourage people to pay attention to considerations such as probabilities and base rates, they often do so. Note, too, that people differ widely from one another in the extent to which they rely on heuristics in situations in which doing so leads to errors (Stanovich, 1999). Also, formal training in statistics and rational decision making can lessen inappropriate reliance on heuristics (Gebotys & Claxton, 1989; Kosonen & Winne, 1995; Nisbett, 1993).

It is also worth noting that apparent errors in reasoning may sometimes be caused by reliance on linguistic conventions rather than by irrationality. Earlier in this chapter, we mentioned that good language users follow certain conversational conventions or maxims, such as "be informative." In view of such maxims, some subjects may reinterpret some decision-making questions. For example, the choice "Linda is a bank teller" versus "Linda is a bank teller and an active feminist" may be understood as a choice between "Linda is a bank teller who is *not* a feminist" and "Linda is a bank teller who *is* a feminist." If so, then there is nothing irrational about selecting the latter alternative (Slugoski & Wilson, 1998). It is clear, however, that such linguistic conventions don't account for all of the reasoning and decision-making errors described in this chapter (Stolarz-Fantino et al., 1996).

Test Yourself 8.4

Check your knowledge about decision making by picking the term that best fits the following statements. Choose your answer from the following: framing; representativeness heuristic; availability heuristic; confirmation bias; illusory correlations. (You will find the answers in Appendix B.)

1. Matt used to fly to visit his parents during the holiday break, but after seeing nonstop coverage of a gory plane accident, he now chooses to drive. _____

2. Chantelle is a firm believer in the herb echinacea; whenever she has a cold she takes lots of echinacea and she always gets over the cold within a few days. _____

3. Larry, a broker, used to tell people that his mutual fund lost money only 3 times in the last 10 years. Now he tells them that the fund has made money in 7 of the last 10 years. He's noticed a marked improvement in sales of the fund. _____

4. Jing has a theory that extroverted people tend to be less bright than introverted people, which she supports with numerous examples of boisterous dullards and reserved scholars. _____

5. Kelley sleeps until noon, parties at night, and carries around a big backpack the rest of the time. Her neighbour Eileen assumes that Kelley must be a university student. _____

Solving the Adaptive Problems

In this chapter, we've discussed how people use their higher mental processes to communicate, categorize, solve problems, and make decisions. Each of these abilities illustrates how the mind draws on its adaptive tool kit to thrive in the human environment.

First, how do we communicate with others? One of the defining characteristics of the human species is that we have a complex, generative linguistic grammar—a system of rules and procedures for combining arbitrary symbols in meaningful ways to express thoughts, feelings, and needs to others. A grammar consists of rules and procedures for combining sounds (phonology), for expressing particular meanings in words (semantics), and for constructing sentences from words to express complex messages (syntax). To understand how language works, it is important to distinguish between the surface structure of a sentence—the literal ordering of words—and its deep structure, which taps the underlying representation of meaning. Human communication also relies on mutual knowledge, or pragmatics, to interpret statements or requests that would otherwise be ambiguous or anomalous (such as, "Can you pass the salt?").

Are we born with a natural blueprint for language, or does language develop exclusively as a product of experience? The sequence of language development is quite universal—it doesn't matter where you look in the world, babies show similar milestones in language development. This and other findings have led most researchers to conclude that people are born ready to learn language in the same way they are born ready to learn to walk.

Second, how do we categorize objects in our world? When people categorize, or put objects or events into meaningful groups, they create a world that is more sensible and predictable. Categorization skills enable us to infer invisible properties about objects—if X is a member of category Y, then X will have at least some of the characteristics of category Y members. As a result, we can make accurate predictions about the things we encounter. How do people identify category membership? Research suggests that the mind uses "family resemblance" to identify the category to which an object or event belongs. Members of the same category tend to share at least some of a set of basic or core features of that category. Categories are remarkably flexible; their boundaries are fuzzy, which enables us to classify things adaptively even when those objects don't share all the typical features of the category members. Any given object or event can be categorized at numerous levels of abstraction, ranging from very broad and general categories (such as "living things") to very narrow and specific ones ("adult female Siamese seal-point cat"). People have a bias toward using basic-level category terms (such as "cat"), which tend to be at intermediate levels of the hierarchy and which communicate a great deal of information very efficiently.

Third, how do we solve problems such as the ticket-scalping-profit problem posed at the beginning of the chapter? When people are faced with a problem, there is a starting point and a goal, and there is some uncertainty over how to move from the former to the latter. Some problems are well defined, others ill defined. What thought processes are involved in finding an appropriate solution? According to the model of the IDEAL problem solver, good problem solving involves five main steps: (1) Identify the problem. (2) Define, or represent, the problem. (3) Explore strategies for a solution. (4) Act on those problem strategies. (5) Look back and learn from the experience. To identify and define a problem correctly, it's important to see the problem in an appropriate way. One of the common pitfalls with problem solving is that people allow their preconceptions to influence how they represent problem information. For example, most people fall prey to functional fixedness, or the tendency to see objects and their functions in certain fixed ways.

People use a variety of problem-solving strategies. Algorithms are procedures that guarantee a solution, but they're often time consuming and cannot always be applied. Heuristics are problem-solving rules of thumb that can be applied quickly but do not always lead to the correct solution. Examples of problem-solving heuristics include means–ends analysis, working backward, and solving through analogies.

Fourth, how do we make decisions when confronted with a set of alternatives? Decision making involves evaluating and choosing from among a set of alternatives. Choice in decision making is usually accompanied by risk, so it's adaptive to evaluate and select from among the alternatives with care. As with problem solving, decision making is influenced by how the alternatives are viewed or represented. For example, the framing or structuring of the alternatives can affect the decision that is made. We reviewed two common decision-making heuristics, representativeness and availability. These strategies sometimes lead us to make errors, but they are quick and easy and often lead to good decisions. Humans have a tendency to focus on evidence that supports their hypotheses, and this confirmation bias can contribute to illusory correlations (i.e., unfounded beliefs about relationships between variables).

Chapter Summary

COMMUNICATING WITH OTHERS

The ability to communicate with others through the use of spoken and written language is one of humanity's greatest success stories. Through language production, we transmit thoughts, feelings, and needs to others; through language comprehension, we learn from and understand one another.

Does Language Determine Thought?

Learning Goal: Be able to evaluate the linguistic relativity hypothesis. The *linguistic relativity hypothesis* proposes that language determines thought; if one lacks words to describe an experience, the experience is literally "out of mind." Cross-cultural evidence suggests that a literal interpretation of this hypothesis cannot be true. But there is little doubt that language influences thought in many ways.

The Structure of Language

Learning Goal: Learn about the structure of language and its basic units. To qualify as true language, a communication system must have rules, collectively termed *grammar.* A grammar specifies how arbitrary symbols can be combined to generate and comprehend any of an infinitely large number of ideas. Grammar has three aspects: *phonology,* the rules for combining sounds to make words; *syntax,* the rules for combining words to make sentences; and *semantics,* the rules used to communicate meaning. Language has a hierarchical structure, ranging from *phonemes* (the smallest significant sound units in speech) to *morphemes* (the smallest units of language that carry meaning) to words, phrases, and sentences. Language is generative, in that the fairly small set of phonemes can be combined to express an infinite number of different sentences. According to Chomsky, sentences have a *surface structure* (superficial appearance) and a *deep structure* (underlying representation of meaning). Language production involves the transformation of deep structure into an acceptable surface structure, and comprehension involves translating a surface structure into the appropriate deep structure.

Language Comprehension

Learning Goal: Appreciate the role of shared knowledge in language comprehension. Effective communication relies heavily on *shared knowledge* among speakers and involves a combination of bottom-up and top-down processing. The term *pragmatics* is used to describe how practical knowledge is used to comprehend the intentions of speakers and to produce appropriate responses.

Language Development

Learning Goal: Be able to identify the major milestones of language development. Researchers believe that human infants are innately prepared to learn language. Crying, cooing, and babbling are important vocalization milestones that are attained in similar ways across cultures. Between 6 and 18 months, experience begins to play a larger role. Simple words are usually uttered by the end of the first year. Two-year-olds develop a *telegraphic grammar* that omits articles and prepositions but that reflects a rudimentary version of adult syntax. As children learn grammatical rules, they pass through a stage during which they *overgeneralize* those rules (e.g., saying things such as "goed").

Language in Nonhuman Species

Learning Goal: Evaluate whether or not nonhuman animals are capable of language. Early attempts to teach chimps to speak were unsuccessful, partly because chimps lack the necessary vocal equipment for speech. Subsequent researchers have taught chimps to communicate with visual mediums, such as American Sign Language. Chimps can associate particular symbols with words and actions, and understand some spoken English, but not all researchers are convinced that the chimps' achievements constitute true language. In any case, it's clear that the linguistic abilities of nonhumans are vastly and qualitatively different from those of *Homo sapiens.*

The Evolution of Language

Learning Goal: Be able to summarize ideas about the evolution of language. If all humans share a "universal grammar" (with the thousands of languages being variants on that underlying shared grammar), how did they acquire it? Presumably, universal grammar evolved gradually by way of natural selection. It is easy to appreciate that possessing language confers great selective advantage. What is amazing is that the gap between humans' and nonhumans' linguistic abilities appears to be so great. Because evolution occurs gradually in small steps, it is likely our prehuman ancestors possessed protogrammars of varying degrees of complexity.

CATEGORIZATION

To make sense of our environment and the objects in it, we carve the world into meaningful chunks called categories. A *category* is a class of objects (people, places, or things) or events that most people agree belong together. The ability to see similarities between different things, to classify objects and events into meaningful categories, allows us to simplify our environment, apprehend nonapparent properties of objects, and make predictions.

Defining Category Membership

Learning Goal: Understand why psychologists have rejected the idea that natural categories have defining features, in favour of the idea that category members share a "family resemblance." What criteria do people use to determine *category membership*? According to the *defining-features* account, things are classified as members of a category if they have certain features that all members of that category share. This works fine for mathematical categories (e.g., triangle), but breaks down for natural categories (e.g., weapon), which tend to have *fuzzy boundaries*. The *family resemblance* view is that members of a category share at least some of a set of core features that are characteristic of that category, but it isn't necessary for each member to have them all. By this view, some members of a category are more typical, or better exemplars, of that category than others.

Do People Store Category Prototypes?

Learning Goal: Be able to compare the prototype and exemplar views of categorization. The notion that categories are defined by family resemblance leads to the concept of a *prototype:* the best or most representative member of a category. Objects may be categorized by comparing them to stored representations of the prototypes of various categories. Alternatively, we may store memories of all of the category examples (*category exemplars*) that we encounter and use these remembered examples to determine category membership.

The Hierarchical Structure of Categories

Learning Goal: Learn about the hierarchical organization of categories. Any object or event can be categorized at numerous levels of abstraction within a hierarchy, ranging from very general to highly specific. *Basic-level category* terms are mid-level in the hierarchy and communicate a wealth of useful and predictive information in an efficient manner. Higher-level *(superordinate)* category terms are less informative, and lower-level *(subordinate)* category terms tend to be longer and deliver only a small amount of additional information over basic-level terms.

SOLVING PROBLEMS

Problem solving refers to situations in which someone wants to reach a goal, but the way to do so is not immediately obvious. The ability to solve problems is important for everyday survival. *Well-defined* problems have a clearly defined starting point and a well-specified goal. *Ill-defined* problems do not have clear starting points or well-specified goals.

The IDEAL Problem Solver

Learning Goal: Be able to list the steps in the IDEAL problem-solving technique. The five major steps in problem solving are (1) identifying the problem, (2) defining (representing) it in the most efficient way, (3) exploring problem strategies, (4) acting on the problem strategy chosen, and (5) looking back to evaluate the effectiveness of the selected strategy.

Identifying and Defining: Problem Representation

Learning Goal: Describe factors that influence how a problem is identified and defined. To identify and define a problem, you must understand exactly what information is given and how that information can potentially be used. One obstacle in representation is *functional fixedness,* the tendency to see objects and their functions in certain fixed and typical ways. People typically rely on well-established patterns of perception and thought *(mental sets);* most of the time this is an effective strategy, but it sometimes leads us astray.

Exploring and Acting: Problem Strategies

Learning Goal: Understand the distinction between algorithms and heuristics as problem-solving strategies, and learn about several commonly used problem-solving heuristics. For some well-defined problems, you can use *algorithms,* step-by-step procedures that guarantee a solution. Algorithms can be used only for certain well-defined problems, and even for such problems they are not always practical. When algorithms are not feasible, we use *heuristics,* or problem-solving "rules of thumb." Three common problem-solving heuristics are *means–ends analysis, working backward,* and *searching for analogies.*

Looking Back and Learning

Learning Goal: Appreciate the importance of looking back and assessing how well a problem was solved for improving future problem solving. The problem-solving process is incomplete unless one looks back and learns from the experience. By analyzing one's performance in detail, one can learn whether the strategy worked for some aspects of the problem but not for others, and gain insight into why a particular heuristic failed or succeeded.

MAKING DECISIONS

Decision making involves choosing from among a set of alternatives. Choosing entails risk because an incorrect decision can have unpleasant consequences.

The Framing of Decision Alternatives

Learning Goal: Learn about framing effects and their influence on decision making. The way alternatives are structured *(framing)* can dramatically influence decision making. When choices are framed in ways that highlight potential gains, people tend to avoid taking risks. If decisions are framed in ways that emphasize potential losses, people are more likely to take a risk that may limit or avoid the loss.

Confirmation Bias and Illusory Correlations

Learning Goal: Understand the human tendency toward confirmation bias and how this bias can contribute to illusory correlations. People have a bias to seek, remember, and emphasize evidence that confirms their hunches, often failing to look for evidence that could potentially disconfirm them. This *confirmation bias* can lead people to have faith in unfounded ideas. Confirmation bias can also contribute to *illusory correlations*, beliefs that two variables are correlated when in truth they are not, because people tend to assess relationships between variables by trying to remember cases in which variables they think should go together (e.g., a patient's diagnosis and unusual characteristics of that patient's drawings) did happen to go together.

Decision-Making Heuristics

Learning Goal: Learn about two common decision-making heuristics: representativeness and availability. When asked to judge the likelihood that something belongs to class A or B, people often rely on a rule of thumb termed the *representativeness heuristic,* which involves comparing the thing in question to beliefs regarding the average member of each class. When asked to estimate the odds of some event occurring, we often rely on the *availability heuristic,* basing estimates on the ease with which examples of the event come to mind. Both heuristics are beneficial most of the time, but they can lead to irrational decisions.

The Value of Heuristics

Learning Goal: Be able to discuss the pros and cons of using heuristics. Although heuristics are imperfect, they are usually effective. Also, heuristics are economical, because they lead to quick decisions with little cost. In any case, we often must rely on heuristics because there are no feasible algorithms for many of the problems and decisions that people confront.

Terms to Remember

Recommended Readings

Bransford, J. D., & Stein, B. S. (1993). *The ideal problem solver* (2nd ed.). New York: Freeman. This fun book, written by a pair of famous cognitive psychologists, is full of great advice on how to solve problems effectively.

Pinker, S. (1994). *The language instinct.* New York: Morrow. In this very readable and insightful book, Canadian psychologist Pinker addresses language, how it evolved, and whether it truly represents a unique human ability.

For additional readings, explore InfoTrac® College Edition, your online library. Go to:

www.adaptivemind2e.nelson.com

Hint: enter the search terms: language development; animal communication; problem solving; decision-making heuristics.

What's on the Web?

Please note that Web addresses are subject to change. Check out the accompanying Web site for updates: www.adaptivemind2e.nelson.com. This site presents practice quiz questions, hypercontent, information on degrees and careers in psychology, study tips, and more.

Creativity Web

www.ozemail.com.au/~caveman/Creative

Billed as "resources for creativity and innovation," this Web site includes all manner of techniques for improving one's creative thinking and problem solving. Read about techniques such as "mind mapping" and "lateral thinking," and try to fit them in with the steps of the IDEAL problem solver. Take a stroll around the "creative genius gallery," or take a "mental workout."

Chimpanzee and Great Ape Language Resources on the Internet

www.brown.edu/Departments/Anthropology/apelang.html

This page includes a wealth of links to information on primates and research on their language abilities. Follow the links to the primate home page or the gorilla home page. Go into the picture gallery and see if you can tell a Drill baboon from a Diana monkey. This is a great resource for finding more information on apes and their communication skills.

Mind/Brain Resources

mind.phil.vt.edu/www/mind.html

You've read a bit about the field of cognitive psychology. Now find out about the exciting interdisciplinary field of cognitive science (mentioned in the chapter introduction), a group of disciplines all working together to explain the mysteries of the mind. Cognitive science includes such diverse areas as philosophy, computer science, psychology, linguistics, and neuroscience. Explore the common threads that these disciplines share.

The Gods do not give all men gifts of grace—nor good looks, nor intelligence.

Homer, ca. 700 B.C.

It's not that I'm so smart, it's just that I stay with problems longer.

Albert Einstein

Chapter 9   Intelligence

L

ate at night, students in the dormitory are arguing about who is the epitome of intelligence. Jennifer, a physics major, argues: "Obviously it's the person who figured out how the universe works—Albert Einstein." Dan, a business major, retorts: "If Einstein was so smart, how come he wasn't rich? I've got to pick Bill Gates 'cause he's the richest person in the world." Alan, a psychology major, says: "It's got to be the person who can charm, control, and entertain anyone she wants: That's Oprah Winfrey." Who's right? Or is it totally a matter of opinion? Given how different the three nominations were, could it be that the students' own majors influenced their choices?

After getting back their marks on the history exam, Larry Knoway argues with his friend: "Sure, we both got the same mark—but I didn't study. That makes me more intelligent." His friend disagrees: "No way, Larry—working hard is part of intelligence." Who's right? Is a person's personality part of their intelligence?

Jane interviews candidates for jobs in a computer software company. She has trouble with the immigrant applicants because they don't seem to catch on to her explanations very well. Her job is important and she doesn't want to hire incompetent applicants. But she wonders whether they are really incompetent or whether their language skills are giving her the wrong impression about their intelligence. Can a person's accent and appearance affect our judgments of their intelligence?

These three anecdotes illustrate that the concept of **intelligence** is an especially elusive one. It seems self-evident to all of us that some people we meet are smarter than others. Yet, as with all psychological concepts, we can't directly see intelligence. Nonetheless, we constantly judge people's intelligence (or lack of it) on the basis of such behaviour as their school grades or the salary they make or the way they talk. The concept is also especially sensitive and the act of labelling arouses people's emotions. Surveys show that the trait is rated as both highly important and highly desirable. This high value placed on intelligence may explain why polls asking people to rate themselves as either "above average" or "below average" in intelligence find an odd result: Virtually everyone reports being above average! Although this result upsets statisti-

intelligence
An internal capacity hypothesized to explain people's ability to solve problems, learn new material, and adapt to new situations. The strength of this capacity must differ across individuals to explain why some people are better at these tasks than other people.

Albert Einstein's name is almost synonymous with intelligence. Is it partly because few people really understand his complex physics and mathematics?

Bill Gates created a business empire based on personal computers. Many others tried to take advantage of the computer revolution, but his technical and business savvy proved incomparable.

Oprah Winfrey also became rich but primarily on the basis of her social skills. Can one decide to be popular, or is it an inborn talent?

340

Previewing the Scientific and Practical Problems

This chapter examines the scientific and practical problems that psychologists face in their efforts to understand intelligence. In each of the chapter sections, you'll find that the concept of intelligence has evolved somewhat over time. There is much agreement among psychologists in how to define and measure intelligence, but there are significant differences as well. Debates tend to focus on three major conceptual and practical problems.

First, how should intelligence be conceptualized? It's normal for people to talk of intelligence as if it's some "thing" that is possessed by a person, such as blue eyes, a thin waist, or large muscles. Yet we cannot see intelligence or measure it directly with a stick. Nonetheless, psychologists assume that there is some underlying biological explanation yet to be identified. Intelligence may not even be best

viewed as a single capacity: It may be better seen as a collection of separate abilities. In other words, there may be multiple intelligences ranging from the more traditional verbal and math skills to musical ability, mechanical ability, and even athletic ability.

Second, how can we measure the individual differences in performance? Regardless of how we may choose to conceptualize intelligence, there is still the practical problem of measuring it. For any particular task, such as getting high grades at school, there is a distribution of abilities. Some people perform extremely well; others struggle. If these abilities can be measured accurately, we should be able to decide how many types of intelligence there are. Then it should be possible to tailor your activities to fit your skills. You can be advised not to enter architecture school if your spatial

abilities are weak, and you can be steered toward a career as a writer or journalist if your verbal abilities are strong.

Third, what are the sources of intelligence? Does intelligent behaviour come primarily from your genetic background or from life experiences? The study of intelligence is also an investigation into the plasticity of the mind. Although genius runs in families, it is not immediately obvious whether these similarities are due to permanent genetic factors or simply to the similarities in their environmental history. Is poor map-reading a permanent condition, resulting from a hard-wired genetic blueprint, or can the ability to read maps be taught? Because of the wiring in your brain, are you doomed forever to have trouble fixing that leaky faucet in the kitchen, or can you be taught mechanical skill?

---

cians, it is quite understandable to psychologists. Research by David Dunning and colleagues explains how this can happen (e.g., Beauregard & Dunning, 1995). Because the concept is so elusive, people can define it the way they want. So they simply define "intelligence" subjectively in such a way that they personally rate highly on it. As a result, we can all be geniuses in our own minds!

Rather than accept a completely **subjective definition** of intelligence, psychologists have expended considerable energy on developing an **objective test**. The former has no fixed meaning and depends on who is doing the judging; the latter yields the same concrete number no matter who calculates the score. Over one hundred years of research has been devoted to developing intelligence tests that are able to predict important consequences, such as school performance and job success.

subjective definition
A definition based on personal opinion. Each person's definition seems designed to suit his or her personal needs and world views.

objective test
A test that is scored in a standardized fashion so that anyone calculating the result gets the same answer.

CONCEPTUALIZING INTELLIGENCE

Learning Goals

1. Comprehend the psychometric approach to conceptualizing intelligence, including Spearman's two-factor theory.
2. Understand cognitive approaches to conceptualizing intelligence.
3. Learn the differences among the various expanded theories.

FROM THE PERSPECTIVE of the adaptive mind, intelligence is simply the degree to which one is successful in adapting. You are considered intelligent if you can solve the particular problems that you confront in your environment (Matthews, 1997; Sternberg, 1997). The adaptive interpretation of intelligence presents many advantages.

For one thing, focusing on adaptation helps to prevent us from thinking that human thoughts and actions are the only proper measuring tools for intelligent behaviour. The fact that the nutcracker bird can efficiently hide and relocate thousands of seeds is certainly intelligent from the standpoint of adapting to the harshness of winter (Kamil & Balda, 1990). From this perspective, University of British Columbia psychologist Stanley Coren (1995) argues that all species are equally intelligent because they are all well adapted to their unique environments. This notion that different species (and cultures) have different survival problems previews the fact that we may need to establish a wide range of criteria for what constitutes intelligence.

However, conceptualizing intelligence simply in terms of adaptability does not tell us much about what produces *individual differences* within our species. People differ in their ability to fit successfully into their environments, even when they're faced with similar problems. We need to understand the factors that account for individual differences. In this section of the chapter, we'll consider three general ways to accomplish this end: (1) the *psychometric* approach, (2) the *cognitive* approach, and (3) *expanded conceptions of intelligence*. Each approach is designed to provide a general framework for conceptualizing intelligence, with the express goal of explaining how people differ in mental ability.

Psychometric Approach: Measuring the Mind

We begin with the psychometric approach, which proposes that intelligence is a mental capacity that can be understood by analyzing performance on mental tests. The word **psychometric** literally means "to measure the mind." A person's intelligence is determined by tests that measure his or her specific mental skills, such as verbal comprehension, memory, or spatial ability. The results are then analyzed statistically and conclusions are drawn about underlying mental abilities.

Englishman Sir Francis Galton (1822–1911) was one of the first researchers to examine intelligence in an experimental fashion. Galton was a half-cousin of Charles Darwin, and, like his famous relative, was deeply committed to the idea of "survival of the fittest." He believed that individual differences in ability had their basis in heredity and could be measured through a series of tests of sensory discrimination and reaction time. For a small fee, visitors to Galton's laboratory were given a variety of psychological and physical tests, measuring such things as visual acuity, grip strength, and reaction time to sounds. At the end of the test session, they were handed a card with a detailed record of their scores (Hilgard, 1987; Johnson et al., 1985).

Galton developed a wide variety of tests that he thought would measure intelligence. He noticed that there were positive correlations among most of the tests. If a

Critical Thinking

Should scientists stick with concrete observations and avoid abstract ideas such as intelligence (and anxiety and gravity)?

psychometrics

The use of psychological tests to measure the mind and mental processes.

Sir Francis Galton (1822–1911) and his "anthropometric" laboratory, which he used to measure intellectual ability.

person tended to score high on a certain test, such as sensory acuity, he or she tended to score high on other measures as well. This pattern suggested to Galton that each test might be tapping into the same general ability—a general factor of intelligence that contributed in some way to each of the different measured skills.

As it turned out, Galton's laboratory investigations into the measurement of intelligence did not pan out. His measurements were crude, and his tests were later shown to be poor predictors of actual intellectual performance, such as academic success (Wissler, 1901). For these and other reasons, his contributions are of interest primarily for historical rather than scientific reasons. But his general approach captured the attention of other researchers, who went on to develop the psychometric approach in a more rigorous way. Among the more influential of those who carried on the Galton tradition was a mathematically inclined psychologist named Charles Spearman.

Spearman and Factor *g*

One problem with Galton's approach was that he didn't know how to combine his multitude of measurements. When British intelligence researcher Charles Spearman (1904) applied a mathematical technique he called **factor analysis** to the testing of mental ability, he discovered evidence for general intellectual ability. Results showed a single common factor in the analysis, which he called *g* for **general intelligence.** Although *g* helped to explain performance on a wide variety of mental tests, it did not explain the unique part of each test. The correlations among the test scores were highly positive but not perfect. He argued, therefore, that it is necessary to acknowledge the **specific factor, *s,*** that is the left-over part of each individual measure (see Figure 9.1). The left-over part of a test of verbal comprehension represents a special aptitude or special experience not captured by *g*. Note that special talents like musical and mechanical ability did not show any connection with *g*.

Hierarchical Models of Intelligence

Over the years, researchers have challenged Spearman's conclusions, especially the overarching concept of *g*. Psychologist Leon Thurstone, for example, applied a somewhat different version of factor analysis, as well as a more extensive battery of tests, and discovered evidence for seven **primary mental abilities:** verbal comprehension, verbal fluency, numerical ability, spatial ability, memory, perceptual speed, and reasoning (Thurstone, 1938). He rejected Spearman's notion of a single general intelligence, *g*, because Thurstone's analysis indicated that these seven primary abilities are sometimes discrepant. Just because someone is good at

factor analysis

A statistical procedure developed by Charles Spearman that groups together related items on tests by analyzing the correlations among test scores. It is often used by psychologists to determine underlying common "factors," that summarize a large number of scores.

_g_ (general factor)

According to Spearman, the general factor, derived from factor analysis, that underlies or contributes to performance on a variety of mental tests.

_s_ (specific factor)

According to Spearman, a specific factor, derived from factor analysis, that is unique to a particular kind of test.

primary mental abilities

The seven distinct forms of intelligence that Thurstone uncovered with modern forms of factor analysis.

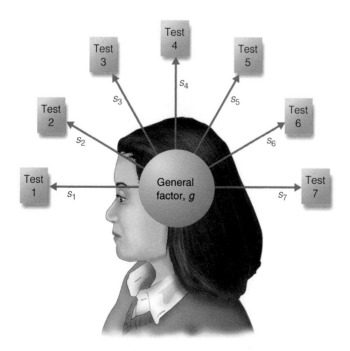

FIGURE 9.1

Spearman's General and Specific Factors

Spearman discovered that, to explain performance on a variety of mental tests, it was necessary to consider (1) a common factor, called *g* for general intelligence, that contributes to performance on all of the tests, (2) specific factors—labelled here as s_1 through s_7—which are specific to the particular tests, and (3) special talents.

Some people seem to be all-round athletes. Deion Sanders performed at the highest levels in both professional football and professional baseball. Do his skills support the existence of a "g factor" of athletic ability?

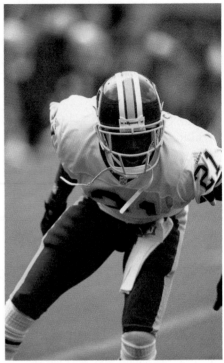

verbal reasoning, for example, doesn't guarantee that he or she will be good at memory or perceptual speed. Although the correlations among the primary abilities tend to be positive, Thurstone did not feel that a general factor was responsible.

Psychologists have argued for decades about (1) the proper way to apply factor analysis, (2) the particular kinds of ability tests that should be used, and (3) whether single or multiple factors are needed to explain the data (Jensen & Weng, 1994). The statistical debates will not be considered here. But the evidence for a central *g* is hard to dismiss completely, at least when intelligence is defined by performance on tests of mental ability. For this reason, most modern psychometric theories of intelligence retain the concept of general intelligence but propose more of a hierarchical structure, such as that shown in Figure 9.2. General intelligence, *g*, occupies a position at the top of the hierarchy, and various subfactors that may or may not operate independently

FIGURE 9.2

Hierarchical Models

Many psychologists now propose hierarchical models of intelligence, which include elements found in the theories of both Spearman and Thurstone. Like Thurstone, hierarchical models propose separate factors that contribute independently to certain types of tests (e.g., factor 1 contributes to tests 1 to 3 but not to tests 4 to 9). But, like Spearman, these models also assume that all factors are influenced by an overall *g*.

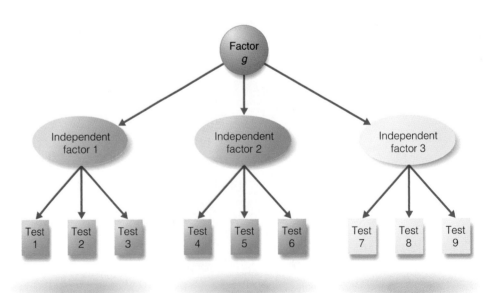

from one another sit at the lower levels. This represents a compromise of sorts between Thurstone's view—that there is more than one primary mental ability—and Spearman's concept of *g*, but it is a compromise that is supported by the data.

Fluid and Crystallized Intelligence Other psychologists believe strongly in the notion of general intelligence, but contend that it should be broken down into two separate dimensions: *fluid* intelligence and *crystallized* intelligence (Cattell, 1963, 1998; Horn & Cattell, 1966). **Fluid intelligence** is the basic ability to solve problems, reason, and remember in ways that are relatively uninfluenced by experience. It's the type of intelligence that is probably determined primarily by biological or genetic factors. **Crystallized intelligence,** on the other hand, refers to knowledge and ability acquired from experience. You might learn things about the world, such as tricks to deal with arithmetic problems, and learn words used only at higher levels of schooling and in certain cultural groups.

The distinction between fluid and crystallized intelligence is important because it helps to explain how mental abilities change with age and across different cultures (Horn & Noll, 1997; Parkin & Java, 2001). As you'll see later in the chapter, there are reasons to expect fluid and crystallized intelligence to change in different ways as we age. It's also common to find striking differences in people's ability to perform on psychometric tests of mental ability across different cultures and socioeconomic classes. Such differences are difficult to explain from the perspective of general intelligence, unless we assume that an important part of general intelligence is acquired from experience. Distinguishing between fluid and crystallized intelligence can help explain how two people born with the same amount of natural (fluid) intelligence can end up performing quite differently on tests of mental ability.

fluid intelligence
The natural ability to solve problems, reason, and remember; fluid intelligence is thought to be relatively uninfluenced by experience.

crystallized intelligence
The knowledge and abilities acquired as a result of experience (as from schooling and cultural influences).

Critical Thinking

Which do you think contributes the most to performance on an essay exam: fluid or crystallized intelligence?

The Cognitive Approach

Psychologists who adopt a cognitive perspective argue that intelligence needs to be understood by clarifying internal mental processes. They analyze how people differ on the complex mental tasks detailed in Chapter 8. This kind of analysis typically comes in two forms: (1) measurement of the speed of mental processing and (2) an analysis of the specific mental operations that produce intelligent thought.

Mental Speed Some cognitive psychologists have suggested that intelligence reflects, in part, the speed of transmission among the neural pathways of the brain (see Hunt, 1985; Jensen, 1993; Vernon, 1983). The faster the brain communicates internally, the higher an individual's intelligence. The reason that communication speed might be important is that the brain has limited resources and must quickly allocate, or divide, its processing in order to perform efficiently (see Chapter 4). In support of this position, Jensen and his colleagues typically find a significant correlation between measures of neural communication speed and performance on mental tests of intelligence (Reed & Jensen, 1992). Similarly, Philip Vernon, Linda Miller, and their colleagues at the University of Western Ontario have found a positive relationship between speed of information processing, working memory, and intelligence; they have also found that this relationship holds true for children as well as adults (Miller & Vernon, 1996, 1997). Other researchers have linked the speed difference to genetic factors (Rijsdijk et al., 1998).

Componential Analysis In addition to measuring the speed of mental processing, cognitive theorists also attempt to identify the specific mental processes that contribute to superior test performance. Robert Sternberg (1997) developed a procedure called *componential analysis* that uses people's reaction times, as well as their error rates, to isolate the mental operations that are tapped by traditional intelligence tests. For example, to isolate the ability to detect relationships between concepts, people might be asked to solve analogies of the following form as quickly as possible: LAWYER is to CLIENT as DOCTOR is to _____? Sternberg argues that intelligent performers are able to infer the relation between the first two components of the analogy quickly (Sternberg & Gardner, 1983). They recognize, for example, that a LAWYER is typically hired by and works for the CLIENT, and they're able to then map and apply this perceived relation to generate the correct answer (PATIENT). Sternberg believes that intelligent people can generate effective overall plans for attacking problems—they represent problems well and then generate and monitor global strategies for problem solution (see Chapter 8).

Like the psychometric theorists, cognitive theorists hope that once they identify the fundamental components and processes of intelligence, those elements can be used to predict and explain individual differences in task performance. If we can get a measure of your ability to analyze analogies, for instance, we might be able to predict how well you will perform on a wide variety of tests of mental ability. One special approach called **artificial intelligence** involves developing computer programs that mimic human intelligence, or at least expert thinking in more narrow domains. We already know, for example, that the famous IBM computer program called "Deep Blue" can defeat the best human chess player, Garry Kasparov. Another program called "Liza" can actually do psychotherapy at a bargain price (free). Other programs under development can diagnose medical conditions and solve physics or engineering problems (Simon, 1969, 1992). By conceptualizing intelligence in terms of underlying mental processes and then modelling those processes using computer programs, cognitive theorists hope to go beyond just measuring intelligent behaviour to understanding and explaining its causes.

Expanded Conceptions of Intelligence

In recent years, several psychologists have argued that the traditional unitary conception of intelligence needs to be expanded to include a wider variety of abilities and talents. They reject the idea that intelligence can be adequately conceptualized through the analysis of test performance or artificial laboratory tasks (as used by the psychometric and cognitive approaches). Criticizing the narrow definition implied by a single underlying *g*, they argue that we should acknowledge a wider variety of human talents and abilities.

Gardner's Multiple Intelligences   Howard Gardner (1983, 1993) has been the most powerful voice in pushing for the expansion of current conceptions of intelligence with his theory of **multiple intelligences.** An *intelligence* (rather than "the" intelligence) is defined as "an ability or set of abilities that permits an individual to solve problems or fashion products that are of consequence in a particular cultural setting" (Walters & Gardner, 1986). (Note that Gardner's treatment of intelligence has an adaptive flavour and fits snugly into our general conception of the adaptive mind.) Although Gardner believes that each of these separate intelligences may be rooted in the biology of the brain, the way that each is manifested may depend on one's culture.

Rather than studying intelligent behaviour in the laboratory, Gardner has used a case study approach. He analyzes reports of particular individuals with special abilities or talents, such as superior musicians, poets, scientists, and savants. He has also looked extensively at the effects of damage to the brain. He has noted, for example, instances in which brain damage can affect one kind of ability, such as reasoning and problem solving, yet leave intact other abilities, such as musical skill. Based on his research, Gardner has identified what he believes to be nine kinds of intelligence.

1. *Musical intelligence:* the type of ability displayed by gifted musicians or child prodigies.

2. *Bodily-kinesthetic intelligence:* the type of ability shown by gifted athletes, dancers, or surgeons who have great control over body movements.

3. *Logical-mathematical intelligence:* the type of ability displayed by superior scientists and logical problem solvers.

artificial intelligence
The attempt to understand the meaning of intelligence by building intelligent machines. Such machines—usually computer programs—can simulate or surpass many human capabilities.

multiple intelligences
The notion proposed by Howard Gardner that people possess a set of separate and independent "intelligences" ranging from musical to linguistic to interpersonal abilities.

Critical Thinking

Do you think the average person on the street thinks that athletic ability or dancing ability qualifies as a type of intelligence? What others could be added to Gardner's list?

4. *Linguistic intelligence:* the type of ability shown by great writers or poets who can express themselves verbally.

5. *Spatial intelligence:* the type of ability shown by those with superior navigation skills or an ability to visualize spatial scenes.

6. *Interpersonal intelligence:* the type of ability shown by those who can easily infer other people's moods, temperaments, or intentions and motivations.

7. *Intrapersonal intelligence:* the ability shown by someone who has great insight into his or her own feelings and emotions.

8. *Naturalist intelligence:* the ability to observe and interact with diverse species in nature; the type of ability shown by a biologist or environmentalist.

9. *Spiritual intelligence:* the ability to sense spiritual aspects of human experience and use them to adapt to the environment.

Notice that some forms of intelligence, as described by Gardner, are covered well by conventional tests of mental ability. The psychometric and cognitive approaches focus extensively on logical-mathematical intelligence and to some extent on linguistic and spatial intelligence. Certainly, some psychometric researchers argued for the need to distinguish between subtypes of intelligence, but they rarely, if ever, included special intelligences such as mechanical ability, musical ability, or athletic skill. As a result, the multiple intelligences approach is a direct challenge to traditional unitary conceptions of intelligence.

Clearly, Gardner's multiple intelligences approach has an adaptive flavour and fits snugly into the textbook's general conception of the adaptive mind. The idea is that everyone has a life niche where they display intelligence. Gardner's framework has been applied successfully in educational settings (Krechevsky & Seidel, 1998). Many grade-school and high-school teachers like the idea of multiple intelligences because it can help rescue the lower self-esteem of the poorer students. Some critics say that Gardner is really talking about multiple talents rather than intelligences, and his theory remains primarily descriptive without much hard scientific evidence. But many psychologists (and real people too!) are coming to agree with Gardner that intelligence should be broadly conceived—it's not simply performance on a battery of primarily verbal-linguistic or sensory tests.

Exemplars of Intelligence Instead of relying on Gardner's case studies, Paulhus and his colleagues simply asked ordinary people to suggest famous individuals whom they consider to be intelligent. These researchers from the University of British Columbia had collected data from thousands of people over many years—1982 to 1997. When the voting was compiled, Albert Einstein topped the list in every year. In the most recent 1997 survey, the rest of the "top 10" were (in order): Bill Gates, Bill Clinton, Stephen Hawking, Isaac Newton, Leonardo Da Vinci, William Shakespeare, Sigmund Freud, Charles Darwin, and Ludwig van Beethoven.

The Canadian who received by far the most nominations over the years was Pierre Trudeau. In fact, in Canadian surveys, Trudeau was the only nominee to ever come close to "beating" Einstein (in 1982). Although over 60% of the participants in this study were female, they nominated only three women to be among the "top 15" over the years: Margaret Thatcher, Madonna, and Oprah Winfrey. Paulhus and his colleagues concluded that there is remarkable consistency in the "exemplars" nominated over the years, that powerful individuals are often seen as intelligent, and that people seem to differentiate several different "subtypes" of intelligence: scientific, communicative, entrepreneurial, moral, and artistic intelligences (Paulhus et al., 2002). These popular subtypes show some overlap with the multiple intelligences arising from Gardner's case study approach.

People possess unique abilities that Gardner views as types of intelligence. For example, the performers from Cirque du Soleil (left) possess high levels of artistic and bodily-kinesthetic intelligence; Jim Carrey (right) rates highly in artistic, interpersonal, and kinesthetic intelligence.

Sternberg's three facets of intelligence

Robert Sternberg's theory of intelligence; it includes three types of intelligence—analytic, creative, and practical.

Sternberg's Three Facets of Intelligence Robert Sternberg has also challenged the unitary notion of intelligence suggested by psychometric researchers. He agrees that it's important to understand the analytic mental operations that are involved in the planning and execution of specialized tasks, but he also believes that any complete account of intelligence must address behaviour outside of the laboratory. For example, what is the form of intelligence that enables people to apply their mental processes creatively to problems that arise in the external environment? Furthermore, how does intelligence relate to the practical experience of the individual? In short, like Gardner, Sternberg sees the need for more than one intelligence. Instead of Gardner's nine types, **Sternberg's three facets of intelligence** include *analytic*, *creative*, and *practical* types (Sternberg, 1985, 1988b).

Sternberg believes that any complete theory of intelligence must refer in some way to basic analytic skills. Some people are simply better than others at processing information—they're good at representing (or seeing) problems in the right way and can generate effective strategies for solutions. People with high degrees of *analytical intelligence* tend to perform well on conventional tests that tap reasoning and logical-mathematical ability—such as the Scholastic Achievement Test (SAT). Because most psychometric tests of intelligence require these kinds of abilities, people who are high in analytic intelligence tend to be assigned a high *g*. If you know someone who performs well in school or who claims to be highly intelligent based on a standardized test, he or she is likely to score highly on analytic intelligence.

Sternberg proposes that *creative intelligence* expresses how well people are able to cope with new or novel tasks. Being analytic and processing information well does not guarantee that you will be creative or be able to apply the skills you've mastered in a new context. The world is full of people who are good at school or who perform well on assigned tasks, but have nothing to contribute when the situation changes. They lack creativity and seem to have trouble applying what they've learned. A child who is motivated to read widely after acquiring the rudiments of language, for example, is said to be high in creative intelligence (Sternberg, 1985).

Finally, people differ in *practical intelligence,* which taps how well they fit into their environments. People with lots of practical intelligence solve the problems that are uniquely posed by their cultural surroundings. They mould themselves well into existing settings, and move to new environments, if required, that provide a better fit or niche for their talents. In a nutshell, these individuals have "street smarts"; they size up situations well and act accordingly. You probably know someone who seems to lack analytic skills—who fails school or drops out—but still manages to succeed quite well in life. Such success involves adapting to the environment and doing what it takes to succeed.

This theory fits the current trend toward a broadening of the concept of intelligence. Like Gardner's approach, Sternberg's theory deals with behaviours and skills that are not normally covered by the psychometric and purely cognitive approaches. Also like Gardner's theory, Sternberg's distinctions can be applied successfully in classroom settings where multiple types of intelligence can be nurtured and developed (Sternberg, 1998; Sternberg et al., 1998). At the same time, breadth is not gained without some cost: Concepts such as practical and creative intelligence are not defined with precision and, consequently, can be somewhat difficult to measure and test (Sternberg et al., 2001). Moreover, even if it is desirable to broaden our conceptualization of intelligence, that doesn't mean that the cognitive or psychometric approaches to intelligence have no value. As you'll see in the next section, psychometric tests are often quite useful in predicting performance, even though they may be measuring only narrow dimensions of intelligence.

Concept Summary

VIEWS OF INTELLIGENCE

Approach	Example(s)	Intelligence Is ...
Psychometric	Spearman's factor g Hierarchical models	A mental capacity that can be understood by analyzing performance on mental tests.
Cognitive	Cognitive strategies Mental speed	Strategies and components of specific mental operations.
Gardner's multiple intelligences	Musical intelligence and spatial intelligence	The speed of mental processing. A variety of abilities that permit an individual to succeed in a particular achievement setting.
Sternberg's three facets of intelligence	Analytic intelligence Creative intelligence Practical intelligence	The ability to process information analytically. The ability to cope with novel tasks. The ability to solve problems uniquely posed by cultural surroundings.

Test Yourself 9.1

For each of the following statements, pick the term that best describes the approach to conceptualizing intelligence. Choose your answers from the following: psychometric; cognitive; Gardner's intelligences; Sternberg's intelligences. (You will find the answers in Appendix B.)

1. Mitsuko has street smarts—she can mould herself successfully into any situation. _____

2. Celia wants to measure her intelligence so she volunteers to participate in a reaction time experiment in the psychology department.

   _____

3. Jeremy flunks most of his classes, but he's a brilliant pianist so he considers himself to be highly intelligent. _____

4. Lucy has just finished an exhaustive battery of mental tests; she's waiting to find out if she has a high g. _____

5.   Natalie wants to understand the concept of intelligence so she has signed up for a class on factor analysis. _____

6.   Verne shows great insight into the feelings of others, which makes him score highly on tests of interpersonal intelligence. _____

7.   Sheila scored a perfect 4.0 GPA in high school, but has trouble applying what she's learned to new situations. She's beginning to feel like she might not be so intelligent after all. _____

MEASURING INDIVIDUAL DIFFERENCES

7a, 7b, 7c, SIM 8

Learning Goals

1.   Recognize the components of a good test: reliability, validity, and standardization.
2.   Understand the intelligence quotient (IQ) and how it is interpreted.
3.   Learn how mental retardation, giftedness, and savant are defined.
4.   Understand the validity of IQ tests.
5.   Be able to explain creativity and emotional intelligence.

WE HAVE NOW DISCUSSED several ways to conceptualize the idea of intelligence. We have yet to discuss how individual differences are actually measured and scored. Although the different conceptions take different approaches, they all acknowledge the need to perform objective measurement. As noted earlier, objective tests give the same number no matter who calculates the score. A scientific analysis of intelligence cannot proceed without collecting objective scores that we can use to compare people.

Of course, there is no guarantee that a test score is useful just because it is objective. We might all agree on how many freckles you have, but this agreement is hardly a good reason for using your freckle score as an indicator of your intelligence. This section of the chapter deals with various ways of distinguishing a good test from a bad one.

First, we have to decide on exactly what we want to measure. It is easy to confuse similar concepts such as intelligence with aptitude, achievement, or achievement motivation. They all have different implications for a person's future. **Achievement motivation tests** evaluate a person's ambition or desire to be successful. Some people devote all their energies toward future achievements and others choose to pass their time entertaining themselves or helping others. **Achievement tests** measure someone's actual level of knowledge or competence in a particular subject (such as math or reading). Researchers and teachers can use the results of an achievement test to assess the effectiveness of a learning procedure or a school curriculum. They are also used to make predictions about the future, such as how well you can be expected to perform in your chosen profession or whether you are likely to succeed at university. **Aptitude tests** measure your ability to learn in a particular area and to acquire new knowledge needed for success in a given domain. Aptitude test results can be used to help choose a career path and to avoid those where your specific lack of ability may hold you back. (You probably don't want to waste 10 years learning a career that you don't have a knack for.) **Intelligence tests** are similar to aptitude tests but they are assumed to measure a more generalized form of aptitude. Intelligence should reveal itself in successful performance in many domains.

achievement motivation tests
Psychological tests that measure your desire to perform challenging tasks and reach difficult goals.

achievement tests
Psychological tests that measure your current level of knowledge or competence in a particular subject.

aptitude tests
Psychological tests that measure your ability to learn and solve problems in a particular subject area.

intelligence tests
Tests that evaluate your overall ability to learn and solve problems.

The Characteristics of a Good Test

7b, SIM 8

We'll begin by discussing the qualities or characteristics of a "good" test (i.e., a dependable test that can be expected to provide a meaningful measure of individual differences). Given that we recognize the need to measure these differences, it's crucial that

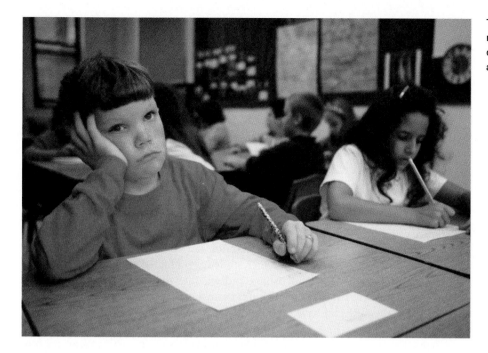

the measurement device yield information that is scientifically useful. Researchers generally agree on three characteristics that are needed for a good test: reliability, validity, and standardization.

Reliability

The first good test characteristic, **reliability,** refers to the consistency of the test results. Reliable tests produce similar scores when the test is administered more than once. Suppose we want to measure creativity and we design a test that produces a score from 0 to 100. On their first try, Al gets a score of 53 and Cynthia scores much higher at 86. It seems that Cynthia is way more creative than Al. To be sure about the results, we administer the test again. This time Al scores 77 and Cynthia 43. Unfortunately, our new creativity test lacks reliability: That is, it does not produce consistent scores from one administration to the next. Cynthia may very well be more creative than Al, but this particular test is not helpful in drawing that conclusion. Either the new test is unreliable or we have to give up on the idea that some people are consistently more creative than others.

It's important for a test to be reliable. Otherwise, we cannot draw firm conclusions from people's scores. One way to measure a test's reliability is to give it to the same group of individuals again after an interval of time, say a month. **Test-retest reliability** is then calculated by comparing the scores across the repeated administrations. Often, a correlation coefficient is computed to put a number on how well scores on the second test can be predicted from scores on the first. The closer the test-retest correlation comes to a perfect +1.00, the better the test is. Another kind of reliability is calculated by correlating people's scores on the first half of the test with their scores on the second half. A high value of this **split-half reliability** is even more important than a high test-retest reliability, because test scores cannot be trusted if they change from the first half of the test to the second half.

Validity

The second good test characteristic, **validity,** refers to how well a test measures what it is supposed to measure. In other words, is the label of the test (intelligence, height, sociability) truly justified? A test can yield reliable numbers (i.e., consistent results across repeated administrations), yet not truly measure the psychological characteristic of interest. If a test of creativity actually measures shoe size, then the data are likely to be quite reliable but not very valid. Shoe size isn't going to change much from one measurement to the next, but it has little to do with creativity.

reliability
A measure of the consistency of test results; reliable tests give people similar scores when the test is repeated.

test-retest reliability
Ability of a test to give consistent scores.

split-half reliability
Ability of a test to give the same scores in the first and second halves of the test.

validity
An assessment of how well a test measures what the label of the test says it is measuring. *Content validity* assesses the degree to which the content of a test samples broadly across the domain of interest; *predictive validity* assesses how well the test predicts an important criterion; *construct validity* assesses how well the test captures all the details of the theoretical construct.

Actually, there are several different forms of validity. *Content validity* measures the degree to which the content of a test samples the entire domain of interest. If you're trying to get a general measure of creativity, your test should not be limited to one kind of creativity, such as artistic creativity. For the test to have a high degree of content validity, it should probably measure artistic, verbal, mechanical, mathematical, and other kinds of creativity.

Sometimes psychologists are interested in designing a test that predicts a particular outcome, such as job performance or success in school. For a test to have *predictive validity*, it needs to predict this outcome adequately. An example of predictive validity is provided by researcher Douglas Symons of Acadia University, in a study of the predictive validity of the Graduate Record Exam (GRE) (Symons, 1999). The GRE is designed to measure the likelihood of success in graduate school, and most graduate schools require applicants to submit scores on the GRE as part of the application process. To examine the predictive validity of the GRE in a master's program in clinical psychology, Symons examined the correlations between GRE scores and success regarding several goals, including whether students graduated on time, whether they received external grants and scholarships, and whether they published their master's theses. Symons concluded that the GRE did correlate highly with these variables and, therefore, that the GRE did have high predictive validity for students in the program that was studied.

There is a more general kind of validity, construct validity, which measures how well a test captures all the details of the theoretical concept or construct. Suppose we have a theory of creativity that is developed well enough to generate a wide variety of predictions—how creative people act, the kinds of books that creative people are interested in, the susceptibility of creative people to mental disorders, and so on. To have high construct validity, our test must show the predicted connections with each of these variables, rather than just one. So if the theory predicts that creative people are more likely to suffer from depression, then people who score highly on the creativity test should have a greater likelihood of being depressed. Finally, the test should also avoid measuring other constructs such as achievement motivation or *g*, if your theory of creativity says that these are different.

Standardization The third characteristic of a good test of individual differences is **standardization.** When you take a test such as the SAT, or any widely used aptitude or achievement test, you quickly learn that the testing procedures are extremely rigid. You can break the test seal only at a certain time, the instructions are read in monotone by a serious administrator, and your yellow number 2 pencil must be put down immediately when the time elapses. Clearly, these tests are *standardized*, which means that the testing, scoring, and interpretation procedures are kept similar across all administrations of the test. Rigid adherence to standardization is important because it ensures that all test takers will be treated the same.

In fact, the proper interpretation of a test score absolutely demands standardization. Remember: We're concerned with individual differences. It doesn't make much sense to compare two people's scores if different amounts of time or scoring procedures were used in the two test sessions. A person's score on a test of individual differences can be understood only with respect to a reference group, often called a *norm group*, and everyone within the group must receive the same test and administration procedures. We'll return to this notion of a norm reference group momentarily, as we consider the concept of the IQ.

Critical Thinking

Do you think the class tests that you've taken so far have been valid? What specific kind of validity are you using as a basis for your answer?

standardization

Keeping the testing, scoring, and interpretation procedures similar across all administrations of a test.

IQ: The Intelligence Quotient

A critical step in developing an objective measure is deciding how to operationalize the concept; that is, how does one assign numbers to people to represent their intelligence? One could use each individual's salary, or school grades, or shoe size. Instead of those questionable operationalizations, psychologists typically administer a test containing

Concept Summary

COMPONENTS OF A GOOD TEST

Component	Description	Example
Reliability	Consistency of test results.	Taking a test twice should yield similar scores each time.
Validity	Does the test measure what it's supposed to?	
— Content	— The degree to which the content of a test samples broadly across the domain of interest.	The items on a test of creativity should cover different types of creativity, such as artistic, mathematical, and verbal.
— Predictive	— The degree to which a test predicts a particular outcome.	Performance on the Scholastic Achievement Test (SAT) should correlate with later performance in university classes.
— Construct	— The total evidence that a test actually measures the intended concept.	Performance on a test of creativity should correlate with other characteristics or indexes thought to be associated with creativity.
Standardization	Testing, scoring, and interpretation procedures are kept similar across all administrations of the test.	Everyone who takes the SAT receives the same instructions, uses a yellow number 2 pencil and standard answer sheet, and has to complete the test within the same specified period of time.

questions of varying difficulty. Most people get the easy questions but very few get the difficult ones. Much research is required to decide on the appropriate questions, to demonstrate that the test has reliability and validity, and to provide large samples of comparison data to standardize the test. Whatever questions are on the test, it has become traditional to convert overall scores to a single number labelled **IQ,** which stands for **intelligence quotient.** You will see in the rest of this section that the calculation of this number can be complicated.

The historical roots of the intelligence quotient trace back about a hundred years to the work of the French psychologist Alfred Binet and his associate, Théopile Simon. Binet and Simon were commissioned by the French government in 1904 to develop a test that would identify children who were considered "dull"—specifically, children who would have a difficult time grasping concepts in school. It was the French government's intention to help these children, once they were identified, through some kind of special education. Thus, the mission of the test was primarily practical, not theoretical; the goal was to develop a test that would accurately assess individual differences in future academic performance.

Mental Age Not surprisingly, Binet and Simon designed their test to measure the kinds of skills that are needed in school—such as memory, reasoning, and verbal comprehension. To form a meaningful scale, they came up with the notion of **mental age,** defined as the chronological age that best describes the child's current level of intellectual performance. Thus it is actually a performance measure in disguise. Mental age is calculated by comparing a child's test score with the average scores for different age groups. For example, let's suppose that 8-year-old Jenny is able to answer the questions that an average 12-year-old can answer. Then Jenny would be assigned a mental age of 12.

Thus individuals may have a mental age that is higher or lower than their chronological age. When averaged over the whole group, they will be the same: By definition, an average 8-year-old solves problems at the average 8-year-old level. By using mental age, Binet and Simon (1916) were able to diagnose the slow and quick learners and recommend appropriate curriculum adjustments.

IQ (intelligence quotient)
A single number calculated to represent a person's intelligence. Originally, mental age divided by chronological age and then multiplied by 100; more recently, defined in terms of deviation from the average score on an IQ test.

mental age
The chronological age that best fits a child's level of performance on a test of mental ability. Mental age is typically calculated by comparing a child's test score with the average scores for different age groups.

Alfred Binet, shown here with an unidentified child, was commissioned by the French government to develop a test that would help teachers identify students who might need special education.

Still, mental age does not allow an easy comparison of the ability of children of different ages. Intuitively, we recognize that an 8-year-old child who has a mental age of 10 is smarter than a 10-year-old with the same mental age.

Ratio Formula for IQ   German psychologist William Stern solved the problem of comparisons across age. He suggested using a formula called IQ that compares a child's mental age to chronological age; that is, their true physical age.

$$\text{Intelligence quotient (IQ)} = \frac{\text{Mental age}}{\text{Chronological age}} \times 100$$

The IQ is a useful scoring system because it establishes an easy-to-understand baseline for "average" intelligence: People of average intelligence will have an IQ of 100 because their mental age will always be equal to their chronological age. People with IQs greater than 100 will be above average in intelligence; those below 100 will be below average in intelligence.

Binet's intelligence test was revised several times and was ultimately translated into English for use in North America. The most popular American version was developed by psychologist Lewis Terman at Stanford University. Thus, it became known as the *Stanford-Binet* test of intelligence. It was also Terman who refined the standardization and conducted large-scale studies of intelligence. With him the term "IQ test" became a short form for intelligence test and it still is today.

Deviation Formula for IQ   Defining IQ simply in terms of the ratio of mental age to chronological age has some problems. The main problem is that performance on mental tests seems to level off around age 16. For example, the number of items one can hold in mind or remember does not increase after that age. Chronological age, however, keeps getting larger. It doesn't seem fair to continue dividing by a bigger and bigger number when the mental age is not growing along with one's chronological age. The ratio formula makes it look like people are getting less and less intelligent with age. One solution has been to divide by 16 for all people age 16 and above.

Another way to overcome this problem is to define IQ in terms of a *deviation*, or difference, rather than as a ratio. A **deviation IQ** still uses 100 as the average, but people are only compared against others of the same age. A particular person's IQ is then calculated by determining where his or her test score lies relative to the average score, in the overall distribution of scores. Figure 9.3 shows the typical **bell curve** of scores that would result from administering an IQ test such as the Stanford-Binet to a large group of people aged 25. The average score of the distribution is converted to 100

deviation IQ
An intelligence score that is derived from determining where your performance sits in an age-based distribution of test scores.

bell curve
The plot of frequencies obtained for many psychological tests. Most people get scores in the middle range, and the decline in frequencies is similar whether scores get higher or lower than the mean.

FIGURE 9.3
The Distribution of IQ Scores

IQ scores for a given age group will typically be distributed in a bell-shaped, or normal, curve. The average and most frequently occurring IQ score is defined as 100. Roughly 68% of the test takers in this age group received IQ scores between 85 and 115, which includes everyone scoring between one *standard deviation* above and below the mean. People labelled as "gifted" (an IQ of 130 and above) or "retarded" (an IQ of 70 or below) occur infrequently in the population—about 2% each.

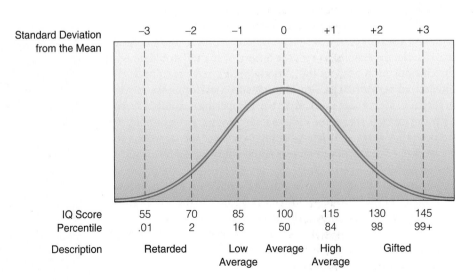

and everyone else's score is converted accordingly. Therefore, half of the test takers will be given scores above 100 and the other half below 100. The standard deviation is 15.

One of the characteristics of modern intelligence tests is that they tend to produce very regular and predictable distributions of scores (see Figure 9.3). This regularity allows us to know the percentages of people scoring in each range of scores. For example, 68% of the people will receive an IQ score between 85 and 115, and 95 percent between 70 and 130. We can also easily calculate the percentage of the population likely to score at or below a particular IQ score. For example, 50 percent of scores fall below 100 (by definition), and about 98% of the people will receive a score at or below 130. Notice once again that IQ in this case is defined in terms of the relative location of a person's score in a frequency distribution of scores gathered from people in the same chronological age group.

Extremes of Intelligence

Tests such as the Stanford-Binet or the related Wechsler Adult Intelligence Scale have been given to many thousands of people. Consequently, we know a great deal about how IQ scores tend to be distributed in the population. All but 5% of people score between 70 and 130. Individuals who fall above or below this range represent extremes in intelligence.

Mental Retardation   A score of 70 or below on a standard IQ test qualifies an individual for a diagnosis of **mental retardation.** It is rare, however, that a single test score leads to a final diagnosis of mental retardation; other factors (such as daily living skills) contribute to the diagnosis (Fredericks & Williams, 1998). A four-level classification scheme, as shown in Table 9.1, has been developed by the American Association on Mental Deficiency. The table shows how each category level for retardation is defined in terms of IQ. It also lists some of the adaptation skills that can be expected, on average, for individuals who meet the diagnostic criteria.

What causes mental retardation? There are many possible sources, some genetic and some environmental. Down syndrome, for example, is typically associated with low IQ scores and is caused by a genetic abnormality—usually an extra chromosome. Environmental factors during development, such as birth trauma, inadequate nutrition, and maternal illness, have also been linked to mental retardation.

Giftedness   At the other end of the IQ scale are people considered **gifted,** with IQs at or above approximately 130. The highest score ever assigned—to Johann Goethe—was

Critical Thinking

Do you see any similarities between the way that deviation IQ is interpreted and the way that you normally interpret your test scores in a class?

mental retardation
A label that is generally assigned to someone who scores below 70 on a standard IQ test. Other factors, such as one's ability to adapt to the environment, are also considered before putting someone in this category.

gifted
A label that is generally assigned to someone who scores above 130 on a standard IQ test.

Table 9.1
Types of Mental Retardation

Type	IQ Range (approximate)	Adaptation Potential
Mild	50 to 70	May develop academic skills comparable to a sixth-grade educational level; with assistance, may develop significant social and vocational skills and be self-supporting.
Moderate	35 to 50	Unlikely to achieve academic skills over the second-grade level; may become semi-independent.
Severe	20 to 35	Speech skills will be limited, but communication is possible; may learn to perform simple tasks in highly structured environments.
Profound	Below 20	Little or no speech is possible; requires constant care and supervision.

Ten-year-old Eddie Bonafe was born with severe physical and mental handicaps. But he could reproduce on the piano every hymn he heard sung in church before he had learned to walk. Individuals with Eddie's intellectual pattern are called savants.

savant

An individual with a special talent despite generally low intelligence.

estimated posthumously at 210 (Cox, 1926). The estimate was based on records confirming that Goethe performed at the level of university students when he was only 5 years old. Unfortunately, we don't have his score on a standard IQ test. Nor do we have the scores of most acknowledged geniuses such as Einstein or Shakespeare.

But several studies have tracked the intellectual and social accomplishments of gifted children. One of the most famous studies was started in the 1920s by Lewis Terman (1925; Terman & Ogden, 1947). Terman was interested in whether children who were identified early in life as gifted would be likely to achieve success throughout their lives. Generally, this turned out to be the case: Terman's gifted subjects earned more college degrees than average, made more money, wrote more books, generated more successful patents, and so on.

Interestingly, these kids also turned out to be both emotionally stable and generally socially adept, which is surprising given the bookworm stereotype that people have of highly intelligent people. Most had successful marriages, and the divorce rate was lower for them than for the general population (Terman, 1954). A more recent study examining gifted children who skipped high school and moved directly to college also found evidence for better-than-average social adjustment (Nobel et al., 1993). On the other hand, if one looks at profoundly gifted children—those with IQs above 180—some different patterns emerge. Ellen Winner (1997) found that profoundly gifted children typically showed only average adult achievement and were more likely to suffer emotional problems and become socially isolated.

Savants Even more fascinating are the cases of **savants** (formerly known as "idiot savants" because they display both retardation and giftedness). They are generally deficient in most standard mental abilities but have some special mental talent such as musical ability, memory for dates, or calculating numbers. The existence of such individuals makes it clear that intelligence cannot be a unitary ability. The neurology of the brain must allow some separation of mental abilities.

The Validity of Popular Intelligence Tests

In the section on characteristics of a good test, we discussed the central importance of validity. Now we can ask the critical question: Are standard tests of intelligence valid? Do IQ scores truly tap some hidden mental power (i.e., cognitive ability) that accounts for individual differences? Do intelligence tests adequately measure the ability to adapt and solve the problems of survival? Remember, the term *validity* has a technical meaning to the psychologist: How well does the test measure the thing that it is supposed to measure? To assess the validity of IQ tests, then, we need to ask: How well do IQ scores predict the appropriate criteria? Let's consider several of the popular tests.

The most widely applied intelligence tests today are the Stanford-Binet, the Wechsler Adult Intelligence Scale (WAIS), and the Wechsler Intelligence Scale for Children, 3rd edition (WISC-III). These are not the only tests, of course. In fact, if we combine intelligence tests with measures of scholastic aptitude, then we can identify at least 120 different tests currently in use (Jensen, 1992). Usually these tests are given for the same reasons that originally motivated Binet and Simon—to predict some kind of academic performance, usually grades in high school or college. From this perspective, IQ passes the validity test with flying colours: IQ, as measured by Stanford-Binet or the Wechsler tests, typically correlates about +0.50 or higher with school grades (Ceci, 1991; Kline, 1991). Notice that the correlation is not perfect, but it is high in comparison to other attempts to predict real-world behaviour from a psychological test. Consider all of the other factors that can affect grades in school (motivation, home environment, participation in extracurricular activities, teacher bias, and so on). IQ is also a reasonable predictor of real-world job performance, although its success in this domain is more modest (see the Practical Solutions box).

Practical Solutions

DOES INTELLIGENCE PREDICT SUCCESS IN THE WORKPLACE?

Theories and measures of intelligence have traditionally focused on school performance. But a much larger part of people's lives is spent at work. How well does the concept apply there? It is essential to employers to have some ability to predict who will function well in the job being filled. Interviews, although widely used, are poor predictors. The research is clear that general cognitive ability (*g*) is the best predictor of overall job performance (Jensen, 1993; Ree & Earles, 1992; Schmidt & Hunter, 1998). Nonetheless, this predictive power is far from perfect and it seems intuitively obvious that other factors such as personality and motivation play a role in people's performance on the job (Hogan et al., 1996).

Even the concept of intelligence has been expanded to deal with workplace performance. Standard intelligence tests contain questions that have right and wrong answers. There is usually only one path or method for solving the problem. But success on a job typically requires knowledge that is not so cut-and-dried. Often there are unspoken rules and strategies that are not taught formally. They help one to think quickly and efficiently in workplace situations. This kind of unspoken practical "know-how" is called **tacit knowledge,** and some psychologists believe that it will turn out to be an even better predictor of job performance than *g* (Wagner & Sternberg, 1985).

Such knowledge is rarely written in books and is not usually taught directly. Instead, it comes primarily from experience—from watching and analyzing the behaviour of others. But some workers pick up tacit knowledge more quickly than others. Some managers learn the rules for maximizing the performance of their subordinates better than others do. Tacit knowledge tests contain "inside knowledge" questions provided by experts.

Here's a multiple-choice question on the tacit knowledge about becoming a famous academic:

What is the best strategy early in one's career?

(a) Publish as many articles as possible in as many places as possible.
(b) Publish your articles in prestigious journals.
(c) Gain good teacher ratings at your school.
(d) Acquire contacts at the higher levels of school administration.

The answer, as judged by successful academics, is (b).

Although the evidence is sparse so far, Sternberg and Wagner (1993) found that tacit knowledge correlates positively with such indicators as salary, performance ratings, and the prestige of the business or institution where the person is employed. They also showed that tacit knowledge improves with work experience, which is what you would expect.

A telling example was provided by a study at the racetrack (Ceci, 1986). A sample of people were asked to spend a day betting on horses. Some were experts on horseracing and some were not. Standard tests were administered to ensure that the experts and nonexperts had the same IQ scores. When the accounts were examined at the end of the day, the experts had won an average of $92 as opposed to the $30 lost by the nonexperts. So IQ is not everything. As with most jobs, racetrack professionals draw on their experience to succeed in their chosen profession.

Let's now take a moment to critique the concept of tacit knowledge. The idea that it's useful to develop and use multiple strategies to perform successfully is almost certain to be true. The adaptive mind soaks up knowledge where it can and, as we've seen in earlier chapters, modelling others is an important vehicle for guiding behaviour. But critics of Wagner and Sternberg's research have questioned whether tacit knowledge is really anything new. It sounds much like job experience or specific knowledge (Schmidt & Hunter, 1993). It may not be some human ability, like *g*, that can be tapped by the appropriate test; instead, measures of tacit knowledge may simply be indexes of what has been learned on the job. Other critics have questioned the claim that tacit knowledge scores really help predict job performance over and above *g* (Jensen, 1993). At this point, the jury is still out on whether tacit knowledge is a separate component of intelligence.

tacit knowledge
The special knowledge in a particular area that allows one to think quickly and efficiently.

Successful managers understand the unspoken rules and strategies—called "tacit knowledge"—that are rarely, if ever, taught directly.

Wechsler Adult Intelligence Scale (WAIS)		
Test	**Description**	**Example**
Verbal scale		
Information	Taps general range of information.	On what continent is France?
Comprehension	Tests understanding of social conventions and ability to evaluate past experience.	Why are children required to go to school?
Arithmetic	Tests arithmetic reasoning through verbal problems.	How many hours will it take to drive 150 miles at 50 miles per hour?
Performance scale		
Block design	Tests ability to perceive and analyze patterns by presenting designs that must be copied with blocks.	Assemble blocks to match this design:
Picture arrangement	Tests understanding of social situations through a series of pictures that must be arranged in the right sequence to tell a story.	Put the pictures in the right order: 1 2 3
Object assembly	Tests ability to deal with part-to-whole relationships by presenting puzzle pieces that must be assembled to form a complete object.	Assemble the pieces into a complete object:

FIGURE 9.4

Examples from the WAIS

The Wechsler Adult Intelligence Scale (WAIS) was designed to measure both verbal and performance aspects of intellectual ability. Included here are samples of the various question types. (From Weiten, 1995.)

Critical Thinking

Do you think it makes sense for elementary schools to use "tracking" systems, that is, to divide children early on into different classes based on early performance on standardized tests?

Critics of IQ tests often argue that they fail to provide a broad enough index of intelligence. This is a complaint about content validity. There are many ways that people can fit successfully into their environments—and it's certain that not all forms of multiple intelligence are tapped by traditional IQ tests. This criticism has been recognized for years by the community of intelligence test researchers, and efforts have been made to develop tests that tap a variety of abilities. The influential tests of David Wechsler, for example, were developed in part to measure nonverbal aspects of intellectual ability. The Wechsler tests include not only verbal-mathematical questions of the type traditionally found on the Stanford-Binet test, but also performance questions requiring physical movement like the completion or rearrangement of pictures (see Figure 9.4). Scores are then broken down into a verbal IQ and a performance IQ.

Again, most intelligence tests were designed to measure g and, therefore, are successful in predicting future academic performance; they were not designed to provide an all-encompassing index of multiple intelligences. So if you develop a test to predict college performance, it probably isn't reasonable to expect it to predict creativity, originality, or the ability for moral insight. For their purpose, then, standard IQ tests have good predictive validity. Whether they have construct validity is a more complex issue: The psychologist's answer will depend on whether IQ tests match that psychologist's concept of intelligence.

As we'll discuss later, this also means that intelligence tests can suffer from cultural limitations—a test designed to measure the abilities of high school students in suburbia may not be valid for students in the inner city or from a different region of the world. This doesn't mean that intelligence tests aren't useful—you just need to be aware of what the tests were designed to measure.

The developer of the WISC test has recently conducted research that compared the performance of American and Canadian children, and the results indicated that Canadian children tend to score slightly higher on certain test items than American children (Beal et al., 1996; Wechsler, 1996). As a result, new tables for interpreting the results of the test have been provided to Canadian psychologists using the WISC-III, so that a valid assessment of each child in comparison to the Canadian norm is possible.

Other Individual Differences Related to Intelligence

To end our discussion of the measurement of individual differences, we'll briefly consider two psychological characteristics that are often aligned with the topic of intelligence: *creativity* and *emotional intelligence*. Neither creativity nor emotional intelligence is necessarily related to general intelligence, but both represent quite adaptive characteristics that can potentially increase our ability to survive.

Creativity The term **creativity** refers to the ability to generate ideas that are original and novel. Creative thinkers think in unusual ways, which means that they can look at the usual and express it in an unusual way. Creative thinkers tend to see the "big picture" and are able to find connections between things that others might not see. Importantly, however, it's not just the generation of new and different ideas that makes one creative; those ideas must also be useful and relevant—they must potentially have adaptive value.

How is creativity measured? Psychologists have devised a number of ways to measure individual differences in creative ability (Cooper, E., 1991; Cropley, 1996). One popular technique is to give someone a group of unrelated words, or unrelated objects in a picture, and then ask him or her to generate as many connections between the items as possible (Mednick, 1962; Torrance, 1981). Try it yourself: Take the words FOOD, CATCHER, and HOT and try to think of a fourth word (or words) that relates to all three. It turns out that measures like these reveal individual differences among people—some find this task to be quite easy; others find it extremely difficult. Moreover, performance on these creativity tests can then be correlated with other abilities, such as IQ or job success, to see if there is a connection.

What's the relation between creativity and intelligence? When intelligence is conceptualized in a broad way, then creativity fits in nicely as a part of general intellectual ability. You'll remember, for instance, that Sternberg's three facets of intelligence include the concept of creative intelligence. However, we noted that IQ tests aimed at *g* show relatively little overlap with measures of creativity. Correlations between creativity and IQ are always positive but modest (Horn, 1976; MacKinnon, 1962). What this means, however, is not clear—traditional IQ tests don't really measure creative thinking, so perhaps it's not surprising that the correlations are not very high. Perhaps being intelligent is a necessary but not sufficient condition for being creative. Furthermore, this issue still suffers from disagreement about which is the best test of creativity.

Emotional Intelligence The second psychological characteristic, emotional intelligence, has recently gained some popularity among psychologists and is worthy of discussion here. **Emotional intelligence** is essentially the ability to perceive, understand, and express emotion (Bar-On & Parker, 2000; Parker, 2000; Salovey & Mayer, 1990). The concept applies to perceiving and understanding the emotions of others, as well as to the understanding and control of one's own emotions. Emotions, as you'll see in Chapter 11, can play a large role in behaviour, so it's clearly adaptive to manage and express them appropriately.

People who score highly on emotional intelligence can read others' emotions well and tend to be empathetic as a result. They're good at managing conflict, both their own and the conflicts of others. Not surprisingly, emotional intelligence is believed to be an excellent predictor of success in career and social settings. In fact, some have argued that emotional intelligence may be a more important predictor of success in life than more traditional conceptions of intelligence (Goleman, 1995). Critics have argued that emotional intelligence is not really a form of intelligence at all but an aspect of personality (e.g., Block, 2002). Research on emotional intelligence is in its infancy, so we'll need to wait before concluding anything about its ultimate usefulness (Pfeiffer, 2001).

creativity
The ability to generate ideas that are original, novel, and useful.

emotional intelligence
The ability to perceive, understand, and express emotion in ways that are useful and adaptive.

Test Yourself 9.2

Check what you know about the measurement of individual differences by answering the following questions. (You will find the answers in Appendix B.)

1. For each of the following statements, pick the test characteristic that is most appropriate. Choose from the following: reliability, standardization, and validity.
    a. Donna performs poorly on the SAT, so she takes it again and finds herself performing poorly again: _____
    b. Larry has devised a new test of intelligence, but he finds that it predicts nothing about school performance or success on the job:
        _____
    c. Chei-Wui wants to see how consistent the scores are on his new intelligence test, so he correlates answers across repeated administrations of the test: _____
    d. Robert's new job is to administer the Graduate Record Exam. He is very careful to keep the testing and scoring procedures the same for everybody who takes the test: _____
2. Decide whether each of the following statements is true or false.
    a. Lucinda has a mental age of 8 and an IQ of 160—this means that she must be 5 years old chronologically. *True or False?*
    b. Average IQ, based on the deviation IQ method, varies with chronological age. *True or False?*
    c. Lewis has just scored below 70 on his IQ test, which means that he will soon be labelled as mentally retarded. *True or False?*
    d. Creativity increases with intellectual ability, as measured by IQ. *True or False?*

DISCOVERING THE SOURCES OF INTELLIGENCE: THE NATURE–NURTURE ISSUE

Learning Goals

1. Understand the stability of IQ, and discuss why IQ might change across the life span.
2. Learn how twin studies are used to evaluate genetic contributions to intelligence.
3. Recognize environmental influences on intelligence.
4. Understand how genetic and environmental factors interact to determine intelligence.

WE'VE SEEN THAT PEOPLE DIFFER, and we've considered some of the ways to measure these individual differences. We've also discussed methods for conceptualizing these differences theoretically—there may be differences in *g*, there may be differences in the speed of brain cells, or people may lack some of the mental operations that are needed for intelligent performance. But what accounts for these differences in the first place? Why is one person's *g* higher or lower than another person's *g*? Is there anything that can be done about these differences, or are they fixed in stone?

There are essentially two ways to explain how differences in intelligence might arise. First, you can appeal to heredity, particularly the internal *genetic code*—those strands of DNA that determine eye colour, thickness of hair, and possibly *g*. According to this view, intellectual potential is established at conception through some particularly fortunate (or unfortunate) combinations of genes. The second way is to appeal to

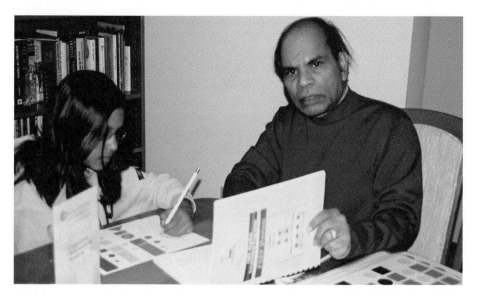

Pictured is intelligence researcher J. P. Das, working with a child at his clinic at the University of Alberta. Although tests are available to measure intelligence in small children, it's difficult to obtain reliable estimates of intelligence before age 4.

an external cause, specifically, the *environment*. Variations in *g* might be attributable to one's past history: A high scorer might have been reinforced for intellectual pursuits or might have gone to an excellent school. Perhaps a low score might be traced to exposure to toxins as a child (such as lead paint). In this section, we'll frame this classic *nature versus nurture* debate and consider the evidence relevant to each position. But first, we have a practical issue to consider: How stable is the IQ measure itself?

The Stability of IQ

One way to answer questions about the origins of intelligence is to ask whether IQ changes significantly over a lifetime. If intelligence is caused by something like a "fast brain," then we might expect intellectual ability to change very little over time until the brain deteriorates along with the rest of the body. On the other hand, if intelligence is determined mainly by the environment, we would probably expect to find variation over time: IQ might rise and fall depending on recent experience or current environmental setting. Neither of these arguments is airtight, however. For instance, your environment might remain constant over time, or the genetic code might express itself differently at different ages. It might also be the case that IQ is determined by early experience and remains fixed after a certain point in development. Still, examination of the stability of the IQ measure is a reasonable place to start the search.

When intelligence is measured in the standard way, through performance on a battery of tests, the stability of the measure depends on when the measuring process begins. Before the age of about 3 or 4, it's difficult to get an accurate assessment of intellectual ability. Infants can't talk or show sustained attention, so conventional testing procedures can't be used. Investigators resort to indirect measures, such as recording whether babies choose to look at old or new pictures presented on a screen. There is some evidence that babies who quickly "habituate," or lose interest, in response to repeated presentations of the same picture, and who prefer to look at novel pictures when they're shown, score higher on intelligence tests later in childhood (Bornstein, 1989; McCall & Carriger, 1993). But in general, it's widely believed that you can't get reliable assessments of IQ until somewhere between ages 4 and 7; from that point onward, IQ scores tend to predict performance on later IQ tests reasonably well (Honzik et al., 1948; Sameroff et al., 1993).

Longitudinal Studies One of the best ways to measure the stability of IQ is through a longitudinal study, which involves testing the same people repeatedly as they age. The most widely known investigation of the stability of adult intelligence is the Seattle

Critical Thinking

Elderly people are often said to possess wisdom. In what ways do you think the label "wise" differs from the label "intelligent"?

Longitudinal Study, which has examined mental test performance for approximately 5000 adults ranging in age from 25 to 88 (Schaie, 1983, 1989, 1993). The subjects have been tested in seven-year cycles, dating back to 1956, using a battery of tests to assess such things as verbal fluency, inductive reasoning, and spatial ability. Schaie and his colleagues have found great stability in intellectual ability throughout adulthood. From age 21 to about age 60, there appears to be no serious decline in general intellectual ability, as measured through the test battery (see Figure 9.5). After age 60, abilities begin to decline a bit, although the losses are not great. There are also large individual differences—some people retain their performance well into their 80s, whereas others do not (Schaie, 1998).

It's difficult to interpret changes in IQ with age because many factors change concurrently with age. Elderly people are more likely to have physical problems, for example, that can affect performance. Declines in intelligence with age also depend on the type of intellectual ability measured. Earlier, we discussed the distinction between fluid intelligence, which taps basic processing skills, and crystallized intelligence, which taps acquired knowledge. The current thinking is that fluid intelligence declines with age—perhaps because the biology of the brain changes—whereas crystallized intelligence remains constant, or perhaps even increases, until late in adulthood (Horn, 1982; Kaufman & Horn, 1996; Schretlen et al., 2000). The brain may become a bit slower with age, but people continue to add knowledge and experiences that are invaluable in their efforts to solve the problems of everyday life.

Nature: The Genetic Argument

A number of pioneers in intelligence testing, including Galton, strongly believed that individual differences in mental ability are inherited. After all, Galton argued, it's easy to demonstrate that intellectual skill runs through family lines. (Remember: His cousin was Charles Darwin; in addition, his grandfather was another famous evolutionist, Erasmus Darwin.) But family-tree arguments do not lead to firm conclusions. Environmental factors, such as social and educational opportunities, can explain why members of the same family might show similar skills. Growing up in a family that

Critical Thinking

Do you think it's possible to separate the relative contributions of nature and nurture to intelligence by studying animals in the laboratory?

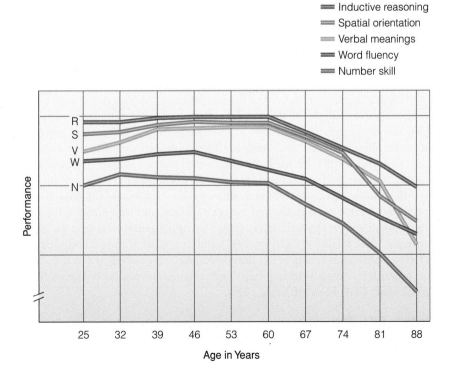

FIGURE 9.5

The Stability of Intellectual Ability

Data from the Seattle Longitudinal Study show how performance changes on a variety of mental tasks between the ages of 25 and 88. Notice that average performance is remarkably stable up to about age 60, at which point some declines are seen. (Data from Schaie, 1983.)

places value on intellectual pursuits determines to some extent what sort of behaviours will be rewarded in a child, or the particular type of role models that will be available. To capture this debate in a phrase, it was Galton who coined the phrase "nature versus nurture" (Galton, 1869, 1883).

To establish a genetic basis for a psychological or physical characteristic, it's necessary to control for the effects of the environment. In principle, if two people are raised in exactly the same environment and receive exactly the same experiences, we can attribute any reliable differences in IQ to inherited factors (*nature*). In this case, you've held any nurturing effects of the environment constant, so any differences must be due to genetics. Alternatively, if two people are born with exactly the same genes but end up with quite different intelligence scores, it must be the environment, not genes, that is responsible (*nurture*). We can't do a true experiment to confirm these arguments, for obvious reasons, but we can look for natural comparisons that are relevant. As we discussed in Chapter 3, psychologists often study identical twins, who share nearly complete genetic overlap, to tease apart the nature and nurture components of mind and behaviour.

Twin Studies In twin studies, researchers search for identical twins who have been raised together in the same household or who have been separated at birth through adoption (Bouchard & McGue, 1981; Bouchard et al., 1990). The effects of the environment are assumed to be similar for the twins raised together but quite different, at least on average, for twins raised apart. If intelligence comes primarily from genetic factors, we would expect identical twins to have very similar intelligence scores, regardless of the environments in which they have been raised. One way to measure similarity is by correlation. More specifically, you can attempt to predict the IQ of one twin when given knowledge about the IQ of the other.

If genes are entirely responsible for intelligence, we would expect to get a strong positive correlation between IQ scores for identical twins. We wouldn't necessarily expect it to be exactly +1.00 because of measurement error or other uncontrolled factors. In reviewing the research literature on this issue, Bouchard and McGue (1981) found strong evidence for the genetic position: The IQ scores of identical twins are indeed quite similar, irrespective of the environment in which the twins have been reared. As shown in Figure 9.6, the IQ scores for twins reared together showed an average correlation of 0.86; even when reared apart, the average correlation remained strongly positive at 0.72 (Bouchard & McGue, 1981).

Some kinds of abilities tend to run in families, such as musical ability in the Rankin family. It's difficult, though, to separate the influences of nature and nurture.

Type of Relationship

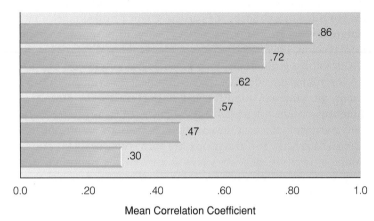

*One or both of the siblings were adopted.

FIGURE 9.6

Nature versus Nurture

The horizontal bars show the mean correlation coefficients for pairs of people with differing amounts of genetic overlap who have been reared in similar or different environments. For example, the top bar shows the average correlation for identical twins who have been reared together in the same environment. The bottom bar shows the correlation coefficient for adopted siblings reared together. Higher correlations mean that the measured IQ scores are more similar. (Data from Bouchard & McGue, 1981.)

heritability

A mathematical index that represents the extent to which IQ differences in a particular population can be accounted for by genetic factors.

Researchers who conduct twin studies are actually interested in many different comparisons. For instance, it's useful to compare intelligence scores for fraternal twins (who are genetically no more similar than normal siblings) and among unrelated people who have been reared together or apart. In general, the impressive finding is that the closer the overlap in genes, the more similar the resulting IQs. Notice, for example, that the average correlation for adopted siblings who have been reared together (0.30) is much lower than the average correlation for identical twins reared apart (0.72). Thus, similarity in environmental history is not as strong a predictor of intelligence as similarity in genetic background.

Adoption Studies Adopted children have two sets of parents: The biological parents have a genetic impact on the child's IQ and the adopting parents have an environmental effect. Who will the child most resemble? Studies show that the child's IQ is correlated with the IQs of both sets of parents; however, the correlation with the biological parents is higher and it increases with time (Plomin et al., 1997). Together, the twin data and the adoption data suggest that genetic background plays an important role in intelligence, at least when intelligence is measured through conventional IQ testing.

Heritability Intelligence researchers often use a concept called heritability to describe the influence of genetic factors on intelligence. **Heritability** is a mathematical index that indicates the extent to which IQ differences within a population can be accounted for by genetic factors. For any group with differences in IQ scores, heritability measures the role that genetic factors play in producing these differences. Its value is expressed as a percentage, so if the heritability of intelligence was 100%, that would mean that all differences in measured IQ could be explained by genetics. Most estimates of the heritability of intelligence, derived from twin studies, hover at around 50%, which means that approximately half of the differences in IQ have a genetic basis (Sternberg & Kaufman, 1998). Other researchers propose values that are higher, perhaps closer to 70% (Bouchard et al., 1990). There is some debate over the fact that heritability estimates are somewhat higher in twin studies than in adoption studies.

It's important to understand that estimates of heritability apply only to groups, not to individuals. A heritability estimate of 70% does not mean that 70% of someone's intelligence is due to his or her genetic blueprint. To see why, imagine two groups of people with the same genetic histories. Group A maintains rigid control of the environment—everyone is treated exactly the same. Group B allows the environment to vary. If IQ scores are influenced by the environment in any way, we would expect the heritability values to be quite different for the two groups, even though the groups' genetic backgrounds are identical. Because the environment is held constant in group A, all of the variability in measured IQ will be due to genes. In group B, the heritability index will be lower because some of the differences in IQ will be due to environmental effects. Heritability tells us only that for a given group, a certain percentage of the differences in intelligence can be explained by genetic factors.

Nurture: The Environmental Argument

You may have noticed in Figure 9.6 that identical twins and siblings reared together have IQs that are more similar than twins or siblings reared apart. This means that individual differences in intelligence cannot be explained completely through genetic background. The environment also plays an important role.

Most psychologists acknowledge that different learning experiences result in different performance on intellectual tasks. Zajonc (1983), for example, details how intellectual stimulation of a child accumulates over childhood to determine adult scores on IQ tests. Chapter 10 provides much more detail on this topic. There are significant economic differences between individuals even within ethnic groups. And these differences correspond well to differences in IQ scores. In other words, poverty may contribute to low scores: The most obvious reason is the reduced access to education among the poor.

The twin studies and adoption studies noted in the section "Nature: The Genetic Argument" also provide evidence for environmental influences on IQ scores. Although it may be lower than the genetic contribution, the environmental influence is significant and well established.

Group Differences Most intelligence researchers agree that different ethnic and socioeconomic groups score, on average, somewhat differently on intelligence tests, and these differences are relatively stable. At the same time, it's very important to understand that group differences are averages. The bell curves always overlap. So the average differences don't tell us anything about single individuals.

Still, the group differences are real and should be explained. How can we account for these differences? Some researchers have suggested that evolutionary and genetic factors are the most important factors in such IQ differences between ethnic and racial groups (e.g., Eysenck, 1991; Jensen, 1992; Rushton, 2000).

A consistent pattern of sex differences remains even in modern samples. Men tend to score higher on spatial ability and women higher on verbal ability (Benbow et al., 2000). The origin of such differences, however, remains controversial. For example, the difference in spatial ability might be traceable to sex differences in the brain or to the fact that boys more often play sports (Halpern, 2000; Kimura, 1999). In sum, the research literature is more certain about the existence of group differences than about their origins in nature or nurture.

Many psychologists suggest that cultural background plays an important role in the measurement of intelligence. The cultural background of this Innu family should be taken into account when assessing intelligence.

Economic Differences There are significant economic differences between racial and ethnic groups that make interpretation of intergroup IQ differences difficult. For example, Black and First Nations Canadians are more likely to live at or below the poverty level than are White Canadians. Poverty, of course, may lead to nutrition problems and difficulties in gaining proper health care, and may hurt one's chances of entering adequate schools. Black and First Nations Canadians are also more likely to experience racial discrimination than are Whites. The impact of these factors on intelligence testing is not completely understood, although they may play an important role. Black, First Nations, and White Canadians also tend to live in somewhat different social worlds; consequently, it is difficult to disentangle the effects of the environment from any genetic differences that might contribute to group differences in intelligence.

Test Bias   There is also some indication that test biases might contribute to group differences in IQ scores (Bernal, 1984). Racial/ethnic group differences depend, to a certain extent, on the type of intelligence test that is administered (Brody, 1992). Most traditional IQ tests of the type that we've discussed in this chapter are written, administered, and scored by White, middle-class psychologists. This raises the very real possibility that cultural biases might be contaminating some of the test questions. For example, if you are asked a question such as "Who wrote *Faust*?" (which once appeared on a Wechsler test), your ability to answer correctly will depend partly on whether your culture places value on exposure to such information. In general, it is most likely that White students of European descent would have been exposed to the information necessary to answer such a question. Therefore, one's failure to answer it might not be a sign of lower intelligence, but rather of a culture that places a higher value on other types of information. Some observers have even argued that because of such problems, conventional intelligence tests have little validity with some populations, such as many First Nations groups, and should not be used (Darou, 1992; Kleinfeld & Nelson, 1991).

Psychologists have worked hard to remove bias from standard intelligence and achievement tests (Raven et al., 1985); in some cases, the development of **"culture-fair" tests** has reduced racial differences in measured ability. However, significant group differences usually remain even after culture-bound questions have been altered or removed. In sum, bias is recognized as a contributor to measured intelligence, although it's unlikely to be the sole determinant of group differences in IQ (Cole, 1981; Kaplan, 1985).

Adoption Studies   A more direct test of environmental explanations of racial/ethnic differences comes from studies looking at the IQs of African-American children who have been reared in White homes. If the average African-American childhood experience puts children at a disadvantage on tests of intelligence (for whatever reason), then African-American children raised in White, middle-class homes should be expected to produce higher IQ scores. In general, this assumption is supported by the data. Scarr and Weinberg (1976) investigated interracial adoptions in Minnesota and found that the average IQ for African-American children reared in economically advantaged White households was significantly higher than the national African-American mean score. This finding was confirmed again in later follow-up studies (Waldman et al., 1994; Weinberg et al., 1992). You should not conclude from this finding that White, middle-class households are better in every way. The results simply imply that certain cultural experiences give one an advantage on the IQ tests currently being used to assess intelligence.

The Interaction of Nature and Nurture

So what are we to conclude about the relative contributions of genetics and the environment to intelligence? Nature–nurture issues are notoriously difficult to resolve, and this is especially true in the politically sensitive area of intelligence. It's extremely difficult to control for the effects of either the environment or genetics. Consider the twin studies—how reasonable is it to assume that twins who have been reared apart have had unrelated environmental experiences? Are children who are adopted really representative of the racial or ethnic populations from which they have been drawn? It's difficult to answer questions like these, because neither the environment nor genetic structure can be manipulated directly in the laboratory (at least for humans).

Critical Thinking

Do you think it's possible to eliminate cultural influences completely from a psychological test?

culture-fair test

Tests that avoid using language (e.g., by using only pictures or symbols) so that the test is fair to all cultures.

Critical Thinking

Genetic and environmental theories are both scientific in origin. Then why is it that different people—even scientists—tend to have an emotional preference for one approach or the other?

The most reasonable position to take at the present time is that your intelligence, like many other psychological attributes, is determined by a mixture of genes and environment. The genes that you inherit from your parents place upper and lower bounds on intellectual ability. Genes may importantly determine how your brain is wired and, possibly, the speed of neural transmission, but the expression of your genetic material is strongly influenced by the environment.

Recall from Chapter 3 that geneticists use the term *genotype* to refer to the genetic message itself and *phenotype* to refer to the observable characteristics that actually result from genetic expression. An analogy that is sometimes used by intelligence researchers compares the development of intelligence to the nurturing of flowering plants (Lewontin, 1976). Imagine that we have a packet of virtually identical seeds and we toss half into a pot containing fertile soil and half into a pot of barren soil (see Figure 9.7). The seeds tossed into the poor soil will undoubtedly grow, but their growth will be stunted relative to that of the group planted in the rich soil. Because these are virtually identical groups of seeds, containing similar distributions of genetic information, any differences in growth between the pots are due entirely to the environment (the soil). So, too, with intelligence—two people can be born with similar genetic potential, but the degree to which their intellectual potential "blossoms" depends critically on the environment.

Consider as well that within each handful of seeds there will be variations in genetic information. Some plants will grow larger than others, regardless of the soil in which they have been thrown. A similar kind of result would be expected for intelligence—variations in the genetic message will produce individual differences in IQ that cannot be adequately explained by environmental variables. In fact, after analyzing the differences within a pot, we might conclude that all of the differences are due to inherited factors. But even if the differences within a group are due to genes, the differences between groups would still be due to the environment (fertile or barren soil). This kind

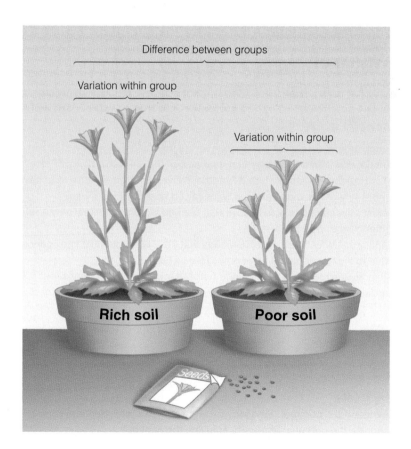

FIGURE 9.7

Between- and Within-Group Variation

In the plant analogy, all of the variation in plant height within a pot is due to genetics, but the overall height difference between the two pots is attributable to the environment (rich soil versus poor soil).

FIGURE 9.8

Reaction Range

Each person may have genes that set limits for intellectual potential, sometimes called a reaction range. In this case, Tom inherited a capacity for obtaining an IQ anywhere between 80 and about 112. The IQ that Tom actually obtains (shown as the dark bar) is determined by the kind of environment in which he is reared. Notice that Miguel inherited a greater IQ potential than Tom, but if Tom is raised in an enriched environment, his IQ may actually turn out to be higher than Miguel's.

of insight might help account, in part, for the racial/ethnic differences in IQ that we discussed earlier. Even though genes may exert a strong influence within a population, between-population differences could still be determined primarily by the environment (Eysenck & Kamin, 1981; Lewontin, 1976).

One other feature of the interaction between nature and nurture is worth noting. Environmental experiences do not occur independently of inherited factors. It's a two-way street. The environment will partly determine how genetic information is expressed, but so too will genetic information determine experience. If you're born with "smart" genes, then early on you're likely to be exposed to opportunities that will help you realize your full intellectual potential; conversely, if you're born "slow," the environment is likely to shape you away from intellectually nurturing experiences (see Figure 9.8). Even in the domain of intelligence, the rich tend to get richer.

Test Yourself 9.3

Check your knowledge about the sources of intelligence by deciding whether each of the following statements is true or false. (You will find the answers in Appendix B.)

1. Longitudinal studies of intelligence reveal that fluid, but not crystallized, intelligence remains largely constant across the life span. *True or False?*
2. Twin studies have shown that fraternal twins raised together tend to have more similar IQs than identical twins raised apart. *True or False?*
3. Most psychologists now believe that genetic factors definitely play a role in intelligence. *True or False?*
4. A heritability estimate of 70% means that 70% of someone's intelligence is due to his or her genetic blueprint. *True or False?*
5. Test bias is recognized as a contributor to measured intelligence, but it's unlikely to be the sole determinant of group differences in IQ. *True or False?*

PERCEPTIONS OF INTELLIGENCE

Learning Goals

1. Understand the common tendency to judge people's intelligence.
2. Recognize the potential abuses in applying the concept.

AT THE BEGINNING OF THE CHAPTER, we noted that the concept of intelligence looms large in people's lives. Its high value in society leads people to have strong opinions about who deserves the label and who does not. Of course, we all believe that we deserve the label: Everyone believes that they are above average in intelligence (Beauregard & Dunning, 1997). However, we do not extend that generosity to other people. Indeed, "stupid" and "idiot" are common terms in some people's daily descriptions of others. Here we discuss our natural human tendency to judge other people's intelligence.

Judging Intelligence

Several times in an average day, we find ourselves commenting on people's intelligence: "Man, he's smart" or "What an idiot!" Typical situations are when a classmate makes a comment in class or when a politician makes a controversial remark. We tend to attribute high intelligence to those who talk fast (Amabile, 1983), those with a confident voice (Reynolds & Gifford, 2001), those who criticize others, and those who wear glasses (McKelvie, 1997; Kellerman & Laird, 1982). But these cues have little validity. We also make complex judgments based on people's accents. In Canada, for example, we tend to make biased judgments against those with "Newfie" accents (Edwards, 1999). On the other hand, when we use cues such as confident voice and careful speech, we are accurate (Borkenau & Liebler, 1995). According to Sternberg (1988), our overall judgment of a person will correspond to the proportion of apparent matches between an individual's characteristics and our **intelligence prototype,** that is, our list of the characteristics of (what we think constitutes) a perfectly intelligent person. Personal prototypes differ from person to person and from situation to situation (we use different prototypes at school versus the business world).

intelligence prototype
The list of characteristics that each person believes are present in the perfectly intelligent person.

But how accurate are people in judging intelligence? When IQ scores are used as the criterion, the correlation with rated intelligence is roughly 0.30 (Paulhus et al., 1998). Does it matter who does the rating? Research shows that your friends are just as accurate as you are in judging your intelligence. Despite this rather modest success in judging others' intelligence, we do it many times a day without ever being proved wrong. Yet decisions influencing our lives and those of others are made on this basis without recourse (Kunda & Thagard, 1996). For each time that we are evaluated by a standard test, our intelligence is evaluated a thousand times by those who meet us.

Ordinary people also differ in their general style of judging people's intelligence. Carol Dweck and her colleagues at Columbia University make the distinction between people who see intelligence as fixed (entity theorists) and people who see intelligence as malleable (incremental theorists). Entity theorists believe that intelligence is a permanent quality that one is born with. Incremental theorists believe that one gradually acquires intelligence through hard work. According to Dweck, it is more adaptive to be an incremental theorist, especially when judging oneself (Dweck, 1999; Dweck et al., 1995). Recent evidence suggests that Asian students tend to be incremental whereas European-heritage students tend to be entity theorists (Tweed & Lehman, 2002).

The Potential for Abuse

Because of our strong tendency to judge others—accurately or not—intelligence testing has the potential for abuse. As noted earlier in the chapter, the high value placed on having the trait and the correspondingly strong emotional reaction to being labelled as unintelligent pose a number of dangers. As with any form of psychological assessment, wrong conclusions might be drawn but the consequences of those conclusions can be more serious with intelligence testing. The pronouncements of an authority figure such as a teacher or psychologist are taken much more seriously than a schoolyard insult.

Consider the potentially serious problem of labelling. Once a child takes an IQ test, his or her performance becomes part of a continuing academic record. A label tends to be applied—you're smart, you're below average, and so on. As a result, your expectations of yourself are altered accordingly. Expectations are also altered in those who have access to your score. Some studies have suggested that intelligence-related labels influence how teachers interact with their students in the classroom. The kids with the "smart" label are exposed to more educational opportunities and are treated with more respect (Oakes, 1985; Rosenthal & Jacobson, 1968). More recent research suggests that such effects are detectable but rather weak (Jussim, 1989). Overall, the effects may be weak because not all teachers react the same way: The most diligent and nurturant teachers might actually increase their assistance once a student is labelled as less able.

Labelling effects were serious in the early decades of the 20th century, when intelligence tests were in their formative stages of development. Tests were widely administered to newly arriving immigrants and all army recruits well before the impact of cultural and educational factors on test performance was widely understood by test administrators. As noted earlier, people can perform poorly on an intelligence test because the test has certain built-in biases with respect to language and cultural lifestyle.

The result was that certain population groups, such as immigrants from southern and eastern Europe, generally performed poorly on these tests. Some psychologists even went so far as to label these immigrant groups as "feeble minded" or "defective" based on their test performance. One result was that immigration laws enacted in the 1920s in the United States discriminated against poorly performing groups. For many years, several Canadian provinces permitted forced sterilization of individuals who performed very poorly on intelligence tests. In modern times, psychologists are more aware of test bias, but its impact on test performance remains controversial to this day.

To be fair, any critique of intelligence tests should answer the question "compared to what"? It is unlikely that society will stop evaluating people—the only question is how. Aptitude and intelligence tests were designed to counter the biases inherent in previous methods of evaluating people (e.g., interviews and letters of recommendation). Compared to the alternatives, intelligence tests seem rather unbiased. Of course, the optimal assessment approach would take advantage of a variety of information sources to minimize the effects of any one bias. Whether or not we use standard IQ tests, people's intelligence will continue to be evaluated in both job situations and everyday interactions.

Test Yourself 9.4

Check your knowledge about perceptions of intelligence by deciding whether each of the following statements is true or false. (You will find the answers in Appendix B.)

1. People show a general tendency to believe that others are above average in intelligence. *True or False?*
2. Our perceptions about others' intelligence are totally inaccurate. *True or False?*
3. Entity theorists believe that intelligence is malleable. *True or False?*
4. Labelling people as intelligent or unintelligent can affect how we treat them. *True or False?*
5. IQ test scores have been used unfairly to mistreat whole groups of people. *True or False?*

Solving the Scientific and Practical Problems

What is intelligence? It is a concept that we use to explain individual differences in life success. No one disputes that people differ in intelligence, and it seems preferable to assess people with objective tests than use our subjective judgments. A century of testing has led to a variety of theories of intellectual functioning. What kinds of mental processes underlie intelligent thought? The most general notion to characterize intelligence is the adaptability of behaviour. From this perspective, the nutcracker bird, in its successful search for a cache of seeds, fits the adaptive view of intelligence just as well as the human achievement of building cities. But there are undeniable differences within species (Coren, 1999). What makes one species member more intelligent than another is a higher level of some chronic ability to adapt to changing environments and solve the problems of survival.

In this chapter, our discussion revolved around three scientific and practical problems that researchers interested in intelligence have attempted to resolve.

First, how should intelligence be conceptualized? Researchers have attempted to conceptualize intelligence in a number of ways. Proponents of the psychometric approach to intelligence try to map out the concept by analyzing performance on a battery of mental tests. They traditionally debate distinctions between a general factor of intelligence, *g*, which applies broadly, and independent sets of abilities. In the psychometric community, the idea that intelligence involves several overlapping types of ability still emphasizes scholastic mental abilities.

Cognitive approaches to intelligence seek to discover the internal processes that account for intelligent behaviour. There's some evidence to suggest that performance on traditional tests of mental ability might be related to the speed of processing among neurons in the brain. Multiple intelligence approaches such as Howard Gardner's and Robert Sternberg's both suggest that the concept of intelligence must be defined broadly. We cannot rely entirely on things such as academic ability to define intelligence—everyday intelligence and "street smarts" also enhance our ability to adapt.

Second, how can we measure the individual differences in performance? To conduct research on intelligence, we need a numerical index of mental performance. IQ test scores provide such a number. A good IQ test has three main characteristics: reliability, validity, and standardization.

Understanding the concept of test validity is crucial because it holds the key to appreciating the widespread use of standardized measures such as IQ or tests such as the SAT. Researchers who study individual differences are often primarily interested in using measured differences to make predictions about future success. Will Jennifer perform well in school? Will Sam make it as a graduate student in psychology? As you've seen, the IQ test was originally developed to measure academic ability and that remains its most successful domain.

Third, what are the sources of intelligence? There are two primary ways to explain how measured differences in intelligence might arise: genetics and the environment. Twin and adoption studies provide convincing evidence that at least some kinds of mental ability are inherited, although how much remains controversial. However, the role of the environment in determining IQ—cultural background, economic status, and even built-in test biases—cannot be discounted. Intelligence, like many psychological attributes, grows out of an interaction between nature and nurture.

Chapter Summary

CONCEPTUALIZING INTELLIGENCE

Psychometric Approach: Measuring the Mind

Learning Goal: Comprehend the psychometric approach to conceptualizing intelligence, including Spearman's two-factor theory. The *psychometric approach* proposes that intelligence is a mental capacity that can be understood by analyzing performance on mental tests. Galton and Spearman are two pioneers of this approach. Spearman used *factor analysis* to analyze the relationships between test scores and isolate the "factors" that account for test performance. Spearman proposed that intelligence derives from *g*, or general intelligence, as well as more specific abilities, *s*. Later models have emphasized more than one kind of ability, as in *hierarchical models*. Some propose that general intelligence is composed of two abilities: *fluid intelligence* (ability to solve problems and reason) and *crystallized intelligence* (acquired knowledge).

The Cognitive Approach

Learning Goal: Understand cognitive approaches to conceptualizing intelligence. The cognitive approach argues that intelligence can be understood by analyzing internal mental processes. This analysis usually involves measuring the speed of mental processing and analyzing the specific mental operations that produce intelligent thought. Some believe that intelligence reflects, in part, the speed of neural processing. Sternberg uses *componential analysis* to isolate the mental processes that are tapped by traditional intelligence tests.

Expanded Conceptions of Intelligence

Learning Goal: Learn the differences among the various expanded theories. Gardner has proposed that traditional views of intelligence should be broadened to include special abilities or talents and that there are *multiple intelligences*. Using a case study approach, Gardner has identified seven kinds of intelligence: *musical, bodily-kinesthetic, logical-mathematical, linguistic, spatial, interpersonal,* and *intrapersonal*. The psychometric and cognitive approaches focus on logical-mathematical, linguistic, and spatial intelligence. Many of Gardner's intelligences match those found by Paulhus and his colleagues when they collected ordinary people's nominations of *intelligent exemplars*.

In contrast, Sternberg's conceptualization of intelligence includes three facets of abilities: *Analytic intelligence* refers to a person's basic ability to process information; *creative intelligence* expresses how well people are able to cope with new or novel tasks; *practical intelligence* taps how well people fit into their environments.

MEASURING INDIVIDUAL DIFFERENCES

Regardless of how psychologists conceptualize intelligence, an important practical consideration is how to measure intelligence. Accurate measurement of abilities through the use of psychological tests allows for the tailoring of people's activities to fit their skills. *Achievement tests* measure someone's current level of knowledge in a particular topic; *aptitude tests* measure the ability to learn in a particular area.

The Characteristics of a Good Test

Learning Goal: Recognize the components of a good test: reliability, validity, and standardization. Three characteristics are needed for a good test. *Reliability* is a measure of the consistency of a test. *Test-retest reliability* is calculated by comparing test scores across repeated administrations. *Validity* tells us whether a test measures what it is supposed to measure. *Content validity* measures the degree to which the content of the test samples broadly across the domain of interest. *Predictive validity* measures the degree to which the test predicts a particular outcome. *Construct validity* measures how well a test captures the whole theme or construct. *Standardization* means that the testing, scoring, and interpretation procedures are similar across all administrations of the test.

IQ: The Intelligence Quotient

Learning Goal: Understand the intelligence quotient (IQ) and how it is interpreted. The *IQ*, or *intelligence quotient*, dates back to Binet and Simon, who were commissioned to develop a test to identify children who might have trouble in school. Their goal was to determine a child's *mental age*, which is typically calculated by comparing a child's test score with the average score for different age groups. The IQ was originally calculated by the *ratio method*—dividing mental age by chronological age and multiplying by 100. Now it is specified in terms of a *deviation IQ*, in which a person's IQ is calculated by determining where his or her test score "sits" relative to the average score.

Extremes of Intelligence

Learning Goal: Learn how mental retardation, giftedness, and savant are defined. A score of 70 or below on a standard IQ test (along with some other factors) is likely to lead to a diagnosis of *mental retardation*. Numerous factors, both genetic and environmental, may cause mental retardation. *Giftedness* is seen in individuals with IQs at or above 130. Terman's longitudinal study of gifted children showed that these kids were likely to achieve later success and were stable emotionally and socially adept, contrary to the "bookworm" stereotype. *Savants* exhibit characteristics of both giftedness and retardation.

The Validity of Popular Intelligence Tests

Learning Goal: Understand the validity of IQ tests. Scores on traditional IQ tests correlate well with school grades. Critics of IQ tests argue that they fail to provide a broad index of intelligence. Also, a particular IQ "label" influences how teachers interact with students. These labelling effects were particularly serious in the early 20th century, when many immigrants were given intelligence tests and labelled as feeble-minded or defective.

Other Individual Differences Related to Intelligence

Learning Goal: Be able to explain creativity and emotional intelligence. *Creativity* refers to the ability to generate ideas that are original and novel and is an important component of broad conceptualizations of intelligence. *Emotional intelligence* is the ability to perceive, understand, and express emotion. According to some, it is also an important component of intelligence.

DISCOVERING THE SOURCES OF INTELLIGENCE: THE NATURE–NURTURE ISSUE

Does intelligent behaviour come primarily from one's genetic background or from life experience? The study of intelligence serves as an investigation into the plasticity of the mind.

The Stability of IQ

Learning Goal: Understand the stability of IQ, and discuss why IQ might change across the life span. The Seattle Longitudinal Study of Adult Intelligence found great stability in intellectual ability throughout adulthood. Current thinking is that *fluid intelligence* (which taps basic reasoning skills) may decline with age, whereas *crystallized intelligence* (which taps acquired knowledge) remains constant, and perhaps even increases.

Nature: The Genetic Argument

Learning Goal: Learn how twin studies are used to evaluate genetic contributions to intelligence. *Twin studies* are one method for addressing the role of heredity in intelligence. The IQ scores of identical twins are quite similar, irrespective of environment. Similarity of genetic background is a stronger predictor of intelligence than similarity of environment. *Heritability* is a mathematical index that tells a researcher the extent to which IQ differences within a population can be accounted for by genetic factors; estimates of heritability apply to groups, not individuals. Estimates of the heritability of intelligence range from 0.50 to 0.70.

Nurture: The Environmental Argument

Learning Goal: Recognize environmental influences on intelligence. Individual differences in intelligence cannot be explained completely through genetic background. Most intelligence researchers agree that there are stable differences in IQ across racial, ethnic, and socioeconomic groups. These differences, however, reflect average *group* differences. Possible sources of these differences could be economic factors and test bias. Adoption studies have supported the role of the environment in explaining group differences.

The Interaction of Nature and Nurture

Learning Goal: Understand how genetic and environmental factors interact to determine intelligence. Intelligence is determined by a mixture of genes and environment. Genes place lower and upper bounds on intellectual ability, but the expression of genetic material is strongly influenced by the environment. The *genotype* is the genetic message itself, and the *phenotype* is the observable characteristic that results from the genetic expression. Genetic expression depends critically on the environment, and genetic background affects how one interacts with the environment.

PERCEPTIONS OF INTELLIGENCE

The importance of the dimension of intelligence guarantees that people frequently judge each other. People have strong reactions to such judgments likely because the consequences can be substantial.

Judging Intelligence

Learning Goal: Understand the common tendency to judge people's intelligence. On a daily basis, we tend to judge other people's intelligence using a variety of cues—some valid and some invalid. Our accuracy is modest at best, but that doesn't stop us. Our judgments may be automatic. People also differ in their tendency to perceive intelligence as fixed or malleable.

The Potential for Abuse

Learning Goal: Recognize the potential abuses in applying the concept. Because we judge other people so readily on this important dimension, the consequences of an official declaration of mental incompetence can be devastating. Being labelled as unintelligent can have continuing negative effects on one's self-esteem and motivation. Low scores obtained by minority groups are sometimes used to justify mistreatment.

Terms to Remember

Recommended Readings

Das, J. P., Naglieri, J. A., & Kirby, J. R. (1994). *Assessment of cognitive processes: The PASS theory of intelligence.* New York: Allyn & Bacon. Co-authored by researchers from the University of Alberta and Queen's University, this book presents a cognitively based theory of intelligence that focuses on planning, attention, simultaneous, and successive processes (PASS). The authors suggest that this theory has a particular application in providing remediation for children with cognitive disabilities.

Bar-On, R., & Parker, J. D. A. (Eds.). (2000). *The handbook of emotional intelligence.* New York: John Wiley/Jossey-Bass. If the idea of emotional intelligence intrigues you, this volume will provide you with a comprehensive review of contemporary research and applications. Edited by the scholar who coined the term "EQ" (emotional quotient), Reuven Bar-On, and James Parker, who conducts research on emotions and emotional intelligence at Trent University.

Gardner, H. (1983). *Frames of mind.* New York: Basic Books. A very readable introduction to Gardner's theory of multiple intelligences.

Neisser, U. (Ed.). (1998). *The rising curve: Long-term gains in IQ and related measures.* Washington, DC: American Psychological Association. A collection of interesting articles written by experts addressing what is known, unknown, and controversial in modern intelligence research.

Sternberg, R. J. (1999). *Thinking styles.* New York: Cambridge University Press. A very readable book, written by a leading intelligence researcher, explaining how aptitude tests, school grades, and classroom performance often fail to identify real ability because of differences in thinking styles.

For additional readings, explore InfoTrac® College Edition, your online library. Go to:

www.adaptivemind2e.nelson.com

Hint: enter the search terms: intelligence tests; general intelligence; mental retardation; giftedness; psychometrics; nature, nurture, and intelligence.

What's on the Web?

Please note that Web addresses are subject to change. Check out the accompanying Web site for updates: www.adaptivemind2e.nelson.com. This site presents practice quiz questions, hypercontent, information on degrees and careers in psychology, study tips, and more.

Mensa Canada
www.canada.mensa.org

Mensa is an organization for people who score in the top 2% on standardized intelligence tests (on the WAIS, that would be over 130). This page explains what the organization is about, how to apply to join, and links to puzzles and tests.

J. P. Das Developmental Disabilities Centre
www.quasar.ualberta.ca/ddc/INDEX.html

Located at the University of Alberta, this centre acts as a research, training, informational, and clinical service for people with disabilities, including intellectual impairments.

Includes links to resources for people with disabilities and related problems.

The Genius Web Site

home8.swipnet.se/~w-80790/Index.htm

This Web site reviews the concept of genius and looks at examples of extremely high intelligence. Detailed histories of geniuses such as Einstein, Goethe, and Marie Curie are reviewed in detail.

The ARC

www.thearc.org

This is the home page of the Association for Retarded Citizens of the United States. The site offers a wide array of information on mental retardation, including "Q & A fact sheets." What do we know about the genetic roots of mental retardation? What is Fragile X syndrome? What issues arise when we consider the relationship between aging and mental retardation? Find answers to all of these questions and many more with a trip to The ARC.

Online IQ Tests

botree.com/iq.htm

www.geocities.com/CapitolHill/1641/iq.html

There seems to be a fascination with intelligence testing. As you were reading the material in the chapter, you may have been thinking, "I wonder what my IQ is?" This site purports to help you find out. (But beware! Consider the standardization, reliability, and validity of these tests.) You'll even find tests of your emotional IQ, "political IQ," and your "jewellery IQ."

Upstream: Issues: Psychology: Intelligence and IQ

www.mugu.com/cgi-bin/Upstream/Issues/psychology/IQ/

The book *The Bell Curve* helped to re-ignite the controversies that revolve around intelligence testing, such as the validity of scores, group differences, and the sources of intelligence. This site provides a wealth of links to the writings of prominent figures in the debate, such as Arthur Jensen and Stephen Jay Gould. The Upstream site also has general information on the controversial book as well as reviews and analyses.

What creature walks in the morning on four feet, at noon upon two,
and in the evening upon three?
The Riddle of the Sphinx
Sophocles, 2000 B.C.

Chapter 10 Human Development

development

The age-related physical, intellectual, social, and personal changes that occur throughout an individual's lifetime.

he famous saying "The apple doesn't fall far from the tree" is a literary way of pointing out that children tend to resemble their parents. The evidence for this claim is overwhelming but, as you saw in Chapter 1, philosophers and scientists have debated for centuries about the relative influences of nature and nurture. If you could rerun your life with control over your environment, would you really end up as a different person? You might, but it's also possible that your personality—your likes and dislikes—simply reflects the genetic material that you inherited from your parents. By now, you probably recognize that there is no simple answer to the classic nature versus nurture debate. The origins of behaviour and knowledge don't lie exclusively in either nature (genes) or nurture (the environment), but most often in both.

Let us define human **development** as the age-related physical, intellectual, and social changes that occur throughout an individual's lifetime. The incredible change from the newborn through the adolescent, adult, and elderly human being is one of nature's most wondrous spectacles. How does it happen? If you listen to the discussions of modern *developmental psychologists*—those who study the developmental process—you will repeatedly hear references to the concept of *interaction*. They believe that to comprehend the origins of any developmental change, it's necessary to understand the interaction of combined social, cultural, and biological forces on the developing human (Sigelman & Shaffer, 1995). This notion first became prominent with Freud's theories, but we will save the details of his theory for Chapter 12. As you saw in Chapter 3, unique genetic messages direct the body to change over time, but the environment modifies how those messages are realized. Understanding the idea of interaction goes beyond realizing that both heredity and the environment contribute to development. It means that you can't understand one without the other. Instead, development is better seen as a series of adjustments that the mind and body make to multiple factors. Moreover, these adjustments occur throughout the life span: From conception to death, the developmental process continues.

Previewing the Adaptive Problems

This chapter focuses on three main developmental problems (see Figure 10.1).

First, how do we go from fertilized eggs to fully functioning adults, capable of producing our own offspring? The environment helps shape the physical process of growth and can determine its ultimate outcome, but most physical changes are surprisingly consistent and predictable. In general, the timing of development is a product of evolutionary history and reflects the problems of survival that the human species has been required to solve.

Second, how do we develop the intellectual tools needed to solve survival problems? The developmental changes that occur in how people think—what is called cognitive development—have been studied extensively by psychologists. Intellectually, the newborn is hardly a miniature adult. You'll discover that infants see and think about the world quite differently from adults.

Third, how do we form the social relationships and sense of personal identity needed for personal protection, nourishment, and continuation of the species? Humans are social animals. They are continually interacting with each other, and these relationships help people adapt successfully to their environments. In this section, we'll consider the milestones of social development, beginning with the formation of attachments to parents and caregivers and ending with a discussion of how relationships change in middle and late adulthood.

378

Developing physically   Developing intellectually   Developing socially and personally

FIGURE 10.1
Adaptive Problems of Development
Humans face three main developmental problems: developing physically, intellectually, and socially/personally.

DEVELOPING PHYSICALLY

Learning Goals

1. Understand the physical changes that occur during prenatal development.
2. Learn about growth from infancy through adolescence.
3. Be able to explain adulthood and the aging body and brain.

TO A CHILD, it seems to take forever to grow up. In fact, humans do take a relatively long time to reach full physical maturity, compared to other species. At birth, for example, the brain of a chimpanzee is at about 60% of its final weight, whereas the brain of a human newborn is only at about 25% of its ultimate weight (Corballis, 1991; Lenneberg, 1967). Humans do a lot of developing outside of the womb. Still, the main components of the body—the nervous system, the networks of glands, and so on—develop at an astonishingly rapid rate from the point of conception.

Guided by the genetic code and influenced by the release of hormones by the endocrine system, individuals in the early years change physically at rates that will never again be matched in their lifetimes. To place the growth rate in some perspective, it's been estimated that if children continued to develop at the rate they show in the first two years of life, adults would end up over 3 metres tall and weighing several thousand kilograms! Fortunately, things slow down considerably after the first few years of life; but they never completely stop—we continue to change physically until the very moment of death.

The Stages of Prenatal Development

The human developmental process begins with the union of egg and sperm at conception. Within the fertilized egg, or **zygote,** the 23 chromosomes from the father and the 23 chromosomes from the mother pair up to form the master genetic blueprint. Over the next 266 days or so (approximately 9 months), the organism undergoes a steady and quite remarkable transformation. It begins as a single cell and ends as an approximately 3-kg newborn composed of literally billions of cells. The period of development

zygote
The fertilized human egg, containing 23 chromosomes from the father and 23 chromosomes from the mother, which pair up to form the master genetic blueprint.

germinal period
The period in prenatal development from conception to implantation of the fertilized egg in the wall of the uterus.

embryonic period
The period of prenatal development lasting from implantation to the end of the eighth week; during this period, the human develops from an unrecognizable mass of cells to a somewhat familiar creature.

fetal period
The period of prenatal development lasting from the ninth week until birth, during which the fetus develops functioning organ systems, and increases are seen in body size and in the size and complexity of brain tissue.

that occurs *prior* to birth is called prenatal development and is divided into three main stages: *germinal, embryonic,* and *fetal.* The **germinal period** lasts approximately two weeks, from conception to when the zygote migrates from the mother's fallopian tubes to implant itself on the wall of the uterus (often called the womb). The **embryonic period,** which comes next, lasts for about six weeks: from implantation to the eighth week after fertilization. In this period, arms, legs, fingers, toes, and a distinctly beating heart appear, and the embryo starts to develop the sexual characteristics of either a male or a female (see Figure 10.2).

At the ninth week of prenatal development, the **fetal period** begins and continues until birth. Early in the period, the bones and muscles of what is now called the *fetus* start to develop. By the end of the third month, the skeletal and muscular systems allow for extensive movement—even somersaults—although the fetus at this point is still only about 7 cm (Apgar & Beck, 1974). The last three months of prenatal development are marked by extremely rapid growth, both in body size and in the size and complexity of brain tissue.

Environmental Hazards   Although the developing child is snugly tucked away within the confines of its mother's womb, it is by no means completely isolated from the effects of the environment. The mother's physical health, as well as exposure to toxins, can seriously affect the developing child. Mother and child are linked physically, so if the mother gets sick, smokes, drinks, or takes drugs, the effects can transfer to the fetus or embryo. Some psychologists believe that the mother's psychological state, such as

FIGURE 10.2
Genetic Determinants of Gender
If the father contributes an X chromosome, the child will be a girl. If he contributes a Y chromosome, the child will be a boy.

her level of anxiety during pregnancy, can exert an effect and may even influence the personality of the child (Dawson et al., 2000; Oldani, 1997).

Environmental agents that can potentially damage the developing child are called **teratogens.** The developing fetus or embryo is generally most susceptible to teratogens during its initial formation. For example, if the mother contracts German measles (rubella) during the first six weeks of pregnancy, the child is at risk for developing heart defects because it is during this period that the structures of the heart are formed. Figure 10.3 shows the periods of greatest susceptibility—called critical periods—for various structures in the body. The embryonic period is the point of greatest susceptibility, although the central nervous system can be affected throughout prenatal development. Evolutionary biologist Margie Profet has suggested that the pregnancy sickness (also called morning sickness) experienced by many pregnant women is especially strong during the first three months of pregnancy because it constitutes an evolutionary adaptation to make women be especially careful about the food they ingest during this critical period of embryonic growth. The food aversions and nausea associated with pregnancy sickness are thought to protect the development of the embryo by influencing the mother toward eating bland foods that are less likely than stronger-tasting foods to contain toxins that could damage or even terminate embryonic development (Profet, 1988, 1992).

teratogens

Environmental agents—such as disease, organisms or drugs—that can potentially damage the developing embryo or fetus.

Growth during Infancy

We've stressed the negative impact of the environment, such as how teratogens can prevent expression of the normal genetic plan. However, the environment usually has a

FIGURE 10.3

Critical Periods of Susceptibility during Prenatal Development

Specific organs and body parts are at greatest risk from teratogens during certain critical periods of prenatal development. The light part of each bar signifies the period of greatest susceptibility. (Adapted from Sigelman & Shaffer, 1995.)

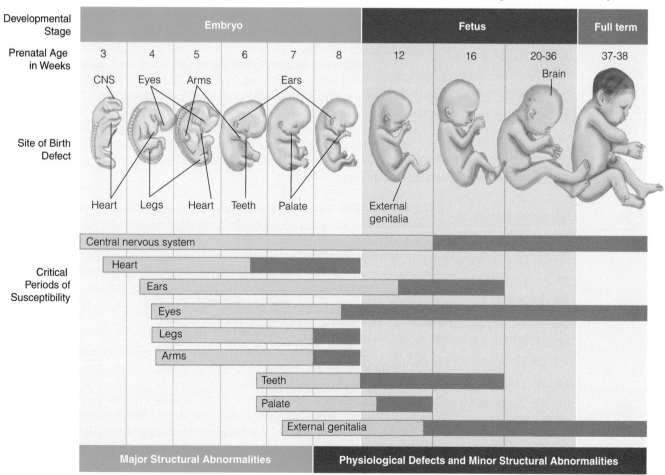

The child on the left is one of thousands born each year with fetal alcohol syndrome. The age of the mother is also a risk factor in pregnancy, but most women over the age of 35, such as the woman on the right, deliver normal, healthy babies.

Critical Thinking

Given that the environment plays such an important role in shaping brain development, what advice would you give new parents to maximize enriched development of their baby's intellectual capabilities?

nurturing effect on the developing organism. The internal conditions of the mother's uterus are perfectly tuned for physical development. The temperature is right, the fetus floats cushioned in a protective fluid, and regular nourishment is provided through the umbilical cord and placenta. More often than not, the result is a healthy baby, with normal physical systems, who is ready to take on the world.

The average newborn weighs in at about 3 kg and is roughly 51 cm in length. Over the next two years, as the child grows from baby to toddler, this weight will quadruple and the child will reach about half of his or her final adult height. Along with the rest of the body, the brain continues its dramatic growth spurt during this period. As mentioned earlier, a newborn enters the world with a brain that is only 25% of its final weight; but by the second birthday, the percentage has increased to 75%. Remarkably, this increase in brain size is not due to the formation of new neurons, since most of the cells that make up the cerebral cortex are in place well before birth (Nowakowski, 1987; Rakic, 1991). Instead, the cells grow in size and complexity, and a number of supporting glial cells are added. Each of us has essentially all the neurons we're going to possess at the moment we're born.

Experience Matters   The fact that substantial numbers of neurons are intact at birth does not mean that the brain of the newborn infant is mature—far from it. The brain still needs to refine its vast internal communication network, and it needs experience to accomplish this task. During the final stages of prenatal development, and especially during the first year or two after birth, tremendous changes occur in the neural circuitry. More branches (dendrites) sprout off from the existing cells, in order to receive information from other cells, and the number of connections, or synapses, greatly increases. There is even a kind of neural pruning process in which neurons that are not used simply atrophy or die (Dawson & Fischer, 1994).

The key principle at work is *plasticity*. The genetic code does not rigidly fix the internal circuitry of the brain; instead, a kind of rough wiring pattern is established during prenatal development that is filled in during the important first few years of life. Studies with animals have shown that the quality of early experience may be extremely important during this period. For example, rats raised in enriched environments (with lots of social contact and environmental stimulation) show significantly more complex and better functioning brain tissue than rats raised in sterile, barren

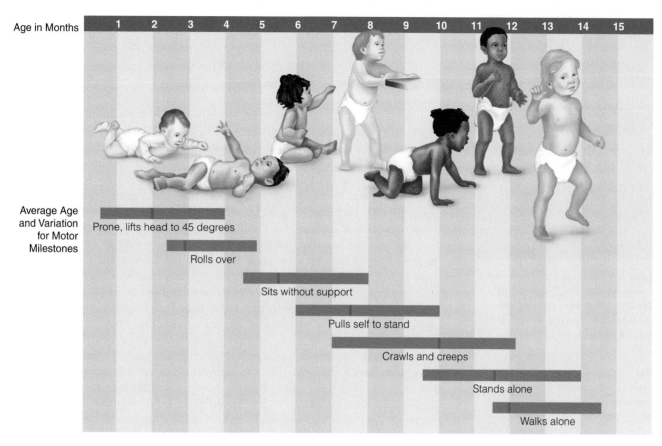

Age in Months

Average Age
and Variation
for Motor
Milestones

Prone, lifts head to 45 degrees

Rolls over

Sits without support

Pulls self to stand

Crawls and creeps

Stands alone

Walks alone

environments. There is also better recovery of function after brain injury if rats spend their recovery time in an enriched environment (van Rijzingen et al., 1997).

From Crawling to Walking

Most children learn to crawl, then stand alone, and walk at predictable ages. Figure 10.4 shows the major stages of an infant's motor development. The sequence of development, from lifting the head to walking alone, is stable, orderly, and predictable. The baby sits before it stands and crawls before it walks partly because of the way that the nervous system develops. The figure also shows the typical range of ages for each stage. Roughly 90% of all babies can roll over at 5 months of age, sit without support at 8 months, and then walk alone by 15 months. However, one baby might stand alone consistently at 9 months, while another might not accomplish the same feat until nearly 14 months of age.

Individual Differences What accounts for individual differences in early motor development? Although environmental and cultural influences play a role, differences attributable to these factors are usually small, and they play little, if any, role in determining final motor development. Hopi babies are traditionally swaddled and bound to cradleboards for much of the first year of life, yet these babies begin walking at roughly the same time as babies who are not bound in this manner (Dennis & Dennis, 1940). To learn to walk at a reasonable age, the infant simply needs to be given the opportunity to move around at some point—to "test the waters" and explore things on his or her own (Bertenthal et al., 1994). Hopi babies are bound to cradleboards for only their first 9 or 10 months; afterward, they are given several months to explore their motor capabilities before they begin to walk (Shaffer, 2002). Evidence such as this suggests that differences

FIGURE 10.4
Major Stages of Motor Development
Approximate time periods are given for the major points in motor development. Although psychologists are reluctant to tie developmental milestones to age, most children learn to crawl, stand alone, and walk at about the same age.

Grace and coordination in motor movements take time to develop. This 2-year-old will probably have little trouble throwing and catching a baseball successfully by the time he enters elementary school.

puberty
The period during which a person reaches sexual maturity and is potentially capable of producing offspring.

in early motor development appear to be more attributable to genetic and other constitutional factors than to environmental differences.

From Toddlerhood to Adolescence

A notable change occurs in hand-to-eye coordination as the child matures. Three-year-olds lack the grace and coordination in movements that are so obvious in a 6-year-old. The brain also continues to mature, although far more slowly than during prenatal development or during the first two years of life. General processing speed—how quickly people think and react to sudden changes in their environment—also increases consistently throughout childhood (Kail & Salthouse, 1994).

Between the end of childhood and the beginning of young adulthood lies an important physical and psychological transition period called *adolescence.* Physically, the two most dramatic changes that occur during this time are the adolescent *growth spurt* and the onset of **puberty,** or sexual maturity (the word *puberty* is from the Latin for "to grow hairy"). As with crawling and walking, it's not possible to pinpoint the timing of these changes exactly, particularly for a specific individual, but changes usually start occurring for girls at around age 11 and for boys at about 13. Hormones released by the endocrine system trigger a rapid increase in height and weight accompanied by the maturation of internal and external sexual organs.

Maturing Sexually Puberty is the developmental period during which individuals mature sexually and acquire the ability to reproduce. For the adolescent female, high levels of estrogen in the body lead to external changes, such as breast development and broadening hips, and eventually to the beginning of *menarche* (the first menstrual flow) at around age 12 or 13. For boys, hormones called *androgens* are released, leading to the appearance of facial hair, a lower voice, and the ability to ejaculate (release semen) at around age 13 or 14. Neither the initial appearance of menarche nor the first ejaculation necessarily means that the adolescent is ready to reproduce—ovulation and sperm production may not occur until months later—but psychologically these "firsts" tend to be highly memorable and emotional events (Golub, 1992).

The onset of puberty is another classic instance of how the master genetic plan interacts with the nurturing effects of the environment. The average onset age for menarche has dropped from about 16 in the 1880s to the current 12 to 13. Physically,

Not all children reach the adolescent growth spurt at the same age. Boys can lag behind girls by two years during this stage.

people are maturing earlier than in past generations, and it's almost certainly not due to genetics. Instead, better nutrition, better living conditions, and improved medical care are responsible for the trend. Even today, in parts of the world where living conditions are difficult, the average age of menarche is later than in industrialized countries such as Canada (Chumlea, 1982). Although the environment does not cause sexual maturation—that's controlled by the genetic code—the environment modulates the expression of the code, either accelerating or delaying the point when changes start to occur (Graber et al., 1995). Research by Mount Allison University developmental psychologist Michelle Surbey indicates an intriguing factor that may influence the age of menarche in girls. Surbey has reported that girls who grow up with high levels of stress and in father-absent homes tend to go through menarche earlier than girls who grow up in less stressful environments and who have fathers present in the home during their childhood (Surbey, 1990, 1998). Surbey suggests that this pattern may reflect evolved psychobiological mechanisms that allow females to unconsciously adjust their rate of pubertal development in ways that would have been adaptive in the evolutionary history of human ancestors. Although this finding needs to be confirmed by further research, it illustrates the range of possible factors that may contribute to the timing of puberty.

Reaching Adulthood

The adolescent years are marked by dramatic changes in appearance and strength. Motor skills, including hand-to-eye coordination, improve to adult levels during the teenage years. As you're undoubtedly aware, there are world-class swimmers and tennis players who are barely into their teens. The brain reaches adult weight by about age 16, although the myelination of the neurons—so critical in early motor development— continues throughout the adolescent years (Benes et al., 1994). The continued maturation of the brain can also be seen in the gradual quickening of reaction times that occurs throughout adolescence.

When do individuals actually cross the threshold to adulthood? That's a difficult question to answer because becoming an adult is, in some sense, a state of mind. There are differences in how the transition from adolescent to adult is defined across the world. Some cultures have specific rites of passage and others do not. And, as you know, not all adolescents are willing to accept the socially defined responsibilities of adulthood at the appropriate time. But by the time people reach their 20s, they are physically mature and at the height of their physical prowess.

The Aging Body It's barely noticeable at the time, but most people begin slowly and steadily to decline physically, at least with respect to their peak levels of strength and agility, at some point during their 20s. Unfortunately, the loss tends to be across the board, which means that it applies to virtually all physical functions, from strength to respiration rate to the heart's pumping capacity (Whitbourne, 1985). Individual differences occur in the rate of decline, of course, depending on such factors as exercise, illness, and heredity. (We're sure you can think of a 40-year-old who is in better physical shape than a 25-year-old.) But wrinkles, age spots, sagging flesh, and loss of muscle tone are all reliable and expected parts of the aging process.

By about age 50, the average woman begins **menopause,** the period during which the menstrual cycle slows down and finally stops. Ovulation also stops, so women at this point lose the ability to bear children. These events are caused by hormonal changes, in particular by a decline in the level of female hormones in the body. Despite what you might have heard, menopause is not disruptive for all women, either physically or psychologically (McKinlay et al., 1992). The main physical symptoms, such as hot flashes, can be controlled by hormone replacement therapy, and the idea that the majority of women undergo a sustained period of depression or crankiness is simply a myth (Matthews, 1992). Men do not experience "male menopause" because they never menstruate, although some men do lose the ability to father children in their later years

menopause
The period during which a woman's menstrual cycle slows down and finally stops.

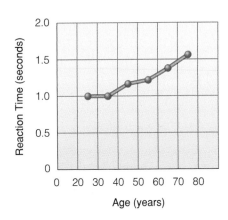

FIGURE 10.5

Age and Reaction Time

This figure shows how average reaction time changes between age 20 and age 80 for a cognitive task requiring subjects to match numbers with symbols on a computer screen. Although there is a gradual quickening of reaction time from childhood through adolescence, after age 20 reaction time gradually slows. (Based on Salthouse, 1994.)

dementia

Physically based losses in mental functioning.

Critical Thinking

How might you test the idea that mental activity or exercise helps to counteract the decline in mental skills that occurs with age? Can you make predictions based on choice of profession? Should people who choose intellectually challenging professions show less mental decline with age?

because of a decline in the production or activity of their sperm. This loss in reproductive capacity, expressed by the term *climacteric* (meaning "critical time"), does not occur in all men.

The Aging Brain With age, the brain undergoes significant physical changes. Some individuals suffer brain degeneration—the loss of brain cells—which can lead to senility and, in some cases, to a disabling condition called Alzheimer's disease. But the good news is that the majority of older people never experience these problems; fewer than 1% of people at age 65 are afflicted with **dementia,** the technical name for physically based loss in mental functioning. Although that percentage may rise to as much as 20% for individuals over age 80 (Cavanaugh & Blanchard-Fields, 2002), significant losses in mental functioning or mental health are still the exception rather than the rule. The bad news is that everyone loses brain cells with age—the extent of the loss depends on the particular site in the brain (Kemper, 1994; Selkoe, 1992)—and associated declines occur in certain kinds of memory, sensory abilities, and reaction time, as shown in Figure 10.5 (Cavanaugh, 1993; Salthouse, 1994). (Later in this chapter, we'll take a closer look at how memory changes with age.)

The physical changes that occur in the aging brain may not be all bad, however. Neurons are lost, and the loss is apparently permanent, but the remaining neurons may in some instances increase in complexity. In a famous autopsy study by Buell and Coleman (1979), it was found that dendrites were significantly longer and more complex in samples of normal brain tissue taken from elderly adults when compared to those of middle-aged adults (see Figure 10.6). It appears that the brain may compensate for the losses it experiences by making better use of the structures that remain intact. Some researchers have even argued that sustained mental activity in later years may help promote neural growth, thereby counteracting some of the normal decline in mental skills (Mirmiran et al., 1996).

FIGURE 10.6

Aging Neurons

Samples of hippocampal neurons taken from people in their 50s, 70s, and 90s and from adults afflicted with Alzheimer's disease. Notice that the dendrites of the samples actually increase in length and complexity from the 50s to the 70s, declining only in late old age or with Alzheimer's disease.

Test Yourself 10.1

Check your knowledge about the physical changes that occur during development by deciding whether the following statements are true or false. (You will find the answers in Appendix B.)

1. The period in prenatal development lasting from implantation of the fertilized egg to the end of the eighth week is called the germinal period. *True or False?*
2. The initial development of arms, legs, fingers, and toes occurs during the embryonic period of prenatal development. *True or False?*
3. The large increases in brain size that occur in the first two years of life are due primarily to increases in the number of neurons in the brain. *True or False?*
4. The timing of motor development—when a baby begins to crawl, walk, and so on—is affected to a small extent by nature (biology) and to a large extent by nurture (the environment). *True or False?*
5. Everyone loses brain cells with age, and roughly half of all people over 70 can expect to develop dementia. *True or False?*

DEVELOPING INTELLECTUALLY

Learning Goals

1. Understand the tools used to study infant perception and memory.
2. Be able to explain the perceptual capabilities of an infant.
3. Comprehend the characteristics of memory loss in the elderly.
4. Understand and evaluate Piaget's theory of cognitive development.
5. Understand and evaluate Kolhberg's theory of moral development.

THROUGHOUT A PERSON'S LIFETIME, the connections between neurons in the brain are continually changing. New pathways are formed and others are abandoned in response to environmental experiences. The brain's *plasticity*—the ability to change and adjust its connections—is extremely adaptive, especially during the early years of development. Because there is no way for the master genetic plan to predict the environments that a person will encounter after birth, the intrinsic capacity for change is built in.

As the brain changes physically in response to the environment, so too do the characteristics of the mind that are of main interest to psychologists. Infants are not born seeing and thinking about the world as adults do. Cognitive processes—how individuals think and perceive—develop over time. As with learning to walk, intellectual development depends on adequate physical maturation within the brain as well as on exposure to the right kinds of experiences. In this section, we'll consider three aspects of intellectual development: How do children learn to perceive and remember the world? How do thought processes change with age? How do individuals develop a sense of right and wrong?

The Tools of Investigation

What does the world look like to a newborn child? Is it like our view—a complex three-dimensional world, full of depth, colour, and texture? Or is it a "blooming, buzzing confusion," as claimed by the early psychologist William James (1890)? Let's stop for a moment and think about how a psychologist might answer these questions. Deciphering the perceptual capabilities of an infant is not a simple matter. Babies can't tell us what they see, nor can they move around in ways that allow us to figure out what they see (e.g., by avoiding some things and knocking into others).

Therefore, it is necessary to devise creative methods to infer perceptual capabilities from immobile, largely uncommunicative infants. Fortunately, babies already possess several capabilities that can be exploited to understand their level of mental development: (1) They show *preferences,* which means they prefer some stimuli over others; (2) they notice *novelty,* which means they notice new or different things in their environment; and (3) they can *learn* to repeat activities that result in a reward.

The Preference Technique   In the "preference technique" developed by Robert Fantz (1961), an infant is presented with two visual displays simultaneously, and the investigator simply records how long the infant looks at each (see Figure 10.7). Suppose that one of the displays shows a male face and the other a female face; and suppose we find that the baby looks at the female face for a significantly longer period of time. By "choosing" to look longer at the female face, the infant has shown a preference. By itself, this preference indicates very little. Perhaps the baby tends to turn its head to the left; or perhaps it prefers to look at smaller faces. To draw clear inferences, it's necessary to repeat the test a number of times with different male and female faces, and switching the male–female relative positions from trial to trial. If the baby continues to look longer at the female face—even when it's larger and on the right—we can infer that the baby has the visual capability to tell the difference between the two displays. The infant "tells" us that he or she can detect differences by exclusively tracking the female face. Notice that we didn't need to ask the baby anything; we simply inferred things about his or her visual system by measuring overt behaviour.

Habituation Techniques   One of the preferences babies consistently show is for novelty—they like to look at new things. But they tend to ignore events that occur repeatedly in their environment without consequence. For instance, if you show newborns a blue-coloured card and track how their eyes move (or how their heart rate changes), you'll find that they spend a lot of time looking at the card when it first appears—it's something new. But if you present the same card over and over again, their interest wanes, and they'll begin to look at something else. This decline in responsiveness to repeated stimulation, called **habituation,** provides an effective tool for researchers seeking to map out the infant's perceptual world (Colombo et al., 1997). By acting bored, which is defined operationally by how long they look at the card, babies reveal that they remember the stimulus from its previous presentation and recognize that it hasn't changed. It's as if the baby is saying, "Oh, it's that blue card again."

Habituation can be used to discover specific information about how babies perceive and remember their worlds (DeSaint et al., 1997; Granrud, 1993). For example, suppose we wanted to discover whether newborns have the capacity to perceive colour. We could show the blue card for a while, then suddenly switch to a green card that matches on all other visual dimensions (such as size and brightness). If the infant shows renewed interest in the card—treating the stimulus as if it were novel—we can infer that the baby can discriminate, or tell the difference, between blue and green. However, if the baby continues to ignore the new green card, it suggests that the baby lacks colour vision at this stage in development. We can also study memory by varying the time that

habituation

The decline in responsiveness to repeated stimulation; habituation has been used to investigate the perceptual capabilities of infants.

Critical Thinking

Why do you think nature built in a tendency to habituate?

FIGURE 10.7

The Preference Technique

Babies prefer some visual stimuli over others. In this case, a preverbal infant is demonstrating a preference for a female face by tracking its location across trials. The preference can be determined by simply recording how long the baby looks at each face.

elapses between presentations of the card. If the baby continues to act bored by the blue card even though we insert long pauses between successive presentations, we know that he or she is remembering the card over those particular time intervals.

Using Rewards   A researcher can also gain insight into what a baby sees, knows, and remembers by *rewarding* a simple motor movement, such as kicking a leg or sucking on an artificial nipple, in the presence of particular kinds of events (Siqueland & DeLucia, 1969). For example, in research by Carolyn Rovee-Collier (1993), 2- and 3-month-old infants were taught that kicking their legs could produce movement of a crib mobile hanging overhead. A moving mobile is quite rewarding to babies at this age, and they'll double or triple their rate of leg kicking in a matter of minutes if it leads to movement. We can then study cognitive abilities—such as memory—by taking the mobile away, waiting for some period of time, and then replacing the mobile. If the baby begins leg kicking again at rates comparable to those produced at the end of training, we can infer that the baby has remembered what he or she has learned. We can also change the characteristics of the mobile after training and learn things about a baby's perceptual abilities. For example, if we train an infant with a blue mobile and then switch to a green one, differences in leg kicking help us infer whether the baby can discriminate between green and blue.

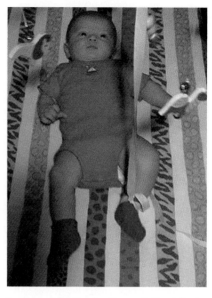

In research by Carolyn Rovee-Collier, infants learn that leg kicking can produce movement of a mobile hanging overhead.

The Growing Perceptual World

Based on such techniques, researchers have discovered that babies greet the world with sensory systems that function reasonably well. Although none of these systems is operating at peak efficiency, because their biological equipment is still maturing, babies still see a world of colour and shape (Banks & Shannon, 1993). They even arrive with built-in preferences for some colours and shapes. One-day-old babies, for example, respond more to patterned stimuli than to unpatterned ones. As shown in Figure 10.8, they even prefer to look at correctly drawn faces rather than scrambled faces with features placed in incorrect positions (Johnson et al., 1991; see also Walton & Bower, 1993).

FIGURE 10.8
Infant Preferences

In the experiment, babies were shown either a blank stimulus, a stimulus with scrambled facial features, or a face. Each stimulus was positioned over the baby's head and then moved from side to side. The dependent variable was the extent to which the baby tracked each stimulus by turning his or her head and eyes. As the results show, the babies tracked the face stimulus more than the others. (Graph adapted from Johnson et al., 1991.)

Experimental Setup

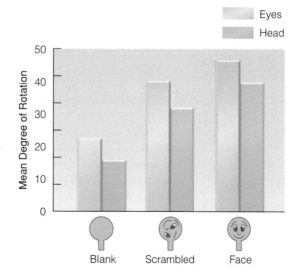

This baby is a few months old, but even newborn infants show distinctive reactions to a variety of tastes (lemon, sugar, and salt are shown here).

Such research indicates that reasonably sophisticated perceptual processing can occur rapidly after birth.

Newborns also hear reasonably well, and they seem to recognize their mothers' voice within a day or two after birth (DeCasper & Fifer, 1980). Remarkably, there is evidence to suggest that newborns can even hear and remember things that happen prior to birth. By week 28, fetuses will close their eyes in response to loud noises presented near the mother's abdomen (Parmelee & Sigman, 1983). Infants will also choose to suck on an artificial nipple that produces a recording of a story that was read aloud to them repeatedly before birth (DeCasper & Spence, 1986). This is an adaptive quality for the newborn to possess, since the newborn needs nourishment and is dependent on others for survival. Consequently, babies born with a visual system that detects shapes and forms and an auditory system tuned to the human voice have an increased likelihood of survival.

In addition to sights and sounds, babies are quite sensitive to touch, smell, pain, and taste. Place a drop of lemon juice in the mouth of a newborn and you'll see a distinctive grimace. Place a small amount of sugar in the baby's mouth, and the baby will smack its lips. These distinctive reactions are present at birth and are found even before the infant has had a single taste of food (Steiner, 1977). A baby's sense of smell is developed well enough that the newborn quickly learns to recognize the odour of its mother's breast (Porter et al., 1992). As for pain and touch, babies will reject a milk bottle that is too hot, and, as every parent knows, the right kind of pat on the baby's back is pleasurable enough to soothe the newborn into sleep.

Babies even seem to recognize the three-dimensional world. When placed on a visual cliff, such as the one shown in the accompanying photo, 6-month-old babies are reluctant to cross over the apparent drop-off, or cliff, to reach a parent (Gibson & Walk, 1960). Even babies as young as 2 months show heart rate changes when they're placed on the glass portion covering the deep side of the visual cliff (Campos et al., 1970).

But these are infant perceptions, and the infant's world is not the same as the one viewed by an adult. Newborn babies cannot see as well as adults. They're not very good at discriminating fine detail in visual patterns: Compared with the ideal acuity level of 20/20, babies see a blurry world that is more on the order of 20/600, meaning that what newborns see at 20 feet (6 metres) is like what adults with ideal vision see at 600 feet (180 metres) (Banks & Salapatek, 1983). In addition, newborns probably cannot perceive shapes and forms in the same way as adults do (Johnson, 1997), nor can they hear as well as adults. For example, infants seem to have some trouble listening selectively for certain kinds of sounds, and infants need sounds to be louder than adults do before they can be detected (Bargones & Werner, 1994).

Infants' perceptual systems improve markedly during the first few months, partly because of continued physical development but also because experience plays a role in the fine-tuning of sensory abilities. Research with nonhuman subjects, such as cats or chimpanzees, has shown that if animals are deprived of visual stimulation during the

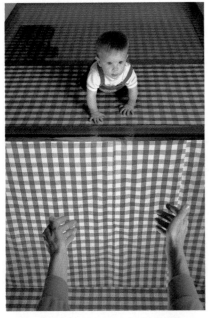

In the visual cliff apparatus, a plate of glass covers the drop-off or "cliff." Beginning at roughly 6 months of age, babies are reluctant to cross over to reach a beckoning parent.

early weeks or months of life, permanent visual impairments can result (Gandelman, 1992). Thus, perceptual development relies on experience as well as on physically mature sensory equipment.

By the time we leave infancy, our perceptual systems are reasonably intact. Most of the changes that occur during childhood and adolescence deal with the ability to use the equipment we have. For example, as children grow older, their attention span improves and they are better able to attend selectively to pertinent information. Memory improves throughout childhood, partly because kids learn strategies for organizing and maintaining information in memory. Moreover, as you saw in Chapters 4 and 7, the way individuals perceive and remember the world depends on what they know about the way the world works. We use our general knowledge about people and events to help us interpret ambiguous stimuli and to remember things that happen in our lives. Perception and memory are influenced by the knowledge gained from experience, which is one of the reasons why perceptual development is really a lifelong process.

Do We Lose Memory with Age?

What happens to memory as we age? Is there an inevitable decline in the ability to remember? It's quite common for the elderly to report memory problems. We know from recent research that there are declines in both prospective memory and retrospective memory (Craik, 1994; Uttl et al., 2001) and both speed and capacity of information processing (Graf & Uttl, 1995). Beyond that, the relationship between aging and memory is rather complex. Some kinds of memory falter badly with age, but other kinds do not. For example, age-related deficits appear to be restricted to tasks that require conscious memory. If memory is tested in ways that do not require conscious awareness (such as testing to see whether your ability to solve a puzzle increases when you've seen it before), age-related differences disappear (Balota et al., 2000).

It is not easy to design studies to accurately measure how people change in their thinking and behaviour as they get older (Muir, 1999). Researchers who study the developmental process typically conduct research using what are called *longitudinal* and *cross-sectional research designs*. In a **longitudinal design,** the same individuals are tested repeatedly over time, at various points in childhood or even on through adulthood. In a **cross-sectional design,** researchers compare people of different ages at the same point in time.

A cross-sectional design was used in a study conducted at the University of Toronto by Craik and McDowd (1987). They used the design to compare recall and recognition memory in two age groups: (1) a "young" group of university students, with an average age of 20.7 years, and (2) an "old" group, volunteers from a senior citizen centre, with an average age of 72.8 years. All the participants were asked to learn memory lists that consisted of short phrases (e.g., "a body of water") presented together with associated target words (e.g., "pond"). The lists were followed by either an immediate recall test, in which the short phrase was given and the subject needed to recall the target word, or a delayed recognition test, which required the subjects to decide whether a word had or had not been presented in one of the earlier lists.

In such experiments, attempts are made to match the participants on as many variables as possible—such as educational level and verbal ability—so that the only difference between the groups is *age.* Any performance differences can then be attributed uniquely to the independent variable (age) and not to some other confounding factor (see Chapter 2). The results of the Craik and McDowd (1987) study are shown in Figure 10.9. As you can see, the young subjects outperformed the old subjects on the test of recall, but the advantage vanished on the recognition test. Measuring memory loss in the elderly therefore depends on how memory is actually tested. Other studies have shown that performance also depends on the types of materials tested. When older subjects are asked to remember materials that fit naturally into their rich knowledge base, they may even perform better than their younger counterparts (Zacks & Hasher, 1994).

longitudinal design

A research design in which the same people are studied or tested repeatedly over time.

cross-sectional design

A research design in which people of different ages are compared at the same time.

FIGURE 10.9

Memory and Aging

In the study by Craik and McDowd (1987), two groups, one with an average age of 20.7 years and one with an average age of 72.8 years, were asked to learn and then recall or recognize target words. Although the "young" subjects recalled more targets than the "old" group, the advantage disappeared for recognition.

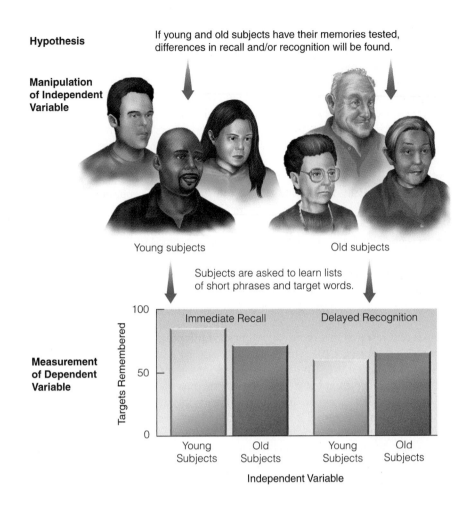

Although many people past age 60 or 70 are able to perform well on certain kinds of memory tests, it is still the case that older people generally perform quite poorly on some kinds of memory tasks, such as those that require recalling lists of newly presented information (Hultsch et al., 1999). UBC researchers are actively trying to determine why these memory deficits occur (Graf & Uttl, 2001). One possibility is that older adults lose the ability to suppress irrelevant thoughts or ignore irrelevant stimuli (Hasher et al., 1991). Because they are unable to focus selectively on the task at hand, they fail to process the to-be-remembered information in ways that are conducive to later recall (Craik, 1994).

One fascinating argument from evolutionary theory is that the deterioration of short-term memory in the elderly is adaptive for our species. The elderly must retain accumulated cultural information that helps prevent hasty decisions made by young people. If they learned everything new that came along during their lives, it would interfere with their function as society's storehouse of wisdom (Pinker, 1997a).

A question that naturally arises in considering memory problems in older people is this: Can anything be done to prevent these age-related memory decrements? This is a question that has been addressed by University of Victoria life-span developmental psychologists David Hultsch and Roger Dixon and their colleagues (Hultsch et al., 1999). These researchers examined data from the Victoria Longitudinal Study, a major Canadian study of age-related changes in people's cognitive functioning, particularly their memory processes. The researchers tested the hypothesis that people who continue to engage in intellectually demanding activities throughout their life span, including old age, may not experience the same decline in memory processes experienced by other older people. (The researchers termed this the "use it or lose it" hypothesis). The results generally supported this idea, with cognitive activities that involved processing novel information, such as playing bridge or learning a language, apparently being particularly related to "buffering" older people against the usual decreases in memory processes in old age. However, the researchers caution that it is difficult to ascertain cause and effect in this kind of study, and it is possible that the results may also be due to a pattern of people who engaged in challenging intellectual tasks throughout their lives continuing to do so well into their later years, until age-related cognitive declines compelled them to stop.

Piaget and the Development of Thought

The close connection between what we see and what we know explains why it's difficult for researchers to get a good grasp on how infants truly perceive the world. It might be possible for a researcher to demonstrate that a newborn can tell the difference between a purring kitten and a block of wood, but does this mean that the infant really sees what we know of as a cat? Babies might coo and smile to the rhythmic sound of music on the radio, but is their internal experience anything close to that of an adult? In some sense, these are philosophical questions rather than scientific ones, but it's important to recognize that it's not easy to talk about a baby's ability to perceive or remember without knowing something about how a baby thinks.

Much of what we know about how thought processes develop during childhood comes from the collective works of a Swiss scholar named Jean Piaget (1929, 1952, 1970). It was Piaget who first convinced psychologists that children think quite differently from adults. Children are not little adults, he argued, who simply lack knowledge and experience; instead, they view the world in a very unique and idiosyncratic way. Piaget believed that everyone is born with a natural tendency to organize the world meaningfully. People construct mental models of the world—called **schemas**—and use these schemas to guide and interpret their experiences. But these schemas are not very adult-like early in development—in fact, they tend not to reflect the true world accurately—so much of early intellectual development is spent modifying our cognitive models of how the world operates. One of Piaget's primary contributions was to demonstrate that mistakes in children's reasoning can illuminate how the schema construction process is proceeding.

For example, consider the two tilted cups shown at right. When young children are asked to draw a line indicating how the water level in a tilted cup might look, they tend to draw a line that is parallel to the top and bottom of the cup, as shown in the cup on the left, rather than parallel to the ground, as shown in the cup on the right. This kind of error is important, Piaget argued, because children can't have learned such a thing directly from experience (water never tilts that way in real life). Instead, the error reflects a fundamental misconception of how the world is structured. Young children simply have an internal schema of that aspect of the world that is inaccurate.

Assimilation and Accommodation As their brains and bodies mature, children build more accurate mental models of the world, based in part on their experiences. Piaget

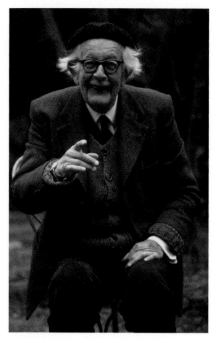

Jean Piaget

schemas
Mental models of the world that people use to guide and interpret their experiences.

Concept Summary

RESEARCH DESIGNS FOR STUDYING DEVELOPMENT

Type of Design	Overview	Advantages and Disadvantages
Cross-sectional	Researchers compare performance of different people of different ages.	A: Faster, more practical than longitudinal. D: Other variables may be confounded with age.
Longitudinal	Researchers test the same individuals repeatedly over time.	A: Can examine changes in individuals. D: Cost intensive; subject loss over time.

assimilation

The process through which people fit—or assimilate—new experiences into existing schemas.

accommodation

The process through which people change or modify existing schemas to accommodate new experiences when they occur.

suggested that this process of cognitive development is guided by two adaptive psychological processes: **assimilation** and **accommodation.** Assimilation is the process through which people fit—or assimilate—new experiences into their existing schemas. For example, suppose a small child who has been raised in a household full of cats mistakenly concludes that the neighbour's new rabbit is simply a kind of kitty. The new experience—the rabbit—has been assimilated into the child's existing view of the world: Small furry things are *cats.* The second function, accommodation, is the process through which one changes or modifies existing schemas to accommodate new experiences when they occur. When the child learns that the new "kitty" hops rather than walks and seems reluctant to purr, he or she will need to modify and revise the existing concept of small furry things; the child is forced to change the existing schema to accommodate the new information. Notice that the child plays an active role in constructing schemas by interacting directly with the world (Piaget, 1929).

Piaget believed that children develop an adult world-view by proceeding systematically through a series of four stages or developmental periods: *sensorimotor, preoperational, concrete operational,* and *formal operational.* Each of these periods is tied roughly to a particular age range—for example, the preoperational period usually lasts from age 2 to about age 7—but individual differences may occur in how quickly children progress from one period to the next. Although the timing may vary from child to child, Piaget believed that the order in which individuals progress through the stages is invariant—it remains the same for everyone. Let's consider these cognitive developmental periods in more detail.

The Sensorimotor Period: Birth to 2 Years

sensorimotor period

Piaget's first stage of cognitive development, lasting from birth to about 2 years of age; schemas revolve around sensory and motor abilities.

object permanence

The ability to recognize that objects still exist when they're no longer in sight.

From birth to about age 2, schemas about the world revolve primarily around the infant's sensory and motor abilities (hence the name **sensorimotor period**). Babies initially interact with the world through a variety of evolved reflexes. For example, they'll start sucking when an object is placed in their mouth (called the *sucking reflex*), and they'll automatically turn their head in the direction of a touch or brush on the cheek (called the *rooting reflex*). This means that when an object comes into a newborn's view, that object is interpreted in terms of how it can be sucked. Of course, this behaviour is far different from an adult's, but it's *adaptive* for a newborn. These reflexes increase the likelihood that adequate nourishment will follow, and attaining adequate nourishment is a significant problem the newborn needs to solve.

Object Permanence As infants develop intellectually over the first year, they begin to use their maturing motor skills to help them understand how they can voluntarily interact with the world. Babies start to vocalize to gain attention; they learn that they can kick their legs to make sounds; they acquire the ability to reach with their arms to touch or grasp objects. The initial stirrings of symbolic thought also begin during the sensorimotor period. The infant gradually develops the ability to represent things internally as mental images or symbols. Early in the first year, for example, babies lack **object permanence,** which means that they fail to recognize that objects exist when they're no longer in sight. The photos on the following page illustrate how psychologists have measured object permanence. Notice that the baby loses interest when the toy is covered, suggesting that the baby is only capable of thinking about objects that are directly in view. Babies at this point

The rooting reflex is adaptive because it helps the newborn receive needed sustenance.

are unable to represent objects symbolically—out of sight equals out of mind. But by the end of the first year, Piaget argued, the child has a different reaction to the disappearance of a favoured toy; as object permanence develops, the child will begin to search actively for the lost toy.

The Preoperational Period: 2 to 7 Years

From about ages 2 through 7, the child's schemas continue to grow in sophistication. Children in the **preoperational period** no longer have difficulty thinking about absent objects, and they can use one sort of object to stand for another. A 4-year-old, for example, can easily use a stick to represent a soaring airplane or a cardboard box for a stove. The child realizes that these are not the real objects, but he or she can imagine them to be real for the purposes of play. However, as Piaget demonstrated in a number of clever ways, the child still thinks about the world quite differently from an adult. The preoperational child lacks the ability to perform certain basic mental *operations*—hence Piaget's use of the term *preoperational* to describe a child's mental abilities during this period.

Conservation Something that children at the preoperational stage often fail to understand is the principle of conservation. To understand **conservation,** one needs to be able to recognize that the physical properties of an object can remain the same despite superficial changes in its appearance (see Figure 10.10). If 4- or 5-year-old children are shown two play dough balls of exactly the same size and we ask them which object contains more play dough, most of the children will say that the two balls contain the same amount. But if one of the balls is then rolled into a long, sausage-like shape, the children are likely to think that the two quantities of play dough are no longer the same, saying that either the sausage or the ball has more play dough. Children at this age simply do not understand that a basic property of an object, in this case its mass, doesn't change as the object changes shape.

Typically, preoperational children will fail to conserve a basic quantity even if they directly observe the change in appearance taking place. Suppose that we ask 5-year-old Sam to pour a cup of water into each of two identical glasses. Sam performs the task and accepts that the two glasses now contain the same amount of water. We then instruct him to pour the water from one of the glasses into another glass that is tall and thin. Do the glasses now contain the same amount of water? "No," Sam explains. "Now the tall one has more water." Sam is not showing any evidence of conservation; he does not yet recognize that how the water looks in the glass has no effect on its volume.

Piaget argued that the reason children in the preoperational period make these kinds of errors is that they still lack the capacity to think in truly adult-like ways. For example, the thinking of preoperational children demonstrates *centration,* the tendency to focus attention on one particular aspect of a situation and to ignore other aspects.

According to Piaget, until object permanence develops, babies fail to understand that objects still exist when they're no longer in view. Notice how this boy loses interest when he can no longer see his favourite toy.

preoperational period
Piaget's second stage of cognitive development, lasting from age 2 to about age 7; children begin to think symbolically but often lack the ability to perform mental operations like conservation.

conservation
The ability to recognize that the physical properties of an object remain the same despite superficial changes in the object's appearance.

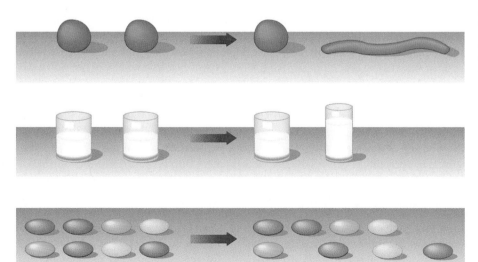

FIGURE 10.10
Examples of Conservation Problems
Understanding conservation means recognizing that the physical properties of objects remain the same even though the objects may superficially change in appearance. Preoperational children often fail conservation problems—they fail to detect, for example, that the objects to the right of the arrows still retain the same volume or number.

Do you think Piaget's insights about cognitive development have any implications for education? For example, should teachers be giving first- and second-grade children abstract math problems to solve?

egocentrism
The tendency to see the world from your own unique perspective only; a characteristic of thinking in the preoperational period of development.

concrete operational period
Piaget's third stage of cognitive development, lasting from age 7 to age 11. Children acquire the capacity to perform a number of mental operations but still lack the ability for abstract reasoning.

Sam believes that the tall glass has more water because he cannot simultaneously consider both the height and width of the glass; he focuses only on the height and is therefore convinced that the taller glass must contain more water. In addition, children at this age have difficulty understanding *reversibility*—they don't understand that one kind of operation can produce change and that another kind of operation can undo that change. For example, Sam is unlikely to consider what will happen if the water from the tall glass is poured back into the original glass. The capacity to understand that operations are reversible doesn't develop until the next stage.

Egocentrism   Piaget also discovered that children in the preoperational period tend to see the world, and the objects in it, from primarily one perspective: their own. Children at this stage have a tough time imagining themselves in another person's position. If you ask a child in the preoperational period to describe what another person will see or think, the child will usually describe what he or she personally sees or thinks. Piaget called this characteristic **egocentrism**—the tendency to view the world from your own unique perspective only.

Children's Theory of Mind   An important aspect of children's cognitive development that occurs during the preoperational stage is the child's development of a "theory of mind." This refers to how children view the process of acquiring knowledge. Developmental researchers Christopher Lalonde of the University of Victoria, Michael Chandler of the University of British Columbia, and Kang Lee of Queen's University have examined this issue (Chandler & Lalonde, 1996; Lalonde & Chandler, 1995; Lee & Homer, 1999). Although infants appear to have mental mechanisms that contribute to a primitive theory of mind (Baron-Cohen, 1994; Muir et al., 1994), Lalonde and Chandler suggest that there is a fundamental shift in children's theory of mind around the age of 6 or 7. Prior to this, 3- to 5-year-olds think of the mind very much as a tape recorder: a passive tool for making copies of whatever is in the environment. At 6 or 7, however, things change: Children begin to realize that the mind can impose meaning on the world and that knowledge is often a matter of interpretation. By realizing that other people can be mistaken, children are (unfortunately) better able to deceive others (Chandler et al., 2000). This is a considerably more sophisticated view of people's thinking processes than that held by preschoolers, and it is another example of the relatively rapid changes in cognitive development in the preoperational stage.

The Concrete Operational Period: 7 to 11 Years

Between the ages of 7 and about 11, children enter the **concrete operational period** and gain the capacity for true mental *operations*. By mental operations Piaget meant the ability to perform mental actions on objects—to verbalize, visualize, and mentally manipulate objects. A child of 8 can consider the consequences of rolling a long strip of play dough into a ball before the action is actually performed. The result is that children in the concrete operational period have fewer difficulties with conservation problems because they are capable of reversing operations on objects; they can mentally consider the effects of both doing and undoing an action.

Children at the concrete operational stage also show the initial stirrings of logical thought, which means they can now mentally order and compare objects and perform more sophisticated classifications. These children can do simple math problems and solve problems that require elementary reasoning. Consider a problem such as the following: Martin is faster than René. René is faster than Conrad. Is Martin faster or slower than Conrad? Children of 9 or 10 have little trouble with this problem because they can keep track of ordered relations in their heads. Younger preoperational children will probably insist on actually seeing Martin and Conrad race—they cannot easily solve the problem in their heads.

Although concrete operational children possess a growing array of mental operations, Piaget believed that they are still limited intellectually in an important way. The mental operations they can perform remain concrete, or tied directly to actual objects in the real world. Children at this age have great difficulty with problems that do not flow directly from everyday experience. Ask an 8-year-old to solve a problem involving four-armed people and barking cats and you're likely to see a blank look on his or her face. Basically, if something can't be seen, heard, touched, tasted, or smelled, it's not going to be something that concrete operational children can easily consider in their heads (although these children can imagine non–real-world objects they have encountered, as in cartoons or fairy tales). The ability to think truly abstractly doesn't develop until the final stage of cognitive development.

The Formal Operational Period: 11 to Adulthood

Piaget repeatedly stressed the idea that children tend to think differently from adults. Children's schemas, or mental models of the world, are limited because they lack the proper amounts of biological maturation and experience. These limitations in turn lead to errors in reasoning or judgment, although the child's view of the world can be adaptive for solving the particular problems that children face (as when a baby's viewing of an object as something to be sucked increases the likelihood of obtaining nourishment). But by the time children reach their teenage years, many of them will be in the formal operational period, during which their thought processes become increasingly more like those of an adult. Neither teenagers nor adults have problems thinking about imaginary or artificial concepts; they can consider hypothetical outcomes and make logical deductions about places they've never visited or that might not even exist. Teenagers as well as adults can develop systematic strategies for solving problems—such as using trial and error—that are beyond the capability of most preteens.

The **formal operational period** is the stage in which individuals start to gain mastery over abstract thinking. Ask a concrete operational child about the meaning of education, and you'll likely hear about teachers and grades. The formal operational adolescent is able to answer the question in a general and abstract way, perhaps describing education as a system organized by parents and the government to foster the acquisition of useful knowledge. Piaget believed that the transition from concrete operational thinking to formal operational thinking probably occurs gradually, over several years, and is not achieved by everyone (Piaget, 1970). Once it is reached, the adolescent is no longer tied to concrete real-world constructs and can invent and experiment with the possible rather than with the here and now alone.

formal operational period
Piaget's last stage of cognitive development; thought processes become adult-like, and people gain mastery over abstract thinking.

Challenges to Piaget's Theory

Most psychologists agree that Piaget's contributions to the understanding of cognitive development have been substantial. He successfully convinced the psychological community that children have unique internal schemas, and he provided convincing demonstrations that those schemas, once formed, tend to change systematically over time. However, not all of Piaget's ideas have withstood the rigours of experimental scrutiny. It's now common for researchers to challenge the specifics of his theory, primarily his assumptions about what children really know and when they know it.

It now seems clear that Piaget was simply wrong in some of his conclusions about the young child's mental capabilities. Children and young infants are considerably more sophisticated in their models of the world than Piaget believed (Flavell et al., 1993; Kuhn, 1992). For example, Piaget stated that object permanence doesn't develop until late in the child's first year. Although it's true that children will not search for a hidden toy in the first few months of life, more sensitive tests have revealed that even 1- to 4-month-old infants are capable of recognizing that vanished objects still exist.

In research by child psychologist T. G. R. Bower (1982), very young infants watched as a screen was moved in front of a toy, blocking it from view (see Figure 10.11). Moments later, when the screen was removed, the infants acted surprised if the toy was absent (it could be secretly removed by the experimenter). If objects no

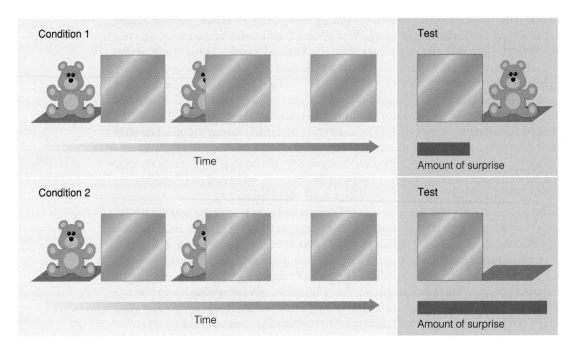

FIGURE 10.11

Re-evaluating Object Permanence

In this experiment by T. G. R. Bower, young infants watched as a screen was moved in front of a toy, blocking it from view. Moments later, the screen was removed and the baby's level of "surprise," defined as a change in heart rate, was measured. In one condition, the toy appeared behind the screen; in a second condition, the toy had vanished. Despite their young age, the babies showed more surprise when the toy was absent, suggesting that object permanence may develop earlier than Piaget suspected.

longer exist when removed from view, then infants shouldn't be surprised by a sudden absence (see also Hofstadter & Reznick, 1996). Other researchers have demonstrated that small infants can show symbolic thought—they understand, for instance, that objects move along continuous paths and do not jump around—and they gain this understanding at points in development far earlier than Piaget imagined (see Mandler, 1992; Spelke et al., 1992).

Problems with the Stage View Piaget has also been criticized for sticking to the notion of distinct stages, or periods of development (Flavell et al., 1993). Piaget recognized that not all children develop cognitively at the same rate, but he remained convinced that a child's thought processes undergo sharp transitions from one qualitative stage to the next. Most modern developmental psychologists believe that cognitive development is better viewed as a process of continual change and adaptation (Siegler, 1996). If we adopted a stage view, as Piaget did, we should expect that once the child undergoes a stage transition—say, from the preoperational stage to the concrete operational stage—the child should relatively quickly show the capacity to perform a variety of new tasks. But this is not usually the case.

Children's thought processes do not seem to undergo rapid transitions; in fact, they often change slowly over long periods of time (Flavell, 1971). For example, it is not uncommon to find a 5-year-old who understands conservation of number but has no idea about conservation of mass or volume. So a given child might show mental schemas that are characteristic of more than one stage. Children are learning to adapt to their world and to tasks and problems that might occur only in particular situations. So it's not surprising that they act in ways that are difficult to fit into any specific cognitive stage or that the transitions from one developmental point to the next are not rapid and well defined (Munakata et al., 1997).

The Role of Culture Piaget was also rather fuzzy about the mechanisms that produce cognitive change. His demonstrations that infants, toddlers, and school-age children think in fundamentally different ways were brilliant, but he never clearly accounted for the psychological processes that produce those changes. He also tended to ignore the importance of social context in explaining individual differences in cognitive ability. Cross-cultural research has shown that children across the world develop cognitively in similar ways, but significant cultural differences occur in the rate of development

PIAGET'S STAGES OF COGNITIVE DEVELOPMENT

Stage	Basic Characteristics	Accomplishments	Limitations
Sensorimotor period (birth to 2 years)	Schemas about the world revolve primarily around sensory and motor abilities.	Children develop object permanence; learn how to vocalize and learn first words.	Schemas are limited primarily to simple sensory and motor function; problems in thinking about absent objects (early).
Preoperational period (2 to 7 years)	Schemas grow in sophistication. Children can think about absent objects and can use one object to stand for another.	Children readily symbolize objects, and imaginary play is common; great strides in language development.	Children are prelogical; they fail to understand conservation, due to centration and a failure to understand reversibility; children show egocentricity in thinking.
Concrete operational period (7 to 11 years)	Children gain the capacity for true mental operations, i.e., verbalizing, visualizing, mental manipulation.	Children understand reversibility and other simple logical operations like categorizing and ordering.	Mental operations remain concrete, tied to actual objects in the real world. Difficulty with problems that do not flow from everyday experience.
Formal operational period (11 years to adulthood)	Mastery is gained over abstract thinking.	Adolescents can think and answer questions in general and abstract ways.	No limitations; development of reasoning is complete. However, not all reach this stage.

(Matsumoto, 1994). For example, children raised in nomadic societies, which move frequently from place to place, seem to acquire spatial skills (the ability to orient themselves in their environment) earlier and better than children raised in single, fixed locales. Schooling may also be a factor: Ample cross-cultural evidence indicates that people who never attend school may have a difficult time reaching the formal operational stage of thinking, at least as measured through the use of traditional Piagetian tasks (Cole, 1992; Segall et al., 1990).

The idea that we cannot fully understand the development of mental processes without considering social and cultural influences was actually promoted by a Russian psychologist, Lev Vygotsky, around the same time that Piaget was developing his theoretical ideas. Vygotsky died in 1934, after only a decade of work in psychology, but his ideas continue to exert a powerful influence on modern developmental psychologists (Duncan, 1995; Wertsch & Tulviste, 1992). Vygotsky argued that cognitive abilities emerge directly out of our social interactions with others. He proposed, for example, that inner speech, which people use to think and plan activities, is simply a natural extension of the outer speech that people use to communicate with others. Vygotsky was convinced that intellectual development is tied to social interaction—it grows out of each person's attempts to master social situations. This means that we cannot understand development by considering the individual alone; we must always consider the individual in his or her social context (Vygotsky, 1978).

This Vygotskyian perspective on inner speech has recently been examined by developmental psychologist Robert Duncan of Mount Allison University and his colleagues from the University of Waterloo (Duncan & Cheyne, 1999; Duncan & Pratt, 1997). Duncan and his colleagues found support for Vygotsky's suggestions that inner speech is an important cognitive "tool," although it is internalized during childhood, and hence it is not readily apparent in adults.

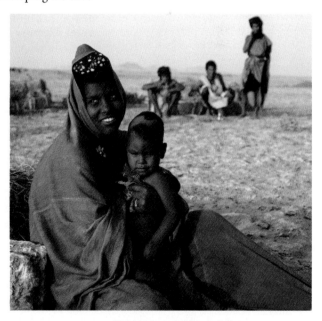

Children in nomadic societies move frequently from place to place and may be able to orient themselves in an environment faster and more efficiently than children raised in fixed locales.

Beyond Formal Operational Thought Another active area of controversy surrounding Piaget's theory concerns the issue of adult cognitive development. Does

399

According to Vygotsky, cognitive abilities arise directly out of the social and verbal interactions that children have with other people, including their friends and relatives.

intellectual development really end with the acquisition of formal operational thinking at some point during adolescence, as claimed by Piaget? A number of researchers believe that mastery over abstract thought, which is the hallmark of the formal operational period, is only one part of a much more extensive process of adult cognitive development (Cavanaugh, 1993; Riegel, 1976). There are probably fundamental differences between adolescent and adult thought processes that cannot be explained without the introduction of new, *postformal* stages of cognitive development.

Currently, there is no general consensus over exactly what these postformal thoughts represent. One popular idea is that postformal cognitive development is characterized by *relativistic thinking*. Adults tend to think about "truth" in a much more relative way than teenagers do; adults recognize, for instance, that the correct answer to a moral dilemma might vary from one situation to the next. Adults are also more tolerant of ambiguity in their thinking than teenagers are (although too much ambiguity in thought is obviously a problem). Adolescent thinking is typically rigid and absolute in the sense that teenagers tend to rely on fixed rules of right and wrong and show little intellectual flexibility (Labouvie-Vief et al., 1987; Perry, 1970).

Other researchers have argued that adolescents are also less capable of thinking about *systems* of ideas. Teenagers who have reached the formal operational stage might be able to deal with abstract ideas, but they will have trouble dealing with higher-order systems of ideas of the type found in a scientific theory (Richards & Commons, 1990). Systematic comparisons among ideas, as in the analysis of the similarities and differences among theories, require postformal thought processes. Ironically, many modern developmental psychologists argue that Piaget himself must have been operating at a level of cognitive development beyond the formal operational stage when he developed his own theory.

Moral Development: Learning Right from Wrong

morality

The ability to distinguish between appropriate and inappropriate actions; a child's sense of morality may be tied to his or her level of cognitive development.

Developing intellectually means more than just learning to think logically and form correct internal models of the world. As children mature intellectually, they also acquire a sense of morality, which provides them with a way to distinguish between appropriate and inappropriate thoughts and actions. Piaget had strong opinions on this topic, arguing that the sense of **morality** is closely tied to one's stage of cognitive development and to one's social experiences with peers. For example, from Piaget's perspective children in the concrete operational stage would not be expected to show sophisticated moral reasoning skills, because morality is basically an abstract concept—something that cannot be handled until the formal operational stage of development. Partly for this reason, researchers have largely focused on the moral development of adolescents and adults, rather than children.

Kohlberg's Stage Theory The most influential theory of moral development is the stage theory proposed by Lawrence Kohlberg. Strongly influenced by the writings of Piaget, Kohlberg framed his theory around the idea that individuals progress through an orderly series of stages of moral development (Kohlberg, 1963, 1986). His investigative technique was to give people of various ages a hypothetical moral dilemma and use their solutions to identify their current state of moral development. Let's consider in detail an example, based on Kohlberg (1969).

A woman is stricken with a rare and deadly form of cancer. There is a drug that can save her, a form of radium recently discovered by a druggist in town. But the druggist is charging an impossible amount for the medicine, in fact, 10 times what the drug cost him to make. The sick woman's husband, Heinz, tries desperately to raise the money but can raise only half the needed amount. He pleads with the druggist to sell him the drug at a reduced cost, or at least to allow him to pay for the drug over time, but the druggist refuses. "No," the druggist says. "I discovered the drug and I'm going to make money from it." Frantic to save his wife, Heinz considers breaking into the druggist's office to steal the drug.

What do you think? Should the husband steal the drug? Why or why not? You probably have an answer to this dilemma. Whether you answer "yes" or "no" doesn't matter to Kohlberg. Instead, it is the reasoning behind your answer, the kind of intellectual justification that you give, that is important. Kohlberg argued that an adult's moral development can be evaluated by matching it against the three levels through which children progress. Few children progress through them all, leaving all adults fixed at one of the three levels: the *preconventional*, the *conventional*, or the *postconventional* level (see the Concept Summary table on page 403).

At the lowest level of moral development—the **preconventional level**—decisions about right and wrong are based primarily on external consequences. Young children will typically interpret the morality of a behaviour in terms of its immediate individual consequences—that is, whether the act will lead directly to a reward or to a punishment: "Heinz shouldn't steal the drug because he might get caught and punished" or

preconventional level
In Kohlberg's theory, the lowest level of moral development, in which decisions about right and wrong are made primarily in terms of external consequences.

Children need to develop a sense of morality, which helps them tell the difference between appropriate and inappropriate actions.

"Heinz should steal the drug because people will get mad at him if his wife dies." Notice the rationale is based on the immediate external consequences of the action rather than on some abstract moral principle.

At the **conventional level** of moral reasoning, people start to justify their actions on the basis of internalized rules. Now an action is right or wrong because it maintains or disrupts the *social order.* Someone at this level might argue that Heinz shouldn't steal the drug because stealing is illegal, whether or not he gets caught. Or, Heinz should steal the drug because husbands have a traditional obligation to protect their wives. Notice here that the moral reasoning has moved away from immediate individual consequences to societal consequences: What if everyone did that? Moral behaviour is conduct that conforms to the rules and conventions of society. In general, individuals at the conventional level of moral reasoning tend to consider the appropriateness of their actions from the perspective of cultural traditions and current authority figures.

At the final level of moral development, the **postconventional level,** morality is based on abstract principles that may even conflict with accepted laws and standards. The individual adopts a moral standard—not to seek approval from others or an authority figure, but to follow some universal ethical principle. "An individual human life is more important than society's dictum against stealing," someone at this level might argue. In this case, moral actions are driven by general and abstract personal codes of ethics that may not agree with societal norms.

Evaluating Kohlberg's Theory   The idea that we progress through periods of moral development, from an early focus on immediate individual consequences toward a final principled code of ethics, remains popular among many developmental psychologists (see Damon & Hart, 1992). A number of observational studies have confirmed aspects of Kohlberg's views. For example, research by University of British Columbia developmental psychologist Lawrence Walker suggests that people do seem to move through the various types of moral reasoning in the sequence suggested by Kohlberg (Walker, 1989). Furthermore, the link that both Piaget and Kohlberg made between moral reasoning and level of cognitive development has clear merit. But Kohlberg's theory has attracted criticism and amendment suggestions from many subsequent researchers—not unlike any major theory in psychology.

A strong competitor to Kohlberg's theory of moral development comes from psychologists who view morality from an evolutionary perspective. Social and developmental psychologist Dennis Krebs of Simon Fraser University reviewed some of the likely factors leading to the evolutionary selection of moral behaviours in humans (Krebs, 1998). This analysis of moral development leads to two main differences from Kohlberg's view. The evolutionary perspective suggests that people's cognitive mechanisms for thinking about morality are probably not as unified as Kohlberg suggested. Indeed, people's minds probably contain relatively unconnected "modules" or submechanisms for thinking about different aspects of morality, such as obeying authority and treating people fairly. Therefore, all modules are there from the beginning and they may sometimes come into conflict in ways not anticipated by Kohlberg.

An evolutionary analysis leads to the second difference from Kohlberg's view: Kohlberg (1984) suggested that people first think about moral dilemmas, then come up with a judgment on a moral way to proceed, and then behave in a way suggested by their moral judgment. Evolutionary psychology suggests that the system evolved the other way around: Certain social tendencies were selected because they proved to be adaptive. For example, it was adaptive to help other humans in distress because the whole group benefited. People often help first and think later. These socialized behaviours become so common and accepted that people get upset with their own and others' deviations from the norm. The bad feeling (e.g., anxiety, disgust) associated with deviations from the norm then tells us that something is immoral (Krebs, 1998).

Other critics of Kohlberg's theory argue that he tied the concept of morality too closely to an abstract code of *justice*—that is, to the idea that moral acts are those that

conventional level

In Kohlberg's theory of moral development, the stage in which actions are judged to be right or wrong based on whether they maintain or disrupt the social order.

postconventional level

Kohlberg's highest level of moral development, in which moral actions are judged on the basis of personal codes of ethics that are general and abstract and that may not agree with societal norms.

Concept Summary

KOHLBERG'S STAGE THEORY OF MORAL DEVELOPMENT

Stage	Basis for Moral Judgment	Possible Response to "Was Heinz Right?"
Preconventional	External consequences	Yes: "He can't be happy without his wife." No: "If he gets caught, he'll be put in jail."
Conventional	Social order	Yes: "Spouses are responsible for protecting one another." No: "Stealing is against the law."
Postconventional	Abstract ethical principles	Yes: "Individual lives are more important than society's law against stealing." No: "Laws are necessary in a civilized society; they need to be followed by all to prevent chaos."

ensure fairness to the individual (Damon & Hart, 1992). For example, suppose that your sense of morality is not based on fairness but rather on concern for the welfare of others. You might believe that the appropriate action is always one that doesn't hurt anyone and takes into account the happiness of the affected individual. This is the view touted by Harvard psychologist Carol Gilligan (1982), who has argued that women in our culture often adopt such a view (a moral code based on caring), whereas men tend to make moral decisions on the basis of an abstract sense of justice. Given the way Kohlberg's scale is scored, however, this socialization difference means that women will tend to be classified at a lower level of moral development than men. Gilligan sees this result as an unfair and unjustified gender bias.

The Role of Culture It now appears that Gilligan may have overstated the evidence for sex differences in moral reasoning. Modern samples of men and women (e.g., college students) show minimal differences on the types of moral dilemmas studied by Kohlberg (Walker, 1989). At the same time, other evidence indicates that important cross-cultural differences occur in moral thinking that are not captured well by Kohlberg's classification system. For example, studies of moral decision making in India reveal striking differences from those typically found in Western cultures. Richard Shweder and his colleagues (1990) found that both Hindu children and adults are likely to find it morally acceptable for a husband to beat a disobedient wife; in fact, keeping disobedient family members in line is considered to be the moral obligation of the head of the family. In Canada, such actions would be widely condemned. The reverse is true about women showing their hair in public. In some cultures, this behaviour is considered to be outrageous sexual display. In Canada, this view seems silly: Here a woman covering her head is probably having a "bad-hair day."

The source of such differences may arise from the tendency of Western cultures to emphasize individual goals more than other cultures, where the emphasis is on collective goals. These differences in cultural values and teachings need to be factored into any complete theory of moral development (Miller, 1994). Moreover, education and the value a culture places on teaching moral values play a role as well, and can affect the speed with which moral development proceeds (e.g., Snarey, 1995).

Our best current integration is this: Evidence supports the cross-cultural consistency in the developmental ordering of moral thought—that is, people in all cultures tend to interpret morality first in terms of external consequences and only later in terms of abstract principles—but, not surprisingly, culture exerts its influence in powerful ways (Saltzstein, 1997). Recently, developmental researchers Joan Grusec of the University of Toronto and Leon Kuczynski of the University of Guelph collected and summarized contemporary views relating to how children acquire values and morality. They emphasize the fact that development of values is a complex process that involves influences from the larger culture, the community in which the child resides, the relationship between the child and the parent, and the child's own personality and disposition (Grusec & Kuczynski, 1997).

Test Yourself 10.2

Check your knowledge of intellectual development by answering these questions. (You will find the answers in Appendix B.)

1. Pick the appropriate research technique from among the following terms: cross-sectional; habituation; longitudinal; preference; reward.
   a. Baby learns to kick her leg when a blue, but not a red, card appears.
      _____
   b. Baby grows bored and stops looking at repeated presentations of the same event. _____
   c. Comparisons are made between three groups of children; each group contains children of a different age. _____
   d. The development of memory is studied by testing the same individual repeatedly throughout his or her lifetime. _____

2. According to Piaget, children develop mental models of the world, called schemas, that change as the child grows. During the preoperational period of development, children often fail to recognize that the physical properties of an object can stay the same despite superficial changes in its appearance (e.g., rolling a ball of dough into a sausage shape doesn't change its mass). Piaget referred to this ability as:
   a. conservation
   b. object permanence
   c. accommodation
   d. relativistic thinking

3. Pick the appropriate level of moral development, as described by Kohlberg. Possible answers include conventional, preconventional, and postconventional.
   a. Actions are justified on the basis of whether or not they disrupt social order. _____
   b. Actions are justified on the basis of abstract moral principles. _____
   c. Actions are justified on the basis of their immediate consequences. _____

DEVELOPING SOCIALLY AND PERSONALLY

Learning Goals

1. Be able to explain the notion of temperament.
2. Understand the short-term characteristics and long-term consequences of early attachments.
3. Comprehend Erik Erikson's stage theory of personal identity development.
4. Understand gender-role development and the role of the family in adult development.
5. Recognize the social and psychological factors the elderly face.
6. Appreciate the psychological issues connected with death and dying.

HUMAN BEINGS DO NOT DEVELOP IN ISOLATION. Children's biological development occurs in a social context. Their social and emotional relationships critically affect how they act and view themselves. For infants, relationships with caregivers—usually their parents—guarantee them adequate nourishment and a safe and secure environment. For children, the social task is to become part of a social group and thereby learn what it means to get along with peers and follow the rules and norms of society. For adults, whose social bonds become increasingly intimate, the task is to learn to accept responsibility for the care and support of others. As with most aspects of development, social and personal development is a continuous process that is shaped by innate biological forces as well as by learned experiences.

Temperament

The child's social and personal development begins with a set of behavioural predispositions called **temperament.** Included are factors such as moodiness, inhibition, and energy level. Most of temperament is genetic in origin but part is due to congenital factors—that is, biological forces (e.g., hormones) that alter the fetus during pregnancy. Afterward, as the child grows, these in-born temperament factors interact with the environment to produce the more complex adult personality (see Chapter 12).

Early work on temperament argued that infants can be categorized into types. As you might guess, some babies are *easy;* they're basically happy, readily establish daily routines, and tend not to get upset very easily. Other babies are *difficult;* they have difficulty accepting new experiences, establishing routines, and maintaining a pleasant mood. Fortunately, only about 10% of babies fall into this difficult group, and about 40% of sampled babies are readily classified as easy (Thomas & Chess, 1977). The remaining 50% are more difficult to categorize. Some babies are *slow to warm up,* which means they roughly fall between easy and difficult and show a mixture of different temperaments.

Modern research on temperament has moved to a more complex dimensional approach. Instead of a few categories, infants can now be scored on as many as 15 different dimensions (Rothbart et al., 2001; Soudino et al., 1996). One dimension attracting attention seems to be the antecedent of adult shyness. Jerome Kagan developed novel techniques to demonstrate how infants differ in terms of being *inhibited* (i.e., fearful of unfamiliar people or new events) versus *uninhibited* (i.e., calm in the face of the unfamiliar or novel). In several longitudinal studies, he showed that the same babies who acted fearful when a complex mobile was activated in front of them (about 20%) later developed into shy adolescents (Kagan, 1997; Kagan & Snidman, 1991).

Research on other dimensions of temperament has also demonstrated stability across childhood (Caspi & Silva, 1995; Eaton & Saudino, 1992; Schwartz et al., 1996). For example, infants who seem very energetic show that same energy later in life. Most important is the evidence that identical twins, who share the same genetic material, show more similarities in temperament than do fraternal twins or regular siblings raised in the same home (Braungart et al., 1992; Jang et al., 1996b). One implication of the power of temperament is that children may be affecting their parents' behaviour rather than the reverse. A tense, angry, hyper-reactive mother may actually be the creation of her difficult child (Johnston, 1988; Johnston & Freeman, 1997).

Forming Bonds with Others

Think again about the problems faced by the newborn infant: limited motor skills, somewhat fuzzy vision, yet a powerful sustained need for food, water, and warmth. As we've noted, to gain the nourishment needed to live, as well as to gain protection from danger, the newborn relies on interactions with others—usually the mother—to stay alive. The newborn forms what psychologists call **attachments,** the strong emotional ties to one or more intimate companions. The need for early attachments is so critical that many researchers believe that innate, biologically driven behavioural systems may be involved in their formation (Bowlby, 1969, 1988; Maestripieri, 2001).

temperament
Behavioural tendencies that have biological origins.

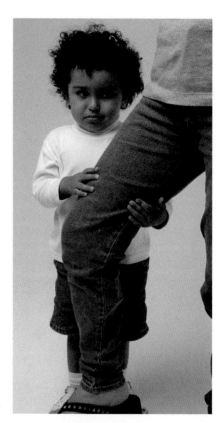

The attachment process involves an interaction between child temperament and parental reactions.

attachments
Strong emotional ties formed to one or more intimate companions.

According to child psychiatrist John Bowlby, both caregiver and infant are preprogrammed from birth to respond to certain environmental signals with attachment behaviour. The newborn typically cries, coos, and smiles, and these behaviours lead naturally to attention and support from the caregiver. It's no accident that adults like to hear babies coo or watch them smile—humans probably evolved to derive pleasure from observing happy babies (Bowlby, 1969; Sigelman & Shaffer, 1995). Parents also seem to derive a great deal of pleasure from singing to their infants (Trehub et al., 1997).

Similarly, newborns are biologically predisposed to respond to nurturance from a caregiver. For example, newborns imitate the facial expressions of their parents (Maratos, 1998), which presumably enhances their social interactions with mom and dad (Bjorklund, 1997). Queen's University infant researchers Lawrence Symons, Sylvia Hains, and Darwin Muir have demonstrated that even 5-month-old infants are quite sensitive to the direction of another person's gaze, and their apparent interest in a social interaction decreases substantially when a person looks away from them even a little bit (Symons et al., 1998). Both the infant and caregiver are active participants in a reciprocal relationship—the attachment is formed because both parties are prepared to respond with bonding to the right kind of environmental events. The bond usually is formed initially between baby and mother because it is the mother who provides most of the early care (Lamb et al., 1992).

The Origins of Attachment

The idea that humans are evolutionarily predisposed to form strong emotional attachments makes sense from an adaptive standpoint—it helps to ensure survival. But what determines the strength and quality of the attachment? Differences clearly exist in the quality of the bond that forms between infant and caregiver—some infants are securely attached to their caregivers; others are not. Research with animal subjects suggests that one very important factor is the amount of actual contact comfort—the degree of warm physical contact—provided by the caregiver.

Contact Comfort In some classic research on early attachment, psychologist Harry Harlow noticed that newborn rhesus monkeys, when separated from their mothers at birth, tended to become attached to soft cuddly things left in their cages, such as baby blankets. If one of these blankets was removed for cleaning, Harlow noticed, the mon-

If forced to choose between two surrogate mothers, baby monkeys prefer a soft and cuddly cloth "mother" to a wire one, even when the wire mother provides the food.

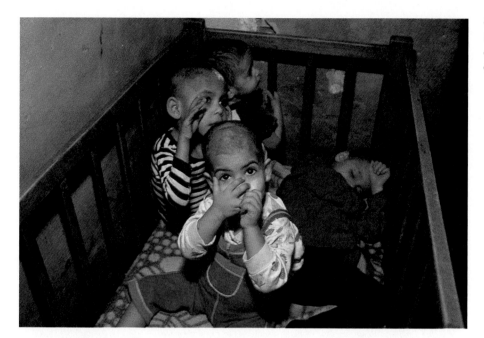

Children orphaned by the 1989 war in Romania were housed in a hospital under conditions that led to its being dubbed "the children's Auschwitz."

keys would become extremely upset and cling to it frantically when it was returned. Intrigued, Harlow began a series of experiments in which he isolated newborn monkeys and raised them in cages with a variety of surrogate, or artificial, "mothers" (Harlow & Zimmerman, 1959). In one experimental condition, baby monkeys were raised with a mother consisting simply of wire mesh fitted with an artificial nipple that delivered food. In another condition, the babies were exposed to a nipple-less cloth mother made of the same wire mesh but wrapped in a soft terry cloth and a padding of foam rubber.

The idea behind the experiment was to see which of the two surrogate mothers the monkeys preferred. If early attachments are formed primarily to caregivers who provide nourishment—that is, infants love the one who feeds them—we would expect the monkeys to prefer and cling to the wire mother, since it provides the food. But in the vast majority of cases, the monkeys actually preferred the cloth mother. If startled in some way, perhaps by the introduction of a foreign object into the cage, the monkeys ran immediately to the cloth mother, hung on tight, and showed no interest in the wire mother that provided the food. Harlow and his colleagues concluded that contact comfort—the warmth and softness provided by the terry cloth—was the primary motivator of attachment (Harlow et al., 1971).

For obvious reasons, similar experiments have never been conducted with human babies. However, it is clear that human infants are like rhesus infants in their desire and need for contact comfort. Many studies have looked at how children fare in institutional settings that provide relatively low levels of contact comfort (e.g., Hodges & Tizard, 1989). Children reared in orphanages with poor infant-to-caregiver ratios (e.g., one caregiver for every 10 to 20 infants), on average, show many more developmental problems than children reared in less deprived environments (Shaffer, 1993). Recent research has looked at orphaned children in Romania who, for some time, were literally "warehoused with minimal food, clothing, heat, or caregivers" (Kaler & Freeman, 1994). When the social and intellectual functioning of these orphans is compared to children reared at home, the orphans show significant and sometimes severe deficits.

Interaction with Temperament   Clearly, the emotional and physical responsiveness of parents to their infants is an important predictor of the quality of the parent–child bond, as suggested by Mary Ainsworth and others (Ainsworth et al., 1978; Cox et al., 1992). The quality of the attachment, in turn, can either enhance or hinder the normal developmental process. Physical contact is a necessary part of a quality attachment, but

How children react when they are in a strange situation provides insight into the type of attachment they've formed with their parent or caregiver.

what determines whether the infant will receive the contact he or she needs? Difficult or fussy babies tend to elicit fewer comforting and responsive reactions, and the quality of the attachment between parent and child suffers as a result (Thomas & Chess, 1977).

Types of Attachment

Once attachments are formed, there are systematic differences in the types of bonds that are formed. To investigate these differences, psychologists have used a technique called the **strange situation test.** This test, which was developed by Mary Ainsworth and her colleagues, can be used to classify 10- to 24-month-old children into three main attachment groups (e.g., Ainsworth & Wittig, 1969; Ainsworth et al., 1978). This experimental situation gradually subjects the child to a stressful situation and notes how his or her behaviour toward the parent changes. After arrival in the lab, the parent and child are ushered into a waiting room filled with toys; the child is encouraged to play with the toys. Various levels of infant stress are then introduced. A stranger enters the room; the parent steps out for a few moments, leaving the child alone. The researchers measure several dependent measures of stress or discomfort: Initially, how willing is the child to move away from the parent and play with the toys? How much crying or distress does the child show when the parent leaves the room? How does the child react to the parent when the parent comes back into the room—does the child greet and cling to the parent, or does he or she move away?

Most infants—approximately 70%—react to the strange situation test with what Ainsworth called *secure attachment.* With the parent present, even if the situation is new and strange, these children play happily and are likely to explore the room looking for interesting toys or magazines to shred. But as the level of stress increases, they become increasingly uneasy and clingy. If the mother leaves the room, the child will probably start to cry but will calm down rapidly if the mother returns.

About 10% of children show a pattern called *resistant attachment.* These children react to stress in an ambiguous way, which may indicate a lack of trust for the parent. Resistant children are wary in a strange situation, refusing to leave their mother's side and explore the room, and they do not deal well with the sudden appearance of strangers. If the mother leaves the room, they cry, yet they are unlikely to greet the

strange situation test
Gradually subjecting a child to a stressful situation and observing his or her behaviour toward the parent or caregiver. This test is used to classify children according to type of attachment—secure, resistant, or avoidant.

Practical Solutions

DO PARENTS REALLY MATTER?

Can any idea in child development be more accepted than the assumption that parents have an influence on the way their children turn out? Indeed, much of the field has been built upon debates and subsequent recommendations about how best to raise children. Nonetheless, several psychologists have recently been bold enough to challenge this almost sacred claim. In her review of the literature, Judith Harris (1995, 1998) concluded that the research literature points to factors other than the parents' child-rearing behaviour as the real causes behind the differences seen in the personal and social behaviour of children and adults. A consequence of the traditional view, she complained, was that parents—especially mothers—were blamed for everything their children did. As we did in our discussion of temperament, she noted that parents are often just reacting to their child's behaviour rather than causing it.

Harris accepts that parents do matter in the limited sense that they pass on their genetic predispositions to their children. In fact, she cites the accumulating evidence for the behavioural genetics of personality. Roughly half of the variation observed in childrens' personality can be attributed to the genes inherited from their parents (e.g., Jang et al., 1996a, 1996b). Of course, that leaves a substantial amount for the environment to explain.

But the evidence about environmental effects is even more surprising. It appears that these effects are primarily within the family (Plomin et al., 1997, 1998). That means that children of the same parents are experiencing different environments. The most obvious difference among siblings is their birth order. The effects of birth order—once thought to be disproved (Ernst & Angst, 1983)—have been rehabilitated by the work of Frank Sulloway (1997). The research now indicates that first-born children are more domineering, dutiful, and conservative in

their political beliefs, while later-born children are more rebellious and open to new ideas. These differences in personality are created, not by parents treating the birth orders differently, but by the siblings treating each other differently. First-borns are always older and, therefore, have physical and status superiority over the later-borns. During childhood, they are constantly trying to reassert their higher status in the sibling community. Later-borns are always trying to break down the hierarchy. So, their adult personalities become structured around these issues of status and dominance. Sulloway's results have been replicated in large samples of students and adults (Paulhus et al., 1999).

Rather than birth order, Judith Harris argues that children in the same family end up with different personalities primarily because they have different friends. She provides evidence that siblings who share friends do end up with personalities that are more similar than siblings who do not share friends. Other environmental factors that could make siblings different are different teachers and various chance

experiences. For example, one child might have the good fortune to be taught by an inspiring teacher while the other child was turned off school by a bullying incident. Note again that these are differences among children with the same parents. The differences between families appear to be explicable by genetics, so that the differences we see in parents' child-rearing styles may not actually be having the effect that psychologists have always asssumed.

As you might expect, many developmental psychologists have reacted negatively to Harris's ideas (Borkowski et al., 2001; Maccoby, 2000). The counterarguments have included that (1) the behaviour genetics studies are flawed, (2) there is evidence that children in different cultures have different personalities, and (3) extreme parental treatment (e.g., child abuse) is known to have long-term effects. Controversies such as these often take years to clarify, but the challenge to re-think such a basic issue always has positive scientific benefits. Stay tuned—there is bound to be more debate about this issue.

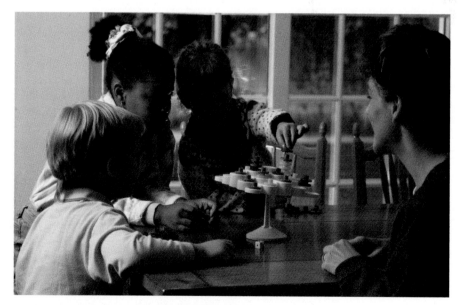

Who affects you more—your parents or your friends?

Do you think the findings of the strange situation test would change if the test were conducted in the child's home? Why or why not?

mother with affection on her return. Instead, these children act ambivalent, scorning their mother by temporarily resisting her affection.

The final group of children—about 20%—show a pattern of *avoidant attachment.* These children demonstrate no strong attachment to the mother in any aspect of the strange situation test. They are not particularly bothered by the appearance of strangers in the room, nor do they show much concern when the mother leaves the room or much interest when she returns. Ainsworth discovered that the parents of these children tend, on average, to be unresponsive and impatient when it comes to the child's needs and may even actively reject the child on a regular basis (Ainsworth, 1979). Why? It's difficult to tell because the parent–child relationship depends on several factors: the particular personality characteristics of the parent, the temperament of the child, and the child-rearing practices of the culture.

Do Early Attachments Matter Later in Life?

Given that infants can be easily divided into these attachment groups by around age one, it's reasonable to wonder about the long-term consequences. For instance, are the avoidant children doomed to a life of insecurity and failed relationships? There is evidence to suggest that children with an early secure attachment do indeed have some social and intellectual advantages. For instance, Acadia University developmental psychologists Douglas Symons and Sharon Clark have reported that 5-year-old children with more secure attachments to their mothers do better at cognitive tasks such as locating objects (Symons & Clark, 2000). In other research, teachers rate securely attached children as more curious and self-directed in school (Waters et al., 1979). By age 10 or 11, securely attached children also tend to have more close and mature relationships with their peers than children who were classified as insecurely attached (Elicker et al., 1992). Other researchers have found that early attachment relationships do predict patterns of social interactions and other behaviours in adulthood (Bartholemew, 1993; Bartholemew et al., 2000).

However, early patterns of attachment are not perfect predictors of later behaviour. One problem is stability: Sometimes a child who appears to be insecurely attached at 12 months can act quite differently in the strange situation test a few months later (Lamb et al., 1992). In addition, a child who has a particular kind of attachment to one parent may show quite a different attachment pattern to the other. It's also important to remember that when psychologists talk about predicting later behaviour based on early attachment patterns, they are referring mainly to correlational studies. As you learned in Chapter 2, it's not possible to draw firm conclusions about causality from simple correlational analyses. The fact that later behaviour can be predicted from early attachment patterns does not mean that early bonding necessarily causes the later behaviour patterns; other factors might be responsible. For instance, children who form secure attachments in infancy typically have caregivers who remain warm and responsive throughout childhood, adolescence, and adulthood. So it could be that securely attached infants tend to have successful and meaningful relationships later in life because they live most of their lives in supportive environments.

Evolutionary Bases of Family Interactions

As discussed above, it is relatively obvious why humans, like other mammals, evolved psychological mechanisms so that babies would tend to become emotionally attached to the adults caring for them. However, there are a number of other types of family interactions that also show evidence of evolved psychological mechanisms for guiding and modifying behaviour. McMaster University psychologists Martin Daly and Margo Wilson have suggested that human parenting behaviour should be considered as a form of "reproductive strategy" and that human parents evolved to "invest resources," including food, protection, and nurturance, in ways that will promote the optimal number of offspring for an individual parent (Daly & Wilson, 1998, 1999). Daly and

Wilson offer an example in the fact that rates of child abuse and neglect are considerably higher in families where there are stepparents as compared to those where there are two biological parents present. They suggest that people may have evolved so that they tend to be more nurturant and protective of children who are biologically related to them, that stepparenting situations involve a decrease in the "buffering" effect that biological relatedness provides against the frustrations and stresses of parenting, and thus stepparents display higher rates of child abuse and neglect than biological parents. Daly and Wilson are quick to point out that many stepparents are excellent parents and that most do not abuse their children. However, they suggest that an evolutionary perspective on this phenomenon provides important insights into the traumatic problem of child abuse and may suggest some targets of programs aimed at preventing such abuse.

In other research, Daly and colleague Catherine Salmon of Simon Fraser University suggest that evolutionary theory predicts that parents should invest more in first-born children and last-born children, and invest the least in middle-born children. First-born children were expected to be favoured partly because they have a higher "reproductive value," which means, all things being equal, favouring older children would have resulted in more descendants for human ancestors. Last-born children are expected to be favoured, to some degree, as well, but for different evolutionary reasons. On average, parents of last-borns are older than parents of first- or middle-borns. Older parents are generally expected to invest more in children, since there is no point in "holding back" resources for future children (unlike the case for parents of first- and middle-borns). But middle-born children have neither the reproductive value advantage of first-borns nor the older parent advantage of younger children. Salmon and Daly found these predictions indirectly confirmed in a sample of Canadian undergraduate students (Salmon & Daly, 1998). When asked what person in the world they felt closest to, 64% of first-borns named a parent, compared to 39% of last-borns and only 10% of middle-borns. Similarly, when asked who they would go to for emotional support after a trauma, 42% of first-borns named a parent, as did 44% of last-borns, compared to only 21% of middle-borns. Instead, middle-borns were five times as likely as first-borns or last-borns to say they would go to a sibling for emotional support, rather than to their parents.

Although these patterns do not directly indicate that parents invested in the ways predicted by Salmon and Daly, they can be interpreted as quite possibly resulting from the predicted patterns of differential parental investment.

An evolutionary view of family relationships does not deny that culture and environment play an important role in influencing parental and other family behaviours (Surbey, 1998). However, it does suggest that people have evolved psychological dispositions that provide a foundation for parenting and other family behaviours and that cultural and other environmental forces interact with these basic evolved dispositions to produce the range of behaviours that we see in contemporary families (Janicki & Krebs, 1998).

It should be noted that infant survival was definitely a prime factor in shaping the evolved psychological adaptations that underlie cultural variations in parenting behaviour (Crawford, 1998b; Daly & Wilson, 1987). Many recent researchers who have examined these issues suggest that variability between cultures in behavioural patterns such as child care are best thought of as deriving from complex interactions between such evolved psychological adaptations and influences from environmental and cultural sources (Barkow et al., 1992; Janicki & Krebs, 1998). This "co-evolutionary" perspective emphasizes the usefulness of considering both biological adaptations and cultural/environmental pressures in understanding differences between cultures in important behaviours such as child-rearing patterns.

Friendships There's no question that early attachments are important. But the relationships formed after infancy, especially during later childhood and adolescence, also significantly affect our social behaviour. Under the right circumstances, there are good reasons to believe that individuals can counteract negative experiences that occur during infancy or childhood (Lamb et al., 1992). The significance of friendship is a case in point. Psychologists now recognize that a child's social network—the number and quality of his or her friends—has a tremendous impact on social development and well-being (Berndt, 1988; Harris, 1998; Hartup & Stevens, 1997).

Children with friends interact more confidently in social situations, they are more cooperative, and they report higher levels of self-esteem (Newcombe & Bagwell, 1995). Children with friends, compared to those without friends, are also less likely to seek help for psychological problems, and they're more likely to be seen as well adjusted by teachers and adult caretakers. Such trends are true for young children and adolescents and continue on into adulthood (Berndt & Keefe, 1995). When you read Chapter 16, which deals with stress and health, you'll find that social support—particularly our network of friends—predicts how well we're able to cope and deal with stressful situations and how well we're able to recover from injury or disease. This is just as true for children as it is for adults (Hartup & Stevens, 1997).

Obviously, general conclusions like these need to be qualified a bit. For example, the quality (or closeness) of the friendship matters, as does the identity of the friends. If you have very close friends who recommend drug use or a life of crime, then the developmental consequences will be less than ideal. It's also unclear at this point what aspects of friendship matter most. For instance, people often share similarities with their friends (such as common attitudes and values). Does this mean that friends merely play the role of reinforcing our values and making us more secure in our attitudes? In-depth research on friendships is ongoing, in part, because psychologists recognize the value of friendship across the life span. When asked to rank what is most important in their lives, children, adolescents, and adults often pick "friends" as the answer (Klinger, 1977).

At adolescence, peer culture becomes increasingly important, and a conflict between family-oriented behaviours and peer-oriented behaviours has often been perceived. Developmental researcher Sherry Beaumont, of the University of Northern British Columbia, examined this issue by focusing on differences between the conversational styles that Canadian adolescent girls adopted with their mothers as compared with their friends. Beaumont found that, with their friends, adolescent girls used a fast-paced conversational style that included many interruptions and considerable mutual talking at the same time, and this pattern increased from preadolescence to mid-adolescence. In contrast, mothers tended to speak more slowly than their daughters, and this resulted in the mothers being interrupted much more by their daughters than the reverse (Beaumont, 1995, 1996). Adolescents also rated their conversations with

The quality of a child's social network—the number and quality of friends—can have a tremendous influence on his or her social development and well-being.

friends as friendlier and more involved than conversations with their mothers. Beaumont suggests that differences in conversational styles may be one of the reasons that adolescents rate their parents as less understanding, less interesting, and more controlling than their friends (Beaumont & Cheyne, 1998).

Unfortunately, there is also a dark side to children's peer relationships, namely, bullying. Developmental psychologists Debra Pepler, of York University and The LaMarsh Centre for Research on Violence and Conflict Resolution, and Wendy Craig, of Queen's University, and their colleagues have extensively studied the development and remediation of bullying in children and adolescents (e.g., Craig et al., 2000; Pepler et al., 1999). Their research has led to "systemic recommendations for anti-bullying interventions," some of which are the following (Connolly et al., 2000):

1. Change must occur in the entire system, that is, with the bully, victim, peers, school staff, parents, and community.

2. Parents of both bullies and victims must intervene.

3. Both bullies and victims must receive counselling.

4. Implementing an anti-bullying program is a complex and prolonged process but can be successful.

Pepler and Craig's research on bullying is a good reminder of the fact that research in developmental psychology is not just of theoretical interest, but can often be applied to important real-world problems.

Forming a Personal Identity: Erikson's Crises of Development

One of the most important parts of social development is the formation of **personal identity**—a sense of self, of who you are as an individual and how well you measure up against peers. We recognize ourselves—that is, that we represent a unique person different from others—quite early in our development. Children as young as 6 months of age will reach out and touch an image of themselves in a mirror; by a year and a half, if they look into a mirror and notice a smudge mark on their nose, they'll reach up and touch their own face (Butterworth, 1992; Lewis & Brooks-Gunn, 1979).

As noted earlier in the chapter, many psychologists are convinced that people use social interactions—primarily the ones with parents during childhood and with peers later in life—to help them come to grips with who they are as individuals. One of the most influential theories of how this process of identity formation proceeds is the stage theory of Erik Erikson. Erikson (1963, 1968, 1982) believed that personal identity is shaped by a series of psychosocial crises that each person must confront at a characteristic stage in development (see the Concept Summary table on the following page).

Infancy and Childhood As you know, for the first few years of life babies are largely at the mercy of others for their survival. According to Erikson, this overwhelming dependency leads infants to their first true psychosocial crisis, usually in the first year of life: *trust versus mistrust*. Psychologically and practically, babies face an important problem: Are there people out there in the world who will meet my survival needs? Resolution of this crisis leads to the formation of an initial sense of either trust or mistrust, and the infant begins to develop some basic knowledge about how people differ. Some people can be trusted and some cannot. It is through social interactions, learning who to trust and who not to trust, that the newborn ultimately resolves the crisis and learns how to deal more effectively with his or her environment.

As the child progresses through toddlerhood and on into childhood, other fundamental conflicts appear and need to be resolved. During the "terrible 2s," the child struggles with breaking his or her dependence on parents. The crisis at this point, according to Erikson, is *autonomy versus shame or doubt:* Am I capable of independent

personal identity
A sense of who one is as an individual and how well one stacks up against peers. Erik Erikson's theory postulates that personal identity is shaped by a series of personal crises that each person confronts at characteristic stages of development.

Part of the process of developing socially and personally is the development of personal identity. This child may be experiencing self-awareness as she examines her reflection in the mirror.

Concept Summary

ERIKSON'S STAGES OF PERSONAL IDENTITY DEVELOPMENT

Life Period	Stage	Conflicts Revolve Around ...
Infancy and childhood	Trust vs. mistrust (first year of life)	Developing a sense of trust in others. Are there others present who will fulfill my needs?
	Autonomy vs. shame or doubt ("terrible 2s")	Developing a sense of self-control. Can I control my own actions?
	Initiative vs. guilt (ages 3 to 6)	Developing a sense of one's own drive and initiative. Can I carry out plans? Should I feel guilty for trying to carry out my own plans?
Adolescence and young adulthood	Industry vs. inferiority (ages 6 to 12)	Developing a sense of personal ability and competence. Can I learn and develop new skills?
	Identity vs. role confusion (adolescence)	Developing a single, unified concept of self, a sense of personal identity. Who am I?
	Intimacy vs. isolation (young adulthood)	Questioning the meaning of our relationships with others. Can I form a committed relationship with another person, or will my personal insecurities lead to isolation?
Adulthood and older adulthood	Generativity vs. stagnation	Concern over whether one has contributed to the success of children and future generations. Older adulthood: Have I contributed to the community at large?
	Integrity vs. despair	Acceptance of one's life—successes and failures. Am I content, looking back on my life?

self-control of my actions, or am I generally inadequate? Between the ages of 3 and 6, the crisis becomes one of *initiative versus guilt:* Can I plan things on my own, with my own initiative, or should I feel guilty for trying to carry out my own bold plans for action? In late childhood, beginning around age 6 and ending around age 12, the struggle is for a basic sense of *industry versus inferiority:* Can I learn and master new skills? Can I be industrious and complete required tasks? Or do I lack fundamental competence?

Again, what's important in determining how these crises will be resolved is the quality of the child's interactions with parents, peers, and other significant role models. If 5-year-old Danielle's parents repeatedly scold her for taking the initiative to get her own drink of milk, she may develop strong feelings of guilt for trying to become independent. According to Erikson, children with highly critical parents or teachers can acquire a self-defeating attitude toward themselves that carries over later in life. Children who resolve these crises positively learn to trust themselves and their abilities and acquire a strong positive sense of personal identity.

Adolescence and Young Adulthood By the time we reach adolescence, our intellectual development has proceeded to the point where we naturally begin to consider personal qualities that are both general and abstract. In particular, Erikson argued, adolescents have to deal with the fundamental crisis of *identity versus role confusion.* They become concerned with testing roles and finding their true identity: Who am I? What kind of person do I really represent? In a very real sense, the teenager acts as a kind of personality theorist, attempting to integrate various self-perceptions about abilities and limitations into a single unified concept of self. Erikson (1968) coined the term *identity crisis* to describe this transition period, which he believed is often filled with turmoil.

Observational studies of how adolescents actually come to grips with the identity crisis reveal many individual differences (Offer & Schonert-Reichl, 1992; Peterson, 1988). Not all teenagers become paralyzed with identity "angst" and anxiety—most, in fact, show no more anxiety during this transition period than at other points in their lives. Simon Fraser University psychologist James Marcia found that individual differences also occur in how young people commit to a particular view of themselves (e.g., Marcia, 1966). Some adolescents choose an identity by modelling others: "I'm honest,

Erik Erikson would probably argue that this young man is concerned with testing roles and finding his true identity.

414

open, and cooperative because that's the way I was brought up by my parents." Others develop a personal identity through a soul-searching evaluation of their feelings and abilities. Some adolescents even reject the crisis altogether, choosing instead not to commit to any particular view of themselves. The specific course or path an individual takes depends on many factors, including his or her level of cognitive development, the quality of the parent–child relationship, and outside experiences (Compas et al., 1995). The ethnic and sociocultural groups that the adolescent is part of and identifies with can also play an important role in identity formation (e.g., Leadbeater & Way, 1996).

Entrance into young adulthood is marked by the crisis of *intimacy versus isolation*. Resolution of the identity crisis causes us to question the meaning of our relationships with others: Am I willing or able to form an intimate, committed relationship with another person? Or will my insecurities and fears about losing independence lead to a lifetime of isolation and loneliness? People who lack an integrated conception of themselves, Erikson argued, cannot commit themselves to a shared identity with someone else. Some have argued that this particular conclusion may be more applicable to men than women (Gilligan, 1982). Historically, women have been forced by societal pressures to deal with intimate commitments—raising a family and running a home—either at the same time as, or before, the process of searching for a stable personal identity. This trend may well be changing, however, because more women are establishing professional careers prior to marriage.

Adulthood, Middle Age, and Beyond With the establishment of career and family arrives the crisis of *generativity versus stagnation*. The focus at this point shifts from resolving intimacy to concern about children and future generations: Am I contributing successfully to the community at large? Am I doing enough to ensure the survival and productivity of future generations? Failure to resolve this crisis can lead to a sense of meaninglessness in middle life and beyond—a condition Erikson calls *stagnation*.

For some people, especially men in their 40s, this point in psychosocial development is marked by soul-searching questions about personal identity reminiscent of those faced in adolescence (Gould, 1978; Levinson et al., 1978). According to psychologists such as Gould and Levinson, the so-called "midlife crisis" arises as people begin to confront their own mortality—the inevitability of death—and as they come to grips with the fact that they may never achieve their lifelong dreams and goals. There is no doubt that this can be an emotionally turbulent period, but recent evidence suggests that the midlife crisis is a relatively rare phenomenon. It gets a lot of attention in the media, and it's certainly consuming for those affected, but probably fewer than 5% of people in middle age undergo anything resembling a turbulent midlife crisis (McCrae & Costa, 1990).

The final stage in the process of psychosocial development, which occurs from late adulthood to the point of death, is the crisis of *integrity versus despair*. It is at this stage in people's lives, Erikson argued, that they strive to accept themselves and their pasts—both failures and successes. Older people undergo a kind of life review in an effort to resolve conflicts in the past and to find meaning in what they've accomplished. If successful in this objective search for meaning, they acquire wisdom; if unsuccessful, they wallow in despair and bitterness (Reker, 1995, 1997). An important part of the process is the preparation for death and dying, which we'll discuss in more detail near the end of the chapter.

Evaluating Erikson's Theory Erikson's stage theory of psychosocial crises has been enormously influential in shaping how psychologists view personal identity development (Steinberg & Morris, 2001). Among its most important contributions is the recognition that personal development is a lifelong process. Individuals don't simply establish a rigid personal identity around the time they reach Piaget's formal operational stage; the way that people view themselves and their relationships changes continually throughout their lives. Erikson's theory is also noteworthy for its emphasis on the role of social and cultural interactions in shaping human psychology (Douvan, 1997).

Erik Erikson

Critical Thinking

How well do Erikson's ideas describe your own personal identity development? Are you going through any fundamental crisis at the moment, or are you aware of having solved one in the past?

Nevertheless, Erikson's theory suffers from the same problems as any stage theory. Although people may confront psychosocial crises in an orderly sequence, overlap occurs across the stages (Whitbourne et al., 1992). As noted earlier, the search for identity is not confined to one turbulent period in adolescence—it is likely to continue throughout a lifetime. Furthermore, like Piaget, Erikson never clearly articulated how a person actually moves from one crisis stage to the next: What are the psychological mechanisms that allow for conflict resolution, and what determines when and how they will operate (Achenbach, 1992)? Finally, Erikson's theory of identity development, although useful as a general organizing framework, lacks sufficient scientific rigour. His concepts are vague enough to make scientific testing difficult.

Additional Issues in Adolescent Development

Developmental researchers have examined many aspects of psychological development during adolescence besides moral development and the development of personal identity. Adolescence has often been considered a period of life when people take greater risks than at other stages of development. To examine the development of risk-taking behaviour in adolescents and young adults, Nancy Galambos and Lauree Tilton-Weaver studied the following four risk-taking behaviours among a sample of almost 2000 young Canadians aged 15 to 24: smoking, binge drinking, sex with multiple partners, and sex without a condom (Galambos & Tilton-Weaver, 1998). Binge drinking was the most common of these risk behaviours among the 15- to 19-year-olds, with 52% of males and 35% of females reporting consuming five or more alcoholic beverages on a single occasion in the previous year. Approximately 5% of both males and females in the sample reported engaging in all four risk behaviours, although far more reported engaging in none of the four risk behaviours: 39% of the females and 32% of the males. The researchers found that multiple-risk behaviour was higher among young people who were not students, as well as among those who did not live with their parents, and those who felt distressed. Adolescents who regularly attended religious services, however, did not engage in risk-taking behaviours as much as other teens.

Adolescents display gender differences in many other behaviours besides risk taking. For example, female teenagers tend to show far more "internalizing" of psychological problems than males, problems such as depression, anxiety, suicidal feelings, and eating disorders. Males, on the other hand, have more "externalizing" problems: oppositional behaviour, delinquency, and school problems (e.g., Leadbeater et al., 1995). Developmental psychologist Bonnie Leadbeater and her colleagues suggest that one factor leading to more internalizing problems in girls is a greater sense of interpersonal vulnerability in teenage girls—a tendency to see themselves as helpless, together with a fear of being abandoned. Leadbeater suggests that even normal pressures during adolescence moving girls toward greater autonomy could result in "interpersonally vulnerable" girls becoming depressed or anxious. Leadbeater also suggests that teenage boys at risk for externalizing problems seem to suffer more from the effects of self-criticism than girls. Such boys tend to view themselves and others negatively, and this leads to difficulties in interpersonal relationships that may be steppingstones to acting out and delinquency. Leadbeater suggests that one avenue for preventing such externalizing problems may be programs that promote interpersonal involvement during adolescence and that give all teenagers opportunities for leadership, valued community service, and caring for others (Leadbeater et al., 1999).

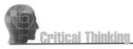

Critical Thinking

Do you think that we as a society should work hard to eliminate specific gender roles? Do you believe that men and women can ever be taught to think and act similarly?

Gender-Role Development

By the time children are in elementary school, gender is seen as a permanent condition—"I'm a boy (or a girl) and always will be." At this point, children tend to act in accordance with reasonably well-established **gender roles**—specific patterns of behaviour consistent with how society dictates males and females should act. Children at this age have strong opinions about how boys and girls should behave, what occupations

gender roles

Specific patterns of behaviour that are consistent with how society dictates males and females should act.

they should have when they grow up, and how they should look. Can you imagine the reaction that a 7-year-old boy might receive if he walked into his second-grade class wearing a dress or with his fingernails polished a bright shade of pink? Indeed, there is much evidence that boys are punished more than girls for deviating from their standard sex role. It is more acceptable to be a "tom-boy" than a "sissy" (Ruble & Martin, 1998).

Nature or Nurture? How do these firm ideas about gender roles develop? Are they the inevitable byproduct of biological differences between male and female brains, or do they grow out of experience? We encountered this issue in Chapter 3, where we considered the evidence supporting gender-based differences in brain anatomy and functioning. Behavioural sex differences such as activity level can be detected even in the womb (Campbell & Eaton, 1999). Hormones released by the endocrine system early in development likely account for some gender differences in behaviour and thought (Kimura, 1999), and it is likely that natural selection has shaped males and females to have evolved psychological adaptations that differ in some respects (Buss, 1999; Miller, 1998). However, many psychologists have focused on environmental factors in gender-role development because they are more subject to modification.

The development of **gender schemas** may play an important role in maintaining gender roles in children and adults (Bem, 1981). A gender schema is an organized set of beliefs and perceptions held about men and women. Once established, these schemas guide and direct how individuals view others, as well as their own behaviour. For example, men's gender schemas might direct them to judge their own behaviour, as well as the behaviour of other men, in terms of "strength," "aggression," and "masculinity." We encountered the concept of schemas earlier in the chapter when we talked about Piaget, and we'll have more to say in later chapters about schemas and the role they play in directing behaviour. For the moment, you can think of schemas as knowledge organizers that people carry around inside their heads. Gender schemas are acquired through learning, they set guidelines for people's behaviour, and they underlie the expectations that people hold about the appropriateness of actions. As you can probably guess, gender schemas are mostly adaptive—they help us interpret the behaviour of others—but they can lead to inaccurate perceptions of specific individuals and even to discrimination.

Growing Old in Society

With the passage of time, and the inevitable physical declines that accompany the aging process, come constant new challenges for the developing individual. Of course, not all the changes that greet us in our older years are negative—far from it. In fact, some kinds of intelligence seem to increase with age (see Chapter 9), marital satisfaction often grows (Carstensen, 1995), and many elderly people remain actively involved in the community and report high levels of contentment. One recent survey found that people in their 70s, on average, report more confidence in their ability to perform tasks than do people in their 50s (Wallhagen et al., 1997).

At the same time, there are definite hurdles in the pathways of the elderly, many related to health care. The elderly need more physical care, require more doctor visits, and can be at an economic disadvantage due to retirement; they also have an elevated rate of depression (Reker, 1997). Although most elderly adults do not live in nursing homes, many are in need of continuing care. Whatever form this care takes, it is likely to be expensive. The scope of the problem should not be underestimated, especially as the "greying of Canada" continues. Over the next 50 years, there is expected to be a large increase (perhaps as much as sixfold) in the number of people over age 85.

Death and Dying

There are many psychological aspects to death, and to the dying process, including how people come to grips with their own mortality and how they grieve and accept the loss

Many negative stereotypes about the elderly are untrue. The majority of elderly people are not sick or disabled; they lead active lives.

of others. One of the most influential approaches to the dying process is the stage theory of Elisabeth Kübler-Ross (1969, 1974).

Kübler-Ross proposed that people progress through five distinct psychological stages as they face death. She based her theory on a set of extensive interviews conducted with hundreds of terminally ill patients. Her fundamental insight was that people appear to react to their own impending death in a characteristic sequence: (1) *denial*—"There must be some terrible mistake"; (2) *anger*—"Why is this happening to me?"; (3) *bargaining*—"What can we do to stop this terrible thing?"; (4) *depression*—"Blot out the sun because all is lost"; and (5) *acceptance*—"I am ready to die." As a stage theorist, Kübler-Ross essentially implied that people move through each of these five stages, from denial to acceptance, as a normal part of their emotional acceptance of death.

Kübler-Ross's views on the dying process have been highly influential, both in psychological and medical circles, primarily because she was one of the first people to treat the topic of dying thoroughly and systematically. She sensitized legions of physicians to the idea that denial, anger, and depression are normal reactions to dying and that they should be treated with respect rather than dismissed. However, most psychologists today are not convinced that people progress through a fixed set of orderly stages in the way Kübler-Ross described. There are simply too many individual differences to support the theory. Not all dying people move through distinct emotional stages, and, even if they do, the stages do not seem to follow any particular set order. Stages might be skipped, might be experienced out of order, or might alternate, with the person being angry one day and accepting the next. In sum, there is no firm evidence to support a stage approach to the process of dying.

Many psychologists find it more appropriate to talk about *dying trajectories*. A dying trajectory is simply the psychological path people travel as they face their impending death. Different people show different trajectories, and the shape of the path depends on the particular illness as well as on the personality of the patient (Bortz, 1990; Glaser & Strauss, 1968). Trajectories are preferred to stages because stages imply that all people react to impending death in fixed and characteristic ways. But there is no right or wrong way to deal with dying—some people may react with anger and denial, others with calm acceptance. The best that witnesses to the dying process can do is offer support and allow the individual to follow his or her own unique path.

End-of-Life Decisions One current topic of particular interest to psychologists is the decision-making processes that surround the end of life. Should people have the right to control how and when they die, especially if they're faced with a poor quality of life (e.g., constant pain, immobility, or dependency)? Is suicide, assisted suicide, or "pulling the plug" justified under any circumstance (Brigham & Pfeifer, 1996)? In some sense, these are legal and ethical questions rather than psychological ones, but questions about controlling the end of life occupy the attention of many people, especially the elderly.

There has been very little research conducted on the psychological factors that influence end-of-life decisions. It seems likely that religious convictions, value systems, life satisfaction, and even fear of death play a role in how people feel about the various end-of-life options. A recent study by Cicirelli (1997) confirms these expectations. Older adults, ranging in age from 60 to 100, were asked their views of various end-of-life options. Each person was given sample decision situations such as the following:

> Mrs. Lee is an elderly widow who has terminal bone cancer. She has had chemotherapy to try to cure the cancer but it has not helped her, and the side effects from the chemotherapy itself have been difficult to deal with. She is slowly getting worse, and the pain is unbearable. Drugs for pain help some, but leave her in a stupor.

The participants were then asked to make judgments about various end-of-life options, such as the following: strive to maintain life, refuse medical treatment or request that it

The shape and form of the final dying trajectory depends on the particular illness, the conditions of care, and the personality of the individual.

be removed, commit suicide, or allow someone else to the make the decision about terminating life. Cicirelli (1997) found that people were often willing to endorse more than one option, but the majority opinion was to strive to continue life (51% of the participants endorsed this view). Psychosocial factors, such as religious convictions and fear of death, played a significant role in the decision-making process. For example, there was a significant minority who favoured the ending of life under these circumstances, but these individuals tended, on average, to be less religious, to value the quality of life more, and to have a greater fear of death.

Test Yourself 10.3

Test your knowledge about social and personal development by answering the following questions. (You will find the answers in Appendix B.)

1. The strange situation test is often used to study attachment. Identify the type of attachment that best characterizes the following reactions: avoidant, resistant, secure.
   a. When Mom leaves the room, the child begins to cry but calms down rapidly when she returns. _____
   b. When Mom leaves the room, the child couldn't care less. There is little reaction or interest when she returns. _____
   c. When Mom leaves the room, the child cries but shows little or no affection on her return. _____
   d. When Mom is in the room, the child refuses to leave her side and does not react well to the sudden appearance of strangers.
   _____

2. According to Erik Erikson, adolescents face a psychosocial crisis called *identity versus role confusion.* Current research suggests that:
   a. This is a time of rebellion for all adolescents.
   b. Erikson made a mistake—no such crisis occurs.
   c. The identity crisis has mostly a genetic basis.
   d. Not all teenagers suffer anxiety during this period.

3. Gender identity doesn't develop until a child enters elementary school—it's only at that point that gender-role curricula begin to exert an effect. *True or False?*
4. Which of the following statements about the elderly and growing old in society are true and which are false?
    a. Most elderly people are sick and disabled. *True or False?*
    b. Stereotypes about the elderly are always harmful. *True or False?*
    c. Most elderly people have little, if any, confidence in their abilities. *True or False?*
    d. The elderly, on average, would rather die than suffer the consequences of a painful and terminal disease. *True or False?*

Solving the Adaptive Problems

As people grow from infancy through childhood and on to adulthood, they experience fundamental changes in physical, intellectual, and social functioning. For the most part, these developmental changes can be viewed as adaptive reactions to environmental change as individuals grow and learn from experience. As with other species, the changes in developing humans seem to show regularities that can be seen as stages of development. At the same time, the exact psychological effects of the stages can vary dramatically according to the environment in which they occur.

First, how do we go from fertilized eggs to fully functioning adults, capable of producing our own offspring? Individuals begin life as a fertilized egg, or zygote, which contains genetic material packed into chromosomes received from the mother and father. Prenatal development—which is divided into the germinal, embryonic, and fetal stages—takes place between conception and birth. The body develops rapidly during this time and is especially susceptible to both positive and negative influences from the environment. Infancy and childhood are marked by rapid growth in height and weight and by a further maturing of the nervous system. One of the

byproducts of nerve cell maturation is motor development. The major milestones in motor development— crawling, standing alone, walking— occur at similar times for most individuals, in part because of the systematic manner in which the nervous system develops.

As people move through adolescence and into early adulthood, their physical systems continue to change. Puberty is the developmental period in which individuals mature sexually, and it's marked by dramatic changes in physical appearance driven primarily by the release of gender-specific hormones. Once people reach their 20s, their bodies become physically mature, and most begin a gradual across-the-board decline in physical ability. Some declines occur in mental ability over time, especially in old age, although significant losses in mental functioning or mental health are still the exception rather than the rule. There is evidence to suggest that losses in the number of brain neurons may be counteracted by increases in the complexity of the remaining nerve cells. In general, there are individual differences in how the aging process proceeds; both the positive and negative consequences of aging are affected by one's genetic blueprint as well as by lifestyle choices (for instance, how much one exercises).

Second, how do we develop the intellectual tools needed to solve survival problems? Psychologists use the term *cognitive development* to refer to the changes in intellectual functioning that accompany physical maturation. Several innovative techniques have been used to map out the internal perceptual world of infants. Newborns have remarkably well-developed tools for investigating the world around them: They can see, hear, smell, feel, and taste, although not at the same level as they will later in childhood. Individuals leave infancy with well-developed perceptual systems and use the experiences of childhood to help fine-tune and use their sensory equipment.

Much of what we know about how thought processes develop during infancy and childhood comes from the work of Jean Piaget. Piaget's theory of cognitive development proposes that children use mental models of the world—called schemas—to guide and interpret ongoing experience. Central to the theory is the idea that as children grow physically and acquire new experiences, their mental models of the world change systematically. Piaget argued that children pass through a series of cognitive stages (sensorimotor, preoperational, concrete operational, and formal operational) characterized by unique ways of thinking. Piaget's theory has been criticized for a number of reasons, but the idea that children do not function as "little adults" continues to be widely accepted among developmental psychologists. Piaget's theory is complemented by Lawrence Kohlberg's theory of moral development. Like Piaget, Kohlberg proposed a stage theory, suggesting that individuals pass through qualitatively different levels of moral development, which differ in the extent to which moral actions are seen as driven by immediate external consequences or by general abstract principles.

Third, how do we form the social relationships and sense of personal identity needed for personal protection, nourishment, and continuation of the species? Humans use relationships with others to help them solve the problems that arise throughout development. Infants, burdened with limited motor skills and immature perceptual systems, form attachments with others to gain the sustenance they need for survival. Both the infant and the caregiver are active participants in the attachment process and are prepared to respond, given the right kinds of environmental events, with mutual bonding. Ainsworth identified three main categories of attachment—secure, resistant, and avoidant—that may have long-term consequences. In general, the responsiveness of the parent early in life is a significant but not inevitable influence on the relationships formed later in life.

Another aspect of social development is the formation of personal identity—a sense of who one is as an individual. Erik Erikson argued that personal identity is shaped by a series of "psychosocial" crises that individuals confront over the life span. During infancy and childhood, individuals address questions about their basic abilities and independence and learn to trust or mistrust others. During adolescence and adulthood, individuals deal with the identity crisis and come to grips with their roles as participants in intimate relationships. In the later years, individuals struggle with questions of accomplishment, concern for future generations, and meaning. Other important aspects of social development include the learning of gender roles—how each person learns to think and act as a member of a gender group—and the critical influences of the family structure. The chapter ended with a discussion of the social and psychological factors that confront the elderly and some of the important stages and decisions that accompany death and dying.

Chapter Summary

DEVELOPING PHYSICALLY

The environment helps shape the physical process of growth and can determine its ultimate outcome, but most physical changes are surprisingly consistent and predictable.

The Stages of Prenatal Development

Learning Goal: Understand the physical changes that occur during prenatal development. The fertilized egg is referred to as the *zygote.* Prenatal development is divided into three main stages. The *germinal period* is the period from conception to implantation. The *embryonic period* occurs over the next six weeks. The *fetal period* goes from the ninth week to birth, and includes the development of skeletal and muscular systems.

Growth during Infancy, Childhood, and Adolescence

Learning Goal: Learn about growth from infancy through adolescence. The average newborn weighs about 3 kg and is approximately 51 cm in length. Over the next two years, there is tremendous physical development and increasing complexity of brain networks. The newborn's brain shows *plasticity;* changes are constantly occurring in neural circuitry. Generally, the nervous system develops from the head down and from the centre out. The sequence of development, from lifting the head to walking alone, is stable and predictable. Both nature and nurture contribute to individual differences. After toddlerhood, general processing speed and coordination improve rapidly. *Adolescence* is an important physical and psychological transition period that features the *growth spurt* and the onset of *puberty.*

Reaching Adulthood

Learning Goal: Be able to explain adulthood and the aging body and brain. By their 20s, people are physically mature and at the height of their physical prowess. A small decline begins to occur in the 20s. Some individuals suffer brain degeneration with age, but fewer than 1% of people at age 65 are afflicted with *dementia*, or physically based loss in mental functioning.

DEVELOPING INTELLECTUALLY

The developmental changes that occur in how people think (cognitive development) are of major importance to psychologists. There are good reasons to believe that infants see and think about the world differently from adults.

The Tools of Investigation

Learning Goal: Understand the tools used to study infant perception and memory. In the *preference technique*, an infant is presented with two visual displays simultaneously, and the researcher notes how long the infant looks at each. Researchers also use *habituation*, the decline in responsiveness to repeated stimulation, by *rewarding* simple motor movements to investigate infants' preferences and abilities.

The Growing Perceptual World

Learning Goal: Be able to explain the perceptual capabilities of an infant. Babies greet the world with sensory systems that function reasonably well. They show preferences for some colours and shapes; they recognize their mothers' voices within a day or two after birth; they are sensitive to smell, taste, and touch; and they seem to perceive a three-dimensional world.

Do We Lose Memory with Age?

Learning Goal: Comprehend the characteristics of memory loss in the elderly. Many memory functions decline but some do not. Least affected are those involving recognition rather than recall and nonconscious rather than conscious testing. Aged individuals who maintain an active intellectual life are less subject to decline.

Piaget and the Development of Thought

Learning Goal: Understand and evaluate Piaget's theory of cognitive development. Piaget believed that everyone is born with a natural tendency to organize the world meaningfully and do so through the use of *schemas.* Cognitive development is guided by *assimilation* (one fits new experiences into existing schemas) and *accommodation* (one modifies existing schemas to accommodate new experiences). Piaget proposed four stages of cognitive development: *sensorimotor, preoperational, operational,* and *formal operational.*

Moral Development: Learning Right from Wrong

Learning Goal: Understand and evaluate Kolberg's theory of moral development. Kohlberg proposed three major levels of development. At the *preconventional level,* decisions about right and wrong are based primarily on external consequences. At the *conventional level,* people start to justify their actions on the basis of internalized rules and whether an action maintains or disrupts the social order. *Postconventional* morality is based on abstract principles that may even conflict with accepted standards. Kohlberg's critics argue that his views lack generality.

DEVELOPING SOCIALLY AND PERSONALLY

Social relationships help people adapt successfully to their environments.

Temperament

Learning Goal: Be able to explain the notion of temperament. In-born behavioural tendencies are called *temperament.* Although originally thought of as categories (e.g., easy or difficult), they are now considered dimensions, including activity level and degree of inhibition.

Forming Bonds with Others

Learning Goal: Understand the short-term characteristics and long-term consequences of early attachments. Newborns form *attachments,* strong emotional ties to one or more intimate companions. Some believe that both caregiver and infant are preprogrammed from the baby's birth to respond to environmental signals with attachment behaviour.

Forming a Personal Identity: Erikson's Crises of Development

Learning Goal: Comprehend Erik Erikson's stage theory of personal identity development. Erikson believed that *personal identity* is shaped by a series of psychosocial crises. During infancy and childhood, the crises experienced include *trust versus mistrust, autonomy versus shame or doubt, initiative versus guilt,* and *industry versus inferiority.* During adolescence and young adulthood, we experience *identity versus role confusion.* Entrance into young adulthood features the crisis of *intimacy versus isolation.* As career and family are established, the conflict is *generativity versus stagnation,* and in later adulthood we face the conflict of *integrity versus despair.*

Gender-Role Development

Learning Goal: Understand gender-role development and the role of the family in adult development. The foundations of gender identity are in place by age 2 or 3, and by the time children are in grade school, they tend to act in accordance with *gender roles. Gender schemas* guide and direct our perceptions and behaviours.

Growing Old in Society

Learning Goal: Recognize the social and psychological factors the elderly face. The elderly face challenges presented by physical decline and society. Some of the more common myths claim that the elderly are sick, in mental decline, or depressed.

Death and Dying

Learning Goal: Appreciate the psychological issues connected with death and dying. Kübler-Ross proposed that people progress through five stages as they face death: denial, anger, bargaining, depression, and acceptance. Many psychologists find it more appropriate to speak in terms of *dying trajectories,* the paths people travel as they face their impending death.

Terms to Remember

development, 378
Developing Physically
zygote, 379
germinal period, 380
embryonic period, 380
fetal period, 380
teratogens, 381
puberty, 384
menopause, 385
dementia, 386
Developing Intellectually
habituation, 388
longitudinal design, 391
cross-sectional design, 391
schemas, 393
assimilation, 394
accommodation, 394
sensorimotor period, 394
object permanence, 394
preoperational period, 395
conservation, 395
egocentrism, 396
concrete operational period, 396
formal operational period, 397
morality, 400
preconventional level, 401
conventional level, 402
postconventional level, 402
Developing Socially and Personally
temperament, 405
attachments, 405
strange situation test, 408
personal identity, 413
gender roles, 416
gender schemas, 417

Recommended Readings

Pinker, S. (2002). *The blank slate.* New York: Viking. Originally from McGill University, MIT psychologist Steven Pinker writes in a persuasive style in decrying the tendency of social scientists to assume that most human behaviour is learned.

Gopnick, A., Meltzoff, A. N., & Kuhl, P. K. (1999). *The scientist in the crib: Minds, brains and how children learn.* New York: William Morrow. A cognitive science perspective on how babies recognize people, interpret the world around them, and develop language and theories about the world, and how these activities help build their brains.

Slater, A., & Muir, D. (Eds.). (1999). *The Blackwell reader in developmental psychology.* Malden, MA: Blackwell. Includes classic readings in child psychology and human development from the likes of Charles Darwin, Jean Piaget, and B. F. Skinner as well as contemporary readings from researchers at Queen's University, the University of British Columbia, McGill University, the University of Toronto, York University, and other centres of developmental research.

Kagan, J. (1998). *Three seductive ideas.* Cambridge, MA: Harvard University Press. Noted developmental psychologist and infancy researcher Jerome Kagan explores whether the first two years of life really determine later development and whether people really have stable traits like fearfulness and intelligence.

Daly, M., & Wilson, M. (1999). *The truth about Cinderella: A Darwinian view of parental love.* New Haven, CT: Yale University Press. McMaster University psychologists Martin Daly and Margo Wilson apply the perspective of evolutionary psychology to human parenting behaviours and illuminate aspects of child abuse and mistreatment.

Hultsch, D. F., Hertzog, C., Dixon, R. A., & Small, B. J. (1998). *Memory change in the aged.* New York: Cambridge University Press. By University of Victoria life span development researchers, reports on data from the Victoria Longitudinal Project, a major Canadian longitudinal study of memory and personality changes in older people.

Austad, S. (1997). *Why we age: What science is discovering about the body's journey through life.* New York: Wiley. An excellent summary of the biological factors involved in the aging process; it's informative and enjoyable reading.

For additional readings, explore InfoTrac® College Edition, your online library. Go to:

www.adaptivemind2e.nelson.com

Hint: enter the search terms: motor development; cognitive development; moral development; psychosocial development; death and dying.

What's on the Web?

Please note that Web addresses are subject to change. Check out the accompanying Web site for updates: www.adaptivemind2e.nelson.com. This site presents practice quiz questions, hypercontent, information on degrees and careers in psychology, study tips, and more.

Canadian Psychological Association Section on Developmental Psychology

www.cpa.ca/developm.html

Provides information on membership, their newsletter, and contacts for Canada's national association of researchers in developmental psychology.

Descriptions of the Developmental/Life Span Programs at Several Canadian Centres of Developmental Research

University of Waterloo

www.arts.uwaterloo.ca/psychology/gradprog/gradhandbook.html#div-developmental

University of Toronto

www.psych.utoronto.ca/grad/develop.htm

University of Victoria

web.uvic.ca/psyc/lifespan

University of British Columbia

www.psych.ubc.ca/graduate/g_devel.pdf

University of Toronto Institute for Human Development, Life Course and Aging

www.utoronto.ca/lifecourse

One of Canada's centres for research in adulthood and aging, this site includes extensive links to Canadian and international sources on aging and human development.

University of Victoria Centre on Aging: Links Page

www.coag.uvic.ca/

This site includes links to many aging-related sites, including research centres such as the University of Manitoba Centre on Aging, the Gerontology Research Centre at Simon Fraser University, the Nova Scotia Centre on Aging, and the McGill University Centre for Studies in Aging.

Child Development Institute

www.cdipage.com

This award-winning site provides information to parents on topics such as care of young infants, improving learning skills, and learning disabilities.

Idealist.com Child Development

www.idealist.com/ then go to psychology link; then child psychology link

This Idealist.com site is "... a meeting place for parents, students of development and early childhood education, and professionals who work with children." It provides a wealth of information related to child development, as well as tutorials

on various theories of development such as Erikson's and
Freud's.

Adolescence: Change and Continuity

www.personal.psu.edu/faculty/n/x/nxd10/adolesce.htm

This site can help you gain some insight into the turbulent
years of adolescence. You can choose to explore basic domains,
such as social transitions that occur in adolescence; you can
explore the important contexts of adolescence, such as schools,
family, and peer groups; and you can explore how certain
issues, such as achievement, sexuality, and delinquency,
interact with this developmental stage.

The emotion creates the idea, which is then more direct and more powerful.

Alfred North Whitehead

Chapter 11 Motivation and Emotion

You sense only rapid movement at first. A glint to your right and the feel of cool metal on your cheek. You exhale, gasping, as a bony arm wraps itself around your neck. "Welcome to your nightmare, my friend," a voice growls. "Your wallet, your watch, or your life." Inside, your sympathetic nervous system jumps into action—releasing epinephrine, targeting the critical organs of the body and the neural communication chains. Your mind, flooded with the arousal, struggles to decide on the best response. But you're in a psychological meltdown—you see only jumbled images of the sidewalk and needle tracks dotting the arm grasping your neck. There is no focused clarity; no clear course of action appears to guide your response. In your mind there is only surprise, confusion, and the smothering grip of fear.

Not a very pleasant scenario. Two people, reacting to circumstance, each in a highly activated state. For psychologists, however, this story raises a variety of questions around the tight interplay of two broad constructs, namely, emotion and motivation. What factors underlie the initiation and direction of behaviour? What causes the criminal to control the victim: Is it the reinforcing value of money? Is it the loss of control driven by the internal need for a "fix"? And what about the emotions that accompany the act—fear, excitement, despair? In what way does an emotion like fear, with its often-paralyzing consequences, enhance the functioning of the adaptive mind? Could it be that emotions themselves motivate and direct behaviour? These are some of the topics we'll consider in this chapter.

Motivation can be defined as the set of factors that *initiate* and *direct* behaviour, usually toward some goal. If you're motivated, your behaviour becomes activated and goal directed. Hunger is a classic example of an internal condition or "state" that stimulates an organism to pursue food. The desire for a fix motivates the drug user to search for the drug of relief. As you saw in Chapter 6, people are also likely to become motivated if they've recently been rewarded for behaving in a particular way—they're likely to act in a similar way again to get the reward. **Emotions** are complex psychological events that are often associated with the initiation and direction of behaviour. They typically involve (1) a *physiological* reaction, usually arousal; (2) some kind of *expressive* reaction, such as a distinctive facial expression; and (3) some kind of *subjective experience*, such as the conscious feeling of being happy or sad.

Most psychologists are convinced that the concepts of motivation and emotion must be closely linked. Both terms, in fact, derive from the Latin *movere*, meaning "to move." Many conditions that are motivating also give rise to the experience of emotion. Consider the case in which your thirst motivates you to put money into a drink machine. You feel excited about the imminent quenching of your desperate thirst. If the money gets stuck, stalling the pursuit of your goal, frustration and anger are likely. Moreover, once aroused, the emotional experience affects your ability to direct your behaviour successfully. If you continue to scream and kick the machine, it's unlikely that your goal—quenching your thirst—will be satisfied anytime soon. For reasons like these, it's difficult to discuss the topic of motivation without also considering emotion.

motivation
The set of factors that initiate and direct behaviour, usually toward some goal.

emotions
Psychological events involving (1) a physiological reaction, usually arousal; (2) some kind of expressive reaction, such as a distinctive facial expression; and (3) some kind of subjective experience, such as the conscious feeling of being happy or sad.

Previewing the Adaptive Problems

To study motivation, we need to ask questions about the fundamental causes of behaviour (Mook, 1995). Obviously, then, the topic is relevant to much of psychology. Each of the preceding chapters connects in one way or another to the question of why behaviour occurs, but we'll focus our discussion in this chapter on a set of specific adaptive problems that relate to motivation.

First, what activates goal-directed behaviour? Any organism seeking to survive in a changing environment must react quickly to its needs. It must anticipate future outcomes and act accordingly, *now,* with vigour and persistence. Much of the time our actions are controlled by *internal* factors that push us in the direction of a goal. For example, if your body is deprived of food or water, a delicate internal balance is disrupted inside your body. A specific need is signalled, which you seek to satisfy in order to restore the internal balance. At other times we're motivated by *external* events, things in our environment that exert powerful pulling effects. The sight of an attractive person or a slice of chocolate cake can be sufficient to initiate and direct your behaviour.

Second, what factors create hunger and control eating? Obviously, we all need to eat—it's a requirement of living. Consequently, there must be mechanisms in the body and mind that make us hungry and interested in eating at regular intervals. To understand how our bodies maintain the proper levels of internal energy, we'll consider the relevant *internal* and *external* cues that activate and control eating. For example, we'll discuss how the body monitors internal physiological states, using brain mechanisms to check up on levels of energy reserves (e.g., the amount of sugar in the blood). We'll also discuss how external cues in the environment compel us to eat and how these cues can influence the food selection process. Whether you like broccoli, reject mushrooms, or happily consume squid depends on a variety of factors, including what you've learned about these foods.

Third, what factors promote sexual behaviour? Although you may know someone who is "consumed" by sex, sexual activity is not necessary for individual survival. In principle, people can live perfectly productive lives without ever once engaging in sexual behaviour or exploring their sexuality. But sexual behaviour is needed for survival of the *species.* It's reasonable to assume, then, that there are internal cues, based in our genetic code and found in active biological systems, that help motivate an interest in sex. We'll discuss some of the biological and psychological mechanisms that motivate sexual behaviour as well as some of the physiological characteristics of the human sexual response.

Fourth, how are emotions expressed and experienced, and what functions do they serve? All psychologists agree that emotions have considerable adaptive significance. Consider an emotion like *anger.* Anger typically arises in response to an environmental event, usually the perceived misdeed of another, and the body enters a highly aroused state. The arousal activates behaviour and leads to reactions that may substantially increase (or decrease) the likelihood of survival. Once the emotion gains hold, overt physical expressions arise, particularly in the form of easy-to-identify facial expressions. From an adaptive perspective, the sight or sound of an angry person carries important signalling properties—others know to shy away and avoid interaction. As you'll see, emotions are easy to identify but difficult to define.

ACTIVATING BEHAVIOUR

Learning Goals

1. Comprehend the role of instincts and drive in activating behaviour.
2. Be able to explain incentive motivation and discuss how it activates behaviour.
3. Understand achievement motivation.
4. Understand intrinsic motivation.
5. Learn about Maslow's hierarchy of needs, and discuss how each need influences behaviour.

LET'S TURN OUR ATTENTION to the first problem: What are the factors that activate and control goal-directed behaviour? At first, psychologists considered the possibility that there might be a single source of motivation, grounded either in the internal workings of the body or in the external environment. It's possible, for example, that people are born with biological machinery that compels them to act in certain ways irrespective of what they learn from experience. But this idea is largely rejected by current psychologists, who believe instead that no single explanation of goal-directed behaviour, based on either biological or environmental factors, is likely to be found. The reason is simple: Virtually all forms of behaviour are determined by multiple

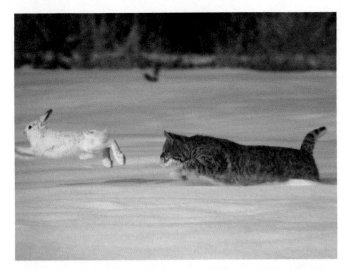

The factors that are initiating and directing this bobcat's behaviour include both internal factors, such as depleted energy resources, and external factors, such as the sight of an attractive meal. As you'll see, internal and external factors often interact to produce motivated behaviour.

The behaviour of many animals is motivated, at least in part, by instincts—unlearned, characteristic patterns of responding that are controlled by specific triggering stimuli in the environment.

causes. Factors both inside and outside the body—internal and external factors—contribute to motivation. In the following sections, we'll consider some examples of these influences.

Internal Factors: Instincts and Drive

Birds don't need to be taught to build nests in the springtime or to fly south in the winter; cats don't need to be taught to show interest in small, rapidly moving creatures. These are unlearned, characteristic patterns of responding—called **instincts**—that are controlled by specific triggering stimuli in the world. Instincts share properties with *reflexes*, which we discussed in Chapter 3, but instincts typically involve more complex patterns of behaviour than those covered by the simple reflexes.

instincts

Unlearned characteristic patterns of responding that are controlled by specific triggering stimuli in the world; they are not thought to be an important factor in explaining goal-directed behaviour in humans.

Human Instincts   It is widely accepted that instincts play a role in nonhuman species. But do instincts play any role in controlling human behaviour? A number of early psychologists followed the lead of Charles Darwin in suggesting that instincts are a central factor in human motivation. Humans don't need to be taught to take care of their young, William James (1890) argued, or to cry as infants, to clean themselves when dirty, or even to play, love, imitate, or be curious. These are ingrained biological "musts" that are as natural to the human as nest building is to the bird.

However, just because a behaviour occurs on a regular basis doesn't guarantee that it's instinctive—that is, unlearned and inflexible in its display. There is no way to open up the body and directly measure an instinct, so it's easy to fall into a trap of circular reasoning: People demonstrate some regular behaviour, such as showing sympathy for a child in need, and the temptation is to propose a corresponding sympathy instinct (Holt, 1931). Over the years, psychologists argued about which behaviours qualify as instinctive. For example, William James (1890) suggested some 20 physical and 17 mental instincts in his writings. William McDougall (1908), on the other hand, was convinced of only 12 (he later changed his mind and upped the number to 17). For these and other reasons, instincts eventually fell out of favour as a widely applied explanation for goal-directed human behaviour. There was simply no agreement about how to confirm or categorize human behaviours as instinctive.

Although psychologists avoid the term, the notion of instinct has been reintroduced by evolutionary psychologists. They argue that our species is born not only with neural "hardware," but also mental "software" that directs and controls at least part of our behaviour. For example, it's possible that we're born with natural reactions to certain types of facial features, or to be on the lookout for people who cheat or engage in deception (Cartwright, 2000; Tooby & Cosmides, 1995). But these "innate" tendencies are not as fixed as traditional instincts, nor are they necessarily automatically triggered by particular stimuli in the environment. Inborn mental software establishes a goal, and may bias us toward a particular kind of strategy, but it allows for multiple ways to achieve that goal.

Drive To replace instinct, psychologists turned to the concept of *drive*. A **primary drive** is a psychological state that arises in response to an internal physiological *need*, such as hunger or thirst. It's clear that the human body is designed to seek fairly stable and constant internal conditions. For example, it's important for the body to maintain an adequate internal supply of fluids or a constant internal temperature. Psychologists use the term **homeostasis** to refer to the process through which the body maintains its steady state, much like the thermostat in a house maintains a constant internal temperature by turning the heat on or off (Cannon, 1929). Once a specific need is detected, drive serves a general activating function: Drive energizes the organism, causing it to seek immediate reduction of the need (Hogan, 1997). So if your water supply is used up, you are driven to drink and restore the appropriate balance. Similar processes are assumed to operate for other biological drives such as hunger and for the maintenance of internal body temperature (see Figure 11.1).

Additional drives are learned by association with primary drives. These **secondary drives** (e.g., money) can eventually act like primary drives. A loss of money, for example, motivates action to relieve the need.

Drive is a considerably more flexible concept than instinct. An organism seeks to reduce drive—to restore homeostatic balance—but it doesn't really matter how balance is restored. People can use what they've learned from experience to help them satisfy the need; they're not stuck with one fixed pattern of behaviour that is triggered only by a restricted set of stimuli. You can think about drive as somewhat analogous to the engine of a car. A properly running engine is necessary for the car to move, as drive is necessary to initiate goal-directed behaviour, but it's not sufficient to get across town. Other factors, such as knowledge about the layout of the town, must be used in conjunction with the operating engine in order to move about. As you'll see shortly, it's also the case that the vigour or intensity with which someone acts depends critically on the value, or incentive, of the goal. You are much more likely to be motivated to eat if

primary drive
A psychological state that arises in response to an internal physiological need, such as hunger or thirst.

homeostasis
The process through which the body maintains a steady state, such as a constant internal temperature or an adequate amount of fluids.

secondary drive
A drive learned by association with a primary drive (e.g., the need for money).

FIGURE 11.1

Homeostasis

It's adaptive for the body to maintain stable and constant internal conditions. If your internal temperature rises above or falls below an optimal level, you are driven to perform actions that will restore the "steady state."

you like the food, even though a wide variety of food options may satisfy the internal need. You sometimes even eat in the absence of an internal need, as in the case in which you have that second brownie just because it looks good.

Ultimate and Proximate Factors in Motivation Evolutionary psychology requires a distinction between *ultimate* and *proximate* levels of explanation. Why do we feel like eating a banana at one time and not at another? An explanation that focuses on changes in our internal body physiology, such as blood glucose level (see the "Internal Factors Controlling Hunger" section later in the chapter), can be referred to as a **proximate** explanation of our eating motivation; that is, an explanation that involves causal factors in the immediate internal or external environment of the person. However, another question we can ask about our motivation for eating bananas is: Why do we eat them in the first place? Why, when we are hungry, are we motivated to eat bananas and not dirt? Answering this question requires attention to the **ultimate factors** that led to the type of motivational systems humans have today. At some point in our evolution, liking the taste of bananas paid off with enhanced likelihood of survival; liking the taste of dirt has never paid off.

Although most psychological explanations of human motivation focus on proximate factors influencing our eating, sexual, and aggressive motivations, human motivational systems are most fully understood when we also consider the ultimate evolutionary factors that led to the construction of our present-day motivational systems (Daly & Wilson, 1995).

proximate factors
Causes of behaviour that derive from the immediate internal or external environment of an organism.

ultimate factors
Causes of behaviour that refer to the evolutionarily adaptive significance and reproductive consequences for the organism.

External Factors: Incentive Motivation

By itself, the concept of drive is insufficient to explain motivated behaviour. Goal-directed behaviour requires connecting the drive reduction with what people learn from experience. External cues tell us when and where to exert our efforts. Generally, whether you will be motivated to perform an action depends on the total value—positive or negative—of the incentive. For this reason psychologists often use the term **incentive motivation** to explain specific goal-directed behaviour. For example, Whitney is motivated to jog for an extra 5 minutes so that she can eat that extra brownie; conversely, Charlie is motivated to avoid the kitchen because of the extra calories (and guilt) that he knows the brownie consumption will produce. Note that the emphasis here is quite different from drive: Drive is an internal push that compels a person to action; incentives are external pulls that tempt or deter people with the prospects of rewards or punishments.

Of course, internal factors interact with external factors in a number of ways. Whether a person is thirsty, for example, clearly affects the incentive value of water; water tastes better and is more rewarding when you've been deprived of it for a while (Blundell & Rogers, 1991; Bolles, 1972). Motivating students with an end-of-chapter test, a good incentive for them to study, has more of an effect when a student is a high procrastinator, that is, someone who finds it difficult to motivate him- or herself to study (Tuckman, 1998). Internal states of deprivation can also act as cues for responding. A person might learn to perform a certain type of action when he or she is thirsty or hungry (Hull, 1943); alternatively, a person might learn that hunger or thirst means that food or water will be especially rewarding (Davidson, 1993, 1998). It's important to remember that motivated behaviour is virtually always jointly determined by internal and external factors. Neither factor alone is sufficient to explain the complexities of human motivation.

incentive motivation
External factors in the environment—such as money, an attractive person, or tasty food—that exert pulling effects on people's actions.

Achievement Motivation

One example of motivated behaviour that clearly depends on both internal and external factors is striving for achievement (Elliot & Thrash, 2001). A number of psychologists have argued that each of us, to varying degrees, has an internally driven need

Concept Summary

GENERAL APPROACHES TO MOTIVATION

Approach	Source of Motivation	Summary and Evaluation
Instinct	Internal	Unlearned, inflexible patterns of responding that are controlled by specific triggering mechanisms in the world. The traditional notion has been rejected as too fixed, but evolutionary psychology has reintroduced a more complex and compelling version.
Drive	Internal	A psychological state that arises in response to a physiological need, such as hunger or thirst. *Homeostasis* is the process through which the body maintains a steady state. A more flexible concept than instinct, but it does not explain behaviour in the absence of need.
Incentive motivation	External	Helps to explain goal-directed behaviour. People are driven by external rewards that exert powerful pulling and guiding effects on their actions.

for achievement (Atkinson, 1957; McClelland et al., 1953; Murray, 1938). The **achievement motive** pushes you to seek challenging tasks and significant accomplishment in your life. People high in achievement motivation tend to work harder and more persistently on tasks, and they tend to achieve more than those who rate low in achievement motivation (Atkinson & Raynor, 1974; Cooper, 1983).

How can the achievement motive be measured? Questionnaire tests simply ask people various questions about their achievement tendencies. But the evidence suggests that measurement is more valid if conducted with projective tests. They examine people's fantasies, wishes, and dreams. This topic is covered in detail in Chapter 12.

Achievement motivation on any particular task depends on (1) your expectations about whether your efforts will be successful and (2) how much you value succeeding at the task (Atkinson, 1957; Molden & Dweck, 2000). This dual requirement means that even people with a high internal need for achievement may not persist at a task either because they do not value success on the task or because they lack confidence in their ability to succeed. For example, young children who experience failure on mathematics problems early in life can develop a negative attitude that prevents them from persisting and succeeding on valued mathematical tasks later in life (Smiley & Dweck, 1994; Wigfield, 1994). Conversely, you may place high value on becoming a professional basketball star but have low expectations because of your height. In both the math and basketball cases, the individual's achievement motivation will be low with respect to that specific task.

achievement motive
A need for achievement that varies in strength across individuals. Its strength on any given task depends on (1) one's expectations about success and (2) how much value one places on succeeding at the task.

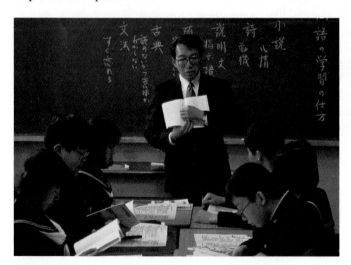

Every society in the world sets standards for achievement—what skills are important and unimportant—and these standards influence what members of the society seek to achieve.

Children who experience failure on mathematical problems early in life can develop a negative attitude that prevents them from persisting and succeeding in mathematics later in life.

433

Parents and teachers play an important part in determining achievement motivation. If a child's parents value a task, it's likely that the child will value it as well and will appear more motivated to succeed (Eccles et al., 1983). What children are told about their performance on a task is also important. For example, if children are praised for their effort, they tend to work harder, report more enjoyment, and show more interest. On the other hand, if they're told that performance is tied to ability, such as natural intelligence, children show less achievement motivation, especially if they fail or perform poorly on the task (Mueller & Dweck, 1998; Ziegert et al., 2001).

Cultural Factors   Every society in the world establishes standards for achievement—what skills and tasks are deemed important and unimportant—and these standards influence what the members of the society seek to achieve and perhaps the level of productivity of the society as a whole (McClelland, 1961). For example, whether a society values individual success or places more of an emphasis on the collective success of the society seems to affect individual levels of achievement motivation (Sagie et al., 1996).

Intrinsic Motivation

Sometimes we choose to engage in actions for which there is no obvious internal or external motivational source. A child spends hours carefully colouring a picture or playing with a doll; you might become transfixed by a crossword puzzle or by a long walk on the beach. Certainly there is no biological *need* that drives colouring or walking. There's also no clear-cut external incentive: Nobody pays the child for colouring or you for finishing the crossword puzzle. Psychologists use the term **intrinsic motivation** to describe situations where behaviour appears to be entirely self-motivated (Sansone & Harackiewicz, 2000). We engage in the action for its own sake, not because someone offers us a reward or because the action restores some internal homeostatic balance.

intrinsic motivation
Goal-directed behaviour that seems to be entirely self-motivated.

What convinced many researchers that intrinsic motivation deserves special status was a counterintuitive finding: It's possible to lower someone's interest in performing a task by giving him or her an external reward. In a classic study by Lepper and colleagues (1973), preschool children who were naturally interested in drawing were asked to draw either for its own sake or to win a "Good Player" certificate. Psychologically, we would expect the external reward to encourage drawing behaviour even more than normal—after all, drawing is now associated with a concrete positive consequence. Instead, the children in the reward condition showed *less* interest in drawing a week later. The reward apparently undermined the children's motivation, making it less rewarding or interesting than it otherwise would have been.

This study has been repeated with other rewards and with activities other than drawing (see Deci & Ryan, 1985). The story is much the same: Externally supplied rewards can lower a person's desire to perform a task. Once someone receives a reward for performing a task, he or she seems less likely to enjoy that task for its own sake in the future. Think about professional athletes. Many sports fans complain that the external reward of money has ruined professional sports. Even baseball players sometimes complain that the game was more fun when they were amateurs—before millions of dollars complicated the motivational chain.

Control and Overjustification   How can a reward lead to a negative effect? One possibility is that people see external rewards as an indirect way of controlling behaviour. Drawing loses its value because it's now something you do to please the person giving you the reward—you're no longer drawing simply

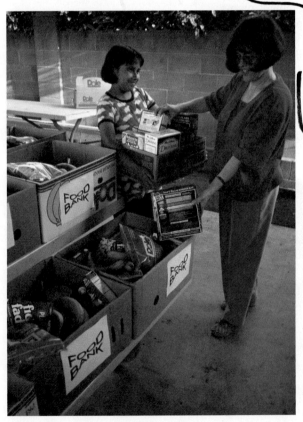

Do you think these two volunteers at a local food bank would feel better about their work if they were also paid for their activities?

because it pleases *you* (Rummel & Feinberg, 1988). Thus, the so-called "reward" is not really a reward at all. When coupled with the loss of control, the consequence loses its reinforcing value and becomes negative.

Another possibility is that external rewards lead to what has been called *overjustification:* When a second motivation is added, it eats away at your intrinsic motivation. Eventually, you conclude that it's the external reward that motivates you to perform the task (Bem, 1972; Deci & Ryan, 1985). Rewarding someone for performing a task in a sense degrades the value of that task (e.g., the baseball player begins to believe that it's the money that makes him play, rather than love of the game). Some researchers have even suggested that things like creativity should never be rewarded, lest the positive internal value of engaging in a creative act be destroyed (Amabile, 1983; Schwartz, 1990).

But not all psychologists are comfortable with these conclusions (Covington & Mueller, 2001; Pittenger, 1996). External reward can enhance creativity under some circumstances, and the negative effects of reward on task motivation may occur only in restricted circumstances (see Dickinson, 1989; Eisenberger, 1992). For example, in the Lepper study, children did indeed choose to draw less frequently when they were rewarded for drawing, but this effect occurred only when the children expected the reward. When children were given an unexpected reward for drawing, they later spent more time drawing than a group who had received no reward. Therefore, the negative effect of reward on intrinsic motivation may be related to the expectation or *promise* of reward rather than to the reward itself (Cameron & Pierce, 1994). In sum, the way we think about rewards strongly influences the way they motivate us.

Maslow's Hierarchy of Needs

Most general theories of motivation rest on a foundation of biological need. The body seeks to maintain a delicate internal balance (homeostasis), and if that balance is disrupted, we're motivated to restore it. But as you've just seen, not all needs are biological in origin—such as the need for achievement (Murray, 1938). For this reason, some psychologists have tried to classify needs and to determine whether some are more important than others.

Among the more influential of these classification systems is the **need hierarchy** introduced by the humanistic theorist Abraham Maslow (see Chapter 12). The essential component of Maslow's theory is the *prioritizing* of needs. Some needs, he argued, have special priority and must be satisfied before others can be addressed. Obviously, if people don't eat or drink water on a regular basis, they'll die. Maslow's theory is usually represented in the form of a pyramid, to emphasize the fact that human motivation rests on a foundation of biological and security "musts" (see Figure 11.2). It is only after satisfying the survival needs—such as hunger and thirst—that we can consider personal security and more social or spiritual needs, such as the need for love or self-esteem. At the top of the structure sits the need for self-actualization, which Maslow believed represented people's desire to reach their full potential as human beings.

The pyramid is an appropriate symbol for Maslow's system because it captures the upward thrust of human motivation. As a humanistic psychologist, Maslow believed that all people have a compelling need to grow, to better themselves as functioning individuals. In his own words: "A musician must make music, an artist must paint, a poet must write if he is ultimately to be at peace with himself" (Maslow, 1954). Maslow was strongly influenced by people who he felt had reached their fullest potential, such as Albert Einstein and Mother Teresa. He used their personality characteristics as a way of defining what it means to sit at the top of the pyramid—to be self-actualized. Some of these characteristics included tolerance, openness to experience, and a high degree of ethical sensitivity (Leclerc et al., 1998; Mook, 1995). (We'll return to humanistic views on personality in Chapter 12.)

It is easy to dispute the specific order of needs that Maslow proposed. There are many daily examples where people sacrifice a lower need to gain a higher one. For

need hierarchy
The idea popularized by Maslow that human needs are prioritized in a hierarchy. Some needs, especially physiological ones, must be satisfied before others, such as the need for achievement or self-actualization, can be pursued.

FIGURE 11.2
A Hierarchy of Needs
Maslow organized his need hierarchy in a pyramid to highlight the fact that the higher needs are built on a foundation of lower, more basic needs.

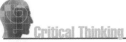

Critical Thinking

Can you think of other examples where Maslow's ordering of needs doesn't hold up?

example, we hear of people going on a hunger strike to gain higher esteem from others. We also hear of people risking their lives for love needs.

Nonetheless, we must acknowledge Maslow's point that how we act is often influenced by unfilled needs. If you have to worry about putting food on the table and consequently steal from others on a regular basis, you might appear to lack moral or ethical values. But this isn't necessarily a permanent fixture of your personality—under different circumstances, with a full stomach, you might be a leader in the promotion of ethical values.

Test Yourself 11.1

Check your knowledge about activating behaviour by answering the following questions. (You will find the answers in Appendix B.)

1. Which of the following statements best captures the difference between an instinct and a drive?
   a. A drive is a reflex; an instinct is not.
   b. Instincts are learned; drives are not.
   c. Instincts lead to fixed response patterns; drives do not.
   d. Instincts restore appropriate internal balance; drives do not.
2. Which type of motivation best describes each of the following behaviours: achievement, incentive, or intrinsic?
   a. Whitney never misses her daily jogging session—she loves the brownie she gives herself at the end: _____
   b. Janice spends hours practising the piano—she just seems to love playing: _____
   c. Candice studies at least six hours a day—she is obsessed with the idea of finishing first in her class: _____
   d. Jerome rarely paints for fun anymore, not since he started teaching art classes at the local college: _____
3. According to Maslow's hierarchy of needs, we can reach our true potential as human beings only after:
   a. restoring a proper level of homeostatic balance.
   b. satisfying basic survival and social needs.
   c. satisfying our need for achievement.
   d. eliminating the need for rewards.

MEETING BIOLOGICAL NEEDS: HUNGER AND EATING

Learning Goals
1. Understand the internal factors that influence when and why we eat.
2. Understand the external factors that influence when and why we eat.
3. Be able to explain how body weight is regulated, including the concept of a set point.
4. Learn about the eating disorders anorexia nervosa and bulimia nervosa.

WE NOW TURN OUR ATTENTION to an important motivational problem that must be dealt with every day: initiating and controlling eating behaviour. Eating is a constant in everybody's life, but we eat for reasons that are more complex than you might think. If asked why we eat, children will explain that we eat "because we're hungry" or "because my tummy hurts." An adult's response will appear more sophisticated, but it usually amounts to much the same thing: "We eat because our bodies need food, internal energy." This is true; eating is a biologically driven behaviour. But eating is a psychologically driven behaviour as well. We sometimes feel hungry when there is no physical need and, as any dieter knows, a strong will can stop consumption even when the physical need is present.

Internal Factors Controlling Hunger

Researchers have spent decades trying to understand the internal mechanisms that influence when and why we eat. We now know, for example, that the body monitors itself, particularly its internal supply of resources, in a number of ways. For example, there is a connection between the volume and content of food in the stomach and the amount that neurons will fire in certain areas of the brain (Sharma et al., 1961). Psychologically, people report little, if any, hunger or interest in food when their stomach is full, and hunger increases in a relatively direct way as the stomach empties (Sepple & Read, 1989).

Chemical Signals It's not only the contents of the stomach that are monitored. The body has several important suppliers of internal energy that it checks regularly. One critical substance is **glucose,** a kind of sugar that cells require for energy production. Receptors in the liver are thought to react to changes in the amount of glucose in the blood or perhaps to how this sugar is being used by the cells, and appropriate signals are communicated upward to the brain (Mayer, 1953; Russek, 1971). When the amount of usable glucose falls below an optimal level, which occurs when you haven't eaten for a while, you start to feel hungry and seek out food (Campfield et al., 1996). If blood glucose levels are high, which occurs after a meal, you lose interest in food. This link between blood sugar levels and hunger is not simply correlational: In the laboratory it is possible to increase or decrease how much an animal will eat by artificially manipulating the amount of glucose in its blood (Smith & Campfield, 1993).

Another key element the body monitors is **insulin,** a hormone released by the pancreas. The body needs insulin to help pump the nutrients present in the blood into the cells, where they can be stored as fat or metabolized into needed energy. At the start of a meal, the brain sends signals to the pancreas to begin the production and release of insulin in preparation for the rise in blood sugar produced by the food. As insulin does its job, the levels of blood sugar go down and you eventually feel hungry once again. It's probably a glucose–insulin interaction that is actually monitored internally because both substances play pivotal roles in the metabolic, or energy-producing, process. If laboratory animals are given continuous injections of insulin, they tend to balloon in weight and grossly overeat—the insulin keeps the blood sugar level low, which tells the animal to start looking for something to eat.

Both glucose and insulin are believed to play key roles in motivating eating behaviour, but it's unlikely that any one single chemical (or even two) completely controls whether you will feel hungry. Other internal stimuli, such as the overall level of body fat (Keesey & Powley, 1975), also play important roles. Of course, ultimately the experience of hunger originates in the brain. It is the activation of brain structures that initiates and directs the search for food. You learned in Chapter 3 that structures in the limbic system are involved in controlling a number of motivational and emotional behaviours. As you'll see momentarily, structures associated with the *hypothalamus* have long been thought to be of central importance in eating.

Brain Regions A number of years ago it was discovered that if a particular portion of the **ventromedial hypothalamus** is lesioned in laboratory animals, a curious transformation occurs. Lesioned animals appear to be hungry all the time and show a striking tendency to overeat. In fact, each animal becomes an eating machine—if allowed, it balloons up to several times its normal weight (Hetherington & Ranson, 1942). If this same area is stimulated electrically, rather than destroyed, the opposite pattern emerges. Electrical stimulation causes the animal to lose all interest in food, even if

glucose
A kind of sugar that cells require for energy production.

insulin
A hormone released by the pancreas that helps pump nutrients in the blood into the cells, where they can be stored as fat or metabolized into needed energy.

ventromedial hypothalamus
A portion of the hypothalamus that, when lesioned, causes an animal to typically overeat and gain a large amount of weight. Once thought to be a kind of "stop eating," or satiety, centre in the brain, its role in eating behaviour is currently unknown.

If a particular portion of the ventromedial hypothalamus is destroyed, rats become eating machines and can balloon up to several times their normal weight.

lateral hypothalamus

A portion of the hypothalamus that, when lesioned, causes an animal to be reluctant to eat; like the ventromedial hypothalamus, it probably plays some role in eating behaviour, but the precise role is unknown.

there is a real need for nutrients in the body. These results suggested to many researchers that the ventromedial hypothalamus functions as a kind of "stop," or *satiety,* centre in the brain. Activation of the region, which presumably occurs whenever we've eaten enough to fulfill the body's energy needs, turns off hunger and eating. This process would be adaptive because it prevents us from accumulating too many nutrients in the blood—more than our bodies can handle.

If activation of the ventromedial hypothalamus stops eating, then what starts the eating process? One logical candidate was the **lateral hypothalamus** because it acts as a kind of mirror image of the ventromedial hypothalamus. In the laboratory, damage to the lateral hypothalamus creates an animal that typically starves itself, even to the point of death. Electrical stimulation of the same area causes the animal to immediately start eating. This suggested that the lateral hypothalamus may act as a kind of eating "start-up" centre to counteract the stop centre located in the ventromedial hypothalamus. This division of labour in the brain paints a cohesive picture—two regions of the hypothalamus working together to initiate and control eating behaviour.

Unfortunately, this simple story turns out to be wrong. Researchers remain convinced that both regions of the hypothalamus help to control eating, but they're uncertain about the precise roles. Part of the problem is that destruction of either area tends to affect the nervous system in a number of ways, so it's difficult to determine the exact causes of the eating changes. Lesions to the ventromedial hypothalamus, for example, may affect the secretion of insulin (Weingarten et al., 1985) or damage the effectiveness of other important pathways in the brain (Kirchgessner & Sclafani, 1988). Moreover, a closer examination of animals with lesions to the ventromedial hypothalamus revealed that they're somewhat picky and won't eat certain foods (Ferguson & Keesey, 1975). They don't just eat anything, as the start–stop hypothesis seems to predict.

Just as the brain monitors the levels of several internal chemicals to determine the need for food, several important locations in the brain besides the hypothalamus help to control eating behaviour (Woods et al., 1998). There is evidence that portions of the brainstem are critical in the initiation of eating (Grill & Kaplan, 1990), and the hippocampus may be involved as well. You may remember from Chapter 7 that we discussed an amnesic called H.M. who was doomed to live in a kind of perpetual present—he could remember nothing of what happened to him moments before. It turns out that H.M., who has damage to his temporal lobes and hippocampus, also has trouble monitoring his need for food. He is sometimes convinced that he's hungry immediately after finishing a meal. He may have simply forgotten that he's eaten; but, as Davidson (1993) points out, he clearly is also unable to use internal signals from his body as cues for hunger or satiety. These data suggest an important role for the hippocampus in feeding behaviour (see also Davidson & Jarrad, 1993).

External Factors

From an adaptive standpoint, it's obviously critical that you eat. You can't let your internal energy sources fall too low; otherwise, you won't have an adaptive mind to consider. But it would be a mistake to think about eating as simply a means of satisfying a variety of internal energy needs. We often eat for reasons that are unrelated to restoring internal homeostatic balance (Capaldi, 1996; Epel et al., 2001). Have you ever eaten to reduce stress or simply to make yourself feel good? Have you ever eaten to promote social interaction, as in going out to dinner with friends? We all have. People even eat at times to make artistic, aesthetic, or moral judgments. For example, some people are vegetarians because they believe it's wrong to eat other animals.

Eating Habits   Most people have established eating habits, which develop through personal experience and by modelling the behaviour of others. These learned habits control much of our decision making about food. For example, you're probably used to eating at certain times and in certain places. If you're offered a tasty snack, how much you eat is determined partly by the time of day—if the offer comes shortly before dinner, you take less than if the offer comes in the middle of the afternoon (Schachter & Gross, 1968). You also know from past experience how much food you can eat and still feel well. You know, for instance, that if you eat a whole pizza you will probably feel sick afterward, even though the pizza probably tasted great at the time.

Your cultural and ethnic background is another powerful influence on when and what you choose to eat (Rozin, 1990). Most people who grow up in Canada will not willingly choose to eat dogs or sheep's eyes, but these are considered delicacies in some parts of the world. Are you hesitant about eating pork or beef? You probably are if you're an Orthodox Jew or a native of India. And it's not just the appearance of food or where it comes from. People around the world often discriminate among whom it is appropriate to eat with. For example, members of some social classes would never consider eating with those that they consider to be social inferiors.

Food Cues   The decision to eat is also strongly influenced by the presence or absence of food cues. Animals know that certain kinds of food signal positive consequences, and the sight of these foods is often enough to make them start eating. Researcher Harvey Weingarten at the University of Calgary has shown that if hungry rats are taught that a flashing light signals food, later on they'll start eating in the presence of the light even if they've been fully fed moments before (Weingarten, 1983). Waiters at fine restaurants push the dessert tray under your nose after a filling meal because they know that the sight (or presentation) of the sugar-filled array will be more likely to break down your reserve than just hearing about what's for dessert. Again, your choice of the cheesecake is not driven by internal need. Your blood contains plenty of appropriate nutrients—the sight of the food, and its associations with past pleasures, acts as an external pull, motivating your choice to consume.

Critical Thinking

Can you think of any factors, besides behaviour modelling, that might help to determine eating habits? What about the availability of food? When was the last time you saw sheep's eyes on a menu?

One's cultural and ethnic background exerts a powerful effect on food selection. Would you be willing to consume the insect delicacies shown in the picture on the right? How about the more traditional desserts shown on the left?

Concept Summary

FACTORS INVOLVED IN HUNGER

Type of Factor	Factor	Its Role in Hunger
Internal	Chemical signals	Receptors in the liver respond to changes in the amount of *glucose* in the blood. The body also monitors *insulin,* a hormone released by the pancreas. The glucose–insulin interaction is monitored internally. Insulin lowers blood glucose levels, leading to hunger.
	Brain	The lateral and ventromedial regions of the hypothalamus help to control eating, but the precise role of each is unclear. Portions of the brainstem also seem important in the initiation of eating.
External	Eating habits	Learned habits develop through personal experience and modelling the behaviour of others. Cultural and ethnic background also plays a critical role in when and what you eat.
	Food cues	Factors such as the attractiveness of food and its association with past pleasures can serve as an external pull, motivating eating behaviour.

Regulating Body Weight

What determines your everyday body weight? Why are some people thin and others obese? Not surprisingly, internal and external factors combine to regulate body weight. It turns out that some factors, such as genetic predisposition, play a particularly important role; this has been demonstrated in animals. For example, Linda Wilson and her colleagues at the University of Manitoba used strains of genetically obese and genetically lean mice to try to tease apart genetic, environmental, and physiological factors involved in obesity (Currie & Wilson, 1993; Wilson et al., 1989).

In humans, we know that when identical twins—those sharing the same genetic material—are fed identical diets, they tend to gain virtually the same amount of weight. But if two unrelated people are given matched diets, the differences in weight gain can be substantial (Bouchard et al., 1990). No doubt you know people who appear to eat continuously and never gain weight; others balloon considerably after only a small daily increase in caloric intake. In short, the amount of food that you eat only partly determines what you normally weigh.

set point

A natural body weight, perhaps produced by genetic factors, that the body seeks to maintain. When body weight falls below the set point, one is motivated to eat; when weight exceeds the set point, one feels less motivated to eat.

Set Point Some earlier researchers suggested that we have a natural body weight, or **set point,** that more or less controls our tendency to gain or lose weight (Keesey & Powley, 1975). Most people show little variation in weight from year to year, presumably because their bodies manipulate the motivation to eat, as needed, to maintain the appropriate set point weight. When people go on a diet and dip below their natural weight, well over 90% of them eventually gain that weight back (Martin et al., 1991). Here again, the idea is that the body adjusts how much it eats, rebounding after a diet, to produce stability in body weight.

Assuming that people do indeed have such set points, what might determine them? Set point theorists have suggested that genetic factors might be responsible: Different people are born with different numbers of fat cells, and this number may constrain just how much weight someone can hope to gain or lose (Faust, 1984). Your metabolic rate—how quickly you burn off calories—could be another important internal factor; again, it's determined in part by your genetic makeup.

Evolutionary Theories of Hunger and Eating However, it should be noted that recently researchers, notably John Pinel and his colleagues from the University of British Columbia and Harvey Weingarten from McMaster University, have criticized set point theory on several grounds (Assanand et al., 1998; Pinel, 1997; Weingarten, 1985). Instead, they propose an evolutionary theory of hunger and eating that suggests that the "mammalian feeding system evolved to anticipate and prevent energy deficits, rather than to merely react to them" (Assanand et al., 1998, p. 1003). These researchers

440

suggest that among most people with adequate access to food, the main cause of hunger is not a decline of energy below fixed set points. According to this view, human food supplies were unpredictable in the human environments of evolutionary adaptedness that forged our eating mechanisms. We could not afford to pass by the opportunity to store significant quantities of sweet, salty, and fatty foods when they were available, so we evolved mechanisms to normatively eat more quantities of such foods if they are available than set point theory would suggest. Although this would be an adaptive mechanism in natural environments, the result in modern societies is what appears to be overeating when compared to our actual ongoing nutritional requirements.

Obesity   What causes **obesity,** the condition characterized by excessive body fat? At one time it was thought that obese people simply lacked sufficient willpower to resist overeating, especially when appealing food was in view (Schachter, 1971). At the University of Toronto, researchers Peter Herman and Janet Polivy conducted studies showing that obese people (but not nonobese people) are more likely to order a specific dish in a restaurant after being given a tasty description (Herman & Polivy, 1988). Obese people are also more likely than nonobese people to report that food still tastes good after a filling meal.

However, to explain obesity by appealing to willpower or to any one psychological factor is simplistic and misleading. The causes of obesity lie in a complex combination of biology and psychology: Metabolic rate, number of fat cells, learned eating habits, cultural role models, level of stress—all contribute in one way or another to weight control (Hill & Peters, 1998; Rodin, 1981).

obesity
A weight problem characterized by excessive body fat.

Eating Disorders

Obviously, it's important to watch your weight by monitoring the nutritional value and volume of your meals. But the pursuit of unrealistic weight goals, ones that you can

Social standards concerning weight "ideals" have changed considerably over the years.

This young woman is suffering from anorexia nervosa, a condition characterized by an intense fear of being overweight.

never hope to reach because of your genetic background, can lead to significant psychological and physical problems. Unhappiness and depression are the all-too-often byproducts of the failure to reach the proper ideal (Rodin et al., 1989).

Interestingly, people's assessments of their own weight, and its relation to these standards, are typically inaccurate. In addition, most people are simply wrong about what members of the opposite sex consider to be an ideal body weight (Fallon & Rozin, 1985). On average, women tend to think men prefer thinner women than men actually do; when men are asked about their own ideal weight, it tends to be heavier than what the average woman rates as most attractive. Not surprisingly, these mistaken beliefs help promote a negative body image. One of the consequences of a negative body image is increased susceptibility to eating disorders, such as *anorexia nervosa* and *bulimia nervosa* (Thompson & Stice, 2001).

Anorexia Nervosa In a recent survey of students in grades 8 and 10 it was discovered that over 60% of the females and 28% of the males were in the midst of dieting (Hunnicutt & Newman, 1993). The concern—some would say obsession—with weight and dieting starts early in Western cultures, and for an unfortunate few the consequences can be life threatening. In the condition called **anorexia nervosa,** an otherwise healthy person refuses to maintain a normal weight level, typically because she or he has an irrational fear of being overweight. In such cases, a person can literally be starving to death and still see an overweight person in the mirror. The condition affects mainly young women between the ages of 12 and 18 (perhaps as many as 1% of female adolescents), and it's been estimated that as many as 20% of those with the disorder will eventually die as a result, either from medical problems or from suicide (Ratnasuriya et al., 1991).

The causes of this disorder are complex and may involve genetic as well as psychological factors (Allison & Faith, 1997; Gorwood et al., 1998). Psychological factors that may contribute include a perfectionistic personality and an exaggerated adherence to some social demand: Such demands could arise from current fashion, athletic competition, or competitive dancing. There is also some evidence of abnormally low levels of certain neurotransmitters. Our lack of understanding makes the disorder very difficult to treat.

The existence of anorexia is a challenge to evolutionary psychology. Michele Surbey of Mount Allison University and Charles Crawford and Judith Anderson of Simon Fraser University have suggested that a disposition toward anorexia may have evolved because it would be adaptive for young women to be able to "automatically" avoid reproduction when they are feeling extreme stress. One of the features of anorexia in women is that menstruation ceases, thus decreasing or eliminating the ability of the woman or girl to conceive. Although the behaviour may have had adaptive roots, it is obviously unnecessary and, indeed, very harmful in modern environments where birth control is available (Anderson & Crawford, 1992; Crawford, 1989; Surbey, 1987).

Bulimia Nervosa In the eating disorder known as **bulimia nervosa,** the principal symptom is *binge eating.* A binge is an episode in which a person consumes large quantities of food, often junk food, in a limited period of time. You might find a person suffering from bulimia locked in a room, surrounded by his or her favourite snacks, eating literally thousands of calories in a single sitting. The condition is marked by a lack of control—the person feels unable to stop the eating or control the content of the food being consumed. A binging episode is often followed by *purging,* in which the person induces vomiting or uses laxatives in an effort to stop potential weight gain. Like anorexia, bulimia primarily affects women and is characterized by an obsessive desire to be thin. It, too, is probably caused by a combination of genetic and psychological factors (Sullivan et al., 1998) but the consequences are seldom life threatening.

anorexia nervosa
An eating disorder diagnosed when an otherwise healthy person refuses to maintain a normal weight level because of an intense fear of being overweight.

bulimia nervosa
An eating disorder in which the principal symptom is binge eating (consuming large quantities of food), followed by purging in which the person voluntarily vomits or uses laxatives to prevent weight gain.

Test Yourself 11.2

Check your knowledge about hunger and eating by deciding whether each of the following statements is true or false. (You will find the answers in Appendix B.)

1. A high level of glucose, or blood sugar, is associated with an increased desire for food. *True or False?*
2. The principal symptoms of anorexia nervosa are binging and purging. *True or False?*
3. The lateral hypothalamus serves as the brain's stop centre for eating. *True or False?*
4. Obesity is primarily caused by poor dietary habits. *True or False?*
5. Destruction of the ventromedial hypothalamus causes a rat to refuse food and dramatically lose weight. *True or False?*

MEETING BIOLOGICAL NEEDS: SEXUAL BEHAVIOUR

Learning Goals

1. Be able to explain the role that hormones play in human and animal sexual behaviour.
2. Understand external influences on sexual behaviour.
3. Recognize the factors that influence mate selection.
4. Learn the possible origins of sexual orientation.

DOES YOUR WORLD revolve around sex? Perhaps not, but there's no denying that sex is a powerful motivator of people around the world. Recent findings by Sandra Byers and Christine Purdon of the University of Waterloo and David Clark of the University of New Brunswick illustrate the powerfully compelling nature of sexual motivation (Byers et al., 1998). These researchers found that 84% of the Canadian university students they surveyed had experienced "intrusive sexual thoughts"—sudden and involuntary sexual images or cognitions that were not part of a consciously determined voluntary fantasy.

To regulate and control this powerful motivation, every culture has rules and guidelines related to courtship, mating, and the sexual act. Why should sex be so important to humans? What adaptive problem is solved by the pursuit and completion of the sex act? People won't die if their goal-directed sexual pursuits fail, as they would from an unsuccessful search for nutrients. But eventually, the species would disappear. Thus the ultimate value of sexual motivation is to encourage people to engage in behaviour that leads to the replication of their genes. Evolution has selected us to be reactive to sexual cues and enjoy sexual activity, because, from an evolutionary point of view, reproduction is even more important than our own survival (Dawkins, 1987).

Of course, sexual motivation has adaptive benefits apart from replicating genes. Besides the pleasurable aspects of sex, sexual desire is often a motivation for people to pursue a mate, thereby opening the door for companionship, protection, and love. We'll first look at the internal and external factors that motivate sexual behaviour, and then conclude with a look at issues involved in mate selection and sexual orientation.

Internal Factors

Hormones and Human Sexuality Humans show regular cyclic variations in the hormones relevant to sex and reproduction. These sets of hormones—*estrogens* in women

Critical Thinking

Is there a connection between the importance of sex for the replication of our genes, and the emphasis that some theorists place on sex in their theories of behaviour and mind (e.g., Freud)?

and *androgens* in men—play a critical role in physical development, affecting everything from the development of the sex organs to the wiring structure of the brain (see Chapter 3). But the initiation and control of adult sexual behaviour does not appear to be simply a matter of mixing and matching the right internal chemicals. We retain a large degree of control over our sexual behaviour, with learned social and cultural factors having an important influence. Instead of instinctive mounting and fixed courtship rituals, people in most human cultures largely choose when and where they engage in sex and the particular manner in which the sexual act is consummated.

Therefore, the role that hormones play in human behaviour is still not well understood. There is some evidence to suggest that a woman's peak of sexual desire occurs in the middle of her menstrual cycle, near the time of ovulation (Adams et al., 1978; Harvey, 1987). There is also evidence that testosterone affects both male and female sexual desire. For example, when testosterone levels are reduced sharply—as occurs, for instance, following removal of the testes (medical castration) in men—there is often a loss of interest in sex. In fact, sex offenders are sometimes treated by administering drugs that block the action of testosterone (Roesler & Witztum, 1998). But neither males nor females are rigidly controlled by these hormones. Some castrated men continue to enjoy and seek out sexual encounters, even without hormone replacement therapy. Similarly, women continue to seek out and enjoy sexual relations after menopause, when the levels of female sex hormones decline (Lamont, 1997; Pedersen, 1998).

External Factors

Rather than appealing to the flow of hormones, an alternative way to explain sexual desire is to appeal to the value, or incentive, of sex. Clearly, there's something about the internal wiring of the brain that makes the sexual stimuli immensely rewarding for most people. We are regular recipients of an ongoing array of sexual signals in our environments, and these signals often stimulate sexual desire. Most men and women are sexually aroused by explicit visual stimuli, although women, if questioned, are less likely to report the arousal (Kelley, 1985; Murnen & Stockton, 1997). If excitement is measured through physiological recording devices attached to sensitive genital regions, men and women show very similar arousal responses to erotic pictures and movies (Meston, 2000; Rubinsky et al., 1987). The argument for external factors suggests that the amount people think about and actually engage in sex is determined by the degree of external stimulation.

Animals often show rigid courtship and mating rituals that are largely under the control of internal hormones.

Touch and Smell Touch is a particularly important external source of sexual arousal. Careful stimulation of certain regions of the body (commonly known as *erogenous zones*) is highly arousing for most people and may be one of the few completely natural, or unlearned, arousal sources (although other "erotic zones" may develop or be influenced by experience). We frequently communicate through touch, and touch is an important source of information regardless of where you look in the world (McDaniel & Anderson, 1998).

In contrast, for many animals it is odour or smell that initiates sexual interest. In Chapter 4, we discussed chemicals called pheromones that are released by the females of many species during periods of receptivity. Pheromones are odour-producing chemicals, and they drive dogs, pigs, and many other creatures into a sexual frenzy. At this point, there's really no solid evidence that human pheromones affect sexual desire, although one recent study reported increased sexual activity for men wearing synthetic human pheromones (compared to a placebo control; Cutler et al., 1998). How a person smells matters—both men and women report that odour is an important factor in selecting a lover (Herz & Cahill, 1997). In all likelihood, however, it is experience rather than biological wiring that is responsible for these reports of sexual triggers.

Mate Selection

The initiation of sexual activity is guided by one very important factor—a person's selection of and acceptance by an appropriate mate. Not surprisingly, what people consider attractive is strongly influenced by sociocultural factors. In our own society, the ideal female body is much thinner than the ideal at the turn of the last century. Societies have unique cultural definitions of attractiveness, their own rules for attracting a mate, and different views on what kinds of sexual behaviour are considered appropriate. In some societies, for example, sexual activity is encouraged at very young ages—even 5- and 6-year-olds are allowed to engage in casual fondling of a willing partner's genitals. In other societies, sexual expression in childhood is strictly prohibited.

Sexual Scripts The sequence of sexual activity between partners tends to unfold according to **sexual scripts.** They are learned programs that instruct people on how, why, and what to do in their interactions with sexual partners (Gagnon & Simon, 1973). These scripts may differ from one culture to the next, and they contribute to many of the differences seen in male and female sexual behaviour. Among other things,

sexual scripts
Learned cognitive programs that instruct us on how, why, and what to do in our interactions with sexual partners; the nature of sexual scripts certainly differs across gender and may vary from one culture to the next.

Besides reproduction, finding an appropriate mate opens the door for companionship, protection, and love.

sexual scripts affect the attitudes we hold toward the sexual act. Boys typically learn, for example, to associate sexual desire with genital fondling; girls are more likely to identify sexuality with romantic love. These scripts affect expectations and sometimes are responsible for miscommunication between the sexes. For instance, over half of teenage girls who engage in premarital sex expect to marry their partners, but this expectation is true for only 18% of the male partners (Coles & Stokes, 1985). York University researcher Michaela Hynie and her colleagues have conducted research exploring how women's sexual scripts relate to their use of condoms (Hynie et al., 1998). They surveyed the sexual scripts of undergraduate students at McGill University and concluded that the women in their sample did indeed hold sexual scripts that were more "relational" in nature than those of men, and that condom use was not an integral part of women's relational sexual scripts. In other words, women generally tended to see sexuality as ideally part of a committed relationship, and condom use did not figure prominently in their scripts for such relationships.

Evolutionary Influences   Despite cultural differences in sexual scripts, there are fundamental similarities among peoples that reflect the evolutionary history of the species. For example, in nearly every culture men are more likely than women to pursue what David Buss and David Schmitt call short-term sexual strategies—brief affairs or one-night stands. In interviews with college students, Buss and Schmitt (1993) confirmed that most men had few qualms about the idea of having sexual intercourse with a woman they'd met only an hour before. For most women, however, the idea of such casual sex was a "virtual impossibility." Across all parts of the world, men seem to value attractiveness in a long-term mating partner and universally tend to prefer to mate with women who are on average younger than themselves (Buss, A. H. 1989). Women, on the other hand, tend to place much greater value on a mating partner's financial prospects than men do—a pattern that is consistent with their preference for older partners (see Figure 11.3).

The fact that these differences are present in virtually every society strongly suggests that these sex differences in mating behaviours might constitute evolutionary adaptations (see Chapter 3). The argument begins with the biological imperative: Only women bear children. Therefore the ideal strategy for ensuring the perpetuation of one's genes necessarily differs between the sexes. Men should have developed a desire for multiple sexual partners in an effort to increase the likelihood of successful reproduction. But why their preference for young and physically attractive women? During human evolutionary history, relative youth (ages 18–30) and physical attractiveness were the best cues as to whether a woman was fertile and healthy enough to bear children. Therefore, men who had these preferences were more likely to successfully reproduce (Buss, 1999).

In contrast, the responsibility of carrying and nurturing a child typically falls on the woman's shoulders. Natural selection should therefore have shaped a preference for males who would be able to contribute resources that would aid in the survival of offspring. The best cues are age, power, and evidence of commitment. From an evolutionary perspective, then, the differing sexual strategies we observe in men and women are not at all surprising (Buss & Schmitt, 1993). Throughout evolutionary history, men and women have faced different reproductive problems; their mating attitudes and behaviours undoubtedly have developed, in part, to solve these different adaptive problems (Miller, 1998, 2000).

As noted before, human sexual behaviour shows considerable flexibility—evolutionary adaptations influence but need not determine our final behaviour. Moreover, it's worth reiterating a point from Chapter 2: Behavioural tendencies that developed during our species' evolutionary history may no longer be adaptive or socially constructive.

Men
Women

FIGURE 11.3
Cross-Cultural Mating Strategies
Men and women in different parts of the world were asked to rate the importance of physical attractiveness and financial prospects in a long-term partner. On average, men rated physical attractiveness as more important than women did, whereas women were more likely than men to consider a partner's financial prospects important. (Data from Buss & Schmitt, 1993.)

Sexual Orientation

When psychologists use the term **sexual orientation,** they are referring to whether a person is sexually and emotionally attracted to members of the same sex or the other sex. The term *homosexual* is applied when the attraction is predominantly to members of the same sex; *heterosexual* refers to the more typical other-sex attraction. Estimates of the number of people in North America who fit the description of homosexual vary, ranging from 2% to perhaps as high as 10% (Rogers & Turner, 1991). Exact numbers are difficult to determine, partly because people are often reluctant to disclose personal information about sexual preference. Moreover, there are some types of sexual orientation (e.g., bisexuality, pedophilia) that do not seem to fit into fixed boundaries. Finally, people who are predominantly homosexual sometimes seek out heterosexual relationships, while many heterosexuals have had sexual experiences with members of the same sex.

But what accounts for a sexual and emotional preference for members of the same sex? The notion of actively choosing our own sexual orientation seems as absurd as choosing whether or not we like the taste of sugar. Even if we could, why would anyone choose the orientation that leads to a lifetime of being mocked, discriminated against, and sometimes beaten up and killed?

But, if the ultimate evolutionary function of sexual desire is procreation, how can homosexuality be considered adaptive? There is no simple answer to this question. For

sexual orientation

A person's sexual and emotional attraction to members of the same sex or the other sex; homosexuality, heterosexuality, and bisexuality are all sexual orientations.

Critical Thinking

If people chose their sexual orientation, how and when would that occur?

many years psychologists were convinced that homosexuality developed as the result of experience, particularly the experiences children have with their parents. Homosexuality was considered to be an abnormal condition that arose from dysfunctional home environments, usually as a consequence of having a domineering mother and a passive father. But this view is no longer widely accepted, primarily because a close examination of family histories revealed that the home environments of heterosexuals and homosexuals are actually quite similar (Bell et al., 1981).

Biological and Environmental Factors Instead, the evidence is accumulating that sexual orientation is at least partly determined by biological factors (Crooks & Baur, 2002; Gladue, 1994). When researcher Simon LeVay (1991) compared the autopsied brains of homosexual and heterosexual men, he discovered that a cluster of neurons associated with the hypothalamus was consistently larger in heterosexual men. Exactly how or why this portion of the brain influences sexual orientation is unknown. But it does fit with new evidence of a genetic basis. For example, twin studies have revealed that if one identical twin is homosexual, there is an approximately 50% chance that the other twin will be homosexual—even when reared apart. This rate is much higher than the 11% rate of homosexuality for fraternal twins or non-twin siblings of homosexuals (Bailey et al., 1993; Bailey & Pillard, 1991). In fact, a systematic analysis of the chromosomes of homosexual brothers suggests evidence for what the researchers believe might be a "gay gene" (Hamer et al., 1993).

Other researchers have provided evidence thought to be consistent with biological influences on the development of homosexuality. J. Hall of the University of Western Ontario and Doreen Kimura of Simon Fraser University have reported that fingerprint "asymmetries" are more pronounced in gay men as compared to heterosexual men (Hall & Kimura, 1994). Martin Lalumière and colleagues at the University of Toronto reviewed 20 studies that compared rates of handedness (primarily left-handedness versus right-handedness) and found that gay men and women had a 39% greater chance of being non–right-handed than heterosexuals, and they suggested that prenatal exposure to sex hormones and maternal immune system reactions may be among the factors that influence developing fetuses toward a homosexual developmental path (Lalumière et al., 2000). Ray Blanchard and his colleagues at the University of Toronto found that the more boys a mother produces, the greater the chance that the next son will be gay (Blanchard, 1997; Bogaert, 2003). The researchers suggest that this pattern may result from a maternal immune response that strengthens after each boy baby. All of these effects are consistent with the notion that homosexuality results from prenatal events that alter the fetal environment.

If there are purely environmental effects such as attachment and learning, they must operate very early in development. Kenneth Zucker and his colleagues have determined that homosexual adults displayed a heightened level of cross-gender characteristics even as young children (Bailey & Zucker, 1995; Zucker, 1987).

Research is accelerating in this field and it's simply too early to be sure what the current data truly mean. They do suggest that biological factors (largely genetic and prenatal) likely play a significant role in the determination of sexual orientation. The biological findings are largely correlational—that is, we know that sexual orientation may be associated with certain brain structures or genetic markers. But these correlational data do not guarantee that the cause of sexual orientation is biological (Bailey & Pillard, 1995). The alternative explanation is that homosexual behaviour somehow alters the biology of the individual. Moreover, it seems unlikely that biological factors alone determine sexual orientation in all cases (after all, 50% of identical twins of homosexuals are straight). The environment likely plays a role, but the nature of that role has yet to be determined.

Test Yourself 11.3

Check your knowledge about the internal and external factors that control sexual behaviour by deciding whether each of the following statements is true or false. (You will find the answers in Appendix B.)

1. It is possible to affect sexual desire in men by altering the natural levels of the hormone testosterone in the body. *True or False?*
2. Condom use plays a role in the sexual scripts of women when they are thinking about committed relationships, but not when they are thinking about more casual sexual encounters. *True or False?*
3. Across the world, men value attractiveness in a long-term mating partner and universally prefer to mate with women who are, on average, younger than themselves. *True or False?*
4. Twin studies have revealed that if one identical twin is homosexual, there is an approximately 50% chance that the other twin will share the same sexual orientation. *True or False?*

EXPRESSING AND EXPERIENCING EMOTION

Learning Goals

1. Be able to identify the basic components of an emotion and discuss their adaptive value.
2. Appreciate the evidence for and against basic emotions.
3. Learn about the role that arousal plays in the emotional experience.
4. Understand the subjective experiences of anger and happiness.
5. Recognize the differences between the James-Lange, Cannon-Bard, and Schachter theories of emotion.

AS WE DISCUSSED at the beginning of this chapter, an emotion is a complex psychological event that involves a mixture of reactions: (1) a *physiological response* (usually arousal), (2) an *expressive reaction* (distinctive facial expression, body posture, or vocalization), and (3) some kind of *subjective experience* (internal thoughts and feelings). Each of these components, which are shown in Figure 11.4, can be measured, although some, especially the subjective-cognitive reaction, are difficult to measure reliably.

What is the function of emotions in the first place? The general belief among psychologists is that emotions help us adapt to rapidly changing environmental conditions. Emotions are powerful motivators of behaviour—they help us prioritize our thoughts, and they force us to focus on finding problem solutions. Physiological arousal, for instance, prepares the body for "fight or flight" and helps us direct and sustain our reactions in the face of danger. Through expressive behaviours, such as the characteristic facial grimace of anger, it's possible to communicate our mental state instantly to others. Emotions can even regulate social behaviours. People perform better and are more likely to help others when they feel happiness (Hoffman, 1986); people are also more likely to volunteer aid after doing something for which they feel guilt (Carlsmith & Gross, 1969).

Are There Basic Emotions?

Most languages contain hundreds of words that relate in one way or another to emotions, but are there hundreds of emotions, or just a basic few? Most emotion researchers agree on about a half-dozen. These lists usually include anger, fear, happiness, and sadness, for example (Ortony & Turner, 1990). Researchers who believe that

Emotion
Body Response (Arousal)
Increased blood pressure, heart rate, muscle tension, respiration
Expressive Reaction
Facial expression, acting out
Subjective Experience
Feeling of happiness, anger, fear, etc.

FIGURE 11.4
The Components of Emotion

Emotions are complex experiences involving (1) a *physiological response*, (2) an *expressive reaction*, and (3) some kind of *subjective experience*.

such emotions are basic, or universal, argue convincingly that certain emotions, such as anger, increase the chances of survival. People also have no trouble recognizing expressions of anger, fear, sadness, and happiness in other people. For example, Paul Ekman and his colleagues asked volunteers to match photographs of grimacing, smiling, or otherwise provocative facial displays to a number of basic emotion labels. There was wide agreement on six fundamental emotions: happiness, surprise, fear, sadness, anger, and disgust combined with contempt (Ekman, 1992; Ekman & Friesen, 1986).

Research by Maxine Wintre at York University also supports the notion of a common understanding of emotions. She found that children as young as 8 already understood emotional situations in the same way as adults (Wintre et al., 1990).

Facial Expressions and Culture Regardless of where you look in the world, people recognize that facial expressions are associated with certain emotional states. For example, a furrowed brow and a square mouth with pursed lips signify anger worldwide (Boucher & Carlson, 1980; Ekman & Friesen, 1975). In one case, Ekman and Friesen (1975) even tested members of a rural, isolated culture in New Guinea. These people had no experience with Western culture, yet they correctly identified the emotions expressed in photographs of Caucasian faces. Similarly, when North American college students were later shown photos of the New Guinea people acting out various emotions, they too were able to identify the emotions with a high degree of accuracy.

Although most researchers are convinced that there is universal recognition of emotion from facial expressions (Ekman, 1994; Izard, 1994), there are some variations on this basic finding. For instance, Manas Mandal of Banara Hindu University and

Different emotions are often associated with particular facial expressions. Can you identify the emotion expressed in each of these photos?

Philip Bryden and Barbara Bulman-Fleming of the University of Waterloo collaborated on a study that compared Canadian and Indian university students in their ability to distinguish Ekman's six basic facial expressions (Mandal et al., 1996). One of their findings was that Indians found fearful and angry expressions to be more unpleasant than did Canadians. Another finding was that happy, sad, and disgusted emotions were judged the most consistently in both cultures and may be the most basic of the basic emotional expressions. Although the ratings of the emotions surprise, anger, and fear were less consistent, the researchers suggest that this does not necessarily mean they are not universal, but that culturally specific "display rules" may influence these basic expressions to some degree.

Babies show a wide range of emotional expressions.

In another cross-cultural study, Michelle Yik of Hong Kong University and James Russell of the University of British Columbia showed Canadian, Chinese, and Japanese respondents the expressions of basic emotions. They found that in addition to showing a considerable degree of agreement regarding the basic emotion expressed, the respondents also tended to agree on other information conveyed in the expressions, such as social messages (Russell & Yik, 1996; Yik & Russell, 1999).

Several researchers have suggested that the expression of emotion may have an evolutionary origin. Babies show a wide range of emotional expressions (Izard, 1994), and even babies who are born blind or hearing impaired and blind show virtually the same facial expressions as sighted babies (Eibl-Eibesfeldt, 1973). It appears, then, that people may purse their lips and furrow their brow when they're mad because these tendencies are built directly into the human genetic code rather than having been learned. The idea that there are universal facial expressions certainly makes adaptive sense; as noted before, facial expressions are excellent signals to others about our current internal state (Ekman & Keltner, 1997).

Interestingly, although basic emotional expressions are likely part of our evolutionary heritage, it appears that the ability to distinguish genuine expressions from faked expressions is not. Researchers Gary Poole, Christine Chambers, and Ken Craig of the University of British Columbia showed undergraduate psychology and nursing students videotaped samples of people experiencing both real pain and faked pain during a physiotherapy examination (Poole & Craig, 1992). They found that the subjects could not reliably distinguish the real pain expressions from the faked pain expressions. They suggest this may be because the human pain expression detection system may be constructed to have a low threshold, which can be easily triggered, because it is more important to register all expressions of possible pain, for instance, including "false positives," than to miss real expressions of pain (Chambers et al., 2002).

The Facial-Feedback Hypothesis Some researchers have argued that feedback from the muscles in the face may even determine the internal emotional experience. According to the **facial-feedback hypothesis,** muscles in the face deliver signals to the brain that are then interpreted, depending on the pattern, as subjective emotional states (Tomkins, 1962). Other researchers point out that there may be direct connections between expressions and physical changes in the brain; for example, smiling can alter the volume of air that is inhaled through the nose. These changes, in turn, can affect the temperature of the brain which, in turn, might affect mood (McIntosh et al., 1997; Zajonc et al., 1993).

The facial-feedback hypothesis makes the unique prediction that if people are asked to copy a particular facial expression, they should experience a corresponding change in emotionality. Indeed, forced smiling, frowning, or grimacing does appear to modulate emotional reports, although the effects may be small (Matsumoto, 1987). You can try this yourself: Try forcing yourself to smile or grimace in an exaggerated

facial-feedback hypothesis
The proposal that muscles in the face deliver signals to the brain that are then interpreted, depending on the pattern, as a subjective emotional state.

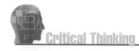
Critical Thinking

Have you ever heard actors talk about how they "become the role" when they're playing emotional parts? What might a psychologist tell an actor to help him or her understand why this happens?

way. Do you feel any different? Some therapists recommend that clients literally force themselves to smile when they are feeling depressed.

How Convincing Is the Evidence?

The link between facial expressions, biology, and emotion seems to support the idea that certain emotions are universal. But does the fact that people have similar facial expressions for fear, anger, or happiness really allow us to conclude that these emotions are somehow more primary or basic than others? Some psychologists think not. Remember: Many psychologists disagree about which emotions belong on the basic list. Does interest, wonder, or guilt belong? How about shame, contempt, or elation? Each of these terms has been identified as basic by at least one prominent emotion researcher. The problem is that humans are capable of an enormous range of emotional experiences. Consider the differences between fear, terror, panic, distress, rage, and anxiety. It is clearly appropriate to use any of these terms in some circumstances and not in others. How can we explain a complex emotion such as terror? If it's not a basic emotion, is it somehow manufactured in the brain by combining or blending more fundamental emotions like fear, surprise, and possibly anger?

Psychologists Andrew Ortony and Terence Turner (1990; Turner & Ortony, 1992) believe that it's not possible to explain the diversity and complexity of human emotional experiences by manipulating and combining a set of basic emotions. Rather than basic emotions, they argue, it's better to think of basic response components that are shared by a wide variety of emotional experiences. For example, the furrowed brow commonly seen in anger is not exclusive to anger but occurs as well when people are frustrated, puzzled, or even just working hard on a task. The furrowed brow may occur in any situation in which a person is somehow blocked from reaching a goal; its appearance, by itself, is not sufficient to infer that the person is angry.

It may help to think about the analogy of human language. There are hundreds of different languages across the world, and each follows certain universal rules (relating to sound and word combinations). But it doesn't make any sense to argue that some of these languages are more basic than others. Human languages are built up from basic components and share many features in common. But the components—the rules of sound and meaning—are not themselves languages (Ortony & Turner, 1990). Similarly, when people are in the grip of an emotion, they may experience many basic and universal conditions (such as a tendency to smile or frown, approach or avoid), but these are merely the components of emotion, not the emotions themselves. Sticking out your tongue, for example, may be a playful sign of resentment in North America; in some regions of China, it indicates surprise.

The Emotional Experience: Arousal

Psychologists may disagree about whether there are basic emotions, but everyone agrees about certain aspects of the emotional *experience*. Virtually all emotions, for instance, lead to *physiological arousal*. Muscles tense, heart rate speeds up, and blood pressure and respiration rates skyrocket. These emotional symptoms arise from activity of the autonomic nervous system as it prepares the body's muscles and organs for a fight-or-flight response. We usually experience emotions in situations that are significant for one reason or another—for instance, the car of a drunken driver swerves sharply into our path, or the sound of breaking glass from the basement window startles us awake. It's adaptive for the body to react quickly in such cases, and the rapid onset of physiological arousal serves that function well. Psychologists have developed instruments for objective measurement of arousal. A device that combines several of these measurements is called the **polygraph.** The Practical Solutions box describes the pros and cons of using this device for lie detection.

Arousal and Performance

The relationship between arousal and performance is not simple and direct—emotional arousal can have a negative side as well. Too much

FIGURE 11.5
Arousal and Task Performance
For a given task, performance tends to be best at intermediate levels of arousal. Too little or too much arousal often leads to a decrease in performance.

polygraph
A device that measures various indexes of physiological arousal in an effort to determine whether someone is telling a lie. The logic behind the test is that lying leads to greater emotionality, which can be picked up through such measures of arousal as heart rate, blood pressure, breathing rate, and perspiring.

Task Performance

Level of Arousal

Practical Solutions

DOES THE POLYGRAPH WORK?

The link between emotions and arousal naturally led to the assumption that arousal could be used as a reliable index of emotional experience. If you're experiencing an emotion, your body ought to show the characteristic patterns of physiological arousal. This assumption lies behind the device commonly called a "lie detector." The technical term is the *polygraph*, a multi-measure of arousal. It is not a mysterious and magical device that measures truth—there's no secret location in the brain, chest, or fingertips that sends up a red flag when you're lying (Lykken, 1998). The polygraph test simply measures mundane things like heart rate, blood pressure, breathing rate, and whether or not you're perspiring. The assumption is that lying leads to greater emotionality, which can then be picked up through measurements of general physiological arousal.

In a polygraph test, the critical comparisons are made between the arousal levels produced by what are called *relevant* and *control* questions. Testers understand that people might become aroused just from taking the test, whether they're lying or not. Therefore, the critical comparison is how arousal levels of the same person change across different question types. During the test, you're typically asked a series of neutral questions (e.g., "What's your name?") to establish a kind of baseline arousal level. Relevant questions are then asked about a specific event (e.g., "Did you change the bank records?"), and the examiner compares the amount of recorded arousal with the various baseline controls.

In the words of Lykken (1998), however, "polygraph pens do no special dance when we are lying." Therefore, this approach has serious problems. First, the person being accused—guilty or not—will naturally react more emotionally to critical questions. Moreover, one can learn to beat the test. If you can control your arousal responses, it's possible to pass the test even if you're lying. Clever criminals can mask lying by increasing their level of arousal on control questions—perhaps by pinching themselves or biting their lip. If arousal levels on the control questions are high, the critical difference between the readings on relevant and control questions will be reduced. If arousal levels are similar across the different question types, the criminal is likely to pass the test. Many hardened criminals may pass the test because they feel little, if any, guilt about their crimes, so their reactions will be minimal anyway.

For these reasons, the polygraph test leads to frequent false positives: That is, innocent people are judged to be lying when, in fact, they are telling the truth. This is a significant problem. Consider that even if testers falsely accused people of lying only 5% of the time, that would still mean 50 out of 1000 people might be falsely accused of a crime. For these reasons, most courtrooms do not allow the results of polygraph tests to be used as evidence for guilt or innocence.

The modern technique that avoids some of these problems is the "guilty knowledge" approach. The polygraph tester can ask about crime scene details that can only be known to someone who was there. A stronger reaction to such details compared to control questions is, therefore, revealing.

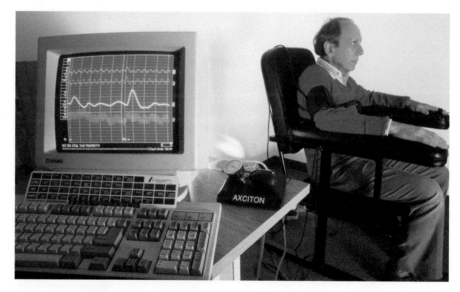

This man is undergoing a polygraph test, which is based on the idea that lying leads to greater emotionality, which can then be picked up through measurements of general physiological arousal.

---

arousal can lead to a breakdown in behavioural, biological, or psychological functioning. Figure 11.5 shows the relationship that exists between level of arousal and task performance. Notice that the pattern looks like an arch or an inverted U. For a given task, as arousal levels increase from low to moderate, performance generally rises. You may perform better on a test if the test is important. But too much pressure, which leads to too much arousal, leads to a sharp drop-off or breakdown in task functioning. You might have more trouble thinking if your entire grade depended on one test. Note

Critical Thinking

Do you think people make distinctive facial expressions when they lie?

that we can also explain individual differences with this idea: Some people perform better under pressure than others because the peak of their arch is closer to the high arousal side of Figure 11.5.

Understanding the relationship between arousal and performance has helped psychologists interpret behaviour in a variety of situations. For example, you may remember from Chapter 7 that people who witness crimes are sometimes inaccurate in their later recollections. One factor that contributes to these inaccuracies is the high level of arousal generated when someone witnesses a crime. If someone is holding a gun to your head, your arousal levels are so high that you are incapable of normal cognitive processing. You are simply too aroused to process the details of the crime scene in a manner that will lead to effective remembering. Moreover, as you'll see in Chapter 13, the relationship between arousal and performance also helps us to understand how our behaviour changes in the presence of other people—our performance is either facilitated or impaired when other people are around, perhaps because the presence of others changes our overall level of arousal.

The Emotional Experience: Subjective Reactions

Experiencing an emotion involves much more than just a facial expression or a flood of physiological arousal. Your thoughts, your perceptions, the things you notice in the environment—these all change when you experience an emotion. But as we discussed before, it's difficult to measure the internal experience accurately and reliably. After all, the emotional experience is by definition personal and subjective. We can ask someone to report what it feels like to be angry, happy, or scared, but the natural constraints of language restrict the answers we receive. Some cultures don't even have a word in their language to describe the concept of an emotion. For example, the Ifaluks of Micronesia have only the word *niferash,* which roughly translates as "our insides" (Lutz, 1982; Matsumoto, 1994).

Anger   What causes *anger?* Not surprisingly the causes are many. If you're restrained in some way, physically or psychologically, you're likely to get angry (Reeve, 1992). More generally, people tend to get angry when their expectations are frustrated. If you're counting on someone to act a certain way or counting on a place or thing to deliver certain rewards, and these expectations are violated, you will probably get angry. This is one of the reasons we are often angry with the ones we love. We tend to expect more from the people we love, which, in turn, increases the chances that our expectations will be violated.

Is the expression of anger healthy psychologically? Psychologists remain undecided about the benefits of "venting" anger, or blowing off steam. On the one hand, expressing your feelings may have a cathartic effect: The expression of anger can lead to an emotional release that is ultimately calming. On the other hand, getting physically angry could well increase the chances that you'll get angry again (Tavris, 1989). When you express anger and feel the calming effect that follows, you reinforce or reward the anger response. Some psychologists have found that encouraging people to express their feelings of anger or hostility leads to more expressions of anger in the future (Ebbesen et al., 1975). The expression of anger can also lead to increased risk taking and other kinds of self-defeating behaviour (Leith & Baumeister, 1996). (We'll return to the effects of anger, specifically on stress and health, in Chapter 16.)

Happiness   The idea that anger arises from violations of expectations also helps account, in part, for the experience of *happiness.* Overall, there is little, if any, relationship between observable characteristics such as age, sex, race, or income and the experience of happiness (Myers & Diener, 1995). Instead, people seem to gain or lose happiness as a result of the comparisons they make—either with others (a well-known tendency called *social comparison*) or with things or experiences from their past. People set standards for satisfaction, and they're happy to the extent that these standards are maintained or surpassed. The trouble is that our standards are constantly changing—Eddie and Lucinda may be able to keep up with the Joneses next door, but there's always the Mendenhalls down the street who just bought that new boat. Once people obtain one level of satisfaction, they set higher goals and thereby immerse themselves in a spiral that never quite leads to utopian bliss.

Actually, many psychological judgments, not just emotions, arise from comparisons with some standard, or *adaptation level*. You may recall from Chapter 4 that whether people will hear one tone as louder than another depends on how loud the standard tone is to begin with. Human judgments are relative—there is no sense in judging whether a tone is "loud," a light is "bright," or a person is "happy" or "sad" without answering the question "Relative to what?" The fact that the subjective experience of happiness is relative helps explain some seemingly inexplicable phenomena. Why is that couple who just won the multimillion-dollar lottery still bickering? How can that homeless man, with only scraps to eat and tattered clothes, wake up every morning with a smile on his face? Happiness is not an absolute Nirvana that can be sought and sometimes found—it's an elusive and fickle condition that depends on constantly changing standards and comparisons.

Disgust As you go to brush your teeth, you notice an unwelcome visitor among the bristles—a cockroach. The mirror captures your reaction: You wrinkle your nose and your mouth drops open in a characteristic gape. Internally, arousal coupled with nausea rise up as your mind plots the exact form of its soon-to-be expressive behaviour. What you are experiencing, of course, is a highly adaptive, usually food-related emotion known as disgust.

Despite what you might think, winning millions of dollars in the lottery does not guarantee future happiness.

If there is a core group of basic emotions, *disgust*, a marked aversion toward something distasteful (literally meaning "bad taste"), is a likely candidate for inclusion. It's easy to appreciate why this emotion is an important tool for the adaptive mind, especially as a mechanism to ensure that we select and reject the appropriate foods. The facial expression that typically accompanies disgust is itself an adaptive reaction to a potentially harmful substance: Wrinkling the nose closes off the air passages, cutting off any offending odour; the gaping expression "causes the contents of the mouth to dribble out" (Rozin & Fallon, 1987).

But in recent years, researchers have come to recognize that there is a psychology to the emotion of disgust that extends beyond its role in food rejection. To illustrate, consider this question: What are the odds that you're going to use that toothbrush again? Suppose you were to drop it into boiling water for a period to ensure sterilization. Would you use it now? Probably not by choice. In a study by Paul Rozin and his colleagues, a dead but sterilized cockroach was dropped into a glass of juice and offered to thirsty subjects. Not surprisingly, few people showed any interest in drinking the juice, even though they knew the roach had been sterilized (Rozin et al., 1986). Most people are also reluctant to consume their favourite soup if they witness the bowl being stirred by a never-used comb or fly swatter (Rozin & Fallon, 1987).

What accounts for these effects? According to some researchers, we are likely to succumb to what has been called *sympathetic magic* (Frazer, 1890/1959; Mauss, 1902/1972; Rozin & Fallon, 1987). People tend to believe that when two objects come in contact, they acquire like properties. The juice acquires some of the disgusting properties of the cockroach, perhaps through a process akin to contagion. The soup becomes associated with flies, even though you know that the fly swatter has never come into contact with a fly. Objects apparently need only to be associated with other disgusting objects to cause an emotional reaction. These are not conscious rational processes at work here, although they may be thought processes that are fundamental

Would you brush your teeth with this toothbrush?

and common to all people (Rozin & Fallon, 1987). (It may also be that classical conditioning is involved—some kind of higher-order association may be formed between the juice, for example, and an object that elicits disgust; see Chapter 6.)

The experience of disgust seems to be universal—appearing cross-culturally—but the emotion takes a while to develop in all of its various forms. For example, if children under age 4 are presented with what adults would consider to be a disgusting odour (feces or synthetic sweat), they tend not to be bothered, or they may even react positively (Stein et al., 1958). Children under age 2, as any parent knows, are happy to put just about anything into their mouths, even "disgusting" objects. In one study, it was found that 62% of tested children under age 2 would put imitation dog feces in their mouth; 31% would mouth a whole, sterilized grasshopper (Rozin et al., 1986). Children simply have no conception that these objects are potentially harmful—they must learn what not to put in their mouths.

It also apparently takes a while for the idea of object contamination to become ingrained in people's minds. You won't brush your teeth with a toothbrush that once housed a cockroach, but a 7-year-old might. Children of this age typically report that a drink has been returned to normal after a disgusting object has been removed (Fallon et al., 1984). In several studies, children under the age of 7 were quite willing to drink a beverage after the experimenter simply removed an object like a fly—they were even willing to drink if a tiny bit of the disgusting object remained in the bottom of the glass (see Rozin, 1990, for a review). Notions about contagion and contamination clearly develop with experience and may even require the child to reach a certain developmental stage.

Theories of Emotion: Body to Mind

We've seen that emotions are complex events. People subjectively experience happiness or sadness, but they also experience important changes in their body and on their face. Questions about how these various components interact have perplexed emotion researchers for decades. For example, what exactly causes the bodily reaction? Is the arousal caused by the internal subjective experience, or is someone happy or sad because his or her body has been induced to react in a particular way?

There are several possible explanations (for an overview, see Figure 11.6). The most commonsense argument is that the subjective experience drives the physiological reaction. People tremble, gasp, and increase their heart rate because some event has

FIGURE 11.7

The Schachter and Singer Experiment

Volunteer subjects were injected with a drug that produced physiological arousal symptoms. Half the subjects were informed about the drug's effects; the other half were not. When placed in a room with either a euphoric or an angry accomplice, only the uninformed subjects adopted the mood of the accomplice. Presumably, the informed subjects interpreted their arousal symptoms as due to the drug, whereas the uninformed subjects interpreted the arousal symptoms as an emotional experience.

injected with either a dose of epinephrine (which produces physiological arousal symptoms) or a dose of saline (which produces no effects). A second manipulated variable was subject expectation: Half the subjects in each of the injection groups were told to expect arousal symptoms ("it's a side effect of the vitamins, you see") and the other half were told to expect no reaction of any kind.

Now let's consider what effect these conditions might be expected to have on emotional reactions. Suppose you're sitting in a room, waiting for further instructions from the experimenter, when suddenly your heart begins to race and your palms begin to sweat. According to James-Lange, this arousal should translate into some kind of emotional experience; you might, for example, expect to become scared or irritated. But what Schachter and Singer (1962) found was that the experience of emotion was determined entirely by expectation. Those subjects who were told to anticipate arousal from the injection showed little emotional reaction to the arousal when it occurred. Only when the arousal was unexpected did people begin to report experiences of emotion. Importantly, participants who were injected with saline experienced no emotion *whether or not* they were told to anticipate arousal.

Even more interesting, Schachter and Singer were able to influence *which* emotion occurred. Joining the subject in the waiting room was an experimental accomplice, introduced as another participant in the experiment. Unknown to the real subject, the accomplice was instructed to act in a fashion that was either playful and euphoric or angry and disagreeable. In later assessments of mood, Schachter and Singer found that aroused but uninformed subjects tended to adopt the mood of the accomplice. If the

Schachter theory

A theory of emotion that argues that the cognitive interpretation, or appraisal, of a body reaction creates the subjective experience of emotion.

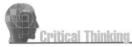

Critical Thinking

If expectations play an important role in determining whether an emotion will be experienced, would you expect to find cultural differences in the expression of emotion?

accomplice was playful, the subjects reported feeling happy; if the accomplice was angry, the subjects reported feeling irritation.

The results of the Schachter and Singer experiment led to the proposal of the **Schachter theory** of emotion, sometimes called the *two-factor theory*. In this theory, autonomic arousal is still a critical determinant of the emotional experience (factor 1). But equally important is the *cognitive appraisal* or *interpretation* of that arousal when it occurs (factor 2). An intense body reaction may be necessary for the full experience of an emotion, but it's not sufficient. It's how you *interpret* the arousal that ultimately determines your subjective emotion. Thus, you're scared when you face an out-of-control bakery truck not only because your body is aroused, but also because your mind understands that the source of the reaction is dangerous. You *label* the arousal and thereby determine the emotion that is experienced.

Like the other theories of emotion we've discussed, the Schachter theory has generated its share of criticism. Some critics have complained that the original Schachter-Singer findings were rather weak (Marshall & Zimbardo, 1979; Reisenzein, 1983). However, the theory produced several key ideas that remain in current thinking about emotion. First, it's reasonably clear that arousal contributes to the experience of emotion. Second, the situation in which the arousal occurs and our expectations about the source of the arousal contribute to the emotional experience. Third, rather than saying that the body reaction creates the emotion or vice versa, it's better to conclude that emotions arise from interactions among several sources: the stimulus event that leads to the reaction, autonomic changes in arousal, and the expectation-based cognitive labels applied to everything involved.

Test Yourself 11.4

Check your knowledge about expressing and experiencing emotion by answering the following questions. (You will find the answers in Appendix B.)

1. For each of the following, pick the component of emotion that best fits the situation: body response, expressive reaction, or subjective experience.
    a. Suzette likes to dance when she's happy: _____
    b. Yolanda grimaces and wrinkles her nose when she sees spaghetti with clam sauce: _____
    c. Mei feels her heart start racing whenever she sees her boyfriend approach:
        _____
    d. Robert would rather use the words "delighted, glad, pleased, and excited" to describe how he feels, instead of the word "happy":
        _____

2. Which of the following situations is most likely to produce happiness?
    a. Receiving a B on a test when you were expecting a C.
    b. Receiving an A on a test when you were expecting an A.
    c. Receiving a C on a test when you were expecting to flunk.
    d. Stimulation of the ventromedial hypothalamus.

3. For each of the following, pick the theory of emotion that best fits the situation: James-Lange, Cannon-Bard, or Schachter.
    a. I love it when my heart starts racing because it makes me feel happy:
        _____
    b. I must be in love because she just gave me a wink and my heart is racing: _____
    c. I really feel happy right now and, by the way, my heart is also racing:
        _____
    d. You're not really in love; you just drank too much coffee this morning:
        _____

Solving the Adaptive Problems

Your adaptive mind is designed to initiate, direct, and control behaviour. Motivation and its intimate companion, emotion, are vehicles that enable you to accomplish these things—to react to sudden changes in the environment, to maintain your internal energy needs, and even to prolong the species. There are certain things that each of us simply must do—consume food, drink liquids, maintain a constant internal temperature—and psychologists have struggled for decades to discover appropriate ways to describe the mechanisms that ensure our accomplishment of them.

First, what activates goal-directed behaviour? As you've seen, motivation depends on an interplay between internal and external factors. Much of the time behaviour is controlled by internal factors that compel us in the direction of a goal. Our bodies are constantly monitoring internal energy levels, and once a disruption in the homeostatic balance is detected, we feel hungry or thirsty and seek to restore the appropriate balance. In these cases, it's likely that motivated behaviour arises directly as a consequence of biological factors and requires no direct experiences with the environment.

But even something as biologically significant as eating or drinking cannot be explained by appealing just to innate internal factors. All forms of motivated behaviour are influenced by external factors as well. External rewards, or incentives, exert powerful pulling and guiding effects on our actions. Understanding motivation then becomes a matter of specifying how these *external* factors interact with *internal* factors to activate and control behaviour. One way in which internal and external factors interact is described by Maslow's notion of a need hierarchy. The essential component of Maslow's theory is the prioritizing of need: Some needs, especially those critical to survival, must be satisfied before others, such as the need for self-actualization, can be pursued.

Second, what factors create hunger and control eating? What are the internal and external sources that initiate and control eating? Internally, the body monitors everything from the amount and content of food in the stomach to the level of glucose in the blood in order to determine its energy needs. If the level of glucose falls below a certain level, for example, you start to feel hungry and seek out food. Although researchers are uncertain about its precise role in controlling eating, the hypothalamus is believed to play an important role in initiating and controlling eating. But we also eat for reasons that appear unrelated to restoring homeostatic balance. People likely evolved to anticipate and prevent energy deficits, rather than to merely react to them. Food, and eating in particular, is clearly reinforcing. People are much more likely to motivate themselves to eat if they like the food—the vigour or intensity with which they respond depends critically on the value, or incentive, of the food. A number of factors, both genetic and environmental, play a role in regulating body weight. Eating disorders such as anorexia nervosa and bulimia nervosa tend to have psychological origins related to body image and to the need for (or lack of) control, and they may also reflect evolutionary adaptations that helped young women delay reproduction when they were feeling extreme stress.

Third, what factors promote sexual behaviour? Why do individuals in sexually reproducing species have such a strong motivation to pursue sexual activity? Sexual activity is necessary for individuals to replicate copies of their genes in the next generation. Humans therefore evolved to find sex to be very reinforcing, and sexual desire compels us to pursue a mate, thereby opening the door for companionship, protection, and love. Hormones apparently influence sexual desire in humans much less than in other animals. Different cultures have different views of attractiveness and different codes of conduct for sexual activity. Many psychologists believe that people acquire sexual scripts that instruct them on how, why, and what to do in their interactions with potential sexual partners. Mate selection and sexual orientation, however, are influenced by biological as well as environmental factors.

Fourth, how are emotions expressed and experienced, and what functions do they serve? Emotions typically involve a mixture of reactions, including a physiological response (arousal), a characteristic expressive reaction (such as a distinctive facial expression), and some kind of subjective experience (such as the feeling of happiness or sadness). The physical expression of an emotion allows us to communicate our feelings to others. The internal components—arousal, for example—prepare us for action. Thoughts become prioritized, and muscles are ready to respond. Emotions are powerful adaptive tools: They not only increase the likelihood of survival, but also, for many, make life itself worth living.

The internal subjective experience of emotion is often relative—whether we feel happy, for example, seems to depend on the comparisons we make with others and with our past experiences. Although a number of theories have tried to explain the relation between arousal and the experience of emotion, most psychologists believe that the experience of emotion depends partly on the presence of a body response—general arousal—and partly on the cognitive appraisals one makes about the origin of arousal when it occurs.

Chapter Summary

ACTIVATING BEHAVIOUR

Any organism that seeks to survive in an ever-changing environment needs motivational mechanisms to be able to react quickly to its needs as well as anticipate future outcomes.

Internal Factors: Instincts and Drive

Learning Goal: Comprehend the role of instincts and drive in activating behaviour. *Instincts* are unlearned, characteristic patterns of responding that are controlled by specific triggering stimuli in the world. Instincts do not adequately explain human behaviour. A *primary drive* is a psychological state that arises in response to a physiological need. *Secondary drives* are learned by association with primary drives. The body is designed to seek stable and constant internal conditions through a process termed *homeostasis*. It is useful to consider both *proximate* and *ultimate* factors in explaining motivational systems.

External Factors: Incentive Motivation

Learning Goal: Be able to explain incentive motivation and discuss how it activates behaviour. External rewards exert powerful "pulling" effects on behaviour. Psychologists use the term *incentive motivation* to explain goal-directed behaviour. Whereas drives serve as an internal "push," incentives serve as an external "pull" toward specific goals. Motivation is determined jointly by both internal and external factors.

Achievement Motivation

Learning Goal: Understand achievement motivation. The *achievement motive* pushes you to seek success and significant accomplishment in your life. People who rate high in achievement motivation tend to work harder and more persistently on tasks. How hard you work on a task depends on your expectations about whether you will be successful and how much you value success on the task. Cultural factors play a role in achievement motivation and gender-related differences.

Intrinsic Motivation

Learning Goal: Understand intrinsic motivation. Psychologists use the term *intrinsic motivation* to describe situations in which behaviour seems to be entirely self-motivated. This form is often contrasted with incentive motivation from externally provided rewards: They can lower a person's intrinsic motivation for a task. One explanation for this is that a reward may be perceived as controlling behaviour. Another account is that external rewards lead to overjustification; you conclude that you're engaging in the

behaviour because of the reward, rather than because you enjoy doing it.

Maslow's Hierarchy of Needs

Learning Goal: Learn about Maslow's hierarchy of needs, and discuss how each need influences behaviour. Maslow's *need hierarchy* provides a prioritizing of needs. Usually represented as a pyramid, the theory proposes that certain fundamental needs (biological "musts") take priority; once fulfilled, we seek to fulfill more personal security, spiritual, and relationship needs. At the top of the hierarchy is the need for self-actualization (reaching one's potential).

MEETING BIOLOGICAL NEEDS: HUNGER AND EATING

Eating is a critical part of living. Both internal and external cues help activate and control eating.

Internal Factors Controlling Hunger

Learning Goal: Understand the internal factors that influence when and why we eat. A number of internal signals influence when and why we eat. The contents of the stomach is one such signal. Also, levels of *glucose* and *insulin* are monitored. It's likely that a glucose–insulin interaction is monitored because both substances play a role in metabolic processes. Brain regions also play a role in signalling hunger. Early research isolating the *ventromedial hypothalamus* and *lateral hypothalamus* as "stop-eating" and "start-eating" centres was overly simplified. Later research indicates that the brainstem and hippocampus are also involved.

External Factors

Learning Goal: Understand the external factors that influence when and why we eat. We often eat for reasons not related to restoring internal homeostatic balance. Our eating behaviour is partially determined by our eating habits and food cues, such as the sight of food and its association with past pleasures.

Regulating Body Weight

Learning Goal: Be able to explain how body weight is regulated, including the concept of a set point. Some researchers suggest that we have a *set point* (natural body weight) that controls our tendency to gain or lose weight. However, more recent researchers have criticized set point theory and suggest that people eat to prevent energy deficits, not in reaction to them. The causes of *obesity* are varied and complex; a combination of biological and psychological factors, including genetics, metabolic rate, and learned eating habits, is likely involved.

Eating Disorders

Learning Goal: Learn about the eating disorders anorexia nervosa and bulimia nervosa. People's assessments of their own weight and its relation to societal standards are typically inaccurate and help promote a negative body image. This increases susceptibility to the eating disorders *anorexia nervosa* (in which a person refuses to maintain a healthy body weight due to a fear of being overweight) and *bulimia nervosa* (binge eating coupled with purging to control body weight). The *reproductive suppression model* suggests that anorexia may constitute part of an evolved disposition for young women to suppress reproduction when under perceived extreme stress.

MEETING BIOLOGICAL NEEDS: SEXUAL BEHAVIOUR

Although sexual activity is not necessary for individual survival, it is necessary to ensure that our genes are represented in the next generation. There are internal and external cues that help motivate an interest in sex.

Internal Factors

Learning Goal: Be able to explain the role that hormones play in human and animal sexual behaviour. For much of the animal kingdom, sexual behaviour is controlled by internal (hormonal) mechanisms. Humans also show cyclic variation in hormones related to sex and reproduction (*estrogens* in females, *androgens* in males). But human sexual behaviour is subject to strong societal regulation as well as self-regulation.

External Factors

Learning Goal: Understand external influences on sexual behaviour. Sexual desire can also be explained by appealing to the incentive value; that is, stimulation by environmental cues. Visual and informational cues are both important. Touch is one important external source of sexual arousal; stimulation of *erogenous zones* is highly arousing for most people under the right circumstances. Also, *pheromones* (chemicals released by the females of many species during periods of receptivity) play a role in producing sexual arousal, but not necessarily in humans.

Mate Selection

Learning Goal: Recognize the factors that influence mate selection. What people consider attractive in a mate is strongly influenced by both cultural and evolutionary factors. Our culture provides men and women with different *sexual scripts* that instruct us on how, why, and what to do in our sexual encounters. Evolutionary factors are implicated by sex differences observed in nearly every culture. Men are more likely than women to pursue short-term sexual strategies and focus on youth and attractiveness. These patterns reflect evolutionary adaptations that were responses to the differing reproductive problems faced by males and females in ancestral environments.

Sexual Orientation

Learning Goal: Learn the possible origins of sexual orientation. *Sexual orientation* refers to whether a person is sexually and emotionally attracted to members of the same sex or the opposite sex. Research suggests that sexual orientation is at least partly determined by biological factors. It is possible that the environment plays a role as well.

EXPRESSING AND EXPERIENCING EMOTION
Are There Basic Emotions?

Learning Goals: Be able to identify the basic components of an emotion and discuss their adaptive value. Appreciate the evidence for and against basic emotions. Most people agree on about a half-dozen basic emotions, typically including anger, fear, happiness, and sadness. Recognition of certain basic facial expressions of emotions seems to be universal, suggesting that expression of emotion may have a biological or genetic origin. Some researchers have argued that the feedback from muscles in the face may determine the internal emotional experience (the *facial-feedback hypothesis*). Some psychologists remain unconvinced that certain emotions are "basic" and "universal." Another idea is that there are basic response components shared by a wide variety of emotional experiences.

The Emotional Experience: Arousal

Learning Goal: Learn about the role that arousal plays in the emotional experience. Emotions are associated with *physiological arousal*. The relationship between arousal and performance is complex. The general relationship is an inverted U function; extremely high or low levels of arousal are likely to disrupt performance. The measurement of arousal serves as the basis for the *polygraph test*. The purpose of a polygraph test is to determine whether someone is being truthful or lying. However, polygraphs are fairly easy to beat and do produce a fair number of false positives.

The Emotional Experience: Subjective Reactions

Learning Goal: Understand the subjective experiences of anger and happiness. The emotional experience is personal and subjective. Anger is typically associated with the violations of one's expectations. The value of "venting" one's anger is a controversial issue. Some psychologists have found that encouraging people to express anger or hostility leads to experiencing more anger in the future, along with increased risk-taking and self-defeating behaviours. *Happiness* seems to rely on the comparisons we make—with others or with things or experiences from our past. Many psychological judgments (like emotions) arise from comparisons with some *adaptation level*.

Theories of Emotion: Body to Mind

Learning Goal: Recognize the differences between the James-Lange, Cannon-Bard, and Schachter theories of emotion. The most natural way to relate emotion to body and mind is to assume that the subjective experience drives the physical reaction. The *James-Lange theory* assumes the opposite, that the body reaction drives the subjective experience of emotion. This theory predicts that unique physical changes should accompany different emotions, and this is typically not the case. The *Cannon-Bard theory* proposes that the subjective experience of emotion and associated body reactions are independent processes that occur together. The *Schachter theory*, formerly known as the *two-factor theory*, assumes that emotion is a product of autonomic arousal and cognitive appraisal of that arousal. Recent data seem to support some version of this theory.

Terms to Remember

Recommended Readings

Capaldi, E. D. (Ed.). (1996). *Why we eat what we eat.* Washington, DC: American Psychological Association. A broad collection of chapters, written by leading researchers, covering all aspects of eating and food selection.

Buss, D. M. (1994). *The evolution of desire: Strategies of human mating.* New York: Basic Books. Evolutionary social psychologist David Buss of the University of Texas presents data from a study with over 10 000 participants that examined cross-cultural similarities in mating and sexual behaviour, and discusses the evolutionary selection pressure that may have moulded human sexual and pair-bonding preferences.

Russell, J. A., & Fernandez-Dols, J. M. (Eds.). (1997). *The psychology of facial expression.* New York: Cambridge University Press. Co-edited by University of British Columbia emotion researcher James Russell, this collection includes reviews of evolutionary, neurobehavioural, and developmental views on facial expression. Included is a chapter by social interaction researchers Janet Beavin Bavelas and Nicole Chovil of the University of Victoria that examines how facial expressions complement the verbal and other nonverbal components of human dialogues.

Bond, M. H. (Ed.). (1996). *The handbook of Chinese psychology.* Hong Kong: Oxford University Press. Includes a chapter on "Emotion among the Chinese" by researchers James Russell from the University of British Columbia and Michelle Yik from the University of Hong Kong.

Johnston, V. S. (1999). *Why we feel: The science of human emotion.* New York: Perseus Books. Draws on recent advances in biology, psychology, and cognitive science to examine how emotions evolve, how they develop over a lifetime, what adaptive purpose they serve, and their physiological bases.

LeDoux, J. E. (1996). *The emotional brain.* New York: Simon & Schuster. A very readable discussion of possible biological mechanisms connected to the experience and display of emotion.

Taylor, G. J., Bagby, R. M., & Parker, J. D. A. (1997). *Disorders of affect regulation: Alexithymia in medical and psychiatric illness.* Cambridge: Cambridge University Press. What happens when people are unable to regulate their emotions in an adaptive way? These people can be said to be suffering from alexithymia, and this volume, by University of Toronto researchers Graeme Taylor and Michael Bagby and Trent University researcher James Parker, explores the possible causes and consequences of this puzzling disorder.

 For additional readings, explore InfoTrac® College Edition, your online library. Go to:

www.adaptivemind2e.nelson.com

Hint: enter the search terms: achievement motivation; intrinsic motivation; eating disorders; sexual drive; sexual orientation; happiness; anger.

What's on the Web?

Please note that Web addresses are subject to change. Check out the accompanying Web site for updates: www.adaptivemind2e.nelson.com. This site presents practice quiz questions, hypercontent, information on degrees and careers in psychology, study tips, and more.

National Eating Disorders Information Centre

www.nedic.ca/

This informative Canadian site provides a great deal of helpful information about eating disorders as well as other health-related issues. Find out the answers to questions such as, How does body image distortion relate to eating disorders? What is the history of eating disorders? What is the relationship between exercise and eating disorders?

American Polygraph Association

www.polygraph.org

This is the home page for the "other APA" (*not* the American Psychological Association or the American Psychiatric Association). This APA is "dedicated to providing a valid and reliable means to verify the truth and establish the highest standards of moral, ethical, and professional conduct in the polygraph field." This is a great site to visit if you're curious about the practice of "lie detecting" with polygraphs. Find answers to the following questions: Who uses polygraph examinations? What factors lead to errors in polygraph results? Is voice stress analysis a valid indicator of lying?

The Kinsey Institute

www.indiana.edu/~kinsey

Everything you wanted to know about sexuality but were afraid to ask. This is the official Web site (housed at Indiana University) of the famous institute, founded by one of the pioneers of human sexuality research. The Institute "supports interdisciplinary research and the study of human sexuality." The site includes a wealth of information about and links to other sites dealing with "sexology."

Human action can be modified to a certain extent, but human nature cannot be changed.

Abraham Lincoln

Chapter 12 Personality

n the most popular books, plays, and films throughout history, it is made clear who are the good characters and who are the bad. The appeal of such stories would be lost without having both decency and evil represented in the cast. Even more appealing to psychologically minded people are stories where good and evil reside within the same person. In his 1886 novel, *The Strange Case of Dr. Jekyll and Mr. Hyde,* Robert Louis Stevenson explored the dual nature of human personality through the characters of Jekyll and Hyde. The good doctor Jekyll could transform himself into the ghastly Mr. Hyde, the personification of evil, by drinking an exotic potion.

As you'll see in this chapter, psychologists such as Sigmund Freud have argued that there are indeed multiple sides to human nature, and that these sides fight a continual internal battle within the mind of the ordinary person. While not as dramatic, other theories of personality accept the idea that people's behaviour can be inconsistent across situations.

Nonetheless, the emphasis in the study of personality is on the aspects of the person's social behaviour that are consistent. If you are sad after a funeral, grouchy after bumping your knee, or elated after hearing good news, we would not describe your personality as sad, grouchy, or elated. The term "mood" or "state" or "feeling" would be more appropriate. In fact, the idea that people are consistent seems to be a necessary assumption of living a normal life. How could we pick friends, get married, or select employees unless we assumed that they will show the same character tomorrow as they do today?

personality

The entire pattern of psychological characteristics—thinking, feeling, and behaving—that differentiates us from others.

trait

A stable predisposition to act or behave in a consistent fashion.

Personality can be defined as the distinguishing pattern of psychological characteristics—thinking, feeling, and behaving—that differentiates us from others and leads us to act consistently across situations. At its core, the study of personality, like the study of intelligence, is first and foremost the study of individual differences (Cronbach, 1957). People seem to differ in lasting ways: Sarah is warm, creative, and energetic; Karla is aggressive in social settings and has an annoying habit of lying. These central elements of personality are called **traits;** that is, predispositions to respond consistently across time and situations. Of course, the full richness of a human's personality cannot be captured by listing his or her traits. Good personality theories must explain how the traits are integrated. They must be able to explain how good and bad qualities, as well as stability and change, can be present in every human being.

The fact that some people are more shy than others is indisputable, but is it a fixed characteristic? Is it even consistent across situations?

468

Previewing the Scientific and Practical Problems

An individual's personality may be viewed as his or her typical way of adapting to life's challenges. Everyone runs into problems in life but, to be successful, we have to cope with such difficult situations. Different people adapt to these problems in different ways. Some people tackle their problems aggressively; others manipulate to get around the problem; others simply fret and hope it goes away. Not surprisingly, then, some personality styles are more adaptive; that is, some people lead more successful and happier lives than others. These adaptive styles may be learned through trial and error or may be imposed by one's temperament.

In one respect, the whole topic of personality represents a challenge to evolutionary theory, which is not designed to explain *differences* within a species (except for sex differences). The theory can certainly explain why the human species is characterized by traits such as cooperativeness, conscientiousness, and even self-deception, because those traits increase the likelihood of survival (Buss, 1988; Kenrick, 1994; Krebs & Denton, 1997). The idea of individual differences, however, requires a more complex version of the theory. Why don't we all have the same optimal trait for our species' niche within the ecosystem? One argument is that different levels of a personality trait (e.g., anxious and calm) stay in the gene pool because each is adaptive in different situations (Buss & Shackelford, 1997). If everyone were calm, who would warn us of possible dangers? Another possible explanation is that personality differences are just random mutations of genes.

As with other chapters, we will show how psychologists have attempted to resolve the scientific and practical problems that are central to the study of personality. As you read this chapter, think back to the issues we considered in Chapter 9—there are many similarities between the study of intelligence and the study of personality.

First, what is the proper way to enumerate and measure the traits that make us both consistent and unique? To understand the concept of personality, it's necessary to summarize across many behaviours. You can't judge someone based on their actions in a restricted situation, or even in several situations. You need to measure the enduring aspects of behaviour—those *traits* that distinguish one person from another consistently across time. Of the traits in the dictionary, we don't want to measure too many or too few. Describing people with only a couple of traits may oversimplify personality. On the other hand, it would be impractical to use hundreds of traits. This chapter outlines various research programs attempting to get the number of important traits just right.

Second, how do personality traits develop? What factors in the individual's development lead to stable and consistent behaviours? It's one thing to identify and measure a person's lasting traits, but quite another to understand their origin. Where do personality traits come from, and what accounts for the individual differences? Why does Karla have that nasty tendency to lie, and why does sweet Sarah always see the romantic side of even dire circumstances? We covered some of these issues in Chapter 10, but it is the study of personality that addresses the most ambitious theories of psychology—the ones that try to put the whole human being together in a unified fashion.

Third, how do personality theories deal with variation and change in the same person's behaviour? Some theorists have gone so far as to say that such situational inconsistencies prove that traits don't even exist (Mischel, 1968). Most psychologists now dismiss that extreme view. Nonetheless, trait theories have trouble explaining any inconsistency because they are designed to explain observed consistency of behaviour. As you know from Chapter 6, the environment not only conditions people but it provides the learned cues to trigger conditioned behaviour. All major theories of personality assume that the environment shapes behaviour; where they differ is in the degree to which the environment is important and in the mechanisms through which the environment exerts its influence. As with intelligence, the data from behavioural genetics indicates large causal portions are attributable to both genetics and environment. In the final section of the chapter, we'll discuss the evidence—and controversy—that bears on this issue.

ENUMERATING AND MEASURING PERSONALITY TRAITS

Learning Goals

1. Appreciate how factor analysis is used to identify basic personality traits.
2. Understand Allport's distinction between cardinal, central, and secondary traits.
3. Be able to explain the advantages and disadvantages of self-report questionnaires, projective tests, and indirect methods.

trait taxonomies
Systems for distinguishing the most important individual differences in personality. These trait taxonomies are usually associated with an inventory of psychometric tests designed to measure these traits.

WE MUST BEGIN with personality measurement before we get to the detailed theories such as psychoanalysis. After all, we need some systematic way of classifying and enumerating the consistent personality differences before we can know what facts need to be explained. **Trait taxonomies** are systems for counting and organizing the important dimensions on which people differ. As a general rule, trait approaches use a psychometric approach; that is, they seek to identify stable individual differences by analyzing the responses of large groups of people.

Three modes of measurement are common in the psychometric approach. The first is self-report: People describe themselves in interviews or questionnaires. The second is observer-report: The person is rated by others who have relevant information (e.g., friends, family, or trained observers such as therapists or job interviewers). The third is actual behaviour: A concrete indicator that can be measured objectively (e.g., speed of initiating conversation, heart rate, number of parties attended in a month).

Whatever the mode of measurement, we have to decide what traits to measure. It's been estimated that comprehensive dictionaries contain approximately 10 000 trait-related terms (Allport & Odbert, 1936). Understandably, most participants in research don't appreciate filling out questionnaires that long. We need a trait taxonomy that reduces these thousands of descriptive terms into a smaller set of more basic terms. We need to find more basic common concepts behind various groups of terms. For example, when you describe someone with words like *kind*, *trusting*, and *warm*, you might really be tapping into specific facets of a general characteristic of the person, such as agreeableness (Goldberg, 1993). But how can we identify the basic traits from among the thousands of personality descriptors in the language?

The Factor Analytic Approach

One way to approach the problem is to use *factor analysis*. Recall from Chapter 9 that it is a mathematical procedure used to analyze the correlations among a large number of variables—in this case trait words. The goal is simplification; that is, to reduce a large set of trait word variables to a small number of factors by lumping together similar traits into subsets called factors. To see how this works in the case of personality, imagine that we ask a group of 500 people to rate themselves on 100 personality characteristics. For example: "On a scale of 1 to 7, how well do you think the term *anxious* is characteristic of you?" To say the least, this large dataset of 50 000 numbers is not easily analyzed by eye—even the trained eyeball of the researcher. Some simplification occurs when you calculate the correlations among the 100 traits: At that point you still have to deal with a huge (100×100) matrix of correlations.

Factor analysis provides an even more dramatic simplification. It examines all the correlations to find subsets of trait words that are highly correlated. People who rate themselves as, say, *kind* also tend to rate themselves as *warm* and *trusting*. High intercorrelations among a group of traits indicate that they are really measuring the same thing. Together, they measure some broader personality characteristic, such as *pleasantness*, which is being tapped by the more specific personality descriptors. This is the logic behind factor analysis—discover the common denominators for personality by noting which terms cluster statistically in a group. The final step is to name each factor in a way that captures the meaning of the whole cluster. Agreeableness or pleasantness seems like an appropriate summary label for the cluster of kind, warm, and trusting. If we end up with only 10 factors instead of the original 100 trait words, we can proceed in a much more efficient way to ask questions about the consistency and validity of personality measures.

Cattell's Source Traits   Raymond Cattell was the first to conduct a factor analysis of all the traits in the English dictionary. This feat became practical around 1960, when university computers became available for this purpose (Cattell, 1963). His analyses yielded 16 basic personality factors from a set of traits that originally numbered in the thousands. Thus an individual's personality could now be summarized by their scores on 16 summary factors: *outgoing, intelligent, dominant, serious, conscientious, venture-some, tough-minded, trusting, imaginative, shrewd, self-assured, conservative, self-sufficient, controlled,* and *relaxed.* The 16 factors were measured by a question-naire—still popular today—that was appropriately labelled the 16 Personality Factors inventory (16PF) (Cattell et al., 1970). To Cattell, all 16 factors were *source traits,* meaning that they represent the underlying causes of behaviour. In contrast, we use the term *surface traits* for the many consistent behavioural tendencies (e.g., interrupts others) that we observe in people. They number far more than 16 and do not neces-sarily map onto the same source for different individuals. For example, the tendency to interrupt might be due to being outgoing for one person, tough-minded for another, and imaginative for a third.

Eysenck's Three Dimensions The major complaint about Cattell's factors was that they overlapped with each other; that is, they were intercorrelated. To solve this problem, Eysenck used a type of factor analysis that produced non-overlapping factors; that is, they should show zero correlations with each other. The three resulting dimen-sions were quite clear: (1) the dimension of *extraversion,* which refers roughly to how outgoing and sociable you are; (2) the dimension of *neuroticism,* which captures your degree of anxiety, worry, or moodiness; and (3) the dimension of *psychoticism,* which represents your tendencies to be irresponsible and nasty toward others (Eysenck, 1991).

With only three primary dimensions (see Figure 12.1), Eysenck's theory is cer-tainly simpler and, therefore, more practical for use in research and testing. Eysenck also theorized about the underlying biological systems required to explain the emer-gence of these three dimensions (Eysenck, 1970). Many have complained about his choice of labels: *neuroticism* and *psychoticism* are extreme terms that other psycholo-gists reserve for clinical disturbances, not normal traits.

The Big Five Who was right—Cattell or Eysenck? A simple answer is that Eysenck and Cattell were operating at different levels of analysis: Eysenck, with his three primary dimensions, is interested in mapping out the more distinct and general aspects of human personality, whereas Cattell's analytic techniques paint a more fine-tuned set of

FIGURE 12.1

Eysenck's Three Primary Dimensions of Personality

Hans Eysenck measured three dimensions of personality: extraversion, neuroticism, and psychoticism. Included in each circle are sample questions of the type used to measure a person's standing on that dimension. (Questions from Eysenck & Eysenck, 1975.)

overlapping traits (see Feist, 1994). But increasingly, researchers seem to be settling on a more intermediate solution: It is now widely believed that the best solution to the factoring problem is the "Big Five"—that is, the five basic personality dimensions (Goldberg, 1993; McCrae & Costa, 1985; Wiggins & Pincus, 1992).

The so-called **Big Five** personality dimensions include *extraversion, agreeableness, conscientiousness, neuroticism,* and *openness to experience.* Each is listed in Figure 12.2 along with some of the descriptors that identify each trait. So, for example, people who score highly on the extraversion dimension tend to see themselves as talkative, sociable, fun-loving, and affectionate. Notice that extraversion and neuroticism are 2 of the 3 primary dimensions suggested by Eysenck, and psychoticism neatly translates into a combination of the reverse of both agreeableness and conscientiousness.

Why 5 factors in the Big Five model instead of 2 or 3 or even 16? Part of the reason is technical, having to do with what current researchers believe is the most appropriate way to apply the factor analytic technique (see Digman, 1990; Goldberg, 1993). But there are other reasons. For example, a number of studies have analyzed trait ratings collected from people around the world. Regardless of the language used—and different languages can have quite different personality descriptors—there still appear to be 5 basic dimensions that best explain the ratings (Digman, 1990; McCrae & Costa, 1997). Many psychologists find the cross-cultural data to be quite convincing; the data suggest that the basic structure of personality may be universal rather than dependent on cultural background (McCrae et al., 1996). At the same time, the fact that 5 factors can be used to categorize people doesn't tell us anything about the internal processes that determine a personality profile. To truly understand personality, some critics argue, you need to understand the ability of people to *change* as well as stay the same across situations (Mischel & Shoda, 1998; Srivastava, 2003). We'll discuss how the environment affects the consistency of behaviour later in the chapter.

The Interpersonal Circle What if we are only interested in dimensions that relate directly to interpersonal behaviour? In that case, personality can be reduced to two primary dimensions of interpersonal behaviour, namely, *agency* and *communion.* Canadian researchers have been especially important in developing this model. The importance of these two dimensions was first pointed out by York University's David Bakan (1966) and later explored in detail by other Canadian researchers, including Ross Broughton and Paul Trapnell of the University of Winnipeg, Jerry Wiggins and

Big Five

The five dimensions of personality— extraversion, agreeableness, conscientiousness, neuroticism, and openness—that have been isolated through the application of factor analysis. It is widely believed that virtually all personality terms in language can be accounted for by appealing to one or more of these basic dimensions.

FIGURE 12.2
The Big Five Dimensions

Many psychologists believe that personality can be summarized in terms of five fundamental personality dimensions: extraversion, agreeableness, conscientiousness, neuroticism, and openness.

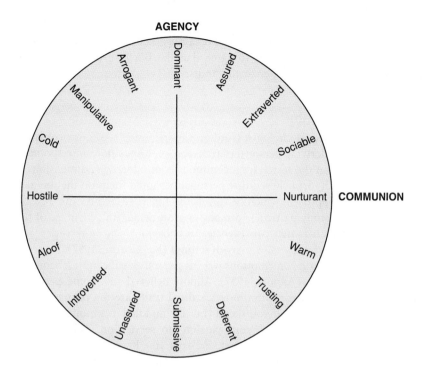

FIGURE 12.3
Wiggins's Interpersonal Circle of Personality Traits

Personality researcher Jerry Wiggins of the University of British Columbia has suggested that this two-dimensional figure provides a useful summary of important personality traits relating to the interpersonal domain. Traits that are close on the circle are those that are most highly correlated.

Del Paulhus of the University of British Columbia, Debbie Moskowitz of McGill University, and Krista Trobst of York University (Moskowitz, 1994; Trapnell & Wiggins, 1990; Trobst, 2000; Wiggins, 1979; Wiggins & Broughton, 1991).

The central idea is that all interpersonal traits form a circle, as in Figure 12.3. The closer two traits are on the circle, the more highly correlated they are. Moreover, any interpersonal trait can be summarized by how much it reflects each of the two basic social values—agency and communion. The concept of agency refers to "getting ahead"; that is, achieving more than others do. The concept of communion refers to "getting along"; that is, fitting in with and supporting others. Of central importance is the idea that they are not mutually exclusive: You can be agentic and communal, too. Successful leaders, for example, require both. Note that four out of the Big Five dimensions can be mapped onto the interpersonal circle (Paulhus & John, 1998; Wiggins & Trapnell, 1997). Extraversion and openness to experience are associated with agency, whereas agreeableness and conscientiousness are associated with communion.

Recent Alternatives to the Big Five Several Canadian psychologists have addressed the limitations of the Big Five factor model. The University of Western Ontario's Sampo Paunonen (1998) wondered how specific lower-order traits (like talkativeness and sociability) would compare with a broader Big Five dimension (extraversion) in predicting observable behaviour. Ninety-six undergraduates completed a general inventory of 22 lower-order trait measures (e.g., affiliation, aggression, dominance, and impulsivity), a measure of the five global factors (e.g., extraversion and agreeableness), and a pool of 14 behavioural criteria like number of dates per month, number of different people dated per month, whether the student was a smoker, choice of liberal arts or non–liberal arts program of major, religiosity, and interest in fraternity or sorority membership. When analyzed together, the lower-order traits offered significantly better prediction of the behavioural criteria, suggesting that specific behaviours may be better predicted by specific (less general) traits. In short, ask a specific question and you will get a specific answer.

Other researchers at the University of Western Ontario have argued that the conscientiousness dimension of the Big Five should be subdivided into two parts: dutifulness and ambition (Jackson et al., 1996). More recently, Michael Ashton of Brock University proposed adding a sixth dimension to the Big Five. In a series of factor analyses, he noted that the next most important dimension was "integrity," or the tendency to be honest and forthright in social relations (Ashton et al., 2000). Nonetheless, most personality researchers tend to agree that the Big Five dimensions provide a useful structure for measuring personality traits.

Allport's Trait Theory

Like the factor analysts, psychologist Gordon Allport (1897–1967) was convinced that all people possess underlying personality traits, or "predispositions to respond." But he was less convinced that the search for a common set of underlying dimensions was the way to go. Instead, Allport believed that personality should focus on the uniqueness of the individual. His approach, which he called *idiographic* (which means "revealing the individual"), was to study particular persons in great detail. An advantage of this kind of case study approach is that consistencies in behaviour can be recorded across an entire lifetime of experiences in a variety of settings (Barenbaum, 1997).

One of Allport's main contributions was his general classification scheme for identifying personality traits (Allport, 1937). Allport believed that some people display what he called *cardinal personality traits.* **Cardinal traits** are the ruling passions that dominate an individual's life. If you spend your life huddled in a mountain monastery, rejecting all worldly possessions, your passion "to serve God" would likely satisfy Allport's description of a cardinal trait. Perhaps you know someone whose every thought or action seems to revolve around the pursuit of wealth, fame, or power. People with cardinal traits do not represent the average—these people are driven and highly focused; every action appears to be motivated by some particular goal. Notice that we can't really capture something like a cardinal trait by applying a technique such as factor analysis, because cardinal traits are uniquely defined by the individual rather than the group.

Allport believed that cardinal traits are rare. Most people have personalities that are controlled by several lasting characteristics, which Allport labelled as *central traits.* **Central traits** are the 5 to 10 descriptive terms that you would use to describe someone you know. Sarah? She's warm and friendly, very trustworthy, sentimental at times, and honest to the core. In addition to central traits, Allport suggested that everyone has **secondary traits,** which are less obvious because they may not always appear in an individual's behaviour. For example, Sarah might also have a secondary trait of *grouchiness*

cardinal traits
Allport's term to describe personality traits that dominate an individual's life, such as a passion to serve others or to accumulate wealth.

central traits
Allport's term to describe the 5 to 10 descriptive traits that you would use to describe someone you know—friendly, trustworthy, and so on.

secondary traits
The less obvious characteristics of an individual's personality that do not always appear in his or her behaviour, such as testiness when on a diet.

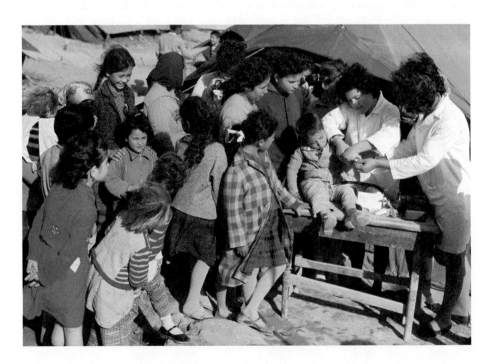

Cardinal traits are the ruling passions that dominate a person's life, such as a compelling need to help others at the expense of personal comfort.

that always shows up in morning meetings. Personality characteristics, therefore, can be appropriately described in terms of levels ranging from dominant (cardinal) to representative (central) to occasional (secondary).

Assessment Methods

We have now covered the best-known systems for organizing traits, the basic dimensions of human personality. They are of scientific interest in our search to find distinguishing patterns of psychological characteristics. But there are also practical reasons why it's important to measure personality traits—they provide an efficient screening process for job selection and clinical diagnosis.

Suppose you're the personnel director at a large nuclear power plant. You need to hire responsible people to run the plant—people who have the right stuff to handle potentially dangerous materials in an emergency. You wouldn't want to hire someone like Karla, with her tendency toward dishonesty. Or even the forgetful Homer Simpson.

But how do you make the proper determination for a given individual? The three modes of measurement mentioned earlier (self-report, observer-rating, behaviour) have led to a wide variety of assessment devices. The trait taxonomies detailed above (e.g., the Big Five factors) were developed primarily from questionnaires. Observer versions of these measures are often the same as the self-report: You are asked to answer the questions about someone else. Behaviours can usually be scored objectively (e.g., counted or measured) but are time-consuming and otherwise difficult to collect.

Of these three modes of measurement, we can discuss only *self-report questionnaires* in detail. We will also discuss two methods that go beyond the three standard modes, namely *projective tests* and *indirect methods*.

Self-Report Questionnaires Sometimes the best way to learn what people are like is to ask them. The questions can be developed and asked by an interviewer or a computer, but are usually posed on a standardized questionnaire. On the latter, responses are scored objectively, and the results are then compared to test averages that have been compiled from the performances of thousands of other test takers. The major advantage of **self-report questionnaires** is their ease of administration: Hundreds of responses can be collected from thousands of people in a short period of time. They paint a reliable picture of how someone differs from the average. Karla's answers, for instance, would probably raise red flags on a number of measures; her answers are likely to show some disdain for others (compared to the average) and a marked tendency toward impulsiveness. If you were the personnel director, you could easily make your hiring decision (presumably "no hire") based on the test results.

Many kinds of self-report questionnaires are employed by professionals. Some tests are based on popular trait theories. For example, to assess normal personality traits you can administer the **16 Personality Factor (16 P-F),** which is a 187-item questionnaire designed to measure the 16 primary personality factors identified by Cattell (Cattell et al., 1970). Alternatively, there is the **NEO-PI-R,** which was designed by Costa and McCrae (1989) to measure the Big Five personality traits identified in Figure 12.2. For clinical purposes, the most widely used self-report inventory is the **Minnesota Multiphasic Personality Inventory (MMPI).** The MMPI requires test takers to answer hundreds of true–false questions about themselves (e.g., "I never get angry"), and it's now available in several revised forms (see Butcher, 1995). An individual's answers are expressed in a personality profile that describes his or her scores on various subscales (see Figure 12.4). Note that all of these self-report questionnaires have been validated by showing significant correlations with alternative measures such as peer-reports and behavioural measurement.

The main advantage of self-report questionnaires is their efficiency. Large numbers of individuals can be scored quickly with objective scoring keys—they're standardized, everyone takes the same test, and they can easily be scored by a computer. This efficiency of questionnaires facilitates research so that hundreds of studies have

self-report questionnaires
Personality tests that ask sets of questions about how the respondent typically thinks, acts, or feels; his or her responses, or self-reports, are then compared to average responses compiled from large groups of prior test takers.

16 Personality Factor (16 P-F)
A self-report inventory developed by Cattell and colleagues to measure 16 primary personality factors.

NEO-PI-R
A self-report inventory developed to measure the Big Five personality dimensions.

Minnesota Multiphasic Personality Inventory (MMPI)
A widely used self-report inventory for assessing personality traits and for diagnosing psychological problems.

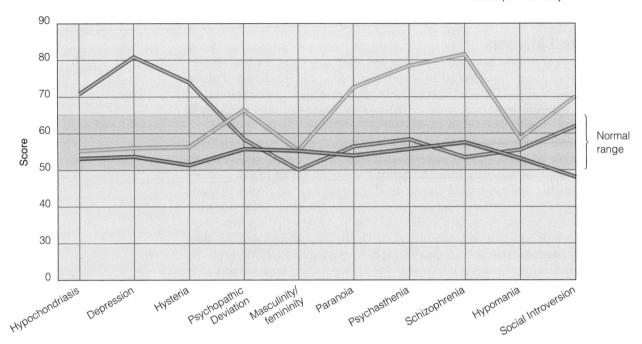

FIGURE 12.4
MMPI Profiles

The MMPI is often used to help psychologists diagnose psychological disorders. A client's scores on the various clinical scales can be compared to average scores from people who are not suffering from psychological problems as well as from people who have been diagnosed with specific problems (such as depression or schizophrenia). (Adapted from Weiten, 1995.)

been conducted on the reliability and validity of the major instruments, especially the MMPI (Butcher & Rouse, 1996; Helmes & Reddon, 1993). At the same time, self-report questionnaires depend on the accuracy of the information provided by the test taker. If people choose to be deceptive on the test or try to make themselves look good in some way, the results can be of limited usefulness (Nichols & Greene, 1997).

Assumptions behind Self-Reports A number of Canadian researchers have either developed or evaluated scales to assess many important personality constructs. These include Ron Norton's work at the University of Winnipeg on social anxiety or shyness (Norton et al., 1997), Ken Cramer's work at the University of Windsor on loneliness and self-concealment (Cramer & Barry, 1999a, 1999b), Gordon Flett's work at York University on perfectionism (Flett, Hewitt, Blankstein, & Gray, 1998; Flett, Hewitt, Blankstein, & Pickering, 1998), Gerald Wilde's work at Queen's University on risk taking (Wilde, 1994), and Donald Saklofske and Peter Greenspoon's work at the University of Saskatchewan on student life satisfaction (Greenspoon & Saklofske, 1998; Saklofske & Greenspoon, 2000). In fact, personality scale construction and evaluation may become easier following an important finding from University of Calgary researchers Karen Pasveer and John Ellard (1998). They found that scale data can be collected on the World Wide Web with the same reliability as when collected traditionally in a classroom or in person; however, these Internet samples tend to be larger and more diverse.

Of course, a researcher using self-report questionnaires typically makes a series of assumptions about the validity of such data. Suppose you asked two friends to fill out a loneliness scale. You hope not only that their answers are honest, but also that they have enough insight to accurately evaluate their own loneliness. Your own knowledge of your friends might make you doubt the accuracy of their questionnaire answers. Given that psychologists often study very sensitive personality variables such as loneliness, depression, authoritarianism, and sexual tendencies, they have devoted considerable energy to evaluating such distortions. For example, questionnaire responses are usually screened for **socially desirable responding,** that is, the tendency of some

socially desirable responding
The tendency to describe oneself as having positive, or at least normal, traits.

people to describe themselves as having positive, or at least normal, traits. Therefore, personality inventories often include extra items that are desirable but very unlikely to be true (e.g., "I have never stolen anything" or "I have no prejudices"). Initial research in this area began decades ago with work by the University of Waterloo's Douglas Crowne (Crowne & Marlowe, 1964) and Western University's Douglas Jackson. More recently, the University of British Columbia's Paulhus and Reid (1991) made the distinction between two forms of desirable responding: One is conscious and based on purposeful distortion (known as *impression management*) and the other is based on an unconscious bias (known as *self-deception*).

For example, University of Saskatchewan researchers Ken Cramer and Kim Neyedley (1998) investigated whether males' and females' reports of their loneliness were influenced by the negative social stigma associated with our perceptions of the lonely individual. Over 250 respondents completed one scale that measured how lonely they felt and another that measured how masculine they felt. The researchers originally found no sex differences in loneliness but after adjusting the data for the fact that males scored higher on masculinity, the results suggested that males were significantly lonelier than females. It seemed that males were not honest about their feelings of loneliness: Their masculinity forced them to deny that they were lonely. Note that this form of "dishonesty" is more likely to involve self-deception than impression management. To avoid such problems, most modern personality scales are evaluated for possible contamination with either form of desirable responding.

Projective Tests

Based on the theories of Sigmund Freud (whom we'll discuss shortly), psychologists sometimes use what are called projective personality tests. In a **projective test,** you're asked to interpret an unstructured or ambiguous stimulus. The underlying idea is that you will "project" your thoughts and true feelings into the stimulus interpretation, thereby revealing elements of your personality. For example, take a look at the inkblot shown in Figure 12.5, which is similar to the kind of unstructured stimulus used on the **Rorschach test.** Can you see how someone's interpretation of such a stimulus might provide insight into aspects of his or her personality? If Karla always sees snakes and dragons in the images, whereas Sarah sees butterflies and flowers, it's not too difficult to infer that they have quite different personality characteristics.

Another popular projective test is the **Thematic Apperception Test (TAT)**. Instead of an inkblot, you're shown an ambiguous picture, such as the one on the following page. You are asked to make up a story about the picture that explains what is happening. Again, the idea is that you will reveal aspects of yourself in the themes of your stories. Both the TAT and the Rorschach test use a standardized set of stimuli, so your responses can be compared to those of thousands of other people who have interpreted the same picture. Many clinical psychologists prefer to use tests like the TAT or the Rorschach, rather than self-report inventories like the MMPI, because projective tests are revealing without being threatening. After all, you are just making up stories about pictures!

But this method requires much interpretation: How do we know what your responses mean? Psychologists have tried to develop reliable standards for interpreting responses in these kinds of tests. Typically, the researcher or clinician is trained to look for common themes in interpretation (such as a tendency to see sex, death, or aggressiveness) or for qualities such as originality (Edberg, 1990; Hurt et al., 1995). The clinician might also look for such things as the realistic nature of the interpretation: Does the response really match the perceptual structure of the stimulus? If you claim to see a dragon in an inkblot like the one in Figure 12.5, your general view of the world may slant toward fantasy rather than reality. The degree to which you seek help in your interpretation may also be instructive. For example, individuals who constantly seek guidance from the clinician before giving an answer are likely to be classified as dependent.

FIGURE 12.5
Projective Tests

In projective tests, we are asked to interpret unstructured or ambiguous stimuli. Our answers are presumed to provide insight into our personalities. What do you see hidden in this inkblot? Is it an angel longing to return to the Garden of Eden—or just a dissected frog? (From Kalat, 1996.)

projective test
A type of personality test in which individuals are asked to interpret unstructured or ambiguous stimuli; the idea is that subjects will project their true thoughts and feelings into the interpretation, thereby revealing elements of their personality.

Rorschach test
A projective test that requires people to interpret ambiguous inkblots.

Thematic Apperception Test (TAT)
A projective personality test that requires people to make up stories about the characters in ambiguous pictures.

Critical Thinking

Do you think there is any connection between the interpretation of projective tests and the interpretation of dreams? Do you think we could use dream interpretation as a way of discovering someone's true personality?

This image, taken from the Thematic Apperception Test, can be interpreted in many ways. What do you think the characters in the picture are thinking and feeling? Your answers may reveal something about your personality. Henry A. Murray, *Thematic Apperception Test,* Cambridge, MA: Harvard University Press, Copyright © 1943 by the President and Fellows of Harvard College, © 1971 by Henry A. Murray.

Even more than the self-report approach, projective tests have been critiqued. The scoring procedures for projective tests still tend to be somewhat unreliable. The same person's answers change from session to session and it's not uncommon for administrators to arrive at quite different interpretations of the same subject's responses (see Beutler & Berren, 1995). Questions about the validity of the interpretations have also been raised (Lilienfeld et al., 2000).

Even with these criticisms, however, projective tests remain extremely popular (Butcher & Rouse, 1996). Some major researchers continue to hold that projective tests are the only valid way to capture such tendencies as power motivation (Winter et al., 1998) and uncertainty motivation (Sorrentino & Roney, 2000).

Indirect Methods To avoid the problems of projective testing and as an alternative to self-report inventories, a number of other indirect methods have been developed. Sampo Paunonen and colleagues at the University of Western Ontario have devised a unique form of nonverbal personality assessment (Paunonen et al., 1990; Paunonen et al., 2000). In this nonverbal assessment method, the items are drawings of a figure performing trait-relevant behaviours in specific situations, like getting angry over a missed tennis volley or returning a lost hat to a stranger (see Figure 12.6). Respondents rate the likelihood that they themselves would engage in similar behaviours. These researchers found that the nonverbal personality scales have compared favourably in reliability and validity to the standard verbal scales, even when administered to diverse samples of university undergraduates from Canada, England, the Netherlands, Finland, Norway, and Israel. In fact, the factor structure of the nonverbal scales is very similar to the familiar Big Five factor model found in more conventional personality assessments. This approach has some advantages in cross-cultural applications and in the assessment of illiterate populations, non-native language groups, dyslexic individuals, young children, and some psychiatric patients with attention problems.

A variety of other indirect methods have recently been developed, including those based on posture, facial photographs, and even Web sites. One novel approach—room analysis—is detailed in the Practical Solutions box on page 481.

FIGURE 12.6
Nonverbal Personality Assessment

In nonverbal personality assessments, respondents are shown line drawings and asked to rate the likelihood that they would act similarly themselves. Panel (a) is meant to portray aggressive behaviour, and (b) portrays thrill-seeking behaviour. (From Paunonen et al., 1990.)

Test Yourself 12.1

Check your knowledge about conceptualizing and measuring personality by answering the following questions. (You will find the answers in Appendix B.)

1. For each of the following, identify the personality dimension of the Big Five that the statement best describes. Choose from the following terms: extraversion; agreeableness; conscientiousness; neuroticism; openness.

   a. Jack is known as a risk taker; he just loves to bungee jump:

   _____

   b. It's difficult to get Mimi to stop talking: _____

   c. Lindsay is very cooperative; she's virtually always sympathetic to my needs: _____

   d. Mark is very insecure; he always seems to feel guilty about something: _____

   e. Elena is very productive and has very high ethical standards:

   _____

2. For each of the following, pick the personality test that the statement best describes. Choose from the following: MMPI; NEO-PI-R; 16 Personality Factor; Rorschach; TAT.

   a. An ambiguous picture is shown and the client is asked to make up a story about its contents: _____

   b. An objective self-report inventory that is often used in clinical settings: _____

c. A test used primarily to measure someone's standing on the Big Five:
_____

d. A projective personality test using standardized inkblots as stimuli:
_____

e. Designed to create a trait profile representing Cattell's source traits: _____

DETERMINING HOW PERSONALITY DEVELOPS

Learning Goals

1. Be able to explain Freud's psychodynamic theory of personality and mind.
2. Understand and evaluate humanistic approaches to personality, including the specific proposals of Carl Rogers and Abraham Maslow.
3. Assess cognitive–behavioural theories of personality, and understand how cognitions and the environment interact to produce behaviour.

AS YOU'VE JUST SEEN, we can describe the personality traits of people like Karla or Sarah—perhaps by their standing on the Big Five—and there is a good chance that our measurements will be reasonably accurate and reliable. But description is not the same thing as explanation. We may know that Sarah has a bright and sunny disposition, but the trait theories provide little insight into the origin of those characteristics. Why do Karla and Sarah differ? What mechanisms in the mind produce and maintain those differences?

In this section we'll consider three quite different approaches to understanding personality development: the psychodynamic theory of Sigmund Freud, humanistic theories, and cognitive–behavioural theories. Each claims that individual uniqueness comes from the operation of general psychological principles. We're not unique or consistent in our behaviour by accident or chance; rather, there are processes at work inside our heads, or in the external environment, that shape and mould our predispositions. In each case, personality is a product of general adaptive processes that help initiate and control behaviour in widely different situations.

The Psychodynamic Approach of Freud

Consider the following scenario. You're a practising clinician and your latest patient, 18-year-old Katarina, complains of persistent physical problems. "I'm often overcome with a frightful choking feeling," she insists. "I have trouble catching my breath, my head begins to spin, and I truly think I must be about to die." Extensive examinations reveal no physical cause and the attacks appear suddenly without warning. Katarina herself provides no insight: "There's nothing in my head when the attacks begin; my mind is a blank." The only additional information you have about Katarina is that she makes a face when the idea of sex is mentioned and she has a persistent dream in which a young child is pursued from room to room by a shadowy figure.

Long before the advent of modern psychology, this sort of clinical case intrigued Sigmund Freud (1856–1939). As you learned in Chapter 1, Freud began as a medical doctor in Vienna, where he dealt with a wide variety of patients. But he was particularly intrigued by patients like Katarina, who reported serious physical symptoms without any discernable physical cause. Explaining such cases seemed to require an entirely new way of thinking. The idea that traumatic life events might be manifested in physical symptoms was the basis for Freud's **psychodynamic theory** of personality, as well as for his method of treatment known as *psychoanalysis*. The theory gradually grew into an extremely complex set of ideas that tried to explain every aspect of

A young Sigmund Freud is shown here in 1891, at a time when he was becoming increasingly convinced that certain physical problems may have psychological origins.

psychodynamic theory

An approach to personality development, based largely on the ideas of Sigmund Freud, which holds that much of behaviour is governed by unconscious forces.

Practical Solutions

DOES YOUR ROOM GIVE AWAY YOUR PERSONALITY?

Does your room give away your personality? Research by Sam Gosling and colleagues investigated this possibility with both college residence rooms and workplace offices (Gosling et al., 2002). They hypothesized that the environments people create around themselves are rich with information about the occupants' personalities. It seems likely, for example, that the pictures a student selects to hang on the walls and the books on the shelf both reflect aspects of his or her personality. One's office could be equally revealing. The way that office furniture is arranged and the items on the worker's desk are likely to reveal some aspect of the occupant's personality.

To conduct a systematic investigation, Gosling arranged for a team of raters to examine the residence rooms of 83 college students and judge their personalities. The raters had no direct contact with the occupants and had to base their judgments solely on the qualities of the room. As a criterion for accuracy, Gosling collected personality ratings of the 83 students from their close friends.

Of course, to get the most accurate information on a student's room, it would have been better to sneak into the rooms without warning. Such a practice would be unethical, however, so the researchers obtained the consent of the students to examine their rooms while they were away. Their roommates reported that the students in the study tidied up a little more than usual for a few days but eventually went back to their typical room habits.

Results showed that the raters were quite confident of all their personality judgments and they agreed with each other. But they were accurate only on a few of the Big Five personality dimensions. They were accurate on judging the occupant's conscientiousness and openness to experience. A valuable cue for the former was the general state of neatness and organization evident in the room. A valuable cue for the latter was the type of books on the shelf. If the books were creative, intellectual, or politically radical, then the individual was judged accurately as higher in openness. Take a look at room photos A and B. Which one is higher in conscientiousness? Which one is higher in openness to experience? (After you guess, see the answer below.)

A parallel investigation of 94 offices and their residents yielded a similar pattern of results, although somewhat weaker. There are several reasons why students' personal living spaces may have provided unusual insight into the minds of their occupants. First, college is a time when individuals are negotiating identity issues, so students may be particularly prone to self-expression. Second, people generally have the freedom to decorate their personal living spaces as they please, but office decor is often restricted by company guidelines. Third, individuals in offices, both voluntarily and because of extrinsic pressure and norms, are typically concerned about the positive and professional image they project. As a result, they may be pressured to arrange and decorate their offices in ways that are contrary to their actual preferences and personalities. Fourth, the observers in both studies were students themselves and perhaps were relatively well versed in the cultural meaning of the possessions and icons found in student living spaces but less so in the meanings of cues in office spaces. Fifth, the rooms in the study of residences were often multipurpose spaces where the occupants spent a great deal of their time, using them for a variety of activities such as working, sleeping, relaxing, and entertaining. Thus the personal living spaces in the study of residence rooms may have been informationally richer environments than the office spaces were.

Gosling's room research is only part of a growing **personality profiling** approach based on the notion that people can be judged by their behavioural residue. People can be judged by the music they listen to (Rentfrow & Gosling, in press), the pets they choose (Coren, 2000), the food they eat (Goldberg & Stycker, 2002), and even their Web sites (Vazire & Gosling, 2003). The most important application to date is criminal profiling: Here details about the perpetrator of a crime are assembled to create a character sketch (Kocsis et al., 2002). The hypothesized character is then used to make predictions about the perpetrator's habits, which could then be used to make an arrest.

(The answer to the room question above is high conscientiousness and low openness for Room A, and vice-versa for Room B.)

personality profiling
Estimating the personality makeup of an individual based on indirect evidence, such as his or her eating habits, room arrangement, and so on.

Residence Room A   Residence Room B
For a more detailed look, go to www.psych.ubc.ca/~dpaulhus/textbook/photos.

humanity. The great creative accomplishments of culture as well as the everyday slip-of-the-tongue all derive from the fascinating recesses of the human mind. Two prominent themes—sex and aggression—were said to play a leading role in all human emotions, thoughts, and behaviour.

The Structure of Mind Freud believed that the human mind was divided into three levels of awareness: the *conscious,* the *preconscious,* and the *unconscious.* The **conscious mind** consists of the contents of current awareness—those things that occupy the focus of your attention at the moment. As you read the words on this page and think about Freud's theory, you are using the processes of the conscious mind. The **preconscious mind** contains inactive but accessible thoughts and memories—those things that you could easily recall, if desired, but are simply not thinking about at the moment. If asked what you had for breakfast, you can summon the information from your preconscious into your conscious mind. Finally, the **unconscious mind** houses all the memories, urges, and conflicts that are beyond awareness.

To Freud, the important contents of the mind are not politics, the sports scores, or the Dow-Jones average, but deep conflicts related to sex and violence. These topics are at once the most alluring and the most disturbing aspects of life. And important psychological events involve the transfer of information among the different levels of awareness. For instance, picture your mother and father having sexual intercourse. Because you exist, your parents must have had sex, but the mental image is still disturbing to most people. The aversiveness of this idea (and others even worse than copulating parents) explains why we might be motivated to push some images out of consciousness. The actual experience of seeing this event as a child—the inexplicable noises and apparent suffering—creates a conflict that the child is motivated to forget.

Even from the depths of the unconscious mind, however, such conflicts continue to exert powerful and enduring influences on behaviour. Indeed, to Freud and subsequent psychoanalysts, the phenomenon of repressed conflicts is thought to be the primary reason for mental illness.

Given these assumptions, if you were Katarina's psychoanalyst, you would try to trace her panic attacks back to memories of sex or aggression recorded in her unconscious. Consider her repetitive dream of being chased through her house by a shadowy figure. She can remember the details of the dream—her appearance as a young child, perhaps the colour and shapes of the rooms—but her conscious memory of the dream is likely to be superficial and misleading. The parts of the dream that she remembers, its *manifest content,* are merely symbolic of the dream's true unconscious meaning, or *latent content.* As we discussed in Chapter 5, according to Freud, dreams represent a mental mechanism for wish fulfillment; dreams are simply one way that the mind attempts to gratify desires or deal with forbidden conflicts that are normally stored in the unconscious. In Katarina's case, the pursuing shadowy figure may well have arisen from a traumatic childhood experience—perhaps sexual abuse by a relative—or even from her own unconscious desire for a forbidden sexual experience. In his early years, Freud relied heavily on such dream interpretation as a technique for mapping out the contents of the unconscious mind. Dreams, Freud argued, represent a "royal road" to the unconscious (Freud, 1900/1990).

The Structure of Personality The two powerful instinctual drives—sex and aggression—are said to motivate and control much of our behaviour. Rather than revealing themselves in fixed traits, however, these two motives are played out in conflicts among the mind's three dynamic elements: the *id, ego,* and *superego* (see Figure 12.7). Freud used the term **id** to represent the portion of personality that seeks immediate satisfaction of innate urges, without concern for the morals and customs of society. It pursues immediate satisfaction of animalistic urges. A central aspect—the *life instinct*—is the desire to explore and enjoy life's pleasures, especially sex. It is this optimistic side of personality that promotes survival of our genes by motivating a desire for sexual con-

---

conscious mind

The contents of awareness—those things that occupy the focus of one's current attention.

preconscious mind

The part of the mind that contains all of the inactive but potentially accessible thoughts and memories.

unconscious mind

The part of the mind that Freud believed housed all the memories, urges, and conflicts that are truly beyond awareness.

Critical Thinking

How do the modern memory concepts of short-term and long-term memory relate to Freud's three-part theory of the mind?

id

In Freud's theory, the portion of personality that is governed by inborn instinctual drives, particularly those related to sex and aggression.

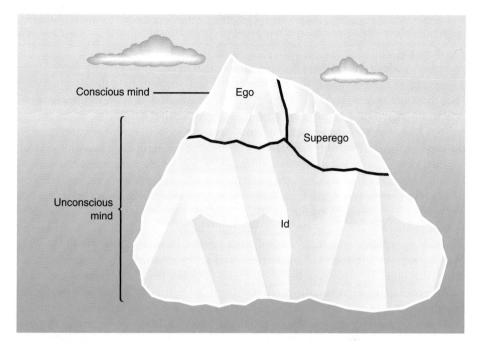

FIGURE 12.7
Freud's View of Personality
Freud believed that our personalities are influenced by three forces. The *id* is the unconscious and unrepentant seeker of pleasure; the *superego* is the moral critic of unacceptable behaviour; and the *ego* is the executive that acts in accordance with reality. Just as most of an iceberg lies beneath the water, much of personality operates at an unconscious level.

tact. A more morbid and bizarre aspect of the id, *the death instinct*, is required to explain suicide and other self-destructive human behaviour. All human societies throughout history have documented such negativistic behaviour. Another aspect of every human society—aggression toward others—was explained by Freud as an indirect display of the death instinct. In short, psychoanalysis specifically acknowledges the dark side of personality.

At the same time, Freud understood that human behaviour involves more than just sexual and aggressive instincts. The forces of the id are appropriately balanced by a moral arm of personality called the superego. The **superego** is the component of our personality that deters us from breaking the moral customs we learned from our parents and other conveyors of culture. The superego is acquired primarily from punishing experiences. But the details of these experiences are mostly forgotten and the superego exerts its influence as a conscience—a self-inflicted punishment mechanism that makes us feel ashamed and guilty when our behaviour strays from accepted standards. Like the id, the superego is essentially irrational—its only goal is to avoid sin. Left to its own devices, the superego would undercut or block satisfaction of the more basic urges, even though those urges benefit fundamental survival needs. In short, the superego follows a *moralistic principle:* Always act in a proper and decent fashion as defined by parents and culture.

Sitting between the forces of the id and superego, and acting as a mediator, is the third component of personality—the **ego.** This component serves a managerial role in Freud's conception of personality and resembles later theories about a "self." The ego encourages you to act with reason and deliberation and helps you conform to the requirements of the external world. Freud suggested that the ego obeys a *reality principle* in that it monitors the real world looking for appropriate outlets for the id's needs. But, to avoid punishments such as guilt, the ego also considers the moralistic preachings of the superego. Its goal is compromise among three demanding masters: the external world, the id, and the superego.

Defence Mechanisms As just noted, Freud argued that we're unaware of most of the conflicts that occur among the id, ego, and superego. We consciously experience only the side effects of these battles. For example, Freud believed that the experience of *anxiety* (an unpleasant feeling of dread) often comes from confrontations between the id

superego
In Freud's theory, the portion of personality that motivates people to act in a proper fashion, that is, in accordance with the moral customs defined by parents and culture.

What are the adaptive qualities of the superego? What would happen to the human species if the superego always controlled behaviour?

ego
In Freud's theory, the portion of personality that induces people to act with reason and deliberation and helps them conform to the requirements of the external world.

defence mechanisms
According to Freud, unconscious processes used by the ego to ward off the anxiety that comes from conflicts between the superego and the id.

denial
A defence mechanism involving the refusal to accept an external reality that creates anxiety.

repression
A defence mechanism used to bury anxiety-producing thoughts and feelings in the unconscious.

projection
A defence mechanism in which unacceptable feelings or wishes are dealt with by attributing them to others.

reaction formation
A defence mechanism used to transform an anxiety-producing wish into a kind of opposite—people behave in a way that counters the way they truly feel.

sublimation
A defence mechanism used to channel unacceptable impulses into socially acceptable activities.

Freud believed that people sometimes deal with unacceptable feelings by attributing them to others through a process called *projection*. Freud might argue that the woman on the left is "projecting" anger from some deeper conflict onto the man on the right. Through *sublimation*, unacceptable impulses, such as a desire to hurt others, are channelled into socially acceptable activities.

and superego. To regain control, the ego must often resort to its most powerful weapon—the ability to alter reality. This task is accomplished with a variety of **defence mechanisms,** which are unconscious processes designed to ward off anxiety.

Most crude of the defences is **denial,** the refusal to accept an external fact because it causes anxiety. It is usually the first reaction when people receive devastating news: "No, that's not true. I can't have cancer." The most powerful weapon in the arsenal of defences is **repression,** a process that actively keeps anxiety-producing thoughts and feelings buried in the unconscious. When a primitive urge from the id conflicts with the superego, the ego actively represses the thought or feeling. The urge is blocked out, jammed down into the dark recesses of the unconscious. Because they are the most common sources of conflict, we are particularly likely to repress sexual or aggressive thoughts or experiences. Unrestricted sexual activity is typically discouraged by parents and society and eventually by our own superego. So sexual thoughts and feelings need to be actively blocked by the reality-driven ego. The type of aggression most likely to cause id–ego conflict is hostility toward one's parents. In contrast, we would probably have few repressed thoughts or memories about eating or drinking, although both are instinctual urges, because these behaviours tend to violate few, if any, societal norms.

Repression is a kind of self-deception—the mind deals with the anxiety-producing impulse by acting as if it isn't there. Different kinds of self-deception occur with the other defence mechanisms that Freud proposed (Sackeim, 1983). For example, through a process called **projection,** you deal with unacceptable feelings or wishes by attributing them to others. A person harbouring strong sexual feelings toward a married neighbour—an impulse likely to cause considerable guilt—might project his or her feelings onto the neighbour: "That woman keeps trying to turn me on—just like all the women at work!" **Reaction formation** occurs when you transform an anxiety-producing wish into a kind of opposite—you actually behave in a way that counters the way you truly feel. For example, a mother who secretly resents the birth of her daughter and unconsciously wishes her to die might smother the child with exaggerated care and affection. The unconscious anti-Semite, who wishes the degradation of all Jews, might become an active and tireless volunteer for organizations championing Jewish causes. Notice that, in each of these cases, the unconscious conflict receives attention, but the attention is disguised in a self-deceptive way.

Note again that the point of the self-deception is to reduce the conscious experience of anxiety. Defence mechanisms allow the ego to deal indirectly with unacceptable psychological thoughts and feelings. Suppose you are an extremely aggressive person who unconsciously would love to hurt others. According to Freud, you might use the defence mechanism of **sublimation,** in which unacceptable impulses are channelled into socially acceptable activity, to deal with the potential anxiety. Perhaps you would pursue a career in professional hockey or even the local police force. Here, the aggressive impulse would be satisfied, but in an indirect and socially acceptable manner.

Similarly, a strong sex drive could be channelled into sensual creative activities such as sculpting figures or even composing symphonies. To Freud, the great artistic accomplishments of human culture are actually a side effect of sublimation.

The idea of defence mechanisms has strongly influenced subsequent psychological research, although psychodynamic labels are often used. Consider the current debate over the consequences of positive illusions. Some researchers have argued that positive illusions about oneself can be beneficial to one's mental health (Taylor & Brown, 1988). The tendency to err on the positive side when evaluating oneself could explain why some people are more optimistic about life and seem to bounce back from failure when others seem paralyzed. Two questionnaires have been developed to measure the tendency of individuals to have positive illusions about themselves. One is a measure of self-deception (Paulhus & Reid, 1991); the other is a measure of narcissism (John & Robins, 1994; Morf & Rhodewalt, 2001). Although they sound different, they both seem to measure people's tendency to exaggerate their positive qualities (Paulhus, 1998).

The research with these new questionnaires has shown that positive illusions are, at best, a mixed blessing. In one study at the University of Manitoba, Edward Johnson, Norah Vincent, and Leah Ross (1997) investigated whether self-deception helps or hurts task performance after failure. Results showed that self-deceivers felt good about themselves but performed poorly on a task that was preceded by a failure experience. It would appear that individuals who have to self-deceive to feel good about themselves after a failure experience are also too distracted to perform well on the next task. A different sort of tradeoff was demonstrated in studies conducted at the University of British Columbia. Delroy Paulhus (1998) arranged for members of discussion groups to rate each other's behaviour over a period of seven meetings. Group members enjoyed the self-deceivers at the first meeting but, after seven weeks, hated them. The results of both of these studies are consistent with Freud's idea that defence mechanisms have advantages and disadvantages.

Psychosexual Development   To Freud, the unconscious mind is a bubbling cauldron of hidden conflicts, repressed memories, and biological urges. In the case of the biological urges, their origin is relatively clear—people are born with instinctual drives for self-preservation and sex. But where do the other conflicts come from? Freud argued that conflicts are almost inevitable as children pass through a series of stages of psychosexual development (Freud, 1905/1962). How children deal with their emerging sexuality importantly affects the way they feel about their family and their other relationships when they reach adulthood.

Each developmental stage is associated with a particular region of pleasure, which Freud called an *erogenous zone*. In the first year or so of life—during the **oral stage**—pleasure is derived primarily from sucking and from placing things in the mouth (such as the mother's breast). The adaptive significance of this first stage is clear—gaining pleasure through sucking or crying for milk or warmth increases the probability that you will get the nourishment and care you need for survival. In the second year of life, the focus of pleasure shifts to the anus. During this **anal stage,** pleasure arises from the process of defecation, the passing of feces, and also marks greater self-control and more autonomous activity of the ego. From ages 3 through 5, in the **phallic stage,** the genital regions of the body receive the focus of attention. The child notices the pleasure obtained from stimulation of the sexual organs. A sense of relationships is also developing, and the emerging sexuality is naturally associated with the currently most prominent individuals—the parents, of course.

Freud argued that we move through these stages for primarily biological reasons. All organisms, including humans, need to learn how to gain nourishment, control the elimination of waste, and satisfy the sexual drive. Unfortunately, it's possible to become stalled, or fixated, at a particular stage, which, in turn, can have important and long-lasting effects on personality. By *fixation*, Freud meant that a person will continue to act in ways that are appropriate for a particular stage, seeking pleasure in

oral stage
The first stage in Freud's conception of psychosexual development, occurring in the first year of life; in this stage, pleasure is derived primarily from sucking and placing things in the mouth.

anal stage
Freud's second stage of psychosexual development, occurring in the second year of life; pleasure is derived from the process of defecation.

phallic stage
Freud's third stage of psychosexual development, lasting from about age 3 to age 5; pleasure is gained from self-stimulation of the sexual organs.

Freud believed that people can become "fixated" at a particular psychosexual stage if activities associated with that stage, such as toilet training during the anal stage, are particularly traumatic or frustrating.

Critical Thinking

Most people deny that they've ever had sexual feelings toward their parents. If you were Freud, how would you explain these denials?

latency period
Freud's period of psychosexual development, from age 5 to puberty, during which the child's sexual feelings are largely suppressed.

genital stage
Freud's final stage of psychosexual development, during which one develops mature sexual relationships with members of the opposite sex.

stage-dependent ways, even after he or she has physically matured. Fixations result from traumatic events, often excessive parental punishment, during a particular stage.

Notice that the oral and anal stages are associated with the potentially traumatic experiences of weaning and toilet training. Freud emphasized these experiences because a child can become easily frustrated during either event. People who are fixated in the oral stage, Freud believed, continue to derive excessive pleasure from oral activities in adulthood. They become smokers or constant eaters, or bite their nails, or chew on pencils. (By the way, are you doing any of these at the moment?) Fixation at the anal stage can lead to either excessive neatness or excessive messiness. The pleasure-seeking activities in these instances are symbolic, of course; compulsive room cleaning might be a symbolic attempt at the gratification a child sometimes receives from the retention of feces. Phallic fixations involve overvaluing the male organ, which translates into narcissism in men and aggressiveness in women. This sampling of Freud's ideas makes it clear that adult personality can be traced back to events that occurred during the first few years of childhood.

Freud's interpretation of the events that surround the phallic stage of psychosexual development remain particularly controversial. He was convinced that small children have intense but unconscious sexual urges that become focused on the parents during this stage. For example, boys become erotically attracted to their mother, a condition Freud called the *Oedipus complex* (after the Greek tragedy of Oedipus, who unknowingly killed his father and married his mother); girls identify with their father in what has been called (but not by Freud) the *Electra complex* (after the mythical Greek Electra, who hated and conspired to murder her mother). Desire for the opposite-sex parent creates enormous unconscious conflicts in the developing child. Freud believed that many adult sexual or relationship problems can be traced back to a failure to resolve these conflicts adequately. Needless to say, the idea of childhood sexuality was considered outrageous in his time, and still remains offensive to most people.

One prediction from Freudian theory is that parent–child conflict should be greater between same-sex combinations (i.e., father–son, mother–daughter) than opposite-sex combinations. This prediction was evaluated by McMaster University researchers Martin Daly and Margo Wilson (1990) in a study looking at same-sex and opposite-sex family homicides. No difference in homicide rates was found. This pattern is consistent with evolutionary theory (see Chapter 10), but fails to support Freudian theory. This one study may not convince those of you who are currently having trouble with your same-sex parent.

After the age of 5 or 6, boys and girls enter a kind of psychosexual lull—called the **latency period**—during which their sexual feelings are largely suppressed. During this period children direct their attention to social concerns, such as developing solid friendships. Finally, beginning with the onset of puberty, one enters the **genital stage.** Here, sexuality reawakens, but in what Freud considered to be a more mature and appropriate fashion. Erotic tendencies now tend to be directed toward members of the opposite sex outside of the family.

The Neo-Freudians: Adler, Jung, and Horney A number of Freud's early disciples became famous in their own right because they extended Freud's theory or disagreed with part of it. One of the first to split from Freud's inner circle was Alfred Adler (1870–1937). Adler strongly disagreed with Freud about the role of early psychosexual experience. Rather than sexual gratification, he believed that it is our natural drive for superiority that explains human motivation (Adler, 1927). But because we grow up with older people, we struggle to compensate for our relative inadequacy: Some never do and their later personalities are centred around an *inferiority complex*. Adler also hypothesized another source of motivation, social interest. This is the desire to help society rather than just ourselves. He was also the first to speculate about the role of birth order in personality development (see Chapter 10).

Adler was not the only dissenting voice. One of the biggest personal blows to Freud was the departure of his disciple Carl Jung (1875–1961), whom Freud had picked as his intellectual heir. Jung, like Adler, was dissatisfied with Freud's narrow reliance on sexuality as the dominant source of human motivation. Jung believed instead in the idea of a "general life force," which he adopted from his extensive study of Eastern religions and mythology. This general life force was sexual in part but included other basic sources of motivation as well, such as the need for creativity (Jung, 1923).

Among Jung's more influential ideas was his concept of the **collective unconscious.** Jung believed that people have a shared unconscious, in addition to the personal unconscious described by Freud. This shared portion is filled with mystical symbols and universal images that have accumulated over the lifetime of the human species. These symbols are inherited—passed genetically from one generation to the next—and tend to represent enduring concepts (or *archetypes*), such as God, evil, Mother, hero, wise old man, earth, and water. Actually, the idea that all humans share certain concepts (like fear of the dark) buried deep in a collective unconscious can also be found in the writings of Freud, but Jung expanded on the idea and assigned it a central focus.

Jung was a charismatic figure whose ideas continue to attract followers. His version of psychodynamic psychology was a predecessor to humanistic psychology (which we'll discuss shortly) and continues to have an almost cultlike following. In fact, most major Western cities still have a Jungian society for advocates to meet regularly.

Another historic blow to Freud was the dissenting voice of Karen Horney (pronounced HORN-eye). She was one of the first women to learn and practise psychodynamic theory. Horney (1885–1952) agreed with Freud's basic approach, but she rebelled against what she felt was Freud's male-dominated view of sexuality. Freud had argued in his writings that women are fundamentally dissatisfied with their gender— they suffer from what he called *penis envy*—a view that Horney found unsatisfactory in many ways. She boldly confronted Freud, both personally and in her writings, and offered revised forms of psychodynamic theory that treated women in a more balanced way (Horney, 1967). One of her more lasting theoretical contributions was her insistence that a link exists between the irrational beliefs people hold about themselves and their psychological problems (Horney, 1945). As you'll see in Chapters 14 and 15, this idea continues to be influential in the conceptualization and treatment of psychological disorders.

Carl Jung believed that all people share a collective unconscious filled with mystical symbols and universal images.

collective unconscious
The notion proposed by Carl Jung that certain kinds of universal symbols and ideas are present in the unconscious of all people.

Evaluating Psychodynamic Theory No psychological theory has been as influential as Freud's. Many of the terms and concepts he introduced—particularly his ideas about the unconscious and defence mechanisms—have become part of modern language and have now been accepted by all psychologists. You were probably familiar with such Freudian terms as *repression, ego,* and *denial* before you opened this psychology text. Moreover, the suggestion that personality is determined in part by how we learn to satisfy basic biological drives, as well as deal with traumatic childhood events, is now undisputed (Buss, 1991; Revelle, 1995). But psychodynamic theory, as envisioned by Freud, has been steadily losing its influence over the past several decades for several reasons.

Part of the problem is that many of the ideas that Freud proposed lack scientific rigour. He never articulated concepts such as the id, superego, and ego with precision. Moreover, he changed his mind on many issues over his 40 years of writing about psychology. As a result, it's been difficult, if not impossible, to subject the ideas to proper scientific testing. Consider the concept of repression, which Freud believed to be the bedrock of psychodynamic theory. If repressed memories are hidden behind the veil of the unconscious, expressing themselves only in masked and largely symbolic ways, can we ever be certain that we have correctly identified and interpreted the source and content of these unconscious influences? Patients of psychoanalysts can feel frustrated when their therapist scolds them: "Well of course, you deny that you're acting defensive. It's all unconscious."

Karen Horney rebelled against what she felt was Freud's male-dominated view of sexuality.

Debates about psychoanalysis often centre on the contradiction between clinical evidence and experimental evidence. Many practising therapists are certain that they regularly see defences like repression operating in their patients. But these are uncontrolled case studies of individuals who are not representative of the general population. In the laboratory, experimental psychologists have been unable to create repression (i.e., the forgetting of threatening events). The consistent finding in lab studies is that threatening events are remembered *better* than nonthreatening events (Loftus, 1993). Therapists reply that, of course, you can't simulate real repression in the lab; it would be unethical to create the severe level of trauma required to send someone into a repression episode.

Besides the problems of testability and lack of scientific rigour, Freud's theory is often criticized for its biases against women. There is no question that Freud viewed women as the weaker sex psychologically. As mentioned earlier, he painted women as unsatisfied with their gender, and more subject to neurosis. Women were even said to be morally inferior, partly because they don't have to overcome as many temptations as men do. Freud also argued that memories of sexual abuse were sometimes false. Instead, they could be a child's confused recollections of sexual feelings toward their parents. Even many modern psychologists consider these ideas to be offensive (Masson, 1984; Vitz, 1988).

But, to give Freud his due, no theory other than psychoanalysis ever postulated that children could forget traumatic events (such as sexual abuse) and yet suffer their negative consequences for the rest of their lives. And what other theory could begin to explain why teenage girls who repeatedly cut themselves almost invariably suffered sexual abuse in their childhood? Although many of Freud's speculations may have been off the mark, it is important to recognize that many modern views of childhood, unconscious processes, dreams, and even the sexual revolution stem in part from his pioneering work.

Humanistic Approaches to Personality

There is another reason why many psychologists simply don't like Freud's psychodynamic approach: They see it as a dark and dismal view of human nature. In particular, they don't like the idea that the mind's primary concerns are the animalistic urges related to sex and aggression. Nor do they like the idea that the unconscious is in charge of the bulk of our behaviour.

Humanistic psychology provides a more optimistic alternative to Freud's pessimistic view of the human spirit. Humanistic psychologists don't talk about battlefields and conflict; instead, they talk about growth and potential. It is not animalistic urges that are stressed in explaining personality; it is the human being's unparalleled capacity for self-awareness, choice, responsibility, and growth. Humanistic psychologists believe that each of us can control our own behavioural destiny—we can consciously rise above whatever animalistic urges might be coded in our genes. We're built and designed for personal growth, to seek our fullest potential, to self-actualize—to become all we are capable of becoming.

To a humanistic psychologist, every human being is considered to be naturally *unique*. People are more than the sum of a set of predictable parts—everyone is a unique and individual *whole*. However, the environment influences the natural growth process. Like plants, people will grow best in fertile and supportive environments; barren environments can't stop the growth process, but they can prevent us from realizing our own true potential (Rogers, 1963).

A central theme in humanistic psychology is the validity of subjective experience. How we act is determined by our unique view of the world—our interpretation of reality. Moreover, our personal view of ourselves and the environment is as genuine and valid as anyone else's view. Nonetheless, some people's subjective experience of reality is not very adaptive. Notice the emphasis is on conscious mental processes. We're assumed to be responsible for our own actions, and accepting this responsibility

humanistic psychology
An approach to personality that focuses on people's unique capacity for choice, responsibility, and growth.

is key to good adjustment. The ideas of two humanistic psychologists, Carl Rogers and Abraham Maslow, have been especially influential.

Carl Rogers and the Self

To Carl Rogers (1902–1987), the essence of personality lies in the concept of the self. He defined the **self-concept** as an organized set of perceptions about one's abilities and characteristics: It amounts to that keen sense of oneself, what it means to be "I" or "me." The self-concept comes primarily from social interactions, particularly the interactions we have with our parents, friends, and other significant role models throughout our lifetimes. The people around us mould and shape our self-image through their ongoing evaluations of our actions.

Rogers argued that we have a basic need for **positive regard.** We value what others think of us and constantly seek others' approval, love, and companionship. Unfortunately, in real life, **conditions of worth** tend to be attached to the level of approval we get from others. For instance, suppose that you come from a family that values education and intellectual pursuits. You, however, couldn't care less about such things—your interests are in popular music and athletics. To gain acceptance from your parents, you may well deny your true feelings and modify your self-concept to bring it more in line with what your parents believe: "I'm not someone who cares about a trivial activity like sports; I'm someone who cares intensely about the pursuit of knowledge."

Rogers called this condition **incongruence,** which he defined as a discrepancy between the image you hold of yourself—your self-concept—and the sum of all your experiences. Incongruence leads to the experience of anxiety and ultimately forms the basis for a variety of psychological problems. True psychological health, Rogers suggested, comes when the self-concept is *congruent* (agrees) with your true feelings and experiences, that is, when your opinions and beliefs about yourself accurately reflect your everyday experiences. The larger the discrepancy is, the greater your anxiety and the lower your self-esteem will be.

Undoubtedly, the greatest influence of Carl Rogers has been to turn psychologists' attention to the study of the self. The topic is now one of the major topics in both personality and social psychology and, in fact, creates a bridge between the two topics (Baumeister, 1997). The self has enduring features, to be sure, but it can also be affected by contextual features (Sorrentino & Higgins, 1996).

Modern laboratory techniques are now being used for teasing apart the complexities of this topic. In a series of studies at the University of Waterloo, Ziva Kunda and

self-concept
An organized set of perceptions that we hold about our abilities and characteristics.

positive regard
The idea that we value what others think of us and constantly seek others' approval, love, and companionship.

conditions of worth
The expectations or standards that we believe others place on us.

incongruence
A discrepancy between the image we hold of ourselves—our self-concept—and the sum of all our experiences.

Carl Rogers proposed that people have an ingrained need for positive regard—we value what others think of us and constantly seek their approval and companionship.

colleagues have shown how the self-concept can be manipulated by altering the value of different attributes. For example, if extraversion is made to sound valuable, participants reported higher levels of that trait (Kunda & Sanitioso, 1989). Even more dramatic was McGill University researcher Mark Baldwin's demonstration of how others' perceived approval affects the experience of self (Baldwin et al., 1990). Baldwin's research participants were graduate students who wrote down recent research ideas they had been working on. Participants were presented with subliminal images of either (a) an approving, smiling face or (b) a disapproving, scowling face (both faces were unfamiliar). The participants then evaluated the research ideas they had indicated earlier. Their ratings of their own research ideas tended to be higher immediately following a presentation of the approving face than following the disapproving face. This experiment demonstrated that self-evaluations can be influenced by very minimal exposures to positive and negative evaluative stimuli, which is in line with the humanistic belief that unconditional positive regard can foster self-esteem development.

With respect to personality and its development, Rogers believed that regularities in behaviour come largely from the structure of the self-concept. We tend to act consistently, Rogers argued, simply because our actions consistently mirror the self-concept we have established. We act in ways that support rather than contradict our beliefs about ourselves. More often than not, we will actively seek to protect our self-image. Given a choice, you might purposely choose to read philosophy rather than watch television because it's consistent with your vision of yourself. If you consistently choose television, at some point, you'll need to reconsider who you really are—exactly the sort of confrontation that people tend to avoid.

The Self in Flux   Although Rogers felt that there was only one "true self," the sense of self can be changed just by putting people in a different context. This effect was shown in simple studies where people were asked to fill out a "Who Am I" questionnaire in different situations. This measure simply asks people to report the most important aspects of who they are. When responding to the questionnaire in a room full of men, women are more likely to mention their gender than when they respond in a room with only 50% men. Similar effects are found for race (McGuire & McGuire, 1988).

A more dramatic claim is that each of us may have multiple internal selves (Kihlstrom & Cantor, 1984). No one would disagree that we act differently in different contexts. When we go home to visit our parents, we show a different set of behavioural reactions from those we show with our friends. Even our self-image changes. But these different selves seem to be triggered so quickly and effortlessly that they become automatic. These different senses of self have been labelled "self-schemas" (Markus, 1977). They are organized packages of information about ourselves. They help us interpret the present, reconstruct the past, and guide our actions.

People commonly adopt different roles, and employ unique "self-schemas," in the various situations of life.

Not surprisingly then, the self-concept can change upon immigration to another country. Canadian researchers have been at the forefront of addressing acculturation effects on the self-concept. Clarry Lay from York University investigated ethnic self-definition in a recent study comparing the level of self-esteem between Canadian-born and foreign-born Chinese adolescents (Lay & Verkuyten, 1999). Because of their greater breadth of experiences in Canada, Canadian-born Chinese adolescents may feel more accepted and less like minority group members compared to their foreign-born counterparts. Therefore Canadian-born Chinese adolescents should attend less to their ethnic origins. As predicted, results showed that foreign-born Chinese adolescents were more likely to label themselves "Chinese" (rather than "Chinese Canadian") and were more likely to make reference to their ethnicity in the "Who Am I" questionnaire.

Recognized as a major figure in cross-cultural psychology, John Berry at Queen's University developed a two-factor system for categorizing various strategies for acculturating to a new country (Berry, 1999). Immigrants can acquire the new culture to varying degrees, and they can lose the old culture to varying degrees. Most important, one change does not necessarily affect the other. Berry hypothesized that the best strategy for bolstering self-esteem was to acquire the new culture without losing the old. When tested on Asian immigrants at the University of British Columbia, Andrew Ryder and colleagues found only partial support for Berry's hypothesis. Acquiring the new culture did boost self-esteem, but retaining the old culture did not matter (Ryder et al., 2000).

The take-home message from all this work is that, despite its central importance to people's sense of well-being, the self seems quite sensitive to external influences. The notion of personality that follows from this view is obviously much more variable and flexible than trait psychology implies.

Abraham Maslow and Self-Actualization

Consistent with the humanistic approach, Abraham Maslow took a very positive perspective on psychology. At our core, he argued, we are all creative individuals yearning to fulfill our personal potential. This idea that everyone has a basic need for **self-actualization**—the need to move forward toward the realization of potential—has already been discussed in Chapter 11, under the topic of motivation. Recall Maslow's explanation that human motivation is grounded in the satisfaction of *need*. And higher-level needs can be addressed only when the lower-level needs have already been satisfied.

self-actualization
The ingrained desire to reach one's true potential as a human being.

Your personality characteristics will reflect where you are positioned in the *hierarchy of needs.* Maslow was convinced that all people are inherently good; a person may consistently act in an unkind, defensive, or aggressive manner, but these personality traits reflect a failure to satisfy basic needs—they will never be fundamental to the human spirit. To support this claim, Maslow pointed to the behaviour of individuals whom he felt had progressed through the entire hierarchy. The characteristics of human personality, he argued, are highly consistent across individuals at the highest levels of the hierarchy. People who are self-actualizing show none of the darker personality traits exhibited by those locked in at lower levels; they tend to be positive, creative, accepting individuals (Leclerc et al., 1998).

Maslow's conclusions were based largely on the study of particular individuals, people whom he knew and admired. He also noted the personality traits of individuals who had reached the pinnacle of success, such as Albert Einstein, Abraham Lincoln, and Mother Teresa. All self-actualizing people, he argued, share certain personality traits. They tend to be accepting of themselves and others, to be self-motivated and problem-oriented, and to have a strong ethical sense and hold democratic values. Self-actualizing people also often undergo what Maslow called *peak experiences*—emotional, often religious, experiences in which one's place in a unified universe becomes clear and meaningful. Notice that these are all quite positive traits; self-actualizing people tend to be at peace with themselves and with the world that surrounds them.

Evaluating Humanistic Theories The humanistic approach, with its optimistic emphasis on positive growth, has had considerable influence in psychology. Concepts such as the *self* are now receiving a great deal of attention among researchers and, as you'll see in Chapter 15, humanistic approaches to psychotherapy are popular and widely applied. The humanistic approach provides a welcome balance to the pessimism of Freud. Rather than ignoring the conscious influences on behaviour, humanists champion personal choice and responsibility. Take a trip to your local bookstore and check the shelves devoted to psychology—you'll find that many of the books emphasize the control *you* can exert over your own behaviour. This is one indication of the humanists' widespread impact, especially in tapping the general population's interest in psychology.

As contributors to scientific psychology, however, humanistic psychologists are often criticized (Funder, 2001). Many of the fundamental concepts we've discussed, such as the potential for growth and self-actualizing tendencies, are vague and difficult to pin down. It's also not clear where these tendencies come from and under which conditions they will fully express themselves. Remember too that the humanists place important emphasis on personal, subjective experience. This means that researchers must often rely on self-reports by individuals to generate data, and we cannot always be sure that these reports are reliable and accurate representations of internal psychological processes (Leclerc et al., 1998). So in addition to problems of conceptual vagueness, the approach lacks adequate testability.

The highlighting of the self in human motivation and cognition is reason enough to recognize the importance of the humanistic approach. Although it may be the most abstract of mental concepts, the self has become a key part of developmental psychology, social cognition (see Chapter 13), and other branches. Research on the self has become much more rigorous as the latest laboratory technology is applied to it. Given the central themes of humanistic psychology, these developments would not necessarily meet Carl Rogers's approval.

The humanistic approach to personality is also criticized for adopting too optimistic a view of human nature. In part, the arguments of humanists like Rogers and Maslow are reactions against the pessimism of Freud and the mechanical depiction of humans outlined by Skinner. Humanistic theorists may have gone too far in the other direction to adopt an extremely optimistic view of human nature: People are basically good, unless constrained in some way by social conditions of worth, and are driven to pursue lofty goals. And self-actualized people seem to be almost God-like in their perfection. Thus, we have the dark view described by Freud (people are all driven by unconscious animalistic urges) countered by the extremely optimistic views of the humanists.

Some humanistic psychologists believe that it's probably better to adopt a more balanced approach: People are neither inherently good nor evil; they sometimes act in self-interested ways that may appear animalistic, but these actions are often adaptive and increase one's likelihood of survival. At the same time, the message of humanistic psychology is that we can exercise considerable conscious control over both good and bad behaviour.

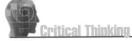

Critical Thinking

Think about how good it makes you feel to talk to a really close friend. From the perspective of humanistic theory, why should this be the case?

Cognitive–Behavioural Approaches to Personality

One particularly important characteristic of both the psychodynamic and humanistic approaches to personality is their emphasis on built-in determinants of behaviour. People are born with animalistic urges that must be satisfied, or they greet the world naturally good with a compelling need for personal growth.

But in Chapter 6, you learned about the power of conditioning. People may simply *learn* to act in consistent ways that differentiate them from others. Isn't it possible that Karla's nasty tendency to lie and Sarah's outgoing and sunny disposition come entirely from experience? Maybe Karla stole candy when she was 4 and was rewarded by not being caught; maybe Sarah learned at an early age that smiles are often met with smiles and that a good deed will be returned in kind. According to **cognitive–behavioural theories** of personality, human experience, not human nature, is the primary cause of personality growth and development. The *behavioural* side of the approach emphasizes the actual experiences delivered by the environment; the *cognitive* side emphasizes how interpretations and expectations about the events we experience play a significant role in determining what we learn.

cognitive–behavioural theories
An approach to personality that suggests it is reward–punishment experiences, and interpretations of those experiences, that determine personality growth and development.

Rewards and Punishments An exclusively behavioural approach to personality development would propose that it is the outside world alone that influences our actions. As we discussed in Chapter 1, behaviourists believe that psychologists should look to observable behaviour for answers to psychological questions; the research goal of most behaviourists is to understand how *observable* behaviour changes when rewards and punishments are applied. Personality, then, might really be nothing more than the collective actions we've learned to produce in various situations. As with all other animals, if our behaviour is rewarded in a particular situation, we will be more likely to perform that behaviour again the next time we encounter the same situation.

There are three main ways in which people acquire situation-specific response tendencies (see Chapter 6). First, through *classical conditioning,* we learn that certain kinds of events signal other events. Imagine that as a small child little Albert is frightened in the presence of a white furry rat; he develops a specific fear, or phobia, of small furry animals that continues on into adulthood. His behaviour is consistent and regular over time—he panics at the sight of anything small and furry—due in large part to this early childhood experience. Second, through *instrumental conditioning,* we learn about the consequences of our behaviour. If we're rewarded in some context for acting aggressively, we will tend to act aggressively in the future. If we are repeatedly put down at parties for acting outgoing, we will learn to be withdrawn and to avoid social situations. Here it is the environment alone—one's past history of rewards and punishments—that is shaping behaviour.

The third way that regularities in behaviour can develop is through observational learning, or *modelling.* We observe the behaviour of others around us—especially role models—and imitate the models' behaviour. As we discussed in Chapter 6, it's adaptive for organisms to mimic the behaviour of others because in this way, they can learn appropriate behaviour without directly experiencing the consequences of an inappropriate action. Rhesus monkeys, for example, learn to show fear in the presence of snakes through modelling their parents' behaviour, not from directly experiencing the negative consequences of a bite (Mineka, 1987). According to **social learning theory,** many important personality traits come from copying the behaviour of others, especially when the behaviour of the model regularly leads to positive, reinforcing outcomes (Bandura, 1986; Mischel, 1968).

social learning theory
The idea that most important personality traits come from modelling, or copying, the behaviour of others.

Expectations and Cognitions Very few psychologists actually believe that the environment *alone* determines personality growth. The reason is that the psychological effect of most experiences—positive or negative—depends crucially on the expectations and beliefs you hold about the experience. For example, suppose we ask two groups of people to perform a relatively difficult task, such as predicting sequences of numbers. We tell one of the groups that performance on the task is based on skill; the other group is told that success or failure is due entirely to chance. (Unknown to the participants, we actually rig the procedure so that people in both groups will succeed and fail the same number of times.) What you'll find in such a situation is that task effort, as well as the amount that is learned, depends on how much control a person thinks he or she has over the outcome. That is, people who believe that their performance is skill based work harder and learn more from the task (Rotter et al., 1961).

The important point here is that the groups perform differently even though everyone receives exactly the same number of rewards and punishments. So it is not only the literal distribution of rewards and punishments that matters; your *beliefs* about the origins of those consequences are equally important. Some psychologists

The way we act and feel often depends on how much control we think we have over the environment. Externals, who perceive little connection between their own actions and the occurrence of rewards, tend to see themselves as powerless and possess low levels of self-esteem.

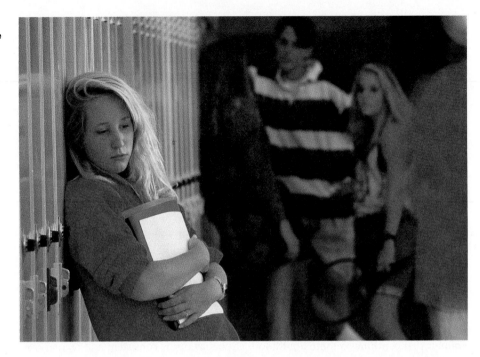

locus of control
The amount of control that a person feels he or she has over the environment.

have suggested that people acquire enduring personality traits based on their perceived **locus of control**—how much control they feel they can actually exert over their environment (Rotter, 1966). People who are oriented externally, known as *externals,* perceive little connection between their own actions and the occurrence of rewards; such people tend to see themselves as powerless and generally have low levels of self-esteem (Lefcourt, 1982). Internally oriented individuals *(internals)* view the world as fundamentally responsive to their actions; they feel confident that they can control the occurrence of rewards and punishment. Internally oriented people display high levels of self-confidence and tend to score higher than externally oriented individuals on a variety of academic and social indices (see Ryckman, 2000).

Researcher Ross Broughton of the University of Winnipeg has investigated one aspect of cognitive personality psychology—*prototypes,* which are defined as the clearest case or best example of a category. Although prototypes do not occur in nature, the prototype approach to personality suggests that scales and factors can be represented by unique words (e.g., demanding, interrupting, bold, pushy). Researchers have recently investigated prototype theory with respect to occupational preferences. For example, after thinking about the prototypical dominant person, what sort of job would best suit that person? Broughton and colleagues (1991) took this approach a step further and considered whether unique occupational clusters exist for specific interpersonal personality types.

Subjects in their study rated occupations according to the extent to which the ideal person in that role had any of the following eight personality traits from Wiggins's Interpersonal Circle: dominant, quarrelsome, submissive, agreeable, arrogant, introverted, unassuming, and gregarious.

Results showed the following features by trait: dominant (business executive, hotel manager); quarrelsome (credit investigator, cost estimator); submissive (bank teller, astronomer); agreeable (playground director, missionary); arrogant (broker, bank examiner); introverted (poet, author); unassuming (concert singer; wildlife specialist); and gregarious (master of ceremonies; drama coach). The results supported the idea that people do show considerable agreement regarding the types of personalities they attribute to people in different professions and that simply by knowing a person's occupational preference, you can predict interpersonal aspects of his or her personality with some degree of accuracy.

The concept of locus of control is related to another psychological concept called **self-efficacy** (Bandura, 1986, 1993). Whereas locus of control refers to your beliefs about how much control you can exert over the environment, self-efficacy is defined as the beliefs you hold about your own ability. For example, Raymond might be convinced that people can control their environments but feels that he personally lacks the skill. In this case, he would be rated as low in self-efficacy, with an internal locus of control. On the other hand, John might be extremely confident in his basic abilities (high self-efficacy) but believes that he can do little to control the things around him (external locus of control). Often a person's degree of self-efficacy is related to particular situations or tasks. You might believe strongly in your ability to excel academically but lack any measure of confidence in your social skills.

Concepts such as locus of control and self-efficacy are important because they indicate that what we learn from the environment depends on more than just the delivery of rewards and punishments. Expectations and beliefs about the world and your abilities influence the types of tasks you will choose to engage in, as well as the effectiveness of rewards and punishments. If you're convinced you have little or no ability in social settings—your self-efficacy is low—you will either tend to avoid going to parties or be nervous and uncomfortable if you do go. If you feel you have no chance of succeeding in your psychology course because the teaching assistant doesn't like you—that is, you've adopted an external locus of control—your motivation to work hard is likely to be low. Note that in these cases your internal beliefs end up affecting your overt behaviour (avoidance of parties or class), which, in turn, affects the likelihood that you will be rewarded. Psychologist Albert Bandura (1986) has referred to this relationship between beliefs, overt behaviour, and the environment as one of **reciprocal determinism**: beliefs, behaviour, and the environment interact to shape what is learned from experience (see Figure 12.8).

The Pure Cognitive Approach The cognitive–behavioural theories just discussed have kept their roots in learned behaviour. The most recent ones have emphasized the cognitive aspect to the exclusion of behaviour. Here the central ingredients are mechanisms such as the particular tasks or problems that the person is trying to solve. Psychologists such as Nancy Cantor and Brian Little suggest thinking about personality as something that a person *does,* rather than something that a person *has* (Cantor,

self-efficacy
The beliefs that we hold about our own ability to perform a task or accomplish a goal.

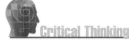
Critical Thinking

Madeline receives an A in her psychology class, but attributes it to the fact that her teacher is easy. Does she have an internal or external locus of control, and how confident do you think she is of her own abilities?

reciprocal determinism
The idea that beliefs, behaviour, and the environment interact to shape what is learned from experience.

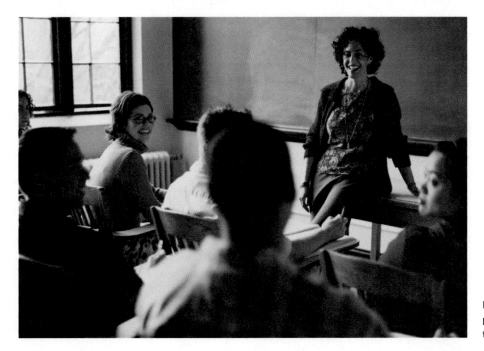

How students cope with the problem of performing well in school depends on the type of "life task" strategy that they adopt.

FIGURE 12.8

Reciprocal Determinism

Bandura proposed that personality is
shaped by complex interactions between
expectations and beliefs, behaviour, and
the rewards and punishments delivered by
the environment. In this case, the
expectation of failure in class
(personal/cognitive factors) affects studying
(behaviour), which in turn affects the
likelihood of success on the test
(environment). Note that the arrows point
both ways, suggesting that these factors
can all interact.

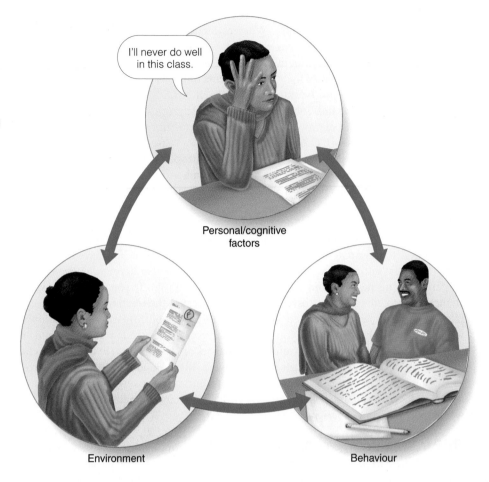

I'll never do well in this class.

Personal/cognitive factors

Environment

Behaviour

1990; Little, 2000). Each person approaches life with a unique set of goals or personal projects. Individuals differ in what is important to them and in their own personal agenda for accomplishment. Karla may be concerned with accumulating wealth and fame; Sarah may be seeking to master her interpersonal skills. To solve these problems or life tasks, we use strategies or characteristic ways of responding that help us meet the challenges that arise (Cantor & Harlow, 1994). The strategies we adopt may cause us to act consistently, but only to the extent that the goal is met or the problem resolved.

The important point to remember is that you cannot understand a person's personality without considering these strategies for solving life tasks. Cantor and her colleagues have found that students in academic settings often adopt quite different strategies to cope with the same task, such as performing well in school. Some students adopt pessimistic strategies, in which they ignore past accomplishments and consistently report low expectations for success on assignments and exams; pessimists spend lots of time thinking and worrying about their academic performance. Other students are optimists, which means they set high expectations for themselves and try not to worry or dwell on negative thoughts. But surprisingly, Cantor has found that these two types of students often perform equally well on exams. They simply have different strategies for meeting the same end. The pessimists are able to confront their anxieties effectively by dwelling on the possibility of failure, whereas the optimists prepare better by accentuating the positive. The pessimists and the optimists seem to have different personalities, but those special characteristics may have arisen simply as a result of the strategies they've adopted to solve a particular life task.

Now let's consider two final points. First, this view of personality predicts that if someone's personal life tasks change, he or she may well adopt new strategies that will affect how he or she behaves. Thus, an individual's personal actions could appear to

Concept Summary

VIEWS OF PERSONALITY DEVELOPMENT

Approach	Description	Example
Psychodynamic	Personality is influenced by forces originating in the unconscious and is made up of three components: the *id* (instinctive urges), *ego* (conscious decision making), and *superego* (conscience).	Laurie is strongly attracted to men, but her parents are very strict about dating, so her sexual feelings are repressed. As a result, she tends to avoid men and is uncomfortable when she is around them.
Humanistic	We all control our own behavioural destiny. Personality reflects our uniqueness and our self-concept as well as our environment and our personal view of the world.	Because of criticism from her parents during childhood, Laurie has developed a poor self-concept. She has not experienced unconditional positive regard. As a result, she feels uncomfortable with who she is.
Cognitive–behavioural	Personality results from an interaction between the experiences delivered by the environment and our interpretations and expectations about those experiences.	Laurie had bad experiences with men in sexual situations although not in other situations. As a result, she's a bit uncomfortable in sexual situations.

change, or be inconsistent, across situations, but only because he or she is trying to solve a different kind of problem. Second, this problem-solving description of personality also predicts that individuals from different cultures or social groups may appear to possess unique personality traits. As the problems of a culture change, so too should the strategies that its people adopt. (We'll have more to say about the relationship between culture and the individual in Chapter 13.)

Evaluating Cognitive–Behavioural Theories All psychologists recognize that behaviour is importantly influenced by what we learn from the environment. Thus, the idea that at least some personality traits might be learned is not considered controversial. Furthermore, the idea that cognitive factors are involved in learning, in the form of expectations and beliefs, has also gained relatively wide acceptance. Critics of the cognitive–behavioural approach simply argue that it is insufficient as a general account of personality development (Feist, 1994; Ryckman, 2000). Cognitive–behavioural theory, for example, tends to neglect the individual as a *whole*, choosing instead to concentrate on how people have learned to respond in particular situations. The pure cognitive theories do move substantially in that direction, however.

The approach has also been criticized for failing to adequately emphasize the role of biological and genetic factors in development. Perhaps ingrained drives and urges are not the main determinants of personality, but biological ancestry cannot be ignored completely. By choosing to focus primarily on the environment, the cognitive–behaviourists sometimes ignore potentially important motivational factors that are controlled largely by biological processes.

Test Yourself 12.2

Check your knowledge of how personality develops by deciding whether each of the following statements is most likely to have been made by a psychodynamic, humanistic, or cognitive–behavioural personality theorist. (You will find the answers in Appendix B.)

1. Estelle talks a lot, but that's only because she's trying to cover up her true feelings of inadequacy: _____
2. Teresa is very demanding, but that's because her boyfriend always gets her what she wants: _____

3. Sally can't help herself—her basic needs are preventing her from realizing her true potential: _____

4. Sharma seems to be a tireless volunteer, but in truth she secretly resents people in need: _____

5. Kevin isn't really an intellectual—he just acts that way because both of his parents are famous academics and he desperately wants to please them: _____

6. Henry is shy because he lacks confidence in his abilities and he's convinced that he cannot really influence or control the people who are around him: _____

7. Ralph sleeps around a lot, but that's because he doesn't have enough moral virtue to control his animalistic nature: _____

RESOLVING THE PERSON–SITUATION DEBATE

Learning Goals

1. Understand both sides of the person–situation debate.
2. Learn the role genetic factors play in personality.
3. Appreciate how the different approaches to personality may not be contradictory.

ACCORDING TO COGNITIVE–BEHAVIOURAL THEORIES, behaviour is primarily the product of the environment. As a result, you might be expected to act somewhat inconsistently from one situation to the next. If you are rewarded for acting bold and aggressive when negotiating a deal (such as buying a car), you will almost certainly act bold and aggressive in such situations in the future. But if similar actions lead to rejection in the classroom or in social situations, you might very well turn meek and mild in class or when you go to a party. If you think about it, you probably know people who seem to change their behaviour at the drop of a hat, acting one way in one situation and quite differently in another.

However, this kind of reasoning really strikes at the core of personality. Remember, personality is defined in terms of lasting qualities—distinguishing patterns of characteristics that differentiate us from others and lead us to act consistently from one situation to the next. Throughout this chapter, we've assumed that such traits exist and that they can be measured and interpreted through the application of psychological principles. But the assumption of cross-situational *consistency* in behaviour has been challenged by some prominent psychologists, notably Walter Mischel, and the issue has come to be known as the **person–situation debate**.

person–situation debate

A controversial debate centring on whether people really do behave consistently across situations.

The Person–Situation Debate

The argument is really a simple one. If people possess unique and enduring personality traits, we should be able to predict their behaviour from one situation to the next. If you believe Karla to be dishonest, perhaps because you witnessed her peering over Sarah's shoulder during a history test, then you also expect her to be dishonest in the future. You predict that she will take a fallen wallet, or jewellery that someone left lying on the counter. In statistical terms, we expect that trait behaviours should *correlate* across situations; that is, given that you know a person's tendency to be extraverted in situation A, you should be able to predict his or her tendency to be extraverted in situation B.

Unfortunately, as Walter Mischel (1968) pointed out over three decades ago, the cross-situational consistency seems weak. If you look carefully at studies reporting correlations between measures of behaviour that tap a particular kind of personality trait (such as honesty), the correlations are virtually always low. While a correlation of 1.00 implies perfect behavioural consistency across situations, Mischel found that actual correlations rarely exceeded 0.30. To say the least, Mischel's conclusions were quite controversial; in fact, they rocked the foundation of personality theory. Without consistency in behaviour, the psychological construct of personality has little meaning.

Situational Consistency Despite those pessimistic data, very few psychologists (including Mischel) reject personality altogether as a viable psychological construct. People may not always act consistently *across* situations, but they do tend to act consistently *within* a situation. For example, in a famous study by Hartshorne and May (1928), the honesty of schoolchildren was tested by placing them in situations in which they could act dishonestly without much likelihood of being caught (money was left on a table, cheating on a test was possible, and so on). Little evidence of cross-situational consistency was found, but the children did tend to act the same way in a similar situation. For instance, kids who cheated on a test were not necessarily more likely to steal money, but they were more likely to cheat on a test again if given the chance. In short, people do act consistently from one situation to the next, as long as the situations are similar (Mischel & Peake, 1982; Mischel & Shoda, 1995). This is exactly the type of finding you would expect if people are simply learning specific kinds of actions in particular circumstances. So the evidence for greater within-situational consistency is often used to support cognitive–behavioural approaches to personality development.

Other psychologists have pointed out that low cross-situational correlations, by themselves, are misleading. Data of the type reported by Hartshorne and May and others (see Mischel, 1968) are based primarily on the observation of single behaviours (did the child steal the money on the table?) rather than on collections of behaviours. But, as we noted earlier, single observations tend to be unreliable indicators of any concept. To get an accurate estimate of a true personality trait, you have to collect lots of observations, not just one (Epstein, 1979). When calculated properly, cross-situational consistency is clear on established traits, such as the Big Five (Kenrick & Funder, 1988).

Self-Monitoring Some psychologists have argued that the tendency to act consistently or haphazardly across different situations may itself be a kind of personality trait. People differ in the extent to which they engage in chameleon-like **self-monitoring,** which can be defined as the tendency to alter your behaviour to fit the situation at hand (Snyder, 1974, 1987). People who are high self-monitors attend closely to their present situation and change their behaviour to best fit their needs. They are likely to alter their behaviour, and even their stated opinions and beliefs, simply to please someone with whom they are currently interacting. People who are low self-monitors are less likely to change their actions or beliefs and therefore are more likely to show consistency in their behaviour across situations (Gangestad & Snyder, 1985).

Scales have been developed to measure self-monitoring tendencies. Typically, you're asked to respond to statements such as the following: "I'm not always the person that I appear to be" or "I might deceive people by acting friendly when I really dislike them." People who score highly on self-monitoring, not surprisingly, are likely to conform to social norms. They also tend to be aware of how their behaviour is affecting others. High self-monitors even seem to remember the actions of others better than low self-monitors, especially when those actions are unexpected or unusual (Beers et al., 1997). Thus, self-monitoring can be quite adaptive: It is usually in our interest to monitor the environment and change our behaviour accordingly (Graziano & Bryant, 1998; Mischel & Shoda, 1998).

The Current Resolution Currently, the majority of psychologists resolve the person–situation debate simply by assuming that it is necessary to take both the person and the situation into account. It is unlikely that either alone, the person or the situation, is going to explain behaviour or allow us to predict consistency. People *interact*

self-monitoring
The degree to which a person monitors a situation closely and changes his or her behaviour accordingly; people who are high self-monitors may not behave consistently across situations.

 Critical Thinking

Decide whether each of your friends is a high or a low self-monitor. Whom do you prefer to be around—the high self-monitors or the low self-monitors?

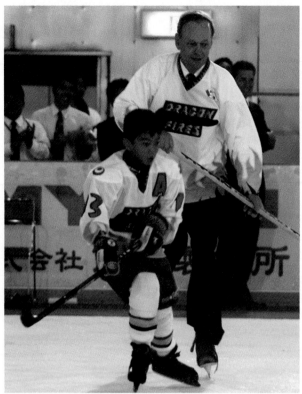

Successful politicians are often high self-monitors, which means they attend closely to the situation and change their behaviour accordingly.

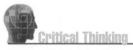

Critical Thinking

Do you think identical twins who are reared apart share totally different environments? How might their environments still be similar?

with situations, and the expression of lasting qualities or traits will depend partly on what's required by current needs. Personality traits will tend to reveal themselves primarily in situations in which they are relevant (Kenrick et al., 1990) and may not otherwise. Similarly, given the right situational demands, each of us can act in ways that seem to violate our basic nature. (We'll return to this issue, and provide some compelling illustrations of the power of the situation, when we take up the general topic of social psychology in Chapter 13.)

Genetic Factors in Personality

As noted in Chapters 9 and 10, the evidence has accumulated that individual differences must be at least partly genetic in origin. People appear to be born with certain genetic predispositions that induce them—but not compel them—to act in an idiosyncratic and regular fashion throughout their lifetime. It is not unusual for family members to show similar personality traits, but normally we cannot rule out the role of experience in producing these similarities. At the same time, as we all know, siblings can show strikingly different personality traits: These differences often appear early in life and can be strong, even for siblings raised under apparently similar environmental conditions. Observations like these indicate that more may be at work in determining personality than the environment.

Special methods such as twin analysis and adoption studies are required to separate the genetic and environmental effects. This approach is called "behavioural genetics." Note that this method does not tell us the details about the biological differences. Likely suspects are different brain structures, different chemical balances, and different speeds of neural transmission. The nature of genetic differences is currently an active area of research. The genome project is currently revealing exciting results, but we are far from being able to point to specific genes that explain personality differences.

Twin Data   As in the study of intelligence, most of the evidence for genetic factors in personality comes from twin studies. Identical twins are compared with fraternal twins under conditions in which the twins have been reared together or apart. Perhaps you've seen reports in the popular media of identical twins who were separated at birth but ended up sharing many of the same personality traits. There is the case of identical twins Oscar and Frank—one raised as a Nazi in Czechoslovakia and the other as a Jew in Trinidad. When they were reunited in 1979, it was discovered that they shared numerous odd but regular behaviours. For example, they both had a habit of sneezing deliberately in elevators to surprise people, and they both liked to flush toilets before and after use.

However, reports like these do not make a convincing scientific case (Horgan, 1993). Coincidences are possible, and some of the more famous reunited twins may have had ulterior motives for manufacturing shared traits (e.g., Oscar and his brother eventually sold the rights to their story in Hollywood). More compelling evidence comes from large-scale studies, in which the personality characteristics of different types of twins are analyzed. In one such study (Tellegen et al., 1988), 217 pairs of identical twins who had been reared together and 44 pairs of twins who had been reared apart were compared with 114 pairs of fraternal twins reared together and 27 pairs reared apart. Each of the participants was administered the MMPI, which, as you remember from our earlier discussion, is a widely used questionnaire for measuring personality traits.

Some of the results of this study are shown in Figure 12.9, for several of the personality traits measured by the MMPI. Of main interest is the similarity between members of a twin pair, expressed in terms of correlation coefficients. In other words, for a

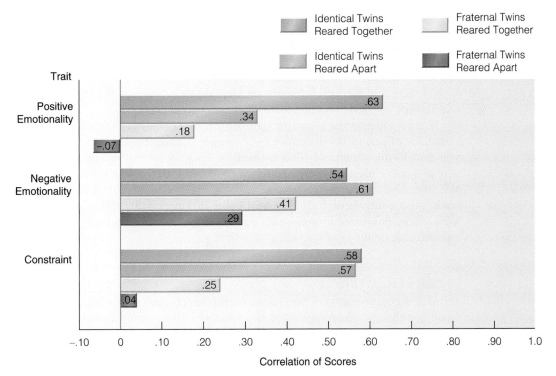

FIGURE 12.9

The Genetics of Personality

Are identical twins more likely to share basic personality traits than fraternal twins? Does the rearing environment matter? These average correlations from the Tellegen and colleagues (1988) study reveal consistent differences between identical and fraternal twins, irrespective of the rearing environment, suggesting that genetics play a role in determining personality. The environment also had a significant effect in some cases, but overall it appeared to be less important. (Adapted from Tellegen et al., 1988.)

trait such as aggressiveness or positive emotionality, can we predict the score that one twin will receive on the MMPI if we know the score of the other twin? Correlations that are close to 1.00 suggest that members of a twin pair share many of the same personality traits. As the figure indicates, identical twins tend to show higher correlations than fraternal twins, regardless of whether they have been reared in the same or different environments. Twins who share the same genes but have been reared in different households tend to have more similar personality traits than fraternal twins who have been reared together.

Data like these have convinced many psychologists that at least some enduring psychological traits have their origins in genetic predispositions present at birth. Of course, as we discussed in Chapter 9, the expression of genetic tendencies depends on the nurturing conditions (the environment): Nature interacts with nurture in determining a person's final physical and psychological makeup. Therefore, although genes may play a critical role in determining how personality develops, environmental factors are also extremely important (Beer et al., 1998; Plomin et al., 1998).

Among the world leaders in the behavioural genetics of personality are the University of Western Ontario's Philip Vernon and the University of British Columbia's Kerry Jang and John Livesley. In one recent study, these researchers considered the role of culture in the heritability of personality across culture (Jang et al., 1998). They reasoned that although culture may affect the expression of a trait, it does not instill those traits in the individual. As a result, basic traits should be heritable in all cultures, and one should expect heritability scores to be similar in Canadian and German twins. These studies examined identical and fraternal Canadian twins from the Vancouver area and German twins sampled from across Germany. Respondents completed the NEO-PI-R, and correlations were calculated to predict one twin's personality score based on the other twin's score. All of the Big Five dimensions showed similar heritabilities—around 0.50. Moreover, both the genetic and environmental effects on personality traits were essentially the same in form and magnitude in Germany and Canada, offering strong support for the idea that the genetic roots of personality are very similar in different cultures. These data are consistent with earlier findings of Jang et al. (1996a) that the correlation among identical twins was significantly and noticeably higher compared to the correlation among fraternal twins.

Using a cross-sectional twin design, Jang et al. (1996b) considered whether the heritability of personality dimensions was consistent across the life span, which would help explain the stability of adult personality. They found that whereas correlations were higher for identical compared to fraternal twins, this was especially true in the older sample. This suggests that genetic influence on personality increases over time, a finding that contradicts the widely held belief that personality should somehow be *more* heavily influenced by genes early in life, with a greater influence from the environment later in life.

Levels of Analysis

At this point in the history of psychology, there is no easy way to integrate all the major theories. Although we can agree that both person and situation variables must play a role in determining personality, the conceptual systems seem too dramatically different to integrate. Each seems to have a different focus and a different method of assessment. One possibility is to think of the different approaches as dealing with different levels of analysis (Little, 1996; McAdams, 2000). High-level issues such as consciousness and goal setting are best dealt with by humanistic and cognitive theories. Middle-level issues such as expectancies seem to be best addressed by cognitive–behavioural theories. Low-level issues such as genetic and unconscious factors seem better addressed by psychoanalysis and evolutionary approaches.

All personality theories are compatible with an evolutionary analysis. We all agree that our species has behavioural tendencies that differ in degree, and likely in kind, from other species. Behavioural geneticists would say that human traits were selected for adaptive reasons and, moreover, we differ because there is more than one way to adapt. Cognitive–behavioural theorists would say that our main adaptive advantage is that we have a superior ability to learn from experience. Humanistic theorists might say that consciousness is our distinctive trait. Psychoanalysis argues that we are gifted with a complex structural system that engages in a symbolic fashion with the environment. In short, all personality theories can be viewed as an answer to the general adaptive question: What allows human beings to adapt so well to our environments?

Finally, the person–situation debate can be resolved by the levels of analysis distinction. People are born with genetically endowed traits that, without counter forces, produce consistent tendencies in behaviour. The higher levels of analysis deal with the varieties of ways in which these traits are channelled by environmental forces or overridden by conditioning. And at the highest level, humans are able to recognize their own tendencies and reflect on them.

Test Yourself 12.3

Check your knowledge about the person–situation debate by deciding whether each of the following statements is true or false. (You will find the answers in Appendix B.)

1. In the Hartshorne and May (1928) study, kids who cheated on a test were not more likely to steal money, but they were more likely to cheat on a test again if given the chance. *True or False?*

2. People do tend to act consistently from one situation to the next, as long as the situations are similar. *True or False?*

3. People who are low self-monitors tend to change their behaviours to fit the situation at hand. *True or False?*

4. Identical twin studies show little evidence for genetic contributions to personality characteristics, as measured by the MMPI. *True or False?*

5. Most psychologists believe that personality traits are revealed in all situations, regardless of the relevance of the trait. *True or False?*

Solving the Scientific and Practical Problems

There is little question in most people's minds about the existence of personality—anyone will tell you that people differ in enduring ways. We all have behavioural quirks that differentiate us from others, and most of us at least give the impression of acting consistently across situations. If asked, people also have little trouble making judgments about the personality of others. Without hesitation, we identify Sarah as agreeable and open and Karla as disagreeable and unbalanced. These differences in personality can be viewed as different adaptive styles. Thus, personality is clearly an important aspect of the adaptive mind.

To psychologists, however, the study of personality has proven to be a source of controversy. As we've seen, questions have even been raised about the validity of the concept itself—how useful is a concept such as personality in describing individual differences in behaviour? (Remember, similar issues were raised about the study of intelligence.) Still, the vast majority of psychologists agree that the concept of personality is needed to describe the full range of human psychological functioning. Personality is indeed something to be studied, and understanding it is both a conceptual and practical problem to be solved by the psychological community.

First, what is the proper way to enumerate and measure the traits that make us both consistent and unique? Trait taxonomies are formal systems for measuring and identifying personality characteristics, such as emotional stability or extraversion. Currently, the trait theorists seem to agree that there are five basic personality dimensions—the so-called Big Five (extraversion, agreeableness, conscientiousness, neuroticism, and openness)—that accurately and reliably describe a person's unique and consistent attributes. Psychometric techniques such as factor analysis, along with the development of personality tests such as the NEO-PI-R and the MMPI, have proven useful in advancing theory and in applying what we've learned about personality to practical settings. For example, the NEO-PI-R has proven itself in business settings as part of the decision-making process for hiring new employees.

Second, how do personality traits develop? Identifying stable personality traits, however, leaves unanswered the general question of how those traits originate. Noted psychologists have developed several grand theories of personality development, including the psychodynamic approach of Freud, the humanistic perspective of Rogers and Maslow, and the cognitive–behavioural approach of Bandura, Mischel, and others. These theoretical frameworks propose very different mechanisms for personality development and offer quite different conceptions of basic human nature. The pessimism of Freud, with his emphasis on battling unconscious biological urges, is counterbalanced by the optimism of the humanists. To the cognitive–behaviourists, the environment and beliefs about controlling that environment underlie the consistent actions that define personality. Each of these perspectives has been enormously influential in the past and remains so today.

Third, how do personality theories deal with variation and change in the same person's behaviour? The concept of personality demands at least some consistency in behaviour across situations. Early worries about low cross-situational consistency have been clarified by aggregation across large numbers of behaviours. The current consensus is that a proper analysis of behaviour requires consideration of the *interaction* between the person and the situation. The growing evidence from behavioural genetics rules out any approach to personality that is focused entirely on situational effects.

Chapter Summary

ENUMERATING AND MEASURING PERSONALITY TRAITS

What is the proper way to conceptualize and measure the *traits* that make us both consistent and unique? Psychologists attempt to measure the enduring aspects of behaviour—those things that distinguish one person from another consistently across time.

The Factor Analytic Approach

Learning Goal: Appreciate how factor analysis is used to identify basic personality traits. Factor analysis is used to analyze correlations among test responses. This approach attempts to determine the degree to which trait ratings correlate with one another, in hopes of discovering common denominators for *personality.* Cattell identified 16 *source traits,* each represented by a dimension marked by an opposing pole. Eysenck argued that personality can be described best by 3 independent factors (extraversion, neuroticism, and psychoticism). Current thinking is that 5 dimensions—the *Big Five* (extraversion, agreeableness, openness, neuroticism, and conscientiousness) best describe personality.

Allport's Trait Theory

Learning Goal: Understand Allport's distinction between cardinal, central, and secondary traits. Allport proposed a classification scheme for identifying personality traits. *Cardinal traits* are ruling passions that dominate an individual's life. *Central traits* are the 5 to 10 descriptive terms you would use to describe someone you know. *Secondary traits* are less obvious traits that do not always appear in an individual's behaviour.

Assessment Methods

Learning Goal: Be able to explain the advantages and disadvantages of self-report questionnaires, projective tests, and indirect methods. The most common method, *self-report questionnaires* use a paper-and-pencil format to identify personality characteristics. Examples are the *16 Personality Factor,* the *NEO-PI-R,* and the *Minnesota Multiphasic Personality Inventory (MMPI).* Self-report questionnaires are objective and standardized. *Projective tests* such as the *Rorschach* and the *Thematic Apperception Test (TAT)* require the test taker to interpret an unstructured or ambiguous stimulus, thereby revealing elements of personality. *Indirect methods* have been developed for use in populations with language difficulties and have been found to provide personality assessments similar to standard verbal scales.

DETERMINING HOW PERSONALITY DEVELOPS

What factors in development lead to stable and consistent behaviours? Where do personality traits come from? What accounts for differences in personality among individuals?

The Psychodynamic Approach of Freud

Learning Goal: Be able to explain Freud's psychodynamic theory of personality and mind. Freud argued the mind could be partitioned into the *conscious,* the *preconscious,* and the *unconscious.* The unconscious mind was said to exert powerful effects on behaviour. Dreams are one window into the unconscious and include a *manifest content* and *latent content* (the hidden meaning). Personality has three components: the *id* (governed by inborn drives and the pleasure principle), the *superego* (the conscience, following the moralistic principle), and the *ego* (the executive of personality, following the reality principle). Conflict between the forces of personality results in anxiety. To cope with the anxiety, we employ *defence mechanisms* such as *denial, repression, projection, reaction formation,* or *sublimation.* Children progress through a series of *psychosexual stages* of development (*oral, anal, phallic, latency,* and *genital*) that help determine later personality. Neo-Freudians such as Jung, Adler, and Horney de-emphasized the role of sexuality in personality, emphasizing other factors as central to the development of personality.

Humanistic Approaches to Personality

Learning Goal: Understand and evaluate humanistic approaches to personality, including the specific proposals of Carl Rogers and Abraham Maslow. *Humanistic psychology* developed partly as a reaction against Freud's pessimistic view of the human spirit. This approach emphasizes self-awareness, choice, responsibility, and growth as important factors in personality. According to Carl Rogers, the essence of personality is tied to the *self-concept.* We have a basic need for *positive regard,* and problems arise when our acceptance by others is tied to *conditions of worth.* Problems may also arise from *incongruence,* a discrepancy between your self-concept and the sum of your experiences. Maslow stressed the drive toward *self-actualization* as important in determining personality. He proposed a need hierarchy, which explains the priority with which needs must be fulfilled. Personality reflects where you are within the hierarchy of needs.

Cognitive–Behavioural Approaches to Personality

Learning Goal: Assess cognitive–behavioural theories of personality, and understand how cognitions and the environment interact to produce behaviour. This approach emphasizes the role of learning in personality. Human experience, not human nature, is the primary cause of personality growth and development. People acquire situation-specific response tendencies through classical conditioning, instrumental conditioning, and modelling. According to *social learning theory*, many personality traits come from copying the behaviour of others. Our interpretation of our experiences also plays a critical role in personality. Perceived *locus of control* (how much control people feel they have over their environment) and *self-efficacy* (the beliefs you have about your own ability) determine how experience is interpreted and how it affects personality.

RESOLVING THE PERSON–SITUATION DEBATE

Are personality characteristics expressed in a way that is independent of the environment? Is behaviour across different situations as consistent as many people, including psychologists, assume?

The Person–Situation Debate

Learning Goal: Understand both sides of the person–situation debate. Do people show cross-situational consistency in their behaviour? This question is at the heart of the *person–situation debate*. According to Mischel, the evidence for consistency looked weak across situations, although reasonable within situations. However, proper aggregation of behaviours indicates a fair degree of consistency in both. Some psychologists have suggested that the tendency to act consistently or inconsistently across different situations may itself be a personality trait. This tendency is termed *self-monitoring*. High self-monitors attend closely to their behaviour and change it to best fit their needs, whereas low self-monitors are less likely to change their actions and beliefs. Current thinking is that both the person and the situation need to be taken into account to explain personality.

Genetic Factors in Personality

Learning Goal: Learn the role genetic factors play in personality. Evidence from twin and adoption studies indicates that genetic factors play a substantial role in determining personality. Correlational studies of personality traits as measured by the MMPI and NEO-PI-R reveal that identical twins tend to show higher correlations than fraternal twins, regardless of being raised in the same or different environments. Data like these have convinced psychologists that there are some enduring psychological traits and that

these have their roots in genetic predispositions. Nonetheless, we know little about the actual biological mechanisms.

Levels of Analysis

Learning Goal: Appreciate how the different approaches to personality may not be contradictory. The field of personality is not yet at a stage where a synthesis of all the theories is possible. The best perspective to date is to consider that different theories are not in conflict but are considering people's personalities at different levels of analysis.

Terms to Remember

Recommended Readings

Dutton, D. G. (1998). *The abusive personality: Violence and control in close relationships.* New York: Guilford. Donald Dutton of the University of British Columbia has studied people with abusive personalities for many years, and this volume addresses issues such as the structure and origins of the abusive personality.

Wiggins, J. S. (Ed.). (1996). *The five-factor model of personality: Theoretical perspectives.* New York: Guilford. Jerry Wiggins of the University of British Columbia is one of Canada's foremost personality researchers, and this collection of articles examines a variety of current issues pertaining to the Big Five.

Hoyle, R. H., Kernis, M. H., Leary, M. R., & Baldwin, M. W. (Eds.). (1999). *Selfhood: Identity, esteem, regulation.* New York: Westview. Co-edited by Mark Baldwin of the University of Winnipeg, this collection summarizes current research and findings pertaining to people's perceptions of themselves and how their self-esteem influences their self-perceptions.

Altemeyer, B., & Hunsberger, B. (1997). *Amazing conversions: Why some turn to faith and others abandon religion.* Amherst, NY: Prometheus. University of Manitoba researcher Bob Altemeyer, together with colleague Bruce Hunsberger of Wilfred Laurier University, surveyed hundreds of Canadian university students in order to understand the backgrounds of people who either became devout believers in spite of nonreligious backgrounds or who became atheist or agnostic although coming from religious families.

Beyerstein, B. L., & Beyerstein, D. F. (Eds.). (1992). *The write stuff: Evaluations of graphology—The study of handwriting analysis.* Amherst, NY: Prometheus. Co-edited by brothers Barry Beyerstein of Simon Fraser University and Dale Beyerstein of Langara College, these articles examine the scientific evidence relating to graphology (the attempt to determine a person's personality based on their handwriting). Along the way, they also review a number of aspects of what constitutes appropriate scientific method in examining such claims.

Coren, S. (2000). *Why we love the dogs we do: How to find the dog that matches your personality.* New York: Fireside. Noted research psychologist and popular psychology author Stanley Coren of the University of British Columbia has researched both the personalities of dogs and the personalities of dog owners. In this book, he uses that research to suggest the matches between breeds of dog and owner personality that are likely to lead to the best outcome.

For additional readings, explore InfoTrac® College Edition, your online library. Go to:

www.adaptivemind2e.nelson.com

Hint: enter the search terms: personality traits; personality tests; Sigmund Freud; defence mechanisms; humanistic psychology; locus of control.

What's on the Web?

Please note that Web addresses are subject to change. Check out the accompanying Web site for updates: www.adaptivemind2e.nelson.com. This site presents practice quiz questions, hypercontent, information on degrees and careers in psychology, study tips, and more.

Freud Museum

www.freud.org.uk

This site provides some very interesting information about the founder of psychoanalysis. You can also look at some fascinating pictures from the museum, including Freud's original couch and "tub chair" that he used in his psychoanalytic sessions.

The Personality Project

personality-project.org/personality.html

This fascinating site serves as a sort of clearinghouse for information related to personality measurement and personality theory. The pages are "meant to guide those interested in personality theory and research to the current personality literature." The site provides pages that allow you to find out more about psychoanalytic theory, behavioural genetics, and evolutionary psychology.

Whatever you may be sure of, be sure of this—that you are dreadfully like other people.
James Russell Lowell

Chapter 13 Social Psychology

t's the annual Christmas party for the Jersey Sanitation Company. Chris M. has worked in the unit for three years now, and he's hoping for a promotion. At one point in the party, Chris and several other ambitious co-workers chat with the head of the unit, Tony S. The topic of conversation is the company's recent disastrous expansion, spearheaded by Tony S., whose shortcomings are recognized by everyone in the group save one—Tony himself.

"My brilliant plan—ruined," spouts Tony, arrogantly. "Not a single one of my managers could do it right. It's amazing how they all screwed it up."

"They're all just stupid," agrees Charlie. "They wouldn't know a good plan if they saw one."

"Absolutely," adds Ralph. "Your plan was brilliant."

The little voice inside Chris's head chimes, "I'm working with spineless yes-men. These guys are wimps—with no sense of personal integrity. Everyone knows that Tony's plan was terrible."

"And what about you, Chris," boss Tony says, looking directly at him. "What do you think?"

"Excellent plan, sir," Chris says, hesitating only slightly. "The work of genius!"

Let's analyze Chris M.'s behaviour. From this brief exchange, can you draw any conclusions about what kind of person he is? He clearly violated his own beliefs and publicly conformed to social pressure. But he was also disgusted by the weakness of his colleagues, concluding that they were wimps. Do you think Chris will now draw the same conclusion about himself? Do you suppose he might have acted differently if the boss had been absent or if the promotion had already been his? How might you have acted in this situation—would you have conformed to the opinions of others? Would you, like Chris M., have left the conversation thinking your co-workers—but not you—have a pathetic personality? All of these questions are studied by social psychologists.

Throughout this text we've stressed that behaviours, as well as internal thoughts and feelings, are influenced by the immediate context. Not only do you behave differently in different situations, but you also think differently. Nor do we judge ourselves by the same standards that we use to judge others. Chris M.'s example is relatively harmless, but other situations can have more far-reaching and disturbing consequences. Suppose, for example, that Tony S. was not simply a company head but a commanding officer in the military, and the situation was a faraway Asian battlefield. Suppose the issue under consideration was not a company expansion campaign, but rather the leader's decision to execute all the inhabitants, including women and children, of a just-captured village. How would you react then? Would you still conform to the opinions of your superior? Clearly, the answers to such questions have powerful implications for society.

Undoubtedly, it's adaptive for us to monitor the environment closely and to change our behaviour accordingly. But the social environment has a unique and, in many ways, more complex effect than other aspects of our environment. The mere presence of other people, as well as their behaviours, can be among the most powerful and pervasive of environmental influences. Our behaviours and thoughts change in systematic ways when we are in the presence of other people, or even thinking about other people. It is this social aspect of psychology that is the focus of this chapter.

510

Previewing the Adaptive Problems

Social psychology studies how people think about, influence, and relate to other people. Social psychologists investigate topics such as persuasion, interpersonal attraction, attitude formation and change, and the behaviour of groups. Understanding people's social behaviour involves three important adaptive problems (see Figure 13.1).

First, how do we think about the social world? As social animals, we're constantly trying to figure out the behaviour of other people. We form impressions of our friends, teachers, and colleagues in the workplace; we even form impressions of the people we meet on the street. We devise theories about *why* people behave the way they do; we form attitudes that advance our interests with particular individuals or groups. At

the same time, as you'll see, we show consistent biases in our interpretation of social events, which sometimes leads us to act in regrettable ways.

Second, how does our behaviour change in the presence of others? Everyone's behaviour is strongly influenced by the social context. For example, sometimes people perform better when others are present; other times their performance falls apart. Human behaviour is also strongly influenced by authority figures and by the opinions of group members. When do people yield to the demands of others, and what implications does such compliance have for the structure of society? We'll expand our psychological analysis of Chris M.'s behaviour and extend it to more situations.

Third, how do we establish relationships—whether positive or negative—with other people? It's certainly adaptive for us to try to understand others' behaviour and to use that information to our benefit. Our attitudes about the social world form the basis for our social actions. On the positive side, attraction and romantic love receive the most media attention, but it is the relationships within the family that protect and nurture us and our offspring. The dark side of relationships, namely aggression, remains both a destructive force in society and a challenge to society.

social psychology
The study of how people think about, influence, and relate to other people.

Thinking about the social world

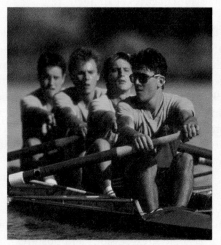

Behaving in the presence of others

Establishing relations with others

FIGURE 13.1
Summarizing the Adaptive Problems
In this chapter we address three main adaptive problems studied by social psychologists.

THINKING ABOUT
THE SOCIAL WORLD: SOCIAL COGNITION

Learning Goals
1. Understand how physical attractiveness, stereotypes, and social schemas influence our impressions of others.
2. Learn how we attribute causality to the behaviour of others, and the biases and errors that we show when making attributions.
3. Appreciate the complexity of attitudes and how they are formed and changed.

social cognition

The study of how people use cognitive processes—such as perception, memory, thought, and emotion—to make sense of other people as well as themselves.

LET'S BEGIN BY DISCUSSING how people think about other people, specifically, how impressions of others are formed, how people attribute causes to behaviour, and what mental mechanisms construct our attitudes about people and things. Together, these topics are labelled **social cognition,** which can be defined as the study of how people use cognitive processes—such as perception, memory, and thought—to help make sense of other people as well as themselves. First is the topic of person perception, which deals specifically with how we form impressions of others.

Person Perception: How Do We Form Impressions of Others?
12d, SIM 10
Psyk.trek

When we first discussed the topic of perception in Chapter 4, we focused on the processes used to interpret elementary sensations as meaningful wholes. In that chapter you learned that perception is driven by a combination of *bottom-up processing*—building the whole from details received by the sensory equipment—and *top-down processing*, which begins with global expectations and beliefs about the world. Either way, we do not simply see what's "out there" in the physical world; our perceptions of objects are also influenced by our *expectations* of what's out there.

A similar process applies when we perceive people. When you encounter a person for the first time, your expectancies tend to be dominated by obvious physical factors—gender, physical attractiveness, skin colour, clothing. If you see a ragged, unshaven man staggering toward you on the street, you would likely form a negative first impression, because past experience has taught you to avoid people who fit this description. You could be wrong about this individual, of course, but in the face of limited information, it's adaptive to use such background knowledge to anticipate the possible consequences of an interaction.

Physical Appearance Of the possible cues for judging people, physical appearance produces the strongest expectancies. A person's gender, race, and physical attractiveness are the most powerful cues. We tend to assume that attractive people are more intelligent, better adjusted, and healthier than those with only average looks (Chia et al., 1998; Eagly et al., 1991; Feingold, 1992; Kalick et al., 1998). These expectancies translate into behavioural reactions: Attractive students are less likely to get "carded" in bars and are less likely to be convicted of crimes (McCall, 1997). Moreover, these tendencies don't diminish as we age: Even the elderly attribute positive personality characteristics to attractive people (Larose & Standing, 1998).

Why do we rely on physical appearance to form a first impression? After all, it seems like a rather shallow way to judge a person. The reason is simple: When you form a *first* impression, you use the most *salient* information, that is, the cues that are most dramatic and available. You can't avoid noticing race, gender, and attractiveness, but also facial expressions and posture. These raw materials are combined with your background knowledge to generate an expectation of what an encounter with that person might be like. Your cultural background may influence your final judgment to a certain extent—some cultures do not rely on attractiveness as much as others (Wheeler & Kim, 1997)—but all people, across cultures, rely on physical appearance as an important part of impression formation.

Obviously, judging a book by its cover is not always an effective long-term strategy for impression formation (Feingold, 1992). Collecting objective facts about a person will generally create more valid judgments (Paulhus & Reynolds, 1995). But because of their speed, appearance-based judgments can be adaptive as a short-term strategy. If the person approaching you on the street appears clean and well dressed, at least you know that he or she follows some of the accepted standards and norms of the culture (Damhorst, 1990). Think about it. If you were in trouble and needed help, whom would you approach—someone with poor personal hygiene and tattered clothes or someone neat, clean, and well dressed?

The physical appearances of these individuals are likely to activate "social schemas" that will direct and guide your behaviour. Social schemas are generally adaptive, but they can lead to inappropriate conclusions or actions under some circumstances.

Social Schemas   Our expectancies about such a huge amount of our background knowledge require substantial organization. The subsets of those expectancies that we use in social situations are called *schemas* (Macrae & Bodenhausen, 2000). They are general knowledge structures about a particular topic in memory, such as knowledge about how houses are constructed or about what to expect at a restaurant or the doctor's office. We use schemas to help reconstruct the past but also to organize and interpret our experiences. A schema can be formed about just about anything—a person, a place, or a thing. When schemas are about social experiences or people, they are commonly called **social schemas** (Fiske, 1993).

Returning to the dirty, ragged man on the street, your initial impression is likely to be negative because his tattered appearance activates one of your social schemas about people. A ragged appearance is associated with negative social characteristics—such as an offensive smell or even criminal behaviour—and his weaving gait signals possible drunkenness. All these things lead you to categorize the man as "trouble" and make it less likely that you will either ask him for help or respond to his requests (Benson et al., 1980). Both the man's physical appearance and his behaviour feed into your existing social schema about seedy characters, and, once he has been categorized, the schema quickly directs you to alter your behaviour accordingly.

Stereotypes   When social schemas concern traits and behaviours of groups and their members, they are called **stereotypes.** We form stereotypes about many kinds of social groups, from car-salesmen to college professors, but three of the most common are based on gender, race, and age (Fiske, 1993). Most people carry around a collection of impressions about men and women, for example, which can importantly influence behaviour: Men are typically seen as strong, dominant, and aggressive; women are typically seen as sensitive, warm, and dependent (Deaux & Lewis, 1984). The central problem with stereotypes is that they lead us to judge individuals on the basis of our expectancies about the group they belong to.

Stereotypes share many of the properties of categories covered in Chapter 8. For example, *prototype theories* of stereotypes assume that we store abstract representations of the typical features of a group; we then judge particular individuals based on their similarity to the prototype (Cantor & Mischel, 1978; Sternberg, 1988a). *Exemplar*

social schema
A general knowledge structure, stored in long-term memory, that relates to social experiences or people.

stereotypes
The collection of beliefs and impressions held about a group and its members; common stereotypes include those based on gender, race, and age.

theories assume instead that we store memories of particular individuals, or exemplars, and these individual memories form the basis for stereotypes (Paulhus et al., 2002; Smith & Zárate, 1992). So, for example, the stereotypic belief that Black people are athletic would be based on information about particular individuals (e.g., Michael Jordan or Tiger Woods) rather than with some abstract representation (Hilton & von Hippel, 1996). Either way, these categories speed up our thinking but can lead to misjudgments about individuals.

Stereotypes tend to be activated if we have recently been exposed to stereotypic beliefs and actions. For example, men are more likely to behave sexually toward a woman if they've recently seen a television commercial in which women were presented as sexual objects (Rudman & Borgida, 1995). In addition, witnessing a Black man engaging in a negative stereotypic behaviour influences how a White male evaluates other Black men (Henderson-King & Nisbett, 1996). Recent exposure to a behaviour relevant to a stereotype apparently activates, or "primes," the stereotype, which in turn affects behaviour (Smith et al., 1992; Stewart et al., 1998). Finally, a stereotype that is easily communicable (e.g., simple and salient) will be more frequently activated and therefore will persist longer within a culture (Schaller et al., 2002).

The Self-Fulfilling Prophecy Effect   Once stereotypes are activated, we expect certain kinds of behaviour from members of groups. These expectations can produce the **self-fulfilling prophecy effect,** which is the power of expectations about a person's actions to cause that person to behave in the expected way (Merton, 1948). If you expect someone to be unreliable, and you act in accordance with your expectations (such as snubbing or avoiding the person), the chance that their future behaviour is unreliable may actually increase.

Let's consider an experiment demonstrating the self-fulfilling prophecy effect. In a study by Mark Snyder and his colleagues (1977), undergraduate men were asked to talk to undergraduate women, whom they had never met, on the telephone. Prior to the conversation, the men were shown a photograph of their prospective telephone partner. The partner appeared as either physically attractive or unattractive. In reality, the photos were not really those of the women participating in the study. The intention of the experimenters was simply to lead the men to *believe* they were talking to a woman who was attractive or unattractive. As for the women, they were not given a photo of their partner, nor were they told that the man was looking at a misleading photo. All the telephone calls were taped, and the quality of the men's and women's conversational styles was then rated by independent judges who were unaware of the misleading photos.

Not surprisingly, if the men thought they were talking to an attractive female, their conversational styles tended to be rated as friendly and positive, more so than if their partner had been depicted as unattractive. But the important finding of the study focused on the women. It turned out that the women's conversational styles also differed, depending on whether or not the man they were talking to thought they were attractive. The women who were presumed by their partners to be attractive were rated by the judges as more friendly, open, and poised and generally more pleasant than the women depicted as unattractive. Remember, these women had no idea that their male partners had pre-formed opinions about their attractiveness. Apparently, the friendly, positive conversational styles of the men were able to elicit similar qualities from the women. This is the self-fulfilling prophecy effect: The expectations that we have toward others, along with our actions, can actually influence them to act in the expected way (see Figure 13.2). This study, and others like it, can be seen as providing support for the old adage "Smile and the world smiles with you!" Interestingly, Jacquie Vorauer of the University of Manitoba and Dale Miller of Princeton University have found that people often seem surprisingly unaware of the fact that their behaviour is influenced by such social influence processes. They also discovered that such "blindness" to social influences seems to be particularly true of people with low self-esteem (Vorauer & Miller, 1997).

self-fulfilling prophecy effect
When our expectations about the actions of another person actually lead that person to behave in the expected way.

Critical Thinking

Do you think the social schemas that were activated in the telephone study were different for the men and the women? If so, in what way?

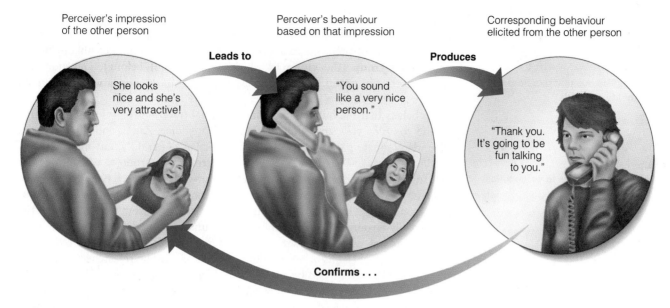

Perceiver's impression of the other person

Perceiver's behaviour based on that impression

Corresponding behaviour elicited from the other person

Leads to

Produces

She looks nice and she's very attractive!

"You sound like a very nice person."

"Thank you. It's going to be fun talking to you."

Confirms . . .

FIGURE 13.2

The Self-Fulfilling Prophecy Effect

Our impressions of another person can affect how that person behaves, leading him or her to act in the expected way. In the study by Snyder and his colleagues, if a male participant thought he was talking to an attractive female, his conversational style was rated as more friendly and positive—but so too was the conversational style of his female telephone partner.

Prejudice: The Canadian Context As you've seen, stereotypes can lead to rigid interpretations of people. Stereotypes can cause us to overgeneralize and focus on the differences *between* groups (for instance, between men and women), rather than acknowledging the differences that exist *within* groups. Not all women are dependent, nor are all men strong. Furthermore, when the beliefs we hold about a group are negative, stereotypes increase the likelihood of **prejudice** (unfair negative feelings) and actual **discrimination** (unfair behaviour). Someone can be excluded from a job, or even criminally assaulted, because of negative beliefs activated by his or her skin colour or sexual orientation.

prejudice
An unrealistic negative evaluation of a group and its members.

discrimination
Behaving in an unfair way toward members of another group.

Concept Summary

FACTORS IN PERSON PERCEPTION

Factor	Role in Person Perception	Example
Physical appearance	We tend to assume that physically attractive individuals are more intelligent, well adjusted, and more socially aware.	Tyrone encounters Michelle at a party. He finds Michelle quite attractive. In addition, he perceives her as very personable, good humoured, and intelligent.
Social schemas	We use schemas (e.g., stereotypes) to organize and interpret experiences.	Tyrone believes most women are very sensitive, warm, and dependent. He finds that Michelle's behaviour fits this pattern.
Self-fulfilling prophecies	The activation of stereotypes leads to expectations of certain behaviours. These expectations can cause the person to behave in the expected way.	Tyrone is very attentive toward Michelle at the party, bringing her refreshments and introducing her to all of his friends. Michelle relaxes; she begins to open up and make witty comments.

out-group

A group of individuals that one does not belong to or identify with.

in-group

A group that one belongs to or identifies with.

However, stereotypes are not the only cause of prejudice. University of Waterloo social psychologist Mark Zanna has suggested that we can distinguish at least three other components of prejudice in addition to stereotypic beliefs: (1) symbolic beliefs about the **out-group** (the group to which one does not belong), (2) emotional responses to the out-group, and (3) past experiences with the out-group (Esses et al., 1993; Zanna, 1994). Zanna and his colleagues define symbolic beliefs about the out-group as beliefs that the out-group violates essential traditions or values. To examine this more complex view about the structure of prejudice, Zanna and his colleagues asked undergraduate participants at the University of Waterloo about their attitudes toward five groups in Canadian society: one **in-group** (the group to which one does belong, in this case English Canadians) and four out-groups (French Canadians, Native Canadians, Pakistanis, and homosexuals). The responses did indicate some degree of prejudice, on average, toward the four out-groups. On a scale from 0 to 100, where 100 was "extremely favourable" and 0 was "extremely unfavourable," the participants rated English Canadians as approximately 81, but rated French Canadians as 69, Native Canadians as 66, Pakistanis as 59, and homosexuals as 44. The researchers also found that, although the stereotyped beliefs of the participants were an important aspect of their prejudice, the participants' emotional reactions to the groups, independent of their cognitive stereotypes of the group, were also a very important aspect of their prejudiced attitudes. Similarly, it was found that the more an individual believed that a group blocked or spurned a cherished value (such as "family values" or "respect for law and order"), the greater the degree of prejudice toward that group, and this "symbolic belief" component was somewhat independent of the "stereotyped belief" and the "emotional" components of prejudice. In other words, a person who held strong negative emotions about an out-group did not always express equally strong negative stereotypes about the group. Zanna and his colleagues suggest these data support their contention that prejudice consists of far more than simple negative stereotypes about out-groups.

Of course, some people are more prejudiced than others. The tendency is higher in those who are rigidly conservative, or authoritarian (Adorno et al., 1950). This tendency is commonly measured with the right-wing authoritarianism (RWA) scale developed by social psychologist Bob Altemeyer of the University of Manitoba (Altemeyer, 1988, 1994, 1996). People high in RWA tend to agree with items on the RWA scale, such as, "Obedience and respect for authority are the most important virtues children should learn" (Adorno et al., 1950). Right-wing authoritarians tend to have especially strong tendencies to favour the in-group over out-groups. Zanna and his colleagues also found that the prejudiced attitudes of people high in RWA tend to be more related to their concern that out-groups are disregarding or even interfering with essential values and traditions ("symbolic beliefs") than to stereotyped beliefs about the out-groups.

How early in life do people begin to display prejudicial attitudes toward out-groups, and what can we do to try to promote tolerance rather than prejudice among children? These are among the questions addressed in a research program by Frances Aboud of McGill University and Anna Beth Doyle of Concordia University (Aboud, 1988, 1993; Aboud & Doyle, 1996; Doyle & Aboud, 1995). In one study (Aboud & Doyle, 1996), prejudice among 8- to 11-year-old White children in Montreal was measured using the Multi-response Racial Attitude measure: It assesses whether a child tended to evaluate White, Black, and Chinese children positively or negatively. Children who scored high in prejudice as measured by this scale were then paired with a friend who had scored low in prejudice, and they were asked to discuss two items that they had disagreed on. In general, high-prejudice children displayed less prejudice following these discussions, particularly when their low-prejudice partner made more statements relating to similarity among groups (e.g., "Everyone can be mean sometimes"). Happily, the low-prejudice children did not become more prejudiced as a result of the discussions. Aboud and Doyle suggest that these results indicate one strategy for decreasing prejudice among children is to systematically arrange for high-prejudice children to engage in such discussions with low-prejudice peers. They also suggest that, although parents and teachers might be hesitant to engage children in any discussions of racial differences and similarities, such discussions might have a positive effect if they are structured to promote tolerance and respect for diversity among children.

At Queen's University, John Berry and Rudolf Kalin have studied Canadians' attitudes toward multiculturalism and ethnic groups within Canada. Much of the research on the psychology of prejudice in the United States has focused on how a majority group (usually Americans of European origin) views minority groups (often African-Americans). Berry and Kalin suggest that in Canada's multicultural environment, a wider perspective is more appropriate, one that involves examining the attitudes of multiple ethnic groups toward each other, not just the attitudes of the majority group toward minority groups (Berry, 1999; Berry & Kalin, 1995; Kalin & Berry, 1996). In one such study, the researchers analyzed a 1991 survey of over 3000 Canadians from across the country. Respondents were asked to rate how comfortable they were being around people from 14 different ethnic groups: British, French, Ukrainians, Sikhs, Indo-Pakistanis, Germans, Chinese, West Indian Blacks, Jews, Arabs, Italians, Portuguese, Aboriginal Canadians, and Moslems. The good news is that people reported being relatively comfortable with all the groups, which could be taken as validation of Canadians' self-schema of being tolerant.

On average, however, these subgroups of Canadians evaluated their own group more positively than other groups, a tendency referred to as *ethnocentrism.* In addition, if one group ranked another group highly, the second group tended to rank the first group highly as well ("reciprocity"). For instance, the British tended to rate Ukrainians highly, and Ukrainians also rated the British highly. Berry and Kalin's multiethnic comparison approach to studying ethnic attitudes provides some clear advantages over the older, more simplistic assessments of majority views of minorities, and provides psychologists and social planners with a detailed analysis of the psychological complexity of the Canadian multicultural experience.

In an additional study, Kalin (1996) reported that people tend to have more positive attitudes toward ethnic groups that they often see around them, compared to groups who are not present in their environment. Kalin suggests that this pattern may be partly a result of the "mere exposure" effect (Zajonc, 1968), discussed later in this chapter. People feel more comfortable with a given ethnic group simply because they have seen members of the group around them more often. Another factor that is possibly at work here is the "contact" effect (Allport, 1954; Hewstone & Brown, 1986), which states that under certain circumstances, repeated interactions between members of ethnic groups are likely to lead to more positive attitudes.

Discrimination: The Personal/Group Discrepancy
Social psychologists have discovered an interesting anomaly regarding how the targets of discrimination perceive their situation. It appears that members of groups that are discriminated against, such as gay people and visible minorities, tend to report that while they believe discrimination against their group is quite significant, they themselves have experienced relatively little discrimination (e.g., Taylor, Wright, Moghaddam, & Lalonde, 1990). Although such a situation might be possible for a few fortunate members of out-groups, it is logically impossible for discrimination to be high against a group as a whole, yet minimal toward most members of the group. Nonetheless, that is what is reported by members of disadvantaged groups in numerous studies. This anomaly has been labelled the **personal/group discrimination discrepancy,** and it has been examined by several Canadian social psychologists (e.g., Dion & Kawakami, 1996; Wright et al., 1996).

McGill University researchers Donald Taylor, Winnifred Louis, and their colleagues suggest that two somewhat-independent psychological processes may be operating to create this discrepancy. One is a tendency for members of discriminated-against groups to minimize discrimination as a possible explanation for failures in their lives. Taylor and colleagues (1996) suggest that, contrary to previous suggestions, this reluctance to invoke an explanation involving discrimination, even when there is

personal/group discrimination discrepancy

The tendency for members of groups experiencing discrimination to minimize discrimination directed toward themselves as individuals, but to agree with other group members that discrimination against the group as a whole is significant.

auto-stereotyping
A belief system about discrimination that is widely shared by group members.

good evidence for such discrimination, may be adaptive for the individual, allowing the individual to distance him- or herself from a potentially unpleasant explanation, and permitting the individual to maintain an adaptive belief that evaluations of his or her performance are largely under his or her control, not resulting from the vagaries of unfair prejudices. Why, then, are members of disadvantaged groups willing to believe that their group as a whole suffers from such discrimination, if they generally minimize such discrimination when it happens to them? Taylor and colleagues (1996) suggest that when asked about discrimination against their group, disadvantaged group members are influenced by an **auto-stereotype** regarding societal discrimination against their group—that is, a belief system about discrimination that is widely shared by group members. And where does this auto-stereotype come from, if it is not a product of perceived instances of discrimination against individuals? The researchers suggest that it is possible that the auto-stereotype is largely created by media portrayals of discrimination against the group that become part of the belief system of the group members, to be automatically invoked when they think about discrimination against their group as a whole.

Another aspect of ethnically based stereotypes that has been recently researched involves assessing the stereotypes that individuals feel that other groups hold about them. Jacquie Vorauer and her colleagues at the University of Manitoba refer to these as **meta-stereotypes.** They found, for instance, that White Canadians believe that Aboriginal Canadians hold a negative stereotype of them (i.e., White Canadians) (Vorauer et al., 1998, 2000). Furthermore, they have also reported the somewhat paradoxical finding that White Canadians who are less prejudiced against Aboriginal Canadians rate Aboriginal Canadians as holding a more negative view of White Canadians than do more prejudiced White Canadians. This research indicates the complex nature of ethnic stereotyping and confirms the need to consider multiple causal factors and processes when attempting to understand and explain prejudice and discrimination.

meta-stereotyping
A person's beliefs regarding the stereotype that out-group members hold about his or her own group.

Attribution Theory: Attributing Causes to Behaviours

It's natural to interpret the behaviour of others. A wife tries to understand why her husband forgot about their anniversary dinner; a student tries to understand why the teacher refuses his plaintive appeal for a grade change. Television viewers try to understand why the bachelor picked that woman. When people assign causes to behaviours, psychologists refer to these inferences as **attributions.** Attribution theories are concerned with the psychological processes that underlie these inferences of cause and effect (Heider, 1944; Jones & Davis, 1965).

attributions
The inference processes people use to assign cause and effect to behaviour.

The Covariation Model Let's consider an example of the attribution process at work. Suppose you notice that your friend Larry's mood improves noticeably on Monday, Wednesday, and Friday afternoons, after he returns from lunch. He smiles a lot, exchanges pleasantries, and offers advice freely. These behaviours contrast sharply with his normal gruff manner and generally sour disposition. What accounts for the behaviour change? you wonder. According to the *covariation model of attribution* (Kelley, 1967), the first thing you'll look for is some factor that happens at the same time as, or *covaries* with, the behaviour change. You will try to identify an event or some other factor that is present when the behaviour change occurs and is absent when the behaviour change does not occur. In this particular example, it turns out that Larry goes to his aerobic exercise class between 12:00 and 1:00 on those three days.

But covariation by itself is not an infallible criterion for attributing causality, for much the same reason that we cannot infer causality from the presence of a correlation (see Chapter 2). Just because Larry's mood improves after he leaves his exercise class does not guarantee that exercise is the cause of the change; other factors could be involved. Perhaps he meets a certain someone at the exercise class. According to the covariation model, we rely on three additional pieces of information to help us make the appropriate inference: *consistency, distinctiveness,* and *consensus.* When assessing *consistency,* we try to determine whether the change occurs regularly when the causal event is present—does Larry's mood consistently improve after exercise class? *Distinctiveness* provides an indication of whether the change occurs uniquely in the presence of the event—does Larry's mood improve after lunch only if he's been exercising? Finally, we look for *consensus,* which tells us whether other people show similar reactions when they are exposed to the same causal event—is elevation of mood a common reaction to exercising?

Internal versus External Attributions   These three factors—consistency, distinctiveness, and consensus—work in combination to help us form an attribution. In the particular example we've been considering, it's likely that we'll assume it's the external event—the exercise class—that is the cause of Larry's mood change. People tend to make an **external attribution,** which appeals to external causes, when the behaviour in question is high in consistency, distinctiveness, and consensus. In the case of Larry's pleasant demeanour, it's highly consistent (it happens every Monday, Wednesday, and Friday afternoon); its occurrence is distinctive (it occurs only after exercise class); and there is a high level of consensus (exercise tends to make other people happy too).

But what if no single event or situation in the environment can be used to explain someone's behaviour? For example, suppose Larry consistently smiles and acts pleasant in the afternoon, but he also smiles during the mornings and on days he has skipped the exercise class. Under these conditions it's doubtful that you will appeal to the environment to explain his behaviour; instead, you'll likely make an **internal attribution,** which means you'll attribute his pleasant behaviour to some *internal* personality trait or disposition: "Larry just has a great personality; he's a friendly, pleasant guy." Internal attributions are common when the consistency of a behaviour is high but its distinctiveness and consensus are low. If Larry is pleasant all the time, his post-lunch behaviour lacks distinctiveness, and you'll be unlikely to appeal to some lunch activity to explain his behaviour. Similarly, if the consensus is low—suppose exercise rarely improves mood for most people—you'll again resist attributing his good mood to this particular event (see Figure 13.3).

The Fundamental Attribution Error   So far, it seems like the attribution process is quite logical and rational, but this characterization is a bit misleading. Social psychologists have discovered that it's common for us to take shortcuts in the attribution process, probably because we're often required to make attribution judgments quickly, and it's effortful and time consuming to consider all potential factors logically (Gilbert, 1989). What happens, however, is that these shortcuts produce consistent biases in the judgment process. One of the most pervasive of these is the **fundamental attribution error:** When we interpret someone's behaviour, we overestimate the influence of internal personal factors and underestimate the role of external situational factors (Jones, 1990; Ross, 1977).

In a classic demonstration of this bias, Jones and Harris (1967) had college students read essays expressing either positive or negative opinions about Fidel Castro's communist regime in Cuba. Before reading the essays, one group of students was told that the person writing the essay had been allowed to write freely and choose the position adopted in the text. A second group was told that the writer had no choice and had been forced to adopt a particular pro or con position. Afterward, the students in both groups were asked to speculate about the writer's true opinion on the topic. Thinking logically, you might assume that if the writer had been given a choice, then the essay position probably reflected his or her true opinion on Castro. Alternatively, if the writer were simply following directions, it would be difficult to tell. To the surprise of the experimenters, however, the students tended to believe that the essay always reflected the writer's true opinion, even when the students knew that the essay writer had been forced to adopt a particular position. This example represents the fundamental attribution error at work: People tend to attribute an individual's activities to

external attribution
Attributing the cause of a person's behaviour to an external event or situation in the environment.

internal attribution
Attributing the cause of a person's behaviour to an internal personality characteristic.

Critical Thinking

Suppose you were forced to make an attribution quickly, without much time for thought. Do you think quickly formed attributions are more likely to be internal or external? Why?

fundamental attribution error
The fact that causal attributions tend to overestimate the influence of internal personal factors and underestimate the role of situational factors.

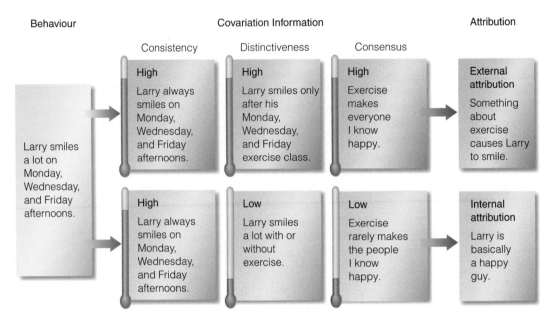

FIGURE 13.3

The Covariation Model of Attribution

When people make internal attributions, they attribute behaviour to internal personality characteristics; external attributions attribute behaviour to factors in the environment. In Kelley's attribution model, whether an internal or external attribution will be made about a particular behaviour depends on *consistency, distinctiveness,* and *consensus.* Generally, consistent behaviours that are highly distinctive and show consensus are attributed to the environment, whereas consistent behaviours that are not distinctive and show little consensus are attributed to internal characteristics.

People often think that popular game show hosts, such as Alex Trebek, are extremely knowledgeable individuals. What attribution processes might underlie such an inference?

actor-observer effect

The tendency to attribute others' behaviour to internal forces and our own behaviour to external forces.

internal personal factors, even when something in the situation (in this case, being compelled to take a certain position) provides a more likely explanation for their behaviour (Jones, 1990; Ross, 1977).

Now consider another example: You're driving down the street at a perfectly respectable speed, when you glance in your rear-view mirror and see a pickup truck bearing down on your bumper. You speed up a bit, only to find the truck mirroring your every move. Being tailgated like this is a relatively common experience. But what kind of attribution do you typically make about the driver? Do you attribute the behaviour to the person or the situation? If you're like most people, your first response is likely to be an internal attribution—you naturally assume that the driver behind you has some severe personality flaw; put simply, the driver is an aggressive jerk. You ignore the possibility that situational factors might be compelling the driver to drive fast. Isn't it possible, for instance, that the driver is late for work or has a sick child in the back seat who is in need of a doctor? These kinds of attributions, which focus on the situation, don't usually enter our minds because our first tendency is to attribute behaviour to an internal personal characteristic. The fundamental attribution error is one of the most powerful aspects of our social thinking, and it is useful for understanding many social phenomena, from prejudice to helping.

Self-Attributions   Most of these biases apply to attributions made about our own behaviour as well as those made about others. But there are some differences. Suppose in the above example, you're the one doing the tailgating. It's extremely unlikely that under these conditions you'll blame your tailgating on the fact that you're a jerk; instead, your attribution will be situation based. You're tailgating, you explain, because you're late for an appointment, or because the driver in front of you is simply driving too slowly. Generally, each of us shows what's called the **actor-observer effect**—we tend to attribute our own behaviour to external sources but the behaviours of others to internal sources.

We also show what's called the **self-serving bias;** that is, people take internal credit for their actions when those actions produce positive outcomes and blame external forces when their behaviour produces negative outcomes (Miller & Ross, 1975). When they receive an A grade on a psychology exam, students attribute the success to their own intelligence. When they fail, however, they tend to say that the exam was too difficult or the teacher was unfair. They seldom say that the exam was "too easy" if they achieve a high mark. Note that people show the same bias even when they are explaining the causes privately and anonymously. So they are not just making excuses to other people. This self-serving bias is adaptive because it allows us to bolster and maintain our self-esteem and project a sense of self-importance and confidence to the world (Greenwald, 1980).

self-serving bias
The tendency to make internal attributions about one's own behaviour when the outcome is positive and to blame the situation when one's behaviour leads to something negative.

Attribution biases can have important implications for society. The tailgating attributions just discussed may sustain the high rate of car accidents because we all tend to believe that we are in the right. When we compare the behaviour of other countries with that of Canada, we will always assume that Canada has the correct perspective. Even broader social values and world-view can be affected. Think about discussions of welfare policy or homelessness. Because of attribution biases, you might naturally attribute someone's receiving welfare or losing a job to laziness, incompetence, or some other negative internal trait. You may not consider that, in many cases, an individual is on welfare or out of work because of situational factors, perhaps because of some catastrophic life event. Attribution biases may have considerable adaptive value—because they allow us to make quick decisions about the causes of behaviour, and they make us feel more comfortable about ourselves and the world as a whole. As usual, however, they do have a downside: They can sometimes lead to incorrect conclusions.

Evolutionary and Cultural Bases of Biases

We noted in Chapter 8 the adaptive value of cognitive biases. The same arguments can be made for the presence of consistent biases and errors in social judgments—including assessments of our own abilities and accomplishments. Social/developmental psychologists Dennis Krebs of Simon Fraser University and Kathy Denton of Douglas College suggest that natural selection may have shaped human minds to process social information in a systematically inaccurate fashion (Krebs & Denton, 1997). In particular, they suggest that humans may have evolved to deceive themselves about their own motives, that we consistently overvalue our own abilities and ignore explanations for our behaviour that are embarrassing or ignoble. Krebs and Denton imply that such adaptive self-deception and overvaluation might have contributed to the reproductive success of our ancestors. People who overvalued their abilities and overlooked their baser motives might have been more successful in encouraging other people to cooperate with them, for instance, or even in exploiting other people, as compared to people who operated with a completely accurate and lesser view of themselves. Research by Joan Lockard and University of Victoria neuropsychologist Catherine Mateer suggests that the brain is capable of storing information in such a way that specific types of information are not easily accessible to other parts of the mind/brain system (Lockard & Mateer, 1988). Such findings suggest a possible neuropsychological basis for adaptive mechanisms of self-deception and social biases (Lockard & Paulhus, 1988). As with mechanisms selected by evolution, there is no guarantee that they are adaptive in all contemporary situations. For example, Edward Johnson of the University of Manitoba showed that self-deception may be useful in certain limited contexts but can interfere with performance after failure in laboratory situations (Johnson, 1995; Johnson et al., 1997).

Other evolutionary psychologists such as Steven Pinker (2002) have suggested that the human tendency to classify people into in-groups and out-groups may be based on the likelihood that our ancestors often had to make critical but immediate life decisions, such as "Is this new person likely to harm me or help me?" Thus evolutionary selection would shape our minds with structures that quickly classify people into "friend or foe" categories—even if mistakes are sometimes tragic. Recent laboratory work on stereotypes has supported such speculations: Differences in brain activation have been detected when individuals are making judgments about a disliked out-group compared to judgments about an in-group (Phelps et al., 2000).

If human tendencies to classify people into in-groups or out-groups did have an evolutionary origin, this would not mean that society could not overcome, or at least modify, people's ethnic or other prejudices. Research has shown that such attitudes can be changed. However, knowledge of the origins of the basic cognitive modules that underlie group categorization will be useful in attempting to eliminate ethnic and other prejudice.

However, these claims for universality of cognitive biases have been challenged by recent work at the University of British Columbia. Steve Heine and Darrin Lehman have demonstrated that the Japanese show little in the way of self-serving biases or any sort of self-enhancement (e.g., Heine & Lehman, 1999). Moreover, Ara Norenzayan and his colleagues have shown that people in Eastern cultures are generally more situationist and, therefore, less susceptible to the fundamental attribution error (Norenzayan et al., 2002). When members of such cultures do consider dispositions, they consider them to be more malleable than do Westerners (Norenzayan & Nisbett, 2000). The field awaits a theory that can integrate the evolutionary and cultural positions.

Attitudes and Attitude Change

The final topic we'll consider in our discussion of social cognition is the study of attitudes and attitude change. An **attitude** is simply a positive or negative evaluation or belief held about something, which in turn may affect behaviour. Like the other forms of social cognition we've discussed, attitudes are beneficial for a number of reasons. When they guide behaviour, attitudes help us remain consistent in our actions and help us use our knowledge about individuals or situations. Attitudes also play an important role in our perception and interpretation of the world. They help us focus our attention on information relevant to our beliefs, particularly information that can help confirm an existing belief. As a result, attitudes may serve as a kind of defensive function, protecting people's basic beliefs about themselves and others (Fazio, 1986).

The Components of an Attitude Typically, social psychologists divide attitudes into three main components: a *cognitive* component, an *affective* component, and a *behavioural* component (Olson & Zanna, 1993). The cognitive component represents what people know or believe about the object of their attitude; the affective component is made up of the feelings that the object engenders; and the behavioural component is a predisposition to act toward the object in a particular way.

To see how these three components work together, let's suppose that you've formed an unfavourable attitude toward your landlord. Your attitude rests on a foundation of facts and beliefs about behaviour. You know, for instance, that the landlord has raised your rent three times in the last year, that he enters your apartment without first asking permission, and that he won't let you keep your pet cat, Mr. Wigglesworth, without a huge pet deposit. These facts and beliefs form the cognitive component of your attitude. Accompanying these facts are your emotional reactions, which make up the affective component: When you see or think about your landlord, you get angry and feel slightly sick to your stomach. Finally, the behavioural component of your attitude predisposes you to act in certain ways. You may continually scan the classified ads looking for a new apartment; you may constantly complain about your landlord to anyone who'll listen. It's these three factors in combination—cognitive, affective, and behavioural—that compose what psychologists mean by an attitude (see Figure 13.4).

Notice that the behavioural component of the attitude is described as a predisposition to act. This is an important point to remember because attitudes do not always directly affect behaviour. As you know, people sometimes act in ways that are inconsistent with their attitudes (Ajzen, 2001; Ajzen & Fishbein, 1977). When talking to your landlord, for instance, you may be all smiles even though underneath you're steaming.

attitude

A positive or negative evaluation or belief held about something, which in turn may affect one's behaviour; attitudes are typically broken down into cognitive, affective, and behavioural components.

Attitude
Cognitive
Knowledge about the object
Affective
Emotional feelings
Behavioural
Predisposition to act

FIGURE 13.4

The Three Components of Attitudes

Social psychologists typically divide attitudes into three main components: cognitive, affective, and behavioural.

Attitudes do not always connect with behaviour because behaviour is usually determined by multiple factors, especially external factors such as the situation. In some situations, it is simply unwise to express true feelings, such as when dealing with the landlord. In other situations, people act quickly and mindlessly without considering the true meaning or ramifications of their behaviour (Langer, 1989). For example, people often sign petitions for activities they may not completely believe in or buy products that they don't really want, simply because they're in a hurry and don't want to be bothered further. For an attitude to guide behaviour, it needs to come to mind—that is, it needs to be accessible—and it should be appropriate or relevant to the situation (Kraus, 1995; Pratkanis & Greenwald, 1989).

How Are Attitudes Formed and Changed?   Where do attitudes come from, and how are they acquired? There are many routes to attitude formation. We use our everyday experiences as the basis for many of our beliefs. How we interpret those experiences depends partly on our inborn intellectual and personality traits (Tesser, 1993). But even something as simple as mere exposure can be sufficient to change your feelings about an object. In a classic study by Robert Zajonc (1968), participants were shown photographs of undergraduate men taken from a school yearbook. Some of the photos were shown only once or twice; others were shown up to 25 times. Following exposure, participants were asked to give an estimate of how much they liked each of the men shown. The results revealed that the more often a photo had been presented, the more the participants claimed to "like" the person shown. It is not clear exactly how to interpret this finding, in part because people's ratings change on a whole host of dimensions following exposure (Mandler et al., 1987). But it demonstrates how easily some attitudes, particularly new ones or those that are not strongly held, can be modified (Zajonc, 2001).

Direct positive or negative experience with an attitude target is generally agreed to be the single most important factor affecting attitude formation. A great deal of evidence suggests that attitudes can be conditioned, through experiences of the type discussed in Chapter 6. Events that occur outside of one's control can acquire signalling properties, through classical conditioning, and then serve as an initial foundation for an attitude (Baldwin et al., 2003; Petty et al., 2001). Advertisers commonly try to manipulate how people feel toward consumer products by pairing the product with something pleasurable, such as an attractive model or a successful athlete. Through

Critical Thinking

Do you think it's likely that all people have an innate attitude, or preference, for pleasurable things over painful things? What other kinds of attitudes might be influenced by genetic factors?

How closely do your attitudes mirror the positions and beliefs of your peer group?

instrumental conditioning, attitudes are influenced by the rewards and punishments people receive for their actions. Certainly if you express a tentative opinion on a subject—"We've got too much big government in this country"—and this opinion is reinforced by people whom you respect, you're likely to express this same attitude again.

Finally, much of what we learn, including attitudes, is the result of *observational learning.* We model significant others—our parents, peers, teachers, and so on—when it comes to both attitudes and behaviour. The political convictions of most people, for example, mirror quite closely the political attitudes of their parents (McGuire, 1985). People also use their peers as a reference group for judging the acceptability of their behaviours and beliefs. Simply observe teenagers in the local mall to see how important modelling behaviour can be. Everything from language to musical taste to hairstyle to shoe type is replicated from one teen to the next. Ask yourself: How differently do you think and act from the people in your immediate circle of friends? Modelling is not the only reason why people act and think like their peers, but it is a large part of the reason.

Established attitudes tend to be fairly stable (Grant et al., 1994), although people can be persuaded to change them. We are particularly likely to change our attitudes when we're motivated and inclined to process an incoming persuasive communication with care and attention, that is, when we listen carefully to the arguments and then judge them according to their merits. Imagine you've recently changed your views on the topic of abortion after listening to a persuasive speaker at your school. If you carefully weighed the quality and strength of the arguments and then changed your attitude accordingly, your attitude change is likely to be stable and long lasting (Olson & Zanna, 1993). This is referred to as the *central route* to persuading someone to change his or her attitude. However, another way that advertisers in particular attempt to change our attitudes is called the *peripheral route* to attitude change. This approach works on the affective component of the attitude and usually involves simply exposing people to the attitude or product to be adopted, without any deep processing of rational arguments. For instance, an advertiser who suggests you buy a Zippo car because it gets good gas mileage is using the central route to persuade you to buy the car; an advertisement that simply shows you attractive actors enjoying themselves in a Zippo car is using the peripheral route.

The Festinger and Carlsmith Study We can also be persuaded to change our attitudes because of our own actions. In an influential study of attitude change conducted by Festinger and Carlsmith (1959), college students were asked to perform some

Critical Thinking

Next time you watch television, notice which commercials rely on logical arguments and which use humour or celebrity endorsers. Do you see any connection between the type of product and the style of persuasion? What kinds of products are more likely to induce us to use central rather than peripheral processing?

In situations in which a person's level of involvement or commitment to a message is low, advertisers tend to capitalize on the peripheral route to persuasion by using celebrity endorsers or humour in the persuasive message.

incredibly boring tasks for a full-hour session. At the end of the hour, some of the participants (the two experimental groups) were asked to tell the next participant that the experiment was actually filled with interesting and enjoyable tasks. To provide an incentive, the experimenter offered participants in one experimental group a monetary reward of $1 and those in the other experimental group a reward of $20.

The point of the offer was to get the members of the two experimental groups to act in a way that contradicted their true feelings, or attitudes, about the experiment. The task was clearly boring, so they were essentially asked to lie for either a small or a large reward. Festinger and Carlsmith were interested in what effect this behaviour would have on participants' attitudes about the experiment. After students accepted the offer and tried to convince the next participant, their attitudes about the boring tasks were assessed through an interview. The researchers found that attitudes about the tasks did indeed change: They became more positive relative to the attitudes of the members of the control group, who had not been asked to lie. Moreover, the positive shift was larger for participants receiving $1 as opposed to $20. The more participants were paid to act inconsistently with their true feelings, the less likely their attitudes were to change (see Figure 13.5).

Cognitive Dissonance The above results may seem perplexing. You would probably have predicted that the students receiving $20 would show the greatest attitude change; after all, wouldn't a large reward have a greater reinforcing effect? The answer, according to Festinger's (1957) theory of **cognitive dissonance,** is that the inconsistent behaviour produces psychological distress, or what he called *dissonance.* Think about it. Which action is going to lead to greater internal turmoil and distress: lying to receive $1 or lying to receive $20? Most people can easily justify a simple white lie when offered a reasonable amount of money, especially when asked by an authority figure (remember that $20 was worth a lot more in the 1950s than it is now). But to lie for a mere $1 is tough to justify—unless, of course, you weren't really lying. Maybe it wasn't so bad after all. According to cognitive dissonance theory, if the discrepancy between what you believe and how you act is great, you will tend to change your beliefs to match the behaviour.

Since cognitive dissonance theory was first introduced in the 1950s, hundreds of follow-up studies have been conducted (Aronson, 1992). Most have confirmed Festinger and Carlsmith's basic finding: When people are induced to act in ways that are inconsistent with their attitudes, those attitudes tend to change as a consequence. For instance, suppose you are asked to eat fried grasshoppers either by an experimenter

cognitive dissonance
The tension produced when people act in a way that is inconsistent with their attitudes; attitude change may occur as a result of attempting to reduce cognitive dissonance.

FIGURE 13.5
Cognitive Dissonance

Festinger proposed that attitudes change when a discrepancy exists between what we believe and how we act. People who lied about the boring experimental task for a mere $1 later claimed to enjoy the task more than did people who lied for $20 or who were not asked to lie. (Data from Festinger & Carlsmith, 1959.)

who behaves in a rude and disrespectful way toward you or by a nice experimenter. If you do eat the grasshoppers offered by the rude experimenter, you are more likely to report later that you actually liked them; otherwise, it is difficult to explain to yourself and others why you would do something you dislike for someone who treated you rudely. It is much easier to explain why you did something you dislike for someone who treated you well.

But not all psychologists are convinced that internal tension, or dissonance, results from acting inconsistently with your beliefs. You might, for example, feel personally responsible for creating an unwanted or negative situation (Blanton et al., 1997; Cooper, 1992). Some psychologists are also uncomfortable with the concept of cognitive dissonance because it seems rather vague and not easy to measure directly. It's also difficult to predict when dissonance will occur and, if it's present, how people will choose to reduce it (Joule, 1986). However, the idea continues to be influential among social psychologists, especially when the motivational and cognitive components of dissonance are taken into account (Aronson, 1997; Petty et al., 1997; Wood, 2000).

Self-Perception Theory One of the best-known alternatives to dissonance theory is psychologist Daryl Bem's (1967, 1972) **self-perception theory.** The idea behind self-perception theory is that we are active interpreters of our own behaviour. We learn from our behaviour and use our actions as a basis for inferring internal beliefs. For example, if I sit down and practise the piano for two hours a day, it must be the case that I like music and think I have at least a bit of musical talent. If I regularly stop for hamburgers and fries for lunch, it must be the case that I like fast food. The basis for the attitude is self-perception—behaviour is observed, and attitudes follow from the behaviour (see Figure 13.6). Note that there is no reference to distress or any kind of emotion in this theory.

Many experimental findings support these basic ideas. For example, the Festinger and Carlsmith study can be interpreted from this perspective. You observe yourself telling someone that a boring task is interesting, for a mere $1, and conclude that since you engaged in this behaviour your attitude toward the task must not have been that negative. Another phenomenon that may be explained this way is the persuasion method known as the *foot-in-the-door technique*. Jonathan Freedman and Scott Fraser (1966) convinced a group of California householders to sign a petition expressing support for safe driving. Several weeks later, the researchers returned with a request that

self-perception theory
The idea that people use observations of their own behaviour as a basis for inferring their internal beliefs.

FIGURE 13.6
Self-Perception Theory

Some psychologists believe that we form attitudes at least in part by observing our own behaviour. If I regularly eat hamburgers, then my attitude about hamburgers must be positive.

Concept Summary

ROOTS OF ATTITUDES AND ATTITUDE CHANGE

Mechanism	Description	Example ("Whom should I vote for?")
Central route	When motivated to process an incoming message, we listen carefully to the arguments given and judge them on their merits.	Jason is not sure whom to vote for in the upcoming federal election. He obtains detailed information on the candidates' views on the major issues, and after considering each, decides on the Liberal candidate.
Peripheral route	When we are unable or unwilling to process a message carefully, our attitudes are more affected by superficial cues or mere exposure.	Yvette hasn't really kept up with the election coverage, but has seen some commercials during her nightly TV viewing. She gets a kick out of the New Democratic Party candidate's humorous ad, so decides to vote for her.
Cognitive dissonance	Behaviour that is inconsistent with attitudes produces psychological tension (i.e., *dissonance*). If this discrepancy is large enough, attitudes or behaviour will change.	Jeremy has always considered himself a Conservative and backs the Conservative candidate for Member of Parliament. Lately he's been dating a woman involved with the Canadian Alliance party. At first, Jeremy feels distressed, but gradually he becomes more favourable toward the Alliance party.
Self-perception	We learn from our behaviour, using our actions as a basis for inferring beliefs. Behaviour is observed, and attitudes follow from the behaviour.	Felicia gets a phone call from the Green Party campaign headquarters pleading for help. The Green Party can't compete with the other campaigns unless it raises more money for its candidate. Felicia agrees to donate $20 to the cause. Looking back on it, she decides she must really favour the Green Party candidate.

the householders now place a large and quite ugly "Drive Safely" billboard in their yards. The petition signers were three times more likely to comply with this new request than a control group of people who were never asked to sign a petition. What's the interpretation? The memory of signing the original petition triggered *self-perception,* which then helped shape the attitude: If I signed the petition, then I must be a strong advocate for safe driving. Another more troublesome outcome of self-perception processes involves the development of prejudiced attitudes. A person who finds him- or herself avoiding a minority group in public places, for instance, may reflect on this pattern and conclude: "I tend to move away from people of that minority group; I suppose this means I must believe they are undesirable."

Of course, there are boundary conditions for these effects—we do not always simply match our attitudes to our behaviours—but monitoring one's own behaviour is clearly an important ingredient of attitude formation and change. It may be that we are particularly likely to use our own actions as a guide when we're unsure of or undecided about our attitude. Or we may use our own behaviour to see if our attitudes or opinions have recently changed: "Do I still like playing video games? Well, let's see. I haven't played a game for a while, so I must not be crazy about them any more." It's adaptive for us to use multiple sources of information for establishing our beliefs, including our own actions.

 Critical Thinking

How might you use cognitive dissonance theory to explain the foot-in-the-door technique?

Test Yourself 13.1

Check your knowledge about how we form impressions of others by answering the following questions. (You will find the answers in Appendix B.)

1. Decide whether each of the following statements about person perception is true or false.
   a. On average, attractive people are assumed to be more intelligent, better adjusted, and more socially aware than people with average looks. *True or False?*

b. Prototype theories assume that we represent stereotypes with particular individuals, or exemplars. *True or False?*

c. The prejudiced attitudes of people who also express authoritarian attitudes appear to be more related to their stereotyped beliefs about out-groups rather than to their concern that such groups disrespect traditional values. *True or False?*

d. The degree of discrimination that people believe is directed toward their group is usually closely correlated with the discrimination that individuals in the group report experiencing personally. *True or False?*

2. For each of the following, decide whether you are most likely to make an internal or an external attribution for the behaviour described.

a. You get a perfect score on your psychology exam: _____

b. Josie always smiles after her psychology lecture, but everyone else in the class leaves angry: _____

c. You get a failing score on your psychology exam: _____

d. Eagerly anticipating your food, you notice your waiter seems to spend a lot of time talking to the hostess: _____

3. Decide whether each of the following statements about attitudes and attitude change is true or false.

a. For an attitude to guide behaviour, it should be appropriate or relevant to the situation. *True or False?*

b. The peripheral route to persuasion operates when our level of involvement in or commitment to a message is high. *True or False?*

c. According to cognitive dissonance theory, it is inconsistencies between internal beliefs and our actions that lead to attitude change. *True or False?*

d. Mere exposure can lead to attitude change, but only if we're processing an incoming communication with care and attention. *True or False?*

BEHAVING IN THE PRESENCE OF OTHERS: SOCIAL INFLUENCE

Learning Goals

1. Understand social facilitation and interference, including the relationship between task difficulty, arousal, and performance.
2. Be able to explain the bystander effect and the concept of diffusion of responsibility.
3. Learn how behaviour changes in a group setting.
4. Understand some aspects of group decision making.
5. Be able to describe the Milgram experiment and discuss its implications for the power of authority.

social influence

The study of how the behaviours and thoughts of individuals are affected by the presence of others.

WE NOW TURN OUR ATTENTION to the topic of **social influence:** How is our behaviour affected by the presence of others? The evidence shows that the presence of other people can cause us to act in new or different ways or to change our attitudes and beliefs. Think back to the ambitious underling, Chris M., whom we met at the beginning of the chapter. His behaviour certainly changed in the presence of others: He violated his beliefs and conformed to the opinions of his colleagues and his arrogant boss.

Social Facilitation and Interference

One of the simplest and most widely documented examples of social influence is the phenomenon of social facilitation. **Social facilitation** is the *enhancement* in performance that is sometimes found when we perform in the presence of others. To demonstrate social facilitation, we need to compare someone's task performance in two conditions: when performing alone and when performing in the presence of other people. The "other people" could be either co-actors (often people performing the same task or a related one), or they could be audience members (for instance, friends and family watching a piano recital). If performance improves when other people are around, you've demonstrated social facilitation. In an early investigation of this effect, Norman Triplett (1898) discovered that adolescents would wind in a fishing line faster when working in pairs than when working alone. Task performance improved in the presence of others, which is the defining characteristic of social facilitation.

Social facilitation is a widespread effect, occurring in many kinds of social environments and for many kinds of tasks (Aiello & Douthitt, 2001). Motorists drive through intersections faster when another car is travelling in the lane beside them (Towler, 1986); people run faster when others are present (Worringham & Messick, 1983); people even eat more when dining out with friends than when eating alone (Clendenen et al., 1994). In fact, the effect is not restricted to humans: Ants will excavate dirt more quickly to build their nests when other ants are present (Chen, 1937); hungry chickens will peck food more when other chickens observe passively through a clear plastic wall (Tolman, 1968); cockroaches will even run faster down an alleyway when a "spectator" roach watches from a small plastic enclosure (Zajonc et al., 1969).

But there is another side to the coin. It's easy to think of examples of how we've "risen to the occasion" and excelled when an audience was present, but the opposite can be the case as well. Sometimes performing in a crowd impairs performance—we "choke," a tendency referred to as **social interference.** Talented Angela, who finally performs Bach's Invention No. 1 perfectly in her last practice session, finds her fingers fumbling helplessly during the piano recital. Confident Eddie, who thought he had learned his lines to perfection, finds that on opening night he's standing embarrassingly silent on centre stage. Social interference is the opposite of social facilitation, but both represent cases in which our ability to perform a task is influenced by the presence of others.

Task Difficulty and Arousal   So what determines whether the presence of others will help or hinder performance? Psychologists have determined that *task difficulty* is one important factor: If the task is relatively easy, the presence of others will spur the person on, and you'll see social facilitation; if the task is new or difficult, the presence of others can have an inhibitory effect, and you'll find social interference.

According to psychologist Robert Zajonc (1965), it's possible to explain the relationship between task difficulty and performance by appealing to how an audience's presence influences *arousal*. When others are watching, Zajonc argued, it's reasonable to assume that our general level of arousal increases. Arousal, in turn, naturally biases us toward engaging in well-learned responses. If the task is a relatively easy one, such as running or solving simple multiplications, then such well-learned responses are likely to be useful and help performance. But when tasks are difficult, we're likely to need new or unusual responses that are less well learned. For difficult tasks, then, performance is likely to be impaired because the high arousal levels will bias us toward responses that are not very useful. For instance, think about trying to perform a complicated jump for the first time in front of your gym class. The high arousal level involved in attempting this difficult task in front of other people would probably decrease your performance compared to trying it by yourself. Evidence shows that home teams tend to lose important hockey games played in their home stadium. Apparently, teams feel more pressure when their own fans are watching (Wright et al., 1995). Thus, the influence that others have on performance is explained by the relationship between general arousal and its effects on task performance.

social facilitation
The enhancement in performance that is sometimes found when an individual performs in the presence of others.

social interference
The impairment in performance that is sometimes found when an individual performs in the presence of others.

Critical Thinking

Under what conditions do you think the presence of an audience might actually lower someone's arousal? What implications does this possibility have for social facilitation?

Demonstrating the phenomenon of social facilitation, people tend to eat more when they're in the presence of others.

When a task is difficult, performing in the presence of others can lead to social interference. What seemed easy in private becomes a nightmare in public.

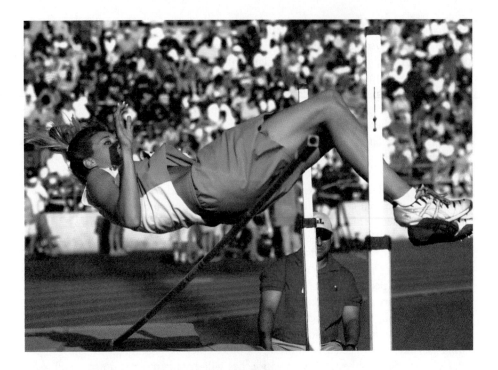

Social Influences on Helping: The Bystander Effect

In addition to task performance, the presence of other people can dramatically influence whether we help others in need. Think about the last time that you were driving on the highway and noticed some poor person standing alongside his or her disabled car by the side of the road. Did you stop and help? Did you at least get off at the nearest exit and telephone the police or highway patrol? If you're like most people, you probably did nothing. In all likelihood, you failed to accept responsibility for helping; you left that job for someone else.

The problem is more serious than you might think. In March 1964, while walking home from work at 3:30 in the morning, Catherine "Kitty" Genovese was stalked and then brutally attacked by a knife-wielding assailant outside her apartment building in New York City. "Oh my god, he stabbed me!" Kitty screamed. "I'm dying! I'm dying!" Inside the apartment building, awakened by the screams, some 38 of her neighbours sat silently listening as the attacker finished the job. Kitty was stabbed repeatedly before she eventually died; in fact, the attacker actually left and came back to assault her again and then kill her. No one in the apartment building came to her aid or called the police until approximately 30 minutes after the first attack. Only in New York, you say? A similar incident happened in Vancouver in December 2002. Fifteen people heard a girl scream as she was murdered, but none responded in a helpful way. Were bystanders simply afraid to get involved in these situations, or was some other more general psychological process at work?

The reluctance to come to someone's aid when other people are present is known generally as the **bystander effect** (Darley & Latané, 1968). Although it's relatively easy to document examples in the news, it's also possible to study the bystander effect in the laboratory. Consider the following scenario. You've volunteered to participate in a psychology experiment that involves groups of students discussing the problems of college life. To minimize embarrassment, you're allowed to sit in a small cubicle where you can communicate with the others using an intercom system. Before the experiment begins, you're told that one, two, or five other people will be participating. The session begins and suddenly one of the group members, who had previously mentioned being prone to epileptic seizures, begins to have a seizure. Over the intercom, his voice begins to garble—"Somebody-er-er-help-er-uh-uh-uh"—followed by silence. What do you do? Do you get up and help or sit where you are?

bystander effect

The reluctance to come to the aid of a person in need when other people are present.

In the actual version of this experiment, of course, no one actually had a seizure; the incident was manufactured by the experimenters to observe the bystander effect. There was also only one real participant in the experiment; the "others" were simply voices recorded on tape. The researchers found that the likelihood that the real participant would offer some kind of help to the imaginary seizure victim depended on how many other people the participant believed to be present. When the participant was convinced that only one other person was participating in the group, he or she almost immediately rose to intervene. But when it was presumed that four others (in addition to the seizure victim) were present, only 62% of the participants offered aid (Darley & Latané, 1968).

Diffusion of Responsibility   Most social psychologists believe that the behaviour of the people in these situations, including the actions of the New York apartment dwellers, is not unusual, nor does it simply reflect widespread societal apathy. Instead, the reluctance to help the needy in the presence of others can be explained by a specific kind of social influence. We avoid helping, or getting involved, because the presence of others leads to **diffusion of responsibility**—we believe that others have already done something to help or will soon get involved. If we know that others are present in the situation, and certainly many occupants of the apartment building heard the terrible screams, we allow our sense of responsibility to *diffuse,* or spread out widely, among the other people presumed to be present.

diffusion of responsibility
The idea that when people know, or think, that others are present in a situation, they allow their sense of responsibility for action to diffuse, or spread out widely, among those who are present.

The bystander effect is a disturbing but powerful example of social influence. The more witnesses there are, the less likely it will be that any one will step forward to offer aid. The effect has been replicated many times in numerous social settings that extend beyond the laboratory. It extends to other social situations where several people have the opportunity to contribute to a worthwhile goal (Latané & Nida, 1981). While you may not have witnessed a murder, you surely have witnessed a messy kitchen. Everyday experience, as well as research, confirms that the more people involved in messing up a communal room, the less likely any one of them will clean it up.

Of course, there are many other social determinants of helping behaviour. For instance, people are more likely to help if they have recently observed others being helpful. It is the counterintuitive nature of the bystander effect—that there is danger in numbers rather than safety in numbers—that makes it a fascinating social phenomenon. In trying to explain the bystander effect, it is tempting (and much more comfortable) to suggest that it was the weak character of the reluctant nonhelpers rather than a complex social effect such as diffusion of responsibility. For instance, in the Kitty Genovese incident, many commentators suggested that this phenomenon is peculiar to New Yorkers, who have a reputation for being collectively callous and indifferent. Such a suggestion can be interpreted as being an example of the fundamental attribution error (discussed earlier in the chapter): The reason for the failure to intervene in the Genovese case was New Yorkers' callousness (an internal explanation) rather than diffusion of responsibility dynamics (a more external attribution). Although local norms regarding helpfulness undoubtedly play a role in interventions and intervention failures, people seem particularly quick to blame such failures on the lack of character in people ("That couldn't happen here in Canada" or "I would never behave that way"), rather than considering the more complex external explanations. Of course, people do not have easy access to the driving forces of social situations. Given our inability to pinpoint the true causes of our own social dynamics, it is understandable that we resort to explanations that make us feel more comfortable.

The Power of the Group

The social context is particularly powerful in well-defined groups. Our behaviour is shaped not only by the characteristics of the group—its size and the unanimity of its members—but even by the mere fact that we're *in* the group. Among the most impressive demonstrations of the power of the group involves its ability to get group members to conform to the behaviour of other people in the group. Also powerful are the tendencies of individuals in groups to shirk responsibility for their own actions. We discuss these group pressures toward conformity in the following section.

social loafing

The tendency to put out less effort when several people are supposed to be working on a task than when only one is working.

Social Loafing   During our discussion of social facilitation you learned that a person's performance often changes when others are present. Whether performance improves or declines depends on factors such as the difficulty of the task or one's general level of arousal. But when participating as a member of a group, most people show a strong tendency to engage in **social loafing,** which means they put out less effort than when the task is theirs alone (Latané et al., 1979). Social loafing is easy to demonstrate in the laboratory. In one study, volunteer subjects were instructed to clap and cheer as loudly as possible while blindfolded and listening to noise over headphones. Just before they began the task, the participants were told they would be clapping either with a group of other subjects or by themselves. When the volunteers believed they were part of a clapping group, their individual output dropped considerably.

Like many of the phenomena we've discussed in this chapter, social loafing is complex. Whether it occurs in a particular situation will depend on many factors, including the importance of the task, the cohesiveness of the group, and the personalities of the group members (Karau & Hart, 1998; Smith et al., 2001). The effect occurs widely across cultures, although it may be especially common in cultures that stress individuality (Karau & Williams, 1993). Some social psychologists make a connection between social loafing and the bystander effect. Bibb Latané (1981), in particular, has argued that both effects result from diffusion of responsibility. In the bystander effect, people suspect that others either will or have become involved; in social loafing, we assume that others will carry the load. In both cases, the fact that we are simply one of many makes us feel less accountable for our behaviour. We fail to step up and take full responsibility, or to work to our fullest capabilities, because the responsibility can be diffused or spread to the other members of the group.

Critical Thinking

What situations are subject to social loafing as opposed to social facilitation?

deindividuation

The loss of individuality, or depersonalization, that comes from being in a group.

Deindividuation   The idea that we feel less accountable for our behaviour when we're in a group setting can lead to a phenomenon called **deindividuation.** Imagine yourself at a particularly lively party: The people around you are acting crazy—they're drinking too much, damaging the furniture, and some are even beginning to shed their clothes. Are you likely to start doing the same? Some psychologists believe that when people are in large groups, they lose their sense of individuality. We can enter a depersonalized state of mind, called deindividuation, that increases the chances of engaging in destructive, aggressive, or deviant behaviour. Under most circumstances, it's highly unlikely that you would trash the furniture in a friend's home. But when you're a part of large rowdy group, deindividuation can lead you to do things that you might not otherwise do.

Once again, diffusion of responsibility is likely to play a role in such situations. When you're in a large group, you're less likely to feel accountable for your actions. You feel anonymous, which lowers your normal restraints on destructive actions. You also feel less self-conscious—you go along with the group, as a whim, because you're not thinking about your normal standards, values, and morals. Whether you truly enter a depersonalized state of mind is debatable, but your actions do differ from your normal tendencies. Some psychologists have argued that deindividuation is simply an example of situation-specific behaviour; your behaviour is being controlled by an unusual situation and your actions probably don't provide much information about how you typically behave (Postmes & Spears, 1998).

conformity

The tendency to go along with the wishes of the group; when people conform, their opinions, feelings, and behaviours generally start to move toward the group norm.

Conformity   One of the most important behavioural consequences of group membership is **conformity,** the tendency of a member's opinions, feelings, and behaviours to move toward the group norm. Its effects are powerful even when that person has not been explicitly asked to behave in the same way as others. Normally conformity is an adaptive function for group success and a cohesive society. We agree to drive on the

People can feel less accountable for their behaviour in a group setting, a phenomenon known as deindividuation.

right side of the road. We go to Aunt Sarah's for the holidays because that's what the family tradition is. If your friends all want to see *Titanic* for the fifth time, why cause a fuss? The downside, of course, is that your group may not always do the right thing. Smoking, racism, shoplifting, violence, and promiscuous sex can often result from pressure to feel part of a group. Studies investigating issues of conformity to group norms are among the oldest and best known of all social psychology experiments.

In one classic study of conformity, psychologist Solomon Asch (1951, 1955) rigged the following experimental setup. Participants were asked to take part in a simple perception experiment that required them to make judgments about line length. Two cards were shown: one displaying a standard line of a particular length and the other showing three comparison lines of differing lengths. The participant was required to state aloud which of the three comparison lines was the same length as the standard line (see Figure 13.7). The task was really quite simple—there was no question as to what the correct answer should be. The catch was that the participant was part of a group and the other members of the group were really *confederates* of the experimenter—they were there to put social pressure on the true participant.

FIGURE 13.7
The Asch Study of Conformity

Do you think you would have any trouble choosing the correct comparison line in this task? Asch found that people often conformed to the group opinion—even when it was clearly wrong. The photo shown here is taken from one of his actual experiments.

Standard
Line

1   2   3
Comparison
Lines

The confederate participants were instructed to lie on some of the trials. They were told to give a response, aloud, that was clearly wrong (such as picking comparison line 1 as the correct answer). Asch was mainly concerned about how often these incorrect answers would affect the answers of the real participant. Imagine yourself in this situation: You know the answer is line 2, but four of your fellow participants have already given line 1 as a response. Do you conform to the opinions of your peers, even though doing so conflicts with what you know to be true? Asch found that in approximately 75% of the sessions, participants conformed on at least one of the trials, and the overall rate of conformity was around 37%. Although peer pressure wasn't always effective in altering the behaviour of the participants—in fact, only 5% of the participants conformed on every trial—its power was surprising.

As you might imagine, the Asch experiments had quite an impact on the psychological community. It was disturbing to many that intelligent college students could be pressured by a group of strangers to agree with a clear falsehood. Similar experiments have been conducted on dozens of occasions in many countries around the world. Generally, Asch's results have held up well, although a number of variables affect the likelihood that conformity will occur. Asch himself found, for example, that the rate of conformity dropped dramatically when one of the confederates dissented from the majority and gave the correct answer. It was also discovered that the size of the group is not as important as you might think. Conformity increases as the size of the pressure group gets larger, but it levels off relatively quickly. The pressure to conform does not increase directly with group size; after a certain point, usually when the majority group contains three to five members, adding even more pressure has a minimal effect (Tanford & Penrod, 1984). Finally, attitudes about the group as a whole also matter; if people have little respect for the group, they're less likely to conform. Conformity is particularly likely when pressure comes from an in-group (Abrams et al., 1990).

Group Decision Making

As you've just seen, members of an in-group can exert considerable pressure on one another to conform to the standards or norms of the group. One of the consequences of these internal pressures is that groups tend to take on behavioural characteristics of their own, especially when group decisions need to be made. Obviously, the psychology of group decision making is critically important—it affects everything from how verdicts are reached by juries, to how families decide where to go on vacation, to decisions made by government cabinet members. Psychologists have identified two important characteristics of group decision making: group polarization and groupthink.

Group Polarization

When members of an in-group arrive at a consensus of opinion, there is a tendency for the group's opinion to polarize. **Group polarization** means that the group's dominant point of view—which is usually determined by the initial views of the majority—becomes stronger and even more extreme with time. If you join a local action group dedicated to exposing corporate corruption and the group tends to believe initially that corporate corruption is a significant and rising problem, it's likely that over time you and the rest of the members of the group will become even more convinced of that position (Moscovici & Zavalloni, 1969; Myers, 1982).

What accounts for group polarization? Not surprisingly, some of the same factors that promote conformity promote polarization. For example, group discussions tend to provide information that consolidates initial opinions. Those who enter the group with strong opinions make strong cases for their viewpoint and dissenting viewpoints are less likely to be heard (Stewart & Stasser, 1995). At the same time, the social aspects of the discussion play an important role. People want to be liked by the other members of the group, so they shift their attitude toward the group consensus. You're more likely to be accepted by the group if you forcefully argue in favour of the group's dominant viewpoint.

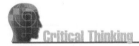

Critical Thinking

Notice that when people conform they often act in ways that are inconsistent with their attitudes. What implications should this have for attitude change?

group polarization
The tendency for a group's dominant point of view to become stronger and more extreme with time.

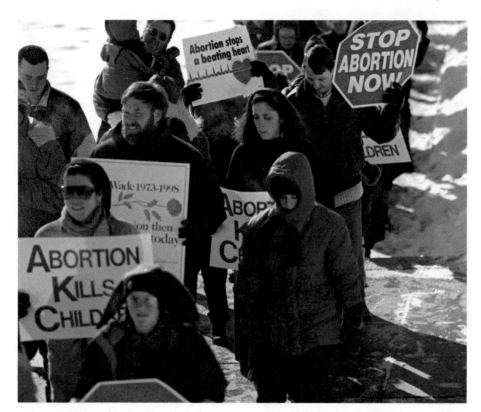

Polarization occurs when a group's majority opinion becomes stronger and more extreme with time. What's the likelihood that people in this group will adopt more tolerant views in the future?

Groupthink The trend toward consensus and polarization of opinion may also be influenced by what psychologist Irving Janis has labelled **groupthink:** Members of a group become so interested in seeking a consensus of opinion that they start to ignore and even suppress dissenting views. Janis (1982, 1989) found evidence for groupthink when he looked at how well-established in-groups arrived at decisions, particularly policy decisions by members of the government. He and others analyzed a number of watershed events in U.S. policymaking, including the decision to escalate the war in Vietnam, the decision by President John F. Kennedy to invade Cuba in 1961, and even the decision by NASA to launch the ill-fated *Challenger* Space Shuttle. Not all psychologists are satisfied with the interpretations that Janis provided for groupthink (e.g., Kramer, 1998), but there is still wide agreement that the phenomenon exists (Esser, 1998).

In an alarming number of cases, Janis discovered that group members systematically sought consensus at the expense of critical analysis. Group members often acted as if they were trying to convince themselves of the correctness of their position. When alternative views were expressed, those views were either suppressed or dismissed. The management at NASA had clear evidence that freezing launch temperatures might pose a problem for the *Challenger* Space Shuttle, but the managers chose to ignore that evidence in the interest of going forward with the mission. The result of groupthink is general closed-mindedness and an overestimation of the uniformity of opinion.

Can groupthink be avoided? According to Janis (1982), it is possible to counteract groupthink by following certain guidelines. For instance, it helps to have a leader who acts impartial, one who does not quickly endorse a particular position. One or more members of the group can also be assigned a kind of "devil's advocate" role in which they are expected and encouraged to represent a dissenting position. Perhaps most important, however, is making the group members aware that social influences such as groupthink are real phenomena that can lead to bad decisions, irrespective of group members' intelligence or commitment to the truth. Groupthink can be avoided, although it requires reconsidering how group decision making is normally conducted.

groupthink
The tendency for members of a group to become so interested in seeking a consensus of opinion that they start to ignore and even suppress dissenting views.

Concept Summary

VARIETIES OF SOCIAL INFLUENCE

Phenomenon	Description
Social facilitation	An improvement in performance is sometimes found when we perform in the presence of others. Especially likely with easy or well-practised tasks.
Social interference	A decline in performance when one is in the presence of others. Especially likely with tasks that are unique or not well learned.
Bystander effect	The reluctance to come to someone's aid when other people are present. Characterized by diffusion of responsibility, the tendency to believe that others will help.
Social loafing	Most people show a strong tendency to put in less effort when they are working in a group compared to when they work alone.
Deindividuation	When in large groups, we can lose our sense of individuality and be more likely to engage in destructive, aggressive, or deviant behaviour.
Conformity	A person's opinions, feelings, and behaviours start to move toward the group norm.

GROUP–DECISION-MAKING EFFECTS

Phenomenon	Description
Group polarization	A group's dominant point of view become stronger and even more extreme with time.
Groupthink	Members of a group become so interested in seeking a consensus of opinion that they ignore and suppress dissenting views.

The Power of Authority: Obedience

Up to this point in our discussion of social influence, we've concentrated on how our behaviour is affected by the presence of others of comparable status to us. But what if those other individuals have higher status than us? Think back once again to our story about Chris M., who opened the chapter. Do you think he would have agreed so readily with his co-workers if the boss had not been standing there, drink in hand, listening intently to his opinions? To what degree was Chris's behaviour influenced because it was someone in a position of authority who had asked him his opinion? The question of how behaviour changes in the presence of authority has produced some of the most intriguing and controversial studies in the history of psychology.

obedience
The form of compliance that occurs when people respond to the orders of an authority figure.

Psychologists use the term **obedience** to refer to the form of compliance that occurs when people respond to the orders of an authority figure. You're of course aware of the fact that during World War II, millions of Jewish men, women, and children were systematically executed by German soldiers working under orders from Nazi officials. In a rural area of Guyana, South America, in 1978, hundreds of converts to the religious teachings of Reverend Jim Jones chose, under his direct orders, to commit mass suicide. Most people find it extremely difficult to understand such events and consider them to be social aberrations committed by people far different from themselves. Admittedly, you might toe the line in front of your boss and do and say things that you don't really believe, but murder innocent people? Drink Kool-Aid laced with cyanide and feed the same lethal concoction to your children (as parents did at Jonestown)? Most people would say, "Not a chance." However, the certainty with which most people answer these questions might partly be another reflection of the fundamental attribution error, which, as you remember, involves a basic unwillingness to fully acknowledge the extraordinary power of situational forces when we explain other people's behaviour.

The Milgram Experiment   In the most famous social psychology experiment ever conducted, psychologist Stanley Milgram (1963) set out to determine how far an average

Obedience to authority reached shocking levels in 1978 when followers of Reverend Jim Jones chose, under his direct orders, to commit mass suicide by drinking Kool-Aid laced with cyanide.

person would go in complying with the directions of an authority figure. He placed a newspaper ad recruiting men for what was described as a study looking at the effects of punishment on learning. The participants were told that they would be paid a small fee to play one of two roles in an experiment: either a *learner*, which required memorizing and then recalling lists of word pairs, or a *teacher*, whose task it would be to administer an electric shock to the learner whenever he made any recall errors. Each session required two participants—one teacher and one learner—and the assignment of roles was decided by drawing slips of paper out of a hat.

But things were not exactly what they appeared to be. In fact, in every case the true volunteer, the one who had actually responded to the ad, was picked to be the teacher. The learner was a confederate of the experimenter, someone who pretended to be another participant. Although it was rigged to look like he was receiving shocks throughout the session, he never actually did. The idea was to see how willing the teacher would be to give the learner electric shocks when the authority figure—the experimenter—told him to do so.

To begin the setup, the two were introduced and the teacher watched as the learner was led away to an adjacent room and hooked up to a shock-administering apparatus. Back in the original room, the teacher was then placed in front of an imposing-looking electrical shock generator, which contained some 30 different switches. It was explained that each switch was able to generate a particular level of shock intensity, ranging from 15 V (slight shock), through 150 V (strong shock), and finally up to 450 V (labelled simply XXX). With the experimenter standing by his side, the teacher was instructed to begin reading and then testing the learner's memory for the words, over an intercom, and to administer a shock whenever the learner failed to call out the correct answer. Moreover, to see how far the teacher would go, he was instructed to increase the voltage level of the shock (by clicking up the switch) after each new mistake.

Remember: No one was actually shocked in this experiment; the learner was in on the experiment, and he was told to make mistakes consistently throughout the session and the apparent "mistakes" were preprogrammed. A tape recording made it seem as if the learner was responding. At first, when the shock levels were low, there wasn't much response. But as the prearranged mistakes continued—which, of course, necessitated the teacher to continue increasing the voltage of the shock—loud protests began to come over the intercom. By the time the mistake-prone learner was receiving 150-V shocks, he was demanding to be released from the experiment. By around 300 V, he was

These photos were taken during one of Milgram's early experiments on obedience to authority. The first photo shows the shock generator used during the experiment; the second photo shows the "learner," who was actually a confederate of the experimenter, being hooked up to the shocking apparatus; the third photo shows the "teacher" with the demanding experimenter (in the lab coat) standing over him.

screaming in pain in response to each delivered shock and pounding on the wall; after the 330-V level, the shocks yielded no response at all—simply silence.

Listening to these disturbing pleas for help did not, of course, make most "teachers" very comfortable. Most expressed concern about the shocks and wanted to discontinue the experiment. But the teacher's concerns were met with resistance from the authoritative experimenter, who demanded that the shocks go on. "Please continue," the experimenter responded. "The experiment must go on." What would you do in this situation? You're participating in an experiment, which is being conducted in the name of science, but the task requires you to inflict pain and suffering on someone else. Do you continue, delivering shocks in compliance with the requests of the authority figure, or do you quit and give the experimenter a piece of your mind? This was exactly the question of interest to Milgram: How obedient would people be to unreasonable requests by an authority figure?

Before the experiment began, Milgram asked several people, including psychological professionals, to predict how much shock participants would be willing to deliver in his task. Most predicted that obedience would be low; the estimates were that only a few people in a thousand would deliver shocks up to 450 V and that most participants would defy the experimenter after discomfort was expressed by the learner. In reality, the results were far different. Milgram found that 65% of the 40 participants who participated were willing to deliver shocks up to 450 V, and no participant quit before the pounding on the wall started (see Figure 13.8). This means that 26 of the 40 participants went all the way to the final switch—the one with the ominous XXX label—despite the agonizing pleas from the learner. (Subsequent research found approximately the same rate of compliance in women participants as in men.) Milgram's remarkable finding rocked the psychological community and initiated a great deal of subsequent research as well as a firestorm of controversy.

Controversies and Ethical Concerns   Milgram's (1963) experiment was controversial for two main reasons. First, the manner in which it was conducted raises serious ethical questions. The participants in his study were misled from the beginning and became severely distressed during their participation. Milgram observed many indications of distress during the experiment: The "teachers" sometimes groaned, bit their lips, trembled, stuttered, and even broke into a sweat. Some critics feel that this kind of psychological manipulation—even though it was conducted to advance knowledge—cannot be justified (Baumrind, 1964; Schlenker & Forsyth, 1977). In response, Milgram (1974) argued that his participants were thoroughly debriefed at the end of the experiment—they were told in detail about the true nature of the experiment—and generally said they were glad they had participated. Follow-up questionnaires sent to the participants months later revealed that only a few felt negative about the experiment.

Other criticisms concerned the validity of conclusions about obedience. Some critics argued that the participants had seen through the cover story and were simply

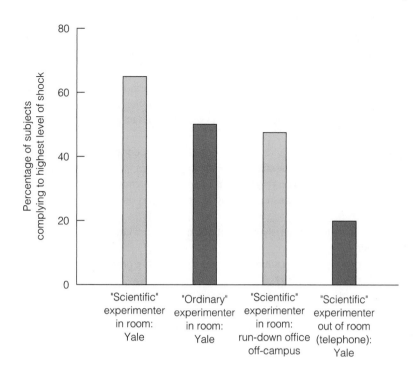

FIGURE 13.8
Milgram's Study of Obedience
Milgram was astonished to discover that 65 percent of the people he tested gave (what they thought was) a life-threatening electric shock to another person simply because a Yale University experimenter told them to. You can see from the lower bars on the graph that obedience was reduced if the experimenter was out of the room or looked non-scientific, or if the location was off-campus in a run-down building.

trying to please the experimenter. They said that participants would assume that the procedure was OK; otherwise, how could such an experiment be allowed? Milgram again pointed out the extreme distress that his participants exhibited: That suggests that they had *not* figured out the hoax. Other critics argued that the results, although interesting, had no general applicability beyond the laboratory. That argument does not seem very comforting when one considers that many important life situations involve the same psychological elements. Think about the plight of soldiers ordered to behave in a barbaric fashion. Think about orders from employers who want you to ignore potential environmental damage caused by the company's new policies.

In the four decades since Milgram's original experiment was conducted, his general procedure has been repeated a number of times, in many countries around the world (see Blass, 2000; Meeus & Raaijmakers, 1987). Few psychologists today question the validity of the basic findings, although it's clear that the degree of compliance that people will show to authority depends on many factors. For example, the Milgram experiment was conducted at a prestigious university (Yale); when the same study was conducted in a less prestigious setting—a run-down office building—compliance dropped (although it remained alarmingly high). People were also less likely to comply if the authority figure left the room after explaining the experiment or if the person giving the orders looked ordinary rather than official or scientific (Milgram, 1974). Thus, obedience to authority is not absolute; it depends on the characteristics of the situation as well as on the characteristics of the person giving the orders.

Critical Thinking

Why might it be adaptive for us to respond so readily to the demands of an authority figure?

Test Yourself 13.2

Check your knowledge about social influence by answering the following questions. (You will find the answers in Appendix B.)

1. Pick the psychological term that best fits each of the statements below. Choose from the following: social facilitation; social interference; bystander effect; social loafing; deindividuation; conformity; group polarization; groupthink; obedience.

a. Sergio is convinced that his study group is dead wrong about their interpretation of the Milgram experiment, but he chooses to nod in agreement with the others in the group: _____

b. Gabriella never calls 911 when she sees a broken-down car by the side of the road; she assumes everyone has a cell phone: _____

c. Teresa notices that she always talks more when she's at a large party: _____

d. Brett is normally shy and polite, but at the rock concert last night he was loud and shouted obscenities at the police: _____

e. Landlord Sang-Woo notices that the grievances coming from his tenant group have become increasingly more rigid and demanding over time: _____

f. Laurie writes extremely well, but she contributes little to group discussions during class: _____

2. Which of the following situations should lead to the greatest reduction in obedience to authority?

a. The authority figure wears a uniform in front of the teacher.

b. The authority figure stands close to the teacher.

c. The experiment is conducted in a federal building.

d. The experiment is conducted in the teacher's home.

RELATIONSHIPS WITH OTHERS: POSITIVE AND NEGATIVE

Learning Goals

1. Understand the factors that influence our perception of facial attractiveness.
2. Distinguish how proximity, similarity, ingratiation, and reciprocity influence liking and loving.
3. Be able to define the components of romantic love and discuss the triangular theory of love.
4. Understand the psychology of aggression and how it can be reduced.

OUR FIRST TWO ADAPTIVE PROBLEMS have dealt with social thought and social influence. We now turn our attention to the third and final component: How do we establish and maintain relationships with others? What differentiates the pleasant ones from the unpleasant ones? For most of us, it is our personal relationships that are the best part of life. We depend on our interactions with colleagues, friends, lovers, and family for protection and inspiration. At the same time, personal hostility and aggression are a major disruption. Both positive and negative relationships give meaning to our lives. Each type of relationship (e.g., parent–child, siblings, friends, lovers, colleagues, competitors, enemies) may invoke quite different schemas to guide our behaviour. In evolutionary terms, these different "mind modules" were selected for dealing with the normal relationships necessary for the continuation of our species (Daly et al., 1997; Daly & Wilson, 1998; Krebs & Denton, 1997).

We've actually encountered the topic of social relationships several times in earlier chapters. In Chapter 10, when we discussed social development, we dealt in detail with the topic of attachment. But in that case we were concerned with the function of social bonds for solving the problems that arise during development. Infants are born with limited motor skills and somewhat immature perceptual systems; consequently, they need to establish strong bonds with their caregivers in order to survive. In Chapter 11, when we discussed motivation and emotion, we saw how people use facial expressions

Our relationships with others protect us, nurture us, and give meaning to our lives.

to communicate their emotions to others and how people are motivated to secure sexual partners. Again, in that discussion we emphasized the adaptive value of the relationship rather than the role that the social context plays in the process. In this section we'll first consider interpersonal attraction, which usually precedes relationship development, and then we'll discuss how psychologists have tackled the mysterious phenomenon of love. We'll also address the darker side of relationships—aggression—and whether it can be reduced.

What Makes a Face Attractive?

We often resent it. We even deny it. Like it or not, beauty is a powerful motivator of human behaviour. Psychologists have confirmed that people's physical attractiveness often shapes how their behaviour is interpreted and how they are treated by others. As you learned earlier in the chapter, the mind utilizes social schemas to form impressions, and physical attractiveness is used as a cue to generate expectations about others (Eagly et al., 1991). The 19th-century German poet Johann Schiller captured the tendency of humans to equate beauty with worthiness when he wrote, "Physical beauty is the sign of an interior beauty, a spiritual and moral beauty." Schiller's contention pervades modern advertisements, but research has shown that physical attractiveness is not actually correlated with people's character or mental health (Hatfield, 1988).

An Evolutionary Perspective What exactly is it that makes a face physically beautiful? What are the qualities that determine whether someone's looks are considered desirable? One way to think about this problem is from the perspective of evolutionary theory. Like other animals, humans likely evolved to prefer mating with someone with a high reproductive capacity or someone who is able to provide protection for offspring and compete successfully for needed resources. This reasoning predicts that people should be attracted to opposite-sex members who are youthful, vigorous, and healthy looking because these qualities are usually correlated with the likelihood of successful reproduction and child rearing (Alley & Cunningham, 1991; Buss, D. M. 1989; Buss & Schmitt, 1993; Johnston, 2000).

Another prediction of evolutionary theory is that features of attractiveness should transcend cultural boundaries. If attractiveness is grounded somewhere deep in our evolutionary heritage, then it shouldn't matter much where you are raised and what experiences you have; in general, there should be worldwide agreement about what constitutes attractiveness. This conclusion contrasts sharply with the generally accepted idea that "beauty is in the eye of the beholder," but it's supported by empirical research. People from quite different cultures rate the same basic structural facial features as attractive (Bernstein et al., 1982; McArthur & Berry, 1987). It's also been discovered that babies, within hours of birth, prefer to look at pictures of attractive faces compared to those that have been rated as unattractive by adults (Langlois et al., 1987; Slater et al., 1998). Culturally based standards of beauty cannot account for this very early human preference.

Attractive Faces May Be Average   Psychologists Judith Langlois and Lori Roggman (1990; Langlois et al., 1994) suggest that the universality of attractiveness may be partly due to the fact that people are programmed to prefer faces that are *average* representations of faces in the population. By average, Langlois and Roggman do not necessarily mean common, typical, or frequently occurring faces. Instead, they mean prototypical faces—that is, faces that are good representations of the category "faces." Back in Chapter 8, we defined category prototypes as the best or most representative members of a category—a robin, for example, is probably close to the prototype for the category "bird." According to Langlois and Roggman, attractive faces are those that are particularly *facelike,* or representative of the category of faces.

They based their conclusions on research in which people were asked to rate the attractiveness of average faces that were generated electronically on a computer. To create these faces, hundreds of individual black and white photographs, composed of either male or female Caucasians, Asians, and Hispanics, were first scanned into a computer and then digitized into matrices of individual grey values. Each of these grey values corresponded to a shade of grey sitting at a particular small location on the scanned face. A whole face was represented by many thousands of these grey values, as they are in a typical newspaper photo or video display. As you probably know, any image you see in a newspaper or on a video monitor is actually a configuration of many rows and columns of individual-intensity dots or pixels. When viewed as a whole, the dots blend together to form a familiar image on the page or screen.

The unique feature of the Langlois and Roggman research was that people were sometimes shown faces that were generated by averaging the grey values across a large collection of individual faces. An individual dot in one of these composite faces was set by averaging the values of all the dots at the same relative location in the face pool. The result was a kind of blended face that did not look exactly like any one of the individual faces but rather represented a kind of prototype face in the population. Volunteer participants were asked to rate these faces for attractiveness, along with the individual faces that had been used to form the composite. The surprising result was that people generally rated the composite faces as more attractive than the individual faces (see also Rhodes & Tremewan, 1996).

Why would people prefer faces that are prototypical? Langlois and Roggman offer several speculative reasons. One possibility is that prototypical faces are easy to identify and classify as human faces. Classifying something as a face may not seem like much of a task for adults, but it could well be for the newborn infant. It is critical for infants to be able to recognize a looming visual configuration as a face because they are dependent on their social interactions with people for survival. Yet the visual acuity of the newborn is limited, so faces that are particularly facelike may make this critical classification process easier. Another possibility is that people are programmed biologically to prefer prototypical faces because individuals with average features may be less likely to harbour potentially harmful genetic mutations. Generally, it is the average or normal characteristics that tend to be preferred over extreme ones in a population.

The Socialized Components   Despite the evidence for universality in how people conceive of attractiveness, most psychologists recognize that there is a strong socialized

The faces shown in each row are composites created by averaging either two individual faces (far left), 8 faces (middle photos in each row), or 32 faces (far right). The stimuli were created using the averaging process employed by Langlois and Roggman. (Courtesy Judith Langlois.)

component to the perception of beauty as well. As we discussed in Chapter 11, standards of beauty have changed over time in most cultures of the world. In Western societies, for instance, our icon of beauty, the fashion model, has ranged from a "curvaceous bustiness" at one point to slender tomboyishness at the next (Silverstein et al., 1986). It's also the case that features considered attractive in one culture—pierced noses, liposuctioned thighs, elongated earlobes—may be considered unattractive in another. Nevertheless, people can generally identify which people from other quite different cultures are considered beautiful by others from within that culture.

Perceptions of attractiveness and beauty also clearly change with experience. We generally rate people we like as more attractive than people we don't like. Moreover, if you've just been shown a picture of a strikingly attractive person, your ratings of average-looking people go down (Kenrick et al., 1989). Beauty is not entirely in the eye of the beholder, as the research of Langlois and Roggman (1990) indicates, but there is indeed a measurable subjective component that cannot be ignored.

Determinants of Liking and Loving

Do we form friendships, or choose marriage partners, based on some relationship equation that sums desirable and undesirable attributes in a logical and rational way?

One of the most important lessons of this textbook, and certainly of this chapter, is that our behaviour is strongly influenced by external forces in the environment. People act the way they do partly because of conscious, internally driven processes, but also because the environment shapes and constrains behaviour in an unconscious fashion. In the case of interpersonal attraction, the environment usually plays a major role in determining both whom you choose to spend time with and whom you consider to be an appropriate mate. As you learned earlier in the chapter, even mere

There are subjective components to the perception of beauty that are culturally dependent.

Critical Thinking

Think about your own relationship experiences. Have you ever felt peer or parental pressure to find a partner who meets a well-defined set of standards? How important were these factors in your decisions?

Birds of a feather do tend to flock together; more often than not, we form lasting relationships with people who are similar to ourselves.

reciprocity
The tendency for people to return in kind the feelings that are shown toward them.

exposure to something can be sufficient to increase its likeability (Zajonc, 1968). People like things that are familiar, even when that familiarity has been created by simple repetition.

Proximity In a classic study conducted 50 years ago, psychologist Leon Festinger and his colleagues (1950) analyzed the friendships that formed among students living in an apartment complex near the Massachusetts Institute of Technology. Festinger and his colleagues found that they could predict the likelihood of a friendship forming by simply noting the *proximity*—defined in terms of the closeness of living quarters—between two people in the building. When the students were asked to list their three closest friends, two-thirds of the time they named students who lived in their same apartment complex. Moreover, when a fellow apartment dweller was listed as a friend, two-thirds of the time he or she lived on the same floor as the respondent. Clearly, the choice of friends is strongly influenced by where one lives. People tend to end up with friends who live nearby.

Of course, it isn't really proximity by itself that leads to liking and loving. When somebody lives close by, you see him or her a lot, and it may be the increased exposure that promotes the attraction. We've already seen that increased exposure leads to an increase in rated likeability, but it also provides the opportunity for interaction. When you consistently interact with someone, mutual feelings of connectedness and belonging tend to follow (Cantor & Malley, 1991). You tend to see each other as members of the same in-group. In fact, you don't even have to interact physically with someone for increased liking to occur. Psychologists John Darley and Ellen Berscheid (1967) found that even the anticipation of an interaction with someone you don't already know can cause you to rate that person as more attractive.

Similarity It's also the case that we tend to like and form relationships with people who are *similar* to us (Byrne, 1971). Friends and intimate partners typically resemble each other in age, social status, education level, race, religious beliefs, political attitudes, intelligence, and even physical attractiveness. People may report preferring physically attractive mates, but most end up marrying someone who is comparable to them in degree of physical attractiveness (Feingold, 1988, 1990). The only case where "opposites attract" is on the vertical dimension of the interpersonal circle (see Chapter 12). Specifically, a couple that differs on the dimension of dominance versus submission is more stable than a couple that does not differ on that dimension (Wiggins, 1979).

Although few psychologists question the finding that similarities attract, there are disagreements about how best to interpret this finding. The fact that similarities are found between the appearance and attitudes of friends and lovers doesn't explain why these similarities exist. As we discussed in Chapter 2, correlations do not imply causality. One possibility is that we like others who share our beliefs and attitudes because they *validate* those beliefs, which further helps convince us that our beliefs are the right ones (Byrne, 1971; Laprelle et al., 1990). Another possibility is that we spend time with others like ourselves because we *dislike* people who hold different views (Rosenbaum, 1986). It's not so much that we want to spend time with those who resemble us; it's that we don't want to spend time with those we despise.

Reciprocity There is also a role in the dynamics of interpersonal attraction for **reciprocity,** or our tendency to return in kind the feelings that are shown toward us. If someone doesn't like you and displays hostility at every turn, you usually have similar negative feelings toward him or her. If someone likes you, or even if you simply *think* the person likes you, then you tend to like that person back (Kelley, 1983). In a study by Curtis and Miller (1986), participants were asked to have a conversation with someone whom they believed had been told either positive or negative information about them (actually, the conversation partner hadn't been told anything). If the participants believed they were talking to someone who perceived them in a positive light, they

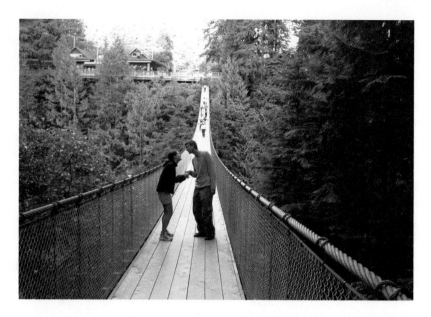

Meeting someone in an exciting place can mislead you into feeling more attracted than you really are.

tended to be friendlier and more open in their conversation; they acted as if they liked their partner more.

Reciprocity helps lead to interpersonal attraction because it is self-fulfilling and because people who like you tend to be reinforcing and accepting of your actions. But it doesn't always work. If you feel that the positive actions of another are motivated for some selfish reason—as part of a con job or to get something such as a promotion—then your reaction will typically be negative (Jones, 1964). **Ingratiation,** in which a person consciously tries to win the affections of another for some ulterior motive, is likely to backfire as a strategy if it is discovered.

ingratiation
The attempt to get someone to like you for some ulterior motive.

General Level of Arousal   We learned in Chapter 11 that our bodies can experience a global feeling of arousal without our understanding what is going on. An example relevant to this chapter is that people can misinterpret arousal due to one source (e.g., exercise or fear) as sexual attraction to someone nearby. Psychologists at the University of British Columbia showed how men's fear of an unsteady suspension bridge could transfer into feelings of attraction for a female interviewer (Dutton & Aron, 1974). As young men finished walking across two kinds of bridges in a Vancouver mountain park, they were interviewed by an attractive young woman. The men were more likely to ask the interviewer for a date if they had just walked across the fear-arousing suspension bridge than if they had just walked across a small non-threatening bridge. This same effect was recently shown by measuring attraction to a female interviewer just after men had experienced a scary ride at the fair (Meston & Frolich, in press). Think about how similar misinterpretations of your feelings could occur if you met someone in an exciting location; for example, a loud, crowded bar with flashing lights.

The Psychology of Romantic Love

When psychologists study a topic such as *interpersonal attraction,* it's likely to be seen as an interesting and important research endeavour by most casual observers. But when psychologists turn to the study of "love," as you might imagine, the reactions are often more skeptical. How, you ask, can someone understand, define, or attempt to measure something like love? Love is a topic to be tackled by the poet or the artist, not the questionnaire-bearing social psychologist. Perhaps. But as you'll soon see, that hasn't stopped psychologists from trying.

passionate love

An intense emotional state characterized by a powerful longing to be with a specific person; passionate love is marked by a combination of intimacy and passion, but commitment may be lacking.

companionate love

A kind of emotional attachment characterized by feelings of trust and companionship; companionate love is marked by a combination of intimacy and commitment, but passion may be lacking.

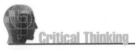

Critical Thinking

If you had to write a recipe for a successful marriage, what priority would you give to the three dimensions of Sternberg's triangle?

Defining Love   Psychologists recognize that love is a complex emotion that can be expressed in many ways. There is the love that exists between parent and child, between lovers, between husband and wife, even between friends. In each case, when it's measured through a questionnaire, the relationship is typically characterized by the giving and receiving of support, mutual understanding, and intense personal satisfaction, according to University of Winnipeg social psychologist Beverley Fehr and her colleagues (Fehr & Russell, 1991; Sternberg & Grajek, 1984). Although there may be fundamental similarities in how love is experienced, the amount of love that is reported depends on the type of relationship studied. Women, for example, often report loving their lover more than a best friend, but liking their best friend more; men, on the other hand, report liking and loving their lover more than they report these feelings for their friends (Sternberg, 1986).

When the relationship between two individuals is romantic, it is possible to distinguish further between passionate love and companionate love. **Passionate love** is an intense emotional state in which the individual is enveloped by a powerful longing to be with the other person (Hatfield, 1988). For many people, passionate love resembles a ride on a kind of emotional roller coaster—they experience intense joy if the feelings are reciprocated and intense pain and despair if their feelings are unrequited. **Companionate love** is less emotional and intense, but its feelings of trust and warmth can be more enduring. Whereas passionate love leads to intense arousal, companionate love leads to self-disclosure—we are willing to reveal our innermost secrets because the relationship sits on a bedrock of trust. It is, of course, possible for both passionate love and companionate love to be present in the same relationship, but this is not always the case.

The Triangular View of Love   Psychologist Robert Sternberg (1986, 1988) has argued for what he calls a triangular view of love. He sees love as triangular because it is composed of three major dimensions—*intimacy, passion,* and *commitment*—that vary in relation to one another (see Figure 13.9). Intimacy is the emotional component that brings closeness, connectedness, and warmth to a relationship. Passion is the motivational component that underlies arousal, physical attraction, and sexual behaviour. Commitment is the decision-making arm of love: How willing are the partners to stick with the relationship in times of trouble? All forms of love can be seen as some combination of these three components. For example, according to Sternberg (1986), *romantic love* is marked by a combination of intimacy and passion (but it may lack the commitment); *companionate love* is high in intimacy and commitment (but without passion); and *empty love* occurs when there is commitment but little or no passion or intimacy. Sternberg has suggested the term *consummate love* for the love relationship in which passion, intimacy, and commitment are all present. While many people might find this the "ideal" kind of love, we should note that people do differ in their preferences for ideal love arrangements and that forms of love relationships other than consummate love are quite satisfying for many people.

In addition to using his triangle as a vehicle for defining love, Sternberg has followed other researchers in attempting to map out how the components of love change over time (see Berscheid, 1985; Hatfield & Rapson, 1993). What patterns have been found? Do couples gain intimacy? Lose passion? Become increasingly willing to commit? It is impossible to predict for any particular relationship, but the theory proposes some general trends. On the average, for example, the passion component of love builds early and rapidly in a relationship—it can even be experienced almost immediately on meeting another—but it's difficult to sustain for long periods. Commitment, on the other hand, is slow to develop but can be quite long lasting. Intimacy, too, is unlikely to be found early in a relationship (there is too much uncertainty), but it grows and maintains itself in most successful relationships. Therefore, the components of love are conceived as fluid, changing over time in ways that reflect the developmental trajectory of the couple and their changing circumstances.

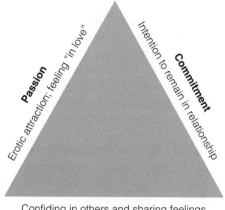

Passion	Intimacy	Commitment	Type of Love That Results
+	−	−	Infatuated love
−	+	−	Liking (friendship)
−	−	+	Empty love
+	+	−	Romantic love
−	+	+	Companionate love
+	−	+	Fatuous love

FIGURE 13.9

The Triangular View of Love

Robert Sternberg has proposed that there are many kinds of love, each defined by the degree of *passion, intimacy,* and *commitment* present in the relationship. For example, "infatuation" is a kind of love with lots of passion but little intimacy or commitment, whereas "empty love" has commitment but little passion or intimacy. (Based on Sternberg, 1986.)

Predicting the Longevity of Love Relationships Predicting whether a specific love relationship will last or not is a topic that is of interest to most people, particularly those embarking on such a relationship. Researchers Tara MacDonald of Queen's University and Michael Ross of the University of Waterloo examined this question in a study that focused on first-year undergraduates at the University of Waterloo who were in dating relationships that had lasted at least one month, but less than a year (at the time of the study) (MacDonald & Ross, 1999). The students, their roommates, and their friends were all asked questions about these relationships, including questions assessing relationship quality (e.g., How satisfied are they with the relationship? How serious is it?) and predictions about the relationship (e.g., What is the likelihood that the relationship will last beyond six months? Two years? Five years? What is the likelihood that the couple will marry? How likely is it that the relationship will last a lifetime?).

MacDonald and Ross found, surprisingly, that the roommates were better at predicting the longevity of the relationship at six months and one year after the original predictions than the lovers themselves. Intriguingly, the students' original *ratings of the quality of the relationship* correlated more highly with the outcome of the relationship than did the student's *predictions* about the relationship. That is, relationships that were rated by the participants as higher quality (e.g., more satisfying, more serious) tended to last compared to those rated as less serious, less satisfying. But evidently, the lovers did not attend very much to those factors in making their predictions about the relationships. MacDonald and Ross suggest that the students' predictions may have reflected their hopes for the relationships to continue, rather than an objective evaluation of that likelihood, and that people in the early stages of love relationships may engage in "tunnel vision" and ignore evidence of current relationship problems when asked to predict the future of the relationship. The researchers conclude by suggesting that to get a more realistic view of what the future holds, lovers should focus more on the quality of the current relationship, rather than being overly sentimental about the prospect of relationship problems improving in the future. And they should pay attention to what their roommates and parents predict; these observers are evidently not as swayed by the "longing in their hearts" that lovers feel and can therefore be a little more accurate in predicting the course of true love.

aggression
Behaviour meant to harm someone.

Aggression

Aggression can be defined as behaviour meant to harm someone. Its manifestation in wars between democratic countries has shown some decline over the last century. But aggression within such modern societies as Canada, Britain, and the United States has not shown any clear reduction. High levels of violent aggression are documented in crime statistics, but aggression is also prominent in business, sports, driving styles, and even everyday interpersonal interactions. Moreover, people seem to be highly entertained by watching violent sports, films, and television, playing violent video games, and car crashes.

In modern, wealthy societies, there are clear links between who actually commits violent aggression and such demographic factors as gender, age, relative poverty, ethnicity, and availability of firearms. But recent news events have highlighted the fact that aggression appears in all human groups—sometimes when we least expect it.

One of the most shocking recent examples is the case of the shootings at Columbine High School in Littleton, Colorado, in 1999. Two intelligent White children of middle-class parents massacred 13 of their schoolmates, and then they committed suicide, bringing the death toll to 15. (Within two years, a series of similar incidents took place in Canada, Australia, and elsewhere in the United States.) So much for the claim that poverty and disadvantaged ethnicity are necessary conditions for violence. In the recent case of the missing Eastside Vancouver women, close to 50 women were murdered without the benefit of firearms. So much for the placidness of Canada and the argument that guns are necessary for the perpetration of widespread murder. Although often rated by the U.N. as the best country in the world to live in, Canada has nonetheless seen a number of serious street riots over relatively trivial events.

Can it be that we are not the civilized species that we claim to be? Our species—supposedly superior—shows the highest rate of within-species murder (Lorenz, 1966). Even harder to explain is why human beings actually enjoy seeing others get hurt. The possible psychological explanations of aggression map onto the various theories of personality outlined in Chapter 12. To Freud, aggression is a natural component of human nature tied to the death instinct. In strict learning theories, aggression is learned by receiving repeated rewards for aggressive behaviour (Skinner, 1938). In cognitive–behavioural theories, aggression is learned by observing others behaving aggressively (e.g., Bandura et al., 1963). Evolutionary theories explain that aggression was an adaptive behaviour—especially for males—that was selected into our gene pool because it led to successful reproduction (Daly & Wilson, 1983). In contrast, humanistic psychologists argue that aggression results from society's perversion of the naturally good selves that we are born with. These traditional theories have guided a variety of attempts to reduce aggression (see the Practical Solutions box).

Research has established sex differences in aggression but they are more complex than one might expect. Physical aggression is certainly higher in males than females but, in some studies, verbal aggression is higher in females (Eagly & Steffen, 1986). By verbal aggression, these studies are usually referring to behaviours such as purposely spreading false rumours about someone you dislike. Observations of greater physical aggression in males are consistent with research on sex differences in testosterone: The effects seem to alter the brain structure as well as physical appearance of the developing fetus (Dabbs, 2000; Halpern, 1989; Mazur & Booth, 1998).

Test Yourself 13.3

Check your knowledge about how we establish relationships with other people by deciding whether each of the following statements is true or false. (You will find the answers in Appendix B.)

1. Babies, within hours of birth, show a preference for attractive over unattractive faces. *True or False?*

Practical Solutions

HOW CAN HOSTILITY AND AGGRESSION BE REDUCED?

Each of the major personality theories has a different recommendation on how to solve the aggression problem. Psychodynamic theory advises that society must recognize the inevitability of some degree of aggression. Its intensity can be minimized via **catharsis,** that is, expending the aggressive energy either (a) directly at the cause of frustration, or (b) indirectly via vigorous exercise or aggressive forms of entertainment. Individuals especially prone to aggression require extensive one-on-one psychotherapy to uncover and repair the conflicts they are playing out against parental symbols. Behaviourist theories argue that punishment for bad behaviour may be necessary at first, but rewards for alternative good behaviour are more effective in the long run. To control society, its priorities must be rearranged to apply such rewards and punishments more systematically. Aggressive individuals must be reconditioned. Cognitive–behavioural theories point to the plethora of bad role modelling in modern society. If we didn't see so much violence in film, television, and sports, then people would not be as aggressive. Humanistic psychologists argue that society must return to its more natural state where people are naturally good to

one another. In the meantime, aggressive individuals should receive warm counselling to raise their self-esteem. Evolutionary theories may be the most pessimistic given their assumption that our general tendencies as well as individual differences are largely driven by our genetic makeup. Individual differences in aggression are similarly explained by genetic differences manifested in our biological makeup. For example, exaggerated levels of testosterone have been linked to aggression both as a cause and an effect (Dabbs, 2000). Accordingly, some have argued for reducing the testosterone levels of violent individuals with antidote drugs, a type of therapy that is sometimes dramatically labelled "chemical castration" (Bain, 1987).

A large amount of laboratory research along with a smaller amount of field research has been directed toward testing these different claims about how to reduce aggression. The results are always complex and subject to debate. But, in most cases, the hypotheses have not been supported (Freedman, 2002). Catharsis does not seem to work: Angered individuals who are given the opportunity to aggress become even more aggressive in a later situation (Wood et al., 1991). Punishment seems to inhibit aggression only as long as the threat

is maintained and represents the worst kind of modelling (Bushman & Anderson, 2001). Violent modelling appears to increase aggression even when it is done by the villain, who gets punished in the end. Violent pornography appears to promote sexual aggression (Malamuth & Check, 1983), but only among those with hostile attitudes toward women. Finally, aggression can be amplified by the presence of authority figures who appear to condone the behaviour (Altemeyer, 1988). Raising the self-esteem of aggressive individuals simply seems to create more confident aggressors (Baumeister et al., 1996). So-called "chemical castration" has some supportive research, but most societies seem very reluctant to use it.

In summary, the research to date has shown us how to increase aggression, but we are still waiting for confirmed and acceptable methods for reducing it. This potential conflict between effective and acceptable approaches will surely become more fierce as we develop gene therapy and accurate methods for identifying aggression-prone individuals at birth.

catharsis
The expending of aggressive energy via direct or indirect means.

---

2. Blending studies of facial attractiveness indicate that faces that are unusual or distinct tend to receive higher ratings of attractiveness than averaged faces. *True or False?*

3. Studies have found that if you've just been shown a picture of a strikingly attractive person, your ratings of an average-looking person go up. *True or False?*

4. Friends and intimate partners typically resemble each other in age, social status, education level, race, religious beliefs, political attitudes, intelligence, and even physical attractiveness. *True or False?*

5. According to the triangular theory of love, infatuated love represents passion without intimacy or commitment. *True or False?*

6. Passionate love typically leads to more feelings of warmth and trust than does companionate love. *True or False?*

7. Aggression can be reduced by catharsis. *True or False?*

Solving the Adaptive Problems

Throughout this text we've repeatedly emphasized that people neither develop nor live in a vacuum. Our actions, thoughts, and feelings arise out of the interactions we have with ever-changing environments. Among the most powerful of environmental forces are social forces—our thoughts and actions are strongly influenced by other people. Social psychology studies how people think about, influence, and relate to others. In recent years, social psychologists have moved beyond the laboratory to examine problems in the real world, such as issues surrounding legal testimony and courtroom procedures (Luus & Wells, 1994; Pfeifer, 1996). In this chapter we tackled the topic areas of social psychology from the perspective of three major adaptive problems.

First, how do we think about the social world? As we move through the social world, it's extremely adaptive for us to try to make sense of the people around us. We form initial impressions of others by using the information we have available—such as the physical appearance of the person—and by relying on pre-existing knowledge structures, called social schemas, which help us interpret that information. Schemas are useful features of the adaptive mind because they help us to direct our actions in uncertain situations. But schemas can also lead to stereotypes—beliefs about people belonging to groups—which, although useful in many ways, can produce prejudice.

Attributions—our inferences about the causes of another's behaviour—form another important part of the overall interpretation process. When searching for reasons why others act the way they do, we look for factors that covary with the behaviour, and we assess the consistency of the behaviour, its distinctiveness, and whether or not there is consensus among people. Whether you decide the cause of a given action is in the external environment or within the person depends on how these factors of consistency, distinctiveness, and consensus work together. There are also basic attribution biases—such as the fundamental attribution error—that help shape the attributions we make.

Attitudes, which are positive or negative evaluations, are typically separated into three components: a cognitive component, an affective component, and a behavioural component. Attitude formation is influenced by several factors, but direct experience is one of the most important. It's clear that when people are induced to act in ways that are inconsistent with their existing attitudes, their attitudes often change as a result.

Second, how does our behaviour change in the presence of others? Psychologists use the term *social influence* to refer to how behaviour is affected by other people in one's environment. Sometimes social influence can produce positive effects, as in social facilitation, and sometimes the presence of others hinders performance, as in social interference. The relationship between arousal and performance might explain some of these patterns. The presence of other people can have an arousing effect, and depending on whether the task is easy or difficult, performance will be facilitated or impaired. The presence of other people can also affect our willingness to help people in need. The bystander effect reveals that we're reluctant to help when other people are present. One interpretation of this effect appeals to diffusion of responsibility: We believe that others have already done something to help or will soon get involved.

Behaviour is also strongly influenced by the social pressures of groups and of authority. Participation as a member of a well-defined group can make us conform, which means that our opinions and behaviours tend to move toward the group norm. Conformity operates on the group level as well. It is common for groups to polarize, which means that the group's dominant point of view tends to become stronger and more extreme with the passage of time. If the phenomenon of groupthink is operating, members have become so interested in seeking a consensus of opinion that dissenting views start to be ignored or suppressed. Milgram's famous experiment on obedience to authority demonstrated that people can be induced by an authority figure to engage in behaviour that they would not engage in otherwise. The degree of compliance is related to characteristics of both the situation and of the person giving the orders.

Third, how do we establish relationships—whether positive or negative—with other people? How are relationships formed? We examined facial attractiveness and discovered that attractiveness may be determined, in part, by innate biological factors. People tend to prefer averaged, or prototypical, faces, contrary to our belief that attractive people are special. Factors that influence liking and loving include familiarity, proximity, similarity, reciprocity, and general level of arousal. We're more likely to be attracted to someone we know, who lives nearby, who is similar to ourselves, and who likes us back. Psychologists have also attempted to understand love, which is typically defined in terms of multiple components—such as intimacy, passion, and commitment—acting together. Whether a person ends up in a relationship based on passionate love or companionate love depends on the relative amounts of each of these three components in the relationship. The dark side of human relationships—hostility and aggression—remains a critical problem despite the many attempts to reduce it.

Chapter Summary

THINKING ABOUT THE SOCIAL WORLD: SOCIAL COGNITION

As social animals, we're constantly trying to interpret the behaviour of other people. We form impressions of people we encounter, and we concoct theories about why people behave the way they do. There are systematic biases in the interpretation processes we use to make these judgments.

Person Perception: How Do We Form Impressions of Others?

Learning Goal: Understand how physical attractiveness, stereotypes, and social schemas influence our impressions of others. Our perception of people is guided by *bottom-up processing* (actual physical sensations) and *top-down processing* (our expectations and beliefs). Physical appearance is a powerful determinant of a first impression. Physically attractive individuals are perceived as superior on a variety of dimensions. *Social schemas,* our schemas about social experiences and people (e.g., *stereotypes*), exert a strong influence on our perception of others. An example is the *self-fulfilling prophecy effect,* in which we expect certain kinds of behaviour from members of groups, and these expectations can cause the person to behave in the expected fashion. Stereotypes can also increase the likelihood of *prejudice* and discriminatory behaviour. People tend to show preferences for their *in-group* and are more likely to display prejudice against *out-groups.* Prejudice can be reduced through repeated exposure to *individuals* in the stereotyped group. People in groups that are discriminated against tend to deny suffering discrimination themselves, but agree that the group as a whole is discriminated against. *Auto-stereotyping* refers to a belief system about discrimination that is widely shared by group members, while *meta-stereotyping* refers to a person's beliefs regarding the stereotype that out-group members hold about his or her own group.

Attribution Theory: Attributing Causes to Behaviours

Learning Goal: Learn how we attribute causality to the behaviour of others, and the biases and errors that we show when making attributions. *Attributions* are the inferences generated when we assign causes to behaviours. The *covariation model* assumes that we look for some factor that covaries with the behaviour we're judging. In addition, we rely on *consistency, distinctiveness,* and *consensus* to make the appropriate inference. We tend to make *external attributions* (appealing to external causes) when a behaviour is high on these three dimensions; we tend to make *internal attributions* (appealing to internal personality traits) when a behaviour is high in consistency but low in consensus and distinctiveness. The *fundamental attribution error* refers to our tendency to overestimate the role of internal factors and underestimate the role of external factors. The *actor-observer effect* is the tendency to make internal attributions for others' behaviour and external attributions for our own. The *self-serving bias* refers to our tendency to take internal credit for actions that produce positive outcomes and to blame the situation when behaviours lead to failure. Evolutionary researchers have suggested that natural selection may have shaped human minds to systematically misrepresent and oversimplify social phenomena because such distortions may have been adaptive for humans during our evolutionary history.

Attitudes and Attitude Change

Learning Goal: Appreciate the complexity of attitudes and how they are formed and changed. *Attitudes* are positive or negative beliefs we hold about something and include a *cognitive, affective,* and *behavioural* component. The behavioural component is a predisposition to act; attitudes do not always directly affect behaviour. Attitudes are formed primarily through experience, through the mechanisms of classical conditioning, instrumental conditioning, and observational learning. According to *cognitive dissonance theory,* inconsistency between behaviour and attitudes results in tension that may be relieved through attitude change. An alternative, *self-perception theory,* states that we use our own actions as the basis for beliefs about ourselves. The *foot-in-the-door technique* provides support.

BEHAVING IN THE PRESENCE OF OTHERS: SOCIAL INFLUENCE

Everyone's behaviour is strongly influenced by the social context. The ability to perform a task might improve or fall apart in the presence of others. How we act is also profoundly influenced by the presence of authority figures and by the opinions of fellow members in a group.

Social Facilitation and Interference

Learning Goal: Understand social facilitation and interference, including the relationship between task difficulty, arousal, and performance. *Social facilitation* is an enhancement in performance sometimes found when we perform in the presence of others. *Social interference* occurs when performing in front of a crowd impairs performance. Task difficulty helps determine when the presence of others will help or hinder performance. When a task is easy, social facilitation is likely; when it's difficult, social interference is likely.

Social Influences on Helping: The Bystander Effect

Learning Goal: Be able to explain the bystander effect and the concept of diffusion of responsibility. The presence of others can affect *helping*, whether we will act in a way that shows unselfish concern for others. The reluctance to come to someone's aid when others are present is termed the *bystander effect*. The presence of others leads to a *diffusion of responsibility;* we believe that others have already done something to help.

The Power of the Group

Learning Goal: Learn how behaviour changes in a group setting. People have a tendency toward *social loafing*, putting out less effort when working with a group than when working alone. *Deindividuation* occurs when we feel less accountable in the presence of others than when we're on our own. *Conformity* occurs when a person's opinions, feelings, or behaviours move toward the group norm and is especially likely when the pressure is coming from an *in-group*.

Group Decision Making

Learning Goal: Understand some aspects of group decision making. When the dominant point of view within a group becomes stronger and more extreme with time, *group polarization* has occurred. When group members become so interested in achieving consensus that they ignore and even suppress dissenting views, *groupthink* has taken over.

The Power of Authority: Obedience

Learning Goal: Be able to describe the Milgram experiment and discuss its implications for the power of authority. *Obedience* refers to following the orders of an authority figure. The Milgram experiment found that a surprisingly high proportion (65%) of research participants were willing to follow an experimenter's orders to deliver shocks, despite pleas from the participant. Milgram's study has been criticized on ethical grounds as well as for the general procedures used.

RELATIONSHIPS WITH OTHERS: POSITIVE AND NEGATIVE

Among our most important social actions are the relationships that we share with others. It's unlikely that the human species would survive without attraction and romantic love. In addition, we rely on our relationships within the family as well as on the social structures in society to help protect and nurture us. At the same time, the worst of human behaviour can be seen in aggression and hostility toward others.

What Makes a Face Attractive?

Learning Goal: Understand the factors that influence our perception of facial attractiveness. An evolutionary perspective on physical attractiveness predicts that we will be attracted to opposite-sex members who are youthful, vigorous, and healthy looking. Also, features of attractiveness should cut across cultural boundaries. The evolutionary view has some research support. The universality of attractiveness may be due to the fact that we seem programmed to prefer faces that are average representations of faces in a population. There is also a strong socialized component to the perception of beauty.

Determinants of Liking and Loving

Learning Goal: Distinguish how proximity, similarity, ingratiation, and reciprocity influence liking and loving. The environment plays a major role in determining interpersonal attraction. Attraction to others is determined by others' *familiarity, similarity, proximity, ingratiation*, and *reciprocity*, our tendency to return in kind the feelings that are shown toward us. We can also misinterpret arousal from other sources as evidence for attraction to someone.

The Psychology of Romantic Love

Learning Goal: Be able to define the components of romantic love and discuss the triangular theory of love. Love is a complex emotion that can be expressed in a variety of forms. *Passionate love* is an intense emotional state in which the individual is enveloped by a powerful longing to be with the other person. *Companionate love* tends to be less intense and is characterized by trust and warmth. According to the *triangular theory*, love is composed of three major dimensions: *intimacy, passion*, and *commitment*. These components are fluid, changing over time.

Aggression

Learning Goal: Understand the psychology of aggression and how it can be reduced. *Aggression* (behaviour meant to harm someone) remains at high levels in crime statistics, but it is also widespread in business, sports, driving styles, and even interpersonal interactions. In modern societies, there are links between rates of aggression and demographic factors, but there remains much that we don't understand about the psychology of aggression. All the major theories of psychology have different perspectives on the nature of aggression and different recommendations about how it can be reduced.

Terms to Remember

Recommended Readings

Taylor, D. M., & Moghaddam, F. M. (1994). *Theories of intergroup relations* (2nd ed.). Westport, CT: Praeger. Co-written by McGill University social psychologist Donald Taylor, this text summarizes a variety of approaches to understanding relations among human groups, especially ethnically defined groups, and offers suggestions for integrating different theoretical approaches.

Zanna, M., & Olson, J. M. (1994). *The psychology of prejudice (Ontario Symposium on Personality and Social Psychology, Vol. 7)*. Mahwah, NJ: Erlbaum. Edited by social psychologists from the universities of Waterloo and Western Ontario, this volume is one in a distinguished series that presents current research and reviews of topics in social and personality psychology. Other volumes in the series cover topics such as the psychology of values and social influence.

Altemeyer, B. (1996). *The authoritarian specter*. Cambridge, MA: Harvard University Press. Based on years of research into the authoritarian personality by University of Manitoba psychologist Bob Altemeyer, this book explores the origins and development of authoritarian attitudes and the social problems related to these attitudes.

Simpson, J. A., & Kenrick, D. T. (1997). *Evolutionary social psychology*. Mahwah, NJ: Erlbaum. The evolutionary bases of social phenomena such as social perception, attraction, and mating; includes articles on social illusions and self-deception by Simon Fraser University psychologists Dennis Krebs and Kathy Denton, and on kinship by McMaster University evolutionary psychologists Martin Daly, Catherine Salmon, and Margo Wilson.

Cialdini, R. B. (1993). *Influence: Science and practice* (3rd ed.). New York: HarperCollins. A fascinating exploration of the psychology of compliance and persuasion; includes many real-world examples (e.g., politicians and con artists) illustrating the power and tactics of influence.

 For additional readings, explore InfoTrac® College Edition, your online library. Go to:

www.adaptivemind2e.nelson.com

Hint: enter the search terms: social cognition; stereotypes; persuasion and attitude change; conformity; interpersonal attraction; romantic love.

What's on the Web?

Please note that Web addresses are subject to change. Check out the accompanying Web site for updates: www.adaptivemind2e.nelson.com. This site presents practice quiz questions, hypercontent, information on degrees and careers in psychology, study tips, and more.

Canadian Psychological Association: Social and Personality Section

www.psych.mcgill.ca/perpg/fac/baldwin/cpa/index.html

This Web site for Canadian social and personality psychologists from across the country includes newsletters, announcements of meetings and presentations, and links to relevant sites.

Descriptions of the Eight Largest Canadian University Psychology Programs

University of British Columbia

www.psych.ubc.ca/~dpaulhus/sparea.htm

University of Calgary

www.psych.ucalgary.ca/Social/

University of Manitoba

www.umanitoba.ca/faculties/arts/psychology/programs/social.html

McGill University

www.psych.mcgill.ca/grad/resar.htm

University of Waterloo

www.arts.uwaterloo.ca/psychology/gradprog/gradhandbook.html#div-social

Simon Fraser University

www.sfu.ca/psychology/groups/researchAreas/social/

University of Saskatchewan

www.usask.ca/psychology/gradhdbk/c4.htm

University of Toronto

www.psych.utoronto.ca/grad/social.htm

York University

www.atkinson.yorku.ca/~hynie/socpers/

Social Psychology Network

www.socialpsychology.org

This is *the* Web site for social psychology. It's a clearinghouse with a tremendous amount of information about social psychology, including areas of study within social psychology, Ph.D. programs in social psychology, and even online experiments that allow you to take part in actual online research. The links to research include student projects on interpersonal relations, social perception, and judgment and decision making.

The Influence at Work Web Site

www.influenceatwork.com

This Web site is devoted to the psychology of persuasion and contains a wealth of information about the dynamics of social influence and how it is implemented in everyday settings. There's even a test to measure your "influence quotient." Cruise to this site to find out how influence relates to courtrooms, cults, Aristotle, and George W. Bush.

Though this be madness, yet there be method in't.

William Shakespeare, *Hamlet*

Chapter 14 Abnormal Psychology

Over the next two chapters, we'll turn our attention to the classification and treatment of abnormal behaviour. But defining abnormality turns out to be more difficult than you might think. Let's suppose you arrive home tonight and find your roommate slumped in a corner with his cap pulled down over his eyes. You ask him to explain, but he tells you to "mind your own business." Later that night, you hear sobbing and crying coming from behind his locked bedroom door. He has never acted this way before and it continues for days. He refuses to respond to questions, he stops going to class, and he refuses to eat or clean himself. He's been hit with some psychological illness, right? Perhaps, but what if we tell you that his father and mother were just killed in an automobile accident? What would your reaction be now? You might well change your mind and conclude that he's simply showing an intense but totally normal grief reaction.

Previewing the Scientific and Practical Problems

To help you understand how psychologists view abnormal behaviour, our discussion will revolve around three basic scientific and practical problems: What is the proper way to conceptualize and define abnormal behaviour? How can the various types be organized in the ideal way to reveal their similarities and differences? Finally, what are the underlying causes?

First, what is the proper way to conceptualize abnormal behaviour? In the psychological literature, various terms such as *abnormal behaviour, mental illness,* and *psychopathology* are used more or less equivalently. No matter which term is chosen, defining it has proved to be a struggle to the psychological community. In this textbook, we use the term **abnormal behaviour** as a broad term for behaviour that is some combination of unusual, dysfunctional, culturally deviant, and accompanied by considerable personal distress. We will see that none of these criteria alone is sufficient to capture the concept. There *is* general agreement on using the term

psychological disorder to refer to the underlying psychological problem (or problems) that is responsible for the abnormal behaviour.

Second, how do we classify the underlying disorders that lead to abnormal behaviour? There are a wide variety of psychological disorders (e.g., depression, schizophrenia, psychopathy), many of which overlap in terms of their symptoms. Therefore it has been a real challenge for psychologists and psychiatrists to develop a rigorous system for the diagnosis and classification of psychological disorders. Classification systems have evolved over the years. We'll consider the current system, which is detailed in the American Psychiatric Association's *Diagnostic and Statistical Manual of Mental Disorders* (4th ed.-Revised), and you'll see how it's used to diagnose a variety of mental problems. The manual provides detailed criteria for diagnosing disorders on the basis of specific symptoms.

Third, what are the underlying causes of each disorder? What causes an

anxiety disorder, a mood disorder such as depression, or schizophrenia? Does abnormal behaviour result from some kind of mental breakdown, or is it simply an adaptive reaction to stress? If it's a breakdown, is the cause biological or environmental? When someone is depressed, for example, is it because of a problem with brain chemistry? Or has the person simply learned to act in depressed ways either through modelling the behaviour of others or because acting depressed has received some reinforcement? We'll consider the major theoretical tools that psychologists use to explain abnormal behaviour. Not surprisingly, the answer to many psychological problems lies in an interaction between biological, cognitive, and environmental factors.

abnormal behaviour
A general term including behaviour that is unusual, maladaptive, socially deviant, and/or accompanied by continuing distress.

psychological disorder
A specific psychological problem that causes abnormal behaviour to occur.

CONCEPTUALIZING ABNORMALITY: WHAT IS ABNORMAL BEHAVIOUR?

Learning Goals

1. Understand and evaluate the various criteria that have been proposed to define abnormality.
2. Understand how the medical and sociological models view disorders.

Psychological distress is a normal reaction to a negative event. But how long and severe must the distress be in order for it to be called abnormal?

IF YOU MEET SOMEONE IN THE STREET who babbles about voices in his head that are warning about a Klingon invasion, you would likely categorize this behaviour as abnormal. Clearly, this person is in trouble and in need of some professional help. But as you've seen, sharp dividing lines don't always exist between normal and abnormal behaviour. Sometimes behaviour that appears abnormal can turn out to be a reasonable reaction to a stressful event, such as the roommate's reaction to the death of his parents. And the Klingon example is a standard plot in science fiction stories: The apparently sick babbler turns out to be telling the truth but no one will listen.

It's certainly true that a behaviour that seems abnormal in one culture can appear to be perfectly normal in another (Castillo, 1997; Marsella & Yamada, 2000). Entering a trance state and experiencing visual hallucinations are considered abnormal in Western cultures, but in other cultures they may not be (Bentall, 1990). Even within a culture, conceptions of abnormality can change over time. For many years homosexuality was considered deviant and abnormal by the psychological community. But this view is rejected by most psychologists today. Fifty years ago, a strong dependence on tobacco would not have raised many eyebrows, but today if you're hooked on tobacco you're likely to be classified as having a substance-related disorder by many professionals (see Chapter 16). As times change, so do conceptions of what are appropriate and inappropriate actions. For these reasons, psychologists are justifiably cautious when it comes to applying the label of abnormality. Many professionals try to stick to clear behavioural criteria so that the diagnosis can be reliably communicated to other professionals (Widiger & Sankis, 2000).

The extreme version of this critique goes so far as to argue that the term *abnormality* is purely in the mind of the beholder and that mental illness does not really exist outside of our arbitrary societal biases (e.g., Szasz, 1961, 1990). Moreover, there is evidence that once an authority labels someone as abnormal, people interpret any behaviour as being more evidence for that abnormality (Rosenhan, 1973). Of course, it would be irresponsible for us to ignore such unusual behaviours as those exhibited in the above examples of your roommate and Mr. Klingon: If such individuals do indeed have a psychological disorder, they can be dangerous to themselves and others.

Criteria for Defining Abnormal Behaviour

Over the years, researchers have proposed a number of approaches to defining abnormality. In each of the four approaches, as you'll see, the proposed criteria capture some but not all of the important features of what is agreed to be abnormal behaviour.

Statistical Deviance   One way to define abnormal behaviour is in terms of **statistical deviance,** or infrequency. For any given behaviour, such as talking to yourself or hearing voices, there is a certain probability that the behaviour will occur in society at large. Most people have talked to themselves at one time or another, but few have actually had an absorbing conversation with a cabbage. According to the concept of statistical deviance, a behaviour is abnormal if it occurs infrequently among the members of a population. As you've learned elsewhere in this text, it's not unusual for psychologists to classify behaviour on the basis of statistical frequency. For example, terms such as *gifted* and *mentally retarded* are defined with respect to statistical frequencies. So it

statistical deviance criterion
A criterion for abnormality based on a low frequency of occurrence among the members of a population.

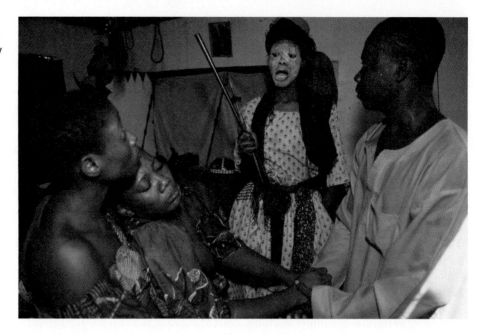

Entering a trance state is likely to be classified as "abnormal behaviour" in Western cultures, but in other cultures it may not be.

should come as no surprise that statistical frequencies have been used to define abnormality.

But statistical deviance cannot be used as the sole criterion for labelling a behaviour as abnormal. It's easy to come up with a list of behaviours or abilities that are statistically infrequent but are not abnormal in a psychological sense. For example, Tiger Woods and Wayne Gretzky have athletic skills that are extreme, and thereby statistically deviant, but to be a great athlete does not make one abnormal. Similarly, only a handful of individuals have reached the intellectual heights of Albert Einstein or Isaac Newton, but superior intelligence is not abnormal in the usual psychological sense of the word. Even restricting the definition to extremely bad or poor performance seems to include far too many people. You might claim to be the world's worst singer or hockey player, but that won't convince your instructor to give you more exam time because you are "abnormal." An additional problem is the establishment of a cut-off point: Just how infrequent or unusual does a behaviour need to be, to be characterized as abnormal? One percent of the population? Ten percent? The statistical deviance approach cannot provide a satisfactory answer to such questions.

Kenneth Thomson (Canada's richest person in 1999, with an estimated worth of $16.1 billion) and actress Pamela Anderson are statistically deviant in some respects, but does that mean they would necessarily be categorized as abnormal in a psychological sense?

Cultural Deviance   Another criterion is **cultural deviance,** which compares behaviour to existing cultural norms. In this case, a behaviour would be considered abnormal if it violates the accepted standards of society. In most cultures, for example, it is not considered normal or acceptable to go to church naked or to defacate in a classroom. These behaviours break the established rules of our culture, and if you engage in either it's likely that people will think you have a serious problem.

But once again, cultural deviance by itself fails as a sufficient criterion. Some people—especially college students—purposely engage in behaviour that is counter-cultural and anti-authority. But it seems clear that their motivation is to express their values and identity as free thinkers: Rarely is such behaviour indicative of a psychological disorder. And many criminals violate the established norms of society—stealing cars or embezzling money, for example. Such behaviour might be abnormal by both statistical and cultural standards, but that doesn't mean all criminals suffer from psychological disorders. As we discussed previously, behaviours that are abnormal in one culture may be considered normal in another. There are cultures in the world, for instance, where nakedness in public breaks no established cultural rules. Views of deviance also change over time in the same society. Twenty years ago, the idea of body piercings (other than earrings) was considered repulsive; today, it is common. Finally, there are exceptions of the opposite sort: Many people suffering psychological problems never violate a law or defy any established standard of society.

Emotional Distress   A third criterion for labelling someone's behaviour as abnormal is the presence of **emotional distress.** People who suffer from psychological disorders often experience great despair and unhappiness. They feel hopeless, lost, out of control, and alienated from others. In fact, it is the emotional distress that usually leads them to seek professional help for their problems. But as you can probably guess, not all disorders make people unhappy. There are people, for example, who have little contact with reality but seem perfectly content in their fantasy world. Likewise, there are many distressed people in the world—for example, those who have recently lost a loved one or a job—who would not be classified as abnormal by the psychological community.

Dysfunction   A final criterion for abnormality considers the general adaptiveness of the individual's behaviour. Is there a breakdown in normal functioning—a **dysfunction**—that prevents the person from functioning successfully in typical daily activities? They may not be able to eat properly, clean themselves, buy groceries, or hold a job. There may be such an impairment in thinking and judgment that it affects their ability to adapt successfully to minor changes in their environment. As you'll see later, the assessment of global functioning—defined as the ability to adapt in social, personal, and occupational environments—plays a large role in the diagnosis and treatment of psychological disorders.

Summarizing the Criteria   You've seen that abnormal behaviour can be defined in terms of statistical or cultural deviance, personal or emotional distress, or dysfunction. Normal behaviour, then, could be any behaviour that is relatively common, is socially acceptable, does not cause personal distress, or generally leads to adaptive consequences. However, psychologists will usually refuse to label any behaviour as normal or abnormal unless it satisfies several of these criteria rather than just one. Crying hysterically for hours at a time may be a normal grief reaction, or it may signal a serious disorder. Even a behaviour that seems to be clearly abnormal—such as a paranoid delusion that people are out to get you—might be adaptive in some environments. To paraphrase comedian Woody Allen, even paranoids are sometimes right.

Even when the criteria are clear, psychologists warn against our natural tendencies to categorize people as "abnormal" and "normal." Each of us can relate in one way or another to the criteria of abnormality we've just discussed. We all know people who have occasionally acted unusually, suffered from emotional distress, or failed to follow an adaptive strategy. Many psychological disorders are characterized by behaviours or

cultural deviance criterion
Behaviour is abnormal if it violates the rules or accepted standards of society.

Critical Thinking

Suppose a 70-year-old entered university and started acting exactly the same way as an 18-year-old first-year student. Would you consider his or her behaviour to be abnormal?

emotional distress criterion
Behaviour is abnormal if it regularly leads to personal distress or emotional upset.

dysfunction criterion
Behaviour is abnormal if it interferes with one's ability to pursue daily activities such as work and relationships.

Concept Summary

CRITERIA FOR DEFINING ABNORMALITY

Criterion	Description	Example
Statistical deviance	Behaviour that occurs infrequently among the members of a population.	Jon goes back to make sure his front door is locked exactly 12 times each morning. As he walks to the door, he mutters over and over, "lock the door...." No one else in the neighbourhood does this.
Cultural deviance	Behaviour that violates the accepted standards of society.	Jon notices that each time he comes back to his front door, talking to himself, his neighbours look at him rather nervously and tend to avoid him at other times.
Emotional distress	Experiencing great despair and unhappiness.	Jon is very distressed by his compulsive behaviour.
Dysfunction	A breakdown in normal everyday functioning.	Jon's routine of checking his front door 12 times every morning has made him late for work a number of times, and his job is in jeopardy.

Normal	Criterion	Abnormal
Common	Statistical Deviance	Rare
Acceptable	Cultural Deviance	Unacceptable
Low	Emotional Distress	High
Adaptive	Dysfunction	Maladaptive

FIGURE 14.1

The Normal-to-Abnormal Continuum

In this view, "abnormal" and "normal" are not fixed and rigid categories. They are better seen as endpoints on a continuum. To a certain degree, everyone has acted unusually, behaved unacceptably, suffered from emotional distress, or failed to follow an adaptive strategy. Abnormality is a matter of degree, not a matter of kind.

medical model
The view that abnormal behaviour is symptomatic of an underlying "disease" that can be "cured" with the appropriate therapy.

sociological model
The view that abnormal behaviour is a label that each society assigns to certain behaviours that it finds unacceptable, even if they are not criminal in nature.

feelings that are merely exaggerations of normal ones, such as anxiety, feelings of sadness, or concerns about one's health. Consequently, it's better to think about normal and abnormal behaviour as endpoints on a *continuum* rather than as nonoverlapping categories (see Figure 14.1). (For a discussion of the legal concept of insanity, which differs from the concept of a psychological disorder, see the Practical Solutions box.)

The Medical Model versus the Sociological Model

When abnormality is present, is it better to think of the person as suffering from a physical problem—that is, something that is broken or not working properly in the body—or is the person simply psychologically unsuited to the environment? We'll discuss the possible causes of psychological disorders in detail later in the chapter, but to understand how disorders are actually classified, you need to understand what is called the *medical model* of diagnosis. According to the **medical model,** abnormal behaviour is caused by an underlying *disease*—a kind of mental *illness*—that can be cured with the appropriate therapy.

This conception of abnormality has been quite influential. As you already know, there are good reasons to believe that behaviour is strongly influenced by biological factors, such as an oversupply or undersupply of neurotransmitters in the brain. In addition, biomedical therapies, such as the administration of psychoactive drugs, are often effective in treating a variety of psychological problems. As you'll see shortly, it's also the case that most psychological disorders can be classified in terms of *symptoms.* Depression, for example, typically leads to one or more of the following: sad mood, diminished interest in pleasure, difficulty in sleeping, and feelings of worthlessness. The medical influence is deeply ingrained in the very language that psychologists use—they talk about mental health, mental illness, or psychopathology in much the same way a physician describes a medical condition.

But is the medical model the only way to view abnormality? Both strep throat and depression lead to a set of reliable symptoms. Strep throat is caused by a physical problem, namely, specific bacteria. Application of the medical model to depression, however, is less convincing because its cause is much more complicated than a single, simple trigger.

The **sociological model** argues that the interpretation of psychological symptoms as abnormal is arbitrary and depends on the particular social or cultural context. We pointed out earlier that some kinds of behaviour thought to be abnormal in one culture could be considered normal in another. In the case of extreme shyness, for

562

Practical Solutions

THE INSANITY DEFENCE

As we've just discussed, it's difficult to find an acceptable scientific definition for abnormal behaviour. Behaviour can mean different things depending on the context in which it occurs—something that is abnormal in one situation may be quite normal in another. Still, regardless of where you travel in the world, some kinds of behaviour are always recognized as abnormal. Consider, for example, the behaviour of Chicago serial killer Jeffrey Dahmer, who admitted butchering and having sex with the dead bodies of over a dozen young men and boys. Then, he went on to eat selected body parts. Everyone, including Dahmer's own lawyers, was in agreement—this was a man who was suffering from serious psychological problems. According to the criteria discussed above, psychologists and psychiatrists agreed that Dahmer suffered from one or more psychological disorders.

But you may be surprised to hear that Jeffrey Dahmer was judged by a jury to be sane! How could this be possible? The answer lies in the fact that *insanity* is a *legal* concept rather than a *psychological* one. Legally, an insane person cannot be guilty. So, Dahmer's lawyers tried to have him declared mentally unfit, and thus not responsible for his crimes. But the prosecution lawyers were successful in having him declared legally sane and, therefore, guilty. Although the legal definition varies somewhat across jurisdictions, **insanity** is usually defined in terms of the defendant's thought processes at the time of the crime. One definition by the president of the Canadian Psychological Association is that a criminal is insane and therefore not guilty by reason of insanity if, because of a "mental disease," he or she fails to appreciate or understand that certain actions are wrong in a legal or moral sense (Ogloff et al., 1993). Often this conclusion can be refuted by showing that the individual was acting in a rational and manipulative fashion in other

respects—such as evading the police and carefully hiding the bodies. It is clear that cases of horrendous crimes put judges and juries in a difficult dilemma: The worse the crime, the more they want to hold the offender responsible, *but* the more likely the offender is actually insane. Jeffrey Dahmer was judged capable of understanding the wrongfulness of his actions; that is, the jury determined that he was fully aware of the fact that his actions were wrong. As a result, he failed the insanity test, even though he was clearly suffering from serious psychological problems.

The concept of legal insanity has generated considerable controversy over the years. But the controversy has not usually come from cases like Dahmer's, in which someone with a disorder has been declared legally sane. Instead, the brunt of the concern has been over instances of acquittal—in which someone who obviously committed a crime has been

From a legal standpoint, Jeffrey Dahmer was considered sane because he was judged capable of understanding the wrongfulness of his actions.

judged not guilty by reason of insanity. The classic case was the landmark trial of Daniel M'Naghten back in 1843. Driven by "voices from God," M'Naghten set out to kill the British prime minister, Sir Robert Peel, but ended up killing Peel's secretary instead. The court acquitted M'Naghten for reasons of insanity. This particular ruling was strongly criticized by the public, even though M'Naghten spent the rest of his life in a mental hospital. But it remains important because the so-called M'Naghten rule for insanity—which focuses on what the criminal understands at the time of the crime—is still the foundation for most current standards of insanity (De Jesus-Zayas et al., 2001).

The insanity defence is not a widely used legal loophole, despite the impressions of the general public. Note that being declared insane does not mean that you can go right home and do what you want: You are put in a mental institution until there is clear evidence that the mental illness has subsided. In many cases, this amounts to a life sentence. Nonetheless, the form of supervision you receive in an institution is likely to be more sensitive to the specific psychological disorder. Most mental health professionals concur with this distinction and agree that people with serious psychological disorders are sometimes incapable of judging the appropriateness of their actions. As this chapter will illustrate, psychological disorders can lead to distorted views of the world—affected individuals not only act in ways that are abnormal, but their very thoughts, beliefs, and perceptions of the world can be wildly distorted as well.

insanity

A legal term usually defined as the inability to understand that certain actions are wrong, in a legal or moral sense, at the time of a crime.

example, it might be cured (based on any of the four criteria discussed above) by moving to an East Asian country, where shyness is more common and modesty is highly valued (Chen et al., 1992).

We will see that some psychotherapies are as simple as changing one's perspective on life. Such flexibility is consistent with the sociological model. Moving to the country or avoiding those irritating relatives may solve your problem. If such simple strategies can make the distress go away, they seem more like a lifestyle choice than a medical cure. A true disease would not go away so easily. In short, the arbitrariness and flexibility of a disorder will help us determine the degree to which the disorder fits the sociological model better than the medical model.

Extreme versions of the sociological model argue that cultural deviance is overemphasized in defining mental illness. In fact, psychological disorders don't even exist except in a totally subjective sense. Society decides that certain behaviours and people are "sick" and need to change (Rosenhan, 1973; Szasz, 1961). From this perspective, psychological disorders are labels for behaviours that society considers to be nonconformist. As we will see below, such an extreme view is refuted by our increasing understanding of the chemical and biological basis of many psychological disorders.

Test Yourself 14.1

Check your knowledge about how abnormality is conceptualized by deciding whether each of the following statements is true or false. (You will find the answers in Appendix B.)

1. When a behaviour occurs infrequently among members of a population, it meets the criterion of cultural deviance. *True or False?*
2. To be diagnosed with a psychological disorder, a person must be suffering from a certain amount of emotional distress. *True or False?*
3. In many cases, abnormal behaviours are simply exaggerated versions of normal behaviours. *True or False?*
4. According to the medical model, psychological disorders can and should be classified in terms of measurable symptoms. *True or False?*

CLASSIFYING PSYCHOLOGICAL DISORDERS: THE DSM-IV

Learning Goals

1. Understand the DSM-IV, and discuss the pros and cons of this multiaxial system.
2. Identify and describe the common anxiety disorders.
3. Identify and describe the somatoform disorders.
4. Identify and describe the common dissociative disorders.
5. Identify and describe the common mood disorders.
6. Identify and describe the characteristics of schizophrenia.
7. Identify and describe the common personality disorders.
8. Understand the debate over cult membership and Internet addiction.

AS MENTIONED IN THE PREVIOUS SECTION, specific psychological disorders are often diagnosed in terms of a set of defining criteria or symptoms. This is the approach used by the *Diagnostic and Statistical Manual of Mental Disorders (DSM)*, published by the American Psychiatric Association. A large committee of psychiatrists and psychologists from Canada and the United States took many years to develop the DSM, and it has been used as the standard diagnostic reference by both psychologists and psychiatrists in North America. (Europe has a somewhat different, less integrated system.)

Because it is in its fourth edition, the manual is currently referred to as the **DSM-IV.** The DSM-IV provides clinicians with a well-defined classification system based on objective and measurable criteria, so that reliable diagnoses of psychological disorders can be produced across the continent (Maser et al., 1991; Spitzer et al., 1994). In a way, the system is like a dictionary that allows a psychologist in Edmonton to communicate with a psychiatrist in Alabama about the nature of a particular individual's psychological disorders. The DSM-IV is intended only for the purposes of diagnosis and classification; it does not suggest therapies or methods of treatment for its various listed disorders. (The manual is continually being revised, and the latest version is labelled DSM-IV-R.)

How does the classification system work? The DSM-IV is composed of five major rating dimensions, or *axes* (see Figure 14.2). We'll focus our attention mainly on the

DSM-IV

The *Diagnostic and Statistical Manual of Mental Disorders* (4th ed.), which is used for the diagnosis and classification of psychological disorders. The DSM-IV is composed of five major rating dimensions, or *axes*.

FIGURE 14.2

The Five Axes of the DSM-IV Diagnostic System

The DSM-IV is composed of five major rating dimensions, or axes. Information collected from each axis is integrated into final diagnosis and treatment decisions. (From DSM-IV, APA, 1994.)

Axis I Clinical Disorders	Axis II Personality Disorders and Mental Retardation	Axis III General Medical Conditions	Axis IV Psychosocial and Environmental Problems
Examples: Substance-related disorders Schizophrenia and other psychotic disorders Mood disorders Anxiety disorders Somatoform disorders Dissociative disorders Sexual and gender identity disorders Eating disorders Sleep disorders	**Examples:** Paranoid personality disorder Schizotypal personality disorder Antisocial personality disorder Borderline personality disorder Narcissistic personality disorder Dependent personality disorder	**Examples:** Infectious and parasitic diseases Endocrine, nutritional, and metabolic diseases and immunity disorders Diseases of the nervous system and sense organs Diseases of the circulatory system Diseases of the respiratory system Diseases of the digestive system Diseases of the genitourinary system Congenital anomalies	**Examples:** Problems with primary support group Problems related to the social environment Educational problems Occupational problems Housing problems Economic problems

Axis V

Global Assessment of Functioning (GAF) Scale

Code	Examples of symptoms:
100	Superior functioning in a wide range of activities
90	Absent or minimal symptoms, good functioning in all areas
80	Symptoms transient and expectable reactions to psychosocial stressors
70	Mild symptoms or impairment in social, occupational, or school functioning, but general functioning is pretty good
60	Moderate symptoms or impairment in social, occupational, or school functioning
50	Serious symptoms or impairment in social, occupational, or school functioning
40	Major impairment in work or school, family relations, judgment, thinking, mood; some communication impairment
30	Influenced by delusions or hallucinations, serious impairment in communication or judgment
20	Some danger of severely hurting self or others, gross impairment in communication, sporadic personal hygiene
10	Persistent danger of severely hurting self or others

first axis, which lists the major clinical disorders (such as depression and schizophrenia), although all five are important to the complete diagnostic process. The clinician uses the criteria outlined in Axis I (Clinical Disorders) and Axis II (Personality Disorders) to classify and label any abnormal behaviour that may be present. Axis III allows the clinician to record any *medical* conditions that the individual is suffering from. It's important for the clinician to know a person's medical history because some medical conditions (such as Alzheimer's disease) can contribute to abnormal behaviour. Axis IV indicates any environmental or psychosocial problems that may be present. For example, is the client going through a difficult divorce, or has he or she recently been fired? Finally, on Axis V, the clinician codes the individual's current level of adaptive or global functioning. Is the client able to function adequately in social, personal, and occupational settings?

The clinician uses this multiaxial classification system to get the widest possible assessment of the individual's current psychological status. It matters to the clinician how someone is functioning in daily life, for example, because it often determines the most effective kind of treatment program. If the person is so severely impaired that he or she cannot hold a job, go to school, or even keep clean, it may be necessary to initiate a period of hospitalization. Our discussion will focus primarily on the diagnostic criteria that are used to classify the most common psychological disorders, as depicted on Axis I. We'll consider the major clinical syndromes and then end the section with a brief discussion of Axis II–based personality disorders. But remember, categorizing the disorder is only part of the diagnostic process; the remaining axes also play an important role in the diagnosis. Figure 14.3 summarizes some of the disorders we'll be discussing and presents data showing how likely each disorder is to occur in the population at large.

FIGURE 14.3

Prevalence Rates for Various Psychological Disorders

Each bar shows the percentage of individuals in a large sample (over 8000 participants) who reported suffering from the listed psychological disorder during the last 12 months or at some point in their lifetime. Note: A given individual might have reported suffering from more than one of these disorders concurrently. (Data from Kessler et al., 1994.)

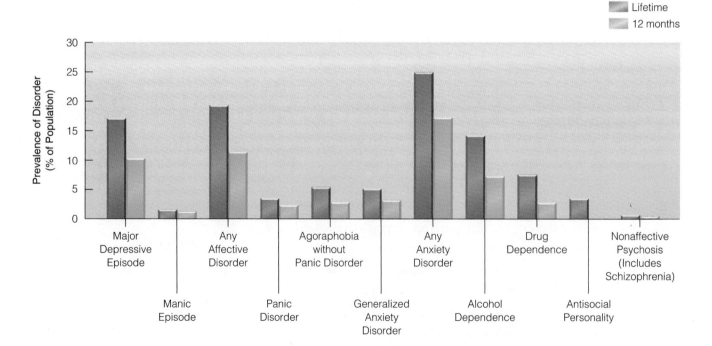

Anxiety Disorders: Beyond Rational Fear

We all understand rational fear, that is, the normal sense of aroused distress we experience when confronting real danger. Anxiety is a similar distressed feeling when the threat is less clear and nonphysical. We may become anxious when meeting strangers, when awaiting an important exam, or upon suddenly remembering that we forgot to pay our taxes for the last five years. Even though the physical and psychological changes that accompany anxiety can seem unpleasant, anxiety is ultimately an *adaptive* human response. The physical changes prepare the body to take action—to fight or flee—and thereby increase the chances of survival. The psychological changes cause us to become attentive—we monitor our environment more closely so we're more apt to notice a potentially dangerous event when it occurs.

But there is a maladaptive extreme to anxiety. When it becomes too persistent and intense, it interferes with your everyday activities. **Anxiety disorders** are diagnosed when the levels of apprehension and worry become so extreme that normal functioning is impaired in some way. For example, if you consistently fail on exams because you cannot collect your thoughts, or if you refuse to leave the house because you're convinced you will experience a frightening panic attack, then you're likely to be suffering from an anxiety disorder. There are several kinds of anxiety disorders, and each is defined by its own set of DSM-IV diagnostic criteria. We'll concentrate on some common ones in this section: *generalized anxiety disorder, panic disorder, obsessive–compulsive disorder, social phobia,* and *specific phobias.*

anxiety disorders
A class of disorders marked by excessive apprehension and worry that in turn impairs normal functioning.

Generalized Anxiety Disorder The defining characteristic of **generalized anxiety disorder** is excessive and chronic worrying that lasts for a period of at least six months. The anxiety is "free floating," as Freud described it, and cannot be attributed to any single identifiable source. People who suffer from this problem tend to worry about very minor things (Brown et al., 2001) as well as life *in general* (Sanderson & Barlow, 1990). To qualify as a disorder, the worrying must be unrealistic; that is, it's not rationally related to the chances that the feared event will actually occur (Brown et al., 1994).

Because anxiety is associated with activity of the autonomic nervous system, generalized anxiety disorder tends to be accompanied by a range of physical symptoms, including high pulse and respiration rates, chronic diarrhea, a need to urinate frequently, and chronic digestive problems. Someone burdened with generalized anxiety disorder is likely to have trouble sleeping and becomes easily irritated; he or she is also likely to spend a lot of time worrying about the future—more so than someone suffering from the other anxiety disorders we'll consider (Dugas et al., 1998). These kinds of symptoms are an understandable result of living in a world of perpetual fear.

generalized anxiety disorder
Excessive worrying, or free-floating anxiety, that lasts for at least six months and cannot be attributed to any single identifiable source.

Panic Disorder In **panic disorder,** people suffer from recurrent episodes, or attacks, of extremely intense fear or dread (Craske & Barlow, 1993). A *panic attack* is a sudden and unexpected event, and it can make a person feel as if he or she is about to die (or, sometimes, go crazy). Panic attacks are brief, but they produce high levels of anxiety and, as a result, are accompanied by a collection of physical symptoms: a pounding heart, shortness of breath, sweating, nausea, chest pains, and so on. These symptoms can be devastating experiences, and they often lead to persistent concern about the possibility of having additional attacks (Barlow, 1988). It's worth noting that a single isolated panic attack is not sufficient for diagnosis of a panic disorder; the attacks need to occur repeatedly and unexpectedly.

Remarkably, panic attacks can even occur while you're asleep, a condition referred to as *nocturnal panic* (Craske & Rowe, 1997). Nocturnal panic attacks usually occur in the middle of the night—between 1:30 a.m. and 3:30 a.m.—and they're associated with slow-wave sleep rather than REM sleep (Barlow & Durand, 1999). This fact suggests that the attacks are not a consequence of bad dreams or nightmares, which tend to be associated with REM sleep (see Chapter 5). Nocturnal panic attacks are poorly understood at the moment, although they may be related to night terrors, which commonly

panic disorder
A condition marked by recurrent discrete episodes or attacks of extremely intense fear or dread.

occur in children, or to a sleep-related breathing problem called *sleep apnea*. Not surprisingly, people who experience nocturnal panic attacks are terrified after an attack and, in some cases, are very reluctant to go to sleep at night.

Panic disorder is sometimes associated with an additional complication, called *agoraphobia,* that arises from the worry that further panic attacks might occur. **Agoraphobia**—which translates from the Greek as "fear of the marketplace"—causes a person to restrict his or her normal activities in an extreme way (Mennin et al., 2000). People who suffer from agoraphobia typically stay away from crowded or public places, such as shopping malls or restaurants, because they're afraid they'll experience a panic attack and be rendered helpless. In severe cases, people with agoraphobia might simply refuse to leave their house. Home, they decide, is the only really safe place in the world. For obvious reasons, panic disorder with accompanying agoraphobia can significantly reduce a person's ability to function successfully in the world.

Obsessive–Compulsive Disorder
In **obsessive–compulsive disorder,** anxiety manifests itself through persistent, uncontrollable thoughts, called *obsessions,* or by the presence of a compelling need to perform one or more actions repeatedly, which is called a *compulsion* (Foa & Franklin, 2001; Swinson et al., 1998). Compulsions are related to obsessions in the sense that the repetitive action is usually performed in response to some kind of obsessive thought (Riggs & Foa, 1993). Have you ever had part of a song or jingle in your head—one that keeps repeating despite your best efforts to stop it? This phenomenon is somewhat like an obsession, although in obsessive–compulsive disorder the obsessions tend to focus on fears (such as being contaminated by germs), doubts (such as forgetting to turn off the stove), and impulses (such as hurting oneself or others) (Jenike et al., 1986; Salkovskis, 1985).

Compulsions consist of such actions as cleaning or checking, or actions that prevent some inappropriate impulse from occurring. For example, someone might repeat the alphabet aloud over and over in an effort to divert his or her thinking away from a frightening or inappropriate aggressive or sexual impulse. In extreme cases, the compulsions are so repetitive and ritualistic that they essentially prevent the sufferer from leading anything resembling a normal life. Some people become housebound, relentlessly cleaning rooms; others feel irresistibly compelled to leave work 10 to 15 times a day to check and make sure the gas wasn't left on in the stove. Interestingly, in the majority of such cases the suffering individuals understand that their actions are irrational and of little adaptive value (Stern & Cobb, 1978). The disorder simply compels the action.

agoraphobia
An anxiety disorder that causes an individual to restrict his or her normal activities; someone suffering from agoraphobia tends to avoid public places out of fear that a panic attack will occur.

obsessive–compulsive disorder
An anxiety disorder that manifests itself through persistent and uncontrollable thoughts, called *obsessions,* or by the compelling need to perform repetitive acts, called *compulsions.*

In panic disorder, a person suffers from recurrent episodes, or attacks, of intense fear or dread.

People who suffer from agoraphobia are often reluctant to leave the house; they're afraid that once outside they will experience a panic attack and be rendered helpless.

A person suffering from obsessive–compulsive disorder may feel the need to engage in a repetitive activity, such as compulsively lining up candies, to reduce anxiety or to avoid thinking inappropriate thoughts.

Social Phobia The most commonly reported fear is **social phobia,** an incapacitating fear of social interactions (Alden, 2001). This fear is maximized with larger audiences, authority figures, and meeting strangers. The very idea of speaking in front of a group is terrifying to many students. They would rather quit school than face such a horror. Its milder form, social anxiety or shyness, appears to be a combination of two normal personality dimensions, namely, introversion and neuroticism (Coplan et al., 1994; Paulhus & Trapnell, 1998). In its extreme form, this tendency to avoid (even important) interactions is considered by some psychologists to be a personality disorder (Widiger, 1998).

social phobia

An incapacitating fear of social interactions.

Specific Phobic Disorder The defining feature of a **specific phobic disorder** is a highly focused fear of a specific object or situation (other than social situations). These include bugs, snakes, heights, animals, closed places, storms, or flying. Like the other anxiety disorders we've discussed, specific phobias are irrational, which means that the level of anxiety the object or situation produces is in no way justified by reality. True, elevators do fall, snakes can bite, and planes do crash, but these events are rare and do not justify daily worry. Many people show mild forms of phobic reactions, but in specific phobic disorder the fear and distress can be severely disabling. To avoid the anxiety-producing object or situation, individuals with a specific phobic disorder might significantly disrupt their normal routines; they might avoid going to work or school or travelling to anywhere different if there is even a slight chance that they will encounter the object of their fear.

specific phobic disorder

A highly focused fear of a specific object or situation.

Specific phobias typically revolve around one of four classes of fear-inducing objects or situations: (1) animals (insects, snakes, dogs, etc.), (2) natural environments (storms, heights, water, etc.), (3) blood-injection-injury (the sight of blood or even the thought of an injection), and (4) specific situations (fears associated with public transportation or closed-in places). These four categories capture the majority of phobic reactions, although there are others—such as fear of choking or fear of costumed characters—that do not fit easily into these established categories. Most people who suffer from specific phobias tend to have more than one, and often more than one type (Hofmann et al., 1997). For a look at how likely the various specific phobias are to occur among the general population, see Figure 14.4.

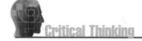

Critical Thinking

Can you think of reasons why it might be adaptive for people to show specific reactions for each of the four classes of phobic stimuli described in the text?

Somatoform Disorders: Body and Mind

A common phenomenon, called the *medical student syndrome,* often plagues medical students as they first learn about the various diseases of the body. The students find

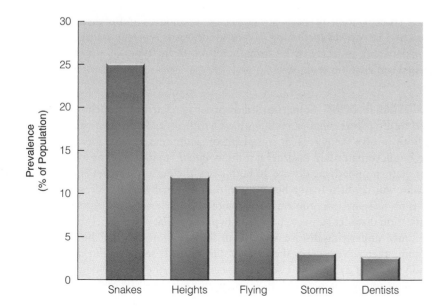

FIGURE 14.4

Prevalence Rates for Various Specific Phobias

Each bar shows the percentage of people in a large sample who reported suffering from a particular kind of phobia. (Data from Agras et al., 1969.)

Concept Summary

ANXIETY DISORDERS

Disorder	Description
Generalized anxiety disorder	Excessive and chronic worrying that lasts for a period of at least six months. Accompanied by excessive autonomic activity (e.g., increased respiration, heart rate).
Panic disorder	Recurrent episodes or "attacks" of extremely intense fear or dread. Sometimes accompanied by agoraphobia, the fear of being in public due to anticipation of another panic attack.
Obsessive–compulsive disorder	Anxiety is manifested through *obsessions* (persistent uncontrollable thoughts) and/or *compulsions* (a compelling need to perform one or more actions repeatedly).
Social phobia	A fear of social interactions so extreme that it interferes with everyday work and relationship requirements.
Specific phobic disorder	A highly focused fear of a specific object or situation. Most revolve around animals, natural environments, blood-injection-injury, or specific situations.

somatoform disorders
Psychological disorders that focus on the physical body.

hypochondriasis
A long-lasting preoccupation with the idea that one has developed a serious disease, based on what turns out to be a misinterpretation of normal body reactions.

somatization disorder
A long-lasting preoccupation with body symptoms that have no identifiable physical cause.

A person suffering from hypochondriasis is prone to misinterpreting normal bodily reactions as symptomatic of a serious disease.

that the symptoms described in class, or in the text, become increasingly familiar and personal. A pain that appears suddenly in the night is interpreted as a signal for a heart attack; that darkening blemish on the forehead becomes the rare form of skin cancer that often accompanies AIDS. In almost every case these students are perfectly healthy, but their mind has started over-interpreting normal physical feedback as some kind of serious physical problem. We all do the same from time to time after seeing a television show or reading an article about some new illness: "Uh-oh, I've got that one, too!"

It can be adaptive for us to pay attention to physical symptoms, but when the preoccupation with bodily functions or symptoms is excessive and not grounded in any physical reality, a true psychological disorder may be indicated (Iezzi et al., 2001). Mental health professionals classify psychological problems that focus on the physical body as **somatoform disorders** (*soma* means "body"). The DSM-IV lists a number of basic somatoform disorders; we'll focus briefly on three: *hypochondriasis, somatization disorder,* and *conversion disorder.*

Hypochondriasis The main symptom of **hypochondriasis** is the persistent preoccupation with the idea that you've developed a serious disease, based on what turns out to be a misinterpretation of normal bodily reactions. The pain in the side, the slight case of indigestion, the occasional irregular heartbeat—these are interpreted as symptomatic of a serious medical condition. Moreover, unlike the situation for the normal medical student, these preoccupations persist for months and often cause significant distress and impaired functioning. Hypochondriasis is typically associated with excessive anxiety and, in fact, may be strongly related to the types of anxiety disorders we discussed earlier (Otto et al., 1998).

Somatization Disorder **Somatization disorder** is related to hypochondriasis; in fact, mental health professionals sometimes have a difficult time distinguishing between the two. Both involve the persistent complaint of symptoms with no identifiable physical cause, but in somatization disorder it is the *symptoms* that receive the focus of attention rather than an underlying disease. In both cases, the person searches endlessly for doctors who will confirm his or her symptoms, but usually with little success (because there is no real physical problem). The major difference between hypochondriasis and somatization disorder seems to be that in hypochondriasis the anxiety arises because of a presumed underlying disease, whereas in somatization disorder the presence of the symptoms themselves causes the anxiety. People with somatization disorder are not typically afraid of dying from a serious disease; rather, they are looking for someone to understand and sympathize with their countless physical problems.

Conversion Disorder

In **conversion disorder,** unlike the other two somatoform disorders we've considered, there appears to be real physical or neurological impairment. Someone suffering from a conversion disorder might report being blind, paralyzed, or unable to speak. The affected person might even experience seizures resembling those found in epilepsy or other neurological disorders (Bowman, 1998). These are not feigned symptoms; that is, these problems are not intentionally invented by the individual to gain sympathy or attention. These are real problems, although no physical cause can be discovered.

Obviously, in such cases there is always the possibility that a true neurological or other physical problem does exist. Indeed, physical problems are sometimes misdiagnosed as conversion disorders (Fishbain & Goldberg, 1991; Slater & Glithero, 1965). But when the reported problems disappear after effective therapy, a psychological origin is usually indicated. You may remember from our discussion of personality in Chapter 12 that Sigmund Freud often used his psychoanalytic techniques to treat patients with conversion disorders (although the problem was known as *hysteria* in his day). In fact, the term *conversion,* as used here, originates from psychodynamic theory and the proposal that unconscious conflicts have been converted into a physical form.

conversion disorder
The presence of real physical problems, such as blindness or paralysis, that seem to have no identifiable physical cause.

Dissociative Disorders: Disruptions of Identity or Awareness

Some of the more colourful types of psychological disorders, at least as seen by Hollywood or the popular press, come from a class of problems called **dissociative disorders.** Dissociative disorders are defined by the separation, or *dissociation,* of conscious awareness from previous thoughts or memories. If you're affected by one of these disorders, you lose memory for some specific aspect of your life, or even your entire sense of identity. The theme of the confused amnesiac, searching for his or her lost identity, has been explored repeatedly in books and films throughout the years. Another fascinating example is the so-called "multiple personality." As usual, the actual clinical versions are more complex than those depicted in popular movies. We'll focus our attention on three types of dissociative disorder: *dissociative amnesia, dissociative fugue,* and *dissociative identity disorder.*

dissociative disorders
A class of disorders characterized by the separation, or dissociation, of conscious awareness from previous thoughts or memories.

Dissociative Amnesia

In Chapter 7, when we tackled remembering and forgetting, we discussed various kinds of *amnesia,* or the inability to remember or retain personal experiences. It was noted that amnesia could result from either physical factors (such as brain damage) or psychological factors (such as traumatic stress). In **dissociative amnesia,** which is assumed to be psychological in origin, the person is unable to remember important personal information. The amnesia can be quite general, as in the failure to remember one's identity or family history, or it can be localized, such as the failure to remember a specific traumatic life experience (Loewenstein, 1996). In dissociative amnesia, the forgetting can last for hours or for years. It often disappears as mysteriously as it arises.

dissociative amnesia
A psychological disorder characterized by an inability to remember important personal information.

Dissociative Fugue

In **dissociative fugue,** there is also a loss of personal identity—people forget who they are—but it's accompanied by an escape or flight from the home environment (*fugue* literally means "flight"). Imagine leaving for work or school as usual only to "awaken" some time later in a different city. One example is Canadian actor Margot Kidder, famous for her film roles as Superman's girlfriend. She disappeared for a week and was found dishevelled, dirty, carrying a knife, and ranting about phantom pursuers. Sometimes the fugue state can last months or even years, and some individuals experiencing this disorder have even adopted different identities in their new locale. Recovery can be sudden and often complete, but affected individuals typically report that they have no knowledge of their activities during the blackout period.

dissociative fugue
A loss of personal identity that is often accompanied by a flight from home.

dissociative identity disorder
A condition in which an individual alternates between what appear to be two or more distinct identities or personalities (also known as *multiple personality disorder*).

Kenneth Bianchi, known as the Hillside Strangler, claimed that he could not be held responsible for the rape and murder of a number of California women because he was suffering from dissociative identity disorder. The evidence presented at trial suggested that Bianchi was "faking" the disorder, and he was later convicted and sentenced to life imprisonment.

Critical Thinking

Can you think of any reason why a client who is seeking help for a psychological problem might want desperately to please the therapist?

Dissociative Identity Disorder In what is perhaps the most baffling of all dissociative disorders, **dissociative identity disorder,** a person alternates between what appear to be two or more distinct identities or personality states (hence the previous label for this condition, *multiple personality disorder*). Some cases of this disorder have been widely publicized. The classic 1950s case was Sybil Dorsett, who was diagnosed with 16 personalities (Schreiber, 1973); she was portrayed by Sally Field in the television movie *Sybil.* Another well-known case is "Eve," who alternated between three personality types (Thigpen & Cleckley, 1957); she was portrayed by Joanne Woodward in the film *The Three Faces of Eve.*

In dissociative identity disorder, the unique personalities or identities appear to take control of the affected person's thoughts and actions, one personality at a time. More important, the personality in control will profess to have only limited awareness of the other personality inhabitants. Commonly, there is inter-personality amnesia, which means that events experienced while the person is inhabited by personality A cannot be remembered when he or she is occupied by personality B (Eich et al., 1997). It is for this reason that the disorder is classified as *dissociative*—there is a separation of current conscious awareness from prior thoughts and memories. Dozens of different identities may be involved, including both males and females, and a given identity will tend to have unique physical attributes, such as a distinct tone of voice, facial expression, handwriting style, or behavioural habit (Putnam et al., 1986).

Dissociative identity disorder is recognized as a legitimate disorder in the DSM-IV, but not all mental health professionals are comfortable with this designation (Fahy, 1988). Controversy often surrounds the diagnosis, for a number of reasons. First, this disorder often co-occurs with other psychological problems (such as depression and somatization disorder), so it's quite difficult to pinpoint the ultimate cause of any particular symptom (Ross et al., 1990). Second, although each of the observed personalities may be distinguished on the basis of personality tests or physiological measures, we still cannot be completely sure about the true origins of these differences—other factors, such as mood or arousal differences, may partly account for the distinct performance patterns (Fahy, 1988; Lilienfeld, 1994).

The third reason for skepticism is that researchers such as Nicholas Spanos of Carleton University have shown that it's relatively easy to fake or simulate multiple personalities (Spanos, 1994; Spanos et al., 1985). This research raises the possibility that people with dissociative identity disorder may actually be role-playing in some fashion, perhaps in a way comparable to those who have been hypnotized. As you might recall from Chapter 5, many psychologists question whether hypnosis really represents some kind of dissociated state; instead, hypnotized people often seem eager to please the hypnotist by acting in accordance with a hypnotized role. This is not necessarily a conscious choice made by those who have been hypnotized; instead, it may represent a kind of unconscious or involuntary compliance (Lynn et al., 1990). Some researchers are convinced that dissociative identity disorder is best interpreted as a kind of self-hypnosis that arises partly to please the therapist. There has been an unusually rapid rise in the number of cases of dissociative identity disorder since the disorder has been publicized in the media, which lends support to the role-playing hypothesis.

Despite the controversy, dissociative identity disorder was retained as a diagnostic disorder in the DSM-IV, which was published in 1994. It does seem clear that not all aspects of the disorder can be consciously faked (Kluft, 1991). Highly specific physiological differences have been reported across personalities—such as differences in visual acuity or eye muscle balance (Miller, 1989)—and it seems unlikely that such things could be easily faked (see Figure 14.5). After all, they are not part of the stereotype. There also appear to be certain similarities in the past histories of affected individuals that have convinced many of the validity of the diagnosis. For example, in a recent study of 97 cases, 95% of the individuals were found to have suffered some form of abuse, usually sexual or physical, most often during childhood (Ross et al., 1990). The diagnosis of dissociative identity disorder remains controversial, but it is considered to be a legitimate disorder by the psychological community at large (Gleaves et al., 2001).

Mood Disorders: Depression and Mania

From time to time everyone experiences depression, that overwhelming feeling that things are completely hopeless and sad. For most, thankfully, the experience is brief; moreover, most of us can usually account for our depressed mood by pointing to a particular experience or event in our lives: We failed a test; our beloved pet died; our once-trusted romantic partner now prefers the affections of another. But when an extreme mood swing is prolonged and accompanied by other symptoms, such as a loss of appetite and a negative self-concept, a mood disorder may be present. **Mood disorders**—which are defined as prolonged and disabling disruptions in emotional state—come in two main varieties: (1) *depressive disorders,* in which the person suffers primarily from depression, and (2) *bipolar disorders,* which are characterized by *mood swings* between extreme highs, called manic states, and the lows of depression. We'll consider each of these types of disorders separately.

Depressive Disorders   The DSM-IV lists specific criteria for the diagnosis of depressive disorders, which are among the most common of all psychological disorders. For something to qualify as a **major depressive episode,** for instance, you must show five or more of the following types of symptoms for a period of at least two weeks:

- Depressed mood for most of the day.
- Loss of interest in normal daily activities.
- A significant change in weight (either a loss or a gain).
- Difficulty sleeping or a desire to sleep all the time.
- A change in activity level (either extreme restlessness or lethargy).
- Daily fatigue or loss of energy.
- A negative self-concept, including feelings of worthlessness or excessive guilt.
- Trouble concentrating or in making decisions.
- Suicidal thoughts.

In a major depressive episode, the world is seen through a kind of dark filter. You feel extremely sad and full of self-doubt, and the environment seems overwhelming, imposing, and full of obstacles that cannot be overcome (Young et al., 1993). This world-view of a depressed person is a particularly grim aspect of the disorder—if you're depressed, the future seems hopeless with little or no possibility of a reprieve. Moreover, depressed people are absolutely convinced about the truth of their hopelessness, which tragically leads some to consider suicide as their only outlet.

It is important to understand that major depression is more than just feeling sad. You literally view and interpret the world differently when you're depressed, which tends to feed and confirm your negative self-concept. Normal activities are interpreted as indicating some dire consequence (e.g., if a friend fails to call, it must mean the friend no longer likes me). As you'll see in the next chapter, one of the goals of therapy in treating depression is to change depressed individuals' thought patterns—to make them see the world in a more realistic way.

Mental health professionals distinguish between several types of depressive disorders, based partly on the length and severity of the depressive episode. For example, a major depressive episode can be classified as *recurrent,* which means that it has occurred more than once in an individual's lifetime (but separated by a period of at least two months). There is also a condition called *dysthymic disorder,* in which the depressive symptoms tend to be milder and less disruptive but more chronic. Most major depressive episodes end after a period of weeks or months and the person returns to normal, but people affected by dysthymic disorder show a relatively continuous depressed mood for a period of at least two years (Akiskal & Cassano, 1997). A major depressive episode can even occur at the same time as dysthymic disorder, in

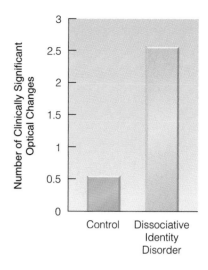

FIGURE 14.5
Optical Changes across Personalities

In a study by Miller (1989), individuals diagnosed with dissociative identity disorder were asked to undergo ophthalmological (eye) exams while "inhabited" by each of three different personalities. Significant differences were found in optical functioning across personalities, whereas there were no differences when normal control subjects were asked to "fake" different personalities. (Data from Miller, 1989.)

mood disorders
Prolonged and disabling disruptions in emotional state.

major depressive episode
A type of mood disorder characterized by depressed mood and other symptoms.

which case the condition is referred to as *double depression* (Hellerstein & Little, 2000; Keller & Shapiro, 1982).

McMaster University researcher David Offord and colleagues have reported that approximately twice as many women as men have suffered a major depressive episode (Offord et al., 1996). However, Simon Fraser University researchers Marlene Moretti, Amy Rein, and Vanessa Wiebe point out that this gender difference is not typically found in university-aged people (Moretti et al., 1998). These researchers also point out a factor that might be involved in explaining some aspects of gender differences in depression. They found that although both men and women experienced considerable unhappiness when their perceived self-image was far from their ideal self-image, only the women in their sample tended to be unhappy when they perceived themselves as not meeting other people's ideal standards for them. Moretti and colleagues suggest that this potential double source of unhappiness relating to women's self-images may be involved in the higher rates of depression found among women in general.

David Zuroff of McGill University has proposed, together with his colleagues, that people who are highly self-critical or dependent on others will tend to be more depressed than people low on those traits (Blatt & Zuroff, 1992; Zuroff & Pilkonis, 1999). Following this suggestion, researchers Jennifer Aubé and Valerie Whiffen of the University of Ottawa found that self-critical people tended to have worse social acuity than other people, and they suggest that a deficit in social acuity (i.e., judging the reactions and feelings of others) may be a factor contributing to the development or continuation of depressive states in self-critical individuals (Aubé & Whiffen, 1996).

Bipolar Disorders   Major depression can be described as unipolar because the disorder is defined by a mood shift in only one direction—toward the negative. In a **bipolar disorder,** you experience mood shifts in two directions: travelling from the depths of depression (a major depressive episode) to a hyperactive, euphoric condition called a **manic state** (Miklowitz, 2001). When you're in a manic state, you act as if you're on top of the world—you're hyperactive, talkative, and seem to have little need for sleep. These symptoms may seem positive and desirable, but they get exaggerated toward grandiosity, distractibility, and risk taking. In a manic state, a person might attempt a remarkable feat—such as climbing a dangerous cliff—or perhaps will go on a sudden spending spree, cashing in all his or her savings. People who are in a manic state report feeling great, even euphoric—but their thinking is far from normal or rational. Their speech can appear disrupted because they shift rapidly from one fleeting thought to another.

To be classified as a manic episode in the DSM-IV, this abnormally elevated mood state must last for at least a week, although it can last for months. Like a depressive episode, the manic state typically goes away, even without treatment, and the person either returns to normal or roller-coasters into another depressive episode. People who suffer from bipolar disorders live lives of extreme highs and lows: As a result, their ability to function normally in society is often severely impaired. Moreover, tragically, it's been estimated that as many as 19% of individuals who are affected with bipolar disorders end up committing suicide, usually during one of their episodes of depression (Jamison, 1986). (For a discussion of the possible connection between bipolar disorders and creativity, see the Practical Solutions box.)

Suicide   As just noted, suicide can be one fatal consequence of suffering from a mood disorder such as bipolar disorder. It's worth pausing for a moment and considering suicide because it's quite a significant problem worldwide; suicide rates have been on the rise for decades, especially among adolescents. It's now the third leading cause of death among adolescents and the eighth leading cause of death overall. Men are four to five times more likely to commit suicide than women. Women are slightly more likely to attempt suicide, but they often use nonlethal methods (Statistics Canada, 1997). It's

bipolar disorder
A type of mood disorder in which the person experiences disordered mood shifts in two directions—from depression to a manic state.

manic state
A disordered state in which the person becomes hyperactive, talkative, and has a decreased need for sleep; a person in a manic state may engage in activities that are self-destructive or dangerous.

Practical Solutions

ARE CREATIVE PEOPLE MAD?

It is commonly believed that inside the hearts and minds of truly creative people lies an element of madness. If you take a journey through history and consider the psychological health of prominent individuals, it's not difficult to find examples of psychological problems. In the 20th century alone, there have been at least five Pulitzer Prize–winning poets (including Sylvia Plath) who have committed suicide in the midst of depression. So, too, have a number of fiction writers (e.g., Ernest Hemingway) and song writers (e.g., Kurt Cobain). It is now recognized that Abraham Lincoln, Cole Porter, and Winston Churchill all probably suffered from bipolar disorder, marked by swings between manic states and depression, and Canadian Prime Minister Mackenzie King may well have had recurrent delusions.

Such examples are intriguing, but they don't constitute solid scientific evidence. More systematic data have come from studies in which pools of highly creative and "average" people are matched on a number of dimensions and the rate of psychological problems is then compared. In one such study, Nancy Andreasen (1987) compared the psychiatric diagnoses of 30 creative writing faculty at the University of Iowa Writers' Workshop (a highly regarded creative writing program) with those of 30 control individuals who were matched to the writers on age, sex, and educational status. Andreasen discovered that the writers had a substantially higher rate of psychological disorders than the controls—in fact, 43% of the writers were found to have experienced the symptoms of a bipolar disorder at some point in their lives. This was the case for only 10% of the controls. Andreasen also found a higher likelihood of mental problems among the writers' first-degree relatives (parents and siblings). According to University of British Columbia psychologist Mark Schaller, the disorder becomes even worse when writers become famous. His argument is that fame increases their self-consciousness to a degree that pushes their already-frenetic minds over the edge (Schaller, 1997).

Kay Redfield Jamison (1989) looked to see whether similarities might exist between creative states and the characteristics of manic states. She interviewed 47 famous British writers and artists—all had won at least one prestigious literary or artistic prize—and asked them to describe their moods, thoughts, and actions during spurts of creative activity. She found striking similarities between their answers and the symptoms found in manic states: Virtually all of the subjects reported experiencing creative states characterized by a decreased need for sleep; increases in energy, enthusiasm, self-confidence, and speed and fluency of thoughts; as well as an elevated mood and sense of well-being. Moreover, when Jamison asked the subjects how important these extremes in mood and thoughts were to the creation of their work, 90% of the participants stated that the moods and feelings were integral, necessary, or very important (Jamison, 1989).

But this kind of evidence does not indicate that the psychological disorder is *causing* the creative activity. Other factors might be involved. For example, one possibility is that when creative individuals are in a manic state, they simply do more work because of their high energy levels. This can make it look like the mania is enhancing creativity, even though it is the *quantity* rather than the *quality* of the work that is really changing. Suppose that you're capable of writing one really good poem for every 10 attempts you make. If you normally make 10 attempts in a month, you will end up with one excellent result. Now suppose you enter a manic state, which increases your output to 30 poems in a month. Even if the mania doesn't affect the quality of your work one bit, it will still look as if you have tripled the number of "great" works that you have produced. Madness and creativity may co-occur, but one is not directly causing the other.

To examine the possibility that it may be the quantity rather than the quality of output that is affected by a mood disorder, Robert Weisberg (1994) conducted a detailed case study of the composer Robert Schumann (1810–1856). Schumann is believed to have suffered from bipolar disorder; throughout his life, he repeatedly entered either manic or depressive states, and he eventually starved himself to death in an institution at age 46. Schumann is an excellent case to study because there are medical records, as well as other data, that pinpoint on a year-by-year basis which kind of mood state he was in. Weisberg found a clear relationship between Schumann's mood state and his productivity as a composer: For the years that he was primarily in a state of depression, he completed, on average, fewer than three compositions per year. On the other hand, his output during manic years was a little over 12 compositions per year (see Figure 14.6).

But were the compositions from his manic years of high quality? To find out, Weisberg (1994) determined the number of times Schumann's compositions had been recorded professionally over the years. If a composition is recorded often by professionals, Weisberg argued, it's reasonable to conclude that the piece is of high quality. Weisberg found that when the quality of Schumann's compositions—defined as the average number of recordings available for each composition in a particular year—was compared across manic and depressive years, no significant differences emerged. Although Schumann composed more during his manic periods, he was not more likely to produce works of extremely high quality. In this particular case, then, madness affected the quantity of creative output but not the quality.

Determining whether there really is a causal relationship between certain kinds of psychological problems and genius or creativity is a difficult thing to do. Obviously, psychologists cannot conduct a well-controlled experiment (creating madness in one randomly sampled group

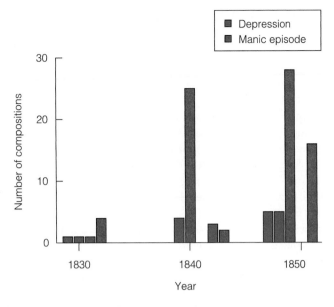

FIGURE 14.6

Musical Productivity and Mood State

The graph shows the number of musical compositions written by Robert Schumann during years in which his mood state was characterized primarily as manic (red) or depressed (blue). (Based on Weisberg, 1994.)

of creative people and not in another), so they are typically forced to rely on correlational studies or anecdotes as the basis for their opinions. Weisberg's research, with its careful and objective separation of quality from quantity, suggests that the anecdotal evidence may be wrong or misleading, at least for people suffering from bipolar disorders. The link between madness and creativity may turn out to be quite weak, despite centuries of belief to the contrary.

Suicide is the third leading cause of death among adolescents.

been estimated that more than 90% of people who kill themselves suffer from some kind of psychological disorder (Garland & Zigler, 1993).

What are the risk factors associated with suicide? Besides the presence of a psychological disorder, many different factors can be involved. Alcohol use and abuse is particularly likely in adolescent suicides, existing in perhaps 50% of suicides (Kelly et al., 2001; Woods et al., 1997). In Canada, First Nations people and people living in remote northern communities have a higher suicide rate than other groups (Statistics Canada, 2000). Another important factor is the sudden occurrence of a very stressful event—something such as the death of a loved one, failure or rejection in a personal relationship, or even a natural disaster. There is convincing evidence suggesting that suicide rates increase after natural disasters, such as floods, hurricanes, or earthquakes (Krug et al., 1998). Suicide may also be contagious: There are increased suicide rates following widely publicized suicides, especially among adolescents, suggesting that imitation or modelling is an important factor (Gould, 1990; Gould & Kramer, 2001).

Among the most significant predictors of suicide, however, are prior suicide attempts and suicidal thoughts. Among adolescents there is a ratio of somewhere between 3:1 and 6:1 between serious suicidal thoughts and an actual suicide attempt. Not everyone who thinks about suicide makes an attempt—and the ratio of attempted suicides to successful suicides is perhaps 50:1 (Garland & Ziegler, 1993)—but suicidal thinking is a serious warning sign. We'll discuss treatment options for the psychological conditions that are associated with suicide in Chapter 15, but there are a variety of intervention programs currently being used to tackle the suicide problem nationally. One suggestion is that teams of mental health professionals be sent to schools, for counselling and screening, whenever a student or visible member of the community commits suicide. Moreover, most cities and towns now have 24-hour suicide hotline services that allow people in need to voice their concerns and learn about alternative ways of dealing with their crises. Most psychologists are optimistic that as the risk factors associated with suicide are identified, and treatment options become more accessible, suicide rates can be slowed or reversed (Holden et al., 1998; Kosky et al., 1998).

Schizophrenia: When Thought Processes Go Awry

Schizophrenia is actually a group or class of disorders. There are different subtypes of schizophrenia, defined by different DSM-IV criteria, but each case is identified with some kind of fundamental disturbance in thought processes, emotion, or behaviour. Schizophrenia is a bit unusual compared to the other disorders we've considered because it doesn't always reveal itself in the same way; whereas everyone who suffers from an anxiety disorder feels apprehensive, or in depression feels sad, each of the symptoms of schizophrenia need not be shared by all affected individuals. Schizophrenia is a complex disorder that is expressed in a variety of complex ways—no single symptom must be present for the diagnosis to be applied (Maj, 1998).

It is important to understand that schizophrenia is not the same thing as a dissociative identity disorder, despite the misleading translation of schizophrenia as "split mind." Schizophrenia leads to faulty thought processes and inappropriate emotions—not to dissociations among distinct personality types. In fact, when the Swiss psychiatrist Eugen Bleuler (1908) originally introduced the term *schizophrenia,* he was referring primarily to the fact that affected individuals have trouble holding on to a consistent line of thought. Their thinking is disorganized; their thought lines and associations seem to split apart and move forward in inconsistent ways. Both schizophrenia and dissociative identity disorder are serious psychological problems, but they fall into completely different categories in the DSM-IV.

Shown here are areas of the brain that appear to be selectively activated during auditory and visual hallucinations. The highlighted areas were captured through the use of a PET scanning procedure, during which a young man who was suffering from schizophrenia was asked to press a button, initiating the scan, every time he experienced a hallucination.

Diagnostic Symptoms There are two main types of symptoms in schizophrenia: *positive symptoms* and *negative symptoms.* Positive symptoms usually include observable expressions of abnormal behaviour, such as delusions or hallucinations; negative symptoms consist of deficits in behaviour, such as an inability to express emotion. The DSM-IV requires that two or more characteristic symptoms be present for the diagnosis of schizophrenia, but a particular person may have only positive symptoms or a combination of both positive and negative symptoms. As with the other disorders we've considered, these symptoms need to last for a significant period of time, they must cause social or job distress, and they cannot be due to the effects of a general medical condition or to the use of a drug or medication.

schizophrenia
A class of disorders characterized by fundamental disturbances in thought processes, emotion, or behaviour.

Let's consider some of the major positive symptoms of schizophrenia in more detail. As noted earlier, one of the main problems in schizophrenia is distorted or disorganized thinking. People with schizophrenia often suffer from delusions, which are thoughts with inappropriate content. If someone sitting next to you in class leaned over and claimed to be Elvis in disguise, or Jesus Christ, or Adolf Hitler, the content of his or her thoughts would clearly be inappropriate or deviant—this individual would be suffering from a delusion. People suffering from schizophrenia sometimes hold a *delusion of grandeur,* which is a belief that they are more famous or important than they actually are, or a *delusion of persecution,* which is a belief that others are conspiring or plotting against them in some way.

It is also not unusual for people with schizophrenia to report distorted perceptions of the world. For them, objects can seem to change their shape or size; distances can be perceived in ways that are different from reality. Frequently, these *hallucinations*—which are perceptions that have no basis in external stimulation—are auditory. People with schizophrenia claim to hear disembodied voices in their heads, giving them commands or commenting on the quality of their activities ("You're an idiot," "You should stay away from that person," and so on). Some researchers believe that these voices may originate from the same areas of the brain that control language production. It may be the case that people with schizophrenia are actually "listening" to their inner voice (see Chapter 7) but fail to recognize the voice as their own. Instead, they falsely attribute the source of the voice to something external (Cleghorn et al., 1992; Evans et al., 2000; McGuire et al., 1993).

Two other positive symptoms of schizophrenia that may be present are *disorganized speech* and *catatonia.* Sometimes the speech patterns of a person with

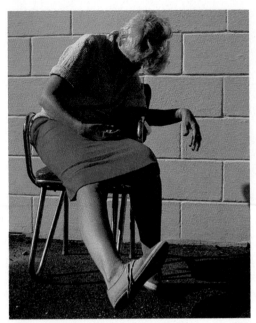

When catatonia is present as a positive symptom of schizophrenia, the affected person might adopt a peculiar stance or position and remain immobile for hours.

schizophrenia appear quite jumbled and incoherent; the affected individual jumps repeatedly from one disconnected topic to another. ("I went to the beach today where the moon pulls the rabbit out of the hat. I'm the world's greatest cook, but that's because volcanic magma heats the glaciers and makes the water and the sand.") It's as if the mind has lost its internal editor—ideas or thoughts no longer flow in a connected way. In addition to displaying speech problems, someone with schizophrenia can behave in ways that are quite disorganized and bizarre. The person might engage in repetitive activities, such as swirling his or her arms repeatedly, or will appear to laugh or cry at inappropriate times. When *catatonia* is present, people will sometimes adopt a peculiar stance or position and remain immobile for hours; or, they may wildly and suddenly change position for no apparent reason.

Negative symptoms of schizophrenia are expressed by the elimination or reduction of normal behaviour. For example, it's quite common for people with schizophrenia to display *flat affect,* which means that they show little or no emotional reaction to events. Show someone with flat affect an extremely funny movie or a tragic, heart-rending photo, and the person is unlikely to crack a smile or shed a tear. People with schizophrenia also often refuse to engage in the most basic and important of everyday activities. They may refuse to wash or clean themselves, eat, or dress themselves. Activities that are pleasurable to most people become unpleasurable or uninteresting to some individuals with schizophrenia.

For obvious reasons, people with schizophrenia are often unable to cope successfully at school or at work. In many cases, their behaviour becomes so maladaptive that hospitalization is required. As you'll see later in the chapter, there are reasons to believe that people with schizophrenia may be suffering from a kind of "broken" brain—fundamental neurological problems may underlie the bizarre thinking and behaviours that plague people affected with the disorder.

Personality Disorders

personality disorders
Chronic or enduring patterns of behaviour that lead to significant impairments in social functioning.

paranoid personality disorder
A personality disorder characterized by pervasive distrust of others.

dependent personality disorder
A personality disorder characterized by an excessive and persistent need to be taken care of by others.

antisocial personality disorder
A personality disorder characterized by repeated offences against social laws, customs, or norms.

All of the psychological disorders we've considered up to now are described on Axis I of the DSM-IV (Clinical Disorders). Axis II describes **personality disorders,** which are essentially chronic or enduring patterns of behaviour that lead to significant impairments in social functioning (Livesley, 2001). People with personality disorders have a tendency to act repeatedly in an inflexible and maladaptive way. They may show an exaggerated distrust of others, as in **paranoid personality disorder,** or they may show an excessive and persistent need to be taken care of by others, as in **dependent personality disorder.** One of the best-known examples of a personality disorder, occurring mainly in males, is the **antisocial personality disorder.** People with this type of disorder show little respect for social customs or norms. They act as if they have no conscience—they lie, cheat, or steal at the drop of a hat and show no remorse for their actions if caught. Someone with antisocial personality disorder is likely to have no qualms about committing criminal acts, even murder. Even among other prison inmates, they stand out because of their long criminal records and the wide variation in the type of crimes they commit (Cunningham & Reidy, 1998).

Research on the closely related concept of *psychopathy* has been led by University of British Columbia psychologist Robert Hare and his colleagues (those in Canada include Stephen Hart, Adelle Forth, Jim Hemphill, Hughes Herve, and Steve Wong). Hare uses the term *psychopath* in preference to antisocial personality disorder because of his belief that personality, not behaviour, is the central feature of the syndrome (Hare, 1996). His most recent elaboration of the syndrome includes four facets: interpersonal manipulation, cold affect (e.g., lack of remorse), social deviance (criminal history), and impulsive thrill seeking (Hare, 1993, 2003). Hare developed the standard instrument for assessing psychopathy entitled the Psychopathy Checklist Revised (PCL-R): It requires that a trained assessor complete a 20-item rating scale, based on a semi-structured interview and detailed information from files or other corroborating sources (Hare, 1991).

Other researchers have also used the PCL-R to advance our knowledge of psychopaths and other violent offenders. Among these are Marnie Rice and Grant Harris of Mental Health Centre, Penetanguishene, Vernon Quinsey of Queen's University, and Martin Lalumière of the Clarke Institute of Psychiatry. One of the surprising findings of these researchers was that group therapy programs designed to rehabilitate violent psychopathic offenders actually increased their rate of re-offending. Perhaps the program raised their self-confidence and, therefore, their subsequent aggression, or it provided them with practice in appearing empathic, which they later used to manipulate other people more effectively (Harris et al., 1994; Rice, 1997). Nonetheless, use of the PCL-R and other data has permitted prediction of the likelihood of violent offenders re-offending with far more accuracy than has ever been possible (Hare, 2003; Harris et al., 1993; Quinsey et al., 1998).

Among the more speculative suggestions is that psychopaths may form a separate category of people and that psychopathy perhaps should not be considered a psychological disorder (e.g., psychopaths show little personal distress or desire to change their behaviour, unlike others afflicted with other disorders). Some experts suggest that psychopathy better fits the criteria of a "cheater life strategy" that evolved during our evolutionary history and is passed along genetically to a small percentage of the human population today (Harris et al., 1994; Lalumière & Quinsey, 1999; Quinsey, 1995). Although this perspective does not de-emphasize the seriousness of offences committed by psychopaths, it does help provide some insights into the difficulty of treating psychopaths as well as their opportunistic nature and their lack of distress regarding their condition.

The **perfectionistic personality disorder** has been elaborated primarily by Canadian researchers Paul Hewitt, of the University of British Columbia, and Gordon Flett, of York University. Perfectionists have an exaggerated need to make things of the highest quality, organization, and/or precision. Instead of handing in a less-than-perfect assignment, they will continue to work on it until they have no time for other necessary tasks. As a result, their lives are full of stress, anxiety, and depression—with no particular successes to show for it (Hewitt & Flett, 2003). The disorder has not yet been given a distinct location in the DSM. Given its overlap with eating disorders, obsessive–compulsive disorder, and narcissism, some experts have argued that it is a combination of symptoms of other known disorders.

What is it about personality disorders that requires them to be placed on their own classification axis? Do personality disorders have characteristics that fundamentally distinguish them from the major clinical syndromes described on Axis I? Most mental health professionals believe that personality disorders are unique primarily because they tend to be more *ingrained* and *inflexible* than the major clinical syndromes outlined on Axis I (Barlow & Durand, 2002). These are not problems that typically appear and disappear over time, which is the case with many psychological disorders. They may not be accompanied by a sense of distress. Instead, these disorders arise from someone's basic personality and, as a result, tend to continue throughout adulthood and are quite resistant to therapy. Personality disorders are placed on a separate axis in the DSM-IV in part to force the clinician to consider the possibility that it is a personality characteristic, rather than a major clinical syndrome, that is contributing to the appearance of abnormal behaviour.

Because personality disorders are linked to an individual's personality, some mental health professionals have argued that it's wrong to think of them as *disorders* in the same sense as something like a specific phobia or depression (Gunderson, 1992; Trull & McCrae, 1994). In Chapter 12, we discussed the idea that personality can be defined by the Big Five personality dimensions (McCrae & Costa, 1985). Some researchers have argued that it is better to think about people with personality disorders as simply extreme or deviant on one or more of these five dimensions—extraversion, agreeableness, conscientiousness, neuroticism, and openness (Clarke &

perfectionistic personality disorder
A personality disorder characterized by an excessive and rigid need to achieve the highest level of quality in achievements.

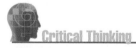
Critical Thinking

Think back to our earlier discussion of how to conceptualize abnormality. Do you think personality disorders should be labelled as "abnormal" behaviours?

Livesley, 1994; Wiggins & Pincus, 1992). For example, the dimension of *agreeableness* measures how kind, warm, and trusting an individual is. It's possible that people classified with a paranoid personality disorder may simply lie at the extreme low end on the agreeableness scale—they trust almost no one. Similarly, perfectionism may be an exaggerated combination of conscientiousness and neuroticism (Alden et al., 2002). At present, questions are still being raised about the proper way to think about personality disorders, and whether the Big Five will be sufficient to account for the complexities of the disorders is still an unresolved question (Widiger, 1998).

Cult Membership and Internet Addiction: Psychological Disorders?

There are some behaviours or situations that are often troubling or problematic to individuals and to those around them, but are not necessarily included in the DSM-IV. This may be because there is insufficient evidence to conclude that the condition should actually be considered as a psychological disorder rather than simply a social or personal problem. There are also conditions that are linked to specific technologies, substances, or social conditions and that may not have existed prior to the development of such innovations. Cult membership and Internet addiction are two such conditions that would definitely be considered to be indications of psychological disorders to some observers, but have not yet received "official" DSM status.

Cult Membership   James Ogloff of Simon Fraser University and Jeffrey Pfeifer of the University of Saskatchewan conducted a survey and examination of Canadian and American university students' attitudes toward cults (Ogloff & Pfeifer, 1992). Only about 2% of the respondents reported ever having been a member of a cult. Students generally reported feeling negative toward cults (including satanic cults) and alternative religious movements, but they expressed the most negative attitudes toward satanic cults and the least toward alternative religious movements. However, the fact that most university students hold negative attitudes toward cult membership does not mean that cult members are necessarily psychologically disordered. Other researchers have examined whether cult membership is generally psychologically harmful (Aronoff et al., 2000), and they conclude that, perhaps surprisingly to many, cult members generally seem to be well adjusted psychologically and show few obvious signs of greater-than-average levels of psychological disorders. The authors caution, however, that the usual cult environment of extreme conformity may mask some underlying psychological problems. They also note that there may be some significant psychological problems (referred to as adjustment difficulties) for former cult members who have recently left cults. Therefore, although cult membership can be problematic and severely stressful, particularly for the family and friends of cult members, current evidence does not indicate that cult membership by itself constitutes a psychological disorder or is highly correlated with such disorders.

Internet Addiction   Many substance-related addictions, such as those to alcohol, nicotine, and cannabis, are considered to be psychological disorders and are described in the DSM-IV. What about addiction to the Internet? Can obsessive interest in and time spent online constitute a "real" addiction? Some psychologists think so, particularly Kimberly Young. She has suggested (1998, 1999) that pathological Internet use can be considered very similar to pathological gambling (which is a disorder listed in the DSM-IV) insofar as it also involves a failure of impulse control without involving an intoxicant. Young has listed several criteria of "pathological Internet use." To be considered Internet addicted, she suggests people would meet four or more of the following criteria:

- Preoccupation with the Internet (thinking about it while offline).
- Inability to control Internet use.

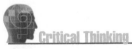

Critical Thinking

What characteristics of the Internet make it likely to facilitate a variety of addictions?

- Using the Internet to escape from problems.
- Going through withdrawal when offline.
- Staying online longer than originally intended.

(See "What's on the Web?" for online information. But don't spend too much time there!)

Pathological Internet use is too recent a phenomenon to be included in the current DSM-IV. Other repetitive behaviours given recent consideration include sexual addiction and videogame addiction. In the meantime, there is no question that some people, particularly adolescents and young adults, have problems with excessive and harmful Internet use, and people with such problems should seek help from psychologists, counsellors, or self-help groups (Cooper et al., 1999).

Test Yourself 14.2

Check your knowledge about classifications of psychological disorders by picking the diagnostic category that best describes each of the following behaviour patterns. Pick from among the following terms: anxiety disorder; somatoform disorder; dissociative disorder; mood disorder; schizophrenia; personality disorder. (You will find the answers in Appendix B.)

1. Sharma is convinced that the ringing in her ears means she has a brain tumour, even though a variety of doctors can find nothing wrong:

   _____

2. Gabriella is a checker—she often drives home five or six times a day to make sure that she hasn't left the oven on: _____
3. Kunal hasn't left his house for six years—it's the only place he really feels safe: _____
4. Otto hates himself. He's convinced that he's worthless, stupid, and unlovable. No one can convince him otherwise: _____
5. Sergio is found wandering aimlessly in the park. When questioned, he can't remember who he is or how he got to the park: _____
6. Sarah is a habitual con artist with little regard for the truth. She steals regularly and feels no guilt or remorse about her actions:

   _____

7. Melissa is convinced that her psychology professor is beaming his thoughts directly into her brain; she feels empowered and ready to complete her takeover of the world: _____
8. Billy shows little or no emotional reaction to events in his world; in fact, he usually stands in the corner for hours at a time with his right arm resting on his head: _____

UNDERSTANDING PSYCHOLOGICAL DISORDERS: BIOLOGICAL, COGNITIVE, OR ENVIRONMENTAL?

11a, 11b, 11c, SIM 9 Psyk.trek

Learning Goals

1. Understand how biological and genetic factors can contribute to psychological disorders.
2. Learn how maladaptive thoughts can contribute to psychological disorders.
3. Be able to explain how environmental factors can contribute to psychological disorders.

THE DSM-IV CLASSIFICATION SYSTEM is designed to provide a reliable way for mental health professionals to diagnose psychological problems. The word *reliable* in this case refers to whether professional clinicians will tend to arrive at the same or similar diagnoses for people with a given set of symptoms. In general, the DSM system is considered to be quite reliable, although agreement is higher for some diagnostic categories than for others (Linde & Clarke, 1998). But it's important to remember that the DSM-IV is only a classification system—it does not indicate anything about the root cause, or *etiology*, of the underlying disorder. What factors, alone or in combination, conspire to produce a major clinical syndrome such as depression, anxiety, or schizophrenia? The answer, in a nutshell, is that we don't know for sure. But most current explanations, as well as most approaches to therapy, appeal to *biological, cognitive,* or *environmental* factors.

The recognition that psychological disorders are influenced by biological, cognitive, and environmental factors is sometimes called the **bio-psycho-social perspective.** Biological factors *(bio)* include physiological problems with the body, particularly the brain, and genetic influences that are present at birth. Cognitive factors *(psycho)* include our beliefs, styles of thought, and any other psychological mechanisms that potentially influence behaviour. Finally, environmental factors *(social)* include what we learn from the environment, cultural influences, and how other people treat us in our daily lives. We'll consider each of these three major factors in greater detail in the following sections.

bio-psycho-social perspective
The idea that psychological disorders are influenced, or caused, by a combination of biological, psychological (cognitive), and social (environmental) factors.

Biological Factors: Genes, Brain, and Hormones

Over the past several decades, there have been significant advances in our understanding of the brain and its functions. Most researchers are now convinced that at least some kinds of abnormal behaviour result directly from brain dysfunction. The disordered thoughts of someone with schizophrenia, for example, may be partly due to a broken or at least malfunctioning brain. What is the evidence? Biological accounts are typically supported by two kinds of findings. First, it's been discovered that abnormal brain chemistry or abnormal brain structures accompany some kinds of mental disorders. Second, through the close study of family histories, it has been determined that a number of psychological disorders may have a powerful genetic component—psychological disorders tend to run in families in ways that cannot be easily explained by environmental histories. We discussed some of these findings in Chapter 3; we'll review and expand on that discussion here.

Neurotransmitter Imbalances   As you may recall from Chapter 3, schizophrenia has been linked to an excess supply of the neurotransmitter *dopamine* (Seeman et al., 1976; Snyder, 1976), or possibly to an interaction between dopamine and the neurotransmitter *serotonin* (Carlsson et al., 2001; Kahn et al., 1993). Support for the link has come primarily from studying how different drugs affect the disorder. Among the most effective treatments for schizophrenia are medications that act as dopamine *antagonists,* which means they reduce or block dopamine use in the brain (Gershon & Reider, 1992). It's also the case that drugs that increase the level of dopamine in the brain can sometimes produce side effects that resemble the symptoms found in schizophrenia (Braff & Huey, 1988; Davidson et al., 1987). Abnormal dopamine levels may not be the only cause of schizophrenia—for example, not all people with schizophrenia are helped by dopamine-reducing medications—but problems in brain neurochemistry are widely believed to be at least partly responsible for the disorder (Csernansky & Bardgett, 1998).

Neurotransmitter imbalances may also contribute to mood disorders, such as manic states and depression. Once again, most of the effective medications for these problems act by altering the actions of neurotransmitters in the brain. Fluoxetine (more commonly known by its brand name, Prozac) is one of the most commonly prescribed treatments for depression; it acts by slowing the reuptake of serotonin, thereby

Some psychological disorders, such as depression, can be effectively treated by administering drugs that correct neurotransmitter imbalances in the brain.

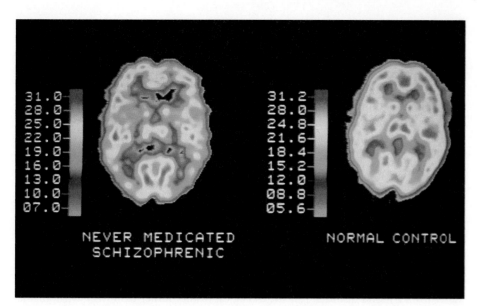

NEVER MEDICATED
SCHIZOPHRENIC

NORMAL CONTROL

People who suffer from disorders such as schizophrenia may possess malfunctioning brains. These two PET scans, taken from a person diagnosed with schizophrenia (left) and one without the disorder (right), show dramatic differences in brain activity levels. The blue and purple colours in the scans show areas of relatively low brain activity.

prolonging the neurotransmitter's effectiveness. More generally, depression and mania have been linked to a group of neurotransmitters called *monoamines,* which include serotonin, norepinephrine, and dopamine. Researchers currently believe that these neurotransmitters are involved in the regulation of mood, although the specifics have yet to be worked out (Okada et al., 1998). It's unlikely that mood disorders are caused by a single neurotransmitter deficit. Instead, a decrease in one may have multiple effects on the others. A decrease in serotonin, for instance, may permit the levels of other neurotransmitters in the brain to vary more widely; these more complex interactions probably work together in some way to alter mood abnormally (Goodwin & Jamison, 1990).

Structural Problems In addition to neurochemical problems, such as imbalances in neurotransmitters, there may also be structural problems in the brains of people suffering from serious psychological problems. In the case of schizophrenia, anatomical and brain-imaging studies have revealed that people with schizophrenia tend to have larger *ventricles,* which are the liquid-filled cavities in the brain. (For reasons that are not yet clear, increased ventricle size tends to be more likely in men who suffer from schizophrenia.) Larger ventricles are associated with the loss, or shrinkage, of brain tissue, and this factor may help explain some instances of schizophrenia (Pahl et al., 1990). There is also evidence that activity in the frontal areas of the brain may be abnormally low in schizophrenia patients (Berman & Weinberger, 1990). Although it's not clear why these activity levels are low, decreased brain activity in certain prefrontal regions may directly or indirectly alter the neural pathways associated with the neurotransmitter dopamine (Davis et al., 1991).

These data are convincing, but it's important to remember that not all people with schizophrenia show these kinds of neurological problems. Not all people with schizophrenia have larger ventricles or show lower frontal lobe activity. Moreover, not all people who have been diagnosed with depression respond to drug therapies that alter the levels or actions of monoamines. So we're left with a somewhat cloudy picture. There's little doubt that psychological disorders are sometimes associated with observable abnormalities in brain chemistry or function. But whether these factors are the true cause of disorders such as schizophrenia or depression, or simply one cause, or even occur as a consequence of having the disorder, is not currently known. For example, larger ventricle size is observed more often in people who have suffered from schizophrenia for a long time, so it's conceivable that the structural abnormality is partly a consequence of the disorder or even of its treatment (DeLisi et al., 1997).

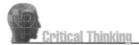

Critical Thinking

Based on our earlier discussion of schizophrenia, why don't all people who are diagnosed with schizophrenia show the same neurological problems?

Genetic Contributions Increasingly, researchers are concluding that people may inherit predispositions toward abnormality. For example, the odds that any particular individual in the population will develop schizophrenia are roughly 1 in 100. But if you have a brother, sister, or parent with the disorder, the odds increase dramatically, perhaps to 1 in 10. If you have an identical twin—someone who has essentially the same genetic information as you do—and your twin has been diagnosed with schizophrenia, the odds that you will develop the disorder during your lifetime jump to about 1 in 2 (Gottesman, 1991) (see Figure 14.7). Notice that the disorder cannot be explained entirely by appealing to genetic factors—otherwise, identical twins would always share the disorder—but these data suggest that genetic background plays a significant role.

A similar pattern emerges with mood disorders. Depression and bipolar disorder tend to run in families, and the *concordance rate,* which measures the likelihood of sharing a disorder, is quite high between identical twins. A number of studies have shown that if one twin is diagnosed with depression, there is a 50% or greater chance that the other twin will also be diagnosed with depression; the concordance rate may be even higher for bipolar disorders (Gershon, 1990). It is also the case that adoptees with biological parents who suffer from a mood disorder are themselves more likely to suffer from a mood disorder. It is the biological history rather than the environmental history that, on average, predicts the chances of becoming affected by the disorder (Wender et al., 1986).

Genetic factors help predict the likelihood that someone will suffer from certain psychological disorders, but genetic factors are not necessarily sufficient to explain abnormal behaviour. Anxiety disorders, for example, are more likely to occur in people born with sensitive temperaments, but experience will influence whether a full-blown disorder actually develops.

FIGURE 14.7

The Genetics of Schizophrenia

Each bar shows the risk of developing schizophrenia when one or more relatives have been diagnosed with the disorder. For example, if one identical twin has schizophrenia, there is a roughly 50% risk that the other will also develop the disorder. In general, the closer the individual is related genetically to the person with schizophrenia, the more likely he or she is to develop the disorder. (Based on Gottesman, 1991.)

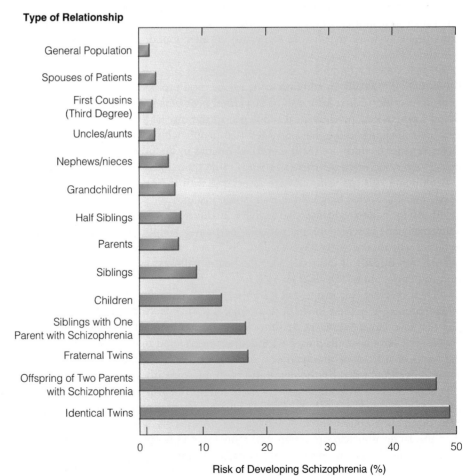

Type of Relationship

Risk of Developing Schizophrenia (%)

Cognitive Factors: Thinking Maladaptive Thoughts

If you look closely into the mind of someone with a psychological disorder, you will often find fixed and disordered styles of thinking. People with anxiety disorders, somatoform disorders, or just about any of the other disorders we've discussed typically believe things about themselves or the world that have little or no basis in reality. Robert, who is depressed, is convinced that he lacks ability and drive, even though he is a successful banker. Jill, who suffers from agoraphobia, refuses to leave her house because she's convinced that something terrible will happen outside, even though she can think of no real reason for this belief.

Many psychologists feel that such faulty beliefs may be more than just symptoms of an underlying disorder—they may contribute to, or even cause, the disorder itself. To see how this might work, suppose we are able to convince you, by feeding you false but convincing reports, that your city was about to be carpet-bombed. Your anxiety level would certainly shoot up, and there's little question that your behaviour would change. You might not leave your house, and you might, in fact, end up spending a lot of time crying and huddled under a table in your basement. This behaviour is not irrational if the belief about the attack is true. Similarly, many people with psychological disorders act the way they do because they have incorrect beliefs. If you're absolutely convinced that you're no good and can never succeed at anything, it's not surprising that you withdraw from social situations and fail to secure steady employment.

Maladaptive Attributions Psychologists use the term *attribution* to refer to the processes involved in assigning causality to a behaviour (see Chapter 13). When you fail at something, such as a test or a new job, you attribute the failure to a cause, such as your own incompetence or the lousy teacher. It turns out that people who have psychological disorders, particularly depression, have relatively distinctive and predictable attributional or explanatory styles. Unfortunately, the attributions that these people make are often maladaptive, which means that they lead to behaviours that are abnormal or unproductive (McFarland & Miller, 1994).

As Figure 14.8 shows, when something bad happens to a person prone to depression, he or she is likely to explain it in terms of *internal* ("I'm to blame rather than the situation"), *stable* (long-lasting), and *global* (widespread) attributions (Abramson et al., 1989; Foersterling et al., 1998). Let's suppose you fail a test at school. If you're depressed, you will probably attribute that failure to some personal inadequacy (internal) that is likely to be long lasting (stable) and that will apply in lots of situations other than school (global). People who are not prone to depression tend to have more flexible explanatory styles. They might attribute the failure to some *external* source ("I've got a rotten teacher") and consider the failure to be *unstable* ("I had a bad day"),

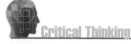

Critical Thinking

Try to identify your own attributional style. Do you tend to attribute outcomes to global, stable, and internal causes?

Stable
"I was born stupid."

Internal
"It's totally my fault."

Global
"I'll probably fail all my courses."

FIGURE 14.8

Maladaptive Thoughts in Depression

Depressed individuals tend to attribute failure to internal, stable, and global conditions.

and they will probably make a *specific* rather than global attribution. Nondepressed people have less of a tendency to overgeneralize from a situation at school to other areas of life. They are also less likely to process every event as having implications for their self-evaluation (Moretti et al., 1996).

Learned Helplessness What produces these different explanatory styles? It's difficult to know whether people who make maladaptive attributions do so because they are depressed or whether it is the unfortunate explanatory style that creates the depression. Some researchers have argued that prolonged experience with failure may be one contributing factor. According to the **learned helplessness** theory of depression (Seligman, 1975), if you repeatedly fail while attempting to control your environment, you acquire a general sense of helplessness. You give up and become passive, which, the theory proposes, leads to depression. Still, it's unlikely that we can account for all forms of depression by appealing simply to repeated failure. Experience with failure may be a necessary condition for acquiring depression, but it is not a sufficient condition. Many people fail repeatedly yet show no tendencies toward depression.

Moreover, it isn't really the failure that leads to depression but rather your attributions about the failure. Instead of learning to be helpless, it is really the sense of *hopelessness*—the belief that things cannot become better because of internal, stable, and global factors—that is more likely to produce depression (Alloy & Clements, 1998; Joiner, 2001). Whether this sense of hopelessness can be explained by appealing to experience alone or to some interaction between experience and biological/genetic predispositions remains to be seen (Alloy et al., 2001). In a recent study, researcher Kenneth Cramer of the University of Windsor and his colleagues demonstrated two important determinants of feeling helpless: believing that you were going to fail in a task and feeling that you have no control over outcomes important to you (Cramer et al., 1997). They also found that an uncertain outcome did not seem to have the same effect in creating a feeling of helplessness; people seem to be able to cope with uncertainty better than with lack of confidence or lack of control.

Environmental Factors: Do People Learn to Act Abnormally?

All theories of psychological disorders ultimately appeal either directly or indirectly to environmental factors. Even if a researcher believes that a disorder such as schizophrenia is primarily caused by a genetically induced brain dysfunction, it is still necessary to explain why identical twins don't always share the disorder. Experience clearly

learned helplessness
A general sense of helplessness that is acquired when people repeatedly fail in their attempts to control their environment; learned helplessness may play a role in depression.

Prolonged exposure to stressful situations may play a role in the onset of psychological disorders.

plays a pivotal role. Similarly, the irrational beliefs and explanatory styles that characterize depression must be learned somewhere, although two people with the same experiences may not always end up with the same set of beliefs. Once again, experience is the bedrock on which the psychological interpretation is built.

Culture's Role Cultural factors also play an obvious and important role (Harper, 2000). Although the symptoms of most serious psychological disorders—such as schizophrenia and depression—are generally similar across the world (Draguns, 1997), there are culture-based differences. For example, the types of delusions found in schizophrenia depend to a certain extent on cultural background (Tateyama et al., 1998). Different cultural groups may also be more or less likely to show symptoms of disorders because of cultural "rules" for expressing emotion and action (Manson, 1995). If you live in a culture, for instance, that discourages the expression of emotion, then depression will be somewhat more difficult to detect and treat.

Your cultural background may also determine the likelihood that you will be exposed to environmental events that could trigger the onset of psychological disorders. Obviously, if you live somewhere in the world where war or extreme poverty is a way of life, you are likely to encounter more stressful events that, in combination with a genetic predisposition, could lead to psychological problems (Bonanno et al., 2002). Cultural goals or ideals can also influence your psychological health. For example, living in a society that places enormous emphasis on weight ideals can increase the chances that you'll suffer from an eating disorder such as bulimia or anorexia nervosa (see Chapter 11). (You'll learn more about how cultural ideals and stressors in everyday life can affect your physical and psychological health in Chapter 16.)

Conditioning Disorders Mental health professionals who follow a social learning model feel that psychological disorders may be essentially *learned*. People can learn to act and think abnormally in perhaps the same way they might learn how to bake a cake, make friends, or avoid talking in class. Experts with this view of abnormality propose that learning principles of the type we discussed in Chapter 6 help explain why psychological disorders develop and how they can be best treated. A specific phobia, for example, could be acquired through *classical conditioning;* you might learn to associate a particular stimulus or event with another event that makes you afraid. Alternatively, you might learn to act abnormally, through *instrumental conditioning,* because you've been reinforced for those actions. Acting in a strange way thus becomes more likely than it was before.

Learning theorists believe that modelling, or observational learning, might play a particularly important role in the development of some psychological disorders. As we discussed in Chapter 6, there are reasons to believe that specific phobias are sometimes acquired through modelling (Bouton et al., 2001). Parents who react in terror to the sight of snakes might easily transfer this reaction to their children in this fashion. Some of the best evidence has come from animal studies, in which it is possible to control how the fear reaction is initially acquired. Rhesus monkeys raised in the wild show an extremely strong fear response to snakes; monkeys reared in the laboratory will show a similar reaction, but only if they've witnessed other monkeys reacting fearfully when snakes are introduced into the cage. This research has made it clear that it is not necessary for the animal to directly experience something negative, such as getting attacked and bitten by the snake; the animal can acquire its fear simply by watching other monkeys act afraid (Cook & Mineka, 1989). Modelling in this case makes adaptive sense because appropriate actions can be learned without directly experiencing negative consequences.

The monkey data are important because they show how modelling can lead to the acquisition of a strong fear response. Obviously, for monkeys in the wild it's quite adaptive to be afraid of snakes. For humans, we know that modelling is also a powerful way to learn, but the evidence that modelling underlies specific phobias—which, after all, are essentially irrational fears—is still largely indirect at this point. Stanley

Critical Thinking

Do you suffer from any kind of specific phobia? Can you trace the fear to any particular experience in your life? Does anyone else in your family share the same fear?

Concept Summary

CAUSES OF PSYCHOLOGICAL DISORDERS

Factor	Description	Example
Biological	Physiological problems, particularly in the brain. Could include neurotransmitter imbalances, structural problems, and genetic influences.	Jennifer feels extremely depressed. She goes to a psychologist, who asks her whether anyone else in her family has suffered from depression. Jennifer reports that her mother and grandmother did have bouts of severe depression.
Cognitive	Our beliefs and styles of thought, such as maladaptive attributions and a sense of hopelessness.	Jennifer is struggling with her studies. She receives a D on a big exam. She is disgusted with herself and keeps thinking, "How could I be so stupid? I am such a loser!"
Environmental	The influence of experience and culture. Cultural background, events, and learning all have an impact on psychological disorders.	Jennifer's family has always struggled financially, and now her parents are going through a nasty divorce. Jennifer acts disruptively because it's one of the few ways she can get any attention from them.

Rachman and Sheila Woody of the University of British Columbia have pointed out that many people with specific phobias cannot remember having a traumatic experience with the object of their fear (Rachman, 1990). It's also the case that specific phobias tend to run in families—if your father was afraid of heights, for instance, there's an increased chance that you too will be afraid of heights (Fyer et al., 1990). This kind of evidence is consistent with a modelling account of specific phobias but it does not preclude alternative accounts (Woody & McLean, 2001). From our adaptive perspective, it's interesting to note that modelling, which is essentially an adaptive process, might under certain conditions lead people to acquire behaviours that are not very adaptive.

As with the biological, genetic, and cognitive factors we've considered, it's unlikely that learning principles alone will be able to account for why people develop psychological disorders. People probably can't learn to be schizophrenic, for example, although stressful events in the environment may play an important role in this disorder. Even with phobias, which may be largely learning based, it is probably necessary to be predisposed to anxiety for a full-blown phobia to develop (Barlow, 1988). Experience plays a significant role in the development of most psychological disorders, but it does not act alone. Behaviour, both normal and abnormal, is virtually always produced by multiple causes.

Test Yourself 14.3

Check your knowledge about how psychologists have attempted to understand psychological disorders by answering the following questions. (You will find the answers in Appendix B.)

1. Which of the following biological conditions is most likely to be a contributing factor in schizophrenia?
   a. slowed reuptake of the neurotransmitter serotonin
   b. excessive amounts of the neurotransmitter dopamine
   c. smaller than normal ventricles in the brain
   d. increased random activity in the frontal lobes

2. Studies examining the genetics of schizophrenia have discovered that:
   a. Schizophrenia is a learned rather than an inherited disorder.
   b. Living with two parents with schizophrenia increases your risk of developing schizophrenia by about 65%.
   c. Identical twins are more likely to develop schizophrenia than fraternal twins.
   d. If your identical twin has schizophrenia, you have about a 50% chance of developing the disorder yourself.

3. Psychologists studying depression have found that depressed people tend to make the following kinds of personal attributions:
   a. external, stable, and global
   b. internal, unstable, and global
   c. internal, stable, and specific
   d. internal, stable, and global

4. Studies examining how monkeys develop a strong fear response to snakes have been used to support which of the following accounts of specific phobias?
   a. instrumental conditioning
   b. observational learning
   c. learned helplessness
   d. classical conditioning

Solving the Scientific and Practical Problems

In this chapter, we've considered the notion of abnormality and its various definitions. The underlying disorders responsible for abnormal behaviour are numerous and diverse: Hence much work has been put into the development of a precise classification system. The adaptive nature of the "normal" mind becomes clearer when we consider the variety of ways in which it can be maladaptive. Each disorder may be relatively rare but many produce destructive consequences. It's important to note that many abnormal behaviours are simply extreme versions of adaptive behaviours. Anxiety, for example, is an adaptive bodily response that prepares us for action and keeps us vigilant for danger. Only when prolonged does it impair normal functioning. Many of the personality disorders are simply extreme versions of normal personality traits. It is worth considering the more radical possibility that some disorders may actually have adaptive value: Some have argued that depression is a mechanism for disengaging from one's current lifestyle; some amnesias may be adaptive in preventing recall of traumatic events. To paraphrase Shakespeare, there may indeed be some method (i.e., a function) in our madness.

First, what is the proper way to conceptualize abnormal behaviour? Conceptualizing abnormal behaviour turns out to be a rather difficult thing to do. A number of criteria have been proposed, including the notions of statistical and cultural deviance. By the term *deviance*, psychologists typically mean behaviour that is essentially unusual in some way, with respect to either its statistical likelihood or the accepted norms of the culture. Abnormality can also be defined in terms of emotional distress or dysfunction. None of these criteria alone is sufficient to capture the concept. Instead, the concept of abnormality is usually defined by some combination of these factors.

Many mental health professionals conceive of abnormal behaviour in terms of a medical model. According to this view, psychological disorders are best described as "illnesses" that can be "cured" through appropriate treatment. The sociological model assumes that calling an individual's behaviour abnormal is more of a declaration that the individual's current society disapproves of the behaviour. The latter model provides a useful warning, but it should not be taken too literally. Given that society is unlikely to change quickly, psychologists must still do their best to alleviate the serious distress experienced by the victims of such disorders.

Second, how do we classify the underlying disorders that lead to abnormal behaviour? Once we recognize that a behaviour is abnormal, is there a reliable way of classifying the underlying problem? Most mental health professionals in North America rely on the DSM-IV, which lists objective criteria for the diagnosis of psychological disorders. The DSM-IV is composed of five major rating dimensions, or axes, which are used to record the presence of clinical or personality disorders, existing medical conditions, environmental problems, and the ability of the individual to function globally. In this chapter we focused our attention primarily on Axis I, which lists the major clinical syndromes.

Anxiety disorders are diagnosed when a person's apprehension and worry become so extreme that behaviour is impaired. Generalized anxiety disorder is characterized by chronic worrying that cannot be attributed to any obvious source. Obsessive–compulsive disorders are characterized by the presence of persistent, uncontrollable thoughts, called *obsessions,* or by compelling needs to perform actions repetitively, called *compulsions.* Specific phobias are highly focused fears of specific objects or events.

In somatoform disorders, the focus of an individual's disorder is the body: The person might have a persistent preoccupation with the possibility that he or she has a serious disease (hypochondriasis), or the individual might appear to suffer from an actual physical problem that has no identifiable physical cause (conversion disorder).

In dissociative disorders, the person appears to separate, or dissociate, previous thoughts and memories from current conscious awareness. These disorders include dissociative amnesia, dissociative fugue states, and the more controversial dissociative identity disorder, in which the person appears to have two or more distinct personalities.

Mood disorders typically come in two forms: depressive disorder, in which the affected individual is mired in depression, and bipolar disorder, in which the individual alternates between the highs of mania and the lows of depression. The final clinical syndrome we discussed, schizophrenia, is characterized by distorted thoughts and perceptions. The positive symptoms of schizophrenia include delusions, hallucinations, and disorganized speech and behaviour. The negative symptoms include flat affect, which means that the person shows little or no emotional reactions to events. Personality disorders are listed in Axis II because they tend to be more ingrained and inflexible than the major clinical syndromes described on Axis I. Cult membership and Internet addiction constitute potentially problematic and disturbing behaviours. However, neither is currently "officially" recognized as a psychological disorder in the DSM-IV.

Third, what are the underlying causes of each disorder? Mental health professionals currently believe that the root cause, or etiology, of most disorders lies in a combination of biological, cognitive, and environmental factors. Some disorders may result from broken or abnormal brains. There is evidence to support the idea that some psychological problems result from neurotransmitter problems in the brain or perhaps from structural problems in brain anatomy. Many psychological disorders also appear to have a genetic basis—individuals may inherit a predisposition for a particular kind of problem.

Psychological disorders are often characterized by maladaptive thinking, and it has been suggested that maladaptive beliefs and attributions contribute to the appearance of abnormal behaviour. Depressed individuals, for example, tend to attribute negative events to internal, stable, and global causes; these attributions are often associated with a sense of hopelessness, or the faulty belief that things cannot get better.

Finally, all theories of psychological disorders consider the environment in one form or another. For example, your cultural background may play a role in the expression of biological or genetic predispositions and may even determine the kinds of personal attributions that you make. Some theories emphasize mechanisms whereby people learn to act abnormally, either through conditioning or through modelling the behaviour of significant people around them.

Chapter Summary

CONCEPTUALIZING ABNORMALITY: WHAT IS ABNORMAL BEHAVIOUR?

The term *abnormal* is often used as roughly equivalent to the term *psychological disorder*. But psychologists have had an ongoing struggle with how to best define the concept of abnormality. No single criterion is sufficient to capture the concept.

Criteria for Defining Abnormal Behaviour

Learning Goal: Understand and evaluate the various criteria that have been proposed to define abnormality. A number of criteria have been proposed to define abnormality. *Statistical deviance* refers to infrequency. *Cultural deviance* compares behaviour to existing cultural norms. Behaviour is considered abnormal if it violates the accepted standards of society. A third criterion for defining abnormality is *emotional distress*. A final criterion is *dysfunction*, a breakdown in the ability to perform daily tasks. *Abnormal* and *normal* are best seen as ends of a continuum rather than distinct categories.

The Medical Model versus the Sociological Model

Learning Goal: Understand how the medical and sociological models view disorders. According to the *medical model*, abnormal behaviour is seen as an underlying disease that can be cured. This conception of abnormality has been quite influential; drugs are effective in treating a variety of disorders, and most disorders can be classified in terms of symptoms. The *sociological model* argues that mental illness does not lie directly in the patient but in the context and perceptions of the individual and society as a whole.

CLASSIFYING PSYCHOLOGICAL DISORDERS: THE DSM-IV

Learning Goal: Understand the DSM-IV, and discuss the pros and cons of this multiaxial system. Even if we successfully define abnormality, we still need a means for naming and classifying the underlying disorders that lead to abnormal behaviour. The purpose of the *Diagnostic and Statistical Manual of Mental Disorders (DSM-IV)*, now in its fourth edition, is to provide clinicians with a well-defined classification system for psychological disorders. Based on objective and measurable criteria, it consists of five major ratings dimensions, or *axes*, that assess clinical and personality disorders, health status, environmental stressors, and the client's ability to cope.

Anxiety Disorders: Beyond Rational Fear

Learning Goal: Identify and describe the common anxiety disorders. *Anxiety disorders* are diagnosed when levels of worry and apprehension become so extreme that behaviour is impaired in some way. *Generalized anxiety disorder* is characterized by excessive and chronic worrying. *Panic disorder* is characterized by sudden "attacks" of extremely intense fear or dread and is sometimes associated with the complication *agoraphobia* (a fear of being in public places). In *obsessive–compulsive disorder,* anxiety manifests itself through persistent uncontrollable thoughts *(obsessions)* or by the compelling need to perform one or more actions repeatedly *(compulsions)*. *Social phobia* is an extreme fear of social interactions. The defining feature of *specific phobic disorder* is a highly focused fear of a specific object or situation.

Somatoform Disorders: Body and Mind

Learning Goal: Identify and describe the somatoform disorders. *Somatoform disorders* are psychological problems that focus on the physical body. *Hypochondriasis* involves a preoccupation with the idea that one has developed a serious disease based on a misinterpretation of normal bodily reactions. A related problem, *somatization disorder,* involves a focus on physical symptoms rather than an underlying disease. In *conversion disorder,* real physical impairment exists in the absence of an apparent physical cause.

Dissociative Disorders: Disruptions of Identity or Awareness

Learning Goal: Identify and describe the common dissociative disorders. *Dissociative disorders* are defined by the dissociation of conscious awareness from previous thoughts or memories. In *dissociative amnesia,* a person is unable to remember certain events after suffering traumatic stress. *Dissociative fugue* involves a loss of personal identity, accompanied by flight from the home environment. In *dissociative identity disorder,* a person alternates between distinct identities or personality states. Controversy surrounds the diagnosis of dissociative identity disorder for a number of reasons.

Mood Disorders: Depression and Mania

Learning Goal: Identify and describe the common mood disorders. *Mood disorders* (prolonged and disabling disruptions in emotional state) come in two varieties: *depressive disorders* and *bipolar disorders*. A *major depressive episode* is characterized by a number of symptoms, including loss of interest in daily activities, daily fatigue or loss of energy, trouble concentrating, and suicidal thoughts. In *dysthymic disorder,* depression tends to be milder but more chronic. In a *bipolar disorder,* one alternates between depression and *mania,* a hyperactive, euphoric condition. *Suicide* is one fatal consequence that can result from a mood disorder. Risk factors for suicide include substance abuse, the sudden occurrence of a very stressful event, and the occurrence of other suicides.

Schizophrenia: When Thought Processes Go Awry

Learning Goal: Identify and describe the characteristics of schizophrenia. People with *schizophrenia* live in an internal world marked by delusions, hallucinations, and generally disordered thinking. Schizophrenia can be expressed in a variety of complex ways. Two major types of symptoms in schizophrenia are *positive symptoms* and *negative symptoms.* Positive symptoms are observable expressions of abnormal behaviour, such as *delusions* (thoughts with inappropriate content), *hallucinations* (perceptions that have no basis in external stimulation), *disorganized speech,* and *catatonia.* Negative symptoms involve the reduction of normal behaviour, as in *flat affect.*

Personality Disorders

Learning Goal: Identify and describe the common personality disorders. *Personality disorders* are chronic or enduring patterns of behaviour that lead to significant impairments in social functioning. They include *paranoid personality disorder* (an exaggerated distrust of others), *dependent personality disorder* (an excessive need to be taken care of by others), *perfectionistic personality disorder* (an excessive need to accomplish tasks that are error-free), and *antisocial personality disorder* (an absence of respect for social customs or norms). Some believe that those with personality disorders are simply extreme or deviant on one or more of the Big Five personality dimensions.

Cult Membership and Internet Addiction: Psychological Disorders?

Learning Goal: Understand the debate over cult membership and Internet addiction. Although most university students have negative attitudes toward cults, there is little evidence that cult members have more psychological disorders than non–cult members. However, they may experience some significant adjustment problems upon leaving the cult. Some psychologists have suggested that Internet

addiction constitutes a psychological disorder much like pathological gambling. However, the phenomenon is too recent to be included in the DSM-IV, and it is too soon to tell whether the problem of excessive Internet use will eventually be found to meet all the criteria to be considered a psychological disorder.

UNDERSTANDING PSYCHOLOGICAL DISORDERS: BIOLOGICAL, COGNITIVE, OR ENVIRONMENTAL?

What are the causes of psychological disorders? The answer to many psychological problems lies in an interaction between biological, cognitive, and environmental factors. This view is sometimes called the *bio-psycho-social perspective.*

Biological Factors: Genes, Brain, and Hormones

Learning Goal: Understand how biological and genetic factors can contribute to psychological disorders. Abnormal brain chemistry accompanies some psychological disorders. Schizophrenia has been linked to an excess supply of dopamine or to an interaction between dopamine and serotonin. Neurotransmitter imbalances may also contribute to mood disorders. Structural problems in the brain are also sometimes associated with some psychological disorders. Also, research indicates that genetic factors probably play a role in psychological disorders. People may inherit predispositions toward certain disorders. The *concordance rate* (likelihood of sharing a disorder) is quite high between identical twins.

Cognitive Factors: Thinking Maladaptive Thoughts

Learning Goal: Learn how maladaptive thoughts can contribute to psychological disorders. People with psychological disorders, particularly depression, have distinctive and predictable attributional or explanatory styles. When something bad happens to someone prone to depression, he or she is likely to make internal, stable, and global attributions. According to the *learned helplessness* theory of depression, people who repeatedly fail to control their environment give up, leading to depression.

Environmental Factors: Do People Learn to Act Abnormally?

Learning Goal: Be able to explain how environmental factors can contribute to psychological disorders. Experience plays a pivotal role in psychological disorders. Culture, for example, can affect how disorders are expressed, and/or the likelihood that you will be exposed to events that could trigger the onset of psychological disorders. Some professionals feel that disorders can be learned through classical or instrumental conditioning, or through modelling.

Terms to Remember

abnormal behaviour, 558
psychological disorder, 558
Conceptualizing Abnormality: What Is Abnormal Behaviour?
statistical deviance criterion, 559
cultural deviance criterion, 561
emotional distress criterion, 561
dysfunction criterion, 561
medical model, 562
sociological model, 562
insanity, 563
Classifying Psychological Disorders: The DSM-IV
DSM-IV, 565
anxiety disorders, 567
generalized anxiety disorder, 567
panic disorder, 567
agoraphobia, 568
obsessive–compulsive disorder, 568
social phobia, 569
specific phobic disorder, 569
somatoform disorders, 570
hypochondriasis, 570
somatization disorder, 570
conversion disorder, 571
dissociative disorders, 571
dissociative amnesia, 571
dissociative fugue, 571
dissociative identity disorder, 572
mood disorders, 573
major depressive episode, 573
bipolar disorder, 574
manic state, 574
schizophrenia, 577
personality disorders, 578
paranoid personality disorder, 578
dependent personality disorder, 578
antisocial personality disorder, 578
perfectionistic personality disorder, 579
Understanding Psychological Disorders: Biological, Cognitive, or Environmental?
bio-psycho-social perspective, 582
learned helplessness, 586

Recommended Readings

Alexander, B. K. (1990). *Peaceful measures: Canada's way out of the war on drugs.* Toronto: University of Toronto Press. An examination of the causes of drug addiction and some suggestions for treating drug addiction as a medical and social problem rather than as a criminal issue. By Simon Fraser University researcher Bruce Alexander.

De Silva, W. P., & Rachman, S. J. (1996). *Panic disorder: The facts.* New York: Oxford University Press. Succinct summaries of research and treatment of several of the anxiety disorders. Co-written by Stanley Rachman of the University of British Columbia.

Flett, G. L., & Hewitt, P. L. (2003). *Perfectionism: Theory, research and treatment.* Washington, DC: American Psychological Association. Co-written by researchers from York University and the University of British Columbia, this volume provides up-to-date summaries of several perspectives on perfectionism.

Mash, E. J., & Wolfe, D. A. (1999). *Abnormal child psychology.* Albany, NY: Wadsworth. Co-written by prominent researchers and clinicians from the universities of Calgary and Western Ontario, this excellent textbook covers a range of childhood disorders, including attentional, conduct, anxiety, and eating disorders, and child abuse.

Peters, R. DeV., & McMahon, R. J. (Eds.). (1996). *Preventing childhood disorders, substance abuse and delinquency.* Thousand Oaks, CA: Sage. Co-written by a clinical child psychologist from Queen's University, this volume examines how early intervention programs can prevent the development of some kinds of psychological disorders and child and adolescent problems.

Hare, R. D. (1993). *Without conscience: The disturbing world of the psychopaths among us.* New York: Pocket Books. University of British Columbia psychologist Robert Hare has been studying psychopaths (i.e., people with antisocial personality disorder), both criminal and noncriminal, for over 30 years and is one of the world's foremost experts on the subject. This volume summarizes his research in a popular format. Detailed sketches include those of Ted Bundy and Clifford Olson.

Roesch, R., Hart, S. D., & Ogloff, J. R. P. (Eds.). (1999). *Psychology and law: The state of the discipline.* New York: Kluwer Academic/Plenum. Edited by researchers from Simon Fraser University's Mental Health, Law, and Policy Institute, this professional-level volume deals with issues such as the psychology of juries, eyewitness testimony, and predicting violence in mentally disordered individuals.

Quinsey, V. L., Harris, G. T., Rice, M. E., & Cormier, C. (1998). *Violent offenders: Appraising and managing risk.* Washington, DC: American Psychological Association. Edited by members of the Forensic/Correctional Studies Program of the Department of Psychology at Queen's University, this text provides an excellent summary of empirical studies, psychological tests, and questionnaires relating to the important issue of attempting to predict violent offenders' risks of re-offending.

Woody, S., & McLean, P. D. (2001). *Anxiety disorders in adults: An evidence based approach to psychological treatment.* New York: Oxford University Press. Co-authored by University of

British Columbia researchers, this volume makes clear recommendations about treating various anxiety disorders.

 For additional readings, explore InfoTrac® College Edition, your online library. Go to:

www.adaptivemind2e.nelson.com

Hint: enter the search terms: diagnosis of mental illness; anxiety disorder; dissociative identity disorder; bipolar disorder; schizophrenia; causes of mental illness.

What's on the Web?

Please note that Web addresses are subject to change. Check out the accompanying Web site for updates: www.adaptivemind2e.nelson.com. This site presents practice quiz questions, hypercontent, information on degrees and careers in psychology, study tips, and more.

Centre for Addiction and Mental Health

www.camh.net

The CAMH is now Canada's most comprehensive organization for all issues relating to psychological disorders. It recently incorporated a number of other institutions, including the Clarke Institute of Psychiatry.

Canadian Mental Health Association

www.cmha.ca

CMHA combats mental health problems and emotional disorders through research and information services, sponsored research projects, workshops, seminars, pamphlets, newsletters, and resource centres. The site includes items such as stress tests and "10 Tips for Mental Health."

Mental Health, Law, and Policy Institute

www.sfu.ca/psychology/groups/mhlpi

Located at Simon Fraser University, this institute promotes collaboration among research practitioners and policymakers working in the area of mental health law and policy. Includes a useful set of links to sites such as the Canadian Supreme Court and Statistics Canada.

Canadian Centre for Substance Abuse

www.ccsa.ca

This nonprofit organization works to combat harm associated with the use of nicotine, alcohol, and other drugs.

Evaluate Your Drinking Online

notes.camh.net/efeed.nsf/feedback

You can test your degree of alcohol abuse using a standard test process online.

Center for On-Line Addiction

www.netaddiction.com

Are you addicted to the Web? Try the "IA Tests" link and see.

The Phobia List

www.phobialist.com

Who thinks these things up? According to the author of this site, "all of the phobia names on this list have been found in some reference book." So find out for yourself what you would call a fear of being forgotten (athazagoraphobia). You probably didn't know that there was such a thing as a fear of gravity (barophobia). Hundreds of phobias are listed at this site.

Dr. Ivan's Depression Central

www.psycom.net/depression.central.html

This site, according to its author (Dr. Ivan), "is the Internet's central clearinghouse for information on all types of depressive disorders and on the most effective treatments" for individuals suffering from various mood disorders. Topics you can find at this site include "famous people with mood disorders," seasonal affective disorder, and postpartum depression.

Internet Mental Health

www.mentalhealth.com/t20a.html

This is one page at the vast Internet Mental Health Web site. It includes an alphabetical list of links for dozens of psychological disorders. Click on each link, and you'll be able to read detailed information about the disorder. The site even has a tool for diagnosis of disorders (although it goes without saying that you should view such a tool with more than a little caution!).

You cannot teach people anything. You can only help them discover it within themselves.
Galileo

The art of medicine consists in amusing the patient while nature cures the disease.
Voltaire

Chapter 15   Therapy

psychotherapy
Treatment designed to help people deal with mental, emotional, or behavioural problems.

f you regularly hear voices in your head, or you have to check everything you've done exactly 333 times, you may well have trouble leading a normal life. You probably can't hold a job or make lasting friendships, and you may even be incapable of carrying on a coherent conversation. Clearly, you need some kind of treatment—**psychotherapy**—to deal with your mental, emotional, and behavioural problems. But as you'll discover in this chapter, even those with less severe disturbances can benefit from the right kind of therapy. What if Ralph, for example, turns down the job of national sales manager because he is afraid of flying? What if Julie spends most of her time alone in her apartment because she's convinced she'll embarrass herself in public? Treatment options are available to tackle these milder personal problems as well as for the severely maladapted few.

Mental health professionals have a variety of tools at their disposal to help people regain their ability to function well in their surroundings. The particular tool used by the therapist depends on a number of factors, including the specific type of psychological disorder being treated and the personality of the person seeking treatment. There are also several ways that a treatment can be administered. Some people respond well to one-on-one encounters with a therapist; others thrive best in group settings. As we discussed in Chapter 1, good therapists are often *eclectic,* meaning they draw on a variety of therapeutic techniques to meet the needs of the particular client. This commitment to eclecticism doesn't mean that therapists must abandon all theoretical orientations (Lazarus & Messer, 1991), but it does require flexibility. Good therapists recognize that a method that proves effective for one patient may not work for another.

Previewing the Scientific and Practical Problems

As you saw in Chapter 14, when researchers study the cause of a psychological disorder, they tend to focus on either biological, cognitive, or environmental factors. Abnormal behaviour can be caused by physical problems in the brain, maladaptive thinking, environmental experiences, or some combination of these factors. As a result, most kinds of psychotherapy are specifically designed to treat either the body, the mind, or the environment (see Figure 15.1). Nonetheless, therapists can draw on any one of these approaches or even combine them. In this chapter, we'll consider the scientific and practical problems associated with the practice and evaluation of psychotherapy.

First, what are the most effective biologically based treatments? As you know, abnormal functioning in the brain is thought to contribute to a number of psychological disorders. Schizophrenia, for example, appears to be traceable in part to imbalances in neurotransmitters. Depression and mania have also been linked to the activities of neurotransmitters. To address these kinds of problems, it makes sense to consider treating the body itself through biomedical therapies. One option might be to administer a drug that restores the proper balance of neurotransmitters in the brain; other options might include surgery to repair damage in a particular region of the brain, or even the use of electric shock treatment.

Second, how can maladaptive thinking be changed? As you know, psychological disorders are often associated with irrational beliefs and faulty attributions. Many psychologists are convinced that the key to improvement lies in insight—you must gain awareness of your own thought processes. When you think of psychotherapy, do you imagine someone lying on a couch and talking about dreams and early childhood experiences? Although this cliché used to be accurate, you'll see in our discussion of insight therapies that most therapists have abandoned the couch as well as the emphasis on dreams and recollections of childhood. What remains strong is the idea that the exploration of one's thought processes can help solve psychological problems.

Third, how can the environment be altered to reduce maladaptive behaviour? In Chapter 14 we discussed the idea that some psychological disorders are learned responses to specific situations. People learn to think and act in abnormal ways in much the same way that they acquire other thoughts and actions—through the experiences of instrumental conditioning, classical conditioning, or modelling the actions of others. Such maladaptive learning is best undone, according to behavioural therapies, by (a) changing the situation or (b) relearning more adaptive behaviour patterns in the current situation. For example, if experience has taught you to associate high places with disabling fear, it might be possible to alter the association either through extinction or by counterconditioning relaxation to replace the fear.

Fourth, how can we evaluate the effectiveness of psychotherapy? Do all forms of therapy work, or are some more effective than others? Therapy can be a costly and time-consuming process, so it's important to evaluate the advantages and disadvantages of the intervention. Many studies have compared people who have undergone therapy with those left untreated. Although most studies clearly demonstrate the effectiveness of psychotherapy, some of the findings may surprise you. We'll also look at factors to consider when choosing a therapist.

Treating the body

Treating the mind

Treating the environment

FIGURE 15.1
Previewing the Problems
Psychologists face three main scientific and practical problems as they seek to administer and evaluate therapy.

TREATING THE BODY: BIOMEDICAL THERAPIES

Learning Goals

1. Learn how drug therapies can be used to treat psychological disorders.
2. Understand and evaluate electroconvulsive therapy.

PSYCHOLOGICAL DISORDERS have afflicted people since the beginning of history. And for almost as long, people have speculated about what causes abnormal behaviour and have offered remedies for its treatment. At one time, people who exhibited bizarre or deviant behaviour were believed to be possessed by evil spirits or demons. Early "therapies" included chaining, drowning, or torturing the sufferer in an effort to drive out the evil inhabitants.

Less barbaric methods have also been around for some time. In fact, over 2000 years ago, Hippocrates (469–377 B.C.) and his followers suggested that psychological disorders should be treated as manifestations of the body. Hippocrates believed that people get depressed or exhibit manic states for much the same reason we fall victim to the common cold—the body and, hence, the mind are affected by some kind of "disease." Hippocrates even went so far as to recommend changes in diet and exercise as a

This engraving from 1598 demonstrates an early form of "therapy" for psychological disorders—drilling holes in the head to promote the release of evil spirits. Believe it or not, this method, called trephination, is still recommended today by certain cult groups.

biomedical therapies
Biologically based treatments, including drug therapies, shock treatments, and, very rarely, psychosurgery.

antipsychotic drugs
Medications that reduce the positive symptoms of schizophrenia; the majority act on the neurotransmitter dopamine.

way of treating depression, a course of action that many modern therapists consider appropriate today.

The medical approach to understanding disorders was placed on firmer scientific ground in the 19th and early 20th centuries as scientists began to establish links between known physical problems and psychological disorders. For example, by the end of the 19th century it was recognized that the venereal disease syphilis is responsible not only for a steady deterioration in physical health (and eventually death) but also for the appearance of paranoia and hallucinations. Establishing a link between syphilis and mental problems was an important step in the eventual development of biologically based therapies.

In this section of the chapter, we'll consider several modern biological approaches to the treatment of psychological disorders. **Biomedical therapies** use physiological interventions in an effort to reduce or eliminate the symptoms of psychological disorders. By far the most popular approach is treatment with drugs, but other biomedical therapies are also available, including electroconvulsive therapy and psychosurgery. We will say very little about psychosurgery (operating on the brain in an attempt to cure or alleviate psychological disorders) because it is now rarely used and then only for quite specific conditions.

Drug Therapies

In the early 1950s two French psychiatrists, Jean Delay and Pierre Deniker, reported success in treating the positive symptoms of schizophrenia with a drug called *chlorpromazine* (now sold under the brand name Thorazine). Patients suffering from severe delusions and hallucinations showed considerable improvement after prolonged use of the drug. Since that time, dozens of other drugs have proven successful in treating a wide variety of psychological disorders. In fact, there are now specific medications available to treat most of the disorders that we considered in Chapter 14—everything from obsessive–compulsive disorder to depression. Unfortunately, these drugs do not work for all people affected with mental problems, and some drugs have disturbing side effects. Nonetheless, they have helped thousands of people, and in many ways they have revolutionized the mental health profession.

The use of medications such as chlorpromazine has greatly reduced the number of patients who require extended stays in mental hospitals or institutions. Prior to the 1950s, hundreds of thousands of people were institutionalized in North America because their symptoms were too severe for them to cope in everyday settings. Partly through the administration of drugs, it is now possible to control the severity of these symptoms, allowing individuals to be treated outside of a hospital or institution. The results have been dramatic: By the 1980s, the number of people institutionalized for psychological problems had dropped to less than 25% of what it had been in the 1950s. Effective medications are not the only reason for the decline in hospitalized patients. Other factors include improvements in alternative forms of therapy (including behavioural and cognitive), cutbacks in government funding needed to maintain adequate institutional care, and stricter laws governing commitment.

Antipsychotic Drugs Medications that treat the positive symptoms of schizophrenia—delusions, hallucinations, disorganized speech—are commonly called **antipsychotic drugs.** Chlorpromazine is an example of such a drug, but others are also effective. Most of these antipsychotic drugs are believed to act on the neurotransmitter

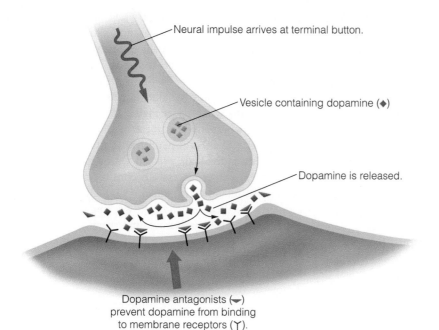

FIGURE 15.2
Dopamine Antagonists
Some antipsychotic medications act as antagonists, which means they block or slow down the action of neurotransmitters in the brain. Here, a dopamine antagonist is binding with the receptor membrane, blocking the neurotransmitter.

Neural impulse arrives at terminal button.

Vesicle containing dopamine (◆)

Dopamine is released.

Dopamine antagonists (�m)
prevent dopamine from binding
to membrane receptors (Υ).

dopamine in the brain. As we discussed in Chapter 14, many researchers believe that schizophrenia is caused by excess supplies of dopamine. Chlorpromazine acts as a dopamine *antagonist,* meaning that it blocks or slows down the use of dopamine in the brain (Gershon & Reider, 1992) (see Figure 15.2). The fact that dopamine antagonists work so well in treating positive symptoms is strong support for the dopamine hypothesis of schizophrenia (Barlow & Durand, 2002).

But dopamine antagonists do not work for all sufferers of schizophrenia. Moreover, these drugs tend to work almost exclusively on positive symptoms. The negative symptoms of schizophrenia, such as the sharp decline in the normal expression of emotions, are not affected very much by the administration of antipsychotic medications. Antipsychotic drugs can also produce unwanted and persistent side effects in some patients, including drowsiness, difficulties in concentrating, blurry vision, and movement disorders (Windgassen, 1992). One particularly serious side effect is a condition called *tardive dyskinesia,* which produces disabling involuntary movements of the mouth and face (Kane et al., 1986). These side effects can be permanent and they act as a two-edged sword: Not only are they extremely uncomfortable for the patient, but they also increase the chances that the patient will stop taking the medication (Tugrul, 1998). Without the medication, of course, it's very likely that the positive symptoms of the disorder will reappear.

Over the past decade or so, a number of new medications, including *clozapine* and *risperidone,* have been introduced that work well for patients who don't respond to the more traditional dopamine antagonists (Chakos et al., 2001). These medications do not produce movement side effects such as tardive dyskinesia, although medical complications can still be a concern in some cases (Hector, 1998). From a research standpoint, the effectiveness of the newer "second-generation" medications is noteworthy because they don't work simply by regulating the amount of dopamine in the brain. It's believed that they affect a number of neurotransmitters, including dopamine, serotonin, and others (Carlsson et al., 2001). Thus dopamine alone, as we noted in Chapter 14, cannot account entirely for schizophrenic disorders.

Antidepressant Drugs Medications for treating manic states and depression were also introduced in the 1950s. Mood disorders have been linked to several neurotransmitters, including norepinephrine and serotonin. **Antidepressant drugs,** like the antipsychotic drugs, act by modulating the availability or effectiveness of these kinds of

Critical Thinking

Just because dopamine antagonists reduce the positive symptoms of schizophrenia does not necessarily mean that dopamine causes schizophrenia. Why not?

antidepressant drugs
Medications that modulate the availability or effectiveness of the neurotransmitters implicated in mood disorders; Prozac, for example, increases the action of the neurotransmitter serotonin.

neurotransmitters. The group of antidepressants called *tricyclics,* for example, alters mood by acting primarily on norepinephrine: They apparently allow norepinephrine to linger in synapses longer than normal, which eventually modulates its effectiveness. A different class of antidepressants called SSRIs (selective serotonin reuptake inhibitors) includes fluoxetine, sold commercially as Prozac, as well as Zoloft and Paxil. These drugs act primarily on serotonin, again by blocking its "reuptake" into the neuron, thereby allowing it to linger in the synapse (see Figure 15.3).

At present, researchers do not know exactly how these medications affect mood, outside of the fact that they alter the effectiveness of neurotransmitters. Fortunately, it's clear that they do work well for many individuals affected with depression. It's been estimated that sustained use of antidepressants successfully controls depression in over 50% of all depressed patients (Depression Guideline Panel, 1993). On the downside, it typically takes several weeks for these medications to begin working (the time periods may differ across the different types of antidepressants), and there are potential side effects that must be monitored. Prozac, for example, can produce agitation or restlessness, difficulty sleeping, as well as diminished sexual desire and performance. A few early reports claimed that Prozac might also induce violent or suicidal tendencies, but these claims were refuted in follow-up research (Dinan, 2000).

Effective medications are also available for treating bipolar disorders, which are characterized by mood swings between depression and hyperactive manic states. Bipolar disorders are usually treated by administering a common salt called *lithium carbonate.* Lithium is more effective for bipolar disorder than the antidepressants because it works well on the manic state; it puts affected individuals on a more "even keel" and helps to prevent the reoccurrence of future manic episodes. But it too needs to be monitored closely because lithium use can lead to a variety of medical complications (Keck, 2000; Moncrieff, 1997).

Antianxiety Drugs   To treat anxiety-related disorders, mental health professionals typically use **antianxiety drugs,** known more generally as *tranquillizers.* Tranquillizers include a class of chemicals called *benzodiazepines*—Valium and Xanax are popular trade names—and they are quite effective for reducing tension and anxiety. In the mid-1970s it was estimated that 10% to 20% of adults in the Western world were "popping" tranquillizers (Greenblatt & Shader, 1978), which gives you some idea of their wide-

antianxiety drugs
Medications that reduce tension and anxiety. Many work on the inhibitory neurotransmitter GABA.

FIGURE 15.3
Reuptake Blockers
Some antidepressant medications block the reabsorption of neurotransmitters, which then linger longer in the synapse and continue to activate receptor neurons. Prozac is in the class of antidepressants that block the reabsorption of serotonin.

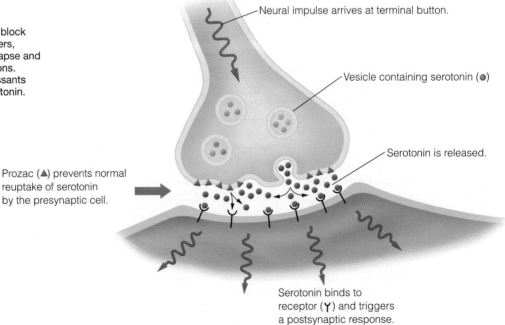

Neural impulse arrives at terminal button.

Vesicle containing serotonin (●)

Serotonin is released.

Prozac (▲) prevents normal reuptake of serotonin by the presynaptic cell.

Serotonin binds to receptor (Υ) and triggers a postsynaptic response.

spread use. In recent years tranquillizer use has been on the decline, primarily because mental health professionals recognize a downside to their continued use.

Most benzodiazepines appear to work on a neurotransmitter in the brain called gamma-amino-butyric acid (GABA), which tends to produce primarily inhibitory effects. The effectiveness of GABA increases after taking the drug, which leads to a lowering of excitation in affected neurons (Lickey & Gordon, 1991). Potential side effects include drowsiness, impaired motor coordination, and possible psychological dependence (Rickels et al., 1990). Tranquillizers can act as a psychological crutch after lengthy use, so most clinicians now recommend that they be used primarily as a short-term remedy for anxiety rather than as a long-term cure. There are some newer antianxiety drugs on the market, such as *buspirone*, that may not produce the same degree of dependency, but whether they will turn out to be as useful as traditional medications remains to be seen (Carrazana et al., 2001).

Electroconvulsive Therapy

When traditional medications for depression fail, clinicians turn to a different form of biomedical therapy: "shock" treatment. At face value, few psychological therapies seem as radical as the idea of strapping someone down on a table and passing 100 V or so of electricity into his or her brain. During this procedure, a brief brain seizure occurs that produces convulsions and loss of consciousness. When **electroconvulsive therapy** **(ECT)** was first introduced in the 1930s, it was a terrifying and hazardous procedure; patients suffered serious side effects that included the occasional broken bone from the convulsions. Thankfully, modern applications of ECT are much less physically traumatic; the patient is given a light anesthetic and medications that relax the muscles so that injuries will not occur (Sackeim et al., 2000).

Most mental health professionals believe that ECT, as currently administered, is a safe and effective treatment for patients who are suffering from severe depression. Some clinicians believe it may benefit other psychological problems as well (Fink, 2001; Krystal & Coffey, 1997). Nonetheless, most professionals consider it to be a treatment of last resort. It is used in cases in which people have shown little or no response to conventional antidepressant drugs or "talk" therapies. Controlled studies have found that ECT is successful some 50% to 70% of the time in lessening the symptoms of depression in patients who have not responded to any other treatment (Prudic et al., 1990; Weiner & Coffey, 1988).

electroconvulsive therapy (ECT)
A treatment used primarily for depression in which a brief electric current is delivered to the brain.

Concept Summary

DRUG THERAPIES

Type of Drug	Used in the Treatment of	Examples and Effects
Antipsychotic	Positive symptoms of schizophrenia, including delusions, hallucinations, and disorganized speech.	*Chlorpromazine* acts by impeding the flow of dopamine in the brain. *Clozapine* has also proven effective in alleviating some symptoms of schizophrenia.
Antidepressants	Mood disorders.	*Tricyclics* alter mood by acting primarily on norepinephrine, allowing it to linger in synapses longer. *Fluoxetine* (e.g., Prozac) works primarily on serotonin, blocking its reuptake into the neuron. *Lithium carbonate* is used to treat bipolar disorder.
Antianxiety	Psychological problems associated with anxiety.	Commonly known as *tranquillizers*. Tranquillizers come from a class of chemicals called *benzodiazepines;* they inhibit excitation in affected neurons, reducing tension and anxiety.

ECT, as currently administered, is a reasonably safe and effective form of treatment for patients suffering from severe depression, but its use is still debated by some mental health professionals and advocates.

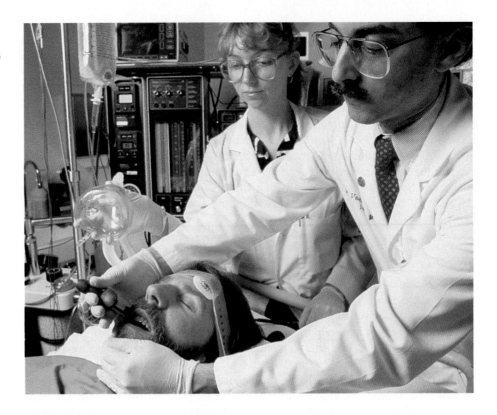

Controversies Despite the demonstrated effectiveness of ECT as a treatment for severe depression, there are several reasons why the procedure remains controversial. First, no one is certain exactly why the treatment works. It's possible that shocking the brain affects the release of neurotransmitters or changes some structural feature of the brain (Mann, 1998), but at present there is no definitive answer to why the procedure changes mood (Kapur & Mann, 1993). Second, ECT produces side effects, particularly confusion and a loss of memory for events surrounding the treatment (Breggin, 1991). These side effects are usually temporary, and they're not serious for most patients, but some observers remain concerned that ECT might cause long-term brain damage. Finally, the third reason for controversy is the emotional revulsion many people feel about putting an electric current through a patient's brain—a treatment not unlike that used to execute convicted murderers.

Is ECT worth the risks? The medical consensus has become more optimistic over the last two decades (Sackeim, 1999). Certainly, for the deeply depressed individual who has tried but received no relief from other treatment options, ECT might literally be a lifesaver. Psychologist Norman Endler of York University definitely would agree. Endler suffered from severe depression himself and found that the only treatment that was effective in alleviating it was ECT, as recounted in his book *Holiday of Darkness* (1990).

Test Yourself 15.1

Check your knowledge about biomedical therapies by answering the following questions. (You will find the answers in Appendix B.)

1. Pick the psychological disorder that is best treated by each of the following therapies or medications. Choose your answers from among the following: depression; manic state; generalized anxiety disorder; schizophrenia; hypochondriasis.

  a. Clozapine: _____
  b. Prozac: _____
  c. ECT: _____
  d. Benzodiazepine: _____
2. Which of the following statements about ECT is false?
  a. ECT is an effective treatment for depression.
  b. Researchers are uncertain why ECT works.
  c. ECT can produce confusion and some memory loss.
  d. ECT is used regularly to treat schizophrenia.

TREATING THE MIND: INSIGHT THERAPIES

Learning Goals
1. Understand and evaluate psychoanalysis as a form of insight therapy.
2. Understand and evaluate cognitive therapies.
3. Understand and evaluate humanistic therapies.
4. Learn about group and family therapy.

PEOPLE WHO SUFFER from psychological disorders often carry around faulty or irrational beliefs about the world and about themselves. Many clinicians are convinced that the role for the therapist is to challenge these irrational thoughts and beliefs directly through what are called insight therapies. **Insight therapies** are designed to give clients self-knowledge, or *insight,* into their psychological problems, usually through extensive one-on-one verbal interactions with the therapist. The hope is that, with insight, the person will adopt a more realistic, adaptive view of the world, and behaviour will change accordingly.

There are many forms of insight therapy available for use by mental health professionals. We'll consider three in this section: *psychoanalysis, cognitive therapies,* and *humanistic approaches.* Most of the other insight therapies are related in one form or another to these three main approaches. The common thread that ties them all together is the belief that cognitive or mental insight can produce significant changes in one's psychological condition. The therapies differ in the kinds of beliefs or memories that are considered of vital importance and in how the client's insight can best be obtained. Finally, we'll end the chapter by briefly discussing the value of group and family therapy.

insight therapies
Treatments designed to give clients self-knowledge, or insight, into their psychological problems, usually through one-on-one interactions with a therapist.

Psychoanalysis: Resolving Unconscious Conflicts

The best-known insight therapy is **psychoanalysis,** an elaborate set of ideas and techniques emanating from the psychodynamic theory of Sigmund Freud and his disciples. As discussed in Chapter 12, Freud emphasized the impact of the *unconscious mind.* We can't directly think about the urges and memories stored in the unconscious mind, but they affect our behaviour nonetheless. Freud argued that through psychoanalysis, these hidden impulses and memories could be brought to the surface of awareness, thereby freeing us from the insidious harm they wreak on our thoughts and behaviours.

Freud based his ideas on two sources: (a) self-analysis, and (b) case studies of individuals he encountered in his private practice. He routinely treated patients with troubling psychological problems, and he discovered that he could often help these people by getting them to recall and relive traumatic experiences that they had apparently forgotten, or repressed. Freud was particularly interested in the emotionally significant experiences of childhood because he believed that during childhood we progress through a number of psychologically "fragile" stages of psychosexual development (see

psychoanalysis
Freud's method of treatment that attempts to bring hidden impulses and memories, which are locked in the unconscious, to the surface of awareness, thereby freeing the patient from disordered thoughts and behaviours.

Some critics argue that Freud based psychoanalysis far too much on the analysis of his own mind.

free association
A technique used in psychoanalysis to explore the contents of the unconscious; patients are asked to relax and freely express whatever thoughts and feelings happen to come into their minds.

dream analysis
A technique used in psychoanalysis; Freud believed that dreams are symbolic and contain important information about the unconscious.

resistance
In psychoanalysis, a patient's unconsciously motivated attempts to subvert the process of therapy.

transference
In psychoanalysis, the patient's expression of thoughts or feelings toward the therapist that are actually representative of the way the patient feels about other significant people in his or her life.

Chapter 12). Traumatic experiences are, by definition, anxiety provoking and therefore difficult for the young mind to deal with. If sufficiently traumatizing, the ideas are buried in the unconscious. Although no longer consciously available, these experiences continue to influence feelings and behaviour in ways that are beyond the person's awareness.

The Tools of Psychoanalysis The goal of psychoanalysis is to help the patient uncover, and thereby relive, these unconscious conflicts. Obviously, because the patient is unaware of the conflicts, the therapist needs certain tools to gain access to the contents of the unconscious mind. Freud liked to compare psychoanalysis to excavating a buried city; but instead of picks and shovels, his tools were the uncensored expressions and feelings of his patients. In the beginning, Freud tried hypnosis and other new techniques of his era. Later he developed a technique called **free association,** in which patients were asked to relax on a couch and freely express whatever thoughts and feelings came into their minds. To the untrained eye, the results were disconnected streams of thought, but to Freud, these free associations represented symbolic clues to the contents of the unconscious.

Another of Freud's important therapeutic tools was **dream analysis:** He felt that it provided a "royal road" to the unconscious. As we discussed in Chapter 5, Freud was convinced that dreams are partly a psychological mechanism for wish fulfillment, a way to satisfy hidden desires that are too anxiety provoking to be allowed to be directly experienced in the conscious state. The story line of dreams, he believed, is largely symbolic—there is a hidden meaning to dreams, a *latent content*, that reveals the unconscious. Freud therefore encouraged his patients to describe their dreams, so he could acquire further clues in the search for hidden psychological truth. A third tool, projective tests, was covered in some detail in Chapter 12.

Resistance and Transference In classic psychoanalysis, the therapist seeks to understand the contents of the unconscious, but ultimately, it is really the patient who needs the insight. The therapist can't simply relay the hidden meanings that are uncovered—explanation is not enough. Instead, the patient needs to face the emotional conflicts directly and relive them, and the therapist can only act as a kind of expert guide. But the journey toward insight is not an easy one, and the therapist must usually navigate around several roadblocks. For example, patients typically go through periods in which they are uncooperative; they show **resistance,** that is, an unconsciously motivated attempt to subvert the therapy (Adler & Bachant, 1998).

Why would people try to block their own therapy? Because the hidden unconscious conflicts are anxiety provoking. As a result, the patient will do almost anything to reduce the anxiety. As Freud (1912/1964) put it, "Resistance accompanies the treatment at every step; every single association, every act of the patient's ... represents a compromise between the forces aiming at cure and those opposing it" (p. 140). The resistance can express itself in a variety of ways; the patient might become inattentive, claim to forget dreams, skip therapy sessions, or argue with the directions suggested by the therapist.

As resistance begins to wane, a new problem develops. **Transference** is the tendency of patients to express thoughts or feelings toward the therapist that are actually representative of the way the patient feels about other significant people in his or her life. The patient "transfers" feelings of love, hate, or dependence onto a substitute figure, the therapist. Depending on the repressed feelings being tapped, the patient might turn the therapist into an object of passionate love or into a hated and despised

Resistance

"I know I'm late. I ... uh... couldn't find my dream notes."

Transference

"You really understand me. I cherish our time together."

FIGURE 15.4
Resistance and Transference
People in therapy typically go through resistance periods in which they are uncooperative—skipping a session, arriving late, or arguing with the therapist. Subsequently, the patient's feelings toward significant others begin to be transferred onto the therapist.

individual (see Figure 15.4). Recent research supports many of these aspects of transference (Andersen & Berk, 1998).

Transference is a significant event in analysis because it means that the patient's hidden memories and conflicts are bubbling up close to the surface of consciousness. The patient is made aware of the strong feelings he or she is experiencing—although the object of those feelings is inappropriate—and the therapist can help the patient work through what those feelings might mean. The patient is no longer in denial of powerful emotional urges—they are now ready to be dealt with. At the same time, it's important for the therapist to recognize that the patient's feelings at this point are symbolic. It's not uncommon for the patient to express feelings of strong sexual desire for the therapist, for example, and it would be inappropriate and unethical for the therapist to respond sexually (Tyler & Tyler, 1997).

Current Applications   Classical psychoanalysis, as practised by Freud and his contemporaries, is a very time-consuming process. It can take years for the analyst to excavate the secrets of the unconscious, and the patient needs to be properly prepared to accept the insights when they are delivered. It is assumed that the patient will set up roadblocks throughout the process. So this kind of therapy is never presented as a quick fix. It's acknowledged to be not only time consuming but also expensive.

For these reasons, modern practitioners of psychoanalysis often streamline the therapeutic process (Coren, 2001). So-called brief forms of psychoanalysis encourage the therapist to take a more active role in the analytic process (Horvath & Luborsky,

Critical Thinking

What do you think Freud would have thought about the value of biomedical therapies? Would he have supported or rejected the idea of treating psychological disorders through medications or ECT?

1993). Rather than waiting for patients to find insight themselves in response to subtle nudgings, the analyst is much more willing to offer interpretations in the early stages of therapy. Rather than waiting for transference to occur on its own, the analyst might actually encourage role playing in an attempt to get the patient to deal with deep-seated feelings. So, rather than requiring years of analysis, progress can occur in weeks or months (Book, 1998).

Besides increasing the speed of treatment, modern versions of psychoanalysis are often tailored to meet the needs of the particular patient (Westen, 1998). No attempt is made to excavate and reconstruct the patient's entire personality; instead, the analyst focuses on selective defence mechanisms or conflicts that are more pertinent to the individual's particular symptoms (Luborsky et al., 1990). There is also often a greater emphasis placed on improving the patient's interpersonal and social skills and less of an emphasis is placed on sexual and aggressive drives. Because these forms of treatment differ from classical psychoanalysis, they sometimes go by the more general name: *psychodynamic therapy*.

Cognitive Therapies: Changing Maladaptive Beliefs

According to Freud's theory, a person's conscious thoughts, beliefs, and feelings are of primary importance only because they provide clues to the inner workings of the unconscious mind. **Cognitive therapies,** in contrast, emphasize the conscious beliefs themselves, rather than what those beliefs may mean symbolically. Cognitive therapists assume that irrational beliefs and inappropriate thoughts are primarily responsible for psychological disorders. If the inappropriate thoughts can be altered, the psychological disorder can be alleviated.

cognitive therapies
Treatments designed to remove irrational beliefs and negative thoughts that are presumed to be responsible for psychological disorders.

Let's take depression as an example. People who are depressed usually do not think constructively. They view themselves as worthless and unlovable, and they see little chance that things will get better in the future. Such negative thinking clouds the interpretation of normal events; everyday experiences are viewed through a negative filter, which means that depressed people often jump to irrational conclusions. For instance, a depressed woman whose husband arrives home slightly late from work might be immediately convinced that her husband is having an affair. The depressed student who fails the test might see the F as confirmation of a fundamental lack of intelligence.

Cognitive therapists argue that it is not direct experience, such as failure on a test, that actually produces depression. Straight thinking tells us that failing a test doesn't tell us much about a student. One can fail a test for many reasons—most of them having nothing to do with one's intrinsic worth as a human being. But in the mind of a depressed person, the event (failing the test) is accompanied by an irrational belief ("I'm incredibly stupid"), and it is this belief that leads to negative emotional consequences (feeling sad and depressed). Thus, it is the *interpretation* of the event, not the event itself, that leads to problems (Beck, 1991; Ellis, 1962, 1993) (see Figure 15.5).

Rational-Emotive Therapy   The goal of cognitive therapy is to remove these irrational beliefs. But how can irrational beliefs be changed? One technique is to challenge the beliefs directly, through active and aggressive confrontation. In **rational-emotive therapy,** developed by Albert Ellis, the therapist acts as a kind of cross-examiner, verbally disputing the client's irrational thought processes. Here's an excerpt from an exchange between a therapist practising rational-emotive therapy and a client showing signs of depressed thinking (from Walen et al., 1992, pp. 204–205):

rational-emotive therapy
A form of cognitive therapy, developed by Albert Ellis, in which the therapist acts as a kind of cross-examiner, verbally disputing the client's irrational thought processes.

Therapist: You really believe that you're an utterly worthless person. By definition, that means that you always do things poorly. Can you prove to me that that's correct?

Client: But I've failed at so many things.

Therapist: Just how many?

FIGURE 15.5

The Cognitive View of Depression

Cognitive therapists believe that it is not direct experience, such as failing a test, that leads to depression. Instead, the depression is caused by one's internal thoughts and beliefs about the event.

Client: I've lost my job, my wife is threatening to leave me, I don't get along with my kids—my whole life's a mess!

Therapist: Well, let me make two points. First of all, that's not every aspect of your life. Second, you seem to take total responsibility for all of those events, rather than only partial responsibility.

Client: But even if I'm not totally responsible, I'm still a failure.

Therapist: No. You've failed at those things. There are other things you haven't failed at.

Client: Like what?

Therapist: You still manage to get up every morning, you keep up appearances, you manage your finances well considering your economic plight—there are lots of things you do well.

Client: But they don't count!

Therapist: They don't count to you right now because you're overly concerned with negative issues, but they certainly do count. There are lots of people who don't do those things well. Are they failures?

Client: No, but ...

Therapist: You know, Jack, you're one of the most conceited people I've ever met!

Client: What do you mean? I've just been telling you how lousy I am!

Therapist: The fact that you hold two different standards tells me how conceited you are. You hold much higher standards for yourself than for anyone else, which implies that you think you're much better than others.

It's okay for those lowly slobs to have problems, but not a terrific person like you. Isn't that contradictory to your notion that you're worthless?

Client: Hmmmmm.

Therapist: How about instead of rating yourself as worthless, you just accept the failings that you do have and try your best to improve them?

Client: That sounds sensible.

Therapist: Let's take one of those problem areas now and see how we can improve things ...

The important part of rational-emotive therapy is the therapist's attack on the reasonableness of the client's beliefs. The therapist's challenge, often confrontational in manner, assumes that such maladaptive beliefs will ultimately be rejected, thereby alleviating their emotional consequences. The creator of rational-emotive therapy, Albert Ellis (1962), identified the major irrational beliefs he has observed in people seeking treatment for psychological disorders. The therapist tries initially to pinpoint which of these beliefs characterize a particular client's thought processes, so they can be changed accordingly. Here are a few examples from Ellis's list of common irrational beliefs:

1. I must be loved and approved of by every significant person in my life, and if I'm not, it's awful.

2. It's awful when things are not the way I'd like them to be.

3. I should be very anxious about events that are uncertain or potentially dangerous.

4. I am not worthwhile unless I am thoroughly competent, adequate, and achieving at all times, or at least most of the time in at least one major area.

5. I need someone stronger than myself on whom to depend or rely.

What makes these beliefs irrational is their inflexibility and absoluteness. I *must* be loved and approved; I *must* be thoroughly competent; I *need* someone stronger than myself. The client firmly believes that things must be a particular way or something awful or catastrophic will happen.

Critical Thinking

Where do you think these irrational beliefs come from? Is it possible that people are taught to think in these absolute and inflexible ways by their parents, by role models, or by the general culture at large?

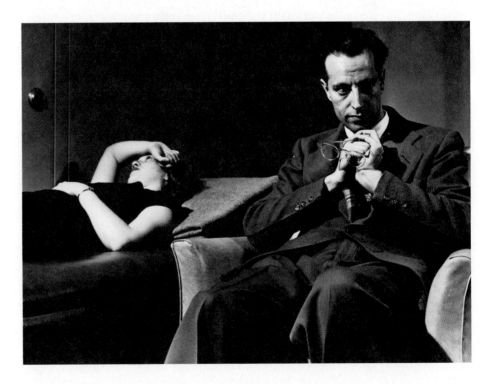

Albert Ellis developed rational-emotive therapy to help people eliminate their irrational thoughts and beliefs.

Beck's Cognitive Therapy Although all forms of cognitive therapy focus on changing irrational thought processes, not all treatments are as direct and harsh as rational-emotive therapy. The rational-emotive therapist will essentially lecture—and in some instances even belittle—the client in an effort to attack faulty beliefs. Other cognitive therapies, such as the treatment procedures pioneered by Aaron Beck, take a more subtle tack. Rather than directly confronting clients with their irrational beliefs, Beck suggests it is more therapeutic to get clients to identify negative forms of thinking themselves. The therapist acts as an adviser, or co-investigator, helping clients discover their own unique kinds of faulty beliefs (Young et al., 2001).

In a sense, clients who undergo Beck's cognitive therapy are asked to become psychological detectives. Part of the therapy involves extensive record keeping, or "homework." Between therapeutic sessions, Beck asks his clients to record their automatic thoughts and emotions in a notebook as they experience various situations during the day. Clients are then asked to write rational responses to those thoughts and emotions, as if they were scientists evaluating data. Is the thought justified by the actual event? What's the evidence for and against the conclusions that I reached? The therapist hopes clients will eventually discover the contradictions and irrationality in their thinking and realign their beliefs accordingly (see Figure 15.6).

Humanistic Therapies: Treating the Human Spirit

In cognitive therapy, the goal is for clients to gain understanding or insight into their faulty and irrational ways of thinking. In classical psychoanalysis, the focus of the insight is on the patient's hidden conflicts and desires. In the final type of insight-based

FIGURE 15.6
Homework from a Cognitive Therapist

During cognitive therapy, people are often asked to record their automatic thoughts and emotions in a notebook. Notice that the daily log requires the person to construct a rational response to the situation and then rerate the emotional reaction. (Adapted from Beck & Young, 1985.)

	Situation	Emotion(s)	Automatic Thought(s)	Rational Response	Outcome
	1. Actual event leading to unpleasant emotion, or 2. Stream of thoughts, daydreams, or recollections, leading to unpleasant emotion.	1. Specify sad/ anxious/ angry, etc. 2. Rate degree of emotion, 1–100.	1. Record automatic thought(s) that preceded emotion(s). 2. Rate belief in automatic thought(s), 0–100%.	1. Write rational response to automatic thought(s). 2. Rate belief in rational response, 0–100%.	1. Rerate belief in automatic thought(s), 0–100%. 2. Specify and rate subsequent emotions, 0–100.
7/15	Audre didn't return my phone call.	Anxious – 75 Sad – 55 Angry – 40	People don't like talking to me – 75% I'm incompetent. 65%	She's out walking the dog so she hasn't had the time to call back. 70%	1. 35% 15% 2. Relieved – 35

Explanation: When you experience an unpleasant emotion, note the situation that seemed to stimulate the emotion. (If the emotion occurred while you were thinking, daydreaming, etc., please note this.) Then note the automatic thought associated with the emotion. Record the degree to which you believe this thought: 0% = not at all, 100% = completely. In rating degree of emotion: 1 = a trace, 100 = the most intense possible.

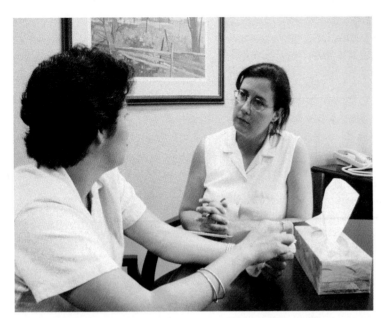

In humanistic therapies, the therapist tries to provide a completely supportive environment that allows clients to rediscover their natural self-worth.

humanistic therapy
Treatments designed to help clients gain insight into their fundamental self-worth and value as human beings; therapy is a process of discovering one's own unique potential.

client-centred therapy
A form of humanistic therapy, developed by Carl Rogers, proposing that it is the client, not the therapist, who holds the key to psychological health and happiness; the therapist's role is to provide genuineness, unconditional positive regard, and empathy.

Critical Thinking

Think about the interactions you've had with a really close friend. Do you see any similarities to the client-centred approach advocated by Carl Rogers?

treatment that we'll consider—**humanistic therapy**— the purpose of therapy is to help the client gain insight into his or her own fundamental *self-worth* and *value* as a human. Therapy is a process of discovering one's own unique potential, one's innate capacity to grow and better oneself as a human being.

Humanistic therapists argue that all people are capable of controlling their behaviour—we can fix our own problems—because each of us ultimately has free will. We sometimes lose sight of our potential because we're concerned about what others think of us and our actions. We let others control how we think and feel. It is the therapist's job to help clients rediscover their natural self-worth—to help them get back in touch with their own true feelings, desires, and needs—by acting as a confidant and friend.

Client-Centred Therapy   Humanistic therapies resemble cognitive therapies in their emphasis on conscious thought processes. But the intention of humanistic therapy is not to criticize or correct irrational thinking; quite the contrary, it's to be totally supportive in all respects. The therapist's proper role is to be nonjudgmental, which means the client should be accepted unconditionally. According to humanistic therapists such as Carl Rogers, the most effective form of therapy is **client-centred**—it is the client, not the therapist, who ultimately holds the key to psychological health and happiness.

We discussed the theoretical ideas of humanistic psychologists, especially Carl Rogers, in some detail in Chapter 12. Rogers was convinced that most psychological problems originate from *incongruence,* which he defined as the discrepancy between people's self-concept and the reality of their everyday experiences. People often hold an inaccurate view of themselves and their abilities, Rogers argued, because of an ingrained need for *positive regard*—they seek the approval, love, and companionship of significant others (such as their parents). But these significant others sometimes attach *conditions of worth* to their approval: They demand that we think and act in ways that may not be consistent with our true inner feelings. The humanistic therapist provides a warm and supportive environment—without conditions of worth—that will encourage clients to accept themselves as they truly are. Attaining this goal may require accepting some disapproval from significant others.

In client-centred therapy, there are three essential core qualities that the therapist seeks to provide to the client: *genuineness, unconditional positive regard,* and *empathy.* As the client's confidant, the therapist must be completely genuine—he or she must act without phoniness and express true feelings in an open and honest way. The second quality, unconditional positive regard, means that the therapist cannot place conditions of worth on the client. The therapist must be totally accepting and respectful of the client at all times, even if the client thinks and acts in a way that seems irrational or inappropriate. Remember, humanists believe that people are essentially good—they simply need to be placed in an environment that will nurture their innate tendencies toward positive growth.

The third quality, empathy, is achieved when the therapist is able to truly understand and accept what the client is feeling—to see things from the client's perspective. Through empathy, the therapist acquires the capacity to reflect those feelings back in a way that helps the client gain insight into himself or herself. Consider the following interaction between Carl Rogers and one of his clients, a woman coming to grips with deep feelings of betrayal and hurt that she's tried to cover up (from Rogers, 1961, p. 94):

Client: I never did really know. But it's—you know, it's almost a physical thing. It's—it's sort of as though I were looking within myself at all kinds of—nerve endings and bits of things that have been sort of mashed.

Rogers: As though some of the most delicate aspects of you physically almost have been crushed or hurt.

Client: Yes. And you know, I do get the feeling, "Oh, you poor thing." (Pause)

Rogers: Just can't help but feel very deeply sorry for the person that is you.

Client: I don't think I feel sorry for the whole person; it's a certain aspect of the thing.

Rogers: Sorry to see the hurt.

Client: Yeah.

Notice that Rogers reflects back the feelings of the client in a completely nonjudgmental fashion. He is seeking to understand and empathize with her feelings, thereby validating their existence and helping her to work through them. Notice also that it is the client, not the therapist, who is doing the analyzing. Client-centred therapy is founded on the idea that it is the clients who understand what truly hurts them psychologically, and it is the clients who have the best sense of how to proceed with therapy. All the therapist can do is provide the right kind of supportive environment and help clients recognize their own self-worth and trust their own instincts.

Other Humanistic Approaches Client-centred therapy is the most popular form of humanistic therapy, but it is not the only one. *Gestalt therapy,* developed by Fritz Perls (1969; Perls et al., 1951), also places the burden of treatment in the hands of a "naturally good" client, but the approach is far less gentle and nondirective than client-centred therapy. In Gestalt therapy, clients are actively encouraged—even forced—to express their feelings openly. The emphasis is on the "here and now," and the therapist uses a variety of techniques to get the client to open up. For example, in the "empty

Concept Summary

INSIGHT APPROACHES TO PSYCHOTHERAPY

Approach	Source of Psychological Problem	Approach to Treatment (Depression)
Psychoanalysis	Problem arises from unconscious conflict, often rooted in childhood trauma.	Debbie is depressed because of repressed fears that her parents don't really love her. They were not very affectionate while she was growing up. Her therapist tries to get Debbie to talk about her childhood relationship with her parents.
Cognitive	Problem arises from conscious processes, including irrational beliefs and negative thoughts.	Troy is having a tough time with his parents. They want him to major in business, which he hates. He feels like a terrible person for not following his parents' wishes. After all, they're paying his tuition. His therapist attempts to show him that disagreeing with his parents over his university major does not reflect badly on him as a person.
Humanistic	Problem arises from incongruence between one's self-concept and reality.	Azra feels guilty. She plans on having only one child, but her parents would like lots of grandchildren, and Azra is an only child. Azra feels bad about herself and about her failure to get acceptance from her parents. Her therapist listens as Azra describes her feelings, and tries to be warm, supportive, and open to what she is saying.

chair" technique, clients are asked to project their feelings onto an empty chair in the room and then, literally, "talk" to the feelings. The idea is that only through fully understanding and overtly expressing oneself as a whole person (the word *Gestalt* roughly translates from the German as "whole") can a person hope to take responsibility for those feelings and change them for the better.

There is another group of humanistic treatments known collectively as *existential therapies* (Yalom, 1980). Existential therapists believe that psychological problems originate from the anxieties created by personal choices, such as whether to stay in school, get married, or quit a job. These fundamental choices—choices that relate to one's daily existence as a human being—are often difficult to face, and individuals may choose not to deal with them directly. Existential therapists encourage their clients to accept responsibility for these decisions, but in a supportive environment that encourages positive growth (Fischer et al., 2000).

Group Therapy

group therapy
A form of therapy in which several people are treated simultaneously in the same setting.

Therapy is most commonly perceived as a one-on-one experience—you and the therapist sit alone in a room discussing your problems. In **group therapy,** you join other people who are undergoing treatment for a similar problem. Typically, group sessions include the therapist and somewhere between 4 and 15 clients, although there are few strict rules for conducting group sessions; for example, in some cases there may be more than one therapist involved in the session (Yalom, 1995).

At first glance, the idea of group therapy seems troubling to most people. After all, who wants to talk about their personal problems in front of others? It's hard enough to open up to one person—the therapist—but at least he or she is a trained professional. Yet there are a number of advantages that groups offer over individual sessions (MacKenzie, 2000). First, group therapy can be much more cost effective because the therapist can meet with multiple clients at the same time (Wolff et al., 1997). Second, hearing other people talk about problems that match your own can be educational (Matano et al., 1997). You can learn about their strategies for coping with problems, and you can see firsthand how their symptoms compare to your own. Third, and perhaps most important, when you hear testimonies from other people it's easier to realize that you're not alone—you're not the only person who is suffering from psychological problems. As you'll discover later in this chapter, empathy is a very important predictor of success in therapy; group settings can improve the trusting relationship you have with your therapist as well as with other people who share your problem (Donigian & Malnati, 1997).

family therapy
A form of group therapy in which the therapist treats the family as a whole, as a kind of social system. The goals of the treatment are often to improve interpersonal communication and collaboration.

Family Therapy   One place in which group therapy can be particularly appropriate is with the family. Rather than just treating an individual, in **family therapy** the therapist treats the family as a whole, as a kind of *social system* (Cox & Paley, 1997; Lebow & Gurman, 1995). Clearly, if one member of a family suffers from a psychological problem, such as depression, all family members tend to be affected and all can benefit from treatment. Moreover, the family environment can play either a positive or a negative role in helping a particular family member recover from a psychological problem. If the family understands the disorder, and what's necessary for treatment, the odds of successful treatment go up considerably. Family therapists work on ways to improve interpersonal communication and collaboration among family members (Rivett, 1998).

The critical role that emotions play in family and couples therapy has been emphasized by Canadian researchers Les Greenberg at York University and Susan Johnson at the University of Ottawa. They have shown how the emotions experienced by patient and therapist alike can be used to understand and improve therapy. Their recommendations to therapists include encouraging patients to fully express their emotions, access previously unacknowledged feelings, and restructure their emotions in a more adaptive way (Greenberg & Paivio, 1997; Johnson, 1996).

Test Yourself 15.2

Check your knowledge about insight therapies by matching each of the following statements to a type of therapy. Choose from among the following: psychoanalysis; Gestalt therapy; rational-emotive therapy; Beck's cognitive therapy; client-centred therapy; family therapy. (You will find the answers in Appendix B.)

1. "You think you're worthless? Well, I'm sitting here spending time with you so how can you be completely worthless? It's a ridiculous idea."
   _____

2. "I want you to keep a record of your thoughts, and the situations that produce them, so that you can judge whether those thoughts are really appropriate given the situation." _____

3. "Don't leave. Sit down and tell me again about the dream you had last night." _____

4. "You feel pain, deep pain, and you just can't get beyond the hurt that you feel inside." _____

5. "Talk to the chair ... be the chair. Open up and let your true feelings come out." _____

6. "It's not just your problem. Each of you needs to communicate better and learn to work together to solve problems and avoid conflicts."
   _____

CHANGING THE ENVIRONMENT: BEHAVIOURAL THERAPIES

Learning Goals
1. Understand how conditioning techniques can be used in therapy.
2. Understand how rewards and punishments can be used to improve behaviour.

INSTEAD OF SEARCHING THE MINDS of their clients for hidden conflicts, faulty beliefs, or damaged self-worth, some approaches to therapy essentially leave the mind alone. Behavioural therapies treat behaviour rather than thoughts or memories. **Behavioural therapies** are designed to change unwanted or maladaptive behaviour through the application of basic learning principles (Spiegler & Guevremont, 1998).

As we discussed in Chapter 14, many psychologists argue that psychological problems are *learned*, that is, acquired as a result of experience. Afraid of snakes? Perhaps you were bitten by one at some point in your life, or you saw someone else get bitten. That experience caused you to associate snakes with a negative emotional consequence. It's not that the snake is symbolic of some hidden sexual conflict—you feel anxious because you have a chance of being bitten again.

If you believe that a psychological problem has been learned, it doesn't make a lot of sense to spend months or years searching for a hidden reason for the problem. It's better to treat the surface symptoms by learning something new. More productive actions need to be rewarded, and the negative associations you've formed need to be extinguished or counteracted. We'll consider several behavioural approaches in this section of the chapter, beginning with an effective technique for treating phobias that is based on the principles of *classical conditioning*.

behavioural therapies
Treatments designed to change behaviour through the use of established learning techniques.

 Critical Thinking

Can you think of a role that reinforcement might play in maintaining a phobia? Isn't it true that every time you stay away from a snake you avoid being bitten?

Conditioning Techniques

In Chapter 6, we discussed how dogs and people learn about the signalling properties of events. In Pavlov's classic experiments, dogs learned that one event, called the

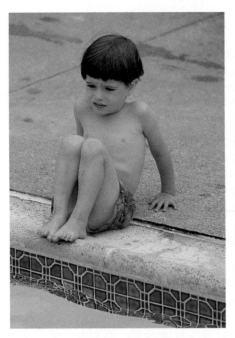

This child's fear of the water might have been acquired as a result of an earlier frightening experience.

Psychologist Mary Cover Jones proposed that intense fear reactions, such as those seen in phobias, could be treated as if they were classically conditioned responses.

conditioned stimulus, signalled the occurrence of a second event, called the *unconditioned stimulus.* After pairing the conditioned stimulus and the unconditioned stimulus together in time, Pavlov found that his dogs responded to the conditioned stimulus in a way that anticipated the arrival of the unconditioned stimulus. For example, if a bell (the conditioned stimulus) was repeatedly presented just prior to food (the unconditioned stimulus), the dogs would begin to salivate (the conditioned response) to the bell in anticipation of the food. Pavlov also showed that this conditioned response, the drooling, was sensitive to a termination of the association between the conditioned stimulus and the unconditioned stimulus: If the bell was rung repeatedly after conditioning but the food was no longer presented, the dog eventually stopped salivating to the bell (a procedure Pavlov called *extinction*).

Now let's consider the case of a specific phobia, such as fear of snakes. Specific phobias are highly focused fears of objects or situations. When the feared object is present, it produces an intense anxiety reaction. In the 1920s, psychologist Mary Cover Jones proposed that intense fear reactions like these can be treated as if they are classically conditioned responses. A snake produces fear because some kind of earlier experience has taught you to associate snakes with something fearful. Perhaps while standing near one as a child, your brother or sister screamed in terror, thereby scaring you. Jones's analysis suggested a treatment: It might be possible to eliminate phobias by conditioning a new association between the feared object and something pleasurable. As she reported in 1924, she was able to use this logic to treat a little boy's fear of rabbits. She fed the boy some tasty food in the presence of the rabbit, which extinguished the association between the rabbit and an earlier negative experience and replaced it with a more pleasurable association (Jones, 1924).

Systematic Desensitization   The treatment pioneered by Mary Cover Jones was later refined by psychiatrist Joseph Wolpe into a technique known as **systematic desensitization** (Wolpe, 1958, 1982). As with Jones's approach, systematic desensitization uses counterconditioning as a way of reducing the fear and anxiety that have become associated with a specific object or event. The therapist attempts to replace the negative asso-

systematic desensitization
A technique that uses counterconditioning and extinction to reduce the fear and anxiety that have become associated with a specific object or event. It's a multistep process that attempts to replace the negative learned association with something relaxing.

ciation with something relaxing and pleasurable. It's a gradual process that involves three major steps:

1. The therapist helps the client construct an anxiety hierarchy, which is an ordered list of situations that lead to fearful reactions. The client is asked to imagine a series of anxiety-provoking situations, beginning with the least fear-arousing situation and ending with the feared situation itself.

2. The therapist spends time teaching the client ways to induce deep muscle relaxation. A state of deep relaxation is inconsistent with the experience of anxiety—you can't be afraid and relaxed at the same time.

3. With the help of the therapist the client then attempts to work through the anxiety hierarchy, forming an image of each of the scenes, while maintaining the state of relaxation. The idea is to pair the images of fearful situations with the pleasurable state of relaxation to extinguish the old negative association and replace it with something relaxing.

Let's imagine you have a deep, irrational fear of flying in an airplane. Treatment starts by having you create a list of flying-related situations that are increasingly frightful. Next, you would receive lessons in how to relax yourself fully. Finally, you would begin working through your hierarchy. Perhaps you might start by simply imagining a picture of an airplane. If you can consistently remain relaxed under these conditions, the therapist will direct you to move up the hierarchy to the next most stressful situation—perhaps imagining the airplane actually taking off. Gradually, over time, you will learn to relax in increasingly more stressful situations, even to the point where you can imagine yourself strapped in the seat as the plane rolls down the runway. The key to the technique is to maintain the relaxation. If you can stay relaxed—which is incompatible with fear and anxiety—the fearful association with planes should extinguish and be replaced by an association that is neutral or positive. Eventually, when you move to a real situation, the learning will generalize and you will no longer be afraid to fly in a plane. This type of therapy is summarized in Figure 15.7, using another specific phobia—the fear of snakes.

Aversion Therapy   Systematic desensitization attempts to eliminate unpleasant associations by replacing them with pleasant ones. In **aversion therapy,** the therapist tries to replace a pleasant reaction to a harmful stimulus with an unpleasant one: For example, make the client feel bad rather than good after smoking a cigarette or having a drink of alcohol. Once again, the idea is to use a kind of counterconditioning, but the goal is to make the target situation something to be avoided rather than approached.

Critical Thinking

In what ways is shaping, which we discussed in Chapter 6, similar to and different from the procedures of systematic desensitization?

aversion therapy

A treatment for replacing a positive reaction to a harmful stimulus, such as alcohol, with something negative, such as feeling nauseated.

FIGURE 15.7

Systematic Desensitization

After learning relaxation techniques, the client works slowly through an anxiety hierarchy. At first she simply imagines the feared object while relaxed. Eventually, the relaxation response can be maintained while she experiences the actual feared situation.

In the case of alcohol dependency, it's possible to give people a drug (Antabuse) that causes the patient to become nauseated and vomit upon taking a drink of alcohol. The drug interacts with alcohol, causing extreme discomfort. Under these conditions, the person who is drinking learns a new association that helps combat the alcohol dependency, namely, that drinking leads to an unpleasant feeling. A similar technique can be used for smoking. There are drugs containing chemicals that leave an extremely bad taste in one's mouth after smoking. The old association connecting pleasure with smoking is replaced by a new association: connecting smoking with a terrible taste.

Aversion therapy can be quite effective, as long as the client takes the aversive drug for a sufficient period of time. The problem is that people who undergo this therapy are often reluctant to continue the treatment unless they're closely supervised. If the client stops the treatment and returns to normal drinking or smoking, the newly learned negative association will extinguish and be replaced by the old, positive association. Ethical concerns have also been raised about this form of treatment. Although those who participate do so voluntarily, they are often people who are desperately seeking a solution to their problems. Because the treatment directly induces extremely unpleasant experiences, many therapists are convinced that it should be used only as a treatment of last resort.

Using Rewards and Punishments to Change Behaviour

As we discussed in Chapter 6, it is possible to change behaviour by teaching people about the direct consequences of their behaviour. You can be shaped, through the application of rewards and punishments, away from abnormal actions and toward more normal behaviours. Although aversion therapy involves elements of punishment (e.g., the act of drinking is followed by an extremely unpleasant consequence), its goal is mainly to replace prior pleasant emotional associations with unpleasant ones. Behavioural therapies that use reward and punishment systems, that is, instrumental conditioning, are designed to modify specific unwanted behaviours by teaching people about the consequences of their actions.

Token Economies Shaping behaviour through the delivery of reward has proven to be particularly effective in institutional settings. When people are confined to mental hospitals or other kinds of institutions, it is usually because they cannot cope successfully without constant supervision. If people cannot care for themselves—if they don't wash properly, eat proper foods, or protect themselves from harm—they need a structured environment around them. In institutional settings, therapists have found that setting up an economic system in which patients are rewarded for behaving appropriately can be quite effective in teaching patients how to cope with the realities of everyday life (Ayllon & Azrin, 1968; Lindsley & Skinner, 1954; Paul & Lentz, 1977).

In a **token economy,** institutionalized patients are rewarded with small tokens (such as poker chips) whenever they engage in an appropriate activity. Certain rules are established and explained to the patient, which determine when tokens are handed out (or taken away). For example, if Bob, who is suffering from schizophrenia, takes his medication without complaint, he is given a plastic token. Sally might receive tokens for getting out of bed in the morning, washing her hair, and brushing her teeth. The tokens can later be exchanged for certain privileges, such as being able to watch a video or buy soft drinks. Similarly, if a patient acts in an inappropriate manner, the therapist might choose to take tokens away as a form of punishment. This technique is called a token *economy* because it represents a voluntary exchange of goods and services—the patient exchanges appropriate behaviour for the privileges that tokens provide.

Token economies are highly successful in helping patients develop the skills they'll need to function well inside and outside of the institution. Not only do the everyday "maintenance" activities of the patients improve, but token rewards can also be used to

token economy

A type of behavioural therapy in which institutionalized patients are rewarded with small tokens when they act in an appropriate way; the token can then be exchanged for certain privileges.

Practical Solutions

SOCIAL SKILLS TRAINING IN SCHIZOPHRENIA

Serious psychological disorders can have a devastating impact on a person's ability to function successfully in virtually all environments, especially social ones. In schizophrenia, for example, social or occupational dysfunction is one of the defining characteristics of the disorder. Patients with schizophrenia tend to isolate themselves from others, and, when they do interact socially, they typically act in odd or peculiar ways.

Consider the conversational speech of David, a 25-year-old with schizophrenia, during an interaction with his therapist (Barlow & Durand, 1999):

> Therapist: I was sorry to hear that your Uncle Bill died a few years ago. How are you feeling about him these days?
>
> David: Yes, he died. He was sick and now he's gone. He likes to fish with me, down at the river. He's going to take me hunting. I have guns. I can shoot you and you'd be dead in a minute.

In the words of his therapist, David's conversational speech "resembled a ball rolling down a rocky hill. Like an accelerating object, his speech gained momentum the longer he went on, and as if bouncing off obstacles, the topics almost always went in unpredictable directions" (Barlow & Durand, 1999, p. 407).

In such cases, therapists face a practical problem: How can they improve the social skills of the person with the disorder? This is a particularly important concern in schizophrenia, which is often difficult to treat. Even with effective medications, many patients suffer relapses of symptoms (Liberman et al., 1994), and some symptoms of the disorder, including social withdrawal and flat affect, are not affected by conventional psychoactive drugs. For these reasons, therapists sometimes turn to social skills training, which is a form of behavioural therapy that uses modelling and reinforcement to shape appropriate adjustment skills (McFall, 1976; Wong et al., 1993).

Social skills training usually consists of a series of steps. To teach conversational skills, for example, the therapist might begin with a discussion of appropriate verbal responses in a conversation, followed by a videotaped demonstration. The patient is then asked to role-play an actual conversation, and the therapist provides either corrective feedback or positive reinforcement. "Homework" might then be assigned, in which the patient is encouraged to practise his or her skills outside of the training session, preferably in new situations. If the training is conducted in an institutional setting, such as a mental hospital, the therapist must monitor the patient's subsequent interactions carefully so that appropriate reinforcement can be delivered (Wallace, 1998).

Let's be clear that social skills training does nothing to cure schizophrenia. But reviews of the research literature indicate that the application of these simple learning principles—positive reinforcement and modelling—can lead to significant improvements in social functioning and in the quality of life for individuals affected with psychological disorders (Benton & Schroeder, 1990; Bustillo et al., 2001). Although a major goal of any therapy is to improve global functioning, improvements in specific symptoms—even something as simple as knowing how to answer a casual question in an appropriate way—can make an enormous difference in the life of a troubled individual.

---

shape social behaviour and even vocational skills (for a closer look, see the Practical Solutions box). Token economies have also been used in classroom settings to reward children for showing appropriate individual and group behaviour (Kazdin, 1982).

Punishment Token economies tend to be based primarily on the application of reward as a way of changing unwanted behaviours. But as we've seen, punishment can also be an effective way to teach people about the consequences of their behaviour. And, indeed, there are instances in which therapists feel that following a behaviour with an aversive stimulus (sometimes even a shock) or removing something pleasant is justified. Consider a patient who is extremely self-destructive—perhaps a disturbed boy who continually bangs his head against the wall. Under these conditions, the safe delivery of an aversive event has been shown to reduce these self-destructive behaviours, thereby preventing serious injury (Lovaas, 1987; Lovaas et al., 1973).

But, for several reasons, punishment is rarely used as the sole kind of behavioural intervention. First, punishment has side effects—for example, it can damage the working relationship between the therapist and the client. Second, punishment by itself only teaches someone what not to do; it doesn't teach someone the appropriate way to act. Third, punishing someone who is in the grips of a psychological disorder raises

619

Concept Summary

BEHAVIOURAL THERAPIES

Conditioning Approaches

Approach	Based on the Idea That:	Therapeutic Approach
Systematic desensitization	Intense anxiety reactions can be reconditioned.	Uses counterconditioning to reduce the fear and anxiety that have become associated with a particular object or event. The therapist attempts to replace a negative association with something relaxing and pleasurable.
Aversion therapy	Unhealthy attractions can be reconditioned.	The therapist tries to replace a pleasant reaction to a harmful stimulus with an unpleasant reaction. For example, the pleasurable reaction associated with smoking is replaced by a new association between smoking and a terrible taste.

Rewards and Punishments

Token economies	Behaviour can be changed by teaching people about the positive consequences of their behaviour.	Therapist and patient have a voluntary exchange of goods and services—the patient exchanges appropriate behaviour for privileges provided by tokens.
Punishment	Behaviour can be changed by teaching people about the negative consequences of their behaviour.	An inappropriate (e.g., self-injurious) behaviour is followed with an aversive stimulus or with the removal of a pleasant stimulus.

ethical concerns. We cannot be sure the person on the receiving end of the aversive event approves of the treatment, even though the therapist and the patient's family may be convinced it's in the patient's best interest.

Test Yourself 15.3

Check your knowledge about behavioural therapies by answering the following questions. (You will find the answers in Appendix B.)

1. According to the classical conditioning account of phobias, the feared stimulus, such as a snake, acts as a(n):
   a. unconditioned stimulus.
   b. conditioned stimulus.
   c. conditioned response.
   d. conditioned reinforcer.

2. In systematic desensitization, the fear that has become associated with a specific object or event is reduced through:
   a. counterconditioning and extinction.
   b. second-order conditioning.
   c. delivery of an aversive consequence.
   d. token rewards.

3. Which of the following is not a major concern in aversion therapy?
   a. Clients cannot truly give informed and voluntary consent.
   b. Effective punishments can't be delivered because pain thresholds are high.
   c. Clients are often reluctant to continue treatment.
   d. Newly learned negative associations can extinguish.

4. In a token economy, the token acts as which of the following?
   a. Conditioned stimulus
   b. Punishment
   c. Conditioned inhibitor
   d. Reinforcement

EVALUATING AND CHOOSING PSYCHOTHERAPY

Learning Goals

1. Understand the major findings of clinical evaluation research.
2. Understand the factors that are common across psychotherapies.
3. Appreciate the important personal and cultural factors that should be considered when choosing a therapist.

WHEN PEOPLE MAKE THE DECISION to enter therapy, they do so because they're badly in need of help. But how do they know what kind of therapy they need? We've now examined the major types of therapy, but we've said little about their relative effectiveness. How well does psychotherapy actually work? Are all forms of therapy equally effective, or do some forms work better than others?

To assess the effectiveness of any therapy requires carefully controlled research. As we discussed in Chapter 2, just because a change occurs after a manipulation does not guarantee that it was the manipulation that caused the change. Someone might enter therapy and leave improved, but the change could have occurred for reasons unrelated to the actual treatment. As Eysenck (1952) pointed out, many patients simply improve spontaneously with the passage of time. Most people who get the flu improve over time—even if they never see a doctor—and it could be that the same kind of thing happens with psychological disorders. A control group—in which no treatment is given—is needed to confirm that the therapy was indeed responsible for the improvement. Fortunately, a number of such controlled research studies have been conducted (Chambless & Ollendick, 2001).

Clinical Evaluation Research

Let's begin by considering a well-known example of a clinical evaluation study (Sloane et al., 1975). In this study, conducted at a Philadelphia psychiatric clinic in the mid-1970s, men and women who were seeking treatment primarily for anxiety disorders were assigned at random to one of three treatment conditions. One group of patients was assigned to therapists experienced in the practice of psychodynamic techniques (the analysis of unconscious conflicts and memories); a second group was assigned to experienced behavioural therapists (using systematic desensitization and other learning-based techniques); and a third group—the *control* group—was placed on a "waiting list" and received no immediate treatment. After four months, an independent team of therapists, who were unaware of the treatment assignments, was called in to evaluate the progress of the patients.

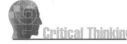
Critical Thinking

Is it ethical to assign patients who are seeking help for their psychological problems to a no-treatment control group?

The results were somewhat surprising. The good news is that the therapies clearly worked. As shown in Figure 15.8, the people who were given either the psychodynamic or the behavioural therapy showed significantly more improvement after four months than the people who were left on the waiting list. Interestingly, the waiting list people also improved slightly. But there were no significant differences between the two treatment conditions—the behavioural approach worked just as well as the psychodynamic approach. Even more surprising was the finding that eight months later, at a year-end follow-up assessment, the patients in the control group had essentially caught up with the treatment patients—they had improved enough to be comparable to the patients in the other two groups. Thus the treatments worked, but it appears that their primary effect was simply to speed up natural improvement. Problems with this interpretation are discussed below.

Meta-Analysis The Philadelphia study is important because it's an example of how evaluation research should be conducted—random assignment to groups, the use of a no-treatment control, and an independent assessment procedure (Wolpe, 1975). Since that study was first reported, hundreds of other studies have been conducted (although

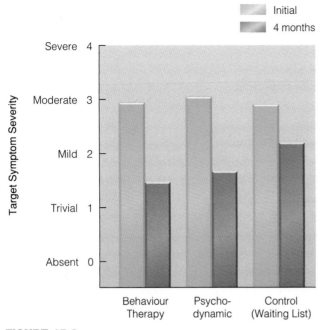

FIGURE 15.8

Evaluating Forms of Treatment

In the study by Sloane and colleagues (1975), men and women seeking treatment for anxiety disorders were randomly assigned to behaviour therapy, psychodynamic therapy, or a control waiting list. After four months, the people receiving therapy showed significantly less severe symptoms than people in the control group, but there were no significant differences between types of therapy (behaviour and psychodynamic). (Data from Sloane et al., 1975.)

meta-analysis

A statistical technique used to accumulate findings across all available studies; comparisons are based on some common evaluation index, such as the numerical difference between the success rate of the treatment and control conditions.

not all have included the same rigorous control procedures). Rather than picking and choosing from among these studies, mental health professionals often rely on a technique called meta-analysis to help them draw conclusions about this research. In a **meta-analysis,** all available studies are combined statistically using some common evaluation measure. The comparison standard is usually something called an *effect size,* which is a standardized measure of the difference in the success rate of the treatment and control conditions (see Robey & Dalebout, 1998). If the average effect size across all available studies is large and positive, then that type of therapy is proved to be effective.

In one of the first extensive meta-analytic studies, Smith and colleagues analyzed the results of 475 research studies designed to evaluate one or more forms of psychotherapy (Smith & Glass, 1977; Smith et al., 1980). Although the individual studies covered a wide range of psychological problems and therapeutic techniques, in each case it was possible to compare a treatment condition to some kind of control condition (usually an untreated group). Smith and colleagues reached two major conclusions from their meta-analysis of the data. First, there was a consistent and large treatment advantage (see Figure 15.9). People who experienced some kind of active psychotherapy were better off, on average, than roughly 80% of the people who were left untreated. Second, when the various kinds of psychotherapy were compared, few, if any, differences were found. It really didn't matter whether the patient was receiving an insight therapy or a behavioural therapy—all produced the same amount of improvement (see also Wampold et al., 1997).

There have been hundreds of other attempts to meta-analyze evaluation studies. Some have sought to exercise more control over the research quality of the studies included (Lipsey & Wilson, 1993); others have attempted to extend the areas of examination to such things as client characteristics, experience of the therapist, or length of the treatment (Lambert & Bergin, 1994). In general, the findings support two main conclusions: Therapy works and the effects of therapy are long lasting. For example, one recent review of meta-analysis studies, which examined some 302 published meta-analyses, found that only 6 produced negative effect sizes (which means that patients undergoing therapy actually got worse than untreated controls), and the vast majority were overwhelmingly positive (Lipsey & Wilson, 1993).

Controversies Psychologists generally agree that psychotherapy works, but how to evaluate the evidence remains the subject of debate. For example, what should consti-

FIGURE 15.9

The Effectiveness of Psychotherapy

In the meta-analysis by Smith and colleagues (1980), which assessed hundreds of clinical evaluation studies, people who experienced psychotherapy were better off, on average, than roughly 80% of the people who were not treated. (Data from Smith et al., 1980.)

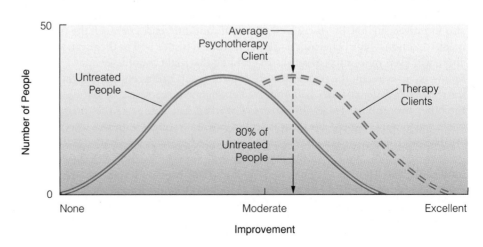

tute the proper evaluation "control"? Let's return to the Philadelphia experiment in which two treatment groups (psychodynamic and behavioural) were compared with a group containing people who were left on a waiting list. Remember, the control patients actually got considerably better over time, to a point in which, after a year, they had improved to the same levels as the treatment groups. Psychologists call this kind of improvement in the absence of treatment **spontaneous remission,** and it's been estimated that psychological disorders may improve on their own as much as 30% or more of the time (Eysenck, 1952; Lambert & Bergin, 1994).

But did the people who were left on the waiting list in the Philadelphia experiment really receive no treatment? This is a difficult question to answer—it depends on how you define "treatment." Although those people received no formal psychotherapy, they were given initial psychological tests and were called frequently and given support. Their participation in the study, along with the expectation that they would be receiving some help, may itself have acted as a kind of therapy. Similar effects are commonly found with many placebo controls, in which clients are given attention and support but no formal therapy. Many critics have argued that these no-treatment conditions actually involve factors—such as social support—that are common to most forms of therapy (Horvath, 1988). Even more serious is the high likelihood that some patients secretly sought out—but didn't report—other treatments from other therapists. After all, their overriding goal was to get better, not to aid science. We'll return to this issue in the next section.

The reported finding that all types of psychotherapy are equally effective has also proven to be controversial (Crits-Christoph, 1997). We know that certain treatments work best for certain kinds of problems. For example, psychotherapy researcher Keith Dobson of the University of Calgary conducted a meta-analysis of 28 studies that looked at the effectiveness of different therapies for the treatment of depression (Dobson, 1989). Dobson concluded that cognitive therapy was more effective for treating depression than other therapies, including drug therapy and behavioural therapy. However, behavioural therapies may be ideal for combating anxiety disorders such as specific phobias (Bowers & Clum, 1988). But even if the treatment is matched to the problem, there are also "client variables" that can influence the effectiveness of the therapy. Not all people have the desire or capacity to respond to rational, verbal arguments of the type used by some cognitive therapists, or to the probing questions of the psychoanalyst. As a result, it is very difficult to conduct an evaluation study that properly takes all of these factors into account (Chambless & Ollendick, 2001).

Recently, many psychologists have come to support a move toward promoting **empirically supported treatments** as recognized foundations of psychological practice and training. This suggestion involves psychologists coming to an agreement about what we can conclude from the research literature regarding which treatments work best with which disorders (Hunsley et al., 1999). This movement also suggests that clinical psychology graduate programs be required to train students in at least two of the "empirically supported treatments." Although there has been some controversy surrounding these suggestions, it is likely that this kind of approach will be a major component guiding the development and application of psychotherapy in the future (McLean & Woody, 1999).

Common Factors across Psychotherapies

Clinical researchers have also considered the possibility that there may be common factors shared by all successful therapies, regardless of surface differences. Although the various therapies we've considered seem to be very different and they're clearly driven by very different assumptions about human psychology, they do share features in common (Grencavage & Norcross, 1990; Rosenzweig, 1936). Michael Lambert and Allen Bergin (1994) have suggested that these common factors can be grouped into three main categories: *support factors, learning factors,* and *action factors.*

spontaneous remission
Improvement in a psychological disorder without treatment—that is, simply as a function of the passage of time.

empirically supported treatments
Treatments or therapies that have been shown, based on extensive and well-validated research, to be effective in treating specific psychological disorders and problems.

therapeutic alliance
The bond formed between the client and therapist in successful psychotherapy that is focused on working together constructively to solve the client's problem.

Support Factors Virtually all therapies that produce positive outcomes provide tangible support for the client. People who enter therapy find themselves face to face with someone who is willing to accept and understand their problems. Both the therapist and the client have a common goal, which is to help the client get better. Regardless of their theoretical orientation—psychodynamic, cognitive, behavioural, or humanistic—effective therapists are clearly interested in listening to and reassuring their clients and in developing a positive, trusting relationship. Many studies have found a strong correlation between the amount of empathy that the therapist establishes with the client and the effectiveness of the treatment (Lafferty et al., 1991; Miller et al., 1980). One aspect of the relationship between therapist and client that appears to be quite important in the success of therapy is referred to as the **therapeutic alliance,** which refers to the extent to which the therapist and client work together constructively to address the client's problems. Psychotherapy researcher David Zuroff of McGill University and his colleagues have found that the more the client perceives the therapeutic alliance to be strong, and the more that the client actively contributes toward making the therapeutic alliance work, the more successful the therapy (Zuroff et al., 2000). Interestingly, one factor that seemed to be detrimental to successful therapy was a perfectionistic personality style on the part of the client. Particularly in the latter stages of therapy, perfectionist clients tended to have little success in improving their conditions, evidently partly because their perfectionism somehow blocked them from forming a strong therapeutic alliance with the therapist (Hewitt & Flett, 2003).

Learning Factors When people go through therapy, they *learn* things about themselves. They learn about their thought processes, about their behaviour, or about important factors in their past that might be contributing to current discomforts. Effective therapists often act as mirrors, reflecting back a client's beliefs and actions in ways that provide critical insight. Regardless of the method of treatment, effective therapists also give feedback about how various experiences relate to one another. They point out connections between experiences—how people might behave and think similarly across different situations. Even if their understanding of the problem is somewhat off the mark, people are often helped because they now have a reason or a rationale for their problems.

Action Factors Finally, all forms of therapy ultimately provide people with a set of specific suggestions for *action*. Troubled clients might be asked to face their fears, take risks, or directly test irrational beliefs. They might be given specific strategies for coping with anxiety or training in how to relax. Irrespective of the specific suggestions, just providing clients with a tangible course of action may be sufficient to give them hope and allow them to feel in control of their problem.

Choosing a Therapist

At some point in your life, you might find yourself in need of a psychotherapist. Perhaps you'll experience a simple problem in living or maybe something more serious. What should you do? Given our discussion about the relative effectiveness of the various treatment options, it might seem that it doesn't make much difference whom you choose. But those overall results mask the fact that for any specific problem there are specific therapists using specific techniques that work best (Dobson, 1989). Given the complexities involved, the task of making the right choice would seem impossible for the average person. Fortunately, there are some consumer-oriented books that can be of assistance (Engler & Gordon, 1992). Part of the judgment is subjective: The level of trust that you feel with the therapist is critical. So don't be afraid to shop around a bit to find the right person.

It used to be the case that therapists would align themselves with a particular approach or "school" (such as psychoanalysis or behavioural therapy), but in a recent survey of 800 therapists, 68% of respondents described their orientation as eclectic

Critical Thinking

What kind of therapeutic approach would you choose if you needed help? Justify your answer based on what you've learned in this chapter.

(Jensen et al., 1990). You can expect most therapists to be flexible in their approach, and if one form of treatment is not yielding results—or if you feel uncomfortable with the approach—you can expect the therapist to be open to trying something different. Effective therapy requires open communication, and the therapist is dependent on your feedback as a client throughout the treatment process.

Cultural Factors Mental health professionals also now recognize that cultural factors are important in both the diagnosis and the treatment of psychological disorders (Gaw, 2001; Sue & Zane, 1987; Tseng & McDermott, 1975). For many years, cultural barriers have made it difficult for members of ethnic minorities to use and benefit from mental health resources. Language differences between the client and the therapist clearly undermine effective communication, as do differences between the therapist's and the client's world-view. For example, many Asians feel uncomfortable with open self-disclosure and the expression of emotions. Indeed, the uniquely Japanese disorder called *taijin kyofusho* is the fear of inappropriately disclosing information to others (Kirmayer, 1991). As a result, it's unlikely that many Japanese patients will benefit from Western therapists who encourage clients to "let it all hang out" (Sue et al., 1994). Instead, there is an increasing availability of traditional Asian therapies such as Morita therapy (Alden, 1988).

Similarly, First Nations people have their own traditions of healing, including treating mental and emotional problems, that share some similarities with psychotherapy (Krippner, 1993) and that are in some ways quite different (McCormick, 1996, 2000). For instance, some researchers have found that the most successful substance abuse programs for First Nations people were "self-generated, led by a healer or shaman, and organized as healing communities" (Weibel-Orlando, 1989; Wyrostok & Paulson, 2000, p. 15). Most First Nations approaches to healing psychological or emotional problems also emphasize a strong spiritual component and focus on the healing powers of nature (McCormick, 1996). Therapists working with First Nations clients are increasingly trying to coordinate their efforts with First Nations' community-based interventions and to respect these traditions as useful aspects of the healing process.

Does this mean you should always seek a therapist with a cultural background identical to your own? Not necessarily. For one thing, there is still a shortage of therapists from ethnic minorities in Canada. This means that finding a cultural match may be difficult. Moreover, with the increased exposure to cultural influences, many therapists are now making concerted efforts to become culturally sensitive, and almost all

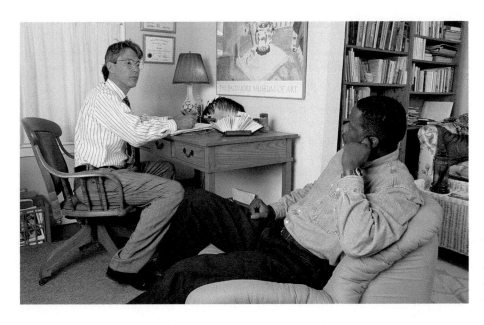

Cultural barriers sometimes prevent members of ethnic minorities from benefiting from mental health resources. It's essential for a therapist to be sensitive to a client's cultural background and general world-view.

clinical psychology graduate programs in Canada have aspects of their curricula devoted to cultural diversity issues (Hertzsprung & Dobson, 2000).

Who Uses Psychotherapy, and When? It is interesting to ask, Who are the people most likely to go to a psychotherapist? Clinical researchers John Hunsley, Catherine Lee, and Tim Aubry of the University of Ottawa addressed this question recently (Hunsley et al., 1999). They found that approximately 2.15% of Canadians had consulted a psychologist in the 12 months preceding the survey. These people were more likely to be middle-aged, female, and separated, divorced, or widowed. They also tended to have higher incomes than average. One interesting aspect of the study was that the majority of Canadians who were diagnosed as depressed (and who could have presumably benefited from psychotherapy) were not being treated by a psychologist. This suggests that psychological services are probably underutilized in Canada, as is the case in many countries, and steps should be taken to increase people's awareness of how such services could help them and their families. This difference between the number of people who could benefit from psychological services and those who actually receive them has sometimes been referred to as the **service gap** (Cramer, 1999).

What are some of the nondemographic factors (i.e., factors unrelated to ethnicity, age, and gender) that increase the likelihood of people seeking psychological help? Kenneth Cramer of the University of Windsor has examined this question by reanalyzing data from two recent studies of psychology undergraduates (Cramer, 1999). As expected, he found that university students tend to seek psychological help when their level of personal distress is quite high; they also have positive attitudes toward counselling. More interesting, however, was the influence of self-concealment on the decision to seek psychological help. Cramer's analysis suggests that university students who tend to keep their problems to themselves and not share their problems with others (i.e., who self-conceal) tend to have more psychological problems than students who more freely disclose their problems to other people. Another finding was that psychological distress tends to be high when students do not have access to a solid social support network (i.e., understanding and attentive friends and family). Cramer suggests that steps to enhance students' social support systems may both decrease their psychological distress and increase their likelihood of seeking appropriate psychological services when needed. He also points out that it may be useful to conduct public education programs aimed at changing students' attitudes about counselling, so that the students who would benefit from such treatment are more likely to seek it.

service gap
The difference between the number of people who could benefit from receiving psychological services and those who receive them.

Test Yourself 15.4

Check your knowledge about evaluating and choosing psychotherapy by deciding whether each of the following statements is true or false. (You will find the answers in Appendix B.)

1. Psychological disorders may improve on their own as much as 30% or more of the time. *True or False?*
2. According to most meta-analytic studies, people who experience active psychotherapy are better off, on average, than roughly 80% of the people who are left untreated. *True or False?*
3. Most evaluation studies show that specific disorders, such as depression, require specific forms of therapy, such as psychoanalysis. *True or False?*
4. One factor that is common to all forms of psychotherapy is the need to investigate the traumatic events of childhood. *True or False?*
5. In choosing a therapist, perhaps the most important factor is empathy—finding someone you trust and with whom you feel comfortable. *True or False?*

Solving the Scientific and Practical Problems

In this chapter, we've discussed the various techniques used to treat psychological disorders. In each case, the therapist's goal is to find a way to improve the client's ability to function successfully in the world. Most forms of therapy are designed to address one or more of the three basic factors thought to contribute to maladaptive behaviour patterns: biological, cognitive, and environmental factors.

First, what are the most effective biologically based treatments? Therapies that use medical interventions to treat psychological problems are called *biomedical therapies*. The most popular form is drug therapy, in which certain medications are given to affect thought and mood by altering the actions of neurotransmitters in the brain. Antipsychotic drugs, for example, reduce the symptoms of schizophrenia by acting as antagonists to the neurotransmitter dopamine in the brain. The antidepressant drug Prozac acts on the neurotransmitter serotonin, and antianxiety drugs (tranquillizers) are believed to act on neurotransmitters in the brain that have primarily inhibitory effects.

In the event that drug therapies fail, therapists treating depression sometimes turn to other forms of biomedical intervention, particularly electroconvulsive therapy (ECT). Such shock therapy is used only if more conventional forms of treatment have failed. No one is completely sure how or why the administration of electric shock affects mood, but there's wide agreement that ECT works for many patients.

Second, how can maladaptive thinking be changed? In *insight therapy*, the psychotherapist attempts to treat psychological problems by helping clients gain insight, or self-knowledge, into the contents of their thought processes. Usually, this insight is obtained through prolonged verbal, one-on-one interactions between the therapist and the client. Perhaps the best-known form of insight therapy is Freudian *psychoanalysis*. The goal of psychoanalysis is to help the client uncover and relive conflicts that have been hidden in the unconscious mind through such techniques as free association and dream analysis. As hidden conflicts begin to surface, the client will typically show *resistance*—an attempt to hinder the progress of therapy—and *transference,* in which the client transfers feelings about others onto the therapist.

Cognitive therapists argue that psychological problems arise primarily from irrational beliefs and thought processes. The therapist attempts to change the client's negative beliefs and thoughts by actively attacking them in verbal exchanges. The therapist points out the irrationality of negative thoughts, using evidence where possible, in the hope that the client will reject the beliefs, thereby lessening their emotional consequences. *Humanistic therapists* attempt to help clients gain insight into their own self-worth. The client, not the therapist, holds the key to self-improvement; therapy is a process of discovering one's natural tendencies toward growth and free will. In *client-centred therapy*, the therapist tries to provide an approving and nonjudgmental environment, thereby allowing the client to recognize and trust his or her own instincts.

Third, how can the environment be altered to reduce maladaptive behaviour? *Behavioural therapies* are designed to treat overt behaviour rather than inner thought processes. Behavioural therapists assume that many kinds of psychological problems have been learned and can be treated through the application of learning principles. With many counterconditioning techniques, for example, the therapist attempts to replace learned negative associations with new, pleasurable associations. Thus, in systematic desensitization, specific phobias are treated by having the subject (1) construct an anxiety hierarchy of fear-inducing situations, (2) learn relaxation techniques, and (3) work through the anxiety hierarchy, imagining each of the scenes while maintaining a feeling of relaxation. Pairing the feared object with relaxation is intended to extinguish the negative association and replace it with something pleasurable. Other behavioural therapies use rewards and punishments to change behaviour. In token economies, patients are rewarded with small tokens when they engage in normal or appropriate behaviours. The tokens can later be exchanged for more tangible rewards or privileges.

Fourth, how can we evaluate the effectiveness of psychotherapy? Evaluating any form of psychotherapy requires controlled research in which treatment groups are compared with appropriate control conditions. Hundreds of such studies have been conducted, and meta-analyses of their results typically reach two main conclusions. First, people who receive psychotherapy do significantly better than those left untreated. Second, there are few overall advantages for one type of psychotherapy over another.

One reason that most forms of treatment are equally effective may be that all psychotherapies have common factors, which can be grouped into three main categories: support, learning, and action. All therapists provide some kind of support for their client, and therapist empathy is important to outcome success. All forms of therapy also help clients learn about themselves and their behaviour, and clients are provided specific prescriptions for action or behaviour change. In choosing a therapist, it's critical that you find someone you trust and feel comfortable interacting with. Cultural factors are also important: For therapy to work the therapist needs to be sensitive to the client's cultural world-view. Women and middle-aged people tend to attend psychotherapy more than men or younger people, and university students tend to use psychological services more if they have positive attitudes toward counselling and are in distress.

Chapter Summary

TREATING THE BODY: BIOMEDICAL THERAPIES

Abnormal functioning in the brain is thought to contribute to a number of psychological disorders. To address these problems, psychologists sometimes consider the use of *biomedical therapies.*

Drug Therapies

Learning Goal: Learn how drug therapies can be used to treat psychological disorders. Medications (such as chlorpromazine) that treat positive symptoms of schizophrenia are termed *antipsychotic drugs* and quite often act on the neurotransmitter dopamine. However, these drugs are limited in their effect and can produce side effects such as *tardive dyskinesia,* which produces disabling involuntary movements. *Clozapine* and *risperidone* are newer medications that serve as an effective alternative. *Antidepressant drugs* also modulate the effectiveness of neurotransmitters, particularly norepinephrine and serotonin. Bipolar disorders are often treated with the common salt *lithium carbonate. Antianxiety drugs,* or *tranquillizers* (e.g., Valium), come from a class of drugs called *benzodiazepines* and work primarily on the neurotransmitter GABA.

Electroconvulsive Therapy

Learning Goal: Understand and evaluate electroconvulsive therapy. Many professionals believe that *electroconvulsive therapy (ECT)* is a reasonably safe and effective treatment for severe depression. Nonetheless, it is typically used as a treatment of "last resort." The treatment remains controversial for a number of reasons. The reasons for its effectiveness are not well understood, and it can produce side effects such as confusion and memory loss.

TREATING THE MIND: INSIGHT THERAPIES

Psychological disorders are often associated with abnormal thoughts and beliefs. Many psychologists believe that the key to improvement lies in insight. *Insight therapies* encourage clients to gain a clearer understanding of their psychological problems, usually through a one-on-one interaction with a therapist.

Psychoanalysis: Resolving Unconscious Conflicts

Learning Goal: Understand and evaluate psychoanalysis as a form of insight therapy. Freud believed that through *psychoanalysis,* hidden impulses and memories can be brought to awareness, freeing us from disordered thoughts and behaviours. The tools used to uncover unconscious conflicts include *free association* and *dream analysis. Resistance* (unconsciously motivated attempts to hinder therapy) and *transference* (expression of thoughts or feelings toward the therapist that are representative of how patients feel about others in their lives) also provide clues about unconscious conflict. Modern versions of psychoanalysis streamline the therapeutic process and are often tailored to meet the specific needs of individuals.

Cognitive Therapies: Changing Maladaptive Beliefs

Learning Goal: Understand and evaluate cognitive therapies. Unlike the psychoanalytic approach, *cognitive therapies* place emphasis on *conscious* beliefs. Psychological problems arise from maladaptive and/or negative interpretations of daily events. In *rational-emotive therapy,* the therapist "cross-examines" the client, disputing irrational thought processes. Beck's cognitive therapy takes a more subtle approach, helping clients discover their own unique kinds of faulty beliefs through record-keeping or other types of "homework."

Humanistic Therapies: Treating the Human Spirit

Learning Goal: Understand and evaluate humanistic therapies. *Humanistic therapies* help the client gain insight into his or her own fundamental self-worth and value as a person. In *client-centred therapy,* the therapist is warm, empathic, and supportive in all respects, accepting the client unconditionally. This unconditional positive regard helps the client overcome *incongruence.* One variation, *Gestalt therapy,* forces clients to express their feelings openly.

Group Therapy

Learning Goal: Learn about group and family therapy. In *group therapy,* you join others who are undergoing treatment for a similar problem. This can be particularly appropriate in the case of families. In *family therapy,* the therapist treats the family as a kind of social system, attempting to improve interpersonal communication and collaboration among family members.

CHANGING THE ENVIRONMENT: BEHAVIOURAL THERAPIES

People may *learn* to feel, think, and act in abnormal ways through the mechanisms of classical and instrumental conditioning and observational learning. *Behavioural therapies* employ basic learning principles to recondition maladaptive behaviour patterns into adaptive behaviour patterns.

Conditioning Techniques

Learning Goal: Understand how conditioning techniques can be used in therapy. Phobias can be eliminated by teaching a new association between the feared object and something pleasurable. *Conditioning techniques* may be used to change the association to something pleasurable. In *systematic desensitization,* the therapist uses counterconditioning, systematically associating relaxation with feared objects as expressed in an *anxiety hierarchy.* In *aversion therapy,* the therapist attempts to replace a pleasant reaction to a harmful stimulus (e.g., alcohol) with something unpleasant.

Using Rewards and Punishments to Change Behaviour

Learning Goal: Understand how rewards and punishments can be used to improve behaviour. People can be shaped, through rewards and punishments, away from abnormal actions and toward more normal behaviours. In a *token economy,* institutionalized patients are rewarded with tokens whenever they engage in an appropriate activity. The tokens are later exchanged for certain privileges. *Punishment* may also be effective in teaching people to understand the consequences of their actions, and is sometimes used to discourage self-injurious behaviour.

EVALUATING AND CHOOSING PSYCHOTHERAPY

Therapy is a costly and time-consuming process, so it's important to determine the advantages and disadvantages of an intervention. One must also take a number of factors into account when choosing a therapist.

Clinical Evaluation Research

Learning Goal: Understand the major findings of clinical evaluation research. One well-known study that compared psychoanalytic and behavioural approaches to therapy with a control condition demonstrated that therapy clearly worked, but there were no reliable differences in the effectiveness of the two approaches. *Meta-analyses* of evaluation studies have shown that therapy works, although some problems may improve on their own through *spontaneous remission.* Overall, no one therapeutic approach seems more effective than others, although particular kinds of therapy may work best for certain problems. Psychologists have recently begun to agree on which treatments are *empirically supported* by research as being effective.

Common Factors across Psychotherapies

Learning Goal: Understand the factors that are common across psychotherapies. Common factors are seen in each therapeutic approach: All therapies provide *support* for the client; all people in therapy *learn* something about themselves; and all forms of therapy provide people with some suggestions for *action.* These common factors may account for the finding that approaches are comparable in their overall effectiveness. Also important is the *therapeutic alliance:* the agreement between therapist and client to work together to solve the client's problem.

Choosing a Therapist

Learning Goal: Appreciate the important personal and cultural factors that should be considered when choosing a therapist. People seeking a psychotherapist should choose someone they trust and feel comfortable with. Most therapists are eclectic in orientation, so that they can adjust their therapeutic approaches. Cultural factors are also important in the diagnosis and treatment of psychological disorders. People who use psychotherapy tend to be middle-aged, female, separated/divorced, wealthier, and better educated than average. University students seek psychological services more if they have positive attitudes toward counselling and are in psychological distress. Unfortunately, there is a *service gap* in psychological services: More people are in need of psychological help than receive it.

Terms to Remember

psychotherapy, 598
Treating the Body: Biomedical Therapies
biomedical therapies, 600
antipsychotic drugs, 600
antidepressant drugs, 601
antianxiety drugs, 602
electroconvulsive therapy (ECT), 603
Treating the Mind: Insight Therapies
insight therapies, 605
psychoanalysis, 605
free association, 606
dream analysis, 606
resistance, 606
transference, 606
cognitive therapies, 608
rational-emotive therapy, 608
humanistic therapy, 612
client-centred therapy, 612
group therapy, 614
family therapy, 614
Changing the Environment: Behavioural Therapies
behavioural therapies, 615
systematic desensitization, 616
aversion therapy, 617
token economy, 618
Evaluating and Choosing Psychotherapy
meta-analysis, 622
spontaneous remission, 623
empirically supported treatments, 623
therapeutic alliance, 624
service gap, 626

Recommended Readings

Endler, N. S. (1990). *Holiday of darkness: A psychologist's personal journey out of his depression.* New York: Wall and Emerson. York University psychologist Norman Endler's personal account of struggling with his own depressive episodes. Endler defends the usefulness of ECT for helping people with his kind of depression.

Mahrer, A. R. (1995). *A complete guide to experiential psychotherapy.* New York: John Wiley. Alvin Mahrer of the University of Ottawa is a distinguished psychotherapy researcher and practitioner. In this volume, he outlines how to conduct experiential psychotherapy (which shares many features with humanistic approaches).

Greenberg, L. S., & Paivio, S. C. (1997). *Working with emotions in psychotherapy.* New York: Guilford. Psychotherapy researchers Leslie Greenberg of York University and Sandra Paivio of the University of Windsor examine the role of emotions in psychotherapy, with many specific examples taken from therapy sessions.

Hays, K. F. (1999). *Working it out: Using exercise in psychotherapy.* Washington, DC: American Psychological Association. Katie Hays is a consultant in Toronto who has been president of the American Psychological Association's Division of Exercise and Sport Psychology. In this book she outlines how physical exercise can be an important component of an integrated, holistic therapy program.

Mash, E. J., & Barkley, R. A. (Eds.). (1998). *Treatment of childhood disorders.* New York: Guilford. Co-edited by University of Calgary clinical researcher Eric Mash, this text provides clear descriptions and discussions of treatments of childhood disorders such as learning disabilities, fears and anxieties, ADHD, anorexia, autism, and adolescent substance abuse problems.

Wolfe, D. A., McMahon, R. J., & Peters, R. D. (Eds.). (1997). *Child abuse: New directions in prevention and treatment across the lifespan.* Thousand Oaks, CA: Sage. Co-edited by clinical researchers from the University of Western Ontario, University of Calgary, and Queen's University, this volume presents recent information on methods and techniques of preventing and treating physical and sexual abuse of children.

Johnson, S. M. (1996). *The practice of emotionally focused marital therapy: Creating connection.* New York: Guilford. Susan Johnson of the University of Ottawa has conducted research on how couples therapy works to repair problematic relationships; she also reviews some practical aspects of this type of therapy in this volume.

Engler, J., & Gordon, B. (1992). *The consumer's guide to psychotherapy.* New York: Simon & Schuster. This book is a good source for discovering the range of available psychotherapies and for help in picking the kind of therapy that might work best for you.

 For additional readings, explore InfoTrac® College Edition, your online library. Go to:

www.adaptivemind2e.nelson.com

Hint: enter the search terms: Prozac; psychotherapy; psychoanalysis; cognitive therapy; behaviour modification; effectiveness of psychotherapy.

What's on the Web?

Please note that Web addresses are subject to change. Check out the accompanying Web site for updates: www.adaptivemind2e.nelson.com. This site presents practice quiz questions, hypercontent, information on degrees and careers in psychology, study tips, and more.

Canadian Psychological Association: Clinical Section Web Page

www.cpa.ca/clinical/

Includes information on psychotherapy effectiveness and reports and conferences on psychotherapy and other aspects of clinical psychology.

Mental Health Evaluation and Community Consultation Unit

www.mheccu.ubc.ca/index.shtml

Based at the University of British Columbia, this organization conducts research, training, and education focused on integrating mental health promotion activities into communities.

Canadian Traumatic Stress Network

www.ctsn-rcst.ca

Resources, support, and advice for people who have suffered traumatic stress, and for practitioners working with such people.

Canadian Journal of Psychiatry and Neuroscience

www.cma.ca/jpn/index.htm

Canada's leading psychiatric journal; contains abstracts and some full-text research articles, many of them examining biomedical approaches to the treatment of mental disorders.

Psychotherapy Links

www.psychiatry.med.uwo.ca/ptherapy/links.htm

From the University of Western Ontario Department of Psychiatry, an extensive collection of well-organized links to almost every type of psychotherapy.

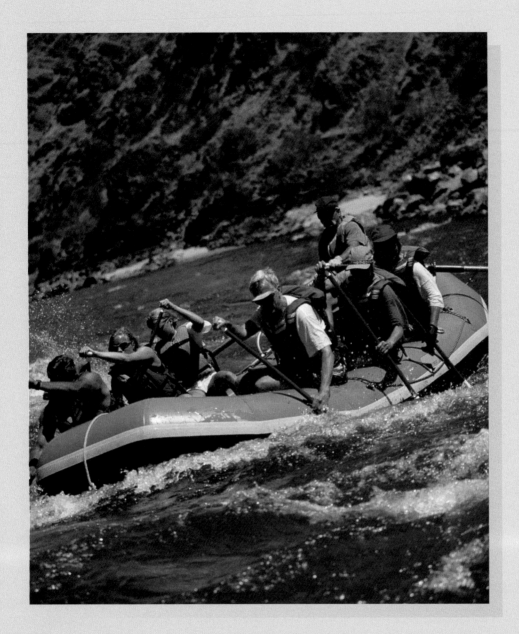

... most commentators believe that ours is the "age of stress," forgetting that the caveman's fear of attack by wild animals or of death from hunger, cold, or exhaustion must have been just as stressful as our fear of a world war, the crash of the stock exchange, or overpopulation.

Hans Selye

Chapter 16 Stress and Health

Like every generation, we tend to claim exclusive rights to the "age of stress." It hits us from all sides—school, work, relationships, family. Everyone expects something from us, and they seem to want it now. Your teachers expect you to read too much material and to write papers before the deadline; your boss expects overtime in addition to your regular hours; your parents expect you to show up for family events—and to act as if you enjoy them. Is it any wonder that you feel tired all the time, can't seem to shake that cough, and feel the need to keep the antacid tablets by your bedside at night? Although we can adapt to stress reasonably well in the short run, there are consequences for our physical health in the long run.

The idea that there is a close relationship between your psychological state and the physical reactions of your body has been around since Freud. The mind and the body interact, and the forces work in both directions. As we've discussed, disruptions in the delicate balance of neurotransmitters in the brain can contribute significantly to psychological problems such as schizophrenia and depression. At the same time, beliefs, expectations, and reactions to the environment affect how those neurotransmitters are manufactured and used in the brain. In this chapter, you'll see that the mind-to-body connection affects not only the way you think, feel, and react; it can affect your overall state of health as well.

Our focus in this chapter is the general topic of **health psychology.** Also known as *behavioural medicine,* this field seeks to understand how biological, psychological, environmental, and cultural factors are involved in the promotion of physical health and the prevention of illness. Not surprisingly, health psychologists are particularly interested in the psychological and environmental contributions (Krantz & McCeney, 2002; Schneiderman et al., 2001; Taylor et al., 1997). They tend to ask questions such as: Are there particular personality characteristics that determine who becomes sick or who will recover from an illness once it is acquired? Can the same theories that have been used successfully to diagnose and treat psychological disorders be applied to the promotion of physical health? Is it possible to identify the kinds of working environments that lead to illness or promote recovery? Are there specific strategies, or lifestyle choices, that reduce the likelihood of getting sick?

health psychology
The study of how biological, psychological, environmental, and cultural factors are involved in physical health and the prevention of illness.

Previewing the Adaptive Problems

Much of our discussion in this chapter will deal with the topic of psychological stress and its effects on health. Our reactions to stress tend to be adaptive, but prolonged exposure to stressful environments can have a negative long-term impact on health. Our discussion in this chapter will focus on four adaptive problems that are related to stress and to health psychology in general.

First, what is stress, and how is it experienced? Everyone has an intuitive sense of what *stress* is, but the term can actually be defined in a variety of ways. We'll discuss some of the meanings of the term, as well as the various components of the stress response. It's best to conceive of stress not as a single reaction, such as a sudden release of activating hormones, but rather as an extended response that occurs over time.

Second, how does the body react when the exposure to stressful situations is prolonged? The human body is usually well equipped to deal with unexpected trauma by activating those systems that are needed to respond to the emergency. But if the threat continues for an extended period of time, the body's defences can begin to break down. We'll consider some of the physical consequences of prolonged exposure to stress, including the role that stress plays in the immune system.

Third, what strategies enable us to reduce and cope with stress? Given that prolonged exposure to stress can have negative long-term consequences, psychologists have developed specific methods of treatment for reducing and controlling stress. A number of techniques are available for managing stress, and we'll consider some of them later in the chapter.

Fourth, what general factors and lifestyle choices promote physical and psychological health? Whether you will remain healthy throughout your life depends importantly on the lifestyle habits you choose. Obviously, if you choose to engage in risky behaviours— such as smoking, failing to get adequate nutrition, or practising unsafe sex— then you increase your likelihood of illness or death. Health psychologists have joined with other professionals, including physicians, to offer prescriptions for a healthy lifestyle. We'll discuss some of these recommendations along with their foundations in psychological theory.

EXPERIENCING STRESS: STRESSORS AND THE STRESS RESPONSE

Learning Goals

1. Understand the stress response.
2. Be able to explain the role of cognitive appraisal in the stress response.
3. Learn about external sources of stress.
4. Learn about internal sources of stress.

"STRESS" IS ONE OF THOSE CONCEPTS that is easy to identify but difficult to define precisely. Part of the problem is that the term can be used to refer to two different aspects of the psychological process. Stress can be an actual *stimulus* (such as an event or a person) that places a demand on us or threatens our well-being ("Four final exams in one week is too much stress"). On the other hand, we're just as likely to describe stress as a physical *response* or reaction that we feel ("I'm really stressed out"). To complicate matters even further, as you'll see later, whether we experience stress depends on how we interpret the situation we're in (Lazarus, 1966, 1991).

For our purposes, we'll define **stress** as the physical and psychological reaction that people have to threatening or demanding situations, and we'll refer to the demanding

stress
People's physical and psychological reactions to demanding or threatening situations.

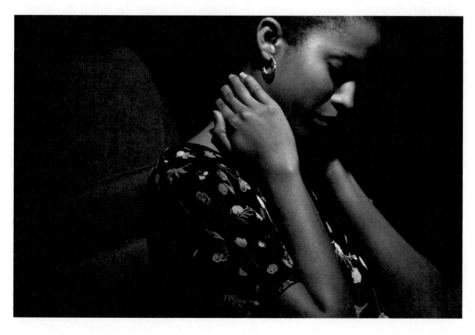

Prolonged exposure to stress can lead to physical and psychological problems.

The early stages of the stress response are clearly adaptive because they help organisms initiate a "fight-or-flight" response.

stressors
The demanding or threatening situations that produce stress.

or threatening situations that produce stress as **stressors.** For example, the traffic jam that blocks your usual route home from school is a stressor, whereas your fuming physical and emotional reaction to such a situation is stress. In this section of the chapter, we'll first consider some of the physical and psychological characteristics of stress; then we'll examine the external and internal factors that create stress.

The Stress Response

If you're like most people, you probably think of stress as a bad thing. Certainly when you're "stressed out," you tend to feel lousy, and there's no question that extended exposure to stressful situations can have long-term negative consequences. But it's important to understand that stress is in many ways an adaptive reaction. When you're in a threatening situation, or when someone is placing demands on you, it's important that your body become activated so you can respond to the threat with energy. The experience of stress does exactly that—it activates you for responses that are quick and intense.

general adaptation syndrome (GAS)
Hans Selye's model of stress as a general, nonspecific reaction that occurs in three phases: alarm reaction, resistance, and exhaustion.

Physiological Reactions In Montreal during the 1930s, a physician named Hans Selye introduced an influential model of stress reaction that he called the **general adaptation syndrome** (**GAS**) (Selye, 1936, 1952, 1974). Selye suggested that our reaction to stressful situations is general and nonspecific, by which he meant that people are biologically programmed to respond to most threats in the same way. He was initially led to this idea as a medical student, when he was struck by the similarities he saw among his patients. Across wildly different illnesses and injuries, his patients seemed to share a "syndrome of just being sick": That syndrome suggested to Selye that the body was reacting to each threatening situation in a very general way (no matter what the illness or the injury). Later, working in the laboratory with rats, he was able to confirm his hypothesis under controlled experimental conditions. Rats subjected to a variety of different kinds of threat—cold, heat, shock, restraint—produced a similar pattern of deteriorating health.

Selye's concept of the GAS proposed that the body reacts to threat or demand in three stages, or phases (see Figure 16.1). The first phase, the *alarm reaction,* corresponds to the adaptive fight-or-flight response we've discussed in previous chapters (Cannon, 1932). The body becomes energized, through activation of the sympathetic division of the autonomic nervous system, and hormones are released by the glands of the endocrine system. Heart rate and respiration rate increase, as does blood flow to the muscles; each of these actions helps prepare the body for immediate defensive or evasive action. The alarm reaction enables one to get out of life-threatening jams, but it

General Adaptation Syndrome

FIGURE 16.1

The General Adaptation Syndrome

Hans Selye proposed that the body reacts to threat or demand in three stages, or phases: (1) an *alarm reaction,* which corresponds to the fight-or-flight response; (2) a *resistance phase*, during which the body adjusts its reaction in an effort to cope with a threat that is still present; and (3) *exhaustion*, which occurs when the body's energy reserves become so depleted that it starts to give up.

is extremely intense and cannot be sustained for long periods without serious negative consequences (even death).

If the threat continues but is not serious enough to demand a continued alarm reaction, the body enters a *resistance phase.* During this phase, the body adjusts its physiological reaction in an effort to reduce, or cope with, the still-present threat. Arousal levels remain higher than normal, but the body is capable of replenishing at least some of its resources. During the resistance phase, people are able to function reasonably well, but they are particularly susceptible to other stressors in the environment and may begin to suffer from health problems, or what Selye called "diseases of adaptation."

Finally, if the person is unable to find a way to neutralize the threat, the body eventually enters the *exhaustion phase* of the GAS. The body simply cannot continue to maintain a high state of readiness for extended periods of time. Eventually, energy reserves become so taxed and depleted that the body starts to give up. During this period, resistance declines to the point at which the stress reaction becomes more and more maladaptive. Irreversible damage and even death become real possibilities.

Selye's notion of the GAS has remained influential over the years (Csermely, 1998). But today, many researchers believe that the body's reaction to threat may not be as general and nonspecific as Selye suggested. Different stressors may well produce somewhat different patterns of response in the body (Krantz & Manuck, 1984; Mason, 1975). Moreover, as you'll see momentarily, the stress reaction depends on the cognitive interpretation, or appraisal, of the threatening situation. But the idea that stress is best conceived as a complex process of adaptation is still widely accepted, as is Selye's discovery of the link between stress and health.

Psychological Reactions Stress is not just a physiological reaction to threat; there are also emotional and behavioural components to the reaction. We will consider the psychological consequences of prolonged exposure to stressful situations later in the chapter, but emotional reactions are an important component of the stress response regardless of when or how long it occurs. *Fear* is a common reaction to threat, as is *anger.* Stressful situations can also lead to feelings of *sadness, dejection,* or even *grief* (Lazarus, 1991). Notice that this diverse set of emotional reactions is another piece of evidence suggesting that the stress reaction is not completely general and nonspecific—people are capable of responding emotionally to different stressors in quite different ways.

The psychological consequences of stress are not always negative. Stress can have significant short-term and long-term psychological benefits (Suedfeld, 1997). For example, one study of people who suffered from frequent illness found them to be more empathic toward others and more tolerant of uncertainty (Haan, 1977). Stressful situations require people to use their skills and to interact with the environment. Those who can successfully resolve a stressful situation can learn from it and gain confidence in their abilities. Even some of the survivors of the Holocaust in World War II appeared

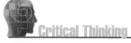

Critical Thinking

Just because two things occur together, such as illness and empathy, doesn't mean that one causes the other. How would you determine whether physical illness truly causes increased empathy?

to gain some long-term benefits, including a more complex world-view (Suedfeld et al., 1997). Experimental laboratory work showed that rats who were allowed to escape from shock, thereby reducing stress, had better-functioning immune systems than rats who received no shock (Laudenslager et al., 1983). A similar reaction may happen to people: Stress may, at times, lead to the release of hormones that are health enhancing, at least in the short term (Epel et al., 1998).

Gender Differences Although the basic physiological stress reaction (e.g., activation of the sympathetic nervous system) doesn't differ much between males and females, some psychologists believe there are important behavioural differences. For example, rather than showing the typical fight-or-flight response that is characteristic of males, females seem predisposed to react to stressors with "tending and befriending" behaviour (Taylor et al., 2000). Because of evolutionary pressures, females may have evolved to respond by tending and protecting offspring (in addition to themselves) rather than fighting or fleeing the scene.

According to Taylor and her colleagues, it's more adaptive for males to react to potential harm by being aggressive or fleeing; females are faced with different pressures, especially the care of the young, and often lack the necessary physical power to ward off threats through aggression. Although women can certainly become physically aggressive in some settings, aggression and flight are secondary reactions to threats. Instead, the first line of defence is to protect and calm offspring, which increases the chances of offspring survival. These reactions are also reflected in longer-term strategies: Females appear more likely to create and maintain social networks that potentially can aid in protecting themselves and their offspring (Haselton & Buss, 2000).

The proposal that males and females differ fundamentally in their behavioural reactions to stressors is new and likely to be controversial—especially the idea that gender-specific stress reactions may be adaptations arising from evolutionary pressures. However, the evidence supporting gender differences appears across the animal kingdom and may have some basis in the biology of male and female brains (Kimura, 1999). As Taylor and her colleagues note, the majority of research on the behavioural components of the stress response has been conducted on one sex at a time, so much remains to be learned about the role of gender in the basic stress response.

Cognitive Appraisal

The experience of stress is critically influenced by the way that people perceive or *appraise* their situation (Lazarus, 1993). To feel stress, it's necessary to (1) perceive there is some kind of demand or threat present and (2) come to the conclusion that you may not have adequate resources available to deal with that threat. If you have a black belt in the martial arts, then the sudden appearance of a school bully is not likely to cause much stress—the threat is there, but you have adequate defensive resources should you need to use them.

This idea—that the experience of stress depends on the **cognitive appraisal** of the situation—is reminiscent of what we know about the experience of emotions. As you may remember from Schachter's work in Chapter 11, the same general physiological reaction can lead to different subjective emotional experiences, depending on how one interprets the arousal experienced. The same is true for stress. Identical environmental events can lead to two very different stress reactions, depending on how the event is interpreted. Consider an upcoming exam: Everyone in the class receives the same test, but not everyone will feel the same amount of stress. Those people who are prepared for the exam—the people (like you) who read the chapter—are likely to feel less stress. You, the diligent student, still perceive the threat, but you have adequate resources to deal with it (see Figure 16.2). The converse is also true—dangerous situations must be perceived as dangerous in order for a stress response to be produced. A small child does not necessarily understand that a loaded gun is dangerous and so may feel no stress while handling it.

cognitive appraisal
The idea that in order to feel stress you need to perceive a threat and come to the conclusion that you may not have adequate resources to deal with the threat.

Event

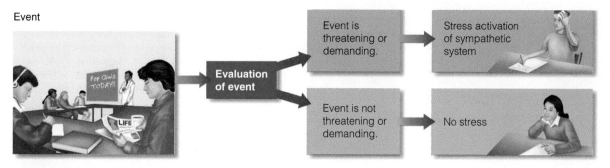

FIGURE 16.2
Cognitive Appraisal
Like emotion, whether an event will create stress depends on how the event is interpreted. A stress reaction is more likely to occur if you feel you have inadequate resources to deal with the potential threat.

A great deal of evidence confirms the role of cognitive appraisal in the experience of stress (Tomaka et al., 1997). In one study of elementary school children, urine samples were taken from the children on both normal school days and on days when they were about to take standardized achievement tests. The urine sample measured the amount of cortisol, an important stress hormone, that each child produced. In formal terms, the authors operationalized stress as the current amount of the hormone in the urine. Not surprisingly, more cortisol was found on test days, suggesting a higher level of stress, but the increase in stress depended on the child's previously recorded overall intelligence score. The children with higher intelligence scores showed less of a stress reaction on test days, presumably because they considered the test to be less of a threat (Tennes & Kreye, 1985).

External Sources of Stress

The fact that the stress reaction depends on one's appraisal of the situation means that it will never be possible to compile an exhaustive list of life's stressors. We can never predict how everyone will react to an environmental event, even though it may seem clearly stressful to the majority. But it is possible to catalogue external situations, or life events, that induce stress reactions in *most* individuals. We'll consider four major classes of external stressors in this section: significant life events, physical pain, daily hassles, and other factors in the environment.

Significant Life Events Certain events in our lives are virtually guaranteed to produce stress. We can all agree that the death of a loved one or getting fired from a job is likely to lead to an extended stress reaction in most people. On a larger scale, catastrophes and natural disasters—such as the terrorist attacks that occurred in the United States on September 11, 2001—unquestionably produce stress that is prolonged and widespread. In the case of the terrorist attacks in 2001, a national phone survey conducted three to five days after the attack found that over 44% reported one or more substantial symptoms of stress, and over 90% reported feeling at least some symptoms (Schuster et al., 2001).

Many studies have found clear relationships between such events and subsequent physical and psychological problems (Dohrenwend, 1998; Goldberger & Breznitz, 1993). Although it's too early to tell what the long-term health consequences of the terrorist attacks will be, other cases suggest the long-term effects will be widespread. For instance, in the seven months following the 1980 volcanic eruption of Mount Saint Helens in Washington State, one nearby town reported a more than 30% increase in the number of hospital emergency room visits, compared to a similar period in the

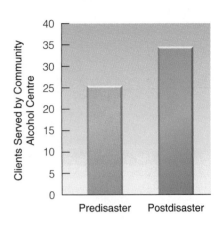

FIGURE 16.3
Reacting to a Natural Disaster

In the seven months following the volcanic eruption of Mount Saint Helens in 1980, the residents of nearby Othello, Washington, showed dramatic increases in a variety of stress-related behaviours. The data shown here present the mean monthly hospital emergency room visits, mental health crisis line calls, and number of clients served by a community alcohol centre for comparable time periods before and after the disaster. (Data from Adams & Adams, 1984.)

year prior to the eruption (Adams & Adams, 1984) (see Figure 16.3). These visits were *not* for injuries directly caused by the eruption but rather for general health problems that may have been created or enhanced by the experience of stress.

Over the years researchers have tried to compile lists of external life stressors. The best-known example is the Social Readjustment Rating Scale, which was put together by researchers Thomas Holmes and Richard Rahe (1967). Holmes and Rahe interviewed thousands of people who were suffering from health problems and then tried to determine whether there were certain kinds of events that preceded the onset of the health problems. The results are shown in Table 16.1. This table lists the various significant life events mentioned by the people who were interviewed, ranked in terms of "life change units" (roughly representing the amount of readjustment that the event caused in the person's life).

There are two interesting things to notice about the results shown in the table. First, most of these life events are associated with some kind of change in a person's day-to-day activities. Thus, it may be that the disruption caused by the event is just as important as the event itself in causing the stress reaction. People get stressed, in part, because something happens that requires them to alter their ways or lifestyle. Second, notice that many of the events listed in the table are actually quite positive. For example, marriage and retirement both make the top ten. Even vacations and Christmas make the list. This is not really too surprising if you think about it, because each is associated with some kind of temporary or long-lasting change or disruption of normal routines.

The results listed in Table 16.1 are over 35 years old, but they continue to be used by researchers as an index for predicting the likelihood of stress. Dozens of studies have shown that there are significant correlations among the rankings shown in the table and various measures of stress, including physical and psychological problems (Derogatis & Coons, 1993; Miller, 1993). However, not all experts are satisfied with the methods that have been used to compile such lists (Brett et al., 1990; Cleary, 1980; Schroeder & Costa, 1984), and recent revisions of the scale have been introduced to take into account factors such as gender, age, and amount of education (Hobson & Delunas, 2001; Miller & Rahe, 1997). Moreover, change by itself will not necessarily lead to stress reactions in all individuals. Remember, it's how you appraise the event that is really important, along with your assessment of whether you have adequate resources to deal with the life change when it occurs.

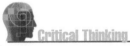

Critical Thinking

Try listing and ranking the life events that cause, or have caused, you the most stress. How do your rank orderings differ from those listed in Table 16.1?

Table 16.1
Social Readjustment Rating Scale

Rank	Life Event	Point Value	Rank	Life Event	Point Value
1	Death of spouse	100	23	Son or daughter leaving home	29
2	Divorce	73	24	Trouble with in-laws	29
3	Marital separation	65	25	Outstanding personal achievement	28
4	Jail term	63	26	Wife begins or stops work	26
5	Death of close family member	63	27	Begin or end school	26
6	Personal injury or illness	53	28	Change in living conditions	25
7	Marriage	50	29	Revision of personal habits	24
8	Fired at work	47	30	Trouble with boss	23
9	Marital reconciliation	45	31	Change in work hours or conditions	20
10	Retirement	45	32	Change in residence	20
11	Change in health of family member	44	33	Change in schools	20
12	Pregnancy	40	34	Change in recreation	19
13	Sex difficulties	39	35	Change in church activities	19
14	Gain of new family member	39	36	Change in social activities	18
15	Business readjustment	39	37	Mortgage or loan less than $20 000	17
16	Change in financial state	38	38	Change in sleeping habits	16
17	Death of close friend	37	39	Change in number of family get-togethers	15
18	Change to different line of work	36	40	Change in eating habits	15
19	Change in number of arguments with spouse	35	41	Vacation	13
20	Mortgage over $20 000	31	42	Christmas	12
21	Foreclosure of mortgage or loan	30	43	Minor violations of the law	11
22	Change in responsibilities at work	29			

Source: Holmes & Rahe, 1967.

Physical Pain For some time, scientific research on pain has been led by Canadian researchers such as Ronald Melzak at McGill University, Ken Craig at the University of British Columbia, and Patrick McGrath at Dalhousie University. Craig and McGrath have developed methods for detecting pain in babies to avoid the possibility that we are inflicting pain on individuals who cannot report it (e.g., Craig, 1988; McGrath, 1992). Recently, research on pain has been advanced by researchers such as Thomas and Heather Hadjistavropoulos at the University of Regina (Hadjistavropoulos, 1999). They have shown, for example, that observers judging someone in pain tend to underestimate pain intensity when judging men and those who are physically attractive (Hadjistavropoulos et al., 1999).

Daily Hassles Psychologists also recognize that it is not just the big events that cause problems. The little things, the daily irritations and hassles of life, also contribute significantly to the experience of stress (Cassidy, 2000). Think about how you feel when you're stuck in a long checkout line at the store, when someone's tailgating you on the highway, or when you're hungry and you've waited a half-hour or more for your order at a restaurant. Some psychologists believe the cumulative effect of these "daily hassles" may actually be more important in creating stress than the kinds of life events that we just considered (Lazarus & Folkman, 1984; Miller, 1993). University of British

Crowded urban environments can be a source of stress for many people.

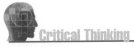

Critical Thinking

Suppose you discover a group of people living in a crowded and noisy environment who show little or no stress reaction. What kind of explanation would you look for?

environmental psychology

A specialty area in psychology devoted to the study of environmental effects on behaviour and health, such as the effects of crowding or noise.

Columbia psychologist Anita DeLongis and her colleagues (1988) have developed what they call a Daily Hassles Scale, and it seems to predict, on average, the likelihood of physical and mental health problems. The more hassles you experience in your daily life, the more likely you are to experience health problems. Included on the scale are such things as concern about one's weight and physical appearance, home maintenance, and worries about misplacing or losing something.

Environmental Factors People are also subjected to stress by their environment. *Noise* is a good example. Think about how difficult it is to study when someone is talking loudly nearby, or how irritated you get when you're roused from sleep by the whirring, clanging sounds of the morning garbage truck. Chronic exposure to noise interferes with everyday activities and it's been linked with the appearance of such stress-related disorders as ulcers and high blood pressure (Evans, 1997; Nagar & Panady, 1987), and with a general decline in the perceived quality of life (Evans et al., 1995). School children experience more stress when they're exposed to chronic noise, and cognitive measures (such as reading comprehension) appear to suffer (Haines et al., 2001). Apparently, it's not the loudness of the noise that really matters; people are bothered most by noises that are new, intermittent, or unpredictable (Graig, 1993).

Another environmental factor that has been linked to stress is *crowding* (Freeman & Stansfeld, 1998). The larger the number of people who live or work around you, the more likely you are to experience a stress reaction (Weiss & Baum, 1987). Living in a crowded environment, on average, makes people more susceptible to health problems and increases the likelihood of aggression. People who live in high-rise apartment buildings, filled with tenants, are more likely to behave aggressively than those who live in apartment buildings with fewer floors (Bell et al., 1990). The effects of crowding on health and aggression have also been studied extensively in prison settings: Again, inmates who live in crowded environments suffer more health problems and are more likely to act aggressively than inmates housed in less crowded environments (Paulus, 1988). Others have argued that total segregation from others is even more damaging (Bonta & Gendreau, 1990).

Crowding and noise are two examples of environmental stressors, but there are many others. For example, stress and health have been closely linked to the family social environment, to peer interactions, conditions in the workplace, and socioeconomic class (Chen & Mathews, 2001; Taylor et al., 1997). There is, in fact, an entire specialty in psychology—called **environmental psychology**—devoted to the study of environmental effects such as these on behaviour and health (Gifford, 1997). Environmental psychologists have shown a particular interest in the psychology of urban living because living in a large city is likely to expose one to a large variety of environmental stressors—especially noise and crowding. Cities such as Tokyo and New York, with a fast-paced life, tend to have higher rates of heart disease and smoking (Levine & Norenzayan, 1999). In general, people succumb to stress when they're forced to live in situations where there is excessive stimulation, constrained movement, or limitations in some important resource (Graig, 1993).

Internal Sources of Stress

As you are now aware, no single event or set of living conditions will automatically lead to stress in everyone. Stress is a very subjective experience, which means we need to know something about the internal characteristics of the individual before we can predict whether he or she will experience stress. Stress arises out of an interaction between individuals and events in the world—neither alone is sufficient to predict the reaction. The notion of the **hardy personality** was hypothesized to explain why some individuals could resist chronic stressors with minimal effects (Kobasa, 1979). Rather than a single personality variable, the hardy personality is currently seen as a collection of adaptive personality traits, attitudes, and skills (Maddi, 2002). We'll consider three in this section: perceived control, explanatory style, and personality characteristics.

Perceived Control To experience stress, you need to perceive a threat or some kind of demand, and you need to feel you lack the resources to deal effectively with that threat. This second part of the appraisal process, the assessment of resources, is influenced by a psychological construct called **perceived control,** which is the amount of influence you feel you have over the situation and your reaction to it. It turns out that perceived control significantly affects the amount of stress you will experience. If you perceive a demand or threat and you think you have no control over the situation, your body is likely to react with arousal and the release of stress hormones, and there will be changes in the activities of your immune system (Brosschot et al., 1998). If the situation continues for a prolonged period, negative physical and psychological consequences are likely to result.

There are many examples, both scientific and anecdotal, that support the link between perceived control and stress. Early in the manned space program, for instance, the Mercury astronauts insisted that manual controls and windows be placed in the orbiting space capsule. Although not necessary from an engineering standpoint, doing so gave the astronauts a "sense of control" over their environment, which reduced their stress. In laboratory studies, animals who are exposed to shocks that they can turn off by turning a wheel are less likely to develop ulcers than animals who receive the same amount of shock but cannot control it (Weiss, 1977).

Explanatory Style The results of the cognitive appraisal process, and therefore susceptibility to stress, are also influenced by one's general style of thinking. At several points in the text, we've discussed the importance of the process of *attribution,* which refers to how we arrive at conclusions about cause and effect. Different kinds of explanations are available for the positive and negative events that occur in the world. For example, use of an *internal, stable,* and *global* attribution for a negative event can lead to a sense of personal inadequacy.

We've seen elsewhere that a maladaptive explanatory style can be altered via cognitive therapy (see Chapter 15). Continued use of this explanatory style can undermine physical health and lead to susceptibility to stress. People who consistently make internal, stable, and global attributions for negative events have been found to suffer from increased stress-related health problems in midlife as well as later in life (Kamen-Siegel et al., 1991; Peterson et al., 1988). In one particularly intriguing study, Peterson and Seligman (1987) analyzed the explanatory styles of 94 members of the Baseball Hall of Fame who had played at some point between 1900 and 1950. Many of these players were dead at the time of the study, so the researchers had to glean the players' explanatory styles from stories and quotations in old newspapers. The players with the negative explanatory styles were found, on average, to have lived shorter lives.

Personality Characteristics Perceptions of control and explanatory styles are more easily modified than long-term personality traits. Consider the personality characteristic *optimism*—the belief that good things will happen—a relatively enduring trait that changes little over a lifetime (Scheier & Carver, 1993). "Optimism scales" have been developed and used to look for a connection between personality and health. In one study, optimism was assessed on the day before a group of men underwent coronary bypass surgery. The optimists reacted physiologically to the surgery in ways that lowered the risk of heart attack, and they also recovered more quickly after the surgery (Scheier et al., 1989). More recent studies have demonstrated links between optimism

hardy personality
The set of traits, attitudes, and skills that make an individual less vulnerable to stress.

perceived control
The amount of influence you feel you have over a situation and your reaction to it.

Type A personalities expose themselves to stressful situations and then react in a hostile fashion; consequently, they are more likely to develop coronary heart problems than Type B personalities.

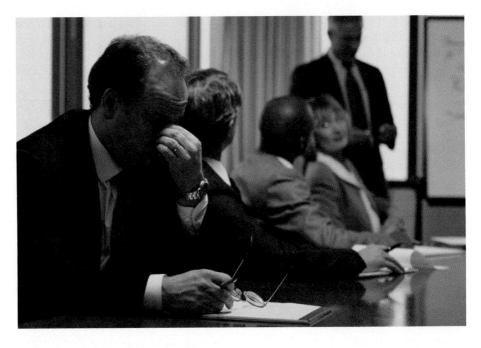

Type A
An enduring pattern of behaviour linked to coronary heart disease: The combination of tendencies to be hard driving, ambitious, easily annoyed, and impatient all seem to derive from the trait hostility.

Type B
People who lack the Type A traits—they experience less stress and, therefore, better health outcomes.

and improved functioning of the immune system (Segerstrom et al., 1998). An optimistic view of life, therefore, appears to reduce stress and its associated health risks (Davidson & Prkachin, 1997).

The best-known personality characteristic linked to *higher* levels of stress is the **Type A** pattern. Traditionally, the syndrome included tendencies such as hard driving, ambitious, easily annoyed, and impatient. Those with a Type A personality seem to be immersed in a sea of perpetual self-imposed stress; they react badly to frustration because they're engaged in a relentless pursuit of success. **Type B** personality types are essentially people who lack the Type A attributes—they put themselves under less pressure and react more calmly when stress does occur.

The connection between behaviour patterns and heart disease was first noted by cardiologists Meyer Friedman and Ray Rosenman (1974). They sought to explain why some people with known risk factors for heart disease (e.g., smoking, obesity, inactivity) do develop heart problems and some don't. Two people can appear to have identical risk profiles but end up healthy in one instance and disease-prone in another. Friedman and Rosenman proposed that the explanation lies in the connection between personality and stress. People who willingly choose a high-stress lifestyle—Type A personalities—will be more susceptible to diseases of the heart.

Over the past several decades, many extensive studies have explored the health consequences of Type A behaviour patterns. The results have generally supported the proposals of Friedman and Rosenman: People who are classified as Type A personality types are at least twice as likely to develop coronary heart problems as Type B personality types (Lyness, 1993).

Recent work has refined the original interpretation of the Type A behaviour pattern or personality. Original diagnoses required that you score high on a number of dimensions—competitiveness, ambition, time urgency, and so on. Some of these turn out to be incidental. It now appears that your overall level of hostility is most responsible for producing subsequent coronary artery disease (Krantz & McCeney, 2002). Chronically high levels of hostility naturally lead to a character that, under stress, will show irritability, impatience, and competitiveness. In terms of the Big Five, these are disagreeable individuals. This proclivity is subject to cultural factors—some occupations, subcultures, and even societies encourage competition and others do not (Thoresen & Powell, 1992). In short, those with the Type A personality have a combination of tendencies making them highly vulnerable to both stress and disease: They immerse themselves in stressful situations and then react badly to them (Friedman et al., 1994).

Concept Summary

SOURCES OF STRESS

External Source	Description
Significant life events	Major life events associated with a change in a person's day-to-day activities; they can be positive (e.g., getting married) or negative (e.g., death of a loved one).
Physical pain	Chronic or frequent repetitive pain that cannot be entirely alleviated (e.g., migraine headaches, arthritis, back pain).
Daily hassles	Daily irritations and hassles of life, such as getting stuck in traffic.
Environmental factors	Stressors present in a person's environment, such as noise and crowding.

Internal Source	Description
Perceived control	The amount of influence you feel you have over a situation. A sense of control often lessens the stress one feels in a situation.
Explanatory style	One's general style of thinking about and explaining events. People who make internal, stable, and global attributions for negative events are more likely to suffer from stress-related health problems.
Personality characteristics	*Optimism* (the belief that good things will happen) generally reduces stress. A *Type A* behaviour pattern (hard driving, ambitious, easily annoyed, impatient) is associated with elevated stress and heart problems.

Test Yourself 16.1

Check your knowledge about the stress response by answering each of the following questions. (You will find the answers in Appendix B.)

1. Hans Selye's concept of the general adaptation syndrome (GAS) proposes that the body reacts to stress in three phases. Which of the following shows the correct sequence of these phases?
   a. Resistance, alarm, exhaustion
   b. Exhaustion, resistance, alarm
   c. Alarm, resistance, exhaustion
   d. Exhaustion, alarm, resistance

2. The experience of stress is related to the experience of emotion in which of the following ways?
   a. The experience of stress, like emotion, is an inevitable reaction to threat.
   b. The experience of stress, like emotion, is accompanied by very distinctive facial expressions.
   c. The experience of stress, like emotion, depends on the appraisal of the event rather than on the event itself.
   d. The experience of different kinds of stress, like emotion, leads to highly specific kinds of body reactions.

3. According to the Social Readjustment Rating Scale, which of the following events is most likely to cause stress-related health problems?
   a. Marriage
   b. Death of a close friend
   c. Sex difficulties
   d. Trouble with your boss

4. Which of the following internal characteristics is least likely to be associated with stress-related health problems?
   a. Low levels of perceived control
   b. Type A behaviour pattern
   c. An optimistic outlook
   d. Internal, stable, and global attributions

REACTING TO PROLONGED STRESS: PHYSICAL AND PSYCHOLOGICAL EFFECTS

Learning Goals

1. Understand the physical consequences of prolonged stress, including the link between stress and the immune system.
2. Understand the psychological consequences of prolonged stress, including posttraumatic stress disorder and burnout.

THERE IS A DEFINITE CONNECTION between prolonged exposure to stress and subsequent physical and psychological health. Stress is an adaptive reaction to threat—it helps us to fight or flee. But when it is prolonged, we're not able to reduce or eliminate the perceived threat and the mind and body start to break down. If the stress reaction is extreme enough, the breakdown can be sudden and may even result in death; in most cases, however, the effects are gradual and reveal themselves slowly through a growing list of physical and psychological problems. In this section of the chapter, we'll consider the nature of these breakdowns and how and why they occur.

Physical Consequences of Stress

Stress has been implicated in a wide variety of health problems. Besides ulcers and heart disease, it has been linked to everything from the common cold to chronic back pain, multiple sclerosis, and even cancer (Schneiderman et al., 2001). Most of the scientific evidence is correlational, which means a statistical relationship has been found between the incidence of a health problem such as heart disease and some measurement of stress. Large numbers of people are interviewed, and health histories as well as stress levels are measured. The net result is that we can predict whether someone, on average, will have an increased chance of developing a particular kind of health problem by knowing the amount of stress that person experiences on a regular basis. But this does not tell us whether a causal relationship exists between stress and illness. To determine such a relationship, we must turn to experimental research.

Ideally, we would randomly divide people into groups, subject some of them to high levels of stress, and then monitor the later consequences of that manipulation on health. Ethically, however, we cannot knowingly subject people to harmful conditions. Instead, studies have been conducted on groups of people who have been previously identified as having either a high or low level of stress in their lives. In one study (Cohen et al., 1993), high- and low-stress people were given nasal drops that either contained or did not contain a common cold virus. It was a double-blind study, so neither the participants nor the researchers were aware during the course of the study who was getting the actual virus and who was not. Afterward, when the subject assignments were "decoded," it was found that the high-stress people who received the virus were the ones most likely to show cold symptoms. Living a stressful life apparently lowers one's ability to fight off disease.

The Immune Response To understand why stress increases susceptibility to illness, you need to understand something about the human immune system. The human body has a complex defence system, called the *immune system*, that is constantly on the lookout for foreign substances, such as viruses or bacteria. The primary weapons of the immune system are **lymphocytes,** which are specialized white blood cells that have the job of attacking and destroying most of these foreign invaders. Stress can increase a person's risk for disease by interfering with white blood cells' ability to eliminate foreign substances that have invaded the body (see Cohen & Herbert, 1996; Gonzalez-Quijano et al., 1998). The underlying mechanisms that produce these changes have not been completely determined, although the prolonged release of stress hormones into the bloodstream probably plays a significant role (Kiecolt-Glaser et al., 2002).

lymphocytes
Specialized white blood cells that have the job of attacking foreign substances, such as viruses and bacteria.

People who are subjected to chronic stress, because of environmental conditions, can show weakened immune system functioning.

Several investigations have shown that stressful life events directly affect the immune response. Medical students, on average, have fewer lymphocytes in their blood during a period of final exams compared to levels found before exams (Kiecolt-Glaser et al., 1984); they are also more likely to get sick during exams. Depressed individuals who have recently had a spouse or loved one die also show suppressed immune responses (Miller et al., 1999). One investigative team tracked the immune response in men married to women with advanced breast cancer. Samples of the men's blood were taken during a period of months preceding and following their wife's death. On average, the existing lymphocytes in blood samples drawn *after* the wives had died showed a weaker response to foreign substances (Schleifer et al., 1983).

The fact that stress weakens the immune system has led researchers to wonder about the effects of stress on more chronic illnesses, such as cancer. In the laboratory it's been shown that stress can increase the growth rate of cancerous tumours in rats, although the particular type of tumour apparently matters (Justice, 1985). There have also been reports that cancer patients who are optimistic or who are given therapy to help reduce anxiety and depression survive longer than patients who are hopeless or depressed (Andersen, 1992; Spiegel et al., 1989). Stress may affect not only the body's ability to fight cancer but also the likelihood that cancer cells will form in the first place (Schneiderman et al., 1992).

At present, however, most researchers remain cautious about the link between psychology, the immune system, and cancer (Cohen & Herbert, 1996). Not all studies have found associations between psychological factors and cancer (Schneiderman et al., 2001), and the fact that data linking cancer to stress have come primarily from correlational studies means that it is difficult to draw conclusions about cause and effect. For example, it's possible that "stressful" people, on average, have a greater risk of acquiring cancer because they tend to engage in unhealthy behaviours—such as smoking—as a way of dealing with the stress. It may also be the case that people who are optimistic about their survival from cancer tend to comply more with the recommendations of their doctors. So, although there may be a statistical association between stress and cancer, that does not necessarily mean that stress is causing cancer by compromising the functioning of the immune system.

Cardiovascular Disease Health psychologists have also intensively studied the well-documented relationship between stress and cardiovascular disease (problems connected with the heart and blood vessels). We discussed the connection between Type A behaviour and heart problems earlier, but we left the mechanisms through which stress undermines cardiovascular health unspecified. The two most important risk factors in heart disease are high cholesterol levels in the blood and high blood pressure. Prolonged exposure to stress increases exposure to both of these risk factors.

Increased blood pressure, a natural byproduct of the stress response, is generally helpful over the short term (as part of the fight-or-flight response). But if the elevated pressure continues, it causes wear and tear on the blood vessels in the body, which can lead to both cardiovascular disease and kidney problems. Stress can also directly affect the level of cholesterol in the blood. For example, when college students are anticipating an upcoming exam, samples of their blood show higher levels of cholesterol (Van Doornen & Van Blokland, 1987). People who display Type A behaviour patterns have also been found, on average, to have higher levels of blood cholesterol. One possibility is that when people sense threat, the body directs the blood flow to the muscles and away from the internal organs that remove fat and cholesterol from the blood.

Interestingly, it is not just Type A individuals who show this pattern of health problems. Depressed individuals are also at higher risk for cardiovascular disease. One study looked at patients in Montreal who had survived a heart attack. It showed that patients who were depressed in the period shortly after their heart attack were four times more likely to die within the next six months, compared with nondepressed patients (Smith et al., 1993). The fact that depressed individuals seem to show the same pattern of health risks as Type A individuals has led researchers to look for common biological mechanisms such as high blood pressure and altered immune function (Miller et al., 2002; Musselman & Nemeroff, 2000).

Psychological Consequences of Stress

The mental and emotional consequences of stress can also be profound. You feel anxious, out of control, emotionally drained, and, after a while, possibly even sad and depressed. Stress is not a pleasant experience, and if the stress reaction is intense enough, or if it continues long enough, serious psychological problems can result.

Most psychologists are convinced that stressful life events play a significant role in the onset of many psychological disorders. If you interview people who have suffered from major depression or a bipolar disorder, you will find that most have experienced some kind of major stressor just before or early into the depressive episode—they got fired from their job, they moved to a new town, they're mired in a nasty divorce, and so on (Barlow & Durand, 2002). Stress tends to deplete one's willpower to resist such unhealthy behaviours as overeating (Vohs & Hetherton, 2000). Stress has also been implicated in the onset of schizophrenia. Several studies have shown that stressful life events tend to immediately precede schizophrenic episodes (Brown & Birley, 1968; Harvey, 2001).

As noted earlier, some hardy individuals are quite resistant to stress. Even some who have endured prolonged imprisonment or torture or survived the horrors of the Holocaust do not show long-term consequences (Bonta & Gendreau, 1990; Suedfeld, 1999). In fact, the majority of people who experience a traumatic life stressor do not subsequently develop psychological disorders. But others seem to have some kind of vulnerability, perhaps rooted in the genetic code, and stress can trigger an extreme disorder such as major depression or schizophrenia. Similar arguments apply to anxiety disorders, such as posttraumatic stress disorder, which we discuss briefly below.

Posttraumatic Stress Disorder You're familiar with the story: A soldier returns home from war, shell shocked, suffering from sleepless nights and flashbacks of traumatic episodes in battle. Hollywood has exploited this image to the point where the "unstable war vet" has become a recurring character in popular books and films. In reality, the vast majority of soldiers who return from war suffer no long-term psychological problems. At the same time, even though the percentages are small, psychologists do recognize that exposure to extreme stress can produce a serious psychological condition known as **posttraumatic stress disorder.** This disorder is not limited to

Critical Thinking

How might the onset of a psychological disorder, such as depression, be an adaptive reaction to prolonged stress?

posttraumatic stress disorder
A trauma-based anxiety disorder characterized by flashbacks, avoidance of stimuli associated with the traumatic event, and chronic arousal symptoms.

battle veterans; it can occur in any individual who has undergone a traumatic episode, such as a physical attack, rape, or a natural disaster (Foa & Riggs, 1995). Canadian researchers have discovered that for some unknown reason women are found to be five times more likely than men to develop posttraumatic stress disorder following exposure to serious trauma (Stein et al., 2000).

In the DSM-IV, posttraumatic stress disorder is classified as an anxiety disorder, and the diagnosis is made if the following three types of symptoms occur for a period lasting longer than one month:

1. *Flashbacks.* When a flashback occurs, the person relives the traumatic event in some way. These flashbacks can take the form of persistent thoughts or images of the traumatic scene, and they can even involve vivid hallucinations; the affected person seems at times to be re-experiencing the event—fighting the battle anew or fending off the attacker.

2. *Avoidance of stimuli associated with the trauma.* People with posttraumatic stress disorder actively try to avoid anything that reminds them of the event. This avoidance behaviour can lead to significant disruptions in normal social functioning, as the affected person turns away from friends and loved ones who in some way remind him or her of the trauma.

3. *Chronic arousal symptoms.* These symptoms can include sleep problems, irritability or outbursts of anger, and difficulties in concentrating.

Obviously, posttraumatic stress disorder is a disabling condition, not only for the individuals who are directly affected but also for family and friends (Sims & Sims, 1998). The cause of the disorder is clear—traumatic stress—but the reason why only some people who experience trauma develop posttraumatic stress disorder remains a mystery. There is evidence that the intensity of the trauma may be important. For example, soldiers who were in heavy combat were significantly more likely to develop posttraumatic stress disorder than those serving in noncombat roles (Goldberg et al., 1990). But, once again, this does not explain why the disorder remains relatively rare even among people who have experienced extreme trauma. If we look to the experience of firefighters, we note that it is certainly not the case that every firefighter

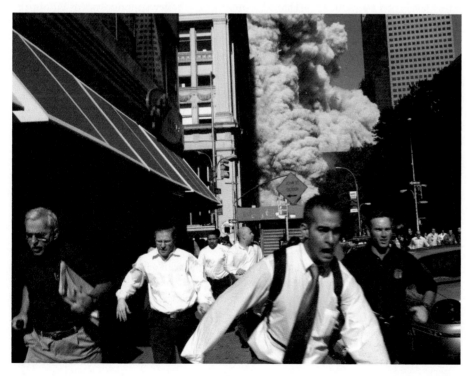

Witnessing or experiencing traumatic events, such as the bombing of the World Trade Center on September 11, 2001, can lead to disabling psychological conditions.

develops the disorder, despite their exposure to duty-related trauma (Corneil et al., 1999). As is the case for most psychological disorders, the likelihood that posttraumatic stress disorder will develop undoubtedly depends on a complex mix of biological and environmental factors (Craske, 1999; O'Shea, 2001).

Burnout   Stress does not need to be extreme to produce unpleasant psychological consequences. In the 1970s, the term "burnout" was introduced by psychologists to describe a syndrome that develops in certain people who are exposed to stressful situations that are demanding but not necessarily traumatic (Freudenberger, 1974; Maslach, 1976). Although the term **burnout** has become a household word, to psychologists it refers to "a state of physical, emotional, and mental exhaustion caused by long-term involvement in emotionally demanding situations" (Pines & Aronson, 1988). When burnout occurs, affected individuals essentially lose their spirit—they become emotionally drained, they feel used up, and they lose their sense of personal accomplishment (Maslach & Jackson, 1981).

As in the case of posttraumatic stress disorder, stress is a necessary component but is not a sufficient condition for producing burnout. Not everyone who has a demanding and stressful job becomes burned out. Burnout seems to occur only in idealistic individuals—people who have entered their careers with a high sense of motivation and commitment. In the words of psychologist Ayala Pines (1993), "You cannot burn out unless you were 'on fire' initially." Because burnout tends to occur only in highly motivated individuals, it can have a high cost for organizations as well as for the individual. People who suffer from burnout lose their edge on the job—they become disillusioned with their work, are frequently absent from the job, and usually are at increased risk for a host of physical problems (Maslach et al., 2001). Healthcare workers seem to be especially vulnerable.

Why does burnout occur? The underlying cause may well be related to a loss of meaning in life (Pines, 1993) or to a loss of control in the workplace (McKnight & Glass, 1995). People who are subject to burnout are usually those who think of their work as a kind of "calling." They use success on the job as a way of validating their existence. They identify so closely with their work that when failure happens, their entire lives lose meaning. This failure could be artistic, financial, or, in the case of healthcare workers, a learned helplessness in their attempts to aid needy patients. If the overall stress levels can be reduced, perhaps by providing a better support system within the work environment, burnout is less likely to occur (Maslach et al., 2001; Pines & Aronson, 1988).

burnout
A state of physical, emotional, and mental exhaustion created by long-term involvement in an emotionally demanding situation.

Test Yourself 16.2

Check your knowledge about reacting to stress by deciding whether each of the following statements is true or false. (You will find the answers in Appendix B.)

1. Lymphocytes are the primary weapons of the human immune system. *True or False?*
2. Much of the data linking cancer and stress have come from correlational studies; researchers are unable, therefore, to draw firm conclusions about cause and effect. *True or False?*
3. Stress is known to affect blood pressure, but no links have been established between stress and cholesterol levels. *True or False?*
4. Posttraumatic stress disorder is a common reaction to experiencing a traumatic event. *True or False?*
5. Burnout is more likely to occur in people who use success on the job as a way of giving life meaning. *True or False?*

Concept Summary

CONSEQUENCES OF STRESS

Physical

Stress Effects	Nature of the Effect
Immune response	Stressful events directly affect the immune response, lowering the number of disease-fighting *lymphocytes.* Some believe that stress also has an effect on more chronic illnesses, such as cancer.
Cardiovascular disease	Increased blood pressure from prolonged stress causes wear and tear on blood vessels, which can lead to cardiovascular disease.

Psychological

Stress Leads To	Nature of the Effect
Posttraumatic stress disorder	A serious psychological condition that can result from exposure to extreme stress. Classified as an anxiety disorder, it's characterized by flashbacks, avoidance of trauma-associated stimuli, and chronic arousal symptoms.
Burnout	A state of physical, emotional, and mental exhaustion caused by long-term involvement in emotionally demanding situations. It seems to occur in idealistic individuals who are highly motivated, perhaps due to a loss of control or a loss of meaning in life.

REDUCING AND COPING WITH STRESS: TECHNIQUES OF STRESS MANAGEMENT

Learning Goals

1. Learn how relaxation techniques can be used to reduce stress.
2. Understand the positive and negative effects of social support.
3. Be able to explain how stress can be managed through cognitive reappraisal of the stressful situation.

BECAUSE STRESS IS ASSOCIATED with so many physical and psychological problems, it is obviously in our best interest to develop techniques for reducing stress. Unfortunately, stressors are often outside of our direct control—you can't prevent the tornado that demolishes the neighbourhood trailer park or the death of a valued friend from accident or illness. But techniques are available for psychological management of stressors when they're present. **Coping** is a term that psychologists use to describe efforts to manage conditions of threat or demand that tax one's resources (Lazarus, 1993).

The variety of coping techniques reported by ordinary people is incredibly diverse. They can be organized into techniques that resolve the stress-inducing situation, deal with the negative emotions, or connect with other people (DeLongis & O'Brien, 1990). Specific examples include distracting oneself from the problem, confronting (or actively avoiding) the person responsible for the stress, improving relevant abilities, and turning to religion. Below, we consider three others in detail: (1) using relaxation techniques, (2) exploiting social support networks, and (3) reappraising the environment in a less threatening way.

coping
Efforts to manage or master conditions of threat or demand that tax one's resources.

Relaxation Techniques

By definition, the stress response is incompatible with relaxation. You cannot be prepared to fight or flee if your body is calm, relaxed, and free from arousal-inducing stress hormones. Studies have shown that high-stress individuals can reduce the physically threatening components of the stress reaction—such as high blood pressure—by simply practising a regimen of relaxation techniques. You may remember that in Chapter 15 we discussed how relaxation can be used effectively in the treatment of anxiety disorders; similar relaxation techniques have proven effective in reducing long-term stress reactions (Stoyva & Carlson, 1993).

651

Several types of relaxation procedures are available to help manage stress. In *progressive muscle relaxation,* you're taught to concentrate on specific muscle groups in the body, to note whether there is any tension, and then to try to relax those specific groups (Jacobson, 1938). Often in progressive relaxation, you learn to address muscle groups in sequence. For example, you might begin with the muscle groups in the neck, move to the shoulders, and so on, first tensing and then relaxing each group. In this way, you learn to pay attention to how muscles in your body feel when tense or relaxed. Progressive relaxation has been used successfully to treat a variety of stress-related health problems, everything from tension headaches (Myers et al., 1998) to posttraumatic stress disorder (Frueh et al., 1997). In a somewhat different technique, called *autogenic relaxation,* you're taught to focus on directing blood flow toward tense muscle groups, "warming" and relaxing each group (Linden, 1990); once again, autogenic relaxation has proven beneficial in treating stress-related conditions (Friedlander et al., 1997).

Relaxation techniques such as these are sometimes accompanied by *meditation* training. We discussed some of the benefits of meditation in Chapter 5. Meditation essentially involves learning how to relax, using techniques similar to progressive muscle relaxation. But you're also taught some time-tested mental exercises, such as repeating a string of words or sounds over and over again in your head. The mental repetition focuses awareness and helps prevent potentially distracting or stress-producing thoughts from interfering with the relaxation response. (For instance, if you're concentrating on repeating the phrase "I'm at one with the universe," you cannot simultaneously be worrying about whether the relaxation technique is working.) Daily meditation sessions clearly help people deal with stress-related arousal (MacLean et al., 1997) and are likely to prevent the later development of health problems such as high blood pressure (Barnes et al., 2001).

There are a variety of ways to reduce and cope with stress, including exercise, meditation, social support, and biofeedback.

Biofeedback The goal of relaxation training is to counteract components of the stress response, such as blood pressure, heart rate, and muscle tension. For example, if stress-related headaches are caused by tension in the muscles of the head and scalp, then people should be able to reduce or eliminate the pain by relaxing these specific muscle groups. Such a feat is made possible by giving people feedback—*biofeedback*—about the effectiveness of their relaxation efforts. With biofeedback, monitoring equipment provides a continuous reading of your physiological state: In the case of tension headaches, the feedback would indicate the tension levels in the muscles of the head; for blood pressure or heart rate, you would be able to read your blood pressure and heart rate directly from appropriate monitoring equipment.

To say the least, biofeedback works. When people are given information about how well their relaxation efforts are succeeding, compared with control subjects who are given no feedback, it's clearly easier to control the relevant physiological response (Blanchard, 1992). But researchers are still debating exactly why biofeedback produces its beneficial effects. Yes, it may well be that the benefits help the affected person gain control over countermeasures to reduce the physiological problem. Another possibility is that it may simply be the *feeling* of control that leads to reductions in the stress response.

For instance, in one study on tension headaches, three groups of subjects were given a feedback signal that they were led to believe indicated a successful lowering of muscle tension in their foreheads. Actually, unknown to the subjects, the signal had three different meanings: In one group, it appeared only when subjects successfully *increased* the amount of tension in their foreheads; in a second group, the signal appeared whenever the amount of tension decreased; in a third group, it appeared when tension levels remained the same. Remarkably, despite the misleading feedback in two of the groups, everyone reported headache improvement (see Figure 16.4). Apparently, feeling that you have some control over your body can be sufficient to lower stress-induced pain (Andrasik & Holroyd, 1980). This finding does not mean that biofeedback is an ineffective way to treat stress. Whether you will experience a stress response depends on a cognitive appraisal of your resources. If you feel you have the ability to control the threat or demand, even if that control is illusory, you're less likely to experience stress.

biofeedback
Specific physiological feedback that people are given about the effectiveness of their relaxation efforts.

FIGURE 16.4
Biofeedback, Perceived Control, and Stress

In the study by Andrasik and Holroyd (1980), subjects in three groups were led to believe that they could lower the amount of muscle tension in their foreheads through biofeedback. Actually, the subjects learned to increase, decrease, or keep the tension levels the same. Yet all three groups showed significant improvement in headache symptoms, compared to subjects who received no biofeedback. (Data from Andrasik & Holroyd, 1980.)

social support

The resources that individuals receive from other people or groups, often in the form of comfort, caring, or help.

Critical Thinking

Do you think it's possible that simply believing that you have social support is more important than actually receiving it?

Social Support

Although it may seem like a cliché, having a good friend or loved one to lean on during a time of stress really does matter. Psychologists use the term **social support** to refer to the resources we receive from other people or groups, often in the form of comfort, caring, or help. A great deal of research has backed up the claim that people blessed with good social support have better psychological and physical health (Cohen & Wills, 1985). For example, Wolfgang Linden, a health psychologist at the University of British Columbia, has investigated the effect of social support on cardiovascular patients. He showed that patients with well-established social support systems have lower rates of morbidity and mortality than those who have less social support (Linden et al., 1996). Quick recovery from real world stressors such as surgery is also linked to good social support (Schroeder et al., 1997). Several studies on depression have established that individuals with better social support are less likely to get depressed and recover more quickly (McLeod et al., 1992).

The association between social support and lower stress has several possible explanations (Sarason et al., 1994). Social contacts should help people maintain a healthy lifestyle. Friends and family push you out the door for your morning jog, force you to take your medications, and encourage you to visit the doctor regularly. Family and friends also bolster your confidence in times of stress, so you're more likely to feel that you have the necessary resources to cope with the demand. In a time of loss, such as immediately after the death of a spouse, social support lowers the likelihood that a grieving person will engage in unhealthy behaviours, such as drinking (Jennison, 1992). (For a discussion of how pets can act as a form of positive social support see the Practical Solutions box.)

But the reverse causal argument is just as convincing. People who are healthier and experience less stress may have more social support. Who wants to hang out with someone who is always sick and stressed out? Fortunately, there is now some experimental evidence to support the claim that social support helps reduce stress. Bill Gerin and his associates have conducted laboratory studies using blood pressure monitors to measure level of stress. They set up a stressful debate between two experimental participants. Debaters were randomly assigned to have a supporter in the room or not to have one. Results showed that debaters with supporters—even if they didn't participate in the debate—showed lower stress levels (Gerin et al., 1992). Other experimental work has shown that simply having someone to talk things over with can help you cope with stress. James Pennebaker (1990) had college students talk about upsetting events in their lives (everything from a divorce in the family to fears about the future). Compared to a control group, those students given the opportunity to talk it over (or just write about it) showed improved immune functioning and were less likely to visit the college health centre over the next several months. Pennebaker has found similar benefits for people who lived through natural disasters (such as earthquakes) or were part of the Holocaust. Opening up, talking about things, and confiding in others really seemed to help these people cope (Pennebaker et al., 2001). Given that research, it seems no surprise that a positive relationship with one's parents can improve the chances of surviving a stressful episode without depression (Mongrain et al., 1998).

On the other hand, psychologists recognize that social support can have a negative side as well. For example, if you've come to depend on another for support and that support is no longer delivered, your ability to cope can be compromised. Social support can also reduce self-reliance in some people, which may produce psychological distress and impair their ability to cope. It's been found that whether people respond favourably to social support and the receipt of aid, or consider it to be a meddling nuisance, depends to some extent on how much control they feel they have over their own actions and the outcomes of their actions (Hobfoll et al., 1991).

Finally, research at York University has shown how the nature of support provided is linked to the personality of the supporter. Using the interpersonal circle (see Chapter 12), Krista Trobst examined how each of the eight personalities provided a different form of

Practical Solutions

PET SUPPORT

Having a loved one or a good friend to talk to about your problems makes a difference, and that friend doesn't even need to be human. The companionship of pets—dogs, cats, even birds—has repeatedly been found to be an effective form of social support. Heart attack victims who own pets, for example, are more likely to survive the first year after the attack than are those who do not own pets. Correlational studies among the elderly have found that pet ownership is inversely related to the severity of psychological problems: People who are attached to their pets are less likely to show the symptoms of depression (Garrity et al., 1989). Ownership of a dog, in particular, is an excellent predictor of whether or not an elderly person will feel the need to visit a doctor (Siegel, 1990).

There's some evidence to suggest that having a pet may even be a more effective buffer against stress than having a human companion. In an experiment conducted by Karen Allen and her colleagues (1991), women dog owners agreed to have several physiological reactions monitored while they tried to solve relatively difficult math problems. Prior to starting the task, the women were randomly divided into three groups. In one group, the women were allowed to have their dog with them in the room while completing the math task. In a second group, no dogs were allowed but each woman was allowed the presence of a close human friend. In the third group, no social support was present during the testing.

A variety of physiological reactions were measured, including heart rate and blood pressure. Not surprisingly, solving difficult math problems led directly to stress-related arousal—heart rate increased, as did blood pressure. But the amount of reactivity depended on the group: The women who were allowed to have their dog with them showed the lowest arousal effects compared to the women in the other two groups (see Figure 16.5). The presence of the pet

Pets are effective buffers against stress for many people.

apparently acted as an effective buffer against stress. The surprise finding of the study was that having a close human friend sit nearby while solving the math problems actually led to the highest relative stress reaction.

Does this mean that pets are more therapeutic than friends or loved ones? For some people in some situations, the answer may well be "Yes." Allen and her colleagues argued that pets are often effective buffers against stress because they are essentially nonevaluative. Pets don't make value judgments about their caretakers. Your dog or cat doesn't care one bit about how well you're doing on some math task, but your close human friend might. A friend's expectations can place added pressure on you as you perform an already stressful task. A woman who participated in the study by Allen and colleagues put it this way: "Pets never withhold their love, they never get angry and leave, and they never go out looking for new owners." Another woman offered the following: "Whereas husbands may come and go, and children may grow up and leave home, a 'dog is forever.'" The opinions of these women may not be shared by everyone, nor do you need to hold these strong views to appreciate the value of pet companionship. The data simply indicate that pets can be an important part of your social network and as such can help you cope with stress.

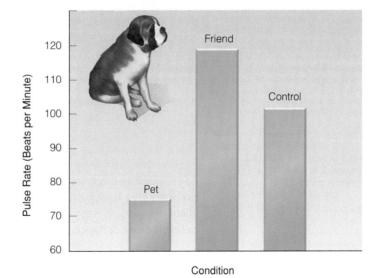

FIGURE 16.5

Pets as Stress Moderators

In one study, a pet's presence during a stressful task significantly lowered the stress reaction (measured here in terms of pulse rate) compared to when a friend was present or to a control condition in which neither a friend nor a pet was present. (Data from Allen et al., 1991.)

support. She showed, for example, that dominant people tended to be highly directive in their support attempts, whereas nurturant individuals tended to give warm and accepting support (e.g., Trobst, 2000). As with Hobfall's conclusions, which type of support is more beneficial will depend on both the nature of the help and how it is received.

Reappraising the Situation

When thinking about how to cope with stress, it's important to remember that the stress reaction is essentially psychological. In most instances, it is not the sudden life event or the daily hassle that leads us to experience stress—it's our *interpretation* of the event that really matters (Lazarus, 1991). Even the death of a spouse or the occurrence of a natural disaster, cruel as it may seem, will create significant stress only if the event is appraised in a negative way (Davis & Nolen-Hoeksema, 2001). Imagine that your spouse was suffering from an incurable disease, one that produced extreme and persistent pain. Under these conditions, death could be seen as a kind of blessing.

Remember, too, that many instances of stress are caused by the little things, the daily hassles of life (DeLongis et al., 1988). Getting stuck in traffic or in the wrong line at the store makes us feel stressed only because we have a tendency to "catastrophize" the situation: "This is absolutely awful ... I can't stand waiting here any longer ... I'm going to get home late and my family will be mad." It's not the delay that creates the stress; it's the things we tell ourselves about the delay that cause the problems. As a result, many psychologists feel that stress can be managed effectively through logical reanalysis and positive reappraisal. If you can interpret the hassle in a more rational and adaptive manner, you can reduce or eliminate the stress reaction (Preece & DeLongis, in press).

Stress management techniques that rely on cognitive reappraisal take a variety of forms. For instance, you can be taught to focus on certain aspects of the situation that distract you from catastrophizing. If you're stuck in the slow checkout line at the supermarket, rather than concentrating on why you "must" get home on time, instead, pick up one of the supermarket tabloids and catch up on the latest celebrity gossip. It may be the only time when you have a good excuse to do so. Alternatively, try using your past experiences to reappraise the consequences: "Let's see, this certainly is not the first time I've been stuck in a checkout line, and it's never led to any tragedies." Another approach would be to analyze the situation logically and derive alternatives for the future: "Every time I come to the store at 5:30, right after work, I get stuck in a line— maybe if I wait and go after dinner, there will be less of a wait."

Some stress management programs recommend that clients keep daily records of the specific situations that have led to stress, as well as the specific symptoms and thoughts that arose (an example is shown in Figure 16.6). The value of a stress record is that it allows the client to recognize any unrealistic thoughts or conclusions on the spot because they need to be written in the record. With time, clients get a pretty good idea of the situations that lead to the highest stress, and they gain insight into the thought processes that underlie their reaction. As each unrealistic thought is recognized, the client can work at reappraising the situation and confronting any negative attitudes or beliefs (Barlow & Rapee, 1991).

Critical Thinking

What's the link between these stress management programs and the techniques used in cognitive therapies, such as rational-emotive therapy?

Test Yourself 16.3

Check your knowledge about stress management techniques by answering the following questions. (You will find the answers in Appendix B.)

1. Relaxation techniques, such as meditation or progressive muscle relaxation, appear to work because:

Sample Daily Stress Record

Week of _____

	8	Extreme stress
	7	
	6	Great stress
	5	
	4	Moderate stress
	3	
	2	Mild stress
	1	
	0	No stress

| | (1) | (2) | (3) | (4) | (5) | (6) |
Date	Starting time	Ending time	Highest stress (0-8)	Triggers	Symptoms	Thoughts
1–5	10:00 am	11:00 am	7	Sales meeting	Sweating, headache	My figures are bad.
1–7	5:15 pm	5:35 pm	6	Traffic jam	Tension, impatience	I'll never get home.
1–8	12:30 pm	12:32 pm	3	Lost keys	Tension	I can't find my keys.
1–9	3:30 pm	4:30 pm	4	Waiting for guests	Sweating, nausea	Are they lost?

FIGURE 16.6

A Daily Stress Record

Stress management programs often recommend that clients keep daily records of situations that lead to stress, along with the specific symptoms and thoughts that arise. (From Barlow & Rapee, 1991.)

    a. They promote a sense of "connectedness" with the therapist.

    b. They lead to positive cognitive reappraisals.

    c. The stress response is incompatible with relaxation.

    d. They cause you to open up and express feelings.

2. Biofeedback may be effective for managing stress because:

    a. It gives you a feeling of control.

    b. It leads to muscle relaxation.

    c. It trains neurons to fire in sequence.

    d. It works well with meditation.

3. Which of the following statements about the influence of social support on stress is false?

    a. Social contacts help you maintain a healthy lifestyle.

    b. Social support increases the chances that you'll open up and express feelings.

    c. Social support can reduce the chances of a second heart attack.

    d. Social support makes it easier to cope if the support is no longer delivered.

4. Bernie no longer fumes when he gets stuck in traffic because he's stopped catastrophizing about the consequences. Which of the following stress management techniques is Bernie probably using?

    a. Cognitive reappraisal

    b. Autogenic relaxation

    c. Progressive muscle relaxation

    d. Cathartic exploration

LIVING A HEALTHY LIFESTYLE

Learning Goals

1. Be able to explain the physical and psychological benefits of aerobic exercise.
2. Understand the value of proper nutrition.
3. Learn the consequences of tobacco use, and explain why it's difficult to quit smoking.
4. Learn the consequences of drinking alcohol, and explain how intoxication leads us to engage in other risky health-related behaviours.
5. Distinguish among the different types of prevention programs and learn how we can reduce unsafe sexual practices.

ONE OF THE CHALLENGES of the health psychology movement is to devise a comprehensive and workable framework for health promotion (Winett, 1995). In a review of the literature, researchers Nancy Adler and Karen Matthews (1994) summed up the goals of the health psychologist by asking three essential questions: "First, who becomes sick and why? Second, among the sick, who recovers and why? Third, how can illness be prevented or recovery be facilitated?" Such questions are appropriately addressed to a psychologist because, as we've seen, a close and intimate connection exists between mind, behaviour, and health.

In offering prescriptions for healthy lifestyles, psychologists recognize that not all risk factors can be controlled. Men, for example, have a much greater risk of developing heart disease than women, and the elderly are at a greater risk of developing a whole host of health-related problems. Obviously, people have no control over heredity and they can't help the fact that they grow old. Even a sex change won't help. But as you are no doubt aware, there are lifestyle choices that can make a difference.

Get Fit: The Value of Aerobic Exercise

Exercise is an excellent example of an activity that can have a substantial positive impact on physical and psychological health, especially if the exercise is sustained and aerobic. **Aerobic exercise** consists of high-intensity activities that increase both heart rate and oxygen consumption, such as fast walking, running, dancing, rowing, swimming, and so on. As you probably know, regular aerobic exercise improves cardiovascular fitness over the long term and, on average, increases the chances that you will live longer (Blair et al., 1989; Villeneuve et al., 1998).

Psychologically, regular exercise improves mood and makes people more resistant to the effects of stressors (Stoyva & Carlson, 1993). For example, in one study (McCann & Holmes, 1984), volunteer female college students who were suffering from mild depression were asked to (1) engage in a regular program of aerobic exercise, (2) learn relaxation techniques, or (3) do nothing. After 10 weeks, the aerobic exercise group showed the largest improvement in mood. More recent work indicates that 30 minutes of moderate exercise daily may be sufficient to increase mood (Hansen et al., 2001). In another experimental study looking at stress resistance, men were randomly assigned to exercise conditions that involved either aerobic activity or nonaerobic strength-and-flexibility training. After 12 weeks of training, the men in the aerobic group showed lower blood pressure and heart rate when they were exposed to situations involving mental stress (Blumenthal et al., 1988).

But researchers have yet to understand fully how or why exercise improves psychological health and functioning. Over the short term, vigorous exercise increases the amount of oxygen that reaches the brain, which undoubtedly improves cognitive functioning, and sustained exercise may alter mood-inducing neurotransmitters in the brain (Sheridan & Radmacher, 1992). It is also clearly the case that aerobic exercise, since it improves cardiovascular health, will lessen the physiological effects of the stress reaction. But there may also be placebo-like effects involved: People who choose to exercise

aerobic exercise
High-intensity activities, such as running and swimming, that increase both heart rate and oxygen consumption.

Regular exercise is an important ingredient in living a healthy lifestyle.

regularly are convinced that they're going to get better, and they subsequently rate themselves as healthier psychologically than they may in fact be (Pierce et al., 1993).

Despite the benefits of exercise, only 56% of men and 58% of women report that they exercise regularly (Statistics Canada, 1999). Obviously, the more people who exercise, the healthier our population will be. Researchers are investigating why people do or do not exercise. Lise Gauvin of Concordia University discovered that regular exercisers differed from individuals with less active lifestyles in a number of ways (Gauvin, 1990). For example, regular exercisers stated that the aspect they enjoyed most about participation was the task itself (e.g., running or weight lifting). In addition, the regular exercisers did not need to do any planning to ensure that they regularly attended their workouts. That is, exercise was part of their routine. In fact, the regular exercisers felt that something was missing in their life when they did not exercise.

In an effort to increase exercise participation, James Olson of the University of Western Ontario and Mark Zanna of the University of Waterloo developed a number of recommendations for motivating people to begin exercising (Olson & Zanna, 1987). Olson and Zanna suggest the following:

1. Specific exercises should be promoted (e.g., jogging, swimming, or walking) and specific personal gains from exercise should be identified (e.g., you'll feel and look better).

2. Negative personal consequences of not exercising should be identified as well as how those consequences can be avoided (e.g., to reduce your risk of cardiovascular disease, you should walk for 15 minutes a day).

3. Perceived social pressure for exercising can be created (communicate that respected others value and engage in regular exercise).

4. Increase perceived control over exercising (demonstrate how exercising regularly is compatible with lifestyle).

5. Provide basic, detailed information about exercising (e.g., how to stretch properly or how much it costs to join exercise facilities).

Eat Right: The Value of Proper Nutrition

In Chapter 11 we dealt with the adaptive problem of how to motivate eating behaviour. Obviously, to maintain proper functioning of body and mind, people need to consume

Critical Thinking

Do you think there's a connection between age and the chances of living a healthy lifestyle? If so, why do you think this is the case?

the necessary amounts of food. In our earlier discussion of eating, we didn't pay too much attention to the quality of the food that people consume; instead, our concern was mainly with the internal and external factors that underlie the motivation to eat. But proper nutrition is vitally important to maintaining a healthy body and mind, and health psychologists are engaged in a vigorous campaign to improve people's dietary habits.

The dietary habits of most North Americans leave much to be desired. Our diet tends to be too high in calories, fat, cholesterol, sugar, protein, and salt (Nolan et al., 1995; Sheridan & Radmacher, 1992). High-fat diets have been linked to heart disease, stroke, and several kinds of cancer, as well as to obesity. Diets that are high in cholesterol contribute to heart disease because the cholesterol can lodge in the walls of arteries, which can lead to hardening and narrowing, which restricts blood flow. Of course, not everyone who maintains a diet high in fat or cholesterol will develop these problems (because genetic predispositions are also a factor), but there's no question that many people eat themselves into an early grave.

Given the overwhelming amount of evidence linking diet to health, why don't people eat better? For many people, it's not the amount of food they eat but their choice of food that creates the problems. Consider the following: A baked potato has 0.5% of its calories as fat; when that same potato is French-fried, it has 42% of its calories as fat (Winikoff, 1983). Everyone has a handy list of reasons for choosing to stop for fast food, including the fact that it tastes good. Few people admit that their choices are influenced by television commercials that emphasize foods low in nutrition (e.g., beer and candy), yet the media undoubtedly influence our choices (Ostbye et al., 1993). From a nutritional standpoint, fast foods tend to come up short because they're packed with fat and sodium. The best advice is to eat a variety of foods and to avoid foods with too much fat, cholesterol, sugar, and sodium. This is not a new message for you, we are sure, but remember: You're now much more sophisticated about the psychological factors that influence your choice of foods (see Chapter 11). So think before you eat—it might make a difference.

Don't Smoke: Tobacco and Health

Virtually everyone knows that smoking or the oral ingestion (chewing) of tobacco is bad for your health. There is no shortage of correlational and experimental studies available to document this fact. Few researchers question, for example, that smoking contributes annually to tens of thousands of deaths in Canada alone from associated heart disease, cancer, stroke, and emphysema (Ellison et al., 1999). And it's not just the smokers who are affected—the babies of women who smoke during pregnancy tend to have lower birth weights and are at increased risk for birth defects; even people who are simply exposed to smoke secondhand may suffer from subsequent health problems (Byrd, 1992). So why, given that it is so damaging to their health, do people smoke?

First, despite what you might have heard on television (especially from tobacco company executives), smoking is recognized to be *addictive* by the vast majority of mainstream researchers in the health-related sciences (Marlatt & VandenBos, 1997). Many people who smoke regularly become dependent on their daily dosage, and when they try to quit, they suffer physical and psychological withdrawal symptoms. The DSM-IV lists criteria for a diagnosis of "nicotine withdrawal" that include insomnia, irritability, difficulty concentrating, and increased appetite or weight gain. The symptoms of withdrawal can be severe enough to cause a significant disruption in normal everyday functioning (Piasecki et al., 1998). This conclusion, of course, comes as no surprise to anyone who has ever tried to quit smoking after prolonged use.

The reinforcing effects of cigarette smoking can be explained by appealing to chemical reactions in the brain and to factors in the culture at large. Within the brain, it takes only seconds for nicotine—the active agent in cigarette smoke—to stimulate the central nervous system, elevating heart rate, blood pressure, and mood. Many smokers report that cigarettes not only improve mood but help alleviate anxiety and

University of British Columbia researcher Rick Pollay has studied the effects of tobacco advertising. He is shown here with examples of cigarette advertising, including some that attempt to associate smoking with healthy, vigorous lifestyles.

stress. At the same time, tobacco companies launch advertising campaigns designed to make smoking appear desirable. Tobacco use is identified with role models—often thin, vigorous, and healthy people on horseback or frolicking on the beach—or is associated with independence and nonconformity. Unfortunately, these types of advertising campaigns are often particularly effective for those in adolescence, which is the time when most smokers begin their habit.

You've probably heard the saying that the best way to stop smoking is never to start. It's undoubtedly true, because once started, tobacco use is a difficult habit to break. The psychological and physical withdrawal symptoms associated with tobacco use make quitting extraordinarily difficult.

In an effort to understand what strategies are most effective in helping people quit smoking, Canadian researchers, including Martin Taylor of McMaster University and Mark Zanna of the University of Waterloo, were involved in the most extensive smoking cessation study ever undertaken in North America (e.g., COMMIT Research Group, 1995a, 1995b; Taylor et al., 1998). This study, the Community Intervention Trial for Smoking Cessation (COMMIT), took place in 11 pairs of matched communities (10 in the United States and one in Canada) and incorporated a variety of smoking cessation techniques that were developed based on psychological principles. For example, smokers were recruited and became part of the "Smokers' Network"; thus social support was provided. In addition, participants took part in a "Quit and Win" contest whereby contest participants who remained smoke-free for 30 days were eligible to win a substantial prize. The smoking cessation interventions took place for four years, from 1989 to 1993, but the results of these interventions were somewhat disappointing. The results revealed that light to moderate smokers in the intervention communities were more likely to quit than those in the comparison communities. The number of heavy smokers in the intervention communities who quit smoking was not significantly different from the number who quit in the comparison communities. On a more positive note, smokers in all groups came to have stronger beliefs about smoking as a serious public health problem.

Changes in attitudes toward smoking and behaviour are occurring throughout North America. There has been a significant drop in the percentage of people who smoke in the United States and Canada, especially over the past two or three decades. Currently, approximately 25% of Canadians over the age of 12 smoke. (Unfortunately, the rate of smoking among First Nations people is about double the overall rate in the

Canadian population as a whole.) Large numbers of people are choosing never to start smoking and more and more people are quitting—although often only after many relapses. In the words of Mark Twain: "To cease smoking is the easiest thing I ever did; I ought to know because I've done it a thousand times."

Problem Drinking: One Risky Behaviour Leads to Another

Drinking is commonplace in North America. Just over half of Canadians drink alcohol at least once per month (Health Canada, 1999). Although rates of drinking for adults have been decreasing over the last couple of decades, there are disturbing indications that the proportion of adolescents who drink to excess is increasing (Canadian Centre on Substance Abuse, 1999). The act of "binge" drinking (i.e., consuming five or more drinks on one occasion) is also more frequent in adolescents than in adults. Psychologists Roger Tonkin at the McCreary Centre Society and David Cox of Simon Fraser University surveyed more than 25 000 adolescents and found that more than 40% of the 12- to 18-year-olds who reported ever having a drink had engaged in a binge at least once during the past month (McCreary Centre Society, 1999). Canadian First Nations adolescents are reported as having a risk that is as much as six times greater than other Canadians for developing alcohol problems (Canadian Centre on Substance Abuse, 1999).

Canadian researchers have also been at the forefront of clarifying the link between personality and drinking behaviour. These researchers include Robert Pihl at McGill, Sherry Stewart at Dalhousie, Patricia Conrod at the University of British Columbia, and Jordan Peterson at the University of Toronto. Together, they have clarified links between personality traits and vulnerability to, as well as choice of, substance abuse (e.g., Conrod et al., 2000). Even for the same substance abuse (e.g., alcohol), there are different motives for use that can be traced to underlying biological vulnerabilities (Stewart et al., 1995).

Excessive use of alcohol can have adverse effects on almost every system of the body. For example, chronic alcohol abuse causes liver disease and damage to the stomach, pancreas, and intestines. Moreover, chronic drinking causes high blood pressure, leads to depression of the immune system, and is associated with coronary artery disease and cancer of the throat, larynx, mouth, esophagus, and liver (Alberta Alcohol and Drug Abuse Commission, 1999).

Excessive use of alcohol can have adverse effects on almost every system of the body. The act of "binge" drinking—that is, consuming five or more drinks on one occasion—is more frequent in adolescents than in adults.

Alcohol is a depressant drug and, like other depressant drugs (e.g., tranquillizers and painkillers), it slows down the nervous system, which may cause drowsiness, induce sleep, or relieve pain. Even the initial apparent stimulant effect actually results from depression of various centres in the brain. At higher doses—even below a blood-alcohol concentration of 0.08%, the legal limit for driving a car in Canada—thinking and judgment are impaired. Thus, engaging in the health-compromising behaviour of drinking may lead one to engage in other risky health-related behaviours.

Psychologists Tara MacDonald of Queen's University and Mark Zanna and Geoffrey Fong of the University of Waterloo have been studying the effects of alcohol on our attitudes and intentions to engage in risky health-related behaviours such as drinking and driving and having unprotected sexual intercourse (MacDonald et al., 1995, 1996, 1998). For example, in a series of experimental laboratory and field studies, MacDonald, Zanna, and Fong discovered that, compared to sober participants, intoxicated participants report a decrease in their intentions to use condoms, even among those participants who claimed to practise safe sex on a regular basis. These researchers believe that the phenomenon of **alcohol myopia** explains their findings. According to this theory, "alcohol causes social behaviours to become more extreme, and the direction of the behaviour will be determined by whatever cues are most salient in the environment" (MacDonald et al., 1998, p. 410). In the case of engaging in unprotected sex, intoxicated individuals likely do not have the requisite cognitive capacity to attend to both the costs and the benefits of their actions. Because the salient cue available to people in a situation described as "a possible sexual encounter" is likely sexual satisfaction and not the threat of pregnancy or sexually transmitted diseases, intoxicated individuals are more apt than sober individuals to participate in unprotected sexual intercourse.

alcohol myopia
A state induced by alcohol intoxication that results in more extreme social behaviours.

Avoid Risky Behaviour: Protect Yourself from Disease

Choosing a healthy lifestyle requires having the right kind of information about how to prevent health-impairing habits. Health psychologists often distinguish between three main types of prevention programs (Winett, 1995):

1. *Primary prevention* is designed to educate the public as a whole in ways to reduce or eliminate a problem before it starts. Teaching children about the potential hazards of smoking or drug use is an example of primary prevention.

2. *Secondary prevention* involves the early identification of risk factors in specific population groups, such as checking for HIV infection in intravenous drug users or looking for early signs of disease through screening.

3. *Tertiary prevention* seeks to handle and contain an illness or habit once it has been acquired.

All three types of prevention programs are needed, but stopping an illness or habit before it starts—primary prevention—obviously has greater long-term significance.

Unsafe Sexual Behaviours   Engaging in unsafe sexual behaviours can lead to serious health consequences, including the contraction of sexually transmitted diseases (STDs) such as human immunodeficiency virus (HIV), the virus that causes acquired immune deficiency syndrome (AIDS). HIV does its damage by attacking cells in the immune system, which leaves the body unable to fight off opportunistic infections that would otherwise be controlled. The disease **AIDS** is diagnosed in the latter stages of HIV infection, when the immune system has been sufficiently compromised. Living in the age of AIDS dramatically underscores the need for primary prevention programs.

Although AIDS and HIV infection are medical conditions, psychologists have two important roles to play. First, the only effective way to control widespread HIV transmission is to prevent risk-taking behaviour—in this case, preventing sexual intercourse

AIDS
Acquired immune deficiency syndrome, a disease that gradually weakens and disables the immune system.

Primary prevention is crucial in battling the AIDS epidemic.

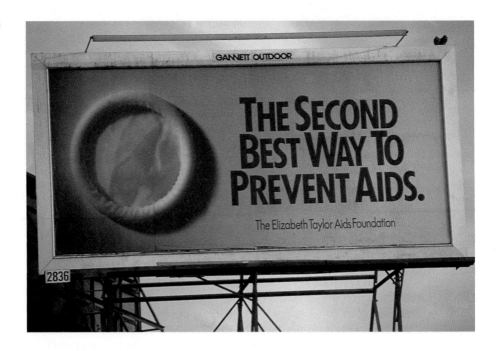

without the use of latex condoms. Second, psychologists also play a therapeutic role with those who have contracted STDs.

To control transmission of STDs, psychologists are attempting to understand why people engage in unsafe sexual behaviours and how best to persuade people not to engage in these behaviours. Certainly a large number of our youth are practising unsafe sex. Results from the 1994/1995 National Public Health Survey indicate that over 50% of female and approximately 35% of male sexually active 15- to 24-year-olds (excluding those with only one sexual partner and those who were married, in a common-law relationship, divorced, or widowed) have had sex without a condom in the past year. These figures are estimated to be even higher for First Nations people (Jolly et al., 1995).

Why do people not use condoms when engaging in sexual intercourse? Researchers attempted to gain insight into this question by conducting a national survey of 5500 first-year Canadian college and university students between the ages of 16 and 24 years (MacDonald et al., 1990). The students reported not using condoms for a number of reasons: They were embarrassed about purchasing them; they had difficulty discussing condom use with their partner; they believed that condoms interfered with sexual pleasure; they already used oral contraceptives. The students also were found not to use condoms because they lacked knowledge about HIV and STDs. The reasons for participating in unsafe sexual behaviours provided by the students in this study are similar to those provided by surveys of the general population (Boroditsky et al., 1996).

In an effort to understand the best method of curtailing the unsafe sexual practices of youth, health psychologist Geoffrey Fong of the University of Waterloo and his colleagues examined which interventions are most effective (Jemmott et al., 1998, 1999). In one study, grade 6 and grade 7 students took part in an 8-hour intervention as part of a Saturday program. The adolescents were randomly assigned to one of three different interventions: an abstinence HIV intervention, which acknowledged that condoms can reduce risks but emphasized abstinence to eliminate the risk of pregnancy and STDs, including HIV; a safer-sex HIV intervention, which indicated that abstinence is the best choice but that condom use is important to reduce the risk of pregnancy and STDs, including HIV, if participants were to have sex; or a health promotion intervention, which focused on behaviours associated with risk of cardiovascular disease, stroke, and certain cancers rather than on AIDS or sexual behaviour. Those adolescents assigned to the health promotion intervention served as the control group. The results of this study suggest that both abstinence and safer-sex interventions can reduce unsafe sexual behaviours, but safer-sex interventions may have longer-lasting effects. Not surprisingly, safer-sex interventions may be especially effective with sexually experienced adolescents.

Taking a somewhat different approach, psychologist William Fisher of the University of Western Ontario researched the psychological determinants of human sexual and reproductive health behaviour. With Jeffrey Fisher of the University of Connecticut he proposed the Information-Motivation-Behavioral Skills (IMB) model (Fisher & Fisher, 1992, 1993, 1998). According to this model, there are three fundamental determinants to successfully achieving safe-sex practices. First, those who are sexually active must be *knowledgeable* about sexual and reproductive health information. If you do not know that STDs exist, or if you do not know what constitutes safe sex, practising safe sex is unlikely. Second, in addition to being knowledgeable about safe-sex practices, you must be *motivated* to act on this information. Finally, you must possess the *behavioural skills* for acting on this information effectively. For example, you must be able to negotiate with your partner to ensure cooperation in safe-sex practices.

The other key role being played by psychologists in the AIDS epidemic is a therapeutic one. Once infected, people with HIV are subjected to an overwhelming amount of stress. Not only are these individuals faced with the prospect of an early death, but they must face the stigma that often accompanies the disease. Psychologists are actively involved in the establishment of treatment programs that can help AIDS patients cope with their disease (Chesney, 1993; Feldman & Christensen, 1997).

Test Yourself 16.4

Check your knowledge about living a healthy lifestyle by deciding whether each of the following statements is true or false. (You will find the answers in Appendix B.)

1. Aerobic exercise improves cardiovascular health and general mood, but produces few changes in the physiological effects of the stress reaction. *True or False?*
2. For many people, it's not the amount of food they eat but their choice of food that creates health problems. *True or False?*
3. Smoking is recognized to be addictive by the vast majority of mainstream researchers in the health-related sciences. *True or False?*
4. Teaching children about the hazards of smoking or drugs would be classified as an example of secondary prevention. *True or False?*

Solving the Adaptive Problems

The close relationship that exists between thoughts and emotions and the physical reactions of the body means that understanding and promoting physical health requires some attention to psychological factors. Health psychology (also called *behavioural medicine*) seeks to understand the medical consequences of the interaction between body and mind. Health psychologists are interested in the psychological and environmental factors—everything from personality characteristics to the work environment—that both produce illness and affect the likelihood of recovery.

First, what is stress, and how is it experienced? Stress has historically been a somewhat tough concept to define. It can be conceived of as a stimulus, as a response, or as a process through which external events are interpreted as threatening or demanding. We chose to define stress as the physical and psychological reaction that is shown in response to demanding situations. The stress response involves an extended reaction that occurs in phases. According to the general adaptation syndrome proposed by Hans Selye, the body initially reacts to threat with a highly adaptive fight-or-flight response (although there may be gender differences in the behavioural response); if the threat continues, the body goes through resistance and exhaustion phases that make it vulnerable to disease.

Our reactions are critically influenced by the way we perceive or appraise a situation. To experience stress, it's necessary to both perceive a threat and feel that you lack the necessary resources to deal with it effectively. This means that identical environmental events can lead to very

different stress reactions, depending on how the situation is interpreted. Overall, however, it is possible to identify some common sources of stress. External sources of stress include significant life events, physical pain, daily hassles, and environmental factors such as noise and crowding. Internal sources of stress include insufficient perceived control over the situation and a maladaptive explanatory style.

Certain personality characteristics have been linked to stress. Type A individuals—those who are hard driving, ambitious, and impatient—appear to be at increased risk for subsequent heart disease. It has become clear that the decisive element in the Type A behaviour pattern is the tendency toward angry, hostile reactions to stressful situations.

Second, how does the body react when the exposure to stressful situations is prolonged? Stress is an adaptive reaction to threat, but if the threat is extended over time, both body and mind can start to break down. Stress has been implicated in a wide variety of health problems, ranging from heart disease to the common cold. A number of studies have shown that prolonged stress can affect immune functioning, which is the body's method for fighting off disease. Stress can compromise the immune response by either lowering the number of specialized white blood cells (lymphocytes) or by somehow suppressing the response of those lymphocytes to foreign substances that have invaded the body.

Two chronic psychological consequences of prolonged stress are posttraumatic stress disorder and burnout. Posttraumatic stress disorder results from exposure to extreme trauma, such as that experienced

during battle or as a result of a physical assault such as rape. The symptoms of the disorder include flashbacks in which the traumatic event is re-experienced, avoidance of stimuli associated with the trauma, and chronic arousal problems. Burnout is a term that psychologists use to describe a state of physical, emotional, and mental exhaustion that sometimes develops after prolonged stress.

Third, what strategies enable us to reduce and cope with stress? The term *coping* describes efforts to manage conditions of threat that tax one's resources. Effective coping techniques include relaxation training, the use of social support, and reappraisal. The stress response is incompatible with relaxation: Therefore relaxation training can help lower components of the stress response (such as blood pressure and heart rate). In progressive relaxation training, the client is taught to concentrate on specific muscle groups in the body, note whether they seem tense, and then relax those specific groups. Sometimes it's useful to provide biofeedback as well.

Additional evidence indicates that social support—the resources received from other people—can also help you cope effectively with stress. Friends and family help us maintain a healthy lifestyle, boost confidence, or simply provide an avenue for us to open up and express our feelings. Talking about things and confiding in others really seem to help people deal with stress. Finally, because stress depends on how you interpret the threatening or demanding situation, it can often be managed effectively through cognitive reappraisal. You can be taught to reinterpret significant life events or daily hassles in a less stressful way. Some stress management programs encourage clients to keep daily stress records. By identifying the kinds of situations that create stress, as well as the negative thoughts those situations induce, you become better prepared to reinterpret those situations and thoughts in a more adaptive manner.

Fourth, what general factors and lifestyle choices promote physical and psychological health? Aerobic exercise is one example of an activity that can have a substantial effect on physical and psychological health. Regular exercise improves mood and makes people more resistant to the effects of stressors. Proper nutrition is another important ingredient in maintaining a healthy body and mind. The North American diet tends to be too high in calories, fat, cholesterol, sugar, protein, and salt. Poor dietary habits can lead to significant long-term health problems. Another lifestyle choice that directly affects physical health is the decision not to smoke. Smoking and other tobacco use contribute to tens of thousands of deaths annually in Canada alone, from associated heart disease, cancer, stroke, and emphysema. Tobacco use stimulates activity in the central nervous system, which is immediately reinforcing, but prolonged use leads to addiction or dependence that can be difficult to overcome. Choosing to drink is a lifestyle choice that affects one's health both immediately and over time. Alcohol is a depressant drug that slows down the nervous system, altering one's judgment and decision-making skills. With excessive use alcohol can have adverse effects on several organs and almost every system of the body, including the liver, stomach, pancreas, intestines, and cardiovascular and immune systems. Finally, maintaining a healthy lifestyle includes avoiding risky behaviours and preventing disease. For example, psychologists are playing an important role in the AIDS epidemic by educating the public about risky behaviour, and through the establishment of treatment programs they are helping AIDS patients cope with the psychological effects of the disease.

Chapter Summary

EXPERIENCING STRESS: STRESSORS AND THE STRESS RESPONSE

How does the body produce stress? How is it experienced? *Stress* is best conceived of as an extended response that occurs over time rather than as a single reaction.

The Stress Response

Learning Goal: Understand the stress response. One influential model of the stress reaction is known as the *general adaptation syndrome (GAS),* which proposes that we respond to threat or demand in three phases. The *alarm reaction* corresponds to a fight-or-flight response; during the *resistance stage,* the threat continues and the body adjusts its reaction to cope; if the person is unable to neutralize the threat, *exhaustion* occurs. Fear, anger, sadness, dejection, and grief are common psychological responses to stress. Despite the negative health consequences, this sequence of reactions to stress seems to have adaptive value. Because of different evolutionary strategies, sex differences in coping behaviour may have evolved.

Cognitive Appraisal

Learning Goal: Be able to explain the role of cognitive appraisal in the stress response. The experience of stress is critically affected by how people appraise the situation they're in. People must feel that there is a threat present and that they may not have adequate resources to deal with the threat. The role of *cognitive appraisal* in the stress response is consistent with what we know about the role of cognition in the experience of emotion.

External Sources of Stress

Learning Goal: Learn about external sources of stress. Significant life events can introduce a good deal of stress into a person's life. Holmes and Rahe developed a life-change stress scale that indicates that stressful events are often associated with some type of change in day-to-day activities, which can be either positive or negative. Pain is an obvious warning signal that the body is being stressed. Less obviously stressful, daily hassles and environmental factors, such as noise, may nonetheless contribute to daily stress. The specialty area of *environmental psychology* is devoted to the study of environmental effects on behaviour and health.

Internal Sources of Stress

Learning Goal: Learn about internal sources of stress. The *hardy personality*—that is, the one resistant to stress—includes a number of adaptive perceptions, styles, and traits. One such factor is *perceived control,* or the amount of influence you feel you have over a situation and your reaction to it. Generally, less perceived control is associated with higher stress. A second factor is *explanatory style,* which is also related to psychological disorders such as depression. In contrast, the higher level of stress and heart disease in *Type A* personalities is linked to their preference for high-stress occupations and activities and a hostile reaction to people and events that interfere with their goals.

REACTING TO PROLONGED STRESS: PHYSICAL AND PSYCHOLOGICAL EFFECTS

The human body is usually able to deal with unexpected trauma, but if the threat continues for an extended period, the body's defences can begin to break down.

Physical Consequences of Stress

Learning Goal: Understand the physical consequences of prolonged stress, including the link between stress and the immune system. Stress has been implicated in a wide variety of health problems. Living a stressful life seems to lower one's ability to fight off disease. The immune system and its primary weapons, *lymphocytes,* are affected by stress. The immune response is lowered, decreasing the number of lymphocytes, or the response of lymphocytes to foreign substances is suppressed. The link between stress and the immune system has led some to speculate about the possible relationship between stress and more chronic illnesses, such as cancer, although researchers remain cautious in their conclusions. Prolonged exposure to stress is also associated with two major risk factors in cardiovascular disease: high blood pressure and high cholesterol.

Psychological Consequences of Stress

Learning Goal: Understand the psychological consequences of prolonged stress, including posttraumatic stress disorder and burnout. Most psychologists believe that stressful life events play a significant role in the onset of many psychological disorders. Psychologists assume that a (perhaps genetic) vulnerability interacts with stress to produce a psychological disorder. One psychological disorder resulting from extreme stress is *posttraumatic stress disorder (PTSD),* which is characterized by flashbacks, avoidance of trauma-associated stimuli, and chronic arousal symptoms. *Burnout,* another effect of prolonged stress, is "a state of emotional and mental exhaustion caused by long-term involvement in emotionally demanding situations" (Pines & Aronson, 1988). Burnout may be caused by loss of control in the workplace or of meaning in life.

REDUCING AND COPING WITH STRESS: TECHNIQUES OF STRESS MANAGEMENT

Given the negative consequences that long-term exposure to stress can have, psychologists have developed specific methods for reducing and controlling stress. *Coping* is the term psychologists use to describe efforts to manage conditions of threat or demand that tax one's resources.

Relaxation Techniques

Learning Goal: Learn how relaxation techniques can be used to reduce stress. Relaxation is an effective stress reducer because of its incompatibility with the stress response. *Progressive muscle relaxation* involves concentrating on specific muscle groups of the body, noting tension, and trying to relax those specific groups. In *autogenic relaxation,* a person is taught to focus on directing blood flow toward specific muscle groups, warming and relaxing them. Relaxation techniques are sometimes accompanied by *meditation* training. Giving people feedback (*biofeedback*) about the effectiveness of their relaxation efforts has proven successful.

Social Support

Learning Goal: Understand the positive and negative effects of social support. *Social support* refers to the resources that we receive from other people or groups, often in the form of comfort, caring, or help. Studies indicate that social support can improve one's psychological and physical health. Social support can also have a negative side if one has come to depend on such support and it is no longer available.

Reappraising the Situation

Learning Goal: Be able to explain how stress can be managed through cognitive reappraisal of the stressful situation. Interpretation of events plays a large role in how stressful the situation is; many stress management techniques involve *cognitive reappraisal.* This might involve focusing on aspects of the situation that distract one from catastrophizing, or analyzing a situation logically and deriving alternatives.

LIVING A HEALTHY LIFESTYLE

Whether you will remain healthy throughout your life depends significantly on your lifestyle habits. Health psychologists and other professionals have offered prescriptions for a healthy lifestyle.

Get Fit: The Value of Aerobic Exercise

Learning Goal: Be able to explain the physical and psychological benefits of aerobic exercise. *Aerobic exercise,* which consists of high-intensity activities that increase both heart rate and oxygen consumption, can have a substantial positive impact on psychological and physical health. It can improve mood and increase resistance to the effects of stressors. Researchers have not yet discovered exactly how or why exercise improves functioning; placebo-like effects may be involved.

Eat Right: The Value of Proper Nutrition

Learning Goal: Understand the value of proper nutrition. Proper nutrition is vital to maintaining a healthy body and mind; yet the foods most North Americans eat tend to be high in calories, cholesterol, fat, and other substances that are damaging in excess. Problems usually involve the type of food that is eaten, not the amount.

Don't Smoke: Tobacco and Health

Learning Goal: Learn the consequences of tobacco use, and explain why it's difficult to quit smoking. A wealth of correlational and experimental evidence has demonstrated the link between tobacco and serious health problems. People continue to smoke because smoking is addictive and associated with withdrawal effects. In addition, smoking seems to produce chemical reactions in the brain that lead to reinforcing effects. Although smoking is a difficult habit to break, rates of smoking do seem to be on the decline.

Problem Drinking: One Risky Behaviour Leads to Another

Learning Goal: Learn the consequences of drinking alcohol, and explain how intoxication leads us to engage in other risky health-related behaviours. Drinking alcohol to the point of intoxication affects brain functioning. *Alcohol myopia* means that judgment and decision-making processes are altered, and this may lead to people engaging in other risky health-related behaviours that they wouldn't partake in if sober (e.g., drinking and driving, engaging in unsafe sex). Excessive and chronic use of alcohol may lead to serious health problems.

Avoid Risky Behaviour: Protect Yourself from Disease

Learning Goal: Distinguish among the different types of prevention programs and learn how we can reduce unsafe sexual practices. Health psychologists distinguish between three types of prevention. *Primary prevention* attempts to reduce or eliminate a problem before it starts. *Secondary prevention* involves early identification of risk factors in specific population groups. *Tertiary prevention* seeks to handle and contain an illness or habit once it has been acquired. The prevalence of STDs such as *AIDS* underscores the importance of primary prevention programs.

Terms to Remember

Recommended Readings

Poole, G. D., Matheson, D. H., & Cox, D. (2001). *The psychology of health and health care: A Canadian perspective.* Toronto, ON: Prentice Hall. The first Canadian health psychology undergraduate textbook. This textbook, written by health psychologists from the University of British Columbia, the University of Victoria, and Simon Fraser University, covers many aspects of stress, health, and behaviour.

Gifford, R. (1997). *Environmental psychology: Principles and practice* (2nd ed.). Needham Heights, MA: Allyn & Bacon. Robert Gifford of the University of Victoria is a leading researcher in the emerging field of environmental psychology. This textbook is a comprehensive overview of contemporary

research, model research, and practical applications in this area.

Neese, R. M., & Williams, G. C. (1996). *Why we get sick: The new science of Darwinian medicine.* Toronto, ON: Random House. The authors of this book suggest that there are evolutionary explanations for why our bodies respond the way they do to injury and disease.

Friedman, H. S. (1991). *The self-healing personality: Why some people achieve health and others succumb to illness.* New York: Holt. An excellent introduction to the link between psychological factors and health.

Pennebaker, J. W. (1990). *Opening up.* New York: William Morrow and Company. An in-depth discussion of the role that oral or written expression of painful experiences might play in reducing stress and improving health.

For additional readings, explore InfoTrac® College Edition, your online library. Go to:

www.adaptivemind2e.nelson.com

Hint: enter the search terms: reactions to stress; causes of stress; stress and illness; coping with stress; posttraumatic stress disorder; health psychology.

What's on the Web?

Please note that Web addresses are subject to change. Check out the accompanying Web site for updates: www.adaptivemind2e.nelson.com. This site presents practice quiz questions, hypercontent, information on degrees and careers in psychology, study tips, and more.

Canadian Institute for Health Information

www.cihi.ca

This is a convenient Web site to use as a starting point when conducting a general search for Canadian health-related information. The main function of the Canadian Institute for Health Information is to bring together health-related information from Statistics Canada, Health Canada, the Hospital Medical Records Institute, and other organizations.

Health Canada

www.hc-sc.gc.ca

This site provides a wealth of information on the health of Canadians. The information is available in the form of statistics, articles, and other documents, all of which are organized alphabetically from "Aboriginal Health" all the way to "Youth."

American Institute of Stress

www.stress.org

Although it doesn't sound too inviting at first blush, this site provides some very useful information about stress, how to avoid it, how to cope with it, and how it can affect your life. It presents some surprising statistics. For example, 75% to 90% of visits to primary care physicians are for stress-related problems, and 78% of Americans describe their jobs as stressful (the majority claim that this has worsened in the last 10 years). Clearly, we are living in stressful times.

National Center for PTSD

www.dartmouth.edu/dms/ptsd/Fact_Sheets.html

This site is devoted to education and research on posttraumatic stress disorder; it provides a wealth of information related to the topic, including information for trauma survivors and veterans and fact sheets on a variety of topics, including PTSD and children, PTSD and community violence, and PTSD and the family.

Appendix A
Statistics

Statistics. The word causes many students to shudder with fear and loathing. One reason for this negative reaction is that many students expect the topic to be incredibly difficult. But, in truth, the basics of statistics are fairly easy to understand, and most students are surprised at how quickly they pick it up. The core concepts can be understood intuitively as well as mathematically, and most of the math is pretty easy. (Adding, subtracting, multiplying, and dividing will get you a long way in statistics.)

Another reason that statistics has a bad reputation is that many people are wary of it—they know that it is easy to lie (or at least mislead) with statistics, and some are uncomfortable with the whole idea of trying to quantify human experience. There are legitimate grounds for these concerns: Statistics can be presented in ways that are misleading, and quantifying psychological phenomena can be done poorly. But far from being good reasons for staying ignorant of statistics, these are excellent reasons for learning about it: Knowledge of statistics can protect you from being bamboozled by misleading uses of statistics, and engaging the problem of quantifying aspects of human experience can enhance your appreciation of the subtlety and complexity of human beings.

This appendix offers only a simplified and limited introduction to statistics, intended to supplement the information presented in Chapter 2. There are many textbooks that provide a more complete and sophisticated introduction to the use of statistics in psychology (e.g., Pagano, 1998).

DESCRIPTIVE STATISTICS

Statistics are used to summarize and make inferences about quantitative measurements of variables. A variable is a dimension or characteristic that can vary across or within individuals (e.g., height, gender, hours of sleep, creativity). Before we quantify a psychological variable, we must think carefully about the qualitative aspects of whatever it is we want to measure (e.g., what *is* creativity, and how can we quantify it?). The development of theoretically sound, methodologically rigorous, and practically useful ways of quantifying psychological variables is a central task for psychology, and one on which considerable progress has been made. Briefly, a good measure is *reliable* (the same result is obtained when the same thing is measured on different occasions or by different investigators), *valid* (it measures what it is intended to measure), and *sensitive* (it detects subtle but real differences).

Nominal Data versus Score Data

Suppose that you wanted to describe the students in your introductory psychology course in terms of their favourite hobbies and their performance on a psychology exam. If they all completed a questionnaire with this information, you would want some way of summarizing the responses. That is, you would want to use *descriptive statistics* to characterize the hobbies and test performance of the class.

Different sorts of variables lend themselves to different sorts of statistical analyses. Statisticians differentiate between several different sorts of variables, but here we focus on the two most common kinds: *nominal data* and *score data*.

"Hobbies" is an example of a "nominal" (name-like) variable: You could put the hobbies that students reported into various categories (e.g., sports, collecting, music), and you could quantify the data by reporting the number or percentage of students reporting the various kinds of hobbies. "Hobbies" in this example is a nominal variable because there is no underlying quantitative scale along which the different categories range (i.e., there isn't a quantitative scale running from "sports" to "collecting" to "music"). Gender and cultural heritage are other examples of nominal variables.

You can quantify nominal data in terms of the number (or percentage or proportion of the total) in the various nominal categories. You can also examine relationships between two different nominal variables; for example, you could compare men's and women's reports of their favourite hobbies. One useful way of depicting the relationship between two nominal variables is by creating a *cross-tabulation table*. Table A.1 presents such a table, with data from the 1996/1997 Canada Census on the number of men and women who reported that they had undertaken various activities to improve their health. Perhaps the most striking thing about these data is that the modal (i.e., most common) response was "nothing." It is also interesting that men more often reported doing nothing to improve their health than did women (60% of men versus 54% of women), and that women more often reported health-related changes to diet than did men (14% of women versus 9% of men).

Nominal categories, such as different hobbies, genders, or activities undertaken to improve health, are not quantitative scales. You couldn't, for example, assign numbers to the different categories of hobbies (e.g., sports = 1, collecting = 2, music = 3), add up all of the respondents' responses, divide by the total number of respondents, and come out with a meaningful "average hobby." This wouldn't make sense because "hobbies" is not a quantitative scale but rather a set of qualitatively different categories.

In contrast, performance on an exam (expressed as number, percentage, or proportion correct) is an example of a "score" variable. Score variables are inherently quantitative in a variety of senses. Most obviously, there is an underlying quantitative dimension, ranging from 0% to 100% correct. Also, the intervals between scores are equal at different parts of the scale; for example, scores of 6 and 8 differ by the same amount as scores of 7 and 9. Because score data have these quantitative properties, one can meaningfully perform mathematical operations on them (e.g., calculate the mean to describe the average score on an exam). Psychologists often use measures that produce score data (e.g., IQ tests, measures of creativity, reaction time).

Normal Distributions of Score Data

Frequency Distribution Tables and Frequency Histograms Chapter 2 introduced you to frequency histograms (graphs that depict the frequency of cases getting various scores on some measurement). We will review them here in greater depth. Suppose that you randomly selected 20 students from your introductory psychology class and gave each of them a test on the material in this textbook. Table A.2 shows the raw data you might obtain, scored in terms of percent correct and sorted into rank order from the lowest to the highest.

A frequency histogram summarizes data graphically in a way that depicts the distribution of the scores. In this case, we want to show how many students got particular scores on the psychology test. To do so, we must first select ranges of scores; once we've done that, we'll simply count up the number of cases with scores falling within each of those ranges. Score ranges are selected such that the total range is sufficient to include all of the data and there are enough different intervals along that total range to depict the distribution of scores in a clear and informative manner.

Let's say we decide to use six ranges of test scores: 41–50, 51–60, 61–70, 71–80, 81–90, and 91–100. Now we can construct a *frequency distribution table* that shows the

Table A.1
Cross-Tabulation of the Number of Canadian Men and Women Reporting Undertaking Various Activities to Improve Health (Data from Canada Census 1996/1997) (in thousands)

	Sex		
Activity	Men	Women	Total
Nothing	6 309	5 904	12 213
Exercise more	3 238	3 594	6 832
Change diet	973	1 507	2 480
Total	10 520	11 005	21 525

Table A.2
Percent Correct on a Psychology Test by 20 Students in an Introductory Psychology Course

Rank	Name	Score (x)
1	Mary	59
2	Betty	68
3	Colleen	69
4	Amy	72
5	Tanya	74
6	René	74
7	Inez	75
8	Pierre	75
9	Petra	76
10	Frances	76
11	Cheryl	76
12	Steve	76
13	Martin	77
14	James	77
15	Belinda	79
16	Helene	80
17	Daphne	80
18	Jean	81
19	Deborah	85
20	Theresa	91

Table A.3
Frequency Distribution Table of the Raw Data Presented in Table A.2 (Percent Correct on a Psychology Test by 20 Students in an Introductory Psychology Course)

Test Score Range	Frequency (Number of Cases)
41–50	0
51–60	1
61–70	2
71–80	14
81–90	2
91–100	1

number of students whose scores fell in each of those ranges. Table A.3 is a frequency distribution table of the data shown in Table A.2. Compare Tables A.2 and A.3, and make sure you understand the relationship between them. Notice, for example, that Table A.2 includes two students (Betty and Colleen) with scores between 61 and 70 and that Table A.3 indicates that the frequency of scores from 61 to 70 is 2 (i.e., Betty and Colleen).

A *frequency histogram* is simply a graphic depiction of the numeric information in a frequency distribution table. There are a variety of styles of frequency histograms, but one of the most common has the ranges of scores along the horizontal axis (called the *abscissa*). The vertical axis (called the *ordinate*) is used to represent the frequency (number) of cases.[1] Vertical bars are used to represent the frequency of cases within each of the ranges of scores, with the height of each bar corresponding to the number of cases within that range, as indexed by the values marked on the ordinate. Figure A.1 is a frequency histogram of the data in Tables A.2 and A.3. Take a look now, and make sure you understand how the data in Tables A.2 and A.3 have been depicted in Figure A.1.

Normal Distributions The distribution of scores depicted in Figure A.1 is an approximately "normal" or "bell curve" distribution: The most frequent or common cases are at or near the mean (arithmetic average), and as score values move below or above the mean, the frequency of cases declines. Note that in a normal distribution the rate of the decline in frequency is approximately symmetrical around the mean; in other words, rarity increases at about the same rate as score values move above or below the mean. Notice also that in a normal distribution the mean, median, and mode are all quite close to one another (indeed, in a perfectly symmetrical normal distribution these three measures of central tendency are identical). Think about this for a moment, and make sure you understand why it makes sense that the mean, median, and mode are similar in a normal distribution (and identical in a perfectly symmetrical normal distribution).

Many physical and psychological variables have approximately normal distributions. For example, if you measured the IQ of the members of your introductory psychology course, there would be some mean IQ and most of the class would be at or near that mean, with fewer students with IQ scores at values farther from the mean. The same would hold for height, weight, creativity, performance on an exam, and numerous other score variables.[2]

Measuring Variability in Distributions: The Standard Deviation Suppose that we once again recruited the same 20 students from your introductory psychology course, this time quizzing them about current events. Introductory psychology students vary a great deal from one another in their knowledge of current events: Some are total media hounds, up on all sorts of news items, others avoid such information like the plague,

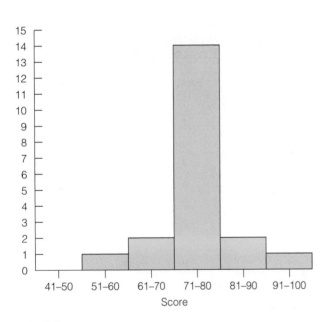

FIGURE A.1

Frequency Histogram of the Data in Tables A.2 and A.3 (Percent Correct on a Psychology Test by 20 Students in an Introductory Psychology Course)

---

1. To remember which of these terms is which, say "abscissa" aloud, and notice that your lips stretch horizontally; then say "ordinate" aloud, noting that your lips purse together somewhat vertically.
2. Not all score variables have normal distributions. For example, the distribution of annual income by Canadian residents is "positively skewed": Most adults in Canada have incomes between $10 000 and $100 000 per year; by definition, none have incomes less than zero, but a few make millions of dollars per year. Other distributions are non-normal in other ways (e.g., negatively skewed, bimodal, etc.). This appendix focuses on normal distributions because they are by far the most common in psychology.

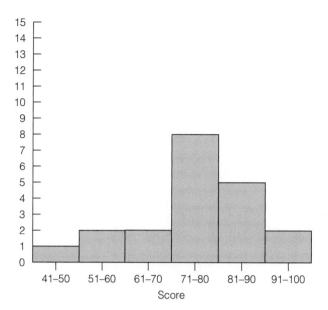

FIGURE A.2
**Frequency Histogram of the Data in Tables A.4 and A.5
(Percent Correct on a Test of Current Events by 20
Students in an Introductory Psychology Course)**

Table A.4
Percent Correct on a Test of Current Events by 20 Students in an Introductory Psychology Course

Rank	Name	Score (x)
1	Tanya	48
2	René	55
3	Colleen	57
4	Amy	61
5	Mary	70
6	Betty	73
7	Frances	74
8	Pierre	75
9	Petra	75
10	Deborah	76
11	Cheryl	77
12	Belinda	79
13	Martin	80
14	James	82
15	Steve	84
16	Jean	84
17	Daphne	88
18	Helene	89
19	Inez	95
20	Theresa	98

and yet others are somewhere between these extremes. We might therefore expect that there would be a lot of variability from one student to another on scores on the current-events test. Table A.4 presents the raw data from the current-events test, and Table A.5 is a frequency distribution table of those same data, using the same score ranges as were used with the psychology test (Table A.3).

Figure A.2 is a frequency histogram of the current-events test scores. Note first that this distribution is approximately normal; that is, the most common cases are at or near the mean, and rarity increases approximately symmetrically as score values move above and below the mean. In this regard, Figure A.2 is similar to Figure A.1. The two figures are also similar in that the mean of each set of scores is 76. The two figures differ, however, in how "flat" versus "narrow" the normal distributions are. The distribution in Figure A.1 is quite narrow because a very large percentage of the students had scores at or quite close to the mean; that is, there is relatively little variability in this data set. The distribution in Figure A.2 is wider because quite a few students had scores that were above or below the mean; that is, there is a fair amount of variability in the current-events data set.

Frequency histograms are very useful because they clearly depict both the mean and the amount of variability around that mean in a set of score data. It is often handy, though, to describe the amount of variability in a set of data quantitatively, that is, with a number that indicates the average extent to which scores in the data set differ from the mean. The most common quantitative index of variability in score data is the *standard deviation* (*SD*). The SD is a standardized measure of the average extent to which scores in a data set deviate or differ from the mean of that data set. To use a somewhat silly but illustrative example, suppose you measured the number of belly-buttons on each of your classmates. What do you think the mean would be? How about the SD? Of course, the mean would be one and the SD would be zero; that is, every student would be exactly at the mean value, so the average amount of deviation from the mean would be zero. The SD would be larger than zero for the scores on the psychology test shown in Figure A.1, and even larger for the scores on the current-events test shown in Figure A.2, because there is more variability around the mean for those measures.

Table A.5
Frequency Distribution Table of the Raw Data Presented in Table A.4 (Percent Correct on a Test of Current Events by 20 Students in an Introductory Psychology Course)

Test Score Range	Frequency (Number of Cases)
41–50	1
51–60	2
61–70	2
71–80	8
81–90	5

To calculate the SD, you first determine the mean for the data set (i.e., add up the scores and divide by the number of scores). Then, for each individual score, you subtract the mean from that score. (See Table A.6, which depicts the steps involved in calculating the SD for the current-events test scores graphed in Figure A.2.) Obviously, if a score is the same as the mean, this difference will be zero; if a score deviates from the mean by a large amount, then this difference will be a lot different from zero. Given that we're trying to measure the average extent to which the scores in the data set differ from the mean, you might think that all you have to do now is add those difference scores up and divide by the number of scores (N), but that wouldn't work. Can you think why? By definition, some scores are above the mean and others below the mean, so some differences will be negative and others positive, and if you simply added up the difference scores you'd get a grand total of zero. Think this through while looking at the difference scores in the third column of Table A.6 and make sure you understand why the difference scores would sum to zero.

To get around this problem, each difference score is squared (multiplied by itself): By the rules of mathematics, a negative number times a negative number equals a positive number, so this eliminates the problem of the differences from the mean adding to zero. Notice that the farther a particular score is from the mean, the larger the squared difference from the mean. The squared differences from the mean are then summed, yielding a measure called *the sum of squared differences from the mean* (or *sum of squares,* for short). The sum of squares is then divided by the number of scores minus one $(N - 1)$ to yield an estimate of the average extent to which scores in the data set deviate from the mean; this measure is called the *variance.*[3] As shown in Table A.6, the sum of squares for the current-events test data is 3210, so the variance of that data set is $3210/(20 - 1) = 168.95$. For reasons that will become at least somewhat clear in a moment, statisticians don't usually use the variance to index variability, but rather go one step further and get the square root of the variance (i.e., the number that, when multiplied by itself, equals the variance). The square root of the variance is the SD. For the current-events test data, the SD is 13.0. (You can assess your understanding of the steps involved in calculating SD by calculating it for the psychology test data in Table A.4; the correct answer is 6.50.)

Whew! That seems like a lot of work! But it's worth it, because the SD has some very cool properties (which is why statisticians usually prefer it to the variance). The

Table A.6
Calculating the Standard Deviation of the Data in Table A.4 (Percent Correct on a Test of Current Events by 20 Students in an Introductory Psychology Course)

Rank	Name	Score (x)	$x - \bar{x}$	$(x - \bar{x})^2$
1	Tanya	48	$48 - 76 = -28$	784
2	René	55	$55 - 76 = -21$	441
3	Colleen	57	$57 - 76 = -19$	361
4	Amy	61	$61 - 76 = -15$	225
5	Mary	70	$70 - 76 = -6$	36
6	Betty	73	$73 - 76 = -3$	9
7	Frances	74	$74 - 76 = -2$	4
8	Pierre	75	$75 - 76 = -1$	1
9	Petra	75	$75 - 76 = -1$	1
10	Deborah	76	$76 - 76 = 0$	0
11	Cheryl	77	$77 - 76 = 1$	1
12	Belinda	79	$79 - 76 = 3$	9
13	Martin	80	$80 - 76 = 4$	16
14	James	82	$82 - 76 = 6$	36
15	Steve	84	$84 - 76 = 8$	64
16	Jean	84	$84 - 76 = 8$	64
17	Daphne	88	$88 - 76 = 12$	144
18	Helene	89	$89 - 76 = 13$	169
19	Inez	95	$95 - 76 = 19$	361
20	Theresa	98	$98 - 76 = 22$	484
$N = 20$		Sum = 1520	Sum = 0	Sum = 3210
		Mean = $\bar{x}$ = 1520/20 = 76		SD = $\sqrt{3210/(20 - 1)}$ = 13.00

---

3. The rationale for dividing by $N - 1$ rather than by N is beyond the scope of this appendix; very briefly, with small samples variability tends to be underestimated if the sum of squares is divided by N; dividing by $N - 1$ corrects for this problem.

marvellous thing about the SD is that for *any* normal distribution (no matter how "narrow" or "wide"), approximately 34.1% of the scores are between the mean and 1 SD above the mean, and 34.1% of the scores are between the mean and 1 SD below the mean (see Figure A.3).[4] Thus, in any normal distribution, approximately 68.2% of the scores are within ±1 SD of the mean. In the current-events test scores, for example, the mean is 76 and the SD is 13.0, so about 68.2% of the scores should be between 63 (1 SD below the mean) and 89 (1 SD above the mean); in fact, 14 of the 20 scores (70%) fall in this range, which is as close to 68.2% as possible given there are only 20 scores. Further, for any normal distribution, approximately 13.6% of the scores are between 1 SD and 2 SD above the mean, and approximately 13.6% are between 1 SD and 2 SD below the mean. So what proportion of the scores in a normal distribution is within ±2 SD of the mean? About 34.1 + 34.1 + 13.6 + 13.6 = 95.4%. Only about 2.1% of the scores in a normal distribution are between 2 SD and 3 SD above the mean (and 2.1% are between 2 SD and 3 SD below the mean), so about 99.6% of the scores are within ±3 SD of the mean.

Figure A.3 shows a particular normal distribution, with a particular mean and a particular SD. There are an infinite number of possible normal distributions, differing from each other in terms of their means and/or SD. Figure A.4 shows four different normal distributions, each with a different mean and a different SD. Note that in a fairly wide distribution, such as that shown in panel (a) of Figure A.4, each SD is fairly wide and short; in contrast, in a relatively narrow distribution, such as that shown in panel (b), each SD is fairly narrow and tall. Thus the proportion of each curve that falls between the mean and a given number of SDs is the same in all four of the distributions.

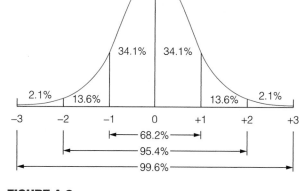

FIGURE A.3

Areas Under the Normal Curve as a Function of Standard Deviation from the Mean[5]

Source: http://qreview.cera.net/Chapters-HTML/Chap4_html/chapter4.htm

Standard Scores (*z*-Scores)   The meaning of any particular score depends not only on how that score compares to the mean, but also on the amount of variability in the distribution of scores. For example, getting a score of 89 on the current-events test would be pretty good (1 SD above the mean) because only about 16% of the scores on that test are 89 or higher. But getting a score of 89 on the psychology test would be superb, because it is 2 SD above the mean, which means that only about 2% of the scores on that test are 89 or higher.

Any particular raw score can be expressed in terms of a *standard score,* sometimes called a *z-score,* which takes into account both how different that score is from the mean and how much variability there is around the mean. To calculate a *z*-score for a particular raw score, you subtract the mean from that score and divide the difference by the SD. Thus the *z*-score is a measure of how much the raw score differs from the mean, expressed in SD units. For example, the *z*-score that corresponds to a raw score of 89 on the current-events test is $(89 - 76)/13 = 1$; that is, a score of 89 on the current-events test is exactly 1 SD unit above the mean. On the psychology test, a raw score of

---

4. The values given here for the percentage of scores falling in various parts of a normal distribution (e.g., 34.1% between the mean and +1 SD) refer to perfectly normal distributions (i.e., those in which frequency declines symmetrically as score values move above and below the mean) of a very large number of scores. They don't work out perfectly for small samples or for distributions that are not perfectly normal, but even in such cases they will be quite close.

5. Unlike the vertical bars used to represent the frequency of particular score ranges in Figures A.1 and A.2, a smooth line is used in Figure A.3 to represent the frequency of cases across the distribution; think of that smooth line as being composed of a large number of points, each of which indicates the frequency of a particular score value.

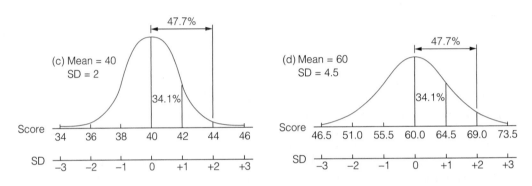

FIGURE A.4

Four Normal Distributions, with Different Means and SDs, Illustrating that the Percentage of the Scores in a Normal Distribution between the Mean and a Given SD Is Always Approximately the Same

Source: Johnson, M. K., & Liebert, R. M. (1977). *Statistics: Tool of the behavioral sciences.* p. 45. Englewood Cliffs, NJ: Prentice-Hall.

89 would correspond to a *z*-score of $(89 - 76)/6.5 = 2$, whereas a raw score of 68 would correspond to a *z*-score of $(68 - 76)/6.5 = -1.23$. Statisticians have created tables that can be used to determine, for any given *z*-score, the percentage of the scores in a normal distribution that are equal to or greater than that *z*-score (of course, because 100% of the scores are in the distribution, the same table can be used to determine the percentage of scores that are equal to or lower than that *z*-score).

INFERENTIAL STATISTICS

Typically, psychologists want to do more than simply describe the data obtained from a sample. Usually we measure a sample because we are interested in some larger population that the sample is supposed to represent. This means we need to estimate the extent to which the sample provides a reliable index of the population. For example, opinion researchers might ask a sample of 100 Canadian teenagers about their views on Web sites such as Napster and its imitators. The point of such a study would not merely be to measure the opinions of those 100 Canadian teenagers, but rather to use them to represent the larger population of some 3 million Canadian teenagers. That is, the sample is used to make inferences about a larger population. *Inferential statistics* are used to estimate the reliability of a sample as a representation of the population on the dependent variable of interest, and to estimate the reliability of relationships between variables observed in one or more samples (i.e., the likelihood that those relationships would be reliably observed in other, similar samples).

Sample Reliability

A sample is *statistically reliable* to the extent that the same results would likely be obtained over and over again if new samples were selected from the same population and measured in the same ways. Obviously, to represent a population accurately a sample must be statistically reliable. Given that proper procedures were used to select a sample (see Chapter 2, pp. 42–44), two factors determine the statistical reliability of the sample: (1) the size of the sample and (2) the amount of variability in the population on whatever dependent variable is measured in the sample.

The size of the sample and the amount of variability on the dependent variable within the population interact with one another to determine the statistical reliability of a sample. The greater the variability, the larger the sample must be to be statistically reliable. To return to our earlier, rather silly example, suppose you wanted to use a sample of students in your introductory psychology class to estimate the number of bellybuttons per student in the whole class. In this case, a sample of one would be perfectly representative because there is no variability in the population (the class) in the number of bellybuttons: Every person in the class has one bellybutton, so any sample will be perfectly representative of the class on this variable. More generally, if there is only a little bit of variability in a population on a particular measure, then even a fairly small sample is likely to be representative of that sample because all or most of the people selected to be in the sample are likely to have scores very close to the mean (because most of the population has scores very close to the mean). The greater the amount of variability in the population, the more opportunities for individuals who differ greatly from the mean to be selected as part of the sample. In other words, as the amount of variability in the population goes up, the reliability of a sample of a given size goes down.

How can we figure out how much variability there is in the population on the dependent variable we want to measure? In theory, we might find out by measuring everyone in the population, but if we did so we'd no longer be concerned about sample reliability. (Who needs a sample if you've measured the whole population?)

Here's a key idea: The variability in a population on a particular dependent variable is estimated by measuring the variability in the sample on that variable. How much variability in bellybuttons would there be in a sample of your classmates? None, and based on that we would estimate the population variability to be low. How much variability would there be in a sample of your classmates on current-events knowledge? Lots, and based on that we would estimate the population variability on that measure to be high. Below we get a bit more specific about this general idea of estimating variability.

95% Confidence Intervals Statisticians estimate the reliability of a sample by (1) ensuring that proper sampling procedures were used (see Chapter 2, pp. 42–44) and (2) using mathematical formulas that simultaneously take into account sample size and variability within the sample. One popular formula is used to calculate what are called *95% confidence intervals*. The formula is slightly beyond the scope of this appendix. For present purposes, the point to understand is that it uses the sample size, variability within the sample, and the sample mean to estimate a range or "interval" of estimates of the population mean, such that there is a 95% probability that the population mean falls somewhere within that range. Given that you have only the one sample, your best estimate of the population mean is the sample mean, but you cannot be sure that the sample mean exactly corresponds to the population mean; by looking at the sample size and the variability within the sample, you can be 95% confident that the population mean falls within a certain range around the sample mean. The larger the sample and/or the less variability in that sample, the smaller the 95% confidence interval. For example, for the psychology test data in Figure A.1 (mean = 76, SD = 6.5), the 95% confidence interval is 73.0 – 79.0, whereas for the current-events test data in Figure A.2 (mean = 76, SD = 13.0), the 95% confidence interval is 69.9 – 82.1. This comparison shows that, all else being equal, the 95% confidence interval increases as variability in the sample increases. Similarly, we could construct another data set that has the same mean and the same SD as one of those data sets but has lots more participants; if we did so, the 95% confidence interval would shrink as the number of participants in the sample increased.

The Single-Sample *t*-Test   Sometimes psychologists are interested in comparing the sample mean to some established value. You might, for example, want to find out if the IQ of the students in your introductory psychology course is greater than 100 (the population mean for IQ). A popular statistical test for this purpose is the *single-sample t-test*. The "single-sample" part of this name is easy to understand: The test is used when you have a single sample and you want to compare it to some established baseline. It's called a *t*-test simply because that's the name given to it by the statistician who created it.

The single-sample *t*-test works something like this: The difference between the sample mean and the baseline value is divided by an estimate of how much the sample mean would be likely to vary by chance alone. The latter measure is related to the SD and is based on the amount of variability within the sample. The logic is as follows: If the difference between the sample mean and the baseline value is no bigger than the extent to which the sample mean would be expected to vary by chance alone, then *t* (the result of dividing the former by the latter) will be about one. As the difference between the sample and the baseline value increases relative to the amount of variability in the sample expected by chance alone, *t* becomes greater than one. Statisticians have created tables of "critical" values of *t*, indexed by sample size: The smaller the sample, the greater the critical value of *t* (because, all else being equal, smaller samples are more likely to be extreme by chance alone). If the obtained value of *t* is as great or greater than the critical value given in the table, then the difference between the sample mean and the baseline value is "statistically significant," meaning it is unlikely that it occurred by chance alone.

Review the preceding paragraph now and note how the single-sample *t*-test simultaneously takes into account (a) the size of the difference between the sample mean and the baseline value, (b) the amount of variability in the sample, and (c) the size of the sample. These three factors are involved in all inferential statistics, and if you can grasp why this makes sense now it will make the rest of this appendix easier.

Estimating the Reliability of Relationships between Variables

Often psychologists are interested in measuring relationships between variables, and we usually want to do so in ways that shed light on the *statistical reliability* of whatever relationships are observed in the sample under investigation. Statistical reliability means just what it sounds like: Would the relationships observed in a particular sample be reliably observed in other, similar samples, or are they likely to have occurred as unreliable flukes of chance?

Correlation   As discussed in Chapter 2 (pp. 50–54), correlations can be used to describe the relationship between pairs of dependent variables. For example, page 52 presents two scatter plots, each of which depicts the relationship between a pair of variables: Number of diapers changed and number of times hands were washed by daycare workers (a positive correlation, meaning that there was a systematic tendency for increases along one of the variables to go along with increases along the other) and number of hours practising piano and number of errors during recital (a negative correlation, meaning that there was a systematic tendency for increases along one of the variables to go along with decreases along the other). Figure A.5 presents scatter plots depicting various directions and strengths of correlation.

Chapter 2 also introduced the correlation coefficient, a value that can range from −1.0 (a perfect negative correlation) to 0 (no relationship) to +1.0 (a perfect positive

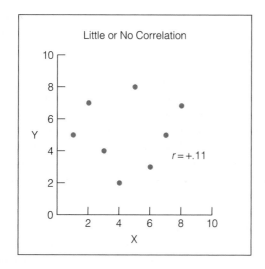

FIGURE A.5
Various Directions and Degrees of Correlation

correlation). We're not going to go through the details of the equation here. Briefly, the correlation coefficient measures how closely the points on a scatter plot conform to a straight line that slopes up (positive) or down (negative) from left to right. For example, if you measured the height of a group of people in inches, then measured their height in centimetres, and then made a scatter plot of those data, all of the data points would fall on a straight, upward-sloping line and the correlation would be +1.0 (assuming accurate measurements). If you also measured each person's weight and made a scatter plot of weight and height, there would still be a positive correlation (because on average, taller people tend to weigh more than shorter people), but the data points would not all perfectly conform to a straight line: The correlation coefficient would be different from zero and it would be positive, but it would be substantially less than +1. Note that the degree of steepness of the line does not affect the size of the correlation coefficient; as long as the line is not flat (i.e., slopes either up or down), what determines the strength of the correlation is how closely points conform to that line.

We remind you that correlation does not necessarily indicate causation (for review, see Chapter 2, pp. 53–54). It is also worth noting here that correlation is only good for measuring the strength of linear relationships, not curvilinear relationships. An example of a curvilinear relationship is the relationship between arousal and memory. At very low levels of arousal (e.g., when people are half asleep), memory tends to be poor (wake up!). As arousal increases from very low levels to moderate levels, memory improves, but as arousal continues to increase (e.g., toward panic), memory may begin to suffer. If you plotted memory performance across a wide range of degrees of arousal, you would therefore expect to see an inverted U-shaped function. Even if the data points conformed to that inverted U-shaped function very well, a correlation coefficient would come out to be fairly low, because correlation coefficients assess how closely the data fit a simple straight line (there are other statistics for measuring the strength of curvilinear relationships, but we will not discuss those here).

Another point to be made about correlation is that the sample that is measured must have a fair amount of variability on both of the dependent variables for a correlation to be detected. For example, the correlation between performance on the Graduate Records Examination (which many graduate schools consider when deciding whether or not to admit applicants for higher degrees) and performance in graduate school is fairly weak (about $r = .33$). This isn't because ability to perform well on the GRE is only weakly related to ability to perform well in graduate school, but rather because only people with fairly good GRE scores get admitted to graduate school. If applicants with very low GREs were admitted more often, they would likely often perform poorly in graduate school and hence the correlation would be stronger. (Note, of course, that it is also the case that GRE scores are imperfect predictors of performance, so the correlation would never be perfect; for research on the GRE as a predictor of success in graduate school, see Kuncel et al., 2001.)

The final point to be made here about correlations is that the correlation coefficient measures the *strength* or consistency of the relationship between two variables, not its statistical reliability. The reliability of a correlation between the two variables is estimated by looking simultaneously at (1) the strength of the relationship as indexed by the correlation coefficient and (2) the sample size. The size of the correlation coefficient is inversely related to the amount of random variability in the relationship (e.g., if the correlation coefficient is −1.0 or +1.0, then there is no variability at all across participants in the relationship; as the correlation coefficient approaches zero, the amount of variability across participants in the relationship increases). Thus, the logic here is the same as in the preceding section on the reliability of sample means: All else being equal, larger samples are more reliable than smaller samples, and samples that have less random variability within them are more reliable than samples that have lots of random variability within them. In the case of correlation, it is the amount of variability in the nature of the relationship between two variables that matters (along with the size of the sample).

Comparing Scores in Two Independent Conditions Many psychological studies compare two independent groups of participants, each in a different condition, to see if they differ on some dependent variable. The conditions are "independent" in that different people are randomly assigned to each; thus, whether or not a particular person gets assigned to a particular condition is independent of what that condition is and of who else gets assigned to it.

Suppose, for example, that at the beginning of the term the students in your introductory psychology class were randomly divided into two groups: Half of the students were required to sit in the front half of the lecture hall throughout the term, whereas the remaining students were required to sit in the back half. Suppose further that we find that the average percentage correct on the midterm exam was 86 for front-sitters and 81 for back-sitters. If all we cared about was this particular sample, measured on this particular midterm, then we could simply report the average scores (and perhaps the SDs) for each group and note that the average score was 5 points higher for front-sitters than for back-sitters.

How could the 5-point difference in average midterm scores between front- and back-sitters be explained? (For research on this subject, see Burda & Brooks, 1996.) There are lots of potential explanations, but for present purposes we put them into two major categories. One category of explanations has to do with causal effects of sitting in the front versus back half of the lecture hall. It could be, for example, that sitting in the front makes it easier to hear the lecture and see whatever visuals the lecturer uses, or that sitting in the front makes it more difficult to chat with neighbours; hence students who sit in the front end up learning more from lectures. Whatever the specific mechanism(s), the important point for now is that there might be something about sitting in the front versus the back of the classroom that tends to *cause* a difference in average marks on the midterm.

Another category of explanations has nothing to do with where people sit. It could be that the difference in midterm scores between front- and back-sitters was a mere fluke of chance. After all, if you had just randomly divided the class into two groups, called X and Y, without regard to where they sit or anything else, the two groups probably wouldn't have come out with exactly identical scores on the midterm. Flukes of chance (such as a few really good test takers having been randomly assigned to condition X, or random errors in how the exams were marked) could easily lead the average score in the two groups to be nonidentical (and the smaller the samples the more likely they would be to differ by chance alone).

How could we estimate the likelihood that the 5-point difference in average midterm scores between front- and back-sitters was a fluke? One approach would be to repeat the experiment several times, with a different class each time. The more times we find a difference favouring front-sitters, the less likely that the difference is a fluke. But this approach would be very time consuming and expensive. The alternative is to use inferential statistics.

To estimate the likelihood that a difference in average scores between two conditions would occur by chance alone, inferential statistics simultaneously takes three considerations into account: how big the difference is, how large the samples are, and how much variability there is in the scores within each condition. It is easy to see that, all else being equal, a large difference between conditions is less likely to occur by chance alone than is a small difference. In other words, a small difference in mean midterm scores is quite likely to occur by chance alone when two random groups are compared, but a large difference is less likely to occur by chance alone. The importance of sample size is also fairly easy to appreciate. As we've already mentioned, the larger the sample, the more likely that it will be a reliable index of the population from which it is drawn: If you randomly selected just one student to represent the population of front-sitters and another student to represent the back-sitters, it would be very likely that the two students would differ on the midterm (not because of where they sit, but because they are different individuals). The more people you randomly assign to the two conditions, the less likely that a mean difference between the conditions has to do with flukes of chance regarding which individuals happened to be assigned to which condition. Finally, the importance of the extent to which scores within each condition vary from one another is also intuitive: All else being equal, the greater the amount of individual differences from one student to another, the greater the likelihood that flukes of random assignment could lead to average differences between the groups.

It is important to grasp that the statistical reliability (or statistical significance) of a difference between conditions depends on all three of these considerations—the size of the difference, the amount of variability within conditions, and sample size—not just on the size of the difference. A difference between conditions that appears to be quite large might turn out to be nonsignificant, or unreliable, if there is a lot of variability within conditions or if sample sizes are very small. Conversely, a very small difference between conditions might turn out to be significant, or reliable, if there is little variability within conditions or the samples are very large. Keep in mind that "significant" means "statistically reliable," or unlikely to be due to chance alone; "significant" does not necessarily mean "large" or "important."

The most popular statistical test for comparing scores in two independent groups of participants is the *independent-samples t-test*. The logic of the independent-samples *t*-test is essentially the same as that for the single-sample *t*-test described above: The difference between the means of the two conditions is divided by a measure of how much the means would be likely to vary by chance alone. The latter measure is related to the SD and is based on the amount of variability within conditions. If the observed difference between conditions is about the same as the extent to which conditions would be likely to vary by chance alone, then the result (t) of dividing the former by the latter will be about one. As the difference between conditions increases relative to the size of the difference expected by chance alone, t becomes greater than one. You would first calculate t, then look up the obtained value in a table, which shows "critical values" of t for various sample sizes: The smaller the sample, the larger the critical value of t. If the obtained value of t is at least as great as the appropriate critical value, then the difference between the conditions is statistically reliable (i.e., unlikely to have occurred by chance alone).

Comparing Scores in Two Dependent Conditions

If an independent variable has only a small effect, and if the variability across participants on the dependent variable of interest is large, then the effect of the independent variable may not be detected when two independent groups of participants are compared (unless the sample sizes are very large). Suppose, for example, that we wish to see if people with myopia gain greater visual acuity from a new kind of contact lens compared to regular contact lenses. We could take a group of people with myopia, randomly assign half of them to wear regular contacts and half to wear the new contacts, and test their visual acuity. But we might well end up with a "null" result (i.e., no statistically significant difference) even if the new lenses do lead to better acuity, because the effect of lens type would probably be small and there would probably be large differences in visual acuity from one participant to another within each condition.

An alternative would be to conduct a dependent-conditions experiment to test the hypothesis that the new lenses give people better visual acuity. The most popular type of dependent-conditions experiment is aptly referred to as a *repeated-measures experiment*. In a repeated-measures experiment, we would test each participant in both conditions (with regular contacts and with the new contacts). In such an experiment, it is important to *counterbalance* the order of the two conditions (i.e., half of the participants are tested first with regular and then with new contacts, whereas the others are tested first with the new contacts and then with regular ones). Counterbalancing the order of conditions eliminates the possibility that differences between the conditions are caused by improvements due to practice on the acuity test or decrements due to fatigue.

In a repeated-measures experiment, individual differences between people cannot lead to a fluke difference between the two conditions (because the same people are in both conditions). The dependent variable that gets analyzed in a repeated-measures *t*-test is a difference score: in this example, the difference (for each participant) between visual acuity with the new contacts and visual acuity with regular contacts. Even if the participants differ wildly from one another in acuity, and even if the size of the advantage of the new contacts is small, if there *is* an advantage then there should be a consistent tendency for the new minus regular difference score to be greater than zero. The formula for calculating *t* for data from a repeated-measures experiment is essentially the same as that used for comparing the mean of a single sample to some *a priori* baseline value; in this case, the baseline value is zero, and the *t*-test estimates the probability that the difference scores would differ from zero as much as and as consistently as they do by chance alone. Repeated-measures experiments are quite sensitive (i.e., they are able to detect small effects even when variability across individuals is large). Unfortunately, they cannot always be used because it is not always possible to test the same individual in different conditions. Imagine, for example, that we are interested in comparing visual acuity in myopic people treated with two different forms of laser surgery. We couldn't test each person in both conditions because once they've had one kind of surgery we cannot undo that surgery and then give them the other.

Comparing Scores in More than Two Conditions: Analysis of Variance The experiments we've described so far all involve comparing two conditions. Often, however, researchers want to examine more than two conditions. You might, for example, want to compare visual acuity in myopic individuals with glasses versus contacts versus laser surgery. You could analyze the data from such an experiment by doing three different *t*-tests (eyeglasses versus contacts, eyeglasses versus surgery, contacts versus surgery), but this is not desirable for two reasons. For one thing, it's a bit of a hassle to have to do so many tests. More importantly, the rationale for using the *t*-test to estimate the probability that a difference between conditions would occur by chance alone is violated when the same set of data is used in several different *t*-tests.

Analysis of variance (ANOVA) is the most popular statistical test for determining if an independent variable reliably affects scores when there are more than two conditions. The equations used by ANOVA look different from those used in *t*-tests, but for present purposes you can think of them as working in similar ways. ANOVA divides a measure of the difference between conditions by a measure of variability within conditions. The result of that division is called the *F statistic*. If there is no effect of the independent variable, then *F* should be approximately one (i.e., the amount of difference between conditions is about the same as the amount of variability within conditions). If there is an effect of the independent variable, then *F* will be greater than one. The larger the *F*, the less likely that the difference between conditions occurred by a fluke of chance. There are statistical tables that give critical values of *F* for various sample sizes. If the obtained value of *F* is at least as great as the critical value, then the difference is statistically reliable (i.e., unlikely to have occurred by chance alone).

Manipulating More than One Independent Variable: Factorial Analysis of Variance So far, we've described only experiments in which there is a single independent variable (e.g., seating position or form of vision correction). Many of the most interesting experiments in psychology involve the simultaneous manipulation of two or more independent variables. For example, Martin and Aggleton (1993) conducted an experiment in which divers studied safety information (printed on plastic sheets) either on land or while under water and were later tested on the studied information either on land or while under water. In that experiment, location of study was one independent variable, and location of test was another. This is an example of what is called a *factorial* experiment: The two independent variables (each with two conditions) were "crossed" to form a total of four conditions (study–dry/test–dry, study–wet/test–dry, study–dry/test–wet, and study–wet/test–wet).

Three different questions are addressed in any experiment in which two independent variables are manipulated: Was there a main effect of independent variable A? Was there a main effect of independent variable B? Was there an interaction between independent variables A and B? "Main effect" means an overall difference between the two conditions of the independent variable in question. For example, was there a reliable main effect of where divers studied? That is, if we ignore where participants were tested and simply compare all of the participants who studied on land with all of those who studied under water, would the scores of those two groups reliably differ? As it turned out, in the Martin and Aggleton (1993) study there was a main effect of study condition, with divers who studied on land tending, on average, to recall more of the studied material than did those who studied under water. Similarly, when we ask if there was a main effect of test condition, we are asking if those tested on land tended, on average, to perform differently from those tested under water. In fact, there was a main effect of test condition, with divers tested on land doing better than those tested under water. Finally, when we ask about the interaction between two independent variables, we are asking whether the effect of one independent variable depended on the level of the other. Two independent variables interact if the effect of one of those independent variables depends upon the level (condition) of the other independent variable. This is the most interesting aspect of the Martin and Aggleton findings: Among divers who studied on land, those tested on land did better than those tested under water, but among divers who studied under water, those tested under water did better than those tested on land. That is, the study and testing conditions interacted, so that the effect of where the diver studied depended on where he or she was tested (and vice versa).

The results of the Martin and Aggleton study provide an example of a "cross-over" interaction, meaning that the *direction* of the effect of one independent variable depended on the other independent variable (e.g., being tested under water helped performance for those who studied under water, but hurt performance for those who studied on land). Not all interactions have this dramatic a pattern. Suppose, for example, that you did a factorial experiment to test the effect of a new form of psychotherapy (compared to a standard form of therapy) on depressed and anxious patients. You might find that the new therapy had superior effects for the depressed patients, but that it did not differ from standard therapy for anxious patients. This too would be an interaction, in that the efficacy of the therapy depended upon the type of disorder, but it would not be a cross-over interaction because the direction of the effect of type of therapy did not reverse as a function of type of patient. (Test yourself by trying to describe a pattern of results from such an experiment that would have yielded a cross-over interaction.)

Inferential Statistics for Nominal Data: The Chi-Square Test At the beginning of this appendix, we differentiated between nominal (name-like) data and score data. Recall that a nominal measure consists of a set of qualitatively different categories, such as sports, collecting, and music hobbies. Recall also that cross-tabulations can be used to summarize the relationship between two nominal measures (e.g., men's versus women's favourite hobbies). The most popular statistical test of the reliability of relationships between nominal variables is called the *chi-square test*. Look again at Table A.1. Notice that 49% of the respondents were men (10 520/21 525) and that 57% of the respondents reported that they had done nothing to improve their health (12 213/21 525). If there was no relationship at all between gender and responding "nothing," then what percentage of the respondents should be men who responded "nothing"? It should just be the percentage of respondents who were men times the percentage of respondents who responded "nothing." Thus if men and women were equally likely to respond "nothing," then the expected frequency of men responding "nothing" is 49% $\times$ 57% = 28% (or 6012). This is substantially lower than the observed frequency (6309). Similarly, given that 51% of the respondents were women and 57% of respondents said "nothing," the expected number of women saying nothing is 51% $\times$ 57% $\times$ 21 525 = 6257, which is substantially higher than the observed frequency of 5904. Chi-square works by weighing the extent to which observed frequencies differ from expected frequencies in each cell; if that difference is sufficiently large, then the relationship between the two nominal variables is statistically significant (i.e., probably not due merely to chance).

CONCLUSION

This appendix introduced many ideas, yet we have barely scratched the surface of statistics. Also, with the exception of the most elementary and foundational statistical procedures (e.g., those used to calculate SD), we have not covered the nitty-gritty of the mathematical formulas involved in performing particular kinds of statistical tests. Again, for a more complete and comprehensive introduction to this important topic, we recommend a good text such as Pagano (1998) (or ask your instructor what text he or she recommends). Despite its brevity and rather abstract nature, we hope that this appendix has sharpened your intuitive grasp of how statistical analyses work and that it has allayed any fears you may have had about the subject.

Appendix B
Answers to the "Test Yourself" Boxes

Chapter 1

Test Yourself 1.1

1. *False.* Psychologists cannot directly observe the thoughts or feelings of other individuals, but they can and do make inferences about them based on other measures (verbal reports of what people think or feel, physiological measures that are indicative of emotions, etc.).
2. *True.*
3. *True.*
4. *False.* Psychiatrists are medical doctors who receive specialized training in psychology, but the psychological problems of their clients are not fundamentally different than those of psychologists. Both clinical psychologists and psychiatrists work on severe psychological problems such as schizophrenia.
5. *False.* The master's degree is a lower-level qualification than the doctoral degree; the latter is the highest level of formal training in psychology.

Test Yourself 1.2

1. *b.* Most psychologists believe that mental events arise entirely from activity in the brain.
2. Functionalists and structuralists used the technique of *introspection* to understand immediate conscious experience. The *structuralists* believed that it was best to break the mind down into basic parts, much like a chemist would seek to understand a chemical compound. The *functionalists* were influenced by Darwin's views on natural selection and focused primarily on the purpose and adaptive value of mental events. *Behaviourism,* founded by John Watson, steered psychology away from the study of immediate conscious experience toward an emphasis on *behaviour.*
3. *d.* Psychoanalysis often places a strong emphasis on hidden urges and memories related to sex and aggression.
4. Mary Salter Ainsworth was a pioneer Canadian woman psychologist, best known for her work (with Bowlby) on how infants develop attachments to their parents.

Test Yourself 1.3

1. *c.* Clinical psychologists who adopt an eclectic approach often consider the preferences of the client, as well as the type of problem presented, in deciding on the most appropriate therapy.
2. Over the past several decades, psychologists have returned to the study of internal mental phenomena such as con-

sciousness. This shift away from strict behaviourism has been labelled the *cognitive* revolution. An important factor that helped fuel this revolution was the development of the *computer,* which became a model of sorts for the human mind. Developments in *biology* are also playing an important role in shaping modern psychology and in creating effective treatments for psychological problems.
3. *b.* Our cultural background can influence how we think, reason, and remember.

Chapter 2

Test Yourself 2.1

1. The *median* is the middle point in an ordered set of scores.
2. The *case study* technique focuses on single instances of behaviour and is criticized for lacking *external validity.*
3. When behaviour changes as a result of the observation process, it's called a problem of *reactivity.*
4. Limited amounts of information are gathered from many people in a *survey.*

Test Yourself 2.2

1. *Negative.*
2. *Positive.*
3. *Positive.*
4. *Zero correlation.*

Test Yourself 2.3

1. In experimental research, the researcher actively manipulates the environment in order to observe its effect on behaviour. The aspect of the environment that is manipulated is called the *independent* variable; the behaviour of interest is measured by the *dependent* variable. To draw conclusions about cause and effect, the experimenter must make certain that the *independent* variable is the only thing changing systematically in the environment.
2. *b.* The independent variable is not the only factor changing across the groups.
3. *c.* Increases the likelihood that subject differences will be equally represented in each group.

Test Yourself 2.4

1. All psychologists have a responsibility to respect the rights and dignity of other people. To ensure that research participants are treated ethically, psychologists use (a) *informed*

688

NEL

consent, which means that all potential participants are fully informed about the potential risks of the project, (b) *confidentiality*, which ensures that the subject's right to privacy will be maintained, and (c) *debriefing*, which is designed to provide participants with more information about the purpose and procedures of the research.

2. *c.* Is justified, but only under some circumstances.

3. *c.* Animals can give no informed consent.

Chapter 3

Test Yourself 3.1

1. The *soma* is the main body of the cell, where excitatory and inhibitory messages combine.

2. The *axon* is the long tail-like part of a neuron that serves as the cell's main transmitter device.

3. The *action potential* is the all-or-none electrical signal that leads to the release of chemical messengers.

4. The *dendrites* are the branch-like fibres that extend outward and receive information from other neurons.

5. *Neurotransmitters.*

6. In a reflex response, *sensory* neurons carry information about a stimulus (such as intense heat) to the *spinal cord*, where they synapse on to *interneurons*, which in turn synapse with *motor* neurons that stimulate muscles to contract.

Test Yourself 3.2

1. The *hindbrain* is the primitive part of the brain that controls basic life support functions such as heart rate and respiration.

2. The *hypothalamus* is a structure thought to be involved in a variety of motivational activities, including eating, drinking, and sexual behaviour.

3. The *frontal lobes* are believed to be involved in higher-order thought processes (such as planning) as well as the initiation of motor movements.

4. The *cerebellum* is a structure near the base of the brain that is involved in coordination of complex activities such as walking.

5. An *EEG* is a device used to monitor gross electrical activity in the brain.

Test Yourself 3.3

1. *Nervous system.*

2. *Endocrine system.*

3. *Endocrine system.*

4. *Endocrine system.*

5. *Nervous system.*

Test Yourself 3.4

1. *Natural selection.*

2. *Trait.*

3. *Recessive.*

4. *Mutation.*

5. To the extent that a trait is inherited, *identical* twins would be expected to be more similar to one another on that trait than *fraternal* twins.

6. To qualify as an evolutionary adaptation, a trait must be *adaptive, heritable,* and *universal.*

7. *Environment of evolutionary adaptedness (EEA).*

Chapter 4

Test Yourself 4.1

1. a. *Fovea.* The "central pit" area where the cone receptors tend to be located.
   b. *Cones.* Receptors that are responsible for visual acuity, or our ability to see fine detail.
   c. *Accommodation.* Process through which the lens changes its shape temporarily in order to help focus light.
   d. *Retina.* The "film" at the back of the eye that contains the light-sensitive receptor cells.
   e. *Cornea.* The protective outer layer of the eye.

2. a. *False.* The majority of visual messages are analyzed in the lateral geniculate and primary visual cortex, although some messages are relayed to the superior colliculus.
   b. *True.*
   c. *True.*
   d. *True.*

3. a. *Top-down processing.* The part of perception that is controlled by our beliefs and expectations about how the world is organized.
   b. *Perceptual constancy.* Perceiving an object, or its properties, to remain the same even though the physical input received by the eyes is changing.
   c. *Convergence.* The depth cue that is based on calculating the degree to which the two eyes have turned inward.
   d. *Recognition by components.* The view that object perception is based on the analysis of simple building blocks, called geons.
   e. *Lower region.*

Test Yourself 4.2

1. *True.*

2. *False.* Place, not frequency, theory proposes that the location of activity on the basilar membrane is a critical cue for determining pitch.

3. *False.* Hair cells are located in the cochlea, not the pinna, and they are "bent" by movement of the basilar membrane.

4. *False.* Figure–ground organization occurs in hearing as well as in vision.

5. *True.*

Test Yourself 4.3

1. *b.* Our perception of temperature is influenced by the changes that occur from one environment to the next.

2. *c.* Psychological factors are thought to somehow block pain messages from reaching higher neural centres.

3. *d.* The vestibular sacs are part of the structures of the inner ear.

Test Yourself 4.4

1. *Chemoreceptors.* The general term for receptor cells that are activated by invisible molecules scattered about in the air or dissolved in liquids.
2. *Olfactory bulb.* One of the main brain destinations for odour stimuli.
3. *Flavour.* A psychological term used to describe the entire gustatory experience.
4. *Olfaction.* The technical name for the sense of smell.
5. *Gustation.* The technical name for the sense of taste.

Test Yourself 4.5

1. *False.* The point on the intensity curve at which an individual reliably detects a stimulus varies over time.
2. *True.*
3. *False.* Detection of a jnd in magnitude depends on the intensity of the standard.
4. *True.*
5. *True.*

Chapter 5

Test Yourself 5.1

1. *False.* The cocktail party effect suggests that we do at least some monitoring of unattended messages. We hear our name when it's spoken from across the room.
2. *True.*
3. *True.*
4. *False.* Damage to the right side of the brain, in visual neglect, means that people will fail to recognize things on the left side of the body.
5. *False.* Although some aspects of attention deficit/hyperactivity disorder may be learned, most researchers believe that some kind of neurological problem also contributes to the disorder.
6. *False.*

Test Yourself 5.2

1. a. *Theta waves.* The characteristic pattern found in stage 1 sleep.
   b. *K complex.* Often triggered by loud noises during stage 2 sleep.
   c. *Delta activity.* Another name for the slow-wave patterns that are found during stage 3 and stage 4 sleep.
   d. *REM.* The characteristic pattern of paradoxical sleep.
2. *c.* Cats sleep more than cows.
3. a. *Insomnia.* Difficulty initiating and maintaining sleep.
   b. *Night terror.* Sleeper awakens suddenly, screaming, but the EEG pattern indicates a period of non-REM sleep.
   c. *Sleep apnea.* Sleeper repeatedly stops breathing during the night, usually for short periods lasting less than one minute.

d. *Nightmare.* A frightening dream that usually occurs during the REM stage of sleep.

Test Yourself 5.3

1. *Stimulant.* Increases central nervous system activity.
2. *Opiate.* Reduces pain by mimicking the brain's own natural pain-reducing chemicals.
3. *Depressant.* Tends to produce inhibitory effects by increasing the effectiveness of the neurotransmitter GABA.
4. *Hallucinogen.* Distorts perception and may lead to flashbacks.
5. *Caffeine.* The active ingredient found in your morning cup of coffee.

Test Yourself 5.4

1. *False.* The EEG patterns of a hypnotized person more closely resemble the patterns found when you're awake, not asleep.
2. *False.* Hypnosis increases the chances of fabrication and does not generally lead to better memory.
3. *True.*
4. *False.* Hilgard's experiments support the idea of hypnotic dissociations.
5. *True.*

Chapter 6

Test Yourself 6.1

1. *Sensitization.*
2. *Orienting response.*
3. *Habituation.*
4. *Habituation.*
5. *Habituation.*

Test Yourself 6.2

1. a. The unconditioned stimulus is the screaming.
   b. The unconditioned response is wincing and covering your ears.
   c. The conditioned stimulus is the sound of running water.
   d. The conditioned response is wincing.
2. a. The unconditioned stimulus is the puff of air.
   b. The unconditioned response is blinking.
   c. The conditioned stimulus is the word "ready."
   d. The conditioned response is the urge to blink.
3. *d. Extinction.* It's likely that the boy looked at the neighbour's yard many times after the neighbours moved, without being frightened by the now-departed dogs. So, the association was extinguished.
4. *e. Inhibitory conditioning.* Your grandmother has become a conditioned stimulus that signals to Rascal that scraps will not be forthcoming and hence inhibits his begging.

Test Yourself 6.3

1. a. *Negative punishment.* Arriving home late is punished by the removal of freedom.

b. *Positive reinforcement.* The bonus is presented to increase the chances of similar sales behaviour again.

c. *Positive punishment.* The ticket is delivered to lower the likelihood of speeding in a school zone.

d. *Positive reinforcement.* Crying increases because Mom delivers a kiss and a story.

e. *Positive punishment.* Dad delivers a stern lecture for crying, which lowers the likelihood of crying in his presence.

2. a. *Variable-ratio.* Reinforcement depends on the number of calls, but the number of calls is not constant or predictable.

b. *Fixed-ratio.* Reinforcement always occurs when she goes to a rally.

c. *Variable-interval.* Reinforcement cannot be predicted and depends on the passage of time rather than the number of responses.

d. *Fixed-ratio.* Reinforcement is delivered after a fixed number of purchases.

e. *Variable-interval.* Reinforcement is not predictable and depends on the passage of time.

Test Yourself 6.4

1. *False.* Observational learning often applies to our own behaviour—we learn to act in a certain way by observing a role model.

2. *True.*

3. *False.* Our beliefs about how well we can perform a task (self-efficacy) play an important role in observational learning.

4. *True.*

5. *True.*

Chapter 7

Test Yourself 7.1

1. *Sensory memory.*
2. *Short-term memory.*
3. *Sensory memory.*
4. *Short-term memory.*
5. *Sensory memory.*
6. *Short-term memory.*
7. *Short-term memory.*
8. *Short-term memory.*

Test Yourself 7.2

1. a. *Semantic.*
   b. *Episodic.*
   c. *Semantic.*
   d. *Procedural.*
   e. *Procedural.*

2. *c.* Form a visual image of each word.

3. a. *Method of loci.* A mnemonic device in which you visualize items sitting in different locations.

b. *Distinctiveness.* The appropriate term to use when you notice how an item is different from other things in memory.

c. *Elaboration.* The formation of connections between an item and other things in memory.

d. *Link-word system.* The French word for "dog," "chien," sounds like the English word "chin," so to learn the French word you might imagine a person's face with a tiny dog sitting on the chin.

e. *Distributed practice.* Spacing practice episodes across time, with other activities between them.

f. *Massed practice.* Opposite of distributed practice.

Test Yourself 7.3

1. *Schema.* An organized structure of knowledge stored in long-term memory.

2. *Implicit memory.* Using memory automatically and without awareness of doing so.

3. *Transfer-appropriate processing.* Studying for a multiple-choice test by writing and answering your own multiple-choice questions.

4. *Encoding specificity principle.* The idea that retrieval cues must match the information stored in the original memory record.

5. *Flashbulb memory.* Very detailed and vivid recollection of an emotionally significant and surprising event, such as hearing the news of the September 11, 2001, attacks.

6. *Free recall.* Remembering material without the aid of any specific external retrieval cues.

Test Yourself 7.4

1. *False.* Most forgetting occurs early and is followed by more gradual loss.

2. *True.*

3. *False.* Proactive interference occurs when prior learning interferes with later remembering.

4. *False.* People with anterograde amnesia can learn new things, but lose the ability to access those memories consciously.

5. *True.*

6. *True.*

Chapter 8

Test Yourself 8.1

1. a. *Phonemes.* The smallest significant sound units in speech.

b. *Pragmatics.* The term used for the practical knowledge that helps us understand the intentions of a speaker and pick an effective response.

c. *Linguistic relativity.* The hypothesis that proposes that language determines the characteristics and content of thought.

d. *Syntax.* The rules that govern how words are combined into sentences.

e. *Morphemes.* The smallest units in a language that carry meaning.

2. a. *True.*

b. *False.* Babies appear to learn language rules implicitly and often produce phrases, and commit errors, that they never hear from their parents.

c. *True.*

d. *True.*

e. *False.* Kanzi appears able to understand and follow spoken requests from this trainers.

f. *True.*

Test Yourself 8.2

1. a. *Defining features.*

b. *Category exemplars.*

c. *Family resemblance.*

d. *Prototype.*

2. *b.* Basic level ("look, it's a cat").

Test Yourself 8.3

1. a. Finding your way to a restaurant is a well-defined problem, because the starting and goal states can be clearly specified.

b. Getting an A in psychology is a well-defined problem; you can specify what your current mark would be, and the criteria for an A are (or at least should be!) clearly defined in the syllabus.

c. Making your lab partner fall madly in love with you is an ill-defined problem, because it would be difficult to precisely define how he or she currently feels and difficult to define "madly in love."

d. Baking a delicious cheesecake is an ill-defined problem, because it is unclear what constitutes "deliciousness."

2. a. *Searching for analogies.*

b. *Algorithm.*

c. *Means–ends analysis.*

d. *Algorithm.*

Test Yourself 8.4

1. *Availability heuristic.*

2. *Confirmation bias.*

3. *Framing.*

4. *Illusory correlation.*

5. *Representativeness heuristic.*

Chapter 9

Test Yourself 9.1

1. *Sternberg's intelligences.* "Street smarts" is an example of practical intelligence.

2. *Cognitive.* Intelligence is defined by the speed of mental processes.

3. *Gardner's intelligences.* Musical ability is considered to be a type of intelligence in Gardner's theory.

4. *Psychometric.* Intelligence is measured by analyzing performance on mental tests.

5. *Psychometric.* Factor analysis is a statistical technique used to analyze test performance.

6. *Gardner's intelligences.* Insight into the feelings of others is a type of intelligence in Gardner's theory.

7. *Sternberg's intelligences.* Applying what's been learned to new situations is a kind of creative intelligence.

Test Yourself 9.2

1. a. *Reliability.* Donna's performance is consistent across testing.

b. *Validity.* Larry's new test doesn't measure what it's supposed to measure.

c. *Reliability.* Chei-Wui is checking on the consistency of test scores.

d. *Standardization.* Robert makes certain that the testing and scoring procedures are the same for everybody who takes the test.

2. a. *True.*

b. *False.* Average IQ, based on the deviation IQ method, is always 100 regardless of age.

c. *False.* The diagnosis of mental retardation depends on many factors, such as one's ability to adapt.

d. *False.* Creativity doesn't correlate very highly with IQ.

Test Yourself 9.3

1. *False.* Fluid intelligence shows declines over the life span.

2. *False.* Identical twins reared apart tend to have more similar IQs than fraternal twins raised together.

3. *True.*

4. *False.* Heritability tells us only that for a given group, a certain percentage of the differences in intelligence can be explained by genetic factors.

5. *True.*

Test Yourself 9.4

1. *False.* No such bias exists.

2. *False.* Our perceptions show a small but significant degree of accuracy.

3. *False.* Entity theorists believe that intelligence is fixed.

4. *True.* Although the effects are small, there is evidence that such labels affect our expectations about people and, consequently, our behaviour toward them.

5. *True.* There are a number of such examples in the history of testing in the 20th century.

Chapter 10

Test Yourself 10.1

1. *False.* The period from implantation to the end of the eighth week is called the embryonic period.

2. *True.*

3. *False.* The cells increase in size and complexity, not in number. The number of glial cells in the brain, however, may increase with age.
4. *False.* The timing of motor development is determined primarily by nature—the genetic code—although the environment may play some role.
5. *False.* We all lose brain cells with age, but the vast majority of people over 70 will not develop dementia.

Test Yourself 10.2

1. a. *Reward.* In the reward technique, the baby is given reinforcement when he or she performs a movement, such as kicking a leg, in response to a presented event.
   b. *Habituation.* The decline in responsiveness to repeated presentations, called habituation, can be used to infer that the baby recognizes that elements of the event have been repeated.
   c. *Cross-sectional.* In a cross-sectional design, different age groups are studied at the same time.
   d. *Longitudinal.* In a longitudinal design, the same individual is tested repeatedly across the life span.
2. *Conservation.* Conservation refers to the ability to recognize that certain physical properties of an object, such as mass, remain the same despite changes in the object's appearance.
3. a. *Conventional.* According to Kohlberg, individuals at the conventional level of moral reasoning decide the correctness of actions on the basis of whether or not the action disrupts the social order.
   b. *Postconventional.* At the postconventional level, moral reasoning is based on abstract principles that may or may not conflict with accepted standards.
   c. *Preconventional.* At the preconventional level, moral decisions are made on the basis of the action's immediate consequences.

Test Yourself 10.3

1. a. *Secure.*
   b. *Avoidant.*
   c. *Resistant.*
   d. *Resistant.*
2. *d.* Not all teenagers suffer anxiety during this period.
3. *False.* Gender identity is already being formed by age 2 or 3.
4. a. *False.* Most elderly people are not sick and disabled, although physical problems certainly do increase with age.
   b. *False.* Some stereotypes about the elderly are positive, such as the belief that all elderly people are wise and kind.
   c. *False.* Research suggests the opposite.
   d. *False.* Research suggests that most elderly people prefer to strive to keep on living in such circumstances.

Chapter 11

Test Yourself 11.1

1. *c.* Instincts lead to fixed response patterns; drives do not.

2. a. *Incentive motivation.* Whitney jogs because of the reward.
   b. *Intrinsic motivation.* Janice's playing is self-motivated.
   c. *Achievement motivation.* Candice studies to satisfy a need for achievement.
   d. *Intrinsic motivation.* Jerome has become less motivated because of the reward.
3. *b.* Satisfying basic survival and social needs.

Test Yourself 11.2

1. *False.* A high level of glucose, or blood sugar, is associated with a decreased desire for food.
2. *False.* Binging and purging are the principal symptoms of bulimia nervosa.
3. *False.* Stimulation of the lateral hypothalamus causes an animal to start eating, not stop eating.
4. *False.* Obesity is caused by many factors, not necessarily poor dietary habits.
5. *False.* Destruction of the ventromedial hypothalamus increases hunger and leads to large weight gains.

Test Yourself 11.3

1. *True.*
2. *False.* Women tend to not include condom use in their sexual scripts.
3. *True.*
4. *True.*

Test Yourself 11.4

1. a. Dancing is an *expressive reaction.*
   b. Grimacing and wrinkling her nose is an *expressive reaction.*
   c. A racing heart is a *body reaction.*
   d. Robert is telling us about his *subjective experience.*
2. *c.* Receiving a C when you expected to flunk is the largest change in expectation (i.e., adaptation level).
3. a. *James-Lange.*
   b. *Schachter.*
   c. *Cannon-Bard.*
   d. *Schachter.*

Chapter 12

Test Yourself 12.1

1. a. *Openness.*
   b. *Extraversion.*
   c. *Agreeableness.*
   d. *Neuroticism.*
   e. *Conscientiousness.*
2. a. *TAT.*
   b. *MMPI.*
   c. *NEO-PI-R.*
   d. *Rorschach.*
   e. *16 Personality Factor.*

Test Yourself 12.2

1. *Psychodynamic.*
2. *Cognitive–behavioural.*
3. *Humanistic.*
4. *Psychodynamic.*
5. *Humanistic.*
6. *Cognitive–behavioural.*
7. *Psychodynamic.*

Test Yourself 12.3

1. *True.*
2. *True.*
3. *False.* High self-monitors tend to adapt their behaviour to the situation.
4. *False.* Genetics appear to play a significant role in personality as measured by the MMPI.
5. *False.* Personality traits may only reveal themselves if they are relevant, or needed, in the situation.

Chapter 13

Test Yourself 13.1

1. a. *True.*
   b. *False.* Exemplar, not prototype, theories assume that we represent stereotypes with particular individuals, or exemplars.
   c. *False.* It is the belief that out-groups are opposed to traditional values that appears to be more of a concern for authoritarian individuals.
   d. *False.* The "personal/group" discrepancy refers to the fact that people tend to report discrimination against their group is high when they themselves report personally experiencing little discrimination.
2. a. *Internal.*
   b. *Internal.*
   c. *External.*
   d. *Internal.*
3. a. *True.*
   b. *False.* The central, not peripheral, route to persuasion operates when our level of involvement in or commitment to a message is high.
   c. *True.*
   d. *False.* Mere exposure is most likely to lead to attitude change when we're processing a message peripherally.

Test Yourself 13.2

1. a. *Conformity.*
   b. *Bystander effect.*
   c. *Social facilitation.*
   d. *Deindividuation.*
   e. *Group polarization.*
   f. *Social loafing,* although conformity is also a possibility.
2. *d.* The experiment is conducted in the teacher's home.

Test Yourself 13.3

1. *True.*
2. *False.* Averaged faces tend to be rated as most attractive.
3. *False.* Your ratings would go down.
4. *True.*
5. *True.*
6. *False.* Companionate love typically leads to more feelings of warmth and trust.
7. *True.*

Chapter 14

Test Yourself 14.1

1. *False.* When a behaviour occurs infrequently among members of a population it meets the criterion of statistical deviance.
2. *False.* Not all people with psychological disorders are emotionally distressed.
3. *True.*
4. *True.*

Test Yourself 14.2

1. *Somatoform disorder* (hypochondriasis or conversion disorder).
2. *Anxiety disorder* (obsessive–compulsive disorder).
3. *Anxiety disorder* (panic disorder, agoraphobia).
4. *Mood disorder* (depressive disorder).
5. *Dissociative disorder* (dissociative fugue).
6. *Personality disorder* (antisocial personality disorder).
7. *Schizophrenia* (paranoia).
8. *Schizophrenia* (catatonia).

Test Yourself 14.3

1. *b.* Excessive amounts of the neurotransmitter dopamine.
2. *d.* If your identical twin has schizophrenia, you have about a 50% chance of developing the disorder yourself.
3. *d.* Internal, stable, and global.
4. *b.* Observational learning.

Chapter 15

Test Yourself 15.1

1. a. *Schizophrenia* (Clozapine).
   b. *Depression* (Prozac).
   c. *Depression* (ECT).
   d. *Generalized anxiety disorder* (Benzodiazepine).
2. *d.* ECT is used regularly to treat schizophrenia.

Test Yourself 15.2

1. *Rational-emotive therapy.*
2. *Beck's cognitive therapy.*
3. *Psychoanalysis.*
4. *Client-centred therapy.*

5. *Gestalt therapy.*
6. *Family therapy.*

Test Yourself 15.3
1. *b.* Conditioned stimulus.
2. *a.* Counterconditioning and extinction.
3. *b.* Effective punishments can't be delivered because pain thresholds are high.
4. *d.* Reinforcement.

Test Yourself 15.4
1. *True.*
2. *True.*
3. *False.* Many evaluation studies show that the particular form of treatment doesn't matter.
4. *False.* Some types of treatment, such as most behavioural therapies, show concern only for the present symptoms.
5. *True.*

Chapter 16

Test Yourself 16.1
1. *c.* Alarm, resistance, exhaustion.
2. *c.* The experience of stress, like emotion, depends on the appraisal of the event rather than on the event itself.

3. *a.* Marriage.
4. *c.* An optimistic outlook.

Test Yourself 16.2
1. *True.*
2. *True.*
3. *False.* Stress has been shown to affect cholesterol levels.
4. *False.* Most people who suffer trauma do not develop post-traumatic stress disorder.
5. *True.*

Test Yourself 16.3
1. *c.* The stress response is incompatible with relaxation.
2. *a.* It gives you a feeling of control.
3. *d.* Social support makes it easier to cope if the support is no longer delivered.
4. *a.* Cognitive reappraisal.

Test Yourself 16.4
1. *False.* Aerobic exercise can lessen the physiological effects of the stress reaction.
2. *True.*
3. *True.*
4. *False.* Teaching children about the hazards of smoking or drugs would be classified as an example of *primary* prevention.

Glossary

abnormal behaviour A general term including behaviour that is unusual, maladaptive, socially deviant, and/or accompanied by continuing distress.

absolute threshold The level of intensity that lifts a stimulus over the threshold of conscious awareness; it's defined as the intensity level at which a person detects the presence of the stimulus 50% of the time.

accommodation (Chapter 4) In vision, the process by which the lens changes shape temporarily to help focus light on the retina. (Chapter 10) The process through which people change or modify existing schemas to accommodate new experiences when they occur.

acetylcholine A neurotransmitter that plays several roles in the central and peripheral nervous systems, including the excitation of muscle contractions.

achievement motivation tests Psychological tests that measure your desire to perform challenging tasks and reach difficult goals.

achievement motive A need for achievement that varies in strength across individuals. Its strength on any given task depends on (1) one's expectations about success and (2) how much value one places on succeeding at the task.

achievement tests Psychological tests that measure your current level of knowledge or competence in a particular subject.

action potential The all-or-none electrical signal that travels down a neuron's axon.

activation-synthesis hypothesis The idea that dreams represent the brain's attempt to make sense out of random patterns of neural activity generated during sleep.

actor-observer effect The tendency to attribute others' behaviour to internal forces and our own behaviour to external forces.

adrenal glands Secrete norepinephrine and epinephrine into the bloodstream.

aerobic exercise High-intensity activities, such as running and swimming, that increase both heart rate and oxygen consumption.

afterimage A sensation experienced after removal of a stimulus. For example, after staring at a red maple leaf for several seconds, when you shift your focus to a blank part of the page you will have a green afterimage.

aggression Behaviour meant to harm someone.

agoraphobia An anxiety disorder that causes an individual to restrict his or her normal activities; someone suffering from agoraphobia tends to avoid public places out of fear that a panic attack will occur.

AIDS Acquired immune deficiency syndrome, a disease that gradually weakens and disables the immune system.

alcohol myopia A state induced by alcohol intoxication that results in more extreme social behaviours.

algorithms Step-by-step rules or procedures that, if applied correctly, guarantee a problem solution eventually.

alpha waves The pattern of brain activity observed in someone who is in a relaxed state with eyes open.

anal stage Freud's second stage of psychosexual development, occurring in the second year of life; pleasure is derived from the process of defecation.

anorexia nervosa An eating disorder diagnosed when an otherwise healthy person refuses to maintain a normal weight level because of an intense fear of being overweight.

anterograde amnesia Memory loss for events that happen after the physical injury.

antianxiety drugs Medications that reduce tension and anxiety. Many work on the inhibitory neurotransmitter GABA.

antidepressant drugs Medications that modulate the availability or effectiveness of the neurotransmitters implicated in mood disorders; Prozac, for example, increases the action of the neurotransmitter serotonin.

antipsychotic drugs Medications that reduce the positive symptoms of schizophrenia; the majority act on the neurotransmitter dopamine.

antisocial personality disorder A personality disorder characterized by repeated offences against social laws, customs, or norms.

anxiety disorders A class of disorders marked by excessive apprehension and worry that in turn impairs normal functioning.

applied psychologists Psychologists who apply the principles of scientific psychology to practical, everyday problems in the world.

aptitude tests Psychological tests that measure your ability to learn and solve problems in a particular subject area.

artificial intelligence The attempt to understand the meaning of intelligence by building intelligent machines. Such machines—usually computer programs—can simulate or surpass many human capabilities.

assimilation The process through which people fit—or assimilate—new experiences into existing schemas.

attachments Strong emotional ties formed to one or more intimate companions.

attention The internal processes people use to set and follow priorities for mental functioning.

attention deficit/hyperactivity disorder A psychological condition marked by difficulties in concentrating or in sustaining attention for extended periods and by high levels of fidgety physical activity; occurs most often in children.

attitude A positive or negative evaluation or belief held about something, which in turn may affect one's behaviour; attitudes are typically broken down into cognitive, affective, and behavioural components.

attributions The inference processes people use to assign cause and effect to behaviour.

automaticity Fast and almost effortless processing that requires little or no focused attention.

autonomic system Nerves that control the more automatic needs of the body, such as heart rate, digestion, blood pressure, and so on; part of the peripheral nervous system.

auto-stereotyping A belief system about discrimination that is widely shared by group members.

availability heuristic The tendency to base estimates of frequency or probability on the ease with which examples come to mind. For example, if you've just heard about a plane crash, your estimate of the likelihood of plane crashes may increase because the recent plane crash easily comes to mind.

aversion therapy A treatment for replacing a positive reaction to a harmful stimulus, such as alcohol, with something negative, such as feeling nauseated.

axon The long tail-like part of a neuron that serves as the cell's transmitter device.

basic-level categories The level in a category hierarchy that most efficiently provides a lot of useful and predictive information; the basic level is usually an intermediate level in a category hierarchy.

basilar membrane A flexible membrane running through the cochlea that, through its movement, displaces the auditory receptor cells (hair cells).

behaviour Observable actions such as moving, talking, gesturing, and so on; behaviours can also refer to the activities of cells, as measured through physiological recording devices, and to thoughts and feelings, as measured through oral and written expression.

behavioural therapies Treatments designed to change behaviour through the use of established learning techniques.

behaviourism A school of psychology proposing that the proper subject matter of psychology is directly observable behaviour and the situations that lead to changes in behaviour, rather than immediate conscious experience.

bell curve The plot of frequencies obtained for many psychological tests. Most people get scores in the middle range, and the decline in frequencies is similar whether scores get higher or lower than the mean.

Big Five The five dimensions of personality—extraversion, agreeableness, conscientiousness, neuroticism, and openness—that have been isolated through the application of factor analysis. It is widely believed that virtually all personality terms in language can be accounted for by appealing to one or more of these basic dimensions.

binocular depth cues Cues for depth that depend on comparisons between the two eyes.

biofeedback Specific physiological feedback that people are given about the effectiveness of their relaxation efforts.

biological clocks Brain structures that schedule rhythmic variations in bodily functions by triggering them at the appropriate times.

biomedical therapies Biologically based treatments, including drug therapies, shock treatments, and, very rarely, psychosurgery.

bio-psycho-social perspective The idea that psychological disorders are influenced, or caused, by a combination of biological, psychological (cognitive), and social (environmental) factors.

bipolar disorder A type of mood disorder in which the person experiences disordered mood shifts in two directions—from depression to a manic state.

blind spot The point where the optic nerve leaves the back of the eye; there are no rods or cones in the blind spot.

bottom-up processing Processing that is driven by the physical input contacting the sensory receptors.

brightness The aspect of the visual experience that changes with light intensity; in general, as the intensity of light increases, so does its perceived brightness.

bulimia nervosa An eating disorder in which the principal symptom is binge eating (consuming large quantities of food), followed by purging in which the person voluntarily vomits or uses laxatives to prevent weight gain.

burnout A state of physical, emotional, and mental exhaustion created by long-term involvement in an emotionally demanding situation.

bystander effect The reluctance to come to the aid of a person in need when other people are present.

Cannon-Bard theory A theory of emotion that argues that body reactions and subjective experiences occur together, but independently.

cardinal traits Allport's term to describe personality traits that dominate an individual's life, such as a passion to serve others or to accumulate wealth.

case study A descriptive research technique in which the research effort is focused on a single case (usually an individual, although case studies can also be conducted on small groups).

catalepsy A hypnotically induced behaviour characterized by an ability to hold one or more limbs of the body in a rigid position for long periods without tiring. Motivated nonhypnotized subjects can enact catalepsy as well as hypnotized subjects.

category A class of objects (people, places, or things) or events that most people in a given culture agree belong together.

category exemplars Specific examples of category members that are stored in long-term memory.

catharsis The expending of aggressive energy via direct or indirect means.

central nervous system The brain and the spinal cord.

central traits Allport's term to describe the 5 to 10 descriptive traits that you would use to describe someone you know—friendly, trustworthy, and so on.

cerebellum A hindbrain structure at the base of the brain that is involved in the coordination of complex motor skills.

cerebral cortex The outer layer of the brain, considered to be the seat of higher mental processes.

chemoreceptors Receptor cells that react to molecules in the air or dissolved in liquids, leading to the senses of smell and taste.

chunking A short-term memory strategy that involves mentally rearranging many pieces of information into a familiar and meaningful pattern. A single chunk can represent a wealth of information.

circadian rhythms Biological activities that rise and fall in a 24-hour cycle.

classical conditioning A set of procedures, initially developed by Pavlov, used to investigate how organisms learn about the signalling properties of events. Classical conditioning leads to the learning of relations between events—conditioned and unconditioned stimuli—that occur outside of one's control.

client-centred therapy A form of humanistic therapy, developed by Carl Rogers, proposing that it is the client, not the therapist, who holds the key to psychological health and happiness; the therapist's role is to provide genuineness, unconditional positive regard, and empathy.

clinical psychologists Professional psychologists who specialize in the diagnosis and treatment of psychological problems.

cochlea The bony, snail-shell–shaped sound processor in the inner ear, where sounds are transduced into nerve impulses.

cocktail party effect The ability to focus on one auditory message, such as a friend's voice at a noisy party, and largely ignore others, yet notice when one's name is spoken among the auditory stimuli that one has been "ignoring."

cognitive appraisal The idea that in order to feel stress you need to perceive a threat and come to the conclusion that you may not have adequate resources to deal with the threat.

cognitive–behavioural theories An approach to personality that suggests it is reward-punishment experiences, and interpretations of those experiences, that determine personality growth and development.

cognitive dissonance The tension produced when people act in a way that is inconsistent with their attitudes; attitude change may occur as a result of attempting to reduce cognitive dissonance.

cognitive revolution The shift away from strict behaviourism, begun in the 1950s, characterized by renewed interest in the study of consciousness and internal mental processes.

cognitive therapies Treatments designed to remove irrational beliefs and negative thoughts that are presumed to be responsible for psychological disorders.

cold fibres Neurons that respond to a cooling of the skin by increasing the production of neural impulses.

collective unconscious The notion proposed by Carl Jung that certain kinds of universal symbols and ideas are present in the unconscious of all people.

companionate love A kind of emotional attachment characterized by feelings of trust and companionship; companionate love is marked by a combination of intimacy and commitment, but passion may be lacking.

computerized tomography scan (CT scan) The use of highly focused beams of X-rays to construct detailed anatomical maps of the living brain.

concrete operational period Piaget's third stage of cognitive development, lasting from age 7 to age 11. Children acquire the capacity to perform a number of mental operations but still lack the ability for abstract reasoning.

conditioned inhibition Learning to associate a previously neutral stimulus with the non-occurrence of an unconditioned stimulus.

conditioned reinforcer A stimulus that has acquired reinforcing properties through prior learning.

conditioned response (CR) The acquired response that is produced to the conditioned stimulus in anticipation of the arrival of the unconditioned stimulus. Often, the conditioned response resembles the unconditioned response, although not always.

conditioned stimulus (CS) A neutral stimulus (one that does not produce the unconditioned response prior to training) that is paired with the unconditioned stimulus during classical conditioning.

conditions of worth The expectations or standards that we believe others place on us.

cones Receptor cells in the central portion of the retina that transduce light energy into neural activity; they operate best when light levels are fairly high, and they are primarily responsible for the ability to sense fine detail and colour.

confidentiality The principle that all personal information obtained from a participant in research or therapy should not be revealed without the individual's permission.

confirmation bias The tendency to emphasize hypothesis-confirming evidence when making decisions.

conformity The tendency to go along with the wishes of the group; when people conform, their opinions, feelings, and behaviours generally start to move toward the group norm.

confounding variable An uncontrolled variable that changes along with the independent variable.

conscious mind The contents of awareness—those things that occupy the focus of one's current attention.

consciousness The subjective awareness of internal and external events.

conservation The ability to recognize that the physical properties of an object remain the same despite superficial changes in the object's appearance.

conventional level In Kohlberg's theory of moral development, the stage in which actions are judged to be right or wrong based on whether they maintain or disrupt the social order.

convergence A binocular cue for depth that is based on the extent to which the two eyes move inward, or converge, when looking at an object.

conversion disorder The presence of real physical problems, such as blindness or paralysis, that seem to have no identifiable physical cause.

coping Efforts to manage or master conditions of threat or demand that tax one's resources.

cornea The transparent and protective outer covering of the eye.

corpus callosum The collection of nerve fibres that connect the two cerebral hemispheres and allow information to pass from one side to the other.

correlation A statistic that indicates whether two variables are related or vary together in a systematic way; correlation coefficients vary from +1.00 (perfect positive relationship) to 0.00 (no relationship) to −1.00 (perfect negative relationship).

counselling psychologist Professional who deals with milder problems such as family and personal adjustment issues.

counsellor An individual who provides some sort of therapy or support to clients, but who (typically) does not have advanced training in providing psychological treatment. Some counsellors (or "therapists") are skilled and effective, but others are not.

creativity The ability to generate ideas that are original, novel, and useful.

cross-sectional design A research design in which people of different ages are compared at the same time.

crystallized intelligence The knowledge and abilities acquired as a result of experience (as from schooling and cultural influences).

cue-dependent forgetting The idea that forgetting is caused by a failure to retrieve memories due to lack of appropriate retrieval cues.

cued recall A testing condition in which subjects are given specific retrieval cues to help them remember. For example, subjects might be given hints or cues such as "some of the words were fruits; others were vegetables."

cultural deviance criterion Behaviour is abnormal if it violates the rules or accepted standards of society.

culture The shared values, customs, and beliefs that are characteristic of a group or community.

culture-fair test Tests that avoid using language (e.g., by using only pictures or symbols) so that the test is fair to all cultures.

dark adaptation The process through which the eyes adjust to dim light.

debriefing At the conclusion of an experimental session, informing the participants about the purpose of the experiment, including any deception that was involved.

decay The proposal that memories are forgotten or lost spontaneously with the passage of time (or with some passive chemical processes that occur over time, akin to rusting).

decision making The thought processes involved in evaluating and choosing from among a set of alternatives; it usually involves some degree of risk.

deep structure The underlying representation of meaning in a sentence.

defence mechanisms According to Freud, unconscious processes used by the ego to ward off the anxiety that comes from conflicts between the superego and the id.

defining features A set of features that define membership in a category, such that all members of that category (and no nonmembers of that category) have all of those features. For example, the defining features of the category "triangle" might be (1) a two-dimensional figure that is (2) composed of three straight lines with (3) each end of each line joined to an end of one of the other lines.

deindividuation The loss of individuality, or depersonalization, that comes from being in a group.

delta activity The pattern of brain activity observed in stage 3 and stage 4 sleep; it's characterized by synchronized slow waves. Also called *slow-wave sleep*.

dementia Physically based losses in mental functioning.

dendrites The branchlike fibres that extend outward from a neuron and receive information from other neurons.

denial A defence mechanism involving the refusal to accept an external reality that creates anxiety.

dependent personality disorder A personality disorder characterized by an excessive and persistent need to be taken care of by others.

dependent variable The behaviour that is measured in an experiment.

depressants A class of drugs that slow or depress the ongoing activity of the central nervous system.

descriptive research The tactics and methods that underlie the direct observation and description of behaviour.

descriptive statistics Mathematical techniques that help researchers describe and summarize their data.

development The age-related physical, intellectual, social, and personal changes that occur throughout an individual's lifetime.

deviation IQ An intelligence score that is derived from determining where your performance sits in an age-based distribution of test scores.

dichotic listening A technique in which two different auditory messages are simultaneously presented, one to each ear. Usually the subject's task is to shadow, or repeat aloud, one of the messages as it goes along while ignoring the other.

difference threshold The smallest difference in the magnitude of two stimuli that an observer can reliably detect.

diffusion of responsibility The idea that when people know, or think, that others are present in a situation, they allow their sense of responsibility for action to diffuse, or spread out widely, among those who are present.

discrimination Behaving in an unfair way toward members of another group.

discriminative stimulus The stimulus situation that sets the occasion for a response to be followed by reinforcement or punishment.

dissociative amnesia A psychological disorder characterized by an inability to remember important personal information.

dissociative disorders A class of disorders characterized by the separation, or dissociation, of conscious awareness from previous thoughts or memories.

dissociative fugue A loss of personal identity that is often accompanied by a flight from home.

dissociative identity disorder A condition in which an individual alternates between what appear to be two or more distinct identities or personalities (also known as *multiple personality disorder*).

distinctiveness A term used to refer to how unique or different a memory record is, compared to other information in memory. Distinctive memory records tend to be recalled well.

distributed practice Spacing the repetitions of to-be-remembered information over time.

dominant versus recessive genes For many traits there are two genes, with one of them being dominant and the other recessive. If the two such genes for a given trait differ, it is the dominant gene that influences the observable characteristic.

dopamine A neurotransmitter that often leads to inhibitory effects; decreased levels have been linked to Parkinson's disease, and increased levels have been linked to schizophrenia.

double-blind study An experimental design in which neither the participants nor the research observers are aware of who has been assigned to the experimental and control groups; it's used to control for both subject and experimenter expectancies.

dream analysis A technique used in psychoanalysis; Freud believed that dreams are symbolic and contain important information about the unconscious.

drug dependency A condition in which an individual experiences a physical or psychological need for continued use of a drug.

DSM-IV The *Diagnostic and Statistical Manual of Mental Disorders* (4th ed.), which is used for the diagnosis and classification of psychological disorders. The DSM-IV is composed of five major rating dimensions, or *axes*.

dysfunction criterion Behaviour is abnormal if it interferes with one's ability to pursue daily activities such as work and relationships.

echoic memory The system that produces and stores auditory sensory memories.

eclectic approach The position adopted by many psychologists that it's useful to integrate information from several sources; one need not rely exclusively on any single theoretical perspective.

ego In Freud's theory, the portion of personality that induces people to act with reason and deliberation and helps them conform to the requirements of the external world.

egocentrism The tendency to see the world from your own unique perspective only; a characteristic of thinking in the preoperational period of development.

elaboration An encoding process that involves the formation of connections between to-be-remembered input and other information in memory.

electroconvulsive therapy (ECT) A treatment used primarily for depression in which a brief electric current is delivered to the brain.

electroencephalograph (EEG) A device used to monitor the electrical activity of the brain by measuring minute changes in the electrical fields on the scalp.

embryonic period The period of prenatal development lasting from implantation to the end of the eighth week; during this period, the human develops from an unrecognizable mass of cells to a somewhat familiar creature.

emotional distress criterion Behaviour is abnormal if it regularly leads to personal distress or emotional upset.

emotional intelligence The ability to perceive, understand, and express emotion in ways that are useful and adaptive.

emotions Psychological events involving (1) a physiological reaction, usually arousal; (2) some kind of expressive reaction, such as a distinctive facial expression; and (3) some kind of subjective experience, such as the conscious feeling of being happy or sad.

empirically supported treatments Treatments or therapies that have been shown, based on extensive and well-validated research, to be effective in treating specific psychological disorders and problems.

empiricism The idea that knowledge comes directly from experience.

encoding The processes that control the acquisition of information into memory.

encoding specificity principle The idea that the effectiveness of retrieval cues depends on the extent to which they match the specifics of the to-be-remembered material; the more similar the cue and the testing situation to the to-be-remembered material and the studying situation, the more likely the memories will be accessed.

endocrine system A network of glands that uses the bloodstream, rather than neurons, to send chemical messages that regulate growth and other internal functions.

endorphins Morphine-like chemicals that act as the brain's natural painkillers.

environmental psychology A specialty area in psychology devoted to the study of environmental effects on behaviour and health, such as the effects of crowding or noise.

environment of evolutionary adaptedness (EEA) Environment, or environments, in which a species' evolutionary adaptations were selected.

episodic memory Remembering a particular past event or episode that happened to you personally, such as recalling having breakfast this morning or where you went on vacation last year.

event-related potentials (ERP) EEG patterns observed shortly after presentation of a stimulus.

evolutionary adaptation A heritable trait that provided an organism with an advantage in surviving and/or reproducing during its evolutionary history.

evolutionary psychology The study of the human mind and behavioural processes as products of natural selection.

experimental method A technique in which the investigator actively manipulates or alters some aspect of the environment (defined broadly) and observes the effect of the manipulation on behaviour.

explicit memory Deliberate uses of memory with conscious awareness of remembering.

external attribution Attributing the cause of a person's behaviour to an external event or situation in the environment.

external validity The extent to which the results of an observation generalize to other situations or are representative of real life.

extinction Presenting a conditioned stimulus repeatedly, after conditioning, without the unconditioned stimulus, resulting in a gradual loss of the conditioned response.

facial-feedback hypothesis The proposal that muscles in the face deliver signals to the brain that are then interpreted, depending on the pattern, as a subjective emotional state.

factor analysis A statistical procedure developed by Charles Spearman that groups together related items on tests by analyzing the correlations among test scores. It is often used by psychologists to determine underlying common "factors" that summarize a large number of scores.

family resemblance The idea that categories are defined by a set of characteristic features, which category members share in varying degrees; each member of the category will have some but not necessarily all of these features.

family studies The similarities and differences between biological (blood) relatives are studied to help discover the role heredity plays in physical or psychological traits. Family studies rarely provide conclusive evidence because genes and the environment are usually entangled.

family therapy A form of group therapy in which the therapist treats the family as a whole, as a kind of social system. The goals of the treatment are often to improve interpersonal communication and collaboration.

feature detectors Cells in the visual cortex that respond to very specific visual events, such as bars of light at particular orientations.

fetal period The period of prenatal development lasting from the ninth week until birth, during which the fetus develops functioning organ systems, and increases are seen in body size and in the size and complexity of brain tissue.

fixed-interval schedule A schedule in which the reinforcement is delivered for the first response that occurs following a fixed interval of time.

fixed-ratio schedule A schedule in which the number of responses required for reinforcement is fixed and does not change from trial to trial.

flashbulb memory Highly detailed and vivid recollections of the circumstances under which one first learned of an emotionally significant and surprising event.

flavour A psychological term used to describe the overall gustatory (eating) experience. Flavour is influenced by taste, smell, the visual appearance of food, and expectations about the food's quality.

fluid intelligence The natural ability to solve problems, reason, and remember; fluid intelligence is thought to be relatively uninfluenced by experience.

forebrain The outer portion of the brain, including the cerebral cortex and the structures of the limbic system.

forgetting The loss in accessibility of previously accessible memory information.

formal operational period Piaget's last stage of cognitive development; thought processes become adult-like, and people gain mastery over abstract thinking.

fovea The "central pit" area in the centre portion of the retina where most of the cone receptors are located.

framing The way the alternatives in a decision-making situation are structured and described.

free association A technique used in psychoanalysis to explore the contents of the unconscious; patients are asked to relax and freely express whatever thoughts and feelings happen to come into their minds.

free recall A testing condition in which a person is asked to remember information without specific retrieval cues. For example, subjects might simply be asked to "recall the words you studied a few minutes ago."

frequency theory The idea that pitch perception is determined partly by the *frequency* of neural impulses travelling up the auditory pathway.

frontal lobe One of four anatomical regions of each hemisphere of the cerebral cortex, located on the top front of the brain; it contains the motor cortex and may be involved in higher-level thought processes.

functional fixedness The tendency to see objects, and their functions, in certain fixed and typical ways, and thereby to fail to see alternative uses of objects that would enable one to solve a problem.

functionalism An early school of psychology; functionalists believe that the proper way to understand mind and behaviour is to analyze their function and purpose. You can only truly understand a mental process, functionalists argue, by first knowing the purpose of that process.

fundamental attribution error The fact that causal attributions tend to overestimate the influence of internal personal factors and underestimate the role of situational factors.

***g* (general factor)** According to Spearman, the general factor, derived from factor analysis, that underlies or contributes to performance on a variety of mental tests.

gamma-amino-butyric acid (GABA) A neurotransmitter that may play a role in the regulation of anxiety; it generally produces inhibitory effects.

gate-control theory The idea that neural impulses generated by pain receptors can be blocked, or gated, in the spinal cord by signals produced in the brain.

gender roles Specific patterns of behaviour that are consistent with how society dictates males and females should act.

gender schemas The organized sets of beliefs and perceptions held about men and women.

generalized anxiety disorder Excessive worrying, or free-floating anxiety, that lasts for at least six months and cannot be attributed to any single identifiable source.

general adaptation syndrome (GAS) Hans Selye's model of stress as a general, nonspecific reaction that occurs in three phases: alarm reaction, resistance, and exhaustion.

genes Segments of chromosomes that contain chemically coded instructions for creating particular hereditary characteristics.

genital stage Freud's final stage of psychosexual development, during which one develops mature sexual relationships with members of the opposite sex.

genotype The genetic information inherited from one's parents.

germinal period The period in prenatal development from conception to implantation of the fertilized egg in the wall of the uterus.

Gestalt principles of organization The organizing principles of perception proposed by the Gestalt psychologists. These principles include the laws of proximity, similarity, closure, continuation, and common fate.

gifted A label that is generally assigned to someone who scores above 130 on a standard IQ test.

glial cells Cells in the nervous system that do not transmit or receive information but perform a variety of functions, such as removing waste, filling in empty space, and helping neurons to communicate efficiently.

glucose A kind of sugar that cells require for energy production.

grammar The rules or procedures of language that allow the communicator to combine arbitrary symbols in an infinite number of ways to convey meaning; grammar includes the rules of phonology, syntax, and semantics.

group polarization The tendency for a group's dominant point of view to become stronger and more extreme with time.

group therapy A form of therapy in which several people are treated simultaneously in the same setting.

groupthink The tendency for members of a group to become so interested in seeking a consensus of opinion that they start to ignore and even suppress dissenting views.

gustation The sense of taste.

habituation The decline in the tendency to respond to an event that has become familiar through repeated exposure; habituation has been used to investigate the perceptual capabilities of infants.

hallucinogens A class of drugs that tend to disrupt normal mental and emotional functioning and produce distorted perceptions.

hardy personality The set of traits, attitudes, and skills that make an individual less vulnerable to stress.

health psychology The study of how biological, psychological, environmental, and cultural factors are involved in physical health and the prevention of illness.

heritability A mathematical index that represents the extent to which IQ differences in a particular population can be accounted for by genetic factors.

heuristics The rules of thumb we often use to solve problems; heuristics are quick and easy, but they do not guarantee a correct solution.

hindbrain A primitive part of the brain that sits at the juncture where the brain and spinal cord merge. Structures in the hindbrain, including the medulla, pons, and reticular formation, act as the basic life-support system for the body.

homeostasis The process through which the body maintains a steady state, such as a constant internal temperature or an adequate amount of fluids.

hormones Chemicals released into the blood by the various endocrine glands to help control a variety of internal regulatory functions.

hue The dimension of light that produces colour; hue is typically determined by the wavelength of light reflecting from an object.

humanistic psychology A movement in psychology that emerged largely as a reaction against the pessimism of Freud. Humanistic psychologists focus on people's unique capacity for choice, responsibility, and growth.

humanistic therapy Treatments designed to help clients gain insight into their fundamental self-worth and value as human beings; therapy is a process of discovering one's own unique potential.

hypersomnia A chronic condition marked by excessive sleepiness.

hypnosis A social interaction between a person perceived to be a hypnotist and a person who perceives himself or herself to be a hypnotic subject; the interaction produces a heightened state of suggestibility in the subject.

hypnotic dissociation A hypothesized, hypnotically induced splitting of consciousness during which two streams of awareness are said to coexist: one that is fully under the sway of the hypnotist's suggestions and one that remains more aloof and objective.

hypnotic hypermnesia The supposed enhancement of memory that is said to occur under hypnosis; there is little evidence to support the existence of this effect.

hypochondriasis A long-lasting preoccupation with the idea that one has developed a serious disease, based on what turns out to be a misinterpretation of normal body reactions.

hypothalamus A forebrain structure thought to play a role in the regulation of various motivational activities, including eating, drinking, and sexual behaviour.

iconic memory The system that produces and stores visual sensory memories.

id In Freud's theory, the portion of personality that is governed by inborn instinctual drives, particularly those related to sex and aggression.

ill-defined problem A problem, such as "becoming a better person," for which the starting point and goal cannot be clearly specified.

illusory correlation Perception of a relationship between variables (e.g., handwriting and personality) that does not really exist.

implicit memory Use of memory that occurs automatically and without conscious awareness of remembering.

incentive motivation External factors in the environment—such as money, an attractive person, or tasty food—that exert pulling effects on people's actions.

incongruence A discrepancy between the image we hold of ourselves—our self-concept—and the sum of all our experiences.

independent variable The aspect of the environment that is manipulated in an experiment. It must consist of at least two conditions.

inferential statistics Mathematical techniques that help researchers estimate the likelihood that recorded behaviours are representative of a population or the likelihood that differences or relationships between observations are due to chance.

informed consent The principle that before consenting to participate in research, people must be fully informed of any significant factors that might affect their willingness to participate.

ingratiation The attempt to get someone to like you for some ulterior motive.

in-group A group that one belongs to or identifies with.

insanity A legal term usually defined as the inability to understand that certain actions are wrong, in a legal or moral sense, at the time of a crime.

insight therapies Treatments designed to give clients self-knowledge, or insight, into their psychological problems, usually through one-on-one interactions with a therapist.

insomnia A chronic condition marked by difficulties in initiating or maintaining sleep, lasting for a period of at least one month.

instincts Unlearned characteristic patterns of responding that are controlled by specific triggering stimuli in the world; they are not thought to be an important factor in explaining goal-directed behaviour in humans.

instrumental conditioning A procedure for studying how organisms learn about the consequences of their own voluntary actions; they learn that their behaviours are instrumental in producing rewards and punishments. Also called *operant conditioning*.

insulin A hormone released by the pancreas that helps pump nutrients in the blood into the cells, where they can be stored as fat or metabolized into needed energy.

intelligence An internal capacity hypothesized to explain people's ability to solve problems, learn new material, and adapt to new situations. The strength of this capacity must differ across individuals to explain why some people are better at these tasks than other people.

intelligence tests Tests that evaluate your overall ability to learn and solve problems.

intelligence prototype The list of characteristics that each person believes are present in the perfectly intelligent person.

internal attribution Attributing the cause of a person's behaviour to an internal personality characteristic.

internal validity The extent to which an experiment has effectively controlled for confounding variables; internally valid experiments allow for the determination of causality.

interneurons Neurons that make no direct contact with the external world but rather convey information from one neuron to another.

intrinsic motivation Goal-directed behaviour that seems to be entirely self-motivated.

IQ (intelligence quotient) A single number calculated to represent a person's intelligence. Originally, mental age divided by chronological age and then multiplied by 100; more recently, defined in terms of deviation from the average score on an IQ test.

iris The ring of coloured tissue surrounding the pupil. If you have brown eyes, your irises are brown.

James-Lange theory A theory of emotion that argues that body reactions precede and drive the subjective experience of emotions.

kinesthesia In perception, the ability to sense the position and movement of one's body parts.

latency period Freud's period of psychosexual development, from age 5 to puberty, during which the child's sexual feelings are largely suppressed.

latent content According to Freud, the true psychological meaning of objects and events in dreams, which are said to represent hidden wishes and desires that are too disturbing to be confronted directly.

lateral hypothalamus A portion of the hypothalamus that, when lesioned, causes an animal to be reluctant to eat; like the ventromedial hypothalamus, it probably plays some role in eating behaviour, but the precise role is unknown.

lateralization Asymmetry in the functions of the right and left hemispheres of the cerebral cortex (e.g., in most individuals, most language skills are lateralized to the left hemisphere).

law of effect The idea that if a response in a particular situation is followed by a satisfying or pleasant consequence, it will be strengthened; if a response in a particular situation is followed by an unsatisfying or unpleasant consequence, it will be weakened.

learned helplessness A general sense of helplessness that is acquired when people repeatedly fail in their attempts to control their environment; learned helplessness may play a role in depression.

learning A relatively permanent change in behaviour, or potential to respond, that results from experience.

lens The flexible, transparent disk of tissue that helps focus light toward the back of the eye.

light The small portion of the electromagnetic spectrum that is processed by the visual system. Light is typically classified in terms of *wavelength* (the physical distance from one energy cycle to the next) and *intensity* (the amount of light falling on an object).

limbic system A system of structures thought to be involved in motivational and emotional behaviours (the amygdala) and memory (the hippocampus).

linguistic relativity hypothesis The proposal that language determines the characteristics and content of thought.

link-word system A mnemonic device for remembering foreign language vocabulary in which you (a) think of an English word that sounds similar to the to-be-learned foreign word and (b) form a visual image connecting the meaning of the to-be-remembered word with the similar-sounding English word.

locus of control The amount of control that a person feels he or she has over the environment.

longitudinal design A research design in which the same people are studied or tested repeatedly over time.

long-term memory The system used to maintain information for extended periods of time, from several seconds to a lifetime.

loudness The psychological experience that results from the auditory processing of a particular *amplitude* of sound.

lower region Bias to perceive the lower part of a visual scene as the "figure" (meaningful object of perception) rather than "ground" (background).

lymphocytes Specialized white blood cells that have the job of attacking foreign substances, such as viruses and bacteria.

magnetic resonance imaging (MRI) A device that uses magnetic fields and radio wave pulses to construct detailed, three-dimensional images of the brain.

major depressive episode A type of mood disorder characterized by depressed mood and other symptoms.

manic state A disordered state in which the person becomes hyperactive, talkative, and has a decreased need for sleep; a person in a manic state may engage in activities that are self-destructive or dangerous.

manifest content According to Freud, the objects and events experienced in a dream.

massed practice Clustering repetitions of to-be-remembered information close together in time.

mean The arithmetic average of a set of scores, obtained by dividing the sum of all scores by the number of scores.

means–ends analysis A problem-solving heuristic that involves devising actions, or means, that reduce the distance between the current starting point and the desired end (the goal).

median The middle point in an ordered set of scores; half the scores fall below the median score, and half fall above the median score.

medical model The view that abnormal behaviour is symptomatic of an underlying "disease" that can be "cured" with the appropriate therapy.

meditation A technique for self-induced manipulation of awareness, often used for relaxation and self-reflection.

memory The capacity to preserve and recover information.

memory span The largest number of items that can reliably be recalled from short-term memory in their proper presentation order.

menopause The period during which a woman's menstrual cycle slows down and finally stops.

mental age The chronological age that best fits a child's level of performance on a test of mental ability. Mental age is typically calculated by comparing a child's test score with the average scores for different age groups.

mental retardation A label that is generally assigned to someone who scores below 70 on a standard IQ test. Other factors, such as one's ability to adapt to the environment, are also considered before putting someone in this category.

mental sets Well-established habits of perception and thought used to solve problems; typically efficient and effective, but sometimes make problem solving more difficult.

meta-analysis A statistical technique used to accumulate findings across all available studies; comparisons are based on some common evaluation index, such as the numerical difference between the success rate of the treatment and control conditions.

meta-stereotyping A person's beliefs regarding the stereotype that out-group members hold about his or her own group.

method of loci A mnemonic device in which you first memorize a series of locations along a familiar real-world pathway, such as the route from your residence to the university, and then form visual images of the to-be-remembered items sitting in the various locations along that pathway. To recall the items, you mentally traverse the pathway, checking each location as a retrieval cue.

midbrain The middle portion of the brain, containing such structures as the tectum, superior colliculus, and inferior colliculus; midbrain structures serve as neural relay stations and may help coordinate reactions to sensory events.

middle ear The portion of the ear between the eardrum and the cochlea containing three small bones (the malleus, incus, and stapes) that intensify and prepare the sound vibrations for passage into the inner ear.

mind The contents and processes of subjective experience: sensations, thoughts, and emotions.

Minnesota Multiphasic Personality Inventory (MMPI) A widely used self-report inventory for assessing personality traits and for diagnosing psychological problems.

mnemonic devices Special mental tricks that help people think about material in ways that improve later memory. Most mnemonic devices use visual imagery and elaboration during encoding and a systematic strategy for searching memory during retrieval.

mode The most frequently occurring score in a set of scores.

modelling See **observational learning**.

monocular depth cues Cues for depth for which input from one eye is sufficient.

mood disorders Prolonged and disabling disruptions in emotional state.

morality The ability to distinguish between appropriate and inappropriate actions; a child's sense of morality may be tied to his or her level of cognitive development.

morphemes The smallest units in a language that carry meaning (words, prefixes, suffixes).

motivation The set of factors that initiate and direct behaviour, usually toward some goal.

motor neurons Neurons that carry information away from the central nervous system to the muscles and glands that directly produce behavioural responses.

multiple intelligences The notion proposed by Howard Gardner that people possess a set of separate and independent "intelligences" ranging from musical to linguistic to interpersonal abilities.

mutation Error in the process by which chromosomes are copied that changes the genotype specified by those chromosomes.

myelin sheath An insulating material that protects the axons of some neurons and helps to speed up neural transmission.

nativism The idea that certain kinds of knowledge and ideas are innate, or present at birth; innate ideas do not need to be learned.

naturalistic observation A research technique that involves recording only naturally occurring behaviour, as opposed to behaviour produced in the laboratory.

natural selection The differential production and survival of offspring by species members with advantageous traits.

need hierarchy The idea popularized by Maslow that human needs are prioritized in a hierarchy. Some needs, especially physiological ones, must be satisfied before others, such as the need for achievement or self-actualization, can be pursued.

negative punishment An event that, when *removed* after a response, lowers the likelihood of that response occurring again.

negative reinforcement An event that, when *removed* after a response in a situation, increases the likelihood of that response occurring in that situation again.

NEO-PI-R A self-report inventory developed to measure the Big Five personality dimensions.

nerves Bundles of axons that make up neural "transmission cables."

neural plasticity Ability of neurons to alter synaptic connections during learning and during recovery from brain injury.

neurons The cells in the nervous system that receive and transmit information by generating an electrochemical signal; neurons are the basic building blocks of the nervous system.

neuroscience An interdisciplinary field of study directed at understanding the brain and its relation to behaviour.

neurotransmitters Chemical messengers that relay information from one neuron to the next. They are released from the terminal buttons into the synapse, where they interact chemically with the cell membrane of the next neuron; the result is either an excitatory or an inhibitory influence on the recipient neuron.

nightmares Frightening dreams that occur primarily during the REM stage of sleep.

night terrors A condition in which the sleeper, usually a child, awakens suddenly in an extreme state of panic; not thought to be associated with dreaming.

nodes of Ranvier Space separating the segments of the myelin covering of the neuron; they help speed the nerve impulse along the axon.

norepinephrine and epinephrine Cause a surge of energy that increases the heart rate; blood is shunted to areas that require it, away from the stomach and intestine; glucose is made available to the muscles.

obedience The form of compliance that occurs when people respond to the orders of an authority figure.

obesity A weight problem characterized by excessive body fat.

objective test A test that is scored in a standardized fashion so that anyone calculating the result gets the same answer.

object permanence The ability to recognize that objects still exist when they're no longer in sight.

observational learning Learning that occurs as a result of observing the experiences of others. Also called *social learning* or *modelling*.

obsessive–compulsive disorder An anxiety disorder that manifests itself through persistent and uncontrollable thoughts, called *obsessions,* or by the compelling need to perform repetitive acts, called *compulsions.*

occipital lobe One of four anatomical regions of each hemisphere of the cerebral cortex, located at the back of the brain; visual processing is controlled here.

olfaction The sense of smell.

operant conditioning See **instrumental conditioning**.

operational definition Concept defined in terms of how it is measured.

opiates A class of drugs that reduce anxiety, lower sensitivity to pain, and elevate mood; opiates often act to depress nervous system activity.

opponent process theory A theory of colour vision proposing that certain cells in the visual pathway increase their activation levels to one colour and decrease their activation levels to another colour (e.g., increasing to red and decreasing to green).

oral stage The first stage in Freud's conception of psychosexual development, occurring in the first year of life; in this stage, pleasure is derived primarily from sucking and placing things in the mouth.

organic amnesia Forgetting that is caused by physical problems in the brain, such as those induced by injury or disease.

orienting response An inborn tendency to shift one's focus of attention toward a novel or surprising event.

out-group A group of individuals that one does not belong to or identify with.

pain An adaptive response by the body to any stimulus that is intense enough to cause tissue damage.

panic disorder A condition marked by recurrent discrete episodes or attacks of extremely intense fear or dread.

parallel processing Processing that occurs in many different brain regions at the same time, in parallel.

paranoid personality disorder A personality disorder characterized by pervasive distrust of others.

parietal lobe One of four anatomical regions of each hemisphere of the cerebral cortex, located roughly on the top middle portion of the brain; it contains the somatosensory cortex, which controls the sense of touch.

partial reinforcement schedule A schedule in which reinforcement is delivered only some of the time after the response has occurred.

passionate love An intense emotional state characterized by a powerful longing to be with a specific person; passionate love is marked by a combination of intimacy and passion, but commitment may be lacking.

perceived control The amount of influence you feel you have over a situation and your reaction to it.

perception The processes used to arrive at a meaningful interpretation of sensations; through perception, the simple component sensations are organized and interpreted into meaningful, recognizable forms.

perceptual constancy Perceiving the properties of an object as remaining the same even though the physical properties of the sensory input are changing.

perceptual illusions Inappropriate interpretations of physical reality. Perceptual illusions often occur as a result of the brain's use of otherwise adaptive organizing principles.

perfectionistic personality disorder A personality disorder characterized by an excessive and rigid need to achieve the highest level of quality in achievements.

peripheral nervous system The network of nerves that link the central nervous system with the rest of the body.

personal/group discrimination discrepancy The tendency for members of groups experiencing discrimination to minimize discrimination directed toward themselves as individuals, but to agree with other group members that discrimination against the group as a whole is significant.

personal identity A sense of who one is as an individual and how well one stacks up against peers. Erik Erikson's theory postulates that personal identity is shaped by a series of personal crises that each person confronts at characteristic stages of development.

personality The entire pattern of psychological characteristics—thinking, feeling, and behaving—that differentiates us from others.

personality disorders Chronic or enduring patterns of behaviour that lead to significant impairments in social functioning.

personality profiling Estimating the personality makeup of an individual based on indirect evidence, such as his or her eating habits, room arrangement, and so on.

person–situation debate A controversial debate centring on whether people really do behave consistently across situations.

phallic stage Freud's third stage of psychosexual development, lasting from about age 3 to age 5; pleasure is gained from self-stimulation of the sexual organs.

phenotype A person's observable characteristics, such as red hair. The phenotype is controlled partly by the genotype and partly by the environment.

phonemes The smallest significant, difference-making sound units in speech.

phonology The rules and procedures for combining sounds to make words in a language.

pinna The external flap of tissue commonly referred to as the "ear"; it helps direct sounds toward the tympanic membrane.

pitch The psychological experience that results from the auditory processing of a particular *frequency* of sound.

pituitary gland A kind of master gland in the body that controls the release of hormones in response to signals from the hypothalamus.

placebo An inactive, or inert, substance or treatment that resembles an experimental substance or treatment.

place theory The idea that the *location* of auditory receptor cells activated by movement of the basilar membrane plays a role in the perception of pitch.

polygraph A device that measures various indexes of physiological arousal in an effort to determine whether someone is telling a lie. The logic behind the test is that lying leads to greater emotionality, which can be picked up through such measures of arousal as heart rate, blood pressure, breathing rate, and perspiring.

positive punishment An event that, when *presented* after a response, lowers the likelihood of that response occurring again.

positive regard The idea that we value what others think of us and constantly seek others' approval, love, and companionship.

positive reinforcement An event that, when *presented* after a response in a certain situation, increases the likelihood of that response occurring again in that situation.

positron emission tomography (PET) A method for measuring how radioactive substances are absorbed in the brain; it can be used to detect how different tasks activate different areas of the living brain.

postconventional level Kohlberg's highest level of moral development, in which moral actions are judged on the basis of personal codes of ethics that are general and abstract and that may not agree with societal norms.

posttraumatic stress disorder A trauma-based anxiety disorder characterized by flashbacks, avoidance of stimuli associated with the traumatic event, and chronic arousal symptoms.

pragmatics The practical knowledge used to comprehend the intentions of a speaker and to produce an appropriate response.

preconscious mind The part of the mind that contains all of the inactive but potentially accessible thoughts and memories.

preconventional level In Kohlberg's theory, the lowest level of moral development, in which decisions about right and wrong are made primarily in terms of external consequences.

prejudice An unrealistic negative evaluation of a group and its members.

preoperational period Piaget's second stage of cognitive development, lasting from age 2 to about age 7; children begin to think symbolically but often lack the ability to perform mental operations like conservation.

primacy effect The better memory seen for items near the beginning of a studied list compared to mid-list items.

primary drive A psychological state that arises in response to an internal physiological need, such as hunger or thirst.

primary mental abilities The seven distinct forms of intelligence that Thurstone uncovered with modern forms of factor analysis.

proactive interference A process in which old memories interfere with the establishment and retrieval of new memories.

procedural memory Memory for how to do things, such as ride a bike or swing a golf club.

projection A defence mechanism in which unacceptable feelings or wishes are dealt with by attributing them to others.

projective test A type of personality test in which individuals are asked to interpret unstructured or ambiguous stimuli; the idea is that subjects will project their true thoughts and feelings into the interpretation, thereby revealing elements of their personality.

prototype The best or most representative member of a category (such as robin for the category "bird").

proximate factors Causes of behaviour that derive from the immediate internal or external environment of an organism.

psychiatrists Medical doctors who specialize in the diagnosis and treatment of psychological problems. Unlike psychologists, psychiatrists are licensed to prescribe drugs.

psychoactive drugs Drugs that affect behaviour and mental processes, and produce alterations of conscious awareness.

psychoanalysis Freud's method of treatment that attempts to bring hidden impulses and memories, which are locked in the unconscious, to the surface of awareness, thereby freeing the patient from disordered thoughts and behaviours.

psychodynamic theory An approach to personality development, based largely on the ideas of Sigmund Freud, which holds that much of behaviour is governed by unconscious forces.

psychological disorder A specific psychological problem that causes abnormal behaviour to occur.

psychology The scientific study of behaviour and mind.

psychometrics The use of psychological tests to measure the mind and mental processes.

psychophysics A field of psychology in which researchers search for ways to describe the transition from the physical stimulus to the psychological experience of that stimulus.

psychotherapy Treatment designed to help people deal with mental, emotional, or behavioural problems.

puberty The period during which a person reaches sexual maturity and is potentially capable of producing offspring.

punishment Consequences that decrease the likelihood of responding in a similar way again.

pupil The hole in the centre of the iris through which light enters the eye; the size of the pupil changes with light intensity.

radical behaviourism A perspective on the analysis of human and animal behaviour that emphasizes explaining behaviour in terms of environmental events and that minimizes the use of internal explanations like thoughts, beliefs, and intentions.

random assignment A technique that ensures that each participant in an experiment has an equal chance of being assigned to any of the conditions in the experiment.

random sampling A procedure for selecting a representative subset of a target population; the procedure guarantees that everyone in the population has an equal likelihood of being selected for the sample.

range The difference between the largest and smallest scores in a distribution.

rational-emotive therapy A form of cognitive therapy, developed by Albert Ellis, in which the therapist acts as a kind of cross-examiner, verbally disputing the client's irrational thought processes.

reaction formation A defence mechanism used to transform an anxiety-producing wish into a kind of opposite—people behave in a way that counters the way they truly feel.

reactivity The extent to which an individual's behaviour changes as a result of being observed; the behaviour is altered in reaction to being observed.

recency effect The better memory seen for items near the end of a studied list compared to mid-list items.

receptive field In vision, the portion of the retina that, when stimulated, causes the activity of a higher-level neuron (such as a ganglion cell or an even higher-level neuron in the visual cortex) to change.

reciprocal determinism The idea that beliefs, behaviour, and the environment interact to shape what is learned from experience.

reciprocity The tendency for people to return in kind the feelings that are shown toward them.

recognition by components The idea proposed by Biederman that people recognize objects perceptually through smaller components called *geons*.

reflex A largely automatic body movement, such as the knee jerk, that is controlled by a simple network of sensory neurons, interneurons in the spinal cord, and motor neurons.

refractory period The period of time following an action potential during which more action potentials cannot be generated.

rehearsal A strategic process that helps maintain short-term memories through the use of internal repetition.

reinforcement Response consequences that increase the likelihood of responding in a similar way again.

reliability A measure of the consistency of test results; reliable tests give people similar scores when the test is repeated.

REM A stage of sleep characterized by rapid eye movements and low-amplitude, irregular EEG patterns similar to those found in the waking brain. REM is typically associated with dreaming.

REM rebound The tendency to increase the proportion of sleeping time spent in REM sleep after a period of REM deprivation.

representativeness heuristic The tendency to base judgments on similarity to an abstract ideal, expectation, or stereotype. For example, when deciding whether a sequence of coin-toss outcomes is random, people using the representativeness heuristic focus on how irregular the sequence looks, because they think short random sequences should look irregular.

research psychologists Psychologists who conduct experiments or collect observations designed to discover the basic principles of behaviour and mind.

resistance In psychoanalysis, a patient's unconsciously motivated attempts to subvert the process of therapy.

resting potential The tiny electrical charge in place between the inside and outside of the resting neuron.

retina The thin layer of tissue that covers the back of the inside of the eye and contains the light-sensitive receptor cells for vision.

retinal disparity A binocular cue for depth that is based on location differences between the images in each eye.

retrieval The processes that control how information is recovered from memory and translated into performance.

retroactive interference A process in which the formation of new memories hurts the retrieval of old memories.

retrograde amnesia Memory loss for events that happened prior to the brain injury.

rods Receptor cells in the retina, located mainly on the periphery of the retina, that transduce light energy into neural inputs; these visual receptors are highly sensitive and are active in dim light.

Rorschach test A projective test that requires people to interpret ambiguous inkblots.

***s* (specific factor)** According to Spearman, a specific factor, derived from factor analysis, that is unique to a particular kind of test.

savant An individual with a special talent despite generally low intelligence.

Schachter theory A theory of emotion that argues that the cognitive interpretation, or appraisal, of a body reaction creates the subjective experience of emotion.

schedule of reinforcement A rule that an experimenter uses to determine when particular responses will be reinforced. A continuous reinforcement schedule is one in which a reward is delivered each and every time the target behaviour is performed. Partial reinforcement schedules, in contrast, can be fixed or variable, and ratio or interval.

schema (Chapter 7) An organized knowledge structure in long-term memory. (Chapter 10) Mental models of the world that people use to guide and interpret their experiences.

schizophrenia A class of disorders characterized by fundamental disturbances in thought processes, emotion, or behaviour.

scientific method A method for acquiring knowledge by combining (a) the principles of rational thought (that is, logic) with (b) information derived from systematic measurements of the object of study (that is, empirical research).

searching for analogies A problem-solving heuristic that involves trying to find a connection between the current problem and some previous problem you have solved successfully.

secondary drive A drive learned by association with a primary drive (e.g., the need for money).

secondary traits The less obvious characteristics of an individual's personality that do not always appear in his or her behaviour, such as testiness when on a diet.

second-order conditioning A procedure in which an established conditioned stimulus is used to condition a second neutral stimulus.

self-actualization The ingrained desire to reach one's true potential as a human being.

self-concept An organized set of perceptions that we hold about our abilities and characteristics.

self-efficacy The beliefs that we hold about our own ability to perform a task or accomplish a goal.

self-fulfilling prophecy effect When our expectations about the actions of another person actually lead that person to behave in the expected way.

self-monitoring The degree to which a person monitors a situation closely and changes his or her behaviour accordingly; people who are high self-monitors may not behave consistently across situations.

self-perception theory The idea that people use observations of their own behaviour as a basis for inferring their internal beliefs.

self-report questionnaires Personality tests that ask sets of questions about how the respondent typically thinks, acts, or feels; his or her responses, or self-reports, are then compared to average responses compiled from large groups of prior test takers.

self-serving bias The tendency to make internal attributions about one's own behaviour when the outcome is positive and to blame the situation when one's behaviour leads to something negative.

semantic memory Knowledge about language and the world, retrieved as abstract facts or beliefs that make little or no reference to any particular episode in one's personal experience.

semantics The rules and procedures for communicating meaning through words and combinations of words.

semicircular canals A receptor system attached to the inner ear that responds to movement and acceleration and to changes in upright posture.

sensations The elementary components, or building blocks, of perception, such as a pattern of light and dark, a bitter taste, or a change in temperature.

sensitization An increase in the tendency to respond to an event that has been repeated; sensitization is more likely when a repeated stimulus is intense.

sensorimotor period Piaget's first stage of cognitive development, lasting from birth to about 2 years of age; schemas revolve around sensory and motor abilities.

sensory adaptation The tendency of sensory systems to reduce sensitivity to a stimulus that remains constant.

sensory memory The capacity to preserve sensory information in a relatively pure, unanalyzed form for a very brief period.

sensory neurons Neurons that make initial contact with the environment and carry the message inward toward the spinal cord and brain.

serotonin A neurotransmitter that has been linked to sleep, dreaming, and general arousal and may also be involved in some psychological disorders such as depression and schizophrenia.

service gap The difference between the number of people who could benefit from receiving psychological services and those who receive them.

set point A natural body weight, perhaps produced by genetic factors, that the body seeks to maintain. When body weight falls below the set point, one is motivated to eat; when weight exceeds the set point, one feels less motivated to eat.

sexual orientation A person's sexual and emotional attraction to members of the same sex or the other sex; homosexuality, heterosexuality, and bisexuality are all sexual orientations.

sexual scripts Learned cognitive programs that instruct us on how, why, and what to do in our interactions with sexual partners; the nature of sexual scripts certainly differs across gender and may vary from one culture to the next.

shaping A procedure in which reinforcement is delivered for successive approximations of the desired response.

short-term memory A limited-capacity "working memory" system that people use to hold information, after it has been perceptually analyzed, for periods usually lasting less than a minute. Short-term memory is the system we use to temporarily store, think about, and reason with new information and with information retrieved from long-term memory.

signal detection A technique that can be used to determine an individual's ability to detect the presence of a stimulus and to measure the individual's response bias.

single-blind study An experimental design in which the participants do not know to which of the conditions they have been assigned (e.g., experimental vs. control); it's used to control for subject expectancies.

16 Personality Factor (16 P-F) A self-report inventory developed by Cattell and colleagues to measure 16 primary personality factors.

sleepwalking A condition in which the sleeper rises during sleep and wanders about; not thought to be associated with dreaming.

social cognition The study of how people use cognitive processes—such as perception, memory, thought, and emotion—to make sense of other people as well as themselves.

social facilitation The enhancement in performance that is sometimes found when an individual performs in the presence of others.

social influence The study of how the behaviours and thoughts of individuals are affected by the presence of others.

social interference The impairment in performance that is sometimes found when an individual performs in the presence of others.

social learning See **observational learning**.

social learning theory The idea that most important personality traits come from modelling, or copying, the behaviour of others.

social loafing The tendency to put out less effort when several people are supposed to be working on a task than when only one is working.

socially desirable responding The tendency to describe oneself as having positive, or at least normal, traits.

social phobia An incapacitating fear of social interactions.

social psychology The study of how people think about, influence, and relate to other people.

social schema A general knowledge structure, stored in long-term memory, that relates to social experiences or people.

social support The resources that individuals receive from other people or groups, often in the form of comfort, caring, or help.

sociological model The view that abnormal behaviour is a label that each society assigns to certain behaviours that it finds unacceptable, even if they are not criminal in nature.

soma The cell body of a neuron.

somatic system Nerves that transmit information from sensory organs to the brain, and from the brain to the skeletal muscles; part of the peripheral nervous system.

somatization disorder A long-lasting preoccupation with body symptoms that have no identifiable physical cause.

somatoform disorders Psychological disorders that focus on the physical body.

sound The physical input to the auditory system, a mechanical energy travelling in waves that requires a medium such as air or water through which to move.

specific phobic disorder A highly focused fear of a specific object or situation.

split-half reliability Ability of a test to give the same scores in the first and second halves of the test.

spontaneous recovery The recovery of an extinguished conditioned response after a period of nonexposure to the conditioned stimulus.

spontaneous remission Improvement in a psychological disorder without treatment—that is, simply as a function of the passage of time.

standard deviation An indication of how much individual scores differ or vary from the mean in a set of scores.

standardization Keeping the testing, scoring, and interpretation procedures similar across all administrations of a test.

statistical deviance criterion A criterion for abnormality based on a low frequency of occurrence among the members of a population.

stereotypes The collection of beliefs and impressions held about a group and its members; common stereotypes include those based on gender, race, and age.

Sternberg's three facets of intelligence Robert Sternberg's theory of intelligence; it includes three types of intelligence—analytic, creative, and practical.

stimulants A class of drugs that increase central nervous system activity, enhancing neural transmission.

stimulus discrimination Responding to a new stimulus differently from the way one responds to an established conditioned stimulus.

stimulus generalization Responding to a new stimulus in a way similar to the response produced by an established conditioned stimulus.

storage The processes that determine how information is maintained over time.

strange situation test Gradually subjecting a child to a stressful situation and observing his or her behaviour toward the parent or caregiver. This test is used to classify children according to type of attachment—secure, resistant, or avoidant.

stress People's physical and psychological reactions to demanding or threatening situations.

stressors The demanding or threatening situations that produce stress.

structuralism An early school of psychology; structuralists attempted to understand the mind by breaking it down into its basic constituent parts, much like a chemist might try to understand a chemical compound.

subjective definition A definition based on personal opinion. Each person's definition seems designed to suit his or her personal needs and world-views.

sublimation A defence mechanism used to channel unacceptable impulses into socially acceptable activities.

superego In Freud's theory, the portion of personality that motivates people to act in a proper fashion, that is, in accordance with the moral customs defined by parents and culture.

surface structure The literal ordering of words in a sentence.

survey A descriptive research technique designed to gather limited amounts of information from many people, usually by administering a questionnaire.

synapse The junction, or small gap, between a terminal button of one neuron and a dendrite of another neuron.

syntax The rules and procedures for combining words to form sentences.

systematic desensitization A technique that uses counterconditioning and extinction to reduce the fear and anxiety that have become associated with a specific object or event. It's a multistep process that attempts to replace the negative learned association with something relaxing.

tacit knowledge The special knowledge in a particular area that allows one to think quickly and efficiently.

taste buds The receptor cells on the tongue involved in taste.

temperament Behavioural tendencies that have biological origins.

temporal lobe One of four anatomical regions of each hemisphere of the cerebral cortex, located roughly on the sides of the brain; it's involved in certain aspects of speech and language perception.

teratogens Environmental agents—such as disease, organisms, or drugs—that can potentially damage the developing embryo or fetus.

terminal buttons The tiny swellings at the end of a neuron's axon that contain chemicals important to neural transmission.

test-retest reliability Ability of a test to give consistent scores.

texture gradient Gradual reduction, with increasing distance, of the apparent coarseness of a surface (such as the ground or floor); provides a powerful cue to the distances of objects located on that surface.

thalamus A relay station in the forebrain thought to be an important gathering point for input from the senses.

Thematic Apperception Test (TAT) A projective personality test that requires people to make up stories about the characters in ambiguous pictures.

therapeutic alliance The bond formed between the client and therapist in successful psychotherapy that is focused on working together constructively to solve the client's problem.

theta waves The pattern of brain activity observed in stage 1 sleep.

thinking The processes that underlie the mental manipulation of knowledge, images, and ideas, often in an attempt to reach a goal such as solving a problem.

token economy A type of behavioural therapy in which institutionalized patients are rewarded with small tokens when they act in an appropriate way; the token can then be exchanged for certain privileges.

tolerance An adaptation that the body makes to compensate for the continued use of a drug such that increasing amounts of the drug are needed to produce the same physical, psychological, and behavioural effects.

top-down processing Processing that is driven by one's beliefs and expectations about how the world is organized.

trait (Chapter 3) A distinguishable characteristic of an organism. (Chapter 12) A stable predisposition to act or behave in a consistent fashion.

trait taxonomies Systems for distinguishing the most important individual differences in personality. These trait taxonomies are usually associated with an inventory of psychometric tests designed to measure these traits.

transcranial magnetic stimulation (TMS) Powerful pulses of magnetic energy applied to the scalp stimulate action potentials in regions of the cortex; behavioural responses cast light on the function of the stimulated brain region.

transduction The process by which external inputs are translated into the internal language of the brain.

transfer-appropriate processing The idea that the likelihood of correct retrieval increases as a function of the similarity between mental processes during encoding and those during test.

transference In psychoanalysis, the patient's expression of thoughts or feelings toward the therapist that are actually representative of the way the patient feels about other significant people in his or her life.

trichromatic theory A theory of colour vision proposing that colour information is extracted by comparing the relative activations of three different types of cone receptors.

twin studies Identical twins, who share genetic material, are compared to fraternal twins in an effort to disentangle the roles of heredity and environment in giving rise to psychological traits.

tympanic membrane The eardrum, which responds to incoming sound waves by vibrating.

Type A An enduring pattern of behaviour linked to coronary heart disease: The combination of tendencies to be hard driving, ambitious, easily annoyed, and impatient all seem to derive from the trait hostility.

Type B People who lack the Type A traits—they experience less stress and, therefore, better health outcomes.

ultimate factors Causes of behaviour that refer to the evolutionarily adaptive significance and reproductive consequences for the organism.

unconditioned response (UR) The observable response that is produced automatically, prior to training, on presentation of an unconditioned stimulus.

unconditioned stimulus (US) A stimulus that automatically produces—or elicits—an observable response prior to any training.

unconscious mind The part of the mind that Freud believed housed all the memories, urges, and conflicts that are truly beyond awareness.

validity An assessment of how well a test measures what the label of the test says it is measuring. *Content validity* assesses the degree to which the content of a test samples broadly across the domain of interest; *predictive validity* assesses how well the test predicts an important criterion; *construct validity* assesses how well the test captures all the details of the theoretical construct.

variability A measure of how much the scores in a distribution of scores differ from one another.

variable-interval schedule A schedule in which the allotted time before a response will yield reinforcement changes from trial to trial.

variable-ratio schedule A schedule in which a certain number of responses is required for reinforcement, but the number of required responses typically changes from trial to trial.

ventromedial hypothalamus A portion of the hypothalamus that, when lesioned, causes an animal to typically overeat and gain a large amount of weight. Once thought to be a kind of "stop eating," or satiety, centre in the brain, its role in eating behaviour is currently unknown.

vestibular sacs Small organs in the inner ear that contain receptors responsible for the sense of balance.

visual acuity The ability to see fine detail.

visual imagery The processes used to construct an internal visual image, using some of the same brain mechanisms as in perception.

visual neglect A complex attention disorder characterized by a tendency to ignore things that appear on one side of the body, usually the left side.

warm fibres Neurons that respond vigorously when the temperature of the skin increases.

Weber's law The principle stating that the ability to notice a difference in the magnitude of two stimuli is a constant proportion of the intensity of the standard stimulus. Psychologically, the more intense a stimulus is to begin with, the more intense it will need to become for a person to notice a difference.

well-defined problem A problem with a clear starting point and a fully specified goal.

withdrawal Clear and measurable physical reactions, such as sweating, vomiting, changes in heart rate, or tremors, that occur when a person stops taking certain drugs after continued use.

working backward A problem-solving heuristic that involves mentally starting at the goal and mentally moving backward toward the starting point to see how the goal can be reached.

zygote The fertilized human egg, containing 23 chromosomes from the father and 23 chromosomes from the mother, which pair up to form the master genetic blueprint.

References

Abdullaev, Y. G., & Posner, M. I. (1998). Time course of activating brain areas in generating verbal associations. *Psychological Science, 8,* 56–59.

Aboud, F. E. (1988). *Children and prejudice.* New York: Blackwell.

Aboud, F. E. (1993). A fifth grade program to reduce prejudice. In K. McLeod (Ed.), *Multicultural education: The state of the art* (pp. 20–27). Toronto: University of Toronto Press.

Aboud, F. E., & Doyle, A. B. (1996). Does talk of race foster prejudice or tolerance in children? *Canadian Journal of Behavioural Science, 28,* 161–170.

Abrams, D., Wetherell, M., Cochrane, S., Hogg, M. A., & Turner, J. C. (1990). Knowing what to think by knowing who you are: Self-categorization and the nature of norm formation, conformity, and group polarization. *British Journal of Social Psychology, 29,* 97–119.

Abramson, L. Y., Metalsky, G. I., & Alloy, L. B. (1989). Hopelessness depression: A theory-based subtype of depression. *Psychological Review, 96,* 358–372.

Achenbach, T. M. (1992). Developmental psychopathology. In M. H. Bornstein & M. E. Lamb (Eds.), *Developmental psychology: An advanced textbook.* Hillsdale, NJ: Erlbaum.

Adair, R., Bauchner, H., Phillip, B., Levenson, S., & Zuckerman, B. (1991). Night waking during infancy: Role of parent presence at bedtime. *Pediatrics, 87,* 500–504.

Adamec, R. E. (2000). Evidence that long-lasting potentiation of amygdala efferents in the right hemisphere underlies pharmacological stressor (FG-7142) induced lasting increases in anxiety-like behaviour: Role of GABA tone in initiation of brain and behavioural changes. *Journal of Psychopharmacology, 14,* 323–339.

Adams, D. B., Gold, A. R., & Burt, A. D. (1978). Rise in female-initiated sexual activity at ovulation and its suppression by oral contraceptives. *New England Journal of Medicine, 299,* 1145–1150.

Adams, P. R., & Adams, G. R. (1984). Mount Saint Helens's ash-fall: Evidence for a disaster stress reaction. *American Psychologist, 39,* 252–260.

Adler, A. (1927). *Understanding human nature.* New York: Greenberg.

Adler, E., & Bachant, J. (1998). Intrapsychic and interactive dimensions of resistance: A contemporary perspective. *Psychoanalytic Psychology, 15,* 451–479.

Adler, N., & Matthews, K. (1994). Health psychology: Why do some people get sick and some stay healthy? *Annual Review of Psychology, 45,* 229–259.

Adorno, T. W., Frenkel-Brunswik, E., Levinson, D. J., & Sanford, R. N. (1950). *The authoritarian personality.* New York: Harpur & Brothers.

Aggleton, J. P. (1993). The contribution of the amygdala to normal and abnormal emotional states. *Trends in Neuroscience, 16,* 328–333.

Agras, W. S., Sylvester, D., & Oliveau, D. (1969). The epidemiology of common fears and phobia. *Comprehensive Psychiatry, 10,* 151–156.

Aiello, J. R., & Douthitt, E. A. (2001). Social facilitation from Triplett to electronic performance monitoring. *Group Dynamics, 5,* 163–180.

Ainsworth, M. D. S. (1979). Attachment as related to mother-infant interactions. In J. S. Rosenblatt, R. A. Hinde, C. Beer, & M. Busnel (Eds.), *Advances in the study of behaviour.* New York: Academic Press.

Ainsworth, M. D. S., & Bowlby, J. (1954). Research strategy in the study of mother-child separation. *Courrier, 4,* 105–131.

Ainsworth, M. D. S., & Wittig, B. A. (1969). Attachment and exploratory behavior of one-year-olds in a strange situation. In B. M. Foss (Ed.), *Determinants of infant behaviour.* London: Methuen.

Ainsworth, M. D. S., Blehar, M., Waters, E., & Wall, S. (1978). *Patterns of attachment.* Hillsdale, NJ: Erlbaum.

Ajzen, I. (2001). Nature and operation of attitudes. *Annual Review of Psychology, 52,* 27–58.

Ajzen, I., & Fishbein, M. (1977). Attitude-behavior relations: A theoretical analysis and review of empirical research. *Psychological Bulletin, 84,* 888–918.

Akiskal, H. S., & Cassano, G. B. (Eds.). (1997). *Dysthymia and the spectrum of chronic depression.* New York: Guilford Press.

Albert, M. S., & Moss, M. B. (1992). The assessment of memory disorders in patients with Alzheimer's disease. In L. R. Squire & N. Butters (Eds.), *Neuropsychology of memory* (2nd ed.). New York: Guilford.

Alberta Alcohol and Drug Abuse Commission (1999). Beyond the ABCs: Information for professionals. www.gov.ab.ca/aadac/addictions/beyond/

Alda, M. (2001). Genetic factors and treatment of mood disorders. *Bipolar Disorders, 3,* 318–324.

Alden, L. E. (1988). Morita therapy with socially avoidant clients. *International Bulletin of Morita Therapy, 1,* 43–51.

Alden, L. E. (2001). Interpersonal perspectives on social phobia. In W. R. Crozier & L. E. Alden (Eds.). *International handbook of social anxiety: Concepts, research and interventions relating to the self and shyness* (pp. 381–404). New York: John Wiley & Sons.

Alden, L. E., Ryder, A. G., & Mellings, T. M. B. (2002). Perfectionism in the context of social fears: Toward a two-component model. In G. L. Flett, & Hewitt, P. L. (Eds.). *Perfectionism: Theory, research, and treatment.* (pp. 373–391). Washington, DC: APA.

Alexander, B. K. (1990). *Peaceful measures: Canada's way out of the war on drugs.* Toronto: University of Toronto Press.

Allan, L. G., & Siegel, S. (1997). Contingent color aftereffects: Reassessing old conclusions. *Perception and Psychophysics, 59,* 129–141.

Allen, K. M., Blascovich, J., Tomaka, J., & Kelsey, R. M. (1991). Presence of human friends and pet dogs as moderators of autonomic responses to stress in women. *Journal of Personality and Social Psychology, 61,* 582–589.

Allen, S. W., & Vokey, J. R. (1998). Directed forgetting and rehearsal on direct and indirect memory tests. In J. M. Golding & C. M. MacLeod (Eds.), *Intentional forgetting: Interdisciplinary approaches* (pp. 173–195). Mahwah, NJ: Erlbaum.

Alley, T. R., & Cunningham, M. R. (1991). Average faces are attractive, but very attractive faces are not average. *Psychological Science, 2,* 123–125.

Allison, D. B., & Faith, M. S. (1997). Issues in mapping genes for eating disorders. *Psychopharmacology Bulletin, 33,* 359–368.

Allison, J. (1989). The nature of reinforcement. In S. B. Klein & R. R. Mowrer (Eds.), *Contemporary learning theories: Instrumental conditioning and the impact of biological constraints on learning.* Hillsdale, NJ: Erlbaum.

Allison, T., & Cicchetti, D. V. (1976). Sleep in mammals: Ecological and constitutional correlates. *Science, 194,* 732–734.

Alloy, L. B., & Clements, C. M. (1998). Hopelessness theory of depression: Tests of the symptom component. *Cognitive Therapy and Research, 22,* 303–335.

Alloy, L. B., Abramson, L. Y., Tashman, N. A., Berrebbi, D. S., Hogan, M. E., Whitehouse, W. G., Crossfield, A. G., & Moroco, A. (2001). Developmental origins of cognitive vulnerability to depression: Parenting, cognitive, and inferential feedback styles of the parents of individuals at high and low cognitive risk for depression. *Cognitive Therapy and Research, 25,* 397–423.

Allport, A. (1989). Visual attention. In M. I. Posner (Ed.), *Foundation of cognitive science.* Cambridge, MA: MIT Press.

Allport, G. W. (1937). *Personality: A psychological interpretation.* New York: Holt.

Allport, G. W. (1954). *The nature of prejudice.* Cambridge, MA: Addison-Wesley.

Allport, G. W., & Odbert, H. H. (1936). Trait-names: A psycho-lexical study. *Psychological Monographs, 47* (1, Whole No. 211).

Altemeyer, B. (1988). *Enemies of freedom: Understanding right-wing authoritarianism.* San Francisco: Jossey-Bass.

Altemeyer, B. (1994). Reducing prejudice in right-wing authoritarians. In M. P. Zanna & J. M. Olson (Eds.), *The psychology of prejudice: The Ontario symposium* (pp. 131–148). Hillsdale, NJ: Erlbaum.

Altemeyer, B. (1996). *The authoritarian specter.* Cambridge, MA: Harvard University Press.

Altemeyer, B., & Hunsberger, B. (1997). *Amazing conversions: Why some turn to faith and others abandon religion.* Amherst, NY: Prometheus.

Amabile, T. M. (1983). *The social psychology of creativity.* New York: Springer-Verlag.

Amzica, F., & Steriade, M. (1996). Progressive cortical synchronization of ponto-geniculo-occipital potentials during rapid eye movement sleep. *Neuroscience, 72,* 309–314.

Anastasi, A. (1985). Psychological testing: Basic concepts and common misconceptions. *G. Stanley Hall Lecture Series, 5,* 87–120.

Andersen, B. L. (1992). Psychological interventions for cancer patients to enhance quality of life. *Journal of Consulting and Clinical Psychology, 60,* 552–568.

Andersen, S. M., & Berk, M. S. (1998). Transference in everyday experience: Implications of experimental research for relevant clinical phenomena. *Review of General Psychology, 2,* 81–120.

Anderson, J. L., & Crawford, C. B. (1992). Modelling the costs and benefits of reproductive suppression. *Human Nature, 3,* 299–334.

Anderson, J. R. (1990). *The adaptive character of thought.* Hillsdale, NJ: Erlbaum.

Anderson, L. E., & Walsh, J. A. (1998). Prediction of adult criminal status from juvenile psychological assessment. *Criminal Justice and Behavior, 25,* 226–239.

Andrasik, F., & Holroyd, K. A. (1980). A test of specific and nonspecific effects in the biofeedback treatment of tension headache. *Journal of Consulting and Clinical Psychology, 48,* 575–586.

Andreasen, N. C. (1987). Creativity and mental illness: Prevalence rates in writers and their first-degree relatives. *American Journal of Psychiatry, 144,* 1288–1292.

Anisman, H., Hayley, S., Staines, W., & Merali, Z. (2001). Cytokines, stress, and neurochemical change: Immediate and proactive effects. In C. A. Shaw & J. C. McEachern (Eds.), *Toward a theory of neuroplasticity* (pp. 301–320). Philadelphia: Taylor & Francis.

Antrobus, J. (1991). Dreaming: Cognitive processes during cortical activation and high afferent thresholds. *Psychological Review, 98,* 96–121.

American Psychiatric Association (1994) *Diagnostic and statistical manual of mental disorders* (4th ed.). Washington, DC: Author.

Apgar, V., & Beck, J. (1974). *Is my baby all right?* New York: Pocket Books.

Araoz, D. L. (1982). *Hypnosis and sex therapy.* New York: Brunner/Mazel.

Arguin, M., & Bub, D. (1993). Modulation of the directional attention deficit in visual neglect by hemispatial factors. *Brain and Cognition, 22,* 148–160.

Arguin, M., Bub, D., & Dudek, G. (1996). Shape integration for visual object recognition and its implication in category-specific visual agnosia. *Visual Cognition, 3,* 221–275.

Aronoff, J., Lynn, S. J., & Malinoski, P. (2000). Are cultic environments psychologically harmful? *Clinical Psychology Review, 20,* 91–111.

Aronson, E. (1992). The return of the repressed: Dissonance theory makes a comeback. *Psychological Inquiry, 3,* 303–311.

Aronson, E. (1997). The theory of cognitive dissonance: The evolution and vicissitudes of an idea. In C. McGarty & S. Haslam (Eds.), *The message of social psychology: Perspectives on mind in society.* Oxford, England: Blackwell.

Arvanitogiannis, A., Riscaldino, L., & Shizgal, P. (1999). Effects of NMDA lesions of the medial basal forebrain on LH and VTA self-stimulation. *Physiology and Behavior, 65,* 805–810.

Asch, S. E. (1951). Effects of group pressure on the modification and distortion of judgments. In H. Guetzkow (Ed.), *Groups, leadership, and men.* Pittsburgh, PA: Carnegie Press.

Asch, S. E. (1955, May). Opinions and social pressures. *Scientific American, 193,* 31–35.

Aschoff, J., & Wever, R. (1981). The circadian system of man. In J. Aschoff (Ed.), *Handbook of behavioral neurobiology: biological rhythms.* New York: Plenum.

Aserinsky, E., & Kleitman, N. (1955). Two types of ocular motility occurring in sleep. *Journal of Applied Physiology, 8,* 1–10.

Ashton, C. H. (2001). Pharmacology and effects of cannabis: A brief review. *British Journal of Psychiatry, 178,* 101–106.

Ashton, M. C., Lee, K., & Son, C. (2000). Honesty as the sixth factor of personality: Correlations with Machiavellianism, primary psychopathy, and social adroitness. *European Journal of Personality, 14,* 359–369.

Assanand, S., Pinel, J. P. J., & Lehman, D. R. (1998). Personal theories of hunger and eating. *Journal of Applied Social Psychology, 28* (11), 998–1015.

Atkinson, J. W. (1957). Motivational determinants of risk-taking behavior. *Psychological Review, 64,* 359–372.

Atkinson, J. W., & Raynor, J. O. (Eds.) (1974). *Motivation and achievement.* Washington, DC: Winston.

Atkinson, R. C., & Shiffrin, R. M. (1968). Human memory: A proposed system and its control processes. In K. W. Spence (Ed.), *The psychology of learning and motivation: Advances in research and theory* (pp. 89–195). New York: Academic Press.

Aubé, J., & Whiffen, V. E. (1996). Depressive styles and social acuity. *Communication Research, 23,* 407–425.

Austad, S. (1997). *Why we age: What science is discovering about the body's journey through life.* New York: Wiley.

Ayllon, T., & Azrin, N. H. (1968). *The token economy: A motivational system for therapy and rehabilitation.* New York: Appleton-Century-Crofts.

Baddeley, A. D. (2000). The episodic buffer: A new component of working memory? *Trends in Cognitive Sciences, 4,* 417–423.

Baddeley, A. D. (1992) Working memory. *Science, 255,* 556–559.

Baddeley, A. D. & Hitch, G. (1974). *Working memory.* In G. H. Bower (Ed.), *The psychology of learning and motivation.* New York: Academic Press.

Baddeley, A. D., & Lieberman, K. (1980). Spatial working memory. In R. Nickerson (Ed.), *Attention and performance VIII.* Hillsdale, NJ: Erlbaum.

Baddeley, A. D., & Longman, D. J. A. (1978). The influence of length and frequency of training sessions on the rate of learning to type. *Ergonomics, 21,* 627–635.

Baddeley, A. D., Gathercole, S. E., & Papagno, C. (1998). The phonological loop as a language device. *Psychological Review, 105,* 158–173.

Baddeley, A. D., Thomson, N., & Buchanan, M. (1975). Word length and the structure of short-term memory. *Journal of Verbal Learning and Verbal Behavior, 14,* 575–589.

Bahrick, H. P. (1984). Semantic memory content in permastore: 50 years of memory for Spanish learned in school. *Journal of Experimental Psychology: General, 113,* 1–29.

Bahrick, H. P., & Hall, L. K. (1991). Lifetime maintenance of high school mathematics content. *Journal of Experimental Psychology: General, 120,* 20–33.

Bailey, J. M., & Pillard, R. C. (1991). A genetic study of male sexual orientation. *Archives of General Psychiatry, 48,* 1089–1096.

Bailey, J. M., & Pillard, R. C. (1995). Genetics of human sexual orientation. *Annual Review of Sex Research, 6,* 126–150.

Bailey, J. M., & Zucker, K. J. (1995). Childhood sex-typed behavior and sexual orientation: A conceptual analysis and quantitative review. *Developmental Psychology, 31* (1), 43–55.

Bailey, J. M., Pillard, R. C., Neale, M. C. I., & Agyei, Y. (1993). Heritable factors influence sexual orientation in women. *Archives of General Psychiatry, 50,* 217–223.

Bain, J. (1987). Hormones and sexual aggression in the male. *Integrative Psychiatry, 5,* 82–89.

Bakan, D. (1996). *The duality of human existence.* Boston, MA: Beacon Press.

Baker, T. B., & Tiffany, S. T. (1985). Morphine tolerance as habituation. *Psychological Review, 92,* 78–108.

Baldo, J. V., & Shimamura, A. P. (1998). Letter and category fluency in patients with frontal lobe lesions. *Neuropsychology, 12,* 259–267.

Baldwin, M.W., Granzberg, A., Pippus, L., & Pritchard, E.T. (2003). Cued activation of relational schemas: Self-evaluation and gender effects. *Canadian Journal of Behavioural Science 35,* 153–163.

Baldwin, M. W., Carrell, S. E., & Lopez, D. F. (1990). Priming relationship schemas: My advisor and the Pope are watching me from the back of my mind. *Journal of Experimental Social Psychology, 26,* 435–454.

Balota, D. A., Dolan, P. O., & Duchek, J. M. (2000). Memory changes in healthy older adults. In E. Tulving & F. I. M. Craik (Eds.), *The Oxford handbook of memory.* Oxford: Oxford University Press.

Banaji, M. R., & Crowder, R. G. (1989). The bankruptcy of everyday memory. *American Psychologist, 44,* 1185–1193.

Bandura, A. (1986). *Social foundations of thought and action.* Englewood Cliffs, NJ: Prentice-Hall.

Bandura, A. (1993). Perceived self-efficacy in cognitive development and functioning. *Educational Psychologist, 28,* 117–148.

Bandura, A., Ross, D., & Ross, S. A. (1963). Imitation of film-mediated aggressive models. *Journal of Abnormal and Social Psychology, 66,* 3–11.

Banks, M. S., & Salapatek, P. (1983). Infant visual perception. In M. M. Haith & J. J. Campos (Eds.), *Handbook of child psychology.* New York: Wiley.

Banks, M. S., & Shannon, E. (1993). Spatial and chromatic visual efficiency in human neonates. In C. E. Granrud (Ed.), *Visual perception and cognition in infancy.* Hillsdale, NJ: Erlbaum.

Barber, T. X. (1976). *Pitfalls in human research: Ten pivotal points.* New York: Pergamon.

Barber, T. X., Spanos, N. P., & Chaves, J. (1974). *Hypnosis, imagination, and human potentialities.* New York: Pergamon.

Barcelo, F., & Gale, A. (1997). Electrophysiological measures of cognition in biological psychiatry: Some cautionary notes. *International Journal of Neuroscience, 92,* 219–240.

Barenbaum, N. B. (1997). The case(s) of Gordon Allport. *Journal of Personality, 65,* 743–755.

Bargones, J. Y., & Werner, L. A. (1994). Adults listen selectively; infants do not. *Psychological Science, 5,* 170–174.

Barkley, R. A. (1997). Behavioral inhibition, sustained attention, and executive functions: Constructing a unified theory of ADHD. *Psychological Bulletin, 121,* 65–94.

Barkow, J. H., Cosmides, L., & Tooby, J. (1992). *The adapted mind: Evolutionary psychology and the generation of culture.* New York: Oxford.

Barlow, D. H. (1988). *Anxiety and its disorders: The nature and treatment of anxiety and panic.* New York: Guilford.

Barlow, D. H., & Durand, V. M. (1999). *Abnormal psychology: An integrative approach* (2nd ed.). Pacific Grove, CA: Brooks/Cole.

Barlow, D. H., & Durand, V. M. (2002). *Abnormal psychology: An integrative approach* (3rd ed.). Pacific Grove, CA: Brooks/Cole.

Barlow, D. H., & Rapee, R. M. (1991). *Mastering stress: A lifestyle approach.* Dallas, TX: American Health.

Barnes, S. J., Floresco, S. B., Kornecook, T. J., & Pinel, J. P. J. (2000). Reversible lesions of the rhinal cortex produce delayed non-matching-to-sample deficits in rats. *Neuroreport: For Rapid Communication of Neuroscience Research, 11,* 351–354.

Barnes, V. A., Treiber, F., & Davis, H. (2001). Impact of Transcendental Meditation (R) on cardiovascular function at rest and during acute stress in adolescents with high normal blood pressure. *Journal of Psychosomatic Research, 51,* 597–605.

Bar-On, R., & Parker, J. D. A. (Eds.) (2000). *The handbook of emotional intelligence.* New York: John Wiley/Jossey-Bass.

Baron-Cohen, S. (1994). Cognitive mechanisms in mind-reading. *Current Psychology of Cognition, 13,* 513–552.

Barsalou, L. W. (1983). Ad hoc categories. *Memory and Cognition, 11,* 211–227.

Bartholomew, K. (1993). From childhood to adult relationships: Attachment theory and research. In S. Duck (Ed.), *Understanding relationship processes 2: Learning about relationships* (pp. 30–62). Beverly Hills: Sage.

Bartholomew, K., Henderson, A. J. Z., & Dutton, D. G. (2000). Insecure attachment and abusive intimate relationships. In C. Clulow (Ed.), *Attachment and couple work: Applying the "secure base" concept in research and practise.* London: Routledge.

Bartlett, F. C. (1932). *Remembering.* Cambridge: Cambridge University Press.

Bassok, M., Wu, L. L., & Olseth, K. L. (1995). Judging a book by its cover: Interpretative effects of content on problem-solving transfer. *Memory and Cognition, 23,* 354–367.

Bastien, C., & Campbell, K. (1992). The evoked K-complex: All or none phenomenon? *Sleep, 15,* 236–245.

Baumeister, R. F. (1997). Identity, self-concept, and self-esteem: The self lost and regained. In R. Hogan, J. Johnson, & S. R. Briggs (Eds.), *Handbook of personality psychology* (pp. 681–711). San Diego: Academic Press.

Baumeister, R. F., Smart, L., & Boden, J. M. (1996). Relation of threatened egotism to violence and aggression: The dark side of high self-esteem. *Psychological Review, 103,* 5–33.

Baumrind, D. (1964). Some thoughts on the ethics of research: After reading Milgram's "Behavioral study of obedience." *American Psychologist, 19,* 421–423.

Baumrind, D. (1985). Research using intentional deception: Ethical issues revisited. *American Psychologist, 40,* 165–174.

Beal, A. L., Dumont, R. P., Cruse, C. L., & Branche, A. H. (1996). Practical implications of differences between the American and Canadian norms for WISC-III and a short form for children with learning disabilities. *Canadian Journal of School Psychology, 12,* 7–14.

Beaubrun, G., & Gray, G. E. (2000). A review of herbal medicines for psychiatric disorders. *Psychiatric Services, 51,* 1130–1134.

Beaumont, S. (1995). Adolescent girls' conversations with mothers and friends: A matter of style. *Discourse Processes, 11,* 325–356.

Beaumont, S. (1996). Adolescent girls' perceptions of conversations with mothers and friends. *Journal of Adolescent Research, 11,* 325–346.

Beaumont, S., & Cheyne, J. A. (1998). Interruptions in adolescent girls' conversations: Comparing mothers and friends. *Journal of Adolescent Research, 13,* 272–292.

Beauregard, K. S., & Dunning, D. (1998). Turning up the contrast: Self-enhancement motives prompt egocentric contrast effects in social judgments. *Journal of Personality and Social Psychology, 74,* 606–621.

Beck, A. T. (1991). Cognitive therapy: A 30-year retrospective. *American Psychologist, 46,* 368–375.

Beck, A. T., & Young, J. E. (1985). Depression. In D. H. Barlow (Ed.), *Clinical handbook of psychological disorders.* New York: Guilford.

Beer, J. M., Arnold, R. D., & Loehlin, J. C. (1998). Genetic and environmental influ-

ences on MMPI factor scales: Joint model fitting to twin and adoption data. *Journal of Personality and Social Psychology, 74,* 818–827.

Beers, M. J., Lassiter, G. D., & Flannery, B. C. (1997). Individual differences in person memory: Self-monitoring and the recall of consistent and inconsistent behavior. *Journal of Social Behavior and Personality, 12,* 811–820.

Begg, I. M., Needham, D. R., & Bookbinder, M. (1993). Do backward messages unconsciously affect listeners? No. *Canadian Journal of Experimental Psychology, 47,* 1–14.

Behrmann, M., Winocur, G., & Moscovitch, M. (1992). Dissociation between mental imagery and object recognition in a brain-damaged patient. *Nature, 359,* 636–637.

Békésy, G. von (1960). *Experiments in hearing.* New York: McGraw-Hill.

Bell, A. P., Weinberg, M. S., & Hammersmith, S. K. (1981). *Sexual preference: Its development in men and women.* Bloomington: Indiana University Press.

Bell, P. A., Fisher, J. D., Baum, A., & Greene, T. E. (1990). *Environmental psychology* (3rd ed.). Fort Worth, TX: Holt, Rinehart and Winston.

Bem, D. J. (1967). Self-perception: An alternative interpretation of cognitive dissonance phenomena. *Psychological Review, 74,* 183–200.

Bem, D. J. (1972). Self-perception theory. In L. Berkowitz (Ed.), *Advances in experimental social psychology.* New York: Academic Press.

Bem, S. L. (1981). Gender schema theory: A cognitive account of sex-typing. *Psychological Review, 88,* 354–364.

Benbow, C. P., Lubinski, D., Shea, D. L., & Eftekhari-Sanjani, H. (2000). Sex differences in mathematical reasoning ability at age 13: Their status 20 years later. *Psychological Science 11,* 474–480.

Benes, F. M., Turtle, M., Khan, Y., & Farol, P. (1994). Myelination of a key relay zone in the hippocampal formation occurs in the human brain during childhood, adolescence, and adulthood. *Archives of General Psychiatry, 51,* 477–484.

Benson, H. (1975). *The relaxation response.* New York: Morrow.

Benson, P. L., Dehority, J., Garman, L., Hanson, E., Hochschwender, M., Lebod, C., Rohr, R., & Sullivan, J. (1980). Intrapersonal correlates of nonspontaneous helping behavior. *Journal of Social Psychology, 110,* 87–95.

Bentall, R. P. (1990). The illusion of reality: A review and integration of psychological research on hallucinations. *Psychological Bulletin, 107,* 82–95.

Benton, M. K., & Schroeder, H. E. (1990). Social skills training with schizophrenics: A meta-analytic evaluation. *Journal of Consulting and Clinical Psychology, 58,* 741–747.

Bergvall, A., Fahlke, C., & Hansen, S. (1996). An animal model for Type 2 alcoholism? Alcohol consumption and aggressive behavior following lesions in the raphe nuclei, medial hypthothalamus, or ventral striatum-septal area. *Physiology and Behavior, 60,* 1125–1135.

Berman, K. F., & Weinberger, D. R. (1990). Lateralization of cortical function during cognitive tasks: Regional cerebral blood flow studies of normal individuals and patients with schizophrenia. *Journal of Neurology, Neurosurgery, and Psychiatry, 53,* 150–160.

Bernal, E. M. (1984). Bias in mental testing: Evidence for an alternative to the heredity-environment controversy. In C. R. Reynolds & R. T. Brown (Eds.), *Perspectives on bias in mental testing.* New York: Plenum.

Berndt, T. J. (1988). The nature and significance of children's friendships. In R. Vasta (Ed.), *Annals of child development.* Greenwich, CT: JAI Press.

Berndt, T. J., & Keefe, K. (1995). Friends' influence on adolescents' adjustments to school. *Child Development, 66,* 1312–1329.

Bernstein, I. H., Lin, T., & McClelland, P. (1982). Cross- vs. within-racial judgments of attractiveness. *Perception and Psychophysics, 32,* 495–503.

Bernstein, I. L. (1978). Learned taste aversions in children receiving chemotherapy. *Science, 200,* 1302–1303.

Berry, J. W. (1999). Intercultural relations in plural societies. *Canadian Psychology, 40,* 12–21.

Berry, J. W., & Kalin, R. (1995). Multicultural and ethnic attitudes in Canada: An overview of the 1991 national survey. *Canadian Journal of Behavioural Science, 27,* 301–320.

Berry, J. W., Poortinga, Y. H., & Pandey, J. (Eds.) (1997). *Handbook of cross-cultural psychology. Theory and method.* Boston: Allyn & Bacon.

Berscheid, E. (1985). Interpersonal attraction. In G. Lindzey & E. Aronson (Eds.), *Handbook of social psychology.* New York: Random House.

Bertenthal, B. I., Campos, J. J., & Kermoian, R. (1994). An epigenetic perspective on the development of self-produced locomotion and its consequences. *Current Directions in Psychological Science, 3,* 140–145.

Best, J. B. (1989). *Cognitive psychology* (2nd ed.). St. Paul, MN: West Publishing.

Beutler, L. E., & Berren, M. R. (Eds.). (1995). *Integrative assessment of adult personality.* New York: Guilford.

Beyerstein, B. L., & Beyerstein, D. F. (Eds.) (1992). *The write stuff: Evaluations of graphology—The study of handwriting analysis.* Amherst, NY: Prometheus.

Biederman, I. (1987). Recognition-by-components: A theory of human image understanding. *Psychological Review, 94,* 115–147.

Biederman, I. (1990). Higher-level vision. In D. H. Osherson, S. M. Kosslyn, & J. M. Hollerbach (Eds.), *An invitation to cognitive science: Visual cognition and action.* Cambridge, MA: MIT Press.

Biederman, I. (2000). Recognizing depth-rotated objects: A review of recent research and theory. *Spatial Vision, 13,* 241–253.

Bigelow, H. J. (1850). Dr. Harlow's case of recovery from the passage of an iron bar through the head. *American Journal of Medical Science, 20,* 13–22.

Binet, A., & Simon, T. (1916; reprinted 1973). *The development of intelligence in children.* New York: Arno Press.

Bisiach, E. (1992). Understanding consciousness: Clues from unilateral neglect and related disorders. In A. D. Milner & M. D. Rugg (Eds.), *The neuropsychology of consciousness.* London: Academic Press.

Bisiach, E., & Rusconi, M. L. (1990). Breakdown of perceptual awareness in unilateral neglect. *Cortex, 26,* 643–649.

Bjork, R. A. (1989). Retrieval inhibition as an adaptive mechanism in human memory. In H. L. Roediger & F. I. M. Craik (Eds.), *Varieties of memory and consciousness: Essays in honor of Endel Tulving.* Hillsdale, NJ: Erlbaum.

Bjorklund, D. F. (1997). The role of immaturity in human development. *Psychological Bulletin, 122,* 153–169.

Blagrove, M. (1996). Problems with the cognitive psychological modeling of dreaming. *Journal of Mind and Behavior, 17,* 99–134.

Blair, H. A., & Sanford, K. (1999). TV and zines: Media and the construction of gender for early adolescents. *Alberta Journal of Educational Research, 45,* 103–105.

Blair, S. N., Kohl, H. W., Paffenbarger, R. S., Clark, K. H., & Gibbons, L. W. (1989).

Physical fitness and all-cause mortality: A prospective study of healthy men and women. *Journal of the American Medical Association, 262,* 2395–2401.

Blake, J., Austin, W., Cannon, M., & Lisus, A. (1994). The relationship between memory span and measures of imitative and spontaneous language complexity in preschool children. *International Journal of Behavioral Development, 17,* 91–107.

Blanchard, E. B. (1992). Psychological treatment of benign headache disorders. *Journal of Consulting and Clinical Psychology, 60,* 537–551.

Blanchard, R. (1997). Birth order and sibling sex ratio in homosexual versus heterosexual males and females. *Annual Review of Sex Research, 8,* 27–67.

Blanchard, R., & Bogaert, A. F. (1996). Homosexuality in men and number of older brothers. *American Journal of Psychiatry, 153,* 27–31.

Blanton, H., Cooper, J., Skurnik, I., & Aronson, J. (1997). When bad things happen to good feedback: Exacerbating the need for self-justification with self-affirmations. *Personality and Social Psychology Bulletin, 23,* 684–692.

Blass, T. (Ed.) (2000). *Obedience to authority: Current perspectives on the Milgram paradigm.* Mahwah, NJ: Lawrence Erlbaum Associates.

Blatt, S. J., & Zuroff, D. C. (1992). Interpersonal relatedness and self-definition: Two prototypes for depression. *Clinical Psychology Review, 12,* 527–562.

Bleuler, E. (1908). Die prognose der Dementia praecox (Schizophreniegruppe). *Allgemeine Zeitschrift für Psychiatrie, 65,* 436–464.

Block, J. (2002). *Ego-resiliency and ego-control through time.* New York: Guilford.

Bloomfield, L. (1933). *Language.* New York: Holt.

Blumenthal, J. A., Emery, C. F., Walsh, M. A., Cox, D. R., Kuhn, C. M., Williams, R. B., & Williams, R. S. (1988). Exercise training in healthy Type A middle-aged men: Effects on behavioral and cardiovascular responses. *Psychosomatic Medicine, 50,* 418–433.

Blundell, J. E., & Rogers, P. J. (1991). Hunger, hedonics, and the control of satiation and satiety. In M. I. Friedman, M. G. Tordoff, & M. R. Kare (Eds.), *Chemical senses.* New York: Marcel Dekker.

Bock, G. R., & Cardew, G. (Eds.) (1997). *Characterizing human psychological adaptations.* New York: Wiley.

Boehnert, J. B. (1993). The psychology of women. In S. Burt, L. Code, & L. Dorney

(Eds.), *Changing patterns: Women in Canada* (2nd ed.). Toronto: McClelland & Stewart.

Boivin, D. B. (2000). Influence of sleep-wake and circadian rhythm disturbances in psychiatric disorders. *Journal of Psychiatry and Neuroscience, 25,* 446–458.

Bolanowski, S. J., Gescheider, G. A., & Verrillo, R. T. (1994). Hairy skin: Psychophysical channels and their physiological substrates. *Somatosensory and Motor Research, 11,* 279–290.

Bolanowski, S. J., Jr. (1989). Four channels mediate vibrotaction: Facts, models, and implications. *Journal of the Acoustical Society of America, 85,* S62.

Bolles, R. C. (1972). Reinforcement, expectancy, and learning. *Psychological Review, 79,* 394–409.

Bolles, R. C. (1993). *The story of psychology: A thematic history.* Pacific Grove, CA: Brooks/Cole.

Bonanno, G.A., Field, N. P., Kovacevic, A., & Kaltman, S. (2002). Self-enhancement as a buffer against extreme adversity: Civil war in Bosnia and traumatic loss in the United States. *Personality and Social Psychology Bulletin 28,* 184–196.

Bond, M. H. (Ed.) (1996). *The handbook of Chinese psychology.* Hong Kong: Oxford University Press.

Bonta, J., & Gendreau, P. (1990). Reexamining the cruel and unusual punishment of prison life. *Law and Human Behavior 14,* 347–372.

Book, H. E. (1998). *How to practice brief psychodynamic psychotherapy: The core conflictual relationship theme method.* Washington, DC: American Psychological Association.

Boone, K. B., & Lu, P. (2000). Gender effects in neuropsychological assessment. In E. Fletcher-Janzen, T. L. Strickland, et al. (Eds.), *Handbook of cross-cultural neuropsychology* (pp. 73–85). Dordrecht, Netherlands: Kluwer Academic Publishers.

Bootzin, R. R., Manber, R., Perlis, M. L., Salvio, M., & Wyatt, J. K. (1993). Sleep disorders and the elderly. In P. B. Sutker & H. F. Adams (Eds.), *Comprehensive handbook of psychopathology* (2nd ed.). New York: Plenum.

Boring, E. G. (1950). *A history of experimental psychology* (2nd ed.). New York: Appleton-Century-Crofts.

Borkenau, P., & Liebler, A. (1995). Observable attributes as manifestations and cues of personality and intelligence. *Journal of Personality, 63,* 1–25.

Borkowski, J. G., Ramey, S. L., & Bristol-Power, M. (Eds.) (2001). *Parenting and the child's world: Influences on academic, intellectual, and social-emotional development.* Mahwah, NJ: Erlbaum.

Bornstein, M. H. (1989). Stability in early mental development: From attention and information processing in infancy to language and cognition in childhood. In M. H. Bornstein & N. A. Krasnegor (Eds.), *Stability and continuity in mental development: Behavioral and biological perspectives.* Hillsdale, NJ: Erlbaum.

Bornstein, M. H. (1992). Perception across the life span. In M. H. Bornstein & M. E. Lamb (Eds.), *Developmental psychology: An advanced textbook* (3rd ed.). Hillsdale, NJ: Erlbaum.

Bornstein, M. H., Kessen, W., & Weiskopf, S. (1976). Color vision and hue categorization in young human infants. *Journal of Experimental Psychology: Human Perception and Performance, 2,* 115–129.

Boroditsky, R., Fisher, W., & Sand, M. (1996). The 1995 Canadian contraception study. *Journal SOGC, 18,* Supplement, 1–31.

Bortz, W. M. (1990). The trajectory of dying: Functional status in the last year of life. *Journal of the American Geriatrics Society, 38,* 146–150.

Bouchard, C., Tremblay, A., Despres, J., Nadeau, A., Lupien, P. J., Theriault, G., Dussault, J., Moorjani, S., Pinault, S., & Fournier, G. (1990). The response to long-term overfeeding in identical twins. *New England Journal of Medicine, 322,* 1477–1487.

Bouchard, T. J., Jr. (1997). IQ similarity in twins reared apart: Findings and responses to critics. In R. J. Sternberg & E. L. Grigorenko (Eds.), *Intelligence, heredity, and environment.* New York: Cambridge University Press.

Bouchard, T. J., Jr., & McGue, M. (1981). Familial studies of intelligence: A review. *Science, 212,* 1055–1059.

Bouchard, T. J., Jr., Lykken, D. T., McGue, M., Segal, N. L., & Tellegean, A. (1990). Sources of human psychological differences: The Minnesota study of twins reared apart. *Science, 250,* 223–228.

Boucher, J. D., & Carlson, G. E. (1980). Recognition of facial expression in three cultures. *Journal of Cross-Cultural Psychology, 11,* 263–280.

Bouton, M. E. (1991). Context and retrieval in extinction and other examples of interference in simple associative learning. In L. Dachowski & C. F. Flaherty (Eds.), *Current topics in animal learning.* Hillsdale, NJ: Erlbaum.

Bouton, M. E., Mineka, S., & Barlow, D. H. (2001). A modern learning theory perspective on the etiology of panic disorder. *Psychological Review, 108,* 4–32.

Bower, G. H. (1973). How to ... Uh ... remember. *Psychology Today, 7,* 63–70.

Bower, T. G. R. (1982). *Development in infancy* (2nd ed.). San Francisco: Freeman.

Bowers, T., & Clum, G. (1988). Relative contributions of specific and nonspecific treatment effects: Meta-analysis of placebo-controlled behavior therapy research. *Psychological Bulletin, 103,* 315–323.

Bowlby, J. (1969). *Attachment and loss:* Vol. 1 *Attachment.* New York: Basic Books.

Bowlby, J. (1988). *A secure base: Parent-child attachment and healthy human development.* New York: Basic Books.

Bowmaker, J. K., & Dartnall, H. J. A. (1980). Visual pigments of rods and cones in a human retina. *Journal of Physiology, 298,* 501–511.

Bowman, E. S. (1998). Pseudoseizures. *Psychiatric Clinics of North America, 21,* 649–657.

Boynton, R. M. (1979). *Human color vision.* New York: Holt, Rinehart & Winston.

Braff, D. L., & Huey, L. (1988). Methylphenidate-induced information processing dysfunction in non-schizophrenic patients. *Archives of General Psychiatry, 45,* 827–832.

Bransford, J. D., & Stein, B. S. (1993). *The ideal problem solver* (2nd ed.). New York: Freeman.

Braungart, J. M., Plomin, R., DeFries, J. C., & Fulker, D. W. (1992). Genetic influence on tester-rated infant temperament as assessed by Bayley's Infant Behavior Record: Nonadoptive and adoptive siblings and twins. *Developmental Psychology, 28,* 40–47.

Breggin, P. R. (1991). *Toxic psychiatry.* New York: St. Martin's.

Bregman, A. S. (1990). *Auditory scene analysis.* Cambridge, MA: Bradford/MIT Press.

Breland, K., & M. (1961). The misbehavior of organisms. *American Psychologist, 16,* 681–684.

Brenneis, C. B. (1994). Can early childhood trauma be reconstructed from dreams? On the relation of dreams to trauma. *Psychoanalytic Psychology, 11,* 429–447.

Brett, J. F., Brief, A. P., Burke, M. J., George, J. M., & Webster, J. (1990). Negative affectivity and the reporting of stressful life events. *Health Psychology, 9,* 57–68.

Brewer, K. R., & Wann, D. L. (1998). Observational learning effectiveness as a function of model characteristics: Investigating the importance of social power. *Social Behavior and Personality, 26,* 1–10.

Briere, J., & Conte, J. (1993). Self-reported amnesia for abuse in adults molested as children. *Journal of Traumatic Stress, 6,* 21–31.

Brigham, J. C., & Pfeifer, J. E. (1996). Euthanasia: An introduction. *Journal of Social Issues, 52,* 1–11.

Broad, W., & Wade, N. (1982). *Betrayers of the truth.* New York: Simon & Schuster.

Broadbent, D. E. (1952). Failures of attention in selective listening. *Journal of Experimental Psychology, 44,* 428–433.

Broadbent, D. E. (1958). *Perception and communication.* London: Pergamon Press.

Broberg, D. J., & Bernstein, I. L. (1987). Candy as a scapegoat in the prevention of food aversions in children receiving chemotherapy. *Cancer, 60,* 2344–2347.

Broca, P. (1861). Remarques sur le siege de la faculté du langage articule, suivies d'une observation d'aphemie (perte de la parole). *Bulletin de la Societé Anatomique (Paris), 36,* 330–357.

Brody, N. (1992). *Intelligence* (2nd ed.). San Diego: Academic Press.

Bromley, D. B. (1986). *The case-study method in psychology and related disciplines.* Chichester, England: Wiley.

Brooks, D. C. (2000). Recent and remote extinction cues reduce spontaneous recovery. *Quarterly Journal of Experimental Psychology, 53B,* 25–58.

Brooks, L. R. (1968). Spatial and verbal components of the act of recall. *Canadian Journal of Psychology, 22,* 349–368.

Brosschot, J. F., Godaert, G. L. R., Benschop, R. J., Olff, M., Ballieux, R. E., & Heijnen, C. J. (1998). Experimental stress and immunological reactivity: A closer look at perceived uncontrollability. *Psychosomatic Medicine, 60,* 359–361.

Broughton, R., Trapnell, P. D., & Boyes, M. C. (1991). Classifying personality types with occupational prototypes. *Journal of Research in Personality, 25,* 302–321.

Brown, A. D., & Murphy, D. R. (1989). Cryptomnesia: Delineating inadvertent plagiarism. *Journal of Experimental Psychology: Learning, Memory, and Cognition, 15,* 432–442.

Brown, D., Scheflin, A. W., & Hammond, D. C. (1998). *Memory, trauma treatment, and the law.* New York: W. W. Norton.

Brown, G. W., & Birley, J. L. T. (1968). Crisis and life change and the onset of schizophrenia. *Journal of Health and Social Behavior, 9,* 203–214.

Brown, J. (1958). Some tests of the decay theory of immediate memory. *Quarterly Journal of Experimental Psychology, 10,* 12–21.

Brown, R. E. (1992). Responses of dominant and subordinate male rats to the odors of male and female conspecifics. *Aggressive Behavior, 18* (2), 129–138.

Brown, R., & Kulick, J. (1977). Flashbulb memories. *Cognition, 5,* 73–99.

Brown, T. A., Barlow, D. H., & Liebowitz, M. R. (1994). The empirical basis of generalized anxiety disorder. *American Journal of Psychiatry, 151,* 1272–1280.

Brown, T. A., O'Leary, T. A., & Barlow, D. H. (2001). Generalized anxiety disorder. In D. H. Barlow (Ed.), *Clinical handbook of psychological disorders: A step-by-step treatment manual* (3rd ed.). New York: Guilford.

Bruce, D. (1985). The how and why of ecological memory. *Journal of Experimental Psychology: General, 114,* 78–90.

Bryden, M. P., & Bulman-Fleming, M. B. (1994). Laterality effects in normal subjects: Evidence for interhemispheric interactions. *Behavior and Brain Research, 64,* 119–129.

Bub, D. N. (2000). Methodological issues confronting PET and MRI studies of cognitive function. *Cognitive Neuropsychology, 17,* 467–484.

Buck, L. (1996). Information coding in the vertebrate olfactory system. *Annual Review of Neuroscience, 19,* 517–544.

Buck, L., & Axel, A. (1991). A novel multigene family may encode odorant receptors: A molecular basis for odor recognition. *Cell, 65,* 175–187.

Buehler, R., Griffin, D., & Ross, M. (1994). Exploring the "planning fallacy": Why people underestimate their task completion times. *Journal of Personality and Social Psychology, 67,* 366–381.

Buell, S. J., & Coleman, P. D. (1979). Dendritic growth in the aged human brain and failure of growth in senile dementia. *Science, 206,* 854–856.

Bulman-Fleming, M. B., & Bryden, M. P. (1994). Simultaneous verbal and affective laterality effects. *Neuropsychologia, 32,* 787–797.

Burda, J. M., & Brooks, C. I. (1996). College classroom seating position and changes in achievement motivation over a semester. *Psychological Reports, 78,* 331–336.

Bushman, B. J., & Anderson, C. A. (2001). Media violence and the American public: Scientific facts versus media misinformation. *American Psychologist, 56,* 477–489.

Buss, A. H. (1988). *Personality: Evolutionary heritage and human distinctiveness.* Hillsdale, NJ: Erlbaum.

Buss, A. H. (1989). Personality as traits. *American Psychologist, 44,* 1378–1388.

Buss, D. M. (1989). Sex differences in human preferences: Evolutionary hypotheses tested in 37 cultures. *Behavioral and Brain Sciences, 12,* 1–49.

Buss, D. M. (1991). Evolutionary personality psychology. *Annual Review of Psychology, 42,* 459–491.

Buss, D. M. (1994). *The evolution of desire: Strategies of human mating.* New York: Basic Books.

Buss, D. M. (1999). *Evolutionary psychology: The new science of the mind.* Needham Heights, MA: Allyn & Bacon.

Buss, D. M. (2000). *The dangerous passion: Why jealousy is as dangerous as love and sex.* New York: Free Press.

Buss, D. M., & Schmitt, D. P. (1993). Sexual strategies theory: An evolutionary perspective on human mating. *Psychological Review, 100,* 204–232.

Buss, D. M., & Shackelford, T. K. (1997). Human aggression in evolutionary psychological perspective. *Clinical Psychology Review, 17,* 605–619.

Bustillo, J. R., Lauriello, J., Horan, W. P., & Keith, S. J. (2001). The psychosocial treatment of schizophrenia: An update. *American Journal of Psychiatry, 158,* 163–175.

Butcher, J. N. (1995). Interpretation of the MMPI-2. In L. E. Beutler & M. R. Berren (Eds.), *Integrative assessment of adult personality.* New York: Guilford.

Butcher, J. N., & Rouse, S. V. (1996). Personality: Individual differences and clinical assessment. *Annual Review of Psychology, 47,* 87–111.

Butler, R. W., Rorsman, I., Hill, J. M., & Tuma, R. (1993). The effects of frontal brain impairment on fluency: Simple and complex paradigms. *Neuropsychology, 7,* 519–529.

Butterworth, G. (1992). Origins of self-perception in infancy. *Psychological Inquiry, 3,* 103–111.

Byers, S. E., Purdon, C., & Clark, D. A. (1998). Sexual intrusive thoughts of college students. *Journal of Sex Research, 35,* 359–369.

Byrd, J. C. (1992). Environmental tobacco smoke: Medical and legal issues. *Medical Clinics of North America, 76,* 377–398.

Byrne, D. (1971). *The attraction paradigm.* New York: Academic Press.

Cacioppo, J. T., Priester, J. R., & Berntson, G. G. (1993). Rudimentary determinants of attitudes. II. Arm flexion and extension have different effects on attitudes. *Journal of Personality and Social Psychology, 65,* 5–17.

Cameron, J., & Pierce, W. D. (1994). Reinforcement, reward, and intrinsic motivation: A meta-analysis. *Review of Educational Research, 64,* 363–423.

Campbell, D. T., & Stanley, J. C. (1966). *Experimental and quasi-experimental designs for research.* Chicago: Rand McNally.

Campbell, D. W., & Eaton, W. O. (1999). Sex differences in the activity level of infants. *Infant and Child Development, 8,* 1–17.

Campfield, L. A., Smith, F. J., Rosenbaum, M., & Hirsch, J. (1996). Human eating: Evidence for a physiological basis using a modified paradigm. *Neuroscience & Biobehavioral Reviews, 20,* 1133–1137.

Campos, J. J., Langer, A., & Krowitz, A. (1970). Cardiac responses on the visual cliff in prelocomotor human infants. *Science, 170,* 196–197.

Canadian Centre on Substance Abuse (1999). www.ccssa.ca/

Canadian Psychological Association (1991). *Canadian code of ethics for psychologists.* Ottawa, ON: Author. Also available at www.cpa.ca/ethics.html.

Canadian Register of Health Service Providers in Psychology (2000). Also available at www.crhspp.ca.

Cannon, W. B. (1927). The James-Lange theory of emotions: A critical examination and an alternative theory. *American Journal of Psychology, 39,* 106–124.

Cannon, W. B. (1929). *Bodily changes in pain, hunger, fear, and rage.* New York: Appleton.

Cannon, W. B. (1932). *The wisdom of the body.* New York: Norton.

Cantor, N. (1990). From thought to behavior: "Having" and "doing" in the study of personality and cognition. *American Psychologist, 45,* 735–750.

Cantor, N., & Harlow, R. E. (1994). Personality, strategic behavior, and daily-life problem solving. *Current Directions in Psychological Science, 3,* 169–172.

Cantor, N., & Malley, J. (1991). Life tasks, personal needs, and close relationships. In G. Fletcher & F. Fincham (Eds.), *Cognition in close relationships.* Hillsdale, NJ: Erlbaum.

Cantor, N., & Mischel, W. (1978). Prototypes in person perception. *Advances in Experimental Social Psychology, 12,* 3–52.

Cantwell, D. P. (1996). Attention deficit disorder: A review of the past 10 years. *Journal of the American Academy of Child and Adolescent Psychiatry, 35,* 978–987.

Capaldi, E. D. (Ed) (1996). *Why we eat what we eat: The psychology of eating.* Washington, DC: American Psychological Association.

Carlsmith, J. M., & Gross, A. E. (1969). Some effects of guilt on compliance. *Journal of Personality and Social Psychology, 11,* 240–244.

Carlsson, N. R., Buskit, W., Enzle, M. E., & Heth, C. D. (1997). The science of behaviour (Canadian ed.). Toronto: Allyn & Bacon.

Carlsson, A., Waters, N., Holm-Waters, S., Tedroff, J., Nilsson, M., & Carlsson, M. L. (2001). Interactions between monoamines, glutamate, and GABA in schizophrenia: New evidence. *Annual Review of Pharmacology and Toxicology, 41,* 237–260.

Carrasco, M., & Ridout, J. B. (1993). Olfactory perception and olfactory imagery: A multidimensional analysis. *Journal of Experimental Psychology: Human Perception and Performance, 19,* 287–301.

Carrazana, E. J., Rivas-Vazquez, R. A., & Rey, G. J. (2001). SSRI discontinuation and buspirone. *American Journal of Psychiatry, 158,* 966–967.

Carstensen, L. L. (1995). Evidence for a life-span theory of socioemotional selectivity. *Current Directions in Psychological Science, 4,* 151–156.

Cartwright, J. (2000). *Evolution and human behavior.* Cambridge, MA: MIT Press.

Cartwright, R. (1991). Dreams that work: The relation of dream incorporation to adaptation to stressful events. *Dreaming, 1,* 2–9.

Caspi, A., & Silva, P. A. (1995). Temperamental qualities at age three predict personality traits in young adulthood: Longitudinal evidence from a birth cohort. *Child Development, 66,* 486–498.

Cassidy, T. (2000). Stress, healthiness and health behaviours: An exploration of the role of life events, daily hassles, cognitive appraisal and the coping process. *Counselling Psychology Quarterly, 13,* 293–311.

Castillo, R. J. (1997). *Culture and mental illness: A client-centered approach.* Pacific Grove, CA: Brooks/Cole Co.

Cattell, R. B. (1963). Theory of fluid and crystallized intelligence: A critical experiment. *Journal of Educational Psychology, 54,* 1–22.

Cattell, R. B. (1998). Where is intelligence? Some answers from the triadic theory. In J. J. McArdle & R. W. Woodcock (Eds.), *Human cognitive abilities in theory and practice.* Mahwah, NJ: Erlbaum.

Cattell, R. B., Eber, H. W., & Tatsuoka, M. M. (1970). *Handbook of the 16 personality factor questionnaire (16PF).* Champaign, IL: Institute for Personality and Ability Testing.

Cavanaugh, J. C. (1993). *Adult development and aging* (2nd ed.). Pacific Grove, CA: Brooks/Cole.

Cavanaugh, J. C., & Blanchard Fields, F. (2002). *Adult development and aging* (4th ed.). Belmont, CA: Wadsworth.

Ceci, S. J. (1991). How much does schooling influence intellectual development and its cognitive components? A reassessment of the evidence. *Developmental Psychology, 27,* 703–722.

Ceci, S. J., & Liker, J. K. (1986). A day at the races: A study of IQ, expertise, and cognitive complexity. *Journal of Experimental Psychology: General, 115,* 255–266.

Cermak, L. S. (1982). The long and the short of it in amnesia. In L. S. Cermak (Ed.), *Human memory and amnesia.* Hillsdale, NJ: Erlbaum.

Chakos, M., Lieberman, J., Hoffman, E., Bradford, D., & Sheitman, B. (2001). Effectiveness of second-generation antipsychotics in patients with treatment-resistant schizophrenia: A review and meta-analysis of randomized trials. *American Journal of Psychiatry, 158,* 518–526.

Challis, B. H. (1993). Spacing effects on cued-memory tests depend on level of processing. *Journal of Experimental Psychology: Learning, Memory, and Cognition, 19,* 389–396.

Chambers, C.T., Craig, K.D., & Bennett, S.M. (2002). The impact of maternal behavior on children's pain experiences: An experimental analysis. *Journal of Pediatric Psychology 27,* 293–301.

Chambless, D. L., & Ollendick, T. H. (2001). Empirically supported psychological interventions: Controversies and evidence. *Annual Review of Psychology, 52,* 685–716.

Chandler, M. J., & Lalonde, C. E. (1996). Shifting toward an interpretive theory of the mind: Five- to seven-year-olds' changing conceptions of mental life. In A. Sameroff & M. Haith (Eds.), *Reason and responsibility: The passage through childhood*

(pp. 111–139). Chicago, IL: University of Chicago Press.

Chandler, M. J., Lalonde, C. E., & Sokol, B. W. (2000). Continuities of selfhood in the face of radical developmental and cultural change. In L. P. Nucci, G. Saze, & E. Turiel (Eds.), *Culture, thought, and development: The Jean Piaget symposium series* (pp. 68–84). Mahwah, NJ: Erlbaum.

Chapman, L. J., & Chapman, J. P. (1967). Genesis of Popular but Erroneous Psychodiagnostic Observations. *Journal of Abnormal Psychology, 72,* 193–204.

Charney, D. S. (2000). The use of placebos in randomized clinical trials of mood disorders: Well justified, but improvements in design are indicated. *Biological Psychiatry, 47,* 687–688.

Chase, W. G., & Simon, H. A. (1973). The mind's eye in chess. In A. L. Glass, K. J. Holyoak, & J. L. Santa, (1979). *Cognition* (p. 422). Reading, MA: Addison-Wesley.

Chase, W. G., & Simon, H. A. (1973). The mind's eye in chess. In W. G. Chase (Ed.), *Visual information processing.* New York: Academic Press.

Chaudhari, N., Landin, A. M., & Roper, S. D. (2000). A metabotropic glutamate receptor variant functions as a taste receptor. *Nature Neuroscience, 3,* 113–119.

Cheesman, J., & Merikle, P. M. (1986). Distinguishing conscious from unconscious perceptual processes. *Canadian Journal of Psychology, 40* (4), 343–367.

Chen, E., & Mathews, K. A. (2001). Cognitive appraisal biases: An approach to understanding the relation between socioeconomic status and cardiovascular reactivity in children. *Annals of Behavioral Medicine, 23,* 101–111.

Chen, S. C. (1937). Social modification of the activity of ants in nest-building. *Physiological Zoology, 10,* 420–436.

Chen, X., Rubin, K. H., & Sun, Y. (1992). Social reputation and peer relationships in Chinese and Canadian children: A cross-cultural study. *Child Development 63,* 1336–1343.

Cherry, E. C. (1953). Some experiments on the recognition of speech with one and with two ears. *Journal of the Acoustical Society of America, 25,* 975–979.

Chesney, M. A. (1993). Health psychology in the 21st century: Acquired immunodeficiency syndrome as a harbinger of things to come. *Health Psychology, 12,* 259–268.

Chia, R. C., Allred, L. J., Grossnickle, W. F., & Lee, G. W. (1998). Effects of attractiveness and gender on the perception of achievement-related variables. *Journal of Social Psychology, 138,* 471–477.

Chomsky, N. (1957). *Syntactic structures.* The Hague: Mouton.

Chomsky, N. (1986). *Knowledge of language: Its nature, origins, and use.* New York: Praeger.

Chumlea, W. C. (1982). Physical growth in adolescence. In B. J. Wolman (Ed.), *Handbook of developmental psychology.* Englewood Cliffs, NJ: Prentice-Hall.

Cialdini, R. B. (1993). *Influence: Science and practice* (3rd ed.). New York: HarperCollins.

Cicirelli, V. G. (1997). Relationship of psychosocial and background variables to older adults' end-of-life decisions. *Psychology and Aging, 12,* 72–83.

Clark, H. H. (1992). *Arenas of language use.* Chicago: University of Chicago Press.

Clarke, L. A., & Livesley, W. J. (1994). Two approaches to identifying the dimensions of personality disorder: Convergence on the five-factor model. In P. T. Costa, Jr., & T. A. Widiger (Eds.), *Personality disorders and the five-factor model of personality.* Washington, DC: American Psychological Association.

Cleary, L. J., Lee, W. L., & Byrne, J. H. (1998). Cellular correlates of long-term sensitization in Aplysia. *Journal of Neuroscience, 18,* 5988–5998.

Cleary, P. J. (1980). A checklist for life event research. *Journal of Psychosomatic Research, 24,* 199–207.

Cleghorn, J. M., Franco, S., Szechtman, B., Kaplan, R., Szechtman, H., Brown, G. M., Nahmias, C., & Garnett, E. S. (1992). Toward a brain map of auditory hallucinations. *American Journal of Psychiatry, 149,* 1062–1069.

Clendenen, V. I., Herman, C. P., & Polivy, J. (1994). Social facilitation of eating among friends and strangers. *Appetite, 23,* 1–13.

Cohen, J. D., & Schooler, J. W. (Eds.) (1997). *Scientific approaches to consciousness.* Mahwah, NJ: Erlbaum.

Cohen, J. S., Simpson, A., Westlake, K., & Hamelin, P. (2002). Integration and representation in rats' serial pattern learning in the T-maze. *Animal Learning and Behavior, 30* (3), 261–274.

Cohen, S., & Herbert, T. B. (1996). Health psychology: Psychological factors and physical disease from the perspective of human psychoneuroimmunology. *Annual Review of Psychology, 47,* 113–142.

Cohen, S., & Wills, T. A. (1985). Stress, social support, and the buffering hypothesis. *Psychological Bulletin, 98,* 310–357.

Cohen, S., Tyrrell, D. A., & Smith, D. A. (1993). Negative life events, perceived stress, negative affect, and susceptibility to the common cold. *Journal of Personality and Social Psychology, 64,* 131–140.

Coile, D. C., & Miller, N. E. (1984). How radical animal activists try to mislead humane people. *American Psychologist, 39,* 700–701.

Cole, M. (1992). Culture in development. In M. H. Bornstein & M. E. Lamb (Eds.), *Developmental psychology: An advanced textbook.* Hillsdale, NJ: Erlbaum.

Cole, N. S. (1981). Bias in testing. *American Psychologist, 36,* 1067–1077.

Coles, R., & Stokes, G. (1985). *Sex and the American teenager.* New York: Harper & Row.

Collins, D. W., & Kimura, D. (1997). A large sex difference on a two-dimensional mental rotation task. *Behavioral Neuroscience, 111,* 845–849.

Colombo, J., Frick, J. E., & Gorman, S. A. (1997). Sensitization during visual habituation sequences: Procedural effects and individual differences. *Journal of Experimental Child Psychology, 67,* 223–235.

Colwill, R. M. (1994). Associative representations of instrumental contingencies. In G. H. Bower (Ed.), *The psychology of learning and motivation.* San Diego: Academic Press.

Colwill, R. M., & Delamater, B. A. (1995). An associative analysis of instrumental biconditional discrimination learning. *Animal Learning and Behavior, 23,* 218–233.

Colwill, R. M., & Rescorla, R. A. (1986). Associative structures in instrumental learning. In G. H. Bower (Ed.), *The psychology of learning and motivation* (pp. 55–104). Orlando, FL: Academic Press.

COMMIT Research Group (1995a). Community intervention trial for smoking cessation (COMMIT): I. Cohort results from a four-year community intervention. *American Journal of Public Health, 85,* 183–192.

COMMIT Research Group (1995b). Community intervention trial for smoking cessation (COMMIT): II. Changes in adult cigarette smoking prevalence. *American Journal of Public Health, 85,* 193–200.

Compas, B. E., Hinden, B. R., & Gerhardt, C. A. (1995). Adolescent development: Pathways and processes of risk and resilience. *Annual Review of Psychology, 46,* 265–293.

Connolly, J., Pepler, D., Craig, W., & Taradash, A. (2000). Dating experiences of bullies in early adolescence. *Journal of the American Professional Society on the Abuse of Children 5,* 299–310.

Conrad, R. (1964). Acoustic confusion in immediate memory. *British Journal of Psychology, 55,* 75–84.

Conrod, P. J., Pihl, R. O., Stewart, S. H., & Dongier, M. (2000). Validation of a system of classifying female substance abusers on the basis of personality and motivational risk factors for substance abuse. *Psychology of Addictive Behaviors, 14,* 243–256.

Conway, M. A. (1995). *Flashbulb memories.* London: Taylor and Francis.

Conway, M. A., Anderson, S. J., Larsen, S. F., Donnelly, C. M., McDaniel, M. A., McClelland, A. G. R., Rawles, R. E., & Logie, R. H. (1994). The formation of flashbulb memories. *Memory and Cognition, 22,* 326–343.

Cook, M., & Mineka, S. (1989). Observational conditioning of fear to fear-relevant versus fear-irrelevant stimuli in rhesus monkeys. *Journal of Abnormal Psychology, 98,* 448–459.

Cook, T. D., & Campbell, D. T. (1979). *Quasi-experimentation: Design and analysis for field settings.* Chicago: Rand McNally.

Cooper, A., Scherer, C. R., Boies, C., & Gordon, B. L. (1999). Sexuality on the Internet: From sexual exploration to pathological expression. *Professional Psychology: Research and Practice, 30,* 154–164.

Cooper, E. (1991). A critique of six measures for assessing creativity. *Journal of Creative Behavior, 25,* 194–204.

Cooper, J. (1992). Dissonance and the return of the self-concept. *Psychological Inquiry, 3,* 320–323.

Cooper, P. E. (1991). Neuroendocrinology. In W. G. Bradley, R. B. Daroff, et al. (Eds.), *Neurology in clinical practice: Principles of diagnosis and management* (pp. 611–625). Boston: Butterworth Heinemann.

Cooper, W. H. (1983). An achievement motivation nomological network. *Journal of Personality and Social Psychology, 44,* 841–861.

Coplan, R.J., Rubin, K.H., Fox, N.A., Calkins, S.D., & Stewart, S. (1994). Being alone, playing alone, and acting alone: Distinguishing among reticence and passive and active solitude in young children. *Child Development 65,* 129-137.

Corballis, M. C. (1991). *The lopsided ape: Evolution of the generative mind.* New York: Oxford University Press.

Coren, A. (2001). *Short-term psychotherapy: A psychodynamic approach.* New York: Palgrave.

Coren, S. (1992). The moon illusion: A different view through the legs. *Perceptual and Motor Skills,* (3, Pt 1), 827–831.

Coren, S. (1995). *The intelligence of dogs.* New York: Bantam Books.

Coren, S. (1996). *Sleep thieves.* New York: The Free Press.

Coren, S. (1999). *Psychology Applied to Animal Learning.* In D.A. Bernstein, A. Stec (Eds.), *Psychology: Fields of Application* (pp. 199–217). Boston: Houghton Mifflin.

Coren, S. (2000). *Why we love the dogs we do: How to find the dog that matches your personality.* New York: Fireside.

Coren, S., Ward, L. M., & Enns, J. T. (1999). *Sensation and perception* (5th ed.). Ft. Worth, TX: Harcourt Brace.

Corneil, W., Beaton, R., Murphy, S., Johnson, C., & Pike, K. (1999). Exposure to traumatic incidents and prevalence of posttraumatic stress symptomatology in urban firefighters in two countries. *Journal of Occupational Health Psychology, 4,* 131–141.

Cosmides, L., & Tooby, J. (1997). Dissecting the computational architecture of social inference mechanisms. In G. R. Bock & G. Cardew (Eds.), *Characterizing human psychological adaptations.* New York: Wiley.

Costa, P. T., & McCraae, R. R. (1989) *NEO/PI/FFI manual supplement.* Odessa, FL: Psychological Assessment Resources.

Cote, K. A., Etienne, L., & Campbell, K. B. (2001). Neurophysiological evidence for the detection of external stimuli during sleep. *Sleep: Journal of Sleep and Sleep Disorders Research, 24,* 791–803.

Covington, M. V., & Mueller, K. J. (2001). Intrinsic versus extrinsic motivation: An approach/avoidance reformulation. *Educational Psychology Review, 13,* 157–176.

Cowan, N. (1995). *Attention and memory: An integrated framework.* New York: Oxford University Press.

Cowan, N., Saults, J. S., & Nugent, L. D. (1997). The role of absolute and relative amounts of time in forgetting within immediate memory: The case of tone-pitch comparisons. *Psychonomic Bulletin and Review, 4,* 393–397.

Cox, C. (1926). *Eminent men and women.* London: Bantam Books.

Cox, M. J., & Paley, B. (1997). Families as systems. *Annual Review of Psychology, 48,* 243–267.

Cox, M. J., Owen, M. T., Henderson, V. K., & Margand, N. A. (1992). Prediction of infant-father and infant-mother attachment. *Developmental Psychology, 28,* 474–483.

Craig, J. C. (1985). Attending to two fingers: Two hands are better than one. *Perception and Psychophysics, 38,* 496–511.

Craig, K. D. (1978). Social disclosure, coactive peer companions, and social modeling determinants of pain communications. *Canadian Journal of Behavioural Science, 10,* 91–104.

Craig, K. D. (1995). From nociception to pain: The role of emotion. In B. Bromm & J. E. Desmedt (Eds.), *Pain and the brain: From nociception to cognition. Advances in pain research and therapy* (pp. 303–317). New York: Raven.

Craig, W., Pepler, D., & Atlas, R. (2000). Observations of bullying in the playground and in the classroom. *School Psychology International, 21,* 22–36.

Craik, F. I. M. (1994). Memory changes in normal aging. *Current Directions in Psychological Science, 5,* 155–158.

Craik, F. I. M., & Jacoby, L. L. (1979). Elaboration and distinctiveness in episodic memory. In L. Nilsson (Ed.), *Perspectives on memory research: Essays in honor of Upsala University's 500th anniversary.* Hillsdale, NJ: Erlbaum.

Craik, F. I. M., & Lockhart, R. S. (1972). Levels of processing: A framework for memory research. *Journal of Verbal Learning and Verbal Behavior, 11,* 671–684.

Craik, F. I. M., & McDowd, J. M. (1987). Age differences in recall and recognition. *Journal of Experimental Psychology: Learning, Memory, and Cognition, 13,* 474–479.

Craik, F. I. M., & Tulving, E. (1975). Depth of processing and the retention of words in episodic memory. *Journal of Experimental Psychology: General, 104,* 268–294.

Cramer, K. M. (1999). Psychological antecedents to help-seeking behavior: A reanalysis using path modeling structures. *Journal of Counseling Psychology, 46,* 381–387.

Cramer, K. M., & Barry, J. E. (1999a). Conceptualizations and measures of loneliness: A comparison of subscales. *Personality and Individual Differences, 27,* 491–502.

Cramer, K. M., & Barry, J. E. (1999b). Psychometric properties and confirmatory factor analysis of the Self-Concealment Scale. *Personality and Individual Differences, 27,* 629–637.

Cramer, K. M., & Neyedley, K. A. (1998). Sex differences in loneliness: The role of masculinity and femininity. *Sex Roles, 38,* 645–653.

Cramer, K. M., Nickels, J. B., & Gural, D. M. (1997). Uncertainty of outcomes, prediction of failure, and lack of control as factors explaining perceived helplessness. *Journal of Social Behavior and Personality, 12* (3), 611–630.

Craske, M. G. (1999). *Anxiety disorders: Psychological approaches to theory and treatment.* Boulder, CO: Westview Press.

Craske, M. G., & Barlow, D. H. (1993). Panic disorder and agoraphobia. In D. H. Barlow (Ed.), *Clinical handbook of psychological disorders* (2nd ed.). New York: Guilford.

Craske, M. G., & Rowe, M. K. (1997). Nocturnal panic. *Clinical Psychology: Science and Practice, 4,* 153–174.

Crawford, C. B. (1989). The theory of evolution: Of what value to psychology? *Journal of Comparative Psychology, 103,* 4–22.

Crawford, C. B. (1998a). The theory of evolution in the study of human behavior: An introduction and overview. In C. B. Crawford & D. L. Krebs (Eds.), *Handbook of evolutionary psychology: Ideas, issues and applications.* Mahwah, NJ: Erlbaum.

Crawford, C. B. (1998b). Environments and adaptations: Then and now. In C. B. Crawford & D. L. Krebs (Eds.), *Handbook of evolutionary psychology: Ideas, issues and applications.* Mahwah, NJ: Erlbaum.

Crits-Christoph, P. (1997). Limitations of the dodo bird verdict and the role of clinical trials in psychotherapy research: Comment on Wampold et al. *Psychological Bulletin, 122,* 216–220.

Croft, R. J., Mackay, A. J., Mills, A. T. D., & Gruzelier, J. G. H. (2001). The relative contributions of ecstasy and cannabis to cognitive impairment. *Psychopharmacology, 153,* 373–379.

Cronbach, L. J. (1957). The two disciplines of scientific psychology. *American Psychologist, 12,* 671–684.

Crooks, R., & Baur, K. (2002). *Our sexuality* (8th ed.). Belmont, CA: Wadsworth.

Cropley, A. J. (1996). Recognizing creative potential: An evaluation of the usefulness of creativity tests. *High Ability Studies, 7,* 203–219.

Crowder, R. G. (1976). *Principles of learning and memory.* Hillsdale, NJ: Erlbaum.

Crowder, R. G., & Neath, I. (1991). The microscope metaphor in human memory. In W. E. Hockley & S. Lewandowsky (Eds.), *Relating* theory and data: Essays on human memory in honor of Bennet B. Murdock. Hillsdale, NJ: Erlbaum.

Crowder, R. G., & Surprenant, A. M. (2000). Sensory memory. In A. E. Kazdin (Ed.), *Encyclopedia of psychology* (pp. 227–229). New York: Oxford University Press and American Psychological Association.

Crowne, D. P., & Marlowe, D. (1964). *The approval motive.* New York: Wiley.

Crowne, D. P., & Wah, L. W. (1998). A comparison of hemispatial neglect from posterior parietal and periarcuate lesions in the monkey. *Psychobiology, 26,* 103–108.

Csermely, P. (Ed.) (1998). *Stress of life: From molecules to man.* New York: New York Academy of Sciences.

Csernansky, J. G., & Bardgett, M. E. (1998). Limbic-cortical neuronal damage and the pathophysiology of schizophrenia. *Schizophrenia Bulletin, 24,* 231–248.

Cunningham, M. D., & Reidy, T. J. (1998). Antisocial personality disorder and psychopathy: Diagnostic dilemmas in classifying patterns of antisocial behavior in sentencing evaluations. *Behavioral Sciences and the Law, 16,* 333–351.

Currie, P. J., & Wilson, L. M. (1993). Central injection of 5-hydroxtryptamine reduces food intake in obese and lean mice. *Neuroreport, 3,* 59–61.

Curtis, R. C., & Miller, K. (1986). Believing another likes or dislikes you: Behaviors making the beliefs come true. *Journal of Personality and Social Psychology, 51,* 284–290.

Cutler, W. B., Friedmann, E., & McCoy, N. L. (1998). Pheromonal influences on sociosexual behavior in men. *Archives of Sexual Behavior, 27,* 1–13.

Czeisler, C. A., Kronauer, R. E., Allen, J. S., Duffy, J. F., Jewett, M. E., Brown, E. N., & Ronda, J. M. (1989). Bright light induction of strong (Type O) resetting of the human circadian pacemaker. *Science, 244,* 1328–1333.

Dabbs, J. M. (2000). *Heroes, rogues, and lovers: Outcroppings of testosterone.* New York: McGraw-Hill.

Daly, M., & Wilson, M. (1983). *Sex, evolution and behavior* (2nd ed.). Boston, MA: PWS Publishers.

Daly, M., & Wilson, M. (1987). The Darwinian psychology of discriminative parental solicitude. In D. W. Leger (Ed.), *Comparative perspectives in modern psychology: Nebraska symposium on motivation, 1987.* New York: John Wiley & Sons.

Daly, M., & Wilson, M. (1990). Is parent–offspring conflict sex-linked? Freudian and Darwinian models. *Journal of Personality, 58,* 163–189.

Daly, M., & Wilson, M. (1995). Discriminative parental solicitude and the relevance of evolutionary models to the analysis of motivational systems. In M. S. Gazzaniga (Ed.), *The cognitive neurosciences.* Cambridge, MA: MIT Press.

Daly, M., & Wilson, M. (1998). The evolutionary social psychology of family violence. In C. Crawford & D. L. Krebs (Eds.), *Handbook of evolutionary psychology: Ideas, issues and applications.* Mahwah, NJ: Erlbaum.

Daly, M., & Wilson, M. (1999). *The truth about Cinderella: A Darwinian view of parental love.* New Haven, CT: Yale University Press.

Daly, M., & Wilson, M. I. (1999). Human evolutionary psychology and animal behaviour. *Animal Behaviour, 57* (3), 509–519.

Daly, M., Salmon, C., & Wilson, M. (1997). Kinship: The conceptual hole in psychological studies of social cognition and close relationships. In J. A. Simpson & D. T. Kenrick (Eds.), *Evolutionary social psychology* (pp. 265–296). Mahwah, NJ: Erlbaum.

Damasio, A. (1999). *The feeling of what happens: Body and emotion in the making of consciousness.* New York: Harcourt Brace.

Damasio, A. R. (1994). *Descartes' error: Emotion, reason, and the human brain.* New York: Grosset/Putnam.

Damhorst, M. L. (1990). In search of a common thread: Classification of information communicated through dress. *Clothing and Textiles Research Journal, 8,* 1–12.

Damon, W., & Hart, D. (1992). Self-understanding and its role in social and moral development. In M. H. Bornstein & M. E. Lamb (Eds.), *Developmental psychology: An advanced textbook.* Hillsdale, NJ: Erlbaum.

Darley, J. M., & Berscheid, E. (1967). Increased liking as a result of the anticipation of personal contact. *Human Relations, 20,* 29–39.

Darley, J. M., & Latané, B. (1968). Bystander intervention in emergencies: Diffusion of responsibilities. *Journal of Personality and Social Psychology, 8,* 377–383.

Darou, W. G. (1992). Native Canadians and intelligence testing. *Canadian Journal of Counselling, 26,* 96–99.

Darwin, C. (1859). *On the origin of species.* London: Murray.

Darwin, C. (1871). *Descent of Man.* London: Murray.

Das, J. P., Naglieri, J. A., & Kirby, J. R. (1994). *Assessment of cognitive processes: The PASS theory of intelligence.* New York: Allyn & Bacon.

Davidson, K., & Prkachin, K. (1997). Optimism and unrealistic optimism have an interacting impact on health-promoting behavior and knowledge changes. *Personality and Social Psychology Bulletin, 23,* 617–625.

Davidson, M., Keefe, R. S. E., Mohs, R. C., Siever, L. J., Losonczy, M. F., Horvath, T. B., & Davis, K. L. (1987). L-dopa challenge and relapse in schizophrenia. *American Journal of Psychiatry, 144,* 934–938.

Davidson, T. L. (1993). The nature and function of interoceptive signals to feed: Toward integration of physiological and learning perspectives. *Psychological Review, 100,* 640–657.

Davidson, T. L. (1998). Hunger cues as modulatory stimuli. In N. A. Schmajuk & P. C. Holland (Eds.), *Occasion setting: Associative learning and cognition in animals.* Washington, DC: American Psychological Association.

Davidson, T. L., & Jarrard, L. E. (1993). A role for hippocampus in the utilization of hunger signals. *Behavioral and Neural Biology, 59,* 167–171.

Davies, I. (1998). A study of colour grouping in three languages: A test of the linguistic relativity hypothesis. *British Journal of Psychology, 89,* 433–452.

Davies, I., & Corbett, G. G. (1997). A cross-cultural study of colour grouping: Evidence for a weak linguistic relativity. *British Journal of Psychology, 88,* 493–517.

Davies, S. N., Pertwee, R. G., & Riedel, G. (2002). Functions of cannabinoid receptors in the hippocampus. *Neuropharmacology, 42,* 993–1007.

Davis, C. G., & Nolen-Hoeksema, S. (2001). Loss and meaning: How do people make sense of loss? *American Behavioral Scientist, 44,* 726–741.

Davis, K. L., Kahn, R. S., Ko, G., & Davidson, M. (1991). Dopamine in schizophrenia: A review and reconceptualization. *American Journal of Psychiatry, 148,* 1474–1486.

Davis, M., & Lee, Y. (1998). Fear and anxiety: Possible roles of the amygdala and bed nucleus of the stria teminalis. *Cognition and Emotion, 12,* 277–305.

Dawkins, R. (1987). *The selfish gene* (new ed.). New York: Oxford University Press.

Dawson, G., & Fischer, K. W. (Eds.) (1994). *Human behavior and the developing brain.* New York: Guilford.

Dawson, G., Ashman, S., & Carver, L. J. (2000). The role of early experience in shaping behavioral and brain development and its implications for social policy. *Development and Psychopathology, 12,* 695–712.

de Boysson-Bardies, B., Sagat, L., & Durand, C. (1984). Discernable differences in the babbling of infants according to target language. *Journal of Child Language, 11,* 1–16.

De Jesus-Zayas, S., Baker, M., Banes, D., & Lozano-Blanco, C. (2001). Opinions on insanity according to federal law, rule 17 and the M'Naghten Standard. *American Journal of Forensic Psychology, 19,* 23–36.

de la Fuente-Fernandez, R., & Stoessl, A. J. (2002). The placebo effect in Parkinson's disease. *Trends in Neurosciences, 25,* 302–306.

de Lacoste-Utamsing, C., & Holloway, R. L. (1982). Sexual dimorphism in the human corpus callosum. *Science, 216,* 1431–1432.

De Silva, W. P., & Rachman, S. J. (1996). *Panic disorder: The facts.* New York: Oxford University Press.

Deaux, K., & Lewis, L. L. (1984). The structure of gender stereotypes: Interrelationships among components and gender label. *Journal of Personality and Social Psychology, 46,* 991–1004.

Debner, J. A., & Jacoby, L. L. (1994). Unconscious perception: Attention, awareness, and control. *Journal of Experimental Psychology: Learning, Memory, and Cognition, 20,* 304–317.

DeCasper, A. J., & Fifer, W. P. (1980). Of human bonding: Newborns prefer their mothers' voices. *Science, 208,* 1174–1176.

DeCasper, A. J., & Spence, M. J. (1986). Prenatal maternal speech influences newborns' perception of speech sounds. *Infant Behavior and Development, 9,* 133–150.

Deci, E. L., & Ryan, R. M. (1985). *Intrinsic motivation and self-determination in human behavior.* New York: Plenum.

DeCola, J. P., & Fanselow, M. S. (1995). Differential inflation with short and long CS-US intervals: Evidence of a nonassociative process in long-delay taste avoidance. *Animal Learning and Behavior, 23,* 154–163.

Deese, J. (1959). On the prediction of occurrence of particular verbal intrusions in immediate recall. *Journal of Experimental Psychology, 58,* 17–22.

DeGrandpre, R. J. (2000). A science of meaning: Can behaviorism bring meaning to psycho-

logical science? *American Psychologist, 55,* 721–773.

Degroot, A., & Parent, M. B. (2001). Infusions of physostigmine into the hippocampus or the entorhinal cortex attenuate avoidance retention deficits produced by intra-septal infusions of the GABA agonist muscimol. *Brain Research, 920,* 10–18.

DeLisi, L. E., Sakuma, M., Tew, W., Kushner, M., Hoff, A. L., & Grimson, R. (1997). Schizophrenia as a chronic active brain process: A study of progressive brain structural change subsequent to the onset of schizophrenia. *Psychiatry Research: Neuroimaging, 74,* 129–140.

DeLongis, A., & O'Brien, T. (1990). An interpersonal framework for stress and coping: An application to the families of Alzheimer's patients. In M. A. P. Stephens, J. H. Crowther, S. E. Hobfall, & D. L. Tennenbaum (Eds.), *Stress and coping in later-life families.* New York: Hemisphere Publishing.

DeLongis, A., Folkman, S., & Lazarus, R. S. (1988). The impact of daily stress on health and mood: Psychological and social resources as mediators. *Journal of Personality and Social Psychology, 54,* 486–498.

Dement, W. C. (1978). *Some must watch while some must sleep.* New York: Norton.

Dement, W. C., & Kleitman, N. (1957). The relation of eye movements during sleep to dream activity: An objective method for the study of dreaming. *Journal of Experimental Psychology, 53,* 339–346.

Dement, W. C., & Vaughan, C. (1999). *The promise of sleep: A pioneer in sleep medicine explores the vital connection between health, happiness, and a good night's sleep.* New York: Delacorte.

DeNelsky, G. Y. (1996). The case against prescription privileges for psychologists. *American Psychologist, 51,* 207–212.

Dennett, D. C. (1991). *Consciousness explained.* Boston: Little, Brown.

Dennett, D. C. (1995). *Darwin's dangerous idea: Evolution and the meanings of life.* New York: Simon & Schuster.

Dennis, W., & Dennis, M. G. (1940). The effect of cradling practices upon the onset of walking in Hopi children. *Journal of Genetic Psychology, 56,* 77–86.

Depression Guideline Panel. (1993). *Depression in primary care: Detection and diagnosis.* Rockville, MD: U.S. Department of Health and Human Services.

Derogatis, L. R., & Coons, H. L. (1993). Self-report measures of stress. In L. Goldberger

& S. Breznitz (Eds.), *Handbook of stress: Theoretical and clinical aspects* (2nd ed.). New York: Free Press.

DeSaint, V., Smith, C., Hull, P., & Loboschefski, T. (1997). Ten-month-old infants' retrieval of familiar information from short-term memory. *Infant Behavior and Development, 20,* 111–122.

DeValois, R. L., & DeValois, K. K. (1980). Spatial vision. *Annual Review of Psychology, 31,* 309–341.

Dewey, J. (1896). The reflex arc concept in psychology. *Psychological Review, 3,* 357–370.

DiBattista, D., & Shepherd, M.-L. (1993). Primary school teachers' beliefs and advice to parents concerning sugar consumption and activity in children. *Psychological Reports, 72,* 47–55.

Dickinson, A. (1989). The detrimental effects of extrinsic reinforcement on "intrinsic motivation." *The Behavior Analyst, 12,* 1–15.

Dickinson, A., & Charnock, D. J. (1985). Contingency effects with a constant probability of instrumental reinforcement. *Quarterly Journal of Experimental Psychology, 37B,* 397–416.

Digman, J. M. (1990). Personality structure: Emergence of the five-factor model. *Annual Review of Psychology, 41,* 417–440.

DiLollo, V., & Bischof, W. F. (1995). Inverse-intensity effect in duration of visible persistence. *Psychological Bulletin, 118,* 223–237.

DiMaggio, P. (1997). Culture and cognition. *Annual Review of Sociology, 23,* 263–287.

Dinan, T. G. (2000). Antidepressants and violence: Cause for concern or media hype? *Human Psychopharmacology, 15,* iii–iv.

Dinges, D. F., Whitehouse, W. G., Orne, E. C., & Powell, J. W. (1992). Evaluating hypnotic memory enhancement (hypermnesia and reminiscence) using multitrial forced recall. *Journal of Experimental Psychology: Learning, Memory, and Cognition, 18,* 1139–1147.

Dion, K., & Kawakami, K. (1996). Ethnicity and perceived discrimination in Toronto: Another look at the personal/group discrimination discrepancy. *Canadian Journal of Behavioural Science, 28,* 203–213.

Dixon, J. A., & Moore, C. F. (1997). Characterizing the intuitive representation in problem solving: Evidence from evaluating mathematical strategies. *Memory and Cognition, 25,* 395–412.

Dixon, M. J., Cudahy, C., Merikle, P. M., & Smilek, D. (2000). Five plus two equals yellow: Mental arithmetic in people with synaesthesia is not coloured by visual experience. *Nature, 406* (6794), 365.

Dobson, K. S. (1989). A meta-analysis of the efficacy of cognitive therapy for depression. *Journal of Consulting and Clinical Psychology, 37,* 414–419.

Dohrenwend, B. P. (Ed.) (1998). *Adversity, stress, and psychopathology.* New York: Oxford University Press.

Domhoff, G. (1996). *Finding meaning in dreams: A quantitative analysis.* New York: Plenum.

Domjan, M. (1998). *The principles of learning and behavior* (4th ed.). Pacific Grove, CA: Brooks/Cole.

Domjan, M., & Purdy, J. E. (1995). Animal research in psychology: More than meets the eye of the general psychology student. *American Psychologist, 50,* 496–503.

Dong, W. K., Chudler, E. H., Sugiyama, K., Roberts, V. J., & Hayashi, T. (1994). Somatosensory, multisensory, and task-related neurons in cortical area 7b (PF) of unanesthetized monkeys. *Journal of Neurophysiology, 72,* 542–564.

Donigian, J., & Malnati, R. (1997). *Systemic group therapy: A triadic model.* Pacific Grove, CA: Brooks/Cole.

Donlon, T. F. (Ed.) (1984). *The College Board technical handbook for the Scholastic Aptitude Test and achievement tests.* New York: College Entrance Examination Board.

Dorward, F. M. C., & Day, R. H. (1997). Loss of 3-D shape constancy in interior spaces: The basis of the Ames-room illusion. *Perception, 26,* 707–718.

Doucet, C., & Stelmack, R. M. (1999). The effect of response execution on P3 latency, reaction time, and movement time. *Psychophysiology, 36,* 351–363.

Douvan, E. (1997). Erik Erikson: Critical times, critical theory. *Child Psychiatry and Human Development, 28,* 15–21.

Doyle, A. B., & Aboud, F. E. (1995). A longitudinal study of White children's racial prejudice as a social cognitive development. *Merrill-Palmer Quarterly, 41,* 210–229.

Draguns, J. G. (1997). Abnormal behavior patterns across cultures: Implications for counseling and psychotherapy. *International Journal of Intercultural Relations, 21,* 213–248.

Drevets, W. C., Burton, H., Videen, T. O., & Snyder, A. Z. (1995). Blood flow changes in human somatosensory cortex during anticipated stimulation. *Nature, 373,* 249–252.

Druckman, D., & Bjork, R. A. (1991). *In the mind's eye: Enhancing human performance.* Washington, DC: National Academy Press.

Druckman, D., & Swets, J. A. (Eds.) (1988). *Enhancing human performance: Issues, theories, and techniques.* Washington, DC: National Academy Press.

Dugas, M. J., Freeston, M. H., Ladouceur, R., Rheaume, J., Provencher, M., & Boisvert, J. (1998). Worry themes in primary GAD, secondary GAD, and other anxiety disorders. *Journal of Anxiety Disorders, 12,* 253–261.

Duncan, R. (1995). Piaget and Vygotsky revisited: Dialogue or assimilation? *Developmental Review, 15,* 458–472.

Duncan, R., & Pratt, M. (1997). Microgenetic change in preschoolers' private speech. *International Journal of Behavioral Development, 20,* 367–383.

Duncan, R. M., & Cheyne, J. A. (1999). Incidence and functions of self-reported private speech in young adults: A self-verbalization questionnaire. *Canadian Journal of Behavioural Science, 31,* 133–136.

Duncker, K. (1945). On problem solving. *Psychological Monographs, 58* (5, Whole No. 270).

Dupont, P., Orban, G. A., De-Bruyn, B., & Verbruggen, A. (1994). Many areas in the human brain respond to visual motion. *Journal of Neurophysiology, 72,* 1420–1424.

Durgin, F. H., Tripathy, S. P., & Levi, D. M. (1995). On the filling in of the visual blind spot: Some rules of thumb. *Perception, 24,* 827–840.

Durie, D. J. (1981). Sleep in animals. In D. Wheatley (Ed.), *Psychopharmacology of sleep.* New York: Raven Press.

Dutton, D. G. (1998). *The abusive personality: Violence and control in close relationships.* New York: Guilford.

Dutton, D. G., & Aron, A. P. (1974). Some evidence for heightened sexual attraction under conditions of high anxiety. *Journal of Personality and Social Psychology, 30,* 510–517.

Dweck, C. S. (1999). *Self-theories: Their role in motivation, personality, and development.* Philadelphia: Psychology Press.

Dweck, C. S., Chiu, C. Y., & Hong, Y. Y. (1995). Implicit theories: Elaboration and extension of the model. *Psychological Inquiry, 6,* 322–333.

Dywan, J., & Bowers, K. (1983). The use of hypnosis to enhance recall. *Science, 222,* 184–185.

Eagly, A. H., & Steffen, F. J. (1986). Gender and aggressive behavior: A meta-analytic review of the social psychological literature. *Psychological Bulletin, 100,* 309–330.

Eagly, A. H., Ashmore, R. D., Makhijani, M. G., & Longo, L. C. (1991). What is beautiful is good, but ...: A meta-analytic review of research on the physical attractiveness stereotype. *Psychological Bulletin, 110,* 109–128.

Easterbrook, M. A., Kisilevsky, B. S., Muir, D. W., & Laplante, D. P. (1999). Newborns discriminate schematic faces from scrambled faces. *Canadian Journal of Experimental Psychology, 53,* 231–241.

Eaton, W. O., & Saudino, K. J. (1992). Prenatal activity level as a temperament dimension? Individual differences and developmental functions in fetal movement. *Infant Behavior and Development, 15,* 57–70.

Ebbesen, E. B., Duncan, B., & Kopnecni, V. J. (1975). Effects of content of verbal aggression on future verbal aggression: A field experiment. *Journal of Experimental Social Psychology, 11,* 192–204.

Ebbinghaus, H. (1885/1964). *Memory: A contribution to experimental psychology.* New York: Dover.

Eccles, J., Adler, T. F., Futterman, R., Goff, S. B., Kaczala, C. M., Meece, J., & Midgley, C. (1983). Expectancies, values, and academic behaviors. In J. T. Spence (Ed.), *Achievement and achievement motives.* San Francisco: Freeman.

Edberg, P. (1990). Rorschach assessment. In A. Goldstein & M. Hersen (Eds.), *Handbook of personality assessment.* New York: Pergamon.

Edelman, G. M. (1987). *Neural Darwinism.* New York: Basic Books.

Edwards, J. (1999). Refining our understanding of language attitudes. *Journal of Language and Social Psychology, 18,* 101–110.

Egan, D., & Schwartz, B. (1979). Chunking in recall of symbolic drawings. *Memory and Cognition, 7,* 149–158.

Ehrlich, S. (1999). Communities of practice, gender, and the representation of sexual assault. *Language and Society, 28,* 239–256.

Eibl-Eibesfeldt, I. (1973). The expressive behavior of the deaf-and-born-blind. In M. von Cranach & I. Vine (Eds.), *Social communication and movement.* San Diego: Academic Press.

Eich, E., & Schooler, J. W. (2000). Cognition/emotion interactions. In E. Eich, J. F. Kihlstrom, et al. (Eds.), *Cognition and emotion* (pp. 3–29). New York: Oxford University Press.

Eich, E., Macaulay, D., Loewenstein, R. J., & Dihle, P. H. (1997). Memory, amnesia, and dissociative identity disorder. *Psychological Science, 8,* 417–422.

Eichenbaum, H., Otto, T., & Cohen, N. J. (1994). Two functional components of the hippocampal memory system. *Behavioral and Brain Sciences, 17,* 449–517.

Eisenberger, R. (1992). Learned industriousness. *Psychological Review, 99,* 248–267.

Ekman, P. (1992). Are there basic emotions? *Psychological Review, 99,* 350–353.

Ekman, P. (1994). Strong evidence for universals in facial expressions: A reply to Russell's mistaken critique. *Psychological Bulletin, 115,* 268–287.

Ekman, P., & Friesen, W. V. (1975). *Unmasking the face.* Englewood Cliffs, NJ: Prentice-Hall.

Ekman, P., & Friesen, W. V. (1986). A new pan-cultural facial expression of emotion. *Motivation and Emotion, 10,* 159–168.

Ekman, P., & Keltner, D. (1997). Universal facial expressions of emotion: An old controversy and new findings. In U. C. Segerstrale & P. Molnar (Eds.), *Nonverbal communication: Where nature meets culture.* Mahwah, NJ: Erlbaum.

Elicker, J., Englund, M., & Sroufe, L. A. (1992). Predicting peer competence and peer relationships in childhood from early parent-child relationships. In R. D. Parke & G. W. Ladd (Eds.), *Family-peer relationships: Modes of linkage.* Hillsdale, NJ: Erlbaum.

Ellard, C. G. (2000). Landmark navigation in gerbils. The role of the posterior parietal cortex. *Psychobiology, 28,* 325–338.

Ellard, J. H., & Rogers, T. B. (1993). Teaching questionnaire construction effectively: The Ten Commandments of question writing. *Contemporary Social Psychology, 17,* 20.

Elliot, A. J., & Thrash, T. M. (2001). Achievement goals and the hierarchical model of achievement motivation. *Educational Psychology Review, 13,* 139–156.

Ellis, A. (1962). *Reason and emotion in psychotherapy.* Secaucus, NJ: Prentice-Hall.

Ellis, A. (1993). Fundamentals of rational-emotive therapy for the 1990s. In W. Dryden & L. K. Hill (Eds.), *Innovations in rational-emotive therapy.* Newbury Park, CA: Sage.

Ellis, R. R., & Lederman, S. J. (1998). The "golf-ball" illusion: Evidence for top-down processing in weight perception. *Perception, 27,* 193–202.

Ellis, R. R., & Lederman, S. J. (1999). The material-weight illusion revisited. *Perception and Psychophysics, 61,* 1564–1576.

Ellison, L. F., Morrison, H. I., de Groh, M., & Villeneuve, P. J. (1999). Health consequences of smoking among Canadian smokers: An update. *Chronic Diseases in Canada, 20,* 36–39.

Ellman, S. J., Spielman, A. J., Luck, D., Steiner, S. S., & Halperin, R. (1991). REM deprivation: A review. In S. J. Ellman & J. S. Antrobus (Eds.), *The mind in sleep* (2nd ed.). New York: Wiley.

Ellsworth, P. C. (1994). William James and emotion: Is a century of fame worth a century of misunderstanding? *Psychological Review, 101,* 222–229.

Elmes, D. G., Kantowitz, B. H., & Roediger, H. L., III (1995). *Research methods in psychology* (5th ed.). St. Paul, MN: West Publishing.

Endler, N. S. (1990). *Holiday of darkness: A psychologist's personal journey out of his depression.* New York: Wall & Emerson.

Engler, J., & Gordon, B. (1992). *The consumer's guide to psychotherapy.* New York: Simon & Schuster.

Epel, E. S., McEwen, B. S., & Ickovics, J. R. (1998). Embodying psychological thriving: Physical thriving in response to stress. *Journal of Social Issues, 54,* 301–322.

Epel, E., Lapidus, R., McEwen, B., & Brownell, K. (2001). Stress may add bite to appetite in women: A laboratory study of stress-induced cortisol and eating behavior. *Psychoneuroendocrinology, 26,* 37–49.

Epstein, S. (1979). The stability of behavior: On predicting most of the people much of the time. *Journal of Personality and Social Psychology, 37,* 1097–1126.

Epstein, S. (1994). Trait theory as personality theory: Can the part be as great as the whole? *Psychological Inquiry, 5,* 120–122.

Erickson, M. A., & Kruschke, J. K. (1998). Rules and exemplars in category learning. *Journal of Experimental Psychology: General, 127,* 107–140.

Erickson, M. H. (1964). A hypnotic technique for resistant patients. *American Journal of Clinical Hypnosis, 7,* 8–32.

Ericsson, K. A., & Simon, H. A. (1993). *Verbal reports as data* (Rev. ed.). Cambridge, MA: MIT Press.

Erikson, E. (1963). *Childhood and society.* New York: Norton.

Erikson, E. (1968). *Identity: Youth and crisis.* New York: Norton.

Erikson, E. (1982). *The life cycle completed: Review.* New York: Norton.

Ernst, C. E., & Angst, J. (1983). *Birth order: Its influence on personality.* Berlin and New York: Springer-Verlang.

Esser, J. K. (1998). Alive and well after 25 years: A review of groupthink research. *Organizational Behavior and Human Decision Processes, 73,* 116–141.

Esses, V. M., Haddock, G., & Zanna, M. P. (1993). Values, stereotypes, and emotions as determinants of intergroup attitudes. In D. M. Mackie & D. L. Hamilton (Eds.), *Affect, cognition, and stereotyping: Interactive processes in group perception* (pp. 137–166). San Diego: Academic Press.

Evans, C. L., McGuire, P. K., & David, A. S. (2000). Is auditory imagery defective in patients with auditory hallucinations? *Psychological Medicine, 30,* 137–148.

Evans, E. F. (1982). Functions of the auditory system. In H. B. Barlow & J. D. Mollon (Eds.), *The senses.* Cambridge: Cambridge University Press.

Evans, G. W. (1997). Environmental stress and health. In A. Baum, T. Revenson, & J. E. Singer (Eds.), *Handbook of health psychology.* Hillsdale, NJ: Erlbaum.

Evans, G. W., Hygge, S., & Bullinger, M. (1995). Chronic noise and psychological stress. *Psychological Science, 6,* 333–338.

Eysenck, H. J. (1952). The effects of psychotherapy: An evaluation. *Journal of Consulting Psychology, 16,* 319–324.

Eysenck, H. J. (1970). *The structure of human personality* (3rd ed.). London: Methuen.

Eysenck, H. J. (1991). Dimensions of personality: 16, 5, or 3? Criteria for a taxonomic paradigm. *Personality and Individual Differences, 12,* 773–790.

Eysenck, H. J., & Eysenck, S. B. G. (1975). *Manual of the Eysenck Personality Questionnaire.* San Diego: EdITS.

Eysenck, H. J., & Kamin, L. (1981). *The intelligence controversy: H. J. Eysenck vs. Leon Kamin.* New York: Wiley.

Fackelmann, K. A. (1993). Marijuana and the brain. *Science News, 143,* 88–94.

Fahy, T. A. (1988). The diagnosis of multiple personality: A critical review. *British Journal of Psychiatry, 153,* 597–606.

Fallon, A. E., & Rozin, P. (1985). Sex differences in perceptions of desirable body shape. *Journal of Abnormal Psychology, 94,* 102–105.

Fallon, A. E., Rozin, P., & Pliner, P. (1984). The child's conception of food: The development of food rejections with special reference to disgust and contamination sensitivity. *Child Development, 55,* 566–575.

Fantz, R. L. (1961, May). The origin of form perception. *Scientific American, 204,* 66–72.

Farah, M. J. (1988). Is visual imagery really visual? Overlooked evidence for neuropsychology. *Psychological Review, 95,* 307–317.

Farah, M. J. (1994). Specialization within visual object recognition: Clues from prosopagnosia and alexia. In M. J. Farah & G. Ratcliff (Eds.), *The neuropsychology of high-level vision.* Hillsdale, NJ: Erlbaum.

Farah, M. J., Wilson, K. D., Drain, M., & Tanaka, J. N. (1998). What is "special" about face perception? *Psychological Review, 105,* 482–498.

Faust, I. M. (1984). Role of the fat cell in energy balance physiology. In A. J. Stunkard & E. Stellar (Eds.), *Eating and its disorders.* New York: Raven.

Fazio, R. H. (1986). How do attitudes guide behavior? In R. M. Sorrentino & E. T. Higgins (Eds.), *Handbook of motivation and cognition: Foundations of social behavior.* New York: Guilford.

Fehr, B., & Russell, J. A. (1991). The concept of love: Viewed from a prototype perspective. *Journal of Personality and Social Psychology, 60,* 425–438.

Feingold, A. (1988). Matching for attractiveness in romantic partners and same-sex friends: A meta-analysis and theoretical critique. *Psychological Bulletin, 104,* 226–235.

Feingold, A. (1990). Gender differences in effects of physical attractiveness on romantic attraction: A comparison across five research paradigms. *Journal of Personality and Social Psychology, 59,* 981–993.

Feingold, A. (1992). Good-looking people are not what we think. *Psychological Bulletin, 111,* 304–341.

Feist, J. (1994). *Theories of personality* (3rd ed.). Fort Worth, TX: Harcourt Brace.

Feldman, M. D., & Christensen, J. F. (Eds.) (1997). *Behavioral medicine in primary care: A practical guide.* Stamford, CT: Appleton & Lange.

Fentress, J. C. (1999). Organization of behaviour revisited. *Canadian Journal of Experimental Psychology, 53,* 8–20.

Fenwick, K. D., & Morrongiello, B. A. (1998). Spatial co-location and infants' learning of auditory-visual associations. *Infant Behavior and Development, 21,* 745–759.

Ferguson, N. B. L., & Keesey, R. E. (1975). Effect of a quinine-adulterated diet upon body weight maintenance in male rats with ventromedial lesions. *Journal of Comparative and Physiological Psychology, 89,* 478–488.

Ferster, C. B., & Skinner, B. F. (1957). *Schedules of reinforcement.* New York: Appleton-Century-Crofts.

Festinger, L. (1957). *A theory of cognitive dissonance.* Stanford, CA: Stanford University Press.

Festinger, L., & Carlsmith, J. M. (1959). Cognitive consequences of forced compliance. *Journal of Abnormal and Social Psychology, 58,* 203–210.

Festinger, L., Riecken, H. W., & Schachter, S. (1956). *When prophecy fails.* Minneapolis: University of Minnesota Press.

Festinger, L., Schachter, S., & Back, K. (1950). *Social pressures in informal groups: A study of human factors in housing.* New York: Harper.

Fiedler, K. (1988). The dependence of the conjunction fallacy on subtle linguistic factors. *Psychological Research, 50,* 123–129.

Fink, M. (2001). Convulsive therapy: A review of the first 55 years. *Journal of Affective Disorders, 63,* 1–15.

Fischer, C. T., McElwain, B., & DuBoise, J. T. (2000). Existential approaches to psychotherapy. In C. R. Snyder and R. E. Ingram (Eds.), *Handbook of psychological change: Psychotherapy processes and practices for the 21st century.* New York: John Wiley & Sons.

Fishbain, D. A., & Goldberg, M. (1991). The misdiagnosis of conversion disorder in a psychiatric emergency service. *General Hospital Psychiatry, 13,* 177–181.

Fisher, C. B., & Younggren, J. N. (1997). The value and utility of the 1992 ethics code. *Professional Psychology—Research and Practice, 28,* 582–592.

Fisher, J. D., & Fisher, W. A. (1992). Changing AIDS risk behavior. *Psychological Bulletin, 111,* 455–474.

Fisher, W. A., & Fisher, J. D. (1993). A general social psychological model for changing AIDS risk behavior. In J. Pryor & G. Reeder (Eds.), *The social psychology of HIV infection* (pp. 127–154). Hillsdale, NJ: Erlbaum.

Fisher, W. A., & Fisher, J. D. (1998). Understanding and promoting sexual and reproductive health behavior: Theory and method. *Annual Review of Sex Research, 9,* 39–77.

Fiske, S. T. (1993). Social cognition and social perception. *Annual Review of Psychology, 44,* 155–194.

Fiss, H. (1991). Experimental strategies for the study of the function of dreaming. In S. J. Ellman & J. S. Antrobus (Eds.), *The mind in sleep* (2nd ed.). New York: Wiley.

Flanagan, O. (2000). *Dreaming souls: Sleep, dreams, and the evolution of the conscious mind.* New York: Oxford University Press.

Flavell, J. H. (1971). Stage-related properties of cognitive development. *Cognitive Psychology, 2,* 421–453.

Flavell, J. H., Miller, P. A., & Miller, S. A. (1993). *Cognitive development* (3rd ed.). Englewood Cliffs, NJ: Prentice-Hall.

Flett, G. L., & Hewitt, P. L. (2003). *Perfectionism: Theory, research and treatment.* Washington, DC: American Psychological Association.

Flett, G. L., Hewitt, P. L., & Hallett, C. J. (1995). Perfectionism and job stress in teachers. *Canadian Journal of School Psychology, 11,* 32–42.

Flett, G. L., Hewitt, P. L., Blankstein, K. R., & Gray, L. (1998). Psychological distress and the frequency of perfectionistic thinking. *Journal of Personality and Social Psychology, 75,* 1363–1381.

Flett, G. L., Hewitt, P. L., Blankstein, K. R., & Pickering, D. (1998). Perfectionism in relation to attributions for success or failure. *Current Psychology: Developmental, Learning, Personality, Social, 17,* 249–262.

Foa, E. B., & Franklin, M. E. (2001). Obsessive-compulsive disorder. In D. H. Barlow (Ed.), *Clinical handbook of psychological disorders: A step-by-step treatment manual* (3rd ed.) New York: The Guilford Press.

Foa, E. B., & Riggs, D. S. (1995). Posttraumatic stress disorder following assault: Theoretical considerations and empirical findings. *Current Directions in Psychological Science, 4,* 61–65.

Foersterling, F., Buehner, M., & Gall, S. (1998). Attributions of depressed persons: How consistent are they with the covariation principle? *Journal of Personality and Social Psychology, 75,* 1047–1061.

Fong, G. T., & Nisbett, R. E. (1991). Immediate and delayed transfer of training effects in statistical reasoning. *Journal of Experimental Psychology: General, 120,* 34–45.

Fong, G. T., Krantz, D. H., & Nisbett, R. E. (1986). The effects of statistical training on thinking about everyday problems. *Cognitive Psychology, 18,* 253–292.

Foulkes, D. (1985). *Dreaming: A cognitive-psychological analysis.* Hillsdale, NJ: Lawrence Erlbaum.

Frazer, J. G. (1890/1959). *The new golden bough: A study in magic and religion* (abridged ed., T. H. Gaster, Ed.). New York: Macmillan.

Fredericks, D. W., & Williams, L. W. (1998). New definition of mental retardation for the American Association of Mental

Retardation. *Image—the Journal of Nursing Scholarship, 30,* 53–56.

Freedman, J. L. (1988). Television violence and aggression: What the evidence shows. In S. Oskamp (Ed.), *Television as a social issue.* Beverly Hills, CA: Sage.

Freedman, J. L. (1992). Television violence and aggression: What psychologists should tell the public. In P. Suedfeld & P. E. Tetlock (Eds.), *Psychology and social policy* (pp. 179–189). Washington, DC: Hemisphere.

Freedman, J.L. (2002). *Media violence and its effects on aggression: Assessing the scientific evidence.* Toronto: University of Toronto Press.

Freedman, J. L., & Fraser, S. C. (1966). Compliance without pressure: The foot-in-the-door technique. *Journal of Personality and Social Psychology, 4,* 195–202.

Freeman, H. L., & Stansfeld, S. A. (1998). Psychosocial effects of urban environments, noise, and crowding. In A. Lundberg (Ed.), *The environment and mental health: A guide for clinicians.* Mahwah, NJ: Erlbaum.

Freud, S. (1900/1990). *The interpretation of dreams.* New York: Basic Books.

Freud, S. (1905/1962). *Three contributions to the theory of sexuality.* New York: Dutton.

Freud, S. (1910). The origin and development of psychoanalysis. *American Journal of Psychology, 21,* 181–218.

Freud, S. (1912/1964). The dynamics of transference. In J. Strachey (Trans. & Ed.), *The standard edition of the complete works of Sigmund Freud.* London: Hogarth Press.

Freud, S. (1940). *An outline of psychoanalysis.* New York: Norton.

Freudenberger, H. J. (1974). Staff burnout. *Journal of Social Issues, 30,* 159–165.

Friedlander, L., Lumley, M. A., Farchione, T., & Doyal, G. (1997). Testing the alexithymia hypothesis: Physiological and subjective responses during relaxation and stress. *Journal of Nervous and Mental Disease, 185,* 233–239.

Friedman, H. S. (1991). *The self-healing personality: Why some people achieve health and others succumb to illness.* New York: Holt.

Friedman, H. S., Hawley, P. H., & Tucker, J. S. (1994). Personality, health, and longevity. *Current Directions in Psychological Science, 3,* 37–41.

Friedman, M., & Rosenman, R. F. (1974). *Type A behavior and your heart.* New York: Knopf.

Friedrich-Cofer, L., & Huston, A. C. (1986). Television violence and aggression: The debate continues. *Psychological Bulletin, 100,* 364–371.

Frueh, B. C., de Arellano, M. A., & Turner, S. M. (1997). Systematic desensitization as an alternative exposure strategy for PTSD. *American Journal of Psychiatry, 154,* 287–288.

Fukuda, T., Kanada, K., & Saito, S. (1990). An ergonomic evaluation of lens accommodation related to visual circumstances. *Ergonomics, 33,* 811–831.

Funder, D. C. (2001). Personality. *Annual Review of Psychology, 52,* 197–221.

Fyer, A. J., Mannuzza, S., Gallops, M. S., Martin, L. Y., Aaronson, C., Gorman, J. M., Liebowitz, M. R., & Klein, D. F. (1990). Familial transmission of simple phobias and fears: A preliminary report. *Archives of General Psychiatry, 47,* 252–256.

Gabrieli, J. D. E. (1998). Cognitive neuroscience of human memory. *Annual Review of Psychology, 49,* 87–115.

Gaetz, M., Weinberg, H., Rzempoluck, E., & Jantzen, K. J. (1998). Neural network classifications and correlational analysis of EEG and MEG activity accompanying spontaneous reversals of the Necker Cube. *Cognitive Brain Research, 6,* 335–346.

Gagnon, J., & Simon, W. (1973). *Sexual conduct: The social sources of human sexuality.* Chicago: Aldine.

Galambos, N. L., & Tilton-Weaver, L. C. (1998). Multiple-risk behavior in adolescents and young adults. *Health Reports, 10,* 9–20.

Galef, B. G., Jr. (1985). Social learning in wild Norway rats. In T. D. Johnston & A. T. Pietrewicz (Eds.), *Issues in the ecological study of learning.* Hillsdale, NJ: Erlbaum.

Gallistel, C. R., & Gibbon, J. (2000). Time, rate, and conditioning. *Psychological Review, 107,* 289–344.

Galton, F. (1869). *Hereditary genius: An inquiry into its laws and consequences.* New York: Appleton.

Galton, F. (1883). *Inquiries into human faculty and development.* London: Macmillan.

Gandelman, R. (1992). *Psychobiology of behavior development.* New York: Oxford University Press.

Gandevia, S. C., McCloskey, D. I., & Burke, D. (1992). Kinaesthetic signals and muscle contraction. *Trends in Neurosciences, 15,* 62–65.

Gangestad, S. W., & Snyder, M. (1985). On the nature of self-monitoring: An examination of latent causal structure. In P. Shaver (Ed.), *Review of personality and social psychology.* Beverly Hills, CA: Sage.

Gardner, E. B., & Costanzo, R. H. (1981). Properties of kinesthetic neurons in somatosensory cortex of awake monkeys. *Brain Research, 214,* 301–319.

Gardner, E. L. (1997). Brain reward mechanisms. In J. H. Lowinson, P. Ruiz, R. B. Millman, & J. G. Langrod (Eds.), *Substance abuse: A comprehensive textbook.* Baltimore: Williams & Wilkins.

Gardner, H. (1983). *Frames of mind: The theory of multiple intelligences.* New York: Basic Books.

Gardner, H. (1993). *Multiple intelligences: The theory in practice.* New York: Basic Books.

Gardner, R. A., & Gardner, B. T. (1969). Teaching sign language to a chimpanzee. *Science, 165,* 664–672.

Gardner, R. A., Gardner, B. T., & Van Cantfort, T. E. (Eds.) (1989). *Teaching sign language to chimpanzees.* Albany, NY: SUNY Press.

Garland, A. F., & Zigler, E. (1993). Adolescent suicide prevention: Current research and social policy implications. *American Psychologist, 48,* 169–182.

Garrity, T. F., Stallones, L., Marx, M. B., & Johnson, T. P. (1989). Pet ownership and attachment as supportive factors in the health of the elderly. *Anthrozoos, 3,* 35–44.

Gauvin, L. (1990). An experiential perspective on the motivational features of exercise and lifestyle. *Canadian Journal of Sport Science, 15,* 51–58.

Gaw, A. C. (2001). *Concise guide to cross-cultural psychiatry.* Washington, DC: American Psychiatric Association.

Gazzaniga, M. S. (1970). *The bisected brain.* New York: Appleton-Century-Crofts.

Gazzaniga, M. S. (1992). *Nature's mind: The biological roots of thinking, emotions, sexuality, and intelligence.* New York: Basic Books.

Gazzaniga, M. S., & LeDoux, J. E. (1978). *The integrated mind.* New York: Plenum.

Gazzaniga, M. S., Bogen, J. E., & Sperry, R. W. (1965). Observations on visual perception after disconnection of the cerebral hemispheres in man. *Brain, 88,* 221–236.

Gazzaniga, M. S., Eliassen, J. C., Nisenson, L., Wessinger, C. Mark, Fendrich, R., & Baynes, K. (1996). Collaboration between the hemispheres of a callosotomy patient: Emerging right hemisphere speech and the left hemisphere interpreter. *Brain, 119,* 1255–1263.

Gebotys, R. J., & Claxton, O. S. P. (1989). Errors in the quantification of uncertainty: A product of heuristics or minimal probability knowledge base? *Applied Cognitive Psychology, 3,* 157–170.

Geiselman, R. E., Fisher, R. P., MacKinnon, D. P., & Holland, H. L. (1985). Eyewitness memory enhancement in the police interview: Cognitive retrieval mnemonics versus hypnosis. *Journal of Applied Psychology, 70,* 401–412.

George, M. S., Lisanby, S. H., & Sackeim, H. A. (1999). Transcranial magnetic stimulation: Applications in neuropsychiatry. *Archives of General Psychiatry, 56,* 300–311.

Gerbner, G., & Gross, L. (1976). Living with television: The violence profile. *Journal of Communications, 26,* 172–199.

Gerin, W., Pieper, C., Levy, R., & Pickering, T. G. (1992). Social support in social interaction: A moderator of cardiovascular reactivity. *Psychosomatic Medicine, 54,* 324–336.

Gershon, E. S. (1990). Genetics. In F. K. Goodwin & K. R. Jamison (Eds.), *Manic-depressive illness.* New York: Oxford University Press.

Gershon, E. S., & Reider, R. O. (1992, April). Major disorders of mind and brain. *Scientific American, 267,* 126–133.

Gianoulakis, C. (2001). Influence of the endogenous opioid system on high alcohol consumption and genetic predisposition to alcoholism. *Journal of Psychiatry and Neuroscience, 26,* 304–318.

Gibbs, R. W., O'Brien, J. E., & Doolittle, S. (1995). Inferring meanings that are not intended: Speakers' intentions and irony comprehension. *Discourse Processes, 20,* 187–203.

Gibson, E. J., & Walk, R. D. (1960, April). The "visual cliff." *Scientific American, 202,* 64–71.

Gibson, J. J. (1966). *The senses considered as perceptual systems.* Boston: Houghton Mifflin.

Gick, M. L., & McGarry, S. J. (1992). Learning from mistakes: Inducing analogous solution failures to a source problem produces later successes in analogical transfer. *Journal of Experimental Psychology: Learning, Memory, and Cognition, 18,* 623–639.

Gifford, R. (1997). *Environmental psychology: Principles and practice* (2nd ed.). Needham Heights, MA: Allyn & Bacon.

Gigerenzer, G. (1996). On narrow norms and vague heuristics: A reply to Kahneman & Tversky. *Psychological Review, 103,* 592–596.

Gigerenzer, G. (1997). Ecological intelligence: An adaptation for frequencies. In D. Cummins & C. Allen (Eds.), *The evolution of mind.* New York: Oxford University Press.

Giguere, C., & Abel, S. M. (1993). Sound localization: Effects of reverberation time, speaker array, stimulus frequency, and stimulus rise/decay. *Journal of Acoustical Society of America, 94,* 769–776.

Gilbert, D. T. (1989). Thinking lightly about others: Automatic components of the social inference process. In J. S. Uleman & J. A. Bargh (Eds.), *Unintended thought.* New York: Guilford.

Gilligan, C. (1982). *In a different voice: Psychological theory and women's development.* Cambridge, MA: Harvard University Press.

Gillin, J. C. (1993). Clinical sleep-wake disorders in psychiatric practice: Dyssomnias. In D. L. Dunner (Ed.), *Current psychiatric therapy.* Philadelphia: Saunders.

Gladue, B. A. (1994). The biopsychology of sexual orientation. *Current Directions in Psychological Research, 3,* 150–154.

Glaser, B. G., & Strauss, A. L. (1968). *Time for dying.* Chicago: Aldine.

Gleaves, D. H., May, M. C., & Cardena, E. (2001). An examination of the diagnostic validity of dissociative identity disorder. *Clinical Psychology Review, 21,* 577–608.

Glucksberg, S. (1998). Understanding metaphors. *Current Directions in Psychological Science, 7* (2), 39–43.

Goldberg, J., True, W. R., Eisen, S. A., & Henderson, W. G. (1990). A twin study of the effects of the Vietnam War on posttraumatic stress disorder. *Journal of the American Medical Association, 263,* 1227–1232.

Goldberg, L. R. (1993). The structure of phenotypic personality traits. *American Psychologist, 48,* 26–34.

Goldberg, L. R., & Stycker, L. A. (2002). Personality traits and eating habits: The assessment of food preferences in a large community sample. *Personality and Individual Differences, 32,* 49–65.

Goldberger, L., & Breznitz, S. (Eds.) (1993). *Handbook of stress: Theoretical and clinical aspects.* New York: Free Press.

Goldstein, B. (1994). *Psychology.* Pacific Grove, CA: Brooks/Cole.

Goldstein, E. B. (1999). *Sensation and perception* (5th ed.). Pacific Grove, CA: Brooks/Cole.

Goldstone, R. L. (1998). Perceptual learning. *Annual Review of Psychology, 49,* 585–612.

Goleman, D. (1995). *Emotional intelligence.* New York: Bantam.

Golub, S. (1992). *Periods: From menarche to menopause.* Newbury Park, CA: Sage.

Gonzalez-Quijano, M. I., Martin, M., Millan, S., & Lopez-Calderon, A. (1998). Lymphocyte response to mitogens: Influence of life events and personality. *Neuropsychobiology, 38,* 90–96.

Goodale, M. A., & Humphrey, G. K. (1998). The objects of action and perception. *Cognition, 67,* 181–207.

Goodale, M. A., & Humphrey, G. K. (2000). Separate visual systems for action and perception. In E. B. Goldstein (Ed.), *Blackwell handbook of perception* (pp. 311–343). Malden, MA: Blackwell.

Goodall, J. (1990). *Through a window: My thirty years with the chimpanzees of Gombe.* Boston: Houghton Mifflin.

Goodenough, D. R. (1991). Dream recall: History and current status of the field. In S. J. Ellman & J. S. Antrobus (Eds.), *The mind in sleep* (2nd ed.). New York: Wiley.

Goodwin, K. F., & Jamison, K. R. (1990). *Manic depressive illness.* New York: Oxford University Press.

Gopnick, A., Meltzoff, A. N., & Kuhl, P. K. (1999). *The scientist in the crib: Minds, brains, and how children learn.* New York: William Morrow.

Gore-Felton, C., Koopman, C., Thoresen, C., Arnow, B., Bridges, E., & Spiegel, D. (2000). Psychologists' beliefs and clinical characteristics: Judging the veracity of childhood sexual abuse memories. *Professional Psychology: Research and Practice, 31* (4), 372–377.

Gorwood, P., Bouvard, M., Mouren-Simeoni, M. C., Kipman, A., & Ades, J. (1998). Genetics and anorexia nervosa: A review of candidate genes. *Psychiatric Genetics, 8,* 1–12.

Gosling, S. D., Ko, S. J., Mannareli, T., & Morris, M. E. (2002). Room with a cue: Personality judgments based on offices and bedrooms. *Journal of Personality and Social Psychology, 82,* 379–398.

Gottesman, I. I. (1991). *Schizophrenia genesis: The origins of madness.* New York: Freeman.

Gould, M. S. (1990). Suicide clusters and media exposure. In S. J. Blumenthal & D. J. Kupfer (Eds.), *Suicide over the life cycle: Risk factors, assessments and treatment of suicidal patients.* Washington, DC: American Psychiatric Press.

Gould, M. S., & Kramer, R. A. (2001). Youth suicide prevention. *Suicide and Life-Threatening Behavior, 31* (Supplement), 6–31.

Gould, R. L. (1978). *Transformations: Growth and change in adult life.* New York: Simon & Schuster.

Gould, S. J. (2000). More things in heaven and earth. In H. Rose & S. Rose (Eds.), *Alas, poor*

Darwin: Arguments against evolutionary psychology. New York: Harmony Books.

Gowing, L. R., Henry-Edwards, S. M., Irvine, R. J., & Ali, R. L. (2002). The health effects of ecstasy: A literature review. *Drug & Alcohol Review, 21,* 53–63.

Graber, J. A., Brooks-Gunn, J., & Warren, M. P. (1995). The antecedents of menarcheal age: Heredity, family environment, and stressful life events. *Child Development, 66,* 346–359.

Graf, P., & Schacter, D. L. (1985). Implicit and explicit memory for new associations in normal and amnesic subjects. *Journal of Experimental Psychology: Learning, Memory, and Cognition, 11,* 501–518.

Graf, P., & Uttl, B. (1995). Component processes of memory: Changes across the adult lifespan. *Swiss Journal of Cognitive Psychology, 6,* 113–129.

Graf, P., Mandler, G., & Haden, P. E. (1982). Simulating amnesic symptoms in normal subjects. *Science, 218,* 1243–1244.

Graf, P., & Uttl, B. (2001). Prospective memory: A new focus for research. *Consciousness and Cognition, 10,* 437–450.

Graffen, N. F., Ray, W. J., & Lundy, R. (1995). EEG concomitants of hypnosis and hypnotic susceptibility. *Journal of Abnormal Psychology, 104,* 123–131.

Grafman, J., & Wassermann, E. (1999). Transcranial magnetic stimulation can measure and modulate learning and memory. *Neuropsychologia, 37,* 159–167.

Graig, E. (1993). Stress as a consequence of the urban physical environment. In L. Goldberger & S. Breznitz (Eds.), *Handbook of stress: Theoretical and clinical aspects* (2nd ed.). New York: Free Press.

Granrud, C. E. (Ed.) (1993). *Visual perception and cognition in infancy.* Hillsdale, NJ: Erlbaum.

Grant, M. J., Button, C. M., & Noseworthy, J. (1994). Predicting attitude stability. *Canadian Journal of Behavioural Sciences, 26,* 68–84.

Granvold, D. K. (Ed.) (1994). *Cognitive and behavioral treatment: Methods and applications.* Pacific Grove, CA: Brooks/Cole.

Graves, R. E., & Jones, B. S. (1992). Conscious visual perceptual awareness vs. non-conscious visual spatial localisation examined with normal subjects using possible analogues of blindsight and neglect. *Cognitive Neuropsychology, 9,* 487–508.

Graziano, W. G., & Bryant, W. H. M. (1998). Self-monitoring and the self-attribution of positive emotions. *Journal of Personality and Social Psychology, 74,* 250–261.

Greenberg, L. S., & Paivio, S. C. (1997). *Working with emotions in psychotherapy.* New York: Guilford.

Greenblatt, D. J., & Shader, R. I. (1978). Pharmacotherapy of anxiety with benzodiazepines and beta-adrenergic blockers. In M. Lipton, A. DiMascio, & F. Killiam (Eds.), *Psychopharmacology: A generation of progress.* New York: Raven.

Greene, R. L. (1992). *Human memory: Paradigms and paradoxes.* Hillsdale, NJ: Erlbaum.

Greenspoon, P. J., & Saklofske, D. H. (1998). Confirmatory factor analysis of the multidimensional Students' Life Satisfaction Scale. *Personality and Individual Differences, 25,* 965–971.

Greenwald, A. G. (1980). The totalitarian ego: Fabrication and revision of personal history. *American Psychologist, 35,* 603–618.

Greenwald, A. G., Schuh, E. S., & Klinger, M. R. (1995). Activation of marginally perceptible ("subliminal") stimuli: Dissociation of unconscious from conscious cognition. *Journal of Experimental Psychology: General, 124,* 22–42.

Greenwald, A. G., Spangenberg, E. R., Pratkanis, A. R., & Eskenazi, J. (1991). Double-blind tests of subliminal self-help audiotapes. *Psychological Science, 2,* 119–122.

Grencavage, L. M., & Norcross, J. C. (1990). Where are the common factors? *Professional Psychology: Research and Practice, 21,* 372–378.

Grice, H. P. (1975). Logic and conversation. In P. Cole & J. L. Morgan (Eds.), *Syntax and semantics: Speech acts.* New York: Seminar Press.

Grill, H. J., & Kaplan, J. M. (1990). Caudal brainstem participates in the distributed neural control of feeding. In E. M. Stricker (Ed.), *Handbook of behavioral neurobiology.* New York: Plenum.

Gronbaek, M. (2002). Alcohol and all-cause and coronary heart disease mortality. *Annals of the New York Academy of Science, 957,* 16–20.

Grove, P. M., Gillam, B., & Ono, H. (2002). Content and context of monocular regions determine perceived depth in random dot, unpaired background and phantom stereograms. *Vision Research, 42,* 1859–1870.

Groves, P. M., & Thompson, R. F. (1970). Habituation: A dual-process theory. *Psychological Review, 77,* 419–450.

Gruneberg, M. M., Sykes, R. N., & Gillett, E. (1994). The facilitating effects of mnemonic strategies on two learning tasks in learning

disabled adults. *Neuropsychological Rehabilitation, 4,* 241–254.

Grusec, J. E., & Kuczynski, L. (Eds.) (1997). *Parenting and children's internalization of values: A handbook of contemporary theory.* New York: John Wiley & Sons.

Gulick, W. L., Gescheider, G. A., & Frisina, R. D. (1989). *Hearing: Physiological acoustics, neural coding, and psychoacoustics.* New York: Oxford University Press.

Gunderson, J. G. (1992). Diagnostic controversies. In A. Tasman & M. B. Riba (Eds.), *Review of psychiatry.* Washington, DC: American Psychiatric Press.

Gurman, E. B. (1994). Debriefing for all concerned: Ethical treatment of human subjects. *Psychological Science, 5,* 139.

Haan, N. (Ed.) (1977). *Coping and defending: Processes of self-environment organization.* New York: Academic Press.

Haber, R. N. (1985). An icon can have no worth in the real world: Comments on Loftus, Johnson, and Shimamura's "How much is an icon worth?" *Journal of Experimental Psychology: Human Perception and Performance, 11,* 374–378.

Hadjistavropoulos, T., McMurtry, B., & Craig, K. D. (1999). Beautiful faces in pain: Biases and accuracy in the perception of pain. *Psychology and Health, 11,* 411–420.

Haerich, P. (1997). Long-term habituation and sensitization of the human acoustic startle response. *Journal of Psychophysiology, 11,* 103–114.

Haines, M. M., Stansfeld, S. A., Job, R. F. S., Berglund, B., & Head, J. (2001). Chronic aircraft noise exposure, stress responses, mental health and cognitive performance in school children. *Psychological Medicine, 31,* 265–277.

Hall, J. A. Y., & Kimura, D. (1994). Dermatoglyphic asymmetry and sexual orientation in men. *Behavioral Neuroscience, 108,* 1203–1206.

Halpern, B. P. (2002). Taste. In H. Pashler & S. Yantis (Eds.), *Steven's handbook of experimental psychology* (3rd ed.): *Vol. 1. Sensation and perception* (pp. 653–690). New York: John Wiley & Sons.

Halpern, D. F. (2000). *Sex differences in cognitive abilities* (3rd ed.). Mahwah, NJ: Erlbaum.

Halpern, D. F. (1989). The disappearance of cognitive gender differences: What you see depends on where you look. *American Psychologist, 44,* 1156–1158.

Hamer, D. H., Hu, S., Magnuson, V. L., Hu, N., & Pattatucci, A. M. L. (1993). A linkage between DNA markers on the X chromosome and male sexual orientation. *Science, 261*, 321–327.

Hansen, C. J., Stevens, L. C., & Coast, J. R. (2001). Exercise duration and mood state: How much is enough to feel better? *Health Psychology, 20*, 267–275.

Hanson, V. L. (1990). Recall of order information by deaf signers: Phonetic coding in temporal order recall. *Memory and Cognition, 18*, 604–610.

Harbluk, J. L., Noy, Y. I, Eizenman, M. (2002). *The impact of cognitive distraction on driver visual behaviour and vehicle control.* Transport Canada. Available: www.tc.gc.ca/roadsafety/tp/tp13889/pdf/tp13889es.pdf

Hare, R. D. (1991). *The Hare Psychopathy Checklist–Revised.* Toronto: Multi-Health Systems.

Hare, R. D. (1993). *Without conscience: The disturbing world of the psychopaths among us.* New York: Pocket Books.

Hare, R. D. (1996). Psychopathy. *Criminal Justice & Behavior, 23*, 25–54.

Hare, R. D. (2003). *Manual for the Psychopathy Check List –Revised (2nd version).* Toronto/Buffalo: Multi-Health Systems.

Harlow, H. F., & Zimmerman, R. R. (1959). Affectional responses in the infant monkey. *Science, 130*, 421–432.

Harlow, H. F., Harlow, M. K., & Meyer, D. R. (1971). From thought to therapy: Lessons from a primate laboratory. *American Scientist, 59*, 538–549.

Harmon, T. M., Hynan, M. T., & Tyre, T. E. (1990). Improved obstetric outcomes using hypnotic analgesia and skill mastery combined with childbirth education. *Journal of Consulting and Clinical Psychology, 58*, 525–530.

Harper, G. (2001). Cultural influences on diagnosis. *Child & Adolescent Psychiatric Clinics of North America, 10*, 711–728.

Harris, G. T., Rice, M. E., & Cormier, C. A. (1994). Psychopaths: Is a therapeutic community therapeutic? *Therapeutic Communities: International Journal for Therapeutic and Supportive Organizations, 15*, 283–299.

Harris, G. T., Rice, M. E., & Quinsey, V. L. (1993). Violent recidivism of mentally disordered offenders: The development of a statistical prediction instrument. *Criminal Justice and Behavior, 20*, 315–335.

Harris, G. T., Rice, M. E., & Quinsey, V. L. (1994). Psychopathy as a taxon: Evidence that psychopaths are a discrete class. *Journal of Consulting and Clinical Psychology, 62* (2), 387–397.

Harris, J. R. (1995). Where is the child's environment? A group socialization theory of development. *Psychological Review, 102*, 458–489.

Harris, J. R. (1998). *The nurture assumption.* New York: Free Press.

Hartshorne, H., & May, A. (1928). *Studies in the nature of character: Studies in deceit.* New York: Macmillan.

Hartup, W. W., & Stevens, N. (1997). Friendships and adaptation in the life course. *Psychological Bulletin, 121*, 355–370.

Harvey, P. D. (2001). Vulnerability to schizophrenia in adulthood. In R. E. Ingram & J. M. Price (Eds.), *Vulnerability to psychopathology: Risk across the lifespan.* New York: Guilford.

Harvey, S. (1987). Female sexual behavior: Fluctuations during the menstrual cycle. *Journal of Psychosomatic Research, 31*, 101–110.

Haselton, M. G., & Buss, D. M. (2000). Error management theory: A new perspective on biases in cross-sex mind reading. *Journal of Personality and Social Psychology 78*, 81–91.

Hasher, L., & Zacks, R. R. (1979). Automatic and effortful processes in memory. *Journal of Experimental Psychology: General, 108*, 356–388.

Hasher, L., Stolzfus, E. R., Zacks, R. T., & Rypma, B. (1991). Age and inhibition. *Journal of Experimental Psychology: Learning, Memory, and Cognition, 17*, 163–169.

Hasselmo, M. E., Rolls, E. T., & Baylis, G. C. (1989). The role of expression and identity in the face-selective responses of neurons in the temporal visual cortex of the monkey. *Behavioral Brain Research, 32*, 203–218.

Hasselmo, M. E., Wyble, B. P., & Wallenstein, G. V. (1996). Encoding and retrieval of episodic memories: Role of cholinergic and GABAergic modulation in the hippocampus. *Hippocampus, 6*, 693–708.

Hatala, R., Norman, G. R., & Brooks, L. R. (1999). Influence of a single example on subsequent electrocardiogram interpretation. *Teaching and Learning in Medicine, 11* (2), 110–117.

Hatfield, E. (1988). Passionate and companionate love. In R. J. Sternberg & M. L. Barnes (Eds.), *The psychology of love.* New Haven, CT: Yale University Press.

Hatfield, E., & Rapson, R. L. (1993). *Love, sex, and intimacy.* New York: HarperCollins.

Hauri, P. (1982). *The sleep disorders.* Kalamazoo, MI: Upjohn.

Hayes, C. (1952). *The ape in our house.* London: Gollacz.

Hays, K. F. (1999). *Working it out: Using exercise in psychotherapy.* Washington, DC: American Psychological Association.

Hayes, K. J., & Hayes, C. (1951). The intellectual development of a home-raised chimpanzee. *Proceedings of the American Philosophical Society, 95*, 105–109.

Hayes, S. C., & Heiby, E. (1996). Psychology's drug problem: Do we need a fix or should we just say no? *American Psychologist, 51*, 198–206.

Health Canada (1999). *Toward a healthy future: Second report on the health of Canadians.* Ottawa: Health Canada Publications.

Hearold, S. (1986). A synthesis of 1043 effects of television on social behavior. In G. Comstock (Ed.), *Public communication and behavior.* New York: Academic Press.

Hearst, E., & Franklin, S. R. (1977). Positive and negative relations between a signal and food: Approach-withdrawal behavior to the signal. *Journal of Experimental Psychology: Animal Behavior Processes, 3*, 37–52.

Hebb, D. O. (1949). *The organization of behaviour.* New York: Wiley-Interscience.

Hebb, D. O. (1949/2002). *The organization of behavior: A neuropsychological theory.* Mahwah, NJ: Lawrence Erlbaum.

Hector, R. I. (1998). The use of clozapine in the treatment of aggressive schizophrenia. *Canadian Journal of Psychiatry, 43*, 466–472.

Hegadoren, K. M., Baker, G. B., & Bourin, M. (1999). 3,4-methylenedioxy analogues of amphetamine: Defining the risks to humans. *Neuroscience and Biobehavioral Reviews, 23* (4), 539–553.

Heider, E. (1972). Universals of color naming and memory. *Journal of Experimental Psychology, 93*, 10–20.

Heider, F. (1944). Social perception and phenomenal causality. *Psychological Review, 51*, 358–374.

Heiman, G. A. (1995). *Research methods in psychology.* Boston: Houghton Mifflin.

Heine, S. J., & Lehman, D. R. (1999). Culture, self-discrepancies, and self-satisfaction. *Personality and Social Psychology Bulletin 25*, 915–925.

Hellerstein, D. J., & Little, S. (2000). Current perspectives on the diagnosis and treatment of double depression. In K. J. Palmer (Ed.), *Managing depressive disorders.* Kwai Chung, Hong Kong: Adis International Publications.

Hellige, J. B. (1990). Hemispheric asymmetry. *Annual Review of Psychology, 41*, 55–80.

Helmes, E., & Reddon, J. R. (1993). A perspective on developments in assessing psychopathology: A critical review of the MMPI and MMPI-2. *Psychological Bulletin, 113,* 453–471.

Henderson-King, E. I., & Nisbett, R. E. (1996). Anti-black prejudice as a function of exposure to the negative behavior of a single Black person. *Journal of Personality and Social Psychology, 71,* 654–664.

Henley, N. M. (1989). Molehill or mountain? What we know and don't know about sex bias in language. In M. Crawford & M. Gentry (Eds.), *Gender and thought: Psychological perspectives.* New York: Springer-Verlag.

Herman, C. P., & Polivy, J. (1988). Studies of eating in normal dieters. In B. T. Walsh (Ed.), *Eating behavior in eating disorders.* Washington, DC: American Psychiatric Press.

Herrmann, D., Raybeck, D., & Gutman, D. (1993). *Improving student memory.* Seattle, WA: Hogrefe & Huber.

Herrmann, D., Yoder, C., & Gruneberg, M. (2000). *Memory and its practical uses.* New York: Allyn & Bacon.

Herz, R. S., & Cahill, E. D. (1997). Differential use of sensory information in sexual behavior as a function of gender. *Human Nature, 8,* 275–286.

Hertzsprung, E. A. M., & Dobson, K.S. (2000). Diversity training: Conceptual issues and practices for Canadian Clinical Psychology Program. *Canadian Psychology, 41,* 184–191.

Hetherington, A. W., & Ranson, S. W. (1942). The relation of various hypothalamic lesions to adiposity in the rat. *Journal of Comparative Neurology, 76,* 475–499.

Hewstone, M., & Brown, R. (1986). *Contact and conflict in intergroup encounters.* Oxford: Basil Blackwell.

Heyes, C. M., & Galef, B. G. (Eds.) (1996). *Social learning in animals: The roots of culture.* London: Academic Press.

Hilgard, E. R. (1965). *Hypnotic susceptibility.* New York: Harcourt, Brace, & World.

Hilgard, E. R. (1986). *Divided consciousness: Multiple controls in human thought and action* (Rev. ed.). New York: Wiley.

Hilgard, E. R. (1987). *Psychology in America: An historical survey.* New York: Harcourt Brace Jovanovich.

Hilgard, E. R. (1992). Dissociation and theories of hypnosis. In E. Fromm & M. Nash (Eds.), *Contemporary hypnosis research.* New York: Guilford.

Hill, J. O., & Peters, J. C. (1998). Environmental contributions to the obesity epidemic. *Science, 280,* 1371–1374.

Hilton, J. L., & von Hippel, W. (1996). Stereotypes. *Annual Review of Psychology, 47,* 237–271.

Hines, M. (1982). Prenatal gonadal hormones and sex differences in human behavior. *Psychological Bulletin, 92,* 56–80.

Hintzman, D. L. (1986). "Schema abstraction" in a multiple-trace memory model. *Psychological Review, 93,* 411–428.

Hirsh, I. J., & Watson, C. S. (1996). Auditory psychophysics and perception. *Annual Review of Psychology, 47,* 461–484.

Hirst, W. (1995). Cognitive aspects of consciousness. In M. S. Gazzaniga (Ed.), *The cognitive neurosciences* (pp. 1307–1319). Cambridge, MA: MIT Press.

Hitch, G. J., & Halliday, M. S. (1983). Working memory in children. *Philosophical Transactions of the Royal Society London B, 302,* 325–340.

Hobfoll, S. E., Shoham, S. B., & Ritter, C. (1991). Women's satisfaction with social support and their receipt of aid. *Journal of Personality and Social Psychology, 61,* 332–341.

Hobson, C. J., & Delunas, L. (2001). National norms and life-event frequencies for the revised Social Readjustment Rating Scale. *International Journal of Stress Management, 8,* 299–314.

Hobson, J. A., & McCarley, R. W. (1977). The brain as a dream state generator: An activation-synthesis hypothesis of the dream process. *American Journal of Psychiatry, 134,* 1335–1348.

Hobson, J. A., Pace-Schott, E. F., & Stickgold, R. (2000). Dreaming and the brain: Toward a cognitive neuroscience of conscious states. *Behavioral and Brain Sciences, 23* (6), 793–842; 904–1018; 1083–1121.

Hodges, J., & Tizard, B. (1989). IQ and behavioral adjustment of ex-institutional adolescents. *Journal of Child Psychology and Psychiatry, 30,* 53–75.

Holden, G. W., Geffner, R., and Jouriles, E. N. (1998). *Children exposed to marital violence.* Washington, DC: American Psychology Association.

Hoff, T. (1992) Psychology in Canada one hundred years ago: James Mark Baldwin at the University of Toronto. *Canadian Psychology, 33,* 683–694.

Hoffman, M. L. (1986). Affect, cognition, motivation. In R. M. Sorrentino & E. T. Higgins (Eds.), *Handbook of motivation and cognition: Foundations of social behavior.* New York: Guilford.

Hoffmann, P. (1997). The endorphin hypothesis. In W. P. Morgan (Ed.), *Physical activity and mental health.* Washington, DC: Taylor & Francis.

Hofmann, S. G., Lehman, C. L., & Barlow, D. H. (1997). How specific are specific phobias? *Journal of Behavior Therapy and Experimental Psychiatry, 28,* 233–240.

Hofstadter, M. C., & Reznick, J. S. (1996). Response modality affects human infant delayed-response performance. *Child Development, 67,* 646–658.

Hogan, J. A. (1997). Energy models of motivation: A reconsideration. *Applied Animal Behaviour Science, 53,* 89–105.

Hogan, R., Hogan, J., & Roberts, B. W. (1996). Personality measurement and employment decisions: Questions and answers. *American Psychologist, 51,* 469–477.

Hohmann, G. W. (1966). Some effects of spinal cord lesions on experienced emotional feelings. *Psychophysiology, 3,* 143–156.

Holden, R.R., Kerr, P.S., Mendonca, J.D., & Velamoor, V.R. (1998). Are some motives more linked to suicide proneness than others? *Journal of Clinical Psychology 54,* 569–576.

Holland, P. C. (1977). Conditioned stimulus as a determinant of the form of the Pavlovian conditioned response. *Journal of Experimental Psychology: Animal Behavior Processes, 3,* 77–104.

Holland, P. C., & Rescorla, R. A. (1975). The effects of two ways of devaluing the unconditioned stimulus after first- and second-order appetitive conditioning. *Journal of Experimental Psychology: Animal Behavior Processes, 1,* 355–363.

Holmes, D. S. (1976). Debriefing after psychological experiments: I. Effectiveness of postdeception dehoaxing. *American Psychologist, 31,* 858–867.

Holmes, D. S. (1987). The influence of meditation versus rest on physiological arousal: A second examination. In M. A. West (Ed.), *The psychology of meditation.* Oxford: Clarendon Press.

Holmes, T. H., & Rahe, R. H. (1967). The Social Readjustment Rating Scale. *Journal of Psychosomatic Research, 11,* 213–218.

Holt, E. B. (1931). *Animal drive and the learning process: An essay toward radical empiricism.* New York: Holt.

Homa, D. (1984). On the nature of categories. In G. H. Bower (Ed.), *The psychology of learning and motivation.* Orlando, FL: Academic Press.

Honzik, M. P., Macfarlane, J. W., & Allen, L. (1948). The stability of mental test performance between two and eighteen years. *Journal of Experimental Education, 17,* 309–324.

Horgan, J. (1993, June). Eugenics revisited. *Scientific American, 268,* 123–131.

Horn, J. L. (1976). Human abilities: A review of research and theory in the early 1970s. *Annual Review of Psychology, 27,* 437–485.

Horn, J. L. (1982). The aging of human abilities. In J. Wolman (Ed.), *Handbook of developmental psychology.* Englewood Cliffs, NJ: Prentice-Hall.

Horn, J. L., & Cattell, R. B. (1966). Refinement and test of the theory of fluid and crystallized ability intelligences. *Journal of Educational Psychology, 57,* 253–270.

Horn, J. L., & Noll, J. (1997). Human cognitive capabilities: Gf-Gc theory. In D. P. Flanagan & J. L. Genshaft (Eds.), *Contemporary intellectual assessment: Theories, tests, and issues.* New York: Guilford.

Horne, J. (2001). State of the art: Sleep. *Psychologist, 14,* 302–306.

Horne, J. A. (1988). *Why we sleep: The functions of sleep in humans and other mammals.* Oxford: Oxford University Press.

Horne, J. A., & Minard, A. (1985). Sleep and sleepiness following a behaviourally "active" day. *Ergonomics, 28,* 567–575.

Horney, K. (1945). *Our inner conflicts: A constructive theory of neurosis.* New York: Norton.

Horney, K. (1967). *Feminine psychology.* New York: Norton.

Horton, K. D., Smith, S. A., Barghout, N. K., & Connolly, D. A. (1992). The use of indirect memory tests to assess malingered amnesia: A study of metamemory. *Journal of Experimental Psychology: General, 121,* 326–351.

Horvath, A. O., & Luborsky, L. (1993). The role of the therapeutic alliance in psychotherapy. *Journal of Consulting and Clinical Psychology, 61,* 561–573.

Horvath, P. (1988). Placebos and common factors in two decades of psychotherapy research. *Psychological Bulletin, 104,* 214–225.

Houle, M., McGrath, P. A., Moran, G., & Garrett, O. J. (1988). The efficacy of hypnosis- and relaxation-induced analgesia on two dimensions of pain for cold pressor and electrical tooth pulp stimulation. *Pain, 33,* 241–251.

Howe, M. L., & Courage, M. L. (1993). Resolving the enigma of infantile amnesia. *Psychological Bulletin, 113,* 305–326.

Hoyle, R. H., Kernis, M. H., Leary, M. R., & Baldwin, M. W. (Eds.) (1999). *Selfhood: Identity, esteem, regulation.* New York: Westview.

Hser, Y., Anglin, M. D., & Powers, K. (1993). A 24-year follow-up of California narcotics addicts. *Archives of General Psychiatry, 50,* 577–584.

Hubbel, J. C. (1990, January). Animal rights war on medicine. *Reader's Digest,* 70–76.

Hubel, D. H., & Wiesel, T. N. (1962). Receptive fields, binocular interaction, and functional architecture in the cat's visual cortex. *Journal of Physiology, 160,* 106–154.

Hubel, D. H., & Wiesel, T. N. (1979, September). Brain mechanisms and vision. *Scientific American, 241,* 150–162.

Hull, C. L. (1943). *Principles of behavior.* New York: Appleton-Century.

Hull, J. G., & Bond, C. F., Jr. (1986). Social and behavioral consequences of alcohol consumption and expectancy: A meta-analysis. *Psychological Bulletin, 99,* 347–360.

Hultsch, D. F., Hertzog, C., Dixon, R. A., & Small, B. J. (1998). *Memory change in the aged.* New York: Cambridge University Press.

Hultsch, D. F., Hertzog, C., Small, B. J., & Dixon, R. A. (1999). Use it or lose it: Engaged lifestyle as a buffer of cognitive decline in aging? *Psychology and Aging, 14,* 245–263.

Humphrey, G. K., James, T. W., Gati, J. S., Menon, R. S., & Goodale, M. A. (1999). Perception of the McCollough effect correlates with activity in extrastriate cortex: A functional magnetic resonance imaging study. *Psychological Science, 10,* 444–448.

Hunnicutt, C. P., & Newman, I. A. (1993). Adolescent dieting practices and nutrition knowledge. *Health Values, 17,* 35–40.

Hunsley, J., Lee, C., & Aubry, T. (1999). Who uses psychological services in Canada? *Canadian Psychology, 40:3.*

Hunt, E. (1985). The correlates of intelligence. In D. K. Detterman (Ed.), *Current topics in human intelligence.* Norwood, NJ: Ablex.

Hunt, M. (1993). *The story of psychology.* New York: Anchor Books.

Hunt, R. R., & Einstein, G. O. (1981). Relational and item-specific information in memory. *Journal of Verbal Learning and Verbal Behavior, 20,* 497–514.

Hunt, R. R., & McDaniel, M. A. (1993). The enigma of organization and distinctiveness. *Journal of Memory and Language, 32,* 421–445.

Hurt, S. W., Reznikoff, M., & Clarkin, J. F. (1995). The Rorschach. In L. E. Beutler & M. R. Berren (Eds.), *Integrative assessment of adult personality.* New York: Guilford.

Hyde, J. S., & Lin, M. C. (1988). Gender differences in verbal ability: A developmental meta-analysis. *Psychological Bulletin, 104,* 53–69.

Hynie, M., Lydon, J. E., Cote, S., & Weiner, S. (1998). Relational sexual scripts and women's condom use: The importance of internalized norms. *Journal of Sex Research, 35,* 370–380.

Iezzi, T., Duckworth, M. P., & Adams, H. E. (2001). Somatoform and factitious disorders. In P. B. Sutker & H. E. Adams (Eds.), *Comprehensive handbook of psychopathology* (3rd ed.). New York: Kluwer Academic/Plenum.

Ingram, J. (1994). *The burning house.* Toronto: Penguin.

Inoue-Nakamura, N., & Matsuzawa, T. (1997). Development of stone tool use by wild chimpanzees (Pan troglodytes). *Journal of Comparative Psychology, 111,* 159–713.

Ishai, A., & Sagi, D. (1997). Visual imagery: Effects of short- and long-term memory. *Journal of Cognitive Neuroscience, 9,* 734–742.

Iverson, G. L., King, R. J., Scott, J. G., & Adams, R. L. (2001). Cognitive complaints in litigating patients with head injuries or chronic pain. *Journal of Forensic Neuropsychology, 2,* 19–30.

Izard, C. E. (1994). Innate and universal facial expressions: Evidence from developmental and cross-cultural research. *Psychological Bulletin, 115,* 288–299.

Jackson, D. N., Paunonen, S. V., Fraboni, M., & Goffin, R. D. (1996). A Five-Factor versus Six-Factor model of personality structure. *Personality and Individual Differences, 20,* 33–45.

Jacobson, E. (1938). *Progressive relaxation.* Chicago: University of Chicago Press.

Jacoby, L. L., & Brooks, L. R. (1984). Nonanalytic cognition: Memory, perception, and concept learning. In G. H. Bower (Ed.), *The psychology of learning and motivation: Advances in research and theory* (pp. 1–47). New York: Academic Press.

Jacoby, L. L., & Dallas, M. (1981). On the relationship between autobiographical memory and perceptual learning. *Journal of Experimental Psychology: General, 110,* 306–340.

Jacoby, L. L., & Witherspoon, D. (1982). Remembering without awareness. *Canadian Journal of Psychology, 36,* 300–324.

Jacoby, L. L., Woloshyn, V., & Kelley, C. M. (1989). Becoming famous without being recognized: Unconscious influences of memory produced by dividing attention. *Journal of Experimental Psychology: General, 118,* 115–125.

James, W. (1884). Some omissions of introspective psychology. *Mind, 9,* 1–26.

James, W. (1890). *The principles of psychology.* New York: Holt. (Reprinted Cambridge, MA: Harvard University Press, 1983).

James, W. (1894). The physical basis of emotion. *Psychological Review, 1,* 516–529.

Jamison, K. R. (1986). Suicide and bipolar disorders. *Annals of the New York Academy of Science, 487,* 301–315.

Jamison, K. R. (1989). Mood disorders and patterns of creativity in British writers and artists. *Psychiatry, 52,* 125–134.

Jang, K. L., Livesley, W. J., & Vernon, P. A. (1996a). Heritability of the Big Five Personality Dimensions and their facets: A twin study. *Journal of Personality, 64,* 577–591.

Jang, K. L., Livesley, W. J., & Vernon, P. A. (1996b). The genetic basis of personality at different ages: A cross-sectional twin study. *Personality and Individual Differences, 21,* 299–301.

Jang, K. L., McCrae, R. R., Angleitner, A., Riemann, R., & Livesley, W. J. (1998). Heritability of facet-level traits in a cross-cultural twin sample: Support for a hierarchical model of personality. *Journal of Personality and Social Psychology, 74,* 1556–1565.

Jang, K. L., Vernon, P. A., Livesley, W. J., Stein, M. B., & Wolf, H. (2001). Intra- and extra-familial influences on alcohol and drug misuse: A twin study of gene-environment correlation. *Addiction, 96* (9), 1307–1318.

Janicki, M. G., & Krebs, D. L. (1998). Evolutionary approaches to culture. In C. Crawford & D. L. Krebs (Eds.), *Handbook of evolutionary psychology: Ideas, issues and applications.* Mahwah, NJ: Erlbaum.

Janis, I. L. (1982). *Victims of groupthink* (2nd ed.). Boston: Houghton Mifflin.

Janis, I. L. (1989). *Crucial decisions: Leadership in policymaking and crisis management.* New York: Free Press.

Jarrad, L. E. (1993). On the role of the hippocampus in learning and memory in the rat. *Behavioral and Neural Biology, 60,* 9–26.

Jasper, J. H., & Tessier, J. (1969). Acetylcholine liberation from cerebral cortex during paradoxical (REM) sleep. *Science, 172,* 601–602.

Jausovec, N. (1997). Differences in EEG activity during the solution of closed and open problems. *Creativity Research Journal, 10,* 317–324.

Jaynes, J. (1976). *The origin of consciousness in the breakdown of the bicameral mind.* Boston: Houghton Mifflin.

Jemmott, J. B. III, Jemmott, L. S., & Fong, G. T. (1998). Abstinence and safer sex HIV risk-reduction interventions for African American adolescents. *Journal of the American Medical Association, 279,* 1529–1536.

Jemmott, J. B. III., Jemmott, L. S., Fong, G. T., & McCaffree, K. (1999). Reducing HIV risk-associated sexual behavior among African American adolescents: Testing the generality of intervention effects. *American Journal of Community Psychology, 27,* 161–187.

Jenike, M. A., Baer, L., & Minichiello, W. E. (Eds.) (1986). *Obsessive-compulsive disorders: Theory and management.* Littleton, MA: PSG Publishing.

Jenkins, H. M., Barrera, F. J., Ireland, C., & Woodside, B. (1978). Signal-centered action patterns of dogs in appetitive classical conditioning. *Learning and Motivation, 9,* 272–296.

Jenkins, J. G., & Dallenbach, K. M. (1924). Obliviscence during sleep and waking. *American Journal of Psychology, 35,* 605–612.

Jenner, P. (1990). Parkinson's disease: Clues to the cause of cell death in the substantia nigra. *Seminars in the Neurosciences, 2,* 117–126.

Jennison, K. M. (1992). The impact of stressful life events and social support on drinking among older adults: A general population survey. *International Journal of Aging and Human Development, 35,* 99–123.

Jensen, A. R. (1992). Commentary: Vehicles of g. *Psychological Science, 3,* 275–278.

Jensen, A. R. (1993). Why is reaction time correlated with psychometric g? *Current Directions in Psychological Science, 2,* 53–56.

Jensen, A. R., & Weng, L. (1994). What is a good g? *Intelligence, 18,* 231–258.

Jensen, J. P., Bergin, A. E., & Greaves, D. W. (1990). The meaning of eclecticism: New survey and analysis of components. *Professional Psychology: Research and Practice, 21,* 124–130.

John, E. R., Prichep, L. S., Fridman, J., & Easton, P. (1988). Neurometrics: Computer-assisted differential diagnosis of brain dysfunction. *Science, 239,* 162–169.

John, O. P., & Robins, R. W. (1994). Accuracy and bias in self-perception: Individual differences in self-enhancement and the role of narcissism. *Journal of Personality and Social Psychology, 66,* 206–219.

Johnson, C. H., & Hastings, J. W. (1986). The elusive mechanism of the circadian clock. *American Scientist, 74,* 29–36.

Johnson, E. A. (1995). Self-deceptive coping: Adaptive only in ambiguous contexts. *Journal of Personality, 63,* 759–191.

Johnson, E. A., Vincent, N., & Ross, L. (1997). Self-deception versus self-esteem in buffering the negative effects of failure. *Journal of Research in Personality, 31,* 385–405.

Johnson, L. M., & Morris, E. K. (1987). Public information on research with nonhumans. *American Psychologist, 42,* 103–104.

Johnson, M. H., Dziurawiec, S., Ellis, H., & Morton, J. (1991). Newborns' preferential tracking of face-like stimuli and its subsequent decline. *Cognition, 40,* 1–19.

Johnson, M. K., & Liebert, R. M. (1977). *Statistics: tool of the behavioural sciences.* Englewood Cliffs, NJ: Prentice-Hall.

Johnson, M. K., Hashtroudi, S., & Lindsay, D. S. (1993). Source monitoring. *Psychological Bulletin, 114,* 3–28.

Johnson, M. K., Nolde, S. F., Mather, M., & Kounios, J. (1997). The similarity of brain activity associated with true and false recognition memory depends on test format. *Psychological Science, 8,* 250–257.

Johnson, R. C., McClearn, C. G., Yuen, S., Nagoshi, C. T., Ahern, F. M., & Cole, R. E. (1985). Galton's data a century later. *American Psychologist, 40,* 875–892.

Johnson, S. M. (1996). *The practice of emotionally focused marital therapy: Creating connection.* New York: Guilford.

Johnson, S. P. (1997). Young infants' perception of object unity: Implications for the development of attentional and cognitive skills. *Current Directions in Psychological Science, 6,* 5–11.

Johnston, V. S. (1999). *Why we feel: The science of human emotion.* Reading, MA: Perseus Books.

Johnston, V. S. (2000). Female facial beauty: The fertility hypothesis. *Pragmatics and Cognition, 8,* 107–122.

Johnson, C., & Freeman, W. S. (1997). Attributions for child behavior in parents of nonproblem children and children with attention deficit hyperactivity disorder. *Journal of Consulting and Clinical Psychology 65*, 636–645 .

Joiner, T. E., Jr., Steer, R. A., Abramson, L. Y., Alloy, L. B., Metalsky, G. I., & Schmidt, N. B. (2001). Hopelessness depression as a distinct dimension of depressive symptoms among clinical and non-clinical samples. *Behaviour Research and Therapy, 39*, 523–536.

Jolly, A. M., Orr, P. H., Hammond, G., & Young, T. K. (1995). Risk factors for infection in women undergoing testing for *Chlamydia trachomatis* and *Neisseria gonorrhoeae* in Manitoba, Canada. *Sexually Transmitted Diseases, 22*, 289–295.

Jones, E. E. (1964). *Ingratiation*. New York: Appleton-Century-Crofts.

Jones, E. E. (1990). *Interpersonal perception*. New York: Freeman.

Jones, E. E., & Davis, K. E. (1965). A theory of correspondent inferences: From acts to dispositions. In L. Berkowitz (Ed.), *Advances in experimental social psychology*. New York: Academic Press.

Jones, E. E., & Harris, V. A. (1967). The attribution of attitudes. *Journal of Experimental Social Psychology, 3*, 1–24.

Jones, E. R., & Childers, R. L. (1993). *Contemporary college physics* (2nd ed.). Reading, MA: Addison-Wesley.

Jones, G. V., & Martin, M. (1992). Misremembering a familiar object: Mnemonic illusions, not drawing bias. *Memory and Cognition, 20*, 211–213.

Jones, L. A. (1988). Motor illusions: What do they reveal about proprioception? *Psychological Bulletin, 103*, 72–86.

Jones, M. C. (1924). A laboratory study of fear: The case of Peter. *Pedagogical Seminary, 31*, 308–315.

Jones, R. T. (1971). Tetrahydrocannabinol and the marijuana-induced social "high" or the effects on the mind of marijuana. In A. J. Singer (Ed.), Marijuana: Chemistry, pharmacology, and patterns of social use. *Annals of the New York Academy of Sciences, 191*, 155–165.

Jonides, J. (2000). Mechanisms of verbal working memory revealed by neuroimaging studies. In B. Landau & J. Sabini (Eds.), *Perception, cognition, and language: Essays in honor of Henry and Lila Gleitman*. Cambridge, MA: The MIT Press.

Joule, R. V. (1986). Twenty-five on: Yet another version of cognitive dissonance theory?

European Journal of Social Psychology, 16, 65–78.

Jung, C. G. (1923). *Psychological types*. New York: Pantheon Books.

Jussim, L. (1989). Teacher expectations: Self-fulfilling prophecies, perceptual biases, and accuracy. *Journal of Personality and Social Psychology, 57*, 469–480.

Justice, A. (1985). Review of the effects of stress on cancer in laboratory animals: Importance of time stress application and type of tumor. *Psychological Bulletin, 98*, 108–138.

Kagan, J. (1997). Temperament and the reactions to unfamiliarity. *Child Development, 68*, 139–143.

Kagan, J. (1998). *Three seductive ideas*. Cambridge, MA: Harvard University Press.

Kagan, J., & Snidman, N. (1991). Temperamental factors in human development. *American Psychologist, 46*, 856–862.

Kahn, R. S., Davidson, M., Knott, P., Stern, R. G., Apter, S., & Davis, K. L. (1993). Effect of neuroleptic medication on cerebrospinal fluid monoamine metabolite concentrations in schizophrenia: Serotonin-dopamine interactions as a target for treatment. *Archives of General Psychiatry, 50*, 599–605.

Kahneman, D. (1973). *Attention and effort*. Englewood Cliffs, NJ: Prentice-Hall.

Kahneman, D., Slovic, P., & Tversky, A. (Eds.) (1982). *Judgment under uncertainty: Heuristics and biases*. Cambridge: Cambridge University Press.

Kail, R., & Salthouse, T. A. (1994). Processing speed as a mental capacity. *Acta Psychologica, 86*, 199–225.

Kalat, J. W. (1992). *Biological psychology* (4th ed.). Belmont, CA: Wadsworth.

Kalat, J. W. (1996). *Introduction to psychology* (4th ed.). Pacific Grove, CA: Brooks/Cole.

Kaler, S. R., & Freeman, B. J. (1994). Analysis of environmental deprivation: Cognitive and social development in Romanian orphans. *Journal of Child Psychology and Psychiatry, 35*, 769–781.

Kales, A., & Kales, J. D. (1984). *Evaluation and treatment of insomnia*. New York: Oxford.

Kalick, S. M., Zebrowitz, L. A., Langlois, J. H., & Johnson, R. M. (1998). Does human facial attractiveness honestly advertise health? Longitudinal data on an evolutionary question. *Psychological Science, 9*, 8–13.

Kalin, R. (1996). Ethnic attitudes as a function of ethnic presence. *Canadian Journal of Behavioural Science, 28*, 171–179.

Kalin, R., & Berry, J. W. (1996). Interethnic attitudes in Canada: Ethnocentrism, consensual hierarchy and reciprocity. *Canadian Journal of Behavioural Science, 28*, 253–261.

Kamen-Siegel, L., Rodin, J., Seligman, M. E. P., & Dwyer, J. (1991). Explanatory style and cell-mediated immunity in elderly men and women. *Health Psychology, 10*, 229–235.

Kamil, A. C., & Balda, R. P. (1990). Differential memory for different cache sites by Clark's nutcrackers (Nucifraga columbiana). *Journal of Experimental Psychology: Animal Behavior Processes, 16*, 162–168.

Kamin, L. J. (1968). "Attention-like" processes in classical conditioning. In M. R. Jones (Ed.), *Miami symposium on the prediction of behavior: Aversive stimulation*. Miami: University of Miami Press.

Kamin, L. J. (1974). *The science and politics of IQ*. Oxford, England: Lawrence Erlbaum.

Kandel, E. R. (1991). Cellular mechanisms of learning and the biological basis of individuality. In E. R. Kandel, J. H. Schwartz, & T. M. Jessel (Eds.), *Principles of neural science* (3rd ed.). New York: Elsevier.

Kane, J. M., Woerner, M., Weinhoold, P., Wegner, J., Kinon, B., & Bernstein, M. (1986). Incidence of tardive dyskinesia: Five-year data from a prospective study. *Psychopharmacology Bulletin, 20*, 387–389.

Kaplan, R. M. (1985). The controversy related to the use of psychological tests. In B. B. Wolman (Ed.), *Handbook of intelligence: Theories, measurements, and applications*. New York: Wiley.

Kapur, S., & Mann, J. J. (1993). Antidepressant action and the neurobiologic effects of ECT: Human studies. In C. E. Coffey (Ed.), *The clinical science of electroconvulsive therapy*. Washington, DC: American Psychiatric Press.

Karau, S. J., & Hart, J. W. (1998). Group cohesiveness and social loafing: Effects of a social interaction manipulation on individual motivation with groups. *Group Dynamics, 2*, 185–191.

Karau, S. J., & Williams, K. D. (1993). Social loafing: A meta-analytic review and theoretical integration. *Journal of Personality and Social Psychology, 65*, 681–706.

Karmiloff-Smith, A., Plunket, K., Johnson, M. H., Elman, J. L., & Bates, E. A. (1998). What does it mean to claim that something is "innate"? Response to Clark, Harris, Lightfoot and Samuels. *Mind and Language, 13* (4), 588–604.

Karni, A., Tanne, D., Rubenstein, B. S., Askenasy, J., & Sagi, D. (1994). Dependence on REM sleep of overnight improvement of a perceptual skill. *Science, 265,* 679–682.

Kauer, J. S. (1987). Coding in the olfactory system. In T. E. Finger & W. L. Silver (Eds.), *Neurobiology of taste and smell.* New York: Wiley.

Kaufman, A. S., & Horn, J. L. (1996). Age changes on tests of fluid and crystallized ability for women and men on the Kaufman Adolescent and Adult Intelligence Test (KAIT) at ages 17–94 years. *Archives of Clinical Neuropsychology, 11,* 97–121.

Kazdin, A. E. (1982). The token economy: A decade later. *Journal of Applied Behavior Analysis, 15,* 431–445.

Keesey, R. E., & Powley, T. L. (1975). Hypothalamic regulation of body weight. *American Scientist, 63,* 558–565.

Keller, M. B., & Shapiro, R. W. (1982). Double depression: Superimposition of acute depressive episodes on chronic depressive disorders. *American Journal of Psychiatry, 139,* 438–442.

Keller, W. C., & Rueda, M. G. (1998). Mechanisms of action in dopaminergic agents in Parkinson's disease. *Neurology, 50,* 511–514.

Kellerman, J. M., & Laird, J. D. (1982). The effect of appearance on self-perception. *Journal of Personality, 50,* 296–315.

Kelley, C. M. (1999). Subjective experience as basis of "objective" judgments: Effects of past experience on judgments of difficulty. In D. Gopher & A. Koriat (Eds.), *Attention and performance XVII: Cognitive regulation of performance: Interaction of theory and application* (pp. 515–536). Cambridge, MA: MIT Press.

Kelley, H. H. (1967). Attribution theory in social interaction. In E. E. Jones, D. E. Kanouse, H. H. Kelley, R. E. Nisbett, S. Valins, & B. Weiner (Eds.), *Attribution: Perceiving the causes of behavior.* Morristown, NJ: General Learning Press.

Kelley, H. H. (1983). Love and commitment. In H. H. Kelley, E. Berscheid, A. Christensen, J. H. Harvey, T. L. Huston, G. Levinger, E. McClintock, L. A. Peplau, & D. R. Peterson (Eds.), *Close relationships.* New York: Freeman.

Kelley, K. (1985). Sex, sex guilt, and authoritarianism: Differences in responses to explicit heterosexual and masturbatory slides. *Journal of Sex Research, 21,* 68–85.

Kellogg, W. N., & Kellogg, L. A. (1933). *The ape and the child.* New York: McGraw-Hill.

Kelly, D. D. (1991). Sleep and dreaming. In E. R. Kandel, J. H. Schwartz, & T. M. Jessell (Eds.), *Principles of neural science* (3rd ed.). New York: Elsevier.

Kelly, T. M., Lynch, K. G., Donovan, J. E., & Clark, D. B. (2001). Alcohol Use Disorders and Risk Factor Interactions for Adolescent Suicidal Ideation and Attempts. *Suicide and Life-Threatening Behavior, 31,* 181–193.

Kemper, T. L. (1994). Neuroanatomical and neuropathological changes during aging and dementia. In M. L. Albert & J. E. Knoefel (Eds.), *Clinical neurology of aging* (2nd ed.). New York: Oxford University Press.

Kenrick, D. T. (1994). Evolutionary social psychology: From sexual selection to social cognition. In M. Zanna (Ed.), *Advances in Experimental Social Psychology* (Vol. 26, pp. 75–122). San Diego: Academic Press.

Kenrick, D. T., & Funder, D. C. (1988). Profiting from controversy: Lessons of the person-situation debate. *American Psychologist, 43,* 23–34.

Kenrick, D. T., Gutierres, S. E., & Goldberg, L. (1989). Influence of erotica on judgments of strangers and mates. *Journal of Experimental Social Psychology, 25,* 159–167.

Kenrick, D. T., McCreath, H. E., Govern, J., King, R., & Bordin, J. (1990). Person-environment intersections: Everyday settings and common trait dimensions. *Journal of Personality and Social Psychology, 58,* 685–698.

Keppel, G., & Underwood, B. J. (1962). Proactive inhibition in short-term retention of single items. *Journal of Verbal Learning and Verbal Behavior, 1,* 153–161.

Kerkhoff, G., Munssinger, U., & Meier, E. K. (1994). Neurovisual rehabilitation in cerebral blindness. *Archives of Neurology, 51,* 474–481.

Kerns, K. A., & Price, K. J. (2001). An investigation of prospective memory in children with ADHD. *Child Neuropsychology, 7,* 162–171.

Kessler, R. C., McGonagle, K. A., Shanyang, Z., Nelson, C. B., Hughes, M., Eshleman, S., Wittchen, H., & Kendler, K. S. (1994). Lifetime and 12-month prevalence of DSM-III-R psychiatric disorders in the United States. *Archives of General Psychiatry, 51,* 8–19.

Key, W. B. (1973). *Subliminal seduction.* Englewood Cliffs, NJ: Prentice-Hall.

Keysar, B., Barr, D. J., Balin, A., & Paekm, T. S. (1998). Definite reference and mutual knowledge: Process models of common ground in comprehension. *Journal of Memory and Language, 39,* 1–20.

Kiecolt-Glaser, J. K., McGuire, L., Robles, T. F., & Glaser, R. (2002). Emotions, morbidity, and mortality: New perspectives from psychoneuroimmunology. *Annual Review of Psychology, 53,* 83–107.

Kiecolt-Glaser, J. K., Garner, W., Speicher, C., Penn, G. M., Holliday, J., & Glaser, R. (1984). Psychosocial modifiers of immunocompetence in medical students. *Psychosomatic Medicine, 46,* 7–17.

Kiernan, J. A., & Hudson, A. J. (1994). Frontal lobe atrophy in motor neuron diseases. *Brain, 117,* 747–757.

Kihlstrom, J. (1985). Hypnosis. *Annual Review of Psychology, 36,* 385–418.

Kihlstrom, J., & Cantor, N. (1984). Mental representations of the self. In L. Berkowitz (Ed.), *Advances in experimental social psychology.* New York: Academic Press.

Kihlstrom, J., & McConkey, K. M. (1990). William James and hypnosis: A centennial reflection. *Psychological Science, 1,* 174–178.

Kilgour, A. R., & Lederman, S. J. (2002). Face recognition by hand. *Perception & Psychophysics, 64* (3), 339–352.

Kimble, G. A. (1993). A modest proposal for a minor revolution in the language of psychology. *Psychological Science, 4,* 253–255.

Kimelberg, H. K., & Norenberg, M. D. (1989, April). Astrocytes. *Scientific American, 260,* 66–76.

Kimura, D. (1999). *Sex and cognition.* Cambridge, MA: Bradford/MIT Press.

Kimura, D., & Hampson, E. (1994). Cognitive pattern in men and women is influenced by fluctuations in sex hormones. *Current Directions in Psychological Science, 3,* 57–61.

King, R. N., & Koehler, D. J. (2000). Illusory correlations in graphological inference. *Journal of Experimental Psychology: Applied, 6,* 336–348.

Kirchgessner, A. L., & Sclafani, A. (1988). PVN-hindbrain pathway involved in the hypothalamic hyperphagia-obesity syndrome. *Physiology and Behavior, 42,* 517–528.

Kirmayer, L. J. (1991). The place of culture in psychiatric nosology: Taijin kyofusho and DSM-III-R. *The Journal of Nervous and Mental Disease, 179,* 19–28.

Kirsch, I. (1999). Automaticity in clinical psychology. *American Psychologist, 54,* 504–515.

Kirsch, I., & Sapirstein, G. (1999). Listening to Prozac but hearing placebo: A meta-analysis of antidepressant medication. In I. Kirsch (Ed.), *How expectancies shape experience* (pp. 303–320). Washington, DC: American Psychological Association.

Kirsch, I., Montgomery, G., & Sapirstein, G. (1995). Hypnosis as an adjunct to cognitive behavioral psychotherapy: A meta-analysis. *Journal of Consulting and Clinical Psychology, 63,* 214–220.

Klatzky, R. L. (1984). *Memory and awareness: An information-processing perspective.* New York: Freeman.

Klatzky, R. L., Lederman, S. J., & Metzger, V. A. (1985). Identifying objects by touch: An "expert system." *Perception and Psychophysics, 37,* 299–302.

Klein, R. M. (1999). Hebb legacy. *Canadian Journal of Experimental Psychology, 53,* 1–3.

Kleinfeld, J., & Nelson, P. (1991). Adapting instruction to Native Americans' learning style. *Journal of Cross-Cultural Psychology, 22,* 273–282.

Kline, P. (1991). *Intelligence: The psychometric view.* New York: Routledge, Chapman, & Hall.

Klinger, E. (1977). *Meaning and void: Inner experience and the incentive in people's lives.* Minneapolis: University of Minnesota Press.

Kluft, R. P. (1991). Multiple personality disorder. In A. Tasman & S. M. Goldfinger (Eds.), *Review of psychiatry.* Washington, DC: American Psychiatric Press.

Kobasa, S. C. (1979). Stressful life events, personality and health: An inquiry into hardiness. *Journal of Personality and Social Psychology, 42,* 168–177.

Kocsis, R. N., Irwin, H. J., Hayes, A. F., & Nunn, R. (2002). Expertise in psychological profiling: A comparative assessment. *Journal of Interpersonal Violence, 15,* 311–331.

Kohlberg, L. (1963). The development of children's orientations toward a moral order: I. Sequence in the development of moral thought. *Vita Humana, 6,* 11–33.

Kohlberg, L. (1969). Stage and sequence: The cognitive-developmental approach to socialization. In D. A. Goslin (Ed.), *Handbook of socialization theory and research.* Chicago: Rand McNally.

Kohlberg, L. (1984). *Essays on moral development: The psychology of moral development.* San Francisco: Harper & Row.

Kohlberg, L. (1986). *The psychology of moral development.* New York: Harper & Row.

Kolb, B. (1995). *Brain plasticity and behavior.* Mahwah, NJ: Erlbaum.

Kolb, B. (1999). Synaptic plasticity and the organization of behaviour after early and late brain injury. *Canadian Journal of Experimental Psychology, 53,* 62–75.

Kolb, B., & Whishaw, I. Q. (2001). *An introduction to brain and behavior.* New York: Worth.

Kolb, B., & Whishaw, I. Q. (2002). *Fundamentals of human neuropsychology* (5th ed.). New York: Freeman.

Konarski, E. A., Jr. (1985). The use of response deprivation to increase the academic performance of EMR students. *The Behavior Therapist, 8,* 61.

Kosky, R. J., Eshkevari, H. S., Goldney, R. D., & Hassan, R. (1998). *Suicide prevention: The global context.* New York: Plenum Press.

Kosonen, P., & Winne, P. H. (1995). Effects of teaching statistical laws on reasoning about everyday problems. *Journal of Educational Psychology, 87,* 33–46.

Kosslyn, S. M., & Koenig, O. (1992). *Wet mind: The new cognitive neuroscience.* New York: Free Press.

Kosslyn, S. M., Ball, T. M., & Reiser, B. J. (1978). Visual images preserve metric spatial information: Evidence from studies of image scanning. *Journal of Experimental Psychology: Human Perception and Performance, 4,* 47–60.

Kosslyn, S. M., Alpert, N. M., Thompson, W. L., & Maljkovic, V. (1993). Visual mental imagery activates topographically organized visual cortex: PET investigations. *Journal of Cognitive Neuroscience, 5,* 263–287.

Kraemer, P. J., & Golding, J. M. (1997). Adaptive forgetting in animals. *Psychonomic Bulletin and Review, 4,* 480–549.

Kramer, P. D. (1993). *Listening to Prozac.* New York: Viking.

Kramer, R. M. (1998). Revisiting the Bay of Pigs and Vietnam decisions 25 years later: How well has the groupthink hypothesis stood the test of time? *Organizational Behavior and Human Decision Processes, 73,* 236–271.

Krank, M. D., & O'Neill, S. (2002). Environmental context conditioning with ethanol reduces the aversive effects of ethanol in the acquisition of self-administration in rats. *Psychopharmacology, 159,* 258–265.

Krantz, D. S., & Manuck, S. B. (1984). Acute psychophysiologic reactivity and risk of cardiovascular disease: A review and methodologic critique. *Psychological Bulletin, 96,* 435–464.

Krantz, D. S., & McCeney, M. K. (2002). Effects of psychological and social factors on organic disease: A critical assessment of research on coronary heart disease. *Annual Review of Psychology, 53,* 341–369.

Kraus, S. J. (1995). Attitudes and the prediction of behavior. *Personality and Social Psychology Bulletin, 21,* 58–75.

Krebs, D. L. (1998). The evolution of moral behaviours. In C. Crawford & D. L. Krebs (Eds.), *Handbook of evolutionary psychology: Ideas, issues and applications.* Mahwah, NJ: Erlbaum.

Krebs, D. L., & Denton, K. (1997). Social illusions and self-deceptions: The evolution of biases in person perception. In J. A. Simpson & J. T. Kenrick (Eds.), *Evolutionary social psychology.* Mahwah, NJ: Erlbaum.

Krechevsky, M., & Seidel, S. (1998). Minds at work: Applying multiple intelligences in the classroom. In R. J. Sternberg & W. M. Williams (Eds.), *Intelligence, instruction, and assessment: Theory into practice.* Mahwah, NJ: Erlbaum.

Kreuz, R. J. (2000). The production and processing of verbal irony. *Metaphor and Symbol, 15* (1–2), 99–107.

Krippner, S. (1993). Some contributions of native healers to knowledge about the healing process. *International Journal of Psychosomatics, 40,* 96–99.

Krug, E. G., Kresnow, M., Peddicord, J., Dahlberg, L., Powell, K., Crosby, A., & Annest, J. (1998). Suicide after natural disasters. *New England Journal of Medicine, 338,* 373–378.

Krystal, A. D., & Coffey, C. E. (1997). Neuropsychiatric considerations in the use of electroconvulsive therapy. *Journal of Neuropsychiatry and Clinical Neurosciences, 9,* 283–292.

Kübler-Ross, E. (1969). *On death and dying.* New York: Macmillan.

Kübler-Ross, E. (1974). *Questions and answers on death and dying.* New York: Macmillan.

Kuhn, D. (1992). Cognitive development. In M. H. Bornstein & M. E. Lamb (Eds.), *Developmental psychology: An advanced textbook.* Hillsdale, NJ: Erlbaum.

Kuhn, W., Winkel, R., Woitalla, D., Meves, S., Przuntek, H., & Mueller, T. (1998). High prevalence of Parkinsonism after exposure to lead-sulfate batteries. *Neurology, 50,* 1885–1886.

Kuncel, N. R., Hezlett, S. A., & Ones, D. S. (2001). A comprehensive meta-analysis of the predictive validity of the graduate record examinations: Implications for graduate student selection and performance. *Psychological Bulletin, 127,* 162–181.

Kunda, Z. (1999). *Social cognition: Making sense of people.* Cambridge, MA: MIT Press.

Kunda, Z., & Sanitioso, R. (1989). Motivated changes in the self-concept. *Journal of Experimental Social Psychology, 25,* 272–328.

Kunda, Z., & Thagard, P. (1996). Forming impressions from stereotypes, traits, and behaviors: A parallel-constraint-satisfaction theory. *Psychological Review, 103,* 284–308.

Labouvie-Vief, G., Hakim-Larson, J., & Hobart, C. J. (1987). Age, ego level, and the life-span development of coping and defense processes. *Psychology and Aging, 2,* 286–293.

Labov, W. (1973). The boundaries of words and their meanings. In C. J. N. Bailey & R. W. Shiny (Eds.), *New ways of analyzing variation in English.* Washington, DC: Georgetown University Press.

Lackner, J. R., & DiZio, P. (1991). Decreased susceptibility to motion sickness during exposure to visual inversion in microgravity. *Aviation, Space, and Environmental Medicine, 62,* 206–211.

Ladd, G. T. (1896). *Psychology: Descriptive and explanatory.* New York: Charles Scribner's Sons.

Lafferty, P., Beutler, L. E., & Crago, M. (1991). Differences between more or less effective psychotherapists: A study of select therapist variables. *Journal of Consulting and Clinical Psychology, 57,* 76–80.

Lakoff, G. (1987). *Women, fire, and dangerous things: What categories reveal about the human mind.* Chicago: University of Chicago Press.

Lalonde, C. E., & Chandler, M. J. (1995). False belief understanding goes to school: On the social-emotional consequences of coming early or late to a first theory of mind. *Cognition and Emotion, 9,* 167–185.

Lalumière, M. L., & Quinsey, V. L. (1999). A Darwinian interpretation of individual differences in male propensity for sexual aggression. *Jurimetrics, 39,* 201–216.

Lalumière, M. L., Blanchard, R., & Zucker, K. J. (2000). Sexual orientation and handedness in men and women: A meta-analysis. *Psychological Bulletin, 126* (4), 575–592.

Lamb, M. E., Ketterlinus, R. D., & Fracasso, M. P. (1992). Parent-child relationships. In M. H. Bornstein & M. E. Lamb (Eds.), *Developmental psychology: An advanced textbook.* Hillsdale, NJ: Erlbaum.

Lambert, M. J., & Bergin, A. E. (1994). The effectiveness of psychotherapy. In A. E. Bergin & S. L. Garfield (Eds.), *Handbook of psychotherapy and behavior change* (4th ed.). New York: Wiley.

Lamont, J. A. (1997). Sexuality. In D. E. Stewart & G. E. Robinson (Eds.), *A clinician's guide to menopause.* Clinical practice. Washington, DC: Health Press International.

Lancet, D., Gross-Isseroff, R., Margalit, T., & Seidemann, E. (1993). Olfaction: From signal transduction and termination to human genome mapping. *Chemical Senses, 18,* 217–225.

Landauer, T. K. (1962). Rate of implicit speech. *Perceptual and Motor Skills, 15,* 646.

Landrum, R. E., & Chastain, G. (1995). Experiment spot-checks: A method for assessing the educational value of undergraduate participation in research. *IRB: A Review of Human Subjects Research, 17,* 4–6.

Lane, R. D., Reiman, E. M., Ahern, G. L., & Schwartz, G. E. (1997). Neuroanatomical correlates of happiness, sadness, and disgust. *American Journal of Psychiatry, 154,* 926–933.

Lang, P. J. (1994). The varieties of emotional experience: A meditation on James-Lange theory. *Psychological Review, 101,* 211–221.

Langer, E. J. (1989). *Mindfulness.* Cambridge, MA: Addison-Wesley.

Langlois, J. H., & Roggman, L. A. (1990). Attractive faces are only average. *Psychological Science, 1,* 115–121.

Langlois, J. H., Roggman, L. A., & Musselman, L. (1994). What is average and what is not average about attractive faces? *Psychological Science, 5,* 214–220.

Langlois, J. H., Roggman, L. A., Casey, R. J., Ritter, J. M., Rieser-Danner, L. A., & Jenkins, V. Y. (1987). Infant preferences for attractive faces: Rudiments of a stereotype? *Developmental Psychology, 23,* 363–369.

Laprelle, J., Hoyle, R. H., Insko, C. A., & Bernthal, P. (1990). Interpersonal attraction and descriptions of the traits of others: Ideal similarity, self similarity, and liking. *Journal of Research in Personality, 24,* 216–240.

Larose, H., & Standing, L. (1998). Does the halo effect occur in the elderly? *Social Behavior and Personality, 26,* 147–150.

Lassonde, M., & Jeeves, M. A. (Eds.), *Callosal agenesis: A natural split brain?* New York: Plenum Press.

Latané, B. (1981). The psychology of social impact. *American Psychologist, 36,* 343–356.

Latané, B., & Nida, S. A. (1981). Ten years of research on group size and helping. *Psychological Bulletin, 89,* 308–324.

Latané, B., Williams, K., & Harkins, S. (1979). Many hands make light the work: The causes and consequences of social loafing. *Journal of Personality and Social Psychology, 37,* 822–832.

Laudenslager, M. L., Ryan, S. M., Drugen, R. L., Hyson, R. L., & Maier, S. F. (1983). Coping and immunosuppression: Inescapable but not escapable shock suppresses lymphocyte proliferation. *Science, 221,* 568–570.

Lay, C., & Verkuyten, M. (1999). Ethnic identity and its relation to personal self-esteem: A comparison of Canadian-born and foreign-born Chinese adolescents. *Journal of Social Psychology, 139,* 288–299.

Lazarus, A. A., & Messer, S. B. (1991). Does chaos prevail? An exchange on technical eclecticism and assimilative integration. *Journal of Psychotherapy Integration, 1,* 143–158.

Lazarus, R. S. (1966). *Psychological stress and the coping process.* New York: McGraw-Hill.

Lazarus, R. S. (1991). *Emotion and adaptation.* New York: Oxford University Press.

Lazarus, R. S. (1993). Why we should think of stress as a subset of emotion. In L. Goldberger & S. Breznitz (Eds.), *Handbook of stress: Theoretical and clinical aspects* (2nd ed.). New York: Free Press.

Lazarus, R. S., & Folkman, S. (1984). *Stress, appraisal and coping.* New York: Springer.

Leach, M. M., & Harbin, J. J. (1997). Psychological ethics codes: A comparison of 24 countries. *International Journal of Psychology, 32,* 181–192.

Leadbeater, B. J., & Way, N. (Eds.) (1996). *Urban adolescent girls: Resisting stereotypes, creating identities.* New York: New York University Press.

Leadbeater, B. J., Blatt, S., & Quinlan, D. M. (1995). Gender-linked vulnerabilities to depressive symptoms, stress, and problem behaviours in adolescents. *Journal of Research on Adolescence, 5,* 1–29.

Leadbeater, B. J., Kuperminc, G. P., Blatt, S. J., & Hertzog, C. (1999). A multivariate model of gender differences in adolescents' internalizing and externalizing problems. *Developmental Psychology, 35,* 1268–1282.

Lebow, J. L., & Gurman, A. S. (1995). Research assessing couple and family therapy. *Annual Review of Psychology, 46,* 27–57.

Leclerc, G., Lefrancois, R., Dube, M., Hebert, R., & Gaulin, P. (1998). The self-actualization concept: A content validation. *Journal of Social Behavior and Personality, 11,* 69–84.

LeDoux, J. E. (1996). *The emotional brain.* New York: Simon & Schuster.

Lee, C. J., & Katz, A. N. (1998). The differential role of ridicule in sarcasm and irony. *Metaphor and Symbol, 13,* 1–15.

Lee, E. K. (1998). Periodic left temporal sharp waves during acute psychosis. *Journal of Epilepsy, 11,* 79–83.

Lee, K., & Homer, B. (1999). Children as folk psychologists: The developing understanding of the mind. In A. Slater & D. Muir (Eds.), *The Blackwell reader in development psychology* (pp. 228–252). Malden, MA: Blackwell.

Lefcourt, H. M. (1982). *Locus of control: Current trends in theory and research.* Waterloo, ON: University of Waterloo.

Leger Marketing (2001). *Canadians and the Use of Cellular Phones.* Available: www.legermarketing.com/documents/spclm/011008eng.pdf

Leith, K. P., & Baumeister, R. F. (1996). Why do bad moods increase self-defeating behavior? Emotion, risk taking, and self-regulation. *Journal of Personality and Social Psychology, 71,* 1250–1267.

Lenneberg, E. H. (1967). *Biological foundations of language.* New York: Wiley.

Lepper, M. R., Greene, D., & Nisbett, R. E. (1973). Undermining children's intrinsic interest with external reward: A test of the "overjustification" hypothesis. *Journal of Personality and Social Psychology, 28,* 129–137.

Lerman, H. G. (1986). From Freud to feminist personality theory: Getting here from there. *Psychology of Women Quarterly, 10,* 1–18.

LeVay, S. (1991). A difference in hypothalamic structure between heterosexual and homosexual men. *Science, 253,* 1034–1037.

Levenson, R. W. (1992). Autonomic nervous system differences among emotions. *Psychological Science, 3,* 23–27.

Levin, I. P., & Gaeth, G. J. (1988). How consumers are affected by the framing of attribute information before and after consuming the product. *Journal of Consumer Research, 15,* 374–378.

Levine, D. N., Warach, J., & Farah, M. J. (1985). Two visual systems in mental imagery: Dissociation of "what" and "where" in imagery disorders due to bilateral posterior cerebral lesions. *Neurology, 35,* 1010–1018.

Levine, G., & Parkinson, S. (1994). *Experimental methods in psychology.* Hillsdale, NJ: Erlbaum.

Levine, R. V., & Norenzayan, A. (1999). The pace of life in 31 countries. *Journal of Cross Cultural Psychology 30,* 178–205.

Levinson, D. J., Darow, C. N., Klein, E. B., Levinson, M. H., & McKee, B. (1978). *The seasons of a man's life.* New York: Knopf.

Lewis, M., & Brooks-Gunn, J. (1979). *Social cognition and the acquisition of self.* New York: Plenum.

Lewontin, R. (1976). Race and intelligence. In N. J. Block & G. Dworkin (Eds.), *The IQ controversy: Critical readings.* New York: Pantheon.

Li, X., Sano, H., & Merwin, J. C. (1996). Perception and reasoning abilities among American, Japanese, and Chinese adolescents. *Journal of Adolescent Research, 11,* 173–193.

Liberman, R. P., Kopelowicz, A., & Young, A. S. (1994). Biobehavioral treatment and rehabilitation of schizophrenia. *Behavior Therapy, 25,* 89–107.

Lickey, M. E., & Gordon, B. (1991). *Medicine and mental illness: The use of drugs in psychiatry.* New York: Freeman.

Liebert, R. M., & Liebert, L. L. (1995). *Science and behavior: An introduction to methods of psychological research* (4th ed.). Englewood Cliffs, NJ: Prentice-Hall.

Lilienfeld, S. O. (1994). Conceptual problems in the assessment of psychopathy. *Clinical Psychology Review, 14,* 17–38.

Lilienfeld, S. O., Wood, J. M., & Garb, H. N. (2000). The scientific status of projective tests. *Psychological Science in the Public Interest, 1,* 27–66.

Linde, J. A., & Clark, L. A. (1998). Diagnostic assignment of criteria: Clinicians and DSM-IV. *Journal of Personality Disorders, 12,* 126–137.

Linden, W. (1990). *Autogenic training: A clinical guide.* New York: Guilford.

Linden, W., Stossel, C., & Maurice, J. (1996). Psychosocial interventions for patients with coronary artery disease. *Archives of Internal Medicine, 156,* 745–752.

Lindsay, D. S. (2002). Children's source monitoring. In H. L. Westcott, G. Davies, & R. H. C. Bull (Eds.), *Children's testimony: Psychological research and forensic practice* (pp. 83–98). Sussex, England: John Wiley and Sons.

Lindsay, D. S., & Kelley, C. M. (1996). Creating illusions of familiarity in a cued recall remember/know paradigm. *Journal of Memory and Language, 35,* 197–211.

Lindsay, D. S., & Poole, D. A. (1998, Fall). The Poole et al. (1995) surveys of therapists: Misinterpretations by both sides of the recovered memories controversy. *Journal of Psychiatry and Law, 26,* 383–399.

Lindsay, D. S., & Read, J. D. (1994). Psychotherapy and memories of childhood sexual abuse: A cognitive perspective. *Applied Cognitive Psychology, 8,* 281–338.

Lindsay, D. S., Wade, K. A., Hunter, M. A., & Read, J. D. (in press). Adults' memories of childhood: Affect, knowing, and remembering. *Memory.*

Lindsley, O. R., & Skinner, B. F. (1954). A method for the experimental analysis of psychotic patients. *American Psychologist, 9,* 419–420.

Linton, M. (1975). Memory for real-world events. In D. A. Norman & D. E. Rumelhart (Eds.), *Explorations in cognition.* San Francisco: Freeman.

Linville, P. W., Fischer, G. W., & Fischhoff, B. (1993). AIDS risk perceptions and decision biases. In J. B. Pryor & G. D. Reeder (Eds.), *The social psychology of HIV infection* (pp. 5–38). Hillsdale, NJ: Erlbaum.

Lipsey, M. W., & Wilson, D. B. (1993). The efficacy of psychological, educational, and behavioral treatment: Confirmation from meta-analysis. *American Psychologist, 48,* 1181–1209.

Lisanby, S. H., Luber, B., Perera, T., & Sackeim, H. A. (2000). Transcranial magnetic stimulation: Applications in basic neuroscience and neuropsychopharmacology. *International Journal of Neuropsychopharmacology, 3,* 259–273.

Little, B. R. (1996). Free traits, personal projects and idio-tapes: Three tiers for personality psychology. *Psychological Inquiry, 7,* 340–344.

Little, B. R. (2000). Persons, contexts, and personal projects: Assumptive themes of a methodological transactionalism. In S. Wapner, J. Demick, T. Yamamoto, & H. Minami (Eds.), *Theoretical perspectives in environment-behavior research: Underlying assumptions, research problems, and methodologies* (pp. 79–88). Dordrecht, Netherlands: Kluwer.

Liu, Z. (1996). Viewpoint dependency in object representation and recognition. *Spatial Vision, 9,* 491–521.

Livesley, W. J. (2001). *Handbook of personality disorders: Theory, research, and treatment.* New York: Guilford.

Livingstone, M., & Hubel, D. H. (1988). Segregation of form, color, movement, and depth: Anatomy, physiology, and perception. *Science, 240,* 740–749.

Lockard, J. S., & Mateer, C. A. (1988). Neural bases of self-deception. In J. S. Lockard & D. L. Paulhus (Eds.), *Self-deception: An adaptive mechanism?* (pp. 23–39). Englewood Cliffs, NJ: Prentice-Hall.

Lockard, J. S., & Paulhus, D. L. (Eds.) (1988). *Self-deception: An adaptive mechanism?* Englewood Cliffs, NJ: Prentice-Hall.

Locke, J. L. (1994). Phases in the child's development of language. *American Scientist, 82,* 436–445.

Loewenstein, R. J. (1996). Dissociative amnesia and dissociative fugue. In L. K. Michelson & W. J. Ray (Eds.), *Handbook of dissociation: Theoretical, empirical, and clinical perspectives.* New York: Plenum Press.

Loftus, E. L. (1979). *Eyewitness testimony.* Cambridge, MA: Harvard University Press.

Loftus, E. L. (1991). *Witness for the defense.* New York: St. Martin's.

Loftus, E. L. (1993). The reality of repressed memories. *American Psychologist, 48,* 518–537.

Loftus, E. L., & Palmer, J. C. (1974). Reconstruction of automobile destruction: An example of the interaction between language and memory. *Journal of Verbal Learning and Verbal Behavior, 13,* 585–589.

Logan, G. D. (1988). Toward an instance theory of automatization. *Psychological Review, 95,* 492–527.

Logan, G. D. (1991). Automaticity and memory. In W. E. Hockley & S. Lewandowsky (Eds.), *Relating theory and data: Essays on human memory in honor of Bennet B. Murdock.* Hillsdale, NJ: Erlbaum.

Looy, H., & Weingarten, H. P. (1992). Facial expressions and genetic sensitivity to 6-n-propylthiouracil predict hedonic response to sweet. *Physiology and Behavior, 52* (1), 75–82.

Lorenz, K. 1966. *On aggression.* New York: Harcourt, Brace & World.

Lorenz, K. Z. (1958, December). The evolution of behavior. *Scientific American, 199,* 67–78.

Lovaas, O. I. (1987). Behavioral treatment and normal educational and intellectual functioning in young autistic children. *Journal of Consulting and Clinical Psychology, 55,* 3–9.

Lovaas, O. I., Koegel, R., Simmons, J. Q., & Long, J. S. (1973). Some generalization and follow-up measures on autistic children in behavior therapy. *Journal of Applied Behavior Analysis, 6,* 131–166.

Loverock, D. S., & Modigliani, V. (1995). Visual imagery and the brain: A review. *Journal of Mental Imagery, 19,* 91–132.

Lowe, J., & Carroll, D. (1985). The effects of spinal cord injury on the intensity of emotional experience. *British Journal of Clinical Psychology, 24,* 135–136.

Luborsky, L., Barber, J. P., & Crits-Cristoph, P. (1990). Theory-based research for understanding the process of dynamic psy-

chotherapy. *Journal of Consulting and Clinical Psychology, 58,* 281–287.

Lucy, J. A. (1997). Linguistic relativity. *Annual Review of Anthropology, 26,* 291–312.

Lutz, C. (1982). The domain of emotion words in Ifaluk. *American Ethnologist, 9,* 113–128.

Luus, C. A. E., & Wells, G. L. (1994). The malleability of eyewitness confidence: Co-witness and perseverance effects. *Journal of Applied Psychology, 79,* 714–723.

Lykken, D. T. (1998). *A tremor in the blood: Uses and abuses of the lie detector.* New York: Plenum Press.

Lyness, S. A. (1993). Predictors of differences between Type A and Type B individuals in heart rate and blood pressure reactivity. *Psychological Bulletin, 114,* 266–295.

Lynn, S. J., Myers, B., & Malinoski, P. (1997). Hypnosis, pseudomemories, and clinical guidelines: A sociocognitive perspective. In J. D. Read & D. S. Lindsay (Eds.), *Recollections of trauma: Scientific evidence and clinical practice* (pp. 305–336). New York: Plenum.

Lynn, S. J., Rhue, J. W., & Weekes, J. R. (1990). Hypnotic involuntariness: A social cognitive analysis. *Psychological Review, 97,* 169–184.

Maccoby, E. (2000). Parenting and its effects on children: On reading and misreading behavioral genetics. *Annual Review of Psychology, 51,* 1–27.

MacDonald, S., Uesiliana, K., & Hayne, H. (2000). Cross-cultural and gender differences in childhood amnesia. *Memory, 8,* 365–376.

MacDonald, T. K., & Ross, M. (1999). Assessing the accuracy of predictions about dating relationships: How and why do lovers' predictions differ from those made by observers? *Personality and Social Psychology Bulletin, 25,* 1417–1429.

MacDonald, T. K., Zanna, M. P., & Fong, G. T. (1995). Decision-making in altered states: The effects of alcohol on attitudes toward drinking and driving. *Journal of Personality and Social Psychology, 68,* 973–985.

MacDonald, N. E., Wells, G. A., Fisher, W. A., Warren, W. K., et al. (1990). High-risk STD/HIV behavior among college students. *Journal of the American Medical Association, 263,* 3155–3159.

MacDonald, T. K., Zanna, M. P., & Fong, G. T. (1996). Why common sense goes out the window: The effects of alcohol on intentions to use condoms. *Personality and Social Psychology Bulletin, 22,* 763–775.

MacDonald, T. K., Zanna, M. P., & Fong, G. T. (1998). Alcohol and intentions to engage in

risky behaviours: Experimental evidence for a causal relationship. In J. G. Adair, D. Belanger, & K. Dion (Eds.), *Advances in Psychological Science: Social, personal, and cultural aspects* (pp. 407–428). East Sussex, England: Psychology Press.

Mackay, D. G. (1983). Prescriptive grammar and the pronoun problem. In B. Thorne, C. Kramarae, & N. Henley (Eds.), *Language, gender, and society.* Rowley, MA: Newbury House.

MacKenzie, K. R. (2000). Current approaches to time-limited group psychotherapy services. In F. Flach (Ed.), *The Hatherleigh guide to psychiatric disorders, Part II.* The Hatherleigh guides series. Long Island City, NY: Hatherleigh Company, Ltd.

MacKinnon, D. W. (1962). The nature and nurture of creative talent. *American Psychologist, 17,* 484–495.

MacLean, C. R. K., Walton, K. G., Wenneberg, S. R., & Levitsky, D. K. (1997). Effects of the transcendental meditation program on adaptive mechanisms: Changes in hormone levels and responses to stress after 4 months of practice. *Psychoneuroendocrinology, 22,* 277–295.

MacLennan, R. N., & Peebles, J. W. E. (1996). Survey of health problems and personality in air traffic controllers. *International Journal of Aviation Psychology, 6,* 43–55.

MacLeod, C. M. (1999). The item and list methods of directed forgetting: Test differences and the role of demand characteristics. *Psychonomic Bulletin and Review, 6,* 123–129.

Macmillan, N. A., & Creelman, C. D. (1991). *Detection theory: A user's guide.* New York: Cambridge University Press.

MacNeill, P., & Webster, I. (1995). *Canada's alcohol and other drugs survey of 1994: A discussion of the findings.* Ottawa, ON: Health Canada.

Macrae, C. N., & Bodenhausen, G. V. (2000). Social cognition: Thinking categorically about others. *Annual Review of Psychology, 51,* 93–120.

Maddi, S. R. (2002). The story of hardiness: Twenty years of theorizing, research, and practice. *Consulting Psychology Journal: Practice and Research, 54,* 175–185.

Maestripieri, D. (2001). Biological basis of maternal attachment. *Current Directions in Psychological Science, 10,* 79–83.

Mahrer, A. R. (1995). *A complete guide to experiential psychotherapy.* New York: John Wiley.

Maier, N. R. F. (1931). Reasoning in humans II: The solution to a problem and its appearance in consciousness. *Journal of Comparative Psychology, 12,* 181–194.

Maier, N. R. F., & Burke, R. J. (1967). Response availability as a factor in the problem-solving performance of males and females. *Journal of Personality and Social Psychology, 5,* 304–310.

Maj, M. (1998). Critique of the DSM-IV operational diagnostic criteria for schizophrenia. *British Journal of Psychiatry, 172,* 458–460.

Malamuth, N. M., & Check, J. V. P. (1983). Sexual arousal to rape depictions: Individual differences. *Journal of Abnormal Psychology, 92,* 55–67.

Malt, B. C., & Smith, E. E. (1984). Correlated properties in natural categories. *Journal of Verbal Learning and Verbal Behavior, 23,* 250–269.

Mandal, M. K., Bryden, M. P., & Bulman-Fleming, M. B. (1996). Similarities and variations in facial expressions of emotions: Cross-cultural evidence. *International Journal of Psychology, 31* (1), 49–58.

Mandler, G., Nakamura, Y., & Van Zandt, B. J. S. (1987). Nonspecific effects of stimuli that cannot be recognized. *Journal of Experimental Psychology: Learning, Memory, and Cognition, 13,* 646–648.

Mandler, J. M. (1992). How to build a baby: II. Conceptual primitives. *Psychological Review, 99,* 587–604.

Mann, J. J. (1998). Neurobiological correlates of the antidepressant action of electroconvulsive therapy. *Journal of ECT, 14,* 172–180.

Mann, T. (1994). Informed consent for psychological research: Do subjects comprehend consent forms and understand their legal rights? *Psychological Science, 5,* 140–143.

Manson, S. M. (1995). Culture and major depression: Current challenges in the diagnosis of mood disorders. *Psychiatric Clinics of North America, 18,* 487–501.

Maratos, O. (1998). Neonatal, early and later imitation: Same order of phenomena? In F. Simion & G. Butterworth (Eds.), *The development of sensory, motor and cognitive capacities in early infancy: From perception to cognition.* Hove, England: Psychology Press/Erlbaum (UK) Taylor & Francis.

Marche, T. A. (1999). Memory strength affects reporting of misinformation. *Journal of Experimental Child Psychology, 73* (1), 45–71.

Marcia, J. E. (1966). Development and validation of ego identity status. *Journal of Personality and Social Psychology, 3,* 551–558.

Markman, A. B., & Wisniewski, E. J. (1997). Similar and different: The differentiation of basic-level categories. *Journal of Experimental Psychology: Learning, Memory, and Cognition, 23,* 54–70.

Markus, H. (1977). Self-schemata and processing information about the self. *Journal of Personality and Social Psychology, 35,* 63–78.

Marlatt, G. A., & VandenBos, G. R. (Eds.) (1997). *Addictive behaviors: Readings on etiology, prevention, and treatment.* Washington, DC: American Psychological Association.

Marquardt, C. J. G., Bonato, R. A., & Hoffmann, R. F. (1996). An empirical investigation into the day-residue and dream-lag effects. *Dreaming: Journal of the Association for the Study of Dreams, 6,* 57–65.

Marsella, A. J., & Yamada, A. M. (2000). Culture and mental health: An introduction and overview of foundations, concepts, and issues. In I. Cuellar & F. A. Paniagua (Eds.), *Handbook of multicultural mental health.* San Diego: Academic Press.

Marsh, R. L., Landau, J. D., & Hicks, J. L. (1997). Contributions of inadequate source monitoring to unconscious plagiarism during idea generation. *Journal of Experimental Psychology: Learning, Memory, and Cognition, 23,* 886–897.

Marshall, G. D., & Zimbardo, P. G. (1979). Affective consequences of inadequately explained physiological arousal. *Journal of Personality and Social Psychology, 37,* 970–988.

Marshall, J. C., & Halligan, P. W. (1988). Blindsight and insight in visuo-spatial neglect. *Nature, 336,* 766–767.

Marson, L., & McKenna, K. E. (1994). Stimulation of the hypothalamus initiates the urethrogenital reflex in male rats. *Brain Research, 638,* 103–108.

Martin, G., & Pear, J. (1999). *Behavior modification: What it is and how to do it* (6th ed.). Upper Saddle River, NJ: Prentice Hall.

Martin, K. M., & Aggleton, J. P. (1993). Contextual effects on the ability of divers to use decompression tables. *Applied Cognitive Psychology, 7,* 311–316.

Martin, P., & Bateson, P. (1993). *Measuring behavior: An introductory guide* (2nd ed.). Cambridge: Cambridge University Press.

Martin, R. J., White, B. D., & Hulsey, M. G. (1991). The regulation of body weight. *American Scientist, 79,* 528–541.

Marx, M. H., & Cronan-Hillix, W. A. (1987). *Systems and theories in psychology.* New York: McGraw-Hill.

Maser, J. D., Kaelber, C., & Weise, R. E. (1991). International use and attitudes toward DSM-III and DSM-III-R: Growing consensus in psychiatric classification. *Journal of Abnormal Psychology, 100,* 271–279.

Mash, D. C., Flynn, D. D., & Potter, L. T. (1985). Loss of M2 muscarine receptors in the cerebral cortex in Alzheimer's disease and experimental cholinergic denervation. *Science, 228,* 1115–1117.

Mash, E. J., & Barkley, R. A. (Eds.) (1998). *Treatment of childhood disorders.* New York: Guilford.

Mash, E. J., & Wolfe, D. A. (1999). *Abnormal child psychology.* Albany, NY: Wadsworth.

Maslach, C. (1976). Burned out. *Human Behavior, 5,* 16–22.

Maslach, C., & Jackson, S. E. (1981). The measurement of experienced burnout. *Journal of Occupational Behavior, 2,* 99–113.

Maslach, C., Schaufeli, W. B., & Leiter, M. P. (2001). Job burnout. *Annual Review of Psychology, 52,* 397–422.

Maslow, A. H. (1954). *Motivation and personality.* New York: Harper.

Mason, J. R., & Reidinger, R. F. (1982). Observational learning of aversions in red-winged blackbirds (Agelaius phoeniceus). *Auk, 99,* 548–554.

Mason, J. W. (1975). A historical view of the stress field. *Journal of Human Stress, 1,* 22–36.

Masson, J. (1984). *The assault on truth: Freud's suppression of the seduction theory.* New York: Farrar, Straus, & Giroux.

Matano, R. A., Yalom, I. D., & Schwartz, K. (1997). Interactive group therapy for substance abusers. In J. L. Spira (Ed.), *Group therapy for medically ill patients.* New York: Guilford.

Mateer, C. A., Kerns, K. A., & Eso, K. L. (1997). Management of attention and memory disorders following traumatic brain injury. In E. D. Bigler & E. Clark (Eds.), *Childhood traumatic brain injury: Diagnosis, assessment, and intervention* (pp. 153–175). Austin, TX: Pro-Ed.

Matsumoto, D. (1987). The role of facial response in the experience of emotion: More methodological problems and a meta-analysis. *Journal of Personality and Social Psychology, 52,* 769–774.

Matsumoto, D. (1994). *People: Psychology from a cultural perspective.* Pacific Grove, CA: Brooks/Cole.

Mattay, V. S., Berman, K. F., Ostrem, J. L., Esposito, G., Van-Horn, J. D., Bigelow, L. B.,

& Weinberger, D. R. (1996). Dextroamphetamine enhances "neural network-specific" physiological signals: A positron-emission tomography rCBF study. *Journal of Neuroscience, 16,* 4816–4822.

Matthews, G. (1997). Intelligence, personality and information-processing: An adaptive perspective. In J. Kingma & W. Tomic (Eds.), *Advances in cognition and educational practice: Reflections on the concept of intelligence.* Greenwich, CT: JAI Press.

Matthews, K. A. (1992). Myths and realities of the menopause. *Psychosomatic Medicine, 54,* 1–9.

Matzel, L. D., Held, F. P., & Miller, R. R. (1988). Information and expression of simultaneous and backward associations: Implications for contiguity theory. *Learning and Motivation, 9,* 317–344.

Mauss, M. (1902/1972). *A general theory of magic* (R. Brain, Trans.). New York: Norton.

Mayberg, H. S., Silva, J. A., Brannan, S. K., Tekell, J. L., Mahurin, R. K., McGinnis, S., & Jerabek, P. A. (2002). The functional neuroanatomy of the placebo effect. *American Journal of Psychiatry, 159,* 728–737.

Mayer, D. J. (1953). Glucostatic mechanism of regulation of food intake. *New England Journal of Medicine, 249,* 13–16.

Mazur, A., & Booth, A. (1998). Testosterone and dominance in men. *Brain and Behavioral Sciences, 21,* 353–397.

McAdams, D. P. (2000). *The person: An integrated introduction to personality psychology.* New York: Harcourt.

McAllister-Williams, R. H., Ferrier, I. N., & Young, A. (1998). Mood and neuropsychological function in depression: The role of corticosteriods and serotonin. *Psychological Medicine, 28,* 573–584.

McArthur, L. Z., & Berry, D. S. (1987). Cross-cultural agreement in perceptions of babyfaced adults. *Journal of Cross-Cultural Psychology, 18,* 165–192.

McCall, M. (1994). Decision theory and the sale of alcohol. *Journal of Applied Social Psychology, 24,* 1593–1611.

McCall, M. (1997). The effects of physical attractiveness on gaining access to alcohol: When social policy meets social decision making. *Addiction, 92,* 597–600.

McCall, R. B., & Carriger, M. S. (1993). A meta-analysis of infant habituation and recognition memory performance as predictors of later IQ. *Child Development, 64,* 57–79.

McCann, I. L., & Holmes, D. S. (1984). Influence of aerobic exercise on depression.

Journal of Personality and Social Psychology, 46, 1142–1147.

McClelland, D. C. (1961). *The achieving society.* Princeton, NJ: Von Nostrand.

McClelland, D. C., Atkinson, J. W., Clark, R. A., & Lowell, E. W. (1953). *The achievement motive.* New York: Appleton-Century-Crofts.

McClelland, J. L., & Elman, J. L. (1986). The TRACE model of speech perception. *Cognitive Psychology, 18,* 1–86.

McCormick, R. (2000). Aboriginal traditions in the treatment of substance abuse: Let only the good spirits guide you. *Canadian Journal of Counselling, 34,* 25–32.

McCormick, R. M. (1996). Culturally appropriate means and ends of counselling as described by the First Nations people of British Columbia. *International Journal for the Advancement of Counselling, 34,* 25–32.

McCrae, R. R., & Costa, P. T., Jr. (1985). Updating Norman's "adequate taxonomy": Intelligence and personality dimensions in natural language and in questionnaires. *Journal of Personality and Social Psychology, 49,* 710–721.

McCrae, R. R., & Costa, P. T., Jr. (1990). *Personality in adulthood.* New York: Guilford.

McCrae, R. R., & Costa, P. T., Jr. (1997). Personality trait structure as a human universal. *American Psychologist, 52,* 509–516.

McCrae, R. R., Costa, P. T., Jr., & Yik, M. S. M. (1996). Universal aspects of Chinese personality structure. In M. H. Bond (Ed.), *The handbook of Chinese psychology.* Hong Kong: Oxford University Press.

McCreary Centre Society (1999). *Healthy connections: Listening to BC Youth.* Burnaby, BC: Author.

McDaniel, E., & Anderson, P. A. (1998). International patterns of interpersonal tactile communication: A field study. *Journal of Nonverbal Behavior, 22,* 59–75.

McDermott, K. B., & Roediger, H. L., III (1994). Effects of imagery on perceptual implicit memory tests. *Journal of Experimental Psychology: Learning, Memory, and Cognition, 20,* 1379–1390.

McDermott, K. B., & Roediger, H. L., III (1998). Attempting to avoid illusory memories: Robust false recognition of associates persists under conditions of explicit warnings and immediate testing. *Journal of Memory and Language, 39,* 508–520.

McDonald, J. J., & Ward, L. M. (2000). Involuntary listening aids seeing: Evidence

from human electrophysiology. *Psychological Science, 11,* 167–171.

McDonald, M. P., & Crawley, J. N. (1997). Galanin-acetylcholine interactions in rodent memory tasks and Alzheimer's disease. *Journal of Psychiatry and Neuroscience, 22,* 303–317.

McDougall, W. (1908). *An introduction to social psychology.* London: Methuen.

McElroy, S. L., & Keck, P. E., Jr. (2000). Pharmacologic agents for the treatment of acute bipolar mania. *Biological Psychiatry, 48,* 539–557.

McFall, R. M. (1976). Behavioral training: A skill-acquisition approach to clinical problems. In J. T. Spence, R. C. Carson, & J. W. Thibaut (Eds.), *Behavioral approaches to therapy.* Morristown, NJ: General Learning Press.

McFarland, C., & Miller, D. T. (1994). The framing of relative performance feedback: Seeing the glass as half empty or half full. *Journal of Personality and Social Psychology, 66,* 1061–1073.

McGrath, P. J., Humphreys, P., Keene, D., & Goodman, J. T. (1992). The efficacy and efficiency of a self-administered treatment for adolescent migrain. *Pain, 49,* 321–324.

McGuire, P. K., Shah, G. M. S., & Murray, R. M. (1993). Increased blood flow in Broca's area during auditory hallucinations. *Lancet, 342,* 703–706.

McGuire, W. J. (1985). Attitudes and attitude change. In G. Lindzey & E. Aronson (Eds.), *Handbook of social psychology.* New York: Random House.

McGuire, W. J., & McGuire, C. V. (1988). Content and process in the experience of the self. In L. Berkowitz (Ed), *Advances in experimental social psychology,* (pp. 97–144). San Diego: Academic Press.

McIntosh, A. R., Grady, C. L., Ungerleider, L. G., & Haxby, J. V. (1994). Network analysis of cortical visual pathways mapped with PET. *Journal of Neuroscience, 14,* 655–666.

McIntosh, D. N., Zajonc, R. B., Vig, P. S., & Emerick, S. W. (1997). Facial movement, breathing, temperature, and affect: Implications of the vascular theory of emotional efference. *Cognition and Emotion, 11,* 171–195.

McIntyre, J. S., & Craik, F. I. (1987). Age differences in memory for item and source information. *Canadian Journal of Psychology, 41* (2), 175–192.

McKenna, S. P., & Glendon, A. I. (1985). Occupational first aid training: Decay in cardiopulmonary resuscitation (CPR) skills.

Journal of Occupational Psychology, 58, 109–117.

McKinlay, S. M., Brambilla, D. J., & Posner, J. G. (1992). The normal menopause transition. *Maturitas, 14,* 103–115.

McKnight, J. D., & Glass, D. C. (1995). Perceptions of control, burnout, and depressive symptomatology: A replication and extension. *Journal of Consulting and Clinical Psychology, 63,* 490–494.

McLean, P. D., & Woody, S. R. (2001). *Anxiety disorders in adults: An evidence-based approach to psychological treatment.* London: Oxford University Press.

McLeod, J. D., Kessler, R. C., & Landis, K. R. (1992). Speed of recovery from major depressive episodes in a community sample of married men and women. *Journal of Abnormal Psychology, 101,* 277–286.

McNeil, B. J., Pauker, S. G., Cox, H. C., Jr., & Tversky, A. (1982). On the elicitation of preferences for alternative therapies. *New England Journal of Medicine, 306,* 1259–1262.

Medin, D. L. (1989). Concepts and conceptual structure. *American Psychologist, 44,* 1469–1481.

Medin, D. L., & Shaffer, M. M. (1978). A context theory of classification learning. *Psychological Review, 85,* 207–238.

Mednick, S. A. (1962). The associative basis of the creative process. *Psychological Review, 69,* 220–232.

Mednick, S. C., Nakayama, K., Cantero, J. L., Atienza, M., Levin, A. A., Pathak, N., & Stickgold, R. (2002). The restorative effect of naps on perceptual deterioration. *Nature Neuroscience, 5,* 677–681.

Meeus, W. H. J., & Raaijmakers, Q. A. W. (1987). Administrative obedience as a social phenomenon. In W. Doise & S. Moscovici (Eds.), *Current issues in European social psychology.* Cambridge, England: Cambridge University Press.

Meisel, A., & Roth, L. H. (1983). Toward an informed discussion of informed consent: A review and critique of the empirical studies. *Arizona Law Review, 25,* 265–346.

Melamed, B. G., & Siegel, L. J. (1975). Reduction of anxiety in children facing hospitalization and surgery by use of filmed modeling. *Journal of Consulting and Clinical Psychology, 43,* 511–521.

Melton, A. W. (1963). Implications of short-term memory for a general theory of memory. *Journal of Verbal Learning and Verbal Behavior, 2,* 1–21.

Melzack, R. (1973). *The puzzle of pain.* New York: Basic Books.

Melzack, R. (1992). Phantom limbs. *Scientific American, 266,* 120–126.

Melzack, R., & Wall, P. D. (1965). Pain mechanisms: A new theory. *Science, 150,* 971–979.

Melzack, R., & Wall, P. D. (1982). *The challenge of pain.* Harmondsworth: Penguin.

Mendez, I., Baker, K. A., & Hong, M. (2000). Simultaneous intrastriatal and intranigral grafting (double grafts) in the rat model of Parkinson's disease. *Brain Research Reviews, 32* (1), 328–339.

Mennin, D. S., Heimberg, R. G., & Holt, C. S. (2000). Panic, agoraphobia, phobias, and generalized anxiety disorder. In M. Hersen & A. S. Bellack (Eds.), *Psychopathology in adulthood* (2nd ed.). Needham Heights, MA: Allyn & Bacon.

Merikle, P. M., & Skanes, H. E. (1992). Subliminal self-help audiotapes: A search for placebo effects. *Journal of Applied Psychology, 77,* 772–776.

Merikle, P. M., Smilek, D., & Eastwood, J. D. (2001). Perception without awareness: Perspectives from cognitive psychology. *Cognition, 79,* 115–134.

Merlin, D. (1999). Proconditions for the evolution of protolanguages. In M. Corballis & S. E. G. Lea (Eds.), *The descent of mind. Psychological perspectives on hominid evolution* (pp. 138–154). New York: Oxford University Press.

Merton, R. (1948). The self-fulfilling prophecy. *Antioch Review, 8,* 193–210.

Meston, C. M., Frohlich, P. F. (in press). Love at first fright: Partner salience moderates roller coaster–induced excitation transfer. *Archives of Sexual Behavior.*

Mesulam, M. M. (1987). Neglect (selective inattention). In G. Adelman (Ed.), *Encyclopedia of neuroscience.* Boston: Birkhauser.

Metcalfe, J. (2002). Is study time allocated selectively to a region of proximal learning? *Journal of Experimental Psychology: General, 131,* 349–363.

Metcalfe, J., & Jacobs, W. J. (2000). "Hot" emotions in human recollection: Toward a model of traumatic memory. In E. Tulving (Ed.), *Memory, consciousness, and the brain: The Tallinn conference* (pp. 228–242). Philadelphia: Psychology Press.

Miklowitz, D. J. (2001). Bipolar disorder. In D. H. Barlow (Ed.), *Clinical handbook of psychological disorders: A step-by-step treatment manual* (3rd ed.). New York: Guilford.

Milgram, S. (1963). Behavioral study of obedience. *Journal of Abnormal and Social Psychology, 67,* 371–378.

Milgram, S. (1974). *Obedience to authority.* New York: Harper & Row.

Miller, D. B. (1977). Roles of naturalistic observation in comparative psychology. *American Psychologist, 32,* 211–219.

Miller, D. T., & Ross, M. (1975). Self-serving biases in the attribution of causality: Fact or fiction? *Psychological Bulletin, 82,* 213–225.

Miller, G. (2000). *The mating mind: How sexual choice shaped the evolution of human nature.* New York: Doubleday.

Miller, G. A. (1956). The magical number seven plus or minus two: Some limits on our capacity for processing information. *Psychological Review, 63,* 81–97.

Miller, G. A., Galanter, E., & Pribram, K. H. (1960). *Plans and the structure of behavior.* New York: Holt.

Miller, G. E., Cohen S., & Herbert, T. B. (1999). Pathways linking major depression and immunity in ambulatory female patients. *Psychosomatic Medicine, 61,* 850–860.

Miller, G. E., Stetler, C. A., Carney, R. M., Freeland, K. E., & Banks, W. A. (2002). Clinical depression and inflammatory risk markers for coronary heart disease. *American Journal of Cardiology, 90,* 1279–1283.

Miller, G. F. (1998). How mate choice shaped human nature: A review of sexual selection and human evolution. In C. Crawford & D. Krebs (Eds.), *Handbook of evolutionary psychology* (pp. 87–129). Mahwah, NJ: Erlbaum.

Miller, J. G. (1994). Cultural diversity in the morality of caring: Individually oriented versus duty-based interpersonal moral codes. *Cross-cultural Research: The Journal of Comparative Social Science, 28,* 3–39.

Miller, L. T., & Vernon, P. A. (1996). Intelligence, reaction time, and working memory in 4- to 6-year-old children. *Intelligence, 22,* 155–190.

Miller, L. T., & Vernon, P. A. (1997). Developmental changes in speed of information processing in young children. *Developmental Psychology, 22,* 549–554.

Miller, M. A., & Rahe, R. H. (1997). Life changes scaling for the 1990s. *Journal of Psychosomatic Research, 43,* 279–292.

Miller, N. E. (1985). The value of behavioral research on animals. *American Psychologist, 40,* 423–440.

Miller, N. E. (1991). Commentary on Ulrich: Need to check truthfulness of statements by opponents of animal research. *Psychological Science, 2,* 422–424.

Miller, S. D. (1989). Optical differences in cases of multiple personality disorder. *Journal of Nervous and Mental Disease, 177,* 480–486.

Miller, T. W. (1993). The assessment of stressful life events. In L. Goldberger & S. Breznitz (Eds.), *Handbook of stress: Theoretical and clinical aspects* (2nd ed.). New York: Free Press.

Miller, W. R., Taylor, C. A., & West, J. C. (1980). Focused versus broad-spectrum behavior therapy for problem drinkers. *Journal of Consulting and Clinical Psychology, 48,* 590–601.

Millsaps, C. L., Azrin, R. L., & Mittenberg, W. (1994). Neuropsychological effects of chronic cannabis use on the memory and intelligence of adolescents. *Journal of Child and Adolescent Substance Abuse, 3,* 47–55.

Milner, A. D., & Rugg, M. D. (Eds.) (1992). *The neuropsychology of consciousness.* London: Academic Press.

Milner, B. (1966). Amnesia following operation on the temporal lobes. In C. W. M. Whitty & O. L. Zangwill (Eds.), *Amnesia.* London: Butterworths.

Milner, B., Corkin, S., & Teuber, H. L. (1968). Further analysis of the hippocampal amnesic syndrome: 14-year follow-up study of H. M. *Neuropsychologia 6,* 215–234.

Mineka, S. (1987). A primate model of phobic fears. In H. Eysenck & I. Martin (Eds.), *Theoretical foundations of behavior therapy.* New York: Plenum.

Mirmiran, M., van Soneren, E. J. W., & Swaab, D. F. (1996). Is brain plasticity preserved during aging and in Alzheimer's disease? *Behavioral Brain Research, 78,* 43–48.

Mischel, W. (1968). *Personality and assessment.* New York: Wiley.

Mischel, W., & Peake, P. K. (1982). Beyond déjà vu in the search for cross-situational consistency. *Psychological Review, 89,* 730–755.

Mischel, W., & Shoda, Y. (1995). A cognitive-affective system theory of personality: Reconceptualizing situations, dispositions, dynamics, and invariance in personality structure. *Psychological Review, 102,* 246–268.

Mischel, W., & Shoda, Y. (1998). Reconciling processing dynamics and personality dispositions. *Annual Review of Psychology, 49,* 229–258.

Mix, J. A., & Crews, W. D. J. R. (2002). A double-blind, placebo-controlled, randomized trial of Ginkgo biloba extract EGb 761(R) in a sample of cognitively intact older adults: Neuropsychological findings. *Human Psychopharmacology Clinical and Experimental, 3,* 267–277.

Molden, D. C., & Dweck, C. S. (2000). Meaning and motivation. In C. Sansone & J. M. Harackiewicz (Eds.), *Intrinsic and extrinsic motivation: The search for optimal motivation and performance.* San Diego: Academic Press.

Moldin, S. Q., & Gottesman, I. I. (1997). Genes, experience, and chance in schizophrenia—Positioning for the 21st century. *Schizophrenia Bulletin, 23,* 547–561.

Moncrieff, J. (1997). Lithium: Evidence reconsidered. *British Journal of Psychiatry, 171,* 113–119.

Mondor, T. A., Zatorre, R. J., & Terrio, N. A. (1998). Constraints on the selection of auditory information. *Journal of Experimental Psychology: Human Perception and Performance, 24,* 66–79.

Mongrain, M. (1998). Parental representations and support-seeking behaviors related to dependency and self-criticism. *Journal of Personality, 66,* 151–173.

Mook, D. G. (1995). *Motivation: The organization of action* (2nd ed.). New York: Norton.

Moore, T. E. (1995). Subliminal self-help auditory tapes: An empirical test of perceptual consequences. *Canadian Journal of Behavioural Science, 27,* 9–20.

Moray, N. (1959). Attention in dichotic listening: Affective cues and the influence of instructions. *Quarterly Journal of Experimental Psychology, 11,* 56–60.

Moray, N., Bates, A., & Barnett, T. (1965). Experiments on the four-eared man. *Journal of the Acoustical Society of America, 38,* 196–201.

Moret, V., Forster, A., Laverriere, M. C., & Lambert, H. (1991). Mechanism of analgesia induced by hypnosis and acupuncture: Is there a difference? *Pain, 45,* 135–140.

Moretti, M. M., Rein, A. S., & Wiebe, V. J. (1998). Relational self-regulation: Gender differences in risk for dysphoria. *Canadian Journal of Behavioural Science, 30* (4), 243–252.

Moretti, M. M., Segal, Z. V., McCann, C. D., & Shaw, B. F. (1996). Self-referent versus other-referent information processing in dysphoric, clinically depressed, and remitted depressed subjects. *Personality and Social Psychology Bulletin, 22,* 68–80.

Morf, C. C., & Rhodewalt, F. (2001). Unraveling the paradoxes of narcissism: A dynamic self-regulatory processing model. *Psychological Inquiry, 12,* 177–196.

Morris, C. D., Bransford, J. D., & Franks, J. J. (1977). Levels of processing versus transfer appropriate processing. *Journal of Verbal Learning and Verbal Behavior, 16,* 519–533.

Morrongiello, B. A., Fenwick, K. D., Hillier, L., & Chance, G. (1994). Sound localization in newborn human infants. *Developmental Psychobiology, 27,* 519–538.

Moscovici, S., & Zavalloni, M. (1969). The group as a polarizer of attitudes. *Journal of Personality and Social Psychology, 12,* 125–135.

Moskowitz, D. S. (1994). Cross-situational generality and the interpersonal circumplex. *Journal of Personality and Social Psychology, 66,* 921–933.

Moskowitz, H. (1985). Marihuana and driving. *Accident Analysis and Prevention, 17,* 323–345.

Moulton, P. L., Boyko, L. N., Fitzpatrick, J. L., & Petros, T. V. (2001). The effect of Ginkgo biloba on memory in healthy male volunteers. *Physiology and Behavior,* 659–665.

Mozell, M. M., Smith, B., Smith, P., Sullivan, R., & Swender, P. (1969). Nasal chemoreception in flavor identification. *Archives of Otolaryngology, 90,* 367–373.

Mueller, C. M., & Dweck, C. S. (1998). Praise for intelligence can undermine children's motivation and performance. *Journal of Personality and Social Psychology, 75,* 33–52.

Muir, D. (1999). Theories and methods in development psychology. In A. Slater & D. Muir (Eds.), *The Blackwell reader in development psychology* (pp. 3–16). Malden, MA: Blackwell.

Muir, D., & Slater, A. (Eds.) (2000). *Infant development: The essential readings.* Malden, MA: Blackwell.

Muir, D., Hains, S. M. J., & Symons, L. A. (1994). Baby and me: Infants need minds to read. *Current Psychology of Cognition, 13,* 669–682.

Mullen, M. (1994). Earliest recollection of childhood: A demographic analysis. *Cognition, 52,* 55–79.

Mumby, D. G., Glenn, M. J., Nesbitt, C., & Kyriazis, D. A. (2002). Dissociation in retrograde memory for object discriminations and object recognition in rats with perirhinal cortex damage. *Behavioural Brain Research, 132,* 215–226.

Munakata, Y., McClelland, J. L., Johnson, M. H., & Siegler, R. S. (1997). Rethinking infant knowledge: Toward an adaptive process account of successes and failures in object permanence tasks. *Psychological Review, 104,* 686–713.

Murdock, B. B. (1995). Primacy and recency in the chunking model. In C. A. Weaver, III, & S. Mannes (Eds.), *Discourse comprehension: Essays in honor of Walter Kintsch* (pp. 49–63). Hillsdale, NJ: Erlbaum.

Murdock, B. B., Jr. (1960). The distinctiveness of stimuli. *Psychological Review, 67,* 16–31.

Murnen, S. K., & Stockton, M. (1997). Gender and self-reported sexual arousal in response to sexual stimuli: A meta-analytic review. *Sex Roles, 37,* 135–153.

Murphy, G. L., & Lassaline, M. E. (1997). Hierarchical structure in concepts and the basic level of categorization. In K. Lamberts & D. R. Shanks (Eds.), *Knowledge, concepts and categories: Studies in cognition.* Cambridge, MA: MIT Press.

Murray, H. A. (1938). *Explorations in personality.* New York: Oxford University Press.

Musselman, D. L., Evans, D. L., & Nemeroff, C. B. (1998). The relationship of depression to cardiovascular disease: Epidemiology, biology, and treatment. *Archives of General Psychiatry, 55,* 580–592.

Muter, P. (1980). Very rapid forgetting. *Memory and Cognition, 8,* 174–179.

Myers, D. G. (1982). Polarizing effects of social interaction. In H. Brandstatter, J. H. Davis, & G. Stocker-Kreichgauer (Eds.), *Group decision making.* New York: Academic Press.

Myers, D. G., & Diener, E. (1995). Who is happy? *Psychological Science, 6,* 10–19.

Myers, T. C., Wittrock, D. A., & Foreman, G. W. (1998). Appraisal of subjective stress in individuals with tension-type headache: The influence of baseline measures. *Journal of Behavioral Medicine, 21,* 469–484.

Nadon, R., Hoyt, I. P., Register, P. A., & Kihlstrom, J. F. (1991). Absorption and hypnotizability: Context effects reexamined. *Journal of Personality and Social Psychology, 60,* 144–153.

Nagar, D., & Panady, J. (1987). Affect and performance on cognitive tasks as a function of crowding and noise. *Journal of Applied Social Psychology, 17,* 147–157.

Nairne, J. S. (1990). A feature model of immediate memory. *Memory and Cognition, 18,* 251–269.

Nairne, J. S. (2002). Remembering over the short term: The case against the standard model. *Annual Review of Psychology, 53,* 53–81.

Nairne, J. S., & Rescorla, R. A. (1981). Second-order conditioning with diffuse auditory reinforcers in the pigeon. *Learning and Motivation, 12,* 65–91.

Naveh-Benjamin, M., & Ayres, T. J. (1986). Digit span, reading rate, and linguistic relativity. *Quarterly Journal of Experimental Psychology, 38A,* 739–751.

Neath, I. (1993). Distinctiveness and serial position effects in recognition. *Memory and Cognition, 21,* 689–698.

Neath, I. (1998). *Human memory: An introduction to research, data, and theory.* Pacific Grove, CA: Brooks/Cole.

Needham, D. R., & Begg, I. M. (1991). Problem-oriented training promotes spontaneous analogical transfer: Memory-oriented training promotes memory for training. *Memory and Cognition, 19,* 543–557.

Neese, R. M., & Williams, G. C. (1996). *Why we get sick: The new science of Darwinian medicine.* Toronto, ON: Random House.

Neisser, U. (1967). *Cognitive psychology.* New York: Appleton-Century-Crofts.

Neisser, U. (1978). Memory: What are the important questions? In M. M. Gruneberg, P. E. Morris, & R. N. Sykes (Eds.), *Practical aspects of memory.* London: Academic Press.

Neisser, U. (Ed.) (1998). *The rising curve: Long-term gains in IQ and related measures.* Washington, DC: American Psychological Association.

Neisser, U., & Harsch, N. (1992). Phantom flashbulbs: False recollections of hearing the news about Challenger. In E. Winograd & U. Neisser (Eds.), *Affect and accuracy in recall: Studies of "flashbulb memories."* Cambridge: Cambridge University Press.

Neisser, U., & Hyman, I. E., Jr. (Eds.) (1999). *Memory observed: Remembering in natural contexts* (2nd ed.). New York: Worth.

Nelson, K. (1973). Structure and strategy in learning to talk. *Monographs of the Society for Research in Child Development, 38* (Serial No. 149).

Nelson, K., & Shaw, L. K. (2002). Developing a socially shared symbolic system. In E. Amsel and J. P. Byrnes (Eds.), *Language, literacy, and cognitive development: The development and consequences of symbolic communication* (pp. 27–57). Mahwah, NJ: Erlbaum.

Newcomb, A. F., & Bagwell, C. L. (1995). Children's friendship relations: A meta-analytic review. *Psychological Bulletin, 117,* 306–347.

Newcombe, N. E., Drummey, A. B., Fox, N. A., Lie, E., & Ottinger-Alberts, W. (2000). Remembering early childhood: How much, how, and why (or why not)? *Current Directions in Psychological Science, 9,* 55–58.

Newell, A., & Simon, H. A. (1972). *Human problem solving.* Englewood Cliffs, NJ: Prentice-Hall.

Nguyen, P. V. (2001). Tracking the cortical signals that mediate visual awareness. *Trends in Neurosciences, 24,* 371–372.

Nichols, D. S., & Greene, R. L. (1997). Dimensions of deception in personality assessment: The example of the MMPI-2. *Journal of Personality Assessment, 68,* 251–266.

Nickerson, R. S. (1999). How we know—and sometimes misjudge—what others know: Imputing one's own knowledge to others. *Psychological Bulletin, 125,* 737–759.

Nickerson, R. S., & Adams, M. J. (1979). Long-term memory for a common object. *Cognitive Psychology, 11,* 287–307.

Nicolaus, L. K., & Nellis, D. W. (1987). The first evaluation of the use of conditioned taste aversion to control predation by mongooses upon eggs. *Applied Animal Behaviour Science, 17,* 329–346.

Nielsen, T. A., & Powell, R. A. (1992). The day-residue and dream-lag effects: A literature review and limited replication of two temporal effects in dream formation. *Dreaming: Journal of the Association for the Study of Dreams, 2,* 67–77.

Nisbett, R. E. (Ed.) (1993). *Rules for reasoning.* Hillsdale, NJ: Erlbaum.

Nisbett, R. E., & Wilson, T. D. (1977). Telling more than we can know: Verbal reports on mental processes. *Psychological Review, 84,* 231–259.

Nobel, K. D., Robinson, N. M., & Gunderson, S. A. (1993). All rivers lead to the sea: A follow-up study of gifted young adults. *Roeper Review, 15,* 124–130.

Nolan, C. C., Gray-Donald, K., Shatenstein, B., & O'Loughlin, J. (1995). Dietary patterns leading to high fat intake. *Canadian Journal of Public Health, 86,* 389–391.

Norenzayan, A., & Nisbett, R. E. (2000). Culture and causal cognition. *Current Directions in Psychological Science, 9,* 132–135.

Norenzayan, A., Choi, I., & Nisbett, R. E. (2002). Cultural similarities and differences in social inference: Evidence from behavioral predictions and lay theories of behavior. *Personality and Social Psychology Bulletin, 28,* 109–120.

Norton, G. R., Cox, B. J., Hewitt, P. L., & McLeod, L. (1997). Personality factors associated with generalized and non-generalized social anxiety. *Personality and Individual Differences, 22,* 655–660.

Nosofsky, R. M. (1992). Exemplar-based approach to relating categorization, identification, and recognition. In G. F. Ashby (Ed.), *Multidimensional models of perception and cognition* (Scientific Psychology Series) (pp. 363–393). Hillsdale, NJ: Erlbaum.

Novick, L. R. (1988). Analogical transfer, problem similarity, and expertise. *Journal of Experimental Psychology: Learning, Memory, and Cognition, 14,* 510–520.

Nowakowski, R. S. (1987). Basic concepts of CNS development. *Child Development, 58,* 568–595.

Oakes, J. (1985). *Keeping track: How schools structure inequality.* New Haven, CT: Yale University Press.

O'Donnell, P., & Grace, A. (1998). Dysfunctions in multiple interrelated systems as the neurobiological bases of schizophrenic symptom clusters. *Schizophrenia Bulletin, 24,* 267–283.

Oezgen, E., & Davies, I. R. L. (2002). Acquisition of categorical color perception: A perceptual learning approach to the linguistic relativity hypothesis. *Journal of Experimental Psychology: General, 131,* 477–493.

Offer, D., & Schonert-Reichl, K. A. (1992). Debunking the myths of adolescence. *Journal of the American Academy of Child and Adolescent Psychiatry, 31,* 1003–1013.

Offord, D. R., Boyle, M. H., Campbell, D., Goering, P., Lin, E., Wong, M., & Racine, Y. A. (1996). One-year prevalence of psychiatric disorder in Ontarians 15 to 64 years of age. *Canadian Journal of Psychiatry, 41* (9), 559–563.

Ogden, J. A., & Corkin, S. (1991). Memories of HM. In W. C. Abraham, M. C. Corballis, & K. G. White (Eds.), *Memory mechanisms: A tribute to G. V. Goddard.* Hillsdale, NJ: Erlbaum.

Ogloff, J. R. P., & Pfeifer, J. E. (1992). Cults and the law: A discussion of the legality of alleged cult activities. *Behavioral Sciences and the Law, 10,* 117–140.

Ogloff, J. R. P., Roberts, C. F., & Roesch, R. (1993). The insanity defense: Legal standards and clinical assessment. *Applied and Preventive Psychology, 2,* 163–178.

Okada, F., Okajima, K., & Tokumitsu, Y. (1998). Contradirect effects on neuronal activity in treating depression. *Human Psychopharmacology, 13,* 455–456.

Oldani, R. (1997). Causes of increases in achievement motivation: Is the personality affected by parental environment? *Personality and Individual Differences, 22,* 403–410.

Olds, J., & Milner, P. (1954). Positive reinforcement produced by electrical stimulation of the septal area and other regions of the rat brain. *Journal of Comparative and Physiological Psychology, 47,* 419–427.

Olson, J. M., & Zanna, M. P. (1987). Understanding and promoting exercise: A social psychological perspective. *Canadian Journal of Public Health, 78,* S1–S7.

Olson, J. M., & Zanna, M. P. (1993). Attitudes and attitude change. *Annual Review of Psychology, 44,* 117–154.

O'Mahony, M. (1978). Smell illusions and suggestion: Reports of smells contingent on tones played on television and radio. *Chemical Senses and Flavor, 3,* 183–187.

Orne, M. T. (1959). The nature of hypnosis: Artifact and essence. *Journal of Abnormal and Social Psychology, 58,* 277–299.

Orne, M. T. (1969). Demand characteristics and the concept of quasi-controls. In R. Rosenthal & R. L. Rosnow (Eds.), *Artifact in behavioral research.* New York: Academic Press.

Ortmann, A., & Hertwig, R. (1997). Is deception acceptable? *American Psychologist, 52,* 746–747.

Ortony, A., & Turner, T. J. (1990). What's basic about basic emotions? *Psychological Review, 97,* 315–331.

Oscar-Berman, M., Shagrin, B., Evert, D. L., & Epstein, C. (1997). Impairments of brain and behavior: The neurological effects of alcohol. *Alcohol Health and Research World, 21,* 65–75.

O'Shea, B. (2001). Post-traumatic stress disorder: A review for the general psychiatrist. *International Journal of Psychiatry in Clinical Practice, 5,* 11–18.

Ostbye, T., Pomerleau, J., White, M., Coolich, M., & McWhinney, J. (1993). Food and nutrition in Canadian "prime time" television commercials. *Canadian Journal of Public Health, 84,* 370–374.

Otto, M. W., Demopulos, C. M., McLean, N. E., Pollack, M. H., & Fava, M. (1998). Additional findings on the association between anxiety sensitivity and hypochondriacal concerns: Examination of patients with major depression. *Journal of Anxiety Disorders, 12,* 225–232.

Pagano, R. R. (1998). *Understanding statistics in the behavioral sciences* (5th ed.). St. Paul, MN: Brooks/Cole.

Pahl, J. J., Swayze, V. W., & Andreasen, N. C. (1990). Diagnostic advances in anatomical and functional brain imaging in schizophrenia. In A. Kales, C. N. Stefanis, & J. A.

Talbott (Eds.), *Recent advances in schizophrenia.* New York: Springer-Verlag.

Paivio, A. (1995). Imagery and memory. In M. S. Gazzaniga (Ed.), *The cognitive neurosciences* (pp. 977–986). Cambridge, MA: MIT Press.

Pappas, B. A., Bayley, P. J., Bui, B. K., Hansen, L. A., & Thal, L. J. (2000). Choline acetyltransferase activity and cognitive domain scores of Alzheimer's patients. *Neurobiology of Aging, 21,* 11–17.

Park, N. W., Moscovitch, M., & Robertson, I. H. (1999). Divided attention impairments after traumatic brain injury. *Neuropsychologia, 37,* 1119–1133.

Parker, J. D. A. (Ed.) (2000). *Emotional intelligence: Clinical and therapeutic implications. The handbook of emotional intelligence.* New York: John Wiley/Jossey-Bass.

Parkes, J. D., & Block, C. (1989). Genetic factors in sleep disorders. *Journal of Neurology, Neurosurgery, and Psychiatry, 52,* 101–108.

Parkin, A. J., & Java, R. (2001). Determinants of age-related memory loss. In T. J. Perfect & E. I. Maylor (Eds.), *Models of cognitive aging.* New York: Oxford University Press.

Parmelee, A. H., & Sigman, M. D. (1983). Perinatal brain development and behavior. In M. M. Haith & J. J. Campos (Eds.), *Handbook of child psychology: Infancy and developmental psychobiology.* New York: Wiley.

Pashler, H. (1992). Attentional limitations in doing two tasks at the same time. *Current Directions in Psychological Science, 1,* 44–48.

Pashler, H. (1998). *The psychology of attention.* Cambridge, MA: MIT Press.

Pasveer, K. A., & Ellard, J. H. (1998). The making of a personality inventory: Help from the WWW. *Behavior Research Methods, Instruments, and Computers, 30,* 309–313.

Patterson, F. G. (1978). The gesture of a gorilla: Language acquisition in another pongid. *Brain and Language, 5,* 72–97.

Paul, G. L., & Lentz, R. J. (1977). *Psychosocial treatment of chronic mental patients: Milieu versus social learning programs.* Cambridge, MA: Harvard University Press.

Paulhus, D. L. (1998). Interpersonal and intrapsychic adaptiveness of trait self-enhancement: A mixed blessing? *Journal of Personality and Social Psychology, 74,* 1197–1208.

Paulhus, D. L., & John, O. P. (1998). Egoistic and moralistic bias in self-perceptions: The interplay of self-deceptive styles with basic traits and motives. *Journal of Personality, 66,* 1024–1060.

Paulhus, D. L., & Morgan, K. (1997). Perceptions of intelligence in leaderless groups: Dynamic effects of shyness and acquaintance. *Journal of Personality and Social Psychology, 72,* 581–591.

Paulhus, D. L., & Reid, D. B. (1991). Enhancement and denial in socially desirable responding. *Journal of Personality and Social Psychology, 60,* 307–317.

Paulhus, D. L., & Reynolds, S. R. (1995). Enhancing target variance in personality impressions: Highlighting the person in person perception. *Journal of Personality and Social Psychology, 69,* 344–354.

Paulhus, D. L., & Trapnell, P. D. (1998). Typological measures of shyness: Additive, interactive, and categorical. *Journal of Research in Personality, 32,* 183–201.

Paulhus, D. L., Lysy, D., & Yik, M. S. M. (1998). Self-report measures of intelligence: Are they useful as proxy measures of IQ? *Journal of Personality, 66,* 525–554.

Paulhus, D. L., Wehr, P., Harms, P. D., & Strasser, D. I. (2002). Use of exemplar surveys to reveal implicit theories of intelligence. *Personality and Social Psychology Bulletin, 28,* 1051–1062.

Paulhus, D. L., Wehr, P., Harms, P. D., & Strasser, D. I. (2002). Use of exemplar surveys to reveal implicit theories of intelligence. *Personality and Social Psychology Bulletin, 28,* 1051–1062.

Paulus, P. B. (1988). *Prison crowding: A psychological perspective.* New York: Springer.

Paunonen, S. V. (1998). Hierarchical organization of personality and prediction of behavior. *Journal of Personality and Social Psychology, 74,* 538–556.

Paunonen, S. V., Jackson, D. N., & Keinonen, M. (1990). The structured nonverbal assessment of personality. *Journal of Personality, 58,* 481–501.

Paunonen, S. V., Zeidner, M., Engvik, H. A., Oosterveld, P., & Maliphant, R. (2000). The nonverbal assessment of personality in five cultures. *Journal of Cross Cultural Psychology, 31,* 220–239.

Pedersen, J. B. (1998). Sexuality and aging. In I. H. Nordhus & G. R. VandenBos (Eds.), *Clinical geropsychology.* Washington, DC: American Psychological Association.

Pelham, B. W. (1999). *Conducting experiments in psychology: Measuring the weight of smoke.* Pacific Grove, CA: Brooks/Cole.

Pendergrast, M. (1996). *Victims of memory: Sex, abuse, accusations and shattered lives* (2nd ed.). Hinesburg, VT: Upper Access Books.

Penfield, W., & Boldrey, E. (1958). Somatic motor and sensory representation in the cerebral cortex as studied by electrical stimulation. *Brain, 60,* 389–443.

Penfield, W., & Perot, P. (1963). The brain's record of auditory and visual experience. *Brain, 86,* 595–696.

Pennebaker, J. W. (1990). *Opening up: The healing power of confiding in others.* New York: Morrow.

Pennebaker, J. W., Zech, E., & Rime, B. (2001). Disclosing and sharing emotion: Psychological, social, and health consequences. In M. S. Stoebe & R. O. Hansson (Eds.), *Handbook of bereavement research: Consequences, coping, and care.* Washington, DC: American Psychological Association.

Pepler, D., Craig, W. M., & O'Connell, P. (1999). Understanding bullying from a dynamic systems perspective. In A. Slater & D. Muir (Eds.), *The Blackwell reader in development psychology* (pp. 440–451). Malden, MA: Blackwell.

Perls, F. S. (1969). *Gestalt therapy verbatim.* Moab, UT: Real People Press.

Perls, F. S., Hefferline, R. F., & Goodman, P. (1951). *Gestalt therapy.* New York: Julian.

Perrett, D. I., & Mistlin, A. M. (1987). Visual neurones responsive to faces. *Trends in Neuroscience, 10,* 358–364.

Perry, W. (1970). *Forms of intellectual and ethical development in the college years.* New York: Holt, Rinehart & Winston.

Pert, C. B., & Snyder, S. H. (1973). The opiate receptor: Demonstration in nervous tissue. *Science, 179,* 1011–1014.

Peters, R. DeV., & McMahon, R. J. (Eds.) (1996). *Preventing childhood disorders, substance abuse and delinquency.* Thousand Oaks, CA: Sage.

Peterson, A. C. (1988). Adolescent development. *Annual Review of Psychology, 39,* 583–607.

Peterson, C., & Seligman, M. E. P. (1987). Explanatory style and illness. *Journal of Personality, 55,* 237–265.

Peterson, C., Seligman, M. E. P., & Vaillant, G. E. (1988). Pessimistic explanatory style is a risk factor for physical illness: A thirty-five-year longitudinal study. *Journal of Personality and Social Psychology, 55,* 23–27.

Peterson, L. R., & Peterson, M. J. (1959). Short-term retention of individual items. *Journal of Experimental Psychology, 58,* 193–198.

Petitto, L. A. (2000). The acquisition of natural signed languages: Lessons in the nature of human language and its biological foundations. In C. Chamberlain, J. P. Morford, & R.

Mayberry (Eds.), *Language acquisition by eye* (pp. 41–50). Mahwah, NJ: Erlbaum.

Petty, R. E., DeSteno, D., & Rucker, D. D. (2001). The role of affect in attitude change. In J. P. Forgas (Ed.), *Handbook of affect and social cognition.* Mahwah, NJ: Lawrence Erlbaum Associates.

Petty, R. E., Wegener, D. T., & Fabrigar, L. R. (1997). Attitudes and attitude change. *Annual Review of Psychology, 48,* 609–647.

Pfeifer, J. E. (1996). Social psychology in the courtroom. In S. W. Sadava & D. R. McCreary (Eds.), *Applied social psychology.* Upper Saddle River, NJ: Prentice Hall.

Pfeiffer, S. I. (2001). Emotional intelligence: Popular but evasive construct. *Roeper Review, 23,* 138–142.

Phelps, E. A., & Anderson, A. K. (1997). Emotional memory: What does the amygdala do? *Current Biology, 7,* 311–314.

Phelps, E. A., O'Connor, K. J., Cunningham, W. A., Funayama, E. S., Gatenby, J. C., Gore, J. C., & Banaji, M. R. (2000). Performance on indirect measures of race evaluation predicts amygdala activation. *Journal of Cognitive Neuroscience, 12,* 729–738.

Piaget, J. (1929). *The child's conception of the world.* New York: Harcourt Brace.

Piaget, J. (1952). *The origins of intelligence in children.* New York: International Universities Press.

Piaget, J. (1970). Piaget's theory. In P. H. Mussen (Ed.), *Carmichael's manual of child psychology.* New York: Wiley.

Piasecki, T. M., Fiore, M. C., & Baker, T. B. (1998). Profiles in discouragement: Two studies of variability in the time course of smoking withdrawal symptoms. *Journal of Abnormal Psychology, 107,* 238–251.

Pickles, J. O. (1988). *An introduction to the physiology of hearing* (2nd ed.). London: Academic Press.

Pierce, T. W., Madden, D. J., Siegel, W. C., & Blumenthal, J. A. (1993). Effects of aerobic exercise on cognitive and psychosocial functioning in patients with mild hypertension. *Health Psychology, 12,* 286–291.

Pinel, J. P. J. (1997). *Biopsychology* (3rd ed.). Boston, MA: Allyn & Bacon.

Pinel, J. P. J., & Edwards, M. E. (1997). *A colorful introduction to the anatomy of the human brain: A brain and psychology coloring book.* Needham Heights, MA: Allyn & Bacon.

Pinel, J. P. J., & Treit, D. (1979). Conditioned defensive burying in rats: Availability of burying materials. *Animal Learning and Behavior, 7,* 392–396.

Pines, A. (1993). Burnout. In L. Goldberger & S. Breznitz (Eds.), *Handbook of stress: Theoretical and clinical aspects* (2nd ed.). New York: Free Press.

Pines, A., & Aronson, E. (1988). *Career burnout: Causes and cures* (2nd ed.). New York: Free Press.

Pinker, S. (1994). *The language instinct.* New York: HarperCollins.

Pinker, S. (1997a). *How the mind works.* New York: Norton.

Pinker, S. (1997b). Language as a psychological adaptation. In G. R. Bock & G. Cardew (Eds.), *Characterizing human psychological adaptations.* New York: John Wiley.

Pinker, S. (2002). *The blank slate.* New York: Viking-Penguin.

Pinker, S., & Bloom, P. (1992). Natural language and natural selection. In J. H. Barkow & L. Cosmides (Eds.), *The adapted mind: Evolutionary psychology and the generation of culture* (pp. 451–493). New York: Oxford University Press.

Piper, A., Jr. (1997). *Hoax and reality: The bizarre world of multiple personality disorder.* Northvale, NJ: Jason Aronson.

Pittenger, D. J. (1996). Reconsidering the over-justification effect: A guide to critical resources. *Teaching of Psychology, 23,* 234–236.

Plomin, R., Fulker, D. W., Corley, R., & DeFries, J. C. (1997). Nature, nurture, and cognitive development from 1 to 16 years: A parent-offspring adoption study. *Psychological Science, 8,* 442–447.

Plomin, R., Corley, R., Caspi, A., Fulker, D. W., & DeFries, J. (1998). Adoption results for self-reported personality: Evidence for non-additive genetic effects? *Journal of Personality and Social Psychology, 75,* 211–218.

Plous, S. (1991). An attitude survey of animal rights activists. *Psychological Science, 2,* 194–196.

Poole, D. A., & Lindsay, D. S. (2002). Reducing child witnesses' false reports of misinformation from parents. *Journal of Experimental Child Psychology, 81,* 117–140.

Poole, D. A., Lindsay, D. S., Memon, A., & Bull, R. (1995). Psychotherapy and the recovery of memories of childhood sexual abuse: U.S. and British practitioners' opinions, practices, and experiences. *Journal of Consulting and Clinical Psychology, 63,* 426–437.

Poole, G. D., & Craig, K. D. (1992). Judgments of genuine, suppressed and faked facial expressions of pain. *Journal of Personality and Social Psychology, 63,* 797–805.

Poole, G. D., Matheson, D. H., & Cox, D. (2000). *The psychology of health and health care: A Canadian perspective.* Toronto, ON: Prentice Hall.

Pope, H. G., Gruber, A. J., Hudson, J. I., Huestis, M. A., & Yurgelun-Todd, D. (2001). Neuropsychological performance in long-term cannabis users. *Archives of General Psychiatry, 58,* 909–915.

Pope, K. S. (1996). Memory, abuse, and science: Questioning claims about the False Memory Syndrome epidemic. *American Psychologist, 51,* 957–974.

Porter, R. H., Makin, J. W., Davis, L. B., & Christensen, K. M. (1992). Breast-fed infants respond to olfactory cues from their own mother and unfamiliar lactating females. *Infant Behavior and Development, 15,* 85–93.

Posner, M. I., & Rothbart, M. K. (1992). Attentional mechanisms and conscious experience. In A. D. Milner & M. D. Rugg (Eds.), *The neuropsychology of consciousness.* London: Academic Press.

Postmes, T., & Spears, R. (1998). Deindividuation and antinormative behavior: A meta-analysis. *Psychological Bulletin, 123,* 238–259.

Potter, W. Z., & Manji, H. K. (1993). Are monoamine metabolites in cerebral spinal fluid worth measuring? *Archives of General Psychiatry, 50,* 653–656.

Pratkanis, A. R., & Greenwald, A. G. (1989). A sociocognitive model of attitude structure and function. *Advances in Experimental Social Psychology, 22,* 245–285.

Pratt, G. J., Wood, D., & Alman, B. M. (1988). *A clinical hypnosis primer.* New York: Wiley.

Preece, M., & DeLongis, A. (in press). Stress, coping, and social support processes in step-families. In T. A. Revenson & K. Kayser (Eds.), *Coping among couples.* Washington, DC: American Psychological Association Press.

Preilowski, B. (1975). Bilateral motor interaction: Perceptual-motor performance of partial and complete split-brain patients. In K. J. Zulch, O. Creutzfeldt, & G. C. Galbraith (Eds.), *Cerebral localization.* New York: Springer-Verlag.

Premack, D. (1962). Reversibility of the reinforcement relation. *Science, 136,* 255–257.

Premack, D. (1976). *Intelligence in ape and man.* Hillsdale, NJ: Erlbaum.

Proctor, R. W., & Van Zandt, T. (1994). *Human factors in simple and complex designs.* Boston: Allyn & Bacon.

Profet, M. (1988). The evolution of pregnancy sickness as protection to the embryo against Pleistocene teratogens. *Evolutionary Theory, 8,* 177–190.

Profet, M. (1992). Pregnancy sickness as adaptation. In J. H. Barkow, L. Cosmides, & J. Tooby (Eds.), *The adapted mind: Evolutionary psychology and the generation of culture.* New York: Oxford University Press.

Prud'homme, M. J. L., Cohen, D., & Kalaska, J. F. (1994). Tactile activity in primate somatosensory cortex during active arm movements: Cytoarchitectonic distribution. *Journal of Neurophysiology, 71,* 173–181.

Prudic, J., Sackeim, H. A., & Devanand, D. P. (1990). Medication resistance and clinical response to electroconvulsive therapy. *Psychiatry Research, 31,* 287–296.

Putnam, F. W., Guroff, J. J., Silberman, E. K., Barban, L., & Post, R. M. (1986). The clinical phenomenology of multiple personality disorder: Review of 100 recent cases. *Journal of Clinical Psychiatry, 47,* 285–293.

Quinsey, V. L. (1995). The prediction and explanation of criminal violence. *International Journal of Law and Psychiatry, 18,* 117–127.

Quinsey, V. L., Harris, G. T., Rice, M. E., & Cormier, C. (1998). *Violent offenders: Appraising and managing risk.* Washington, DC: American Psychological Association.

Quirion, R. (1993). Cholinergic markers in Alzheimer's disease and the autoregulation of acetylcholine release. *Journal of Psychiatry and Neuroscience, 18,* 226–234.

Rachman, S. J. (1990). *Fear and courage.* New York: Freeman.

Raichle, M. E. (1994). Visualizing the mind. *Scientific American, 270,* 58–64.

Raij, T. (1999). Patterns of brain activity during visual imagery of letters. *Journal of Cognitive Neuroscience, 11,* 282–299.

Rakic, P. (1991). Plasticity of cortical development. In S. E. Brauth, W. S. Hall, & R. J. Dooling (Eds.), *Plasticity of development.* Cambridge, MA: Bradford/MIT Press.

Ralph, M. R., Foster, R. G., Davis, F. C., & Menaker, M. (1990). Transplanted suprachiasmatic nucleus determines circadian period. *Science, 247,* 975–978.

Ramachandran, V. S. (1992). Filling in gaps in perception: I. *Current Directions in Psychological Science, 1,* 199–205.

Raskin, S. A., & Mateer, C. A. (Eds.) (2000). *Neuropsychological management of mild traumatic brain injury.* London: Oxford University Press.

Ratnasuriya, R. H., Eisler, I., Szmuhter, G. I., & Russell, G. F. (1991). Anorexia nervosa: Outcome and prognostic factors after 20 years. *British Journal of Psychiatry, 158,* 495–502.

Raugh, M. R., & Atkinson, R. C. (1975). A mnemonic method for learning a second-language vocabulary. *Journal of Educational Psychology, 67,* 1–16.

Raven, J. C., Court, J. H., & Raven, J. (1985). *A manual for Raven's progressive matrices and vocabulary scales.* London: H. K. Lewis.

Rea, C. P., & Modigliani, V. (1988). Educational implications of the spacing effect. In M. M. Gruneberg & P. E. Morris (Eds.), *Practical aspects of memory: Current research and issues: Memory in everyday life* (pp. 402–406). New York: John Wiley & Sons.

Read, J. D. (1996). From a passing thought to a false memory in 2 minutes: Confusing real and illusory events. *Psychonomic Bulletin and Review, 3,* 105–111.

Read, J. D., & Lindsay, D. S. (2000). "Amnesia" for summer camps and high school graduation: Memory work increases reports of prior periods of remembering less. *Journal of Traumatic Stress, 13,* 129–147.

Rechtschaffen, A., Bergmann, B. M., Everson, C. A., Kushida, C. A., & Gilliland, M. A. (2002). Sleep deprivation in the rat: X integration and discussion of the findings. *Sleep: Journal of Sleep and Sleep Disorders Research, 25,* 68–87.

Redelmeier, D. A., & Tibshriani, R. J. (1997). Association between cellular-telephone calls and motor vehicle collisions. *New England Journal of Medicine, 336,* 543–548.

Ree, M. J., & Earles, J. A. (1992). Intelligence is the best predictor of job performance. *Current Directions in Psychological Science, 1,* 86–89.

Reed, T. E., & Jensen, A. R. (1992). Conduction velocity in a brain nerve pathway correlates with intelligence. *Intelligence, 16,* 259–272.

Reeve, J. (1992). *Understanding motivation and emotion.* Fort Worth, TX: Harcourt Brace Jovanovich.

Reisberg, D. (2001). *Cognition: The science of the mind* (2nd ed.). New York: W. W. Norton.

Reisberg, D., & Chambers, D. (1991). Neither pictures nor propositions: What can we learn from a mental image? *Canadian Journal of Psychology, 45,* 336–352.

Reisenzein, R. (1983). The Schachter theory of emotion: Two decades later. *Psychological Bulletin, 94,* 239–264.

Reker, G. T. (1995). Quantitative and qualitative methods. In M. Kimble, S. McFadden, J. W. Ellor, & J. Seeber (Eds.), *Aging, spirituality,*

and religion: A handbook (pp. 568–588). Minneapolis: Fortress Press.

Reker, G. T. (1997). Personal meaning, optimism and choice: Existential problems of depression in community and institutional elderly. *The Gerontologist, 37,* 709–716.

Rentfrow, P. J., & Gosling, S. D. (2003). The do-re-mi's of everyday life: Examining the structure and personality correlates of music preferences. *Journal of Personality and Social Psychology, 84,* 1236–1256.

Rescorla, R. A. (1980). Simultaneous and successive associations in sensory preconditioning. *Journal of Experimental Psychology: Animal Behavior Processes, 6,* 207–216.

Rescorla, R. A. (1988). Pavlovian conditioning: It's not what you think it is. *American Psychologist, 43,* 151–160.

Rescorla, R. A. (1992). Hierarchical associative relations in Pavolvian conditioning and instrumental training. *Current Directions in Psychological Science, 1,* 66–70.

Resnick, S. M., Berenbaum, S. A., Gottesman, I. I., & Bouchard, T. J. (1986). Early hormonal influences on cognitive functioning in congenital adrenal hyperplasia. *Developmental Psychology, 22,* 191–198.

Revelle, W. (1995). Personality processes. *Annual Review of Psychology, 46,* 295–328.

Revonsuo, A. (2000). Did ancestral humans dream for their lives? *Behavioral and Brain Sciences, 23,* 1063–1082; 1083–1121.

Revonsuo, A. (2001). Can functional brain imaging discover consciousness in the brain? *Journal of Consciousness Studies, 8* (3), 3–23.

Reynolds, D. J., & Gifford, R. (2001). The sounds and sights of intelligence: A lens model channel analysis. *Personality and Social Psychology Bulletin, 27,* 187–200.

Rhodes, G., & Tremewan, T. (1996). Averageness, exaggeration, and facial attractiveness. *Psychological Science, 7,* 105–110.

Ribaupierre, F. de. (1997). Acoustical information processing in the auditory thalamus and cerebral cortex. In G. Ehret & R. Romand (Eds.), *The central auditory system.* New York: Oxford University Press.

Ricaurte, G. A., Yuan, J., Hatzidimitriou, G., Cord, B. J., & McCann, U. D. (2002). Severe dopaminergic neurotoxicity in primates after a common recreational dose regimen of MDMA ("ecstasy"). *Science, 297,* 2260–2263.

Rice, M. E. (1997). Violent offender research and implications for the criminal justice system. *American Psychologist, 52* (4), 414–423.

Richards, F. A., & Commons, M. L. (1990). Postformal cognitive-developmental theory and research: A review of its current status. In C. N. Alexander & E. J. Langer (Eds.), *Higher stages of human development: Perspectives on adult growth.* New York: Oxford University Press.

Rickels, K., Schweizer, E., Case, W. G., & Greenblatt, D. J. (1990). Long-term therapeutic use of benzodiazepines. I. Effects of abrupt discontinuation. *Archives of General Psychiatry, 47,* 899–907.

Ridley, M. (2000). *Genome: The autobiography of a species in 23 chapters.* New York: HarperCollins.

Rieber, R. W. (1999). Hypnosis, false memory and multiple personality: A trinity of affinity. *History of Psychiatry, 10* (37, Pt 1), 3–11.

Riegel, K. F. (1976). The dialectics of human development. *American Psychologist, 31,* 689–700.

Riggs, D. A., & Foa, E. B. (1993). Obsessive-compulsive disorder. In D. H. Barlow (Ed.), *Clinical handbook of psychological disorders* (2nd ed.). New York: Guilford.

Rijsdijk, F. V., Vernon, P. A., & Boomsma, D. I. (1998). The genetic basis of the relation between speed-of-information processing and IQ. *Behavioural Brain Research, 95,* 77–84.

Rivett, M. (1998). The family therapy journals in 1997: A thematic review. *Journal of Family Therapy, 20,* 423–430.

Robins, R. W., Gosling, S. D., & Craik, K. H. (1999). An empirical analysis of trends in psychology. *American Psychologist, 54,* 117–128.

Robbins, T. W. (1997). Arousal systems and attentional processes. *Biological Psychology, 45,* 57–71.

Robey, R. R., & Dalebout, S. D. (1998). A tutorial on conducting meta-analyses of clinical outcome research. *Journal of Speech Language and Hearing Research, 41,* 1227–1241.

Robinson, J. O., Rosen, M., Revill, S. I., David, H., & Rus, G. A. D. (1980). Self-administered intravenous and intramuscular pethidine. *Anaesthesia, 35,* 763–770.

Rodin, J. (1981). Current status of the internal-external hypothesis for obesity: What went wrong? *American Psychologist, 36,* 361–372.

Rodin, J., Schank, D., & Striegal-Moore, R. H. (1989). Psychological features of obesity. *Medical Clinics of North America, 73,* 47–66.

Roediger, H. L., III, & McDermott, K. B. (1993). Implicit memory in normal human subjects.

In F. Boller & J. Grafman (Eds.), *Handbook of neuropsychology*. Amsterdam: Elsevier.

Roediger, H. L., III, & McDermott, K. B. (1995). Creating false memories: Remembering words not presented in lists. *Journal of Experimental Psychology: Learning, Memory, and Cognition, 21*, 803–814.

Roediger, H. L., III, Weldon, M. S., & Challis, B. H. (1989). Explaining dissociations between implicit and explicit measures of retention: A processing account. In H. L. Roediger & F. I. M. Craik (Eds.), *Varieties of memory and consciousness: Essays in honour of Endel Tulving* (pp. 355–389). Hillsdale, NJ: Erlbaum.

Roediger, H. L., III, Weldon, M. S., Stadler, M. L., & Riegler, G. L. (1992). Direct comparison of two implicit memory tests: Word fragment and word stem completion. *Journal of Experimental Psychology: Learning, Memory, and Cognition, 18*, 1251–1269.

Roesch, R., Hart, S. D., & Ogloff, J. R. P. (Eds.) (1999). *Psychology and law: The state of the discipline*. New York: Kluwer Academic/ Plenum.

Roesler, A., & Witztum, E. (1998). Treatment of men with paraphilia with a long-acting analogue of gonadotropin-releasing hormone. *New England Journal of Medicine, 338*, 416–422.

Rogers, C. R. (1951). *Client-centered therapy*. Boston: Houghton Mifflin.

Rogers, C. R. (1961). *On becoming a person: A therapist's view of psychotherapy*. Boston: Houghton Mifflin.

Rogers, C. R. (1963). The actualizing tendency in relation to "motives" and to consciousness. In M. R. Jones (Ed.), *Nebraska symposium on motivation*. Lincoln: University of Nebraska.

Rogers, S. M., & Turner, C. F. (1991). Male-male sexual contact in the U.S.A.: Findings from five sample surveys, 1970–1990. *Journal of Sex Research, 28*, 491–519.

Roitblat, H. L., & von Ferson, L. (1992). Comparative cognition: Representations and processes in learning and memory. *Annual Review of Psychology, 43*, 671–710.

Rolls, E. T. (1995). Central taste anatomy and neurophysiology. In R. L. Doty (Ed.), *Handbook of olfaction and gustation*. New York: Dekker.

Rosch, E., & Mervis, C. B. (1975). Family resemblances: Studies in the internal structure of categories. *Cognitive Psychology, 7*, 573–605.

Rosch, E., Mervis, C. B., Gray, W. D., Johnson, D. M., & Bayes-Braem, P. (1976). Basic objects in natural categories. *Cognitive Psychology, 8*, 382–439.

Rosen, D. L., & Singh, S. (1992). An investigation of subliminal embed effect on multiple measures of advertising effectiveness. *Psychology and Marketing, 9*, 157–173.

Rosenbaum, M. E. (1986). The repulsion hypothesis: On the nondevelopment of relationships. *Journal of Personality and Social Psychology, 51*, 1156–1166.

Rosenhan, D. L. (1973). On being sane in insane places. *Science, 179*, 250–258.

Rosenthal, R. (1966). *Experimenter effects in behavioral research*. New York: Appleton-Century-Crofts.

Rosenthal, R. (1994). Science and ethics in conducting, analyzing, and reporting psychological research. *Psychological Science, 5*, 127–134.

Rosenthal, R., & Jacobson, L. (1968). *Pygmalion in the classroom: Teachers' expectations and pupils' intellectual development*. New York: Holt, Rinehart & Winston.

Rosenthal, R., & Rosnow, R. L. (Eds.) (1969). *Artifact in behavioral research*. New York: Academic Press.

Rosenthal, R., & Rosnow, R. L. (1975). *The volunteer subject*. New York: Wiley.

Rosenthal, R., & Rosnow, R. L. (1991). *Essentials of behavioral research: Methods and data analysis* (2nd ed.). New York: McGraw-Hill.

Rosenzweig, S. (1936). Some implicit common factors in diverse methods of psychotherapy. *American Journal of Orthopsychiatry, 6*, 422–425.

Rosnow, R. L., & Rosenthal, R. (1996). *Beginning behavioral research: A conceptual primer* (2nd ed.). New York: Macmillan.

Ross, C. A., Miller, S. D., Reagor, P., Bjornson, L., Fraser, G. A., & Anderson, G. (1990). Structured interview data on 102 cases of multiple personality disorder from four centers. *American Journal of Psychiatry, 147*, 596–601.

Ross, L. (1977). The intuitive psychologist and his shortcomings: Distortions in the attribution process. In L. Berkowitz (Ed.), *Advances in experimental social psychology*. New York: Academic Press.

Ross, M., & Wilson, A. E. (2000). Constructing and appraising past selves. In D. L. Schacter & E. Scarry (Eds.), *Memory, brain, and belief* (pp. 231–258). Cambridge, MA: Harvard University Press.

Rothbart, M. K., Ahadi, S. A., Hershey, K., & Fisher, P. (2001). Investigations of temperament at three to seven years: The children's behavior questionnaire. *Child Development, 72* (5), 1394–1408.

Rothbart, A. & Hershey (1994). Temperament and social behavior in children. *Merrill-Palmer Quarterly*, 21–39.

Rotter, J. B. (1966). Generalized expectancies for internal versus external locus of control of reinforcement. *Psychological Monographs, 80* (Whole No. 609).

Rotter, J. B., Liverant, S., & Crowne, D. P. (1961). The growth and extinction of expectancies in change controlled and skilled tasks. *Journal of Psychology, 52*, 161–177.

Rovee-Collier, C. (1993). The capacity for long-term memory in infancy. *Current Directions in Psychological Science, 2*, 130–135.

Rozin, P. (1990). Development in the food domain. *Developmental Psychology, 26*, 555–562.

Rozin, P., & Fallon, A. E. (1987). A perspective on disgust. *Psychological Review, 94*, 23–41.

Rozin, P., Hammer, L., Oster, H., Horowitz, T., & Marmara, V. (1986). The child's conception of food: Development of categories of accepted and rejected substances. *Journal of Nutrition Education, 18*, 75–81.

Rubinsky, H., Eckerman, D., Rubinsky, E., & Hoover, C. (1987). Early-phase physiological response patterns to psychosexual stimuli: Comparisons of male and female patterns. *Archives of Sexual Behavior, 16*, 45–55.

Ruble, D. N., & Martin, C. L. (1998). Gender development. In W. Damon & N. Eisenberg (Eds.), *Handbook of child psychology: Social, emotional, and personality development*. New York: Wiley.

Ruble, D. N., Balaban, T., & Cooper, J. (1981). Gender constancy and the effects of sex-typed televised toy commercials. *Child Development, 52*, 667–673.

Rudman, L. A., & Borgida, E. (1995). The afterglow of construct accessibility: The behavioral consequences of priming men to view women as sexual objects. *Journal of Experimental Social Psychology, 31*, 493–517.

Rumbaugh, D. M. (Ed.) (1977). *Language learning by a chimpanzee: The Lana project*. New York: Academic Press.

Rummel, A., & Feinberg, R. (1988). Cognitive evaluation theory: A meta-analytic review of the literature. *Social Behavior and Personality, 16*, 147–164.

Rushton, J. P. (2000). *Race, evolution, and behavior: A life-history perspective* (3rd ed.). Port Huron, MI: Charles Darwin Research Institute.

Russek, M. (1971). Hepatic receptors and the neurophysiological mechanisms controlling feeding behavior. In S. Ehrenpreis (Ed.), *Neuroscience research.* New York: Academic Press.

Russell, J. A., & Fernandez-Dols, J.-M. (Eds.) (1997). *The psychology of facial expression.* New York: Cambridge University Press.

Russell, J. A., & Yik, M. S. M. (1996). Emotion among the Chinese. In M. H. Bond (Ed.), *The handbook of Chinese psychology* (pp. 166–188). Hong Kong: Oxford University Press.

Ryckman, R. M. (2000). *Theories of personality* (7th ed.). Belmont, CA: Wadsworth.

Ryder, A. G., Alden, L., & Paulhus, D. L. (2000). Is acculturation unidimensional or bidimensional? A head-to-head comparison in the prediction of demographics, personality, self-identity, and adjustment. *Journal of Personality and Social Psychology, 79,* 49–65.

Sackeim, H. A. (1983). Self-deception, self-esteem, and depression: The adaptive value of lying to oneself. In J. Masling (Ed.), *Empirical studies of psychoanalytic theories* (pp. 101–157). Hillsdale, NJ: Erlbaum.

Sackeim, H. (1999). The anticonvulsant hypothesis of the mechanisms of action of ECT. Current status. *Journal of ECT, 15,* 5–26.

Sackeim, H. A., Prudic, J., Devanand D. P., Nobler, M. S., Lisanby, S. H., Peyser, S., Fitzsimons, L., Moody, B. J., & Clark, J. (2000). A prospective, randomized, double-blind comparison of bilateral and right unilateral electroconvulsive therapy at different stimulus intensities. *Archives of General Psychiatry, 57,* 425–434.

Sacks, O. (1985). *The man who mistook his wife for a hat.* New York: Summit Books.

Sagie, A., Elizur, D., & Yamauchi, H. (1996). The structure and strength of achievement motivation: A cross-cultural comparison. *Journal of Organizational Behavior, 17,* 431–444.

Saitoh, T., Kang, D., Mallory, M., DeTeresa, R., & Masliah, E. (1997). Glial cells in Alzheimer's disease. Preferential effect of APOE risk on scattered microglia. *Gerontology, 43,* 109–118.

Sakai, F., Stirling Meyer, J., Karacan, I., Yamaguchi, F., & Yamamoto, M. (1979). Narcolepsy: Regional cerebral blood flow during sleep and wakefulness. *Neurology, 29,* 61–67.

Saklofske, D. H., & Greenspoon, P. J. (2000). Confirmatory factor analysis of the MSLSS: A reply to Shevlin et al. *Personality and Individual Differences, 28,* 187–190.

Sales, B. D., & Folkman, S. (Eds.) (2000). *Ethics in research with human participants.* Washington, DC: American Psychological Association.

Salkovskis, P. M. (1985). Obsessional compulsive problems: A cognitive behavioral analysis. *Behaviour Research and Therapy, 23,* 571–577.

Salmon, C. A., & Daly, M. (1998). Birth order and familial sentiment: Middleborns are different. *Evolution and Human Behavior, 19,* 299–312.

Salovey, P., & Mayer, J. D. (1990). Emotional intelligence. *Imagination, Cognition, and Personality, 9,* 185–211.

Salthouse, T. A. (1994). The nature of the influence of speed on adult age differences in cognition. *Developmental Psychology, 30,* 240–259.

Saltzstein, H. D. (Ed.) (1997). *Culture as a context for moral development: New perspectives on the particular and the universal.* San Francisco: Jossey-Bass.

Sameroff, A. J., Seifer, R., Baldwin, A., & Baldwin, C. (1993). Stability of intelligence from preschool to adolescence: The influence of social and family risk factors. *Child Development, 64,* 80–97.

Sammons, M. T., Gorny, S. W., Zinner, E. S., & Allen, R. P. (2000). Prescriptive authority for psychologists: A consensus of support. *Professional Psychology–Research and Practice, 31,* 604–609.

Sanders, R. J. (1989). Sentence comprehension following agenesis of the corpus callosum. *Brain and Language, 37,* 59–72.

Sanderson, W. C., & Barlow, D. H. (1990). A description of patients diagnosed with a DSM-II-R anxiety disorder. *Journal of Nervous and Mental Disease, 178,* 588–591.

Sanson, A., & di-Muccio, C. (1993). The influence of aggressive and neutral cartoons and toys on the behaviour of preschool children. *Australian Psychologist, 28,* 93–99.

Sansone, C., & Harackiewicz, J. M. (Ed.) (2000). *Intrinsic and extrinsic motivation: The search for optimal motivation and performance.* San Diego: Academic Press.

Santi, A., Weise, L., & Kuiper, D. (1995). Memory for event duration in rats. *Learning and Motivation, 26,* 83–100.

Sarason, I. G., Sarason, B. R., & Pierce, G. R. (1994). Social support: Global and relationship-based levels of analysis. *Journal of Social and Personal Relationships, 11,* 295–312.

Sarbin, T. R., & Coe, W. C. (1972). *Hypnosis: A social psychological analysis of influence communication.* New York: Holt, Rinehart & Winston.

Saron, C. D., & Davidson, R. J. (1989). Visual evoked potential measures of interhemispheric transfer times in humans. *Behavioral Neuroscience, 103,* 1115–1138.

Saunders, B. A. C., & van Brakel, J. (1997). Are there nontrivial constraints on colour categorization? *Behavioral and Brain Sciences, 20* (2), 167–228.

Savage-Rumbaugh, S., McDonald, D., Sevcik, R., Hopkins, W., & Rupert, E. (1986). Spontaneous symbol acquisition and communicative use by pygmie chimpanzees. *Journal of Experimental Psychology: General, 115,* 211–235.

Savage-Rumbaugh, S., Murphy, J., Sevcik, R., Brakke, K., Williams, S., & Rumbaugh, D. M. (1993). Language comprehension in ape and child. *Monographs of the Society for Research in Child Development, 58* (3–4, Serial No. 233).

Scarborough, E., & Furumoto, L. (1987). *Untold lives: The first generation of American women psychologists.* New York: Columbia University Press.

Scarr, S., & Weinberg, R. A. (1976). IQ test performance of black children adopted by white families. *American Psychologist, 31,* 726–739.

Schachter, S. (1971). *Emotion, obesity, and crime.* New York: Academic Press.

Schachter, S., & Gross, L. (1968). Manipulated time and eating behavior. *Journal of Personality and Social Psychology, 10,* 98–106.

Schachter, S., & Singer, J. E. (1962). Cognitive, social, and physiological determinants of emotional state. *Psychological Review, 69,* 379–399.

Schacter, D. L. (1996). *Searching for memory.* New York: Basic Books.

Schacter, D. L. (2001). *The seven sins of memory: How the mind forgets and remembers.* Boston: Houghton Mifflin.

Schacter, D. L., Norman, K. A., & Koutstaal, W. (1998). The cognitive neuroscience of constructive memory. *Annual Review of Psychology, 49,* 289–318.

Schaie, K. W. (1983). The Seattle Longitudinal Study: A twenty-one-year exploration of psychometric intelligence in adulthood. In K. W. Schaie (Ed.), *Longitudinal studies of adult psychological development.* New York: Guilford.

Schaie, K. W. (1989). The hazards of cognitive aging. *Gerontologist, 29,* 484–493.

Schaie, K. W. (1993). The Seattle Longitudinal Studies of Adult Intelligence. *Current Directions in Psychological Science, 2,* 171–175.

Schaie, K. W. (1998). The Seattle Longitudinal Studies of Adult Intelligence. In M. P. Lawton & T. A. Salthouse (Eds.), *Essential papers on the psychology of aging. Essential papers in psychoanalysis.* New York: New York University Press.

Schaller, M. (1997). The psychological consequences of fame: Three tests of the self-consciousness hypothesis. *Journal of Personality, 65,* 291–309.

Schaller, M., Conway, L. G., & Tanchuk, T. L. (2002). Selective pressures on the once and future contents of ethnic stereotypes: Effects of the communicability of traits. *Journal of Personality and Social Psychology, 82,* 861–877.

Schedlowski, M., Fluge, T., Richter, S., & Tewes, U. (1995). b-Endorphin, but not substance-P, is increased by acute stress in humans. *Psychoneuroendocrinology, 20,* 103–110.

Scheich, H., & Zuschratter, W. (1995). Mapping of stimulus features and meaning in gerbil auditory cortex with 2–deoxyglucose and c-fos antibodies. *Behavioural Brain Research, 66,* 195–205.

Scheier, M. F., & Carver, C. S. (1993). On the power of positive thinking: The benefits of being optimistic. *Current Directions in Psychological Science, 2,* 26–30.

Scheier, M. F., Matthews, K. A., Owens, J. F., Magovern, G. J., Sr., Lefebvre, R. C., Abbott, R. A., & Carver, C. S. (1989). Dispositional optimism and recovery from coronary artery bypass surgery: The beneficial effects on physical and psychological well-being. *Journal of Personality and Social Psychology, 57,* 1024–1040.

Schiller, P. H. (1996). On the specificity of neurons and visual areas. *Behavioural Brain Research, 76,* 21–35.

Schiller, P. H., Logothetis, N. K., & Charles, E. R. (1990). Functions of the colour-opponent and broad-channels of the visual system. *Nature, 343,* 68–70.

Schleifer, S. J., Keller, S. E., Meyerson, A. T., Raskin, M. J., Davis, K. L., & Stein, M. (1983). Suppression of lymphocyte stimulation following bereavement. *Journal of the American Medical Association, 250,* 374.

Schlenker, B. R., & Forsyth, D. R. (1977). On the ethics of psychological research. *Journal of Experimental Social Psychology, 13,* 369–396.

Schmahmann, J. D., & Sherman, J. C. (1998). The cerebellar cognitive affective syndrome. *Brain, 121,* 561–579.

Schmidt, F. L., & Hunter, J. E. (1993). Tacit knowledge, practical intelligence, general mental ability, and job knowledge. *Current Directions in Psychological Science, 2,* 8–9.

Schmidt, F. L., & Hunter, J. E. (1998). The validity and utility of selection methods in personnel psychology: Practical and theoretical implications of 85 years of research findings. *Psychological Bulletin, 124,* 262–274.

Schmidt, S. R. (1991). Can we have a distinctive theory of memory? *Memory and Cognition, 19,* 523–542.

Schmuckler, M. A., & Proffitt, D. R. (1994). Infants' perception of kinetic depth and stereokinetic displays. *Journal of Experimental Psychology: Human Perception and Performance, 20,* 122–130.

Schnapf, J. L., & Baylor, D. A. (1987, April). How photoreceptor cells respond to light. *Scientific American, 256,* 40–47.

Schneider, J. S., Sun, Z. Q., & Roeltgen, D. P. (1994). Effects of dopamine agonists on delayed response performance in chronic low-dose MPTP-treated monkeys. *Pharmacology, Biochemistry, and Behavior, 48,* 235–240.

Schneiderman, N., Antoni, M. H., Saab, P. G., & Ironson, G. (2001). Health psychology: Psychosocial and biobehavioral aspects of chronic disease management. *Annual Review of Psychology, 52,* 555–580.

Schneiderman, N., Antoni, M. H., Ironson, G., Laperriere, A., & Fletcher, M. A. (1992). Applied psychological science and HIV-1 spectrum disease. *Applied and Preventive Psychology, 1,* 67–82.

Schooler, J. W. (2002). Verbalization produces a transfer inappropriate processing shift. *Applied Cognitive Psychology, 16* (8), 989–997.

Schreiber, F. (1973). *Sybil.* New York: Warner Books.

Schretlen, D., Pearlson, G. D., Anthony, J. C., Ayward, E. H., Augustine, A., Davis, A., & Barta, P. (2000). Elucidating the contributions of processing speed, executive ability, and frontal lobe volume to normal age-related differences in fluid intelligence. *Journal of the International Neuropsychological Society, 6,* 52–61.

Schroeder, D. H., & Costa, P. T. (1984). Influence of life event stress on physical illness: Substantive effects or methodological flaws? *Journal of Personality and Social Psychology, 46,* 853–863.

Schroeder, K. E., Schwarzer, R., & Endler, N. S. (1997). Predicting cardiac patients' quality of life from the characteristics of their spouses. *Journal of Health Psychology, 2,* 231–244.

Schuster, M. A., Stein, B. D., Jaycox, L. H., Collins, R. L., Marshall, G. N., Elliott, M. N., Zhou, A. J., Kanouse, D. E., Morrison, J. L., & Berry, S. H. (2001). A national survey of stress reactions after the September 11, 2001, terrorist attacks. *New England Journal of Medicine, 345,* 1507–1512.

Schwartz, B. (1990). The creation and destruction of value. *American Psychologist, 45,* 7–15.

Schwartz, C. E., Snidman, N., & Kagan, J. (1996). Early childhood temperament as a determinant of externalizing behavior in adolescence. *Development and Psychopathology, 8,* 527–537.

Schwartz, W. J. (1996). Internal timekeeping. *Science and Medicine, 3,* 44–53.

Schweickert, R., Guentert, L., & Hersberger, L. (1990). Phonological similarity, pronunciation rate, and memory span. *Psychological Science, 1,* 74–77.

Schweinberger, S. R., & Stief, V. (2001). Implicit perception in patients with visual neglect: Lexical specificity in repetition priming. *Neuropsychologia, 39,* 420–429.

Sclafani, A. (1994). Eating rates in normal and hypothalamic hyperphagic rats. *Physiology and Behavior, 55,* 489–494.

Scott, T. R., Plata-Salamn, C. R., & Smith-Swintosky, V. L. (1994). Gustatory neural coding in the monkey cortex: The quality of saltiness. *Journal of Neurophysiology, 71,* 1692–1701.

Searle, J. R., Dennet, D. C., & Chalmers, D. J. (1997). *The Mystery of Consciousness.* New York: New York Review of Books Press.

Sebrechts, M. M., Marsh, R. L., & Seamon, J. G. (1989). Secondary memory and very rapid forgetting. *Memory and Cognition, 17,* 693–700.

Seeman, P., Lee, T., Chau Wong, M., & Wong, K. (1976). Antipsychotic drug doses and neuroleptic/dopamine receptors. *Nature, 261,* 717–719.

Seer, P. (1979). Psychological control of essential hypertension: Review of the literature and methodological critique. *Psychological Bulletin, 86,* 1015–1043.

Segall, M. H., Dasen, P. R., Berry, J. W., & Poortinga, Y. (1990). *Human behavior in global perspective.* New York: Pergamon.

Segerstrom, S. C., Taylor, S. E., Kemeny, M. E., & Fahey, J. L. (1998). Optimism is associated with mood, coping, and immune change in response to stress. *Journal of Personality and Social Psychology, 74,* 1646–1655.

Seidenberg, M. S., & Petitto, L. A. (1987). Communication, symbolic communication, and language: Comment on Savage-Rumbaugh, McDonald, Sevcik, Hopkins, and Rupert (1986). *Journal of Experimental Psychology: General, 116* (3), 279–287.

Sekular, R., & Blake, R. (1990). *Perception* (2nd ed.). New York: McGraw-Hill.

Sekuler, A. B. (1994). Local and global minima in visual completion: Effects of symmetry and orientation. *Perception, 23,* 529–545.

Seligman, M. E. P. (1975). *Helplessness: On depression, development, and death.* San Francisco: Freeman.

Selkoe, D. J. (1992, September). Aging brain, aging mind. *Scientific American, 267,* 135–142.

Selye, H. (1936). A syndrome produced by diverse nocuous agents. *Nature, 138,* 32.

Selye, H. (1952). *The story of the adaptation syndrome.* Montreal: Acta.

Selye, H. (1974). *Stress without distress.* Philadelphia: Lippincott.

Sepple, C. P., & Read, N. W. (1989). Gastrointestinal correlates of the development of hunger in man. *Appetite, 13,* 183–191.

Servos, P., & Goodale, M. A. (1995). Preserved visual imagery in visual form agnosia. *Neuropsychologia, 33* (11), 1383–1394.

Servos, P., Wilson, D., Gati, J., & Lederman, S. (2001). fMRI-derived cortical maps for haptic shape, texture, and hardness. *Cognitive Brain Research, 12* (2), 307–313.

Shaffer, D. R. (1993). *Developmental psychology: Childhood and adolescence* (3rd ed.). Pacific Grove, CA: Brooks/Cole.

Shaffer, D. R. (2002). *Developmental psychology: Childhood and adolescence* (6th ed.). Pacific Grove, CA: Brooks/Cole.

Shapiro, A. K. (1960). A contribution to a history of the placebo effect. *Behavioral Science, 5,* 109–135.

Shapiro, K. L., & Raymond, J. E. (1994). Temporal allocation of visual attention: Inhibition or interference? In D. Dagenbach & T. H. Carr (Eds.), *Inhibitory processes in attention, memory, and language* (pp. 151–188). San Diego: Academic Press.

Shapley, R. (1990). Visual sensitivity and parallel retinocortical channels. *Annual Review of Psychology, 41,* 635–658.

Sharma, K. N., Anand, B. K., Due, S., & Singh, B. (1961). Role of stomach in regulation of activities of hypothalamic feeding centers. *American Journal of Physiology, 201,* 593–598.

Sharpe, D., & Adair, J. G. (1993). Reversibility of the hindsight bias: Manipulation of experimental demands. *Organizational Behavior and Human Decision Processes, 56,* 233–245.

Shaw, C. A., & McEachern, J. C. (Eds.) (2001). *Toward a theory of neuroplasticity.* Philadelphia: Psychology Press.

Shaywitz, S. E., Fletcher, J. M., & Shaywitz, B. A. (1994). Issues in the definition and classification of attention deficit disorder. *Topics in Language Disorders, 14,* 1–25.

Shepard, R. N. (1990). *Mind sights.* New York: W. H. Freeman.

Shepard, R. N., & Cooper, L. A. (1986). Mental images and their transformations. Cambridge, MA: MIT Press.

Sheridan, C. L., & Radmacher, S. A. (1992). *Health psychology: Challenging the biomedical model.* New York: Wiley.

Shields, S. A. (1975). Functionalism, Darwinism, and the psychology of women: A study in social myth. *American Psychologist, 30,* 739–754.

Shiffrin, R. M., & Schneider, W. (1977). Controlled and automatic human information processing II: Perceptual learning, automatic attending, and a general theory. *Psychological Review, 84,* 127–190.

Shirley, S. G., & Persaud, K. C. (1990). The biochemistry of vertebrate olfaction and taste. *Seminars in the Neurosciences, 2,* 59–68.

Shweder, R. A., Mahapatra, M., & Miller, J. G. (1990). Culture and moral development. In J. W. Stigler, R. A. Shweder, & G. Herdt (Eds.), *Cultural psychology.* New York: Cambridge University Press.

Siegel, J. M. (1983). A behavioral approach to the analysis of reticular formation unit activity. In T. E. Robinson (Ed.), *Behavioral approaches to brain research.* New York: Oxford University Press.

Siegel, J. M. (1990). Stressful life events and use of physician services among the elderly: The moderating role of pet ownership. *Journal of Personality and Social Psychology, 58,* 1081–1086.

Siegel, S. (1988). State dependent learning and morphine tolerance. *Behavioral Neuroscience, 102,* 228–232.

Siegel, S. (1989). Pharmacological conditioning and drug effects. In A. J. Goudie & M. W. Emmett-Oglesby (Eds.), *Psychoactive drugs: Tolerance and sensitization.* Clifton, NJ: Humana Press.

Siegel, S. (1999). Drug anticipation and drug addiction. *Addiction, 94,* 1113–1124.

Siegel, S., & Allan, L. G. (1998). Learning and homeostasis: Drug addiction and the McCollough effect. *Psychological Bulletin, 124,* 230–239.

Siegler, R. S. (1996). *Children's thinking: Beyond the immaculate transition.* New York: Oxford University Press.

Sigelman, C. K., & Shaffer, D. R. (1995). *Lifespan human development* (2nd ed.). Pacific Grove, CA: Brooks/Cole.

Sigmundson, H. K. (1994). Pharmacotherapy of schizophrenia: A review. *Canadian Journal of Psychiatry, 39,* 570–575.

Silber, M. H. (2001). Sleep disorders. *Neurologic Clinics, 19,* 173–186.

Silverman, I., & Eals, M. (1992). Sex differences in spatial ability: Evolutionary theory and data. In J. H. Barkow, L. Cosmides, & J. Tooby (Eds.), *The adapted mind: Evolutionary psychology and the generation of culture.* New York: Oxford University Press.

Silverman, I., & Phillips, K. (1998). The evolutionary psychology of spatial sex differences. In C. B. Crawford & D. L. Krebs (Eds.), *Handbook of evolutionary psychology: Ideas, issues and applications.* Mahwah, NJ: Erlbaum.

Silverstein, B., Perdue, L., Peterson, B., & Kelly, E. (1986). The role of the mass media in promoting a thin standard of bodily attractiveness for women. *Sex Roles, 14,* 519–532.

Simon, H. A. (1969). *The sciences of the artificial.* Cambridge, MA: MIT Press.

Simon, H. A. (1992). What is an "explanation" of behavior? *Psychological Science, 3,* 150–161.

Simpson, J. A., & Kenrick, D. T. (1997). *Evolutionary social psychology.* Mahwah, NJ: Erlbaum.

Sims, A. C. P., & Sims, D. (1998). The phenomenology of post-traumatic stress disorder: A symptomatic study of 70 victims of psychological trauma. *Psychopathology, 31,* 96–112.

Single, E., Robson, L., Xie, X., Rehm, J., Moore, R., Cho, B., et al. (1996). *The cost of substance abuse in Canada.* Available: www.ccsa.ca/docs/costhigh.htm

Siqueland, E. R., & DeLucia, C. A. (1969). Visual reinforcement of nonnutritive sucking in human infants. *Science, 165,* 1144–1146.

Sivian, L. S., & White, S. D. (1933). On minimum audible sound fields. *Journal of Acoustical Society of America, 4,* 288–321.

Skinner, B. F. (1938). *The behavior of organisms: An experimental analysis.* New York: Appleton-Century.

Skinner, B. F. (1948). "Superstition" in the pigeon. *Journal of Experimental Psychology, 38,* 168–172.

Skinner, B. F. (1956). A case history in scientific method. *American Psychologist, 11,* 221–233.

Skinner, B. F. (1969). *Contingencies of reinforcement: A theoretical analysis.* New York: Appleton-Century-Crofts.

Skinner, B. F. (1974). *About behaviorism.* New York: Knopf.

Slater, A., & Muir, D. (Eds.) (1999). *The Blackwell reader in developmental psychology.* Malden, MA: Blackwell.

Slater, A., Von der Schulenburg, C., Brown, E., Badenoch, M., Butterworth, G., Parsons, S., & Samuels, C. (1998). Newborn infants prefer attractive faces. *Infant Behavior and Development, 21,* 345–354.

Slater, E., & Glithero, E. (1965). A follow-up of patients diagnosed as suffering from hysteria. *Journal of Psychosomatic Research, 9,* 9–13.

Sloane, R. B., Staples, F. R., Cristol, A. H., Yorkston, N. J., & Whipple, K. (1975). *Psychotherapy versus behavior therapy.* Cambridge, MA: Harvard University Press.

Slovic, P., Fischoff, B., & Lichtenstein, S. (1982). Facts versus fears: Understanding perceived risk. In D. Kahneman, P. Slovic, & A. Tversky (Eds.), *Judgment under uncertainty: Heuristics and biases.* Cambridge: Cambridge University Press.

Slugoski, B. R., & Wilson, A. E. (1998). Contribution of conversation skills to the production of judgmental errors. *European Journal of Social Psychology, 28* (4), 575–601.

Smiley, P. A., & Dweck, C. S. (1994). Individual differences in achievement goals among young children. *Child Development, 65,* 1723–1743.

Smith, B. N., Kerr, N. A., Markus, M. J., & Stasson, M. F. (2001). Individual differences in social loafing: Need for cognition as a motivator in collective performance. *Group Dynamics: Theory, Research, and Practice, 5,* 150–158.

Smith, D. V., & Margolskee, R. F. (2001). Making sense of taste. *Scientific American, 284,* 32–39.

Smith, E. E. (1989). Concepts and induction. In M. Posner (Ed.), *Foundations of cognitive science.* Cambridge, MA: MIT Press.

Smith, E. E., Patalano, A. L., & Jonides, J. (1998). Alternative strategies of categorization. *Cognition, 65,* 167–196.

Smith, E. R., & Zárate, M. A. (1992). Exemplar-based model of social judgment. *Psychological Review, 99,* 3–21.

Smith, E. R., Stewart, T. L., & Buttram, R. T. (1992). Inferring a trait from a behavior has long-term, highly-specific effects. *Journal of Personality and Social Psychology, 62,* 753–759.

Smith, F. J., & Campfield, L. A. (1993). Meal initiation occurs after experimental induction of transient declines in blood glucose. *American Journal of Physiology, 265,* R1423–R1429.

Smith, M. L., & Glass, G. V. (1977). Meta-analysis of psychotherapy outcome studies. *American Psychologist, 32,* 752–760.

Smith, M. L., Glass, G. V., & Miller, T. I. (1980). *The benefits of psychotherapy.* Baltimore, MD: Johns Hopkins University Press.

Smuts, B. B., Cheney, D. L., Seyfarth, R. M., Wrangham, R. W., & Struhsaker, T. T. (Eds.) (1987). *Primate societies.* Chicago, IL: University of Chicago Press.

Snarey, J. R. (1995). In a communitarian voice: The sociological expansion of Kohlbergian theory, research, and practice. In W. M. Kurtines & J. L. Gewirtz (Eds.), *Moral development: An introduction.* Boston: Allyn & Bacon.

Snodgrass, J. G., Levy-Berger, G., & Haydon, M. (1985). *Human experimental psychology.* New York: Oxford University Press.

Snyder, F. (1967). In quest of dreaming. In H. A. Witkin & H. B. Lewis (Eds.), *Experimental studies of dreaming.* New York: Random House.

Snyder, M. (1974). The self-monitoring of expressive behavior. *Journal of Personality and Social Psychology, 30,* 526–537.

Snyder, M. (1987). *Public appearances/private realities: The psychology of self-monitoring.* New York: Freeman.

Snyder, M., Tanke, E. D., & Berscheid, E. (1977). Social perception and interpersonal behavior: On the self-fulfilling nature of social stereotypes. *Journal of Personality and Social Psychology, 35,* 656–666.

Snyder, S. H. (1976). The dopamine hypothesis of schizophrenia: Focus on the dopamine receptor. *American Journal of Psychiatry, 133,* 197–202.

Snyder, S. H., & D'Amato, R. J. (1986). MPTP: A neurotoxin relevant to the pathology of Parkinson's disease. *Neurology, 36,* 250–258.

Solomon, P. R., Adams, F., Silver, A., Zimmer, J., & DeVeaux, R. (2002). Gingko for memory enhancement: A randomized control trial. *JAMA: Journal of the American Medical Association, 288,* 835–840.

Solowij, N., Stephens, R. S., Roffman, R. A., Babor, T., Kadden, R., Miller, M., Christiansen, K., McRee, B., Vendetti, J., & Numerous, C. (2002). Cognitive functioning of long-term heavy cannabis users seeking treatment. *JAMA: Journal of the American Medical Association, 287,* 1123–1131.

Sorrentino, R. M., & Higgins, E. T. (Eds.)(1996). *Handbook of motivation and cognition: The interpersonal context.* (pp. 570–590). New York: Guilford.

Sorrentino, R. M., & Roney, C. J. R. (2000). *The uncertain mind: Individual differences in facing the unknown.* Philadelphia: Psychology Press.

Soudino, K. J., Plomin, R., & DeFries, J. C. (1996). Tester-rated temperament at 14, 20, and 24 months: Environmental change and genetic continuity. *British Journal of Developmental Psychology, 14,* 129–144.

Spanos, N. P. (1982). Hypnotic behavior: A cognitive, social psychological perspective. *Research Communications in Psychology, Psychiatry, and Behavior, 7,* 199–213.

Spanos, N. P. (1986). Hypnotic behavior: A social psychological interpretation of amnesia, analgesia, and "trance logic." *The Behavioral and Brain Sciences, 9,* 449–502.

Spanos, N. P. (1994). Multiple identity enactments and multiple personality disorder: A sociocognitive perspective. *Psychological Bulletin, 116,* 143–165.

Spanos, N. P. (1996). *Multiple identities and false memories: A sociocognitive perspective.* Washington, DC: American Psychological Association.

Spanos, N. P., Weeks, J. R., & Bertrand, L. D. (1985). Multiple personality: A social psychological perspective. *Journal of Abnormal Psychology, 92,* 362–376.

Sparks, D. L. (1988). Neural cartography: Sensory and motor maps in the mammalian superior colliculus. *Brain, Behavior, and Evolution, 31,* 49–56.

Spearman, C. (1904). "General intelligence," objectively determined and measured. *American Journal of Psychology, 15,* 201–293.

Spelke, E., Hirst, W., & Neisser, U. (1976). Skills of divided attention. *Cognition, 4,* 215–230.

Spelke, E. S., Breinlinger, K., Macomber, J., & Jacobson, K. (1992). Origins of knowledge. *Psychological Review, 99,* 605–632.

Spence, S., Shapiro, D., & Zaidel, E. (1996). The role of the right hemisphere in the physiological and cognitive components of emotional processing. *Psychophysiology, 33,* 112–122.

Sperling, G. (1960). The information available in brief visual presentations. *Psychological Monographs, 74* (Whole No. 48).

Spetch, M. L., & Grant, D. S. (1993). Pigeons' memory for event duration in choice and successive matching-to-sample tasks. *Learning and Motivation, 24,* 156–174.

Spiegel, D. (1995). Hypnosis and suggestion. In D. L. Schacter (Ed.), *Memory distortion.* Cambridge, MA: Harvard University Press.

Spiegel, D. (1998). Social psychological theories cannot fully account for hypnosis: The record was never crooked. *American Journal of Clinical Hypnosis, 41,* 158–161.

Spiegel, D., Bloom, J. R., Kramer, H. C., & Gotheil, E. (1989). Effect of psychosocial treatment on survival of patients with metastatic breast cancer. *Lancet, 14,* 888–891.

Spiegler, M. D., & Guevremont, D. C. (1998). *Contemporary behavior therapy* (3rd ed.). Pacific Grove, CA: Brooks/Cole.

Spitzer, R. L., Gibbon, M., Skodol, A. E., Williams, J. B., & First, M. B. (Eds.) (1994). *DSM-IV casebook.* Washington, DC: American Psychiatric Press.

Sponheim, S. R., Clementz, B. A., Iacono, W. G., & Beiser, M. (1994). Resting EEG in first episode and chronic schizophrenia. *Psychophysiology, 31,* 37–43.

Spreen, O., & Strauss, E. (1998). *A compendium of neuropsychological tests: Administration, norms, and commentary* (2nd ed.). London: Oxford University Press.

Springer, S. P., & Deutsch, G. (1989). *Left brain, right brain* (3rd ed.). New York: Freeman.

Squire, L. R. (1992). Memory and the hippocampus: A synthesis of findings with rats, monkeys, and humans. *Psychological Review, 99,* 195–231.

Squire, L. R., Ojemann, J. G., Miezin, F. M., Petersen, S. E., Videen, T. O., & Raichle, M. E. (1992). Activation of the hippocampus in normal humans: A functional anatomical study of memory. *Proceedings of the National Academy of Sciences, 89,* 1837–1841.

Srivastava, S., John, O. P., Gosling, S. D., & Potter, J. (2003). Development of personality in early and middle adulthood: Set like plaster or persistent change? *Journal of Personality and Social Psychology 84,* 1041–1053.

Staddon, J. E. R. (1998). The dynamics of memory in animal learning. In M. Sabourin et al. (Eds.), *Advances in psychological science: Biological and cognitive aspects.* Hove, England: Psychology Press/Erlbaum.

Standing, L., & Curtis, L. (1989). Subvocalization rate versus other predictors of the memory span. *Psychological Reports, 65,* 487–495.

Stanovich, K. E. (1999). *Who is rational? Studies of individual differences in reasoning.* Mahwah, NJ: Erlbaum.

Stanovich, K. E. (2001). *How to think straight about psychology* (6th ed.). Reading, MA: Addison-Wesley.

Statistics Canada (1997). *Suicides, and suicide rates, by sex, by age group.* Ottawa, ON: Author. Available: www.statcan.ca/english/ Pgdb/People/Health/health01.htm.

Statistics Canada (1999). *Toward a healthy future: Second report on the health of Canadians.* Ottawa, ON: Author.

Statistics Canada (2000, March 31). Health reports: How healthy are Canadians? *The Daily.* Ottawa, ON: Author.

Steblay, N. M., & Bothwell, R. K. (1994). Evidence for hypnotically refreshed testimony: The view from the laboratory. *Law and Human Behavior, 18,* 635–651.

Steele, C. M., & Josephs, R. A. (1990). Alcohol myopia: Its prized and dangerous effects. *American Psychologist, 45,* 921–933.

Stein, M., Ottenberg, P., & Roulet, N. (1958). A study of the development of olfactory preferences. *American Medical Association Archives of Neurology and Psychiatry, 80,* 264–266.

Stein, M. B., Walker, J. R., & Forde, D. R. (2000). Gender differences in susceptibility to post-traumatic stress disorder. *Behaviour Research and Therapy, 38,* 619–628.

Stein, R. M., & Ellinwood, E. H. (1993). Stimulant use: Cocaine and amphetamine. In D. L. Dunner (Ed.), *Current psychiatric therapy.* Philadelphia: W. B. Saunders.

Steinberg, L., & Morris, A. S. (2001). Adolescent development. *Annual Review of Psychology, 52,* 83–100.

Steiner, J. E. (1977). Facial expressions of the neonate infant indicating the hedonics of food-related chemical stimuli. In J. M. Weiffenbach (Ed.), *Taste and development.* Bethesda, MD: Department of Health, Education, and Welfare.

Stern, R. S., & Cobb, J. P. (1978). Phenomenology of obsessive-compulsive neurosis. *British Journal of Psychiatry, 132,* 233–234.

Sternberg, R. J. (1985). *Beyond IQ: A triarchic theory of human intelligence.* New York: Cambridge University Press.

Sternberg, R. J. (1986). A triangular theory of love. *Psychological Review, 93,* 119–135.

Sternberg, R. J. (1988a). Triangulating love. In R. J. Sternberg & M. L. Barnes (Eds.), *The psychology of love.* New Haven, CT: Yale University Press.

Sternberg, R. J. (1988b). *The triarchic theory of mind: A new theory of human intelligence.* New York: Viking Press.

Sternberg, R. J. (1997). The concept of intelligence and its role in lifelong learning and success. *American Psychologist, 52,* 1030–1037.

Sternberg, R. J. (1998). Principles of teaching for successful intelligence. *Educational Psychologist, 33,* 65–72.

Sternberg, R. J. (1999). *Thinking styles.* New York: Cambridge University Press.

Sternberg, R. J., & Gardner, M. K. (1983). Unities in inductive reasoning. *Journal of Experimental Psychology: General, 112,* 80–116.

Sternberg, R. J., & Grajek, S. (1984). The nature of love. *Journal of Personality and Social Psychology, 47,* 312–329.

Sternberg, R. J., & Kaufman, J. C. (1998). Human abilities. *Annual Review of Psychology, 49,* 479–502.

Sternberg, R. J., & Wagner, R. K. (1993). The g-ocentric view of intelligence and job performance is wrong. *Current Directions in Psychological Science, 2,* 1–5.

Sternberg, R. J., Torff, B., & Grigorenko, E. L. (1998). Teaching triarchically improves school achievement. *Journal of Educational Psychology, 90,* 374–384.

Sternberg, R. J., Castejon, J. L., Prieto, M. D., Hautamaeki, J., & Grigorenko, E. L. (2001). Confirmatory factor analysis of the Sternberg Triarchic Abilities Test in three international samples: An empirical test of the triarchic theory of intelligence. *European Journal of Psychological Assessment, 17,* 1–16.

Stevens, S. S. (1939). Psychology and the science of science. *Psychological Bulletin, 36,* 221–263.

Stewart, D. D., & Stasser, G. (1995). Expert role assignment and information sampling during collective recall and decision making.

Journal of Personality and Social Psychology, 69, 619–628.

Stewart, S. H., Peterson, J. B., & Pihl, R. O. (1995). Anxiety sensitivity and self-reported alcohol consumption rates in university women. *Journal of Anxiety Disorders, 9,* 283–292.

Stewart, T. L., Doan, K. A., Gingrich, B. E., & Smith, E. R. (1998). The actor as context for social judgments: Effects of prior impressions and stereotypes. *Journal of Personality and Social Psychology, 75,* 1132–1154.

Stickgold, R., Hobson, J. A., Fosse, R., & Fosse, M. (2001). Sleep, learning, and dreams: Off-line memory reprocessing. *Science, 294,* 1052–1057.

Stock, S. L., Werry, J. S., & McClellan, J. M. (2001). Pharmacological treatment of pediatric anxiety. In W. K. Silverman & P. D. Treffers (Eds.), *Anxiety disorders in children and adolescents: Research, assessment, and intervention.* New York: Cambridge University Press.

Stolarz-Fantino, S., Fantino, E., & Kulik, J. (1996). The conjunction fallacy: Differential incidence as a function of descriptive frames and educational context. *Contemporary Educational Psychology, 21* (2), 208–218.

Storm, C., & Gurevich, M. (2001). Looking forward, looking back: Women in psychology. *Canadian Psychology, 42,* 245–248.

Stoyva, J. M., & Carlson, J. G. (1993). A coping/rest model of relaxation and stress management. In L. Goldberger & S. Breznitz (Eds.), *Handbook of stress: Theoretical and clinical aspects* (2nd ed.). New York: Free Press.

Strassman, R. J. (1992). Human hallucinogen interactions with drugs affecting serotonergic neurotransmission. *Neuropsychopharamacology, 7,* 241–243.

Strauss, E., Slick, D. J., Levy-Bencheton, J., Hunter, M., MacDonald, S. W. S., & Hultsch, D. F. (2002). Intraindividual variability as an indicator of malingering in head injury. *Archives of Clinical Neuropsychology, 17,* 423–444.

Strayer, D. L., & Johnston, W. A. (2001). Driven to distraction: Dual task studies of simulated driving and conversing on a cellular telephone. *Psychological Science, 6,* 462–466.

Stricker, L. J., Rock, D. A., & Burton, N. W. (1996). Using the SAT and high school record in academic guidance. *Educational and Psychological Measurement, 56,* 626–641.

Strough, C., Clarke, J., Lloyd, J., & Nathan, P. J. (2001). Neuropsychological changes after 30-day Ginkgo biloba administration in healthy participants. *International Journal of Neuropsychopharmacology, 4* (2), 131–134.

Stuss, D. T., Winocur, G., & Robertson, I. H. (Eds.) (1999). *Cognitive neurorehabilitation.* New York: Cambridge University Press.

Sue, S., & Zane, N. (1987). The role of culture and cultural techniques in psychotherapy: A critique and reformulation. *American Psychologist, 42,* 37–45.

Sue, S., Zane, N., & Young, K. (1994). Research on psychotherapy with culturally diverse populations. In A. E. Bergin & S. L. Garfield (Eds.), *Handbook of psychotherapy and behavior change* (4th ed.). New York: Wiley.

Suedfeld, P. (1997). Reactions to societal trauma: Distress and/or eustress. *Political Psychology, 18,* 849–861.

Suedfeld, P. (2001). Theories of the Holocaust: Trying to explain the unimaginable. In D. Chirot, & M.E. Seligman (Eds.), *Ethnopolitical warfare: Causes, consequences, and possible solutions* (pp. 51–70). Washington, DC: American Psychological Association.

Suedfeld, P., Krell, R., Wiebe, R. E., & Steel, G. D. (1997). Coping strategies in the narratives of Holocaust survivors. *Anxiety, Stress and Coping: An International Journal, 10,* 153–179.

Sullivan, J. M. (2000). Cellular and molecular mechanisms underlying learning and memory impairments produced by cannabinoids. *Learning and Memory, 7,* 132–139.

Sullivan, P. F., Bulik, C. M., & Kendler, K. S. (1998). Genetic epidemiology of binging and vomiting. *British Journal of Psychiatry, 173,* 75–79.

Sulloway, 1997. *Born to rebel: Birth order, family dynamics, and creative lives.* New York: Pantheon.

Surbey, M. K. (1987). Anorexia nervosa, amenorrhea, and adaptation. *Ethology and Sociobiology, 8,* 47S–61S.

Surbey, M. K. (1990). Family composition, stress and human menarche. In T. E. Ziegler & F. B. Bercovitch (Eds.), *The socioendocrinology of primate reproduction.* New York: Wiley.

Surbey, M. K. (1998). Developmental psychology and modern Darwinism. In C. Crawford & D. L. Krebs (Eds.), *Handbook of evolutionary psychology: Ideas, issues and applications.* Mahwah, NJ: Erlbaum.

Sutton, D. A., Moldofsky, H., & Badley, E. M. (2001). Insomnia and health problems in Canadians. *Sleep: Journal of Sleep & Sleep Disorders Research, 24,* 665–670.

Suzdak, P. D., Glowa, J. R., Crawley, J. N., Schwartz, R. D., Skolnick, P., & Paul, S. M. (1986). A selective imidazobenzodiazepine antagonist of ethanol in the rat. *Science, 234,* 1243–1247.

Swinson, R. P., Antony, M. M., Rachman, S., & Richter, M. A. (Eds.) (1998). *Obsessive-compulsive disorder: Theory, research, and treatment.* New York: Guilford.

Symons, D. K. (1999). GRE predictive validity in a master's program. *Canadian Psychology, 40,* 71–73.

Symons, D. K., & Clark, S. E. (2000). A longitudinal study of mother-child relationships and theory of mind in the preschool period. *Social Development, 9,* 3–23.

Symons, L. A., Hains, S. M. J., & Muir, D. (1998). Look at me: Five-month-old infants' sensitivity to very small deviations in eye-gaze during social interactions. *Infant Behavior and Development, 21,* 531–536.

Szasz, T. (1961). *The myth of mental illness: Foundations of a theory of personal conduct.* New York: Hoeber-Harper.

Szasz, T. (1990). Law and psychiatry: The problems that will not go away. *The Journal of Mind and Behavior, 11,* 557–564.

Tanaka, J. W. (2001). The entry point of face recognition: Evidence for face expertise. *Journal of Experimental Psychology: General, 130* (3), 534–543.

Tanford, S., & Penrod, S. (1984). Social influence model: A formal integration of research on majority and minority influence processes. *Psychological Bulletin, 95,* 189–225.

Tateyama, M., Asai, M., Hashimoto, M., Bartels, M., & Kasper, S. (1998). Transcultural study of schizophrenic delusions: Tokyo versus Vienna versus Tuebingen (Germany). *Psychopathology, 31,* 59–68.

Tavris, C. (1989). *Anger: The misunderstood emotion* (rev. ed.). New York: Touchstone Books/Simon & Schuster.

Taylor, D. M., & Moghaddam, F. M. (1994). *Theories of intergroup relations* (2nd ed.). Westport, CT: Praeger.

Taylor, D. M., Ruggiero, K. M., & Louis, W. R. (1996). Personal/group discrimination discrepancy: Towards a two-factor explanation. *Canadian Journal of Behavioural Science, 28,* 193–202.

Taylor, D. M., Wright, S. C., Moghaddam, F. M., & Lalonde, R. N. (1990). The personal/group discrimination discrepancy: Perceiving my group but not myself to be a target for discrimination. *Personality and Social Psychology Bulletin, 16,* 256–262.

Taylor, F. K. (1965). Cryptomnesia and plagiarism. *British Journal of Psychiatry, 111,* 1111–1118.

Taylor, F. W. (1911). *Principles of scientific management.* New York: Harper.

Taylor, G. J., Bagby, R. M., & Parker, J. D. A. (1997). *Disorders of affect regulation: Alexithymia in medical and psychiatric illness.* Cambridge: Cambridge University Press.

Taylor, H. (1997). The very different methods used to conduct telephone surveys of the public. *Journal of the Marketing Research Society, 39,* 421–432.

Taylor, S. E., Klein, L. C., Lewis, B. P., Gruenewald, T. L., Gurung, R. A. R., & Updegraff, J. A. (2000). Biobehavioral responses to stress in humans: Tend-and-befriend, not fight-or-flight. *Psychological Review, 107,* 411–429.

Taylor, S. E., Repetti, R., & Seeman, T. (1997). Health psychology: What is an unhealthy environment and how does it get under the skin? *Annual Review of Psychology, 48,* 411–447.

Taylor, S. E., & Brown, J. D. (1988). Illusion and well-being: A social psychological perspective on mental health. *Psychological Bulletin, 103,* 193–210.

Taylor, S. M., Ross, N. A., Cummings, K. M., Glasgow, R. E., Goldsmith, C. H., Zanna, M. P., & Corle, D. K. (1998). Community intervention trial for smoking cessation (COMMIT): Changes in community attitudes toward cigarette smoking. *Health Education Research, 13,* 109–122.

Teeter, J. H., & Brand, J. G. (1987). Peripheral mechanisms of gustation: Physiology and biochemistry. In T. E. Finger & W. L. Silver (Eds.), *Neurobiology of taste and smell.* New York: Wiley.

Telford, L., & Frost, B. J. (1993). Factors affecting the onset and magnitude of linear vection. *Perception and Psychophysics, 53,* 682–692.

Tellegen, A., Lykken, D. T., Bouchard, T. J., Jr., Wilcox, K. J., Segal, N. L., & Rich, S. (1988). Personality similarity in twins reared apart and together. *Journal of Personality and Social Psychology, 54,* 1031–1039.

Templeton, J. J. (1998). Learning from others' mistakes: A paradox revisited. *Animal Behaviour, 55,* 79–85.

Tennes, K., & Kreye, M. (1985). Children's adrenocortical responses to classroom activities and tests in elementary school. *Psychosomatic Medicine, 47,* 451–460.

Terman, L. M. (1925). *Mental and physical traits of a thousand gifted children.* Stanford, CA: Stanford University Press.

Terman, L. M. (1954). The discovery and encouragement of exceptional talent. *American Psychologist, 9,* 221–238.

Terman, L. M., & Ogden, M. (1947). *Genetic studies of genius. The gifted child grows up.* Stanford, CA: Stanford University Press.

Terrace, H. S. (1986). *Nim: A chimpanzee who learned sign language.* New York: Columbia University Press.

Tesser, A. (1993). The importance of heritability in psychological research: The case of attitudes. *Psychological Review, 100,* 129–142.

Thibos, L. N., Bradley, A., Still, D. L., & Zhang, X. (1990). Theory and measurement of ocular chromatic aberration. *Vision Research, 30,* 33–49.

Thigpen, C. H., & Cleckley, H. A. (1957). *Three faces of Eve.* New York: McGraw-Hill.

Thomas, A., & Chess, S. (1977). *Temperament and development.* New York: Bruner/Mazel.

Thompson, J. K., & Stice, E. (2001). Thin-ideal internalization: Mounting evidence for a new risk factor for body-image disturbance and eating pathology. *Current Directions in Psychological Science, 10,* 181–183.

Thomsen, P. H. (1994). Obsessive-compulsive disorder in children and adolescents: A review of the literature. *European Child and Adolescent Psychiatry, 3,* 138–158.

Thomsen, P. H. (1998). Obsessive-compulsive disorder in children and adolescents: Clinical guidelines. *European Child and Adolescent Psychiatry, 7,* 1–11.

Thoresen, C. E., & Powell, L. H. (1992). Type A behavior pattern: New perspectives on theory, assessment and intervention. *Journal of Consulting and Clinical Psychology, 60,* 595–604.

Thorndike, E. L. (1898). Animal intelligence: An experimental study of the associative processes in animals. *Psychological Review, Monograph Supplements, 2* (Serial No. 8).

Thurstone, L. L. (1938). *Primary mental abilities.* Chicago: University of Chicago Press.

Tiffany, S. T. (1990). A cognitive model of drug urges and drug-use behavior: Role of automatic and nonautomatic processes. *Psychological Review, 97,* 147–168.

Timberlake, W. (1980). A molar equilibrium theory of learned performance. In G. H. Bower (Ed.), *The psychology of learning and motivation.* New York: Academic Press.

Timberlake, W., & Silva, F. J. (1994). Observation of behavior, inference of func-tion, and the study of learning. *Psychonomic Bulletin and Review, 1,* 73–88.

Tinbergen, N. (1951). *The study of instinct.* London: Oxford University Press.

Titchener, E. B. (1899). Structural and functional psychology. *Philosophical Review, 8,* 290–299.

Tolman, C. W. (1968). The role of the companion in social facilitation of animal behavior. In E. C. Simmel, R. A. Hoppe, & G. A. Milton (Eds.), *Social facilitation and imitative behavior.* Boston: Allyn & Bacon.

Tomaka, J., Blascovich, J., Kibler, J., & Ernst, J. M. (1997). Cognitive and physiological antecedents of threat and challenge appraisal. *Journal of Personality and Social Psychology, 73,* 63–72.

Tombaugh, T. N. (1997). The Test of Memory Malingering (TOMM): Normative data from cognitively intact and cognitively impaired individuals. *Psychological Assessment, 9,* 260–268.

Tomkins, S. S. (1962). *Affect, imagery, and consciousness.* New York: Springer.

Tooby, J., & Cosmides, L. (1995). Mapping the evolved functional organization of mind and brain. In M. S. Gazzaniga (Ed.), *The cognitive neurosciences* (pp. 1185–1197). Cambridge, MA: The MIT Press.

Torrance, E. P. (1981). Empirical validation of criterion-referenced indicators of creative ability through a longitudinal study. *Creative Child and Adult Quarterly, 6,* 136–140.

Towler, G. (1986). From zero to one hundred: Coaction in a natural setting. *Perceptual and Motor Skills, 62,* 377–378.

Trapnell, P. D., & Wiggins, J. S. (1990). Extension of the Interpersonal Adjective Scales to include the Big Five dimensions of personality. *Journal of Personality and Social Psychology, 59,* 781–790.

Travis, C. B., Phillippi, R. H., & Tonn, B. E. (1989). Judgment heuristics and medical decisions. *Patient Education and Counseling, 13,* 211–220.

Travis, F., & Wallace, R. K. (1999). Autonomic and EEG patterns during eyes-closed rest and transcendental meditation (TM) practice: The basis for a neural model of TM practice. *Consciousness and Cognition: An International Journal, 8,* 302–318.

Trehub, S. E., Hill, D. S., & Lamenetsky, S. B. (1997). Parents' sung performances for infants. *Canadian Journal of Experimental Psychology, 51,* 385–396.

Treisman, A. (1960). Contextual cues in selective listening. *Quarterly Journal of Experimental Psychology, 12,* 242–248.

Treit, D., & Menard, J. (2000). The septum and anxiety. In R. Numan (Ed.), *The behavioral neuroscience of the septal region* (pp. 210–233). New York: Springer-Verlag.

Tri-Council Policy Statement (1999). *Ethical conduct for research involving humans.* Ottawa, ON: Medical Research Council of Canada. Also available at www.nserc.ca/programs/ethics/english/policy.htm

Triplett, N. (1898). The dynamogenic factors in pacemaking and competition. *American Journal of Psychology, 9,* 507–533.

Trobst, K. K. (2000). An interpersonal conceptualization and quantification of social support transactions. *Personality and Social Psychology Bulletin, 26,* 971–986.

Trull, T. J., & McCrae, R. R. (1994). A five-factor perspective on personality disorder research. In P. T. Costa, Jr., & T. A. Widiger (Eds.), *Personality disorders and the five-factor model of personality.* Washington, DC: American Psychological Association.

Tseng, W., & McDermott, J. F. (1975). Psychotherapy: Historical roots, universal elements, and cultural variations. *American Journal of Psychiatry, 132,* 378–384.

Tuckman, B. W. (1998). Using tests as an incentive to motivate procrastinators to study. *Journal of Experimental Education, 66,* 141–147.

Tugrul, K. (1998). Newer antipsychotic agents: Impact on quality of life and alternative applications. *Journal of the American Psychiatric Nurses Association, 4,* S35–S41.

Tulving, E. (1983). *Elements of episodic memory.* New York: Oxford University Press.

Tulving, E., & Pearlstone, Z. (1966). Availability versus accessibility of information in memory for words. *Journal of Verbal Learning and Verbal Behavior, 5,* 381–391.

Tulving, E., & Thomson, D. M. (1973). Encoding specificity and retrieval processes in episodic memory. *Psychological Review, 80,* 352–373.

Turner, T. J., & Ortony, A. (1992). Basic emotions: Can conflicting criteria converge? *Psychological Review, 99,* 566–571.

Tversky, A., & Kahneman, D. (1973). On the psychology of prediction. *Psychological Review, 80,* 237–251.

Tversky, A., & Kahneman, D. (1974). Decision making under uncertainty: Heuristics and biases. *Science, 185,* 1124–1131.

Tversky, A., & Kahneman, D. (1983). Extensional versus intuitive reasoning: The conjunction fallacy in probability judgment. *Psychological Review, 90,* 293–315.

Tversky, A., & Kahneman, D. (1987). Rational choice and the framing of decisions. In R. M. Hogarth & M. W. Reder (Eds.), *Rational choice: The contrast between economics and psychology* (pp. 67–94). Chicago: University of Chicago Press.

Tychsen, L. (2001). Critical periods for the development of visual acuity, depth perception, and eye tracking. In D. Bailey & J. Bruer (Eds.), *Critical thinking about critical periods.* Baltimore, MD: Paul H. Brookes.

Tyler, J. M., & Tyler, C. L. (1997). Ethics in supervision: Managing supervisee rights and supervisor responsibilities. *Hatherleigh Guide to Ethics in Therapy, 10,* 75–95.

Ulrich, R. E. (1991). Commentary: Animal rights, animal wrongs and the question of balance. *Psychological Science, 2,* 197–201.

Uttl, B., Graf, P., Miller, J., McIsaac, H., & Tuokko, H. (2001). Age-related changes in pro- and retrospective memory. *Consciousness and Cognition, 10,* 451–472.

Valenstein, E. S. (1986). *Great and desperate cures: The rise and decline of psychosurgery and other radical treatments for mental illness.* New York: Basic Books.

van Dongen, M. C. J. M., van Rossum, E., Kessels, A. G. H., Sielhorst, H. J. G., & Knipschild, P. G. (2000). The efficacy of ginkgo for elderly people with dementia and age-associated memory impairment: New results of a randomized clinical trial. *Journal of the American Geriatrics Society, 48* (10), 1183–1194.

Van Doornen, L. J., & Van Blokland, R. (1987). Serum-cholesterol: Sex-specific psychological correlates during rest and stress. *Journal of Psychosomatic Research, 31,* 239–249.

Van Loocke, P. (Ed.) (2001). *The physical nature of consciousness.* New York: Benjamins.

van Rijzingen, I. M. S., Gispen, W. H., & Spruijt, B. M. (1997). Postoperative environmental enrichment attenuates fimbria-fornix lesion-induced impairments in Morris maze performance. *Neurobiology of Learning and Memory, 67,* 21–28.

Vazire, S., & Gosling, S. D. (2003). *www.knowingmeknowingyou.com: Judging personality from web sites.* Paper presented at the meeting of the Western Psychological Association, Vancouver.

Vecera, S. P., Vogel, E. K., & Woodman, G. F. (2002). Lower region: A new cue for figure-ground assignment. *Journal of Experimental Psychology: General, 131* (2), 194–205.

Vernon, P. E. (1983). Speed of information processing and general intelligence. *Intelligence, 7,* 53–70.

Verschueven, S., Cordo, P. J., & Swinnen, S. P. (1998). Representation of wrist joint kinematics by the ensemble of muscle spindles from synergistic muscles. *Journal of Neurophysiology, 79,* 2265–2276.

Vertes, R. P., & Eastman, K. E. (2000). The case against memory consolidation in REM sleep. *Behavioral & Brain Sciences, 23,* 867–876; 904–1018; 1083–1121.

Victor, M. (1996). Conflicting communicative behavior in a split-brain patient: Support for dual consciousness. In S. Hameroff & A. W. Kaszniak (Eds.), *Toward a science of consciousness: The first Tucson discussions and debates.* Cambridge, MA: MIT Press.

Villeneuve, P. J., Morrison, H. I., Craig, C. L., & Schaubel, D. E. (1998). Physical activity, physical fitness, and risk of dying. *Epidemiology, 9,* 626–631.

Vitz, P. C. (1988). *Sigmund Freud's Christian unconscious.* New York: Guilford.

Vogel, G. W., Buffenstein, A., Minter, K., & Hennessey, A. (1990). Drug effects on REM sleep and on endogenous depression. *Neuroscience and Biobehavioral Reviews, 14,* 49–63.

Vohs, K.D., & Heatherton, T.F. (2000). Self-regulatory failure: A resource-depletion approach. *Psychological Science 11,* 249–254.

Vokey, J. R., & Read, J. D. (1985). Subliminal messages: Between the media and the devil. *American Psychologist, 40,* 1231–1239.

von Frisch, K. (1967). *The dance language and orientation of bees.* Cambridge, MA: Belknap Press.

Vorauer, J. D., & Miller, D. T. (1997). Failure to recognize the effect of implicit social influence on the presentation of self. *Journal of Personality and Social Psychology, 73,* 281–295.

Vorauer, J. D., Main, K. J., & O'Connell, G. B. (1998). How do individuals expect to be viewed by members of lower status groups? Content and implications of meta-stereotypes. *Journal of Personality and Social Psychology, 75,* 917–937.

Vorauer, J. D., Hunter, A. J., Main, K. J., & Roy, S. A. (2000). Meta-stereotype activation: Evidence from indirect measure for specific evaluative concerns experienced by members of dominant groups in intergroup interaction. *Journal of Personality and Social Psychology, 78,* 690–707.

Vygotsky, L. S. (1978). *Mind in society: The development of higher psychological processes.* Cambridge, MA: Harvard University Press.

Wada, J. A. (Ed.) (1991). *Kindling, 4.* New York: Plenum Press.

Waddill, P. J., & McDaniel, M. A. (1998). Distinctiveness effects in free recall: Differential processing or privileged retrieval? *Memory and Cognition, 26,* 108–120.

Wagenaar, W. A. (1986). My memory: A study of autobiographical memory over six years. *Cognitive Psychology, 18,* 225–252.

Wagner, A. R. (1981). SOP: A model of automatic memory processing in animal behavior. In N. E. Spear & R. R. Miller (Eds.), *Information processing in animals: Memory mechanisms.* Hillsdale, NJ: Erlbaum.

Wagner, R. K., & Sternberg, R. J. (1985). Practical intelligence in real-world pursuits: The role of tacit knowledge. *Journal of Personality and Social Psychology, 49,* 436–458.

Waldman, I. D., Weinberg, R. A., & Scarr, S. (1994). Racial-group differences in IQ in the Minnesota Transracial Adoption Study: A reply to Levin and Lynn. *Intelligence, 19,* 29–44.

Walen, S. T., DiGuiseppe, R., & Dryden, W. (1992). *A practitioner's guide to rational-emotive therapy.* New York: Oxford University Press.

Walker, L. J. (1989). A longitudinal study of moral reasoning. *Child Development, 60,* 157–166.

Wallace, C. J. (1998). Social skills training in psychiatric rehabilitation: Recent findings. *International Review of Psychiatry, 10,* 9–10.

Wallhagen, M. I., Strawbridge, W., & Shema, S. (1997). *Perceived control: Mental health correlates in a population-based aging cohort.* Paper presented at the 50th Annual Scientific Meeting of the Gerontological Society of America.

Walters, J. M., & Gardner, H. (1986). The theory of multiple intelligences: Some issues and answers. In R. J. Sternberg & R. K. Wagner (Eds.), *Practical intelligence: Nature and origins of competence in the everyday world.* New York: Cambridge University Press.

Walton, G. E., & Bower, T. G. R. (1993). Newborns form "prototypes" in less than 1 minute. *Psychological Science, 4,* 203–205.

Wampold, B. E., Mondin, G. W., Moody, M., Stich, F., Benson, K., & Ahn, H. (1997). A meta-analysis of outcome studies comparing bona fide psychotherapies: Empiricially, "all must have prizes." *Psychological Bulletin, 122,* 203–215.

Washburn, M. F. (1908). *The animal mind.* New York: Macmillan.

Wasow, T. (1989). Grammatical theory. In M. I. Posner (Ed.), *Foundations of cognitive science.* Cambridge, MA: MIT Press.

Wasserman, E. A., & Miller, R. R. (1997). What's elementary about associative learning? *Annual Review of Psychology, 48,* 573–607.

Waters, E., Wippman, J., & Sroufe, L. A. (1979). Attachment, positive affect, and competence in the peer group: Two studies in construct validation. *Child Development, 50,* 821–829.

Watkins, O. C., & Watkins, M. J. (1980). The modality effect and echoic persistence. *Journal of Experimental Psychology: General, 109,* 251–278.

Watson, J. B. (1913). Psychology as a behaviorist views it. *Psychological Review, 20,* 158–177.

Watson, J. B. (1919). *Psychology from the standpoint of a behaviorist.* Philadelphia: Lippincott.

Watson, S. J., Benson, J. A., Jr., & Joy, J. E. (2000). Marijuana and medicine: Assessing the science base. A summary of the 1999 Institute of Medicine Report. *Archives of General Psychiatry, 57,* 547–552.

Webb, E. J., Campbell, D. T., Schwartz, R. D., Sechrist, L., & Grove, J. B. (1981). *Nonreactive research in the social sciences.* Boston: Houghton Mifflin.

Webb, W. B. (1981). The return of consciousness. *G. Stanley Hall Lecture Series, 1,* 129–152.

Webb, W. B. (1992). *Sleep: The gentle tyrant.* Bolton, MA: Anker Publishing.

Wechsler, D. (1996). *WISC-III Manual Canadian Supplement.* Toronto: The Psychological Corporation.

Weibel-Orlando, J. (1989). Treatment and prevention of Native American alcoholism. In T. D. Watts & R. Wright (Eds.), *Alcoholism in minority populations* (pp. 121–139). Springfield, IL: Charles C Thomas.

Weinberg, R. A., Scarr, S., & Waldman, I. D. (1992). The Minnesota Transracial Adoption Study: A follow-up of IQ test performance at adolescence. *Intelligence, 16,* 117–135.

Weiner, R. D., & Coffey, C. E. (1988). Indications for use of electroconvulsive therapy. In A. J. Frances & R. E. Hales (Eds.), *Review of Psychiatry.* Washington, DC: American Psychiatric Press.

Weingarten, H. P. (1983). Conditioned cues elicit feeding in sated rats: A role for learning in meal initiation. *Science, 220,* 431–433.

Weingarten, H. P. (1985). Stimulus control of eating: Implications for a two-factor theory of hunger. *Appetite, 6,* 387–401.

Weingarten, H. P., Chang, P. K., & McDonald, T. J. (1985). Comparison of the metabolic and behavioral disturbances following paraventricular and ventro-medial-hypothalamic lesions. *Brain Research Bulletin, 14,* 551–559.

Weinstein, L. N., Schwartz, D. G., & Arkin, A. M. (1991). Qualitative aspects of sleep mentation. In S. J. Ellman & J. S. Antrobus (Eds.), *The mind in sleep* (2nd ed.). New York: Wiley.

Weinstein, S., & Graves, R. E. (2002). Are creativity and schizotypy products of a right hemisphere bias? *Brain and Cognition, 49* (1), 138–151.

Weisberg, H. F., Krosnick, J. A., & Bowen, B. D. (1989). *An introduction to survey research and data analysis* (2nd ed.). Glenview, IL: Scott, Foresman.

Weisberg, R. W. (1994). Genius and madness? A quasi-experimental test of the hypothesis that manic-depression increases creativity. *Psychological Science, 5,* 361–367.

Weiskrantz, L. (1992). Introduction: Dissociated issues. In A. D. Milner & M. D. Rugg (Eds.), *The neuropsychology of consciousness.* London: Academic Press.

Weiss, J. M. (1977). Psychological and behavioral influences on gastrointestinal lesions in animal models. In J. D. Maser & M. E. P. Seligman (Eds.), *Psychopathology: Experimental models.* San Francisco: Freeman.

Weiss, L., & Baum, A. (1987). Physiological aspects of environment-behavior relationships. In E. Zube & G. Morre (Eds.), *Advances in environmental psychology.* New York: Plenum.

Weiten, W. (1995). *Psychology: Themes and variations* (3rd ed.). Pacific Grove, CA: Brooks/Cole.

Welder, A. N., & Graham, S. A. (2001). The influences of shape similarity and shared labels on infants' inductive inferences about nonobvious object properties. *Child Development, 72,* 1653–1673.

Weldon, M. S., & Roediger, H. M., III (1987). Altering retrieval demands reverses the picture superiority effect. *Memory and Cognition, 15,* 269–280.

Wender, P. H., Kety, S. S., Rosenthal, D., Schlusinger, F., Ortmann, J., & Lunde, I. (1986). Psychiatric disorders in the biological and adoptive families of adopted individuals with affective disorders. *Archives of General Psychiatry, 43,* 923–929.

Wenner, A. (1998). Honey bee "dance language" controversy. In G. Greenberg & M. M. Haraway (Eds.), *Comparative psychology: A handbook.* New York: Garland.

Werker, J. F., & Desjardins, R. N. (2001). Listening to speech in the 1st year of life. In M. Tomasello & E. Bates (Eds.), *Language development: The essential readings* (pp. 26–33). Malden, MA: Blackwell.

Werker, J. F., & Tees, R. C. (1999). Influences on infant speech processing: Toward a new synthesis. *Annual Review of Psychology, 50,* 509–535.

Wernicke, C. (1874). *Der Aphasische Symptomenkomplex.* Breslau, Poland: Cohn & Weigert.

Wertheimer, M. (1987). *A brief history of psychology* (3rd ed.). New York: Holt, Rinehart & Winston.

Wertsch, J. V., & Tulviste, P. (1992). L. S. Vygotsky and contemporary developmental psychology. *Developmental Psychology, 28,* 548–557.

Wesnes, K. A., Ward, T., McGinty, A., & Petrini, O. (2000). The memory enhancing effects of a Ginkgo bilboa/Panax ginseng combination in healthy middle-aged volunteers. *Psychopharmacology, 152,* 353–361.

Westen, D. (1998). The scientific legacy of Sigmund Freud: Toward a psychodynamically informed psychological science. *Psychological Bulletin, 124,* 333–371.

Wheeler, L., & Kim, Y. (1997). What is beautiful is culturally good: The physical attractiveness stereotype has different content in collectivistic cultures. *Personality and Social Psychology Bulletin, 23,* 795–800.

Wheeler, M. A., Stuss, D. T., & Tulving, E. (1997). Toward a theory of episodic memory: The frontal lobes and autonoetic consciousness. *Psychological Bulletin, 121,* 331–354.

Whishaw, I. Q., Hines, D. J., & Wallace, D. G. (2001). Dead reckoning (path integration) requires the hippocampal formation: Evidence from spontaneous exploration and spatial learning tasks in light (allothetic) and dark (idiothetic) tests. *Behavioural Brain Research, 127,* 49–69.

Whitbourne, S. K. (1985). *The aging body.* New York: Springer.

Whitbourne, S. K., Zuschlag, M. K., Elliot, L. B., & Waterman, A. S. (1992). Psychosocial development in adulthood: A 22-year sequential study. *Journal of Personality and Social Psychology, 63,* 260–271.

White, L., Tursky, B., & Schwartz, G. E. (1985). *Placebo: Theory, research, and mechanisms.* New York: Guilford.

Whittlesea, B. W. A., & Leboe, J. P. (2000). The heuristic basis of remembering and classification: Fluency, generation, and resemblance. *Journal of Experimental Psychology: General, 129,* 84–106.

Whittlesea, B. W. A., & Williams, L. D. (2000). The source of feelings of familiarity: The discrepancy-attribution hypothesis. *Journal of Experimental Psychology: Learning, Memory, and Cognition, 26,* 547–565.

Whittlesea, B. W. A., Brooks, L. R., & Westcott, C. (1994). After the learning is over: Factors controlling the selective application of general and particular knowledge. *Journal of Experimental Psychology: Learning, Memory, and Cognition, 20* (2), 259–274.

Whorf, B. L. (1956). *Language, thought, and reality: Selected writings of Benjamin Lee Whorf.* New York: Wiley.

Wickelgren, W. A. (1999). Webs, cell assemblies, and chunking in neural nets: Introduction. *Canadian Journal of Experimental Psychology, 53,* 118–131.

Widiger, T. A. (1998). Personality disorders. In D. F. Barone & M. Hersen (Eds.), *Advanced personality. The Plenum series in social/clinical psychology.* New York: Plenum Press.

Widiger, T. A., & Sankis, L. M. (2000). Adult psychopathology: Issues and controversies. *Annual Review of Psychology, 51,* 377–404.

Wigfield, A. (1994). Expectancy-value theory of achievement motivation: A developmental perspective. *Educational Psychology Review, 6,* 49–78.

Wiggins, J. S. (1979). A psychological taxonomy of trait descriptive terms: The interpersonal domain. *Journal of Personality and Social Psychology, 37,* 395–412.

Wiggins, J. S. (Ed.) (1996). *The five-factor model of personality: Theoretical perspectives.* New York: Guilford.

Wiggins, J. S., & Broughton, R. (1991). A geometric taxonomy of personality scales. *European Journal of Personality, 5,* 343–365.

Wiggins, J. S., & Pincus, A. L. (1992). Personality: Structure and assessment. *Annual Review of Psychology, 43,* 473–504.

Wiggins, J. S., & Trapnell, P. D. (1997). Personality structure: The return of the Big Five. In R. Hogan, J. A. Johnson, & S. R. Briggs (Eds.), *Handbook of personality psychology* (pp. 737–764). San Diego: Academic Press.

Wilde, G. J. S. (1994). *Target risk: Dealing with the danger of death, disease and damage in everyday decisions.* Toronto, ON: PDE Publications.

Williams, D. A., Frame, K. A., & LoLordo, V. M. (1991). Reexamination of contextual conditioning with massed versus distributed unconditioned stimuli. *Journal of Experimental Psychology: Animal Behavior Processes, 17,* 202–209.

Williams, L. M. (1994). Recall of childhood trauma: A prospective study of women's memories of child sexual abuse. *Journal of Consulting and Clinical Psychology, 62,* 1167–1176.

Willoughby, T., Wood, E., McDermott, C., & McLaren, J. (2000). Enhancing learning through strategy instruction and group interaction: Is active generation of elaborations critical? *Applied Cognitive Psychology, 14* (1), 19–30.

Wilson, E. O. (1963, May). Pheromones. *Scientific American, 208,* 100–114.

Wilson, L. M., Stewart, M. L., & McAnanama, E. P. (1989). Milk intakes of genetically obese (ob/ob) and lean mouse pups differ with enhanced milk supply. *Physiology and Behavior, 46,* 823–827.

Wilson, M., & Daly, M. (1997). Relationship-specific social psychological adaptations. In G. R. Bock & G. Cardew (Eds.), *Characterizing human psychological adaptations.* New York: John Wiley.

Wilson, M., & Daly, M. (1990). Killing the competition: Female/female and Male/male homicide. *Human Nature, 1,* 53–79.

Windgassen, K. (1992). Treatment with neuroleptics: The patient's perspective. *Acta Psychiatrica Scandinavica, 86,* 405–410.

Winett, R. A. (1995). A framework for health promotion and disease prevention programs. *American Psychologist, 50,* 341–350.

Winikoff, B. (1983). Nutritional patterns, social choices, and health. In D. Mechanic (Ed.), *Handbook of health, health care, and the health professions.* New York: Free Press.

Winner, E. (1997). Exceptionally high intelligence and schooling. *American Psychologist, 52,* 1070–1081.

Winter, D. G., John, O. P., Stewart, A. J., Klohnen, E. C., & Duncan, L. E. (1998). Traits and motives: Toward an integration of two traditions in personality research. *Psychological Review, 105,* 230–250.

Wise, R. A., & Bozarth, M. A. (1987). A psychomotor theory of addiction. *Psychological Review, 94,* 469–492.

Wise, R. A., & Rompre, P. P. (1989). Brain dopamine and reward. *Annual Review of Psychology, 40,* 191–225.

Wissler, C. (1901). The correlation of mental and physical tests. *Psychological Review, Monograph Supplement 3* (No. 6).

Witelson, S. F. (1992). Cognitive neuroanatomy: A new era. *Neurology, 42,* 709–713.

Wixted, J. T., & Ebbesen, E. B. (1991). On the form of forgetting. *Psychological Science, 2,* 409–415.

Wolfe, D. A., McMahon, R. J., & Peters, R. D. (Eds.) (1997). *Child abuse: New directions in prevention and treatment across the lifespan.* Thousand Oaks, CA: Sage.

Wolff, N., Helminiak, T. W., & Tebes, J. K. (1997). Getting the cost right in cost-effectiveness analyses. *American Journal of Psychiatry, 154,* 736–743.

Wollberg, Z., & Newman, J. D. (1972). Auditory cortex of squirrel monkey: Response patterns of single cells to species-specific vocalizations. *Science, 175,* 212–214.

Wolpe, J. (1958). *Psychotherapy by reciprocal inhibition.* Stanford, CA: Stanford University Press.

Wolpe, J. (1975). Foreword. In B. Sloane, F. Staples, A. Cristol, N. Yorkston, & K. Whipple (Eds.), *Psychotherapy versus behavior therapy.* Cambridge, MA: Harvard University Press.

Wolpe, J. (1982). *The practice of behavior therapy.* New York: Pergamon.

Wong, S. E., Martinez-Diaz, J. A., Massel, H. K., Edelstein, B. A., Wiegand, W., Bowen, L., & Liberman, R. P. (1993). Conversational skills training with schizophrenic inpatients: A study of generalization across settings and conversants. *Behavior Therapy, 24,* 285–304.

Wood, J. M., Bootzin, R. R., Kihlstrom, J. F., & Schacter, D. L. (1992). Implicit and explicit memory for verbal information presented during sleep. *Psychological Science, 3,* 236–239.

Wood, W. (2000). Attitude change: Persuasion and social influence. *Annual Review of Psychology, 51,* 539–570.

Wood, W., Wang, F. Y., & Chacherie, J. G. (1991). Effects of media violence on viewers' aggression in unconstrained social situations. *Psychological Bulletin, 109,* 371–383.

Woods, D. L., Alain, C., & Ogawa, K. H. (1998). Auditory and visual feature conjunction during high-rate serial presentation: Processing two features can be faster than processing one. *Perception and Psychophysics, 60,* 239–249.

Woods, E. R., Lin, Y. G., Middleman, A., Beckford, P., Chase, L., & DuRant, R. (1997). The associations of suicide attempts in adolescents. *Pediatrics, 99,* 791–796.

Woods, S. C., Seeley, R. J., Porte, D., & Schwartz, M. W. (1998). Signals that regulate food intake and energy homeostasis. *Science, 280,* 1378–1383.

Woodward, T. S., Dixon, M. J., Mullen, K. T., Christensen, K. M., & Bub, D. N. (1999). Analysis of errors in color agnosia: A single-case study. *Neurocase, 5* (2), 95–108.

Woody, G. E., & Cacciola, J. (1997). Diagnosis and classification: DSM-IV and ICD-10. In J. H. Lowinson, P. Ruiz, R. B. Millman, & J. G. Langrod (Eds.), *Substance abuse: A comprehensive textbook.* Baltimore: Williams & Wilkins.

Woody, S., & McLean, P. D. (2001). *Anxiety disorders in adults: An evidence based approach to psychological treatment.* New York: Oxford University Press.

Worringham, C. J., & Messick, D. M. (1983). Social facilitation of running: An unobtrusive study. *Journal of Social Psychology, 121,* 23–29.

Wright, E. F., Voyer, D., Wright, R. D., & Roney, C. (1995). Supporting audiences and performance under pressure: The home-ice disadvantage in hockey championships. *Journal of Sport Behavior, 18,* 21–28.

Wright, M. J. (1992). Women ground-breakers in Canadian psychology: World War II and its aftermath. *Canadian Psychology, 33,* 675–682.

Wright, R. (1994). *The moral animal.* New York: Pantheon/Toronto: Random House.

Wundt, W. (1896). *Outlines of psychology* (C. M. Judd, Trans.). New York: Stechart.

Wyrostok, N., & Paulson, B. (2000). Traditional healing practices among First Nations students. *Canadian Journal of Counselling, 34* (1), 14–24.

Yalom, I. D. (1980). *Existential psychotherapy.* New York: Basic Books.

Yalom, I. D. (1995). *The theory and practice of group psychotherapy* (4th ed.). New York: Basic Books.

Yamaguchi, S., Tsuchiya, H., & Koboyashi, S. (1998). Visuospatial attention shift and motor responses in cerebellar disorders. *Journal of Cognitive Neuroscience, 10,* 95–107.

Yamamoto, T., Yuyama, N., & Kawamura, Y. (1981). Central processing of taste perception. In Y. Katsuki, R. Norgren, & M. Sato (Eds.), *Brain mechanisms of sensation.* New York: Wiley.

Yapko, M. D. (1994). Suggestibility and repressed memories of abuse: A survey of psychotherapists' beliefs. *American Journal of Clinical Hypnosis, 36,* 163–179.

Yates, F. A. (1966). *The art of memory.* Chicago: University of Chicago Press.

Yik, M. S. M., & Russell, J. A. (1999). Interpretation of faces: A cross-cultural study of a prediction from Fridlund's Theory. *Cognition and Emotion, 13,* 93–104.

Yin, R. K. (1998). The abridged version of case study research: Design and method. In L. Bickman & Debra J. Rog (Eds.), *Handbook of applied social research methods.* Thousand Oaks, CA: Sage.

Yonelinas, A. P., & Jacoby, L. L. (1995). The relation between remembering and knowing as bases for recognition: Effects of size congruency. *Journal of Memory and Language, 34,* 622–643.

Young, J. E., Beck, A. T., & Weinberger, A. (1993). Depression. In D. H. Barlow (Ed.), *Clinical handbook of psychological disorders* (2nd ed.). New York: Guilford.

Young, J. E., Weinberger, A. D., & Beck, A. T. (2001). Cognitive therapy for depression. In D. H. Barlow (Ed.), *Clinical handbook of psychological disorders* (3rd ed.). New York: Guilford.

Young, K. S. (1998). *Caught in the net.* New York: John Wiley & Sons.

Young, K. S. (1999). Internet addiction: Symptoms, evaluation and treatment. In L. VandeCreek & T. Jackson (Eds.), *Innovations in clinical practice: A source book.* Sarasota, FL: Professional Resource Press.

Young, L. R., & Shelhamer, M. (1990). Microgravity enhances the relative contribution of visually-induced motion sensation. *Aviation and Space Environmental Medicine, 61,* 525–530.

Yuille, J. C. (1993). We must study forensic eyewitnesses to know about them. *American Psychologist, 48,* 572–573.

Zacks, R. T., & Hasher, L. (1994). Directed ignoring: Inhibitory regulation of working memory. In D. Dagenbach & T. H. Carr (Eds.), *Inhibitory processes in attention, memory, and language.* San Diego: Academic Press.

Zahorik, D. M., Houpt, K. A., & Swartzman-Andert, J. (1990). Taste-aversion learning in three species of ruminants. *Applied Animal Behaviour Science, 26,* 27–39.

Zajonc, R. B. (1965). Social facilitation. *Science, 149,* 269–274.

Zajonc, R. B. (1968). Attitudinal effects of mere exposure. *Journal of Personality and Social Psychology, 9* (Monograph Suppl. 2, Pt 2).

Zajonc, R. B. (1983). Validating the confluence model. *Psychological Bulletin, 93* (3), 457–480.

Zajonc, R. B. (2001). Mere exposure: A gateway to the subliminal. *Current Directions in Psychology Science, 10,* 224–228.

Zajonc, R. B., Heingartner, A., & Herman, E. M. (1969). Social enhancement and impairment of performance in the cockroach. *Journal of Personality and Social Psychology, 13,* 83–92.

Zajonc, R. B., Murphy, S. T., & McIntosh, D. N. (1993). Brain temperature and subjective emotional experience. In M. Lewis & J. M. Haviland (Eds.), *Handbook of emotions.* New York: Guilford.

Zametkin, A. J., Nordahl, T., Gross, M., King, A. C., Semple, W. E., Rumsey, J., Hamburger, S., & Cohen, R. M. (1990). Cerebral glucose metabolism in adults with hyperactivity of childhood onset. *New England Journal of Medicine, 323,* 1361–1366.

Zanna, M., & Olson, J. M. (1994). *The psychology of prejudice (Ontario Symposium on Personality and Social Psychology).* Mahwah, NJ: Erlbaum.

Zanna, M. P. (1994). On the nature of prejudice. *Canadian Psychology, 35,* 11–23.

Zatorre, R. J., Evans, A. C., & Meyer, E. (1994). Neural mechanisms underlying melodic perception and memory for pitch. *Journal of Neuroscience, 14,* 1908–1919.

Zeki, S. (1992, September). The visual image in mind and brain. *Scientific American, 267,* 68–76.

Ziegert, D. I., Kistner, J. A., Castro, R., & Robertson, B. (2001). Longitudinal study of young children's responses to challenging achievement situations. *Child Development, 72,* 609–624.

Zotterman, Y. (1959). Thermal sensations. In J. Fields, H. W. Magoun, & V. E. Hall (Eds.), *Handbook of physiology: Section I. Neurophysiology, 1* (pp. 431–458). Washington, DC: Physiological Society.

Zucker, K. J. (1987). Commentary on Kohlberg, Ricks, and Snarey's (1984) "Childhood development as a predictor of adaptation in adulthood." *Genetic, Social, and General Psychology Monographs, 113* (1), 127–130.

Zuroff, D. C., Blatt, S. T., Sanislow, C. A., III, Bondi, C. M., & Pilkonis, P. A. (1999). Vulnerability to depression: Reexamining state dependence and relative stability. *Journal of Abnormal Psychology, 108,* 76–89.

Zuroff, D. C., Sotsky, S. M., Martin, D. J., Sanislow, C. A., Blat, S. J., Krupnick, J. L., & Simmens, S. (2000). Relation of therapeutic alliance and perfectionism to outcome in brief outpatient treatment of depression. *Journal of Consulting and Clinical Psychology, 68,* 114–124.

Copyright Acknowledgments

These pages constitute an extension of the copyright page. We have made every effort to trace the ownership of all copyrighted material and to secure permission from copyright holders. In the event of any question arising as to the use of any material, we will be pleased to make the necessary corrections in future printings. Thanks are due to the following authors, publishers, and agents for permission to use the material indicated.

CHAPTER 3
107: Figure 3.15 (The Endocrine System): Reprinted by permission of www.KidsHealth.org, the Nemours Foundation.

CHAPTER 4
147: Figure 4.22 (Illusion of Depth): From *Mind Sights,* by Roger N. Shepard. Copyright © 1990 by Roger N. Shepard. Reprinted by permission of Henry Holt and Company, LLC.

CHAPTER 5
189: Figure 5.6 (EEG Patterns Associated with Sleeping and Wakefulness): From *Current Concepts: The Sleep Disorders,* by Hauri. Copyright © 1982. The Upjohn Company, Kalamazoo, Michigan. Reprinted by permission of the author.

CHAPTER 6
216: From *Once in a Lifetime,* by David Byrne, Brian Eno, George Peter, Chris Frantz, Jeffy Harrison, Tina (Martina) Weymouth. Reprinted by permission of WB Music Corporation 235: Figure 6.9 (Instrumental Conditioning): From *Psychology: Themes and Variations,* Third Edition, by Weiten. Copyright © 1995. Reprinted with permission of Wadsworth, a division of Thomson Learning: www.thomsonrights.com. Fax 800 730-2215.

CHAPTER 8
315: Figure 8.5 (Fuzzy Category Boundaries): From *Introduction to Psychology,* First Edition, by Goldstein. Copyright © 1994. Reprinted with permission of Wadsworth, a division of Thomson Learning: www.thomsonrights.com. Fax 800 730-2215.

CHAPTER 9
358: Figure 9.4 (Examples from WAIS): From *Psychology: Themes and Variations,* Third Edition, by Weiten. Copyright © 1995. Reprinted with permission of Wadsworth, a division of Thomson Learning: www.thomsonrights.com. Fax 800 730-2215.

CHAPTER 10
381: Figure 10.3 (Critical Periods of Susceptibility during Prenatal Development): From *Life-Span Human Development,* Second Edition, by Sigelman/Shaffer. Copyright © 1995. Reprinted with permission of Wadsworth, a division of Thomson Learning: www.thomsonrights.com. Fax: 800 730-2215; **389:** Figure 10.8 (Infant Preferences): From Johnson, "Newborns' preferential tracking of…" in *Cognition, 40,* p 1-19. Copyright © 1991. With permission from Elsevier.

CHAPTER 11
447: Figure 11.3 (Cross-Cultural Mating Strategies): From "Cross-Cultural Mating Tendencies" from *Psychological Review 100,* by Buss & Schmitt, p 204-232. Copyright © 1993 by the American Psychological Association. Reprinted with permission.

CHAPTER 12
479: Figure 12.6 (Nonverbal Personality Assessment): Figure taken from Paunonen, et al. "The structured Nonverbal Assessment" from *Journal of Personality, 58,* 1990, p 481-501. Reprinted by permission of Blackwell Publishers; **483:** Figure 12.7 (Freud's View of Personality): From *Psychology: The Science of Behaviour,* Second Canadian Edition, by Carlson, Buskist, Enzie and Heth. Copyright © 2002. Reprinted with permission by Pearson Education Canada Inc.

CHAPTER 14
565: Figure 14.2 (The Five Axes of the DSM-IV Diagnostic System): Reprinted with permission from the *Diagnostic and Statistical Manual of Mental Disorders,* Fourth Edition. Copyright © 1994 American Psychiatric Association; **584:** Figure 14.7 (The Genetics of Schizophrenia): From *Schizophrenia Genius* by Irving Gottesman. Copyright © 1991 by W.H. Freeman & Company. Used with permission.

CHAPTER 15
609-610: Dialogue: From *A Practitioner's Guide to Rational-Emotive Therapy,* Second Edition, by Susan Walen, Raymond Digiuseppe and Windy Dryden. Copyright © 1992 by Oxford University Press, Inc. Used by permission of Oxford University Press. Reprinted with permission from the *Diagnostic and Statistical Manual of Mental Disorders,* Fourth Edition. Copyright © 1994 American Psychiatric Association; **611:** Figure 15.6 (Homework from a Cognitive Therapist): From Beck et al., "Daily Record of Dysfunctional Thoughts" from *Cognitive Therapy of Depression.* Copyright © 1979; **622:** Figure 15.9 (The Effectiveness of Psychotheraphy): From *The Benefits of Psychotherapy,* by Smith, Mary Lee, Gene V. Glass

and Thomas I. Miller. Copyright © 1980. Reprinted with permission of The Johns Hopkins University Press.

CHAPTER 16

641: Table 16.1 (Social Readjustment Rating Scale): Reprinted from Publication: Figure "The Social Readjustment Rating Scale" from *Journal of Psychosomatic Research, 11,* p 218-231. Copyright © 1967 Elsevier Inc. Reprinted with permission from Elsevier Science; **657:** Figure 16.6 (A Daily Stress Record): From D.H. Barlow & R.M. Rapee, "Daily Stress Record," *Mastering Stress 2001: A Lifestyle Approach,* 12. Copyright © 2001. Reproduced with permission of American Health Publishing Company, Dallas, Texas. All rights reserved. For ordering information call 1-800-736-7323.

APPENDIX

677: Figure A.3 (Areas Under the Normal Curve as a Function of Standard Deviation from the Mean): From http://qreview.cera.net/Chapters-HTML/Chap4_html/ chapter4.htm. Reprinted by permission of Carl D. Nocera; **678:** Figure A.4 (Four Normal Distributions, with Different Means and SDs, Illustrating that the Percentage of the Scores in a Normal Distribution between the Mean and a Given SD Is Always Approximately the Same): From *Statistics: Tool of the Behavioural Sciences* by Johnson/Leibert. Copyright © 1997. Reprinted by permission of Prentice-Hall, Inc., Upper Saddle River, NJ.

PHOTOS

CHAPTER 1

2: Corel Solitude 233039; **5:** (bottom left) Suza Scalora/PhotoDisc, (bottom center) Suza Scalora/PhotoDisc, (bottom right) Suza Scalora/PhotoDisc; **8:** (top left) SW Productions/PhotoDisc, (top center) Nelson Photo, (top right) Lawrence Berkely/National Library/PhotoDisc; **11:** (top right) John Livzey, (center) John Livzey, (center bottom) John Livzey; **15:** (top right) Wadsworth Photo, (bottom right) ©Bettman/Corbis/ Magma; **16:** (top) © H. Stanley Johnson/ SuperStock, (bottom left) ©Bettman/Corbis/ Magma; **17:** (top right) Princeton University Library, (bottom right) ©Bettman/Corbis/ Magma; **18:** (top left) ©Underwood and Underwood/Corbis/ Magma, (center left) ©Bettman/ Corbis/Magma; **19:** ©Bettman/Corbis/ Magma; **20:** ©Bettman/Corbis/ Magma; **21:** (top right) Courtesy of Wellesley College Archives/ © Notman, (center right) Dan Grogan Photography; **24:** McGill University Archives; **25:** (bottom left) Barbara Penoyer/PhotoDisc, (bottom center) Kevin Frayer/CP Picture Archive, (bottom right) Andrew Vaughan/CP Picture Archive.

CHAPTER 2

34: © Jeff Greenberg/ PhotoEdit; **38:** (bottom left) Scott Audette/CP Picture Archive, (bottom right) Karl

Weatherly/PhotoDisc; **39:** (top right) Laura Dwight Photography, (bottom left) Dan McCoy/Rainbow; **44:** Copyright © 1998, Multi-Health Systems Inc. All rights reserved. In the USA, O. Box 950, North Tonawanda, NY 14120-0950, 1-800-456-3003. In Canada, 3770 Victoria Park Ave., Toronto, ON M2H 3M6, 1-800-268-6011. Internationally, +1-416-492-2627. Fax, +1-416-492-3343. Reproduced with permission; **51:** (top left) Eyewire/Getty Images, (top center) ©Bob Rowan; Progressive Image/ Corbis/ Magma; **54:** Corbis Royalty Free/Magma; **61:** Nelson Photo; **65:** Hans Deryk /CP Picture Archive; **66:** (bottom left) Jacob Halaska/ Index Stock Imagery, (bottom right) Doug Mazell/ Index Stock Imagery.

CHAPTER 3

74: © David Job/Stone/Getty Images; **77:** (bottom left) Randy Allbritton/PhotoDisc, (bottom right) PhotoLink/PhotoDisc; **84:** ©Bettman/Corbis/ Magma; **85:** (center left) S. Meltzer/ PhotoLink/PhotoDisc, (center left) ©Alison Wright/Corbis/ Magma, (bottom left) Patrick Johns/Corbis/Magma; **89:** Mitch Hrdlicka/PhotoDisc/Getty Images; **92:** Courtesy of Cindy Bukach, University of Victoria, Cognitive Neuropsychology Laboratory; **93:** Montreal Neurological Institute; **94:** Courtesy of Professor Sid Segalowitz; **95:** (top) CEA/IRSAY/CNRI/ PhotoResearchers, (bottom left) Rick Chard/MacLean's, (bottom right) ©Roger Ressmeyer/Corbis/ Magma; **98:** Peter Bregg/MacLean's; **100:** Warren Museum/Harvard Medical School; **104:** Geoff Manasee/PhotoDisc; **105:** Kalat, 1996; **110:** (top left) Corel 3 Children of the World, (top right) Corel 3 Children of the World; **112:** (top center) Corel 3, (top right) Courtesy of Dr. Martin Smith; **113:** Courtesy of Dr. Martin Smith.

CHAPTER 4

122: © Alan Oddie/PhotoEdit; **129:** Omrikon/Photo Researchers; **133:** Wadsworth Photo; **134:** Patrick Dupont; **135:** Fritz Goro/Time Warner; **140:** © Bev Doolittle, "The Forest Has Eyes," The Greenwich Workshop; **142:** (bottom left) Donovan Reese/PhotoDisc, (bottom center) Edmond Van Hoorick/PhotoDisc; (bottom right) Kim Steele/PhotoDisc; **147:** Richard Nowitz/Phototake; **149:** Courtesy of Dr. Mark A. Schmuckler; **152:** © Kevin Radford/SuperStock; **153:** Associated Press/George Widman; **156:** Skip Nall/PhotoDisc; **157:** Associated Press/Don Heupel; **160:** ©Michael Boys/ Corbis/ Magma; **161:** Omrikon/Photo Researchers; **165:** (top left) © Brownie Harris/Corbis/ Magma; (top center) Jules Frazier/PhotoDisc.

CHAPTER 5

172: © Raymond Forbes/SuperStock; **174:** Courtesy of Dr. Jim Tanaka; **175:** (bottom left) PhotoLink/PhotoDisc, (bottom center 1) Don Tremain/PhotoDisc, (bottom center 2) Nancy R. Cohen/PhotoDisc, (bottom right) Joaquin Palting/ PhotoDisc/ Getty Images; **179:** Ryan McVay/PhotoDisc; **181:**

Name Index

Subject Index